Websites for Major Companies and Organizations Cited in the Text

Company	Web Address
Interface Inc.	www.interfaceinc.com
IRS	www.irs.gov
International Paper Company	www.internationalpaper.com
JetBlue Airways	www.jetblue.com
Kellogg's	www.kelloggs.com
Kmart	www.kmart.com
Kodak	www.kodak.com
KPMG	www.kpmg.com
Lands' End	www.landsend.com
Levi Strauss	www.levi.com
Lincoln Electric	www.lincolnelectric.com
LoanCity.com	www.loancity.com
Lockheed Martin	www.lockheedmartin.com
Marriot Hotels	www.marriott.com
Massachusetts General Hospital	www.mgh.harvard.edu
Mayo Clinic	www.mayo.edu
McDonalds	www.mcdonalds.com
Mercedes-Benz	www.mercedes-benz.com
Merck	www.merck.com
MGM	www.mgm.com
Mobil	www.mobil.com
Motorola	www.motorola.com
NationsBank	www.nationsbank.com
Nationwide Insurance	http://nwinsurance.nationwide.com
NBC	www.nbc.com
Nestle	www.nestle.com
New York Yankees	www.yankees.com
Nintendo	www.nintendo.com
Northrup	www.northgrum.com
Northwest Airlines	www.nwa.com
Office Depot	www.officedepot.com
Overture Services	www.overture.com
Parker Hannifin	www.parker.com
Pfizer	www.pfizer.com
Philips Electronics	www.philips.com
Pizza Hut	www.pizzahut.com
Procter and Gamble	www.pg.com
Prudential Insurance Company	www.prudential.com
Qwest	www.qwest.com
Ramada Inn	www.ramada.com
Rockwell International	www.rockwell.com
Royal Bank of Canada	www.royalbank.com
Sabena	www.sabena.com
Sears	www.sears.com
Sheraton Hotels	www.sheraton.com
Siemens	http://siemens.com/index.jsp
Southwest Airlines	www.southwestair.com
Starbucks	www.starbucks.com
State of Florida	www.ebudget.state.fl.us
Taco Bell	www.tacobell.com
Texas Instruments	www.ti.com
Toyota	www.toyota.com
Tyco	www.tyco.com
U.S. Marine Corps	www.usmc.mil
U. S. Postal Service	www.usps.com
U.S. Treasury	www.ustreas.gov
U-Haul	www.uhaul.com
United Airlines	www.united.com
United Parcel Service	www.ups.com
US Airways	www.usairways.com
Wal-Mart	www.wal-mart.com
The Wall Street Journal	www.wallstreetjournal.com
The Walt Disney Company	www.disney.com
Warner Brothers	www.warnerbros.com
Weyerhaeuser	www.weyerhaeuser.com
Worldcom	www.worldcom.com
Xerox	www.xerox.com
Yamanouchi Pharmaceutical	www.yamanouchi.com

MANAGERIAL ACCOUNTING

MANAGERIAL ACCOUNTING

Creating Value in a Dynamic Business Environment

Sixth Edition

Ronald W. Hilton
Cornell University

Boston Burr Ridge, IL Dubuque, IA Madison, WI New York San Francisco St. Louis
Bangkok Bogotá Caracas Kuala Lumpur Lisbon London Madrid Mexico City
Milan Montreal New Delhi Santiago Seoul Singapore Sydney Taipei Toronto

MANAGERIAL ACCOUNTING

CREATING VALUE IN A DYNAMIC BUSINESS ENVIRONMENT

Published by McGraw-Hill/Irwin, a business unit of The McGraw-Hill Companies, Inc. 1221 Avenue of the Americas, New York, NY, 10020.

Some ancillaries, including electronic and print components, may not be available to customers outside the United States.

This book is printed on acid-free paper.

1 2 3 4 5 6 7 8 9 0 WCK/WCK 0 9 8 7 6 5 4 3

ISBN 0-07-250287-8

Publisher: *Stewart Mattson*
Sponsoring editor: *Steve DeLancey*
Managing developmental editor: *Gail Korosa*
Marketing manager: *Katherine Mattison*
Lead producer, Media technology: *Beth Cigler*
Senior project manager: *Christine A. Vaughan*
Production supervisor: *Debra R. Sylvester*
Lead designer: *Matthew Baldwin*
Photo research coordinator: *Jeremy Cheshareck*
Photo researcher: *David Tietz*
Senior supplement producer: *Carol Loreth*
Senior digital content specialist: *Brian Nacik*
Cover and interior design: *Jennifer McQueen*
Cover images: © *GettyImages,* © *Image Works,* © *Masterfile,* © *Stock Boston*
Typeface: *11/12 Times Roman*
Compositor: *GAC Indianapolis*
Printer: *Quebecor World Versailles Inc.*

Library of Congress Cataloging-in-Publication Data

Hilton, Ronald W.
Managerial accounting : creating value in a dynamic business environment / Ronald W. Hilton—6th ed.
p. cm.
Includes index.
ISBN 0-07-250287-8 (alk. paper)
1. Managerial accounting. I. Title.
HF5657.4.H55 2005
658.15′11—dc22

2003066495

INTERNATIONAL EDITION ISBN 0-07-111313-4

www.mhhe.com

To my wife, Meg, and our sons, Tim and Brad.

A MARKET LEADER FOR FIVE EDITIONS, HILTON CONTINUES THAT TRADITION OF MANAGERIAL ACCOUNTING INNOVATION AND EXCELLENCE.

ABOUT THE AUTHOR

Ronald W. Hilton is a Professor of Accounting at Cornell University. With bachelor's and master's degrees in accounting from The Pennsylvania State University, he received his Ph.D. from The Ohio State University.

A Cornell faculty member since 1977, Professor Hilton also has taught accounting at Ohio State and the University of Florida, where he held the position of Walter J. Matherly Professor of Accounting. Prior to pursuing his doctoral studies, Hilton worked for Peat, Marwick, Mitchell and Company and served as an officer in the United States Air Force.

Professor Hilton is a member of the Institute of Management Accountants and has been active in the American Accounting Association. He has served as associate editor of *The Accounting Review* and as a member of its editorial board. Hilton also has served on the editorial board of the *Journal of Management Accounting Research.* He has been a member of the resident faculties of both the Doctoral Consortium and the New Faculty Consortium sponsored by the American Accounting Association.

With wide-ranging research interests, Hilton has published articles in many journals, including the *Journal of Accounting Research, The Accounting Review, Management Science, Decision Sciences, The Journal of Economic Behavior and Organization, Contemporary Accounting Research,* and the *Journal of Mathematical Psychology.* He also has published a monograph in the *AAA Studies in Accounting Research* series, and he is a co-author of *Cost Management: Strategies for Business Decisions, Budgeting: Profit Planning and Control,* and *Cost Accounting: Concepts and Managerial Applications.* Professor Hilton's current research interests focus on contemporary cost management systems and international issues in managerial accounting. In recent years, he has toured manufacturing facilities and consulted with practicing managerial accountants in North America, Europe, Asia, and Australia.

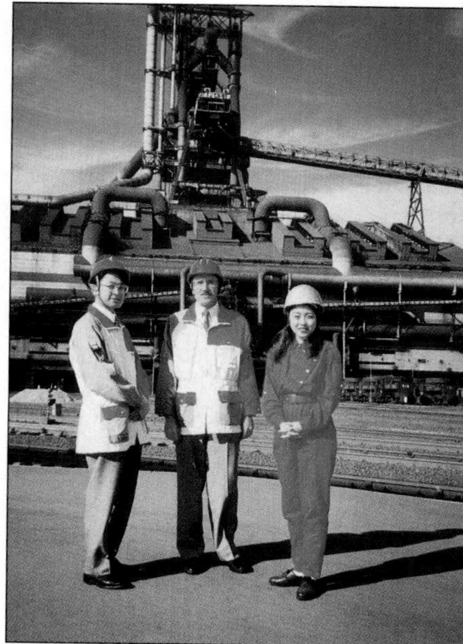

Guided by former students, Professor Hilton tours one of the world's largest steel mills, which is located near Tokyo. In recent years, Professor Hilton has consulted with practicing managerial accountants throughout the world.

BRINGING REAL-WORLD FOCUS TO

Managerial Accounting.

The world of business is changing dramatically. As a result, the role of managerial accounting is very different than it was even a decade ago. Today, managerial accountants serve as internal business consultants, working side-by-side in cross-functional teams with managers from all areas of the organization. For a thorough understanding of managerial accounting, students should not only be able to produce accounting information, but also understand how managers are likely to use and react to the information.

The goal of **Managerial Accounting** is to acquaint students of business with the fundamental tools of management accounting and to promote their understanding of the dramatic ways in which the field is changing. The emphasis throughout the text is on using accounting information to help manage an organization.

"Major strength is how it relates managerial accounting to the general management function and reveals the managerial accountant as an important member of the management team."

— Linda C. Bowen,

University of North Carolina – Chapel Hill

YOUR MANAGERIAL ACCOUNTING CLASS

Focus Companies.

Focus Companies provide a powerful strategy for fostering learning, and Hilton's integration of focus companies throughout the text is unmatched by any other managerial accounting book. Each chapter introduces important managerial accounting topics within the context of a realistic company. Students see the immediate impact of managerial accounting decisions on companies and gain exposure to different types of organizations.

> *"Perhaps what sets Hilton apart from the competition is its recognition that the world consists of more than manufacturing firms, and that managerial accounting plays a significant role in service and not-for-profit organizations."*
> — Lanny Solomon,
> University of Missouri – Kansas City

Balanced.

Hilton's *Managerial Accounting* offers the most balanced coverage of manufacturing and service companies. He recognizes that students will be working in a great variety of business environments and will benefit from exposure to diverse types of companies. Hilton uses a wide variety of examples from retail, service, manufacturing, and nonprofit organizations.

> *"The author has done an excellent job both in placing Managerial Accounting's role in the context of the firm and in presenting contemporary changes affecting the profession (e.g., e-Business, Global Competition, Customer Focus, JIT, TQM, etc.)."*
> — Stephen J. Dempsey,
> University of Vermont

Contemporary.

Hilton continues to be the leader in presenting the most contemporary coverage of managerial accounting topics. The traditional tools of managerial accounting such as product costing and budgeting have been updated with current approaches. New topics such as environmental cost management have been added.

> *"Easily readable, full of relevant up-to-date material, contains all the traditional manufacturing methods, and ABC and ABManagement integrated throughout the textbook."*
> —Marilyn Okleshen,
> Minnesota State University – Mankato

Flexible.

Hilton writes *Managerial Accounting* in a modular format that allows you to cover managerial accounting topics in the order you want. Throughout the development process reviewers of the text continued to stress that flexibility was important. Through this flexible approach your students will get the maximum benefit of learning managerial accounting in the order you determine.

How Does *Managerial Accounting: Creating Value in a Dynamic Business Environment* Bring the Real World into Your Classroom?

FOCUS COMPANIES

Students need to see the relevance of managerial accounting information in order to actively engage in learning the material. Ron Hilton found that by using focus companies to illustrate concepts, students immediately saw the significance of the material and became excited about the content. Hilton's integration of focus companies throughout the text is unmatched by any other managerial accounting textbook. Each chapter introduces important managerial topics within the context of a realistic company. Students see the immediate impact of managerial accounting decisions on companies and gain exposure to different types of organizations.

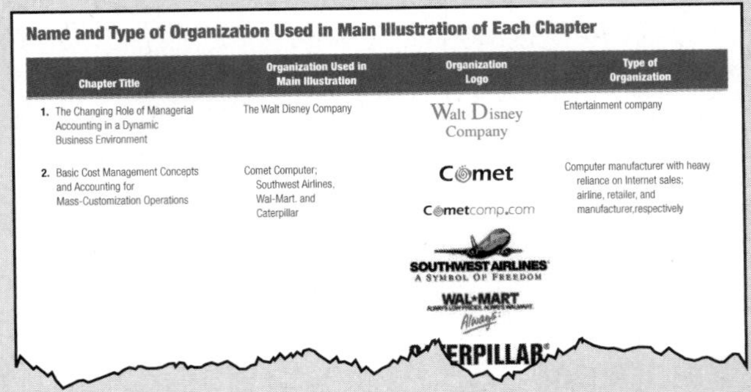

Name and Type of Organization Used in Main Illustration of Each Chapter

Chapter Title	Organization Used in Main Illustration	Organization Logo	Type of Organization
1. The Changing Role of Managerial Accounting in a Dynamic Business Environment	The Walt Disney Company	Walt Disney Company	Entertainment company
2. Basic Cost Management Concepts and Accounting for Mass-Customization Operations	Comet Computer; Southwest Airlines, Wal-Mart. and Caterpillar	Comet; Cometcomp.com; SOUTHWEST AIRLINES A SYMBOL OF FREEDOM; WAL★MART Always; ERPILLAR	Computer manufacturer with heavy reliance on Internet sales; airline, retailer, and manufacturer,respectively

Each chapter begins with a simulated news article highlighting the company featured in the chapter.

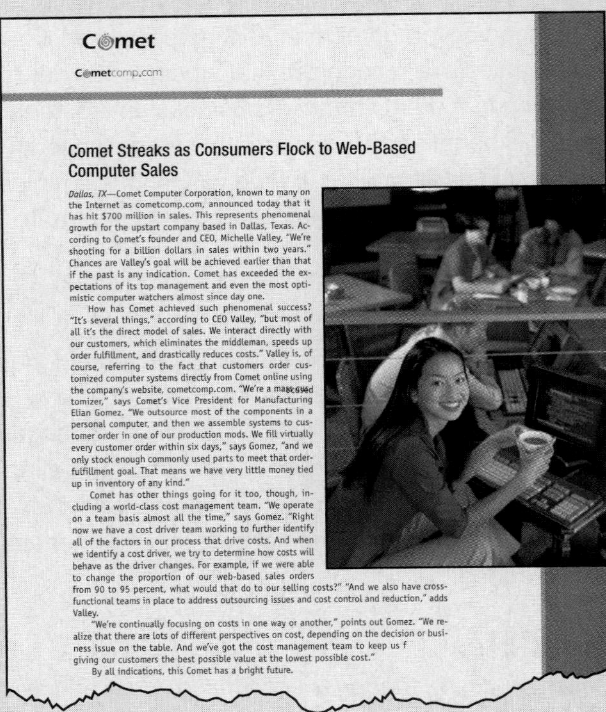

Comet

Cometcomp.com

Comet Streaks as Consumers Flock to Web-Based Computer Sales

Dallas, TX—Comet Computer Corporation, known to many on the Internet as cometcomp.com, announced today that it has hit $700 million in sales. This represents phenomenal growth for the upstart company based in Dallas, Texas. According to Comet's founder and CEO, Michelle Valley, "We're shooting for a billion dollars in sales within two years." Chances are Valley's goal will be achieved earlier than that if the past is any indication. Comet has exceeded the expectations of its top management and even the most optimistic computer watchers almost since day one.

How has Comet achieved such phenomenal success? "It's several things," according to CEO Valley, "but most of all it's the direct model of sales. We interact directly with our customers, which eliminates the middleman, speeds up order fulfillment, and drastically reduces costs." Valley is, of course, referring to the fact that customers order customized computer systems directly from Comet online using the company's website, cometcomp.com. "We're a mass customizer," says Comet's Vice President for Manufacturing Elian Gomez. "We outsource most of the components in a personal computer, and then we assemble systems to customer order in one of our production mods. We fill virtually every customer order within six days," says Gomez, "and we only stock enough commonly used parts to meet that order-fulfillment goal. That means we have very little money tied up in inventory of any kind."

Comet has other things going for it too, though, including a world-class cost management team. "We operate on a team basis almost all the time," says Gomez. "Right now we have a cost driver team working to further identify all of the factors in our process that drive costs. And when we identify a cost driver, we try to determine how costs will behave as the driver changes. For example, if we were able to change the proportion of our web-based sales orders from 90 to 95 percent, what would that do to our selling costs?" "And we also have cross-functional teams in place to address outsourcing issues and cost control and reduction," adds Valley.

"We're continually focusing on costs in one way or another," points out Gomez. "We realize that there are lots of different perspectives on cost, depending on the decision or business issue on the table. And we've got the cost management team to keep us f giving our customers the best possible value at the lowest possible cost."

By all indications, this Comet has a bright future.

Whenever the focus company is presented in the chapter, its logo is shown so the student sees its application to the text topic.

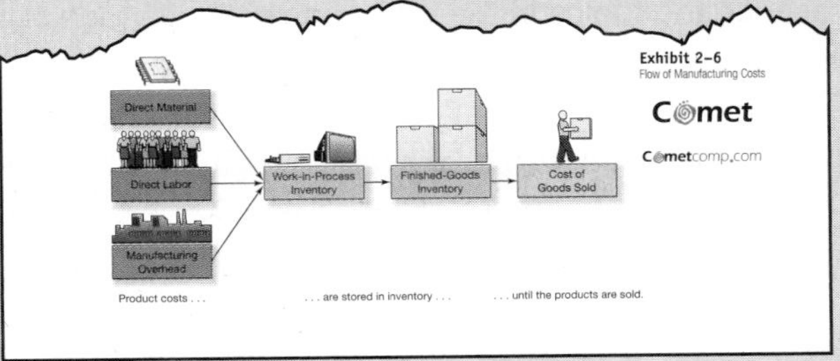

Exhibit 2–6
Flow of Manufacturing Costs

"The text consistently includes the most current topics from the real world and presents them in a well developed model."

—Edward S. Goodhart,
Shippensburg University

REAL-WORLD FOCUS

The Ethical Climate of Business and the Role of the Accountant

Who among us is not shocked and dismayed by the seemingly endless stream of corporate scandals that we have experienced over the past few years. The headlines keep on coming—Enron, Arthur Andersen, Worldcom, AOL, Global Crossing, Rite Aid, Tyco, Xerox, KPMG, Conseco—and the list goes on. Many of the cases involve mismanagement, some are characterized by alleged ethical lapses, and in some instances there is alleged criminal behavior. Who is to blame? According to most observers, there is plenty of blame to go around: greedy corporate executives, managers who make overreaching business deals, lack of oversight by various companies' boards of directors (particularly the boards' audit committees), shoddy work by external auditors, lack of sufficient probing by Wall Street analysts and the financial press, and some accountants who have been all too willing to push the envelope on aggressive accounting to (or beyond) the edge. Billions of dollars have been lost in employee pension funds, several states' investment portfolios, and the private investment accounts of the public. It will no doubt take many years to sort out the mess. Companies have gone bankrupt;

LO 8

Understand the ethical responsibilities of a managerial accountant.

Topic 1–2

Real-World Examples

The Hilton text provides a variety of thought-provoking, real-world examples to focus students on managerial accounting as an essential part of the management process. Featured organizations include FedEx, Ford, JCPenney, Amazon.com, Habitat for Humanity, and many others. These companies are highlighted in blue in the text.

The role of managerial accounting is very different now than it was even a decade ago. In the past, managerial accountants operated in a strictly staff capacity, usually physically separated from the managers for whom they provided reports and information. Nowadays, managerial accountants serve as internal business consultants, working side-by-side in cross-functional teams with managers from all areas of the organization. Rather than isolate managerial accountants in a separate accounting department, companies now tend to locate them in the operating departments where they are working with other managers to make decisions and resolve operational problems. Managerial accountants take on leadership roles on their teams and are sought out for the valuable information they provide. The role of the accountant in leading-edge companies "has been transformed from number cruncher and financial historian to being business partner and trusted advisor."[2]

An organization's management team, on which managerial accountants play an integral role, seeks to create value for the organization by managing resources, activities, and people to achieve the organization's goals effectively.

"We are looked upon as business advisors, more than just accountants, and that has a lot to do with the additional analysis and the forward-looking goals we are setting." (1a)[1]

Caterpillar

Management Accountants: In Their Own Words

Quotes from practicing managerial accountants are included in the margins throughout the text. These actual quotes show how the field of management accounting is changing, emphasize how the concepts are actually used, and demonstrate that management accountants are key players in most companies' management teams.

THE BALANCED SCORECARD

According to a recent survey by Bain & Company, approximately 50 percent of Fortune 1000 companies in North America and roughly 40 percent in Europe use some version of the balanced scorecard (often abbreviated as BSC). Among those is Philips Electronics, a worldwide conglomerate with over 250,000 employees in some 150 countries. Philips' top management believes that its BSC helps the management team streamline the complicated process of running a complex international company with diverse product lines and divisions. The BSC tool has helped Philips Electronics focus on factors critical for its business success and align hundreds of indicators that measure their markets, operations, and laboratories. With reference to the four BSC "compass points" in Exhibit 1–1, examples of the performance measures in the scorecard used by each of Philips' business units are as follows:

Financial perspective

Income from operations
Working capital

Management Accounting Practice

Philips Electronics

Management Accounting Practice

The managerial accounting practices of well-known, real-world organizations are highlighted in these boxes. They stimulate student interest and provide a springboard for classroom discussion.

Focus on Ethics

WAS WORLDCOM'S CONTROLLER JUST FOLLOWING ORDERS?

Through a series of mergers and acquisitions, WorldCom, Inc. grew to become the nation's second-largest long-distance telecommunications company. WorldCom's core communication services included network data transmission over public and private networks. Trouble arose for WorldCom because of the immense overcapacity in the telecommunications industry due to overly optimistic growth projections during the internet boom. The combination of overcapacity, decreased demand, and high fixed costs still pose a serious problem for many of the major players in the industry.

In June 2002, the company disclosed that it had overstated earnings for 2001 and the first quarter of 2002 to the tune of \$3.8 billion. The overstatement arose because the company incorrectly classified period expenses as capital expenditures. This

Focus on Ethics

This new feature is included in most chapters. Focus on Ethics poses an ethical dilemma, then asks tough questions that underscore the importance of ethical management. Some of these are based on real-world issues while others are fictional but based on well-established anecdotal evidence.

A FOCUS ON EXCEPTIONAL END-OF-CHAPTER MATERIAL

Managerial Accounting is known for its comprehensive and reliable end-of-chapter material.

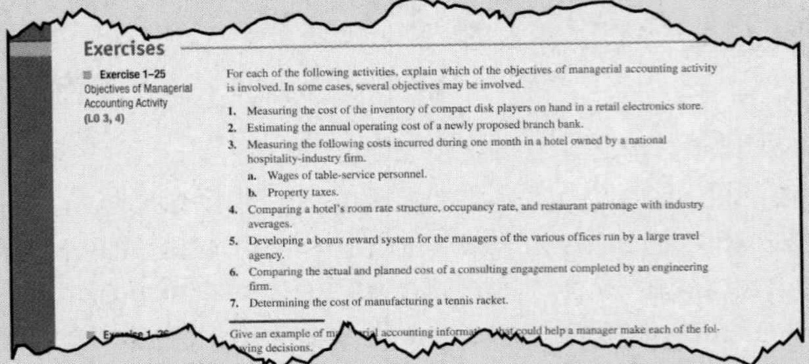

Exercises

Exercise 1–25
Objectives of Managerial Accounting Activity
(LO 3, 4)

For each of the following activities, explain which of the objectives of managerial accounting activity is involved. In some cases, several objectives may be involved.

1. Measuring the cost of the inventory of compact disk players on hand in a retail electronics store.
2. Estimating the annual operating cost of a newly proposed branch bank.
3. Measuring the following costs incurred during one month in a hotel owned by a national hospitality-industry firm.
   a. Wages of table-service personnel.
   b. Property taxes.
4. Comparing a hotel's room rate structure, occupancy rate, and restaurant patronage with industry averages.
5. Developing a bonus reward system for the managers of the various offices run by a large travel agency.
6. Comparing the actual and planned cost of a consulting engagement completed by an engineering firm.
7. Determining the cost of manufacturing a tennis racket.

Each chapter includes an extensive selection of assignment material ranging across review questions, exercises, problems, and cases. Most end-of-chapter material has been revised this edition.

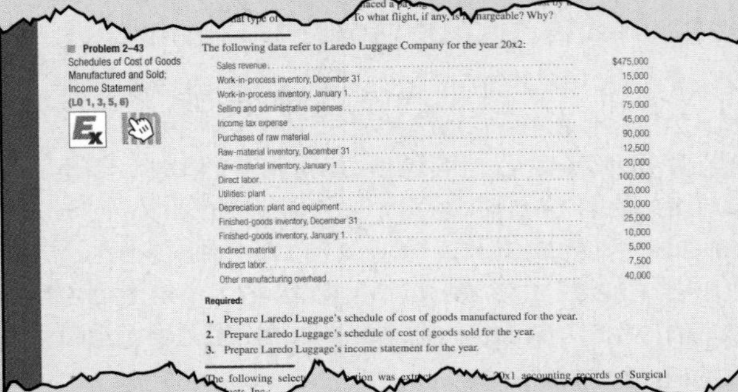

Problem 2–43
Schedules of Cost of Goods Manufactured and Sold; Income Statement
(LO 1, 3, 5, 6)

The following data refer to Laredo Luggage Company for the year 20x2:

Sales revenue	$475,000
Work-in-process inventory, December 31	15,000
Work-in-process inventory, January 1	20,000
Selling and administrative expenses	75,000
Income tax expense	45,000
Purchases of raw material	90,000
Raw-material inventory, December 31	12,500
Raw-material inventory, January 1	20,000
Direct labor	100,000
Utilities: plant	20,000
Depreciation: plant and equipment	30,000
Finished-goods inventory, December 31	25,000
Finished-goods inventory, January 1	10,000
Indirect material	5,000
Indirect labor	7,500
Other manufacturing overhead	40,000

Required:

1. Prepare Laredo Luggage's schedule of cost of goods manufactured for the year.
2. Prepare Laredo Luggage's schedule of cost of goods sold for the year.
3. Prepare Laredo Luggage's income statement for the year.

Many exercises and problems can be solved using the Excel spreadsheet templates contained on the Student Success CD and the text's Online Learning Center at www.mhhe.com/hilton6e. An Excel logo appears in the margin next to these exercises and problems for easy identification.

Numerous adapted CMA and CPA problems are included in the text to prepare students for these exams.

> *"One of the key reasons I selected this book is the great problems."*
> —Lynda Thoman, Purdue University

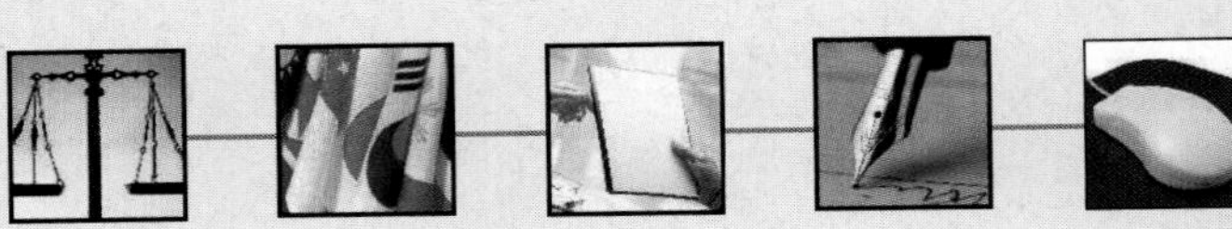

Every chapter in the text includes problems and cases exploring ethical issues, international matters and foreign currency questions, group work, and the requirements of good business communication. There are also exercises requiring students to use the Internet. Logos next to the exercise or problem identify these topics.

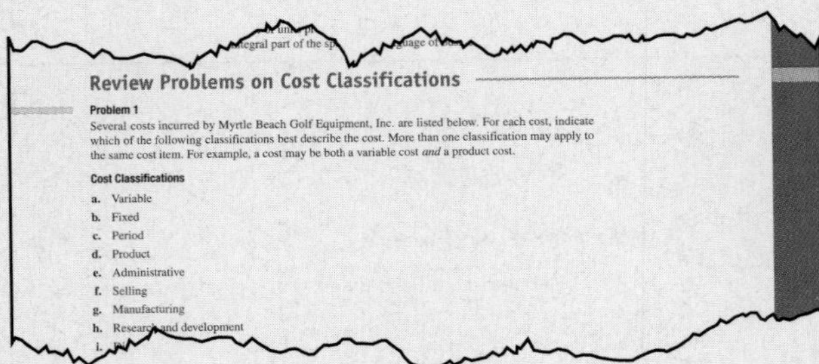

Review Problems on Cost Classifications

Problem 1
Several costs incurred by Myrtle Beach Golf Equipment, Inc. are listed below. For each cost, indicate which of the following classifications best describe the cost. More than one classification may apply to the same cost item. For example, a cost may be both a variable cost *and* a product cost.

Cost Classifications

a. Variable
b. Fixed
c. Period
d. Product
e. Administrative
f. Selling
g. Manufacturing
h. Research and development

Most chapters include a review problem along with its solution to provide students with a way to review their understanding of the material.

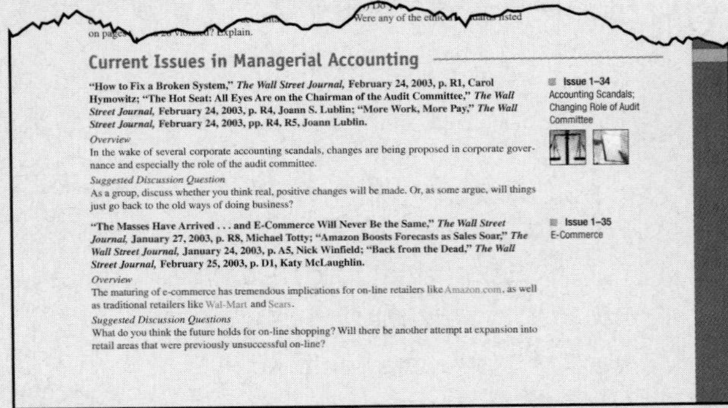

Current Issues in Managerial Accounting

Issue 1–34
Accounting Scandals; Changing Role of Audit Committee

"How to Fix a Broken System," *The Wall Street Journal,* February 24, 2003, p. R1, Carol Hymowitz; "The Hot Seat: All Eyes Are on the Chairman of the Audit Committee," *The Wall Street Journal,* February 24, 2003, p. R4, Joann S. Lublin; "More Work, More Pay," *The Wall Street Journal,* February 24, 2003, pp. R4, R5, Joann Lublin.

Overview
In the wake of several corporate accounting scandals, changes are being proposed in corporate governance and especially the role of the audit committee.

Suggested Discussion Question
As a group, discuss whether you think real, positive changes will be made. Or, as some argue, will things just go back to the old ways of doing business?

Issue 1–35
E-Commerce

"The Masses Have Arrived . . . and E-Commerce Will Never Be the Same," *The Wall Street Journal,* January 27, 2003, p. R8, Michael Totty; "Amazon Boosts Forecasts as Sales Soar," *The Wall Street Journal,* January 24, 2003, p. A5, Nick Winfield; "Back from the Dead," *The Wall Street Journal,* February 25, 2003, p. D1, Katy McLaughlin.

Overview
The maturing of e-commerce has tremendous implications for on-line retailers like Amazon.com, as well as traditional retailers like Wal-Mart and Sears.

Suggested Discussion Questions
What do you think the future holds for on-line shopping? Will there be another attempt at expansion into retail areas that were previously unsuccessful on-line?

Current Issues in Managerial Accounting questions ask students to discuss articles related to *Managerial Accounting.* These articles are from *The Wall Street Journal, Business Week, Fortune,* and *The New York Times.*

> *"The use of the Excel spreadsheet in the text illustrations shows the application of technology to the student early on. These students have been raised with the computer and the use of the spreadsheet makes the text 'real world' to them."*
> —Edward S. Goodhart, Shippensburg University

WHAT'S NEW IN THE SIXTH EDITION

Redesigned pedagogy, new assignment material, and a new design reinforce important managerial accounting concepts.

STREAMLINING

In order to streamline this edition, Chapters 16 and 17 were shortened and combined into the new Chapter 16. The concept of present value has been moved to an appendix for those students who need this review.

Topic Tackler

This tutorial offers a virtual helping hand in understanding the most challenging topics in the managerial accounting course. Through a step-by-step sequence of video clips, PowerPoint slides, interactive practice exercises, and self-tests, Topic Tackler offers help on two key topics for each chapter. These topics are indicated by a logo in the text.

Focus on Ethics

Focus on Ethics is included in most chapters. This feature raises hard-hitting issues and asks tough questions that remind us of the importance of ethical management. Some of these are based on real-world issues reported in the press; others are fictional but based on well-established anecdotal evidence.

Current Issues in Managerial Accounting and Management Accounting Practice

These popular features have been revised and updated this edition and reflect the latest practices and issues in managerial accounting.

End-of-Chapter Material

Hilton has made significant changes to the end-of-chapter material. Most of the exercises, problems, and cases contain different data from that found in the fifth edition.

Significant Content Changes

Chapters 1 and 10: Coverage of the balanced scorecard is expanded.

Chapter 3: Introduction to Activity-based costing (ABC) is moved to the appendix and a discussion of supply-chain management added.

Chapter 6: Activity-based management (ABM) discussion is shortened and consolidated in Chapter 6.

Appendix 7: Microsoft Excel is now used to do linear regression analysis and added to the appendix.

Chapter 12: Completely new coverage of environmental cost management and Six Sigma.

SUPPLEMENTS

Hilton's instructor and student support materials are comprehensive, providing you with superior classroom support and bringing out the best in your students.

"The technology supplements and instructor resources are top notch, and very appropriate for our students."
—Marilyn Okleshen,
Minnesota State University – Mankato

Instructor Supplements

Instructor's Resource Manual

ISBN 0072866241
(Also available on the password-protected Instructor's Edition Online Learning Center (OLC) and Instructors Resource CD)

This comprehensive manual includes chapter outlines, summaries, and teaching overviews. A homework grid provides estimated time for each assignment and its learning objective. The manual also cross-references all the key supplements including the Test Bank, Managerial Accounting Video Series, and PowerPoint slides. Prepared by Lanny Solomon of University of Missouri – Kansas City.

Solutions Manual

ISBN 0072866284
(Also available on the password-protected Instructor's Edition OLC and Instructor Resource CD)

Prepared by the author, the manual contains complete solutions to all the text's end-of-chapter exercises, problems, cases, and Current Issues in Managerial Accounting.

Printed Test Bank

ISBN 007286625X
(Also available on the Instructor's Resource CD)

This test bank in Word format contains multiple-choice questions, essay, and short problems. Each test item is coded for level of difficulty, learning objective, and type. Type refers to whether the problem is a recall, an application, or an analysis problem based on Bloom's taxonomy. Prepared by Lanny Solomon.

Computerized Test Bank

(Available on the Instructor's Resource CD)

The electronic test bank is delivered in the latest version of Diploma, from Brownstone. It can be used to make different versions of the same test, change the answer order, edit and add questions, and conduct online testing.

Solutions Transparencies

ISBN 0072866292

Acetate overhead transparencies for every exercise, problem and case are provided in a large, readable typeface.

PowerPoint Slides

(Available on the Online Learning Center (OLC) and Instructor's Resource CD)

There are two complete PowerPoint packages, each having a student and instructor version.

- One set, by Michael Blue of Bloomsburg University, is for students to complete on their own with an instructor's version to use in the classroom for discussion.
- Another set covers key chapter topics, with an expanded version for instructors. These were prepared by Jon A. Booker and Charles W. Caldwell of Tennessee Technological University.

Instructor Resource CD-ROM

ISBN 0072866217

This CD includes electronic versions of the Resource Manual, Solutions Manual, Test Bank, as well as PowerPoint slides for instructor and students, video clips, exhibits in the text, spreadsheet templates with solutions, and chapters on Process Costing: The First-in, First-Out Method, The Statement of Cash Flows, and Financial Statement Analysis and their Solutions Manuals.

Managerial Accounting Video Library

ISBN 0072376171

These short videos, developed by Dallas County Community College, provide for classroom discussion. The focus is on the preparation, analysis, and use of accounting information for business decision making.

Student Supplements

Study Guide

ISBN 0072866276

This guide incorporates many of the accounting skills essential to student success. Each chapter contains chapter focus suggestions, read and recall questions, self-test questions and exercises, and ideas for study groups. In addition to reinforcing and applying the key concepts in the text, the study guide coaches students on how to study individually and in groups. Prepared by Douglas deVidal of the University of Texas at Austin.

Student Success with Topic Tackler CD-ROM

Packaged free with each new copy of the text, this CD includes two sets of PowerPoint slides, video clips, Topic Tackler tutorial, and additional chapters on Process Costing: The First-in, First-Out Method, The Statement of Cash Flows, and Financial Statement Analysis.

Topic Tackler

Included on the Student Success CD-ROM, this tutorial offers a virtual helping hand in understanding the most challenging topics in the managerial accounting course. Through a step-by-step sequence of video clips, PowerPoint slides, interactive practice exercises, and self-tests, Topic Tackler offers help on two key topics for each chapter. These topics are indicated by a logo in the text.

PowerPoint Notes

ISBN 0072866268

These slides cover key concepts found in each chapter, printed three per page with space for student note taking.

Check Figures

(Available on the Online Learning Center (OLC))

These provide key answers for selected problems in the text.

PowerPoint Slides

(Available on the Online Learning Center (OLC) and on the Student Success CD))

There are two complete PowerPoint packages each having a student and instructor version.

- One set, by Michael Blue of Bloomsburg University, is for students to complete on their own with an instructor's version to use in the classroom for discussion.
- Another set covers key chapter topics. These were prepared by Jon A. Booker and Charles W. Caldwell of Tennessee Technological University.

Excel Templates

(Available on the Online Learning Center (OLC))

These spreadsheets allow students to develop skills by using templates to solve selected assignments identified by an icon in the end-of-chapter material.

Online Learning Center (OLC)

www.mhhe.com/hilton6e

See the next page for details.

A New Focus on Technology

Our technology resources help students and instructors focus on learning success. By using the Internet and multimedia, students get book-specific help at their convenience. Teaching aids make in-class presentations easy and stimulating. These aids give you more power than ever to teach your class the way you want.

www.mhhe.com/hilton6e

More and more students are studying online. That's why we offer an Online Learning Center (OLC) that follows ***Managerial Accounting*** chapter by chapter. It doesn't require any building or maintenance on your part. It's ready to go the moment you type in the URL. The OLC includes:

- Excel Spreadsheets
- Glossary
- Chapter Objectives
- Interactive Quizzes
- Lecture PowerPoint slides
- Interactive PowerPoint slides
- Chapter on Process Costing: The First-in, First-Out Method
- Chapter on The Statement of Cash Flows
- Chapter on Financial Statement Analysis
- Web Links to companies listed in text
- Check figures

For instructors, the book's password-protected Instructor's Edition OLC contains the Instructor's Resource Guide, Solutions Manual, Instructor PowerPoint slides, Excel templates and solutions, video notes, and updates. Instructors can pull all of this material into their PageOut course syllabus or use it as part of another online course management system.

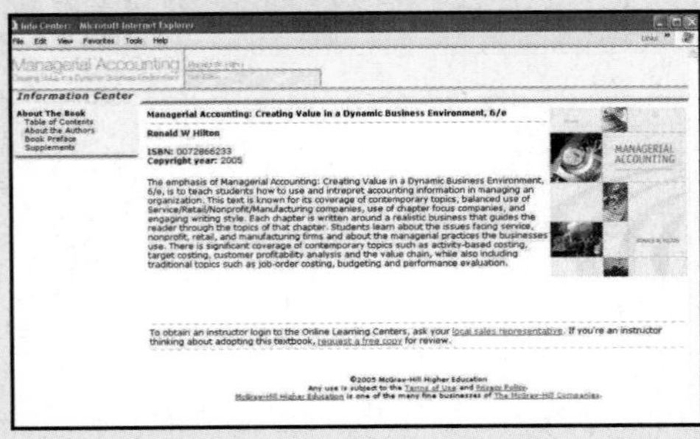

NetTutor™

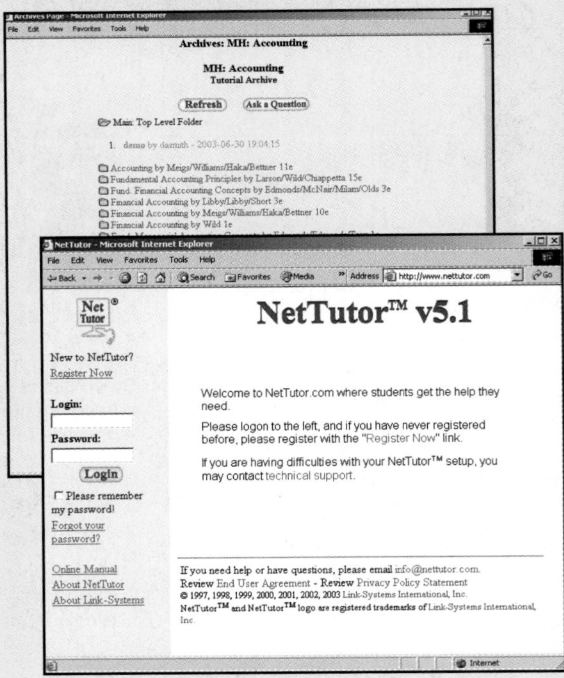

NetTutor is a live, online tutor that guides students through their accounting problems step-by-step. They can also watch other students' problems answered, giving them an opportunity to constantly improve their accounting skills.

NetTutor allows students to communicate with live tutors in a variety of ways: Through a Live Tutor Center, a Q&A Center, and an Archive Center. The Live Tutor Center enables a tutor to hold an interactive on-line tutorial for several students. The Q&A center allows students to submit questions and retrieve answers within 24 hours. The Archive center lets students browse previously asked questions for their answers. They can also search for questions pertinent to a particular topic.

Students are issued 10 hours of free NetTutor time when they purchase a new copy of the text.

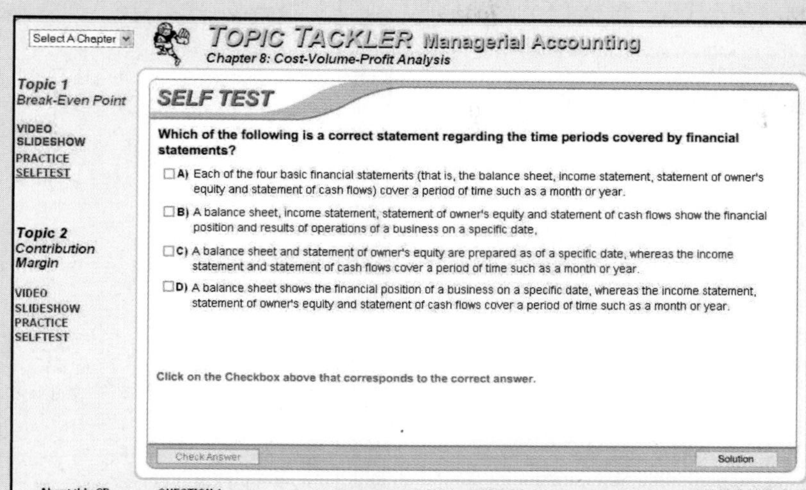

Topic Tackler

This tutorial offers a virtual helping hand in understanding the most challenging topics in the managerial accounting course. Through a step-by-step sequence of video clips, PowerPoint slides, interactive practice exercises, and self-tests, Topic Tackler offers help on two key topics for each chapter. These topics are indicated by a logo in the text.

Student Success with Topic Tackler CD-ROM

Available free with each new text purchase, the CD contains the Topic Tackler tutorial, video clips tied to specific text chapters, PowerPoint slides, and chapters on Process Costing: The First-in, First-Out Method, The Statement of Cash Flows, and Financial Statement Analysis.

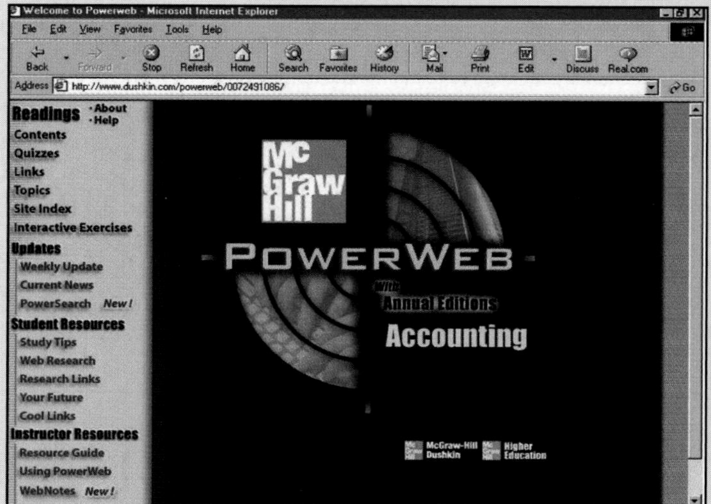

PowerWeb

Keeping your accounting course timely can be a job in itself, and now McGraw-Hill/Irwin does that job for you. PowerWeb is a site where you can access the latest news and developments pertinent to your course without all the clutter and dead links of a typical online search.

PowerWeb offers these course-specific features:

- Current articles related to managerial accounting.
- Daily and weekly updates with assessment tools.
- Referenced Web links.

Students can visit PowerWeb to take a self-grading quiz or check a daily news feed analyzed by an expert in managerial accounting. They can also access interactive glossaries and exercises, obtain study tips, and conduct online research.

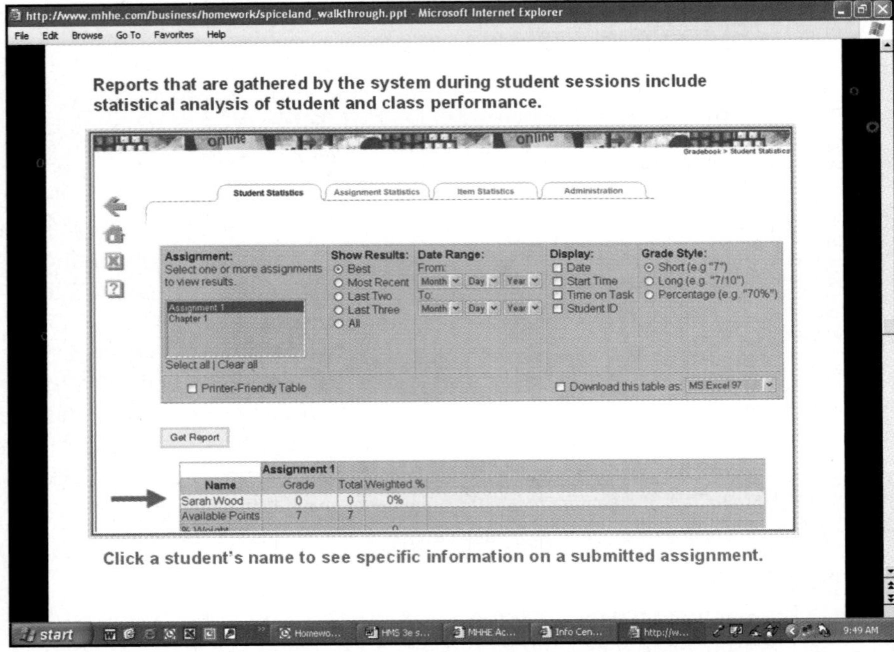

McGraw-Hill's Homework Manager

Homework Manager is an exciting, new Web-based supplement available with *Managerial Accounting.* It will help your students learn managerial accounting by duplicating selected problem structures from each chapter and presenting the problems with new data an infinite number of times. Each student also receives immediate scoring and feedback from the program to guide their studies.

Homework Manager can be used for practice, allowing students to work as many iterations of each problem as they like without their score being recorded. In the homework and exam modes, Homework Manager records all the individual responses, grades the exams, and registers the grades in the online grade book. You not only know how your class performed on the exam, but also which topics or learning objectives your students struggled with.

The problem structures available in Homework Manager can be easily identified in the text by the Homework Manager logo found in the margin. It can be packaged with the text for a small additional charge.

Homework Manager is powered by Brownstone.

Online Course Management

(WebCT, eCollege, and TopClass)

We offer *Managerial Accounting* content for complete online courses. You can customize the Online Learning Center content and author your own course materials. No matter which online course solution you choose, you can count on the highest level of support. Our specialists offer free training and answer any question you have through the life of your adoption.

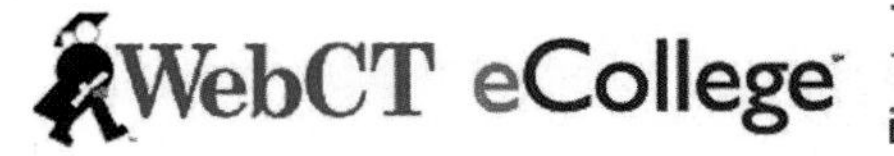

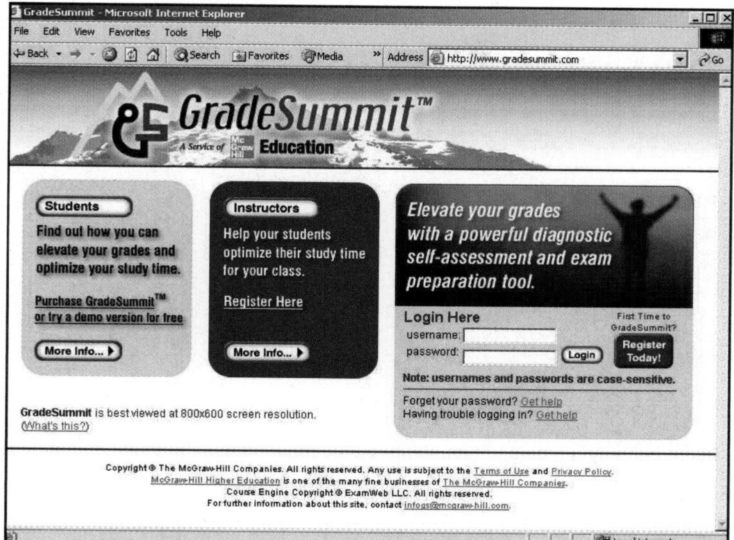

GradeSummit

GradeSummit is an online diagnostic, self-assessment, and exam preparation tool for students. As a student answers questions, diagnostic results provide invaluable feedback. This feedback helps students identify their strengths and weaknesses, enabling them to target their study time more efficiently. It is available as a package with the text for a small additional charge.

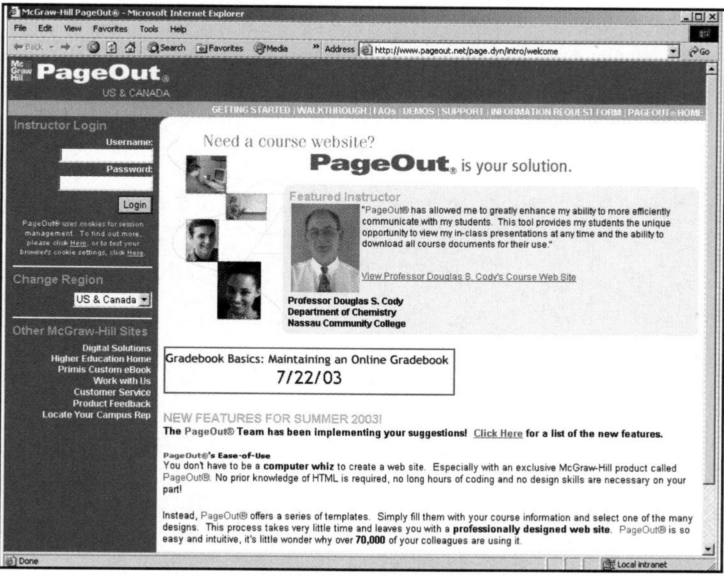

PageOut

McGraw-Hill's Course Management System, PageOut, is the easiest way to create a website for your accounting course. There's no need for HTML coding, graphic design, or a thick how-to book. Just fill in a series of boxes and click on one of our professional designs. In no time your course is online with a website that contains your syllabus. If you need help, our team of product specialists is ready to take your course materials and build a custom website to your specifications.

Knowledge Gateway

Knowledge Gateway is an all-purpose service and resource center for instructors teaching online. While training programs from WebCT and Blackboard will help teach you their software, only McGraw-Hill/Irwin has services to help you actually manage and teach your online course, as well as run and maintain the software. To see how these platforms can assist your online course, visit www.mhhe.com/solutions.

> *"This textbook and technology is superior to others because (of) the presentation CD, the student success CD, and website resources."*
> —Marilyn Okleshen, Minnesota State University – Mankato

Acknowledgments

I Am Grateful
I would like to express my appreciation to people who have provided assistance in the development of this textbook. First, my gratitude goes to the thousands of managerial accounting students I have had the privilege to teach over many years. Their enthusiasm, comments, and questions have challenged me to clarify my thinking about many topics in managerial accounting.

Second, I express my sincere thanks to the following professors who provided extensive reviews for the sixth edition:

REVIEWERS

Denise Guithues Amrhein, *Saint Louis University*

Florence Atiase, *University of Texas at Austin*

Rowland Atiase, *University of Texas at Austin*

K. R. Balachandran, *New York University,*

Frederick Bardo, *Shippensburg University*

Linda Bowen, *University of North Carolina*

Wayne Bremser, *Villanova University*

Richard Brody, *University of New Haven*

Gyan Chandra, *Miami University*

Paul Copley, *University of Georgia*

Maureen Crane, *California State University, Fresno*

Stephen Dempsey, *University of Vermont*

Martha Doran, *San Diego State University*

Allan Drebin, *Northwestern University*

James Emig, *Villanova University*

Michael Flores, *Wichita State University*

Kimberly Frank, *University of Nevada at Las Vegas*

Alan Friedberg, *Florida Atlantic University*

Edward Goodhart, *Shippensburg University*

Paul Juras, *Wake Forest University*

Stacey Konesky, *Kent State University*

James Lasseter, Jr. *University of South Florida*

Angelo Luciano, *Columbia College*

Ana Marques, *University of Texas at Austin*

Sanjay Mehrotra, *Northwestern University*

Cynthia Nye, *Bellevue University*

Marilyn Okleshen, *Minnesota State University*

Mohamed Onsi, *Syracuse University*

Samuel Phillips, *Shenandoah University*

Frederick Rankin, *Washington University*

Lanny Solomon, *University of Missouri at Kansas City*

Lynda Thoman, *Purdue University*

Wendy Tietz, *Kent State University*

Ralph Tower, *Wake Forest University*

Mark Turner, *Stephen F. Austin State University*

Bill Wempe, *Texas Christian University*

James Williamson, *San Diego State University*

Priscilla Wisner, *Graduate School of International Management*

I once again thank those individuals whose input over the last edition has helped the book to evolve to its present form: Noah Barsky, Villanova University; Mohamed Bayou, University of Michigan, Dearborn; Bruce Bradford, Fairfield University; Dan Daly, Boston College; Theresa Hammond, Boston College; and Clifford Nelson, University of Connecticut.

I want to thank Kim Temme of Maryville University, Catherine Usoff of Bentley College, and Beth Woods for their thorough checking of the text and solutions manual for accuracy and completeness. I also want to thank Jim Emig of Villanova University for his accuracy checking of various supplements that accompany the book.

Lanny Solomon of the University of Missouri at Kansas City prepared the Test Bank and Instructors Resource Guide. Michael Blue of Bloomsburg University authored the Interactive PowerPoint slides. Jon A. Booker and Charles W. Caldwell of Tennessee Technological University prepared the lecture PowerPoint slides. Jack Terry of ComSource Associates, Inc. prepared the Excel spreadsheets. Douglas deVidal of the University of Texas at Austin wrote the Study Guide. Linda Schain of Hofstra University prepared Topic Tackler. Leland Mansuetti authored the online quizzes. The supplements are a great deal of work to write and I appreciate their efforts that make teaching the course easier for everyone who uses the text.

I acknowledge the Institute of Management Accountants for permission to use problems from Certified Management Accountant (CMA) examinations. I also acknowledge the American Institute of Certified Public Accountants for permission to use problems from the Uniform CPA Examinations, Questions, and Unofficial Answers. I am indebted to Professors Roland Minch and David Solomons for allowing the use of their case materials in the text. The source for the actual company information in Chapters 1 and 2 regarding The Walt Disney Company, Caterpillar, Wal-Mart, and Southwest Airlines was the companies' published annual reports.

Finally, I wish to express my gratitude to the fine people at McGraw-Hill/Irwin who so professionally guided this book through the publication process. In particular, I wish to acknowledge Steve DeLancey, Gail Korosa, Katherine Mattison, Christine Vaughan, Matthew Baldwin, Debra Sylvester, Beth Cigler, Jeremy Cheshareck, and Carol Loreth.

Ronald W. Hilton

Contents in Brief

Contents

Part I
Fundamentals and Cost Accumulation Systems

Note: Entries printed in blue denote topics that emphasize contemporary cost management issues.

Part II
Cost Management Systems, Activity-Based Costing, and Activity-Based Management

Part III
Planning, Control, and Cost Management Systems

Part IV
Using Accounting Information in Decision Making

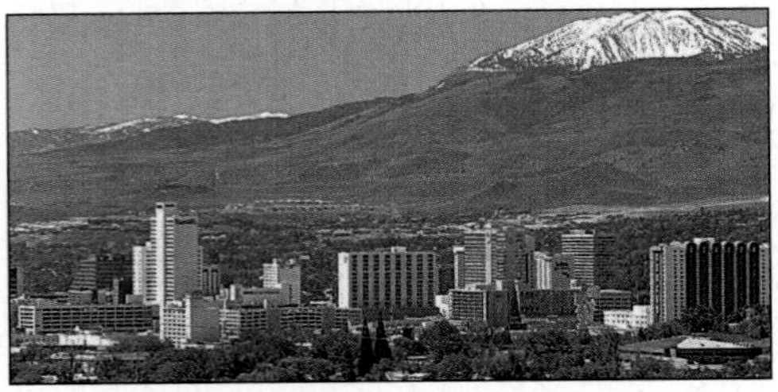

Part V
Selected Topics for Further Study

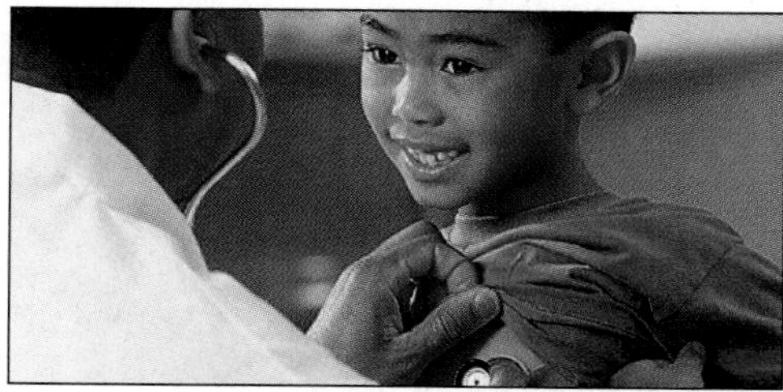

MANAGERIAL ACCOUNTING

Chapter One

The Changing Role of Managerial Accounting in a Dynamic Business Environment

After completing this chapter, you should be able to:

1 Define managerial accounting and describe its role in the management process.

2 Explain four fundamental management processes that help organizations attain their goals.

3 List and describe five objectives of managerial accounting activity.

4 Explain the major differences between managerial and financial accounting.

5 Explain where managerial accountants are located in an organization, in terms of formal organization, deployment in cross-functional teams, and physical location.

6 Describe the roles of an organization's chief financial officer (CFO) or controller, treasurer, and internal auditor.

7 Briefly describe some of the major contemporary themes in managerial accounting.

8 Understand the ethical responsibilities of a managerial accountant.

9 Discuss the professional organizations, certification process, and ethical standards in the field of managerial accounting.

Learning Objectives highlight the key topics to be covered in the chapter. They are repeated in the margin of the text where they are discussed. Also, each end-of-chapter assignment lists its learning objective in the margin.

Walt Disney
Company

Disney Excels with Creative Talent and Sound Management

Burbank, CA—The past few years have seen a significant expansion for Walt Disney Parks and Resorts. With the opening of Disney's Animal Kingdom, Disney's California Adventure, and Tokyo Disney Sea, crowds of tourists are flocking in ever-greater numbers to Disney's entertainment destinations on three continents. In the words of Disney's chairman, "Our overall corporate mission is to offer quality entertainment that people will seek out. At Disney, we are dedicated to creating entertainment of such excellence that people will choose to spend some of their valuable time with us." And spending time they are, as more and more kids, teenagers, and adults visit Disney's Animal Kingdom, Magic Kingdom, Epcot, and Disney–MGM Studios in Florida, as well as California's Disneyland Resort, Disneyland Paris Resort, and Tokyo Disneyland Resort.

In recent years, The Walt Disney Company has invested millions of dollars in major additions to its entertainment lineup. The company has made investments in a new Tomorrowland at Disneyland Park, the Disney Cruise Line, new Disney channels in Italy and Spain, the Disney Ambassador Hotel, its Buena Vista Internet Group, and many others.

The Walt Disney Company has long been widely admired as a visionary and well-managed company. But how does Disney continually make the right calls in terms of investment capital, providing new attractions that appeal to its audience while earning a superior return for its shareholders? In the words of Disney's chief financial officer, "The Walt Disney Company strives to maximize value to its shareholders by leveraging the strength of its brand, character, and entertainment franchises through a commitment to creative excellence and guest service coupled with strict financial discipline. The company evaluates its existing businesses and new initiatives based on their ability to contribute to Disney's long-term cash flow and earnings growth and to provide returns that exceed Disney's cost of capital."

Through strategic planning, sound decision making, and creative and disciplined management, The Walt Disney Company promises to continue providing quality entertainment to its customers and attractive financial returns to its investors for decades to come.

Chapters begin with a simulated newspaper article that introduces the issues to be addressed in the chapter. These focus companies are fictional (except in this case with the Walt Disney Company), but are based on actual practices of real companies. Whenever this focus company is discussed in the chapter, the company logo appears in the margin.

Many different kinds of organizations affect our daily lives. Manufacturers, retailers, service industry firms, agribusiness companies, nonprofit organizations, and government agencies provide us with a vast array of goods and services. All of these organizations have two things in common. First, every organization has a set of *goals* or objectives. An airline's goals might be profitability and customer service. A city police department's goals would include public safety and security coupled with cost minimization. Second, in pursuing an organization's goals, managers need *information*. The information needs of management range across financial, production, marketing, legal, and environmental issues. Generally, the larger the organization is, the greater is management's need for information.

LO 1

Define managerial accounting and describe its role in the management process.

Managerial accounting is the process of identifying, measuring, analyzing, interpreting, and communicating information in pursuit of an organization's goals. Managerial accounting is an integral part of the management process, and managerial accountants are important strategic partners in an organization's management team.

In this chapter, we will explore the role of managerial accounting within the overall management process. In the remaining chapters, we will expand our study by exploring the many concepts and tools used in managerial accounting.

Managerial Accounting: A Business Partnership with Management

The role of managerial accounting is very different now than it was even a decade ago. In the past, managerial accountants operated in a strictly staff capacity, usually physically separated from the managers for whom they provided reports and information. Nowadays, managerial accountants serve as internal business consultants, working side-by-side in cross-functional teams with managers from all areas of the organization. Rather than isolate managerial accountants in a separate accounting department, companies now tend to locate them in the operating departments where they are working with other managers to make decisions and resolve operational problems. Managerial accountants take on leadership roles on their teams and are sought out for the valuable information they provide. The role of the accountant in leading-edge companies "has been transformed from number cruncher and financial historian to being business partner and trusted advisor."[2]

"We are looked upon as business advisors, more than just accountants, and that has a lot to do with the additional analysis and the forward-looking goals we are setting." (1a)[1]
Caterpillar

An organization's management team, on which managerial accountants play an integral role, seeks to create value for the organization by managing resources, activities, and people to achieve the organization's goals effectively.

Managing Resources, Activities, and People

Walt Disney Company

The owners, directors, or trustees of an organization set its goals, often with the help of management. For example, The Walt Disney Company's goals are set by its board of directors, who are elected by the company's stockholders. The overall goal of The Walt Disney Company, according to a recent annual report, may be expressed as a

[1]*Management Accountants: In Their Own Words* Throughout the text, you will find these quotes from practicing management accountants. Collectively they show how the field of managerial accounting is changing, and the important role it plays in today's dynamic business environment. The references for these quotes appear at the end of the text, beginning on page 783. The references are organized by chapter; thus reference (1a) relates to the first quote in Chapter 1, and so forth.

[2]Gary Siegel, "The Image of Corporate Accountants," *Strategic Finance* 82, no. 2 (August 2000), p. 71.

commitment to creative excellence and guest service coupled with strict financial discipline in order to maximize value to the company's shareholders.[3]

LO 2

Explain four fundamental management processes that help organizations attain their goals.

In pursuing its goals, an organization acquires *resources*, hires *people*, and then engages in an organized set of *activities*. It is up to the management team to make the best use of the organization's resources, activities, and people in achieving the organization's goals. The day-to-day work of the management team comprises four activities:

- Decision making.
- Planning.
- Directing operational activities.
- Controlling.

Decision Making

Several years ago, Disney's board of directors decided as one of the company's growth objectives to expand its theme park operations in Florida. It was not immediately clear, however, what would be the best way to accomplish that goal. Would it be best to expand one of the company's three existing theme parks—the Magic Kingdom, Epcot, or Disney-MGM Studios? Or should the company branch out in an entirely new direction with a brand new theme park attraction? How would each of these alternative courses of action mesh with the company's other goals of bringing the best in creative entertainment to its customers and maintaining sound financial discipline? Disney's top management team had to *make a decision* about the best way to expand the company's Florida operations, which entailed *choosing among the available alternatives.*

Planning

Disney's top management team decided to expand the company's Florida operations by building an entirely new theme park named Disney's Animal Kingdom. Created and designed by Walt Disney's Imagineering Division, this 500-acre theme park would offer guests wide-ranging adventures and tell the fascinating stories of all animals—ancient and present-day, real and imagined. Now the detailed planning phase began. How would the Animal Kingdom's many attractions designed by the Imagineering Division be laid out and organized? What food and beverage operations would be appropriate? How many employees would be needed on a day-to-day basis? What supplies would be required to run the park? How much would electricity and other utilities cost? How much would running the park during a typical year cost? Finally, how should the park's admission be priced given predicted patronage? Disney's management team had to *plan* for running the Animal Kingdom, which meant *developing a detailed financial and operational description of anticipated operations.*

"The accounting people are expected to do things that are much more strategic and much more forward looking than [they] have been expected to do in the past." (1b)

Caterpillar

Directing Operational Activities

Now the theme park has been built, equipped, and staffed. How many cashiers should be on duty on Saturday morning? How much food should be ordered each day? How much cash will be needed to meet the payroll, pay the utility bills, and buy maintenance supplies next month? All of these questions fall under the general heading of *directing operational activities*, which means *running the organization on a day-to-day basis.*

[3]The Walt Disney Company, which is discussed in this chapter, is, of course, a real company. However, the subsequent focus organizations around which chapters are built are not real organizations. They are, however, realistic settings in which to discuss business and managerial accounting issues. In most cases they are based on real organizations. Similarly, the news articles in the chapter openers are not real newspaper articles, but most of them are based on real events. These realistic illustrations and scenarios are intended to help students connect the business and managerial accounting issues discussed in this book to everyday life.

Controlling

The theme park has operated for several years now. Is the company's goal being accomplished? More specifically, have the theme park's operations adhered to the plans developed by management for achieving the goal? In seeking to answer these questions, management is engaged in *control*, which means *ensuring that the organization operates in the intended manner and achieves its goals.*

How Managerial Accounting Adds Value to the Organization

Managers need information for all of the managerial activities described in the preceding section. That information comes from a variety of sources, including economists, financial experts, marketing and production personnel, and the organization's managerial accounting system.

Objectives of Managerial Accounting Activity

LO 3

List and describe five objectives of managerial accounting activity.

Managerial accountants add value to an organization by pursuing five major objectives:

1. Providing information for decision making and planning, and proactively participating as part of the management team in the decision-making and planning processes.
2. Assisting managers in directing and controlling operational activities.
3. Motivating managers and other employees toward the organization's goals.
4. Measuring the performance of activities, subunits, managers, and other employees within the organization.
5. Assessing the organization's competitive position, and working with other managers to ensure the organization's long-run competitiveness in its industry.

"In five years [we will become] even more strategic. Really understanding the ins and outs of all the organizations, and really trying to be visionary—understanding what is happening to our business." (1c)
Hewlett-Packard

Nowadays managerial accounting analysis is considered so crucial in managing an enterprise that in most cases managerial accountants are integral members of the management team. Far from playing a passive role as information providers, managerial accountants take a proactive role in both the strategic and day-to-day decisions that confront an enterprise.

Although much of the information provided by the managerial accounting system is financial, there is a strong trend toward the presentation of substantial nonfinancial data as well. Managerial accountants supply all kinds of information to management and act as strategic business partners in support of management's role in decision making and managing the organization's activities. As we will see in subsequent chapters, contemporary managerial accounting systems are focusing more and more on the activities that occur on all levels of the organization. Measuring, managing, and continuously improving operational activities are critical to an organization's success.

To illustrate the objectives of managerial accounting activity, let us continue with the example of Disney's Animal Kingdom.

Providing Information for Decision Making and Planning, and Proactively Participating as Part of the Management Team in the Decision-Making and Planning Processes

For virtually all major decisions, Disney's management team would rely largely on managerial accounting information. For example, the *decision* to establish the new theme park would be influenced heavily by estimates of the costs of building the Animal Kingdom and maintaining it throughout its life. The theme park's managers also would rely on managerial accounting data in formulating plans for the park's operations. Prominent in those *plans* would be a budget detailing the projected revenues and costs of providing entertainment.

While Disney's top management contemplated its decision about the theme park, the company's managerial accountants could not simply gather information and then sit on the sidelines. The managerial accountants were key participants in the management team as decisions were made and plans formulated for the theme park's operations.

> "What we're seeing is less transactional and more decision support type of work. More analytical, more . . . option analysis. Looking at the whole spectrum of options in helping management make decisions." (1d)
>
> **Boeing**

Assisting Managers in Directing and Controlling Operational Activities Directing and controlling day-to-day operations requires a variety of data about the process of providing entertainment services. For example, in *directing* operational activities, the park's management team would need data about customer food-service demand patterns in order to make sure appropriate staffing was provided in the theme park's various food venues. In *controlling* operations, management would compare actual costs incurred with those specified in the budget.

Managerial accounting information often assists management through its **attention-directing function.** Managerial accounting reports rarely solve a decision problem. However, managerial accounting information often directs managers' attention to an issue that requires their skills. To illustrate, suppose Disney's Animal Kingdom incurred electricity costs that significantly exceeded the budget. This fact does not explain why the budget was exceeded, nor does it tell management what action to take, but it does direct management's attention to the situation. Suppose that upon further investigation, the accounting records reveal that the local electric rates have increased substantially. This information will help management in framing the decision problem. Should steps be taken to conserve electricity? Should the park's hours be curtailed? Perhaps management should consider switching to a lower-cost method of air conditioning.

Motivating Managers and Other Employees toward the Organization's Goals Organizations have goals. However, organizations comprise people who have goals of their own. The goals of individuals are diverse, and they do not always match those of the organization. A key purpose of managerial accounting is to motivate managers and other employees to direct their efforts toward achieving the organization's goals. One means of achieving this purpose is through budgeting. In establishing a budget for Disney's Animal Kingdom, top management indicates how resources are to be allocated and what activities are to be emphasized. When actual operations do not conform to the budget, the theme park's managers will be asked to explain the reasons for the deviation.

One way in which employees can be motivated toward the organization's goals is through *empowerment*. Employee **empowerment** is the concept of encouraging and authorizing workers to take the initiative to improve operations, reduce costs, and improve product quality and customer service. At The Walt Disney Company's theme parks, for example, employees are routinely asked for suggestions about ways to improve service to the parks' millions of visitors.

Measuring the Performance of Activities, Subunits, Managers, and Other Employees within the Organization One means of motivating people toward the organization's goals is to measure their performance in achieving those goals. Such measurements then can be used as the basis for rewarding performance through positive feedback, promotions, and pay raises. For example, most large corporations compensate their executives, in part, on the basis of the profit achieved by the subunits they manage. In other companies, executives are rewarded on the basis of operational measures, such as product quality, sales, or on-time delivery. At Disney's Animal Kingdom, for example, management could be rewarded, in part, on the basis of growth in attendance at the theme park.

In addition to measuring the performance of people, the managerial accounting system measures the performance of an organization's subunits, such as divisions, product lines, geographical territories, and departments. These measurements help the subunits' managers obtain the highest possible performance level in their units. Such measurements also help top management decide whether a particular subunit is a viable economic investment. For example, it may turn out that a particular attraction at Disney's Animal Kingdom is too costly an activity to continue, despite the efforts of a skilled management team.

> "You want to be on the team. You want to be the business consultant. You want to be thought of as a value-adding department versus just someone who closes the books." (1e)
>
> **Qwest** (formerly US West)

Assessing the Organization's Competitive Position, and Working with Other Managers to Ensure the Organization's Long-Run Competitiveness in Its Industry Nowadays the business environment is changing very rapidly. These changes are reflected in global competition, rapidly advancing technology, and improved communication systems, such as the Internet. The activities that make an enterprise successful today may no longer be sufficient next year. A crucial role of managerial accounting is to continually assess how an organization stacks up against the competition, with an eye toward continuously improving. Among the questions asked in assessing an organization's competitive position are the following:

- How well is the organization doing in its internal operations and business processes?
- How well is the organization doing in the eyes of its customers? Are their needs being served as well as possible?
- How well is the organization doing from the standpoint of innovation, learning, and continuously improving operations? Is the organization a trendsetter that embraces new products, new services, and new technology? Or is it falling behind?
- How well is the organization doing financially? Is the enterprise viable as a continuing entity?

The Balanced Scorecard

The questions listed in the preceding section are so important for any organization's management to address, that they have been organized into a management framework called the *balanced scorecard,* which is depicted in Exhibit 1–1 for The Walt Disney

Exhibit 1–1
Hypothetical Balanced Scorecard for The Walt Disney Company

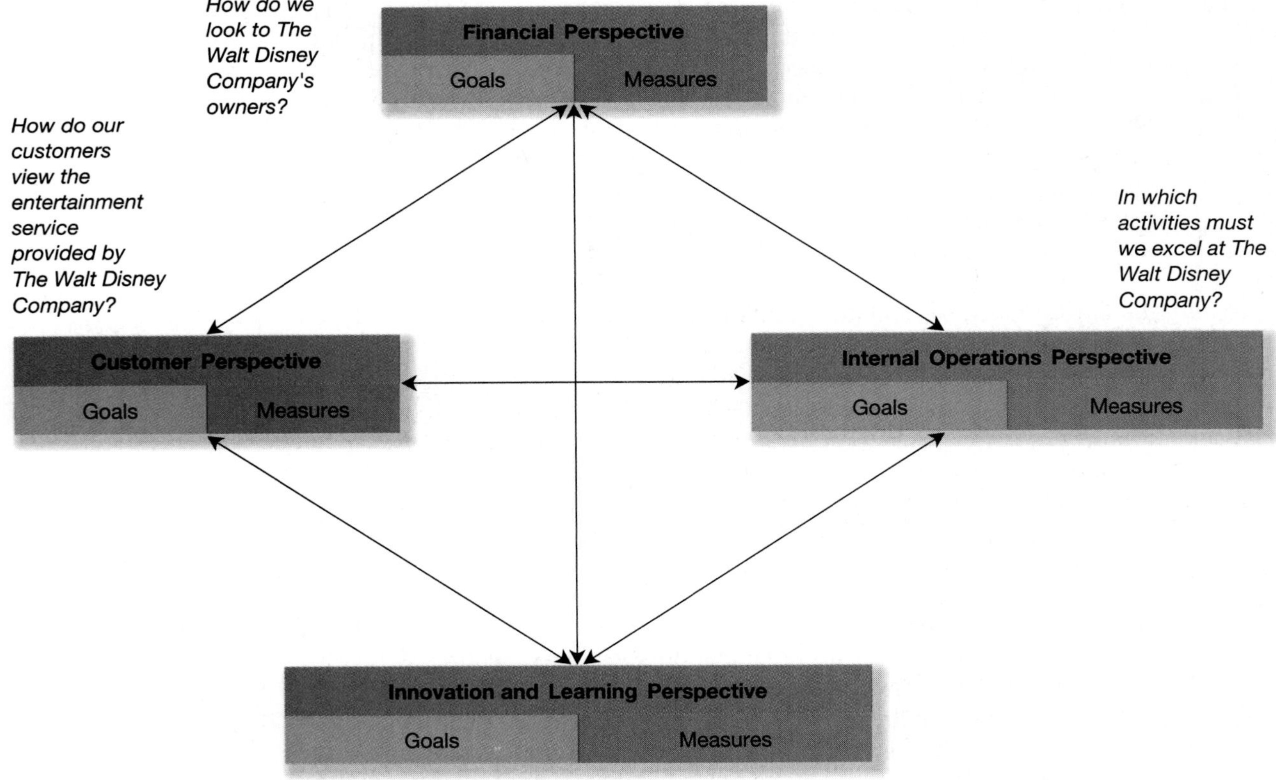
How do we look to The Walt Disney Company's owners?
Financial Perspective
Goals
Measures
How do our customers view the entertainment service provided by The Walt Disney Company?
In which activities must we excel at The Walt Disney Company?
Customer Perspective
Goals
Measures
Internal Operations Perspective
Goals
Measures
Innovation and Learning Perspective
Goals
Measures
How can we continually improve and create value in The Walt Disney Company?

Company.[4] The **balanced scorecard** is a model of business performance evaluation that balances measures of financial performance, internal operations, innovation and learning, and customer satisfaction.

THE BALANCED SCORECARD

According to a recent survey by Bain & Company, approximately 50 percent of Fortune 1000 companies in North America and roughly 40 percent in Europe use some version of the balanced scorecard (often abbreviated as BSC). Among those is Philips Electronics, a worldwide conglomerate with over 250,000 employees in some 150 countries. Philips' top management believes that its BSC helps the management team streamline the complicated process of running a complex international company with diverse product lines and divisions. The BSC tool has helped Philips Electronics focus on factors critical for its business success and align hundreds of indicators that measure their markets, operations, and laboratories. With reference to the four BSC "compass points" in Exhibit 1–1, examples of the performance measures in the scorecard used by each of Philips' business units are as follows:

Financial perspective

- Income from operations
- Working capital
- Cash flow from operations
- Inventory turns

Internal operations perspective

- Reduction in process cycle time
- Number of engineering changes
- Capacity utilization
- Order response time

Customer perspective

- Rank (of Philips) in customer surveys
- Market share
- Repeat order rate
- Customer complaints

Learning and growth perspective (referred to as competence in Philips' scorecard)

- Leadership competence
- Percentage of patent-protected turnover
- Training days per employee
- Quality improvement team participation

"Philips' underlying belief in creating their balanced scorecard is that understanding what drives present performance is the basis for determining how to achieve future results." This is really the key to the BSC concept. By measuring current performance in the organization's critical success areas, management can drive results *now* that will result in financial success in *the future*.[5]

Management Accounting Practice

Philips Electronics

The managerial accounting practices of well-known, real-world organizations are highlighted in these boxes. You'll see how topics in the chapter are actually used.

Actual companies are indicated in blue whenever they are referenced.

"Strategic performance management concerns . . . translating our strategy into action using the balanced scorecard process." (1f)
General Motors Europe

[4]The balanced scorecard concept was developed by Robert S. Kaplan and David D. Norton. See Robert S. Kaplan and David D. Norton, *The Strategy-Focused Organization: How Balanced Scorecard Companies Thrive in the New Business Environment* (Boston: Harvard Business School Press, 2001).

[5]Andra Gumbus and Bridget Lyons, "The Balanced Scorecard at Philips Electronics," *Strategic Finance* 84, no. 5 (November 2002), pp. 45–49.

"[We are] a partner with all of the other functions in the business here. We are an equal partner with our product groups, with the engineering and manufacturing cohorts in making sure this business is a success." (1g)
Caterpillar

If an organization is to remain viable in a changing and ever more competitive business environment, its managers need to continually ask the questions emphasized in the balanced scorecard. The Walt Disney Company is no exception. Disney's management team must be concerned with the cost effectiveness of the company's business processes as well as its entertainment services. Management must continually monitor the needs of its customers and assess their level of satisfaction with the services provided. The company's overall financial strength must also be prominent in management's thinking. Finally, are the company's entertainment attractions "keeping up with the times" in terms of popular culture and technology? Are the company's employees providing the innovation that is critical to the company's future success?

We will hold off on an extensive discussion of the balanced scorecard until Chapter 10. However, let's briefly consider the goals and measures that Disney's top management might consider for the balanced scorecard depicted in Exhibit 1–1. According to the company's website, The Walt Disney Company's "primary financial goals are to maximize earnings and cash flow, and to allocate capital profitably toward growth initiatives that will drive long-term shareholder value." So Disney's *financial perspective* would include such measures as earnings, earnings per share, and cash flow.

Included on the Student Success CD, Topic Tackler offers a helping hand in understanding the most challenging topics in the chapter. It provides help through video clips, PowerPoint slides, practice exercises, and self tests. These topics are indicated by a logo in the text.

Now the question is, for Disney to achieve its *financial goals* in *the future,* what does the company need to be doing *now* in the balanced scorecard's *other three perspectives*? For its *customer perspective,* Disney might use surveys to access customer satisfaction with its theme parks, movies, and products, as well as collect more objective data such as the number of visitors per day at its theme parks, attendance at its feature films, and customer traffic through the many Disney stores. For the *learning and growth perspective,* Disney could focus on new theme parks opened, new theme park attractions, new feature film releases, and new media outlets. For its *internal operations perspective,* Disney could focus on measures such as operating expense per theme park attendee, meals served per attendee, number of visitors at each attraction, rate of employee retention, and so forth.

The key point of the balanced scorecard concept is that by focusing on measures of performance *now* in these three key perspectives, Disney can achieve its financial goals in the *future*. We will come back to the balanced scorecard in Chapter 10.

Topic 1–1

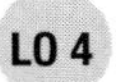

Managerial versus Financial Accounting

LO 4

Explain the major differences between managerial and financial accounting.

Take another look at the major objectives of managerial accounting activity. Notice that the focus in each of these objectives is on *managers*. Thus, the focus of *managerial accounting* is on the needs of managers *within* the organization, rather than interested parties outside the organization.

Financial accounting is the use of accounting information for reporting to parties outside the organization. The annual report distributed by McDonald's Corporation to its stockholders is an example of the output from a financial accounting system. Users of financial accounting information include current and prospective stockholders, lenders, investment analysts, unions, consumer groups, and government agencies.

There are many similarities between managerial accounting information and financial accounting information because they both draw upon data from an organization's basic *accounting system.* This is the system of procedures, personnel, and computers used to accumulate and store financial data in the organization. One part of the overall accounting system is the **cost accounting system,** which accumulates cost data for use in both managerial and financial accounting. For example, production cost data typically are used in helping managers set prices, which is a managerial accounting use. However, production cost data also are used to value inventory on a manufacturer's balance sheet, which is a financial accounting use.

Exhibit 1–2 depicts the relationships among an organization's basic accounting system, cost accounting system, managerial accounting, and financial accounting.

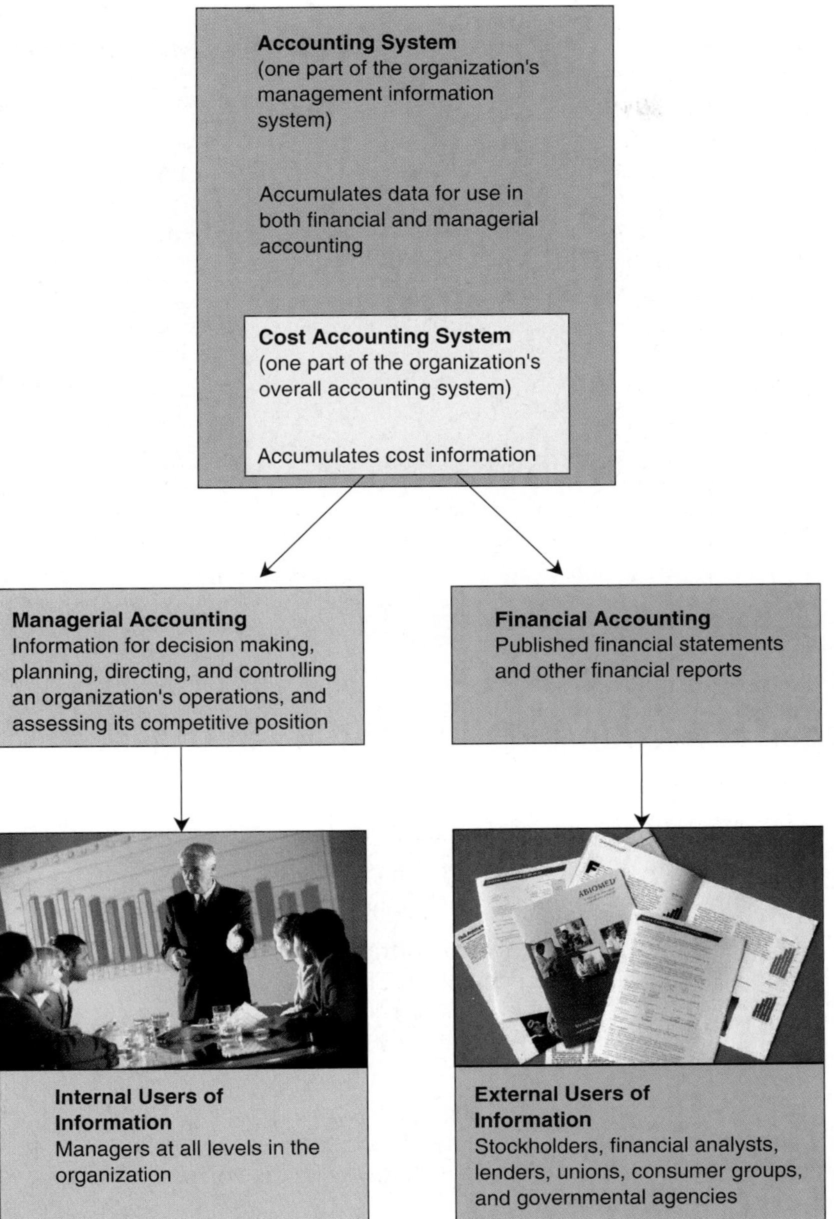

Exhibit 1–2
Managerial Accounting, Financial Accounting, and Cost Accounting

Although similarities do exist between managerial and financial accounting, the differences are even greater. Exhibit 1–3 lists the most important differences.

Managerial Accounting in Different Types of Organizations

All organizations need information, whether they are profit-seeking or nonprofit enterprises and regardless of the activities they pursue. As a result, managerial accounting information is vital in all organizations. Ford, Lands' End, American Airlines, Marriott Hotels, Prudential Insurance, American Express, Cornell University, The United Way, Mayo Clinic, the City of Los Angeles, and the Department of Defense all have managerial accountants who provide information to management. Moreover, the five basic purposes of managerial accounting activity are relevant in each of these organizations.

Exhibit 1–3
Differences between Managerial and Financial Accounting

	Managerial Accounting	**Financial Accounting**
Users of Information	Managers, *within the organization.*	Interested parties, *outside the organization.*
Regulation	*Not required* and *unregulated,* since it is intended only for management.	*Required* and must conform to generally accepted accounting principles. *Regulated* by the Financial Accounting Standards Board, and, to a lesser degree, the Securities and Exchange Commission.
Source of Data	The organization's *basic accounting system, plus various other sources,* such as rates of defective products manufactured, physical quantities of material and labor used in production, occupancy rates in hotels and hospitals, and average take-off delays in airlines.	Almost exclusively drawn from the organization's *basic accounting system,* which accumulates financial information.
Nature of Reports and Procedures	*Reports often focus on subunits* within the organization, such as departments, divisions, geographical regions, or product lines. Based on a combination of historical data, estimates, and projections of future events.	*Reports focus on the enterprise in its entirety.* Based almost exclusively on historical transaction data.

Where Are Managerial Accountants Located in an Organization?

LO 5

Explain where managerial accountants are located in an organization, in terms of formal organization, deployment in cross-functional teams, and physical location.

This question can be interpreted in three different ways:

- Where are managerial accountants *located in an organization chart?*
- How are managerial accountants *deployed?*
- In what *physical location* do managerial accountants actually do their work?

Take a look at Exhibit 1–4, which portrays the organization, deployment, and physical location of managerial accountants in The Walt Disney Company.

Organization Chart

First, let's focus on panel A of the exhibit, which depicts The Walt Disney Company's organization structure.[6] Notice that the company's top management group consists of the board of directors, chairman and chief executive officer (CEO), vice chairman, and chief of corporate operations.

> "[Management accountants] need to be strongly partnered with the line management. They need to be proactive. They need to have a broad sense of business. It's not strictly accounting. It's looking at the full spectrum and range of business." (1h)
> **Boeing**

Line and Staff Positions The other positions in Disney's organization chart are of two types: line positions and staff positions. Managers in **line positions** are *directly* involved in the provision of goods or services. For example, Disney's line positions include the chairman and president of Disney Consumer Products, the chairman and president of Walt Disney Feature Animation, and the chairman and president of Walt Disney Attractions, which is the division responsible for the company's theme parks in Florida, California, and Japan. Also in line positions would be the thousands of managers in the various operating units of the divisions shown in the organization chart. For example, the general manager of Disney's Animal Kingdom, the manager of food and beverage services at the Magic Kingdom, and the manager of the Disney Store in the Carousel Mall in Syracuse, New York, would all be in line positions.

[6]The information for the organization chart comes from a recent annual report for The Walt Disney Company.

Managers in **staff positions** supervise activities that support Disney's overall mission, but they are only *indirectly* involved in operational activities. Disney's staff positions include the general counsel, the executive VP for government relations, and the chief financial officer (CFO), among others.

CFO or Controller In many organizations, the designation given to the top managerial *and* financial accountant is the **chief financial officer (CFO).** In other organizations, this individual is called the **controller** (or sometimes the **comptroller,** particularly in nonprofit or governmental organizations).

LO 6

Describe the roles of an organization's chief financial officer (CFO) or controller, treasurer, and internal auditor.

The CFO or controller usually is responsible for supervising the personnel in the accounting department and for preparing the information and reports used in both managerial and financial accounting. As the organization's chief managerial accountant, the CFO or controller often interprets accounting information for line managers and participates as an integral member of the management team. Most controllers are involved in planning and decision making at all levels and across all functional areas of the enterprise. This broad role has enabled many managerial accountants to rise to the top of their organizations. Former accountants have served as top executives in such companies as General Motors, Singer, General Electric, and Fruehauf.

In addition to the CFO or controller for the entire corporation, most companies, including The Walt Disney Company, have divisional controllers. Thus Disney's detailed organization chart would show a controller for ABC, Inc., Disneyland Paris, Walt Disney Studios, and so forth.

Treasurer The **treasurer** typically is responsible for raising capital and safeguarding the organization's assets. In addition, the treasurer is responsible for the organization's assets, the management of its investments, its credit policy, and its insurance coverage.

Internal Auditor Most large corporations and many governmental agencies have an internal auditor. An organization's **internal auditor** is responsible for reviewing the accounting procedures, records, and reports in both the controller's and the treasurer's areas of responsibility. The auditor then expresses an opinion to top management regarding the effectiveness of the organization's accounting system. In some organizations, the internal auditor also makes a broad performance evaluation of middle and lower management.

Cross-Functional Deployment

On a formal organization chart, accountants generally are in a staff capacity, as explained in the preceding section. However, managerial accountants are increasingly being *deployed* in cross-functional management teams. Managerial accountants work with executives from top management, marketing and sales personnel, design engineers, operations managers, legal experts, quality-control personnel, and virtually every other specialized type of employee in an organization. Managerial teams are formed to make decisions, engage in planning exercises, or address operational problems from many perspectives. Since financial and other managerial accounting issues often are critically important in addressing business problems, managerial accountants routinely play a major role in these cross-functional teams. Panel B of Exhibit 1–4 depicts several plausible cross-functional teams formed to address a variety of hypothetical business problems at The Walt Disney Company. Notice that each of these teams pulls together individuals from a variety of specialties, such as marketing, operations, general management, customer relations, and the general counsel's office (legal issues). Given Disney's overall business strategy, creative talent is almost always present in these cross-functional teams; moreover, managerial accountants play an important role as well.

"Actually, most of the people . . . are decentralized and actually are co-located with the people that they support. That's our approach and we're moving more and more toward that and less and less toward a central group that provides information." (1i)

Boeing

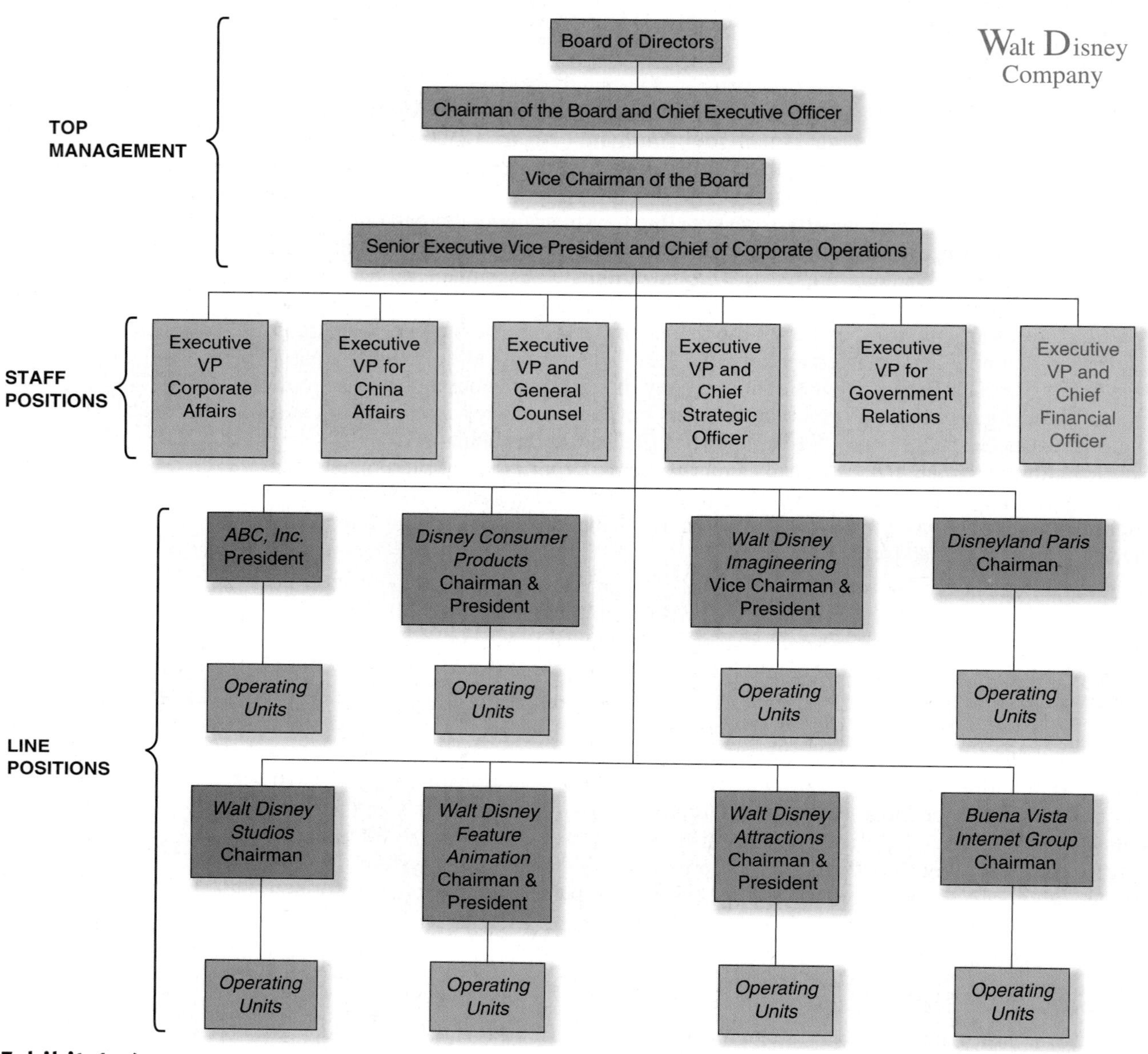

Exhibit 1–4
Managerial Accountants in The Walt Disney Company

Physical Location

Finally, where do managerial accountants actually do their work? The answer is "just about everywhere." As Panel C of Exhibit 1–4 highlights, managerial accountants are not sequestered in some remote corner of the business. To the contrary, they are located in every part of an enterprise, from corporate headquarters to the locations where goods and services are being produced. At Disney, for example, managerial accountants would be present on location when a feature film is being produced, near the ABC news room when decisions are made about deploying journalistic resources, and in the various Disney hotels, such as the Disney Ambassador Hotel in Tokyo.

B. Deployment of Managerial Accountants in Cross-Functional Management Teams

Hypothetical Planning Team for Disney's Animal Kingdom

Marketing Manager, Walt Disney Attractions	Creative Talent, Walt Disney Imagineering	Operations Manager, Disney's Magic Kingdom	Managerial Accountants, Walt Disney Attractions and The Magic Kingdom

Hypothetical Planning Team for New Attractions at California's Disneyland Resort

Assistant General Manager, Disneyland	Operations Manager, Disneyland	Manager of Customer Relations, Magic Kingdom	Creative Talent, Walt Disney Imagineering	Managerial Accountants, Walt Disney Attractions and Disneyland

Hypothetical Decision Making Team for a New Line of Disney Products to Be Sold at Disney Stores

Marketing Manager, Disney Consumer Products	Operations Manager, Disney Consumer Products	Creative Talent, Walt Disney Imagineering	Marketing Personnel, Buena Vista Internet Group	Managerial Accountants, Disney Consumer Products

Hypothetical Decision Making Team for New Hotel to Be Built Near the Tokyo Disneyland Resort

Assistant General Manager, Tokyo Disneyland	Assistant General Manager for Disney Hotel near Magic Kingdom	Creative Talent, Walt Disney Imagineering	Staff Lawyers, General Counsel's Office	Managerial Accountants, Walt Disney Attractions and Tokyo Disneyland

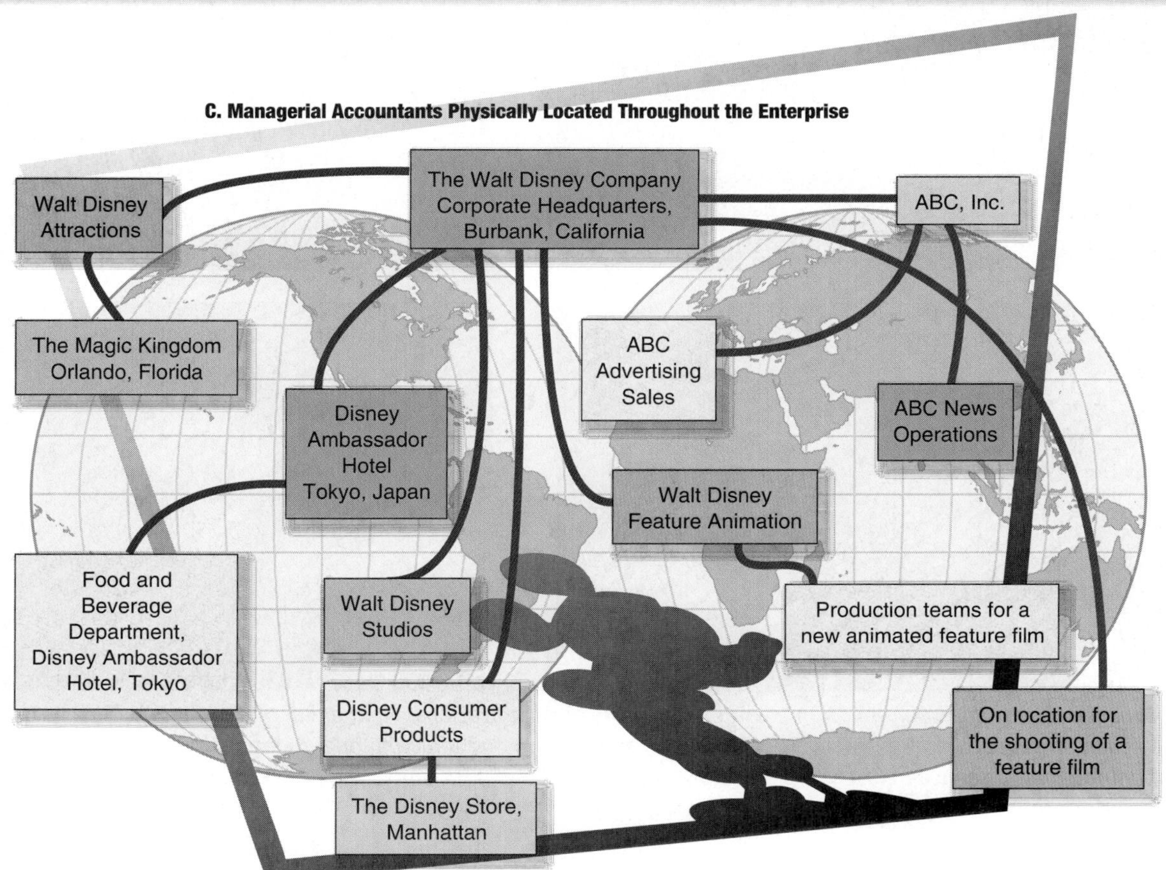

Major Themes in Managerial Accounting

LO 7

Briefly describe some of the major contemporary themes in managerial accounting.

Several major themes influence virtually all aspects of managerial accounting. We will briefly introduce these themes now, and they will be apparent throughout the text.

Information and Incentives

The need for information is the driving force behind managerial accounting. However, managerial accounting information often serves two functions: a *decision-facilitating* function and a *decision-influencing* function. Information usually is supplied to a decision maker to assist that manager in choosing an alternative. Often, that information is also intended to influence the manager's decision.

To illustrate, let us consider The Walt Disney Company's annual budget. Although the budget is prepared under the direction of the CFO, it must be approved by the chairman of the board and CEO and, ultimately, by the board of directors. As part of the budget approval process, the CEO and the board of directors will make important decisions that determine how the company's resources will be allocated. Throughout the year, the decisions of management will be facilitated by the information contained in the budget. Management decisions also will be influenced by the budget, since at year-end actual expenditures will be compared with the budgeted amounts. Explanations will then be requested for any significant deviations.

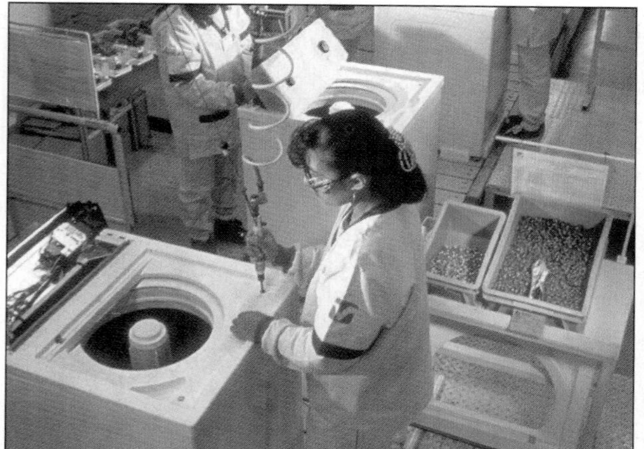

Managerial accounting information is vital in all types of organizations. Managerial accountants act as strategic business partners in support of management's roles in decision making and directing operational activities. Pictured here are a manufacturer, a service-industry firm, a retailer, and a governmental unit. How would managerial accounting be important in each of these organizations?

Behavioral Issues

The reactions of both individuals and groups to managerial accounting information will significantly affect the course of events in an organization. How will the general manager of Disney's Animal Kingdom react to a budget? How will data regarding the cost of providing entertainment services affect the way the theme park's management prices those services? How much detail should be included in the quarterly accounting reports to the general manager? If too much detail is provided, will the manager be overloaded with information and distracted from the main points?

All of these questions involve the behavioral tendencies of people and their cognitive limitations in using information. The better a managerial accountant's understanding of human behavior is, the more effective he or she will be as a provider of information.

Costs and Benefits

Information is a commodity, much like wheat or corn. Like other goods, information can be produced, purchased, and consumed. It can be of high or low quality, timely or late, appropriate for its intended use or utterly irrelevant. As is true of all goods and services, information entails both costs and benefits. The costs of providing managerial accounting information to the managers in Disney's Animal Kingdom include the cost of compensation for the theme park's controller and Accounting Department personnel, the cost of purchasing and operating computers, and the cost of the time spent by the information users to read, understand, and utilize the information. The benefits include improved decisions, more effective planning, greater efficiency of operations at lower costs, and better direction and control of operations.

Thus, there are both costs and benefits associated with managerial accounting information. The desirability of any particular managerial accounting technique or information must be determined in light of its costs and benefits. We will reinforce this cost-benefit trade-off throughout the text by pointing out areas where managerial accounting information could be improved, but only at too great a cost.

Evolution and Adaptation in Managerial Accounting

LO 7

Briefly describe some of the major contemporary themes in managerial accounting.

Compared to financial accounting, managerial accounting is a young discipline. As a result, managerial accounting concepts and tools are still evolving as new ways are found to provide information that assists management. Moreover, the business environment is changing rapidly. For managerial accounting to be as useful a tool in the future as it has been in the recent past, managerial accounting information must be adapted to reflect those changes. Several changes in the business environment that are especially pertinent to managerial accounting are discussed briefly here. The effect of these changes on various topics in managerial accounting will be explored in subsequent chapters.

E-Business E-commerce, e-business, e-tailing! Our ever-expanding e-vocabulary is testimony to the rapid electronic transformation of the business environment. Most of us have gone online to order a book from Amazon.com, an airline reservation from expedia.com, or possibly a computer from dellcomputer.com. We are all aware of the many dot-com companies that populate the electronic-retailing landscape. We're also aware that these companies appear and often disappear at an alarming pace. Nevertheless, the electronic revolution in the marketplace is here to stay.

Perhaps what we're less aware of, though, is the depth of the e-commerce impact throughout the spectrum of the business environment. Just as we can order books, CDs or clothing online in *consumer-to-business* e-commerce channels, businesses can order raw materials and supplies using *business-to-business* networks. *Supply-chain management,* which encompasses the coordination of order generation, order taking, order fulfillment, and distribution of products and services, is increasingly an electronic, online process.[7] *E-commerce* may be defined as buying and selling over digital media.[8] E-business is a broader concept. In addition to encompassing e-commerce, *e-business* includes the business processes that form the engine for modern business.

How does the e-business phenomenon affect the practice of managerial accounting? This is an evolving story, but just as managerial accountants participate as business partners in decisions about a company's product mix or its investment in robotic equipment, they also are active participants in decisions to go online with a company's business processes. The cost management opportunities presented by e-business are sometimes astounding in magnitude. Michael Dell built Dell Computer Corporation into a computer giant with the simple philosophy of managing the supply chain to minimize inventory and fill customer orders in record time. Moreover, managerial accountants are not only quantifying the cost-management benefits of e-business, they are rapidly moving toward *e-accounting* themselves. Managerial accountants are harnessing the power of online communications to streamline the procedures of managerial accounting. For example, *e-budgeting* is now used by hundreds of companies to quickly and effectively transmit the information needed to construct a budget from far-flung business units around the globe.

E-business is here to stay, and it will affect our lives and our jobs in ways we can't even imagine today.

"The pace of change in technology is becoming much faster, and accounting and finance people are very heavy users of technology, more so than a lot of the other functions." (1j)
Hewlett-Packard

Service versus Manufacturing Firms The service sector occupies a growing role in the United States economy. Moreover, several key service industries have been deregulated by the government. The telecommunications, financial services, and airline industries are among them. As more and more companies provide financial, medical, communication, transportation, consulting, and hospitality services, managerial accounting techniques must be adapted to meet the needs of managers in those industries. The key difference between service and manufacturing firms is that most services are consumed as they are produced. Most services cannot be inventoried like manufactured goods. Service organizations also tend to be more labor-intensive than manufacturing firms. Many of the techniques developed for measuring costs and performance in manufacturing companies have been adapted successfully to service industry firms. Throughout the text, you will notice that roughly two-thirds of the illustrations of managerial accounting techniques involve service industry firms and nonprofit organizations.

Emergence of New Industries Scientific discoveries are opening up whole new industries that were not even contemplated a short time ago. Such discoveries as hybrid automobiles, genetic engineering, and superconductivity have spawned business activities in which managers face new challenges. Managerial accountants also face new challenges as they seek to provide relevant information in these new high-tech industries.

Global Competition "It's a small world!" Although this cliché has been around a long time, it concisely sums up today's business environment. Nowadays the marketplace is truly a global one. A firm is just as likely to be in competition with a company from Japan, Germany, or Korea as from across town. Intense international competition is forcing companies to strive for excellence in product quality and service more than ever before.

Moreover, new economic arrangements and potential trade agreements are constantly in the news, as national economies become more and more intertwined.

---

[7]Ravi Kalakota and Andrew B. Whinston, *Electronic Commerce: A Manager's Guide* (Reading, MA: Addison-Wesley, 1997), p. 287.

[8]Ravi Kalakota and Marcia Robinson, *e-Business: Road Map for Success* (Reading, MA: Addison-Wesley, 1999), p. 4.

Today's marketplace is a global one. Many U.S. firms have operations worldwide, and a vast array of international goods are available in most countries. Pictured here are a Mercedes-Benz dealership in the U.S. and Kellogg's corn flakes on sale in Tokyo, Japan.

Organizations such as the European Union (EU) and the World Trade Organization (WTO), as well as international agreements like the North American Free Trade Agreement (NAFTA), all have the potential to dramatically change international commerce.

A *multinational* company is an organization that has operational subunits, such as manufacturing plants or sales facilities, in two or more countries. Multinational firms face several challenges that do not confront domestic companies. Political systems, accounting rules for external reporting, legal systems, and cultural norms vary widely among countries. Managers of multinationals must be aware of these differences to successfully carry out operations across international boundaries. Income tax systems differ among countries also. In planning international operations, managers of multinationals must take into account the different tax laws and rates in the countries where they do business.

Monetary systems also differ among countries, and multinationals must continually monitor the fluctuating values of foreign currencies. The price at which one country's currency can be converted into that of another country is called an *exchange rate.* For example, on the day this paragraph is being written, it takes $.59 in U.S. dollars to buy one Australian dollar. Yesterday, however, the U.S. -Australia exchange rate was $.58. Thus, the exchange rate can fluctuate daily as various forces shape the world economy. An American planning a vacation in Australia would be sensible to time the trip to take advantage of a favorable U.S.-Australia exchange rate. Managers of multinationals face the same kinds of challenges on a much larger scale as they sign contracts, buy and sell goods, and conduct business operations in many countries.

Focus on the Customer "The customer is always right," a traditional saying in the retail industry, has never been more pertinent. To succeed in this era, businesses of all types must continually focus on their customers. Managers are increasingly aware of their product's value to the customer, which is the customer's perceived difference between the benefits the customer receives and the sacrifice the customer incurs to receive the product. The value of a product or service to the customer is affected by such diverse attributes as product price, quality, functionality, user-friendliness, customer service, warranty, and maintenance costs. In response to this heightened customer focus, managerial accounting systems now often measure various attributes of customer value.

Cross-Functional Teams In years past, managers tended to stick to their own turf. Production managers focused on how best to manufacture a product or produce a service. Marketing managers concentrated on selling the product or service. Design engineers often emphasized engineering elegance rather than designing a product for manufacturability. Managerial accountants provided information for decision making, planning, control, and performance evaluation.

Today a cross-functional approach has replaced this narrow managerial perspective. Cross-functional managerial teams bring together production and operations managers, marketing managers, purchasing and material-handling specialists, design engineers, quality management personnel, and managerial accountants to focus their varied expertise and experience on virtually all management issues. If products are to be designed and manufactured with the customers' needs in mind, a cross-functional approach is crucial. Marketing managers have the best feel for customer needs, and production managers are up on the latest in manufacturing technology. Design engineers know how to build the functionality into a product that customers demand, and purchasing managers can acquire the materials, parts, and services necessary to get the job done. Managerial accounting information is the glue that holds the cross-functional team together. The managerial accountant designs an information system and provides data ranging across all aspects of the organization's internal operations and external environment. Then the managerial accountant works as an integral member of the cross-functional team, interpreting information and analyzing the implications of decision alternatives. Working together, the cross-functional team creates value for the organization by meeting the customer's needs in the most effective manner possible.

Computer-Integrated Manufacturing Over a long period of time, manufacturing processes have evolved from labor-intensive methods to more automated processes, in which most of the work is accomplished by machines. This trend continues today, as *computer-integrated-manufacturing* (or *CIM*) systems become more common. A CIM process is fully automated, with computers controlling the entire production process. In CIM systems, the types of costs incurred by the manufacturer are quite different from those in traditional manufacturing environments.

Product Life Cycles and Diversity One impact of highly automated manufacturing systems has been to enable manufacturers to produce an ever-more diverse set of products. Moreover, the rate at which technology is changing means that the life cycles of most products are becoming shorter. In the computer industry, for example, product models are used only a few years before they are replaced by more powerful versions. To be competitive, manufacturers must keep up with the rapidly changing marketplace. Managers must have timely information about production costs and other product characteristics in order to respond quickly and effectively to the competition.

Time-Based Competition *Response time, lead time, on time*, and *downtime* are among the many time-based phrases that dot the conversations of today's managers. Why are managers so concerned with time? In the global competitive environment, time has become a crucial element in many companies' strategies for success. By reducing the time it takes to develop a new product and getting the product on the market more quickly, a company can gain an important advantage over its competitors. Thus, the *time to market* becomes a critical objective for many companies. Reducing the time elapsed from the new product concept stage to having the product in Wal-Mart requires careful time management at each stage of a product's development. The product must be designed with the customer's needs in mind and with a view toward manufacturability. Delays between product development stages must be reduced or eliminated. The production process must be efficient and product quality must be high. A cross-functional approach to management is crucial in managing the time to market. Once again managerial accounting information is critical for the cross-functional

Management Accounting Practice

Harrah's Casino, DuPont, Bank of America, and Herman Miller Company

THE INTERNET AS A LIFELINE

In a tough economic environment, the Internet can be a lifeline. "Companies in a sales squeeze are looking to the Net as a tool for cutting costs, generating new revenue streams, trimming inventories, and serving customers and employees more efficiently." Here are some examples of how companies are using the Web to their advantage.[9]

Harrah's Casino "For years, casino operator Harrah's has had a database of customers it woos with cheap hotel rooms. Harrah's linked the database to its Web site, allowing customers to go online and book rooms at discount prices based on their past spending habits." *The payoff:* After the terrorist attacks of September 11, 2001, occupancy at Harrah's flagship Las Vegas hotel fell by 25 percent. "The chain sent e-mails with bargain offers, filling 4,000 rooms that otherwise would have stayed empty and bringing the hotel back to near-100 percent occupancy by September 30."

DuPont With the chemical industry in a slump, DuPont needed to cut costs in order to prevent a precipitous drop in earnings. One $15 million initiative streamlined DuPont's purchasing of everything from software to sulphur dioxide. "The project eliminates faxes and purchase orders, moving procurement online, where employees can order goods from suppliers that sell to DuPont at a discount." *The payoff:* The company has cut procurement costs by $200 million—a 5 percent reduction in the program's first year—and expects another $200 million in annual savings in the next year. "Now, a typical order is processed in one day instead of five."

Bank of America "Bank of America was spending nearly $100 million annually on human resources paperwork such as enrollment for its retirement programs. The company moved those programs to the Web. Managers now log on to record promotions and raises. All 140,000 employees can change doctors, monitor retirement accounts, and submit travel expenses online. *The payoff:* The bank is saving with the system. Some processes, such as benefits enrollment, now take just minutes to process because they're online. That's down from months under the old system."

Herman Miller Company "Dealers for office furniture maker Herman Miller had to phone company reps to track orders, get shipping dates, or product information." The company recently completed a million dollar project that links it to its 400 dealers via the Web, giving them easy access to information. "*The payoff:* Dealers say it helps them better serve customers by giving them instant access to order and shipping information without having to call. The company says facilitating access by dealers will encourage them to recommend its products over those of other manufacturers."

management team. Information about the trade-offs between time and cost in all phases of a product's development is particularly important. For example, how much more would it cost to get a new product to market six months earlier? Can these cost increases be reflected in the product's price? How much higher would sales be if our company beats the competition by six more months? The answers to these and similar questions are increasingly important to managers as they are ever more likely to find themselves competing against time.

Information and Communication Technology We are all confronted with the breakneck pace of technological change. Just as we learn how to get the most out of our personal computers or to set up our cell phones, they are replaced by new and better models. It would be hard to overestimate the impact of technological innovation

[9]The information and quotations in this inset are from David Rocks, "The Net as a Lifeline," *Business Week,* October 29, 2001.

on the business environment. Although large mainframe computers still perform certain kinds of tasks, businesses now make heavy use of personal computers. In most offices, virtually every employee has a personal computer for such tasks as word processing, data analysis, report generation, presentation preparation, and communication. These PCs are usually linked together in a network that enables employees to electronically transfer files and reports, share data, and communicate via e-mail. Often called an *intranet*, these networked PCs are invaluable tools in the era of cross-functional management teams. Moreover, these intranets are not confined to the walls of a building, as the World Wide Web or *Internet* allows computer-to-computer interface anywhere in the world.

Managerial accounting analyses that in years past would have to be scheduled on a mainframe computer are now done on PCs using a variety of software products. Spreadsheet programs, such as EXCEL® or LOTUS® 1-2-3®, are in wide use for data analysis.[10] Software packages specifically designed for accounting applications are also widely available. Many businesses are adopting integrated business software packages that handle a broad range of computing needs, such as customer and supplier databases, personnel and payroll functions, production scheduling and management, inventory records, and financial and managerial accounting functions. Among the integrated software packages in wide use are SAP, which stands for Systems Applications and Products in Data Processing, and PeopleSoft. Managerial accountants often play significant roles in selecting software for their organizations or designing in-house software to meet the organization's unique needs.

Other innovations have also served to speed communications and link business parties around the world. Global cellular phone technology now enables voice and e-mail communications from the most remote locations. The global positioning satellite system (GPS) now enables trucking, railroad, shipping, and rental car companies to more easily track vehicles. This virtual explosion in data availability has enabled managerial accounting systems to provide information that would have been impossible to supply only a few years ago.

Just-in-Time Inventory Management In traditional manufacturing settings, inventories of raw materials and parts, partially completed components, and finished goods were kept as a buffer against the possibility of running out of a needed item. However, large buffer inventories consume valuable resources and generate hidden costs. Consequently, many companies have completely changed their approach to production and inventory management. These manufacturers have adopted a strategy for controlling the flow of manufacturing in a multistage production process. In a **just-in-time (JIT) production system,** raw materials and parts are purchased or produced just in time to be used at each stage of the production process. This approach to inventory and production management brings considerable cost savings from reduced inventory levels.

The key to the JIT system is the "pull" approach to controlling manufacturing. To visualize this approach, look at Exhibit 1–5, which displays a simple diagram of a multistage production process. The flow of manufacturing activity is depicted by the solid arrows running across the page from one stage of production to the next. However, the signal that triggers more production activity in each stage comes from the *next* stage of production. These signals, depicted by the dashed-line arrows, run from right to left. We begin with sales at the right-hand side of the exhibit. When sales activity warrants more production of finished goods, the goods are "pulled" from production stage III by sending a signal that more goods are needed. Similarly, when production employees in stage III need more inputs, they send a signal back to stage II. This triggers production activity in stage II. Working our way back to the beginning of the process, purchases of

---

[10]EXCEL® is a registered trademark of Microsoft Corporation; LOTUS® 1-2-3® is a registered trademark of Lotus Development Corporation.

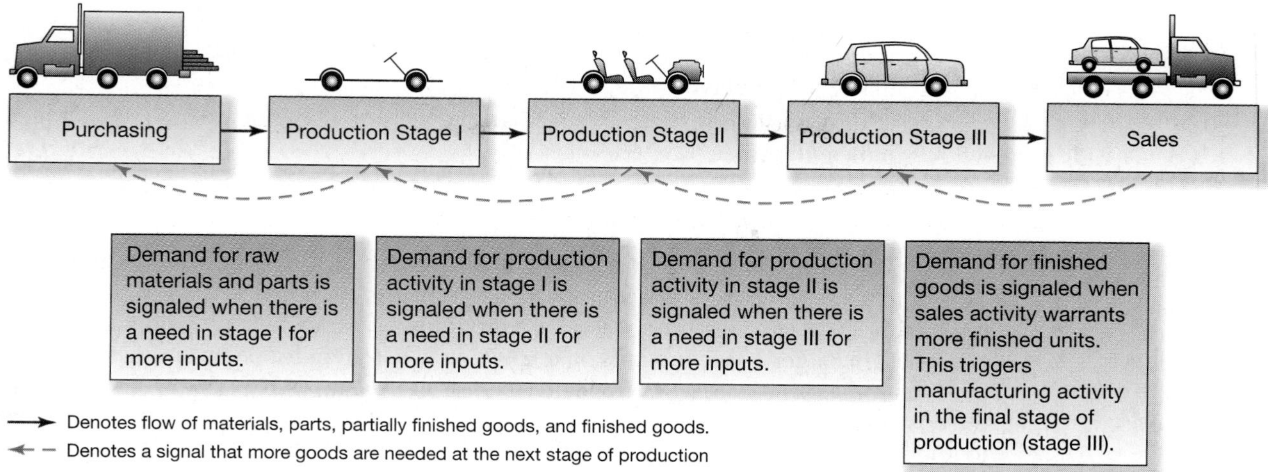
Purchasing
Production Stage I
Production Stage II
Production Stage III
Sales
Demand for raw materials and parts is signaled when there is a need in stage I for more inputs.
Demand for production activity in stage I is signaled when there is a need in stage II for more inputs.
Demand for production activity in stage II is signaled when there is a need in stage III for more inputs.
Demand for finished goods is signaled when sales activity warrants more finished units. This triggers manufacturing activity in the final stage of production (stage III).
Denotes flow of materials, parts, partially finished goods, and finished goods.
Denotes a signal that more goods are needed at the next stage of production

Exhibit 1–5
Just-in-Time (JIT) Production and Inventory Management System

raw materials and parts are triggered by a signal that they are needed in stage I. This pull system of production management, which characterizes the JIT approach, results in a smooth flow of production and significantly reduced inventory levels. The result is considerable cost savings for the manufacturer.

Further details of the JIT production system and other changes in the manufacturing environment will be covered in subsequent chapters. The impact of these changes will be a recurrent theme throughout the book.

Total Quality Management One implication of a just-in-time inventory philosophy is the need to emphasize product quality. If a component is to be produced just in time for the next production stage, it must be "just right" for its intended purpose. One flawed component can shut down the entire production line, entailing considerable cost. Therefore, managerial accountants have become involved increasingly in monitoring product quality and measuring the costs of maintaining quality. This information helps companies maintain programs of **total quality management,** or **TQM.** This refers to the broad set of management and control processes designed to focus the entire organization and all of its employees on providing products or services that do the best possible job of satisfying the customer.

Continuous Improvement Global competition is forcing companies to continuously improve their operations. **Continuous improvement** is the constant effort to eliminate waste, reduce response time, simplify the design of both products and processes, and improve quality and customer service. Managerial accountants are contributing to the continuous improvement programs of many organizations through the development of cost management systems, which are discussed next.

Cost Management Systems

The explosion in technology we are experiencing, coupled with increasing worldwide competition, is forcing managers to produce high-quality goods and services, provide outstanding customer service, and do so at the lowest possible cost. These demands are placing ever-greater requirements on the information provided by managerial accounting systems. Many companies have moved away from a historical cost accounting perspective and toward a proactive *cost management* perspective. A **cost management system** is a management planning and control system with the following objectives.

- To measure the cost of the resources consumed in performing the organization's significant *activities.*

- To identify and eliminate **non-value-added costs.** These are the costs of *activities* that can be eliminated with no deterioration of product quality, performance, or perceived value.
- To determine the efficiency and effectiveness of all major *activities* performed in the enterprise.
- To identify and evaluate new *activities* that can improve the future performance of the organization.

Notice the emphasis of a cost management system on the organization's activities. This emphasis, sometimes called **activity accounting,** is crucial to the goal of producing quality goods and services at the lowest possible cost. In keeping with the focus on activities, managerial accountants have developed a system for determining the cost of producing goods or services called **activity-based costing (ABC).** In an ABC system, the costs of the organization's significant activities are accumulated and then assigned to goods or services in accordance with how the activities are used in the production of those goods and services. An ABC system helps management to understand the causal linkages between activities and costs.

Using an activity-based costing system to improve the operations of an organization is called **activity-based management** or **ABM.** We will have considerably more to say about activity-based costing, activity-based management, and the role of cost management systems throughout the text.

Strategic Cost Management and the Value Chain

LO 7

Briefly describe some of the major contemporary themes in managerial accounting.

How are the goods and services that we all consume created? Usually many activities are involved in securing basic raw materials and turning them into valuable products or services. The set of linked, value-creating activities, ranging from securing basic raw materials and energy to the ultimate delivery of products and services, is called the **value chain.** Although there may be only one organization involved in a particular value chain, usually there are many. For example, the Mayo Clinic's value chain would include not only the hospital but also the suppliers of pharmaceutical products and medical supplies, the manufacturers of diagnostic equipment, the private-practice physicians whose patients use the Mayo Clinic, and the ambulance services that transport patients to the hospital. The major steps in the value chain of a manufacturing firm are depicted in Exhibit 1–6.

In order for any organization to most effectively achieve its goals, it is important for its managers to understand the *entire* value chain in which their organization participates. This understanding can help managers ask, and answer, important questions about their organization's strategy. Should the company concentrate on only a narrow link in the value chain, such as manufacturing and assembly? Or should it expand its operational scope to include securing the raw materials or distributing the final product to end users? Are there opportunities to form beneficial linkages with suppliers, which come earlier in the value chain? Or with customers?

These questions involve fundamental, strategic issues about how an organization can best meet its goals. Although many factors affect such decisions, one important factor concerns the costs incurred in creating value in each link in the value chain. In order for a company to achieve a sustainable competitive advantage, it must either (1) perform one or more activities in the value chain at the same quality level as its competitors, but at a lower cost, or (2) perform its value chain activities at a higher quality level than its competitors, but at no greater cost. Understanding the value chain, and the factors that cause costs to be incurred in each activity in the value chain, is a crucial step in the development of a firm's strategy. These cost-causing factors are called **cost drivers,** and we will have much more to say about them throughout the text. The overall recognition of the importance of cost relationships among the activities in the value chain, and the

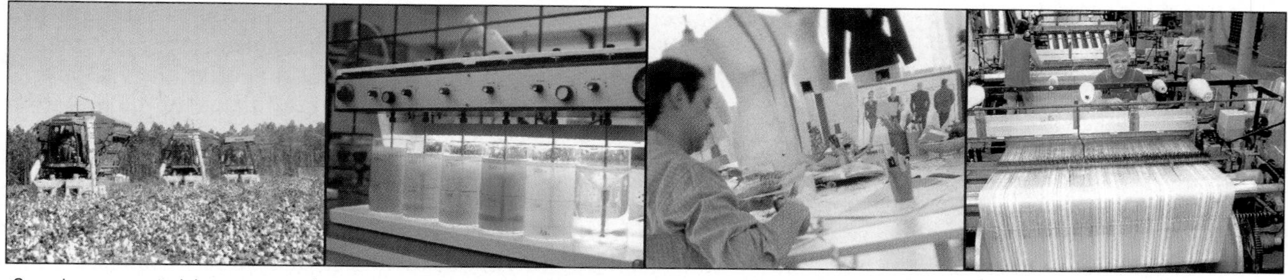
Securing raw materials, energy, and other resources — Research and development — Product design — Production

Marketing — Distribution — Customer service

Exhibit 1–6
Manufacturer's Value Chain

Gap's value chain consists of a myriad of activities, from securing raw materials through distribution and customer service.

process of managing those cost relationships to the firm's advantage, are called **strategic cost management.** Issues in strategic cost management will arise in a variety of contexts as we pursue our study of managerial accounting.

Theory of Constraints Along with a value-chain analysis, managers should carefully examine the chain of linked activities with a view toward identifying the constraints that prevent their organization from reaching a higher level of achievement. Sometimes called the **theory of constraints,** this approach seeks to find the most cost-effective ways to alleviate an organization's most limiting constraints. When binding constraints are relaxed, the organization can reach a higher level of goal attainment. For example, a sequential manufacturing process may include a *bottleneck operation,* which slows down production. By expanding the capacity of a single machine, which is causing the bottleneck, the entire manufacturing process's output may be dramatically increased.

The Ethical Climate of Business and the Role of the Accountant

LO 8

Understand the ethical responsibilities of a managerial accountant.

Topic 1–2

Who among us is not shocked and dismayed by the seemingly endless stream of corporate scandals that we have experienced over the past few years. The headlines keep on coming—Enron, Arthur Andersen, Worldcom, AOL, Global Crossing, Rite Aid, Tyco, Xerox, KPMG, Conseco—and the list goes on. Many of the cases involve mismanagement, some are characterized by alleged ethical lapses, and in some instances there is alleged criminal behavior. Who is to blame? According to most observers, there is plenty of blame to go around: greedy corporate executives, managers who make overreaching business deals, lack of oversight by various companies' boards of directors (particularly the boards' audit committees), shoddy work by external auditors, lack of sufficient probing by Wall Street analysts and the financial press, and some accountants who have been all too willing to push the envelope on aggressive accounting to (or beyond) the edge. Billions of dollars have been lost in employee pension funds, several states' investment portfolios, and the private investment accounts of the public. It will no doubt take many years to sort out the mess. Companies have gone bankrupt;

fortunes have been lost; careers have been ruined; and more of the same is yet to come. Some of those involved will likely end up in jail. Several financial executives have filed guilty pleas on felony charges. Six members of the audit subcommittee of Enron's board have resigned. Some observers have wondered if the confidence of the investing public can ever be regained.

One important lesson from these scandals is that not only is unethical behavior in business wrong in a moral sense, but it can also be disastrous from the standpoint of the economy. We cannot have businesspeople lying, stealing, perpetrating frauds, and making up accounting rules as they go without seriously disrupting business. Thus, ethical behavior by businesspeople in general, and accountants in particular, is not a luxury or a discretionary "good thing to do." It is an absolute necessity to the smooth functioning of the economy.

Sorting out the details of the major scandals mentioned above, as well as others, would require a book (or books) in itself and would take us well beyond the subject matter of this text. Most of the purely accounting issues in these cases involve financial accounting (external reporting) rather than managerial accounting (internal reporting). In most companies, however, many of the same individuals are involved in both types of accounting. In the Enron case, for example, which is perhaps the most notorious of all, investigators allege that a massive fraud was perpetrated on the investing public by creating so-called related parties with names like Raptor for the sole purpose of hiding debt and overstating earnings. Yet the same alleged fraud must have been perpetrated on many at Enron itself. Surely not all of the company's thousands of employees knew of these accounting schemes. So ultimately, what may have been largely financial (external) accounting misstatements, almost certainly resulted in misstated managerial (internal) accounting reports as well.

There will no doubt be reforms that come out of this chaos in corporate governance and accounting. For example, Congress has already passed the *Sarbanes-Oxley Act,* which, among other things, establishes the Public Company Accounting Oversight Board (PCAOB) to establish auditing standards and provide for an audit quality review process. The law also limits the types of nonaudit work that auditing firms can do for their audit clients. For many in the accounting profession, the scandals have served as a wake-up call to concentrate more on ethical issues in practicing and teaching accounting.[11] To this end, in this edition, a significant *ethical issue in managerial accounting* will be addressed at the end of most chapters. The goal of these *Focus on Ethics* pieces is to raise the consciousness of students that legitimate ethical issues do arise in the daily practice of managerial accounting.

In the last section of this chapter, we will turn our attention to managerial accounting as a profession. In the context of that discussion, the *Focus on Ethics* piece for this chapter will be a summary of the *Standards of Ethical Conduct for Practitioners of Managerial Accounting and Financial Management.*

Managerial Accounting as a Career

Discuss the professional organizations, certification process, and ethical standards in the field of managerial accounting.

Managerial accountants serve a crucial function in virtually any enterprise. As the providers of information, they are often in touch with the heartbeat of the organization. In most businesses, managerial accountants interact frequently with sales personnel, finance specialists, production people, and managers at all levels. To perform their duties effectively, managerial accountants must be knowledgeable not only in accounting but in the other major business disciplines as well. Moreover, strong oral and written communication skills are becoming increasingly important for success as a managerial accountant.

[11]Andrew J. Felo and Steven A. Solieri, "New Laws, New Challenges: Implications of Sarbanes-Oxley," *Strategic Finance* 84, no. 8 (February 2003), pp. 31–34.

Professional Organizations

To keep up with new developments in their field, managerial accountants often belong to one or more professional organizations. The largest of these is the Institute of Management Accountants (IMA). The IMA publishes two journals entitled *Management Accounting Quarterly* and *Strategic Finance*, and it also has published many research studies on managerial accounting topics. Other professional organizations in which managerial accountants hold membership include the Financial Executives Institute, the American Institute of Certified Public Accountants, the Institute of Internal Auditors, and the American Accounting Association.

The primary professional association for managerial accountants in Canada is the Society of Management Accountants of Canada (La Société des Comptables en Management du Canada). Great Britain's main professional organization is the Institute of Chartered Management Accountants, and Australia's organization is the Institute of Chartered Accountants in Australia. In all, over 75 countries have professional organizations for their practicing accountants.

"You've got to know how to talk to people, express yourself. And that's oral and written. You also have to be able to understand a lot of different areas, not necessarily just accounting. You've got to understand the business itself." (1k)
Qwest

Professional Certification

In keeping with the importance of their role and the specialized knowledge they must have, managerial accountants can earn a professional certification. In the United States, the IMA administers the Certified Management Accountant (CMA) program. The requirements for becoming a **Certified Management Accountant** include meeting specified educational requirements and passing the CMA examination.[12] In Canada, a managerial accountant may be certified as a Registered Industrial Accountant (RIA) by the Society of Management Accountants of Canada. Great Britain and many other countries also have professional certification programs for their managerial accountants.

Professional Ethics

As professionals, managerial accountants have an obligation to themselves, their colleagues, and their organizations to adhere to high standards of ethical conduct. In recognition of this obligation, the IMA has developed the following ethical standards for practitioners of managerial accounting and financial management.[13] Note: *Various problems and cases at the end of each chapter in this text include ethical issues to be resolved. In addressing those issues, readers will need to refer to these ethical standards.*

[12]For information about the CMA program, write to the Institute of Management Accountants, 10 Paragon Drive, Montvale, NJ 07645-0405, or visit their website at imanet.org.

[13]In 1997, the Institute of Management Accountants (IMA) revised its statement of the standards of ethical conduct for practitioners of managerial accounting and financial management. See *Management Accounting* 79, no. 1 (July 1997), pp. 20, 21.

Focus on Ethics

STANDARDS OF ETHICAL CONDUCT FOR PRACTITIONERS OF MANAGERIAL ACCOUNTING AND FINANCIAL MANAGEMENT

Competence Practitioners of managerial accounting and financial management have a responsibility to:

- Maintain an appropriate level of professional competence by ongoing development of their knowledge and skills.
- Perform their professional duties in accordance with relevant laws, regulations, and technical standards.
- Prepare complete and clear reports and recommendations after appropriate analyses of relevant and reliable information.

Confidentiality Practitioners of managerial accounting and financial management have a responsibility to:

- Refrain from disclosing confidential information acquired in the course of their work except when authorized, unless legally obligated to do so.
- Inform subordinates as appropriate regarding the confidentiality of information acquired in the course of their work and monitor their activities to assure the maintenance of that confidentiality.
- Refrain from using or appearing to use confidential information acquired in the course of their work for unethical or illegal advantage either personally or through third parties.

Integrity Practitioners of managerial accounting and financial management have a responsibility to:

- Avoid actual or apparent conflicts of interest and advise all appropriate parties of any potential conflict.
- Refrain from engaging in any activity that would prejudice their ability to carry out their duties ethically.
- Refuse any gift, favor, or hospitality that would influence or appear to influence their actions.
- Refrain from either actively or passively subverting the attainment of the organization's legitimate and ethical objectives.
- Recognize and communicate professional limitations or other constraints that would preclude responsible judgment or successful performance of an activity.
- Communicate unfavorable as well as favorable information and professional judgments or opinions.
- Refrain from engaging in or supporting any activity that would discredit the profession.

Objectivity Practitioners of managerial accounting and financial management have a responsibility to:

- Communicate information fairly and objectively.
- Disclose fully all relevant information that could reasonably be expected to influence an intended user's understanding of the reports, comments, and recommendations presented.

In resolving an ethical problem, the managerial accountant should discuss the situation with his or her immediate supervisor, assuming that individual is not involved in the problem. If the supervisor is involved in the ethical problem, the accountant should discuss the matter with the next higher level of management.

Chapter Summary

All organizations have goals, and their managers need information as they strive to attain those goals. Information is needed for the management functions of decision making, planning, directing operations, and controlling. Managerial accounting is the process of identifying, measuring, analyzing, interpreting, and communicating information in pursuit of an organization's goals. Managerial accounting is an integral part of the management process, and managerial accountants are important strategic partners in an organization's management team.

Managerial accounting is an important part of any organization's management information system. The five objectives of managerial accounting activity are: (1) providing information for decision making and planning, and proactively participating as part of the management team in the decision-making and planning processes; (2) assisting managers in directing and controlling operations; (3) motivating managers and other employees toward the organization's goals; (4) measuring the performance of activities, subunits, managers, and other employees within the organization; and (5) assessing the organization's competitive position and working with other managers to ensure the organization's long-run competitiveness in its industry.

Managerial accounting differs from financial accounting in several ways. The users of managerial accounting information are managers inside the organization. Managerial accounting information is not mandatory, is unregulated, and draws on data from the basic accounting system as well as other data sources. The users of financial accounting information are interested parties outside the organization, such as investors and creditors. Financial accounting information is required for publicly held companies, is regulated by the Financial Accounting Standards Board, and is based almost entirely on historical transaction data.

In a formal organization chart, managerial accountants are in a staff capacity. However, managerial accountants are increasingly being deployed as members of cross-functional teams, which address a variety of managerial decisions and business issues. More than ever before, managerial accountants are physically located throughout an enterprise alongside the managers with whom they work closely.

Managerial accounting continually evolves and adapts as the business environment changes. The growth of international competition and dramatic changes in technology are placing ever-greater demands on the information provided by managerial accounting systems. Many organizations have moved away from a historical cost accounting perspective and toward a proactive cost management perspective. Under this approach, the managerial accountant is part of a cross-functional management team that seeks to create value for the organization by managing resources, activities, and people to achieve the organization's goals.

Managerial accounting is a profession with a certification process and a code of ethical standards. Managerial accountants are highly trained professionals, who can contribute significantly to the success of any enterprise.

Key Terms

For each term's definition refer to the indicated page, or turn to the glossary at the end of the text.

activity accounting, 24
activity-based costing (ABC), 24
activity-based management (ABM), 24
attention-directing function, 7
balanced scorecard, 9
Certified Management Accountant (CMA), 27
chief financial officer (CFO), 13
continuous improvement, 23
controller (or comptroller), 13
cost-accounting system, 10
cost driver, 24
cost management system, 23
empowerment, 7
financial accounting, 10
internal auditor, 13
just-in-time (JIT) production system, 22
line positions, 12
managerial accounting, 4
non-value-added costs, 24
staff positions, 13
strategic cost management, 25
theory of constraints, 25
total quality management (TQM), 23
treasurer, 13
value chain, 24

Review Questions

1–1. According to some estimates, the volume of electronic commerce transactions exceeds $3 trillion. Business-to-business transactions account for almost half of this amount. What changes do you believe are in store for managerial accounting as a result of the explosion in e-commerce?

1–2. List two plausible goals for each of these organizations: Amazon.com, American Red Cross, General Motors, Wal-Mart, the City of Seattle, and Hertz.

1–3. List and define the four basic management activities.

1–4. Give examples of each of the four primary management activities in the context of a national fast-food chain.

1–5. Give examples of how each of the objectives of managerial accounting activity would be important in an airline company.

1–6. List and describe four important differences between managerial and financial accounting.

1–7. Distinguish between cost accounting and managerial accounting.

1–8. Distinguish between line and staff positions. Give two examples of each in a university setting.

1–9. Distinguish between the following two accounting positions: controller and treasurer.

1–10. How could your college or university use the concepts in the balanced scorecard? List two possible performance measures that would be relevant to a college or university, for each of the balanced scorecard's four areas.

1–11. What does the following statement by a managerial accountant at Caterpillar imply about where in the organization the managerial accountants are located? "[We] are a partner with all of the other functions in the business here." (Reference 11 at end of text.)

1–12. What is meant by the following statement? "Managerial accounting often serves an attention-directing role."

1–13. What is the chief difference between manufacturing and service industry firms?

1–14. Define the following terms: just-in-time, computer-integrated manufacturing, cost management system, empowerment, and total quality management.

1–15. Explain the difference between e-business and e-commerce.

1–16. Define and explain the significance of the term *CMA*.

1–17. Briefly explain what is meant by each of the following ethical standards for managerial accountants: competence, confidentiality, integrity, and objectivity.

1–18. What is meant by the term *non-value-added costs*?

1–19. Managerial accounting is an important part of any enterprise's management information system. Name two other information systems that supply information to management.

1–20. Can managerial accounting play an important role in a nonprofit organization? Explain your answer.

1–21. A large manufacturer of electronic machinery stated the following as one of its goals: "The company should become the low-cost producer in its industry." How can managerial accounting help the company achieve this goal?

1–22. What do you think it means to be a professional? In your view, are managerial accountants professionals?

1–23. Name several activities in the value chain of (*a*) a manufacturer of cotton shirts and (*b*) an airline.

1–24. Define the term *strategic cost management.*

Exercises

Exercise 1–25
Objectives of Managerial Accounting Activity
(LO 3, 4)

For each of the following activities, explain which of the objectives of managerial accounting activity is involved. In some cases, several objectives may be involved.

1. Measuring the cost of the inventory of compact disk players on hand in a retail electronics store.
2. Estimating the annual operating cost of a newly proposed branch bank.
3. Measuring the following costs incurred during one month in a hotel owned by a national hospitality-industry firm.
   a. Wages of table-service personnel.
   b. Property taxes.
4. Comparing a hotel's room rate structure, occupancy rate, and restaurant patronage with industry averages.
5. Developing a bonus reward system for the managers of the various offices run by a large travel agency.
6. Comparing the actual and planned cost of a consulting engagement completed by an engineering firm.
7. Determining the cost of manufacturing a tennis racket.

Exercise 1–26
Managerial Accounting and Decision Making
(LO 2, 3)

Give an example of managerial accounting information that could help a manager make each of the following decisions.

1. The production manager in an automobile plant is deciding whether to have routine maintenance performed on a machine weekly or biweekly.
2. The manager of a discount department store is deciding how many security personnel to employ for the purpose of reducing shoplifting.
3. The county board of representatives is deciding whether to build an addition onto the county library.
4. The president of a rental car agency is deciding whether to add luxury cars to the rental car fleet.

Exercise 1–27
Contributions of Managerial Accounting; Use of Internet
(LO 1, 3, 5)

This logo indicates use of the Internet.

Use the Internet to access the website for one of the following companies, or any other company of your choosing.

American Airlines	www.americanair.com
Coca-Cola	www.cocacola.com
Deere and Company	www.deere.com
IBM	www.ibm.com
Lands' End	www.landsend.com

Required: Find the management discussion and analysis portion of the firm's most recent on-line annual report. Then briefly discuss how managerial accounting can contribute to the company's financial goals.

Problems

Problem 1–28
Role of the Division Controller
(LO 4, 6)

The balance logo identifies an ethical issue.
The pen logo indicates a written response is needed.

A division manager is responsible for each of Resolute Electronics Corporation's (REC) divisions. Each division's controller, assigned by the corporate controller's office, manages the division's accounting system and provides analysis of financial information for the division manager. The division manager evaluates the performance of the division controller and makes recommendations for salary increases and promotions. However, the final responsibility for promotion evaluation and salary increases rests with the corporate controller.

Each of REC's divisions is responsible for product design, sales, pricing, operating expenses, and profit. However, corporate management exercises tight control over divisional financial operations. For example, all capital expenditures above a modest amount must be approved by corporate management. The method of financial reporting from the division to corporate headquarters provides further evidence of the degree of financial control. The division manager and the division controller submit to corporate headquarters separate and independent commentary on the financial results of the division. Corporate management states that the division controller is there to provide an independent view of the division's operations, not as a spy.

Required:

1. Discuss the concepts of line and staff activities, using REC as a context for the discussion.
2. The division manager for Resolute Electronics Corporation has a "dual reporting" responsibility. The controller is responsible both to the division manager, who makes recommendations on salary and promotion, *and* to the corporate controller, who has the final say in such matters.
   a. Identify and discuss the factors that make the division controller's role difficult in this type of situation.
   b. Discuss the effect of the dual reporting relationship on the motivation of the division controller.

(CMA, adapted)

Problem 1–29
Managing a Business; Cross-Functional Teams; E-Commerce
(LO 5, 6, 7)

This logo indicates group work.

Jay Maxey retired a few years ago at age 48, courtesy of the numerous stock options he had been granted while president of e-shops.com, an Internet start-up company. He soon moved to Montana to follow his dream of living in the mountains and Big-Sky country. Maxey, always the entrepreneur, began a sporting goods store shortly after relocating. The single store soon grew to a chain of four outlets throughout the sparsely populated state. As Maxey put it, "I can't believe how fast we've expanded. It's basically uncontrolled growth—growth that has occurred in spite of what we've done."

Although business has been profitable, the chain did have its share of problems. Store traffic was somewhat seasonal, with a slowdown occurring as winter approached. Maxey therefore added ski equipment and accessories to his product line. The need to finance required inventories, which seemed to be bulging, left cash balances at very low levels, occasionally giving rise to short-term bank loans.

Part of Maxey's operation focused on canoe building and white-water rafting trips. Reports from the company's financial accounting system seemed to indicate that these operations were losing money because of increasing costs, although Maxey could not be sure. "The traditional income statement is not too useful in assessing the problem," he noted. "Also, my gut feeling is that we are not dealing with the best suppliers in terms of quality of goods, delivery reliability, and prices." Additional complications were caused by an increasingly competitive marketplace, with many former customers now buying merchandise and booking river excursions via the Internet, through catalogs received in the mail, or through businesses that advertised heavily in outdoor magazines.

Maxey's background is marketing, and he appeared somewhat puzzled on how to proceed. The company's chief financial officer (CFO) would be an obvious asset in terms of addressing these problems. Unfortunately, she knew her numbers but lacked key knowledge of general business operations. The same could be said for other executives who managed somewhat in "silos," becoming experts in a narrow facet of the company but, in general, lacking a big-picture outlook for the firm.

Required:

1. As a group, discuss how the CFO and managerial accounting could assist Maxey in addressing the company's problems.
2. Would a cross-functional team be useful here? Briefly discuss.
3. Does e-commerce appear to be a viable option for the firm? Explain, citing the difference between business-to-consumer and business-to-business channels. Which of the two channels, if any, would you recommend? Why?

Problem 1–30
Quality Control; Ethical Behavior
(LO 6, 7, 8, 9)

Stereo Technology, Inc. manufactures printed circuits for stereo amplifiers. A common product defect is a "drift" caused by failure to maintain precise heat levels during the production process. Rejects from the 100 percent testing program can be reworked to acceptable levels if the defect is drift. However, in a recent analysis of customer complaints, Marie Allen, the assistant controller, and the quality control engineer determined that normal rework does not bring the circuits up to standard. Sampling showed that about half of the reworked circuits will fail after extended amplifier operation. The incidence of failure in the reworked circuits is projected to be about 10 percent over five years.

Unfortunately, there is no way to determine which reworked circuits will fail, because testing will not detect the problem. The rework process could be changed to correct the problem, but the cost-benefit analysis for the suggested change indicates that it is not economically feasible. Stereo Technology's marketing analyst has indicated that this problem will have a significant impact on the company's reputation and customer satisfaction. Consequently, the board of directors would interpret this problem as having serious negative implications for the company's profitability.

Allen included the circuit failure and rework problem in her report prepared for the upcoming quarterly meeting of the board of directors. Due to the potential adverse economic impact, Allen followed a long-standing practice of highlighting this information. After reviewing the reports to be presented, the plant manager and his staff complained to the controller that he should control his people better. "We can't upset the board with this kind of material. Tell Allen to tone that down. Maybe we can get it by the board in this meeting and have some time to work on it. People who buy those cheap systems and play them that loud shouldn't expect them to last forever."

The controller called Allen into his office and said, "Marie, you'll have to bury this one. The probable failure of reworks can be mentioned briefly in the oral presentation, but it should not be mentioned or highlighted in the advance material mailed to the board."

Allen feels strongly that the board will be misinformed on a potentially serious loss of income if she follows the controller's orders. Allen discussed the problem with the quality control engineer, who simply remarked, "That's your problem, Marie."

Required:

1. Discuss the ethical considerations that Marie Allen should recognize in deciding how to proceed.
2. Explain what ethical responsibilities should be accepted by: (*a*) the controller, (*b*) the quality control engineer, and (*c*) the plant manager.
3. What should Marie Allen do? Explain your answer.

(CMA, adapted)

Problem 1–31
Balanced Scorecard
(LO 3, 7)

Angella Lopez, a consultant with Deloitte & Young, has just begun an engagement at Olympic Airways, which is based in Seattle. The company has fallen on hard times of late despite record profits for the rest of the airline industry. Management is somewhat set in its ways and could probably use some "new blood," as the most recent hire to the firm's executive team was 12 years ago.

In Lopez's first meeting with the team, Olympic's chief executive officer commented that "all that mattered in this industry were load factors—the percentage of seats sold on scheduled flights. If load factors were adequate, everything else would take care of itself." Lopez noted that while this measure was important, other, broader facets of operation were significant as well. She asked if any of the management team had heard of the balanced scorecard, and received dead silence as a response.

Based on her experiences with other engagements, including two that involved airlines, Lopez was convinced that the balanced scorecard could provide benefits in helping to solve Olympic's woes. After a presentation about the philosophy of the balanced scorecard, Olympic's management team accepted her idea, feeling that a shift in operating philosophy was needed for survival.

Required:

1. What is a balanced scorecard, and what are its typical key elements?
2. Lopez wants to assemble a committee to prepare the airline's balanced scorecard. List several of the company's functional areas (e.g., marketing) that should be represented on the committee.
3. Identify a number of measures to evaluate the key elements that you specified in requirement (1). Measures would include items such as load factors, number of passenger complaints, percentage of on-time arrivals, and so forth.
4. Do you see any problems with management's prior focus on only one measure (i.e., load factor)? Briefly explain.

Cases

Case 1–32
Disclosure of Confidential Information; Ethics
(LO 1, 3, 6, 8, 9)

SofTech, Inc. a developer and distributor of business applications software, has been in business for five years. SofTech's sales have increased steadily to the current level of $25 million per year. The company has 250 employees. Jennifer Nolan joined SofTech approximately one year ago as accounting manager. Nolan's duties include supervision of the company's accounting operations and preparation of the company's financial statements. No one has noticed that in the past six months SofTech's sales have ceased to rise and have actually declined in the two most recent months. This unexpected downturn has resulted in cash shortages. Compounding these problems, SofTech has had to delay the introduction of a new product line due to delays in documentation preparation.

SofTech contracts most of its printing requirements to Web Graphic Inc., a small company owned by Rob Borman. Borman has dedicated a major portion of his printing capacity to SofTech's requirements because SofTech's contracts represent approximately 50 percent of Web Graphic's business. Nolan has known Borman for many years; as a matter of fact, she learned of SofTech's need for an accounting manager through Borman.

While preparing SofTech's most recent financial statements, Nolan became concerned about the company's ability to maintain steady payments to its suppliers; she estimated that payments to all vendors, normally made within 30 days, could exceed 75 days. Nolan is particularly concerned about payments to Web Graphic; she knows that SofTech had recently placed a large order with Web Graphic for the printing of the new product documentation, and she knows that Web Graphic will soon be placing an order for the special paper required for SofTech's documentation. Nolan is considering telling Borman about SofTech's cash problems; however, she is aware that a delay in the printing of the documentation would jeopardize SofTech's new product.

Required:

1. As a group, discuss Nolan's ethical responsibilities in this situation.
2. Independent of your answer to requirement (1), assume that Nolan learns that Borman of Web Graphic has decided to postpone the special paper order required for SofTech's printing job; Nolan believes Borman must have heard rumors about SofTech's financial problems from some other source because she has not talked to Borman. Should Nolan tell the appropriate SofTech officials that Borman has postponed the paper order? Explain your answer.
3. Independent of your answers to the first two requirements, assume that Borman has decided to postpone the special paper order because he has learned of SofTech's financial problems from some source other than Nolan. In addition, Nolan realizes that Jim Grason, SofTech's purchasing manager, knows of her friendship with Borman. Now Nolan is concerned that Grason may suspect she told Borman of SofTech's financial problems when Grason finds out Borman has postponed the order. Describe the steps that Nolan should take to resolve this situation.

(CMA, adapted)

Case 1–33
The Ethical Climate in Business
(LO 8, 9)

Choose one of the companies mentioned in the discussion of ethical lapses on page 25. Research what happened by using library resources or the Internet.

Required: As a group, make a presentation to the class, which addresses the following points:

(1) Describe the company's situation prior to the ethical problem. (2) Explain what happened with questionable ethics. (3) Was there any alleged illegal activity? (4) Do you see any implications in the case for the company's managerial accountants? Explain. (5) Were any of the ethical standards listed on pages 27 and 28 violated? Explain.

Current Issues in Managerial Accounting

Issue 1–34
Accounting Scandals; Changing Role of Audit Committee

"How to Fix a Broken System," ***The Wall Street Journal,*** **February 24, 2003, p. R1, Carol Hymowitz; "The Hot Seat: All Eyes Are on the Chairman of the Audit Committee,"** ***The Wall Street Journal,*** **February 24, 2003, p. R4, Joann S. Lublin; "More Work, More Pay,"** ***The Wall Street Journal,*** **February 24, 2003, pp. R4, R5, Joann Lublin.**

Overview

In the wake of several corporate accounting scandals, changes are being proposed in corporate governance and especially the role of the audit committee.

Suggested Discussion Question

As a group, discuss whether you think real, positive changes will be made. Or, as some argue, will things just go back to the old ways of doing business?

Issue 1–35
E-Commerce

"The Masses Have Arrived . . . and E-Commerce Will Never Be the Same," ***The Wall Street Journal,*** **January 27, 2003, p. R8, Michael Totty; "Amazon Boosts Forecasts as Sales Soar,"** ***The Wall Street Journal,*** **January 24, 2003, p. A5, Nick Winfield; "Back from the Dead,"** ***The Wall Street Journal,*** **February 25, 2003, p. D1, Katy McLaughlin.**

Overview

The maturing of e-commerce has tremendous implications for on-line retailers like Amazon.com, as well as traditional retailers like Wal-Mart and Sears.

Suggested Discussion Questions

What do you think the future holds for on-line shopping? Will there be another attempt at expansion into retail areas that were previously unsuccessful on-line?

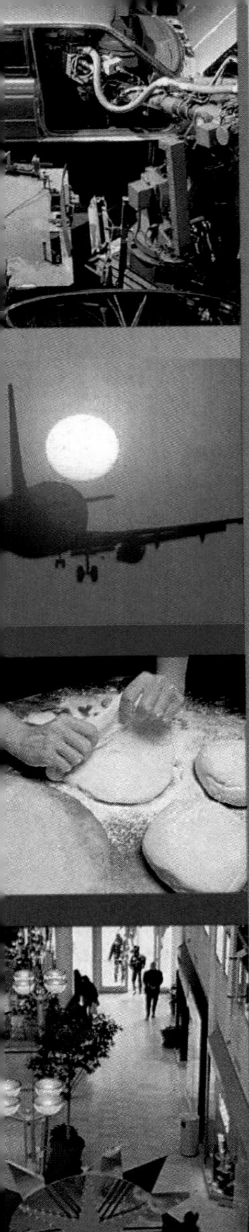

Chapter Two

Basic Cost Management Concepts and Accounting for Mass Customization Operations

After completing this chapter, you should be able to:

1. Explain what is meant by the word "cost."
2. Distinguish among product costs, period costs, and expenses.
3. Describe the role of costs on published financial statements.
4. List five types of manufacturing operations and describe mass customization.
5. Give examples of three types of manufacturing costs.
6. Prepare a schedule of cost of goods manufactured, a schedule of cost of goods sold, and an income statement for a manufacturer.
7. Understand the importance of identifying an organization's cost drivers.
8. Describe the behavior of variable and fixed costs, in total and on a per-unit basis.
9. Distinguish among direct, indirect, controllable, and uncontrollable costs.
10. Define and give examples of an opportunity cost, an out-of-pocket cost, a sunk cost, a differential cost, a marginal cost, and an average cost.

Cometcomp.com

Comet Streaks as Consumers Flock to Web-Based Computer Sales

Dallas, TX—Comet Computer Corporation, known to many on the Internet as cometcomp.com, announced today that it has hit $700 million in sales. This represents phenomenal growth for the upstart company based in Dallas, Texas. According to Comet's founder and CEO, Michelle Valley, "We're shooting for a billion dollars in sales within two years." Chances are Valley's goal will be achieved earlier than that if the past is any indication. Comet has exceeded the expectations of its top management and even the most optimistic computer watchers almost since day one.

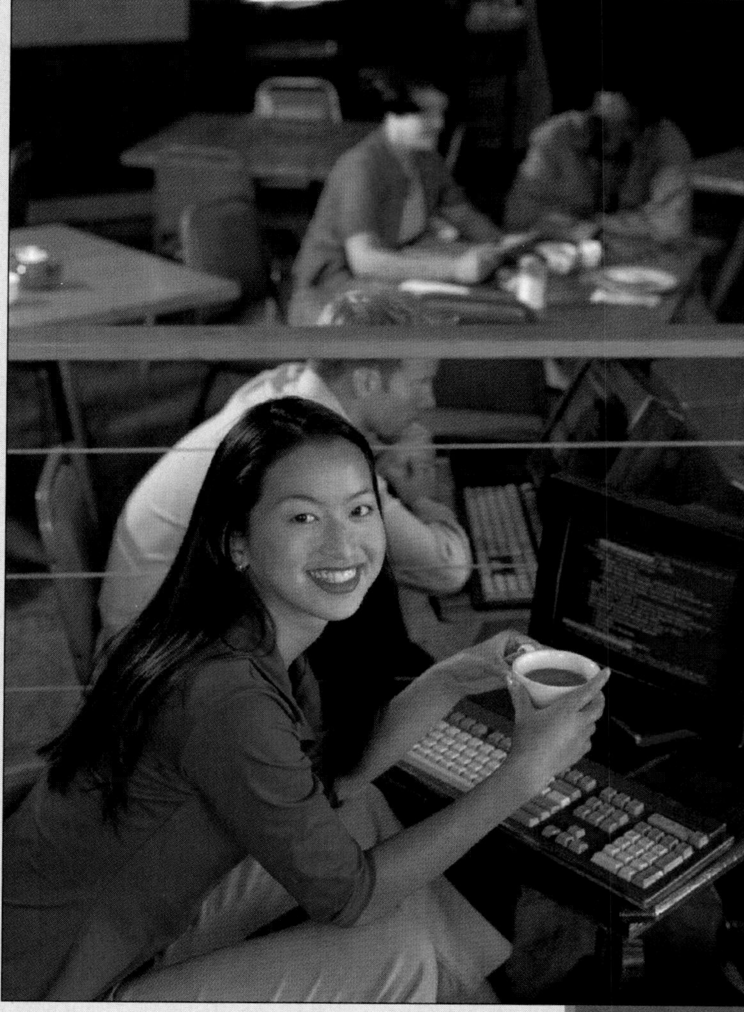

How has Comet achieved such phenomenal success? "It's several things," according to CEO Valley, "but most of all it's the direct model of sales. We interact directly with our customers, which eliminates the middleman, speeds up order fulfillment, and drastically reduces costs." Valley is, of course, referring to the fact that customers order customized computer systems directly from Comet online using the company's website, cometcomp.com. "We're a mass customizer," says Comet's Vice President for Manufacturing Elian Gomez. "We outsource most of the components in a personal computer, and then we assemble systems to customer order in one of our production mods. We fill virtually every customer order within six days," says Gomez, "and we only stock enough commonly used parts to meet that order-fulfillment goal. That means we have very little money tied up in inventory of any kind."

Comet has other things going for it too, though, including a world-class cost management team. "We operate on a team basis almost all the time," says Gomez. "Right now we have a cost driver team working to further identify all of the factors in our process that drive costs. And when we identify a cost driver, we try to determine how costs will behave as the driver changes. For example, if we were able to change the proportion of our web-based sales orders from 90 to 95 percent, what would that do to our selling costs?" "And we also have cross-functional teams in place to address outsourcing issues and cost control and reduction," adds Valley.

"We're continually focusing on costs in one way or another," points out Gomez. "We realize that there are lots of different perspectives on cost, depending on the decision or business issue on the table. And we've got the cost management team to keep us focused on giving our customers the best possible value at the lowest possible cost."

By all indications, this Comet has a bright future.

The process of management involves formulating strategy, planning, control, decision making, and directing operational activities. Managers can perform each of these functions more effectively with managerial accounting information. Much of this information focuses on the costs incurred in the organization. For example, in *formulating its overall strategy,* Southwest Airlines' management team considered the cost savings that result from being a low-cost, no-frills airline. In *planning* Southwest's routes and flight schedules, managers must consider aircraft fuel costs, salaries of flight crews, and airport landing fees. *Controlling* the costs of manufacturing heavy equipment requires that Caterpillar's managerial accountants carefully measure and manage production costs. In *making decisions* about locating a new store, Wal-Mart managers need information about the cost of building, maintaining, equipping, and staffing the store. Finally, to *direct operational activities,* managers in all three of these companies need information about the cost of salaries, utilities, security, and a host of other goods and services.

What Do We Mean by a Cost?

Explain what is meant by the word "cost."

> "We are expected to say, 'Here are the costs, and this is why the costs are what they are, and this is how they compare to other things, and here are some suggestions where we could possibly improve.'" (2a)
> **Caterpillar**

Each of the examples in the preceding paragraph focuses on costs of one type or another. An important first step in studying managerial accounting is to gain an understanding of the various types of costs incurred by organizations and how those costs are actively managed.

At the most basic level, a **cost** may be defined as the sacrifice made, usually measured by the resources given up, to achieve a particular purpose. If we look more carefully, though, we find that the word *cost* can have different meanings depending on the context in which it is used. Cost data that are classified and recorded in a particular way for one purpose may be inappropriate for another use. For example, the costs incurred in producing gasoline last year are important in measuring Mobil's income for the year. However, those costs may not be useful in planning the company's refinery operations for the next year if the cost of oil has changed significantly or if the methods of producing gasoline have improved.

The important point is that different cost concepts and classifications are used for different purposes. Understanding these concepts and classifications enables the managerial accountant to provide appropriate cost data to the managers who need it. The purpose of this chapter is to enable the users of this textbook to gain a firm grasp of the cost terminology used in managerial accounting, which will be used throughout the book.

Product Costs, Period Costs, and Expenses

Distinguish among product costs, period costs, and expenses.

Topic 2–1

An important issue in both managerial and financial accounting is the timing with which the costs of acquiring assets or services are recognized as expenses. An **expense** is defined as the cost incurred when an asset is used up or sold for the purpose of generating revenue. The terms *product cost* and *period cost* are used to describe the timing with which various expenses are recognized.

A **product cost** is a cost assigned to goods that were either purchased or manufactured for resale. The product cost is used to value the inventory of manufactured goods or merchandise until the goods are sold. In the period of the sale, the product costs are recognized as an expense called **cost of goods sold.** The product cost of merchandise inventory acquired by a retailer or wholesaler for resale consists of the purchase cost of the inventory plus any shipping charges. The product cost of manufactured inventory includes all of the costs incurred in its manufacture. For example, the labor cost of a production employee at Texas Instruments is included as a product cost of the calculators manufactured. Exhibit 2–1 illustrates the relationship between product costs and cost-of-goods-sold expense.

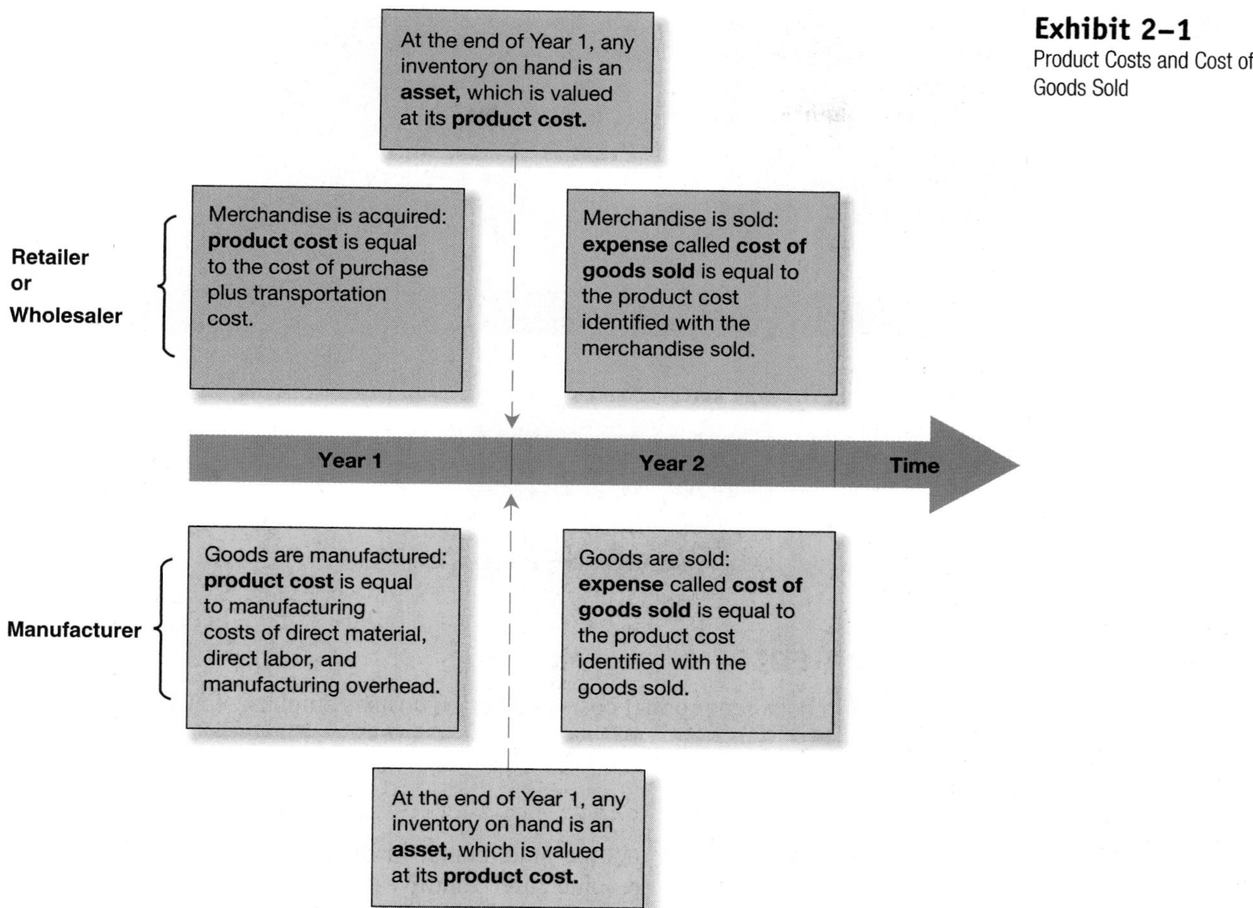

At the end of Year 1, any inventory on hand is an **asset,** which is valued at its **product cost.**
Retailer or Wholesaler
Merchandise is acquired: **product cost** is equal to the cost of purchase plus transportation cost.
Merchandise is sold: **expense** called **cost of goods sold** is equal to the product cost identified with the merchandise sold.
Year 1
Year 2
Time
Manufacturer
Goods are manufactured: **product cost** is equal to manufacturing costs of direct material, direct labor, and manufacturing overhead.
Goods are sold: **expense** called **cost of goods sold** is equal to the product cost identified with the goods sold.
At the end of Year 1, any inventory on hand is an **asset,** which is valued at its **product cost.**

Exhibit 2–1
Product Costs and Cost of Goods Sold

Another term for product cost is **inventoriable cost,** since a product cost is stored as the cost of inventory until the goods are sold. In addition to retailers, wholesalers, and manufacturers, the concept of product cost is relevant to other producers of inventoriable goods. Agricultural firms, lumber companies, and mining firms are examples of nonmanufacturers that produce inventoriable goods. Apples, timber, coal, and other such goods are inventoried at their product cost until the time period during which they are sold.

All costs that are not product costs are called **period costs.** These costs are identified with the period of time in which they are incurred rather than with units of purchased or produced goods. Period costs are recognized as expenses during the time period in which they are incurred. All research and development, selling, and administrative costs are treated as period costs. This is true in manufacturing, retail, and service industry firms.

Research and development costs include all costs of developing new products and services. The costs of running laboratories, building prototypes of new products, and testing new products are all classified as research and development (or R&D) costs. *Selling costs* include salaries, commissions, and travel costs of sales personnel and the costs of advertising and promotion. *Administrative costs* refer to all costs of running the organization as a whole. The salaries of top-management personnel and the costs of the accounting, legal, and public relations activities are examples of administrative costs.

Exhibit 2–2 illustrates the nature of period costs.

Exhibit 2–2
Period Costs

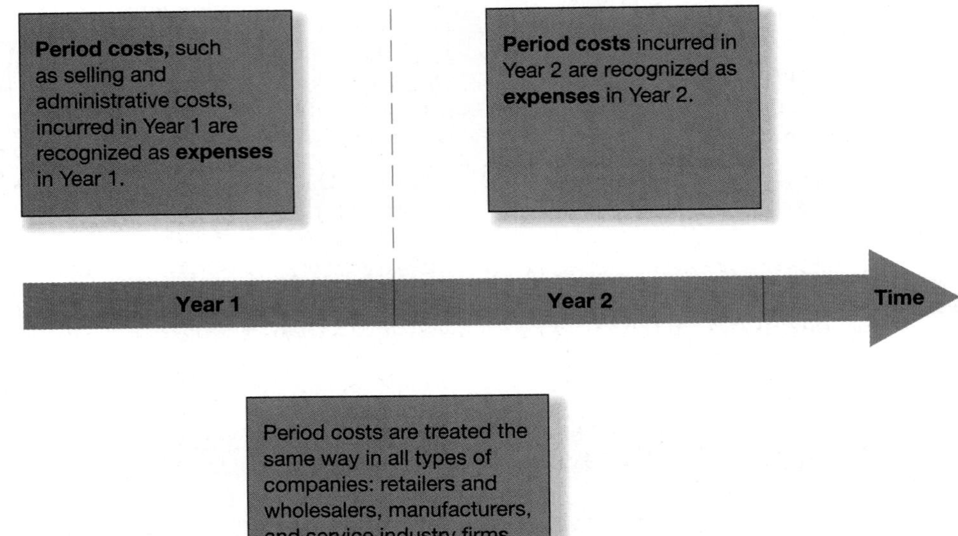
Period costs, such as selling and administrative costs, incurred in Year 1 are recognized as **expenses** in Year 1.
Period costs incurred in Year 2 are recognized as **expenses** in Year 2.
Year 1
Year 2
Time
Period costs are treated the same way in all types of companies: retailers and wholesalers, manufacturers, and service industry firms.

Costs on Financial Statements

LO 3

Describe the role of costs on published financial statements.

The distinction between product costs and period costs is emphasized by examining financial statements from three different types of firms.

Income Statement

Exhibit 2–3 displays recent income statements, in highly summarized form, from Caterpillar, Inc., Wal-Mart Stores, Inc., and Southwest Airlines Company. These companies are from three different industries. Caterpillar is a heavy equipment manufacturer. Wal-Mart Stores is a large retail firm with merchandising operations throughout

Exhibit 2–3
Income Statements from Three Different Industries (all figures in thousands of dollars)

CATERPILLAR®

CATERPILLAR, INC.
Statement of Income for a Recent Year

Value measured by product costs → Less: Cost of goods sold

Sales revenue		$ 20,450,000
Less: Cost of goods sold		14,752,000
Gross profit		$ 5,698,000
Operating costs:		
Selling, general, and administrative expenses	$ 2,567,000	
Research and development expenses	696,000	
Interest expense of financial products	657,000	
Other operating expenses	467,000	
Total operating costs		$ 4,387,000
Operating profit		$ 1,311,000
Less: Other interest expense		285,000
Add: Other income		143,000
Profit before taxes		$ 1,169,000
Less: Provision for income taxes		367,000
Add: Equity in earnings of unconsolidated affiliated companies		3,000
Net income		$ 805,000

(continues)

most of the nation. Representing the service industry is Southwest Airlines, a major airline based in the southwestern United States.

Selling and administrative costs are period costs on all three income statements shown in Exhibit 2–3. For example, Caterpillar lists $2.567 billion of selling, general, and administrative expenses. Travel agency commissions, a selling expense on Southwest Airlines' income statement, amount to $103.014 million.

Exhibit 2–3
(concluded)

WAL-MART STORES, INC.
Statement of Income for a Recent Year

Value measured by product costs →	Sales revenue	$193,295,000
	Less: Cost of goods sold	150,255,000
	Gross profit	$ 43,040,000
	Less: Selling, general, and administrative expenses	31,550,000
	Operating income	$ 11,490,000
	Less: Interest expense	(1,374,000)
	Income before income taxes	$ 10,116,000
	Provision for income taxes	(3,692,000)
	Minority interest	(129,000)
	Net income	$ 6,295,000

SOUTHWEST AIRLINES COMPANY
Statement of Income for a Recent Year

Operating revenue:	
Passenger	$ 5,378,702
Freight	91,270
Other	85,202
Total operating revenue	$ 5,555,174
Less: Operating expenses:	
Salaries, wages, and benefits	$ 1,856,288
Fuel and oil	770,515
Maintenance materials and repairs	397,505
Agency commissions	103,014
Aircraft rentals	192,110
Landing fees and other rentals	311,017
Depreciation	317,831
Other operating expenses	975,772
Total operating expenses	$ 4,924,052
Operating income	$ 631,122
Other expenses (income):	
Interest expense	$ 69,827
Capitalized interest	(20,576)
Interest income	(42,562)
Other (gains) losses, net	(203,226)
Total other expenses, (gains) and losses	$ (196,537)
Income before income taxes	$ 827,659
Provision for income taxes	316,512
Net income	$ 511,147

For Caterpillar, the costs of manufactured inventory are product costs. All costs incurred in manufacturing finished products are stored in inventory until the time period when the products are sold. Then the product costs of the inventory sold become cost of goods sold, an expense on the income statement.

Product costs for Wal-Mart include all costs of acquiring merchandise inventory for resale. These product costs are stored in inventory until the time period during which the merchandise is sold. Then these costs become cost of goods sold.

There are no inventoried product costs at Southwest Airlines. Although this firm does engage in the production of air transportation services, its service output is consumed as soon as it is produced. Service industry firms, such as Southwest Airlines, Chase Manhattan Bank, Sheraton Hotels, Nationwide Insurance, and Burger King, generally refer to the costs of producing services as **operating expenses.** Operating expenses are treated as period costs and are expensed during the period in which they are incurred. Southwest Airlines includes costs such as employee wages, aviation fuel, and aircraft maintenance in operating expenses for the period.

"What we should become in the future is a business partner who helps people understand what the financials are saying and helps them design their businesses." (2b)
Qwest

"Now the accountants are not only the interpreters. They drive management toward the proper response to what the numbers are telling us." (2c)
ITT Automotive

Balance Sheet

Since retailers, wholesalers, and manufacturers sell inventoriable products, their balance sheets are also affected by product costs. Exhibit 2–4 displays the current-assets section from recent balance sheets of Caterpillar and Wal-Mart. Included in the current-assets section of each of these balance sheets is inventory. Manufacturers, such as Caterpillar, have three types of inventory. **Raw-material** inventory includes all materials before they are placed into production. **Work-in-process** inventory refers to manufactured products that are only partially completed at the date when the balance sheet is prepared. **Finished-goods** inventory refers to manufactured goods that are complete and ready for sale. The values of the work-in-process and finished-goods inventories are measured by their product costs.

On the Wal-Mart balance sheet, the cost of acquiring merchandise is listed as the value of the merchandise inventories.

Exhibit 2–4
Partial Balance Sheets for a Manufacturer and a Retailer (all figures in thousands of dollars)

CATERPILLAR®

CATERPILLAR, INC.
Partial Balance Sheet at the End of a Recent Year

	Current assets:	
	Cash and cash equivalents	$ 400,000
	Accounts receivable (net)	8,441,000
Value measured by product costs →	Inventories	2,925,000
	Other current assets	1,634,000
	Total current assets	$13,400,000

WAL-MART STORES, INC.
Partial Balance Sheet at the End of a Recent Year

	Current assets:	
	Cash and cash equivalents	$ 2,054,000
	Receivables (net)	1,768,000
Value measured by product costs →	Inventories	21,442,000
	Other current assets	1,291,000
	Total current assets	$26,555,000

Manufacturing Operations and Manufacturing Costs

List five types of manufacturing operations and describe mass customization.

Although there are tens of thousands of manufacturing firms, their basic production processes can be classified into five generic types. The nature of the manufacturing process can affect the manufacturing costs incurred. Therefore, the management team is in a better position to manage these costs if the relationship of the production process to the types of costs incurred is understood. Exhibit 2–5 defines and describes the five generic manufacturing processes.[1]

We will study the role of managerial accounting and cost management in four of these manufacturing processes. This chapter will focus on a mass customization operation, similar to that used by Dell Computer. Chapter 3 will examine managerial accounting techniques used in job-shop and batch-processing operations. Chapter 4 will focus on the cost accumulation and cost management processes in a continuous-flow manufacturing environment.

"[Management accountants] will be more analytical . . . and more of a partner with the operational side of the business." (2d)
ITT Automotive

Exhibit 2–5
Types of Production Processes

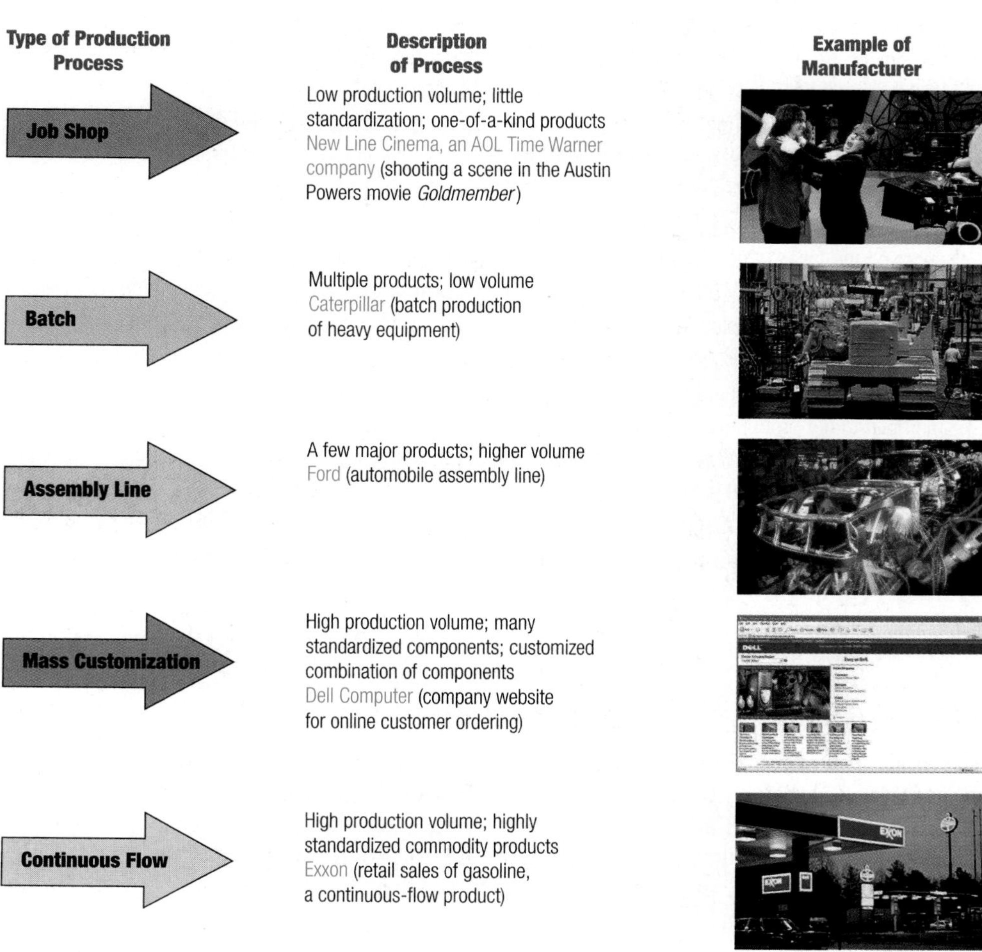

Type of Production Process
Description of Process
Example of Manufacturer
Job Shop
Low production volume; little standardization; one-of-a-kind products
New Line Cinema, an AOL Time Warner company (shooting a scene in the Austin Powers movie Goldmember)
Batch
Multiple products; low volume
Caterpillar (batch production of heavy equipment)
Assembly Line
A few major products; higher volume
Ford (automobile assembly line)
Mass Customization
High production volume; many standardized components; customized combination of components
Dell Computer (company website for online customer ordering)
Continuous Flow
High production volume; highly standardized commodity products
Exxon (retail sales of gasoline, a continuous-flow product)
DELL
EXXON

[1]Based on the well-known and widely used Hayes-Wheelwright production process matrix, with the exception of mass customization, which postdates the Hayes-Wheelwright formulation. See Robert H. Hayes and Steven C. Wheelwright, *Restoring Our Competitive Edge* (New York: John Wiley and Sons), 1984, p. 209.

Management Accounting Practice

Dell Computer

MASS CUSTOMIZATION

"There is no better way to make, sell, and deliver PCs than the way Dell Computer does it, and nobody executes that model better than Dell." The company's machines are made to order and delivered directly to customers, who get the exact machines they want cheaper than they can get them from Dell's competition. "Dell has some 24 facilities in and around Austin and employs more than 18,000 local workers. Dell is improving its earnings and gaining market share even in tough economic times.[2] Nevertheless, Michael Dell, the company's restless founder, is constantly looking for ways to improve the company's operations." In one year alone, Dell has wrung $1 billion out of its costs—half from manufacturing—and Dell executives vowed to cut another $1 billion.

"Visit the Topfer Manufacturing Center in Austin, and it's hard to conceive how Dell could be any more efficient. Workers already scuttle about in the 200,000-square-foot plant like ants on a hot plate. Gathered in cramped six-person 'cells,' they assemble computers from batches of parts that arrive via a computer-directed conveyor system overhead. If a worker encounters a problem, that batch can instantly be shifted to another cell, avoiding the stoppages that plague conventional assembly lines. Dell is constantly tinkering with factory layout and product design to move computers through at a higher velocity. So far they've done extraordinarily well. Dell has increased production by one-third over two years while cutting manufacturing space in half. Workers in the six-person cells assemble 18 units an hour, double the pace of a couple of years ago.

"Can Dell keep it up? The manager of the Topfer factory explains how. He points to places where Dell can shave off a few seconds of assembly time or move completed products out the door a couple of minutes faster. A robot is being tested to pack computers into cartons, eliminating a human-staffed line doing the same thing, freeing up space for more assembly cells. Elsewhere Dell plans to combine the tasks of downloading software and testing computers, eliminating a step—and valuable seconds of worker time. Subtle changes in product design simplify assembly or reduce the number of people needed to complete a product. Other gains are harder to quantify. Dell builds each unit to order, for example, so flexibility is essential. Every change on the factory floor that allows workers to adapt to sudden shifts in demand reduces the excess capacity of people and plant space Dell must maintain to get products out on time. Dell's purchasing managers are working equally hard with suppliers to watch parts inventories on an hour-by-hour basis, making sure Dell has just enough parts to meet expected demand without clogging the system with excess inventory."[3]

In spite of the economic woes widely experienced in the computer technology industry, most observers believe Dell's business model will allow the company to continue its phenomenal success.[4]

Mass-Customization Manufacturing

In a **mass-customization** manufacturing environment, many standardized components are combined in different ways to produce custom-made products to customer order. Dell Computer Corporation and Gateway 2000 are prime examples of mass customizers. Such companies are characterized by high production volume and often use a *direct-sales* approach, in which the consumer orders directly from the manufacturer often via the Internet.

---

[2]Andy Serwer, "Dell Does Domination," *Fortune,* January 21, 2002, p. 70–75.

[3]"The Best Little Factory in Texas," *Forbes,* June 10, 2002, p. 110.

[4]Steve Lohr, "On a Roll, Dell Enters Uncharted Territory," *The New York Times,* August 25, 2002, p. 1 (section 3).

Cometcomp.com

To illustrate a mass-customization environment, let's focus on Comet Computer Corporation, a manufacturer of computers and peripheral devices.[5] Comet purchases computer parts such as motherboards, computer chips, and power units and then assembles these parts into customized personal computers to customer specifications. A finished computer is then packaged with the monitor, keyboard, printer, and cables ordered by the customer, all of which are purchased by Comet.

The direct-sales model, which was popularized by Dell Computer, is used. Ninety percent of Comet's orders are placed on the company's website, cometcomp.com, and 10 percent are taken on an 800 phone number. No sales are made through retail channels.

Comet's production process is triggered when a customer places an order, either on the company's website, cometcomp.com, or its 800 phone line. The customer specifies every aspect of the desired computer system, including the type of processor and amount of memory in the hard drive, the size of the monitor and type of printer, and finally any preinstalled software. Either a Web or a phone sales representative transmits the order electronically to the appropriate production cell module.[6] A production cell module, or *mod,* is responsible for manufacturing a particular product line, such as a desktop computer, laptop, or server. When the order is received in the appropriate mod, the assembly process begins. Memory and processor chips are installed in the motherboard, which is then mounted on the chassis. Then such components as the CD rom drive, hard drive, and power supply are placed into the chassis. After all of the components are chassis-mounted, the computer's hood (cover) is installed, and the finished unit moves to a test and inspection mod. After the unit checks out for reliability, it goes to the software installation mod, where the software ordered by the customer is preinstalled. From the software mod, the unit goes to the shipping mod where it is boxed and prepared for shipping. Comet strives to ship every customer order within six days.

Before we discuss Comet's production process further, let's turn our attention to the types of manufacturing costs incurred by Comet and other manufacturers.

Manufacturing Costs

LO 5

Give examples of three types of manufacturing costs.

To assist managers in planning, decision making, and cost management, managerial accountants classify costs by the functional area of the organization to which costs relate. Some examples of functional areas are manufacturing, marketing, administration, and research and development. Manufacturing costs are further classified into the following three categories: direct material, direct labor, and manufacturing overhead.

Direct Material Raw material that is consumed in the manufacturing process, is physically incorporated in the finished product, and can be traced to products conveniently is called **direct material.** Examples include the sheet metal in a Ford automobile and the semiconductors in a Comet computer.

Some students are confused by the seemingly interchangeable use of the terms *raw material* and *direct material.* However, there is a difference in the meaning of these terms. *Before* material is entered into the production process, it is called *raw* material. *After* it enters production, it becomes *direct* material.

Direct Labor The cost of salaries, wages, and fringe benefits for personnel who work directly on the manufactured products is classified as **direct-labor cost.** Exam-

[5]As mentioned at the beginning of Chapter 1, the focus organizations around which Chapters 2 through 18 are built are not real organizations. They are, however, realistic settings in which to discuss business and managerial accounting issues. In most cases they are based on real organizations. Similarly, the news articles in the chapter openers are not real newspaper articles, but most of them are based on real events. These realistic illustrations and scenarios are intended to help students connect the business and managerial accounting issues discussed in this book to everyday life.

[6]The description of the manufacturing process is based on that used by Dell Computer Corporation.

ples include the wages of personnel who assemble Comet computers and who operate the equipment in an Exxon refinery.

The cost of fringe benefits for direct-labor personnel, such as employer-paid health-insurance premiums and the employer's pension contributions, should also be classified as direct-labor costs.

Manufacturing Overhead All other costs of manufacturing are classified as **manufacturing overhead,** which includes three types of costs: indirect material, indirect labor, and other manufacturing costs.

Indirect Material The cost of materials that are required for the production process but do not become an integral part of the finished product are classified as **indirect material** costs. An example is the cost of drill bits used in a metal-fabrication department at Ford Motor Company. The drill bits wear out and are discarded, but they do not become part of the product. Materials that do become an integral part of the finished product but are insignificant in cost are also often classified as indirect material. Materials such as glue or paint may be so inexpensive that it is not worth tracing their costs to specific products as direct materials.

"If you just simply have [an employee] performing an [assembly] operation, that's direct labor. But when you put in a robot to do the job, which we're all doing, then you've got to have an engineer to make sure the [robot] is programmed right. So now it becomes indirect labor." (2e)

DaimlerChrysler

Indirect Labor The costs of personnel who do not work directly on the product, but whose services are necessary for the manufacturing process, are classified as **indirect labor.** Such personnel include production department supervisors, custodial employees, and security guards.

Other Manufacturing Costs All other manufacturing costs that are neither material nor labor costs are classified as manufacturing overhead. These costs include depreciation of plant and equipment, property taxes, insurance, and utilities such as electricity, as well as the costs of operating service departments. **Service departments** or **support departments** are those that do not work directly on manufacturing products but are necessary for the manufacturing process to occur. Examples include equipment-maintenance departments and computer-aided-design (CAD) departments. In some manufacturing firms, departments are referred to as *work centers.*

Other manufacturing overhead costs include overtime premiums and the cost of idle time. An **overtime premium** is the extra compensation paid to an employee who works beyond the time normally scheduled. Suppose a technician who assembles Comet computers earns $16 per hour. The technician works 48 hours during a week instead of the scheduled time of 40 hours. The overtime pay scale is time and a half, or 150 percent of the regular wage. The technician's compensation for the week is classified as follows:

Direct-labor cost ($16 × 48)	$768
Overhead (overtime premium: ½ × $16 × 8)	64
Total compensation paid	$832

Only the *extra* compensation of $8 per hour is classified as overtime premium. The regular wage of $16 per hour is treated as direct labor, even for the eight overtime hours.

Idle time is time that is not spent productively by an employee due to such events as equipment breakdowns or new setups of production runs. Such idle time is an unavoidable feature of most manufacturing processes. The cost of an employee's idle time is classified as overhead so that it may be spread across all production jobs, rather than being associated with a particular production job. Suppose that during one 40-hour shift, a machine breakdown resulted in idle time of 1½ hours and a power failure idled workers for an additional ½ hour. If an employee earns $14 per hour, the employee's wages for the week will be classified as follows:

Direct-labor cost ($14 × 38)	$532
Overhead (idle time: $14 × 2)	28
Total compensation paid	$560

Both overtime premiums and the cost of idle time should be classified as manufacturing overhead, rather than associated with a particular production job, because the particular job on which idle time or overtime may occur tends to be selected at random. Suppose several production jobs are scheduled during an eight-hour shift, and the last job remains unfinished at the end of the shift. The overtime to finish the last job is necessitated by all of the jobs scheduled during the shift, not just the last one. Similarly, if a power failure occurs during one of several production jobs, the idle time that results is not due to the job that happens to be in process at the time. The power failure is a random event, and the resulting cost should be treated as a cost of all of the department's production.

To summarize, manufacturing costs include direct material, direct labor, and manufacturing overhead. Direct labor and overhead are often called **conversion costs,** since they are the costs of "converting" raw material into finished products. Direct material and direct labor are often referred to as **prime costs.**

Manufacturing Cost Flows

Direct material, direct labor, and manufacturing overhead are the three types of production costs incurred by manufacturers. These costs are product costs because they are stored in inventory until the time period when the manufacturer's products are sold. Manufacturers have product-costing systems to keep track of the flow of these costs from the time production begins until finished products are sold. This flow of manufacturing costs is depicted in Exhibit 2–6. As direct material is consumed in production, its cost is added to work-in-process inventory. Similarly, the costs of direct labor and manufacturing overhead are accumulated in work in process.

> "In my mind, cost accountants are going to be business analysts." (2f)
> **Boeing**

When products are finished, their costs are transferred from work-in-process inventory to finished-goods inventory. The total cost of direct material, direct labor, and manufacturing overhead transferred from work-in-process inventory to finished-goods inventory is called the **cost of goods manufactured.** The costs then are stored in finished goods until the time period when the products are sold. At that time, the product costs are transferred from finished goods to cost of goods sold, which is an expense of the period when the sale is made. Exhibit 2–6 concentrates on the conceptual basis of

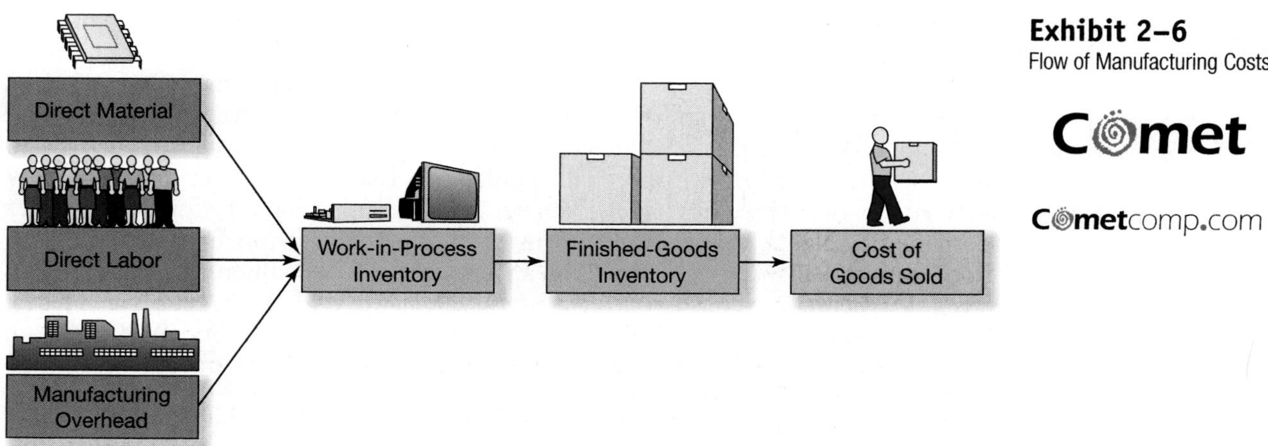

Exhibit 2–6
Flow of Manufacturing Costs

Comet

Cometcomp.com

Exhibit 2–7
Manufacturing Cost Schedules

Cometcomp.com

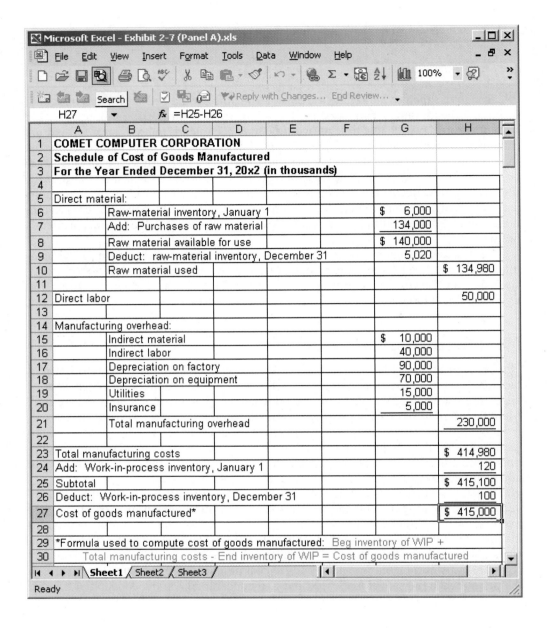

Microsoft Excel - Exhibit 2-7 (Panel A).xls

H27 =H25-H26

	A	B	C	D	E	F	G	H
1	**COMET COMPUTER CORPORATION**							
2	**Schedule of Cost of Goods Manufactured**							
3	**For the Year Ended December 31, 20x2 (in thousands)**							
4								
5	Direct material:							
6		Raw-material inventory, January 1					$ 6,000	
7		Add: Purchases of raw material					134,000	
8		Raw material available for use					$ 140,000	
9		Deduct: raw-material inventory, December 31					5,020	
10		Raw material used						$ 134,980
11								
12	Direct labor							50,000
13								
14	Manufacturing overhead:							
15		Indirect material					$ 10,000	
16		Indirect labor					40,000	
17		Depreciation on factory					90,000	
18		Depreciation on equipment					70,000	
19		Utilities					15,000	
20		Insurance					5,000	
21		Total manufacturing overhead						230,000
22								
23	Total manufacturing costs							$ 414,980
24	Add: Work-in-process inventory, January 1							120
25	Subtotal							$ 415,100
26	Deduct: Work-in-process inventory, December 31							100
27	Cost of goods manufactured*							$ 415,000
28								
29	*Formula used to compute cost of goods manufactured: Beg inventory of WIP +							
30	Total manufacturing costs - End inventory of WIP = Cost of goods manufactured							

Sheet1 / Sheet2 / Sheet3

Ready

LO 6

Prepare a schedule of cost of goods manufactured, a schedule of cost of goods sold, and an income statement for a manufacturer.

a product-costing system. The detailed procedures and accounts used to keep track of product costs are covered in Chapters 3 and 4.

Manufacturers generally prepare a **schedule of cost of goods manufactured** and a **schedule of cost of goods sold** to summarize the flow of manufacturing costs during an accounting period. These schedules are intended for internal use by management and are generally not made available to the public. The Excel spreadsheets in Exhibit 2–7 show these two schedules along with an income statement for Comet Computer Corporation.[7] Notice the extremely low inventories of raw material, finished goods, and work in process in these schedules. With annual sales of $700 million, Comet's year-end inventory of raw material is only $5,020,000, which is less than 1 percent of sales. Work-in-process inventory ($100,000) and finished-goods inventory ($190,000) are even lower. These low inventories, relative to sales volume, are characteristic of mass customizers using the direct-sales approach.

[7]Some numerical displays in the text will be presented as Excel spreadsheets, since this tool is widely used in business.

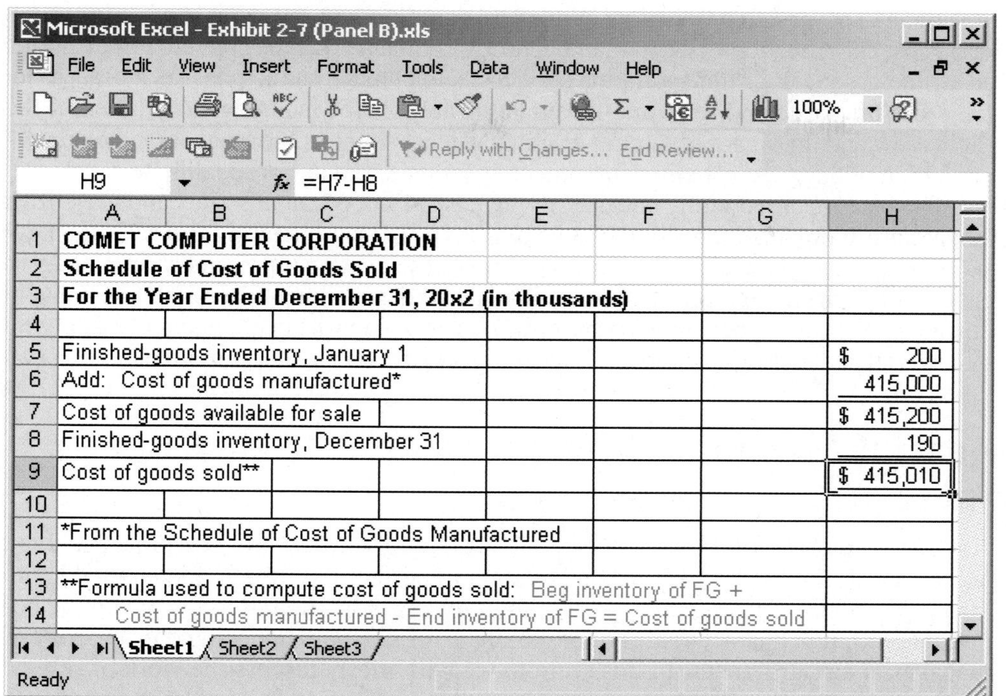

Microsoft Excel - Exhibit 2-7 (Panel B).xls

H9 =H7-H8

	A	H
1	**COMET COMPUTER CORPORATION**	
2	**Schedule of Cost of Goods Sold**	
3	**For the Year Ended December 31, 20x2 (in thousands)**	
4		
5	Finished-goods inventory, January 1	$ 200
6	Add: Cost of goods manufactured*	415,000
7	Cost of goods available for sale	$ 415,200
8	Finished-goods inventory, December 31	190
9	Cost of goods sold**	$ 415,010
10		
11	*From the Schedule of Cost of Goods Manufactured	
12		
13	**Formula used to compute cost of goods sold: Beg inventory of FG +	
14	Cost of goods manufactured - End inventory of FG = Cost of goods sold	

Exhibit 2–7
(concluded)

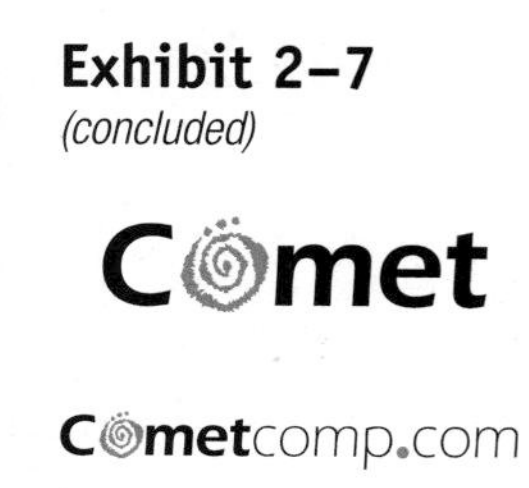

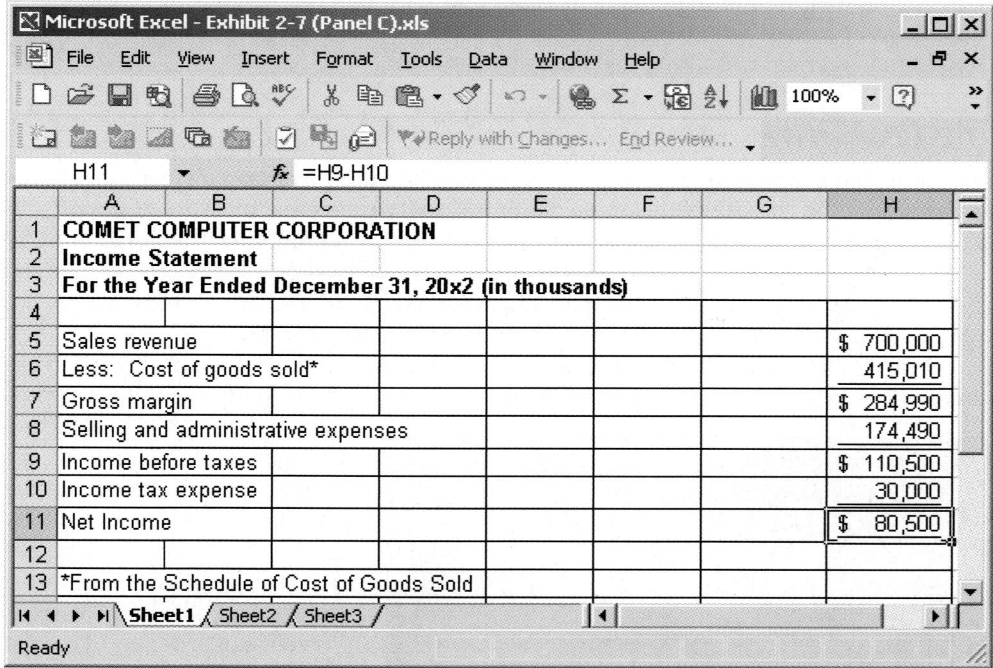

Microsoft Excel - Exhibit 2-7 (Panel C).xls

H11 =H9-H10

	A	H
1	**COMET COMPUTER CORPORATION**	
2	**Income Statement**	
3	**For the Year Ended December 31, 20x2 (in thousands)**	
4		
5	Sales revenue	$ 700,000
6	Less: Cost of goods sold*	415,010
7	Gross margin	$ 284,990
8	Selling and administrative expenses	174,490
9	Income before taxes	$ 110,500
10	Income tax expense	30,000
11	Net Income	$ 80,500
12		
13	*From the Schedule of Cost of Goods Sold	

Production Costs in Service Industry Firms and Nonprofit Organizations

Service industry firms and many nonprofit organizations are also engaged in production. What distinguishes these organizations from manufacturers is that a service is consumed as it is produced, whereas a manufactured product can be stored in inventory. Such businesses as hotels, banks, airlines, professional sports franchises, and automotive repair shops are in the business of producing services. Similarly, nonprofit organizations such as the American Red Cross or the Greater Miami Opera Association also are engaged in service production. While less commonly observed in service firms, the same cost classifications used in manufacturing companies can be applied. For example, an airline produces air transportation services. Direct material includes such costs as jet fuel, aircraft parts, and food and beverages. Direct labor includes the salaries of the flight crew and the wages of aircraft-maintenance personnel. Overhead costs include depreciation of baggage-handling equipment, insurance, and airport landing fees.

The process of recording and classifying costs is important in service industry firms and nonprofit organizations for the same reasons as in manufacturing firms. Cost analysis is used in pricing banking and insurance services, locating travel and car-rental agencies, setting enrollment targets in universities, and determining cost reimbursements in hospitals. As such organizations occupy an ever-growing role in our economy, applying managerial accounting to their activities will take on ever-greater importance.

Basic Cost Management Concepts: Different Costs for Different Purposes

An understanding of cost concepts is absolutely critical to cost management. Moreover, different perspectives on costs are important in different managerial situations. The phrase *different costs for different purposes* is often used to convey the notion that different characteristics of costs can be important to understand in a variety of managerial circumstances. In this section, we will briefly discuss the work of several cross-functional management teams at Comet Computer Corporation, each of which is focusing on a particular management challenge. Through our discussion of these cost management teams' work, we will explore some of the key cost terms and concepts used in managerial accounting and cost management.

The Cost Driver Team

LO 7

Understand the importance of identifying an organization's cost drivers.

One of the most important cost classifications involves the way a cost changes in relation to changes in the activity of the organization. **Activity** refers to a measure of the organization's output of products or services. The number of automobiles manufactured by General Motors, the number of days of patient care provided by Massachusetts General Hospital, and the number of insurance claims settled by Allstate are all measures of activity. The activities that cause costs to be incurred are also called *cost drivers.*

One of Comet Computer Corporation's cost management teams was formed to examine the various costs incurred by Comet. The team consisted of an engineer, a production manager, a purchasing manager, and a managerial accountant. After identifying the various costs incurred by Comet, the team was charged to go on to identify the cost drivers upon which various types of costs depend.[8] A **cost driver** is a characteristic of an activity or event that causes costs to be incurred by that activity or event. In most organizations different types of costs respond to widely differing

Cost drivers in the airline industry are complex. The capacity of an airplane and its passenger load drive costs, but so do a variety of other factors related to the airline's operations.

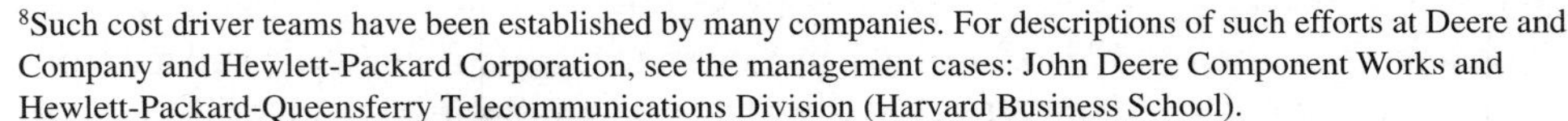

[8]Such cost driver teams have been established by many companies. For descriptions of such efforts at Deere and Company and Hewlett-Packard Corporation, see the management cases: John Deere Component Works and Hewlett-Packard-Queensferry Telecommunications Division (Harvard Business School).

cost drivers. For example, in a manufacturing firm the cost of assembly labor would be driven by the quantity of products manufactured as well as the number of parts in each product. In contrast, the cost of machine setup labor would be driven by the number of production runs. The cost of material-handling labor would be driven by material-related factors such as the quantity and cost of raw material used, the number of parts in various products, and the number of raw-material shipments received.

In identifying a cost driver, the managerial accountant should consider the extent to which a cost or pool of costs varies in accordance with the cost driver. The higher the correlation between the cost and the cost driver, the more accurate will be the resulting understanding of cost behavior. Another important consideration is the cost of measuring the cost driver. Thus, there is a cost-benefit trade-off in the identification of cost drivers. As the number of cost drivers used in explaining an organization's cost behavior increases, the accuracy of the resulting information will increase. However, the cost of the information will increase also. The concept of a cost driver will be an important aspect of many of the topics discussed in subsequent chapters.

Topic 2–2

Variable and Fixed Costs

Describe the behavior of variable and fixed costs, in total and on a per-unit basis.

After identifying costs and cost drivers for Comet Computer Corporation's operations, the cost driver team went on to examine the relationship of various costs to the activities performed. Such a relationship is referred to as *cost behavior* and will be the focus of Chapter 7. At this juncture, though, let's look at two types of cost behavior identified at Comet Computer Corporation: *variable* and *fixed costs.*

Variable Costs A **variable cost** changes in total in direct proportion to a change in the level of activity (or cost driver). If activity increases by 20 percent, total variable cost increases by 20 percent also. For example, the cost of sheet metal used by DaimlerChrysler will increase by approximately 5 percent if automobile production increases by 5 percent. The cost of napkins and other paper products used at a Pizza Hut will increase by roughly 10 percent if the restaurant's patronage increases by 10 percent.

At Comet Computer Corporation, the cost management team identified direct material as a variable cost. One purchased component, a power bus assembly, costs $100 per computer manufactured. The cost behavior for this direct material cost is graphed and tabulated in Exhibit 2–8.

Panel A of Exhibit 2–8 displays a graph of this variable cost. As this graph shows, *total* variable cost increases proportionately with activity. When activity doubles, from 10 to 20 units, total variable cost doubles, from $1,000 to $2,000. However, the variable cost *per unit* remains the same as activity changes. The variable cost associated with each unit of activity is $100, whether it is the first unit, the fourth, or the eighteenth. The table in panel B of Exhibit 2–8 illustrates this point.

To summarize, as activity changes, total variable cost increases or decreases proportionately with the activity change, but unit variable cost remains the same.

Fixed Costs A **fixed cost** remains unchanged in total as the level of activity (or cost driver) varies. If activity increases or decreases by 20 percent, total fixed cost remains the same. Examples of fixed costs include depreciation of plant and equipment at a Nike factory, the cost of property taxes at a Ramada Inn, and the salary of a subway train operator employed by the New York Transit Authority.

Comet Computer Corporation's cost driver team identified the salary of the manager of Web sales operations as a fixed cost. Her $150,000 annual salary does not vary with the number of units produced or sold.

This fixed cost is graphed in panel A of Exhibit 2–9.

From the graph in Exhibit 2–9, it is apparent that *total* fixed cost remains unchanged as activity changes. When activity triples, from 10 to 30 units, total fixed cost

Exhibit 2–8
Variable Cost

Cometcomp.com

A. Graph of Total Variable Cost

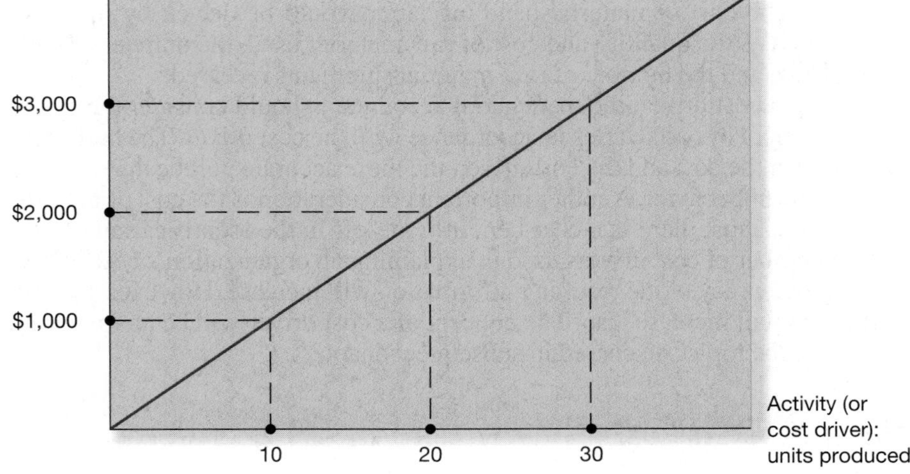

B. Tabulation of Variable Cost

Activity (or cost driver)	Variable Cost per Unit	Total Variable Cost
1	$100	$ 100
4	100	400
18	100	1,800
30	100	3,000

remains constant at $150,000. However, the fixed cost *per unit* does change as activity changes. If the activity level is only 1 unit, then the fixed cost per unit is $150,000 per unit ($150,000 ÷ 1). If the activity level is 10 units, then the fixed cost per unit declines to $15,000 per unit ($150,000 ÷ 10). The behavior of total fixed cost and unit fixed cost is illustrated by the table in panel B of Exhibit 2–9.

Another way of viewing the change in unit fixed cost as activity changes is in a graph, as shown in panel C of Exhibit 2–9. Unit fixed cost declines steadily as activity increases. Notice that the decrease in unit fixed cost when activity changes from 1 to 2 units is much larger than the decrease in unit fixed cost when activity changes from 10 to 11 units or from 20 to 21 units. Thus, the amount of the change in unit fixed cost declines as the activity level increases.

To summarize, as the activity level increases, total fixed cost remains constant but unit fixed cost declines. As you will see in subsequent chapters, it is vital in managerial accounting to thoroughly understand the behavior of both total fixed costs and unit fixed costs.

The Cost Management and Control Team

An important objective of managerial accounting is to assist managers in managing and controlling costs. Sometimes cost management is facilitated by tracing costs to the department or work center in which the cost was incurred. Such tracing of costs to departments is known as *responsibility accounting.*

Comet Computer Corporation formed a cost management and control team to refine the company's responsibility accounting system. The team consisted of an engineer, the production scheduling manager, the assistant manager of quality control, the manager of human resources, and a managerial accountant. The ultimate objective of the team was to develop a responsibility accounting system that would assist management in managing

Exhibit 2–9
Fixed Cost

Cømet

Cømetcomp.com

A. Graph of Total Fixed Cost

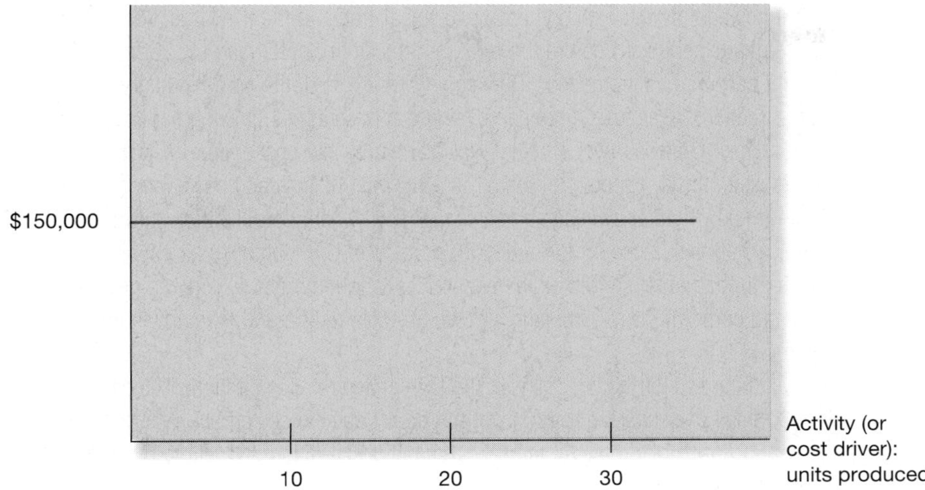

B. Tabulation of Fixed Cost

Activity (or cost driver)	Fixed Cost per Unit	Total Fixed Cost
1	$150,000	$150,000
2	75,000	150,000
5	30,000	150,000
10	15,000	150,000
11	13,636*	150,000
20	7,500	150,000
21	7,143*	150,000
30	5,000	150,000

*Rounded.

C. Graph of Unit Fixed Cost

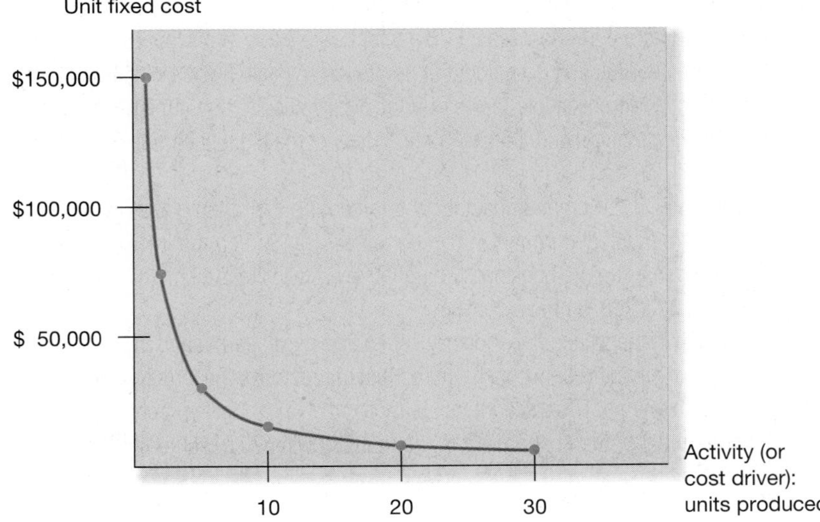

and controlling costs as well as reducing costs whenever possible. We will study cost management systems and cost reduction in considerable detail in Chapters 5 and 6, and responsibility accounting is covered in Chapter 12. For now, let's focus on a couple of cost concepts that are useful in these areas of managerial accounting.

Management Accounting Practice

US Airways, Continental, American, United, Delta, JetBlue, Frontier, and Air-Tran

AIRLINE INDUSTRY: COST STRUCTURE, COST DRIVERS, AND A SHIFTING BUSINESS MODEL

A recent study showed that although domestic passenger traffic at the five largest U.S. airlines has declined from highs experienced before the terrorist attacks of September 11, 2001, traffic at the top five discount carriers has increased. "How could two wings of the same industry be tipping in such different directions? Because American business has changed its flying habits, possibly forever. The bottom line: business travel is being 'Wal-Marted' by low-cost operators. Just as Wal-Mart Stores did in retailing, the discounters of the air—Southwest Airlines and newcomers such as JetBlue Airways—are proving that even some of the most finicky corporate fliers can't resist a bargain.

Low-cost carriers now account for nearly 20 percent of U.S. domestic air capacity. A second force behind the fundamental shift in airline economics is the Internet, which has given travelers, travel agents, and corporate travel managers powerful tools to find and take advantage of deeply discounted fares.

The shift is dire news for the big airliners, the full-service retailers of flight. The carriers, which are bleeding red ink, have massive fixed costs that aren't easy to scale back. Most of them have built expensive hub-and-spoke route systems and signed costly labor contracts that they had hoped to finance by charging high-margin business fares. But now, there is 'a low-fare network in this country that did not exist previously.' A senior vice president at Continental Airlines, told a recent aviation conference, 'We've finally reached the point, perhaps, where [its] penetration may be fatal' to the major carriers' high-cost business models.

Some carriers, including American Airlines and United Airlines, are now rethinking their entire operations, even considering whether they should cut back their high-cost route systems." At American, "a special task force is hunting for immediate money-saving ideas and another is studying longer-range restructuring. Already, the airline has decided to speed up its deployment of self-service check-in kiosks and other technology designed to automate more of its airport operations. US Airways is negotiating with its employees for huge pay cuts in a last-ditch effort to stay in the air. United reached a tentative agreement with its pilots' union on a deal aimed at reducing labor costs."

It won't be easy, however, for major airlines to cut their costs. "Consider the current advantages low-fare carriers have over full-service rivals. They tend to have younger fleets, which require less maintenance, and younger labor forces that aren't tied to complicated, inefficient labor contracts. That's why labor costs are equivalent to just 25 percent of revenue at discounters Air-Tran Airways, Frontier Airlines, and Jet Blue and 30 percent at Southwest. At United and Delta, labor costs exceed 40 percent of revenue. Moreover, low-fare carriers typically stick to one airplane model, thus minimizing maintenance, operating, and training costs." Many of the biggest carriers still fly six or seven types of aircraft.

"The Internet is also having an impact. Low-fare carriers that often got short shrift from travel agencies or corporate travel departments have gotten easy to find on the Internet. Southwest now gets more than 40 percent of its bookings through its own website. American and United both sell only 5 percent of their tickets on their websites."[9]

The bottom line is that the airline industry is undergoing a sea-change in its business model, and it is driven by the very different cost structures that characterize the largest carriers versus their smaller discount competitors. The discounters are more flexible and have proportionately lower fixed costs. An understanding of the cost drivers in the industry will be crucial to the survival of the big airlines.

[9]Melanie Trottman and Scott McCartney, "The Age of Wal-Mart Airlines Crunches the Biggest Carriers," *The Wall Street Journal,* June 18, 2002, pp. A1 and A8. See also Alan Cowell, "Low-Cost Airlines Grow and Compete in Europe," *The New York Times,* July 28, 2002, p. 3.

Direct and Indirect Costs A cost that can be traced to a particular department is called a **direct cost** of the department.

For example, the salary of an auto mechanic is a direct cost of the automotive service department in a Sears department store. The cost of paint used in the painting department of a Toyota plant is a direct cost of the painting department.

LO 9

Distinguish among direct, indirect, controllable, and uncontrollable costs.

A cost that is not directly traceable to a particular department is called an **indirect cost** of the department. The costs of national advertising for Walt Disney World are indirect costs of each of the departments or subunits of the recreational complex, such as the Magic Kingdom and Epcot. The salary of a General Electric Company plant manager is an indirect cost of each of the plant's production departments. The plant manager's duties are important to the smooth functioning of each of the plant's departments, but there is no way to trace a portion of the plant manager's salary cost to each department.

"The flight crew's salaries on a flight, say from Atlanta to St. Louis, would be considered a direct cost of that flight. The salaries of the flight scheduling folks, on the other hand, would be an indirect cost of any given flight." (2g)
Delta Air Lines

Whether a cost is a direct cost or an indirect cost of a department often depends on which department is under consideration. A cost can be a direct cost of one department or subunit in the organization but an indirect cost of other departments. While the salary of a General Electric Company plant manager is an *indirect* cost of the plant's departments, the manager's salary is a *direct* cost of the plant.

Comet Computer Corporation's cost management and control team determined that many of the company's costs were traceable to various departments or to specific activities of those departments. In the purchasing department, for example, costs were traced not just to the department, but to the specific activities of identifying vendors, qualifying vendors, securing design specifications from the engineering design department, negotiating prices, placing orders, expediting orders, receiving materials and components, inspecting materials, and releasing materials to the material-handling operation.

An important objective of a cost management system is to trace as many costs as possible directly to the activities that cause them to be incurred. Sometimes called *activity accounting,* this process is vital to management's objective of eliminating *non-value-added costs.* These are costs of activities that can be eliminated without deterioration of product quality, performance, or perceived value. (We will study the elimination of non-value-added costs in greater detail in Chapter 6.)

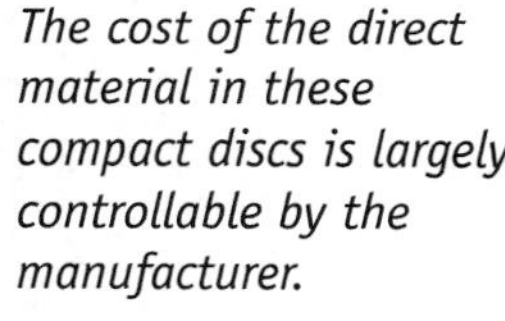

The cost of the direct material in these compact discs is largely controllable by the manufacturer.

Controllable and Uncontrollable Costs Another cost classification that can be helpful in cost control involves the controllability of a cost item by a particular manager. If a manager can control or heavily influence the level of a cost, then that cost is classified as a **controllable cost** of that manager. Costs that a manager cannot influence significantly are classified as *uncontrollable costs* of that manager. Many costs are not completely under the control of any individual. In classifying costs as controllable or uncontrollable, managerial accountants generally focus on a manager's ability to influence costs. The question is not, Who controls the cost? but, Who is in the best position to influence the level of a cost item? Exhibit 2–10 lists several cost items along with their typical classification as controllable or uncontrollable.

Comet Computer's cost management and control team was able to designate many of Comet's costs as controllable or uncontrollable by various managers. Take the cost of raw materials and components, for example. The team determined that the *quantity* of materials used was largely controllable by the production supervisor, but the *price* of the materials was influenced more by the purchasing manager.

Exhibit 2–10
Controllable and Uncontrollable Costs

Cost Item	Manager	Classification
Cost of raw material used to produce computer chips in an Intel factory	Supervisor of the production department for computer chips	Controllable (The production supervisor can exercise some control over the quantity of material used by ensuring that waste and defective units are minimized.)
Cost of food used in a Subway restaurant	Restaurant manager	Controllable (The restaurant manager exercises some control over the quantity of food used by scheduling production to ensure that excess food is not produced and wasted.)
Cost of national advertising for the Alamo car rental company	Manager of the Alamo rental agency at the Orlando airport	Uncontrollable
Cost of national accounting and data processing operations for Target	Manager of a Target store in Gainesville, Florida	Uncontrollable

The Outsourcing Action Team

LO 10

Define and give examples of an opportunity cost, an out-of-pocket cost, a sunk cost, a differential cost, a marginal cost, and an average cost.

Another of Comet Computer Corporation's interdisciplinary management teams was formed to take a close look at which of the raw materials and components used in Comet's products should be manufactured by Comet and which ones should be outsourced (purchased from outside vendors).[10] This team consisted of the assistant manager of purchasing, a product design engineer, a product group sales manager, and a managerial accountant. As the team pursued its assignment, its members soon found that they were once again dealing with several different cost concepts.

In addition to accounting cost classifications, such as product costs and period costs, the team's members also found themselves using economic concepts in classifying costs. Such concepts are often useful in helping managerial accountants decide what cost information is relevant to the decisions faced by the organization's managers. Several of the most important economic cost concepts are discussed next.

Opportunity Costs An **opportunity cost** is defined as the benefit that is sacrificed when the choice of one action precludes taking an alternative course of action. If beef and fish are the available choices for dinner, the opportunity cost of eating beef is the forgone pleasure associated with eating fish.

Opportunity costs arise in many business decisions. For example, suppose a baseball manufacturer receives a special order for softballs from the city of Boston. If the firm accepts the softball order, it will not have enough productive capacity (labor and machine time) to produce its usual output of baseballs for sale to a large chain of sporting-goods stores. The opportunity cost of accepting the softball order is the forgone benefit from the baseball production that cannot be achieved. This forgone benefit is measured by the potential revenue from the baseball sales minus the cost of manufacturing the baseballs.

Opportunity costs also arise in personal decisions. The opportunity cost of a student's college education includes the salary that is forgone as a result of not taking a full-time job during the student's years in college.

From an economic perspective, a dollar of opportunity cost associated with an action should be treated as equivalent to a dollar of out-of-pocket cost. **Out-of-pocket costs** are those that require the payment of cash or other assets as a result of their incurrence. The out-of-pocket costs associated with the softball order consist of the manufacturing costs required to produce the softballs. In making the decision to accept or reject the softball order, the firm's management should consider *both* the out-of-pocket cost and the opportunity cost of the order.

[10]The outsourcing decision, as well as several other common management decisions, is covered in detail in Chapter 14.

Studies by behavioral scientists and economists have shown that many people have a tendency to ignore or downplay the importance of opportunity costs. For example, in one study people were asked if they would pay $500 for two tickets to the Super Bowl. Most people responded that they would not. However, many of the same people said that they would not sell the Super Bowl tickets for $500 if they were given the tickets free of charge. These people refused to incur the $500 *out-of-pocket cost* of buying the Super Bowl tickets. However, they were willing to incur the $500 *opportunity cost* of going to the game rather than sell the tickets. In each case a couple that attends the game ends up $500 poorer than a couple that does not attend the game. (Try surveying your friends with this scenario.)

Behavior such as that illustrated in the Super Bowl example is economically inconsistent. Ignoring or downplaying the importance of opportunity costs can result in inconsistent and faulty business decisions.

Comet Computer's outsourcing action team found that the opportunity cost of using constrained production resources (such as space, machine time, and employee time) to produce a computer component in-house was an important factor to consider in deciding whether to outsource the component.[11]

Sunk Costs **Sunk costs** are costs that have been incurred in the past. Consequently, they do not affect future costs and cannot be changed by any current or future action. Examples of such costs include the acquisition cost of equipment previously purchased and the manufacturing cost of inventory on hand. Regardless of the current usefulness of the equipment or the inventory, the costs of acquiring them cannot be changed by any prospective action. Hence these costs are irrelevant to all future decisions.

Suppose, for example, that a university's traffic department purchased a desktop computer to assist in the vehicle registration process. A year has passed, the computer's warranty has expired, and the computer is not working well. An investigation reveals that this brand of computer is very sensitive to humidity and temperature changes. The traffic department is located in an old building with poor heating and no air-conditioning. As a result, the computer works only intermittently, repair bills have been high, and the office staff is fed up. The office manager requests that the department director junk the computer and instruct the staff to return to the old manual registration system. The director responds by insisting, "We can't afford to junk the computer! We paid $3,400 for it."

This illustration is a typical example of the inappropriate attention paid to sunk costs. The $3,400 paid for the computer is sunk. No future decision about the computer or the office's procedures can affect that cost. Future decisions should be based on future costs, such as the computer repair bills or the costs of upgrading the building's heating and air-conditioning systems.

Although it is incorrect, from an economic perspective, to allow sunk costs to affect future decisions, people often do so. It is human nature to attempt to justify past decisions. When there is a perceived need to demonstrate competence, either to themselves or to others, managers may seek to justify their decisions. The response of the traffic department director that "We can't afford to junk the computer!" may represent the director's need to justify the past decision to purchase the computer. It is important for managerial accountants to be aware of such behavioral tendencies. Such an awareness enables the accountant to prepare the most relevant data for managers' decisions and, sometimes, to assist the managers in using the information.

Comet Computer's outsourcing action team encountered a sunk cost as it considered outsourcing production of a component called a monitor interface unit (MIU). The

---

[11]The details of the outsourcing decision, including its relevant costs and the role of opportunity costs, are covered in Chapter 14.

team discovered that the automatic insertion robot used to insert components into the MIU was difficult to maintain and expensive to operate. Nevertheless, the department supervisor was inclined to keep the robot and continue in-house production of the MIU, because, as he put it, "Comet paid an arm and a leg for this robot." The team was able to demonstrate that the robot's acquisition cost was a sunk cost and was irrelevant to the outsourcing decision. We will explore sunk costs in more detail in Chapter 14.

LO10

Define and give examples of an opportunity cost, an out-of-pocket cost, a sunk cost, a differential cost, a marginal cost, and an average cost.

Differential Costs A **differential cost** is the amount by which the cost differs under two alternative actions. Suppose, for example, that a county government is considering two competing sites for a new landfill. If the northern site is chosen, the annual cost of transporting refuse to the site is projected at $85,000. If the southern site is selected, annual transportation charges are expected to be $70,000. The annual differential cost of transporting refuse is calculated as follows:

Annual cost of transporting refuse to northern site	$85,000
Annual cost of transporting refuse to southern site	70,000
Annual differential cost	$15,000

The increase in cost from one alternative to another is called an **incremental cost.** In the landfill example, the annual incremental cost of refuse transportation is $15,000 if the site is moved from the southern location to the northern location. Differential or incremental costs are found in a variety of economic decisions. The additional cost incurred by Gulliver's Travels, a travel agency, in locating a new office in the suburbs is the incremental cost of the new business location. The difference in the total cost incurred by the travel agency with or without the suburban location is the differential cost of the decision whether to establish the new office. Decisions about establishing new airline routes, adding additional shifts in a manufacturing firm, or increasing the nursing staff in a hospital all involve differential costs.

At Comet Computer, the outsourcing action team estimated that the differential cost between outsourcing the production of the MIU (monitor interface unit) and producing it in-house would be $200,000 annually in favor of outsourcing, based on current projections of annual production.

Marginal Costs and Average Costs A special case of the differential-cost concept is the **marginal cost,** which is the extra cost incurred when one additional unit is produced. The additional cost incurred by Comet Computer when one additional high-performance laptop computer is made is the marginal cost of manufacturing the computer. The table in Exhibit 2–11 shows how marginal cost can change across different ranges of production quantities.

Exhibit 2–11
Marginal Cost of Producing Laptop Computers at Comet Computer Corporation

Cometcomp.com

Number of Laptop Computers Produced	Total Cost of Producing Laptops		Marginal Cost of Producing a Laptop
1	$ 2,000	Difference is $1,900 →	Marginal cost of 2nd laptop is $1,900
2	3,900		
10	18,000	Difference is $1,690 →	Marginal cost of 11th laptop is $1,690
11	19,690		
100	150,000	Difference is $995 →	Marginal cost of 101st laptop is $995
101	150,995		

Marginal costs typically differ across different ranges of production quantities because the efficiency of the production process changes. At Comet Computer the marginal cost of producing a laptop computer declines as output increases. It is much more efficient for the company to manufacture 101 computers than to make only one.

It is important to distinguish between *marginal costs* and *average costs.* In the Comet Computer example, the marginal cost of the second computer is $1,900. However, the average cost per unit when two laptops are manufactured is $3,900 divided by 2, or $1,950. Similarly, the marginal cost of the eleventh laptop is $1,690, but the average cost per unit when 11 laptops are produced is $1,790 (calculated by dividing $19,690 by 11). What is the marginal cost of the 101st laptop computer? The average cost per unit when 101 laptops are manufactured?[12]

To summarize, the marginal cost of production is the extra cost incurred when one more unit is produced. The **average cost per unit** is the total cost, for whatever quantity is manufactured, divided by the number of units manufactured. Marginal costs and average costs arise in a variety of economic situations. A Princeton University administrator might be interested in the marginal cost of educating one additional student, and a Toyota executive might want to know the marginal cost of producing one more Toyota van. A Greyhound route manager might be interested in the average cost per mile on the Pittsburgh to New York City route.

Costs and Benefits of Information

Many different cost concepts have been explored in this chapter. An important task of the managerial accountant is to determine which of these cost concepts is most appropriate in each situation. Then the accountant strives to *communicate* the cost information to the user in the most effective manner possible. The accountant attempts to structure the organization's accounting information system to record data that will be useful for a variety of purposes. The benefits of measuring and classifying costs in a particular way are realized through the improvements in planning, control, and decision making that the information facilitates.

"If you can't communicate information to the individual, then the information is . . . lost. So, your communication skills are very important." (2h)
Abbott Labs

Another important task of the managerial accountant is to weigh the benefits of providing information against the costs of generating, communicating, and using that information. Some accountants, eager to show that they have not overlooked anything, tend to provide too much information. But when managers receive more data than they can utilize effectively, *information overload* occurs. Struggling to process large amounts of information, managers may be unable to recognize the most important facts. In deciding how much and what type of information to provide, managerial accountants should consider these human limitations.

[12]Marginal cost of 101st laptop computer is $995 (from Exhibit 2–11). Average cost per unit when 101 laptops are produced is $1,495 ($150,995 ÷ 101).

Focus on Ethics

WAS WORLDCOM'S CONTROLLER JUST FOLLOWING ORDERS?

Through a series of mergers and acquisitions, WorldCom, Inc. grew to become the nation's second-largest long-distance telecommunications company. WorldCom's core communication services included network data transmission over public and private networks. Trouble arose for WorldCom because of the immense overcapacity in the telecommunications industry due to overly optimistic growth projections during the Internet boom. The combination of overcapacity, decreased demand, and high fixed costs still pose a serious problem for many of the major players in the industry.

In June 2002, the company disclosed that it had overstated earnings for 2001 and the first quarter of 2002 to the tune of $3.8 billion. The overstatement arose because the company incorrectly classified period expenses as capital expenditures. This maneuver had two major effects on the company's financial statements: the company's assets were artificially inflated, and the capitalization allowed the company to spread the recognition of its expenses into the future which increased net income in the current period. The expenses in question related to line costs—the fees that WorldCom pays outside providers for access to their communications networks. In addition, the company announced in July 2002 that it had also manipulated reserve accounts, which affected another $3.8 billion in earnings in 1999 and 2000.

The problems at WorldCom were discovered during an internal audit and brought to the attention of the company's new auditors, KPMG. Arthur Andersen, the auditing firm accused of wrongdoing with Enron, served as WorldCom's auditors during the period covered by the alleged accounting scandal. Arthur Andersen maintained that the details of the accounting fraud were kept from them by senior WorldCom management. The firm's controller and chief financial officer (CFO), who was a former KPMG employee, were fired after the alleged accounting frauds were revealed. Still at issue is how much WorldCom's CEO knew about the alleged fraud. He maintained that he knew nothing of the accounting decisions made by the CFO, but many observers question how almost $8 billion in expenses could slip by senior management.[13]

According to an Associated Press article that ran on September 27, 2002, "the former controller of WorldCom, Inc. pleaded guilty to securities fraud charges, saying he was instructed by 'senior management,' to falsify records. His plea was the first admission of guilt to fall from the largest corporate accounting scandal in U.S. history." In addition to the controller, WorldCom's CFO has also been charged in the alleged massive fraud and other charges are pending.

The CFO and controller were the top two financial and managerial accountants in the WorldCom organization. They were ultimately responsible for all of the company's financial and managerial accounting reports. (Note that this case also involves the alleged intentional misclassification of period costs.) What ethical issues are involved here? What do you make of the controller's assertion that he was just following orders given by senior management? What steps should WorldCom's controller have taken?[14] (Review the Institute of Management Accountants' standards for ethical conduct on pages 27 and 28.)

Chapter Summary

The term *cost* is familiar to everyone. We all discuss the cost of a sweater, a movie ticket, or a semester's tuition. Yet, as we have seen in this chapter, the word *cost* can have a variety of meanings in different situations. Managerial accountants often find it useful to classify costs in different ways for different purposes. An understanding of cost terms, concepts, and classifications is fundamental in any study of managerial accounting.

Several cost management terms are defined and illustrated in the chapter. A cost driver is any activity or event that causes costs to be incurred. Fixed and variable costs are defined by the behavior of total cost as the organization's activity level changes. Direct and indirect costs refer to the ability of the accountant to trace costs to various departments in the organization. The terms *controllable* and *uncontrollable* are used to describe the extent to which a manager can influence a cost. Costs are classified into such functional categories as manufacturing costs, selling costs, and administrative costs. Manufacturing costs are further subdivided into direct-material, direct-labor, and manufacturing-overhead costs. The terms *product cost* and *period cost* refer to the timing with which costs become expenses.

There are five basic types of manufacturing operations: job shop, batch, assembly line, mass customization, and continuous flow. In a mass-customization production environment, many standardized components are used to manufacture customized products to customer order. The direct-sales method often is used, with a large portion of sales orders often taken over the Internet. Raw material and parts

[13]Jared Sandberg, Rebecca Blumenstein, and Shawn Young, "WorldCom Admits $3.8 Billion Error in Its Accounting—Firm Ousts Financial Chief and Struggles for Survival; SEC Probe Likely to Widen," *The Wall Street Journal,* June 26, 2002, p. A1; Jared Sandberg, Deborah Solomon, and Rebecca Blumenstein, "Disconnected: Inside WorldCom's Unearthing of a Vast Accounting Scandal," *The Wall Street Journal,* June 27, 2002, p. A1; and Jared Sandberg, "Leading the News: Was Ebbers Aware of Accounting Move at His WorldCom?" *The Wall Street Journal,* July 1, 2002, p. A3.

[14]Devlin Barrett, "Ex-WorldCom Exec Pleads Guilty," *Associated Press,* September 27, 2002 (as it appeared in the *Ithaca Journal*). See also Kurt Eichenwald and Simon Romero, "Plea Deals Are Seen for Three Wor!dCom Executives," *The New York Times,* August 29, 2002, pp. C1, C4.

inventories, work-in-process inventories, and finished-goods inventories are very low. Cost driver analysis, cost management, and outsourcing decisions are very important in this production environment.

Economic concepts are also important in describing costs. An opportunity cost is the benefit forgone because the choice of one action precludes another action. Sunk costs are costs incurred in the past that cannot be altered by a current or future decision. The term *differential cost* or *incremental cost* refers to the difference in the costs incurred under two alternative actions. Marginal cost is defined as the cost of producing one additional unit. Finally, the average cost per unit is the total cost for whatever quantity is produced, divided by the number of units produced.

These cost terms are an integral part of the specialized language of business.

Review Problems on Cost Classifications

Problem 1

Several costs incurred by Myrtle Beach Golf Equipment, Inc. are listed below. For each cost, indicate which of the following classifications best describe the cost. More than one classification may apply to the same cost item. For example, a cost may be both a variable cost *and* a product cost.

Cost Classifications

a. Variable
b. Fixed
c. Period
d. Product
e. Administrative
f. Selling
g. Manufacturing
h. Research and development
i. Direct material
j. Direct labor
k. Manufacturing overhead

Cost Items

1. Metal used in golf clubs.
2. Salary of the plant manager.
3. Cost of natural gas used to heat factory.
4. Commissions paid to sales personnel.
5. Wages paid to employees who assemble golf bags.
6. Salary of an engineer who is working on a prototype of a new solar-powered golf cart.
7. Depreciation on the word processing equipment used by the company president's secretary.

Problem 2

Listed below are several costs incurred in the loan department of Suwanee Bank and Trust Company. For each cost, indicate which of the following classifications best describe the cost. More than one classification may apply to the same cost item.

Cost Classifications

a. Controllable by the loan department manager
b. Uncontrollable by the loan department manager
c. Direct cost of the loan department
d. Indirect cost of the loan department
e. Differential cost
f. Marginal cost
g. Opportunity cost
h. Sunk cost
i. Out-of-pocket cost

Cost Items

1. Salary of the loan department manager.
2. Cost of office supplies used in the loan department.
3. Cost of the department's personal computers purchased by the loan department manager last year.
4. Cost of general advertising by the bank, which is allocated to the loan department.
5. Revenue that the loan department would have generated for the bank if a branch loan office had been located downtown instead of in the next county.
6. Difference in the cost incurred by the bank when one additional loan application is processed.

Solutions to Review Problems

Problem 1

1. a, d, g, i **2.** b, d, g, k **3.** a, d, g, k **4.** a, c, f **5.** a, d, g, j
6. b, c, h **7.** b, c, e

Problem 2

1. b, c, i **2.** a, c, i **3.** a, c, h **4.** b, d, i **5.** g **6.** e, f

Key Terms

For each term's definition refer to the indicated page, or turn to the glossary at the end of the text.

activity, 48
average cost per unit, 57
controllable cost, 53
conversion costs, 45
cost, 36
cost driver, 48
cost of goods manufactured, 45
cost of goods sold, 36
differential cost, 56
direct cost, 53
direct-labor cost, 43
direct material, 43
expense, 36
finished goods, 40
fixed costs, 49
idle time, 44
incremental cost, 56
indirect cost, 53
indirect labor, 44
indirect material, 44
inventoriable cost, 37
manufacturing overhead, 44
marginal cost, 56
mass customization, 42
operating expenses, 40
opportunity cost, 54
out-of-pocket costs, 54
overtime premium, 44
period costs, 37
prime costs, 45
product cost, 36
raw material, 40
schedule of cost of goods manufactured, 46
schedule of cost of goods sold, 46
service departments (or support departments), 44
sunk costs, 55
variable cost, 49
work in process, 40

Review Questions

2–1. Distinguish between product costs and period costs.

2–2. Why are product costs also called inventoriable costs?

2–3. What is the most important difference between a manufacturing firm and a service industry firm, with regard to the classification of costs as product costs or period costs?

2–4. List, describe, and give an example of each of the five different types of production processes.

2–5. "The words *mass* and *customization* in the term *mass customization* seem contradictory." Do you agree or disagree? Explain.

2–6. Why is the cost of idle time treated as manufacturing overhead?

2–7. Explain why an overtime premium is included in manufacturing overhead.

2–8. What is meant by the phrase "different costs for different purposes"?

2–9. Give examples to illustrate how the city of Tampa could use cost information in planning, controlling costs, and making decisions.

2–10. Distinguish between fixed costs and variable costs.

2–11. How does the fixed cost per unit change as the level of activity (or cost driver) increases? Why?

2–12. How does the variable cost per unit change as the level of activity (or cost driver) increases? Why?

2–13. Distinguish between volume-based and operations-based cost drivers in the airline industry.

2–14. Would each of the following characteristics be a volume-based or an operations-based cost driver in a college: (*a*) number of students, (*b*) number of disciplines offered for study, and (*c*) urban versus rural location?

2–15. List three direct costs of the food and beverage department in a hotel. List three indirect costs of the department.

2–16. List three costs that are likely to be controllable by a city's airport manager. List three costs that are likely to be uncontrollable by the manager.

2–17. Which of the following costs are likely to be controllable by the chief of nursing in a hospital?

a. Cost of medication administered.

b. Cost of overtime paid to nurses due to scheduling errors.

c. Cost of depreciation of hospital beds.

2–18. Distinguish between out-of-pocket costs and opportunity costs.

2–19. Define the terms *sunk cost* and *differential cost.*

2–20. Distinguish between marginal and average costs.

2–21. Think about the process of registering for classes at your college or university. What additional information would you like to have before you register? How would it help you? What sort of information might create information overload for you?

2–22. Two years ago the manager of a large department store purchased new bar code scanners costing $39,000. A salesperson recently tried to sell the manager a new computer-integrated checkout system for the store. The new system would save the store a substantial amount of money each year. The recently purchased scanners could be sold in the secondhand market for $19,000. The store manager refused to listen to the salesperson, saying, "I just bought those scanners. I can't get rid of them until I get my money's worth out of them."

What type of cost is the cost of purchasing the old bar code scanners? What common behavioral tendency is the manager exhibiting?

2–23. Indicate whether each of the following costs is a direct cost or an indirect cost of the restaurant in a hotel.

a. Cost of food served.

b. Chef's salary and fringe benefits.

c. Part of the cost of maintaining the grounds around the hotel, which is allocated to the restaurant.

d. Part of the cost of advertising the hotel, which is allocated to the restaurant.

Exercises

Exercise 2–24
Cost Classifications
(LO 2, 5, 8, 9)

Consider the following costs that were incurred during the current year:

1. Advertising costs of Nike.
2. Straight-line depreciation on factory machinery of Airbus Industrie.
3. Wages of assembly-line personnel of Amana.
4. Delivery costs on customer shipments of Ben & Jerry's ice cream.
5. Newsprint consumed in printing the *Philadelphia Inquirer.*
6. Plant insurance costs of Levi Strauss.
7. Glass costs incurred in light-bulb manufacturing of General Electric.
8. Tire costs incurred by Subaru.
9. Sales commissions paid to the sales force of Dell Computer.
10. Wood glue consumed in the manufacture of Thomasville furniture.
11. Hourly wages of refinery security guards employed by Exxon Corporation.
12. The salary of a financial vice president of Microsoft.

Required: Evaluate each of the preceding and determine whether the cost is (*a*) a product cost or a period cost, (*b*) variable or fixed in terms of behavior, and (*c*) for the product costs only, whether the cost is properly classified as direct material, direct labor, or manufacturing overhead. Item 8 is done as an example:

Tire costs: Product cost, variable, direct material

Exercise 2–25
Cost of Goods Manufactured and Sold; Missing Data
(LO 1, 3, 6)

For each case below, find the missing amount.

	Case I	Case II	Case III
Beginning inventory of finished goods	?	$ 18,000	$ 3,500
Cost of goods manufactured during period	$104,750	142,500	?
Ending inventory of finished goods	24,500	12,000	10,500
Cost of goods sold	101,250	?	152,000

Exercise 2–26
Idle Time
(LO 5)

An employee of Scioto Foundry, Inc. worked a normal 40-hour shift, but four hours were idle due to a small fire in the plant. The employee earns $16 per hour.

Required:

1. Calculate the employee's total compensation for the week.
2. How much of this compensation is a direct-labor cost? How much is overhead?

Exercise 2–27
Overtime Cost
(LO 5)

A loom operator in a Carolina Textiles factory earns $17 per hour. The employee earns $22 for overtime hours. The operator worked 43 hours during the first week of May, instead of the usual 40 hours.

Required:

1. Compute the loom operator's compensation for the week.
2. Calculate the employee's total overtime premium for the week.
3. How much of the employee's total compensation for the week is direct-labor cost? How much is overhead?

Exercise 2–28
Schedules of Cost of Goods Manufactured and Sold; Income Statement
(LO 1, 3, 6)

Alhambra Aluminum Company, a manufacturer of recyclable soda cans, had the following inventory balances at the beginning and end of 20x1.

Inventory Classification	January 1, 20x1	December 31, 20x1
Raw material	$ 55,000	$ 75,000
Work in process	110,000	125,000
Finished goods	160,000	155,000

During 20x1, the company purchased $240,000 of raw material and spent $420,000 on direct labor. Manufacturing overhead costs were as follows:

Indirect material	$ 12,000
Indirect labor	22,000
Depreciation on plant and equipment	110,000
Utilities	23,000
Other	35,000

Sales revenue was $1,210,000 for the year. Selling and administrative expenses for the year amounted to $105,000. The firm's tax rate is 35 percent.

Required:

1. Prepare a schedule of cost of goods manufactured.
2. Prepare a schedule of cost of goods sold.
3. Prepare an income statement.

Exercise 2–29
Mass Customization; Use of Internet
(LO 4)

Find Dell Computer's website on the Internet, www.dell.com.

Required: Read on the company's website about how Dell operates and serves its customers. Then briefly explain whether you believe mass customization to be the best type of manufacturing process for Dell.

Exercise 2–30
Fixed and Variable Costs; Automobile Service; Missing Data
(LO 1, 8)

Mighty Muffler, Inc. operates an automobile service facility that specializes in replacing mufflers on compact cars. The following table shows the costs incurred during a month when 700 mufflers were replaced.

	Muffler Replacements		
	600	700	800
Total costs:			
Fixed costs	a	$56,000	b
Variable costs	c	28,000	d
Total costs	e	$84,000	f
Cost per muffler replacement:			
Fixed cost	g	h	i
Variable cost	j	k	l
Total cost per muffler replacement	m	n	o

Required: Fill in the missing amounts, labeled (*a*) through (*o*), in the table.

Exercise 2–31
Economic Characteristics of Costs
(LO 1, 10)

Thomas Cleverly purchased a vacant lot outside of London for £17,200, because he heard that a shopping mall was going to be built on the other side of the road. He figured that he could make a bundle by putting in a fast-food outlet on the site. As it turned out, the rumor was false. A sanitary landfill was located on the other side of the road, and the land was worthless. (£ denotes the British monetary unit, pounds sterling. Although the new monetary unit, the Euro, has now been introduced in European markets, day-to-day business in the United Kingdom is still conducted in pounds sterling.)

Required: What type of cost is the £17,200 that Thomas paid for the vacant lot?

Exercise 2–32
Fixed, Variable, Marginal, and Average Costs; Hotel
(LO 1, 8, 10)

A hotel pays the phone company $200 per month plus $.15 for each call made. During January 7,000 calls were made. In February 8,000 calls were made.

Required:

1. Calculate the hotel's phone bills for January and February.
2. Calculate the cost per phone call in January and in February.
3. Separate the January phone bill into its fixed and variable components.
4. What is the marginal cost of one additional phone call in January?
5. What was the average cost of a phone call in January?

Exercise 2–33
Computing Costs; Government Agency
(LO 1, 9, 10)

The state Department of Education owns a computer system, which its employees use for word processing and keeping track of education statistics. The governor's office recently began using this computer also. As a result of the increased usage, the demands on the computer soon exceeded its capacity. The director of the Department of Education was soon forced to lease several personal computers to meet the computing needs of her employees. The annual cost of leasing the equipment is $12,500.

Required:

1. What type of cost is this $12,500?
2. Should this cost be associated with the governor's office or the Department of Education? Why?

Exercise 2–34
Economic Characteristics of Costs
(LO 1, 10)

Suppose you paid $75 for a ticket to see your university's football team compete in a bowl game. Someone offered to buy your ticket for $100, but you decided to go to the game.

Required:

1. What did it really cost you to see the game?
2. What type of cost is this?

Exercise 2–35
Differential Cost
(LO 1, 10)

Global Communications, Inc. manufactures communications satellites used in TV signal transmission. The firm currently purchases one component for its satellites from a European firm. A Global Communications engineering team has found a way to use the company's own component, part number A200, instead of the European component. However, the Global Communications component must be modified at a cost of $650 per part. The European component costs $9,100 per part. Global Communications' part number A200 costs $4,900 before it is modified. Global Communications currently uses 15 of the European components per year.

Required: Calculate the annual differential cost between Global Communications' two production alternatives.

Exercise 2–36
Marginal Costs
(LO 1, 10)

List the costs that would likely be included in each of the following marginal-cost calculations.

1. The marginal cost of adding a flight from Syracuse to Miami.
2. The marginal cost of keeping a travel agency open one additional hour on Saturdays.
3. The marginal cost of manufacturing one additional pair of water skis.
4. The marginal cost of one additional passenger on a jet flight.
5. The marginal cost of serving one additional customer in a restaurant.

Problems

Problem 2–37
Cost Terminology
(LO 2, 5, 10)

The following cost data for the year just ended pertain to Heart Strings, Inc., a greeting card manufacturer:

Service department costs*	$ 50,000
Direct labor: fringe benefits	47,500
Indirect labor: fringe benefits	15,000
Fringe benefits for production supervisor	4,500
Total overtime premiums paid	27,500
Cost of idle time: production employees	20,000
Administrative costs	75,000
Rental of office space for sales personnel†	7,500
Sales commissions	2,500
Product promotion costs	5,000
Direct material	1,050,000
Advertising expense	49,500
Depreciation on factory building	57,500
Direct labor: wages	242,500
Cost of finished goods inventory at year-end	57,500
Indirect labor: wages	70,000
Production supervisor's salary	22,500

*All services are provided to manufacturing departments.

†The rental of sales space was made necessary when the sales offices were converted to storage space for raw material.

Required:

1. Compute each of the following costs for the year just ended: (*a*) total prime costs, (*b*) total manufacturing overhead costs, (*c*) total conversion costs, (*d*) total product costs, and (*e*) total period costs.
2. One of the costs listed above is an opportunity cost. Identify this cost, and explain why it is an opportunity cost.
3. One of the costs listed above is a sunk cost. Identify this cost, and explain why it is a sunk cost.

Problem 2–38
Direct and Indirect Labor
(LO 1, 3, 5, 9)

Kaleidoscope Cutlery manufactures kitchen knives. One of the employees, whose job is to cut out wooden knife handles, worked 49 hours during a week in January. The employee earns $14 per hour for a 40-hour week. For additional hours the employee is paid an overtime rate of $19 per hour. The employee's time was spent as follows:

Regular duties involving cutting out knife handles	41 hours
General shop cleanup duties	6 hours
Idle time due to power outage	2 hour

Required:

1. Calculate the total cost of the employee's wages during the week described above.
2. Determine the portion of this cost to be classified in each of the following categories:
   a. Direct labor
   b. Manufacturing overhead (idle time)
   c. Manufacturing overhead (overtime premium)
   d. Manufacturing overhead (indirect labor)

Problem 2–39
Content of Financial Statements and Reports; Mass Customization
(LO 3, 4)

Consider the following cost items:

1. Current year's depreciation on a ship owned by a cruise line.
2. The cost of chemicals and paper used during the period by a producer of film products.
3. Assembly-line wage cost incurred by a bicycle manufacturer.
4. Year-end production in process of a computer manufacturer.
5. The cost of products sold to customers of a department store.
6. The cost of products sold to distributors of a carpet manufacturer.

7. Salaries of players on a professional baseball club.
8. Year-end completed goods of a clothing manufacturer.
9. Executive compensation costs of a mass-market retailer.
10. Advertising costs of an electronics manufacturer.
11. Costs incurred during the period to insure a manufacturing plant against fire and flood losses.

Required:

1. Evaluate the costs just cited, and determine whether the associated dollar amounts would be found on the firm's balance sheet, income statement, or schedule of cost-of-goods-manufactured. (*Note:* In some cases, more than one answer will apply.)
2. What major asset will normally be insignificant for service enterprises and relatively substantial for retailers, wholesalers, and manufacturers? Briefly discuss.
3. Briefly explain the major differences between income statements of service enterprises versus those of retailers, wholesalers, and manufacturers.
4. Picture the operations of a firm such as Comet Computer, one that is involved in direct sales and mass customization of products. What would be the major difference in the balance sheet of this type of organization versus the balance sheet of a company that engages in more traditional manufacturing activities, that is, producing goods and waiting for customer orders to arrive?

Problem 2–40
Product Costs and Period Costs
(LO 1, 2, 3)

Indicate for each of the following costs whether it is a product cost or a period cost.

1. Cost of grapes purchased by a winery.
2. Depreciation on pizza ovens in a pizza restaurant.
3. Cost of plant manager's salary in a computer production facility.
4. Wages of security personnel in a department store.
5. Cost of utilities in a manufacturing facility.
6. Wages of aircraft mechanics employed by an airline.
7. Wages of drill-press operators in a manufacturing plant.
8. Cost of food in a microwavable dinner.
9. Cost incurred by a department store chain to transport merchandise to its stores.

Problem 2–41
Direct, Indirect, Controllable, and Uncontrollable Costs
(LO 1, 9)

For each of the following costs, indicate whether the amount is a direct or indirect cost of the equipment maintenance department. Also indicate whether each cost is at least partially controllable by the department supervisor.

1. Cost of electricity used in the maintenance department.
2. Depreciation on the building space occupied by the maintenance department.
3. Idle time of maintenance department employees.
4. Cost of plant manager's salary, which is allocated to the maintenance department.
5. Cost of property taxes allocated to the maintenance department.

Problem 2–42
Overtime Premiums and Fringe Benefit Costs; Airline
(LO 1, 5, 9)

LaJolla Airways operates commuter flights in California. Due to a political convention held in San Diego, the airline added several extra flights during a two-week period. Additional cabin crews were hired on a temporary basis. However, rather than hiring additional flight attendants, the airline used its current attendants on overtime. Monica Gaines worked the following schedule on August 10. All of Gaines's flights on that day were extra flights that the airline would not normally fly.

Regular time:	2 round-trip flights between San Diego and Fresno (8 hours)
Overtime:	1 one-way flight from San Diego to Sacramento (3 hours)

Gaines earns $14 per hour plus time and a half for overtime. Fringe benefits cost the airline $4 per hour for any hour worked, regardless of whether it is a regular or overtime hour.

Required:

1. Compute the direct cost of compensating Gaines for her services on the flight from San Diego to Sacramento.
2. Compute the cost of Gaines's services that is an indirect cost.

3. How should the cost computed in requirement (2) be treated for cost accounting purposes?
4. Gaines ended her workday on August 10 in Sacramento. However, her next scheduled flight departed San Diego at 11:00 a.m. on August 11. This required Gaines to "dead-head" back to San Diego on an early-morning flight. This means she traveled from Sacramento to San Diego as a passenger, rather than as a working flight attendant. Since the morning flight from Sacramento to San Diego was full, Gaines displaced a paying customer. The revenue lost by the airline was $87. What type of cost is the $87? To what flight, if any, is it chargeable? Why?

Problem 2–43
Schedules of Cost of Goods Manufactured and Sold; Income Statement
(LO 1, 3, 5, 6)

The following data refer to Laredo Luggage Company for the year 20x2:

Sales revenue	$475,000
Work-in-process inventory, December 31	15,000
Work-in-process inventory, January 1	20,000
Selling and administrative expenses	75,000
Income tax expense	45,000
Purchases of raw material	90,000
Raw-material inventory, December 31	12,500
Raw-material inventory, January 1	20,000
Direct labor	100,000
Utilities: plant	20,000
Depreciation: plant and equipment	30,000
Finished-goods inventory, December 31	25,000
Finished-goods inventory, January 1	10,000
Indirect material	5,000
Indirect labor	7,500
Other manufacturing overhead	40,000

Required:

1. Prepare Laredo Luggage's schedule of cost of goods manufactured for the year.
2. Prepare Laredo Luggage's schedule of cost of goods sold for the year.
3. Prepare Laredo Luggage's income statement for the year.

Problem 2–44
Financial-Statement Elements: Manufacturer
(LO 5, 6)

The following selected information was extracted from the 20x1 accounting records of Surgical Products, Inc.:

Raw material purchases	$ 350,000
Direct labor	508,000
Indirect labor	218,000
Selling and administrative salaries	266,000
Building depreciation*	160,000
Other selling and administrative expenses	380,000
Other factory costs	688,000
Sales revenue ($260 per unit)	2,990,000

*Seventy-five percent of the company's building was devoted to production activities; the remaining 25 percent was used for selling and administrative functions.

Inventory data:

	January 1	December 31
Raw material	$ 31,600	$ 36,400
Work in process	71,400	124,200
Finished goods*	222,200	195,800

*The January 1 and December 31 finished-goods inventory consisted of 1,350 units and 1,190 units, respectively.

Required:

1. Calculate Surgical Products' manufacturing overhead for the year.
2. Calculate Surgical Products' cost of goods manufactured.
3. Compute the company's cost of goods sold.
4. Determine net income for 20x1, assuming a 40% income tax rate.
5. Determine the number of completed units manufactured during the year.

Problem 2–45
Incomplete Data; Manufacturing Costs
(LO 2, 5)

Determine the missing amounts in each of the following independent cases.

	Case A	Case B	Case C
Sales	?	?	$240,000
Beginning inventory, raw material	?	$ 60,000	7,500
Ending inventory, raw material	$ 180,000	?	15,000
Purchases of raw material	200,000	255,000	?
Direct material used	140,000	285,000	?
Direct labor	?	300,000	62,500
Manufacturing overhead	500,000	?	80,000
Total manufacturing costs	1,040,000	1,035,000	170,000
Beginning inventory, work in process	70,000	60,000	?
Ending inventory, work in process	?	105,000	2,500
Cost of goods manufactured	1,050,000	?	175,000
Beginning inventory, finished goods	100,000	120,000	?
Cost of goods available for sale	?	?	185,000
Ending inventory, finished goods	?	?	12,500
Cost of goods sold	1,090,000	990,000	?
Gross margin	510,000	510,000	?
Selling and administrative expenses	?	225,000	?
Income before taxes	300,000	?	45,000
Income tax expense	80,000	135,000	?
Net income	?	?	27,500

Problem 2–46
Financial-Statement Elements; Cost Behavior
(LO 5, 6, 8)

Scranton Refrigeration Corporation began operations at the beginning of the current year. One of the company's products, a compressor, sells for $370 per unit. Information related to the current year's activities follows.

Variable costs per unit:	
Direct material	$ 40
Direct labor	74
Manufacturing overhead	96
Annual fixed costs:	
Manufacturing overhead	$1,200,000
Selling and administrative	1,720,000
Sales and production activity:	
Sales (units)	20,000
Production (units)	24,000

Scranton Refrigeration carries its finished-goods inventory at the average unit cost of production and is subject to a 40% income tax rate. There was no work in process at year-end.

Required:

1. Determine the cost of the December 31 finished-goods inventory.
2. Compute Scranton Refrigeration's net income for the current year ended December 31.
3. If next year's production decreases to 22,500 units and general cost behavior patterns do not change, what is the likely effect on:
   a. The direct-labor cost of $74 per unit? Why?
   b. The fixed manufacturing overhead cost of $1,200,000? Why?
   c. The fixed selling and administrative cost of $1,720,000? Why?
   d. The average unit cost of production? Why?

Problem 2–47
Inventory Estimates; Partial Data
(LO 5, 6)

On May 10, after the close of business, Fresno Furniture Company had a devastating fire that destroyed the company's work-in-process and finished-goods inventories. Fortunately, all raw materials escaped damage because materials owned by the firm were stored in another warehouse. The following information is available:

Sales revenue through May 10	$495,000
Income before taxes through May 10	102,000
Direct labor through May 10	180,000
Cost of goods available for sale, May 10	412,500
Work-in-process inventory, January 1	31,500
Finished-goods inventory, January 1	55,500

Fresno Furniture Company's accountants determined that the cost of direct materials used normally averages 25 percent of prime costs (i.e., direct material + direct labor). In addition, manufacturing overhead is 50 percent of the firm's total production costs. The gross margin is 30 percent of sales.

Required: The company is in the process of negotiating a settlement with its insurance company. Prepare an estimate of the cost of work-in-process and finished-goods inventories that were destroyed by the fire.

Problem 2–48
Fixed Costs; Graphical and Tabular Analyses
(LO 7, 8)

Thermal Technology, Inc. manufactures a special chemical used to coat certain electrical components that will be exposed to high heat in various applications. The company's annual fixed production cost is $500,000.

Required:

1. Draw a graph of the company's fixed production cost showing the total cost at the following production levels of the chemical: 50,000 liters, 100,000 liters, 150,000 liters, and 200,000 liters.
2. Prepare a table that shows the unit cost and the total cost for the firm's fixed production costs at the following production levels: 1 liter, 50 liters, 50,000 liters, and 200,000 liters.
3. Prepare a graph that shows the unit cost for the company's fixed production cost at the following production levels: 50,000 liters, 100,000 liters, 150,000 liters, and 200,000 liters.

Problem 2–49
Variable Costs; Graphical and Tabular Analyses
(LO 7, 8)

Air Frame Technology, Inc. incurs a variable cost of $16 per kilogram for raw material to produce a special alloy used in manufacturing aircraft.

Required:

1. Draw a graph of the firm's raw material cost, showing the total cost at the following production levels: 50,000 kilograms, 100,000 kilograms, and 150,000 kilograms.
2. Prepare a table that shows the unit cost and total cost of raw material at the following production levels: 1 kilogram, 50 kilograms, and 5,000 kilograms.

Problem 2–50
Cost Classifications; Manufacturer
(LO 5, 8, 9)

Nantucket Tee manufactures T-shirts and decorates them with custom designs for retail sale on the premises. Several costs incurred by the company are listed below. For each cost, indicate which of the following classifications best describe the cost. More than one classification may apply to the same cost item.

Cost Classifications

- **a.** Variable
- **b.** Fixed
- **c.** Period
- **d.** Product
- **e.** Administrative
- **f.** Selling
- **g.** Manufacturing
- **h.** Research and development
- **i.** Direct material
- **j.** Direct labor
- **k.** Manufacturing overhead

Cost Items

1. Wages of T-shirt designers and painters.
2. Salaries of sales personnel.
3. Depreciation on sewing machines.

4. Rent on the building. Part of the building's first floor is used to make and paint T-shirts. Part of it is used for the retail sales shop. The second floor is used for administrative offices and storage of raw material and finished goods.
5. Cost of daily advertisements in local media.
6. Salaries of designers who experiment with new fabrics, paints, and T-shirt designs.
7. Cost of hiring a pilot to fly along the beach pulling a banner advertising the shop.
8. Salary of the owner's secretary.
9. Cost of repairing the gas furnace.
10. Cost of health insurance for the production employees.
11. Cost of fabric used in T-shirts.
12. Wages of shirtmakers.
13. Cost of new sign in front of retail T-shirt shop.
14. Wages of the employee who repairs the firm's sewing machines.
15. Cost of electricity used in the sewing department.

Problem 2–51
Interpretation of Accounting Reports
(LO 1, 3)

Refer to Exhibit 2–3, and answer the following questions.

Required:

1. List the major differences between the income statements shown for Caterpillar, Inc., Wal-Mart Stores, Inc., and Southwest Airlines Company.
2. Explain how cost-accounting data were used to prepare these income statements.
3. On the income statement for Southwest Airlines Company, where would the ticket agents' salaries be shown? Where would the costs of the computer equipment used to keep track of reservations be included on the statement?
4. On the income statement for Wal-Mart Stores, Inc., where would the cost of newspaper advertising be shown? How about the cost of merchandise?
5. Refer to the income statement for Caterpillar, Inc. Where would the salary of the brand manager who plans advertising for Caterpillar equipment be shown? How about the salary of a production employee? Where would the cost of the raw materials used in the company's products be included on the statement?

Problem 2–52
Cost Classifications; Government Agency
(LO 8, 9, 10)

The Department of Natural Resources is responsible for maintaining the state's parks and forest lands, stocking the lakes and rivers with fish, and generally overseeing the protection of the environment. Several costs incurred by the agency are listed below. For each cost, indicate which of the following classifications best describe the cost. More than one classification may apply to the same cost item.

Cost Classifications

a. Variable
b. Fixed
c. Controllable by the department director
d. Uncontrollable by the department director
e. Differential cost
f. Marginal cost
g. Opportunity cost
h. Sunk cost
i. Out-of-pocket cost
j. Direct cost of the agency
k. Indirect cost of the agency
l. Direct cost of providing a particular service
m. Indirect cost of providing a particular service

Cost Items

1. Cost of the fish purchased from private hatcheries, which are used to stock the state's public waters.
2. The difference between (*a*) the cost of purchasing fish from private hatcheries and (*b*) the cost of running a state hatchery.

3. Cost of producing literature that describes the department's role in environmental protection. This literature is mailed free, upon request, to schools, county governments, libraries, and private citizens.
4. Cost of sending the department's hydroengineers to inspect one additional dam for stability and safety.
5. Cost of operating the state's computer services department, a portion of which is allocated to the Department of Natural Resources.
6. Cost of administrative supplies used in the agency's head office.
7. Cost of providing an 800 number for the state's residents to report environmental problems.
8. The cost of replacing batteries in sophisticated monitoring equipment used to evaluate the effects of acid rain on the state's lakes.
9. Cost of a ranger's salary, when the ranger is giving a talk about environmental protection to elementary school children.
10. Cost of direct-mailing to 1 million state residents a brochure explaining the benefits of voluntarily recycling cans and bottles.
11. The cost of producing a TV show to be aired on public television. The purpose of the show is to educate people on how to spot and properly dispose of hazardous waste.
12. Cost of the automobiles used by the department's rangers. These cars were purchased by the state, and they would otherwise have been used by the state police.
13. Cost of live-trapping and moving beaver that were creating a nuisance in recreational lakes.
14. The department director's salary.
15. Cost of containing naturally caused forest fires, which are threatening private property.

Problem 2–53
Fixed and Variable Costs; Forecasting
(LO 7, 8)

Toledo Toy Company incurred the following costs during 20x4. The company sold all of its products manufactured during the year.

Direct material	$4,500,000
Direct labor	3,300,000
Manufacturing overhead:	
Utilities (primarily electricity)	210,000
Depreciation on plant and equipment	345,000
Insurance	240,000
Supervisory salaries	450,000
Property taxes	315,000
Selling costs:	
Advertising	292,500
Sales commissions	135,000
Administrative costs:	
Salaries of top management and staff	558,000
Office supplies	60,000
Depreciation on building and equipment	120,000

During 20x4, the company operated at about half of its capacity, due to a slowdown in the economy. Prospects for 20x5 are slightly better. Jared Lowes, the marketing manager, forecasts a 30 percent growth in sales over the 20x4 level.

Required: Categorize each of the costs listed above as to whether it is most likely variable or fixed. Forecast the 20x5 cost amount for each of the cost items listed above.

Problem 2–54
Cost Classifications; Hotel
(LO 1, 3, 9, 10)

Several costs incurred by Cape Cod Hotel and Restaurant are given in the following list. For each cost, indicate which of the following classifications best describe the cost. More than one classification may apply to the same cost item.

Cost Classifications

a. Direct cost of the food and beverage department
b. Indirect cost of the food and beverage department

c. Controllable by the kitchen manager
d. Uncontrollable by the kitchen manager
e. Controllable by the hotel general manager
f. Uncontrollable by the hotel general manager
g. Differential cost
h. Marginal cost
i. Opportunity cost
j. Sunk cost
k. Out-of-pocket cost

Cost Items

1. The wages earned by table-service personnel.
2. The salary of the kitchen manager.
3. The cost of the refrigerator purchased 14 months ago. The unit was covered by a warranty for 12 months, during which time it worked perfectly. It conked out after 14 months, despite an original estimate that it would last five years.
4. The hotel has two options for obtaining fresh pies, cakes, and pastries. The goodies can be purchased from a local bakery for approximately $1,550 per month, or they can be made in the hotel's kitchen. To make the pastries on the premises, the hotel will have to hire a part-time pastry chef. This will cost $500 per month. The cost of ingredients will amount to roughly $850 per month. Thus, the savings from making the goods in the hotel's kitchen amount to $200 per month.
5. The cost of dishes broken by kitchen employees.
6. The cost of leasing a computer used for reservations, payroll, and general hotel accounting.
7. The cost of a pool service that cleans and maintains the hotel's swimming pool.
8. The wages of the hotel's maintenance employees, who spent nine hours (at $13.50 per hour) repairing the dishwasher in the kitchen.
9. The cost of general advertising by the hotel, which is allocated to the food and beverage department.
10. The cost of food used in the kitchen.
11. The difference in the total cost incurred by the hotel when one additional guest is registered.
12. The cost of space (depreciation) occupied by the kitchen.
13. The cost of space (depreciation) occupied by a sauna next to the pool. The space could otherwise have been used for a magazine and bookshop.
14. The profit that would have been earned in a magazine and bookshop, if the hotel had one.
15. The discount on room rates given as a special offer for a "Labor Day Getaway Special."

Problem 2–55
Marginal Costs and Average Costs
(LO 7, 10)

Maria Chavez makes custom mooring covers for boats. Each mooring cover is hand sewn to fit a particular boat. If covers are made for two or more identical boats, each successive cover generally requires less time to make. Chavez has been approached by a local boat dealer to make mooring covers for all of the boats sold by the dealer. Chavez has developed the following cost schedule for mooring covers made to fit 17-foot outboard power boats.

Mooring Covers Made	Total Cost of Covers
1.	$ 675
2.	1,275
3.	1,815
4.	2,310
5.	2,775

Required: Compute the following:

1. Marginal cost of second mooring cover.
2. Marginal cost of fourth mooring cover.
3. Marginal cost of fifth mooring cover.

4. Average cost if two mooring covers are made.
5. Average cost if four mooring covers are made.
6. Average cost if five mooring covers are made.

Problem 2–56
Economic Characteristics of Costs
(LO 4, 10)

The following terms are used to describe various economic characteristics of costs.

a. Opportunity cost
b. Out-of-pocket cost
c. Sunk cost
d. Differential cost
e. Marginal cost
f. Average cost

Required: Choose one of the terms listed above to characterize each of the amounts described below.

1. The management of a high-rise office building uses 3,100 square feet of space in the building for its own management functions. This space could be rented for $335,000. What economic term describes this $335,000 in lost rental revenue?
2. The cost of building an automated assembly line in a factory is $700,000. The cost of building a manually operated assembly line is $475,000. What economic term is used to describe the difference between these two amounts?
3. Referring to the preceding question, what economic term is used to describe the $700,000 cost of building the automated assembly line?
4. The cost incurred by a mass customizer such as Dell Computer to produce one more unit in its most popular line of laptop computers.
5. The cost of feeding 400 children in a public school cafeteria is $740 per day, or $1.85 per child per day. What economic term describes this $1.85 cost?
6. The cost of including one extra child in a day-care center.
7. The cost of merchandise inventory purchased two years ago, which is now obsolete.

Problem 2–57
Variable and Fixed Costs; Make or Buy a Component
(LO 8, 10)

Piedmont Industries currently manufactures 40,000 units of part JR63 each month for use in production of several of its products. The facilities now used to produce part JR63 have a fixed monthly cost of $165,000 and a capacity to produce 74,000 units per month. If the company were to buy part JR63 from an outside supplier, the facilities would be idle, but its fixed costs would continue at $45,000. The variable production costs of part JR63 are $12 per unit.

Required:

1. If Piedmont Industries continues to use 40,000 units of part JR63 each month, it would realize a net benefit by purchasing part JR63 from an outside supplier only if the supplier's unit price is less than what amount?
2. If Piedmont Industries is able to obtain part JR63 from an outside supplier at a unit purchase price of $14, what is the monthly usage at which it will be indifferent between purchasing and making part JR63?

(CMA, adapted)

Problem 2–58
Unit Costs; Profit-Maximizing Output
(LO 7, 8)

The controller for Oneida Vineyards, Inc. has predicted the following costs at various levels of wine output.

	Wine Output (.75 Liter Bottles)		
	10,000 Bottles	**15,000 Bottles**	**20,000 Bottles**
Variable production costs	$ 42,000	$ 63,000	$ 84,000
Fixed production costs	120,000	120,000	120,000
Variable selling and administrative costs	2,400	3,600	4,800
Fixed selling and administrative costs	48,000	48,000	48,000
Total	$212,400	$234,600	$256,800

The company's marketing manager has predicted the following prices for the firm's fine wines at various levels of sales.

	Wine Sales		
	10,000 Bottles	15,000 Bottles	20,000 Bottles
Sales price per .75 liter bottle.	$21.60	$18.00	$14.40

Required:

1. Calculate the unit cost of wine production at each level of output. At what level of output is the unit cost minimized?
2. Calculate the company's profit at each level of production. Assume that the company will sell all of its output. At what production level is profit maximized?
3. Which of the three output levels is best for the company?
4. Why does the unit cost of wine decrease as the output level increases? Why might the sales price per bottle decline as sales volume increases?

Cases

Case 2–59
Understanding Cost Concepts
(LO 7, 8, 10)

You just started a summer internship with the successful management consulting firm of Kirk, Spock, and McCoy. Your first day on the job was a busy one, as the following problems were presented to you.

Required: Supply the requested comments in each of the following independent situations.

1. Alderon Enterprises is evaluating a special order it has received for a ceramic fixture to be used in aircraft engines. Alderon has recently been operating at less than full capacity, so the firm's management will accept the order if the price offered exceeds the costs that will be incurred in producing it. You have been asked for advice on how to determine the cost of two raw materials that would be required to produce the order.
   a. The special order will require 900 gallons of endor, a highly perishable material that is purchased as needed. Alderon currently has 1,300 gallons of endor on hand, since the material is used in virtually all of the company's products. The last time endor was purchased, Alderon paid $10.00 per gallon. However, the average price paid for the endor in stock was only $9.50. The market price for endor is quite volatile, with the current price at $11.00. If the special order is accepted, Alderon will have to place a new order next week to replace the 900 gallons of endor used. By then the price is expected to reach $11.50 per gallon.
   Using the cost terminology introduced in Chapter 2, comment on each of the cost figures mentioned in the preceding discussion. What is the real cost of endor if the special order is produced?
   b. The special order would also require 1,400 kilograms of tatooine, a material not normally required in any of Alderon's regular products. The company does happen to have 1,900 kilograms of tatooine on hand, since it formerly manufactured a ceramic product that used the material. Alderon recently received an offer of $28,000 from Solo Industries for its entire supply of tatooine. However, Solo Industries is not interested in buying any quantity less than Alderon's entire 1,900-kilogram stock. Alderon's management is unenthusiastic about Solo's offer, since Alderon paid $40,000 for the tatooine. Moreover, if the tatooine were purchased at today's market price, it would cost $22.00 per kilogram. Due to the volatility of the tatooine, Alderon will need to get rid of its entire supply one way or another. If the material is not used in production or sold, Alderon will have to pay $2,000 for each 500 kilograms that is transported away and disposed of in a hazardous waste disposal site.
   Using the cost terminology introduced in Chapter 2, comment on each of the cost figures mentioned in the preceding discussion. What is the real cost of tatooine to be used in the special order?
2. CopyFast Company, a specialist in printing, has established 500 convenience photo copying centers throughout the country. In order to upgrade its services, the company is considering three new models of laser copying machines for use in producing high-quality copies. These high-quality copies would be added to the growing list of products offered in the CopyFast shops. The selling price to the customer for each laser copy would be the same, no matter which machine is installed in the shop. The three models of laser copying machines under consideration are: 1500S, a small-

volume model; 1500M, a medium-volume model; and 1500L, a large-volume model. The annual rental costs and the operating costs vary with the size of each machine. The machine capacities and costs are as follows:

	Photocopier Model		
	1500S	1500M	1500L
Annual capacity (copies)	80,000	300,000	600,000
Costs:			
Annual machine rental	$ 4,000	$ 5,500	$ 10,000
Direct material and direct labor per copy	.010	.010	.010
Variable overhead costs per copy	.060	.035	.015

a. Calculate the volume level in copies where CopyFast Company would be indifferent to acquiring either the small-volume model laser copier, 1500S, or the medium-volume model laser copier, 1500M.

b. The management of CopyFast Company is able to estimate the number of copies to be sold at each establishment. Present a decision rule that would enable management to select the most profitable machine without having to make a separate cost calculation for each establishment. (*Hint:* To specify a decision rule, determine the volume at which CopyFast Company would be indifferent between the small and medium copiers. Then determine the volume at which the company would be indifferent between the medium and large copiers.)

3. A local PBS station has decided to produce a TV series on state-of-the-art manufacturing. The director of the TV series, Justin Tyme, is currently attempting to analyze some of the projected costs for the series. Tyme intends to take a TV production crew on location to shoot various high-tech manufacturing scenes as they occur. If the four-week series is shown in the 8:00–9:00 P.M. prime-time slot, the station will have to cancel a wildlife show that is currently scheduled. Management projects a 10 percent viewing audience for the wildlife show, and each 1 percent is expected to bring in donations of $20,000. In contrast, the manufacturing show is expected to be watched by 15 percent of the viewing audience. However, each 1 percent of the viewership will likely generate only $10,000 in donations. If the wildlife show is canceled, it can be sold to network television for $50,000.

Using the cost terminology introduced in Chapter 2, comment on each of the financial amounts mentioned in the preceding discussion. What are the relative merits of the two shows regarding the projected revenue to the station?

(CMA, adapted)

Case 2–60
Economic Characteristics of Costs; Closing a Department; Ethics
(LO 10)

Pensacola Printer Company manufactures printers for use with home computing systems. The firm currently manufactures both the electronic components for its printers and the plastic cases in which the devices are enclosed. Jim Cassanitti, the production manager, recently received a proposal from Universal Plastics Corporation to manufacture the cases for Pensacola's printers. If the cases are purchased outside, Pensacola Printer Company will be able to close down its Printer Case Department. To help decide whether to accept the bid from Universal Plastics Corporation, Cassanitti asked Pensacola's controller to prepare an analysis of the costs that would be saved if the Printer Case Department were closed. Included in the controller's list of annual cost savings were the following items:

Building rental (The Printer Case Department occupies one-sixth of the factory building, which Pensacola rents for $180,600 per year.)	$30,100
Salary of the Printer Case Department supervisor	$48,000

In a lunchtime conversation with the controller, Cassanitti learned that Pensacola Printer Company was currently renting space in a warehouse for $41,000. The space is used to store completed printers. If the Printer Case Department were discontinued, the entire storage operation could be moved into the factory building and occupy the space vacated by the closed department. Cassanitti also learned that the supervisor of the Printer Case Department would be retained by Pensacola even if the department were closed. The supervisor would be assigned the job of managing the assembly department, whose supervisor recently gave notice of his retirement. All of Pensacola Printer Company's department supervisors earn the same salary.

Required:

1. You have been hired as a consultant by Cassanitti to advise him in his decision. Write a memo to Cassanitti commenting on the costs of space and supervisory salaries included in the controller's cost analysis. Explain in your memo about the "real" costs of the space occupied by the Printer Case Department and the supervisor's salary. What types of costs are these?

2. Independent of your response to requirement (1), suppose that Pensacola Printer Company's controller had been approached by his friend Jack Westford, the assistant supervisor of the Printer Case Department. Westford is worried that he will be laid off if the Printer Case Department is closed down.

   Westford has asked his friend to understate the cost savings from closing the department, in order to slant the production manager's decision toward keeping the department in operation. Comment on the controller's ethical responsibilities.

Current Issues in Managerial Accounting

"IBM Gets $2 Billion Outsourcing Job," ***The Wall Street Journal,*** **February 12, 2003, p. B3, John Hechinger.**

Issue 2–61
Outsourcing

Overview
IBM will take over the computer operations of auto-parts manufacturer, Visteon Corporation, a spin-off from Ford Motor Company.

Suggested Discussion Questions
Why is outsourcing such a popular business strategy these days? What are its costs and benefits?

"HP and Compaq: It's Showtime," ***Business Week,*** **June 17, 2002, p. 76, Cliff Edwards and Andrew Park; "On a Roll, Dell Enters Uncharted Territory,"** ***The New York Times,*** **August 25, 2002, Steve Lohr.**

Issue 2–62
Mass Customization; Direct-Sales Business Model

Overview
Dell Computer has been amazingly successful with its build-to-order, direct-sales business model.

Suggested Discussion Questions
Will the Hewlett-Packard and Compaq merger be successful in emulating Dell's approach? Do you think the merger will enable HP to cut costs by $3 billion annually, as HP's CEO predicted?

"Year of the Outsourcer," ***Business Week,*** **January 8, 2001, Pete Engardio and Peter Burrows.**

Issue 2–63
Outsourcing

Overview
An expected slowdown in the overall demand for tech products is putting pressure on companies like Hewlett-Packard, Lucent, and Motorola to cut costs. One way to cut costs is "getting rid of factories." Outsourcing, a business method widely used by mass customizers like Dell Computer, also figures prominently in cost management for many companies.

Suggested Discussion Questions
What will be the likely impact, according to the article, of outsourcing in the tech industry? What will be the likely impact on electronics-sector companies like Solectron, Flextronics and Celestica?

"Getting Rid of Guesswork," ***Business Week,*** **August 28, 2000, Adrian J. Slywotzky.**

Issue 2–64
Mass Customization; Changing Technology in Manufacturing Operations

Overview
Mass customization, is it possible? For years, manufacturers have guessed what their customers wanted. Sometimes manufacturers were correct, sometimes they were wrong and inventories built up. Choiceboards are beginning to permit customers to custom-design products.

Suggested Discussion Questions
Explain the concept of a choiceboard. Name some industries currently developing choiceboard systems.

"Hospitals in NH Post More Losses," ***The Wall Street Journal,*** **April 26, 2000, James Bandler.**

Issue 2–65
Fixed Costs

Overview
Recently seven of New Hampshire's 23 hospitals that reported financial results disclosed losses, up from two in the previous year. Six of the seven hospitals are in rural areas. Medicare cuts and managed-care insurance reductions have cut into the pockets of hospitals and doctors. Les MacLeod, chairman of the New Hampshire Rural Health Coalition, states that rural hospitals are hit harder than urban hospitals since rural hospitals serve a higher percentage of elderly patients. This translates into less revenue for rural hospitals, even though their fixed costs are higher as a percentage of total expenses.

Suggested Discussion Question
Assume you have been charged by Les MacLeod to develop some viable methods for reducing fixed costs for New Hampshire's rural hospitals. Work as a group to prepare a written response.

Chapter Three

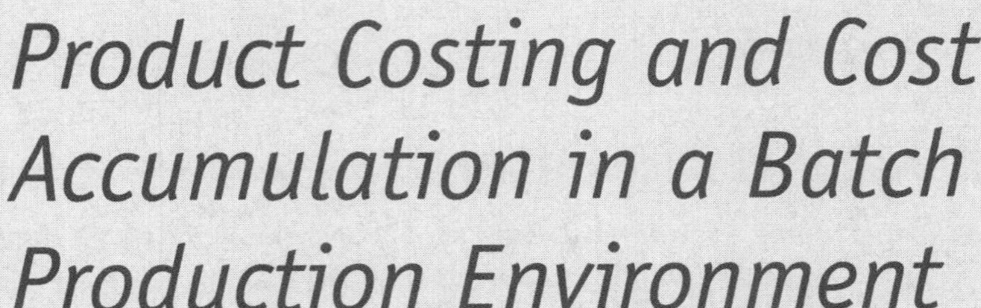

Product Costing and Cost Accumulation in a Batch Production Environment

After completing this chapter, you should be able to:

1. Discuss the role of product and service costing in manufacturing and nonmanufacturing firms.
2. Diagram and explain the flow of costs through the manufacturing accounts used in product costing.
3. Distinguish between job-order costing and process costing.
4. Compute a predetermined overhead rate, and explain its use in job-order costing for job-shop and batch-production environments.
5. Prepare journal entries to record the costs of direct material, direct labor, and manufacturing overhead in a job-order costing system.
6. Prepare a schedule of cost of goods manufactured, a schedule of cost of goods sold, and an income statement for a manufacturer.
7. Describe the two-stage allocation process used to compute departmental overhead rates.
8. Describe the process of project costing used in service industry firms and nonprofit organizations.
9. Diagram and describe the two-stage allocation process used in activity-based costing (appendix).

Making Canoes Is an Art Form in This Adirondack Community

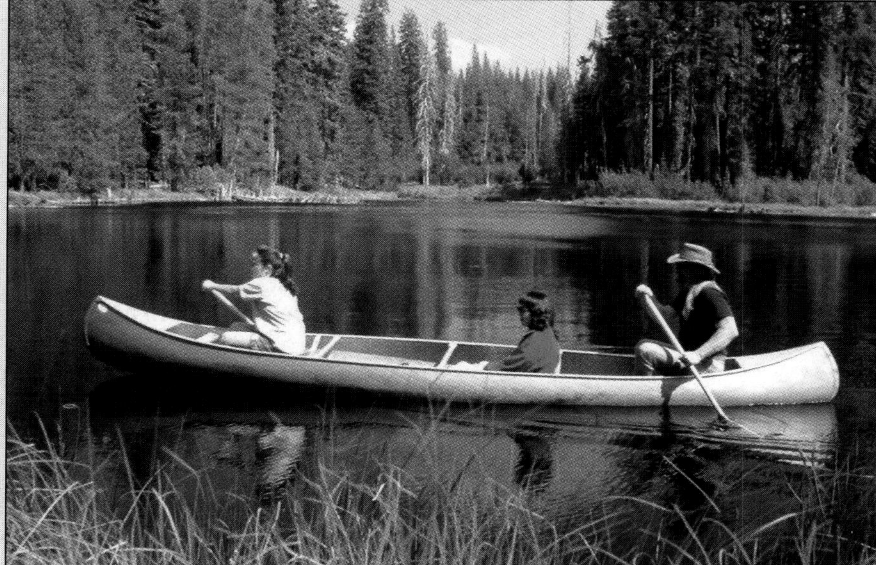

Lake Placid, NY—As we skimmed across the lake, gliding almost effortlessly in our canoe, I was struck by the beauty of the Adirondack Mountains. "Many people don't realize it," said my host, "but New York's Adirondack Park is the largest state park in the nation. There are thousands of acres of unspoiled beauty." We made our way to shore and pulled our 16-foot canoe out of the water. My host was Meg Wilmore, founder of Adirondack Outfitters. Wilmore's company, which produces some of the finest canoes in the Northeast, is located several miles from Lake Placid. Scene of the 1932 and 1980 Winter Olympic Games, Lake Placid is known for its scenic beauty. Nestled in the hills outside this quaint community is Wilmore's highly successful business. "Making canoes is an art," said Wilmore. "I learned it from my grandfather, who made them as a hobby. My goal was to form a small company to make high-quality canoes and small boats in an environmentally friendly way. If you do things right—and we do—it's a nonpolluting industry."

After testing an Adirondack Outfitters' canoe, I returned with Wilmore to her production facility. Giving me a brief tour, Wilmore explained that the company was currently working on two production jobs. "Our production is organized by production jobs," explained Wilmore. "Right now we're making deluxe wooden canoes and deluxe aluminum fishing boats. Both models are good sellers throughout the northeastern states and eastern Canada." Wilmore pointed out that a number of machines were used in the production process, but all were hand operated. In many cases, one employee was able to tend several machines simultaneously. "We strive for a balance between being competitive, requiring machine production, and keeping a hands-on feel to the process. Basically we're a small, traditional job shop. Each job is relatively small in terms of the number of units, and the differences between jobs are significant. There's not much similarity between a wooden canoe and an aluminum fishing boat." Asked what accounted for her company's success, Wilmore's answer was, "quality and price."

"In today's business environment, you have to be price competitive, whether you're into canoes or microchips. To give people a high-quality boat or canoe at the right price means that we have to know our costs inside and out. Since production jobs are so different, we track costs on a job-by-job basis. As in any manufacturing operation, you've got material, labor, and overhead. We accumulate these three costs for each production job. Dividing by the number of units in the job gives us our unit cost."

As we talked, it was clear that Wilmore relished her role as an entrepreneur. I ended the interview by asking her if there was anything she'd rather do than make canoes. "Yes," was her swift reply, "paddle them!"

Product and Service Costing

LO 1

Discuss the role of product and service costing in manufacturing and nonmanufacturing firms.

A **product-costing system** accumulates the costs incurred in a production process and assigns those costs to the organization's final products. Product costs are needed for a variety of purposes in financial accounting, managerial accounting, and cost management.

Use in Financial Accounting In financial accounting, product costs are needed to value inventory on the balance sheet and to compute cost-of-goods-sold expense on the income statement. Under generally accepted accounting principles, inventory is valued at its cost until it is sold. Then the cost of the inventory becomes an expense of the period in which it is sold.

Use in Managerial Accounting In managerial accounting, product costs are needed to help managers with planning and to provide them with data for decision making. Decisions about product prices, the mix of products to be produced, and the quantity of output to be manufactured are among those for which product cost information is needed.

Use in Cost Management It is hard to imagine how management can control or reduce production costs if management does not have a clear idea of how much it costs to make its product. Thus, product costs provide crucial data for a variety of cost management purposes. Many of the cost management uses of product-costing information will be covered throughout this book.

"We recognized that our key competitors were overseas. We realized that in order to compete, we had to be extremely cost conscious." (3a)
MiCRUS (joint venture of IBM and Cirrus Logic)

Use in Reporting to Interested Organizations In addition to financial statement preparation and internal decision making, there is an ever-growing need for product cost information in relationships between firms and various outside organizations. Public utilities, such as electric and gas companies, record product costs to justify rate increases that must be approved by state regulatory agencies. Hospitals keep track of the costs of medical procedures that are reimbursed by insurance companies or by the federal government under the Medicare program. Manufacturing firms often sign cost-plus contracts with the government, where the contract price depends on the cost of manufacturing the product.

Product Costing in Nonmanufacturing Firms

The need for product costs is not limited to manufacturing firms. Merchandising companies include the costs of buying and transporting merchandise in their product costs. Producers of inventoriable goods, such as mining products, petroleum, and agricultural products, also record the costs of producing their goods. The role of product costs in these companies is identical to that in manufacturing firms. For example, the pineapples grown and sold by Dole are inventoried at their product cost until they are sold. Then the product cost becomes cost-of-goods-sold expense.

"The closer we get to the client physically, the more likely it is that we're going to have an opportunity to participate in what's going on in the business. The more remote you are from where the business decision makers are, the less likely they are to think about you." (3b)
Qwest

Service Firms and Nonprofit Organizations The production output of service firms and nonprofit organizations consists of services that are consumed as they are produced. Since services cannot be stored and sold later like manufactured goods, there are no inventoriable costs in service industry firms and nonprofit organizations. However, such organizations need information about the costs of producing services. Banks, insurance companies, restaurants, airlines, law firms, hospitals, and city governments all record the costs of producing various services for the purposes of planning, cost control, and decision making. For example, in making a decision about adding a flight from Chicago to Los Angeles, United Airlines' management needs to know the cost of flying the proposed route. A manager can make a better decision as

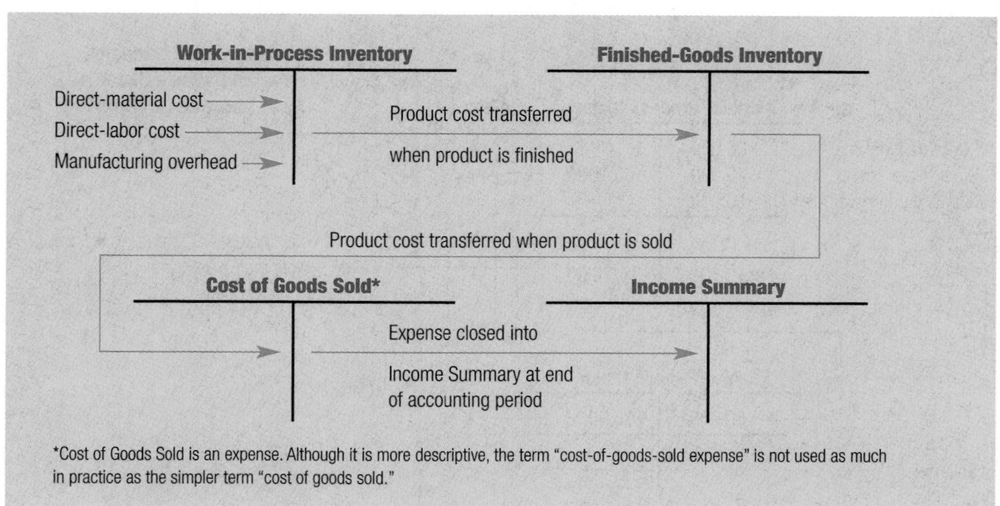

Exhibit 3–1
Flow of Costs through Manufacturing Accounts

to whether a university or city government should begin a drug counseling program if the cost of providing similar, existing services is known.

Flow of Costs in Manufacturing Firms

LO 2 Diagram and explain the flow of costs through the manufacturing accounts used in product costing.

Manufacturing costs consist of direct material, direct labor, and manufacturing overhead. The product-costing systems used by manufacturing firms employ several manufacturing accounts. As production takes place, all manufacturing costs are added to the *Work-in-Process Inventory* account. Work in process is partially completed inventory. A debit to the account increases the cost-based valuation of the asset represented by the unfinished products. As soon as products are completed, their product costs are transferred from Work-in-Process Inventory to *Finished-Goods Inventory.* This is accomplished with a credit to Work in Process and a debit to Finished Goods. During the time period when products are sold, the product cost of the inventory sold is removed from Finished Goods and added to *Cost of Goods Sold,* which is an expense of the period in which the sale occurred. A credit to Finished Goods and a debit to Cost of Goods Sold completes this step. Cost of Goods Sold is closed into the Income Summary account at the end of the accounting period, along with all other expenses and revenues of the period. Exhibit 3–1 depicts the flow of costs through the manufacturing accounts.

Example of Manufacturing Cost Flows Suppose that the Bradley Paper Company incurred the following manufacturing costs during 20x1.

Direct material	$30,000
Direct labor	20,000
Manufacturing overhead	40,000

During 20x1, products costing $60,000 were finished and products costing $25,000 were sold for $32,000. Exhibit 3–2 shows the flow of costs through the Bradley Paper Company's manufacturing accounts and the effect of the firm's product costs on its balance sheet and income statement.

Types of Product-Costing Systems

The detailed accounting procedures used in product-costing systems depend on the type of industry involved. Two basic sets of procedures are used.

Exhibit 3–2
Example of Manufacturing Cost Flows for Bradley Paper Company

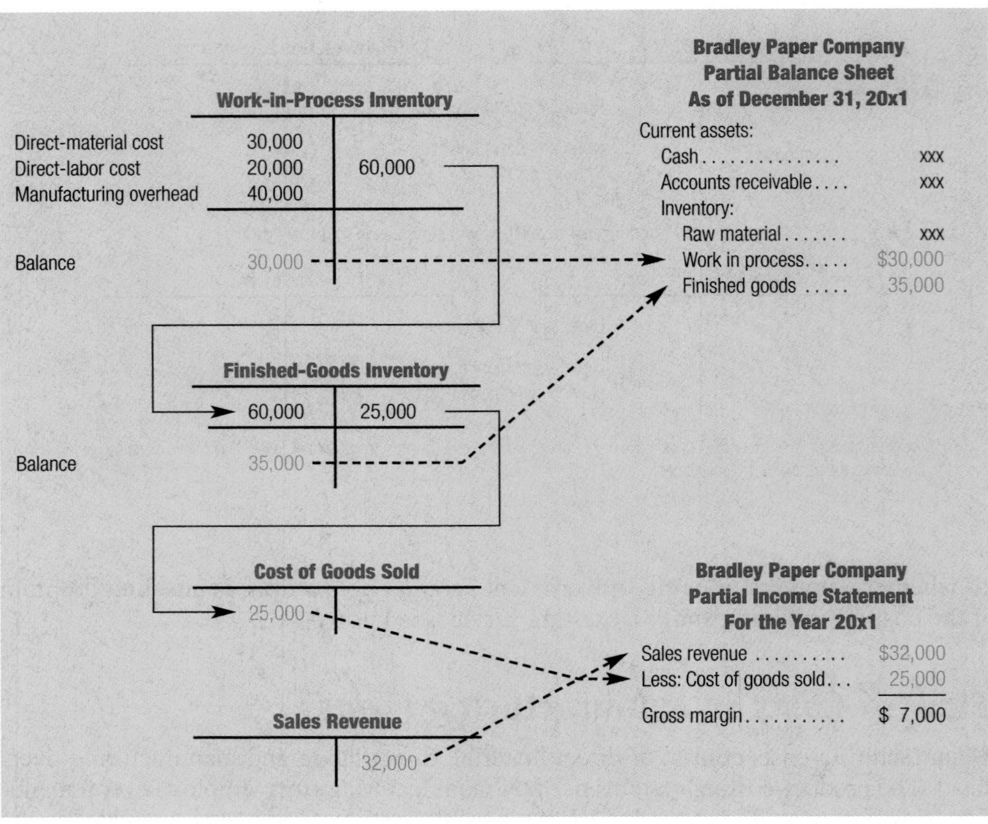

Job-Order Costing Systems

LO 3
Distinguish between job-order costing and process costing.

Job-order costing is used by companies with *job-shop* operations or *batch-production* operations. In a job-shop environment, products are manufactured in very low volumes or one at a time. Examples of a job-shop environment include feature film production, custom house building, ship building, aircraft manufacture, and custom machining operations. In a batch-production environment, multiple products are produced in batches of relatively small quantity. Examples include furniture manufacture, printing, agricultural equipment, and pleasure boat production.

Topic 3–1

In **job-order costing,** each distinct batch of production is called a *job* or *job order.* The cost-accounting procedures are designed to assign costs to each job. Then the costs assigned to each job are averaged over the units of production in the job to obtain an average cost per unit. For example, suppose that AccuPrint worked on two printing jobs during October, and the following costs were incurred.

	Job A27 (1,000 campaign posters)	Job B39 (100 wedding invitations)
Direct material	$100	$ 36
Direct labor	250	40
Manufacturing overhead	150	24
Total manufacturing cost	$500	$100

The cost per campaign poster is $.50 per poster ($500 divided by 1,000 posters), and the cost per wedding invitation is $1.00 ($100 divided by 100 invitations).

Procedures similar to those used in job-order costing are also used in many service industry firms, although these firms have no work-in-process or finished-goods inventories. In a public accounting firm, for example, costs are assigned to audit engagements

The cost-accounting system keeps track of production costs as they flow from work-in-process inventory through finished-goods inventory and into cost of goods sold.

in much the same way they are assigned to a batch of products by a furniture manufacturer. Similar procedures are used to assign costs to "cases" in health care facilities, to "programs" in government agencies, to research "projects" in universities, and to "contracts" in consulting and architectural firms.

> "We have to be the best in cost throughout the world." (3c)
> **MiCRUS** (joint venture of IBM and Cirrus Logic)

Process-Costing Systems

Process costing is used by companies that produce large numbers of identical units. Firms that produce chemicals, microchips, gasoline, beer, fertilizer, textiles, processed food, and electricity are among those using process costing. In these kinds of firms, there is no need to trace costs to specific batches of production, because the products in the different batches are identical. A **process-costing system** accumulates all the production costs for a large number of units of output, and then these costs are averaged over all of the units. For example, suppose the Silicon Valley Company produced 40,000 microchips during November. The following manufacturing costs were incurred in November.

Direct material	$1,000
Direct labor	2,000
Manufacturing overhead	3,000
Total manufacturing cost	$6,000

The cost per microchip is $.15 (total manufacturing cost of $6,000 ÷ 40,000 units produced).

Summary of Alternative Product-Costing Systems

The distinction between job-order and process costing hinges on the type of production process involved. Job-order costing systems assign costs to distinct production jobs that are significantly different. Then an average cost is computed for each unit of product in each job. Process-costing systems average costs over a large number of identical (or very similar) units of product.

The remainder of this chapter examines the details of job-order costing. The next chapter covers process costing.

Accumulating Costs in a Job-Order Costing System

To illustrate job-order costing, we will focus on Adirondack Outfitters, Inc. This small company, nestled in the hills outside Lake Placid, New York, manufactures canoes and small boats.

Exhibit 3–3
Job-Cost Record: Adirondack Outfitters, Inc.

JOB-COST RECORD

Job Number F16 **Description** 80 deluxe aluminum fishing boats
Date Started Nov. 1, 20x1 **Date Completed** Nov. 22, 20x1
Number of Units Completed 80

Direct Material				
Date	**Requisition Number**	**Quantity**	**Unit Price**	**Cost**
11/1	803	7,200 sq ft	$2.50	$18,000

Direct Labor				
Date	**Time Card Number**	**Hours**	**Rate**	**Cost**
Various dates	Various time cards	600	$20	$12,000

Manufacturing Overhead				
Date	**Cost Driver (Activity Base)**	**Quantity**	**Application Rate**	**Cost**
11/30	Machine hours	2,000	$9.00	$18,000

Cost Summary	
Cost Item	**Amount**
Total direct material	$18,000
Total direct labor	12,000
Total manufacturing overhead	18,000
Total cost	$48,000
Unit cost	$600

Shipping Summary			
Date	**Units Shipped**	**Units Remaining in Inventory**	**Cost Balance**
11/30	60	20	$12,000

In a job-order costing system, costs of direct material, direct labor, and manufacturing overhead are assigned to each production job. These costs comprise the *inputs* of the product-costing *system.* As costs are incurred, they are added to the Work-in-Process Inventory account in the ledger. To keep track of the manufacturing costs assigned to *each job,* a subsidiary ledger is maintained. The subsidiary ledger account assigned to each job is a document called a **job-cost record.**

Job-Cost Record

An example of a job-cost record is displayed in Exhibit 3–3. At this juncture, just focus on the major sections and headings, which are printed in blue. (For now just ignore the detailed entries, printed in black, which will be explained in due course.)

Exhibit 3–4
Material Requisition Form

Material-Requisition Number 352 Date 1/28/x1
Job Number to Be Charged J621 Department Painting
Department Supervisor Timothy Williams

Item	Quantity	Unit Cost	Amount
White enamel paint	8 gallons	$14.00	$112
Clear lacquer	2 gallons	11.00	22

This job-cost record is for job F16 consisting of 80 deluxe aluminum fishing boats, which was produced during November 20x1. Three major sections on the job-cost record are used to accumulate the costs of direct material, direct labor, and manufacturing overhead assigned to the job. The other two sections are used to record the total cost and average unit cost for the job, and to keep track of units shipped to customers. A job-cost record may be a paper document upon which the entries for direct material, direct labor, and manufacturing overhead are written. Increasingly, it is a computer file where entries are made using a computer.

The procedures used to accumulate the costs of direct material, direct labor, and manufacturing overhead for a job constitute the *set of activities* performed by the job-order costing *system.* These procedures are discussed next.

Direct-Material Costs

As raw materials are needed for the production process, they are transferred from the warehouse to the production department. To authorize the release of materials, the production department supervisor completes a **material requisition form** and presents it to the warehouse supervisor. A copy of the material requisition form goes to the cost-accounting department. There it is used as the basis for transferring the cost of the requisitioned material from the Raw-Material Inventory account to the Work-in-Process Inventory account, and for entering the direct-material cost on the job-cost record for the production job in process. A document such as the material requisition form, which is used as the basis for an accounting entry, is called a **source document.** Exhibit 3–4 shows an example of a material requisition form.

In many factories, material requisitions are entered directly into a computer by the production department supervisor. The requisition is automatically transmitted to computers in the warehouse and in the cost-accounting department. Such automation reduces the flow of paperwork, minimizes clerical errors, and speeds up the product-costing process.

Supply Chain Management An organization's **supply chain** refers to the flow of all goods, services, and information into and out of the organization. Thus, Adirondack Outfitters' supply chain looks like this:

A supply chain often includes many companies and other organizations. *Supply chain management* means proactively working with some or all of the organizations in a company's supply chain to improve service and to manage or reduce costs. For example, Adirondack Outfitters' managers might work with the vendor supplying aluminum sheet metal to improve delivery schedules or reduce material costs. Adirondack Outfitters' managers might also consult with retailers about more effective displays for the company's products or more timely information about the retailers' restocking needs.

Material-Requirements Planning For products and product components that are produced routinely, the required materials are known in advance. For these products and components, material requisitions are based on a **bill of materials** that lists all of the materials needed.

In complex manufacturing operations, in which production takes place in several stages, *material-requirements planning* (or *MRP*) may be used. MRP is an operations-management tool that assists managers in scheduling production in each stage of the manufacturing process. Such careful planning ensures that, at each stage in the production process, the required subassemblies, components, or partially processed materials will be ready for the next stage. MRP systems, which are generally computerized, include files that list all of the component parts and materials in inventory and all of the parts and materials needed in each stage of the production process.

Adirondack Outfitters' operations are too limited to need an MRP system.

Direct-Labor Costs

The assignment of direct-labor costs to jobs is based on time records filled out by employees. A **time record** is a form that records the amount of time an employee spends on each production job. The time record is the source document used in the cost-accounting department as the basis for adding direct-labor costs to Work-in-Process Inventory and to the job-cost records for the various jobs in process. In some factories, a computerized time-clock system may be used. Employees enter the time they begin and stop work on each job into the time clock. The time clock is connected to a computer, which records the time spent on various jobs and transmits the information to the accounting department.

Exhibit 3–5 displays an example of a time record. As the example shows, most of the employee's time was spent working on two different production jobs. In the accounting department, the time spent on each job will be multiplied by the employee's wage rate, and the cost will be recorded in Work-in-Process Inventory and on the appropriate job-cost records. The employee also spent one-half hour on shop cleanup duties. This time will be classified by the accounting department as indirect labor, and its cost will be included in manufacturing overhead.

Manufacturing-Overhead Costs

It is relatively simple to trace direct-material and direct-labor costs to production jobs, but manufacturing overhead is not easily traced to jobs. By definition, manufacturing

Exhibit 3–5
Time Record

Employee Name Ron Bradley Date 12/19/x1
Employee Number 12 Department Painting

Time Started	Time Stopped	Job Number
8:00	11:30	A267
11:30	12:00	Shop cleanup
1:00	5:00	J122

overhead is a heterogeneous pool of indirect production costs, such as indirect material, indirect labor, utility costs, and depreciation. These costs often bear no obvious relationship to individual jobs or units of product, but they must be incurred for production to take place. Therefore, it is necessary to assign manufacturing-overhead costs to jobs in order to have a complete picture of product costs. This process of assigning manufacturing-overhead costs to production jobs is called **overhead application** (or sometimes **overhead absorption**).

Management Accounting Practice

Campbell Soup, Procter & Gamble, and the U.S. Marine Corps

SUPPLY CHAIN MANAGEMENT

Supply chain management has become a critically important issue in many companies and other organizations. Here are several examples of how organizations are managing their supply chains to get or provide better service at lower costs.

Campbell Soup "Campbell Soup uses an automatic replenishment program (ARP) to ship products from its manufacturing plant warehouses to retailer distribution centers from which stores are restocked. Every weekday morning retail customers send their current inventory positions and sales data to Campbell Soup via electronic data interchange (EDI). Based on this information, Campbell Soup then sends out resupply shipments to the retail distribution centers."[1]

Procter & Gamble P&G saved its retail customers more than $65 million over an 18-month period, primarily by using an automatic replenishment program to collaborate with retailers about restocking their inventories. The program "helps P&G achieve greater integration within its operations, and closer customer linkages have enhanced trade relations."[2]

U.S. Marine Corps "The Marines knew they had problems. When a soldier at Camp Pendleton would put in an order for a spare part, it took him a week to get it—from the other side of the base. Worse, the force had 207 computer systems worldwide. Referred to as the Rat's Nest by Marine techies, most didn't talk to each other, meaning soldiers would have to resort to phone or fax to place orders, leading to errors and lost time. Private companies, meanwhile, were greasing their supply chains to provide just-in-time delivery, and the Marines knew they could do better. So the Corps sketched a 10-year tech strategy in logistics, to ensure that 173,000 Marines have what they need when they need it. To execute, the Corps hired consultants and studied companies like Wal-Mart Stores and United Parcel Service."

The Corps "aims to reduce inventory by half, saving up to $200 million. By replacing inventory with information, the Corps won't have to stockpile tons of supplies—the so-called Iron Mountain—near the battlefield. Taking a page from Unilever and Swissair, the Corps is developing better relations with suppliers to make sure they have access to hard-to-get items like tank parts. And with advice from Caterpillar, the Marines have been upgrading warehouses, adding gadgets like handheld wireless scanners for real-time inventory placement and tracking."[3]

Overhead Application For product-costing information to be useful, it must be provided to managers on a timely basis. Suppose the cost-accounting department waited until the end of an accounting period so that the *actual* costs of manufacturing overhead could be determined before applying overhead costs to the firm's products.

---

[1]Noah P. Barsky and Alexander E. Ellinger, "Unleashing the Value in the Supply Chain," *Strategic Finance* 82, no. 7 (January 2001), pp. 33–37.

[2]Ibid.

[3]Faith Keenan, "The Marines Learn New Tactics—From Wal-Mart," *Business Week,* December 24, 2001, p. 74.

The result would be very accurate overhead application. However, the information might be useless because it was not available to managers for planning, control, and decision making during the period.

LO 4

Compute a predetermined overhead rate and explain its use in job-order costing for job-shop and batch-production environments.

Topic 3–2

Predetermined Overhead Rate The solution to this problem is to apply overhead to products on the basis of estimates made at the beginning of the accounting period. The accounting department chooses some measure of productive activity to use as the basis for overhead application. In traditional product-costing systems, this measure is usually some **volume-based cost driver** (or **activity base**), such as direct-labor hours, direct-labor cost, or machine hours. An estimate is made of (1) the amount of manufacturing overhead that will be incurred during a specified period of time and (2) the amount of the cost driver (or activity base) that will be used or incurred during the same time period. Then a **predetermined overhead rate** is computed as follows:

$$\text{Predetermined overhead rate} = \frac{\text{Budgeted manufacturing-overhead cost}}{\text{Budgeted amount of cost driver (or activity base)}}$$

For example, Adirondack Outfitters has chosen machine hours as its cost driver (or activity base). For the year 20x1, the firm estimates that overhead cost will amount to \$360,000 and that total machine hours used will be 40,000 hours. The predetermined overhead rate is computed as follows:

$$\text{Predetermined overhead rate} = \frac{\$360{,}000}{40{,}000 \text{ hours}} = \$9.00 \text{ per machine hour}$$

In our discussion of the predetermined overhead rate, we have emphasized the term *cost driver,* because increasingly this term is replacing the more traditional term *activity base.* Furthermore, we have emphasized that *traditional* product-costing systems tend to rely on a *single, volume-based cost driver.* We will discuss more elaborate product-costing systems based on multiple cost drivers later in this chapter. This topic is examined in even greater detail in Chapter 5.

Applying Overhead Costs The predetermined overhead rate is used to apply manufacturing overhead costs to production jobs. The quantity of the cost driver (or activity base) required by a particular job is multiplied by the predetermined overhead rate to determine the amount of overhead cost applied to the job. For example, suppose Adirondack Outfitters' job number D22 requires 30 machine hours. The overhead applied to the job is computed as follows:

Predetermined overhead rate	\$ 9
Machine hours required by job D22	× 30
Overhead applied to job D22	\$270

The \$270 of applied overhead will be added to Work-in-Process Inventory and recorded on the job-cost record for job D22. The accounting entries made to add manufacturing overhead to Work-in-Process Inventory may be made daily, weekly, or monthly, depending on the time required to process production jobs. Before the end of an accounting period, entries should be made to record all manufacturing costs incurred to date in Work-in-Process Inventory. This is necessary to properly value Work-in-Process Inventory on the balance sheet.

Summary of Event Sequence in Job-Order Costing

The flowchart in Exhibit 3–6 summarizes the sequence of activities performed by the job-order costing system. The role of the various documents used in job-order costing is also emphasized in the flowchart.

Exhibit 3–6

Summary of Event Sequence in a Job-Order Costing System

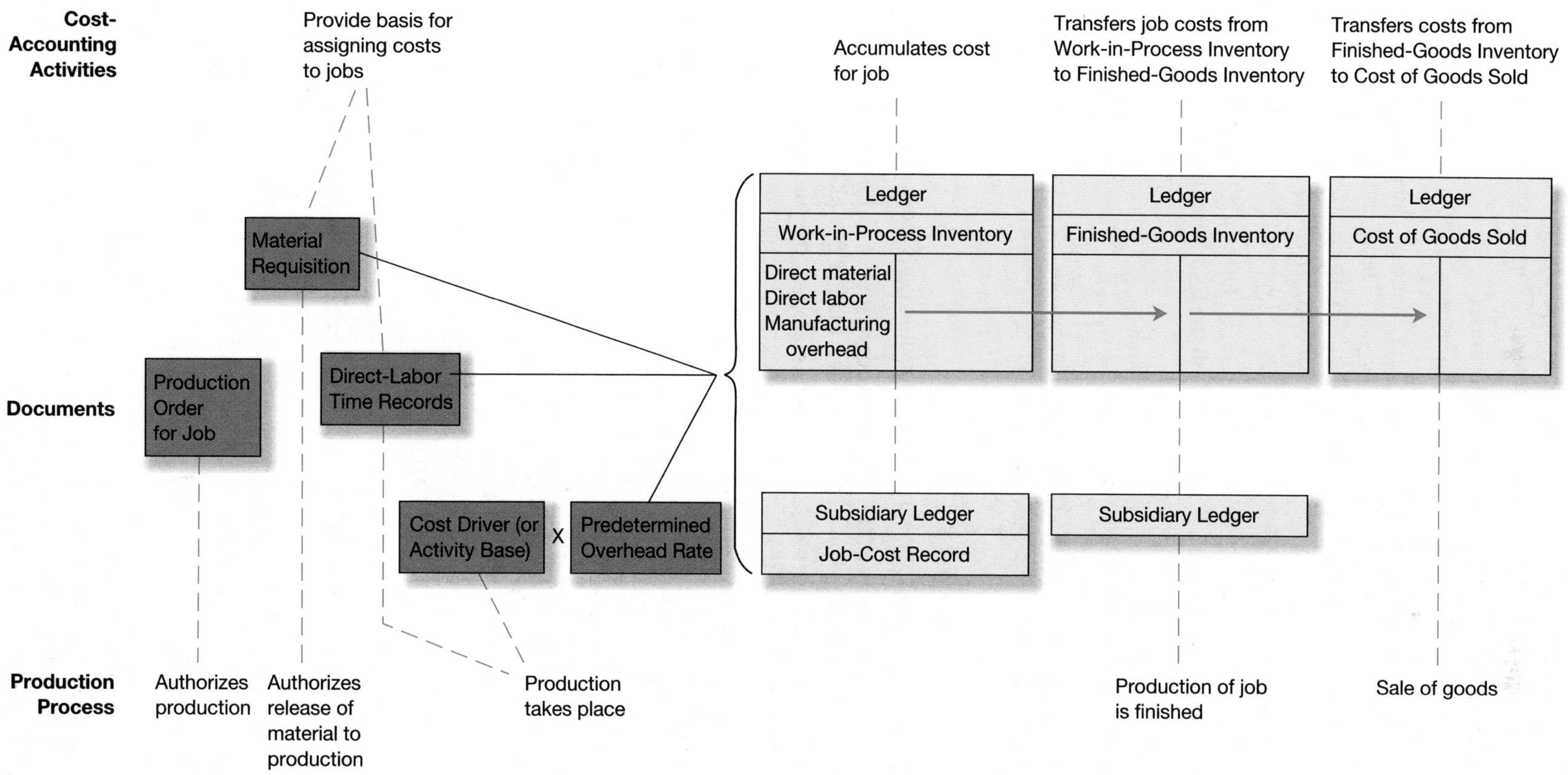

Cost-Accounting Activities

Provide basis for assigning costs to jobs

Accumulates cost for job

Transfers job costs from Work-in-Process Inventory to Finished-Goods Inventory

Transfers costs from Finished-Goods Inventory to Cost of Goods Sold

Documents

Production Order for Job

Material Requisition

Direct-Labor Time Records

Cost Driver (or Activity Base) X Predetermined Overhead Rate

Ledger: Work-in-Process Inventory — Direct material, Direct labor, Manufacturing overhead

Subsidiary Ledger: Job-Cost Record

Ledger: Finished-Goods Inventory

Subsidiary Ledger

Ledger: Cost of Goods Sold

Production Process

Authorizes production

Authorizes release of material to production

Production takes place

Production of job is finished

Sale of goods

Illustration of Job-Order Costing

LO 5

Prepare journal entries to record the costs of direct material, direct labor, and manufacturing overhead in a job-order costing system.

Now let's examine the accounting entries made by Adirondack Outfitters, Inc. during November of 20x1. The company worked on two production jobs:

Job number C12, 80 deluxe wooden canoes
Job number F16, 80 deluxe aluminum fishing boats

The job numbers designate these as the 12th canoe production job and the 16th fishing boat production job undertaken during the year. The events of November are described below along with the associated accounting entries.

Purchase of Material

Four thousand square feet of rolled aluminum sheet metal were purchased on account for $10,000. The purchase is recorded with the following journal entry.

(1) Raw-Material Inventory	10,000	
Accounts Payable		10,000

The postings of this and all subsequent journal entries to the ledger are shown in Exhibit 3–11 which appears on page 97.

Use of Direct Material

On November 1, the following material requisitions were submitted.

Requisition number 802: (for job number C12)	8,000 board feet of lumber, at $2 per board foot, for a total of $16,000
Requisition number 803: (for job number F16)	7,200 square feet of aluminum sheet metal, at $2.50 per square foot, for a total of $18,000

The following journal entry records the release of these raw materials to production.

(2) Work-in-Process Inventory	34,000	
Raw-Material Inventory		34,000

The associated ledger posting is shown in Exhibit 3–11. These direct-material costs are also recorded on the job-cost record for each job. The job-cost record for job number F16 is displayed in Exhibit 3–3 on page 82. Since the job-cost record for job number C12 is similar, it is not shown.

Use of Indirect Material

On November 15, the following material requisition was submitted.

Requisition number 804:	5 gallons of bonding glue, at $10 per gallon, for a total cost of $50

Small amounts of bonding glue are used in the production of all classes of boats manufactured by Adirondack Outfitters. Since the cost incurred is small, no attempt is made to trace the cost of glue to specific jobs. Instead, glue is considered an indirect material, and its cost is included in manufacturing overhead. The company accumulates all manufacturing-overhead costs in the Manufacturing Overhead account. All actual overhead costs are recorded by debiting this account. The account is debited when indirect materials are requisitioned, when indirect-labor costs are incurred, when utility bills are paid, when depreciation is recorded on manufacturing equipment, and so forth. The journal entry made to record the usage of glue is as follows:

(3) Manufacturing Overhead	50	
Manufacturing Supplies Inventory		50

The posting of this journal entry to the ledger is shown in Exhibit 3–11. No entry is made on any job-cost record for the usage of glue, since its cost is not traced to individual production jobs.

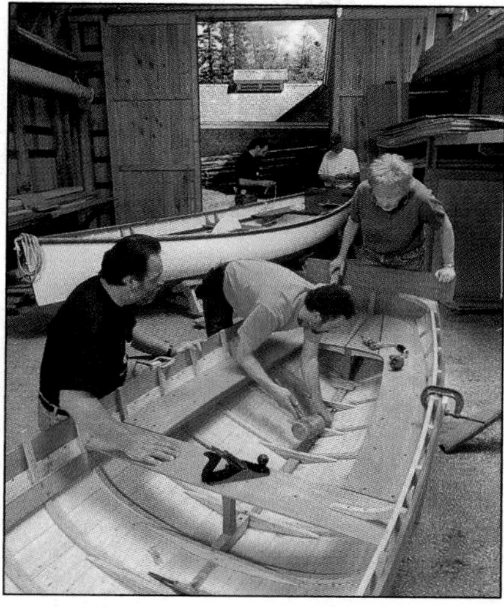

This small production facility records the cost of manufacturing canoes and other boats, which are manufactured in small batches. Direct material, direct labor, and manufacturing overhead costs are tracked.

Use of Direct Labor

At the end of November, the cost-accounting department uses the labor time records filed during the month to determine the following direct-labor costs of each job.

Direct labor: job number C12	$ 9,000
Direct labor: job number F16	12,000
Total direct labor	$21,000

The journal entry made to record these costs is as follows:

(4) Work-in-Process Inventory	21,000	
Wages Payable		21,000

The associated ledger posting is shown in Exhibit 3–11. These direct-labor costs are also recorded on the job-cost record for each job. The job-cost record for job number F16 is displayed in Exhibit 3–3 on page 82. Only one direct-labor entry is shown on the job-cost record. In practice, there would be numerous entries made on different dates at a variety of wage rates for different employees.

Use of Indirect Labor

The analysis of labor time records undertaken on November 30 also revealed the following use of indirect labor:

Indirect labor: not charged to any particular job, $14,000

This cost comprises the production supervisor's salary and the wages of various employees who spent some of their time on maintenance and general cleanup duties during November. The following journal entry is made to add indirect-labor costs to manufacturing overhead:

(5) Manufacturing Overhead	14,000	
Wages Payable		14,000

No entry is made on any job-cost record, since indirect-labor costs are not traceable to any particular job. In practice, journal entries (4) and (5) are usually combined into one compound entry as follows:

Work-in-Process Inventory	21,000	
Manufacturing Overhead	14,000	
Wages Payable		35,000

Incurrence of Manufacturing-Overhead Costs

The following manufacturing-overhead costs were incurred during November.

Manufacturing overhead:	
Rent on factory building	$ 3,000
Depreciation on equipment	5,000
Utilities (electricity and natural gas)	4,000
Property taxes	2,000
Insurance	1,000
Total	$15,000

The following compound journal entry is made on November 30 to record these costs.

	Debit	Credit
(6) Manufacturing Overhead	15,000	
Prepaid Rent		3,000
Accumulated Depreciation—Equipment		5,000
Accounts Payable (utilities and property taxes)		6,000
Prepaid Insurance		1,000

The entry is posted in Exhibit 3–11. No entry is made on any job-cost record, since manufacturing-overhead costs are not traceable to any particular job.

Application of Manufacturing Overhead

Various manufacturing-overhead costs were incurred during November, and these costs were accumulated by debiting the Manufacturing-Overhead account. However, no manufacturing-overhead costs have yet been added to Work-in-Process Inventory or recorded on the job-cost records. The application of overhead to the firm's products is based on a predetermined overhead rate. This rate was computed by the accounting department at the beginning of 20x1 as follows:

$$\text{Predetermined overhead rate} = \frac{\text{Budgeted total manufacturing overhead for 20x1}}{\text{Budgeted total machine hours for 20x1}}$$

$$= \frac{\$360{,}000}{40{,}000} = \$9.00 \text{ per machine hour}$$

Factory machine-usage records indicate the following usage of machine hours during November:

Machine hours used: job number C12	1,200 hours
Machine hours used: job number F16	2,000 hours
Total machine hours	3,200 hours

The total manufacturing overhead applied to Work-in-Process Inventory during November is calculated as follows:

	Machine Hours		Predetermined Overhead Rate		Manufacturing Overhead Applied
Job number C12	1,200	×	$9.00	=	$10,800
Job number F16	2,000	×	$9.00	=	18,000
Total manufacturing overhead applied					$28,800

The following journal entry is made to add **applied manufacturing overhead** to Work-in-Process Inventory.

(7) Work-in-Process Inventory	28,800	
Manufacturing Overhead		28,800

The entry is posted in Exhibit 3–11, and the manufacturing overhead applied to job number F16 is entered on the job-cost record in Exhibit 3–3 on page 82.

Summary of Overhead Accounting

As the following time line shows, three concepts are used in accounting for overhead. Overhead is *budgeted* at the *beginning* of the accounting period, it is *applied during* the period, and *actual* overhead is measured at the *end* of the period.

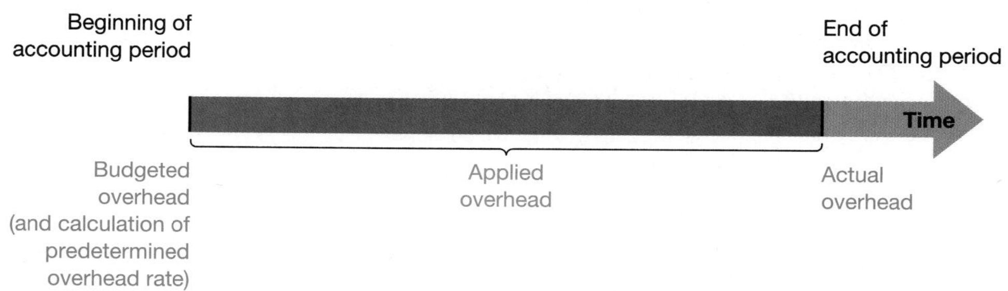

Exhibit 3–7 summarizes the accounting procedures used for manufacturing overhead. The left side of the Manufacturing Overhead account is used to accumulate **actual manufacturing-overhead** costs as they are incurred throughout the accounting period. The actual costs incurred for indirect material, indirect labor, factory rental, equipment depreciation, utilities, property taxes, and insurance are recorded as debits to the account.

The right side of the Manufacturing Overhead account is used to record overhead *applied* to Work-in-Process Inventory.

While the left side of the Manufacturing Overhead account accumulates *actual* overhead costs, the right side applies overhead costs using the predetermined overhead rate, based on *estimated* overhead costs. The estimates used to calculate the predetermined overhead rate will generally prove to be incorrect to some degree. Consequently, there will usually be a nonzero balance left in the Manufacturing Overhead account at the end of the year. This balance is usually relatively small, and its disposition is covered later in this illustration.

"As production processes are becoming more automated, manufacturing overhead is becoming a greater and greater portion of total manufacturing costs. This is true of almost all manufacturing firms." (3d)

DaimlerChrysler

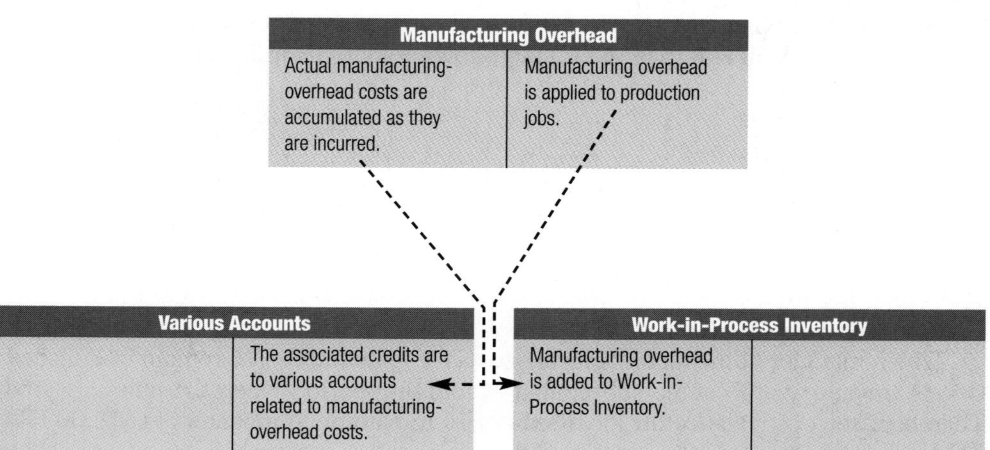

Exhibit 3–7
Manufacturing Overhead Account

Selling and Administrative Costs

During November, Adirondack Outfitters incurred selling and administrative costs as follows:

Rental of sales and administrative offices	$ 1,500
Salaries of sales personnel	4,000
Salaries of management	8,000
Advertising	1,000
Office supplies used	300
Total	$14,800

Since these are not manufacturing costs, they are not added to Work-in-Process Inventory. Selling and administrative costs are period costs, not product costs. They are treated as expenses of the accounting period in which they are incurred. The following journal entry is made.

(8) Selling and Administrative Expenses	14,800	
Wages Payable		12,000
Accounts Payable		1,000
Prepaid Rent		1,500
Office Supplies Inventory		300

The entry is posted in Exhibit 3–11.

Completion of a Production Job

Job number F16 was completed during November, whereas job number C12 remained in process. As the job-cost record in Exhibit 3–3 (page 82) indicates, the total cost of job number F16 was $48,000. The following journal entry records the transfer of these job costs from Work-in-Process Inventory to Finished-Goods Inventory.

(9) Finished-Goods Inventory	48,000	
Work-in-Process Inventory		48,000

The entry is posted in Exhibit 3–11.

Sale of Goods

Sixty deluxe aluminum fishing boats manufactured in job number F16 were sold for $900 each during November. The cost of each unit sold was $600 as shown on the job-cost record in Exhibit 3–3 (page 82). The following journal entries are made.

(10) Accounts Receivable	54,000	
Sales Revenue		54,000

(11) Cost of Goods Sold	36,000	
Finished-Goods Inventory		36,000

These entries are posted in Exhibit 3–11.

The remainder of the manufacturing costs for job number F16 remain in Finished-Goods Inventory until some subsequent accounting period when the units are sold. Therefore, the cost balance for job number F16 remaining in inventory is $12,000 (20 units remaining times $600 per unit). This balance is shown on the job-cost record in Exhibit 3–3 (page 82).

Underapplied and Overapplied Overhead

During November, Adirondack Outfitters incurred total *actual* manufacturing-overhead costs of $29,050, but only $28,800 of overhead was *applied* to Work-in-Process Inventory. The amount by which actual overhead exceeds applied overhead, called **underapplied overhead,** is calculated below.

Actual manufacturing overhead*	$29,050
Applied manufacturing overhead†	28,800
Underapplied overhead	$ 250

*Sum of debit entries in the Manufacturing-Overhead account: $50 + $14,000 + $15,000 = $29,050. See Exhibit 3–11.

†Applied overhead: $9.00 per machine hour × 3,200 machine hours.

If actual overhead had been less than applied overhead, the difference would have been called **overapplied overhead.** Underapplied or overapplied overhead is caused by errors in the estimates of overhead and activity used to compute the predetermined overhead rate. In this illustration, Adirondack Outfitters' predetermined rate was underestimated by a small amount.

Disposition of Underapplied or Overapplied Overhead At the end of an accounting period, the managerial accountant has two alternatives for the disposition of underapplied or overapplied overhead. Under the most common alternative, the underapplied or overapplied overhead is closed into Cost of Goods Sold. This is the method used by Adirondack Outfitters, and the required journal entry is shown below.

(12) Cost of Goods Sold	250	
Manufacturing Overhead		250

This entry, which is posted in Exhibit 3–11, brings the balance in the Manufacturing-Overhead account to zero. The account is then clear to accumulate manufacturing-overhead costs incurred in the next accounting period. Journal entry (12) has the effect of increasing cost-of-goods-sold expense. This reflects the fact that the cost of the units sold had been underestimated due to the slightly underestimated predetermined overhead rate. Most companies use this approach because it is simple and the amount of underapplied or overapplied overhead is usually small. Moreover, most firms wait until the end of the year to close underapplied or overapplied overhead into Cost of Goods Sold, rather than making the entry monthly as in this illustration.

Proration of Underapplied or Overapplied Overhead Some companies use a more accurate procedure to dispose of underapplied or overapplied overhead. This approach recognizes that underestimation or overestimation of the predetermined overhead rate affects not only Cost of Goods Sold, but also Work-in-Process Inventory and Finished-Goods Inventory. As the following diagram shows, applied overhead passes through all three of these accounts. Therefore, all three accounts are affected by any inaccuracy in the predetermined overhead rate.

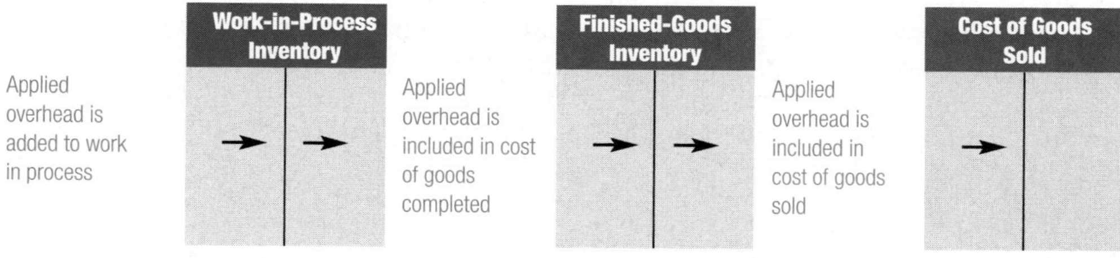

When underapplied or overapplied overhead is allocated among the three accounts shown above, the process is called **proration.** The amount of the current period's applied overhead remaining in each account is the basis for the proration procedure. In the Adirondack Outfitters illustration, the amounts of applied overhead remaining in the three accounts on November 30 are determined as follows:

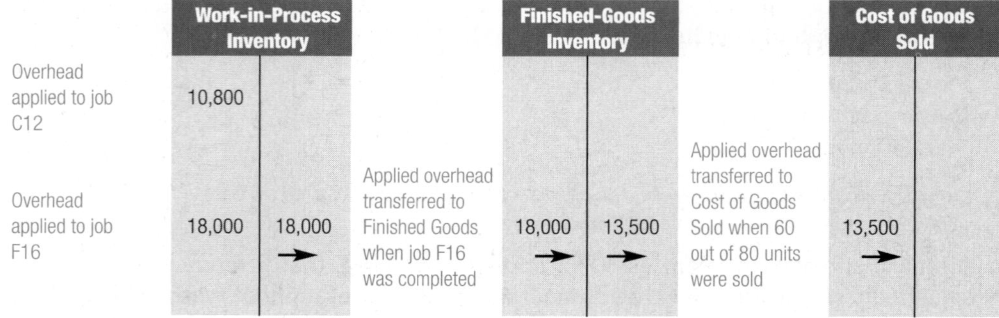

Applied Overhead Remaining in Each Account on November 30

Account	Explanation	Amount	Percentage	Calculation of Percentages
Work in Process	Job C12 only	$10,800	37.5%	10,800 ÷ 28,800
Finished Goods	¼ of units in job F16	4,500	15.6%*	4,500 ÷ 28,800
Cost of Goods Sold	¾ of units in job F16	13,500	46.9%*	13,500 ÷ 28,800
Total overhead applied in November		$28,800	100.0%	

*Rounded

Using the percentages calculated above, the proration of Adirondack Outfitters' underapplied overhead is determined as follows:

Account	Underapplied Overhead	×	Percentage	=	Amount Added to Account
Work in Process	$250	×	37.5%	=	$ 93.75
Finished Goods	250	×	15.6%	=	39.00
Cost of Goods Sold	250	×	46.9%	=	117.25
Total underapplied overhead prorated					$250.00

If Adirondack Outfitters had chosen to prorate underapplied overhead, the following journal entry would have been made.

Work-in-Process Inventory	93.75	
Finished-Goods Inventory	39.00	
Cost of Goods Sold	117.25	
Manufacturing Overhead		250.00

Since this is *not* the method used by Adirondack Outfitters in our continuing illustration, this entry is *not* posted to the ledger in Exhibit 3–11.

Proration of underapplied and overapplied overhead is used by a small number of firms that are required to do so under the rules specified by the *Cost Accounting Standards Board (CASB).* This federal agency was chartered by Congress in 1970 to develop cost-accounting standards for large government contractors. The agency was discontinued by Congress in 1980, but it was recreated in 1990. The standards set forth by the agency apply to significant government contracts and have the force of federal law.

LO 6

Prepare a schedule of cost of goods manufactured, a schedule of cost of goods sold, and an income statement for a manufacturer.

Schedule of Cost of Goods Manufactured

The Excel spreadsheet in Exhibit 3–8 displays the November **schedule of cost of goods manufactured** for Adirondack Outfitters. The schedule details the costs of direct material, direct labor, and manufacturing overhead *applied* to work in process

Exhibit 3–8
Schedule of Cost of Goods Manufactured

Microsoft Excel - Exhibit 3-8

File Edit View Insert Format Tools Data Window Help

H33 =H31-H32

	A–F	G	H
1	**ADIRONDACK OUTFITTERS, INC.**		
2	**Schedule of Cost of Goods Manufactured**		
3	**For the Month of November, 20x1**		
4			
5	Direct material:		
6	Raw-material inventory, November 1	$ 30,000	
7	Add: November purchases of raw material	10,000	
8	Raw material available for use	$ 40,000	
9	Deduct: Raw-material inventory, November 30	6,000	
10	Raw material used		$ 34,000
11			
12			
13	Direct labor		21,000
14			
15	Manufacturing overhead:		
16	Indirect material	$ 50	
17	Indirect labor	14,000	
18	Rent on factory building	3,000	
19	Depreciation on equipment	5,000	
20	Utilities	4,000	
21	Property taxes	2,000	
22	Insurance	1,000	
23	Total actual manufacturing overhead	$ 29,050	
24	Deduct: Underapplied overhead*	250	
25	Overhead applied to work in process		28,800
26			
27			
28	Total manufacturing costs		$ 83,800
29	Add: Work-in-process inventory, November 1		4,000
30			
31	Subtotal		$ 87,800
32	Deduct: Work-in-process inventory, November 30		39,800
33	Cost of goods manufactured		$ 48,000
34			
35	*The schedule of cost of goods manufactured lists the manufacturing costs *applied* to work in		
36	process. Therefore, the underapplied overhead, $250, must be deducted from total actual overhead		
37	to arrive at the amount of overhead *applied* to work in process during November. If there had been		
38	overapplied overhead, the balance would have been *added* to total manufacturing overhead.		

Sheet1 / Sheet2 / Sheet3

Ready

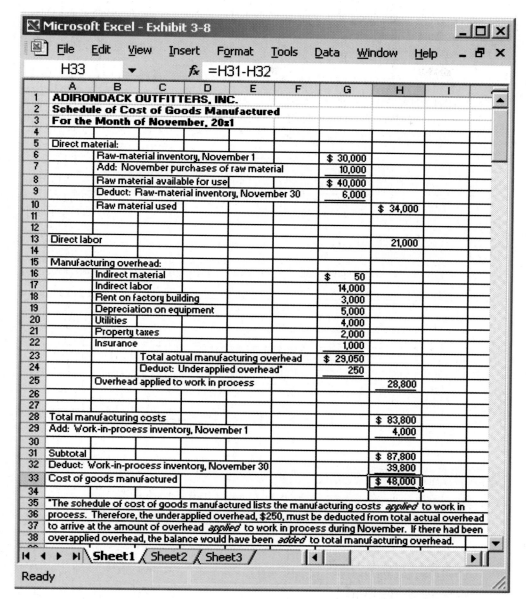

during November and shows the change in Work-in-Process Inventory. The **cost of goods manufactured,** shown in the last line of the schedule, is $48,000. This is the amount transferred from Work-in-Process Inventory to Finished-Goods Inventory during November, as recorded in journal entry number (9).

Schedule of Cost of Goods Sold

A **schedule of cost of goods sold** for Adirondack Outfitters is displayed as an Excel spreadsheet in Exhibit 3–9. This schedule shows the November cost of goods sold and details the changes in Finished-Goods Inventory during the month. The Excel spreadsheet in Exhibit 3–10 displays the company's November income statement.

Posting Journal Entries to the Ledger

All of the journal entries in the Adirondack Outfitters illustration are posted to the ledger in Exhibit 3–11. An examination of these T-accounts provides a summary of the cost flows discussed throughout the illustration.

Exhibit 3–9
Schedule of Cost of Goods Sold

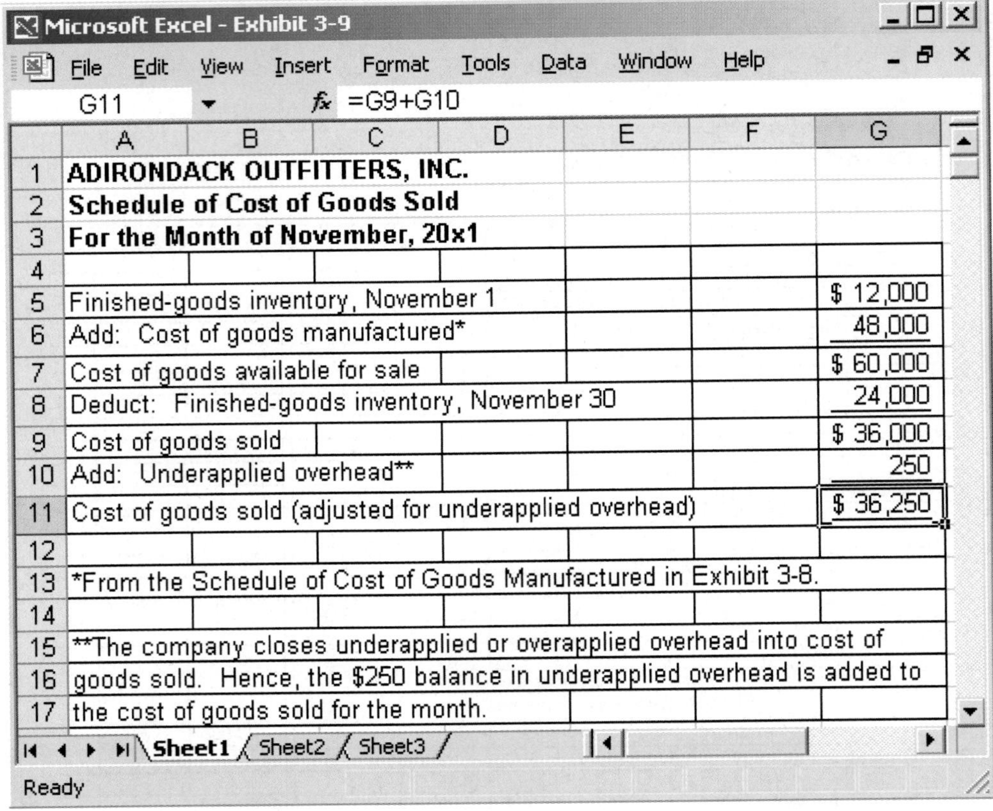

	A	B	C	D	E	F	G
1	**ADIRONDACK OUTFITTERS, INC.**						
2	**Schedule of Cost of Goods Sold**						
3	**For the Month of November, 20x1**						
4							
5	Finished-goods inventory, November 1						$ 12,000
6	Add: Cost of goods manufactured*						48,000
7	Cost of goods available for sale						$ 60,000
8	Deduct: Finished-goods inventory, November 30						24,000
9	Cost of goods sold						$ 36,000
10	Add: Underapplied overhead**						250
11	Cost of goods sold (adjusted for underapplied overhead)						$ 36,250
12							
13	*From the Schedule of Cost of Goods Manufactured in Exhibit 3-8.						
14							
15	**The company closes underapplied or overapplied overhead into cost of						
16	goods sold. Hence, the $250 balance in underapplied overhead is added to						
17	the cost of goods sold for the month.						

Exhibit 3–10
Income Statement

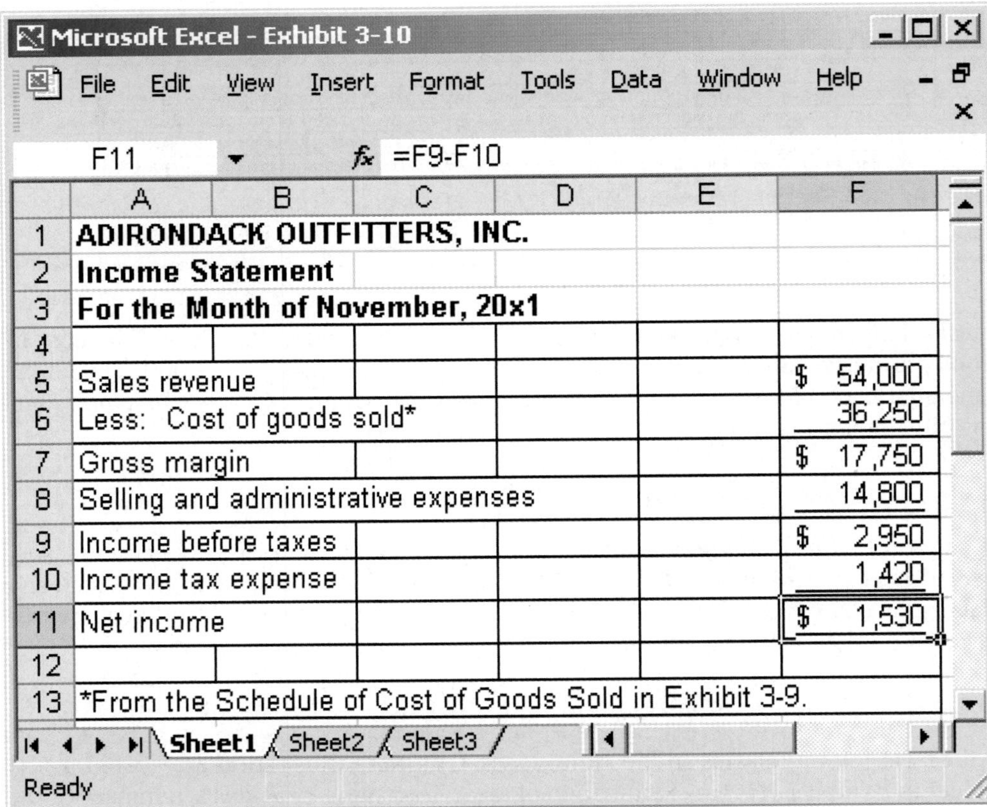

	A	B	C	D	E	F
1	**ADIRONDACK OUTFITTERS, INC.**					
2	**Income Statement**					
3	**For the Month of November, 20x1**					
4						
5	Sales revenue					$ 54,000
6	Less: Cost of goods sold*					36,250
7	Gross margin					$ 17,750
8	Selling and administrative expenses					14,800
9	Income before taxes					$ 2,950
10	Income tax expense					1,420
11	Net income					$ 1,530
12						
13	*From the Schedule of Cost of Goods Sold in Exhibit 3-9.					

Exhibit 3–11
Ledger Accounts for Adirondack Outfitters Illustration*

ADIRONDACK OUTFITTERS

Accounts Receivable

	Debit	Credit	
Bal.	11,000		
(10)	54,000		

Accounts Payable

	Debit	Credit	
		3,000	Bal.
		10,000	(1)
		6,000	(6)
		1,000	(8)

Prepaid Insurance

	Debit	Credit	
Bal.	2,000	1,000	(6)

Wages Payable

	Debit	Credit	
		10,000	Bal.
		21,000	(4)
		14,000	(5)
		12,000	(8)

Prepaid Rent

	Debit	Credit	
Bal.	5,000		
		3,000	(6)
		1,500	(8)

Office Supplies Inventory

	Debit	Credit	
Bal.	900	300	(8)

Manufacturing Supplies Inventory

	Debit	Credit	
Bal.	750	50	(3)

Accumulated Depreciation: Equipment

	Debit	Credit	
		105,000	Bal.
		5,000	(6)

Raw-Material Inventory

	Debit	Credit	
Bal.	30,000	34,000	(2)
(1)	10,000		

Manufacturing Overhead

	Debit	Credit	
(3)	50	28,800	(7)
(5)	14,000	250	(12)
(6)	15,000		

Work-in-Process Inventory

	Debit	Credit	
Bal.	4,000	48,000	(9)
(2)	34,000		
(4)	21,000		
(7)	28,800		

Cost of Goods Sold

	Debit	Credit	
(11)	36,000		
(12)	250		

Finished-Goods Inventory

	Debit	Credit	
Bal.	12,000	36,000	(11)
(9)	48,000		

Selling and Administrative Expenses

	Debit	Credit	
(8)	14,800		

Sales Revenue

	Debit	Credit	
		54,000	(10)

*The numbers in parentheses relate T-account entries to the associated journal entries. The numbers in color are the November 1 account balances.

Further Aspects of Overhead Application

Accuracy versus Timeliness of Information: A Cost-Benefit Issue

One of the themes of managerial accounting mentioned in Chapter 1 is the theme of costs and benefits. The issue of overhead application illustrates the importance of the cost-benefit theme. A product-costing system could be designed to use an **actual**

overhead rate instead of a *predetermined overhead rate.* An actual overhead rate could be computed as follows:

$$\text{Actual overhead rate} = \frac{\text{Actual overhead for the accounting period}}{\text{Actual amount of cost driver (or activity base)}}$$

"We use an actual costing system for the costs incurred in producing a feature film." (3e)
The Walt Disney Company

An actual overhead rate can be computed only at the end of the accounting period. The result is more accurate, but rather untimely, product-costing information. A trade-off exists between accuracy and timeliness. Accurate information is useful when decisions are based on the information. Better pricing or cost-control decisions may result from more accurate product costs. However, late information entails a cost in terms of missed opportunities and late responses to events. Therefore, managers and managerial accountants must weigh the costs and benefits of the following choices.

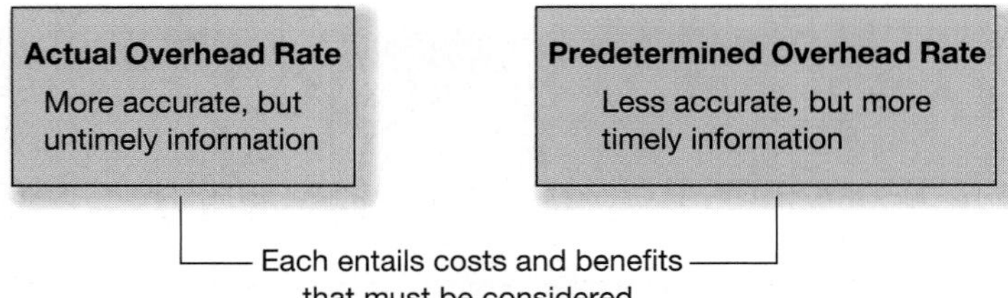

When designing product-costing systems, accountants generally recommend predetermined overhead rates.

It might be tempting to solve the overhead rate problem by using an actual rate and recomputing the rate frequently to provide more timely information. For example, the rate could be recomputed monthly. The problem with this approach is that some manufacturing-overhead costs are seasonal. For example, heating costs are higher in the winter, and air-conditioning costs are higher in the summer. Since overhead costs are incurred unevenly throughout the year, the monthly overhead rate would fluctuate widely. Moreover, the level of a volume-based cost driver, used as the denominator of the overhead rate, also may vary from period to period. Fluctuations in the number of workdays in a month and seasonal fluctuations in production volume can cause such variations. These activity variations can add to the fluctuations in the overhead rate. The resulting inconsistency in product costs could give misleading signals for product pricing and other decisions that may depend on product-cost information.

Accountants generally choose to smooth out fluctuations in the predetermined overhead rate by computing the rate over a long period of time. One-, two-, and three-year periods are common. A predetermined overhead rate computed in this fashion is called a **normalized overhead rate.** The use of a relatively long time period forces the accountant to face the trade-off between accuracy and timeliness that was discussed above. (Problem 3–56 illustrates the effects of using different time periods to compute overhead rates.)

Actual and Normal Costing Most firms use a predetermined overhead rate, based on overhead and activity estimates for a relatively long time period. When direct material and direct labor are added to Work-in-Process Inventory at their actual amounts, but overhead is applied to Work-in-Process Inventory using a *predetermined overhead rate,* the product-costing system is referred to as **normal costing.** This approach, which takes its name from the use of an overhead rate that is *normalized* over a fairly long period, is used in the Adirondack Outfitters illustration.

A few companies use **actual costing,** a system in which direct material and direct labor are added to work in process at their actual amounts, and actual overhead is allocated to work in process using an *actual overhead rate* computed at the *end* of each accounting period. Note that even though an actual overhead rate is used, the amount of overhead assigned to each production job is still an allocated amount. Overhead costs, which are by definition indirect costs, cannot be traced easily to individual production jobs. Actual and normal costing may be summarized as follows:

ACTUAL COSTING Work-in-Process Inventory	
Actual direct-material costs Actual direct-labor costs Overhead allocated: *Actual* overhead rate (computed at *end* of period) × Actual amount of cost driver used (e.g., direct-labor hours)	

NORMAL COSTING Work-in-Process Inventory	
Actual direct-material costs Actual direct-labor costs Overhead applied: *Predetermined* overhead rate (computed at *beginning* of period) × Actual amount of cost driver used (e.g., direct-labor hours)	

Choosing the Cost Driver for Overhead Application

Manufacturing overhead includes various indirect manufacturing costs that vary greatly in their relationship to the production process. If a single, volume-based cost driver (or activity base) is used in calculating the predetermined overhead rate, it should be some productive input that is common across all of the firm's products. If, for example, all of the firm's products require direct labor, but only some products require machine time, direct-labor hours would be a preferable activity base. If machine time were used as the base, products not requiring machine time would not be assigned any overhead cost.

In selecting a volume-based cost driver (or activity base), the goal is to choose an input that varies in a pattern that is most similar to the pattern with which overhead costs vary. Products that indirectly cause large amounts of overhead costs should also require large amounts of the cost driver, and vice versa. During periods when the cost driver is at a low level, the overhead costs incurred should be low. Thus, there should be a correlation between the incurrence of overhead costs and use of the cost driver.

> "As we continue to automate our production processes, direct labor is becoming less and less appropriate as a basis for the application of manufacturing overhead." (3f)
> **DaimlerChrysler**

Limitation of Direct Labor as a Cost Driver In traditional product-costing systems, the most common volume-based cost drivers are direct-labor hours and direct-labor cost. However, there is a trend away from using direct labor as the overhead application base. Many production processes are becoming increasingly automated, through the use of robotics and computer-integrated manufacturing systems. Increased automation brings two results. First, manufacturing-overhead costs represent a larger proportion of total production costs. Second, direct labor decreases in importance as a factor of production. As direct labor declines in importance as a productive input, it becomes less appropriate as a cost driver. For this reason, some firms have switched to machine hours, process time, or throughput time as cost drivers that better reflect the pattern of overhead cost incurrence. **Throughput time** (or **cycle time**) is the average amount of time required to convert raw materials into finished goods ready to be shipped to customers. Throughput time includes the time required for material handling, production processing, inspection, and packaging.

Departmental Overhead Rates

In the Adirondack Outfitters illustration presented earlier in this chapter, all of the firm's manufacturing overhead was combined into a single cost pool. Then the overhead was applied to products using a single predetermined overhead rate based on machine hours. Since only one overhead rate is used in Adirondack Outfitters' entire factory, it is known as a **plantwide overhead rate.** In some production processes, the relationship between overhead costs and the firm's products differs substantially across production departments. In such cases, the firm may use **departmental overhead rates,** which differ across production departments. This usually results in a more accurate assignment of overhead costs to the firm's products. An even more accurate assignment of overhead costs can be achieved with *activity-based costing (ABC).* ABC is introduced in this chapter's appendix, and it is covered extensively in Chapter 5.

Management Accounting Practice

Boeing Company

ARE LAYOFFS A GOOD WAY TO CUT COSTS DURING AN ECONOMIC DOWNTURN?

"At many companies, bolstering the bottom line by cutting jobs is the favored method for coping with a downturn. Yet layoffs often prove to be a flawed strategy. Companies that capriciously cut key employees often lose the talent they need to compete effectively. Those that cut too many positions may also end up paying hefty severance packages and then have to spend even more to find replacements once the recovery occurs. Rather than plan ahead in good times for what they will do if the economy slows, executives typically wait until they feel their backs are against the wall. Then they decide 'let's take out 2 percent or 5 percent of labor costs across divisions,' says David Kieffer, a principal at consultant William M. Mercer. 'They say this is the fairest way, but in taking this approach they focus only on the cost of labor rather than the value created by labor.'"[4]

As an example, consider the case of Boeing. "Just a week after the September 11 attacks, Boeing responded with some grim news of its own. The Chicago-based aerospace giant said it would cut 30,000 jobs from its commercial aircraft division in Seattle and slash jet deliveries by nearly 50 percent over the next two years. The company was responding to a 'dramatically altered market,' Boeing's CEO told analysts." However, "top company and union officials say privately that Boeing had been quietly drawing up plans to slice employment in its commercial-aircraft business by 10,000 to 15,000 jobs over several years, or some 15 percent. The factors pushing the decision included slower sales, sliding market share, and management's efforts to lift productivity and hand work off to subcontractors. The idea was to rely on efficiency gains to assemble jets faster with fewer people."

Is Boeing moving too fast? "A recent study suggests that the steep layoffs could leave Boeing woefully short of skilled workers if orders rebound substantially over the next few years."[5]

Two-Stage Cost Allocation

LO 7

Describe the two-stage allocation process used to compute departmental overhead rates.

When a company uses departmental overhead rates, the assignment of manufacturing-overhead costs to production jobs is accomplished in two stages comprising what is called **two-stage cost allocation.** In the first stage, all manufacturing-overhead costs are assigned to the production departments, such as machining and assembly. In the second stage, the overhead costs that have been assigned to each production department are applied to the production jobs that pass through the department. Let's examine this two-stage process in more detail.

Stage One In the first stage all manufacturing-overhead costs are assigned to the firm's production departments. However, stage one often involves two different types of allocation processes. First, all manufacturing-overhead costs are assigned to **departmental overhead centers.** This step is called **cost distribution** (or sometimes **cost allocation**). For example, the costs of heating a factory with natural gas would be distributed among all of the departments in the factory, possibly in proportion to the cubic feet of space in each department. In the cost distribution step, manufacturing-overhead costs are assigned to *both* production departments and service departments.

[4]Carol Hymowitz, "Using Layoffs to Battle Downturns Often Costs More than It Saves," *The Wall Street Journal,* July 24, 2001, p. B1.

[5]Stanley Holmes, "Is Boeing Cutting Too Close to the Bone?" *Business Week,* November 26, 2001, pp. 108, 109.

Service departments, such as equipment-maintenance and material-handling departments, are departments that do not work directly on the firm's products but are necessary for production to take place.

Second, all service department costs are reassigned to the production departments through a process called **service department cost allocation.** In this step, an attempt is made to allocate service department costs on the basis of the relative proportion of each service department's output that is used by the various production departments. For example, production departments with more equipment would be allocated a larger share of the maintenance department's costs.

> "We're going to have much more general knowledge of how the business works." (3g)
> **Boeing**

At the conclusion of stage one, all manufacturing-overhead costs have been assigned to the production departments.

Stage Two In the second stage all of the manufacturing-overhead costs accumulated in each production department are assigned to the production jobs on which the department has worked. This process is called overhead application (or sometimes overhead absorption). In stage two, each production department has its own predetermined overhead rate. These rates often are based on different cost drivers.

The two-stage process of assigning overhead costs to production jobs is portrayed in Exhibit 3–12. Notice the roles of cost distribution, service department cost allocation,

Exhibit 3–12
Developing Departmental Overhead Rates Using Two-Stage Allocation

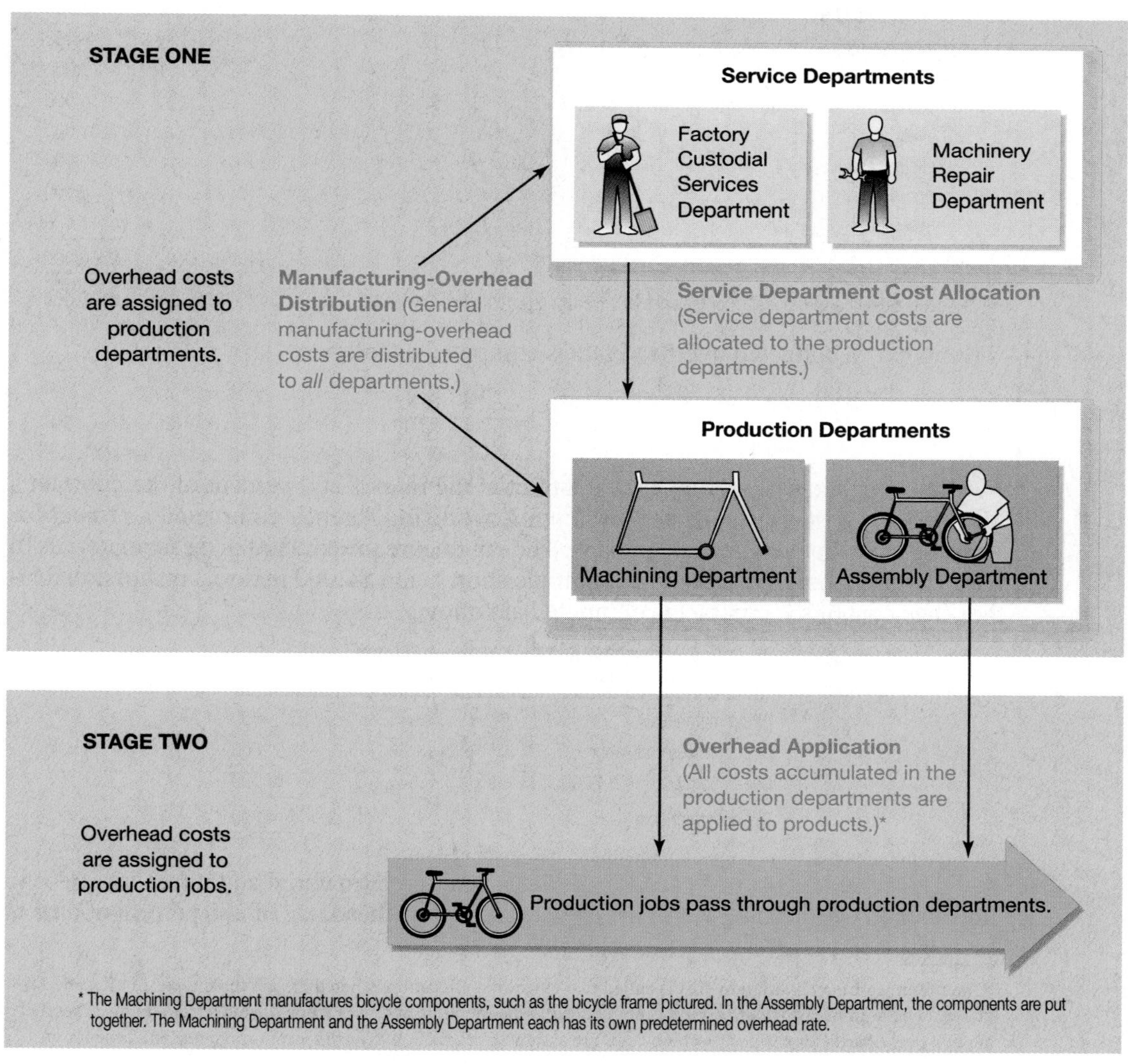
STAGE ONE
Service Departments
Factory Custodial Services Department
Machinery Repair Department
Overhead costs are assigned to production departments.
Manufacturing-Overhead Distribution (General manufacturing-overhead costs are distributed to *all* departments.)
Service Department Cost Allocation (Service department costs are allocated to the production departments.)
Production Departments
Machining Department
Assembly Department
STAGE TWO
Overhead Application (All costs accumulated in the production departments are applied to products.)*
Overhead costs are assigned to production jobs.
Production jobs pass through production departments.
* The Machining Department manufactures bicycle components, such as the bicycle frame pictured. In the Assembly Department, the components are put together. The Machining Department and the Assembly Department each has its own predetermined overhead rate.

and overhead application in the exhibit. The techniques of overhead distribution and service department cost allocation will be covered later in the text. In this chapter we are focusing primarily on the process of overhead application.[6]

Project Costing: Job-Order Costing in Nonmanufacturing Organizations

LO 8

Describe the process of project costing used in service industry firms and nonprofit organizations.

Job-order costing also is used in nonmanufacturing organizations. However, rather than referring to production "jobs," such organizations use terminology that reflects their operations. Hospitals and law firms assign costs to "cases," consulting firms and advertising agencies have "contracts," and governmental agencies often refer to "programs" or "missions." The need for cost accumulation exists in these and similar organizations for the same reasons found in manufacturing firms. For example, a NASA mission to launch a commercial satellite is assigned a cost for the purposes of planning, cost control, and pricing of the launch service.

To illustrate the cost-accumulation system used in a service industry firm, the following information is given for Midtown Advertising Agency, Inc.

Annual budgeted overhead:	
Indirect labor (secretarial and custodial)	$120,000
Indirect materials	15,000
Photocopying	4,000
Computer leasing	17,000
Supplies	14,000
Utilities	21,000
Building rental	90,000
Insurance	8,000
Postage	11,000
Total	$300,000
Budgeted direct professional labor (salaries of advertising account executives)	$120,000

"Every research contract negotiated between Cornell and the federal government includes an overhead component to cover the university's indirect costs." (3h)
Cornell University

The agency's budgeted overhead rate is computed as follows:

$$\frac{\text{Budgeted overhead}}{\text{Budgeted direct professional labor}} = \frac{\$300{,}000}{\$120{,}000} = 250\%$$

Overhead is assigned to each contract at the rate of 250 percent of the contract's direct-labor cost. During June, Midtown Advertising Agency completed a project for the Super Scoop Ice Cream Company. The contract required $800 in direct materials to build an advertising display to use in trade shows, and $4,000 in direct professional labor. The cost of the contract is computed as follows:

Contract B628: Advertising Program for Super Scoop Ice Cream Company

Direct material	$ 800
Direct professional labor	4,000
Overhead (250% × $4,000)	10,000
Total contract cost	$14,800

The contract cost of $14,800 includes actual direct-material and direct-labor costs, and applied overhead based on the predetermined overhead rate of 250 percent of direct-

[6]One might legitimately ask why this is called two-stage cost allocation, when there are three types of allocation involved. The term *two-stage allocation* is entrenched in the literature and in practice. It stems from the fact that there are two *cost objects,* or entities to which costs are assigned: production *departments* in stage one and production *jobs* in stage two.

labor cost. The contract cost can be used by the firm in controlling costs, for planning cash flows and operations, and as one informational input in its contract-pricing decisions. In addition to the contract cost, the firm should also consider the demand for its advertising services and the prices charged by its competitors.

The discussion above provides only a brief overview of cost-accumulation procedures in service industry and nonprofit organizations. The main point is that job-order costing systems are used in a wide variety of organizations, and these systems provide important information to managers for planning, decision making, and control.

Project costing is used to measure the cost of launching a commercial satellite for the purposes of planning, cost control, and pricing of the launch service.

Changing Technology in Manufacturing Operations

The technology of manufacturing is changing rapidly. These technological changes often affect the managerial accounting procedures used to collect data and transmit information to the intended users. Two such technological changes are electronic data interchange (or EDI) and the use of bar codes.

Electronic Data Interchange

Electronic data interchange (or *EDI*) is the direct exchange of data between organizations via a computer-to-computer interface. EDI is used to transmit such documents as purchase orders, shipping notices, receiving notices, invoices, and a host of other production-related data. This eliminates the need for paperwork, speeding up the flow of information and substantially reducing errors. EDI is now in widespread use. For example, Wal-Mart places most of its merchandise orders to its suppliers using this information technology.

Management Accounting Practice

Bank of America and Office Depot

ONLINE PURCHASING

One way in which companies in both the manufacturing and service industries are cutting costs is through online purchasing for supplies of all types. For the past decade, "Bank of America executives have been letting employees order supplies from their desktop computers, but they were using an old-fashioned system that was expensive and difficult to operate. The bankers knew there had to be a better way. 'We weren't ready for the Net,' says the Charlotte (N.C.) bank's senior vice president for strategic sourcing." However, "Office Depot's chief of e-commerce explained how the office-supply retailer could easily plug its online store into Bank of America's internal network. Bank of America managers would be able to set it up to recognize who had clearance to buy an executive chair or a box of pencils. It was a winning pitch. Today, Bank of America orders 85 percent of its office supplies online through Office Depot and is saving millions of dollars a year. Today, 40 percent of Office Depot's major customers are using the online network to buy everything from cherry conference-room tables to paper clips."[7]

[7] Charles Haddad, "Office Depot's E-Diva," *Business Week,* August 6, 2001, pp. 22–24.

Many manufacturers use bar code technology to track orders through every stage of the production process. Pictured here is an employee of McKesson scanning a shipment of pharmaceutical products. The device on this employee's arm includes a bar code scanner, minicomputer, and two-way radio.

"Each production job, from beginning to end, can take several weeks. Bar code technology is used extensively. The container that carries the work in process is bar-coded, and we use that to track each job." (3i)
MiCRUS (joint venture of IBM and Cirrus Logic)

Use of Bar Codes

We all have seen bar codes used to record inventory and sales information in retail stores. This efficient means of recording data is also becoming widely used in recording important events in manufacturing processes. Production employees can record the time they begin working on a particular job order by scanning the bar code on their employee ID badge and a bar code assigned to the production job order. When raw materials arrive at the production facility, their bar code is scanned and the event is recorded. Inventory records are updated automatically. Raw materials and partially completed components are assigned bar codes, and their movement throughout the production process is efficiently recorded. For example, raw materials may be requisitioned by a production employee simply by scanning the bar code assigned to the needed raw materials. When the materials are sent from the warehouse to the requisitioning production department, the bar code is scanned again. Inventory records are updated instantly. Bar codes represent one more instance where technology is changing both the production environment and the procedures used in accounting for production operations.

Focus on Ethics

DID BOEING EXPLOIT ACCOUNTING RULES TO CONCEAL COST OVERRUNS AND PRODUCTION SNAFUS?

Aircraft manufacturers use job-order costing to determine the cost of an airplane. As this chapter discusses, supply chain management and production controls are also important tools used by manufacturers to manage production costs. As *Business Week* reports, however, things don't always go according to plan.

For three years Boeing's top management had been seeking a merger with McDonnell-Douglas Corporation, whose board of directors was reluctant to approve the deal. Finally, the deal went through, and the world's largest aerospace company was born—"the first manufacturer ever with the ability to build everything that flies, from helicopters and fighter jets to space stations."

Unfortunately, "a disaster was quietly unfolding inside Boeing's sprawling factories—one that would ultimately wind up costing billions of dollars, cause several executives to lose their jobs, and lead to claims of accounting fraud. Facing an unprecedented surge in orders because of a booming economy, workers were toiling around the clock, pushing the assembly line to the breaking point. At the same time, the company was struggling to overhaul outdated production methods. These pressures were building up to what was, in essence, a manufacturing nervous breakdown. In the weeks after the merger announcement, parts shortages and overtime approached all-time highs. As costs went through the roof, the profitability of airliners such as the 777 swooned. A special team formed to study the crisis issued a report with a blunt conclusion: 'Our production system is broken.'"

Had investors "understood the scope of the problems, the stock would probably have tumbled and the McDonnell deal—a stock swap that hinged on Boeing's ability to maintain a lofty share price—would have been jeopardized."

In May of 2002, *Business Week* reported the results of its three-month investigation, which "reconstructed this hidden chapter in the company's history—and analyzed its current implications." The *Business Week* article alleges that "new details supplied by several inside witnesses indicate that Boeing did more than simply fail to tell investors about its production disaster. It also engaged in a wide variety of aggressive accounting techniques that papered over the mess. Critics say the company should have taken charges for the assembly-line disaster in the first half of 1997, even if it meant jeopardizing the McDonnell merger. They also claim that Boeing took advantage of the unusual flexibility provided by *program accounting*—a system that allows the huge upfront expense of building a plane to be spread out over several years—to cover up cost overruns and to book savings from efficiency initiatives that never panned out. 'Boeing managed its earnings to the point where it got caught,' says Debra A. Smith, a partner at Constraints Management, a Seattle-area manufacturing consultancy, and a former senior auditor at Deloitte & Touche who worked on the company's account during the early 1980s. 'Boeing basically decided in the short run that [managing earnings] was a lesser evil than losing the merger,' adds Smith. At a time when investors are asking themselves how far Corporate America can be trusted, the Boeing saga provides rich new evidence that companies have much greater leeway to manipulate their numbers than most people suspect."[8]

Boeing allegedly used a system they called *program accounting* to spread their huge cost overruns across several years, thereby propping up earnings and the company's share price. After the merger with McDonnell-Douglas, however, the truth came out in the form of much lower earnings.

What is your view of how Boeing handled its cost overruns, production problems, and the merger with McDonnell-Douglas? Did the company's top executives act ethically? How about their accountants?

Chapter Summary

Product costing is the process of accumulating the costs of a production process and assigning them to the firm's products. Product costs are needed for three major purposes: (1) to value inventory and cost of goods sold in financial accounting; (2) to provide managerial accounting information to managers for planning, cost control, and decision making; and (3) to provide cost data to various organizations outside the firm, such as governmental agencies or insurance companies. Information about the costs of producing goods and services is needed in manufacturing companies, service industry firms, and nonprofit organizations.

Two types of product-costing systems are used, depending on the type of product manufactured. Process costing is used by companies that produce large numbers of nearly identical products, such as canned dog food and motor oil. Job-order costing, the topic of this chapter, is used by firms that engage in either job-shop or batch-production operations. Such firms produce relatively small numbers of dissimilar products, such as feature films, custom furniture, and major kitchen appliances.

In a job-order costing system, the costs of direct material, direct labor, and manufacturing overhead are first entered into the Work-in-Process Inventory account. When goods are completed, the accumulated manufacturing costs are transferred from Work-in-Process Inventory to Finished-Goods Inventory. Finally, these product costs are transferred from Finished-Goods Inventory to Cost of Goods Sold when sales occur. Direct material and direct labor are traced easily to specific batches of production, called job orders. In contrast, manufacturing overhead is an indirect cost with respect to job orders or units of product. Therefore, overhead is applied to production jobs using a predetermined overhead rate, which is based on estimates of manufacturing overhead and the level of some cost driver (or activity base). The most commonly used volume-based cost drivers are direct-labor hours, direct-labor cost, and machine hours. Since these estimates will seldom be completely accurate, the amount of overhead applied during an accounting period to Work-in-Process Inventory will usually differ from the actual costs incurred for overhead items. The difference between actual overhead and applied overhead, called overapplied or underapplied overhead, may be closed out into Cost of Goods Sold or prorated among Work-in-Process Inventory, Finished-Goods Inventory, and Cost of Goods Sold.

The accuracy of product costs often can be increased by the use of departmental overhead rates instead of a single, plantwide overhead rate. Even greater accuracy can be achieved through the use of activity-based costing, which is covered in the appendix.

Job-order costing methods also are used in a variety of service industry firms and nonprofit organizations. Accumulating costs of projects, contracts, cases, programs, or missions provides important information to managers in such organizations as hospitals, law firms, and government agencies.

[8]Stanley Holmes and Mike France, "Boeing's Secret: Did the Aircraft Giant Exploit Accounting Rules to Conceal a Huge Factory Snafu?" *Business Week,* May 20, 2002, pp. 110–120.

Key Terms

For each term's definition refer to the indicated page, or turn to the glossary at the end of the text.

activity base, 86
activity-based costing (ABC) system,* 106
actual costing, 98
actual manufacturing overhead, 91
actual overhead rate, 97
applied manufacturing overhead, 90
bill of materials, 84
cost distribution (sometimes called cost allocation), 100
cost of goods manufactured, 95
cycle time, 99
departmental overhead centers, 100
departmental overhead rate, 100
job-cost record, 82
job-order costing, 80
material requisition form, 83
normal costing, 98
normalized overhead rate, 98
overapplied overhead, 93
overhead application (or absorption), 85
plantwide overhead rate, 99
predetermined overhead rate, 86
process-costing system, 81
product-costing system, 78
proration, 93
schedule of cost of goods manufactured, 94
schedule of cost of goods sold, 95
service departments, 101
service department cost allocation, 101
source document, 83
supply chain, 83
throughput time, 99
time record, 84
two-stage cost allocation, 100
underapplied overhead, 93
volume-based cost driver, 86

*Term appears in the appendix.

Appendix to Chapter 3

Activity-Based Costing: An Introduction

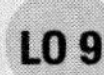

LO 9

Diagram and describe the two-stage allocation process used in activity-based costing.

> "We wanted to find a way that we could determine the profitability of every product, the profitability of every customer we serve, and the profitability of our processes. Activity-based costing has allowed us to do that." (3j)
>
> **Gemico**

As manufacturing processes become more highly automated and the pressures of international competition increase, many manufacturers are introducing even more elaborate product-costing systems. Although departmental overhead rates provide more accurate product costs than a single plantwide rate, it is possible to achieve even greater accuracy by focusing on the many activities that comprise the production process. In an **activity-based costing** (or **ABC**) **system,** the two-stage cost allocation process is retained. However, instead of assigning overhead costs only to departments in stage one, overhead costs are assigned to a larger number of cost pools that represent the most significant *activities* comprising the production process. The activities identified vary across manufacturers, but such activities as engineering support, material handling, machine setup, production scheduling, inspection, receiving, shipping, and purchasing provide examples.

After assigning costs to the activity cost pools in stage one, cost drivers are identified that are appropriate for each cost pool. Then in stage two the overhead costs are allocated from each activity cost pool to each production job in proportion to the amount of activity consumed by the job. For example, the number of inspections might be the cost driver used to assign overhead costs from the inspection activity cost pool to the various production jobs. If job A required twice as many inspections as job B, it would be assigned twice as much overhead cost from the inspection activity cost pool.

Exhibit 3–13 portrays the two-stage allocation process used in activity-based costing systems. The increased product-costing accuracy in activity-based costing comes from (1) the identification of a large number of activity cost pools and (2) the specification of an appropriate cost driver for each activity.

The trend in today's highly automated manufacturing environments is toward greater use of multiple cost drivers for overhead application. Activity-based costing systems are coming into greater use as managers see the strategic importance of having highly accurate product-cost information. Activity-based costing is a relatively new and very important topic in managerial accounting. It cannot be covered adequately in a few pages; we will examine activity-based costing in much greater detail in Chapter 5.

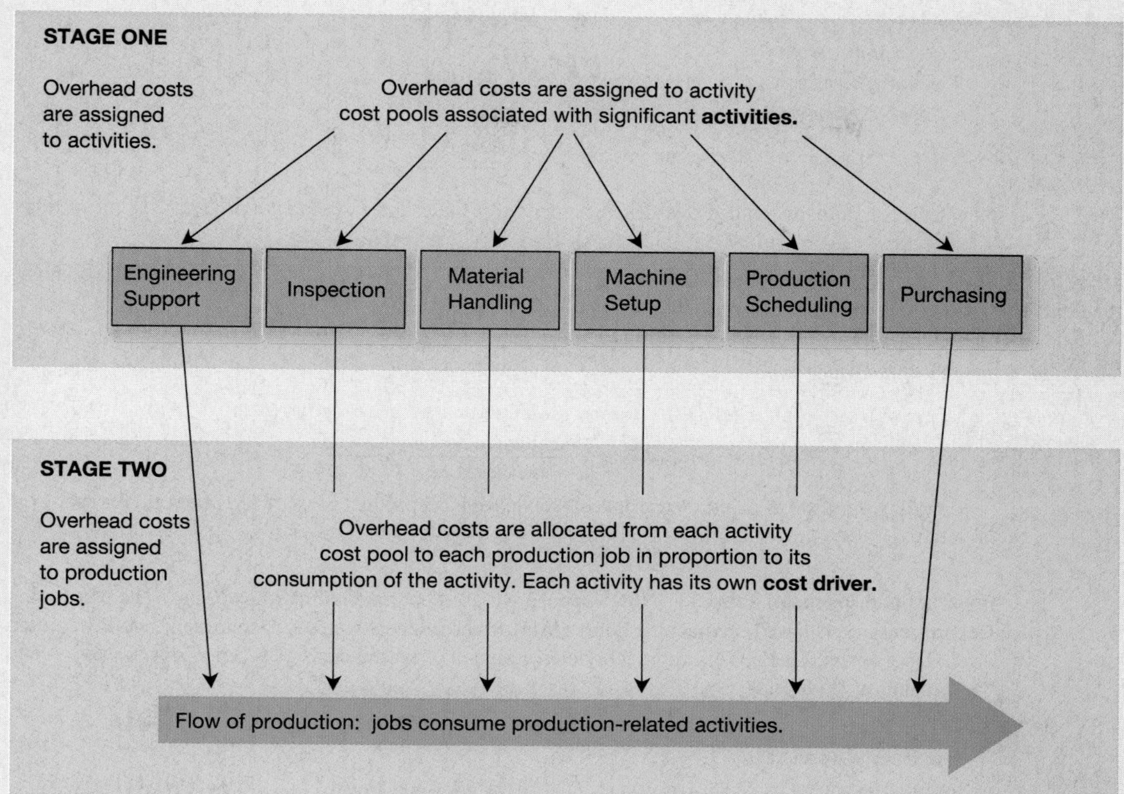
STAGE ONE
Overhead costs are assigned to activities.
Overhead costs are assigned to activity cost pools associated with significant **activities.**
Engineering Support
Inspection
Material Handling
Machine Setup
Production Scheduling
Purchasing
STAGE TWO
Overhead costs are assigned to production jobs.
Overhead costs are allocated from each activity cost pool to each production job in proportion to its consumption of the activity. Each activity has its own **cost driver.**
Flow of production: jobs consume production-related activities.

Exhibit 3–13
Activity-Based Costing System

Different Overhead Rates under Plantwide, Departmental, and Activity-Based Costing Systems

The accuracy of a product-costing system is affected by the number of cost drivers and overhead rates. A single, plantwide overhead rate based on only one volume-related cost driver generally is the least accurate. It is also the simplest system, however, and is the most commonly used method. A two-stage allocation process resulting in multiple departmental overhead rates typically will improve the accuracy of the product-costing system. This is particularly true when the production technology differs markedly among the departments. If, for example, one department relies chiefly on manual labor, while another department makes heavy use of machinery, departmental overhead rates with different cost drivers generally will increase product-costing accuracy. Even greater accuracy can be achieved with an activity-based costing system, with its multiple cost drivers and overhead rates.

DELTA
CONTROLS
CORPORATION

Let's examine the effects of three alternative product-costing systems at Delta Controls Corporation, which manufactures two types of sophisticated control valves used in the food processing industry. Valve A has been Delta's main product for 15 years. It is used to control the flow of milk in various food processing operations, such as the production of cookies. Valve B, a more recently introduced product, is a specialty valve used to control the flow of thicker foods such as jelly and applesauce. The basic data for the illustration follow:

	Valve A	Valve B
Annual production and sales	30,000 units	5,000 units
Direct material	$140	$140
Direct labor:		
Machining Department	30 (1.5 hr. at $20)	30 (1.5 hr. at $20)
Assembly Department	30 (1.5 hr. at $20)	30 (1.5 hr. at $20)
Total prime costs	$200	$200
Machine time in Machining Department	1 hr.	3 hr.

(continues)

(concluded)

Budgeted overhead costs:	
Machining Department	$630,000
Assembly Department	315,000
Total	$945,000

Now let's compute the applied overhead cost per valve under three alternative product-costing systems.

Plantwide Overhead Rate Using a single, plantwide overhead rate based on direct-labor hours (DLH), each product is assigned $27 of overhead per unit.

	Valve A	Valve B
Applied overhead per unit*	$27 (3 DLH at $9 per DLH)	$27 (3 DLH at $9 per DLH)

*Total budgeted DLH = (30,000 units of A)(3 DLH per unit) + (5,000 units of B)(3 DLH per unit) = 105,000 DLH

$$\text{Predetermined overhead rate} = \frac{\text{Total budgeted overhead}}{\text{Total budgeted DLH}} = \frac{\$945{,}000}{105{,}000} = \$9 \text{ per DLH}$$

Adding the $200 of prime costs for each valve, we have product costs of $227 per unit for each type of valve.

Departmental Overhead Rates Now suppose we use departmental overhead rates. The Machining Department rate is based on machine hours (MH), whereas the Assembly Department rate is based on direct-labor hours (DLH). This approach yields assigned overhead costs of $23 per unit of valve A and $51 per unit of valve B.

	Valve A	Valve B
Applied overhead per unit:		
Machining Department*	$14 (1 MH at $14 per MH)	$42 (3 MH at $14 per MH)
Assembly Department†	9 (1.5 DLH at $6 per DLH)	9 (1.5 DLH at $6 per DLH)
Total	$23	$51

*Total budgeted MH = (30,000 units of A)(1 MH per unit) + (5,000 units of B)(3 MH per unit) = 45,000 MH

$$\text{Machining Department overhead rate} = \frac{\text{Machining Department overhead}}{\text{Budgeted MH}} = \frac{\$630{,}000}{45{,}000} = \$14 \text{ per MH}$$

†Total budgeted DLH in Assembly Department = (30,000 units of A)(1.5 DLH) + (5,000 units of B)(1.5 DLH) = 52,500 DLH

$$\text{Assembly Department overhead rate} = \frac{\text{Assembly Department overhead}}{\text{Budgeted DLH}} = \frac{\$315{,}000}{52{,}500} = \$6 \text{ per DLH}$$

Adding the $200 of prime costs for each valve, we have product costs of $223 for each unit of valve A and $251 for each unit of valve B. Valve A, which spends considerably less time in the more costly Machining Department than valve B, is now assigned a lower product cost than it was when a plantwide overhead rate was used. In contrast, valve B's assigned product cost has increased.

Activity-Based Costing (ABC) Finally, let's see what happens to the assigned overhead costs under activity-based costing. Suppose Delta's accountants have established the following activity cost pools and cost drivers in stage one of the ABC method.

Activity	Activity Cost Pool	Quantity of Cost Driver	Cost per Unit of Cost Driver
Machine setups	$ 6,000	120 setups	$50 per setup
Engineering and design	210,000	7,000 engineering hr.	$30 per engineering hr.
Material handling	22,000	220,000 lb. of material	$.10 per lb.
Quality control	32,000	800 inspections	$40 per inspection
Machinery-related costs	675,000	45,000 machine hr.	$15 per machine hr.
Total	$945,000		

In stage two of the ABC method, Delta's accountants estimated how much of each cost driver is consumed by each *product line.* The ABC system then assigned overhead costs of $16.80 per unit of valve A and $88.20 per unit of valve B as follows:

	Valve A	Valve B
Applied overhead *per product line:*		
Setup ($50 per setup)	$ 1,000 (20 setups)	$ 5,000 (100 setups)
Engineering and design ($30 per hr.)	30,000 (1,000 hr.)	180,000 (6,000 hr.)
Material handling ($.10 per lb.)	17,000 (170,000 lb.)	5,000 (50,000 lb.)
Quality control ($40 per inspection)	6,000 (150 inspections)	26,000 (650 inspections)
Machinery-related costs ($15 per MH)	450,000 (30,000 MH)	225,000 (15,000 MH)
	$504,000*	$441,000*
Applied overhead per unit:	$16.80 $\left(\frac{\$504,000}{30,000 \text{ units}}\right)$	$88.20 $\left(\frac{\$441,000}{5,000 \text{ units}}\right)$

*Total applied overhead = $504,000 + $441,000 = $945,000

Adding the $200 of prime costs for each valve, we have product costs of $216.80 for each unit of valve A and $288.20 for each unit of valve B. Valve A, a high-volume and relatively simple product, is considerably less expensive to produce than valve B, a low-volume and relatively complex product.

Summary The following table compares the total reported product costs of each product under the three alternative product-costing systems.

	Valve A	Valve B
Plantwide overhead rate	$227.00	$227.00
Departmental overhead rates	223.00	251.00
Activity-based costing	216.80	288.20

Activity-based costing yields the most accurate product cost for each valve. Notice that both the plantwide and departmental overhead costing systems significantly overcost the high-volume and relatively simple valve A, and undercost the low-volume and complex valve B.

Review Questions

3–1. List and explain four purposes of product costing.

3–2. Explain the difference between job-order and process costing.

3–3. How is the concept of product costing applied in service industry firms?

3–4. What are the purposes of the following documents: (*a*) material requisition form, (*b*) labor time record, and (*c*) job-cost record.

3–5. Why is manufacturing overhead applied to products when product costs are used in making pricing decisions?

3–6. Explain the benefits of using a predetermined overhead rate instead of an actual overhead rate.

3–7. Describe one advantage and one disadvantage of prorating overapplied or underapplied overhead.

3–8. Describe an important cost-benefit issue involving accuracy versus timeliness in accounting for overhead.

3–9. Explain the difference between actual and normal costing.

3–10. When a single, volume-based cost driver (or activity base) is used to apply manufacturing overhead, what is the managerial accountant's primary objective in selecting the cost driver?

3–11. Describe some costs and benefits of using multiple overhead rates instead of a plantwide overhead rate.

3–12. Describe the process of two-stage cost allocation in the development of departmental overhead rates.

3–13. Define each of the following terms, and explain the relationship among them: (*a*) overhead cost distribution, (*b*) service department cost allocation, and (*c*) overhead application.

3–14. Describe how job-order costing concepts are used in professional service firms, such as law practices and consulting firms.

3–15. What is meant by the term *cost driver?* What is a *volume-based cost driver?*

3–16. Describe the flow of costs through a product-costing system. What special accounts are involved, and how are they used?

3–17. Give an example of how a hospital might use job-order costing concepts.

3–18. Why are some manufacturing firms switching from direct-labor hours to machine hours or throughput time as the basis for overhead application?

3–19. What is the cause of overapplied or underapplied overhead?

3–20. Briefly describe two ways of closing out overapplied or underapplied overhead at the end of an accounting period.

3–21. Describe how a large retailer such as Wal-Mart could use EDI.

3–22. Explain how a Texas Instruments engineer might use bar code technology to record the time she spends on various activities.

Exercises

Exercise 3–23
Job-Order versus Process Costing
(LO 1, 3)

For each of the following companies, indicate whether job-order or process costing is more appropriate.

1. Manufacturer of household cleaning solutions.
2. Manufacturer of custom hot tubs and spas.
3. Architectural firm.
4. Manufacturer of ceramic tile.
5. Producer of yogurt.
6. Manufacturer of custom tool sheds.
7. Manufacturer of papers clips.
8. Engineering consulting firm.
9. Manufacturer of balloons.
10. Manufacturer of custom sailboats.

Exercise 3–24
Job-Order Costing Basics
(LO 2, 4, 6)

Rexford Company manufactures finger splints for kids who get tendonitis from playing video games. The firm had the following inventories at the beginning and end of the month of January.

	January 1	January 31
Finished goods	$162,500	$152,100
Work in process	305,500	326,300
Raw material	174,200	161,200

The following additional manufacturing data pertains to January operations.

Raw material purchased	$248,300
Direct labor	390,000
Actual manufacturing overhead	227,500

Rexford Company applies manufacturing overhead at the rate of 70 percent of direct-labor cost. Any overapplied or underapplied manufacturing overhead is accumulated until the end of the year.

Required: Compute the following amounts.

1. The company's prime cost for January.
2. The total manufacturing cost for January.
3. The cost of goods manufactured for January.
4. The cost of goods sold for January.
5. The balance in the Manufacturing Overhead account on January 31. Debit or credit?

(CMA, adapted)

Exercise 3–25
Job-Cost Record
(LO 2, 3, 4)

Shawn Toy Company incurred the following costs to produce job number TB78, which consisted of 1,000 teddy bears that can walk, talk, and play cards.

Direct material:
  8/11/x0 Requisition number 201: 500 yards of fabric at $.90 per yard
  8/12/x0 Requisition number 208: 600 cubic feet of stuffing at $.40 per cubic foot
Direct labor:
  8/15/x0 Time card number 82: 550 hours at $14 per hour
Manufacturing overhead:
  Applied on the basis of direct-labor hours at $3.00 per hour.

Job number TB78 was finished on August 20. On August 30, 800 of the bears were shipped to a local toy store.

Required: Prepare a job-cost record using the information given above. (Use Exhibit 3–3 as a guide.)

Exercise 3–26
Cost Relationships; Normal Costing System
(LO 2, 6)

Cherry Hill Glass Company employs a normal costing system. The following information pertains to the year just ended.

- Total manufacturing costs were $1,250,000.
- Cost of goods manufactured was $1,212,500.
- Applied manufacturing overhead was 30 percent of total manufacturing costs.
- Manufacturing overhead was applied to production at a rate of 80 percent of direct-labor cost.
- Work-in-process inventory on January 1 was 75 percent of work-in-process inventory on December 31.

Required:

1. Compute Cherry Hill's total direct-labor cost for the year.
2. Calculate the total cost of direct material used during the year.
3. Compute the value of the company's work-in-process inventory on December 31.

(CMA, adapted)

Exercise 3–27
Basic Journal Entries in Job-Order Costing
(LO 5)

Dewitt Educational Products started and finished job number RM67 during June. The job required $5,100 of direct material and 40 hours of direct labor at $18 per hour. The predetermined overhead rate is $6 per direct-labor hour.

Required: Prepare journal entries to record the incurrence of production costs and the completion of job number RM67.

Exercise 3–28
Fixed and Variable Costs; Overhead Rate; Agribusiness
(LO 1, 4)

The controller for Tender Bird Poultry, Inc. estimates that the company's fixed overhead is $150,000 per year. She also has determined that the variable overhead is approximately $.15 per chicken raised and sold. Since the firm has a single product, overhead is applied on the basis of output units, chickens raised and sold.

Required:

1. Calculate the predetermined overhead rate under each of the following output predictions: 100,000 chickens, 200,000 chickens, and 300,000 chickens.
2. Does the predetermined overhead rate change in proportion to the change in predicted production? Why?

Exercise 3–29
Job-Order Costing; Feature Film Production; Use of Internet
(LO 1, 3)

Visit the website of a film producer, such as Disney, MGM, or Warner Brothers.

Walt Disney Studios	www.disney.com
MGM	www.mgm.com
Warner Brothers	www.warnerbros.com

Required: Read about one of the company's recent (or upcoming) film releases. Then discuss why or why not job-order costing would be an appropriate costing method for feature film production. Would your answer be any different depending on the type of film being produced (e.g., animation in a studio versus filming on location in Timbuktu)?

Exercise 3–30
Manufacturing Cost Flows
(LO 2, 5, 6)

Jay Sports Equipment Company, Inc. incurred the following costs during 20x2.

Direct material used	$226,200
Direct labor	421,200
Manufacturing overhead applied	234,000

During 20x2, products costing $156,000 were finished, and products costing $171,600 were sold on account for $253,500. There were no purchases of raw material during the year. The beginning balances in the firm's inventory accounts are as follows:

Raw material	$295,100
Work in process	23,400
Finished goods	39,000

Required:

1. Prepare T-accounts to show the flow of costs through the company's manufacturing accounts during 20x2.
2. Prepare a partial balance sheet and a partial income statement to reflect the information given above. (*Hint:* See Exhibit 3–2.)

Exercise 3–31
Basic Manufacturing Cost Flows
(LO 2, 6)

Selected data concerning the past year's operations of the Lone Star Leather Company are as follows:

	Inventories	
	Beginning	Ending
Raw material	$142,000	$ 162,000
Work in process	160,000	60,000
Finished goods	180,000	220,000
Other data:		
Direct material used		$ 652,000
Total manufacturing costs charged to production during the year (includes direct material, direct labor, and manufacturing overhead applied at a rate of 60% of direct-labor cost)		1,372,000
Cost of goods available for sale		1,652,000
Selling and administrative expenses		63,000

Required:

1. What was the cost of raw materials purchased during the year?
2. What was the direct-labor cost charged to production during the year?
3. What was the cost of goods manufactured during the year?
4. What was the cost of goods sold during the year?

(CMA, adapted)

Exercise 3–32
Schedule of Cost of Goods Manufactured
(LO 2, 6)

Crunchem Cereal Company incurred the following actual costs during 20x4.

Direct material used	$412,500
Direct labor	180,000
Manufacturing overhead	378,000

The firm's predetermined overhead rate is 210 percent of direct-labor cost. The January 1 inventory balances were as follows:

Raw material	$45,000
Work in process	58,500
Finished goods	63,000

Each of these inventory balances was 10 percent higher at the end of the year.

Required:

1. Prepare a schedule of cost of goods manufactured for 20x4.
2. What was the cost of goods sold for the year?

Exercise 3–33
Predetermined Overhead Rate; Various Cost Drivers
(LO 4)

The following data pertain to the Aquarius Hotel Supply Company for the year just ended.

Budgeted manufacturing overhead	$650,000
Budgeted machine hours	20,000
Budgeted direct-labor hours	25,000
Budgeted direct-labor rate	$13
Actual manufacturing overhead	$690,000
Actual machine hours	22,000
Actual direct-labor hours	26,000
Actual direct-labor rate	$14

Required:

1. Compute the firm's predetermined overhead rate for the year using each of the following common cost drivers: (*a*) machine hours, (*b*) direct-labor hours, and (*c*) direct-labor dollars.
2. Calculate the overapplied or underapplied overhead for the year using each of the cost drivers listed above.

Exercise 3–34
Actual versus Normal Costing
(LO 4, 5)

Refer to the data for the preceding exercise for Aquarius Hotel Supply Company. Prepare a journal entry to add to work-in-process inventory the total manufacturing overhead cost for the year, assuming:

1. The firm uses actual costing.
2. The firm uses normal costing, with a predetermined overhead rate based on machine hours.

Exercise 3–35
Overapplied or Underapplied Overhead
(LO 4, 5)

The following information pertains to Paramus Metal Works for the year just ended.

Budgeted direct-labor cost: 77,000 hours at $17 per hour	
Actual direct-labor cost: 79,000 hours at $18 per hour	
Budgeted manufacturing overhead: $993,300	
Actual manufacturing overhead:	
Depreciation	$225,000
Property taxes	19,000
Indirect labor	79,000
Supervisory salaries	210,000
Utilities	58,000
Insurance	32,000
Rental of space	295,000
Indirect material (see data below)	79,000
Indirect material:	
Beginning inventory, January 1	46,000
Purchases during the year	95,000
Ending inventory, December 31	62,000

Required:

1. Compute the firm's predetermined overhead rate, which is based on direct-labor hours.
2. Calculate the overapplied or underapplied overhead for the year.
3. Prepare a journal entry to close out the Manufacturing Overhead account into Cost of Goods Sold.

Exercise 3–36
Proration of Underapplied Overhead
(LO 5)

Happy Days Balloon Company incurred $167,000 of manufacturing overhead costs during the year just ended. However, only $145,000 of overhead was applied to production. At the conclusion of the year, the following amounts of the year's applied overhead remained in the various manufacturing accounts.

	Applied Overhead Remaining in Account on December 31
Work-in-Process Inventory	$29,000
Finished-Goods Inventory	50,750
Cost of Goods Sold	65,250

Required: Prepare a journal entry to close out the balance in the Manufacturing Overhead account and prorate the balance to the three manufacturing accounts.

Exercise 3–37
Project Costing; Interior Decorating
(LO 1, 8)

Contemporary Trends is an interior decorating firm in Munich. The following costs were incurred in the firm's contract to redecorate the mayor's offices.

Direct material used	4,100 euros
Direct professional labor	7,000 euros

The firm's budget for the year included the following estimates:

Budgeted overhead	510,000 euros
Budgeted direct professional labor	300,000 euros

Overhead is applied to contracts using a predetermined overhead rate calculated annually. The rate is based on direct professional labor cost.

Required: Calculate the total cost of the firm's contract to redecorate the mayor's offices. (Remember to express your answer in terms of euros. On the day this exercise was written the euro was valued at 1.077 U.S. dollars.)

Exercise 3–38
Cost Drivers; Different Production Methods
(LO 4, 5)

Rocky Mountain Leatherworks, which manufactures saddles and other leather goods, has three departments. The Assembly Department manufactures various leather products, such as belts, purses, and saddlebags, using an automated production process. The Saddle Department produces handmade saddles and uses very little machinery. The Tanning Department produces leather. The tanning process requires little in the way of labor or machinery, but it does require space and process time. Due to the different production processes in the three departments, the company uses three different cost drivers for the application of manufacturing overhead. The cost drivers and overhead rates are as follows:

Department	Cost Driver	Predetermined Overhead Rate
Tanning Department	Square feet of leather	$4 per square foot
Assembly Department	Machine time	$11 per machine hour
Saddle Department	Direct-labor time	$5 per direct-labor hour

The company's deluxe saddle and accessory set consists of a handmade saddle, two saddlebags, a belt, and a vest, all coordinated to match. The entire set uses 110 square feet of leather from the Tanning Department, 4 machine hours in the Assembly Department, and 45 direct-labor hours in the Saddle Department.

Required: Job number DS-25 consisted of 25 deluxe saddle and accessory sets. Prepare journal entries to record applied manufacturing overhead in the Work-in-Process Inventory account for each department.

Exercise 3–39
Choice of a Cost Driver for Overhead Application
(LO 1, 4)

Suppose you are the controller for a company that produces handmade glassware.

1. Choose a volume-based cost driver upon which to base the application of overhead. Write a memo to the company president explaining your choice.
2. Now you have changed jobs. You are the controller of a microchip manufacturer that uses a highly automated production process. Repeat the same requirements stated above.

Exercise 3–40
Two-Stage Allocation
(LO 1, 7)

Refer to Exhibit 3–12, which portrays the three types of allocation procedures used in two-stage allocation. Give an example of each of these allocation procedures in a hospital setting. The ultimate cost object is a patient-day of hospital care. This is one day of care for one patient. (*Hint:* First think about the various departments in a hospital. Which departments deal directly with patients; which ones are service departments and do not deal directly with patients? What kinds of costs does a hospital incur that should be distributed among all of the hospital's departments? Correct hospital terminology is not important here. Focus on the *concepts* of cost allocation portrayed in Exhibit 3–12.)

Exercise 3–41
Activity-Based Costing (Appendix)
(LO 1, 9)

Service industry firms can make effective use of ABC systems as well as manufacturers. For each of the following businesses, list five key activities that are important in the provision of the firm's service. For each activity cost pool, suggest an appropriate cost driver to use in assigning costs from the activity cost pool to the services provided to customers.

1. Bank
2. Hotel
3. Hospital
4. Airline
5. Restaurant
6. Fitness club

Problems

Problem 3–42
Basic Job-Order Costing; Journal Entries
(LO 4, 5)

Vermont Clock Works manufactures fine, handcrafted clocks. The firm uses a job-order costing system, and manufacturing overhead is applied on the basis of direct-labor hours. Estimated manufacturing overhead for the year is $260,000. The firm employs 10 master clockmakers, who constitute the direct-labor force. Each of these employees is expected to work 2,000 hours during the year. The following events occurred during October.

a. The firm purchased 2,900 board feet of mahogany veneer at $12 per board foot.

b. Twenty brass counterweights were requisitioned for production. Each weight cost $27.

c. Five gallons of glue were requisitioned for production. The glue cost $25 per gallon. Glue is treated as an indirect material.

d. Depreciation on the clockworks building for October was $7,000.

e. A $300 utility bill was paid in cash.

f. Time cards showed the following usage of labor:

Job number G60: 12 grandfather's clocks, 950 hours of direct labor

Job number C81: 15 cuckoo clocks, 500 hours of direct labor

The master clockmakers (direct-labor personnel) earn $22 per hour.

g. The October property tax bill for $890 was received but not yet paid in cash.

h. The firm employs laborers who perform various tasks such as material handling and shop cleanup. Their wages for October amounted to $3,100.

i. Job number G60, which was started in July, was finished in October. The total cost of the job was $15,100.

j. Nine of the grandfather's clocks from job number G60 were sold in October for $1,600 each.

Required:

1. Calculate the firm's predetermined overhead rate for the year.
2. Prepare journal entries to record the events described above.

Problem 3–43
Job-Order Costing; Focus on Manufacturing Overhead
(LO 2, 4)

Birmingham Bowling Ball Company (BBBC) uses a job-order costing system to accumulate manufacturing costs. The company's work-in-process on December 31, 20x3, consisted of one job (no. 3088), which was carried on the year-end balance sheet at $78,400. There was no finished-goods inventory on this date.

BBBC applies manufacturing overhead to production on the basis of direct-labor cost. Budgeted totals for 20x4 for direct labor and manufacturing overhead are $2,100,000 and $2,730,000, respectively. Actual results for the year follow.

Direct material used	$2,800,000
Direct labor	2,175,000
Indirect material used	32,500
Indirect labor	1,430,000
Factory depreciation	870,000
Factory insurance	29,500
Factory utilities	415,000
Selling and administrative expenses	1,080,000
Total	$8,832,000

Job no. 3088 was completed in January 20x4; there was no work in process at year-end. All jobs produced during 20x4 were sold with the exception of job no. 3154, which contained direct-material costs of $78,000 and direct-labor charges of $42,500. BBBC charges any under- or overapplied overhead to Cost of Goods Sold.

Required:

1. Determine the company's predetermined overhead application rate.
2. Determine the additions to the Work-in-Process Inventory account for direct material used, direct labor, and manufacturing overhead.

3. Compute the amount that BBBC would disclose as finished-goods inventory on the December 31, 20x4, balance sheet.
4. Prepare the journal entry needed to record the year's completed production.
5. Compute the amount of under- or overapplied overhead at year-end, and prepare the necessary journal entry to record its disposition.
6. Determine BBBC's 20x4 cost of goods sold.
7. Would it be appropriate to include selling and administrative expenses in either manufacturing overhead or cost of goods sold? Briefly explain.

Problem 3–44
Schedules of Cost of Goods Manufactured and Sold; Income Statement
(LO 6)

The following data refer to Mister Munchie, Inc. for the year 20x4.

Work-in-process inventory, 12/31/x3	$ 24,300	Utilities for sales and administrative offices	7,500
Selling and administrative salaries	41,400	Other selling and administrative expenses	12,000
Insurance on factory and equipment	10,800	Indirect-labor cost incurred	87,000
Work-in-process inventory, 12/31/x4	24,900	Depreciation on factory building	11,400
Finished-goods inventory, 12/31/x3	42,000	Depreciation on cars used by sales personnel	3,600
Indirect material used	14,700	Direct-labor cost incurred	237,000
Depreciation on factory equipment	6,300	Raw-material inventory, 12/31/x4	33,000
Raw-material inventory, 12/31/x3	30,300	Rental for warehouse space to store raw material	9,300
Property taxes on factory	7,200	Rental of space for company president's office	5,100
Finished-goods inventory, 12/31/x4	46,200	Applied manufacturing overhead	174,000
Purchases of raw material in 20x4	117,000	Sales revenue	617,400
Utilities for factory	18,000	Income tax expense	15,300

Required:

1. Prepare Mister Munchie's schedule of cost of goods manufactured for 20x4.
2. Prepare the company's schedule of cost of goods sold for 20x4. The company closes overapplied or underapplied overhead into Cost of Goods Sold.
3. Prepare the company's income statement for 20x4.

Problem 3–45
Manufacturing Cost Flows; Analysis of T-Accounts
(LO 2, 5)

Dessert Delite Company produces frozen microwavable desserts. The following accounts appeared in the ledger as of December 31.

Raw-Material Inventory

Bal. 1/1	29,400	
	?	?
Bal. 12/31	50,400	

Accounts Payable

	3,500	Bal. 1/1
191,100	?	
	1,400	Bal. 12/31

Work-in-Process Inventory

Bal. 1/1	23,800	
Direct material	?	?
Direct labor	?	
Manufacturing overhead	?	
Bal. 12/31	26,600	

Finished-Goods Inventory

Bal. 1/1	16,800	
	?	?
Bal. 12/31	28,000	

Manufacturing Overhead

?	?

Cost of Goods Sold

994,000	

Wages Payable

	2,800	Bal. 1/1
205,800	?	
	7,000	Bal. 12/31

Sales Revenue

	?

	Accounts Receivable	
Bal. 1/1	15,400	
	?	1,128,400
Bal. 12/31	21,000	

Additional information:

a. Accounts payable is used only for direct-material purchases.

b. Underapplied overhead of $3,500 for the year has not yet been closed into cost of goods sold.

Required: Complete the T-accounts by computing the amounts indicated by a question mark.

Problem 3–46
Job-Order Costing; Journal Entries
(LO 2, 5)

Southwestern Fashions, Inc. which uses a job-order costing system, had two jobs in process at the start of the year: job no. 101 ($168,000) and job no. 102 ($107,000). The following information is available:

a. The company applies manufacturing overhead on the basis of machine hours. Budgeted overhead and machine activity for the year were anticipated to be $1,680,000 and 32,000 hours, respectively.

b. The company worked on four jobs during the first quarter. Direct materials used, direct labor incurred, and machine hours consumed were as follows:

Job No.	Direct Material	Direct Labor	Machine Hours
101	$42,000	$ 70,000	2,400
102	—	44,000	1,400
103	88,000	130,000	4,000
104	30,000	17,600	1,000

c. Manufacturing overhead during the first quarter included charges for depreciation ($68,000), indirect labor ($120,000), indirect materials used ($10,000), and other factory costs ($279,000).

d. Southwestern Fashions completed job no. 101 and job no. 102. Job no. 102 was sold on account, producing a profit of $69,400 for the firm.

Required:

1. Determine the company's predetermined overhead application rate.
2. Prepare journal entries for the first quarter to record the following. (*Note:* Use summary entries where appropriate by combining individual job data.)
   a. The issuance of direct material to production and the direct labor incurred.
   b. The manufacturing overhead incurred during the quarter.
   c. The application of manufacturing overhead to production.
   d. The completion of jobs no. 101 and no. 102.
   e. The sale of job no. 102.
3. Determine the cost of the jobs still in production as of March 31.
4. Did the finished-goods inventory increase or decrease during the first quarter? By how much?
5. Was manufacturing overhead under- or overapplied for the first quarter of the year? By how much?

Problem 3–47
Job-Order Costing; Focus on Overhead and Cost Drivers
(LO 2, 4, 7)

Juarez, Inc. uses a job-order costing system for its products, which pass from the Machining Department, to the Assembly Department, to finished-goods inventory. The Machining Department is heavily automated; in contrast, the Assembly Department performs a number of manual-assembly activities. The company applies manufacturing overhead by the use of machine hours in the Machining Department and direct-labor cost in the Assembly Department. The following information relates to the year just ended:

	Machining Department	Assembly Department
Budgeted manufacturing overhead	$2,000,000	$1,540,000
Actual manufacturing overhead	2,130,000	1,525,000
Budgeted direct-labor cost	750,000	2,800,000
Actual direct-labor cost	725,000	2,890,000
Budgeted machine hours	200,000	50,000
Actual machine hours	212,500	55,000

The data that follow pertain to job no. DC66, the only job in production at year-end.

	Machining Department	Assembly Department
Direct material	$12,250	$ 3,350
Direct labor	13,950	29,300
Machine hours	180	75

Required:

1. Assuming the use of normal costing, determine the predetermined overhead rates used in the Machining Department and the Assembly Department.
2. Compute the cost of the company's year-end work-in-process inventory.
3. Determine whether overhead was under- or overapplied during the year in the Machining Department.
4. Repeat requirement (3) for the Assembly Department.
5. If Juarez disposes of under- or overapplied overhead as an adjustment to Cost of Goods Sold, would the company's Cost of Goods Sold account increase or decrease? Explain.
6. How much overhead would have been charged to the company's Work-in-Process account during the year?
7. Comment on the appropriateness of the company's cost drivers (i.e., the use of machine hours in Machining and direct-labor cost in Assembly).

Problem 3–48
Job-Order Costing in a Consulting Firm
(LO 1, 2, 4, 8)

Golden State Enterprises provides consulting services throughout California and uses a job-order costing system to accumulate the cost of client projects. Traceable costs are charged directly to individual clients; in contrast, other costs incurred by Golden State, but not identifiable with specific clients, are charged to jobs by using a predetermined overhead application rate. Clients are billed for directly chargeable costs, overhead, and a markup.

Golden State's director of cost management, Brent Dean, anticipates the following costs for the upcoming year:

	Cost	Percentage of Cost Directly Traceable to Clients
Professional staff salaries	$3,750,000	80%
Administrative support staff	450,000	60%
Photocopying	75,000	90%
Travel	375,000	90%
Other operating costs	150,000	50%
Total	$4,800,000	

The firm's partners desire to make a $960,000 profit for the firm and plan to add a percentage markup on total cost to achieve that figure.

On March 10, Golden State completed work on a project for Davis Manufacturing. The following costs were incurred: professional staff salaries, $61,500; administrative support staff, $3,900; photocopying, $750; travel, $6,750; and other operating costs, $2,100.

Required:

1. Determine Golden State Enterprises' total traceable costs for the upcoming year and the firm's total anticipated overhead.
2. Calculate the predetermined overhead rate. The rate is based on total costs traceable to client jobs.
3. What percentage of cost will the firm add to each job to achieve its profit target?
4. Determine the total cost of the Davis Manufacturing project. How much would Davis be billed for services performed?
5. Notice that only 50 percent of Golden State's other operating cost is directly traceable to specific client projects. Cite several costs that would be included in this category and difficult to trace to clients.
6. Notice that 80 percent of the professional staff cost is directly traceable to specific client projects. Cite several reasons that would explain why this figure isn't 100 percent.

Problem 3–49
Schedules of Cost of Goods Manufactured and Sold; Income Statement
(LO 6)

The following data refers to Superior Metals Corporation for the year 20x4.

Raw-material inventory, 12/31/x3	$ 66,750	Depreciation on factory equipment	45,000
Purchases of raw material in 20x4	548,250	Insurance on factory and equipment	30,000
Raw-material inventory, 12/31/x4	44,250	Utilities for factory	52,500
Direct-labor cost incurred	355,500	Work-in-process inventory, 12/31/x3	-0-
Selling and administrative expenses	201,750	Work-in-process inventory, 12/31/x4	30,000
Indirect labor cost incurred	112,500	Finished-goods inventory, 12/31/x3	26,250
Property taxes on factory	67,500	Finished-goods inventory, 12/31/x4	30,000
Depreciation on factory building	93,750	Applied manufacturing overhead	433,125
Income tax expense	18,750	Sales revenue	1,578,750
Indirect material used	33,750		

Required:

1. Prepare Superior Metals' schedule of cost of goods manufactured for 20x4.
2. Prepare the company's schedule of cost of goods sold for 20x4. The company closes overapplied or underapplied overhead into Cost of Goods Sold.
3. Prepare the company's income statement for 20x4.

Problem 3–50
Interpreting the Schedule of Cost of Goods Manufactured
(LO 2, 6)

Refer to the schedule of cost of goods manufactured prepared for Superior Metals Corporation in the preceding problem.

Required:

1. How much of the manufacturing costs incurred during 20x4 remained associated with work-in-process inventory on December 31, 20x4?
2. Suppose the company had increased its production in 20x4 by 30 percent. Would the direct-material cost shown on the schedule have been larger or the same? Why?
3. Answer the same question as in requirement (2) for depreciation on the factory building.
4. Suppose only half of the $45,000 in depreciation on equipment had been related to factory machinery, and the other half was related to selling and administrative equipment. How would this have changed the schedule of cost of goods manufactured?

Problem 3–51
Journal Entries in Job-Order Costing
(LO 4, 5)

Seaway, Inc. manufactures outboard motors and an assortment of other marine equipment. The company uses a job-order costing system. Normal costing is used, and manufacturing overhead is applied on the basis of machine hours. Estimated manufacturing overhead for the year is $1,520,200, and management expects that 69,100 machine hours will be used.

Required:

1. Calculate the company's predetermined overhead rate for the year.
2. Prepare journal entries to record the following events, which occurred during April.
   - **a.** The firm purchased marine propellers from Peninsula Marine Corporation for $8,240 on account.
   - **b.** A requisition was filed by the Gauge Department supervisor for 280 pounds of clear plastic. The material cost $.70 per pound when it was purchased.
   - **c.** The Motor Testing Department supervisor requisitioned 320 feet of electrical wire, which is considered an indirect material. The wire cost $.10 per foot when it was purchased.
   - **d.** An electric utility bill of $900 was paid in cash.
   - **e.** Direct-labor costs incurred in April were $73,500.
   - **f.** April's insurance cost was $2,100 for insurance on the cars driven by sales personnel. The policy had been prepaid in March.
   - **g.** Metal tubing costing $2,800 was purchased on account.
   - **h.** A cash payment of $1,850 was made on outstanding accounts payable.
   - **i.** Indirect-labor costs of $19,000 were incurred during April.
   - **j.** Depreciation on equipment for April amounted to $8,500.
   - **k.** Job number G22, consisting of 60 tachometers, was finished during April. The total cost of the job was $1,200.

l. During April, 6,500 machine hours were used.

m. Sales on account for April amounted to $181,000. The cost of goods sold in April was $142,500.

Problem 3–52
Ethical Issues; Underapplication of Manufacturing Overhead
(LO 1, 2, 4, 6)

Marc Jackson has recently been hired as a cost accountant by Offset Press Company, a privately held company that produces a line of offset printing presses and lithograph machines. During his first few months on the job, Jackson discovered that Offset has been underapplying factory overhead to the Work-in-Process Inventory account, while overstating expenses through the General and Administrative Expense account. This practice has been going on since the start of the company, which is in its sixth year of operation. The effect in each year has been favorable, having a material impact on the company's tax position. No internal audit function exists at Offset, and the external auditors have not yet discovered the underapplied factory overhead.

Prior to the sixth-year audit, Jackson had pointed out the practice and its effect to Mary Brown, the corporate controller, and had asked her to let him make the necessary adjustments. Brown directed him not to make the adjustments, but to wait until the external auditors had completed their work and see what they uncovered.

The sixth-year audit has now been completed, and the external auditors have once again failed to discover the underapplication of factory overhead. Jackson again asked Brown if he could make the required adjustments and was again told not to make them. Jackson, however, believes that the adjustments should be made and that the external auditors should be informed of the situation.

Since there are no established policies at Offset Press Company for resolving ethical conflicts, Jackson is considering one of the following three alternative courses of action:

- Follow Brown's directive and do nothing further.
- Attempt to convince Brown to make the proper adjustments and to advise the external auditors of her actions.
- Tell the Audit Committee of the Board of Directors about the problem and give them the appropriate accounting data.

Required:

1. As a group, discuss the situation at Offset. For each of the three alternative courses of action that Jackson is considering, discuss whether or not the action is appropriate.
2. Independent of your answer to requirement (1), assume that Jackson again approaches Brown to make the necessary adjustments and is unsuccessful. Discuss the steps that Jackson should take in proceeding to resolve this situation.

(CMA, adapted)

Problem 3–53
Cost of Goods Manufactured; Prime and Conversion Costs
(LO 2, 6)

Marvelous Marshmallow Company's cost of goods sold for January was $690,000. January 31 work-in-process inventory was 90 percent of January 1 work-in-process inventory. Manufacturing overhead applied was 50 percent of direct-labor cost. Other information pertaining to the company's inventories and production for the month of January is as follows:

Beginning inventories, January 1:	
Raw material	$ 34,000
Work in process	80,000
Finished goods	204,000
Purchases of raw material during January	226,000
Ending inventories, January 31:	
Raw material	52,000
Work in process	?
Finished goods	210,000

Required:

1. Prepare a schedule of cost of goods manufactured for the month of January.
2. Prepare a schedule to compute the prime costs (direct material and direct labor) incurred during January.
3. Prepare a schedule to compute the conversion costs (direct labor and manufacturing overhead) charged to work in process during January.

(CPA, adapted)

Problem 3–54
Proration of Overapplied or Underapplied Overhead
(LO 2, 4, 5, 6)

Biloxi Billiards Company uses normal costing, and manufacturing overhead is applied to work in process on the basis of machine hours. On January 1 of the current year there were no balances in work-in-process or finished-goods inventories. The following estimates were included in the current year's budget.

Total budgeted manufacturing overhead	$306,000
Total budgeted machine hours	51,000

During January, the firm began the following production jobs:

M07:	1,200 machine hours
T28:	3,000 machine hours
B19:	1,800 machine hours

During January, job numbers M07 and T28 were completed, and job number M07 was sold. The actual manufacturing overhead incurred during January was $38,000.

Required:

1. Compute the company's predetermined overhead rate for the current year.
2. How much manufacturing overhead was applied to production during January?
3. Calculate the overapplied or underapplied overhead for January.
4. Prepare a journal entry to close the balance calculated in requirement (3) into Cost of Goods Sold.
5. Prepare a journal entry to prorate the balance calculated in requirement (3) among the Work-in-Process Inventory, Finished-Goods Inventory, and Cost of Goods Sold accounts.

Problem 3–55
Overhead Application Using a Predetermined Overhead Rate
(LO 2, 4, 6)

Tiana Shar, the controller for Caesar Glassware Company, is in the process of analyzing the overhead costs for the month of November. She has gathered the following data for the month.

Labor	
Direct-labor hours:	
Job 57	7,000
Job 58	6,000
Job 59	4,000
Labor costs:	
Direct-labor wages	$102,000
Indirect-labor wages	30,000
Supervisory salaries	12,000
Material	
Inventories, November 1:	
Raw material and supplies	$ 21,000
Work in process (job 57)	108,000
Finished goods	125,000
Purchases of raw material and supplies:	
Raw material	$270,000
Supplies (indirect material)	30,000
Direct material and supplies requisitioned for production:	
Job 57	$ 90,000
Job 58	75,000
Job 59	51,000
Supplies (indirect material)	24,000
Total	$240,000
Other	
Building occupancy costs (heat, light, depreciation, etc.)	
Factory facilities	$ 12,800
Sales offices	3,200
Administrative offices	2,000
Total	$ 18,000

(continues)

(concluded)

Production equipment costs:	
Power	$ 8,200
Repairs and maintenance	3,000
Depreciation	3,000
Other	2,000
Total	$ 16,200

The firm's job-order costing system uses direct-labor hours as the cost driver for overhead application. In December of the preceding year, Shar had prepared the following budget for direct-labor and manufacturing-overhead costs for the current year. The plant is capable of operating at 140,000 direct-labor hours per year. However, Shar estimates that the normal usage is 115,000 hours in a typical year.

	Manufacturing Overhead	
Direct-Labor Hours	**Variable**	**Fixed**
100,000	$300,000	$230,000
115,000	345,000	230,000
130,000	390,000	230,000

During November the following jobs were completed:

Job 57	10 oz. water glasses
Job 58	5 oz. juice glasses

Required: Assist Shar by making the following calculations.

1. Calculate the predetermined overhead rate for the current year.
2. Calculate the total cost of job 57.
3. Compute the amount of manufacturing overhead applied to job 59 during November.
4. What was the total amount of manufacturing overhead applied during November?
5. Compute the actual manufacturing overhead incurred during November.
6. Calculate the overapplied or underapplied overhead for November.

(CMA, adapted)

Problem 3–56
Predetermined Overhead Rate; Different Time Periods; Pricing
(LO 4)

Rochester Heating Systems, Inc. calculates its predetermined overhead rate on a quarterly basis. The following estimates were made for the current year.

	Estimated Manufacturing Overhead	Estimated Direct-Labor Hours	Quarterly Predetermined Overhead Rate (per direct-labor hour)
First quarter	$ 400,000	50,000	?
Second quarter	320,000	32,000	?
Third quarter	200,000	25,000	?
Fourth quarter	280,000	28,000	?
Total	$1,200,000	135,000	

The firm's main product, part number SC71, requires $600 of direct material and 20 hours of direct labor per unit. The labor rate is $17 per hour.

Required:

1. Calculate the firm's *quarterly* predetermined overhead rate for each quarter.
2. Determine the cost of one unit of part number SC71 if it is manufactured in February versus May.
3. Suppose the company's pricing policy calls for a 10 percent markup over cost. Calculate the price to be charged for a unit of part number SC71 if it is produced in February versus May.
4. Calculate the company's predetermined overhead rate for the year if the rate is calculated *annually.*
5. Based on your answer to requirement (4), what is the cost of a unit of part number SC71 if it is manufactured in February? In May?
6. What is the price of a unit of part SC71 if the predetermined overhead rate is calculated annually?

Problem 3–57
Flow of Manufacturing Costs; Incomplete Data
(LO 2, 4, 5)

Conundrum, Inc. manufactures puzzles. Due to a fire in the administrative offices, the accounting records for September of the current year were partially destroyed. You have been able to piece together the following information from the ledger.

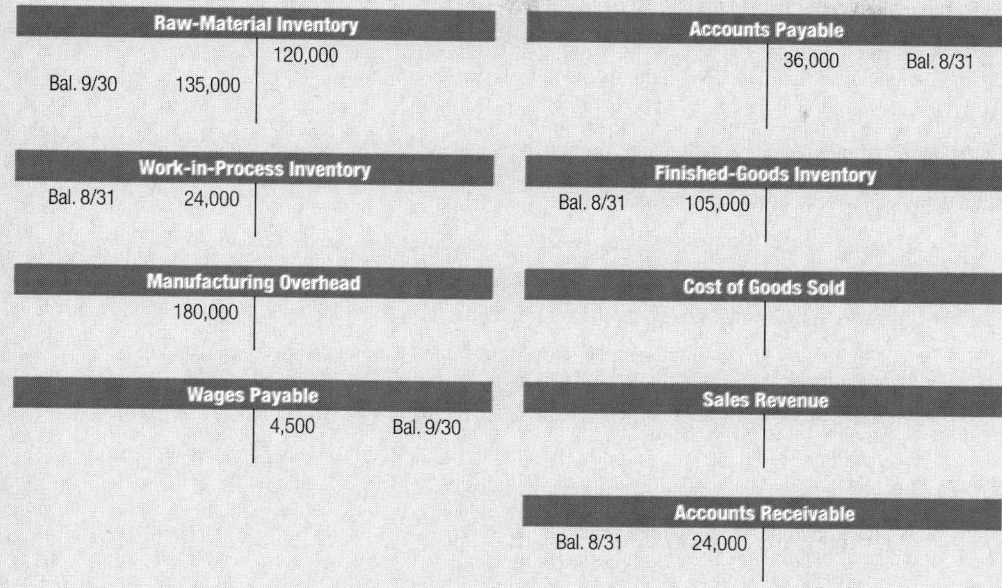

Raw-Material Inventory
120,000
Bal. 9/30
135,000
Accounts Payable
36,000
Bal. 8/31
Work-in-Process Inventory
Bal. 8/31
24,000
Finished-Goods Inventory
Bal. 8/31
105,000
Manufacturing Overhead
180,000
Cost of Goods Sold
Wages Payable
4,500
Bal. 9/30
Sales Revenue
Accounts Receivable
Bal. 8/31
24,000

Upon examining various source documents and interviewing several employees, you were able to gather the following additional information.

a. Collections of accounts receivable during September amounted to $615,000.

b. Sales revenue in September was 120 percent of cost of goods sold. All sales are on account.

c. Overhead is applied using an annual predetermined overhead rate based on direct-labor hours.

d. The budgeted overhead for the current year is $2,160,000.

e. Budgeted direct-labor cost for the current year is $2,880,000. The direct-labor rate is $20 per hour.

f. The accounts payable balance on September 30 was $3,000. Only purchases of raw material are credited to accounts payable. A payment of $243,000 was made on September 15.

g. September's cost of goods sold amounted to $540,000.

h. The September 30 balance in finished-goods inventory was $15,000.

i. Payments of $238,500 were made to direct-labor employees during September. The August 31 balance in the Wages Payable account was $3,000.

j. The *actual* manufacturing overhead for September was $180,000.

k. An analysis of the puzzles still in process on September 30 revealed that so far these items have required 1,500 hours of direct labor and $61,500 of direct material.

Required: Calculate the following amounts. Then complete the T-accounts given in the problem.

1. Sales revenue for September.
2. September 30 balance in accounts receivable.
3. Cost of raw material purchased during September.
4. September 30 balance in work-in-process inventory.
5. Direct labor added to work in process during September.
6. Applied overhead for September.
7. Cost of goods completed during September.
8. Raw material used during September.
9. August 31 balance in raw-material inventory.
10. Overapplied or underapplied overhead for September.

Problem 3–58
Comprehensive Job-Order Costing Problem
(LO 2, 4, 5, 6)

Bandway Company manufactures brass musical instruments for use by high school students. The company uses a normal costing system, in which manufacturing overhead is applied on the basis of direct-labor hours. The company's budget for the current year included the following predictions.

Budgeted total manufacturing overhead	$462,000
Budgeted total direct-labor hours	21,000

During October, the firm worked on the following two production jobs:

Job number T79, consisting of 76 trombones
Job number C41, consisting of 110 cornets

The events of October are described as follows:

a. One thousand square feet of rolled brass sheet metal was purchased on account for $6,000.

b. Four hundred pounds of brass tubing was purchased on account for $5,200.

c. The following requisitions were submitted on October 5:

Requisition number 112: 260 square feet of brass sheet metal at $5.50 per square foot (for job number T79)
Requisition number 113: 1,100 pounds of brass tubing, at $9.00 per pound (for job number C41)
Requisition number 114: 10 gallons of valve lubricant, at $12 per gallon

All brass used in production is treated as direct material. Valve lubricant is an indirect material.

d. An analysis of labor time cards revealed the following labor usage for October.

Direct labor: Job number T79, 850 hours at $20 per hour
Direct labor: Job number C41, 950 hours at $20 per hour
Indirect labor: General factory cleanup, $4,500
Indirect labor: Factory supervisory salaries, $9,600

e. Depreciation of the factory building and equipment during October amounted to $13,000.

f. Rent paid in cash for warehouse space used during October was $1,340.

g. Utility costs incurred during October amounted to $2,400. The invoices for these costs were received, but the bills were not paid in October.

h. October property taxes on the factory were paid in cash, $2,370.

i. The insurance cost covering factory operations for the month of October was $2,900. The insurance policy had been prepaid.

j. The costs of salaries and fringe benefits for sales and administrative personnel paid in cash during October amounted to $7,500.

k. Depreciation on administrative office equipment and space amounted to $4,500.

l. Other selling and administrative expenses paid in cash during October amounted to $1,150.

m. Job number T79 was completed on October 20.

n. Half of the trombones in job number T79 were sold on account during October for $720 each.

The October 1 balances in selected accounts are as follows:

Cash	$ 11,000
Accounts Receivable	20,000
Prepaid Insurance	6,000
Raw-Material Inventory	150,000
Manufacturing Supplies Inventory	600
Work-in-Process Inventory	89,000
Finished-Goods Inventory	223,000
Accumulated Depreciation: Buildings and Equipment	99,000
Accounts Payable	14,500
Wages Payable	8,500

Required:

1. Calculate the company's predetermined overhead rate for the year.
2. Prepare journal entries to record the events of October.

3. Set up T-accounts, and post the journal entries made in requirement (2).
4. Calculate the overapplied or underapplied overhead for October. Prepare a journal entry to close this balance into Cost of Goods Sold.
5. Prepare a schedule of cost of goods manufactured for October.
6. Prepare a schedule of cost of goods sold for October.
7. Prepare an income statement for October.

Problem 3–59
Job-Cost Record; Continuation of Preceding Problem
(LO 2, 4, 5)

Refer to the preceding problem regarding Bandway Company. Complete the following job-cost record for job number T79. (Assume that all of the labor hours for job T79 occurred during the week of 10/8 through 10/12.)

JOB-COST RECORD

Job Number T79 **Description** ____
Date Started ____ **Date Completed** ____
Number of Units Completed ____

Direct Material				
Date	**Requisition Number**	**Quantity**	**Unit Price**	**Cost**

Direct Labor				
Date	**Time Card Number**	**Hours**	**Rate**	**Cost**
10/8 to 10/12	10-08 to 10-12			

Manufacturing Overhead				
Date	**Cost Driver (Activity Base)**	**Quantity**	**Application Rate**	**Cost**
10/8 to 10/12				

Cost Summary	
Cost Item	**Amount**
Total direct material Total direct labor Total manufacturing overhead	
Total cost	
Unit cost	

Shipping Summary			
Date	**Units Shipped**	**Units Remaining in Inventory**	**Cost Balance**

Problem 3–60
Plantwide versus Departmental Overhead Rates; Product Pricing
(LO 1, 7)

ColorTech Corporation manufactures two different color printers for the business market. Cost estimates for the two models for the current year are as follows:

	Basic System	Advanced System
Direct material	$ 450	$ 900
Direct labor (20 hours at $16 per hour)	320	320
Manufacturing overhead*	420	420
Total	$1,190	$1,640

*The predetermined overhead rate is $21 per direct-labor hour.

Each model of printer requires 20 hours of direct labor. The basic system requires 5 hours in department A and 15 hours in department B. The advanced system requires 15 hours in department A and 5 hours in department B. The overhead costs budgeted in these two production departments are as follows:

	Department A	Department B
Variable cost	$17 per direct-labor hour	$5 per direct-labor hour
Fixed cost	$210,000	$210,000

The firm's management expects to operate at a level of 21,000 direct-labor hours in each production department during the current year.

Required:

1. Show how the company's predetermined overhead rate was determined.
2. If the firm prices each model of printer at 10 percent over its cost, what will be the price of each model?
3. Suppose the company were to use departmental predetermined overhead rates. Calculate the rate for each of the two production departments.
4. Compute the product cost of each model using the departmental overhead rates calculated in requirement (3).
5. Compute the price to be charged for each model, assuming the company continues to price each product at 10 percent above cost. Use the revised product costs calculated in requirement (4).
6. Write a memo to the president of ColorTech Corporation making a recommendation as to whether the firm should use a plantwide overhead rate or departmental rates. Consider the potential implications of the overhead rates and the firm's pricing policy. How might these considerations affect the firm's ability to compete in the marketplace?

Problem 3–61[9]
Activity-Based Costing Calculations; Continuation of Problem 3–60 (Appendix)
(LO 1, 7, 9)

Refer to the data given in the preceding problem for ColorTech Corporation. The company has implemented an activity-based costing system with the following activity cost pools and cost drivers:

		Cost Drivers		
Activity	Activity Cost	Total	Basic System Product Line	Advanced System Product Line
Machine setup	$102,000	200 setups	45 setups	155 setups
Material receiving	80,000	80,000 lb.	30,000 lb.	50,000 lb.
Inspection	80,000	1,600 inspections	690 inspections	910 inspections
Machinery-related	480,000	60,000 machine hr.	20,000 machine hr.	40,000 machine hr.
Engineering	140,000	7,000 engineering hr.	2,800 eng. hr.	4,200 eng. hr.
Total overhead	$882,000			

ColorTech plans to produce 1,000 units of each model of color printer.

Required:

1. Compute the cost rate per unit of each cost driver (e.g., the cost per setup).
2. Determine the total overhead to be assigned to each product line under activity-based costing.

[9]Additional problems covering activity-based costing are available in Chapter 5. In particular, the following problems could be assigned after completing the Appendix to Chapter 3: 5–22, 5–25, 5–35, 5–38, and 5–39.

3. Calculate the overhead assigned per unit of each type of printer under ABC.
4. Prepare a table comparing the total product cost assigned to each type of printer using a plantwide overhead rate, departmental overhead rates, and activity-based costing. (This requirement relies on the solution to the preceding problem.)

Cases

Case 3–62
Interpreting Information from a Job-Order Costing System
(LO 1, 2, 3, 4, 6)

KidCo, Inc. is a manufacturer of furnishings for children. The company uses a job-order costing system. KidCo's work-in-process inventory on November 30 consisted of the following jobs.

Job No.	Description	Units	Accumulated Cost
CBS102	Cribs	20,000	$ 900,000
PLP086	Playpens	15,000	420,000
DRS114	Dressers	25,000	250,000
Total			$1,570,000

The company's November 30 finished-goods inventory, which is valued using the FIFO (first-in, first-out) method, consisted of five items.

Item	Quantity and Unit Cost	Accumulated Cost
Cribs	7,500 units @ $64 each	$ 480,000
Strollers	13,000 units @ $23 each	299,000
Carriages	11,200 units @ $102 each	1,142,400
Dressers	21,000 units @ $55 each	1,155,000
Playpens	19,400 units @ $35 each	679,000
Total		$3,755,400

KidCo applies manufacturing overhead on the basis of direct-labor hours. The company's overhead budget for the year totals $4,500,000, and the company plans to use 600,000 direct-labor hours during this period. Through the first 11 months of the year, a total of 555,000 direct-labor hours were worked, and total overhead amounted to $4,273,500.

At the end of November, the balance in KidCo's Raw-Material Inventory account, which includes both raw material and purchased parts, was $668,000. Additions to inventory and requisitions from inventory during December included the following.

	Raw Material	Purchased Parts
Purchases	$242,000	$396,000
Requisitions:		
Job CBS102	51,000	104,000
Job PLP086	3,000	10,800
Job DRS114	124,000	87,000
Job STR077 (10,000 strollers)	62,000	81,000
Job CRG098 (5,000 carriages)	65,000	187,000

During December, KidCo's factory payroll consisted of the following:

CBS102	12,000 hr.	$122,400
PLP086	4,400 hr.	43,200
DRS114	19,500 hr.	200,500
STR077	3,500 hr.	30,000
CRG098	14,000 hr.	138,000
Indirect labor	3,000 hr.	29,400
Supervision		57,600
Total		$621,100

The following list shows the jobs that were completed and the unit sales for December.

Production			Sales	
Job No.	**Items**	**Quantity Completed**	**Items**	**Quantity Shipped**
CBS102	Cribs	20,000	Cribs	17,500
PLP086	Playpens	15,000	Playpens	21,000
STR077	Strollers	10,000	Strollers	14,000
CRG098	Carriages	5,000	Dressers	18,000
			Carriages	6,000

Required:

1. Explain when it is appropriate for a company to use a job-order costing system.
2. Calculate the dollar balance in KidCo's Work-in-Process Inventory account as of December 31.
3. Calculate the dollar amount related to the playpens in KidCo's Finished-Goods Inventory account as of December 31.

(CMA, adapted)

Case 3–63
Cost Flows in a Job-Order Costing System; Schedule of Cost of Goods Manufactured; Automation
(LO 2, 4, 6)

Opticom, Inc. a manufacturer of fiber optic communications equipment, uses a job-order costing system. Since the production process is heavily automated, manufacturing overhead is applied on the basis of machine hours using a predetermined overhead rate. The current annual rate of $30 per machine hour is based on budgeted manufacturing overhead costs of $2,400,000 and a budgeted activity level of 80,000 machine hours. Operations for the year have been completed, and all of the accounting entries have been made for the year except the application of manufacturing overhead to the jobs worked on during December, the transfer of costs from Work in Process to Finished Goods for the jobs completed in December, and the transfer of costs from Finished Goods to Cost of Goods Sold for the jobs that have been sold during December. Summarized data as of November 30 and for the month of December are presented in the following table. Jobs T11-007, N11-013, and N11-015 were completed during December. All completed jobs except Job N11-013 had been turned over to customers by the close of business on December 31.

	Work-in-Process	December Activity		
Job No.	**Balance November 30**	**Direct Material**	**Direct Labor**	**Machine Hours**
T11-007	$174,000	$ 3,000	$ 9,000	300
N11-013	110,000	8,000	24,000	1,000
N11-015	-0-	51,200	53,400	1,400
D12-002	-0-	75,800	40,000	2,500
D12-003	-0-	52,000	33,600	800
Total	$284,000	$190,000	$160,000	6,000

Operating Activity	**Activity through November 30**	**December Activity**
Actual manufacturing overhead incurred:		
Indirect material	$ 250,000	$ 18,000
Indirect labor	690,000	60,000
Utilities	490,000	44,000
Depreciation	770,000	70,000
Total overhead	$2,200,000	$192,000
Other data:		
Raw-material purchases*	$1,930,000	$196,000
Direct-labor costs	$1,690,000	$160,000
Machine hours	73,000	6,000

Account Balances at Beginning of Year	**January 1**
Raw-material inventory*	$210,000
Work-in-process inventory	120,000
Finished-goods inventory	250,000

*Raw-material purchases and raw-material inventory consist of both direct and indirect materials. The balance of the Raw-Material Inventory account as of December 31 of the year just completed is $170,000.

Required:

1. Explain why manufacturers use a predetermined overhead rate to apply manufacturing overhead to their jobs.
2. How much manufacturing overhead would Opticom have applied to jobs through November 30 of the year just completed?
3. How much manufacturing overhead would have been applied to jobs during December of the year just completed?
4. Determine the amount by which manufacturing overhead is overapplied or underapplied as of December 31 of the year just completed.
5. Determine the balance in the Finished-Goods Inventory account on December 31 of the year just completed.
6. Prepare a Schedule of Cost of Goods Manufactured for Opticom, Inc. for the year just completed. (*Hint:* In computing the cost of direct material used, remember that Opticom includes both direct and indirect material in its Raw-Material Inventory account.)

(CMA, adapted)

Current Issues in Managerial Accounting

Issue 3–64
Supply Chain Management

"General Mills Inc. Boosts Target for Savings Project to $1 Billion," *The Wall Street Journal,* February 14, 2003, p. B4, Patricia Callahan.

Overview

General Mills has set a $1 billion savings goal over 10 years from productivity increases.

Suggested Discussion Questions

How is General Mills using supply chain management to achieve this goal? In particular, how is the company saving $1.5 million annually on its cake mix line?

Issue 3–65
Supply Chain Management

"Tidying Up at Home Depot," *Business Week,* November 26, 2001, p. 102, Aixa M. Pascual: "Nike Net Rises 30% on Corrected Glitch to Its Supply Chain," *The Wall Street Journal,* March 22, 2002, Maureen Tkacik.

Overview

Retailer, Home Depot, and athletic shoe manufacturer, Nike, are predicting large cost savings from improvements in their supply chain management.

Suggested Discussion Question

As a group, discuss why supply chain management is so important in cost management.

Issue 3–66
Use of Product Costing Information to Support Marketing Promotions

"'Business-Method' Patents, Key to Priceline, Draw Growing Protest," *The Wall Street Journal,* October 3, 2000, Julia Angwin.

Overview

A new promotional gimmick called "upselling," introduced by Walker Digital Corp., has caught on in the retail industry. (Walker Digital Corp. is one of Jay Walker's companies. He also founded Priceline.com.) Kentucky Fried Chicken, for example, uses the promotional tool to get its customers to increase their food order size. If a customer orders chicken with macaroni and cheese, for a total of $6.48, the cashier might offer an additional small soda or a chicken strip to bring the customer's total up to an even seven bucks. The small soda normally sells for $1.29, but the customer gets "a deal" by paying only $.52 for it. Meanwhile, KFC's sales have increased as well.

Suggested Discussion Questions

Could a manufacturing company use upselling? How would product costing be important to a company engaged in upselling? What kind of software system would be useful in tying a company's product-costing database together with its sales operation to make upselling profitable for the company? As explained in the article, every time a company makes a sale using upselling, Jay Walker will get a royalty cut because his company holds a patent on this particular form of the "business method" called upselling. Some observers are questioning the appropriateness of issuing patents on business methods, such as upselling or Amazon.com's patented 1-Click shopping. Do you believe such business-method patents are ethical?

Chapter Four

Process Costing and Hybrid Product-Costing Systems

After completing this chapter, you should be able to:

1. List and explain the similarities and important differences between job-order and process costing.
2. Prepare journal entries to record the flow of costs in a process-costing system with sequential production departments.
3. Prepare a table of equivalent units under weighted-average process costing.
4. Compute the cost per equivalent unit under the weighted-average method of process costing.
5. Analyze the total production costs for a department under the weighted-average method of process costing.
6. Prepare a departmental production report under weighted-average process costing.
7. Describe how an operation costing system accumulates and assigns the costs of direct-material and conversion activity in a batch manufacturing process.
8. After completing the appendix, prepare process-costing calculations for a sequential manufacturing process (appendix).

Local Sports Hero Continues Winning Ways in Business

Milwaukee, WI—It was another outstanding season for local sports phenom Tim Bradley. But this time he wasn't on the pitcher's mound. Bradley's company, MVP Sports Equipment, just topped $10 million in annual revenue for the first time. Bradley, who starred in three sports at Central High and went on to play college and professional baseball, started MVP Sports Equipment Company eight years ago. Bradley's savings from a highly successful baseball career, along with the financial backing of two local banks, got MVP off and running. And there has been no looking back for Bradley.

I interviewed Bradley in his Milwaukee office yesterday. "I was disappointed when my shoulder injury ended my ball career early," Bradley said. "But I realized I had the skills and knowledge to do other things with my life besides throw a baseball."

Bradley feels his business degree prepared him well to take on the corporate world. "It's amazing how much running a business is like playing a sport," he observed. "When I started MVP, I was a little nervous, just like I was before a big game in high school. But after awhile, you get a sense of the rhythm of the business environment you're in. I knew I wanted to get into manufacturing, and sports equipment was a natural thing to choose."

We left Bradley's office for a tour of the Milwaukee plant where MVP manufactures baseball gloves. I was impressed by how Bradley gave details about the manufacturing operation. "Producing baseball gloves is a two-step process," he explained. "Our operation is organized into two production departments. In the Cutting Department, we cut out the necessary pieces for the gloves from roll stock of imitation leather. Then in the Stitching Department, we sew the pieces together and stamp the label." Bradley's explanation of manufacturing was interspersed with comments about running the business. "One thing I learned early on was the absolute necessity of keeping track of costs. Our aim is to manufacture a quality ball glove that kids and scholastic sports programs can afford. Affordability means keeping the price down, and that means cost awareness and control. Our process-costing system accumulates the production costs as the gloves move through each manufacturing department. As materials are used and labor and other costs are incurred, we accumulate the costs. This gives us good information on our unit costs. And that's the whole ball game . . . so to speak."

Smiling at the pun, and risking another one, I asked Tim Bradley if he had any final comments on the transition from the pitcher's mound to the board room. "Running a business is like mounting a successful pennant campaign," he said seriously. "They both take team work."

We have seen that a product-costing system performs two primary functions:

1. Accumulating production costs.
2. Assigning those production costs to the firm's products.

Product costs are needed for the purposes of planning, cost management, decision making, and reporting to various outside organizations, such as governmental regulatory agencies.

Job-order costing was described in Chapter 3. This type of product-costing system is used when relatively small numbers of products are produced in distinct batches or job orders and these products differ significantly from each other. This chapter covers **process-costing systems.** Process costing is used in **repetitive production** environments, where large numbers of identical or very similar products are manufactured in a continuous flow. Industries using process costing include paper, petroleum, chemicals, textiles, food processing, lumber, and electronics.

Comparison of Job-Order Costing and Process Costing

LO 1

List and explain the similarities and important differences between job-order and process costing.

In many ways, job-order costing and process costing are similar. Both product-costing systems have the same ultimate purpose—assignment of production costs to units of output. Moreover, the flow of costs through the manufacturing accounts is the same in the two systems.

Flow of Costs

"In the early days with the company, the accounting organization typically ended up on one floor, . . . but over time we've physically dispersed ourselves more to get closer to the clients." (4a)

Qwest

Exhibit 4–1 displays the flow of costs in two process-costing situations: one with a single production department and one with two production departments used in sequence. The same accounts are used in this process-costing illustration as were used in job-order costing in the preceding chapter. As the illustration shows, direct-material, direct-labor, and manufacturing-overhead costs are added to a Work-in-Process Inventory account. As goods are finished, costs are transferred to Finished-Goods Inventory. During the period when goods are sold, the product costs are transferred to Cost of Goods Sold. In the two-department case, when goods are finished in the first production department, costs accumulated in the Work-in-Process Inventory account for production department A are transferred to the Work-in-Process Inventory account for production department B.

The journal entries for the case of two sequential production departments, as illustrated in Exhibit 4–1, are as follows. (The numbers used in the journal entries are assumed for the purpose of showing the form of the entries.)

1. As direct material and direct labor are used in production department A, these costs are added to the Work-in-Process Inventory account for department A. Overhead is applied using a predetermined overhead rate. The predetermined overhead rate is computed in the same way in job-order and process costing.

LO 2

Prepare journal entries to record the flow of costs in a process-costing system with sequential production departments.

Work-in-Process Inventory: Production Department A	100,000	
Raw-Material Inventory		50,000
Wages Payable		20,000
Manufacturing Overhead		30,000

2. When production department A completes its work on some units of product, these units are transferred to production department B. The costs assigned to these goods are transferred from the Work-in-Process Inventory account for department A to the Work-in-Process Inventory account for department B. In department B, the costs assigned to these partially completed products are called **transferred-in costs.**

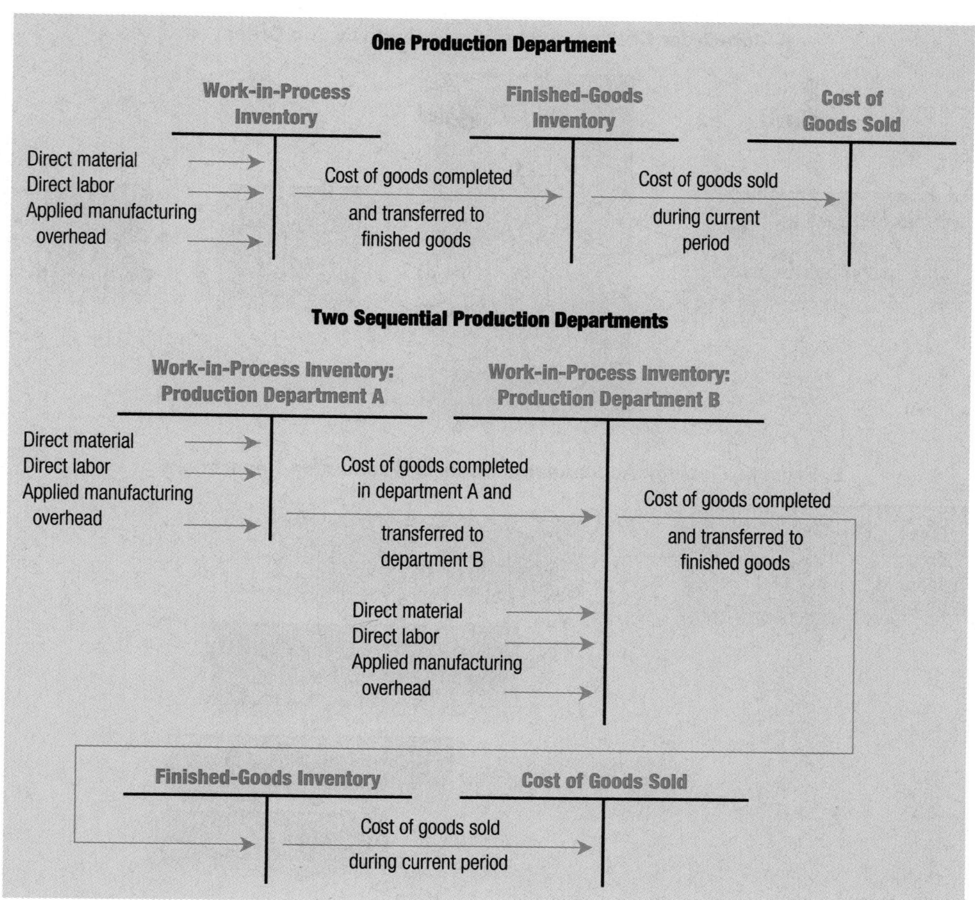

Exhibit 4–1
Flow of Costs in Process-Costing Systems

Work-in-Process Inventory: Production Department B	80,000	
Work-in-Process Inventory: Production Department A		80,000

3. Direct material and direct labor are used in production department B, and manufacturing overhead is applied using a predetermined overhead rate.

Work-in-Process Inventory: Production Department B	75,000	
Raw-Material Inventory		40,000
Wages Payable		15,000
Manufacturing Overhead		20,000

"Process-based costing provided our first opportunity to convert the functional budget into process costing. It allowed us to look at what drives the costs of the individual processes." (4b)
John Deere Health Care, Inc.

4. Goods are completed in production department B and transferred to the finished-goods warehouse.

Finished-Goods Inventory	130,000	
Work-in-Process Inventory: Production Department B		130,000

5. Goods are sold.

Cost of Goods Sold	125,000	
Finished-Goods Inventory		125,000

Exhibit 4–2
Comparison of Job-Order and Process Costing

A. Job-Order Costing: Accumulates Costs by Job Order

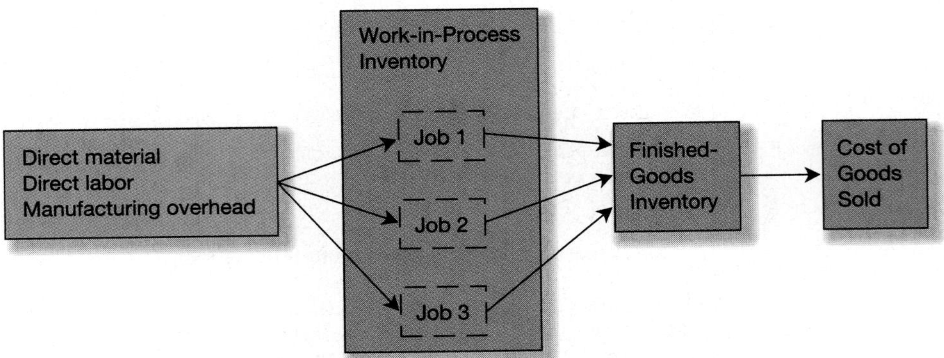

B. Process Costing: Accumulates Costs by Production Department

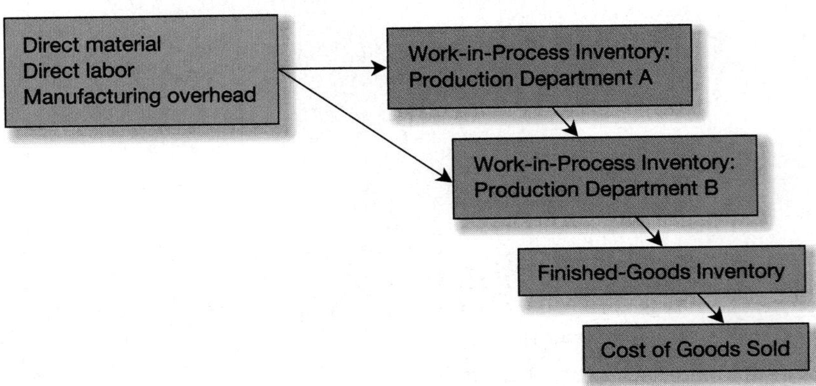

Differences between Job-Order and Process Costing

LO 1

List and explain the similarities and important differences between job-order and process costing.

In job-order costing, *costs are accumulated by job order* and recorded on job-cost records. The cost of each unit in a particular job order is found by dividing the total cost of the job order by the number of units in the job.

In process costing, *costs are accumulated by department*, rather than by job order or batch. The cost per unit is found by averaging the total costs incurred over the units produced. Exhibit 4–2 summarizes this key difference between job-order and process costing.

Equivalent Units: A Key Concept

LO 3

Prepare a table of equivalent units under weighted-average process costing.

Topic 4–1

Material, labor, and overhead costs often are incurred at different rates in a production process. Direct material is usually placed into production at one or more discrete points in the process. In contrast, direct labor and manufacturing overhead, called *conversion costs*, usually are incurred continuously throughout the process. When an accounting period ends, the partially completed goods that remain in process generally are at different stages of completion with respect to material and conversion activity. For example, the in-process units may be 75 percent complete with respect to conversion, but they may already include all of their direct materials. This situation is portrayed in Exhibit 4–3.

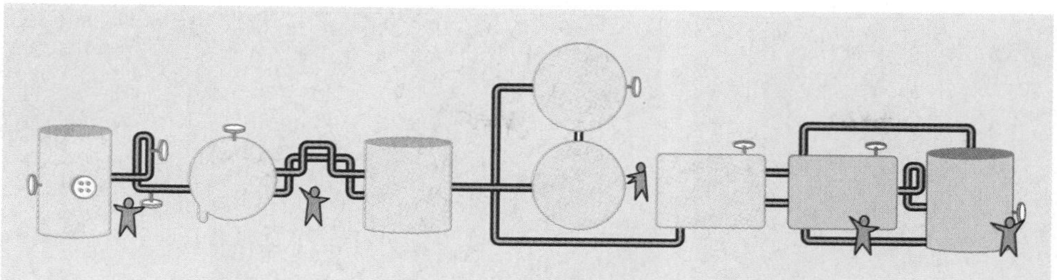
Production Process (e.g., chemical refining process)
Conversion activity (direct labor and manufacturing overhead) applied uniformly throughout the process
Direct material is placed into production at the beginning of the production process.
When the accounting period ends, the partially completed goods are 75% complete with respect to conversion. The goods are 100% complete with respect to direct material.

Exhibit 4–3
Direct Material and Conversion Activity in a Typical Production Process

Equivalent Units

The graphical illustration in Exhibit 4–3 supposes there are 1,000 physical units in process at the end of an accounting period. Each of the physical units is 75 percent complete with respect to conversion (direct labor and manufacturing overhead). How much conversion activity has been applied to these partially completed units? Conversion activity occurs uniformly throughout the production process. Therefore, the amount of conversion activity required to do 75 percent of the conversion on 1,000 units is *equivalent* to the amount of conversion activity required to do all of the conversion on 750 units. This number is computed as follows:

$$\begin{matrix}\text{1,000 partially completed} \\ \text{physical units in process}\end{matrix} \times \begin{matrix}\text{75\% complete with} \\ \text{respect to conversion}\end{matrix} = \text{750 equivalent units}$$

The term **equivalent units** is used in process costing to refer to the amount of manufacturing activity that has been applied to a batch of physical units. The *1,000 physical units* in process represent *750 equivalent units* of conversion activity.

The term *equivalent units* is also used to measure the amount of direct materials represented by the partially completed goods. Since direct materials are incorporated at the beginning of the production process, the *1,000 physical units* represent *1,000 equivalent units of direct material* (1,000 physical units × 100% complete with respect to direct materials).

The most important feature of process costing is that the costs of direct material and conversion are assigned to equivalent units rather than to physical units. Refer again to Exhibit 4–3. For simplicity, suppose that the only production activity of the current accounting period was to start work on the 1,000 physical units and complete 75 percent of the required conversion activity. Assume that the costs incurred were $1,500 for conversion (direct labor and manufacturing overhead) and $5,000 for direct material. These costs would then be assigned as follows:

$$\frac{\text{\$1,500 conversion cost}}{\text{750 equivalent units of conversion}} = \begin{matrix}\text{\$2.00 per equivalent unit} \\ \text{for conversion}\end{matrix}$$

$$\frac{\text{\$5,000 direct-material cost}}{\text{1,000 equivalent units of direct material}} = \begin{matrix}\text{\$5.00 per equivalent unit} \\ \text{for direct material}\end{matrix}$$

"Operations [managers] have a keen interest in cost management. To truly manage costs, you must look at the processes involved." (4c)

John Deere Health Care, Inc.

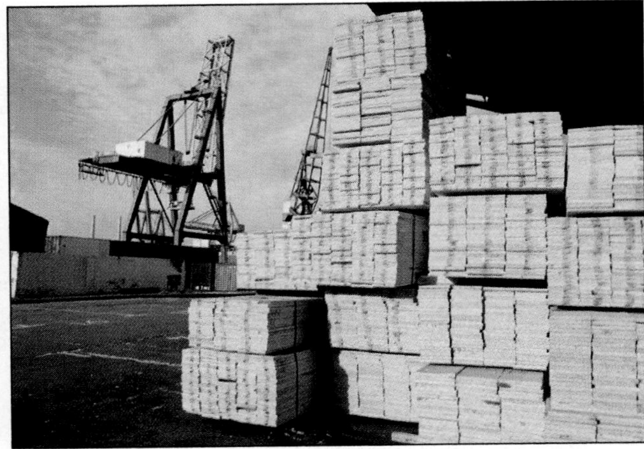

Process costing is used in the timber industry. First, raw material (in this case, logs) are harvested and entered into production. Then conversion costs are incurred in the production process. At the end of the accounting period, partially completed units of building lumber often remain in process.

This is a highly simplified example because there is no work-in-process inventory at the beginning of the accounting period and no goods were completed during the period. Nevertheless, it illustrates the important concept that under process costing, costs are assigned to equivalent units rather than physical units.

Illustration of Process Costing

Topic 4–2

The key document in a typical process-costing system is the **departmental production report**, prepared for each production department at the end of every accounting period. This report replaces the job-cost record, which is used to accumulate costs by job in a job-order costing system. The departmental production report summarizes the flow of production quantities through the department, and it shows the amount of production cost transferred out of the department's Work-in-Process Inventory account during the period. The following four steps are used in preparing a departmental production report.

1. Analysis of physical flow of units.
2. Calculation of equivalent units (for direct material and conversion activity).
3. Computation of unit costs (i.e., the cost per equivalent unit for direct material and conversion).
4. Analysis of total costs (determine the cost to be removed from work in process and transferred either to the next production department or to finished goods).

The method of process costing that we will focus on in this chapter is called the **weighted-average method.** *This method is almost always used in practice* by companies using process costing. There is another process-costing method called the *first-in, first-out*, or *FIFO, method.* This method is covered in some cost accounting courses, but it is rarely used in practice.

Basic Data for Illustration

The Wisconsin Division of MVP Sports Equipment Company manufactures baseball gloves in its Milwaukee plant. Two production departments are used in sequence: the Cutting Department and the Stitching Department. In the Cutting Department, direct

Exhibit 4–4
Basic Data for Illustration—Cutting Department

Microsoft Excel - Exhibit 4-4

B20 =SUM(B18:B19)

	A	B	C
1	Work in process, March 1 - 20,000 units		
2	Direct material: 100% complete, cost of*	$ 50,000	
3	Conversion: 10% complete, cost of*	7,200	
4	Balance in work in process, March 1*	$ 57,200	
5			
6	Units started during March	30,000	units
7			
8	Units completed during March and transferred out of the Cutting Department	40,000	units
9			
10	Work in process, March 31	10,000	units
11	Direct material: 100% complete		
12	Conversion: 50% complete		
13			
14	Costs Incurred during March:		
15	Direct material	$ 90,000	
16			
17	Conversion costs:		
18	Direct labor	$ 86,000	
19	Applied manufacturing overhead**	107,500	
20	Total conversion costs	$ 193,500	
21			
22	*These costs were incurred during the prior month, February		
23			
24	**(Predetermined overhead rate) x (Direct labor cost) = 125% x $86,000 = $107,500		

Sheet1 / Sheet2 / Sheet3

Ready

material consisting of imitation leather is placed into production at the beginning of the process. Direct-labor and manufacturing overhead costs are incurred uniformly throughout the process. The material is rolled to make it softer and then cut into the pieces needed to produce baseball gloves. The predetermined overhead rate used in the Cutting Department is 125 percent of direct-labor *cost*.

The Excel spreadsheet in Exhibit 4–4 presents a summary of the activity and costs in the Cutting Department during March. The direct-material and conversion costs listed in Exhibit 4–4 for the March 1 work in process consist of costs that were incurred during February. These costs were assigned to the units remaining in process at the end of February.

Based on the data in Exhibit 4–4, the Cutting Department's Work-in-Process Inventory account has the following balance on March 1:

Work-in-Process Inventory: Cutting Department		
March 1 balance	57,200	

The following journal entry is made during March to add the costs of direct material, direct labor, and manufacturing overhead to Work-in-Process Inventory.

Work-in-Process Inventory: Cutting Department	283,500	
Raw-Material Inventory		90,000
Wages Payable		86,000
Manufacturing Overhead		107,500

Management Accounting Practice

International Paper Company

PROCESS COSTING STEPS IN PAPER MANUFACTURING

"With 18.3 million tons of capacity, International Paper is the world's largest paper and forest products company. Its businesses include paper, packaging, and forest products. The company's global headquarters is located in Stamford, Connecticut. The company has operations in nearly 50 countries, employs more than 100,000 people, and exports its products to more than 130 nations. Global operations are located primarily in Asia, Canada, Europe, and Latin America."[1]

Paper production is the sort of manufacturing process that uses process costing. Here is a list of the processes typically involved in making paper.[2]

- Harvested trees arrive by rail and are stored outside the plant.
- Logs are moved by a flume into the plant where they pass through a debarker and are cut into chips.
- The chips are stored in large bins near the chipping machines.
- The chips are transported via conveyor system to another building and are placed in a digester, a large pressure cooker where heat, steam, and chemicals convert the chips into moist fibers.
- The fibers are stored near the digester.
- The fibers are moved via conveyor system to a depressurized blow tank, in which the fibers are separated.
- The separated fibers are transferred to the refining area, where the fibers are washed, refined, and treated with chemicals and caustic substances until they become pulp.
- The wood pulp then enters the paper machines through a headbox, which distributes pulp evenly across a porous belt of forming fabric.
- Water is removed from the pulp by passing it over a wire screen.
- Additional water is removed from the pulp in a series of presses.
- Dryers then remove any remaining water from the pulp.
- The thin, dry sheets of pulp are then smoothed and polished by large rollers called *calenders*.
- The paperboard is wound into large rolls, and workers place the rolls on wooden pallets.
- Forklifts are used to move the rolls of paperboard to the labeling building.
- The rolls are labeled and stored for shipment.
- The rolls of paperboard are shipped to customers.

Weighted-Average Method of Process Costing

We now present the four steps used to prepare a departmental production report using weighted-average process costing.

Step 1: Analysis of Physical Flow of Units The first step is to prepare a table summarizing the physical flow of production units during March. The table is shown in Exhibit 4–5 and reflects the following inventory formula.

$$\begin{pmatrix}\text{Physical units}\\\text{in beginning}\\\text{work in process}\end{pmatrix} + \begin{pmatrix}\text{Physical}\\\text{units}\\\text{started}\end{pmatrix} - \begin{pmatrix}\text{Physical units}\\\text{completed and}\\\text{transferred out}\end{pmatrix} = \begin{pmatrix}\text{Physical units}\\\text{in ending work}\\\text{in process}\end{pmatrix}$$

[1]Company website, www.internationalpaper.com.

[2]Based on the author's research.

	Physical Units
Work in process, March 1	20,000
Units started during March	30,000
Total units to account for	50,000
Units completed and transferred out during March	40,000
Work in process, March 31	10,000
Total units accounted for	50,000

Exhibit 4–5
Step 1: Analysis of Physical Flow of Units—Cutting Department

	Physical Units	Percentage of Completion with Respect to Conversion	Equivalent Units	
			Direct Material	Conversion
Work in process, March 1	20,000	10%		
Units started during March	30,000			
Total units to account for	50,000			
Units completed and transferred out during March	40,000	100%	40,000	40,000
Work in process, March 31	10,000	50%	10,000	5,000
Total units accounted for	50,000			
Total equivalent units			50,000	45,000

Exhibit 4–6
Step 2: Calculation of Equivalent Units—Cutting Department (weighted-average method)

Step 2: Calculation of Equivalent Units The second step in the process-costing procedure is to calculate the equivalent units of direct material and conversion activity. A table of equivalent units, displayed in Exhibit 4–6, is based on the table of physical flows prepared in step 1 (Exhibit 4–5). The 40,000 physical units that were completed and transferred out of the Cutting Department were 100 percent complete. Thus, they represent 40,000 equivalent units for both direct material and conversion. The 10,000 units in the ending work-in-process inventory are complete with respect to direct material, and they represent 10,000 equivalent units of direct material. However, they are only 50 percent complete with respect to conversion. Therefore, the ending work-in-process inventory represents 5,000 equivalent units of conversion activity (10,000 physical units × 50% complete).

LO 3 Prepare a table of equivalent units under weighted-average process costing.

As Exhibit 4–6 indicates, the total number of equivalent units is calculated:

$$\begin{pmatrix}\text{Equivalent units of}\\ \text{activity in units completed}\\ \text{and transferred out}\end{pmatrix} + \begin{pmatrix}\text{Equivalent units of}\\ \text{activity in ending}\\ \text{work in process}\end{pmatrix} = \begin{pmatrix}\text{Total}\\ \text{equivalent units}\\ \text{of activity}\end{pmatrix}$$

Note that the total equivalent units of activity, for both direct material and conversion, exceeds the activity accomplished in the current period alone. Since only 30,000 physical product units were started during March and direct material is added at the beginning of the process, only 30,000 equivalent units of direct material were actually placed into production during March. However, the total number of equivalent units of direct material used for weighted-average process costing is 50,000 (see Exhibit 4–6). The other 20,000 equivalent units of direct material were actually entered into production during the preceding month. *This is the key feature of the weighted-average method. The number of equivalent units of activity is calculated without making a distinction as to whether the activity occurred in the current accounting period or the preceding period.*

Exhibit 4–7
Step 3: Computation of Unit Costs—Cutting Department (weighted-average method)

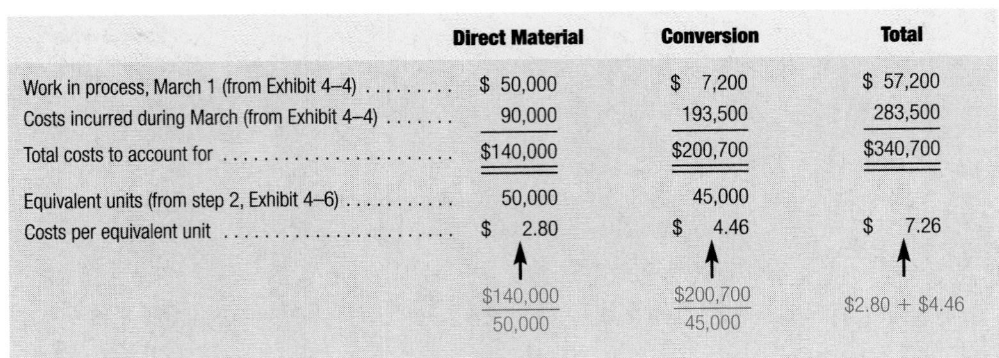

	Direct Material	Conversion	Total
Work in process, March 1 (from Exhibit 4–4)	$ 50,000	$ 7,200	$ 57,200
Costs incurred during March (from Exhibit 4–4)	90,000	193,500	283,500
Total costs to account for	$140,000	$200,700	$340,700
Equivalent units (from step 2, Exhibit 4–6)	50,000	45,000	
Costs per equivalent unit	$ 2.80	$ 4.46	$ 7.26
	↑ $140,000 / 50,000	↑ $200,700 / 45,000	↑ $2.80 + $4.46

LO 4 Compute the cost per equivalent unit under the weighted-average method of process costing.

Step 3: Computation of Unit Costs The third step in the process-costing procedure, calculating the cost per equivalent unit for both direct material and conversion activity, is presented in Exhibit 4–7. The cost per equivalent unit for direct material is computed by dividing the total direct-material cost, including the cost of the beginning work in process *and* the cost incurred during March, by the total equivalent units (from step 2, Exhibit 4–6). An analogous procedure is used for conversion costs.

LO 5 Analyze the total production costs for a department under the weighted-average method of process costing.

Step 4: Analysis of Total Costs Now we can complete the process-costing procedure by determining the total cost to be transferred out of the Cutting Department's Work-in-Process Inventory account and into the Stitching Department's Work-in-Process Inventory account. Exhibit 4–8 provides the required calculations. For convenience, the computations in step 3 are repeated in Exhibit 4–8. At the bottom of Exhibit 4–8, a check is made to be sure that the total costs of $340,700 have been fully accounted for in the cost of goods completed and transferred out and the balance remaining in work-in-process inventory.

The calculations in Exhibit 4–8 are used as the basis for the following journal entry to transfer the cost of goods completed and transferred out to the Stitching Department.

Work-in-Process Inventory: Stitching Department	290,400	
Work-in-Process Inventory: Cutting Department		290,400

On March 31, the Cutting Department's Work-in-Process Inventory account appears as follows. The March 31 balance in the account agrees with that calculated in Exhibit 4–8.

Work-in-Process Inventory: Cutting Department			
March 1 balance	57,200		
March cost of direct material, direct labor, and applied manufacturing overhead	283,500	290,400	Cost of goods completed and transferred out of Cutting Department
March 31 balance	50,300		

LO 6 Prepare a departmental production report under weighted-average process costing.

Departmental Production Report We have now completed all four steps necessary to prepare a production report for the Cutting Department. The report, which is displayed in Exhibit 4–9, simply combines the tables presented in Exhibits 4–6 and 4–8. The report provides a convenient summary of all of the process-costing calculations made under the weighted-average method.

Why is this process-costing method called the *weighted-average* method? Because the cost per equivalent unit for March, for both direct material and conversion activity, is computed as a weighted average of the costs incurred during two different accounting

Exhibit 4–8
Step 4: Analysis of Total Costs—Cutting Department (weighted-average method)

	Direct Material	**Conversion**	**Total**
Work in process, March 1 (from Exhibit 4–4)	$ 50,000	$ 7,200	$ 57,200
Costs incurred during March (from Exhibit 4–4)	90,000	193,500	283,500
Total costs to account for	$140,000	$200,700	$340,700
Equivalent units (from step 2, Exhibit 4–6)	50,000	45,000	
Costs per equivalent unit	$ 2.80	$ 4.46	$ 7.26
	↑ $140,000 / 50,000	↑ $200,700 / 45,000	↑ $2.80 + $4.46

Cost of goods completed and transferred out of the Cutting Department during March:		
(Number of units transferred out) × (Total cost per equivalent unit)	40,000 × $7.26	$290,400
Cost remaining in March 31 work-in-process inventory in the Cutting Department:		
Direct material:		
(Number of equivalent units of direct material) × (Cost per equivalent unit of direct material)	10,000 × $2.80	$ 28,000
Conversion:		
(Number of equivalent units of conversion) × (Cost per equivalent unit of conversion)	5,000 × $4.46	22,300
Total cost of March 31 work in process		$ 50,300
Check: Cost of goods completed and transferred out		$290,400
Cost of March 31 work-in-process inventory		50,300
Total costs accounted for		$340,700

periods, February and March. To demonstrate this fact, we will focus on direct material. Since direct material is placed into production at the beginning of the process, the 20,000 physical units in the March 1 work in process already have their direct material. The direct-material cost per equivalent unit in the March 1 work in process is $2.50 ($50,000 ÷ 20,000, from Exhibit 4–4). This cost was actually incurred in *February*.

In March, 30,000 physical units were entered into work in process and received their direct material. The direct-material cost incurred in March was $90,000. Thus, the direct-material cost per equivalent unit experienced in *March* was $3.00 ($90,000 ÷ 30,000).

Under the weighted-average method of process costing, the cost per equivalent unit for direct material was calculated in Exhibit 4–7 to be $2.80. *This $2.80 unit-cost figure is a weighted average*, as the following calculation shows.

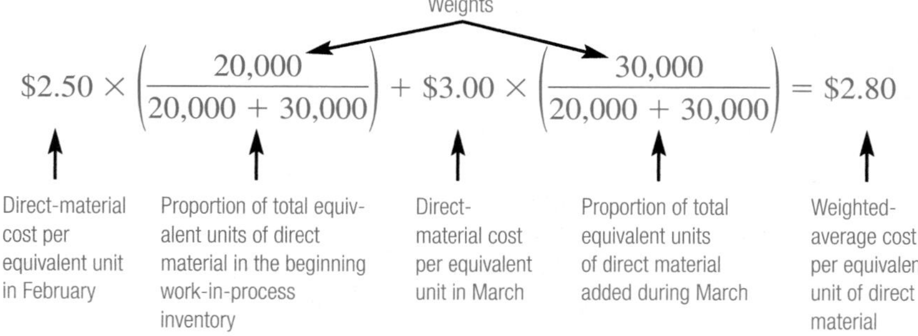

The point of this demonstration is that under weighted-average process costing, unit-cost figures are weighted averages of costs incurred over two or more accounting periods.

"The goal is for management to use the [cost] information daily. We want to . . . make sure that people have the information they need to make more informed decisions." (4d)
John Deere Health Care, Inc.

Exhibit 4–9
Production Report: Cutting Department (weighted-average method)

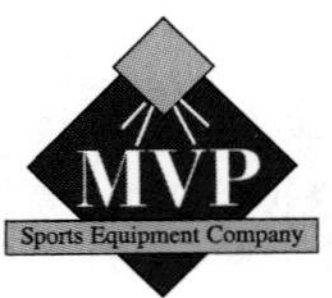

MVP SPORTS EQUIPMENT COMPANY
Production Report: Cutting Department

	Physical Units	Percentage of Completion with Respect to Conversion	Equivalent Units: Direct Material	Equivalent Units: Conversion
Work in process, March 1	20,000	10%		
Units started during March	30,000			
Total units to account for	50,000			
Units completed and transferred out during March	40,000	100%	40,000	40,000
Work in process, March 31	10,000	50%	10,000	5,000
Total units accounted for	50,000			
Total equivalent units			50,000	45,000

	Direct Material	Conversion	Total
Work in process, March 1 (from Exhibit 4–4)	$ 50,000	$ 7,200	$ 57,200
Costs incurred during March (from Exhibit 4–4)	90,000	193,500	283,500
Total costs to account for	$140,000	$200,700	$340,700
Equivalent units (from step 2, Exhibit 4–6)	50,000	45,000	
Costs per equivalent unit	$ 2.80	$ 4.46	$ 7.26
	$\frac{\$140,000}{50,000}$	$\frac{\$200,700}{45,000}$	$2.80 + $4.46

Cost of goods completed and transferred out of the Cutting Department during March:

(Number of units transferred out) × (Total cost per equivalent unit)	40,000 × $7.26	$290,400

Cost remaining in March 31 work-in-process inventory in the Cutting Department:

Direct material:		
(Number of equivalent units of direct material) × (Cost per equivalent unit of direct material)	10,000 × $2.80	$ 28,000
Conversion:		
(Number of equivalent units of conversion) × (Cost per equivalent unit of conversion)	5,000 × $4.46	22,300
Total cost of March 31 work in process		$ 50,300

Check:		
	Cost of goods completed and transferred out	$290,400
	Cost of March 31 work-in-process inventory	50,300
	Total costs accounted for	$340,700

Other Issues in Process Costing

Several other issues related to process costing are worth discussion.

Actual versus Normal Costing

Our illustration of process costing assumed that *normal costing* was used. As explained in Chapter 3, in a normal costing system, direct material and direct labor are applied to Work-in-Process Inventory at their *actual* amounts, but manufacturing overhead is applied to Work-in-Process Inventory using a predetermined overhead rate. In contrast, under an *actual-costing* system, the actual costs of direct material, direct labor, *and manufacturing overhead* are entered into Work-in-Process Inventory.

Either actual or normal costing may be used in conjunction with a process-costing system. Our illustration used normal costing since a predetermined overhead rate was used to compute applied manufacturing overhead in Exhibit 4–4. This resulted in applied overhead for March of $107,500 (125% × $86,000). If actual costing had been used, the manufacturing overhead cost for March would have been the actual overhead cost incurred instead of the applied overhead amount given in Exhibit 4–4. In all other ways, the process-costing procedures used under actual and normal costing are identical.

When normal costing is used, there may be overapplied or underapplied overhead at the end of the period. This amount is either closed into Cost of Goods Sold or prorated, as explained in Chapter 3.

Other Cost Drivers for Overhead Application

Our illustration used a predetermined overhead rate based on direct-labor cost. Since the application of manufacturing overhead was based on direct-labor cost, direct labor and manufacturing overhead were combined into the single cost element *conversion costs*. This procedure is quite common in practice. If some cost driver (or activity base) other than direct labor had been used to apply manufacturing overhead, then overhead costs would be accounted for separately from direct-labor costs in the process-costing calculations.

Suppose, for example, that manufacturing overhead is applied on the basis of machine hours. A group of 100 physical units is 100 percent complete as to direct material, 60 percent complete as to direct labor, and 40 percent complete as to machine time. This situation could arise in a production process that is labor-intensive in its early stages but more automated in its later stages. In this case, the 100 physical units represent the following quantities of equivalent units:

	Equivalent Units		
Physical Units	**Direct Material**	**Direct Labor**	**Manufacturing Overhead**
100	100	60	40
	↑	↑	↑
	100 × 100%	100 × 60%	100 × 40%

Throughout the entire process-costing procedure, there will now be three cost elements (direct material, direct labor, and manufacturing overhead) instead of only two (direct material and conversion). In all other respects, the process-costing calculations will be identical to those illustrated earlier in the chapter.

Subsequent Production Departments

In our illustration, production requires two sequential production operations: cutting and stitching. Although the process-costing procedures for the second department are similar to those illustrated for the first, there is one additional complication. The cost of goods completed and transferred out of the Cutting Department must remain assigned to the partially completed product units as they undergo further processing in the Stitching Department. Process-costing procedures for subsequent production departments are covered in the appendix at the end of this chapter, which may be studied now.

Hybrid Product-Costing Systems

Job-order and process costing represent the polar extremes of product-costing systems. But some production processes exhibit characteristics of both job-order and process-costing environments. Examples of such production processes include some clothing and food processing operations. In these production processes, the conversion

Exhibit 4–10
Operation Costing

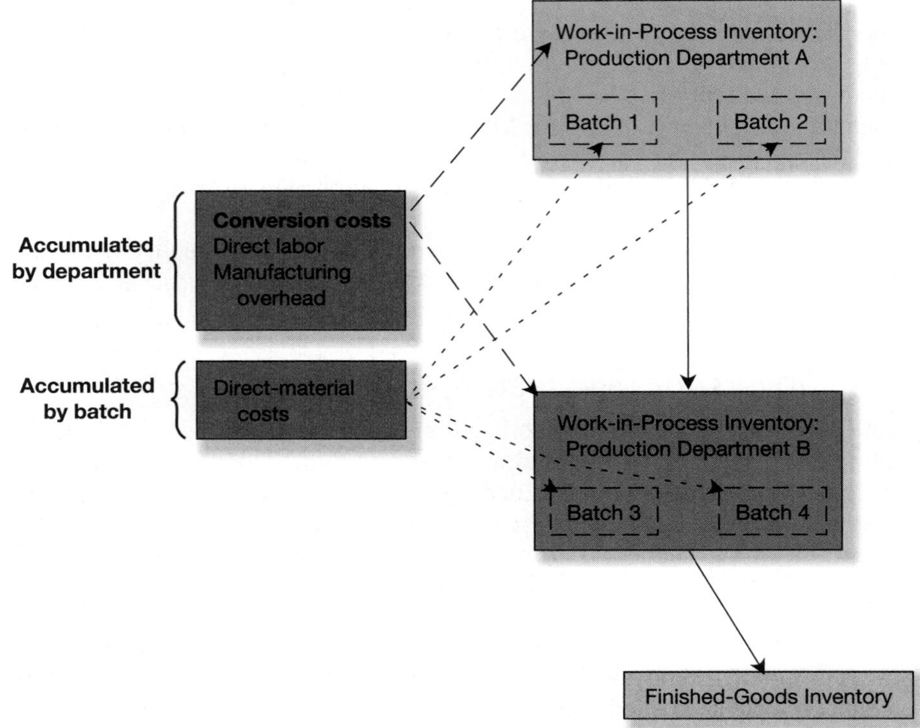

activities may be very similar or identical across all of the firm's product lines, even though the direct materials may differ significantly. Different clothing lines require significantly different direct materials, such as cotton, wool, or polyester. However, the conversion of these materials, involving direct labor and manufacturing overhead, may not differ much across product types. In the food industry, production of economy-grade or premium applesauce differs with regard to the quality and cost of the direct-material input, apples. However, the cooking, straining, and canning operations for these two product lines are similar.

Operation Costing for Batch Manufacturing Processes

LO 7

Describe how an operation costing system accumulates and assigns the costs of direct-material and conversion activity in a batch manufacturing process.

The production processes described above often are referred to as **batch manufacturing** processes. Such processes are characterized by high-volume production of several product lines that differ in some important ways but are nearly identical in others. Since batch manufacturing operations have characteristics of both job-order costing and process-costing environments, a **hybrid product-costing system** is required. One common approach is called **operation costing.** This product-costing system is used when conversion activities are very similar across product lines, but the direct materials differ significantly. *Conversion costs* are accumulated by *department*, and process-costing methods are used to assign these costs to products. In contrast, *direct-material costs* are accumulated by *job order or batch*, and job-order costing is used to assign material costs to products.

The main features of operation costing are illustrated in Exhibit 4–10. Notice in the exhibit that products pass sequentially through production departments A and B. Direct-material costs are traced directly to each batch of goods, but conversion costs are applied on a departmental basis. Direct labor and manufacturing overhead are combined in a single cost category called conversion costs, rather than separately identify-

Exhibit 4–11

Basic Data for Illustration of Operation Costing

Direct-material costs:			
Batch P19 (1,000 professional balls)	$20,000	(includes $1,000 for packaging material)	
Batch S28 (3,000 scholastic balls)	30,000		
Total direct-material costs	$50,000		
Conversion costs (budgeted):			
Preparation Department			$ 30,000
Finishing Department			24,000
Packaging Department			500
Total costs:			
Direct material			50,000
Conversion: Preparation	$30,000		
Finishing	24,000		
Packaging	500		
Total conversion costs			54,500
Total			$104,500

Predetermined application rates for conversion costs:*

Preparation Department

$$\frac{\text{Budgeted conversion costs}}{\text{Budgeted production}} = \frac{\$30{,}000}{4{,}000 \text{ units}} = \$7.50 \text{ per unit}$$

Finishing Department

$$\frac{\text{Budgeted conversion costs}}{\text{Budgeted production}} = \frac{\$24{,}000}{4{,}000 \text{ units}} = \$6.00 \text{ per unit}$$

Packaging Department

$$\frac{\text{Budgeted conversion costs}}{\text{Budgeted units packaged}} = \frac{\$500}{1{,}000 \text{ units}} = \$.50 \text{ per unit}$$

*The cost driver (or activity base) is the number of units processed.

ing direct labor. Moreover, under operation costing, conversion costs are applied to products using a *predetermined application rate*. This predetermined rate is based on *budgeted conversion costs*, as follows:

$$\begin{array}{c}\text{Predetermined application} \\ \text{rate for conversion costs}\end{array} = \frac{\begin{array}{c}\text{Budgeted conversion costs} \\ \text{(direct labor and manufacturing overhead)}\end{array}}{\text{Budgeted cost driver (or activity base)}}$$

As an illustration of operation costing, we will focus on the Minnesota Division of MVP Sports Equipment Company. This division manufactures two different grades of basketballs: professional balls, which have genuine leather exteriors; and scholastic balls, which use imitation leather. The cutting and stitching operations for the two different products are identical. Scholastic balls are sold without special packaging, but professional balls are packaged in an attractive cardboard box.

During October two batches were entered into production and finished. There was no beginning or ending inventory of work in process for October. Cost and production data are given in Exhibit 4–11. Notice in Exhibit 4–11 that the direct-material costs are identified by *batch*. The conversion costs, however, are associated with the two production departments and the Packaging Department.

The product cost for each of the basketballs is computed as follows:

	Professional	Scholastic
Direct material:		
Batch P19 ($20,000 ÷ 1,000)	$20.00	
Batch S28 ($30,000 ÷ 3,000)		$10.00
Conversion: Preparation Department (conversion costs of $30,000 ÷ 4,000 units produced)*	7.50	7.50
Conversion: Finishing Department (conversion costs of $24,000 ÷ 4,000 units produced)*	6.00	6.00
Conversion: Packaging Department (conversion costs of $500 ÷ 1,000 units packaged)*	.50	–0–
Total product cost	$34.00	$23.50

*The two production departments each worked on a total of 4,000 balls, but the Packaging Department handled only the 1,000 professional balls.

Notice in the preceding display that each ball receives the same conversion costs in the Preparation Department and the Finishing Department, since these operations are identical for the two products. Direct-material costs and packaging costs, though, differ for the products. The total costs of $104,500 (Exhibit 4–11) are accounted for in the product costs, as shown below.

Professional balls: 1,000 × $34.00	$ 34,000
Scholastic balls: 3,000 × $23.50	70,500
Total	$104,500

The following journal entries are made to record the Minnesota Division's flow of costs. The first entry is made to record the requisition of raw material by the Preparation Department, when batch P19 is entered into production. (This amount excludes the $1,000 in packaging costs to be incurred subsequently for batch P19.)

Work-in-Process Inventory: Preparation Department	19,000	
Raw-Material Inventory		19,000

The following entry is made to record the requisition of raw material by the Preparation Department, when batch S28 is entered into production.

Work-in-Process Inventory: Preparation Department	30,000	
Raw-Material Inventory		30,000

Conversion costs are applied in the Preparation Department with the following journal entry.

Work-in-Process Inventory: Preparation Department	30,000	
Applied Conversion Costs		30,000

The following entry records the transfer of the partially completed professional and scholastic basketballs to the Finishing Department.

Work-in-Process Inventory: Finishing Department	79,000	
Work-in-Process Inventory: Preparation Department		79,000

The conversion costs applied in the Finishing Department are recorded as follows:

Work-in-Process Inventory: Finishing Department	24,000	
Applied Conversion Costs		24,000

Next, the professional balls are transferred to the Packaging Department, and the scholastic balls are transferred to finished goods.

Work-in-Process Inventory: Packaging Department	32,500	
Finished-Goods Inventory.	70,500	
Work-in-Process Inventory: Finishing Department		103,000

Raw-material (packaging) costs and conversion costs are recorded in the Packaging Department as follows:

Work-in-Process Inventory: Packaging Department	1,500	
Raw-Material Inventory		1,000
Applied Conversion Costs		500

Finally, the professional basketballs are transferred to finished goods.

Finished-Goods Inventory.	34,000	
Work-in-Process Inventory: Packaging Department		34,000

Suppose that at the end of an accounting period, applied conversion costs differ from the actual conversion costs incurred. Then the difference, called overapplied or underapplied conversion costs, would be closed into Cost of Goods Sold. This accounting treatment is similar to that described in Chapter 3 for overapplied or underapplied overhead.

Chapter Summary

Process costing is used in production processes where relatively large numbers of nearly identical products are manufactured. The purpose of a process-costing system is the same as that of a job-order costing system—to accumulate costs and assign these costs to units of product. Product costs are needed for planning, cost management, decision making, and reporting to various outside organizations.

The flow of costs in process-costing systems and job-order costing systems is the same. Costs of direct material, direct labor, and manufacturing overhead are added to a Work-in-Process Inventory account. Direct labor and manufacturing overhead are often combined into a single cost category termed *conversion costs*. When products are completed, the costs assigned to them are transferred either to Finished-Goods Inventory or to the next production department's Work-in-Process Inventory account. In sequential production processes, the cost of the goods transferred from one production department to another is called transferred-in cost.

There are some important differences between job-order and process-costing systems. Chief among these is that job-order costing systems accumulate production costs by job or batch, whereas process-costing systems accumulate costs by department. Another important difference is the focus on equivalent units in process costing. An equivalent unit is a measure of the amount of productive input that has been applied to a fully or partially completed unit of product. In process costing, production costs per equivalent unit are calculated for direct-material and conversion costs.

The key document in a process-costing system is the departmental production report, rather than the job-cost record used in job-order costing. There are four steps in preparing a departmental production report: (1) analyze the physical flow of units, (2) calculate the equivalent units, (3) compute the cost per equivalent unit, and (4) analyze the total costs of the department.

In the weighted-average method of process costing, the cost per equivalent unit, for each cost category, is a weighted average of (1) the costs assigned to the beginning work-in-process inventory and (2) the costs incurred during the current period.

Job-order and process costing represent the polar extremes of product-costing systems. Operation costing is a hybrid of these two methods. It is designed for production processes in which the direct material differs significantly among product lines but the conversion activities are essentially the same. Direct-material costs are accumulated by batches of products using job-order costing methods. Conversion costs are accumulated by production departments and are assigned to product units by process-costing methods.

Key Terms

For each term's definition refer to the indicated page, or turn to the glossary at the end of the text.

batch manufacturing, 144
departmental production report, 136
equivalent units, 135
hybrid product-costing system, 144
operation costing, 144
process-costing system, 132
repetitive production, 132
transferred-in costs, 132
weighted-average method, 136

Appendix to Chapter 4

Process Costing in Sequential Production Departments

LO 8

After completing the appendix, prepare process-costing calculations for a sequential manufacturing process.

In manufacturing operations with sequential production departments, the costs assigned to the units transferred out of one department remain assigned to those units as they enter the next department. In our illustration, the partially completed baseball gloves transferred out of the Cutting Department go next to the Stitching Department. There the cut-out pieces are stitched together. Since the cost of the thread used in the stitching is very small, it is treated as an indirect-material cost and included in manufacturing overhead. At the end of the process in the Stitching Department, rawhide lacing is woven through the fingers and along some edges of each baseball glove. The rawhide lacing is treated as a direct material.

The cost of goods completed and transferred out of the Cutting Department is transferred as shown below.

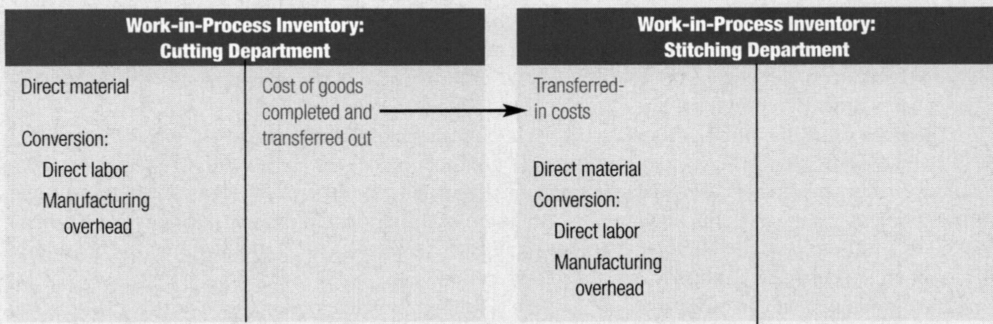

As the T-accounts show, the Cutting Department has two cost elements: direct-material and conversion costs. However, the Stitching Department has three cost elements: direct-material, conversion, and *transferred-in costs*. Transferred-in costs are the costs assigned to the units transferred from the Cutting Department to the Stitching Department. Transferred-in costs are conceptually similar to direct-material costs. The only difference is that direct-material costs relate to raw materials, whereas transferred-in costs relate to partially completed products.

Exhibit 4–12 presents the basic data for our illustration of process costing in the Stitching Department. The March 1 work-in-process inventory in the department consists of 10,000 units that received some work in the Stitching Department during February but were not completed. The $61,000 of transferred-in costs in the March 1 work-in-process inventory are costs that were transferred into the

Exhibit 4–12
Basic Data for Illustration—Stitching Department

Work in process, March 1—10,000 units:	
Transferred-in: 100% complete, cost of	$61,000*
Direct material: none	–0–
Conversion: 20% complete, cost of	7,600*
Balance in work in process, March 1	$68,600*
Units transferred in from Cutting Department during March	40,000 units
Units completed during March and transferred out to finished-goods inventory	30,000 units
Work in process, March 31	20,000 units
Transferred in: 100% complete	
Direct material: none	
Conversion: 90% complete	
Costs incurred during March:	
Transferred in from Cutting Department (assumes that weighted-average method was used for Cutting Department)	$290,400
Direct material	$7,500
Conversion costs:	
Direct labor	$115,000
Applied manufacturing overhead	115,000†
Total conversion costs	$230,000

*These costs were incurred during the prior month, February.
†(Predetermined overhead rate) × (Direct-labor cost) = 100% × $115,000 = $115,000

Stitching Department's Work-in-Process Inventory account during February. Note that any partially completed baseball glove in the Stitching Department must have received all of its transferred-in input, or it would not have been transferred from the Cutting Department. The March 1 work-in-process inventory has not yet received any direct material in the Stitching Department, because the direct material (rawhide lacing) is not added until the end of the process.

As Exhibit 4–12 shows, 40,000 units were transferred into the Stitching Department during March. This agrees with Exhibit 4–4, which shows that 40,000 units were completed and transferred out of the Cutting Department during March. The Stitching Department completed 30,000 units during March and transferred them to finished-goods inventory. This left 20,000 units in the Stitching Department's March 31 work-in-process inventory.

Exhibit 4–12 shows that the costs incurred in the Stitching Department during March were $7,500 for direct material, $115,000 for direct labor, and $115,000 for *applied* manufacturing overhead. The predetermined overhead rate in the Stitching Department is 100 percent of direct-labor cost. Note that the predetermined overhead rates are different in the two production departments.

The March transferred-in cost in the Stitching Department is the cost of goods completed and transferred out of the Cutting Department. The amount shown in Exhibit 4–12, $290,400, comes from Exhibit 4–8.

Exhibit 4–13 presents a completed production report for the Stitching Department using weighted-average process costing. Steps 1 through 4 are identified in the exhibit. The process-costing procedures used for the Stitching Department are identical to those used for the Cutting Department, except for one important difference. While there were only two cost elements (direct material and conversion) in the Cutting Department, there are three cost elements in the Stitching Department. In each of the four steps in Exhibit 4–13, transferred-in costs are listed along with direct material and conversion as a separate cost element.

The analysis of the physical flow of units (step 1 in Exhibit 4–13) is like the analysis for the Cutting Department. Now focus on step 2. In calculating equivalent units, we add a "transferred-in" column. Both the 30,000 units completed and transferred out of the Stitching Department and the March 31 work-in-process inventory are 100 percent complete as to transferred-in activity. Thus, the number of equivalent units is the same as the number of physical units. The calculation yields 50,000 total equivalent units of transferred-in activity for March. The equivalent units of direct material and conversion are determined as described earlier for the Cutting Department.

MVP SPORTS EQUIPMENT COMPANY
Production Report: Stitching Department

	Step 1		Step 2		
			Equivalent Units		
	Physical Units	**Percentage of Completion with Respect to Conversion**	**Transferred in**	**Direct Material**	**Conversion**
Work in process, March 1	10,000	20%			
Units transferred in during March	40,000				
Total units to account for	50,000				
Units completed and transferred out during March	30,000		30,000	30,000	30,000
Work in process, March 31	20,000	90%	20,000	–0–	18,000
Total units accounted for	50,000				
Total equivalent units			50,000	30,000	48,000

Step 3

	Transferred in	**Direct Material**	**Conversion**	**Total**
Work in process, March 1 (from Exhibit 4–12)	$ 61,000	–0–	$ 7,600	$ 68,600
Costs incurred during March (from Exhibit 4–12)	290,400*	$ 7,500	230,000	527,900
Total costs to account for	$351,400	$ 7,500	$237,600	$596,500
Equivalent units	50,000	30,000	48,000	
Costs per equivalent unit	$ 7.028	$ .25	$ 4.95	$ 12.228
	↑ $351,400 / 50,000	↑ $7,500 / 30,000	↑ $237,600 / 48,000	↑ $7.028 + $.25 + $4.95

Step 4

Cost of goods completed and transferred out of the Stitching Department during March:		
(Number of units transferred out) × (Total cost per equivalent unit)	30,000 × $12.228	$366,840
Cost remaining in March 31 work-in-process inventory in the Stitching Department:		
Transferred-in costs:		
(Number of equivalent units of transferred-in costs) × (Cost per equivalent unit of transferred-in cost)	20,000 × $7.028	$140,560
Direct material:		
None		
Conversion:		
(Number of equivalent units of conversion) × (Cost per equivalent unit of conversion)	18,000 × $4.95	89,100
Total		$229,660

*Cost of goods completed and transferred out of Cutting Department during March, under the *weighted-average* method (calculated in Exhibit 4–8).

Check:		
	Cost of goods completed and transferred out	$366,840
	Cost of March 31 work-in-process inventory	229,660
	Total costs accounted for	$596,500

Exhibit 4–13
Production Report—Stitching Department (weighted-average method)

Costs per equivalent unit are computed in step 3. Since we are using the weighted-average method, the transferred-in costs in the March 1 work-in-process inventory are added to the March transferred-in costs before dividing by the equivalent units. Direct material and conversion costs are handled like those for the Cutting Department.

The analysis of total costs is done in step 4. The 30,000 units completed and transferred out of the Stitching Department are assigned a total weighted-average cost per unit of $12.228. This unit cost includes the transferred-in cost per equivalent unit of $7.028 calculated in step 3. The cost remaining in the work-in-process inventory on March 31 consists of two cost elements: transferred-in costs (20,000 equivalent units × $7.028 per equivalent unit) and conversion costs (18,000 equivalent units × $4.95 per equivalent unit). The March 31 work-in-process inventory has not yet received any direct material in the Stitching Department.

The following journal entry is made to transfer the cost of the units completed to the Finished-Goods Inventory account.

Finished-Goods Inventory	366,840	
Work-in-Process Inventory: Stitching Department		366,840
To transfer the cost of goods completed, as computed under the weighted-average method.		

Summary of Transferred-in Costs

When manufacturing is done in sequential production departments, the cost assigned to the units completed in each department is transferred to the next department's Work-in-Process Inventory account. This cost is termed *transferred-in cost,* and it is handled as a distinct cost element in the process-costing calculations. In this way, the final cost of the product is built up cumulatively as the product progresses through the production sequence.

Review Questions

4–1. Explain the primary differences between job-order and process costing.

4–2. List five types of manufacturing in which process costing would be an appropriate product-costing system. What is the key characteristic of these products that makes process costing a good choice?

4–3. List three nonmanufacturing businesses in which process costing could be used. For example, a public accounting firm could use process costing to accumulate the costs of processing clients' tax returns.

4–4. What are the purposes of a product-costing system?

4–5. Define the term *equivalent unit* and explain how the concept is used in process costing.

4–6. List and briefly describe the purpose of each of the four process-costing steps.

4–7. Show how to prepare a journal entry to enter direct-material costs into the Work-in-Process Inventory account for the first department in a sequential production process. Show how to prepare the journal entry recording the transfer of goods from the first to the second department in the sequence.

4–8. What are *transferred-in costs*?

4–9. A food processing company has two sequential production departments: mixing and cooking. The cost of the January 1 work in process in the cooking department is detailed as follows:

Direct material	$ 79,000
Conversion	30,000
Transferred-in costs	182,000

During what time period and in what department were the $182,000 of costs listed above incurred? Explain your answer.

4–10. Explain the reasoning underlying the name of the weighted-average method.

4–11. How does process costing differ under normal or actual costing?

4–12. How would the process-costing computations differ from those illustrated in the chapter if overhead were applied on some activity base other than direct labor?

4–13. Explain the concept of *operation costing*. How does it differ from process or job-order costing? Why is operation costing well suited for batch manufacturing processes?

4–14. What is the purpose of a departmental production report prepared using process costing?

4–15. (Appendix) Referring to Exhibit 4–12, explain why the cost of direct material in the March 1 work in process is zero.

Exercises

Exercise 4–16
Physical Flow of Units
(LO 1, 3)

In each case below, fill in the missing amount.

1.	Work in Process, June 1	10,000 pounds
	Units started during June	?
	Units completed during June	16,000 pounds
	Work in process, June 30	3,000 pounds
2.	Work in process, April 1	12,000 yards
	Units started during April	22,000 yards
	Units completed during April	21,500 yards
	Work in process, April 30	?
3.	Work in process, January 1	50,000 liters
	Units started during the year	67,000 liters
	Units completed during the year	?
	Work in process, December 31	45,000 liters

Exercise 4–17
Physical Flow and Equivalent Units; Weighted-Average
(LO 1, 3)

The Milwaukee plant of Healthy Life Styles, Inc. produces low-fat salad dressing. The following data pertain to the year just ended.

		Percentage of Completion	
	Units	**Direct Material**	**Conversion**
Work in process, January 1	30,000 gal.	70%	50%
Work in process, December 31	25,000 gal.	75%	20%

During the year the company started 140,000 gallons of material in production.

Required: Prepare a schedule analyzing the physical flow of units and computing the equivalent units of both direct material and conversion for the year. Use weighted-average process costing.

Exercise 4–18
Equivalent Units; Weighted-Average
(LO 1, 3)

PetroTech Company refines a variety of petrochemical products. The following data are from the firm's Amarillo plant.

Work in process, July 1	1,900,000 liters
Direct material	100% complete
Conversion	30% complete
Units started in process during July	750,000 liters
Work in process, July 30	250,000 liters
Direct material	100% complete
Conversion	70% complete

Required: Compute the equivalent units of direct material and conversion for the month of July. Use the weighted-average method of process costing.

Exercise 4–19
Equivalent Units; Weighted-Average
(LO 1, 3)

Andromeda Glass Company manufactures decorative glass products. The firm employs a process-costing system for its manufacturing operations. All direct materials are added at the beginning of the process, and conversion costs are incurred uniformly throughout the process. The company's production schedule for August follows.

	Units
Work in process on August 1 (60% complete as to conversion)	2,000
Units started during August	3,500
Total units to account for	5,500
Units from beginning work in process, which were completed and transferred out during August	2,000
Units started and completed during August	1,800
Work in process on August 31 (20% complete as to conversion)	1,700
Total units accounted for	5,500

Required: Calculate each of the following amounts using weighted-average process costing.

1. Equivalent units of direct material during August.
2. Equivalent units of conversion activity during August.

(CMA, adapted)

Exercise 4–20
Process Costing; Use of Internet
(LO 1)

Use the Internet to access the website for Weyerhaeuser (www.weyerhaeuser.com), International Paper (www.internationalpaper.com), or Boise Cascade (www.boisecascade.com).

Required: Skim over the information presented on the website about the company's products and operations. Then discuss why process costing is an appropriate product-costing method for this company.

Exercise 4–21
Cost per Equivalent Unit; Weighted-Average
(LO 1, 4)

Duluth Glass Company manufactures window glass for automobiles. The following data pertain to the Plate Glass Department.

Work in process, February 1:	
Direct material	$ 43,200
Conversion	40,300
Costs incurred during February:	
Direct material	$135,000
Conversion	190,000

The equivalent units of activity for February were as follows: 16,500 equivalent units of direct material, and 47,000 equivalent units of conversion activity.

Required: Calculate the cost per equivalent unit, for both direct material and conversion, during February. Use weighted-average process costing.

Exercise 4–22
Cost per Equivalent Unit; Weighted-Average
(LO 1, 4)

Montana Lumber Company grows, harvests, and processes timber for use in construction. The following data pertain to the firm's sawmill during June.

Work in process, June 1:	
Direct material	$ 74,900
Conversion	167,000
Costs incurred during June:	
Direct material	$380,700
Conversion	625,000

The equivalent units of activity for June were as follows: 6,700 equivalent units of direct material, and 1,600 equivalent units of conversion activity.

Required: Calculate the cost per equivalent unit, for both direct material and conversion, during June. Use weighted-average process costing.

Exercise 4–23
Analysis of Total Costs; Weighted-Average
(LO 4, 5)

The following data pertain to Tuscaloosa Paperboard Company, a manufacturer of cardboard boxes.

Work in process, March 1	10,000 units*
Direct material	$ 10,900
Conversion	28,950
Costs incurred during March	
Direct material	$112,700
Conversion	160,200

*Complete as to direct material; 35% complete as to conversion.

The equivalent units of activity for March were as follows:

Direct material (weighted-average method)	103,000
Conversion (weighted-average method)	97,000
Completed and transferred out	89,000

Required: Compute the following amounts using weighted-average process costing.

1. Cost of goods completed and transferred out during March.
2. Cost of the March 31 work-in-process inventory.

Exercise 4–24
Analysis of Total Costs; Weighted-Average
(LO 4, 5)

Raleigh Textiles Company manufactures a variety of natural fabrics for the clothing industry. The following data pertain to the Weaving Department for the month of November.

Equivalent units of direct material (weighted-average method)	62,500
Equivalent units of conversion (weighted-average method)	49,000
Units completed and transferred out during November	47,000

The cost data for November are as follows:

Work in process, November 1	
Direct material	$ 85,750
Conversion	16,900
Costs incurred during November	
Direct material	$158,000
Conversion	267,300

There were 19,000 units in process in the Weaving Department on November 1 (complete as to direct material, and 38% complete as to conversion).

Required: Compute each of the following amounts using weighted-average process costing.

1. Cost of goods completed and transferred out of the Weaving Department.
2. Cost of the November 30 work-in-process inventory in the Weaving Department.

Exercise 4–25
Operation Costing
(LO 7)

The November production of MVP's Minnesota Division consisted of batch P25 (2,000 professional basketballs) and batch S33 (4,000 scholastic basketballs). Each batch was started and finished during November, and there was no beginning or ending work in process. Costs incurred were as follows:

Direct material:

Batch P25, $42,000, including $2,500 for packaging material; batch S33, $45,000.

Conversion costs:

Preparation Department, predetermined rate of $7.50 per unit; Finishing Department, predetermined rate of $6.00 per unit; Packaging Department, predetermined rate of $.50 per unit. (Only the professional balls are packaged.)

Required:

1. Draw a diagram depicting the division's batch manufacturing process. Refer to Exhibit 4–10 for guidance.
2. Compute the November product cost for each type of basketball.
3. Prepare journal entries to record the cost flows during November.

Exercise 4–26
Cost Flows in Sequential Production; Journal Entries (Appendix)
(LO 2, 8)

Toledo Tile Company produces ceramic tile used in the housing industry. The process takes place in two sequential departments. The following cost data pertain to the month of October.

	Preparation Department	Finishing Department
Direct material entered into production	$ 105,000	$ 37,500
Direct labor	510,000	420,000
Applied manufacturing overhead	1,020,000	630,000
Cost of goods completed and transferred out	1,350,000*	600,000†

*Cost of goods transferred to the Finishing Department.
†Cost of goods transferred to finished goods.

Required: Prepare journal entries to record the following events.

1. Incurrence of costs for direct material and direct labor and application of manufacturing overhead in the Preparation Department.
2. Transfer of goods from Preparation to Finishing.
3. Incurrence of costs for direct material and direct labor and application of manufacturing overhead in the Finishing Department.
4. Transfer of goods from the Finishing Department to finished-goods inventory.

Problems

Problem 4–27
Straightforward Weighted-Average Process Costing, Step-by-Step Approach
(LO 3, 4, 5)

Toronto Titanium Corporation manufactures a highly specialized titanium sheathing material that is used extensively in the aircraft industry. The following data have been compiled for the month of June. Conversion activity occurs uniformly throughout the production process.

Work in process, June 1—40,000 units:	
Direct material: 100% complete, cost of	$110,500
Conversion: 38% complete, cost of	22,375
Balance in work in process, June 1	$132,875
Units started during June	190,000
Units completed during June and transferred out to finished-goods inventory	180,000
Work in process, June 30:	
Direct material: 100% complete	
Conversion: 55% complete	
Costs incurred during June:	
Direct material	$430,000
Conversion costs:	
Direct labor	$128,000
Applied manufacturing overhead	192,000
Total conversion costs	$320,000

Required: Prepare schedules to accomplish each of the following process-costing steps for the month of June. Use the weighted-average method of process costing.

1. Analysis of physical flow of units.
2. Calculation of equivalent units.
3. Computation of unit costs.
4. Analysis of total costs.

Problem 4–28*
Straightforward Weighted-Average Process Costing; Step-by-Step Approach
(LO 3, 4, 5)

Moravia Company processes and packages cream cheese. The following data have been compiled for the month of April. Conversion activity occurs uniformly throughout the production process.

Work in process, April 1—10,000 units:	
Direct material: 100% complete, cost of	$ 22,000
Conversion: 20% complete, cost of	4,500
Balance in work in process, April 1	$ 26,500
Units started during April	100,000
Units completed during April and transferred out to finished-goods inventory	80,000
Work in process, April 30:	
Direct material: 100% complete	
Conversion: 33⅓% complete	
Costs incurred during April:	
Direct material	$198,000
Conversion costs:	
Direct labor	$ 52,800
Applied manufacturing overhead	105,600
Total conversion costs	$158,400

Required: Prepare schedules to accomplish each of the following process-costing steps for the month of April. Use the weighted-average method of process costing.

**Note to instructors:* This problem relates to problem 12 in the supplement, *Process Costing: The First-in, First-Out Method.* Assigning these two problems together facilitates a comparison of the weighted-average and FIFO methods.

1. Analysis of physical flow of units.
2. Calculation of equivalent units.
3. Computation of unit costs.
4. Analysis of total costs.

Problem 4–29
Step-by-Step Weighted-Average Process Costing
(LO 3, 4, 5)

Jupiter Corporation manufactures home security devices. During 20x4, 1,000,000 units were completed and transferred to finished-goods inventory. On December 31, 20x4 there were 310,000 units in work in process. These units were 48 percent complete as to conversion and 100 percent complete as to direct material. Finished-goods inventory consisted of 250,000 units. Materials are added to production at the beginning of the manufacturing process, and overhead is applied to each product at the rate of 100 percent of direct-labor costs. There was no finished-goods inventory on January 1, 20x4. A review of the inventory cost records disclosed the following information:

		Costs	
	Units	Materials	Labor
Work in process, January 1, 20x4 (83% complete as to conversion)	210,000	$300,000	$310,400
Units started in production	1,100,000		
Direct-material costs		$1,403,000	
Direct-labor costs			$1,700,000

Required: Prepare schedules as of December 31, 20x4 to compute the following:

1. Physical flow of units.
2. Equivalent units of production using the weighted-average method.
3. Costs per equivalent unit for material and conversion.
4. Cost of the December 31, 20x4 finished-goods inventory and work-in-process inventory.

(CPA, adapted)

Problem 4–30*
Partial Production Report; Journal Entries; Weighted-Average Method
(LO 2, 3, 4, 5)

Atlantic City Taffy Company produces various kinds of candy, but salt-water taffy is by far its most important product. The company accumulates costs for its product using process costing. Direct material is added at the beginning of the production process, and conversion activity occurs uniformly throughout the process.

Production Report
For August 20x1

			Equivalent Units	
	Physical Units	Percentage of Completion with Respect to Conversion	Direct Material	Conversion
Work in process, August 1	40,000	80%		
Units started during August	80,000			
Total units to account for	120,000			
Units completed and transferred out during August	100,000		100,000	100,000
Work in process, August 31	20,000	30%	20,000	6,000
Total units accounted for	120,000			

	Direct Material	Conversion	Total
Work in process, August 1	$ 42,000	$ 305,280	$ 347,280
Costs incurred during August	96,000	784,400	880,400
Total costs to account for	$138,000	$1,089,680	$1,227,680

Required: Use weighted-average process costing in completing the following requirements.

**Note to instructors:* This problem relates to problem 14 in the supplement, *Process Costing: The First-In, First-Out Method.* Assigning these two problems together facilitates a comparison of the weighted-average and FIFO methods.

1. Prepare a schedule of equivalent units.
2. Compute the costs per equivalent unit.
3. Compute the cost of goods completed and transferred out during August.
4. Compute the cost remaining in the work-in-process inventory on August 31.
5. Prepare a journal entry to record the transfer of the cost of goods completed and transferred out.

Problem 4–31
Partial Production Report; Journal Entries; Weighted-Average Method
(LO 2, 3, 4, 5)

CircleD Fastener Corporation accumulates costs for its single product using process costing. Direct material is added at the beginning of the production process, and conversion activity occurs uniformly throughout the process. A partially completed production report for the month of June follows.

Production Report
For the Month of June

	Physical Units	Percentage of Completion with Respect to Conversion	Equivalent Units: Direct Material	Equivalent Units: Conversion
Work in process, June 1	30,000	35%		
Units started during June	34,000			
Total units to account for	64,000			
Units completed and transferred out during June	40,000		40,000	40,000
Work in process, June 30	24,000	75%	24,000	18,000
Total units accounted for	64,000			

	Direct Material	Conversion	Total
Work in process, June 1	$147,600	$ 623,400	$ 771,000
Costs incurred during June	201,200	2,221,500	2,422,700
Total costs to account for	$348,800	$2,844,900	$3,193,700

Required:

1. Complete each of the following process-costing steps using the weighted-average method:
   a. Calculation of equivalent units.
   b. Computation of unit costs.
   c. Analysis of total costs.
2. Prepare a journal entry to record the transfer of the cost of goods completed and transferred out during June.

Problem 4–32
Determination of Production Costs; Analysis of Equivalent Units
(LO 3, 4, 5)

Texarkana Corporation assembles various components used in the computer industry. The company's major product, a disk drive, is the result of assembling three parts: JR1163, JY1065, and DC0766. The following information relates to activities of April:

- Beginning work-in-process inventory: 3,000 units, 80 percent complete as to conversion; cost, $293,940 (direct material, $230,000; conversion, $63,940).
- Production started: 27,000 units.
- Production completed: 26,000 units.
- Ending work-in-process inventory: 4,000 units, 45 percent complete as to conversion.
- Direct material used: JR1163, $225,000; JY1065, $710,000; DC0766, $455,000.
- Hourly wage of direct laborers, $21; total direct-labor payroll, $134,274.
- Overhead application rate: $69 per direct-labor hour.

All parts are introduced at the beginning of the manufacturing process; conversion cost is incurred uniformly throughout production.

Required:

1. Calculate the total cost of direct material and conversion during April.
2. Determine the cost of goods completed during the month.

3. Determine the cost of the work-in-process inventory on April 30.
4. With regard to the ending work-in-process inventory:
   a. How much direct-material cost would be added to these units in May?
   b. What percentage of conversion would be performed on these units in May?
5. Assume that the disk drive required the addition of another part (TH55) at the 75 percent stage of completion. How many equivalent units with respect to part TH55 would be represented in April's ending work-in-process inventory?

Problem 4–33
Missing Data; Production Report; Weighted-Average
(LO 3, 4, 5, 6)

The following data pertain to the Fantasia Flour Milling Company for the month of October.

Work in process, October 1 (in units)	?
Units started during October	70,000
Total units to account for	80,000
Units completed and transferred out during October	?
Work in process, October 31 (in units)	5,000
Total equivalent units: direct material	80,000
Total equivalent units: conversion	?
Work in process, October 1: direct material	$112,000
Work in process, October 1: conversion	?
Costs incurred during October: direct material	?
Costs incurred during October: conversion	900,000
Work in process, October 1: total cost	142,225
Total costs incurred during October	1,500,000
Total costs to account for	1,642,225
Cost per equivalent unit: direct material	8.90
Cost per equivalent unit: conversion	?
Total cost per equivalent unit	20.75
Cost of goods completed and transferred out during October	?
Cost remaining in ending work-in-process inventory: direct material	?
Cost remaining in ending work-in-process inventory: conversion	41,475
Total cost of October 31 work in process	85,975

Additional Information:

a. Direct material is added at the beginning of the production process, and conversion activity occurs uniformly throughout the process.
b. Fantasia uses weighted-average process costing.
c. The October 1 work in process was 15 percent complete as to conversion.
d. The October 31 work in process was 70 percent complete as to conversion.

Required: Compute the missing amounts, and prepare the firm's October production report.

Problem 4–34
Analysis of Work-in-Process Inventory Account; T-Accounts
(LO 3, 4, 5)

Lawncraft, Inc. manufactures wooden lawn furniture using an assembly-line process. All direct materials are introduced at the start of the process, and conversion cost is incurred evenly throughout manufacturing. An examination of the company's Work-in-Process Inventory account for June revealed the following selected information:

Debit side:

June 1 balance: 200 units, 25% complete as to conversion, cost $18,000*

Production started: 800 units

Direct material used during June: $43,000

June conversion cost: $30,000

Credit side:

Production completed: 600 units

*Supplementary records revealed direct-material cost of $12,000 and conversion cost of $6,000.

Conversations with manufacturing personnel revealed that the ending work-in-process inventory was 75 percent complete as to conversion.

Required:

1. Determine the number of units in the June 30 work-in-process inventory.
2. Calculate the cost of goods completed during June and prepare the appropriate journal entry to record completed production.
3. Determine the cost of the June 30 work-in-process inventory.
4. Briefly explain the meaning of equivalent units. Why are equivalent units needed to properly allocate costs between completed production and production in process?

Problem 4–35
Process Costing in a Public Accounting Firm
(LO 3, 4, 5)

Beowulf and Grendel, a public accounting firm in London, is engaged in the preparation of income tax returns for individuals. The firm uses the weighted-average method of process costing for internal reporting. The following information pertains to February. (£ denotes the British monetary unit, pounds sterling.)*

Returns in process, February 1:	
(20% complete)	300
Returns started in February	900
Returns in process, February 28:	
(75% complete)	400
Returns in process, February 1:	
Labor	£ 3,500
Overhead	4,000
Labor, February (4,500 hours)	90,000
Overhead, February	51,000

*Although the monetary unit, the Euro, has been introduced in European markets, day-to-day business in the United Kingdom continues to be conducted in pounds sterling.

Required:

1. Compute the following amounts for labor and for overhead:
   a. Equivalent units of activity.
   b. Cost per equivalent unit. (Remember to express your answer in terms of the British pound sterling, denoted by £.)
2. Compute the cost of returns in process as of February 28.

(CMA, adapted)

Problem 4–36
Missing Data; Production Report; Weighted-Average
(LO 3, 4, 5, 6)

The following data pertain to the Canandaigua Carpet Company for January.

Work in process, January 1 (in units)	25,000
Units started during January	?
Total units to account for	80,000
Units completed and transferred out during January	?
Work in process, January 31 (in units)	20,000
Total equivalent units: direct material	80,000
Total equivalent units: conversion	?
Work in process, January 1: direct material	$232,000
Work in process, January 1: conversion	?
Costs incurred during January: direct material	?
Costs incurred during January: conversion	820,000
Work in process, January 1: total cost	342,600
Total costs incurred during January	1,220,000
Total costs to account for	1,562,600
Cost per equivalent unit: direct material	7.90
Cost per equivalent unit: conversion	?
Total cost per equivalent unit	22.00
Cost of goods completed and transferred out during January	?
Cost remaining in ending work-in-process inventory: direct material	?
Cost remaining in ending work-in-process inventory: conversion	84,600
Total cost of January 31 work in process	242,600

Additional Information:

a. Direct material is added at the beginning of the production process, and conversion activity occurs uniformly throughout the process.

b. The company uses weighted-average process costing.

c. The January 1 work in process was 25 percent complete as to conversion.

d. The January 31 work in process was 30 percent complete as to conversion.

Required: Compute the missing amounts, and prepare the firm's January production report.

Problem 4–37
Process Costing; Production Report; Journal Entries; Weighted-Average Method
(LO 2, 3, 4, 5, 6)

SolarTech Company manufactures a special lacquer, which is used in the aeronautical and space industries. Two departments are involved in the production process. In the Mixing Department, various chemicals are entered into production. After processing, the Mixing Department transfers a chemical called CXX to the Finishing Department. There the product is completed, packaged, and shipped under the brand name Solarfast.

In the Mixing Department, the raw material is added at the beginning of the process. Labor and overhead are applied continuously throughout the process. All direct departmental overhead is traced to the departments, and plant overhead is allocated to the departments on the basis of direct labor. The plant overhead rate for 20x5 is $1.50 per direct-labor dollar.

The following information relates to production during November 20x5 in the Mixing Department.

a. Work in process, November 1 (5,000 pounds, 70 percent complete as to conversion):

Raw material	$31,600
Direct labor	18,000
Departmental overhead	10,220
Allocated plant overhead	27,000

b. Raw material:

Inventory, November 1, 3,000 pounds	16,000
Purchases, November 3, 9,000 pounds	44,000
Purchases, November 18, 12,000 pounds	60,000
Released to production during November, 17,000 pounds	

c. Direct-labor cost during November, $70,000

d. Direct departmental overhead costs, $35,000

e. Transferred to Finishing Department, 16,000 pounds

f. Work in process, November 30, 6,000 pounds, 30 percent complete as to conversion

The company uses weighted-average process costing to accumulate product costs. However, for raw-material inventories the firm uses the FIFO inventory method.

Required:

1. Prepare a production report for the Mixing Department for November 20x5. The report should show:
   a. Equivalent units of production by cost factor (i.e., direct material and conversion).
   b. Cost per equivalent unit for each cost factor.
   c. Cost of CXX transferred to the Finishing Department.
   d. Cost of the work-in-process inventory on November 30, 20x5, in the Mixing Department.
2. Prepare journal entries to record the following events:
   a. Release of direct material to production during November.
   b. Incurrence of direct-labor costs in November.
   c. Application of overhead costs for the Mixing Department (direct departmental and allocated plant overhead costs).
   d. Transfer of CXX out of the Mixing Department.

(CMA, adapted)

Problem 4–38
Operation Costing; Unit Costs
(LO 7)

(Based on a problem contributed by Roland Minch.) Celestial Glass Company manufactures a variety of glass windows in its Charleston plant. In department I clear glass sheets are produced, and some of these sheets are sold as finished goods. Other sheets made in department I have metallic oxides added in department II to form colored glass sheets. Some of these colored sheets are sold; others are moved to department III for etching and then are sold. The company uses operation costing.

Celestial Glass Company's production costs applied to products in August are given in the following table. There was no beginning or ending inventory of work in process for August.

Cost Category	Dept. I	Dept. II	Dept. III
Direct material	$900,000	$144,000	–0–
Direct labor	76,000	44,000	$ 76,000
Manufacturing overhead	460,000	136,000	147,500

Products	Units	Dept. I Dir. Mat.	Dept. II Dir. Mat.
Clear glass, sold after dept. I	5,500	$495,000	–0–
Unetched colored glass, sold after dept. II	2,000	180,000	$64,000
Etched colored glass, sold after dept. III	2,500	225,000	80,000

Each sheet of glass requires the same steps within each operation.

Required: Compute each of the following amounts.

1. The conversion cost per unit in department I.
2. The conversion cost per unit in department II.
3. The cost of a clear glass sheet.
4. The cost of an unetched colored glass sheet.
5. The cost of an etched colored glass sheet.

Problem 4–39
Operation Costing; Unit Costs; Journal Entries
(LO 7)

Plattsburg Plastics Corporation manufactures a variety of plastic products including a series of molded chairs. The three models of molded chairs, which are all variations of the same design, are Standard (can be stacked), Deluxe (with arms), and Executive (with arms and padding). The company uses batch manufacturing and has an operation-costing system. The production process includes an extrusion operation and subsequent operations to form, trim, and finish the chairs. Plastic sheets are produced by the extrusion operation, some of which are sold directly to other manufacturers. During the forming operation, the remaining plastic sheets are molded into chair seats and the legs are added; the Standard model is sold after this operation. During the trim operation, the arms are added to the Deluxe and Executive models and the chair edges are smoothed. Only the Executive model enters the finish operation where the padding is added. All of the units produced receive the same steps within each operation. The March production run had a total manufacturing cost of $1,347,000. The units of production and direct-material costs incurred were as follows:

	Units Produced	Extrusion Materials	Form Materials	Trim Materials	Finish Materials
Plastic sheets	10,000	$ 90,000			
Standard model	12,000	108,000	$36,000		
Deluxe model	6,000	54,000	18,000	$13,500	
Executive model	4,000	36,000	12,000	9,000	$18,000
Total	32,000	$288,000	$66,000	$22,500	$18,000

Manufacturing costs applied during the month of March were as follows:

	Extrusion Operation	Form Operation	Trim Operation	Finish Operation
Direct labor	$228,000	$ 90,000	$45,000	$27,000
Manufacturing overhead	360,000	108,000	58,500	36,000

Required:

1. For each product produced by Plattsburg Plastics Corporation during the month of March, determine the (*a*) unit cost and (*b*) total cost. Be sure to account for all costs incurred during the month. (Carry out unit costs to three decimal places, i.e., a tenth of a cent.)

2. Prepare journal entries to record the flow of production costs during March.

(CMA, adapted)

■ **Problem 4–40**
Operation Costing; Unit Costs; Cost Flow; Journal Entries
(LO 7)

Orbital Industries of Canada, Ltd. manufactures a variety of materials and equipment for the aerospace industry. A team of R&D engineers in the firm's Winnipeg plant has developed a new material that will be useful for a variety of purposes in orbiting satellites and spacecraft. Tradenamed Ceralam, the material combines some of the best properties of both ceramics and laminated plastics. Ceralam is already being used for a variety of housings in satellites produced in three different countries. Ceralam sheets are produced in an operation called rolling, in which the various materials are rolled together to form a multilayer laminate. Orbital Industries sells many of these Ceralam sheets just after the rolling operation to aerospace firms worldwide. However, Orbital also processes many of the Ceralam sheets further in the Winnipeg plant. After rolling, the sheets are sent to the molding operation, where they are formed into various shapes used to house a variety of instruments. After molding, the sheets are sent to the punching operation, where holes are punched in the molded sheets to accommodate protruding instruments, electrical conduits, and so forth. Some of the molded and punched sheets are then sold. The remaining units are sent to the dipping operation, in which the molded sheets are dipped in a special chemical mixture to give them a reflective surface.

During the month of November, the following products were manufactured at the Winnipeg plant. The direct-material costs are also shown.

	Units	Direct Materials Used in Ceralam Sheets	Direct Materials Used in Dipping
Ceralam sheets (sold after the rolling operation)	6,000	$ 960,000	
Nonreflective housings (sold after the punching operation)	2,500	400,000	
Reflective housings (sold after the dipping operation)	1,500	240,000	$60,000
Total	10,000	$1,600,000	$60,000

The costs incurred in producing the various Ceralam products in the Winnipeg plant during November are shown in the following table. Manufacturing overhead is applied on the basis of direct-labor dollars at the rate of 150 percent.

	Rolling	Molding	Punching	Dipping
Direct material	$1,600,000	–0–	–0–	$ 60,000
Direct labor	600,000	$224,000	$256,000	90,000
Manufacturing overhead	900,000	336,000	384,000	135,000
Total	$3,100,000	$560,000	$640,000	$285,000

Orbital Industries of Canada uses operation costing for its Ceralam operations in the Winnipeg plant. (There were no inventories of work in process or finished goods on November 1 or November 30.)

Required:

1. Prepare a table that includes the following information *for each of the four operations*.
   - Total conversion costs.
   - Units manufactured.
   - Conversion cost per unit.
2. Prepare a second table that includes the following information *for each product* (i.e., rolled Ceralam sheets, nonreflective Ceralam housings, and reflective Ceralam housings).
   - Total manufacturing costs.
   - Units manufactured.
   - Total cost per unit.
3. Prepare journal entries to record the flow of all manufacturing costs through the Winnipeg plant's Ceralam operations during November. (Ignore the journal entries to record sales revenue.)

■ **Problem 4–41**
Transferred-in Costs; Weighted-Average Method (Appendix)
(LO 2, 4, 5, 8)

Toronto AutoFab, Inc. manufactures a variety of aluminum parts for the automotive industry. The company uses a weighted-average process-costing system. A unit of product passes through three departments—molding, assembly, and finishing—before it is completed.

The following activity took place in the Finishing Department during February.

	Units
Work-in-process inventory, February 1	700
Units transferred in from the Assembly Department	7,000
Units completed and transferred out to finished-goods inventory	5,950

Raw material is added at the beginning of processing in the Finishing Department. The work-in-process inventory was 60 percent complete as to conversion on February 1 and 30 percent complete as to conversion on February 28. The equivalent units and current period costs per equivalent unit of production for each cost factor are as follows for the Finishing Department.

	Equivalent Units	Current Period Costs per Equivalent Unit
Transferred-in costs	7,700	$ 6.00
Raw material	7,700	3.00
Conversion cost	6,475	7.00
Total		$16.00

Required:

1. Calculate the following amounts:
   a. Cost of units completed and transferred out to finished-goods inventory during February.
   b. Cost of the Finishing Department's work-in-process inventory on February 28.
2. The total costs of prior departments included in the work-in-process inventory of the Finishing Department on February 1 amounted to $14,500. Prepare the journal entry to record the transfer of goods from the Assembly Department to the Finishing Department during February.

(CMA, adapted)

Cases

Case 4–42
Sequential Production Departments; Weighted-Average (Appendix)
(LO 3, 4, 5, 6)

AgriTech, Inc. manufactures a canine nutrient known as Healthy Pet, which is then sold to dog food manufacturers. The manufacturing process begins in the Mixing Department when raw materials are started in process. Upon completion of processing in the Mixing Department, the output is transferred to the Saturating Department for the final phase of production. Here the product is saturated with water and then dried again. There is no weight gain in the process, and the water is virtually cost-free. The following information is available for the month of September.

	September 1		September 30
Work-in-Process Inventories	**Quantity (pounds)**	**Cost**	**Quantity (pounds)**
Mixing Department	None	—	None
Saturating Department	2,000	$65,600*	3,000

*Includes $24,600 in Saturating Department conversion costs.

The work-in-process inventory in the Saturating Department is estimated to be 40 percent complete both at the beginning and end of September. Costs of production for September are as follows:

Costs of Production	Material Used	Conversion
Mixing Department	$304,000	$95,000
Saturating Department	—	90,000

The material used in the Mixing Department weighed 38,000 pounds.

Required: Use the weighted-average method to prepare production reports for both the Mixing and Saturating Departments for the month of September. The answer should include:

1. Equivalent units of production (in pounds)
2. Total manufacturing costs
3. Cost per equivalent unit (pounds)
4. Cost of ending work-in-process inventory
5. Cost of goods completed and transferred out

(CPA, adapted)

Case 4–43
Weighted-Average Process Costing; Ethics
(LO 3, 4, 5, 6)

Lycoming Leather Company manufactures leather goods in central Pennsylvania. The company's profits have declined during the past nine months. In an attempt to isolate the causes of poor profit performance, management is investigating the manufacturing operations of each of its products.

One of the company's main products is leather belts. The belts are produced in a single, continuous process in the Harrisburg Plant. During the process, leather strips are sewn, punched, and dyed. The belts then enter a final finishing stage to conclude the process. Labor and overhead are applied continuously during the manufacturing process. All materials, leather strips, and buckles are introduced at the beginning of the process. The firm uses the weighted-average method to calculate its unit costs.

The leather belts produced at the Harrisburg Plant are sold wholesale for $22.95 each. Management wants to compare the current manufacturing costs per unit with the market prices for leather belts. Top management has asked the plant controller to submit data on the cost of manufacturing the leather belts for the month of October. These cost data will be used to determine whether modifications in the production process should be initiated or whether an increase in the selling price of the belts is justified. The cost per belt used for planning and control is $11.50.

The work-in-process inventory consisted of 500 partially completed units on October 1. The belts were 30 percent complete as to conversion. The costs included in the inventory on October 1 were as follows:

Leather strips	$1,650
Buckles	350
Conversion costs	2,500
Total	$4,500

During October 8,000 leather strips and buckles were placed into production. A total of 8,100 leather belts were completed. The work-in-process inventory on October 31 consisted of 400 belts, which were 40 percent complete as to conversion.

The costs charged to production during October were as follows:

Leather strips	$ 41,000
Buckles	8,000
Conversion costs	55,320
Total	$104,320

Required: In order to provide cost data regarding the manufacture of leather belts in the Harrisburg Plant to the top management of Lycoming Leather Company, compute the following amounts for the month of October.

1. The equivalent units for material and conversion.
2. The cost per equivalent unit of material and conversion.
3. The assignment of production costs to the October 31 work-in-process inventory and to goods transferred out.
4. The weighted-average unit cost of leather belts completed and transferred to finished goods. Comment on the company's cost per belt used for planning and control.
5. Lycoming Leather Company's production manager, Jack Murray, has been under pressure from the company president to reduce the cost of conversion. In spite of several attempts to reduce conversion costs, they have remained more or less constant. Now Murray is faced with an upcoming meeting with the company president, at which he will have to explain why he has failed to reduce conversion costs. Murray has approached his friend, Jeff Daley, who is the corporate controller, with the following request: "Jeff, I'm under pressure to reduce costs in the production process. There is no way to reduce material cost, so I've got to get the conversion costs down. If I can show just a little progress in next week's meeting with the president, then I can buy a little time to try some other cost-cutting measures I've been considering. I want you to do me a favor. If we raise the estimate of the percentage of completion of October's inventory to 50 percent, that will increase the number of equivalent units. Then the unit conversion cost will be a little lower." By how much would Murray's suggested manipulation lower the unit conversion cost? What should Daley do? Discuss this situation, citing specific ethical standards for managerial accountants. (These standards are listed in Chapter 1.)

(CMA, adapted)

Current Issues in Managerial Accounting

"DuPont Tries to Unclog a Pipeline: Can It Move New Products out of the Lab Faster?" ***Business Week,*** **January 27, 2003, pp. 103, 104, Amy Barrett.**

Issue 4–44
Process Costing and R&D

Overview

DuPont is refocusing its research and development (R&D) spending toward new products.

Suggested Discussion Questions

Would a chemical giant like DuPont be likely to use process costing? Why? How would you account for DuPont's R&D expenditures in a process-costing system?

"International Paper Shutting Plants to Cut Supply," ***The Wall Street Journal,*** **October 19, 2000, Allanna Sullivan.**

Issue 4–45
Paper Industry; Product Costing

Overview

One of the world's largest paper companies, International Paper, announced that it would close four plants in order to reduce the supply of paper.

Suggested Discussion Questions

What type of product-costing system would be most appropriate for International Paper: job-order or process costing? Why? How would the plant closing described in the article be likely to affect product costs?

"Bottled Up: Profits Aren't Flowing Like They Used to at Packaged-Goods Companies. Green Ketchup and Tuna in a Pouch Save Heinz?" ***Fortune,*** **September 18, 2000, Julie Creswell.**

Issue 4–46
Other Issues in Process Costing

Overview

For years packaged goods companies such as Heinz, Gillette, Kellogg, and Coca-Cola didn't worry about making a profit. The packaged goods industry was not growing. National retail chains have more buying power and many have introduced their own private labels. Coupled with mismanagement and lackadaisical innovation, the packaged goods industry has suffered.

Suggested Discussion Questions

Would process costing be an appropriate product-costing system for Heinz? Describe some of the new innovations to old products Heinz is preparing to launch.

"There's a New Economy Out There, and It Looks Nothing Like the Old One," ***The Wall Street Journal,*** **January 1, 2000, Thomas Petzinger, Jr.**

Issue 4–47
Changes in the Business Environment; Effect on Managerial Accounting Information

Overview

One of the author's claims in the article is that the structure of decision making may have changed fundamentally because the economy has experienced a breakup of the massive, monolithic companies of the past, giving way to smaller, more agile, and more focused companies. The downsizing and outsourcing trends of the past decade have speeded up this process. "People, departments and divisions that once marched to a single drummer inside a single company became widely scattered across the economy, each making its own decisions on the basis of local information."

Suggested Discussion Questions

How would the trend described in the article affect the role of managerial accounting information in businesses in general? Would this information be more important? Less important? How would the trend affect the role of product-costing information specifically?

Chapter Five

Activity-Based Costing and Cost Management Systems

After completing this chapter, you should be able to:

1. Explain the key characteristics of a traditional manufacturing process and plant layout.
2. Compute product costs under a traditional, volume-based product-costing system and an activity-based costing system.
3. Explain how an activity-based costing system operates, including the use of a two-stage procedure for cost assignment, the identification of activity cost pools, and the selection of cost drivers.
4. Explain why traditional, volume-based costing systems tend to distort product costs.
5. Discuss several key issues in activity-based costing, including criteria for choosing cost drivers, data collection, storyboarding, and indicators that a new costing system is needed.
6. Describe the key features of a cost management system, including the elimination of non-value-added costs.

Aerotech Announces New Pricing Scheme—Accountants to the Rescue?

Phoenix, AZ—Aerotech Corporation yesterday announced a major shake-up in its product pricing structure. The Phoenix-based company, which manufactures circuit boards used in aircraft radar and communications systems, has been facing stiff competition from both Asian and European firms. According to Kristin Scott, Aerotech's president, "For the past several years our competitors have been undercutting Aerotech's price on our Mode II circuit board. That's our highest-volume product, and we felt that our production process was as efficient as anyone's. We simply couldn't figure out how our competitors' costs could be any lower than ours. At the same time, we seemed to have captured a nice little niche all to ourselves for our Mode III board. The Mode III circuit board is our most complex product, and the demand is much lower than that for our Mode I or Mode II boards. The Mode III is a highly specialized product. Our competitors didn't seem to want to touch the Mode III market. Even though we had raised prices several times on the Mode IIIs, our customers didn't balk."

"We found the whole situation pretty puzzling," added John Stone, Aerotech's vice president for manufacturing. "Puzzling and troubling both. How can you be producing a high-volume product as efficiently as possible, charging a mark-up that is modest for the industry, and still be undercut on the price? We were all getting concerned. The Mode II board is our bread and butter product."

So what happened, and what's behind Aerotech's radical price restructuring? "This is a genuine case of the accountants coming to the rescue," said Scott. "Our controller got wind of a new approach to product costing, which gives much more accurate results. It focuses on the activities that the company engages in to manufacture each of its products. It also measures the resources consumed by those activities. We did a pilot study using this method, called activity-based costing. We found that we had been overcosting our high-volume, relatively simple products. That would be the Mode I and Mode II boards. But we were drastically undercosting our Mode III circuit boards. The complexity and low volume of the Mode IIIs result in a disproportionate share of our support costs. Activities like engineering and material handling were much more costly than we realized for the Mode III boards."

Scott went on to explain that the new costing system showed Aerotech's management that they could easily afford to lower the price on the Mode II boards and be competitive with the Asians and Europeans. At the same time, though, a substantial price increase would be necessary on the Mode III boards in order to cover costs.

A revolution is transforming the manufacturing industry. Not since the mid-nineteenth century have we seen changes as sweeping and dramatic. The growth of international competition, the breakneck pace of technological innovation, and startling advances in computerized systems have created a new playing field for manufacturers around the globe. Some manufacturers have emerged as world-class producers, while others have fallen by the wayside.

What is behind these dramatic changes in the manufacturing industry? And what is the role of managerial accounting in this rapidly changing environment? These questions are the focus of this chapter and the next one. To explore these issues, we will review recent events in the life of Aerotech Corporation, an electronics manufacturer in the southwest.

Aerotech Corporation: A Tale of Two Cities

Aerotech Corporation manufactures complex printed circuit boards used in aircraft radar and communications equipment. The company has operated its Phoenix plant for 20 years. Within the past year, Aerotech opened a new production facility in Bakersfield, California. While the Phoenix plant utilizes a traditional plant layout and production process, the Bakersfield plant employs the latest in advanced manufacturing technology. In this chapter, we will begin by describing the production process used in the Phoenix facility. Then we will describe the adaptations Aerotech's controller has made in the managerial-accounting system used in the Phoenix plant.

In the next chapter, we will examine the production process and managerial-accounting system used in the Bakersfield plant. Then we will study several contemporary accounting and management techniques used by Aerotech to achieve success in its competitive environment.

Aerotech's Phoenix Plant: Traditional Production Process

LO 1

Explain the key characteristics of a traditional manufacturing process and plant layout.

Three complex printed circuit boards are manufactured in Aerotech's Phoenix plant. These products are referred to as Mode I, Mode II, and Mode III boards. Mode I is the simplest of the three circuit boards, and Aerotech sells 10,000 units of the product each year. The Mode II circuit board, which is only slightly more complex, has a high sales volume compared to the other two boards. Aerotech sells 20,000 Mode II boards each year. The Mode III circuit board, which is the most complicated, is a low-volume product with annual sales of 4,000 units.

Production Process

The production process for all three printed circuit boards involves the attachment of various electrical components to a raw circuit board. Aerotech purchases the raw boards and all of the electrical components from other electronics manufacturers. Most of the electrical devices are small axial-lead components, such as diodes and resistors. These components are attached to a circuit board by bending the two lead wires at 90-degree angles and inserting the leads into predrilled holes in the raw boards. A few of the electrical components are large or oddly shaped instruments that require special handling in the production process.

The sequence of production steps is the same for all three boards.

1. *Sequencing*. The small axial-lead components are placed in the proper sequence for insertion into the board. Each type of axial-lead component is purchased in taped reels. The individual components can be peeled off the reel one at a time, just as a piece of tape can be peeled off a roll. A

sequencing machine is programmed to select the components from the proper reels in the sequence required for each type of circuit board.

2. *Auto-insertion.* The sequenced axial-lead components are fed into an auto-inserter machine, which bends the leads and inserts them into the predrilled holes in the raw boards.
3. *Hand-insertion.* The large or oddly shaped components are manually attached to the boards.
4. *Wave soldering.* The boards pass through a wave-solder machine. Here a wave of molten solder passes under each board, and the components' leads are secured.
5. *Wash/dry.* The wash/dry cycle is similar to the operation of a home dishwasher. The boards are washed to remove foreign particles; then they are dried with warm air.
6. *Hand-insertion.* The next step is to insert manually any components that could not withstand either the wave-solder or wash-dry operation.
7. *Bed of nails.* Each completed circuit board then is placed on a bed-of-nails tester. This machine consists of a set of vertical probes that make contact with the lead wires from each component on the circuit board. Each individual component then is tested independently. The bed-of-nails tester can be programmed so that its probes make contact with the different patterns of lead wires on the Mode I, Mode II, and Mode III circuit boards.
8. *Burn-in.* The final step is a burn-in test wherein electrical power is applied to each circuit board. The entire board is tested for functionality. If problems are detected, it is sent immediately to engineering for a full checkout procedure.
9. *Packaging.* The printed circuit boards are packaged and sent to finished-goods storage.

Plant Layout

The layout of Aerotech's Phoenix plant is shown in Exhibit 5–1. Colored arrows depict the flow of production from one operation to the next. Notice that each production operation is performed in a separate department. A storage area for work-in-process inventory is located next to each department. Here, partially completed circuit boards are stored until the next production department is ready for them.

This plant layout is referred to as a **process** (or **functional**) **layout,** since similar processes and functions are grouped together. For example, all auto-insertion activities are performed in one plant area (number 2 in Exhibit 5–1).

Traditional electronics manufacturing operations required considerable "touch labor," which refers to manual operations by production employees.

Traditional, Volume-Based Product-Costing System

Topic 5–1

Until recently, Aerotech's Phoenix plant used a job-order product-costing system similar to the one described in Chapter 3 for Adirondack Outfitters. The cost of each product was the sum of its actual direct-material cost, actual direct-labor cost, and

Exhibit 5–1
Aerotech Corporation's Phoenix Plant

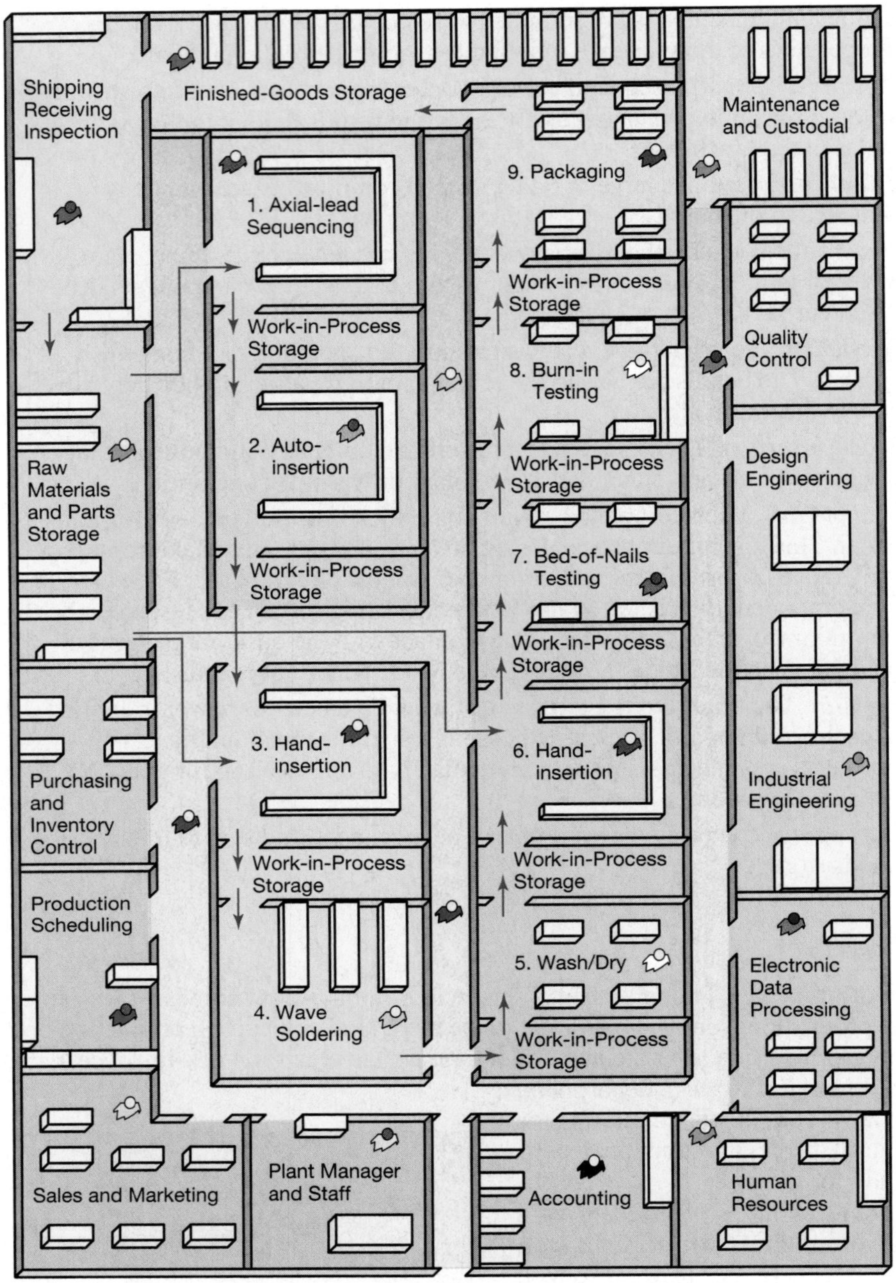

applied manufacturing overhead. Overhead was applied using a predetermined overhead rate based on direct-labor hours. Exhibit 5–2 provides the basic data upon which the traditional costing system was based.

LO 2

Compute product costs under a traditional, volume-based product-costing system and an activity-based costing system.

The Excel spreadsheet in Exhibit 5–3 shows the calculation of the product cost for each of the three circuit boards. Overhead is applied to the products at the rate of $33 per direct-labor hour. Notice that all of the Phoenix plant's budgeted manufacturing overhead costs are lumped together in a single cost pool. This total budgeted overhead amount ($3,894,000) then is divided by the plant's total budgeted direct-labor hours (118,000 hours).

Aerotech's labor-hour-based product-costing system is typical of many manufacturing companies. Labor hours are related closely to the volume of activity in the factory, which sometimes is referred to as *throughput*. Consequently, these traditional

	Mode I Boards	Mode II Boards	Mode III Boards
Production:			
Units	10,000	20,000	4,000
Runs	1 run of 10,000	4 runs of 5,000 each	10 runs of 400 each
Direct material			
(raw boards and components)	$50.00	$90.00	$20.00
Direct labor*			
(not including setup time)	3 hours per board	4 hours per board	2 hours per board
Setup time*	10 hours per run	10 hours per run	10 hours per run
Machine time	1 hour per board	1.25 hours per board	2 hours per board

*Direct labor and setup labor costs $20 per hour, including fringe benefits.

Exhibit 5–2

Basic Production and Cost Data: Aerotech Corporation's Phoenix Plant

Microsoft Excel - Exhibit 5-3.xls

G9 =SUM(G5:G8)

	A	B	C	D	E	F	G	H
1			Mode I		Mode II		Mode III	
2			Boards		Boards		Boards	
3								
4	Direct material							
5	(raw boards and components		$ 50.00		$ 90.00		$ 20.00	
6	Direct labor							
7	(not including set-up time)		60.00	(3 hr. at $20)	80.00	(4 hr. at $20)	40.00	(2 hr. at $20)
8	Manufacturing overhead*		99.00	(3 hr. at $33)	132.00	(4 hr. at $33)	66.00	(2 hr. at $33)
9	Total		$209.00		$302.00		$126.00	
10								
11								
12	*Calculation of predetermined-overhead rate:							
13								
14	Budgeted manufacturing overhead			$3,894,000				
15								
16	Direct labor, budgeted hours:							
17	Mode I: 10,000 units x 3 hours			30,000				
18	Mode II: 20,000 units x 4 hours			80,000				
19	Mode III: 4,000 units x 2 hours			8,000				
20	Total direct-labor hours			118,000	hours			
21								
22	Predetermined overhead rate:							
23	(Budgeted manufacturing overhead / Budgeted direct-labor hours) = $3,894,000 / 118,000 = $33 per hour							

Exhibit 5–3

Product Costs from Traditional, Volume-Based Product-Costing System: Aerotech Corporation's Phoenix Plant

product-costing systems often are said to be **volume-based** (or **throughput-based**) **costing systems.**

Trouble in Phoenix

The profitability of Aerotech's Phoenix operation has been faltering in recent years. The company's pricing policy has been to set a target price for each circuit board equal to 125 percent of the full product cost. Thus, the target prices were determined as shown in Exhibit 5–4. Also shown are the actual prices that Aerotech has been obtaining for its products.

Mode I circuit boards were selling at their target price of $261.25. However, price competition from foreign companies had forced Aerotech to lower its price on Mode II boards to $328, well below the target price of $377.50. Even at this lower price, Aerotech was having difficulty getting orders for its planned volume of Mode II

Exhibit 5–4
Target and Actual Selling Prices: Aerotech Corporation's Phoenix Plant

	Mode I Boards	Mode II Boards	Mode III Boards
Production cost under traditional, volume-based system (Exhibit 5–3)	$209.00	$302.00	$126.00
Target selling price (cost × 125%)	261.25	377.50	157.50
Actual selling price	261.25	328.00	250.00

circuit-board production. Fortunately, the lower profitability of the Mode II boards was offset partially by greater-than-expected profits on the Mode III circuit boards. Aerotech's sales personnel had discovered that the company was swamped with orders for the Mode III boards when the target price of $157.50 was charged. Consequently, Aerotech had raised the price on its Mode III boards several times, and eventually the product was selling at $250 per board. Even at this price, customers did not seem to hesitate to place orders. Moreover, Aerotech's competitors did not mount a challenge in the Mode III market. Aerotech's management was pleased to have a niche for the Mode III circuit boards, which appeared to be a highly profitable, low-volume specialty product. Nevertheless, concern continued to mount in Phoenix about the difficulty with the Mode II boards. After all, the Mode II board was the Phoenix plant's bread-and-butter product, with projected annual sales of 20,000 units.

Activity-Based Costing System

LO 2

Compute product costs under a traditional, volume-based product-costing system and an activity-based costing system.

Aerotech Corporation's controller, Chuck Dickens, had been thinking for some time about a refinement in the Phoenix plant's product-costing system. He wondered if the traditional, volume-based system was providing management with accurate data about product costs. Dickens had read about **activity-based costing (ABC) systems,** which follow a two-stage procedure to assign overhead costs to products. The first stage identifies significant activities and assigns overhead costs to each activity depending on the proportion of the organization's resources it uses. The overhead costs assigned to each activity comprise an **activity cost pool.**

After assigning overhead costs to activity cost pools in stage one, cost drivers are identified that are appropriate for each cost pool. Then in stage two, the overhead costs are allocated from each activity cost pool to each product line in proportion to the amount of the cost driver consumed by the product line.

Dickens discussed activity-based costing with Anne Marley, the assistant controller. Together they met with all of Aerotech's production departments to discuss development of an ABC system. After initial discussion, an ABC proposal was made to Aerotech's top management. Approval was obtained, and an ABC project team was formed, which included Dickens, Marley, and representatives of various functional departments. Through several months of painstaking data collection and analysis, the project team was able to gather the data necessary to implement an ABC system.

LO 3

Explain how an activity-based costing system operates, including the use of a two-stage procedure for cost assignment, the identification of activity cost pools, and the selection of cost drivers.

Stage One Aerotech's ABC project team identified eight activity cost pools, which fall into four broad categories. These are shown in Exhibit 5–5.

- *Unit level.* This type of activity must be done for each unit of production. Aerotech's machine-related activity cost pool represents a **unit-level activity** since every product unit requires machine time.
- *Batch level.* These activities must be performed for each batch of products, rather than each unit. Aerotech's **batch-level activities** include the setup, receiving and inspection, material-handling, packaging and shipping, and quality-assurance activity cost pools.
- *Product-sustaining level.* This category includes activities that are needed to support an entire product line but are not always performed every time a new

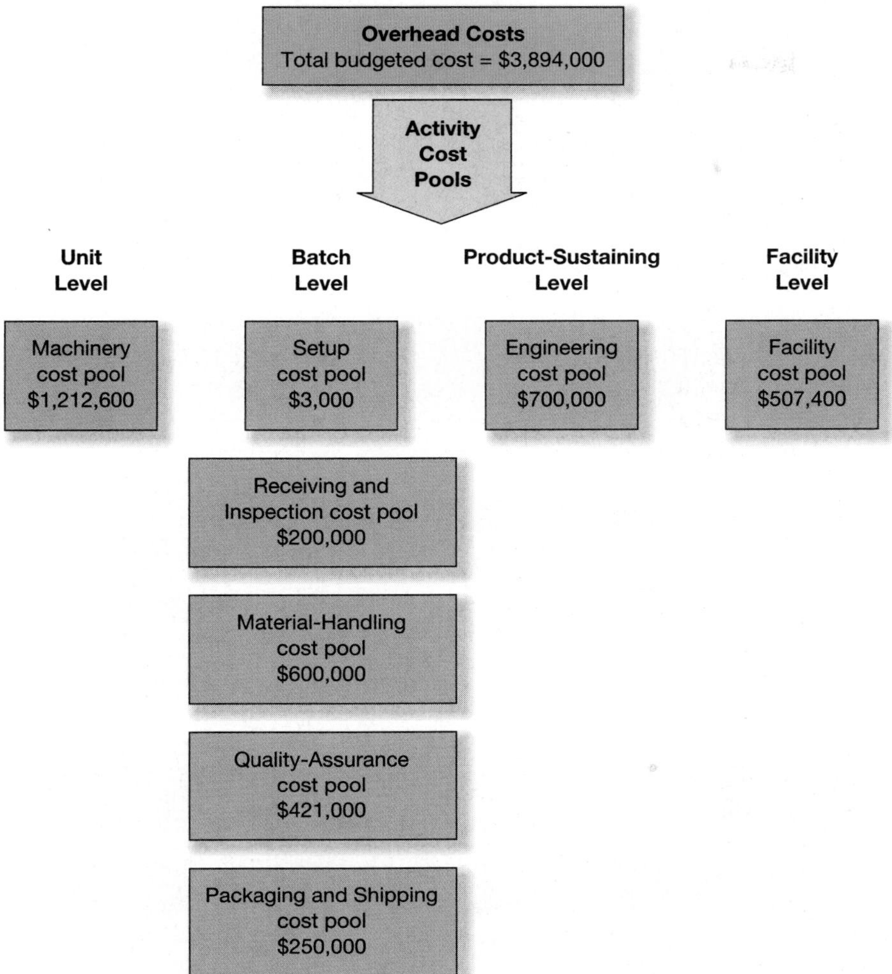

Exhibit 5–5
Stage One of Activity-Based Costing: Identification of Activity Cost Pools

unit or batch of products is produced. Aerotech's project team identified engineering costs as a **product-sustaining-level activity** cost pool.

- *Facility (or general operations) level.* **Facility-level activities** are required in order for the entire production process to occur. Examples of such activity costs include plant management salaries, plant depreciation, property taxes, plant maintenance, and insurance.

Stage Two In stage two of the activity-based costing project, Dickens and Marley identified cost drivers for each activity cost pool. Then they assigned the costs in each activity cost pool to Aerotech's three product lines according to the proportion of each cost driver consumed by each product line. In the following sections, we will discuss in detail how stage two of the ABC project was carried out for four of the activity cost pools identified in stage one. Then we will complete the ABC project by developing new product costs for each of Aerotech's three circuit boards.

LO 3
Explain how an activity-based costing system operates, including the use of a two-stage procedure for cost assignment, the identification of activity cost pools, and the selection of cost drivers.

Machinery Cost Pool The machinery cost pool, a unit-level activity, totals $1,212,600 and includes the costs of machine maintenance, depreciation, computer support, lubrication, electricity, and calibration. Dickens and Marley selected machine hours for the cost driver, since a product that uses more machine hours should bear a larger share of machine-related costs. Exhibit 5–6 shows how machinery costs

Topic 5–2

STAGE ONE

Various overhead costs related to machinery → Activity cost pool

Maintenance, Depreciation, Computer support, Lubrication, Electricity, Calibration → Machinery cost pool
Total budgeted cost = $1,212,600

STAGE TWO

Calculation of pool rate

$$\frac{\text{Total budgeted machinery cost}}{\text{Total budgeted machine hours}} = \frac{\$1{,}212{,}600}{43{,}000 \text{ machine hours}}$$

= $28.20 per machine hour

Cost assignment:
Pool rate per machine hour
× Machine hours per unit

Mode I:	Mode II:	Mode III:
$28.20 per machine hr.	$28.20 per machine hr.	$28.20 per machine hr.
× 1 hr. per unit	× 1.25 hr. per unit	× 2 hr. per unit
$28.20 per unit	$35.25 per unit	$56.40 per unit

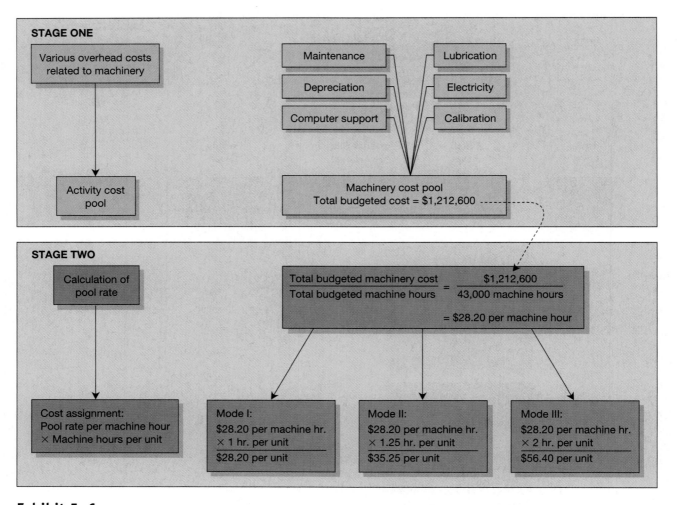

Exhibit 5–6
Activity-Based Costing: Machinery Cost Pool

are assigned to products in stage two of the ABC analysis. Budgeted machinery costs ($1,212,600) are divided by budgeted machine hours (43,000) to obtain a *pool rate* of $28.20 per machine hour. The **pool rate** is the cost per unit of the cost driver for a particular activity cost pool. Next, the pool rate of $28.20 per machine hour is multiplied by the number of machine hours required per unit of each product. For example, each Mode II circuit board is assigned a cost of $35.25 ($28.20 per machine hour × 1.25 machine hours per circuit board).

Setup Cost Pool Setting up production runs is an example of a batch-level activity. The ABC calculations for the setup cost pool are displayed in Exhibit 5–7. In stage one the total setup cost is determined to be $3,000. The cost driver used to assign setup costs to the three product lines in stage two is the number of production runs. The pool rate is determined to be $200 per production run. Finally, the setup cost per circuit board is computed for each product line by dividing the setup cost per production run by the number of units in a run.[1]

Engineering Cost Pool Engineering is classified as a product-sustaining-level activity. Although engineering activities are crucial in supporting each product line, they

[1]Aerotech's setup cost pool, $3,000, is relatively small compared to the other cost pools. Often such a small cost pool is combined with another larger pool. However, the setup cost pool is identified separately in our example for two reasons. First, a setup cost pool is common in the ABC systems observed in practice. Second, it is worthwhile to see how the ABC calculations are done for the setup cost pool.

STAGE ONE

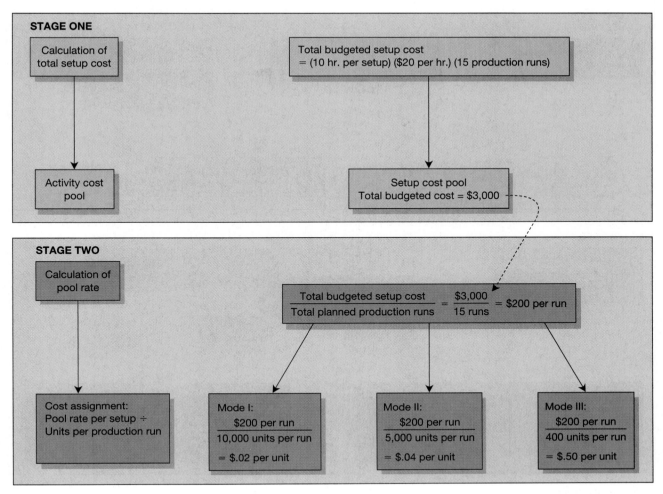

Calculation of total setup cost	Total budgeted setup cost = (10 hr. per setup) ($20 per hr.) (15 production runs)
↓	↓
Activity cost pool	Setup cost pool Total budgeted cost = $3,000

STAGE TWO

Calculation of pool rate

$$\frac{\text{Total budgeted setup cost}}{\text{Total planned production runs}} = \frac{\$3{,}000}{15 \text{ runs}} = \$200 \text{ per run}$$

Cost assignment: Pool rate per setup ÷ Units per production run	Mode I: $\frac{\$200 \text{ per run}}{10{,}000 \text{ units per run}}$ = $.02 per unit	Mode II: $\frac{\$200 \text{ per run}}{5{,}000 \text{ units per run}}$ = $.04 per unit	Mode III: $\frac{\$200 \text{ per run}}{400 \text{ units per run}}$ = $.50 per unit

Exhibit 5–7

Activity-Based Costing: Setup Cost Pool

typically are not carried out for each unit or batch of products. Exhibit 5–8 displays the ABC calculations for the engineering cost pool. In stage one, the total engineering cost is determined to be $700,000.

The cost driver selected in stage two is the number of engineering transactions, such as design specifications and change orders, relating to each product line. The calculations are slightly different here from those used in stage two for the machinery and setup cost pools. Instead of computing the engineering cost per transaction, the ABC project team estimated the percentage of engineering activity related to each product line. For example, since 25 percent of all engineering activity is related to the Mode I circuit boards, 25 percent of the engineering cost pool is assigned to the Mode I product line. Finally, the engineering cost per unit is computed by dividing the engineering cost assigned to each product line by the number of units produced in that line.

This technician is setting up a robot used in manufacturing the circuit boards used in high-definition TVs. Machine setup is a batch-level activity.

This approach to activity-based costing is sometimes called transaction-based costing. Under this method, costs are assigned from an activity cost pool to various product

STAGE ONE

Various overhead costs related to engineering → Activity cost pool

Engineers' salaries

Engineering supplies

Engineering software

Depreciation on engineering equipment

Engineering cost pool
Total budgeted cost = $700,000

STAGE TWO

Allocation to product lines based on proportion of engineering transactions → Cost assignment: Cost allocated to each product line ÷ Number of units of each product

Total budgeted engineering cost = $700,000

25% of transactions	45% of transactions	30% of transactions
Mode I:	Mode II:	Mode III:
$\frac{25\% \times \$700{,}000}{10{,}000 \text{ units}}$	$\frac{45\% \times \$700{,}000}{20{,}000 \text{ units}}$	$\frac{30\% \times \$700{,}000}{4{,}000 \text{ units}}$
= $17.50 per unit	= $15.75 per unit	= $52.50 per unit

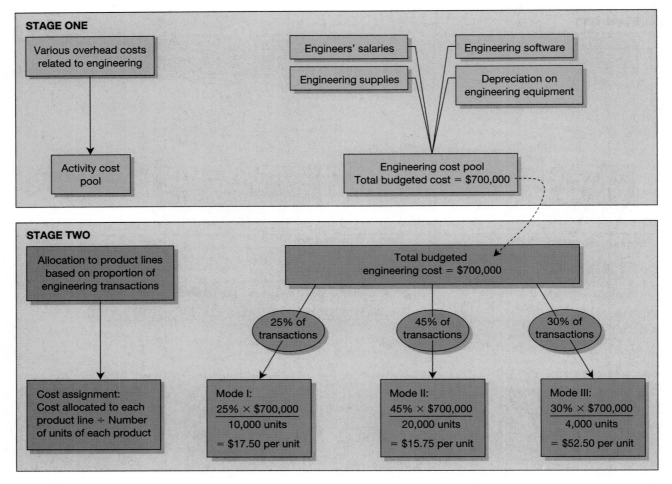

Exhibit 5–8
Activity-Based Costing: Engineering Cost Pool

AEROTECH CORPORATION

lines based on the relative proportion of the activity consumed by each product line, as measured by transactions. Here the term *transaction* is used in a general sense to mean a unit of activity that concludes in some well-defined result, such as a design spec or change order. In most cases, these transactions result in documents of some type, either in hard copy or computer form.

Facility Cost Pool The facility-level (or general-operations-level) activity cost pool includes such costs as plant depreciation, plant management salaries, plant maintenance, property taxes, and insurance. The ABC calculations are displayed in Exhibit 5–9. The total cost, determined in stage one, is $507,400. The cost driver selected in stage two is direct-labor hours. The pool rate is $4.30 per direct-labor hour. Finally, facilities costs are assigned to products by multiplying the pool rate by the number of direct-labor hours required by each circuit board.

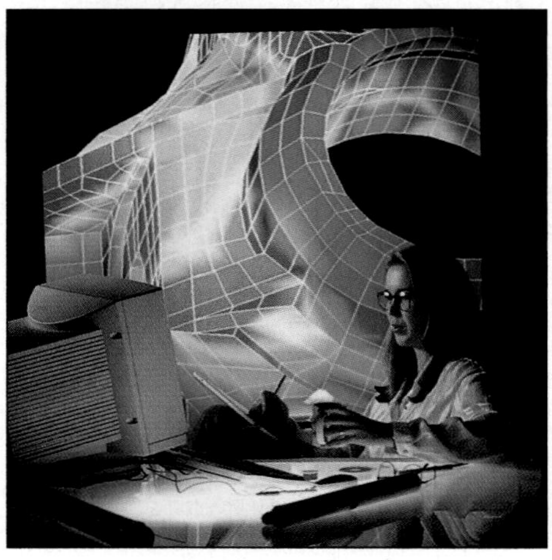

This engineer is using a computer-aided design (CAD) system for engineering design. This is an example of a product-sustaining-level cost.

Product Costs under Activity-Based Costing The ABC calculations for the four remaining cost pools—receiving and inspection, material handling, quality assurance, and

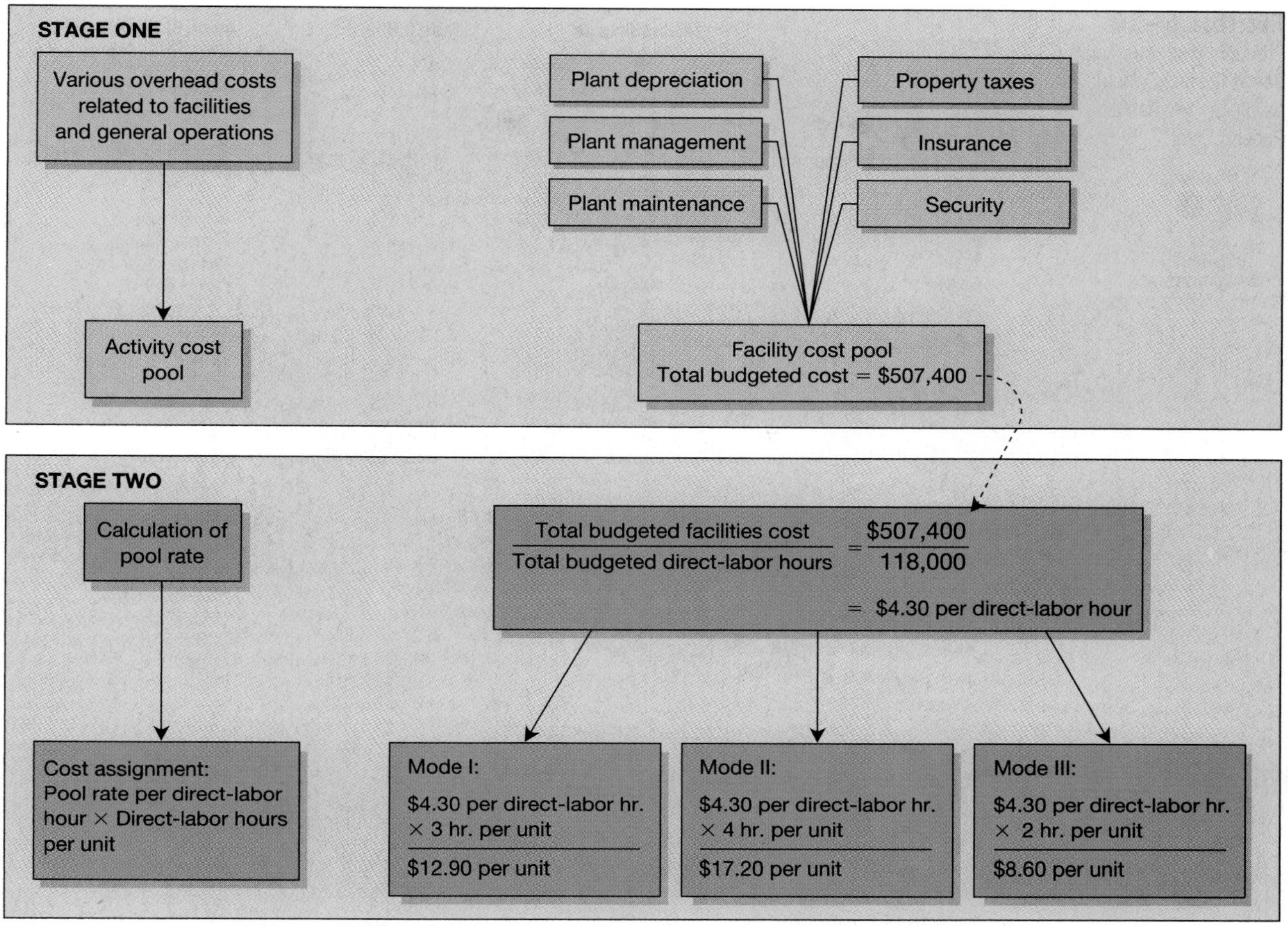

STAGE ONE

Various overhead costs related to facilities and general operations	Plant depreciation Plant management Plant maintenance Property taxes Insurance Security
↓	↓
Activity cost pool	Facility cost pool Total budgeted cost = $507,400

STAGE TWO

Calculation of pool rate	$\frac{\text{Total budgeted facilities cost}}{\text{Total budgeted direct-labor hours}} = \frac{\$507,400}{118,000}$ = $4.30 per direct-labor hour		
Cost assignment: Pool rate per direct-labor hour × Direct-labor hours per unit	**Mode I:** $4.30 per direct-labor hr. × 3 hr. per unit = $12.90 per unit	**Mode II:** $4.30 per direct-labor hr. × 4 hr. per unit = $17.20 per unit	**Mode III:** $4.30 per direct-labor hr. × 2 hr. per unit = $8.60 per unit

Exhibit 5–9
Activity-Based Costing: Facility Cost Pool

packaging and shipping—follow the approach for the engineering cost pool. A transaction-based costing approach is used, assigning each activity's costs to the three product lines on the basis of the relative proportion of the activity consumed by each product line. Exhibit 5–10 completes the calculation of the ABC product costs by totaling the costs assigned from each activity cost pool to each product line.

Examine Exhibit 5–10 carefully, as it details all the results of the activity-based costing system. Notice that the costs of direct material and direct labor remain the same as those in the traditional, volume-based costing system (Exhibit 5–3). However, there are big differences in the assignment of overhead costs to the three product lines under the ABC system.

Interpreting the ABC Product Costs

LO 3

Explain how an activity-based costing system operates, including the use of a two-stage procedure for cost assignment, the identification of activity cost pools, and the selection of cost drivers.

Chuck Dickens was amazed to see the product costs reported under the activity-based costing system. Both the Mode I and Mode II circuit boards exhibited much lower product costs under the ABC system than under the traditional system. This could explain the price competition Aerotech faced on its Mode II circuit boards. Aerotech's competitors could sell their Mode II boards at a lower price because they realized it cost less to produce a Mode II board than Aerotech's traditional costing system had indicated. However, as Dickens scanned the new product costs shown in Exhibit 5–10 he was alarmed by the substantial increase in the reported cost of a Mode III circuit board. The cost of a Mode III board had skyrocketed to over three times the company's original estimate. The complexity of the Mode III boards, and its impact on costs, was

Exhibit 5–10
Product Costs from Activity-Based Costing System: Aerotech Corporation's Phoenix Plant

AEROTECH CORPORATION

	Mode I Boards	Mode II Boards	Mode III Boards
Direct material (raw boards and components) . . .	$ 50.00	$ 90.00	$ 20.00
Direct labor (not including setup time)	60.00 (3 hr. at $20)	80.00 (4 hr. at $20)	40.00 (2 hr. at $20)
Machinery[a]	28.20	35.25	56.40
Setup[b]	.02	.04	.50
Engineering[c]	17.50	15.75	52.50
Facility[d]	12.90	17.20	8.60
Receiving and inspection[e]	1.20	2.40	35.00
Material handling[f]	4.20	9.00	94.50
Quality assurance[g]	8.42	8.42	42.10
Packaging and shipping[h]	1.00	3.75	41.25
Total	$183.44	$261.81	$390.85

[a] Machinery Cost Pool (details in Exhibit 5–6):
Mode I: ($1,212,600 ÷ 43,000 machine hr.) × 1 machine hr. = $28.20
Mode II: ($1,212,600 ÷ 43,000 machine hr.) × 1.25 machine hr. = $35.25
Mode III: ($1,212,600 ÷ 43,000 machine hr.) × 2 machine hr. = $56.40

[b] Setup Cost Pool (details in Exhibit 5–7):
Mode I: ($3,000 ÷ 15 runs) ÷ 10,000 units per run = $.02
Mode II: ($3,000 ÷ 15 runs) ÷ 5,000 units per run = $.04
Mode III: ($3,000 ÷ 15 runs) ÷ 400 units per run = $.50

[c] Engineering Cost Pool (details in Exhibit 5–8):
Mode I: ($700,000 × 25%) ÷ 10,000 units = $17.50
Mode II: ($700,000 × 45%) ÷ 20,000 units = $15.75
Mode III: ($700,000 × 30%) ÷ 4,000 units = $52.50

[d] Facility Cost Pool (details in Exhibit 5–9):
Mode I: ($507,400 ÷ 118,000 direct-labor hr.) × 3 direct-labor hr. = $12.90
Mode II: ($507,400 ÷ 118,000 direct-labor hr.) × 4 direct-labor hr. = $17.20
Mode III: ($507,400 ÷ 118,000 direct-labor hr.) × 2 direct-labor hr. = $ 8.60

[e] Receiving and Inspection Cost Pool:
Mode I: ($200,000 × 6%) ÷ 10,000 units = $ 1.20
Mode II: ($200,000 × 24%) ÷ 20,000 units = $ 2.40
Mode III: ($200,000 × 70%) ÷ 4,000 units = $35.00

[f] Material-Handling Cost Pool:
Mode I: ($600,000 × 7%) ÷ 10,000 units = $ 4.20
Mode II: ($600,000 × 30%) ÷ 20,000 units = $ 9.00
Mode III: ($600,000 × 63%) ÷ 4,000 units = $94.50

[g] Quality-Assurance Cost Pool:
Mode I: ($421,000 × 20%) ÷ 10,000 units = $ 8.42
Mode II: ($421,000 × 40%) ÷ 20,000 units = $ 8.42
Mode III: ($421,000 × 40%) ÷ 4,000 units = $42.10

[h] Packaging and Shipping Cost Pool:
Mode I: ($250,000 × 4%) ÷ 10,000 units = $ 1.00
Mode II: ($250,000 × 30%) ÷ 20,000 units = $ 3.75
Mode III: ($250,000 × 66%) ÷ 4,000 units = $41.25

The percentages in these calculations are the proportions of each activity consumed by each product line, as estimated by the ABC project team.

hidden completely by the traditional, volume-based costing system. To compare the results of the two alternative costing systems, Dickens prepared Exhibit 5–11.

The Mode I boards emerged as an extremely profitable product, selling for over 142 percent of their reported cost under the activity-based costing system ($261.25 ÷ $183.44). The Mode II boards were selling at approximately 125 percent of their new reported product cost ($328 ÷ $261.81). "No wonder we couldn't sell the Mode II boards at $377.50," said Dickens to Marley, as they looked over the data. "Our

	Mode I Boards	Mode II Boards	Mode III Boards
Reported product costs:			
Traditional, volume-based costing system (from Exhibit 5–3)	$209.00	$302.00	$126.00
Activity-based costing system (from Exhibit 5–10)	183.44	261.81	390.85
Sales price data:			
Original target price (based on traditional, volume-based costing system; Exhibit 5–4)	261.25	377.50	157.50
New target price (based on activity-based costing system: 125% of reported ABC product costs)	229.30	327.26	488.56
Actual selling price (Exhibit 5–4)	261.25	328.00	250.00

Exhibit 5–11

Comparison of Product Costs from Alternative Product-Costing Systems: Aerotech Corporation's Phoenix Plant

competitors probably knew the Mode II boards cost around $262, and they priced them accordingly." When he got to the Mode III column, Dickens was appalled. "We thought those Mode III's were a winner," lamented Dickens, "but we've been selling them at a loss of over $140 per board!" After looking over the data, Dickens almost ran to the president's office. "We've got to get this operation straightened out," he thought.

"Before the industry really became wide open in long-distance competition [as the result of deregulation], you could get by with knowing less. You could get by with having price structures that were not based on the underlying activities and the costs associated with those activities, but were instead based on broad averages. It was okay. It worked. It's not good enough anymore. We have to get more precise in our costs. We have to deliver the kinds of prices to our customers that they're willing to pay." (5a)

TELUS (formerly British Columbia Telecommunications)

The Punch Line

What has happened at Aerotech's Phoenix plant? The essence of the problem is that the traditional, volume-based costing system was overcosting the high-volume product lines (Mode I and Mode II) and undercosting the complex, low-volume product line (Mode III). The high-volume products basically subsidized the low-volume line. The activity-based costing system revealed this problem by more accurately assigning overhead costs to the three product lines.

Exhibit 5–12 summarizes the effects of the cost distortion under the traditional product-costing system. Aerotech's traditional system *overcosted* each Mode I circuit board by $25.56, for a total of $255,600 for the Mode I product line on a volume of 10,000 units. Each Mode II board was *overcosted* by $40.19, for a total of $803,800 on a volume of 20,000 units for the Mode II product line. These excess costs had to come from somewhere, and that place was the Mode III product line. Each Mode III board was *undercosted* by $264.85, for a total of $1,059,400 for the Mode III product line on a volume of 4,000 units. Notice that the *total* amount by which the Mode I and II boards were overcosted equals the *total* amount by which the Mode III boards were undercosted.

Why Traditional, Volume-Based Systems Distort Product Costs

LO 4

Explain why traditional, volume-based costing systems tend to distort product costs.

Why did Aerotech's traditional product-costing system distort its product costs? The answer lies in the use of a single, volume-based cost driver. Aerotech's old costing system assigned overhead to products on the basis of their relative usage of direct labor. Since the Mode I and Mode II circuit boards use more direct labor than the Mode III boards, the traditional system assigned them more overhead costs. A review of Exhibit 5–3 confirms this conclusion. Notice, for example, that each Mode II board is assigned twice as much overhead cost as a Mode III board, because each Mode II board requires twice as much direct labor as a Mode III board.

The problem with this result is that for several of Aerotech's overhead activities, the proportion of the activity actually consumed by the Mode III boards is greater than

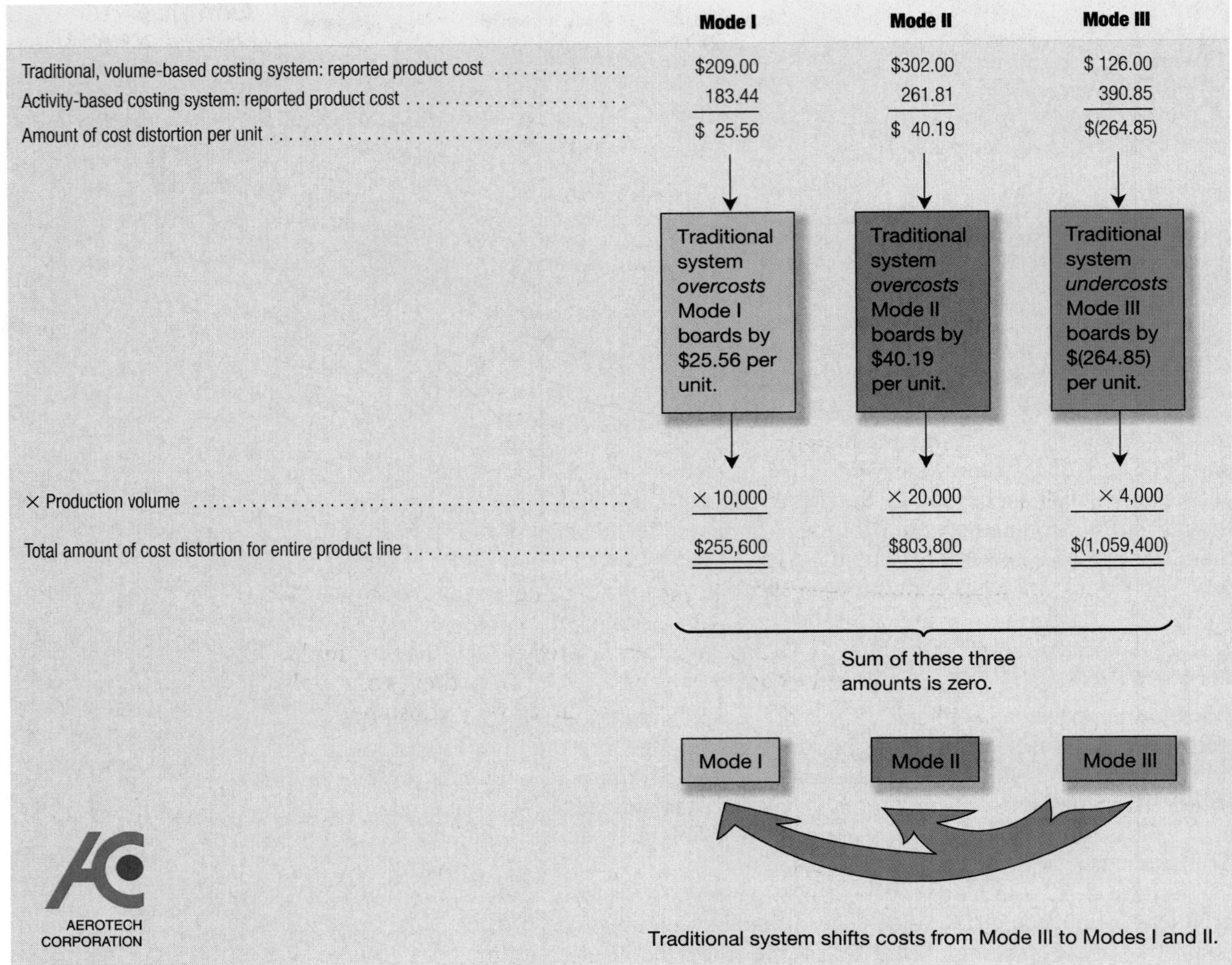

Mode I
Mode II
Mode III
Traditional, volume-based costing system: reported product cost $209.00 $302.00 $ 126.00
Activity-based costing system: reported product cost 183.44 261.81 390.85
Amount of cost distortion per unit $ 25.56 $ 40.19 $(264.85)
Traditional system overcosts Mode I boards by $25.56 per unit.
Traditional system overcosts Mode II boards by $40.19 per unit.
Traditional system undercosts Mode III boards by $(264.85) per unit.
× Production volume × 10,000 × 20,000 × 4,000
Total amount of cost distortion for entire product line $255,600 $803,800 $(1,059,400)
Sum of these three amounts is zero.
Mode I
Mode II
Mode III
AEROTECH CORPORATION
Traditional system shifts costs from Mode III to Modes I and II.

Exhibit 5–12
Cost Distortion under Aerotech's Traditional Product-Costing System

that consumed by the Mode I or II boards. Examine the ABC calculations in Exhibit 5–10. Notice that for many of the overhead activities, the Mode III boards consume the largest share of the activity. The heavy consumption of overhead activities by the Mode III product line is due to its greater complexity and small production runs. We must conclude, therefore, that direct labor is not a suitable cost driver for Aerotech's overhead costs. Usage of direct labor does not drive most overhead costs in this company.

There are actually two factors working against Aerotech's old product-costing system. First, many of the activities that result in Aerotech's overhead costs are *not unit-level activities*. Second, Aerotech manufactures a *diverse set of products*.

"ABC is not a magic bullet, but it is a tool to help you understand your business better." (5b)
Braas Company

Nonunit-Level Overhead Costs When Aerotech's ABC project team designed the activity-based costing system, only the machine-related overhead cost pool was classified as a unit-level activity. All of the other activities were classified as batch-level, product-sustaining level, or facility-level activities. This means that many of Aerotech's overhead costs are not incurred every time a unit is produced. Instead, many of these overhead costs are related to starting new production batches, supporting an entire product line, or running the entire operation. Since direct labor is a unit-level cost driver, it fails to capture the forces that drive these other types of costs. In Aerotech's new ABC system, cost drivers were chosen that were appropriate for each activity cost pool. For example, since setting up machinery for a new production run is a batch-level activity, the number of production runs is an appropriate batch-level cost driver.

In the manufacture of diverse product lines, a single cost driver cannot capture the widely differing usage of production-related activities by the different product lines.

Product Diversity Aerotech manufactures three different products. Although all three are circuit boards used in aircraft radar and communications equipment, the three boards are quite different. The Mode I and II boards are high-volume, relatively simple boards. The Mode III board is a highly complex, low-volume product. As a result of this *product diversity,* Aerotech's three products consume overhead activities in different proportions. For example, compare the consumption ratios for the engineering and material-handling cost pools shown below. The **consumption ratio** is the proportion of an activity consumed by a particular product.

	Consumption Ratios*		
Activity Cost Pool	**Mode I**	**Mode II**	**Mode III**
Engineering	25%	45%	30%
Material handling	7%	30%	63%

*From the ABC calculations in Exhibit 5–10.

These widely varying consumption ratios result from Aerotech's product diversity. A single cost driver will not capture the widely differing usage of these activities by the three products. The activity-based costing system uses two different cost drivers to assign these costs to Aerotech's diverse products.

Two Key Points To summarize, each of the following characteristics will undermine the ability of a volume-based product-costing system to assign overhead costs accurately.

- *A large proportion of nonunit-level activities.* A unit-level cost driver, such as direct labor, machine hours, or throughput, will not be able to assign the costs of nonunit-level activities accurately.
- *Product diversity.* When the consumption ratios differ widely between activities, no single cost driver will accurately assign the resulting overhead costs.

When either of these characteristics is present, a volume-based product-costing system is likely to distort product costs.

Management Accounting Practice

Rockwell International

COST DISTORTION AT ROCKWELL INTERNATIONAL

When managers at Rockwell International noticed erratic sales in one of the company's lines of truck axles, they investigated. One of the company's best axle products was losing market share. A special cost study revealed that the firm's costing system, which applied costs to products in proportion to direct-labor costs, had resulted in major distortions. The reported product costs for high-volume axles were approximately 20 percent too high, and the low-volume axles were being undercosted by roughly 40 percent. The firm's practice of basing prices on reported product costs resulted in the overpricing of the high-volume axles. As a consequence, Rockwell's competitors entered the market for the high-volume axle business.[2]

Does the sort of product-cost distortion experienced by Aerotech occur in other companies? The answer is yes, as illustrated by the examples from Rockwell International (above) and Compaq (next page).[3]

Activity-Based Costing: Some Key Issues

LO 5

Discuss several key issues in activity-based costing, including criteria for choosing cost drivers, data collection, storyboarding, and indicators that a new costing system is needed.

Aerotech Corporation's movement toward activity-based costing is typical of changes currently underway in many companies. Added domestic and foreign competition is forcing manufacturers to strive for a better understanding of their cost structures. Moreover, the cost structures of many manufacturers have changed significantly over the past decade. Years ago, a typical manufacturer produced a relatively small number of products which did not differ much in the amount and types of manufacturing support they required. Labor was the dominant element in such a firm's cost structure. Nowadays, it's a different ball game. Products are more numerous, are more complicated, and vary more in their production requirements. Perhaps most important, labor is becoming an ever-smaller component of total production costs. All these factors mean manufacturers must take a close look at their traditional, volume-based costing systems and consider a move toward activity-based costing.

Another factor in the move toward ABC systems is related to the information requirements of such systems. The data required for activity-based costing are more readily available than in the past. Increasing automation, coupled with sophisticated real-time information systems, provides the kind of data necessary to implement highly accurate product-costing systems. Some key issues related to activity-based costing systems are discussed in the following sections.

Cost Drivers

A **cost driver** is a characteristic of an event or activity that results in the incurrence of costs. In activity-based costing systems, the most significant cost drivers are identified. Then a database is created, which shows how these cost drivers are distributed across products. Three factors are important in selecting appropriate cost drivers.

1. *Degree of correlation.* The central concept of an activity-based costing system is to assign the costs of each activity to product lines on the basis of how each product line consumes the cost driver identified for that activity. The

[2]Ford S. Worthy, "Accounting Bores You? Wake Up," *Fortune* 116, no. 8 (October 12, 1987), pp. 43–53.

[3]S. L. Mintz, "Compaq's Secret Weapon," *CFO* 10, no. 10, pp. 93–97.

idea is to *infer* how each product line consumes the activity by *observing* how each product line consumes the cost driver. Therefore, the accuracy of the resulting cost assignments depends on the *degree of correlation* between consumption of the activity and consumption of the cost driver.

Say that inspection cost is selected as an activity cost pool. The objective of the ABC system is to assign inspection costs to product lines on the basis of their consumption of the inspection activity. Two potential cost drivers come to mind: number of inspections and hours of inspection time. If every inspection requires the same amount of time for all products, then the number of inspections on a product line will be highly correlated with the consumption of inspection activity by that product line. On the other hand, if inspections vary significantly in the time required, then simply recording the number of inspections will not adequately portray the consumption of inspection activity. In this case, hours of inspection time would be more highly correlated with the actual consumption of the inspection activity.

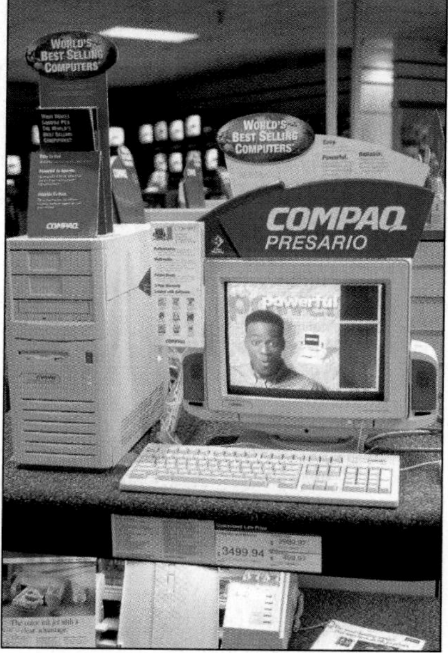

2. *Cost of measurement.* Designing any information system entails cost-benefit trade-offs. The more activity cost pools there are in an activity-based costing system, the greater will be the accuracy of the cost assignments. However, more activity cost pools also entail more cost drivers, which results in greater costs of implementing and maintaining the system.

   Similarly, the higher the correlation between a cost driver and the actual consumption of the associated activity, the greater the accuracy of the cost assignments. However, it may also be more costly to measure the more highly correlated cost driver. Returning to our example of the inspection activity, it may be that inspection hours make a more accurate cost driver than the number of inspections. It is likely, however, that inspection hours also will be more costly to measure and track over time.

3. *Behavioral effects.* Information systems have the potential not only to facilitate decisions but also to influence the behavior of decision makers. This can be good or bad, depending on the behavioral effects. In identifying cost drivers, an ABC analyst should consider the possible behavioral consequences. For example, in a JIT production environment a key goal is to reduce inventories and material-handling activities to the absolute minimum level possible. The number of material moves may be the most accurate measure of the consumption of the material-handling activity for cost assignment purposes. It may also have a desirable behavioral effect of inducing managers to reduce the number of times materials are moved, thereby reducing material-handling costs.

   Dysfunctional behavioral effects are also possible. For example, the number of vendor contacts may be a cost driver for the purchasing activity of vendor selection. This could induce purchasing managers to contact fewer vendors, which could result in the failure to identify the lowest-cost or highest-quality vendor.

Compaq recently merged with Hewlett-Packard. Both companies have made considerable use of ABC. Compaq executives were convinced that they were more efficient in producing computers than other companies, but they were mystified as to how their competitors could sell similar equipment at lower prices and still be profitable. However, an ABC analysis revealed that Compaq's cost-accounting system was overcosting high-volume products, while low-volume products were being undercosted. Low-volume accessories also were being undercosted by a substantial amount.

"After the initial run-through, we completed a separate analysis detailing how many times a [cost] driver was used. We performed a sort of cost-benefit analysis. We gave each [cost] driver a grade, such as how easy would the driver be to collect." (5c)

John Deere Health Care, Inc.

Homogeneous Activity Cost Pools

In deciding how many activity cost pools (and their associated cost drivers) are needed, the ABC analyst should look carefully at the *homogeneity* of each potential cost pool. A **homogeneous cost pool** is a grouping of overhead costs in which each cost component is consumed in roughly the same proportion by each product line. A homogeneous cost pool can be allocated using a single cost driver. To illustrate, suppose Aerotech's receiving and inspection cost pool has the following characteristics.

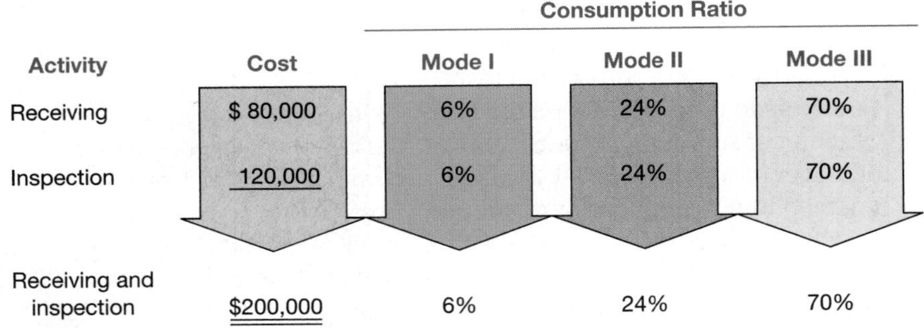

Activity	Cost	Consumption Ratio: Mode I	Mode II	Mode III
Receiving	$ 80,000	6%	24%	70%
Inspection	120,000	6%	24%	70%
Receiving and inspection	$200,000	6%	24%	70%

The combined receiving and inspection cost pool is homogeneous because the consumption ratios are the same for its components. As a result, Aerotech's ABC project team combined receiving and inspection costs into a single cost pool. Slight deviations from homogeneity can be tolerated without significant effects on cost assignment accuracy. However, the greater the deviations become, the greater is the chance of distorted product costs.

Management Accounting Practice

Hospice of Central Kentucky

ACTIVITY COST DRIVERS IN THE HEALTH CARE INDUSTRY

The Hospice of Central Kentucky (HCK) is a Medicare and Medicaid certified hospice serving 10 counties in central Kentucky. "It provides all medical needs to the terminally ill, including nursing care, medical equipment, medications, and palliative treatment so patients can live their last days at home with their family."

In a detailed study of the hospice's costs, the following cost drivers were among those identified for some of the organization's key activities.

Activity	*Cost driver*	*Activity*	*Cost driver*
Prereferral	Indexed referrals*	Reception	Number of calls
Referral	Indexed referrals*	Accounting/finance	Indexed patient days*
Admission	Number of admissions	Management	Indexed patient days*
Post admission	Number of admissions	Information systems	Indexed patient days*
Post death	Number of deaths	Billing	Number of billings
Medical services	Number of service calls	Volunteer services	Number of volunteers

*Patient cases are assigned an index number, which captures the severity of the case. For example, a patient who is in slow decline is assigned an index of 1. A rapidly declining patient is assigned a 2. A patient who is facing imminent death is assigned a 3. This system of indexing the number of referrals and patient days reflects the fact that the more severe the patient case, the more costly is the treatment.

The cost-driver information has given management a much better understanding of the hospice's costs. "Quantifiable information confirmed that management and staff hunches were correct—the cost of care increases as the level of acuity (patient case severity) increases. The surprise was the amount." Armed with the cost-driver information, the hospice's management now is in a better position to negotiate contracts with private insurance carriers.[4]

[4]Sidney J. Baxendale and Victoria Dornbusch, "Activity-Based Costing for a Hospice," *Strategic Finance* 81, no. 9 (March 2000), pp. 65–70.

Collecting ABC Data

The output of an organization's various departments consists of the activities performed by personnel or machines in those departments. Activities usually result in paperwork or the generation of computer documents. For example, engineering departments typically deal with documents such as specification sheets and engineering change orders. Purchasing departments handle requisitions and orders, which may be either hard-copy or computer documents. In an ABC system, analysis of documents such as these can be used to assign the costs of activities to product lines on the basis of the amount of activity generated by each product.

Interviews and Paper Trails The information used in Aerotech's ABC system came initially from extensive interviews with key employees in each of the organization's support departments and a careful review of each department's records. In Aerotech's engineering area, for example, ABC project team members interviewed each engineer to determine the breakdown of time spent on each of the three products. They also examined every engineering change order completed in the past two years. The team concluded that engineering costs were driven largely by change orders and design specs, and that the breakdown was 25 percent for Mode I, 45 percent for Mode II, and 30 percent for Mode III.

Storyboarding As Aerotech's project team delved further into the ABC analysis, they made considerable use of another technique for collecting activity data. **Storyboarding** is a procedure used to develop a detailed process flowchart, which visually represents activities and the relationships among the activities. A storyboarding session involves all or most of the employees who participate in the activities oriented toward achieving a specific objective. A facilitator helps the employees identify the key activities involved in their jobs. These activities are written on small cards and placed on a large board in the order they are accomplished. Relationships among the activities are shown by the order and proximity of the cards. Other information about the activities is recorded on the cards, such as the amount of time and other resources that are expended on each activity and the events that trigger the activity. After several storyboarding sessions, a completed storyboard emerges, recording key activity information vital to the ABC project. Historically, storyboards have been used by

Interviews with department personnel and storyboarding sessions are often used by activity-based costing project teams to accumulate the data needed for an ABC study. In the interview sessions, an ABC project team member asks departmental employees to detail their activities, as well as the time and other resources consumed by the activities. Storyboards, like the one depicted here, visually show the relationships between the activities performed in an organization.

Walt Disney and other film producers in the development of plots for animated films. More recently, storyboarding has been used by advertising agencies in developing event sequences for TV commercials.

Storyboarding provides a powerful tool for collecting and organizing the data needed in an ABC project. Aerotech's ABC project team used storyboarding very effectively to study each of the firm's activity cost pools. The team concluded that receiving and inspection costs were driven by the number of shipments received and inspected. Material-handling costs were driven by the number of times materials and partially completed units were moved, and by the length of time they remained in storage between production operations. Quality-assurance costs were driven by the number of production lots to be tested and the complexity of the product being tested. Packaging and shipping costs were driven by the number of production runs to be packed and the number of shipments made, in addition to the total number of circuit boards being shipped.

In summary, the ABC project team conducted painstaking and lengthy analysis involving many employee interviews, the examination of hundreds of documents, and storyboarding sessions. The final result was the data used in the ABC calculations displayed in Exhibit 5–10.

"We wanted the front-line managers involved, so we took the original activity dictionary to them to validate. This step was key to getting an accurate activity dictionary. It was also essential to gaining additional buy-in for the project." (5d)
John Deere Health Care, Inc.

Multidisciplinary ABC Project Teams In order to gather information from all facets of an organization's operations, it is essential to involve personnel from a variety of functional areas. A typical ABC project team includes accounting and finance people as well as engineers, marketing personnel, production and operations managers, and so forth. A multidisciplinary project team not only designs a better ABC system but also helps in gaining credibility for the new system throughout the organization.

Activity Dictionary and Bill of Activities

Many organizations' ABC teams compile an **activity dictionary,** which is a complete listing of the activities identified and used in the ABC analysis. An activity dictionary helps in the implementation of activity-based costing across several divisions of an organization, because it provides for consistency in the ABC system terminology and the complexity of the ABC analyses in the various divisions.

A **bill of activities** is another commonly used element in an ABC analysis. A bill of activities for a product or service is a complete listing of the activities required for the product or service to be produced. As a familiar analogy, think about a recipe for chocolate chip cookies. The *bill of materials* for the cookies is the list of ingredients provided in the recipe. The *bill of activities* is the list of steps given in the recipe for making the cookies (e.g., combine ingredients in a bowl, stir in chocolate chips, place spoon-size globs of dough on greased cookie sheet, bake at 375° for 10 minutes or until done).

"Having a plant-level activity dictionary allows the plant to manage its activities locally and serves as a standard reference that employees can use to see which activities roll up into which processes." (5e)
Navistar International Corporation

Direct versus Indirect Costs

In traditional, volume-based costing systems, only direct material and direct labor are considered direct costs. All other production costs are lumped together in one (or a few) overhead cost pool and applied to products on the basis of a volume-related measure such as direct labor. Thus, all of these costs are treated as indirect costs with respect to the firm's products. In contrast, under an activity-based costing system, an effort is made to account for as many costs as possible as direct costs of production. Any cost that can possibly be traced to a particular product line is treated as a direct cost of that product. A good example is setup time in Aerotech's Phoenix plant. Under the traditional costing system, the cost of setup time is included in manufacturing overhead and applied to products on the basis of direct-labor hours. Under the activity-based costing system, setup time is measured for each product line, and setup costs are assigned as *direct costs* to each type of circuit board.

When Is a New Product-Costing System Needed?

The redesign of a firm's product-costing system is a significant decision that requires the approval of top management and involves a major effort to accomplish. For this reason, many organizations shy away from such a major change. Yet most organizations that have implemented activity-based costing have found the benefits to be well worth the costs. Nevertheless, it bears emphasizing that designing an optimal information system involves trade-offs between the costs and benefits of increased accuracy. Exhibit 5–13 depicts this trade-off graphically. The optimal information system minimizes the total cost of designing, implementing, and maintaining the system, along with the costs of inferior decisions caused by faulty information.[5]

> "We were negotiating fees, and the customer was under the impression that they were paying more than they should. . . . To make this customer comfortable with the pricing, we needed a [more accurate] costing system." (5f)
>
> **Dana Commercial Credit Corporation**

Indicators for ABC When should management consider incurring the considerable cost of designing and implementing an activity-based costing system? Some indicators can signal the need for a new costing system.[6]

- Line managers do not believe the product costs reported by the accounting department.

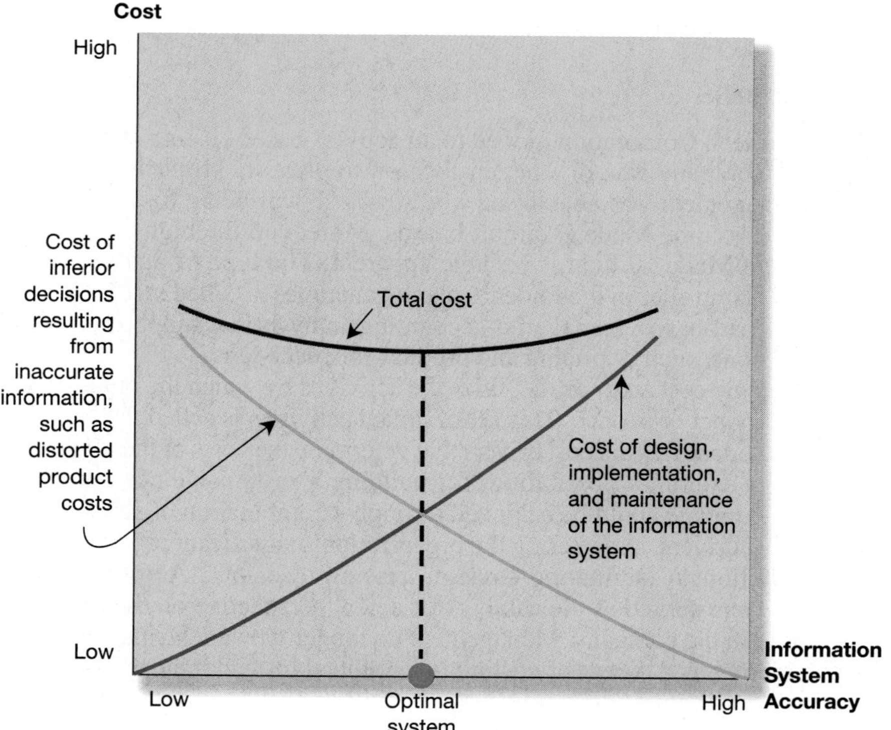

Exhibit 5–13
The Optimal Product-Costing System: A Cost-Benefit Trade-Off

[5]See Robin Cooper, "The Rise of Activity-Based Costing—Part Two: When Do I Need an Activity-Based Costing System?" *Journal of Cost Management* 2, no. 3 (Fall 1988), pp. 41–48.

[6]Robin Cooper, "Does Your Company Need a New Cost System?" *Journal of Cost Management* 1, no. 1 (Spring 1987), pp. 45–49, and Robin Cooper, "You Need a New Costing System When . . . ," *Harvard Business Review* 67, no. 1 (1989), pp. 77–82. See also Peter B. B. Turney, *Common Cents: The ABC Performance Breakthrough* (Hillsboro, OR: Cost Technology, 1991).

- Marketing personnel are unwilling to use reported product costs in making pricing decisions.
- Complex products that are difficult to manufacture are reported to be very profitable, although they are not priced at a premium.
- Product-line profit margins are difficult to explain.
- Sales are increasing, but profits are declining.
- Line managers suggest that apparently profitable products be dropped.
- Marketing or production managers are using "bootleg costing systems," which are informal systems they designed, often on a personal computer.
- Some products that have reported high profit margins are not sold by competitors.
- The firm seems to have captured a highly profitable product niche all for itself.
- Overhead rates are very high, and increasing over time.
- Product lines are diverse.
- Direct labor is a small percentage of total costs.
- The results of bids are difficult to explain.
- Competitors' high-volume products seem to be priced unrealistically low.
- The accounting department spends significant amounts of time on special costing projects to support bids or pricing decisions.

Cost Management Systems

Describe the key features of a cost management system, including the elimination of non-value-added costs.

When Aerotech Corporation moved to an activity-based costing system in its Phoenix plant, the company was in a better position to price its products competitively. The firm's management was able to see why Aerotech was being forced to lower the price on its high-volume Mode II circuit boards. Moreover, the high cost of the complex, low-volume Mode III boards became apparent. The type of analysis undertaken by Aerotech's controller in the Phoenix plant sometimes is called **strategic cost analysis.** This is a broad-based, managerial-accounting analysis that supports strategic management decisions, such as pricing and product-mix decisions.

A strategic cost analysis identifies the activities by which the organization creates a valuable product or service. This set of linked activities is called the *value chain.* Then the analysis identifies the cost drivers that determine the costs of these activities. Finally, the analysis examines possibilities for building a sustainable competitive advantage. Such an advantage could be achieved through a combination of strategic pricing, controlling cost drivers, and altering the organization's significant production activities.[7]

In addition to facilitating strategic pricing decisions, Aerotech's new product-costing system served as the catalyst for a new perspective on the role of managerial accounting in the company. Management no longer viewed the managerial-accounting system merely as a means of costing its products. Instead, management came to view the firm's managerial-accounting function as a **cost management system (CMS).** A cost management system is a management planning and control system with the following objectives.[8]

---

[7]Vijay Govindarajan and John K. Shank, "Strategic Cost Analysis: The Crown Cork and Seal Case," *Journal of Cost Management* 2, no. 4 (Winter 1989), p. 6.

[8]Callie Berliner and James A. Brimson, *Cost Management for Today's Advanced Manufacturing* (Boston: Harvard Business School Press, 1988), pp. 3, 10, 13–15.

- To measure the cost of the resources consumed in performing the organization's significant *activities*.
- To identify and eliminate **non-value-added costs.** These are the costs of *activities* that can be eliminated with no deterioration of product quality, performance, or perceived value.
- To determine the efficiency and effectiveness of all major *activities* performed in the enterprise.
- To identify and evaluate new *activities* that can improve the future performance of the organization.

A cost management system takes a more comprehensive role in an organization than a traditional cost-accounting system. "While cost accounting takes an historical perspective and focuses on reporting costs, cost management takes a proactive role in planning, managing and reducing costs."[9]

Non-Value-Added Costs

The emphasis of a cost management system on activities can help management to identify non-value-added costs and eliminate the activities that cause them. To see how this might occur, let's return to our illustration of Aerotech Corporation's Phoenix plant. How is the time spent in Aerotech's production process from the moment raw material arrives at the Phoenix plant until a finished circuit board is shipped to a customer? As in most manufacturing operations, the time is spent in the following five ways.

- *Process time:* The time during which a product is undergoing conversion activity.
- *Inspection time:* The amount of time spent ensuring that the product is of high quality.
- *Move time:* The time spent moving raw materials, work in process, or finished goods between operations.
- *Waiting time:* The amount of time that raw materials or work in process spend waiting for the next operation.
- *Storage time:* The time during which materials, partially completed products, or finished goods are held in stock before further processing or shipment to customers.

Keep these five types of activities in mind as you reexamine the layout of Aerotech's Phoenix plant (Exhibit 5–1). **Process time** is the amount of time the circuit boards actually are being worked on in one of the production operations (departments 1 through 6) or the packaging operation (department 9). **Inspection time** is the time spent on the bed-of-nails or burn-in testing procedures (departments 7 and 8). **Move time** includes the following activities: receiving raw materials and moving them into storage; moving raw materials and components to the axial-lead sequencing operation (department 1) or the two hand-insertion operations (departments 3 and 6); moving partially completed products from one department to the next; and moving packaged circuit boards to finished-goods storage. **Waiting time** includes the time that partially completed circuit boards spend in the holding areas located next to each department waiting for the next production operation. **Storage time** includes the time spent by raw materials and parts in storage, and the time spent by packaged circuit boards in finished-goods storage.

---

[9]Ibid., p. 3.

Identifying Non-Value-Added Costs in the Phoenix Plant

Can you identify any activities in Exhibit 5–1 that potentially could result in non-value-added costs? The identification of non-value-added activities will vary from company to company, but each of the five types of activities mentioned above has at least some potential for causing non-value-added costs.

Storage Time Perhaps the most obvious is storage time. Manufacturers traditionally have stored large inventories of materials, parts, and finished goods in order to avoid running out. In recent years, however, that philosophy has been challenged. More and more manufacturers are adopting a *just-in-time* approach, where nothing is purchased or produced until it is needed. In Aerotech's Phoenix operation, the large amounts of space devoted to storage activities are indicative of potentially large non-value-added costs of storage.

Waiting Time Refer again to Exhibit 5–1. Notice the large amount of space devoted in the factory to partially completed circuit boards waiting for the next operation. This is again indicative of potentially large non-value-added costs. The firm's working capital is tied up in work in process, and space is unnecessarily wasted on numerous production queues.

Move Time Think about the amount of time Aerotech's Phoenix employees must spend just moving materials and products around in the plant. Every product must be moved 17 times between the axial-lead sequencing operation (department 1) and finished-goods storage. In addition, raw materials and parts must be moved to three different production operations (departments 1, 3, and 6). Once again, we find the potential for significant non-value-added costs associated with the Phoenix plant's material-handling operations.

Inspection Time Aerotech employs three inspection operations. As Exhibit 5–1 indicates, raw materials and components are inspected upon arrival. Later, the circuit boards are tested in the bed-of-nails procedure (department 7) and the burn-in test (department 8). It is difficult to say whether inspection procedures result in non-value-added costs without detailed knowledge of the production technology and inspection procedures. Certainly some type of inspection is necessary to assure product quality. However, many manufacturers are striving to reduce the costs of maintaining product quality and virtually eliminate the costs of reworking defective products.

Process Time The actual production process that transforms raw material into finished products is certainly a value-added activity *overall*. However, this does not preclude the possibility that some non-value-added activities exist within the overall production process. The goal of the cost management system is to evaluate the efficiency of every part of the production process. Is each step necessary? Is each operation being accomplished in the most efficient way? Should some production operations be outsourced?

Conclusion Aerotech's management concluded that substantial non-value-added costs were being incurred in the Phoenix operation. The following activities were identified in a memo from Aerotech's president to key management personnel.

- *Storage:* A considerable reduction in storage space and time is both possible and essential.
- *Waiting:* Circuit boards should be processed through each operation only as they are required in the subsequent operation. Thus, the amount of time products spend waiting for the next operation should be virtually eliminated.
- *Moving:* The time devoted to moving raw material and work in process is excessive. Ways must be found to reduce the costs of these material-handling activities.
- *Inspection:* The bed-of-nails and burn-in tests appear to be necessary and efficiently conducted. Nevertheless, management should continually reassess the need for these inspection operations.
- *Processing:* The manual insertion of components in departments 3 and 6 can be performed by industrial robots. The desirability of this change should be explored.

We will study the elimination of non-value-added costs further in the next chapter.

Activity-Based Costing in the Service Industry

We conclude this chapter with the important point that activity-based costing has found widespread usage in the service industry as well as in manufacturing. There have been many ABC success stories in such diverse organizations as airlines, insurance companies, banks, hospitals, financial services firms, hotels, and railroads. The overall objectives of ABC in service firms are no different than they are in manufacturing companies. Managers want more accurate information about the cost of producing the services they are selling. Moreover, they want to use this information to improve operations and to better meet the needs of their customers in a more cost-effective manner. The general approach of identifying activities, activity cost pools, and cost drivers may be used in the service industry as well as in manufacturing. The classification of activities into unit-level, batch-level, product-sustaining level, and facility-level activities also applies in service industry settings. For example Pennsylvania Blue Shield used these activity classifications in its ABC system.[10] Examples from the Blue Shield system are as follows:

> "As bankers become more familiar with the [ABC] numbers and start to embrace them, their decision making improves, their profitability increases, and the growth of the business improves." (5g)
>
> **Summit Bancorp**

- *Unit level:* Entering initial claim data into the computer (for each claim received).
- *Batch level:* Moving a batch of claims from one processing step to the next.
- *Product-sustaining level:* Maintenance of the medical-services provider network (i.e., maintaining relationships with physicians and hospitals providing medical care to claimants).
- *Facility (general operations) level:* General administration of the claims business unit.

> "The need for better information about product costs for managed care led BCBSNC to an ABM [activity-based management] pilot project." (5h)
>
> **BlueCross BlueShield of North Carolina**

[10]Angela Norkiewicz, "Nine Steps to Implementing ABC," *Management Accounting* 75, no. 10 (April 1994), pp. 28–33.

Management Accounting Practice

DSL Client Services

ACTIVITY-BASED COSTING IN THE SERVICE INDUSTRY

"DSL Client Services is a marketing consulting company specializing in mobile event marketing programs using large-scale exhibit properties. DSL develops, implements, and operates turnkey event marketing programs from start to finish for its clients, which include Sony Electronics and Microsoft among others."[11] DSL uses activity-based costing to "obtain an accurate view of the cost-generating activities undertaken by DSL in producing its marketing programs." Then DSL management uses the ABC data for pricing and bidding on marketing programs for its clients. Some of the activities and cost drivers identified by DSL's ABC analysis are displayed in the following table. For example, the cost of scheduling marketing tours is driven by (i.e., depends on) the number of schedule changes. The cost of answering phones is driven by the number of calls. The cost of approving accounts payable is driven by the number of bills processed.

Activity	*Cost driver*
Tour scheduling	Number of schedule changes
Client inventory monitoring (at DSL)	Number of outgoing shipments
Premium inventory	Number of events/number of premiums used
Web page creation	Number of events/days
Web page database cleaning	Number of input errors
Check writing	Number of bills per month
DSL invoice copying and filing	Number of clients
Travel planning	Number of trips/level of travel
Phone answering	Number of calls
Program development	Number of programs/complexity
Exhibit building	Complexity of program
Exhibit maintenance and repair	Number of problems
Exhibit upgrades	Number of product upgrades
Technical support/on-site staff supervision	Number of problems
Event scheduling/review and approval	Number of events
New business solicitation	Number of prospective clients
Client liaison	Number of clients/level of involvement
Event planning/scheduling	Number of events/number of changes
Event evaluation and reporting	Number of events/trips
Expense report generation	Number of business trips
Strategic marketing planning: program development	Number of and complexity of programs
Schedule/event approval	Number of events
Budget monitoring and reporting	Number of programs
Accounts payable approval	Number of bills processed
Accounts receivable approval	Number of clients

[11]Barb Gauharou, "Activity-Based Costing at DSL Client Services," *Management Accounting Quarterly,* Summer 2000, pp. 4–11.

Focus on Ethics

ETHICAL ISSUES SURROUNDING ACTIVITY-BASED COSTING

The cost study conducted by Aerotech's ABC team seemed to go quite smoothly, as reported in the chapter. Nevertheless, the implications of the analysis are quite significant. When major changes are needed, things don't always go that smoothly. Consider the following hypothetical meeting involving Kristin Scott, Aerotech's president (P), Chuck Dickens, the controller (C), and Tom Reston, the Mode III product line manager (M).

Scott (P): "Chuck, the ABC analysis that you and your team put together was a terrific effort. I was shocked at how inaccurate our product costs were."

Dickens (C): "I must admit that I was pretty surprised myself. From what I've read, though, our experience isn't all that unusual. Most companies adopting ABC find a lot of cost distortion."

Scott (P): "Cost distortion?"

Dickens (C): "Cost distortion is the shifting of costs from one product line to another. In our case, our high-volume products—the Mode I and Mode II boards—were subsidizing the Mode III board, making it appear to be profitable when it wasn't."

Scott (P): "Well, it's certainly no wonder that we were losing bids right and left on the Mode IIs."

Dickens (C): "Yeah, and it also explains why we were easily getting orders for the Mode IIIs. At that price, we were losing our shirt!"

Scott (P): "So what do you think we should do? Before I ask Tom Reston to come in, I'd like your opinion."

Dickens (C): "Well it's clear that we can lower our target price on the Mode II boards to $328, which is what we were getting anyway. As for the Mode I boards, we can either keep the current price of $261.25, or reduce it to the new target of $229.30."

Scott (P): "Why do that if we can get the higher price?"

Dickens (C): "We'd probably sell more at the lower price. Whether it'd be enough more to justify the lower price, I don't know."

Scott (P): "What about the Mode IIIs?"

Dickens (C): "Well, we either drastically increase the price, or we discontinue the line."

Scott (P): "That's a dilemma, Chuck. I'm not convinced that we can get your new target price of, what was it, around $489? And, if we discontinue the line, we're shooting ourselves in the foot."

Dickens (C): "How so?"

Scott (P): "Our bonuses, Chuck! They're tied to our sales revenue. If we jettison a whole product line, I think we'll lose sales on the Mode I and II boards, too, and our revenue will go down."

Dickens (C): "Well, that could be a legitimate concern, but I don't think it's right to carry a line at a huge loss, just to increase our bonuses. And besides, the decline would be temporary. Eventually, we'd fill that capacity with a new product."

Scott (P): "That would take a while, though. I'm also concerned about the impact on Tom Reston. After all, we just hired him a year ago to manage the Mode III line. Let's see what he has to say."

Scott phones Reston, and asks him to join the meeting.

Scott (P): "You've seen the ABC analysis, Tom. What do you think?"

Reston (M): "Frankly, I don't buy it! A product doesn't go from very profitable to very unprofitable overnight."

Dickens (C): "You're missing the point, Tom. The ABC analysis shows that the Mode III wasn't profitable to begin with."

Reston (M): "I've studied your analysis, Chuck. I simply don't buy some of the cost driver estimates. I don't believe that 40 percent of our quality assurance activity is for the Mode IIIs. They do require inspections, but they're quick and straightforward. And I especially question the 63 percent of material-handling activity on the Mode III line. That can't be right. Where'd you get those estimates anyway?"

Dickens (C): "We began by interviewing the department heads. Then we followed up by looking at the number of inspections on each product line, the number of purchase orders, material requisitions. That sort of thing."

Reston (M): "The Mode III inspections are numerous but quick. I'll bet you'd get different results if you used the number of inspection hours instead of the number of inspections. Looks to me like you can manipulate the results by how you choose the cost drivers. And another thing I can tell you is that those two department heads are always complaining about the Mode IIIs. How much of their own time they take, and so on. I think they skewed those estimates up to make the Mode III line look like a loser."

Dickens (C): "You really think they would do that intentionally, Tom? That wouldn't exactly be ethical!"

Reston (M): "Intentional or unintentional? I don't know. I just don't believe the numbers. And if you want to get into ethics, where's the ethics in hiring me to manage a supposedly highly profitable product line—to give it a higher profile you said—and then a year later you tell me the product's a dog! And it's not just me either. What about the people who work on that line?"

Scott (P): "Okay, okay, gentlemen! Relax. Tom, I can see why you're upset. Chuck, let's recheck these numbers. If we have to take drastic action, we need to make sure we're right."

Dickens (C): "I agree. We'll go over everything again, and we'll collect more data on the two departments Tom's worried about. Tom, how about joining our ABC team?"

What ethical issues do you see in this scenario? How would you resolve them?

Chapter Summary

Sweeping changes are revolutionizing the manufacturing industry. Global competition coupled with rapid technological innovation are changing manufacturing in a dramatic way. Along with manufacturing systems, the role of managerial accounting is changing also. Many firms are moving from a traditional cost-accounting approach toward a more proactive cost management system perspective. A cost management system (CMS) measures the cost of significant activities, identifies non-value-added costs, and identifies activities that will improve organizational performance. The CMS emphasis on activities helps a company gain a competitive edge by facilitating production of a high-quality product at the lowest cost possible.

As the manufacturing environment has changed, many managers have come to believe that traditional, volume-based product-costing systems do not accurately reflect product costs. Product-costing systems structured on single, volume-based cost drivers, such as direct labor or machine hours, often tend to overcost high-volume products and undercost low-volume or complex products. These cost distortions can have serious effects on pricing and other decisions. To alleviate these problems, more and more firms are adopting an activity-based costing system based on multiple cost drivers. Such costing systems provide better information for strategic management decisions and help in the identification of non-value-added costs.

Activity-based costing has also found widespread successful implementation in the service industry.

Review Problem on Cost Drivers and Product-Cost Distortion

Edgeworth Box Corporation manufactures a variety of special packaging boxes used in the pharmaceutical industry. The company's Dallas plant is semiautomated, but the special nature of the boxes requires some manual labor. The controller has chosen the following activity cost pools, cost drivers, and pool rates for the Dallas plant's product-costing system.

Activity Cost Pool	Overhead Cost	Cost Driver	Budgeted Level for Cost Driver	Pool Rate
Purchasing, storage, and material handling	$ 200,000	Raw-material costs	$1,000,000	20% of material cost
Engineering and product design	100,000	Hours in design department	5,000 hr.	$20 per hour
Machine setup costs	70,000	Production runs	1,000 runs	$70 per run
Machine depreciation and maintenance	300,000	Machine hours	100,000 hr.	$3 per hour
Factory depreciation, taxes, insurance, and utilities	200,000	Machine hours	100,000 hr.	$2 per hour
Other manufacturing-overhead costs	150,000	Machine hours	100,000 hr.	$1.50 per hour
Total	$1,020,000			

Two recent production orders had the following requirements.

	20,000 Units of Box C52	10,000 Units of Box W29
Direct-labor hours	42 hr.	21 hr.
Raw-material cost	$40,000	$35,000
Hours in design department	10	25
Production runs	2	4
Machine hours	24	20

Required

1. Compute the total overhead that should be assigned to each of the two production orders, C52 and W29.
2. Compute the overhead cost per box in each order.
3. Suppose the Dallas plant were to use a single predetermined overhead rate based on direct-labor hours. The direct-labor budget calls for 4,000 hours.

a. Compute the predetermined overhead rate per direct-labor hour.

b. Compute the total overhead cost that would be assigned to the order for box C52 and the order for box W29.

c. Compute the overhead cost per box in each order.

4. Why do the two product-costing systems yield such widely differing overhead costs per box?

Solution to Review Problem

1.

	Box C52	Box W29
Purchasing, storage, and material handling	$8,000 (20% × $40,000)	$7,000 (20% × $35,000)
Engineering and product design	200 (10 × $20/hr.)	500 (25 × $20/hr.)
Machine setup costs	140 (2 × $70/run)	280 (4 × $70/run)
Machine depreciation and maintenance	72 (24 × $3/hr.)	60 (20 × $3/hr.)
Factory depreciation, taxes, insurance, and utilities	48 (24 × $2/hr.)	40 (20 × $2/hr.)
Other manufacturing overhead costs	36 (24 × $1.50/hr.)	30 (20 × $1.50/hr.)
Total overhead assigned to production order	$8,496	$7,910

2. Overhead cost per box: $.4248 per box $\left(\frac{\$8{,}496}{20{,}000}\right)$ $.791 per box $\left(\frac{\$7{,}910}{10{,}000}\right)$

3. Computations based on a single predetermined overhead rate based on direct-labor hours:

a. $\frac{\text{Total budgeted overhead}}{\text{Total budgeted direct-labor hours}} = \frac{\$1{,}020{,}000}{4{,}000} = \$255/\text{hr.}$

b. Total overhead assigned to each order:

Box C52 order: 42 direct-labor hours × $255/hr. = $10,710

Box W29 order: 21 direct-labor hours × $255/hr. = $5,355

c. Overhead cost per box:

Box C52: $10,710 ÷ 20,000 = $.5355 per box

Box W29: $5,355 ÷ 10,000 = $.5355 per box

4. The widely differing overhead costs are assigned as a result of the inherent inaccuracy of the single, volume-based overhead rate. The relative usage of direct labor by the two production orders does not reflect their relative usage of other manufacturing support services.

Key Terms

For each term's definition refer to the indicated page, or turn to the glossary at the end of the text.

activity-based costing (ABC) system, 172
activity-cost pool, 172
activity dictionary, 186
batch-level activity, 172
bill of activities, 186
consumption ratio, 181
cost driver, 182
cost management system (CMS), 188
facility- (or general-operations-) level activity, 173
homogeneous cost pool, 184
inspection time, 189
move time, 189
non-value-added costs, 189
pool rate, 174
process (or functional) plant layout, 169
process time, 189
product-sustaining-level activity, 173
storage time, 189
storyboarding, 185
strategic cost analysis, 188
unit-level activity, 172
volume-based (or throughput-based) costing system, 171
waiting time, 189

Review Questions

5–1. Briefly explain how a traditional, volume-based product-costing system operates.

5–2. Why was Aerotech Corporation's management being misled by the traditional product-costing system? What mistakes were being made?

5–3. Explain how an activity-based costing system operates.

5–4. What are cost drivers? What is their role in an activity-based costing system?

5–5. List and briefly describe the four broad categories of activities identified in stage one of an activity-based costing system.

5–6. How can an activity-based costing system alleviate the problems Aerotech was having under its traditional, volume-based product-costing system?

5–7. Why do product-costing systems based on a single, volume-based cost driver tend to overcost high-volume products? What undesirable strategic effects can such distortion of product costs have?

5–8. How is the distinction between direct and indirect costs handled differently under volume-based versus activity-based costing systems?

5–9. List four objectives of a cost management system.

5–10. What is meant by the term *non-value-added costs?* Give four examples.

5–11. List and define the five ways that time is spent in a manufacturing process. Which of these types of activities are likely candidates for non-value-added activities? Why?

5–12. Briefly explain two factors that tend to result in product cost distortion under traditional, volume-based product-costing systems.

5–13. List three factors that are important in selecting cost drivers for an ABC system.

5–14. What is meant by a *homogeneous cost pool?*

5–15. What is the role of an *activity dictionary* in an ABC project?

5–16. Explain briefly why multidisciplinary ABC project teams are used.

5–17. List eight indicators that suggest management should consider implementing a new product-costing system.

5–18. Explain why a new product-costing system may be needed when line managers suggest that an apparently profitable product be dropped.

5–19. Explain why a manufacturer with diverse product lines may benefit from an ABC system.

5–20. Are activity-based costing systems appropriate for the service industry? Explain.

5–21. Explain why the maintenance of the medical-services provider network is treated as a product-sustaining-level activity by Pennsylvania Blue Shield.

Exercises

Exercise 5–22
Volume-Based Cost Driver versus ABC
(LO 2, 3, 4)

Precision Lens Company manufactures sophisticated lenses and mirrors used in large optical telescopes. The company is now preparing its annual profit plan. As part of its analysis of the profitability of individual products, the controller estimates the amount of overhead that should be allocated to the individual product lines from the following information.

	Mirrors	Lenses
Units produced	30	30
Material moves per product line	4	16
Direct-labor hours per unit	250	250

The total budgeted material-handling cost is $90,000.

Required:

1. Under a costing system that allocates overhead on the basis of direct-labor hours, the material-handling costs allocated to one mirror would be what amount?
2. Answer the same question as in requirement (1), but for lenses.
3. Under activity-based costing (ABC), the material-handling costs allocated to one mirror would be what amount? The cost driver for the material-handling activity is the number of material moves.
4. Answer the same question as in requirement (3), but for lenses.

(CMA, adapted)

Exercise 5–23
Cost Drivers; Activity Cost Pools
(LO 3, 5)

Digitech, Ltd. manufactures various computer components in its Tokyo plant. The following costs are budgeted for January. (Yen is the Japanese monetary unit.)

Insurance, plant	780,000 *yen*
Electricity, machinery	156,000
Electricity, light	78,000
Engineering design	793,000
Depreciation, plant	910,000
Depreciation, machinery	1,820,000
Custodial wages, plant	52,000
Equipment maintenance, wages	195,000
Equipment maintenance, parts	39,000
Setup wages	52,000
Inspection	39,000
Property taxes	156,000
Natural gas, heating	39,000
Raw materials and components	3,835,000

Required: Divide these costs into activity cost pools, and identify a cost driver for assigning each pool of costs to products.

Exercise 5–24
Categorizing Activity Cost Pools
(LO 3)

Refer to the information given in the preceding exercise. For each of the activity cost pools identified, indicate whether it represents a unit-level, batch-level, product-sustaining level, or facility-level activity.

Exercise 5–25
Activity-Based Costing; Quality Control Costs
(LO 2, 3, 4)

Rainbow Spray Paints, Inc. has used a traditional cost accounting system to apply quality-control costs uniformly to all products at a rate of 16 percent of direct-labor cost. Monthly direct-labor cost for the enamel paint line is $98,000. In an attempt to more equitably distribute quality-control costs, Rainbow is considering activity-based costing. The monthly data shown in the following chart have been gathered for the enamel paint line.

Activity Cost Pool	Cost Driver	Pool Rates	Quantity of Driver for Enamel Paint
Incoming material inspection	Type of material	$ 23.00 per type	24 types
In-process inspection	Number of units	.28 per unit	35,000 units
Product certification	Per order	144.00 per order	50 orders

Required:

1. Calculate the monthly quality-control cost to be assigned to the enamel paint line under each of the following product-costing systems.
   a. Traditional system which assigns overhead on the basis of direct-labor cost.
   b. Activity-based costing.
2. Does the traditional product-costing system overcost or undercost the enamel paint line with respect to quality-control costs? By what amount?

(CMA, adapted)

Exercise 5–26
Distortion of Product Costs
(LO 4, 5)

Wheelco, Inc. manufactures automobile and truck wheels. The company produces four basic, high-volume wheels used by each of the large automobile and pickup truck manufacturers. Wheelco also has two specialty wheel lines. These are fancy, complicated wheels used in expensive sports cars.

Lately, Wheelco's profits have been declining. Foreign competitors have been undercutting Wheelco's prices in three of its bread-and-butter product lines, and Wheelco's sales volume and market share have declined. In contrast, Wheelco's specialty wheels have been selling steadily, although in relatively small numbers, in spite of three recent price increases. At a recent staff meeting, Wheelco's president made the following remarks: "Our profits are going down the tubes, folks. It costs us 31 dollars to manufacture our DC16 wheel. That's our best seller, with a volume last year of 19,000 units. But our chief competitor is selling basically the same wheel for 28 bucks. I don't see how they can do it. I think it's just one more example of foreign dumping. I'm going to write my senator about it! Thank goodness for our specialty wheels. I think we've got to get our sales people to push those wheels more and more. Take the JY16 model, for example. It's a complicated thing to make, and we don't sell many. But look at the profit margin. Those wheels cost us 52 dollars to make, and we're selling them for 110 bucks each."

Required: What do you think is behind the problems faced by Wheelco? Comment on the president's remarks. Do you think his strategy is a good one? What do you recommend, and why?

Exercise 5–27
Key Features of Activity-Based Costing
(LO 3, 4, 5)

Refer to the description given for Wheelco, Inc. in the preceding exercise. Suppose the firm's president has decided to implement an activity-based costing system.

Required:

1. List and briefly describe the key features that Wheelco's new product-costing system should have.
2. What impact will the new system be likely to have on the company's situation?
3. What strategic options would you expect to be suggested by the product-costing results from the new system?

Exercise 5–28
Winery; Classification of Activities
(LO 3)

Seneca Falls Winery is a small, family-run operation in upstate New York. The winery produces two varieties of wine: riesling and chardonnay. Among the activities engaged in by the winery are the following:

1. *Trimming:*	At the end of a growing season, the vines are trimmed, which helps prepare them for the next harvest.
2. *Tying:*	The vines are tied onto wires to help protect them from the cold. (This also occurs at the end of the season.)
3. *Hilling:*	Dirt is piled up around the roots to help protect them from frost.
4. *Conditioning:*	After the snow melts in the spring, dirt is leveled back from the roots.
5. *Untying:*	The vines are untied from the wires to allow them freedom to grow during the spring and summer months.
6. *Chemical spraying:*	The vines are sprayed in the spring to protect them from disease and insects.
7. *Harvesting:*	All of the grapes of both varieties are picked by hand to minimize damage.
8. *Stemming and crushing:*	Batches of grapes are hand-loaded into a machine, which gently removes the stems and mildly crushes them.
9. *Pressing:*	After removal from the stemmer/crusher, the juice runs freely from the grapes.
10. *Filtering:*	The grapes are crushed mechanically to render more juice from them.
11. *Fermentation:*	The riesling grape juice is placed in stainless steel tanks for fermentation. The chardonnay grape juice undergoes a two-stage fermentation process in oak barrels.
12. *Aging:*	The riesling wines are aged in the stainless steel tanks for approximately a year. The chardonnays are aged in the oak barrels for about two years.
13. *Bottling:*	A machine bottles the wine and corks the bottles.
14. *Labeling:*	Each bottle is manually labeled with the name of the vintner, vintage, and variety.
15. *Packing:*	The bottles are manually packed in 12-bottle cases.
16. *Case labeling:*	The cases are hand-stamped with the same information that the bottles received.
17. *Shipping:*	The wine is shipped to wine distributors and retailers, mainly in central New York. Generally, about 100 cases are shipped at a time.
18. *Maintenance on buildings:*	This is done during the slow winter months.
19. *Maintenance on equipment:*	This is done when needed, and on a routine basis for preventive maintenance.

Required: Classify each of the activities listed as a unit, batch, product-sustaining, or facility-level activity.

Exercise 5–29
ABC; Selling Costs
(LO 2, 3, 4)

Zodiac Model Rocketry Company sells model rocketry kits and supplies to retail outlets and through its catalog. Some of the items are manufactured by Zodiac, while others are purchased for resale. For the products it manufactures, the company currently bases its selling prices on a product-costing system that accounts for direct material, direct labor, and the associated overhead costs. In addition to these product costs, Zodiac incurs substantial selling costs, and Jack Maxey, controller, has suggested that these selling costs should be included in the product pricing structure.

After studying the costs incurred over the past two years for one of its products, rocket motors, Maxey has selected four categories of selling costs and chosen cost drivers for each of these costs. The selling costs actually incurred during the past year and the cost drivers are as follows:

Cost Category	Amount	Cost Driver
Sales commissions	$ 675,000	Boxes of rocket motors sold to retail stores
Catalogs	295,400	Catalogs distributed
Costs of catalog sales	105,000	Rocket motors sold through catalogs
Credit and collection	60,000	Number of retail orders
Total selling costs	$1,135,400	

The rocket motors are sold to retail outlets in boxes, each containing 12 motors. The sale of partial boxes is not permitted. Commissions are paid on sales to retail outlets but not on catalog sales. The cost of catalog sales includes telephone costs and the wages of personnel who take the catalog orders. Maxey believes that the selling costs vary significantly with the size of the order. Order sizes are divided into three categories as follows:

Order Size	Catalog Sales	Retail Sales
Small	1–10 rocket motors	1–10 boxes of motors
Medium	11–20 rocket motors	11–20 boxes of motors
Large	Over 20 rocket motors	Over 20 boxes of motors

An analysis of the previous year's records produced the following statistics.

	Order Size			
	Small	Medium	Large	Total
Retail sales in boxes (12 motors per box)	2,000	45,000	178,000	225,000
Catalog sales in units (i.e., motors)	79,000	52,000	44,000	175,000
Number of retail orders	485	2,415	3,100	6,000
Catalogs distributed	254,300	211,300	125,200	590,800

Required:

1. Prepare a schedule showing Zodiac Model Rocketry Company's total selling cost for each order size and the per-rocket motor selling cost within each order size.
2. Explain how the analysis of the selling costs for rocket motors is likely to impact future pricing and product decisions at Zodiac Model Rocketry Company.

(CMA, adapted)

Exercise 5–30
United Technologies; Classification of Activities
(LO 3, 5)

United Technologies Corporation is using activity-based costing in two of its subsidiaries: Otis Elevator Company and Carrier Corporation. The following table shows 27 activities and eight accounts identified at Carrier, along with the classification determined by the ABC project team.[12]

Name of Activity or Account	Classification by Activity Level	Name of Activity or Account	Classification by Activity Level
Acquiring material	Batch	Maintaining/improving production processes	Sustaining
Inspecting incoming materials	Batch	Managing human resources	Sustaining
Moving materials	Batch	Managing waste disposal	Sustaining
Planning production	Batch	Processing payroll	Sustaining
Processing special orders	Batch	Processing production information	Sustaining
Processing supplier invoices	Batch	Providing product cost	Sustaining
Receiving material	Batch	Setting manufacturing methods	Sustaining
Scheduling production	Batch	Supervising production	Sustaining
Inspecting production processes	Batch	Sustaining accounting	Sustaining
Processing purchase orders	Batch	Maintaining production equipment	Sustaining
Building occupancy	Facility	Direct-labor allowances	Unit
Depreciation	Facility	Direct-labor fringes	Unit
General management	Facility	Utilities (equipment)	Unit
Maintaining facilities	Facility	Overtime (hourly)	Unit
Managing the environment	Facility	Rework	Unit
Assuring quality	Sustaining	Shift differential	Unit
Expediting	Sustaining	Spoilage	Unit
Maintaining tools and dies	Sustaining		

[12]Robert Adams and Ray Carter, "United Technologies' Activity-Based Accounting Is a Catalyst for Success," *As Easy as ABC* 18 (1995), p. 4. United Technologies uses the term "*structural*-level activity," instead of "*facility*-level activity" as we have done in the chapter and in the table presented here.

Required: Choose two activities or accounts from each of the four classifications and explain why you agree or disagree with the ABC project team's classification.

Exercise 5–31
Classification of Activities in a University; Cost Drivers
(LO 3, 5)

As a group, discuss the activities of your college or university (e.g., admission, registration, etc.). List as many activities as you can.

Required: Make a presentation to your class that includes the following:

1. Your list of activities.
2. The classification of each activity (e.g., unit level).
3. An appropriate cost driver for each activity.

Exercise 5–32
Activity-Based Costing in a Government Agency; Use of Internet
(LO 3, 5)

Visit the website of a city, state, or Canadian province of your choosing (e.g., the City of Los Angeles, www.losangeles.com).

Required: Read about the services offered to the public by this governmental unit. Then discuss how activity-based costing could be used effectively by the governmental unit to determine the cost of providing these services.

Problems

Problem 5–33
Activity-Based Costing; Analysis of Operations
(LO 2, 3, 4, 5)

Clark and Shiffer LLP perform activities related to e-commerce consulting and information systems in Vancouver, British Columbia. The firm, which bills $140 per hour for services performed, is in a very tight local labor market and is having difficulty finding quality help for its overworked professional staff. The cost per hour for professional staff time is $50. Selected information follows.

- Billable hours to clients for the year totaled 6,000, consisting of: information systems services, 3,600; e-commerce consulting, 2,400.
- Administrative cost of $381,760 was (and continues to be) allocated to both services based on billable hours. These costs consist of staff support, $207,000; in-house computing, $145,000; and miscellaneous office charges, $29,760.

A recent analysis of staff support costs found a correlation with the number of clients served. In-house computing and miscellaneous office charges varied directly with the number of computer hours logged and number of client transactions, respectively. A tabulation revealed the following data:

	E-Commerce Consulting	Information Systems Services	Total
Number of clients	60	240	300
Number of computer hours	2,100	2,900	5,000
Number of client transactions	720	480	1,200

Required:

1. Activity-based costing (ABC) is said to result in improved costing accuracy when compared with traditional costing procedures. Briefly explain how this improved accuracy is attained.
2. Assume that the firm uses traditional costing procedures, allocating total costs on the basis of billable hours. Determine the profitability of the firm's e-commerce and information systems activities, expressing your answer both in dollars and as a percentage of activity revenue.
3. Repeat requirement (2), using activity-based costing.
4. Stephen Shiffer, one of the firm's partners, doesn't care where his professionals spend their time because, as he notes, "many clients have come to expect both services and we need both to stay in business. Also, information systems and e-commerce professionals are paid the same hourly rate." Should Shiffer's attitude change? Explain.
5. Is an aggressive expansion of either service currently desirable? Briefly discuss.

Problem 5–34
Activity-Based Costing; Cost Distortion; Product Promotion
(LO 2, 3, 4, 5)

Wilmington Office Equipment Corporation manufactures two types of filing cabinets—Deluxe and Executive—and applies manufacturing overhead to all units at the rate of $80 per machine hour. Production information follows.

	Deluxe	Executive
Direct-material cost	$40	$65
Direct-labor cost	25	25
Budgeted volume (units)	16,000	30,000

The controller, who is studying the use of activity-based costing, has determined that the firm's overhead can be identified with three activities: manufacturing setups, machine processing, and product shipping. Data on the number of setups, machine hours, and outgoing shipments, which are the activities' three respective cost drivers, follow.

	Deluxe	Executive	Total
Setups	100	60	160
Machine hours	32,000	45,000	77,000
Outgoing shipments	200	150	350

The firm's total overhead of $6,160,000 is subdivided as follows: manufacturing setups, $1,344,000; machine processing, $3,696,000; and product shipping, $1,120,000.

Required:

1. Compute the unit manufacturing cost of Deluxe and Executive filing cabinets by using the company's current overhead costing procedures.
2. Compute the unit manufacturing cost of Deluxe and Executive filing cabinets by using activity-based costing.
3. Is the cost of the Deluxe filing cabinet overstated or understated (i.e., distorted) by the use of machine hours to allocate total manufacturing overhead to production? By how much?
4. Calculate the aggregate amount by which the Deluxe cabinet line is undercosted by the company's current traditional overhead costing procedures. Then calculate the aggregate amount by which the traditional system overcosts the Executive cabinet line.
5. Assume that the current selling price of a Deluxe filing cabinet is $270 and the marketing manager is contemplating a $30 discount to stimulate volume. Is this discount advisable? Briefly discuss.

Problem 5–35
Overhead Application; Activity-Based Costing
(LO 1, 2, 3, 4, 5)

Digital Light Corporation has just completed a major change in its quality control (QC) process. Previously, products had been reviewed by QC inspectors at the end of each major process, and the company's 10 QC inspectors were charged as direct labor to the operation or job. In an effort to improve efficiency and quality, a computerized video QC system was purchased for $500,000. The system consists of a minicomputer, 15 video cameras, other peripheral hardware, and software. The new system uses cameras stationed by QC engineers at key points in the production process. Each time an operation changes or there is a new operation, the cameras are moved, and a new master picture is loaded into the computer by a QC engineer. The camera takes pictures of the units in process, and the computer compares them to the picture of a "good" unit. Any differences are sent to a QC engineer who removes the bad units and discusses the flaws with the production supervisors. The new system has replaced the 10 QC inspectors with two QC engineers.

The operating costs of the new QC system, including the salaries of the QC engineers, have been included as factory overhead in calculating the company's plantwide manufacturing-overhead rate, which is based on direct-labor dollars. The company's president is confused. His vice president of production has told him how efficient the new system is. Yet there is a large increase in the overhead rate. The computation of the rate before and after automation is as follows:

	Before	After
Budgeted manufacturing overhead	$3,800,000	$4,200,000
Budgeted direct-labor cost	2,000,000	1,400,000
Budgeted overhead rate	190%	300%

"Three hundred percent," lamented the president. "How can we compete with such a high overhead rate?"

Required:

1. a. Define "manufacturing overhead," and cite three examples of typical costs that would be included in manufacturing overhead.
   b. Explain why companies develop predetermined overhead rates.
2. Explain why the increase in the overhead rate should not have a negative financial impact on the company.
3. Explain how management could change its overhead application system to eliminate confusion over product costs.
4. Discuss how an activity-based costing system might benefit Digital Light Corporation.

(CMA, adapted)

Problem 5–36
Activity-Based Costing; Cost Analysis
(LO 2, 3, 4, 5)

Meditech, Inc. manufactures two types of medical devices, Medform and Procel, and applies overhead on the basis of direct-labor hours. Anticipated overhead and direct-labor time for the upcoming accounting period are $710,000 and 20,000 hours, respectively. Information about the company's products follows.

Medform:

Estimated production volume, 2,500 units
Direct-material cost, $30 per unit
Direct labor per unit, 3 hours at $15 per hour

Procel:

Estimated production volume, 3,125 units
Direct-material cost, $45 per unit
Direct labor per unit, 4 hours at $15 per hour

Meditech's overhead of $710,000 can be identified with three major activities: order processing ($120,000), machine processing ($500,000), and product inspection ($90,000). These activities are driven by number of orders processed, machine hours worked, and inspection hours, respectively. Data relevant to these activities follow.

	Orders Processed	Machine Hours Worked	Inspection Hours
Medform	350	23,000	4,000
Procel	250	27,000	11,000
Total	600	50,000	15,000

Management is very concerned about declining profitability despite a healthy increase in sales volume. The decrease in income is especially puzzling because the company recently undertook a massive plant renovation during which new, highly automated machinery was installed—machinery that was expected to produce significant operating efficiencies.

Required:

1. Assuming use of direct-labor hours to apply overhead to production, compute the unit manufacturing costs of the Medform and Procel products if the expected manufacturing volume is attained.
2. Assuming use of activity-based costing, compute the unit manufacturing costs of the Medform and Procel products if the expected manufacturing volume is attained.
3. Meditech's selling prices are based heavily on cost.
   a. By using direct-labor hours as an application base, which product is overcosted and which product is undercosted? Calculate the amount of the cost distortion for each product.
   b. Is it possible that overcosting and undercosting (i.e., cost distortion) and the subsequent determination of selling prices are contributing to the company's profit woes? Explain.

Problem 5–37
Automation; Robotics; Overhead Application; Activity-Based Costing
(LO 2, 3, 4, 5)

John Patrick has recently been hired as controller of Valdosta Vinyl Company (VVC), a manufacturer of vinyl siding used in residential construction. VVC has been in the vinyl siding business for many years and is currently investigating ways to modernize its manufacturing process. At the first staff meeting Patrick attended, Jack Kielshesky, chief engineer, presented a proposal for automating the Molding Department. Kielshesky recommended that the company purchase two robots that would have the capability of replacing the eight direct-labor employees in the department. The cost savings outlined in the

proposal include the elimination of direct-labor cost in the Molding Department plus a reduction of manufacturing overhead cost in the department to zero, because VVC charges manufacturing overhead on the basis of direct-labor dollars using a plantwide rate. The president of VVC was puzzled by Kielshesky's explanation: "This just doesn't make any sense. How can a department's overhead rate drop to zero by adding expensive, high-tech manufacturing equipment? If anything, it seems like the rate ought to go up."

Kielshesky responded by saying "I'm an engineer, not an accountant. But if we're charging overhead on the basis of direct labor, and we eliminate the labor, then we eliminate the overhead."

Patrick agreed with the president. He explained that as firms become more automated, they should rethink their product-costing systems. The president then asked Patrick to look into the matter and prepare a report for the next staff meeting. Patrick gathered the following data on the manufacturing-overhead rates experienced by VVC over the years. Patrick also wanted to have some departmental data to present at the meeting and, by using VVC's accounting records, he was able to estimate the following annual averages for each manufacturing department over the five decades since VVC's formation.

Historical Plantwide Data

Decade	Average Annual Manufacturing-Overhead Cost	Average Annual Direct-Labor Cost	Average Manufacturing-Overhead Application Rate
1st	$ 2,200,000	$2,000,000	110%
2nd	6,240,000	2,400,000	260
3rd	13,600,000	4,000,000	340
4th	24,600,000	6,000,000	410
5th	38,710,000	7,900,000	490

Annual Averages during Recent Years

	Cutting Department	Finishing Department	Molding Department
Manufacturing overhead	$22,000,000	$14,000,000	$4,000,000
Direct labor	4,000,000	3,500,000	500,000

Required:

1. Disregarding the proposed use of robots in the Molding Department, describe the shortcomings of the system for applying overhead that is currently used by Valdosta Vinyl Company.
2. Explain the misconceptions underlying Kielshesky's statement that the manufacturing-overhead cost in the Molding Department will be reduced to zero if the automation proposal is implemented.
3. Recommend ways to improve VVC's method for applying overhead by describing how it should revise its product-costing system for each of the following departments:
   a. In the Cutting and Finishing Departments.
   b. To accommodate automation in the Molding Department.

(CMA, adapted)

Problem 5–38
Activity Cost Pools; Cost Drivers; Pool Rates
(LO 2, 3, 4)

Rapid City Radiology, Inc. manufactures chemicals used in radiological imaging systems. The controller has established the following activity cost pools and cost drivers.

Activity Cost Pool	Budgeted Overhead Cost	Cost Driver	Budgeted Level for Cost Driver	Pool Rate
Machine setups	$1,000,000	Number of setups	250	$4,000 per setup
Material handling	300,000	Weight of raw material	75,000 lb.	$4 per pound
Hazardous waste control	100,000	Weight of hazardous chemicals used	10,000 lb.	$10 per pound
Quality control	300,000	Number of inspections	2,000	$150 per inspection
Other overhead costs	800,000	Machine hours	40,000	$20 per machine hour
Total	$2,500,000			

An order for 1,000 boxes of radiological development chemicals has the following production requirements.

Machine setups	6 setups
Raw material	9,000 pounds
Hazardous materials	2,100 pounds
Inspections	8 inspections
Machine hours	550 machine hours

Required:

1. Compute the total overhead that should be assigned to the development-chemical order.
2. What is the overhead cost per box of chemicals?
3. Suppose Rapid City Radiology, Inc. were to use a single predetermined overhead rate based on machine hours. Compute the rate per hour.
4. Under the approach in requirement (3), how much overhead would be assigned to the development-chemical order?
   a. In total.
   b. Per box of chemicals.
5. Explain why these two product-costing systems result in such widely differing costs. Which system do you recommend? Why?

Problem 5–39
Overhead Cost Drivers
(LO 2, 3, 4)

Refer to the original data given in the preceding problem for Rapid City Radiology, Inc.

Required: Calculate the unit cost of a production order for 100 specially coated plates used in radiological imaging. In addition to direct material costing $210 per plate and direct labor costing $60 per plate, the order requires:

Machine setups	4
Raw material	800 pounds
Hazardous materials	400 pounds
Inspections	4
Machine hours	60

Problem 5–40
Activity-Based Costing; Activity Cost Pools; Pool Rates; Calculation of Product Costs; Cost Distortion
(LO 2, 3, 4, 5)

Knickknack, Inc. manufactures two products: odds and ends. The firm uses a single, plantwide overhead rate based on direct-labor hours. Production and product-costing data are as follows:

	Odds	Ends
Production quantity	1,000 units	5,000 units
Direct material	$160	$240
Direct labor (not including setup time)	120 (4 hr. at $30)	180 (6 hr. at $30)
Manufacturing overhead*	384 (4 hr. at $96)	576 (6 hr. at $96)
Total cost per unit	$664	$996

*Calculation of predetermined overhead rate:

Manufacturing overhead budget:

Machine-related costs	$1,800,000
Setup and inspection	720,000
Engineering	360,000
Plant-related costs	384,000
Total	$3,264,000

Predetermined overhead rate:

$$\frac{\text{Budgeted manufacturing overhead}}{\text{Budgeted direct-labor hours}} = \frac{\$3,264,000}{(1,000)(4) + (5,000)(6)} = \$96 \text{ per direct-labor hour}$$

Knickknack, Inc. prices its products at 120 percent of cost, which yields target prices of $796.80 for odds and $1,195.20 for ends. Recently, however, Knickknack has been challenged in the market for ends by a European competitor, Bricabrac Corporation. A new entrant in this market, Bricabrac has been selling ends for $880 each. Knickknack's president is puzzled by Bricabrac's ability to sell ends at such a low cost.

She has asked you (the controller) to look into the matter. You have decided that Knickknack's traditional, volume-based product-costing system may be causing cost distortion between the firm's two products. Ends are a high-volume, relatively simple product. Odds, on the other hand, are quite complex and exhibit a much lower volume. As a result, you have begun work on an activity-based costing system.

Required:

1. Let each of the overhead categories in the budget represent an activity cost pool. Categorize each in terms of the type of activity (e.g., unit-level activity).
2. The following cost drivers have been identified for the four activity cost pools.

Activity Cost Pool	Cost Driver	Budgeted Level of Cost Driver
Machine-related costs	Machine hours	18,000 hr.
Setup and inspection	Number of production runs	80 runs
Engineering	Engineering change orders	200 change orders
Plant-related costs	Square footage of space	3,840 sq. ft.

You have gathered the following additional information:

- Each odd requires 8 machine hours, whereas each end requires 2 machine hours.
- Odds are manufactured in production runs of 25 units each. Ends are manufactured in 125 unit batches.
- Three-quarters of the engineering activity, as measured in terms of change orders, is related to odds.
- The plant has 3,840 square feet of space, 80 percent of which is used in the production of odds.

For each activity cost pool, compute a pool rate.

3. Determine the unit cost, for each activity cost pool, for odds and ends.
4. Compute the new product cost per unit for odds and ends, using the ABC system.
5. Using the same pricing policy as in the past, compute prices for odds and ends. Use the product costs determined by the ABC system.
6. Show that the ABC system fully assigns the total budgeted manufacturing overhead costs of $3,264,000.
7. Show how Knickknack's traditional, volume-based costing system distorted its product costs. (Use Exhibit 5–12 for guidance.)

Problem 5–41
Activity-Based Costing
(LO 2, 3, 4, 5)

Gourmet Specialty Coffee Company (GSCC) is a distributor and processor of different blends of coffee. The company buys coffee beans from around the world and roasts, blends, and packages them for resale. GSCC currently has 12 different coffees that it offers to gourmet shops in one-pound bags. The major cost is raw materials; however, there is a substantial amount of manufacturing overhead in the predominantly automated roasting and packing process. The company uses relatively little direct labor.

Some of the coffees are very popular and sell in large volumes, while a few of the newer blends have very low volumes. GSCC prices its coffee at full product cost, including allocated overhead, plus a markup of 30 percent. If prices for certain coffees are significantly higher than market, adjustments are made. The company competes primarily on the quality of its products, but customers are price-conscious as well.

Data for the 20x5 budget include manufacturing overhead of $12,000,000, which has been allocated on the basis of each product's direct-labor cost. The budgeted direct-labor cost for 20x5 totals $1,200,000. Based on the sales budget and raw-material budget, purchases and use of raw materials (mostly coffee beans) will total $5,800,000.

The expected prime costs for one-pound bags of two of the company's products are as follows:

	Jamaican	Colombian
Direct material	$2.90	$3.90
Direct labor	.40	.40

GSCC's controller believes the traditional product-costing system may be providing misleading cost information. She has developed an analysis of the 20x5 budgeted manufacturing-overhead costs shown in the following chart.

Activity	Cost Driver	Budgeted Activity	Budgeted Cost
Purchasing	Purchase orders	2,316	$ 2,316,000
Material handling	Setups	3,600	2,880,000
Quality control	Batches	1,440	576,000
Roasting	Roasting hours	192,200	3,844,000
Blending	Blending hours	67,200	1,344,000
Packaging	Packaging hours	52,000	1,040,000
Total manufacturing-overhead cost			$12,000,000

Data regarding the 20x5 production of Jamaican and Colombian coffee are shown in the following table. There will be no raw-material inventory for either of these coffees at the beginning of the year.

	Jamaican	Colombian
Budgeted sales	2,000 lb.	100,000 lb.
Batch size	500 lb.	20,000 lb.
Setups	3 per batch	3 per batch
Purchase order size	500 lb.	50,000 lb.
Roasting time	1 hr. per 200 lb.	1 hr. per 200 lb.
Blending time	.5 hr. per 200 lb.	.5 hr. per 200 lb.
Packaging time	.1 hr. per 200 lb.	.1 hr. per 200 lb.

Required:

1. Using GSCC's current product-costing system:
   a. Determine the company's predetermined overhead rate using direct-labor cost as the single cost driver.
   b. Determine the full product costs and selling prices of one pound of Jamaican coffee and one pound of Colombian coffee.
2. Develop a new product cost, using an activity-based costing approach, for one pound of Jamaican coffee and one pound of Colombian coffee.
3. What are the implications of the activity-based costing system with respect to:
   a. The use of direct labor as a basis for applying overhead to products?
   b. The use of the existing product-costing system as the basis for pricing?

(CMA, adapted)

Problem 5–42
Activity-Based Costing; Forecasting; Ethics
(LO 2, 3, 4)

Pensacola Air Industries (PAI) manufactures aircraft parts for small aircraft. Over the past decade, PAI's management has met its goal of reducing its reliance on government contract work to 50 percent of total sales. Thus, PAI's sales are now roughly evenly split between government and commercial sales.

Traditionally, the costs of the Material-Handling Department have been allocated to direct material as a percentage of direct-material dollar value. This was adequate when the majority of the manufacturing was homogeneous and related to government contracts. Recently, however, government auditors have rejected some proposals, stating that "the amount of Material-Handling Department costs allocated to these proposals is disproportionate to the total effort involved."

Kara Lindley, the newly hired cost-accounting manager, was asked by the manager of the Government Contracts Unit, Paul Anderson, to find a more equitable method of allocating Material-Handling Department costs to the user departments. Her review has revealed the following information.

- The majority of the direct-material purchases for government contracts are high-dollar, low-volume purchases, while commercial materials represent low-dollar, high-volume purchases.
- Administrative departments such as marketing, finance and administration, human resources, and maintenance also use the services of the Material-Handling Department on a limited basis but have never been charged in the past for material-handling costs.
- One purchasing manager with a direct phone line is assigned exclusively to purchasing high-dollar, low-volume material for government contracts at an annual salary of $54,000. Employee benefits are estimated to be 20 percent of the annual salary. The annual dedicated phone line costs are $4,200.

The components of the Material-Handling Department's budget for 20x4, as proposed by Lindley's predecessor, are as follows:

Payroll	$ 270,000
Employee benefits	54,000
Telephone	57,000
Other utilities	33,000
Materials and supplies	9,000
Depreciation	9,000
Direct-material budget:	
Government contracts	3,009,000
Commercial products	1,311,000

Lindley has estimated the number of purchase orders to be processed in 20x4 to be as follows:

Government contracts*	120,000
Commercial products	234,000
Marketing	2,700
Finance and administration	4,050
Human resources	750
Maintenance	1,500
Total	363,000

*Exclusive of high-dollar, low-volume materials.

Lindley recommended to Anderson that material-handling costs be allocated on a per purchase order basis. Anderson realizes that the company has been allocating to government contracts more material-handling costs than can be justified. However, the implication of Lindley's analysis could be a decrease in his unit's earnings and, consequently, a cut in his annual bonus. Anderson told Lindley to "adjust" her numbers and modify her recommendation so that the results will be more favorable to the Government Contracts Unit.

Being new in her position, Lindley is not sure how to proceed. She feels ambivalent about Anderson's instructions and suspects his motivation. To complicate matters for Lindley, the company's new president has asked her to prepare a three-year forecast of the Government Contracts Unit's results, and she believes that the newly recommended allocation method would provide the most accurate data. However, this would put her in direct opposition to Anderson's directives.

Lindley has assembled the following data to project the material-handling costs.

- The number of purchase orders increases 5 percent per year.
- The ratio of government purchase orders to total purchase orders remains at 33 percent.
- Total direct-material costs increase 2.5 percent per year.
- Material-handling costs remain the same percentage of direct-material costs.
- Direct government costs (payroll, employee benefits, and direct phone line) remain constant.
- In addition, she has assumed that government material in the future will be 70 percent of total material.

Required:

1. Calculate the material-handling rate that would have been used by Kara Lindley's predecessor at Pensacola Air Industries.
2. **a.** Calculate the revised material-handling costs to be allocated on a per purchase order basis.
   b. Discuss why purchase orders might be a more reliable cost driver than the dollar amount of direct material.
3. Calculate the difference due to the change to the new method of allocating material-handling costs to government contracts.
4. Prepare a forecast of the cumulative dollar impact over a three-year period from 20x4 through 20x6 of Kara Lindley's recommended change for allocating Material-Handling Department costs to the Government Contracts Unit. Round all calculations to the nearest whole number.

5. Referring to the standards of ethical conduct for management accountants:
   a. Discuss why Kara Lindley has an ethical conflict.
   b. Identify several steps that Lindley could take to resolve the ethical conflict.

(CMA, adapted)

Problem 5–43
Activity-Based Costing; Activity-Based Management
(LO 2, 3, 4, 5, 6)

Queensland Electronics Company manufactures two large-screen television models, the Novelle which has been produced for 10 years and sells for $910, and the Zodiac, a new model introduced in early 20x3, which sells for $1,160. Based on the following income statement for 20x4, a decision has been made to concentrate Queensland's marketing resources on the Zodiac model and to begin to phase out the Novelle model.

QUEENSLAND ELECTRONICS COMPANY
Income Statement
For the Year Ended December 31, 20x4

	Zodiac	Novelle	Total
Sales	$4,640,000	$20,020,000	$24,660,000
Cost of goods sold	3,232,000	13,024,000	16,256,000
Gross margin	$1,408,000	$ 6,996,000	$ 8,404,000
Selling and administrative expenses	980,000	5,700,000	6,680,000
Net income	$ 428,000	$ 1,296,000	$ 1,724,000
Units produced and sold	4,000	22,000	
Net income per unit sold	$107.00	$58.91*	

*Rounded.

The standard unit costs for the Zodiac and Novelle models are as follows:

	Zodiac	Novelle
Direct material	$579	$211
Direct labor:		
Zodiac (3.5 hr. × $14)	49	
Novelle (1.5 hr. × $14)		21
Machine usage:		
Zodiac (4 hr. × $19)	76	
Novelle (8 hr. × $19)		152
Manufacturing overhead*	104	208
Standard cost	$808	$592

*Manufacturing overhead was applied on the basis of machine hours at a predetermined rate of $26 per hour.

Queensland Electronics Company's controller is advocating the use of activity-based costing and activity-based management and has gathered the following information about the company's manufacturing-overhead costs for 20x4.

		Number of Events		
Activity Center (cost driver)	Traceable Costs	Zodiac	Novelle	Total
Soldering (number of solder joints)	$ 880,000	400,000	1,200,000	1,600,000
Shipments (number of shipments)	836,000	3,800	15,200	19,000
Quality control (number of inspections)	1,170,000	21,060	56,940	78,000
Purchase orders (number of orders)	1,110,000	105,450	79,550	185,000
Machine power (machine hours)	47,500	15,200	174,800	190,000
Machine setups (number of setups)	948,500	4,500	4,985	9,485
Total traceable costs	$4,992,000			

Required:

1. Briefly explain how an activity-based costing system operates.
2. Using activity-based costing, determine if Queensland Electronics should continue to emphasize the Zodiac model and phase out the Novelle model.

(CMA, adapted)

Problem 5–44
Activity-Based Costing
(LO 3, 4, 5)

Ultratech, Inc. manufactures several different types of printed circuit boards; however, two of the boards account for the majority of the company's sales. The first of these boards, a television circuit board, has been a standard in the industry for several years. The market for this type of board is competitive and price-sensitive. Ultratech plans to sell 65,000 of the TV boards in 20x4 at a price of $300 per unit. The second high-volume product, a personal computer circuit board, is a recent addition to Ultratech's product line. Because the PC board incorporates the latest technology it can be sold at a premium price. The 20x4 plans include the sale of 40,000 PC boards at $600 per unit.

Ultratech's management group is meeting to discuss how to spend the sales and promotion dollars for 20x4. The sales manager believes that the market share for the TV board could be expanded by concentrating Ultratech's promotional efforts in this area. In response to this suggestion, the production manager said, "Why don't you go after a bigger market for the PC board? The cost sheets that I get show that the contribution from the PC board is more than double the contribution from the TV board. I know we get a premium price for the PC board. Selling it should help overall profitability."

The cost-accounting system shows that the following costs apply to the PC and TV boards.

	PC Board	TV Board
Direct material	$280	$160
Direct labor	4 hr.	1.5 hr.
Machine time	1.5 hr.	.5 hr.

Variable manufacturing overhead is applied on the basis of direct-labor hours. For 20x4, variable overhead is budgeted at $2,240,000, and direct-labor hours are estimated at 280,000. The hourly rates for machine time and direct labor are $20 and $28, respectively. The company applies a material-handling charge at 10 percent of material cost. This material-handling charge is not included in variable manufacturing overhead. Total 20x4 expenditures for direct material are budgeted at $21,200,000.

Andrew Fulton, Ultratech's controller, believes that before the management group proceeds with the discussion about allocating sales and promotional dollars to individual products, it might be worthwhile to look at these products on the basis of the activities involved in their production. Fulton has prepared the following schedule to help the management group understand this concept.

"Using this information," Fulton explained, "we can calculate an activity-based cost for each TV board and each PC board and then compare it to the standard cost we have been using. The only cost that remains the same for both cost methods is the cost of direct material. The cost drivers will replace the direct labor, machine time, and overhead costs in the old standard cost figures."

Budgeted Cost		Cost Driver	Budgeted Annual Activity for Cost Driver
Procurement	$ 800,000	Number of parts	4,000,000 parts
Production scheduling	440,000	Number of boards	110,000 boards
Packaging and shipping	880,000	Number of boards	110,000 boards
Total	$ 2,120,000		
Machine setup	$ 892,000	Number of setups	278,750 setups
Hazardous waste disposal	96,000	Pounds of waste	16,000 pounds
Quality control	1,120,000	Number of inspections	160,000 inspections
General supplies	132,000	Number of boards	110,000 boards
Total	$ 2,240,000		
Machine insertion	$ 2,400,000	Number of parts	3,000,000 parts
Manual insertion	8,000,000	Number of parts	1,000,000 parts
Wave-soldering	264,000	Number of boards	110,000 boards
Total	$10,664,000		

Required per Unit	PC Board	TV Board
Parts:	55	26
Machine insertions	36	25
Manual insertions	19	1
Machine setups	3	2
Hazardous waste disposal	.40 lb.	.03 lb.
Inspections	2	1

Required:

1. Identify at least four general advantages associated with activity-based costing.
2. On the basis of Ultratech's unit cost data given in the problem, calculate the total amount that each of the two product lines will contribute toward covering fixed costs and profit in 20x4. (In other words, for each product line calculate the total sales revenue minus the total *variable* costs. This amount is often referred to as a product's total *contribution margin.*)
3. Repeat requirement (2) but now use the cost data from the activity-based costing system.
4. Explain how a comparison of the results of the two costing methods may impact the decisions made by Ultratech's management group.

(CMA, adapted)

Problem 5–45
Activity-Based Costing; Production and Pricing Decisions
(LO 2, 3, 4, 5)

Scott Manufacturing produces two items in its Virginia Beach plant: Tuff Stuff and Ruff Stuff. Since inception, Scott has used only one manufacturing-overhead cost pool to accumulate costs. Overhead has been allocated to products based on direct-labor hours. Until recently, Scott was the sole producer of Ruff Stuff and was able to dictate the selling price. However, last year Marvella Products began marketing a comparable product at a price below the cost assigned by Scott. Market share has declined rapidly, and management must now decide whether to meet the competitive price or to discontinue the product line. Recognizing that discontinuing the product line would place an additional burden on its remaining product, Tuff Stuff, management is using activity-based costing to determine if it would show a different cost structure for the two products.

The two major indirect costs for manufacturing the products are power usage and setup costs. Most of the power is used in fabricating, while most of the setup costs are required in assembly. The setup costs are predominantly related to the Tuff Stuff product line.

The plant manager, Kati Scott, has decided to separate the Manufacturing Department costs into two activity cost pools as follows:

Fabricating: machine hours will be the cost driver.
Assembly: number of setups will be the cost driver.

Jack Riley, the controller, has gathered the following information.

MANUFACTURING DEPARTMENT
Annual Budget before Separation of Overhead

	Total	Product Line	
		Tuff Stuff	**Ruff Stuff**
Number of units		20,000	20,000
Direct-labor hours*		2 hours per unit	3 hours per unit
Total direct-labor cost	$2,400,000		
Direct material		$15.00 per unit	$9.00 per unit
Budgeted overhead:			
Indirect labor	72,000		
Fringe benefits	15,000		
Indirect material	93,000		
Power	540,000		
Setup	225,000		
Quality assurance	30,000		
Other utilities	30,000		
Depreciation	45,000		

*Direct-labor hourly rate is the same in both departments.

MANUFACTURING DEPARTMENT
Cost Structure after Separation of Costs into Activity Cost Pools

	Fabricating	Assembly
Direct-labor cost	74%	26%
Direct material (no change)	100%	0%
Indirect labor	76%	24%
Fringe benefits	80%	20%
Indirect material	$60,000	$33,000
Power	$480,000	$60,000
Setup	$15,000	$210,000
Quality assurance	80%	20%
Other utilities	50%	50%
Depreciation	78%	22%

(continues)

(concluded)

Cost driver:

	Product Line	
	Tuff Stuff	**Ruff Stuff**
Machine-hours per unit	4.4	6.0
Setups	1,000	272

Required:

1. Assigning overhead based on direct-labor hours, calculate the following:
   a. Total budgeted cost of the Manufacturing Department.
   b. Unit cost of Tuff Stuff and Ruff Stuff.
2. After separation of overhead into activity cost pools, compute the total budgeted cost of each department: fabricating and assembly.
3. Using activity-based costing, calculate the unit costs for each product. (In computing the pool rates for the fabricating and assembly activity cost pools, round to the nearest cent. Then, in computing unit product costs, round to the nearest cent.)
4. Discuss how a decision regarding the production and pricing of Ruff Stuff will be affected by the results of your calculations in the preceding requirements.

(CMA, adapted)

Problem 5–46
Traditional versus Activity-Based Costing Systems
(LO 2, 3, 4, 5)

Gigabyte, Inc. manufactures three products for the computer industry:

Gismos (product G): annual sales, 8,000 units
Thingamajigs (product T): annual sales, 15,000 units
Whatchamacallits (product W): annual sales, 4,000 units

The company uses a traditional, volume-based product-costing system with manufacturing overhead applied on the basis of direct-labor dollars. The product costs have been computed as follows:

	Product G		Product T		Product W	
Raw material	$105.00		$157.50		$ 52.50	
Direct labor	48.00	(2.4 hr. at $20)	36.00	(1.8 hr. at $20)	24.00	(1.2 hr. at $20)
Manufacturing overhead*	420.00	($48 × 875%)	315.00	($36 × 875%)	210.00	($24 × 875%)
Total product cost	$573.00		$508.50		$286.50	

*Calculation of predetermined overhead rate:

Manufacturing overhead budget:

Machinery	$3,675,000
Machine setup	15,750
Inspection	1,575,000
Material handling	2,625,000
Engineering	1,034,250
Total	$8,925,000

Direct-labor budget (based on budgeted annual sales):

Product G:	8,000 × $48.00	=	$ 384,000
Product T:	15,000 × $36.00	=	540,000
Product W:	4,000 × $24.00	=	96,000
Total			$1,020,000

$$\text{Predetermined overhead rate} = \frac{\text{Budgeted overhead}}{\text{Budgeted direct labor}} = 875\%$$

Gigabyte's pricing method has been to set a target price equal to 150 percent of full product cost. However, only the thingamajigs have been selling at their target price. The target and actual current prices for all three products are the following:

	Product G	Product T	Product W
Product cost	$573.00	$508.50	$286.50
Target price	859.50	762.75	429.75
Actual current selling price	639.00	762.75	600.00

Gigabyte has been forced to lower the price of gismos in order to get orders. In contrast, Gigabyte has raised the price of whatchamacallits several times, but there has been no apparent loss of sales. Gigabyte, Inc. has been under increasing pressure to reduce the price even further on gismos. In contrast, Gigabyte's competitors do not seem to be interested in the market for whatchamacallits. Gigabyte apparently has this market to itself.

Required:

1. Is product G the company's least profitable product?
2. Is product W a profitable product for Gigabyte, Inc.?
3. Comment on the reactions of Gigabyte's competitors to the firm's pricing strategy. What dangers does Gigabyte, Inc. face?
4. Gigabyte's controller, Nan O'Second, recently attended a conference at which activity-based costing systems were discussed. She became convinced that such a system would help Gigabyte's management to understand its product costs better. She got top management's approval to design an activity-based costing system, and an ABC project team was formed. In stage one of the ABC project, each of the overhead items listed in the overhead budget was placed into its own activity cost pool. Then a cost driver was identified for each activity cost pool. Finally, the ABC project team compiled data showing the percentage of each cost driver that was consumed by each of Gigabyte's product lines. These data are summarized as follows:

Activity Cost Pool	Cost Driver	Product G	Product T	Product W
Machinery	Machine hours	24%	50%	26%
Machine setup	Number of setups	22%	30%	48%
Inspection	Number of inspections	16%	44%	40%
Material handling	Raw-material costs	25%	69%	6%
Engineering	Number of change orders	35%	10%	55%

Show how the controller determined the percentages given above for raw-material costs. (Round to the nearest whole percent.)

5. Develop product costs for the three products on the basis of an activity-based costing system. (Round to the nearest cent. For guidance, you may wish to refer to Exhibits 5–8 and 5–10.)
6. Calculate a target price for each product, using Gigabyte's pricing formula. Compare the new target prices with the current actual selling prices and previously reported product costs.

Problem 5–47
Strategic Cost Analysis; Continuation of Preceding Problem
(LO 4, 5, 6)

Refer to the new target prices for Gigabyte's three products, based on the new activity-based costing system.

Required: Write a memo to the company president commenting on the situation Gigabyte, Inc. has been facing regarding the market for its products and the actions of its competitors. Discuss the strategic options available to management. What do you recommend, and why?

Problem 5–48
Cost Distortion; Continuation of Problem 5–46
(LO 4)

Refer to the product costs developed in requirement (5) of Problem 5–46. Prepare a table showing how Gigabyte's traditional, volume-based product-costing system distorts the product costs of gismos, thingamajigs, and whatchamacallits. (You may wish to refer to Exhibit 5–12 for guidance. Because of rounding in the calculation of the product costs, there will be a small rounding error in this cost distortion analysis as well.)

Cases

Case 5–49
Activity-Based Costing; Budgeted Operating Margin
(LO 2, 3, 5)

Cincinnati Cycle Company produces two subassemblies, JY-63 and RX-67, used in manufacturing motorcycles. The company is currently using an absorption costing system that applies overhead based on direct-labor hours. The budget for the current year ending December 31, 20x4 is as follows:

CINCINNATI CYCLE COMPANY
Budgeted Statement of Operating Margin for 20x4

	JY-63	RX-67	Total
Sales in units	5,000	5,000	10,000
Sales revenue	$3,400,000	$4,400,000	$7,800,000
Cost of goods manufactured and sold:			
Beginning finished-goods inventory	$ 480,000	$ 600,000	$1,080,000
Add: Direct material	2,000,000	3,500,000	5,500,000
Direct labor	370,370	185,186	555,556
Applied manufacturing overhead*	1,088,050	544,026	1,632,076
Cost of goods available for sale	$3,938,420	$4,829,212	$8,767,632
Less: Ending finished-goods inventory	480,000	600,000	1,080,000
Cost of goods sold	$3,458,420	$4,229,212	$7,687,632
Gross margin	$ (58,420)	$ 170,788	$ 112,368

*Applied on the basis of direct-labor hours:

Machining	$ 849,056
Assembly	433,962
Material handling	113,208
Inspection	235,850
Total	$1,632,076

Jay Rexford, Cincinnati Cycle's president, has been reading about a new type of costing method called activity-based costing. Rexford is convinced that activity-based costing will cast a new light on future profits. As a result, Jack Canfield, the company's director of cost management, has accumulated cost pool information for this year shown on the following chart. This information is based on a product mix of 5,000 units of JY-63 and 5,000 units of RX-67.

Cost Pool Information for 20x4

Cost Pool	Activity	JY-63	RX-67
Direct labor	Direct-labor hours (per product line)	10,000	5,000
Material handling	Number of parts (per unit)	5	10
Inspection	Inspection hours (per product line)	5,000	7,500
Machining	Machine hours (per product line)	15,000	30,000
Assembly	Assembly hours (per product line)	6,000	5,500

In addition, the following information is projected for the next calendar year, 20x5.

	JY-63	RX-67
Sales (in units)	5,100	4,900
Beginning inventory, finished goods (in units)	800	600
Ending inventory, finished goods (in units)	700	700

On January 1, 20x5, Rexford is planning to increase the prices of JY-63 to $710 and RX-67 to $910. Material costs are not expected to increase in 20x5, but direct labor will increase by 8 percent, and all manufacturing overhead costs will increase by 6 percent. Due to the nature of the manufacturing process, the company does not have any beginning or ending work-in-process inventories.

Cincinnati Cycle Company uses a just-in-time inventory system and has materials delivered to the production facility directly from the vendors. The raw-material inventory both at the beginning and the end of the month is immaterial and can be ignored for the purposes of a budgeted income statement. The company uses the first-in, first-out (FIFO) inventory method.

Required:

1. Explain how activity-based costing differs from traditional product-costing methods.
2. Using activity-based costing, calculate the total cost for 20x5 for the following activity cost pools: material handling, inspection, machining, and assembly. (For the total costs, round to the nearest dollar.) Then, calculate the pool rate per unit of the appropriate cost driver for each of the four activities.

3. Prepare a table showing for each product line the estimated 20x5 cost for each of the following cost elements: direct material, direct labor, machining, assembly, material handling, and inspection. (Round to the nearest dollar.)
4. Prepare a budgeted statement showing the operating margin for Cincinnati Cycle Company for 20x5, using activity-based costing. The statement should show each product and a total for the company. Be sure to include detailed calculations for the cost of goods manufactured and sold. (Round each amount in the statement to the nearest dollar.)

(CMA, adapted)

Case 5–50
Traditional versus Activity-Based Costing Systems
(LO 2, 3, 4, 5)

Madison Electric Pump Corporation manufactures electric pumps for commercial use. The company produces three models, designated as regular, advanced, and deluxe. The company uses a job-order cost-accounting system with manufacturing overhead applied on the basis of direct-labor hours. The system has been in place with little change for 25 years. Product costs and annual sales data are as follows:

	Regular Model		Advanced Model		Deluxe Model	
Annual sales (units)	20,000		1,000		10,000	
Product costs:						
Direct material	$ 20		$ 50		$ 84	
Direct labor	20	(1 hr. at $20)	40	(2 hr. at $20)	40	(2 hr. at $20)
Manufacturing overhead*	170	(1 hr. at $170)	340	(2 hr. at $170)	340	(2 hr. at $170)
Total product cost	$210		$430		$464	

*Calculation of predetermined overhead rate:

Manufacturing-overhead budget:	
Depreciation, machinery	$2,960,000
Maintenance, machinery	240,000
Depreciation, taxes, and insurance for factory	600,000
Engineering	700,000
Purchasing, receiving and shipping	500,000
Inspection and repair of defects	750,000
Material handling	800,000
Miscellaneous manufacturing overhead costs	590,000
Total	$7,140,000

Direct-labor budget:	
Regular model:	20,000 hours
Advanced model:	2,000 hours
Deluxe model:	20,000 hours
Total	42,000 hours

Predetermined overhead rate: $\frac{\text{Budgeted overhead}}{\text{Budgeted direct-labor hours}} = \frac{\$7,140,000}{42,000 \text{ hours}} = \$170$ per hour

For the past 10 years the company's pricing formula has been to set each product's target price at 110 percent of its full product cost. Recently, however, the regular-model pump has come under increasing price pressure from offshore competitors. The result was that the price on the regular model has been lowered to $220.

The company president recently asked the controller, "Why can't we compete with these other companies? They're selling pumps just like our regular model for $212. That's only two bucks more than our production cost. Are we really that inefficient? What gives?"

The controller responded by saying, "I think this is due to an outmoded product-costing system. As you may remember, I raised a red flag about our system when I came on board last year. But the decision was to keep our current system in place. In my judgment, our product-costing system is distorting our product costs. Let me run a few numbers to demonstrate what I mean."

Getting the president's go-ahead, the controller compiled the basic data needed to implement an activity-based costing system. These data are displayed in the following table. The percentages are the proportion of each cost driver consumed by each product line.

Activity Cost Pool	Cost Driver	Product Lines		
		Regular Model	Advanced Model	Deluxe Model
I: Depreciation, machinery Maintenance, machinery	Machine time	39%	13%	48%
II: Engineering Inspection and repair of defects	Engineering hours	47%	6%	47%
III: Purchasing, receiving, and shipping Material handling	Number of material orders	47%	8%	45%
IV: Depreciation, taxes, and insurance for factory Miscellaneous manufacturing overhead	Factory space usage	42%	15%	43%

Required:

1. Compute the target prices for the three pump models, based on the traditional, volume-based product-costing system.
2. Compute new product costs for the three products, based on the new data collected by the controller. Round to the nearest cent. (You may find it helpful to refer to Exhibits 5–8 and 5–10 for guidance.)
3. Calculate a new target price for the three products, based on the activity-based costing system. Compare the new target price with the current actual selling price for the regular model pump.
4. Write a memo to the company president explaining what has been happening as a result of the firm's traditional volume-based product-costing system.
5. What strategic options does management have? What do you recommend, and why?

Case 5–51
Cost Distortion; Continuation of Preceding Case
(LO 4)

Refer to the product costs developed in requirement (2) of the preceding problem. Prepare a table showing how Madison Electric Pump Corporation's traditional, volume-based product-costing system distorts the product costs of the three pump models. (You may wish to refer to Exhibit 5–12 for guidance. Because of rounding in the calculation of the product costs, there will be a small rounding error in this cost distortion analysis as well.)

Case 5–52
Ethical Issues Related to Product-Cost Distortion; Activity-Based Costing; Continuation of Case 5–50
(LO 3, 5)

Madison Electric Pump Corporation's controller, Erin Jackson, developed new product costs for the three pump models using activity-based costing. It was apparent that the firm's traditional product-costing system had been undercosting the advanced model electric pump by a significant amount. This was due largely to the low volume of the advanced model. Before she could report back to the president, Jackson received a phone call from her friend, Alan Tyler. He was the production manager for the advanced model electric pump. Tyler was upset, and he let Jackson know it. "Erin, I've gotten wind of your new product cost analysis. There's no way the advanced model costs anywhere near what your numbers say. For years and years this line has been highly profitable, and its reported product cost was low. Now you're telling us it costs more than twice what we thought. I just don't buy it."

Jackson briefly explained to her friend about the principles of activity-based costing and why it resulted in more accurate product costs. "Alan, the advanced model really is losing money. It simply has too low a volume to be manufactured efficiently."

Tyler was even more upset now. "Erin, if you report these new product costs to the president, he's going to discontinue the advanced model. My job's on the line, Erin! How about massaging those numbers a little bit. Who's going to know?"

"I'll know, Alan. And you'll know," responded Jackson. "Look, I'll go over my analysis again, just to make sure I haven't made an error."

Required: Discuss the ethical issues involved in this scenario.

1. Is the controller, Erin Jackson, acting ethically?
2. Is the production manager, Alan Tyler, acting ethically?
3. What are Jackson's ethical obligations? To the president? To her friend?

Note: Due to space limitations, there are no Current Issues in Managerial Accounting included in Chapter 5. However, Issue 6–60 (page 253) may be assigned at this time.

Chapter Six

Activity-Based Management and Today's Advanced Manufacturing Environment

After completing this chapter, you should be able to:

1 Describe the key features of a production facility employing advanced manufacturing technology.

2 List and explain eight important features of just-in-time inventory and production management systems.

3 Explain the concept of activity-based management (ABM).

4 Explain the concept of two-dimensional activity-based costing.

5 List and explain the steps in using ABM to eliminate non-value-added costs.

6 Explain and execute a customer-profitability analysis.

7 Define and give an example of target costing.

8 Explain the concept of kaizen costing, and prepare a kaizen costing chart.

9 Briefly explain the concepts of total quality control, continuous improvement, benchmarking, reengineering, and the theory of constraints.

Aerotech to Build New Plant in Bakersfield

Bakersfield, CA—There's a new kid in the park. The industrial park, that is. The mayor announced this week that Aerotech Corporation, the Phoenix-based aerospace company, would build a new plant in Bakersfield's five-year-old industrial park. A simultaneous announcement by Aerotech's president, Kristin Scott, cited Bakersfield's location as a prime factor in the decision. "Bakersfield is much closer to both our suppliers and our customers than is Phoenix. We're looking forward to our new partnership with the people of the Bakersfield area. But I want to emphasize, however, that our Phoenix employees are loyal and talented. Many of them will have the opportunity to come with the company to Bakersfield when we eventually close down our Phoenix operation."

Asked if the Bakersfield plant would be modeled after the Phoenix plant, Scott said, "The Bakersfield plant will be completely different than the Phoenix facility. The Phoenix plant represents a very traditional plant layout, which emphasizes individual manufacturing functions and departments. In contrast, the Bakersfield plant will employ what is called a flexible manufacturing system or FMS. The FMS approach is highly automated, both in terms of production machinery and material-handling equipment. Much of the production process will be computer controlled."

Scott went on to explain that the Bakersfield plant will employ a JIT production and inventory management system. JIT, which stands for "just in time," is becoming more and more widely used globally as a highly efficient system for manufacturing high-quality products while stocking only minimal inventories of materials, parts, and finished products.

According to Scott, "JIT goes hand in hand with several other desirable traits of a production process. A multi-skilled workforce, flexible facilities, an atmosphere of teamwork, and high-quality output are among the hallmarks of a JIT system."

Scott also talked enthusiastically about the new cost management system that would be installed in the Bakersfield plant. "We've learned a lot in our Phoenix operation these past two years. We learned how to really focus on the activities in which we engage to produce our products. We learned how to ask which activities add value and which ones don't. How can our processes be improved by eliminating or combining activities? The bottom-line is getting the most out of every dollar we spend on resources to manufacture the very best product we can."

To achieve and maintain a competitive advantage in today's global marketplace, many companies are investing heavily in new technology. In addition, many organizations are implementing new cost management systems to better meet the needs of management. These new systems, coupled with efforts at continuous improvement, are helping some companies achieve success as world-class competitors. In this chapter, we continue our discussion of Aerotech Corporation to address these important issues.

Aerotech's Bakersfield Plant: Advanced Manufacturing Technology

AEROTECH CORPORATION

LO 1

Describe the key features of a production facility employing advanced manufacturing technology.

After a careful study, Aerotech's board of directors decided to build a new production facility. The site chosen for the new plant was Bakersfield, California, which is much nearer to Aerotech's material suppliers and customers. Initially, the plants in both Phoenix and Bakersfield would manufacture Aerotech's three lines of circuit boards. Eventually, however, all of Aerotech's production would be moved to Bakersfield.

The Bakersfield plant was designed to employ state-of-the-art manufacturing technology. When the new plant was designed, Aerotech's management insisted on a plant layout and production processes that would reduce or eliminate the non-value-added costs incurred in the Phoenix operation. The two key features of the Bakersfield operation are a *just-in-time (JIT)* inventory and production management system and a *flexible manufacturing system (FMS)*. These key features of the Bakersfield plant are discussed next.

Just-in-Time Inventory and Production Management

A **just-in-time (JIT) inventory and production management system** is a comprehensive inventory and manufacturing control system in which no materials are purchased and no products are manufactured until they are needed. Raw materials and parts are purchased only as they are needed in some phase of the production process. Component parts and subassemblies are not manufactured in any stage of production until they are required in the next stage. Finished goods are manufactured only as they are needed to fill customer orders. A primary goal of a JIT production system is to *reduce or eliminate inventories* at every stage of production, from raw materials to finished goods. The JIT philosophy, made famous by Toyota, has been credited with the success of many of the world's leading manufacturers. Tremendous cost savings have been realized by many companies that have adopted the JIT approach.

Ford Motor Company's Valencia, Spain, plant employs a JIT system. Key suppliers located in an adjacent industrial park supply parts, such as these bumpers, just in time for production.

LO 2

List and explain eight important features of just-in-time inventory and production management systems.

How does a JIT system achieve its vast reductions in inventory and associated cost savings? A production-systems expert lists the following key features of the JIT approach.[1]

[1]James B. Dilworth, *Production and Operations Management*, 3d ed. (New York: Random House, 1996), pp. 354–61.

1. *A smooth, uniform production rate.* An important goal of a JIT system is to establish a smooth production flow, beginning with the arrival of materials from suppliers and ending with the delivery of goods to customers. Widely fluctuating production rates result in delays and excess work-in-process inventories. These non-value-added costs are to be eliminated.

2. *A pull method of coordinating steps in the production process.* Most manufacturing processes occur in multiple stages. Under the **pull method,** goods are produced in each manufacturing stage only as they are needed at the next stage. This approach reduces or eliminates work-in-process inventory between production steps. The result is a reduction in waiting time and its associated non-value-added cost.

   The pull method of production begins at the last stage of the manufacturing process.[2] When additional materials and parts are needed for final assembly, a message is sent to the immediately preceding work center to send the amount of materials and parts that will be needed over the next few hours. Often this message is in the form of a **withdrawal Kanban,** a card indicating the number and type of parts requested from the preceding work center. The receipt of the withdrawal Kanban in the preceding work center triggers the release of a **production Kanban,** which is another card specifying the number of parts to be manufactured in that work center. Thus, the parts are "pulled" from a particular work center by a need for parts in the subsequent work center. This *pull approach* to production is repeated all the way up the manufacturing sequence toward the beginning. Nothing is manufactured at any stage until its need is signaled from the subsequent process via a Kanban. As a result, no parts are produced until they are needed, no inventories build up, and the manufacturing process exhibits a smooth, uniform flow of production.[3]

3. *Purchase of materials and manufacture of subassemblies and products in small lot sizes.* This is an outgrowth of the pull method of production planning. Materials are purchased and goods are produced only as required, rather than for the sake of building up stocks. The result is a reduction in storage and waiting time, and the related non-value-added costs.

4. *Quick and inexpensive setups of production machinery.* In order to produce in small lot sizes, a manufacturer must be able to set up production runs quickly. Advanced manufacturing technology aids in this process, as more and more machines are computer-controlled.

5. *High quality levels for raw material and finished products.* If raw materials and parts are to arrive "just in time" for production, they must be "just right" for their intended purpose. Otherwise, the production line will be shut down and significant non-value-added costs of waiting will result. Moreover, if very small stocks of finished goods are to be maintained, then finished products must be of uniform high quality. For this reason, a **total quality control (TQC)** program often accompanies a just-in-time production environment.

6. *Effective preventive maintenance of equipment.* If goods are to be manufactured just in time to meet customer orders, a manufacturer cannot afford significant production delays. By strictly adhering to routine maintenance schedules, the firm can avoid costly down time from machine breakdowns.

7. *An atmosphere of teamwork to improve the production system.* A company can maintain a competitive edge in today's worldwide market only if it is

"We are managing change on top of change on top of change all the time. That means new processes and having to try to improve the efficiency of the old processes." (6a)

Caterpillar

---

[2]You may find it helpful to review Exhibit 1–5 on page 23, which depicts the pull method of the JIT system.

[3]Toyota's ground-breaking JIT system originally was referred to as *Kanban*, a Japanese word meaning "signboard." See Takeo Tanaka, "Kaizen Budgeting: Toyota's Cost Control System under TQC," *Journal of Cost Management* 8, no. 3 (Fall 1994), p. 57.

constantly seeking ways to improve its product or service, achieve more efficient operations, and eliminate non-value-added costs. My favorite football coach often says that a team must improve from one week to the next. Otherwise the team will get worse, because it rarely will stay at the same level. So it goes in business as well. If a company's employees are not constantly seeking ways to improve the firm's performance, before long its competitors will pass it by. Many organizations encourage employees to make suggestions for improvement. Rewards are given when cost-saving suggestions are implemented.

8. *Multiskilled workers and flexible facilities.* To facilitate just-in-time production, manufacturing equipment must be flexible enough to produce a variety of components and products. Otherwise, if a particular production line can produce only one item, bottlenecks may result. A bottleneck can hold up production in subsequent manufacturing stages and result in the non-value-added costs associated with waiting time. As high-tech production equipment becomes more versatile, production employees must be capable of handling a variety of machines and operations. By grouping machines into *cells* that produce a variety of items requiring similar production technology, multiskilled workers are able to operate several machines. This approach is called *group technology.*

JIT Purchasing In addition to a JIT production approach, Aerotech implemented *JIT purchasing* in its Bakersfield plant. Under this approach, materials and parts are purchased from outside vendors only as they are needed. This avoids the costly and wasteful buildup of raw-material inventories. The following are five key features of **JIT purchasing.**

1. *Only a few suppliers.* This results in less time spent on vendor relations. Only highly reliable vendors, who can invariably deliver high-quality goods on time, are used.
2. *Long-term contracts negotiated with suppliers.* This eliminates costly paperwork and negotiations with each individual transaction. The need for delivery can be communicated via a telephone call or computer message. The long-term contracts state the price, quality, and delivery terms of the goods.
3. *Materials and parts delivered in small lot sizes immediately before they are needed.* This is the essence of the just-in-time philosophy. Costly inventories are avoided by having supplies arrive "just-in-time" to be placed into production.
4. *Only minimal inspection of delivered materials and parts.* The long-term contracts clearly state the quality of material required. Vendors are selected on the basis of their reliability in meeting these stringent standards and in delivering the correct amount of materials on time.
5. *Grouped payments to each vendor.* Instead of paying for each delivery, payments are made for batches of deliveries according to the terms of the contract. This reduces costly paperwork for both the vendor and the purchaser.

> "What I rapidly discovered is that technology was rolling over in months rather than years, maybe even in weeks, and decision processes that affected what we were doing were measured in hours and days." (6b)
>
> **Boeing**

JIT purchasing is widely used in a variety of organizations. In manufacturing firms, it goes hand in hand with JIT production. In retail and service industry firms, JIT purchasing reduces costly warehouse inventories and streamlines the purchasing function.

LO 1

Describe the key features of a production facility employing advanced manufacturing technology.

Flexible Manufacturing System

To achieve the objectives of a just-in-time production environment listed in the preceding section, many manufacturers are moving toward more highly automated manufacturing systems. As you may know if you have recently shopped for a VCR, compact disk system, or personal computer, electronic and computer technology is changing at a breathtaking pace. Even as manufacturing facilities are built, engineering breakthroughs make even more efficient operations possible. As a result, a range of automation can be observed even among the most recent production facilities. Before describing Aerotech's Bakersfield plant, let's go over some of the terminology used to describe today's manufacturing environment.

Automated material-handling system (AMHS). Computer-controlled equipment that automatically moves materials, parts, and products from one production stage to another.

Flexible manufacturing system (FMS). An integrated system of computer-controlled machines and automated material-handling equipment, which is capable of producing a variety of technologically similar products.

FMS cell. A particular grouping of machines and personnel within a flexible manufacturing system.

Cellular manufacturing. The organization of a production facility into FMS cells.

Computer-integrated manufacturing (CIM) system. The most advanced level of automated manufacturing. Virtually all parts of the production process are accomplished by computer-controlled machines and automated material-handling equipment. Moreover, the entire production system is an integrated network centrally controlled via a computer.

Plant Layout at Aerotech's Bakersfield Facility

The layout of Aerotech's Bakersfield plant is shown in Exhibit 6–1. This facility is designed around the following advanced manufacturing features.

1. *Flexible manufacturing system.* The Bakersfield plant has three FMS cells. Each cell includes seven computer-controlled machines that are capable of performing almost all of the manufacturing operations on *any* of Aerotech's three circuit boards. With a minor setup operation, each of these FMS cells can be readied for a new production run. The hand-insertion operations used in the Phoenix plant have been replaced by robots, which are programmed to insert odd-shaped or delicate electrical components.
2. *Automated material-handling system.* The Bakersfield plant uses an AMHS for two purposes: to move circuit boards between operations in each FMS cell, and to move completed circuit boards from each cell to the burn-in testing work center. The AMHS includes a conveyor that carries the boards while the burn-in testing procedure is completed on the way to the packaging work center. Bakersfield's AMHS has resulted in substantial reductions in the non-value-added costs of move time.
3. *Computer-aided design (CAD).* The Bakersfield plant utilizes a CAD system in its design department. Notice its location next to the computer department.

Observations on the Bakersfield Layout Several features of the new plant's layout are noteworthy. Notice that the raw-material and parts storage area is located so that materials are easily accessible to each FMS cell. The space devoted to storage of raw materials and finished goods is much smaller in the Bakersfield plant than in the Phoenix facility. This reflects the JIT philosophy of little or no inventory and results in elimination of non-value-added storage costs. Notice that the holding areas next to the production departments in the Phoenix plant have been eliminated in Bakersfield. Now the circuit boards flow continuously through each FMS cell. This eliminates the non-value-added cost of waiting time. Orders that required days to complete in Phoenix, due to delays between operations, are completed in a few hours in Bakersfield.

Describe the key features of a production facility employing advanced manufacturing technology.

Exhibit 6–1
Aerotech Corporation's Bakersfield Plant

Shipping
Receiving
Inspection
Finished-Goods
Storage
Packaging
Work
Center
FMS
Cell
Raw
Materials
and Parts
Storage
Burn-in
Testing
Work
Center
Maintenance
and Custodial
Quality
Control
Engineering
Design
Computer
Center
Purchasing
and Inventory
Control
Production
Scheduling
Human
Resources
Sales and Marketing
Plant Manager
and Staff
Accounting

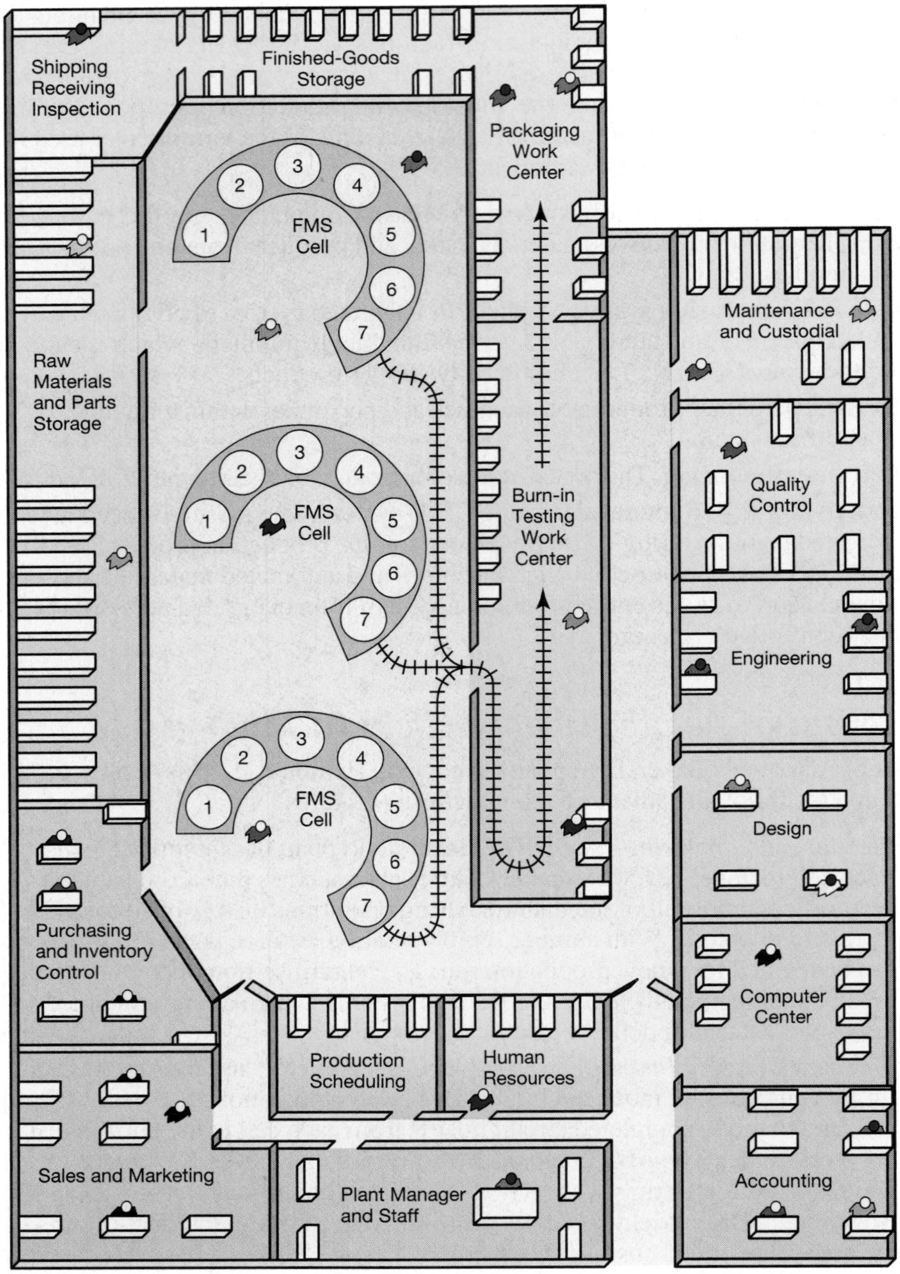

The amount of space devoted to the computer department is greater in Bakersfield than in Phoenix. This reflects the significantly greater role of computer-aided manufacturing (CAM) in the Bakersfield operation. A large amount of space in Bakersfield also is devoted to design, engineering, and quality control. The JIT philosophy demands strict adherence to high-quality standards. These three departments are located near each other to implement **off-line quality control.** This refers to activities during the product design and engineering phases that will improve the manufacturability of the product, reduce production costs, and ensure high quality.

Cost Management System in Bakersfield

The cost management system developed for the Bakersfield operation is an integral part of Aerotech's effort to regain a competitive edge in the market for its products. Several features of the CMS are discussed in this section.

Elimination of Non-Value-Added Costs We have discussed the features of the Bakersfield production system that enabled Aerotech to reduce or eliminate non-value-added costs. Chief among these is the elimination of storage and waiting time and the significant reduction in move time. The AMHS has virtually eliminated material-handling costs. Added to these cost reductions is a significant decrease in indirect-labor costs. Many manufacturing support jobs that were considered indirect labor (and thus overhead) in the Phoenix plant are performed by direct-labor personnel in the Bakersfield facility. In the new plant, direct-labor employees now operate each FMS cell. These workers are trained in the setup, operation, and routine maintenance of several machines. When a machine broke down in Phoenix, an entire production department could be shut down while maintenance department personnel were called in to do repairs. In the meantime, the direct-labor personnel in the department were idled. In contrast, the FMS cell operators in Bakersfield are trained to perform routine maintenance and repairs and spot other, more serious machinery problems before they get out of hand. The result of this multiskilled labor force is the reduction of manufacturing support costs in Bakersfield.

This Kenway automated material-handling system has fully automated storage and retrieval capability. This technician is responsible for programming the computer that controls the system.

A crucial step in bringing about the significant reduction in non-value-added costs in the *Bakersfield plant* was the institution of *activity-based costing in the Phoenix plant.* It was this system of identifying costs with the key activities in the production process that first alerted Aerotech's management to the possibilities for cost reduction. The ABC system developed for the Phoenix operation has now been instituted in the Bakersfield plant. Cost drivers have been identified for each significant product cost. Management's attitude is one of never being complacent about the existence of non-value-added costs. There is a continuing effort to identify and eliminate these barriers to maintaining the firm's competitive edge.

Direct versus Indirect Costs In the Bakersfield plant almost all production costs are traced directly to an FMS cell. Very few costs are considered to be general factory overhead as in more traditional cost-accounting systems. Direct-material costs are traced directly to products. Direct-labor costs have been reduced substantially, due to the advanced level of automation in the Bakersfield plant. In fact, direct labor has been reduced to the point where it is combined with other conversion costs traceable to each FMS cell. Depreciation on the computers and machinery in an FMS cell is traceable directly to the cell. The salaries of computer programmers and maintenance personnel also are traceable to each FMS cell. Conversion costs that have been traced directly to an FMS cell then are assigned to the products that are produced in the cell.

> "The idea of continuous improvement is just paramount. People have a sense of purpose. They have a real sense of 'I'm adding value to the company by reducing this waste.'" (6c)
>
> **Caterpillar**

Shift in the Cost Structure Aerotech's Bakersfield plant is **capital-intensive**, which means that the production process is accomplished largely by machinery rather than by manual labor. In contrast, the Phoenix plant is only *semiautomated*, with all the material handling and several significant production steps performed manually. Thus, the Phoenix plant is more **labor-intensive** than the Bakersfield facility.

A capital-intensive plant, such as the one in Bakersfield, generally has a *cost structure* with a much larger proportion of fixed costs than would be observed in a labor-intensive plant. Direct-labor costs, often a variable cost, are much lower. Depreciation on plant and equipment generally is much higher.

Two-Dimensional ABC and Activity-Based Management

LO 3

Explain the concept of activity-based management.

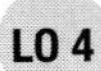

LO 4

Explain the concept of two-dimensional activity-based costing.

Topic 6–1

Using activity-based costing information to improve operations and eliminate non-value-added costs is called **activity-based management (ABM).** We have already caught a glimpse of Aerotech's utilization of ABM in its use of the ABC information from both Phoenix and Bakersfield to improve operations and reduce costs. One way of picturing the relationship between ABC and ABM is in terms of the **two-dimensional activity-based costing model** depicted in Exhibit 6–2.[4] The vertical dimension of the model depicts the cost assignment view of an ABC system. From the *cost assignment viewpoint*, the ABC system uses two-stage cost allocation to *assign* the costs of resources to the firm's cost objects. These cost objects could be products manufactured (such as Aerotech's Mode I, II, and III circuit boards), services produced, or customers served.

Now focus on the horizontal dimension of the model. Depicted here is the *process view* of an ABC system. The emphasis now is on the activities themselves, the various processes by which work is accomplished in the organization. The left-hand side of Exhibit 6–2 depicts **activity analysis**, which is the detailed identification and description of the activities conducted in the enterprise. Activity analysis entails identification not only of the activities but also of their *root causes*, the events that *trigger* activities, and the *linkages* among activities. The right-hand side of Exhibit 6–2 depicts the evaluation of activities through performance measures. It is these processes of *activity analysis and evaluation* that comprise activity-based management. Notice that the *activities*, which appear in the center of both dimensions in Exhibit 6–2, are the focal point of ABC and ABM.

Using ABM to Eliminate Non-Value-Added Activities and Costs

LO 5

List and explain the steps in using ABM to eliminate non-value-added costs.

An important goal of activity-based management is to identify and eliminate non-value-added activities and costs. **Non-value-added activities** are operations that are either (1) unnecessary and dispensable or (2) necessary, but inefficient and improvable.[5] **Non-value-added costs,** which result from such activities, are the costs of activities that can be eliminated without deterioration of product quality, performance, or perceived value. The following five steps provide a strategy for eliminating non-value-added costs in both manufacturing and service industry firms.

---

[4]This section draws on Lewis J. Soloway, "Using Activity-Based Management in Aerospace and Defense Companies," *Journal of Cost Management* 6, no. 4 (Winter 1993), pp. 56–66, and Peter B. B. Turney, "What an Activity-Based Cost Model Looks Like," *Journal of Cost Management* 5, no. 4 (Winter 1992), pp. 54–60.

[5]This definition, as well as other material in this section, is drawn from James A. Brimson, "Improvement and Elimination of Non-Value-Added Costs," *Journal of Cost Management* 2, no. 2 (Summer 1988), pp. 62–65.

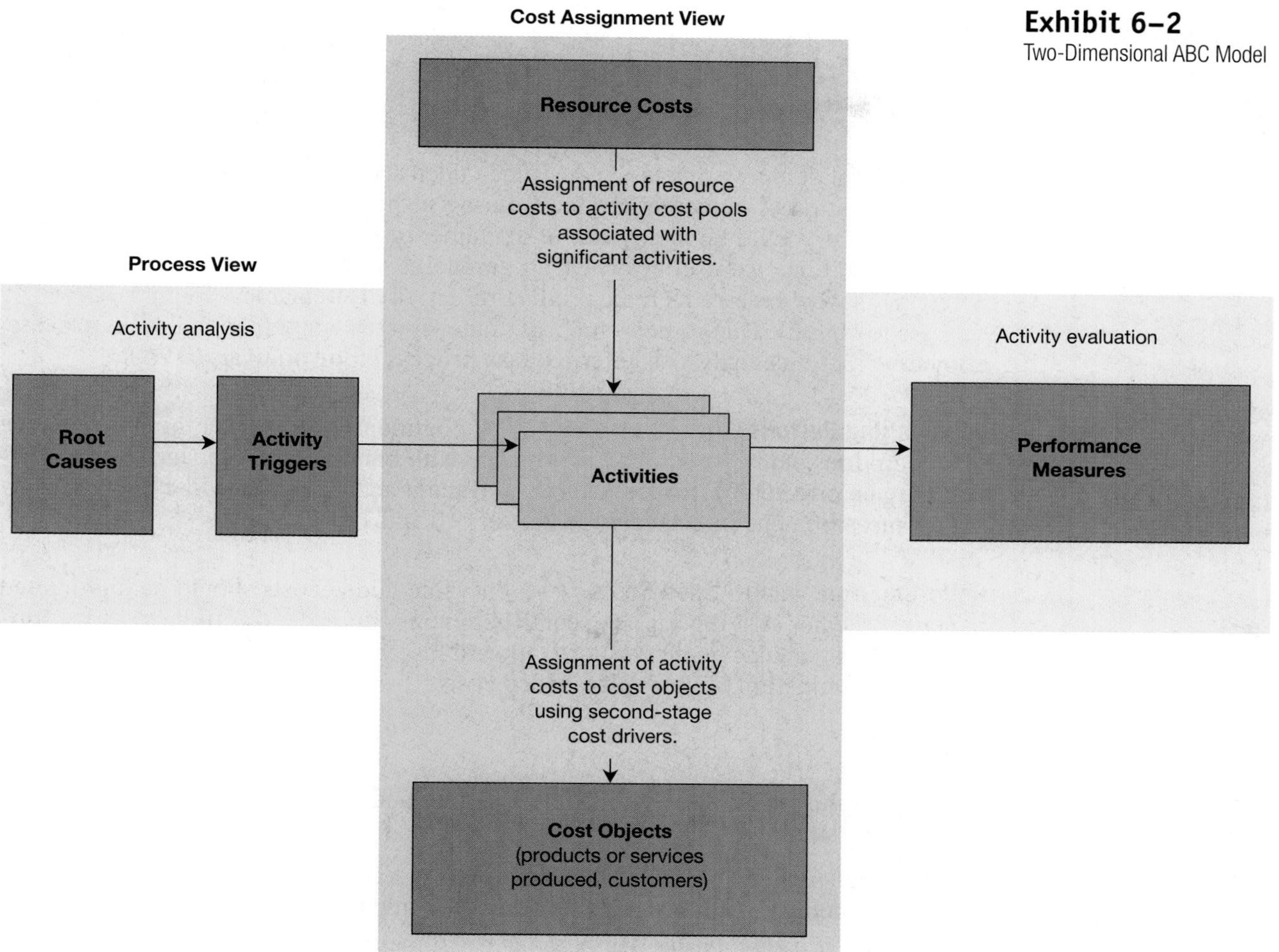

Exhibit 6–2
Two-Dimensional ABC Model

Identifying Activities The first step is activity analysis, which identifies all of the organization's significant activities. The resulting activity list should be broken down to the most fundamental level practical. For example, rather than listing purchasing as an activity, the list should break down the purchasing operation into its component activities, such as obtaining part specifications, compiling vendor lists, vendor selection, negotiation, ordering, and expediting.

Identifying Non-Value-Added Activities Three criteria for determining whether an activity adds value are as follows:

- *Is the activity necessary?* If it's a duplicate or nonessential operation, it is non-value-added.
- *Is the activity efficiently performed?* In answering this question, it is helpful to compare the actual performance of the activity to a value-added baseline established using budgets, targets, or external benchmarks.
- *Is an activity sometimes value-added and sometimes non-value-added?* For example, it may be necessary to move work-in-process units between production operations, but unnecessary to move raw materials around while in storage.

"Putting a spotlight on non-value-added activities, such as [correcting] errors in procurement, provided the focus for ultimately implementing process improvements." (6d)
GTE Supply (currently a part of Verizon)

Understanding Activity Linkages, Root Causes, and Triggers In identifying non-value-added activities, it is critical to understand the ways in which activities are linked together. The following chain of activities provides an example:

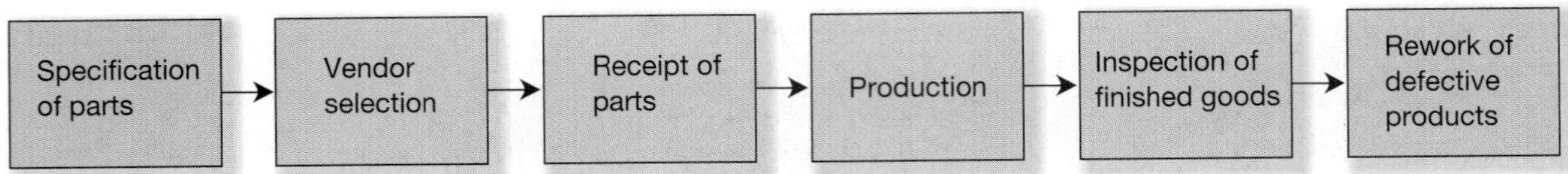

The rework of defective units is a non-value-added activity. The rework is *triggered* by the identification of defective products during inspection. The *root cause* of the rework, however, could lie in any one of a number of preceding activities. Perhaps the part specifications were in error. Or an unreliable vendor was selected. Maybe the wrong parts were received. Or the production activity is to blame.

A set of linked activities (such as that depicted above) is called a **process.** Sometimes activity analysis is referred to as **process value analysis (PVA).**

Establishing Performance Measures By continually measuring the performance of all activities, and comparing performance with benchmarks, management's attention may be directed to unnecessary or inefficient activities. We will explore performance measurement extensively in Chapters 10 and 11.

Reporting Non-Value-Added Costs Non-value-added costs should be highlighted in activity center cost reports. By identifying non-value-added activities, and reporting their costs, management can strive toward the ongoing goals of process improvement and elimination of non-value-added costs.

Achieving Cost Reduction

LO 5

List and explain the steps in using ABM to eliminate non-value-added costs.

Once non-value-added activities have been identified, four techniques may be used to reduce the resulting non-value-added costs.[6]

1. *Activity reduction.* This technique simply scales back the activity, by reducing the time or other resources devoted to it.
2. *Activity elimination.* This approach assumes the activity is utterly unnecessary.
3. *Activity selection.* Under this strategy, the most efficient activity is selected from a set of alternatives.
4. *Activity sharing.* This technique finds ways to get more mileage out of an existing activity by combining functions in a more efficient manner. An example is the use of common parts in several related products, rather than designing each product to use unique parts.

Customer-Profitability Analysis

LO 6

Explain and execute a customer-profitability analysis.

Topic 6–2

It is quite possible for a company to have profitable products and, at the same time, incur customer-related costs that make certain customer relationships unprofitable. **Customer-profitability analysis** uses activity-based costing to determine the activities, costs, and profit associated with serving particular customers. Suppose, for example, that customer X frequently changes its orders after they are placed, but customer Y typically does not. Then the costs incurred in updating sales orders for changes should be recorded in a manner that reflects the fact that customer X is more responsible for those activities and costs than is customer Y. An effective cost management system should allow managers to derive such cost details.

Many factors can result in some customers being more profitable than others. Customers that order in small quantities, order frequently, often change their orders,

[6]Peter B. B. Turney, "How Activity-Based Costing Helps Reduce Cost," *Journal of Cost Management* 4, no. 4 (Winter 1991), pp. 29–35.

require special packaging or handling, demand faster delivery, or need special parts or engineering design generally are less profitable than customers who demand less in terms of customized services. If managers have a good understanding of which customers are generating the greatest profit, they can make more-informed decisions about customer service. Moreover, this allows customers to be educated as to the costs they are causing when demanding special services. In many cases, customers' behavior can be changed in a way that reduces costs to the supplier. Then these cost savings can be shared by the supplier and the customer.

The task of assigning costs to customers is a challenge. A system must be in place that enables the company to identify which customers are using customer support services and how frequently they do so. How much time must the company spend on a customer to make the sale and to provide ongoing support services? These costs are in addition to the cost of manufacturing the product or initially providing a service for the customer.

"When we saw what some of our customers were costing us, we were quite surprised. We shared this information with them, and they were also surprised to see how much work went into servicing them. At this point, we negotiated with them to eliminate certain discounts they were receiving." (6e)

Pfizer (formerly Warner Lambert)

Illustration of Customer-Profitability Analysis

To illustrate customer-profitability analysis, let's focus again on Aerotech Corporation. Two more years have passed, and the company has successfully implemented its activity-based costing system in its new Bakersfield plant. At a recent strategy meeting with her senior management team, Aerotech's president and CEO expressed interest in assessing the profitability of the company's various customer relationships. She found support for the idea from the controller, who had been reading about customer-profitability analysis in some of his professional journals. The company's marketing manager also expressed interest in customer-profitability analysis, since he was concerned about the profitability of a couple of Aerotech's customers in particular. "We have a few customers who seem to want the moon and the stars when it comes to customer service," he complained. "I know the customer is always right and all, but you really have to wonder if we're making any money from a couple of these customers, what with all the extra design and packaging they demand. And some of our other customers seem to require an awful lot of extra attention in sales calls, order processing, and billing. If we had a better idea of each customer's profitability, it would help our marketing and sales staffs to focus their efforts."

The controller soon had his cost management staff attacking the customer-profitability analysis that the president had requested. The first step required an activity-based costing analysis of certain *customer-related costs* that could seriously affect a customer's profitability. Recall that ABC analysis relies on a cost hierarchy with cost levels, such as unit-level, batch-level, product-line level, customer-level, and facility- or general-operations-level costs. In this use of activity-based costing, the cost management team is focusing on the customer-related costs. After an extensive analysis and several interviews with personnel throughout Aerotech Corporation, the cost management team came up with the following ABC analysis.[7]

Customer-Related Activities	Cost Driver Base	Cost Driver Rate
Order processing	Purchase orders	$ 150
Sales contacts (phone calls, faxes, etc.)	Contacts	100
Sales visits	Visits	1,000
Shipment processing	Shipments	200
Billing and collection	Invoices	160
Design/engineering change orders	Engineering/design changes	4,000
Special packaging	Units packaged	40
Special handling	Units handled	60

[7]An important point that could be overlooked here is that activity-based costing analysis can be used in a very specific, targeted manner to address a particular management problem. In this case, the ABC focus is customer-profitability analysis. This is the essence of activity-based management, using the results of an ABC analysis to manage an enterprise more effectively.

Exhibit 6–3
Customer-Profitability Analysis for Five Designated Customers: Aerotech Corporation

	Customer 106	Customer 107	Customer 112	Customer 113	Customer 119
	Designated Customers (By 3-Digit Customer Code)				
Sales revenue	$ 4,320,000	$ 3,480,000	$ 6,500,000	$ 4,490,000	$ 1,960,000
Cost of goods sold	3,220,000	2,810,000	4,890,000	3,380,000	1,480,000
Gross margin	$ 1,100,000	$ 670,000	$ 1,610,000	$ 1,110,000	$ 480,000
Selling and administrative costs:					
General selling costs	$ 362,000	$ 220,000	$ 530,000	$ 366,000	$ 160,000
General administrative costs	181,000	110,000	265,000	183,000	80,000
Customer-related costs					
Order processing	11,100	80,250	16,050	22,200	38,400
Sales contacts	22,000	13,400	32,000	24,100	28,800
Sales visits	44,000	20,000	47,000	38,000	32,000
Shipment processing	33,000	27,800	64,200	44,600	19,200
Billing and collection	33,600	14,000	80,480	22,400	9,600
Design/engineering changes	93,000	96,000	84,000	112,000	68,000
Special packaging	88,000	27,200	64,440	44,480	76,800
Special handling	33,000	80,400	48,300	33,300	86,400
Total selling and administrative cost	$ 900,700	$ 689,050	$ 1,231,470	$ 890,080	$ 599,200
Operating income	$ 199,300	$ (19,050)	$ 378,530	$ 219,920	$ (119,200)

Based on the activity-based costing information, the cost management team assessed the profitability of each of Aerotech's customer relationships. Detailed information from that analysis for five of Aerotech's customers appears in the Excel spreadsheet in Exhibit 6–3. These five customers were singled out because three of them are key Aerotech customers (i.e., customers 106, 112, and 113), and two of them (107 and 119) were suspected by the marketing manager to be at best marginally profitable. As it turned out, suspicions about customers 107 and 119 were well founded. Both customers were found to be unprofitable; in fact, customer 119 had caused Aerotech losses of almost $120,000 during the year.

The customer-profitability analysis for the same five customers is summarized in the bar graph displayed in Exhibit 6–4. Such a graph is a common means of conveying customer-profitability information to management.

To gain further insight into the profitability of the five customers included in Exhibits 6–3 and 6–4, Aerotech's cost management staff prepared the spreadsheet in Exhibit 6–5. In this exhibit, each of the eight key customer-related costs is shown as a percentage of each customer's gross margin. Also displayed in the exhibit is the norm percentage (three-year average percentage across all customers) for each of the eight cost items. For example, the norm percentage for the cost of order processing is 1.1 percent of gross margin. Customers 106, 112, and 113 fall within a percent of the norm for the cost of order processing. However, customer 119's order processing costs were 8.0 percent of its gross margin, and customer 107's were a whopping 12.0 percent!

Look down the column of percentages for each customer, and compare them with the norm for each cost item. It is easy to see why customers 107 and 119 are unprofitable. For each of these customers, several of their customer-related costs are way out of line with the norm. For customer 107, the costs of order processing, design/engineering changes, and special handling are significantly above the norm. In the case of customer 119, all but two of its customer-related costs are out of control. Its special-packaging costs are four times the norm, and its special-handling costs are almost six times the norm!

Are these difficulties with the customer-related costs of certain customers a recent event, or an ongoing problem? Are they getting worse? Insight into these questions is

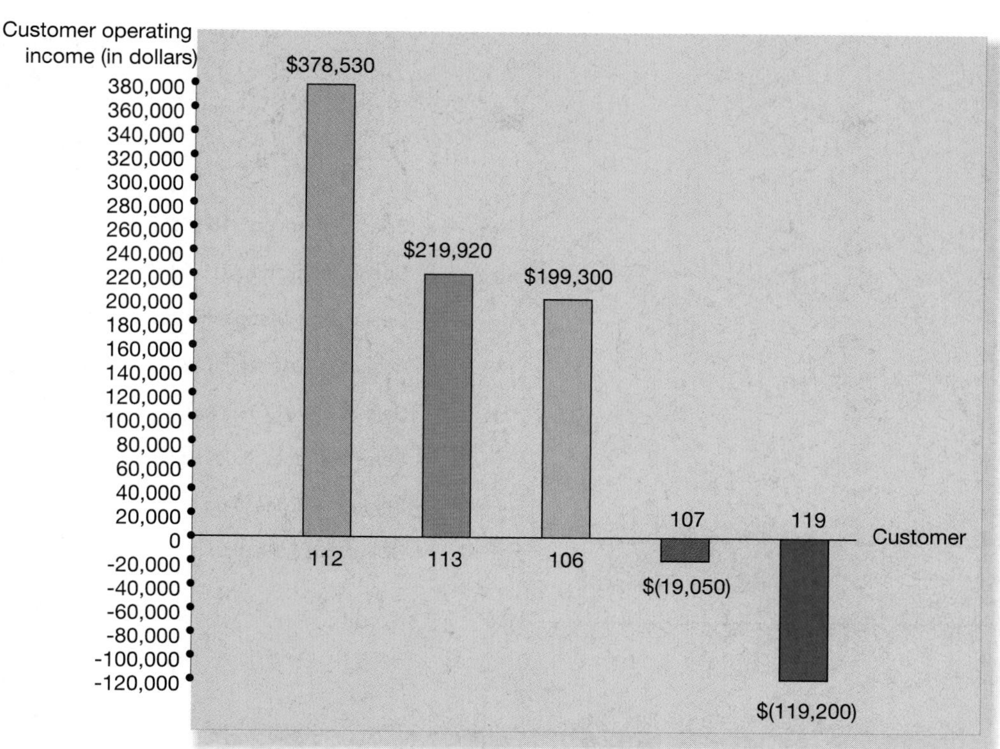

Exhibit 6–4
Customer-Profitability Graphs for Five Designated Customers: Aerotech Corporation

Microsoft Excel - Exhibit 6-5.xls

B11 fx 3.1%

	A	B	C	D	E	F	G
1			Designated Customers (by 3-Digist Customer Code)				
2	**Customer-related cost**	**Norm***	**Customer 106**	**Customer 107**	**Customer 112**	**Customer 113**	**Customer 119**
3							
4	Order processing	1.1%	1.0%	12.0%	1.0%	2.0%	8.0%
5	Sales contacts	1.9%	2.0%	2.0%	2.0%	2.2%	6.0%
6	Sales visits	3.0%	4.0%	3.0%	2.9%	3.4%	6.7%
7	Shipment processing	4.1%	3.0%	4.1%	4.0%	4.0%	4.0%
8	Billing and collection	2.0%	3.1%	2.1%	5.0%	2.0%	2.0%
9	Design/engineering changes	4.9%	8.5%	14.3%	5.2%	10.1%	14.2%
10	Special packaging	4.0%	8.0%	4.1%	4.0%	4.0%	16.0%
11	Special handling	3.1%	3.0%	12.0%	3.0%	3.0%	18.0%
12							
13	Operating income**		18.1%	(2.8)%	23.5%	19.8%	(24.8)%
14							
15	*Norm: Average percentage of gross margin for this cost, across all customers over the past three years.						
16							
17	**Operating income as a percentage of gross margin; negative percentage denotes unprofitable customer						
18	relationship.						

Sheet1 / Sheet2 / Sheet3

Ready

Exhibit 6–5
Customer-Related Costs as a Percentage of Gross Margin for Five Designated Customers: Aerotech Corporation

gleaned from a trend analysis, as depicted in Exhibit 6–6 for customer 119. Special-handling costs have been too high for three years, whereas the cost of design/engineering changes seems to be a one-year spike. Special-packaging costs have been steadily on the rise, while the cost of sales visits has been about twice the norm for all five years. In contrast, customer 119's costs of processing shipments and billing have been close to the norm for all five years.

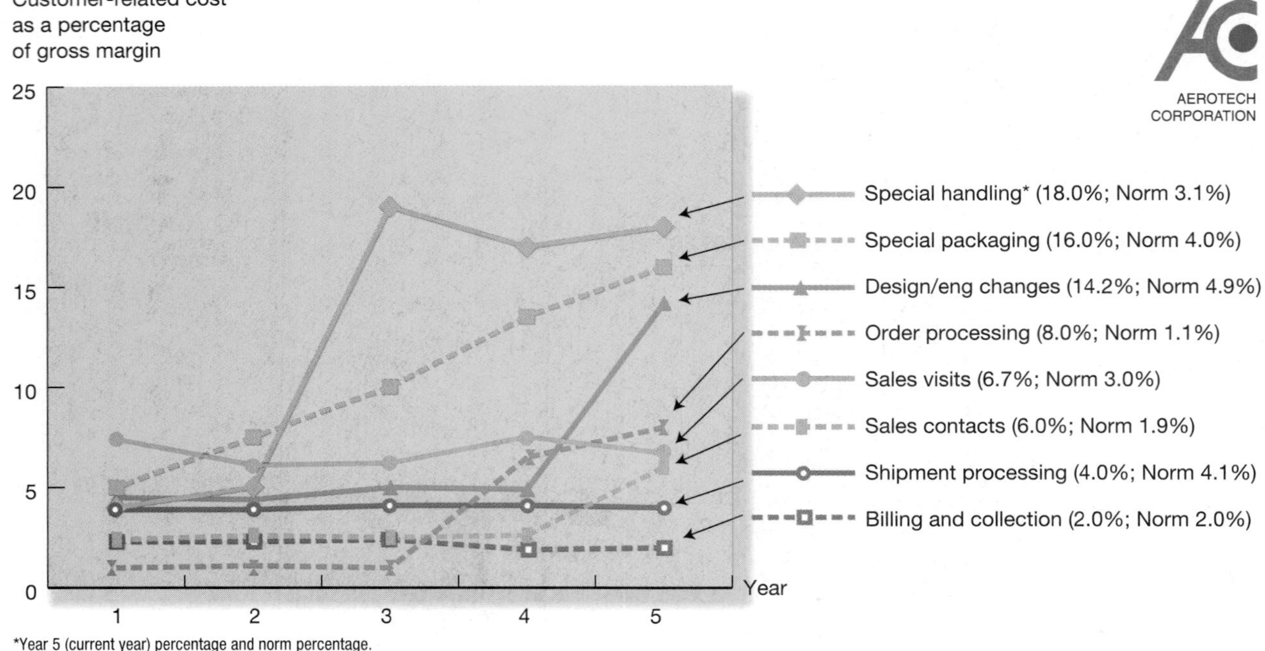

Exhibit 6–6
Trend Analysis for Customer-Related Costs for Customer 119: Aerotech Corporation

A trend analysis like this one can help management decide which customer-related costs need their attention most urgently, and which customers need the most attention. Perhaps even better than comparing the customer-related costs to the norms for Aerotech Corporation would be to compare them to industrywide norms, or the norms for the industry's best performers. Such information can sometimes be generated from *benchmarking studies,* which focus on the best practices of organizations both within the industry and beyond.

Management Accounting Practice

DHL

DHL, an air express transport company, used ABC to do a customer-profitability analysis after an examination of its traditional cost data raised some concerns on the part of management. Using its original cost system, "banks appeared to be very unprofitable customers, whereas heavy manufacturers appeared to be very profitable. This was bad news because we had a lot more banking customers than heavy manufacturing customers."

"A detailed review of the costs showed that the drivers being used (such as the number of shipments) were distorting the true cost picture. These drivers failed to reflect key causal factors such as the impact of package weights. . . . So misleading costs were reported." As a result of these findings, DHL's management decided to do a more robust customer profitability analysis based on ABC.[8]

A complete, but less detailed, customer-profitability analysis for all of Aerotech's customers appears in the spreadsheet in Exhibit 6–7. This exhibit reveals several interesting aspects of Aerotech's customer-profitability scenario. Seventeen of Aerotech's 20 customers are profitable. The three unprofitable customers (107, 134, and 119) resulted in losses of over $240,000 in operating income for Aerotech in a single year!

[8]Steve Player and Carol Cobble, *Cornerstones of Decision Making: Profiles of Enterprise ABM* (Greensboro, NC: Oakhill Press, 1999), p. 133.

Management Accounting Practice

Bank One Corp. and FedEx

An article in *The Wall Street Journal* described how Bank One Corp. and FedEx are using customer-profitability analysis to guide decisions about customer service.[9]

At Bank One Corp., the fifth-largest bank in the U.S., "the line in the sand between preferred and nonpreferred customers has become strikingly obvious." The bank is redesigning its 218 branches in Louisiana so its "Premier One" customers can be whisked away to a special teller window with no wait or to the desk of an appropriate bank officer. "Customers qualify by keeping at least $2,500 in a checking account or a total of $25,000 in a combination of certain bank accounts," or by paying a $17 monthly fee. "Bank One estimates that the extra attention will go only to the top 20 percent of its customers."

"The story is similar at FedEx. Two years ago, the shipping giant began analyzing the returns on its business for about 30 large customers that generate 10 percent of its total volume. It found that certain customers, including some requiring lots of residential deliveries, weren't bringing in as much revenue as they had promised when they first negotiated discounted rates with FedEx." So FedEx demanded that some of these customers pay higher rates. "A couple of big customers who refused to budge were told they could take their shipping business elsewhere. 'We were willing to risk a point or two of market share to correct the problem,' said a spokesman for FedEx. 'You have to be willing to suck it up and walk away.'"

Exhibit 6–7

Customer-Profitability Analysis with Customers Ranked by Operating Income: Aerotech Corporation

Microsoft Excel - Exhibit 6-7.xls

E25 =SUM(D6:D25)

	A	B	C	D	E	F
1						Cumulative Operating
2	3-Digit	Customer	Customer	Customer	Cumulative	Income as a
3	Customer	Sales	Gross	Operating	Operating	Percentage of Total
4	Code	Revenue	Margin	Income	Income	Operating Income
5						
6	**112**	$ 6,500,000	$ 1,610,000	$ 378,530	$ 378,530	8.8%
7	108	6,964,000	1,570,000	370,000	748,530	17.3%
8	114	6,694,000	1,484,300	351,000	1,099,530	25.5%
9	116	5,846,000	1,461,600	340,000	1,439,530	33.4%
10	110	5,602,000	1,430,000	336,070	1,775,600	41.1%
11	121	5,400,000	1,413,000	331,000	2,106,600	48.8%
12	124	5,601,000	1,405,520	330,000	2,436,600	56.5%
13	127	5,090,000	1,280,020	300,000	2,736,600	63.4%
14	128	4,760,000	1,160,200	281,400	3,018,000	69.9%
15	125	5,000,200	1,181,000	276,000	3,294,000	76.3%
16	135	4,431,000	1,150,000	270,000	3,564,000	82.6%
17	133	4,008,000	1,059,800	251,400	3,815,400	88.4%
18	**113**	4,490,000	1,110,000	219,920	4,035,320	93.5%
19	111	4,200,000	875,220	205,000	4,240,320	98.2%
20	**106**	4,320,000	1,100,000	199,300	4,439,620	102.9%
21	136	1,920,000	351,200	82,000	4,521,620	104.8%
22	137	1,641,000	139,400	35,600	4,557,220	105.6%
23	**107**	3,480,000	670,000	(19,050)	4,538,170	105.1%
24	134	2,820,000	582,000	(102,600)	4,435,570	102.8%
25	**119**	1,960,000	480,000	(119,200)	4,316,370	100.0%

Chart1 | **Sheet1** | Sheet2 | Sheet3

Ready

[9] "Alienating Customers Isn't Always a Bad Idea Many Firms Discover," *The Wall Street Journal*, January 7, 1999.

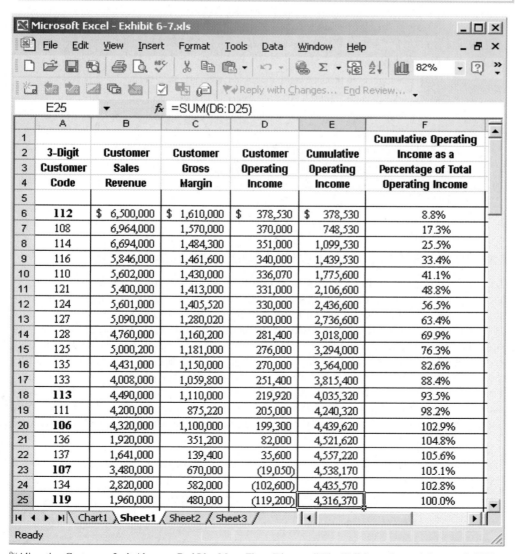

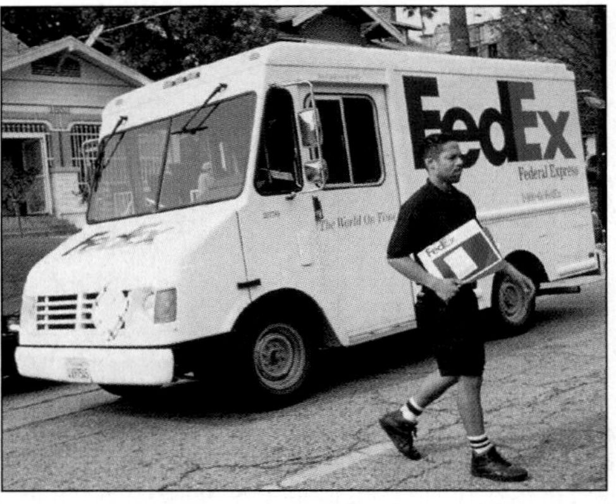

FedEx is using customer profitability analysis to analyze the costs of serving its customers.

> "Almost any person in any organization that implements ABM has some real surprises when they start seeing the data about customer profitability and product profitability." (6f)
> **Sliloh Industries, Inc.**

Notice that over 25 percent of Aerotech's profit is generated by its top three customers. Almost half the company's profit comes from its top six customers, and fully three-quarters of its profit is generated by half its customers. This sort of customer-profitability scenario is quite typical for manufacturers. The lion's share of most companies' profits come from a handful of their customers. Such an insight is important for management as it determines where to devote the company's resources in serving customers.[10]

A graphical portrayal of Aerotech's complete customer-profitability analysis is given in Exhibit 6–8. This graph is called a **customer-profitability profile,** and it is a common and useful way of presenting a customer-profitability analysis to management.

Management Accounting Practice

Dow Chemical Company

At Dow Chemical Company, activity-based costing enables managers to understand the costs of products as well as the costs of serving individual customers.[11] "With this information, the managers are better equipped to make decisions that will best serve the company, its customers, its employees, and its shareholders." Among the decisions addressed by Dow's ABC cost data are the following:

- Which products and services should be produced?
- What does it cost to produce a product or service?
- How profitable is each product or service?
- What are the costs on a plant-by-plant basis?
- Which costs can be reduced?
- Which customers are profitable and should be pursued?
- Where should resources be invested to maximize shareholder value?
- How can Dow improve its performance to maintain its competitive advantage?

Target Costing, Kaizen Costing, and Continuous Improvement

To remain competitive in today's global market, businesses must continually improve. Moreover, this continuous improvement needs to apply across the spectrum of business activity: from product design and quality, through production operations and cost management, to customer service. **Continuous improvement** may be defined as the constant effort to eliminate waste, reduce response time, simplify the design of both products and processes, and improve quality and customer service. One compelling reason for the need for continuous improvement is the *price down/cost down concept.* This refers to the tendency of prices to fall over the life cycle of a newly introduced product. Think, for example, about the prices of hand-held calculators, VCRs, personal listening devices, and CD players. When each of these products was first introduced,

[10]In a conversation with a vice president from a large consumer-products manufacturer, the author was struck by the executive's statement that, "You can bet we pay a lot of attention to the needs and desires of the 'Mart Brothers,' K and Wal."

[11]James W. Damitio, Gary W. Hayes, and Philip L. Kintzele, "Integrating ABC and ABM at Dow Chemical," *Management Accounting Quarterly* 1, no. 2 (Winter 2000), pp. 22–26.

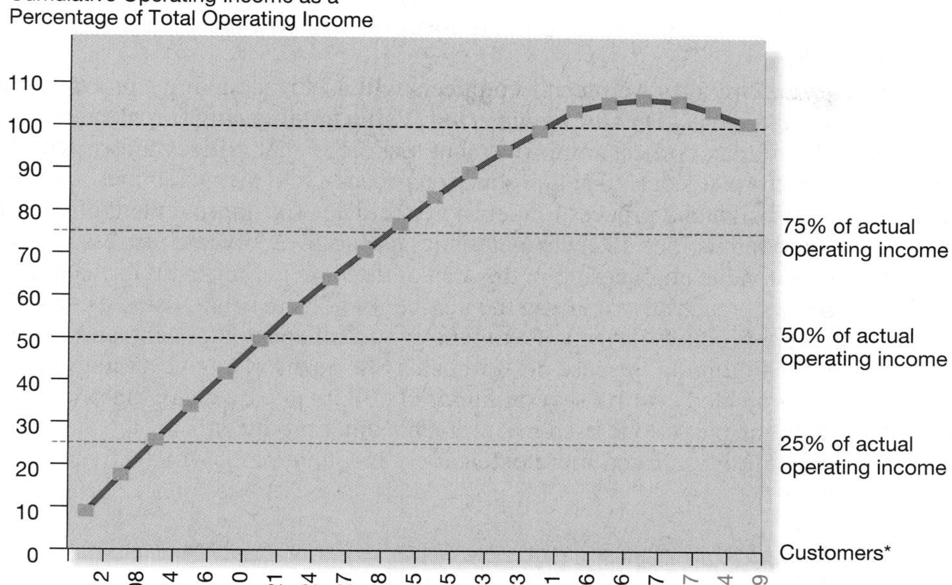

*Customers ranked by operating income.

Exhibit 6–8

Customer-Profitability Profile in Terms of Cumulative Operating Income as a Percentage of Total Operating Income: Aerotech Corporation

prices were quite high. However, as manufacturers gained experience in producing them, prices fell and the products became accessible to a much wider customer pool. However, if prices are to fall over time, manufacturers must continually reduce costs as well.

Two approaches to continuous improvement (i.e., reduction) in production costs are now in widespread use. These techniques are called *target costing* and *kaizen costing*.

Target Costing

LO 7 Define and give an example of target costing.

Target costing refers to the design of a product, and the processes used to produce it, so that ultimately the product can be manufactured at a cost that will enable the firm to make a profit when the product is sold at an estimated market-driven price. This estimated price is called the *target price*, the desired profit margin is called the *target profit,* and the cost at which the product must be manufactured is called the *target cost.*

To illustrate, suppose Aerotech's engineers have developed a new airborne device for detecting wind shear, which is a sudden change in wind direction and speed. Aerotech's management estimates that after a few years on the market, assuming the firm's competitors come out with comparable devices, its Shearsensor will sell for a *target price* of approximately $5,500. Moreover, management desires a *target profit* on its Shearsensor of $500. The *target cost,* then, for the manufacture of a Shearsensor is $5,000 ($5,500 − $500). The task faced by Aerotech's

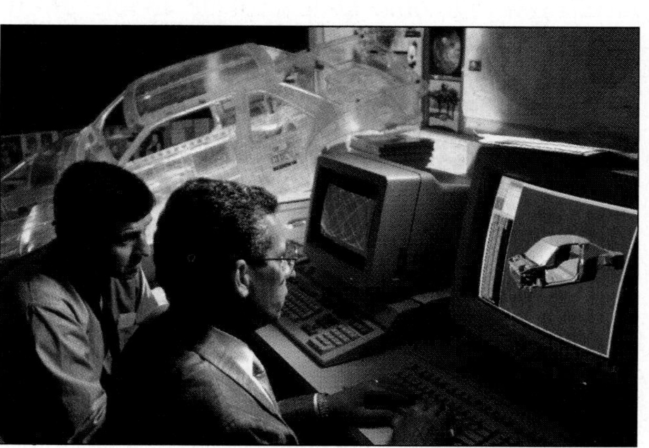

Design engineers play a crucial role in target costing by designing a product that can be manufactured at its target cost and sold at its target price.

engineers now is to refine the Shearsensor's product design, and the processes that will be used to manufacture it, so that ultimately it will cost no more than $5,000 to produce.

One of the techniques Aerotech's engineers will use in achieving a product design that meets the target cost is *value engineering*. **Value engineering** (or **value analysis**) is a cost-reduction and process-improvement technique that utilizes information collected about a product's design and production process, and then examines various attributes of the design and process to identify candidates for improvement efforts. The attributes examined include such characteristics as part diversity and process complexity. Examples of value engineering in the area of direct materials include changing the quality or grade of materials, reducing the number of bolts in a part, using a component common to other products instead of a unique or specialized component, and changing the method of painting. In the case of Aerotech's Shearsensor, engineers might be able to reduce the projected cost by several hundred dollars just by changing one component from a unique part to one used in Aerotech's other products.

Target costing is explored more extensively in Chapter 15, which covers pricing decisions.

Kaizen Costing

LO 8

Explain the concept of kaizen costing, and prepare a kaizen costing chart.

Target costing applies to the *design* of a new product or model and the *design* of its production process. In contrast, **kaizen costing** is the process of cost reduction during the manufacturing phase of an existing product. The Japanese word *kaizen* refers to continual and gradual improvement through small betterment activities, rather than large or radical improvement made through innovation or large investments in technology. The idea is simple. Improvement is the goal and responsibility of every worker, from the CEO to the manual laborers, in every activity, every day, all the time! Through the small but continual efforts of everyone, significant reductions in costs can be attained over time.

To help achieve the continuous cost reduction implied by the kaizen costing concept, an annual (or monthly) *kaizen cost goal* is established. Then, actual costs are tracked over time and compared to the kaizen goal. A kaizen costing chart used by Daihatsu (a Japanese auto manufacturer owned in part by Toyota) is shown in Exhibit 6–9.[12] Notice that the cost base or reference point is the actual cost performance at the end of the prior year. A kaizen goal is established for the cost-reduction rate and amount during the current year. Actual cost performance throughout the year is compared with the kaizen goal. At the end of the current year, the current actual cost becomes the cost base or reference point for the next year. Then, a new (lower) kaizen goal is established, and the cost-reduction effort continues.

How are kaizen costing goals met? The continual and relentless reduction of non-value-added activities and costs, the elimination of waste, and improvements in manufacturing cycle time all contribute to the effort. In addition, the improvement suggestions and kaizen efforts of all employees are taken seriously and implemented when appropriate. The result is a continually more efficient and cost-effective production process.

A good example of the successful use of both target costing and kaizen costing in bringing about continuous improvement is provided by Toyota, as the next section illustrates.

Toyota: Target Costing and Kaizen Costing in Action

Toyota Motor Corporation, Japan's largest automaker, is second in size only to General Motors on a worldwide basis. Toyota uses both target costing and kaizen costing to

---

[12]Yasuhiro Monden and John Lee, "How a Japanese Auto Maker Reduces Costs," *Management Accounting* 75, no. 2 (August 1993), p. 24.

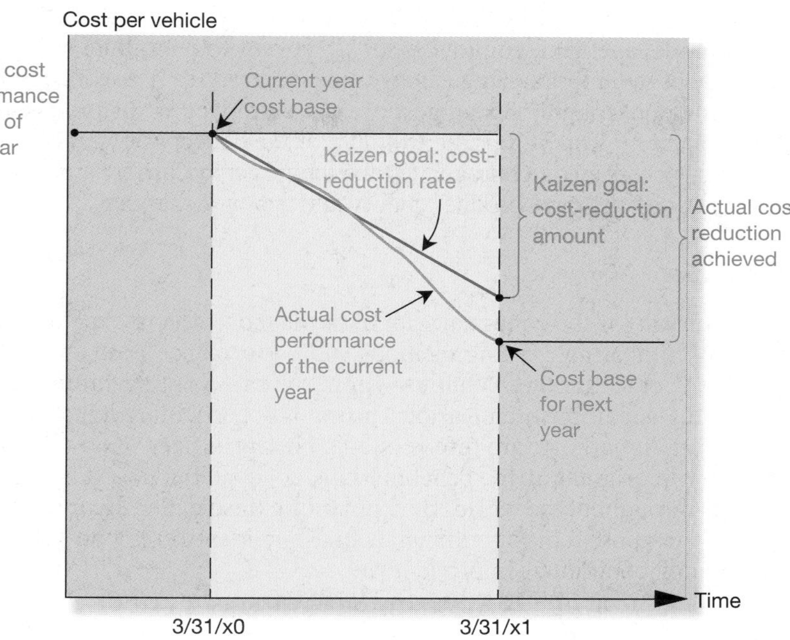

Exhibit 6–9
Kaizen Costing Chart Used by Daihatsu Motor Company (Osaka, Japan)

maintain its strong competitive position. "Cost planning at Toyota is mainly an effort to reduce cost at the design stage. Toyota sets goals for cost reduction, and then seeks to achieve those goals through design changes. To correctly assess the gains made, the exact amount of cost reduction through redesign is measured. Setting goals and assessing the results based on cost differences between old and new models constitute the essence of cost control at Toyota."[13]

Toyota also has achieved significant cost reduction through the redesign of production processes. For example, "over a five-year period, Toyota reduced the setup time for its 800-ton stamping presses from more than one hour to under 12 minutes."[14] Time savings such as this significantly reduce costs.

This Toyota factory shows the company's state-of-the-art manufacturing process. In addition to its advanced manufacturing system, Toyota uses target costing and kaizen costing to maintain its strong competitive position.

In addition to the cost savings realized in the design phase, Toyota aggressively pursues kaizen costing to reduce costs in the manufacturing phase. "In July and January, plant managers submit six-month plans for attaining their kaizen goals. Methods for achieving these goals include cutting material costs per unit and improvements in standard operating procedures. These are pursued based on employee suggestions. For improvements involving industrial engineering or value engineering, employees often receive

[13]Takao Tanaka, "Target Costing at Toyota," *Journal of Cost Management* 7, no. 1 (Spring 1993), p. 4.

[14]Peter B. B. Turney and James M. Reeve, "The Impact of Continuous Improvement on the Design of Activity-Based Cost Systems," *Journal of Cost Management* 4, no. 2 (Summer 1990), p. 44.

support from the technical staff. To draw up a kaizen plan after kaizen goals have been set by top management, employees look for ways to contribute to kaizen in their daily work. About two million suggestions were received from Toyota employees in one recent year alone (roughly 35 suggestions per employee). Ninety-seven percent of them were adopted."[15] This is a prime example of the concept of employee **empowerment**, in which workers are encouraged to take their own initiative to improve operations, reduce costs, and improve product quality and customer service.

Benchmarking

LO 9

Briefly explain the concepts of total quality control, continuous improvement, benchmarking, reengineering, and the theory of constraints.

Benchmarking is the continual search for the most effective method of accomplishing a task, by comparing existing methods and performance levels with those of other organizations or with other subunits within the same organization. The most effective methods of accomplishing various tasks in a particular industry, often discovered through benchmarking, are referred to as **best practices.** Xerox Corporation often is credited with originating the benchmarking concept, but now it is widely used by organizations throughout the world. Benchmarking (also called *competitive benchmarking*) provides one more tool for companies to use in identifying non-value-added activities and pursuing continuous improvement.

Reengineering

In contrast to the concept of kaizen, which involves small, incremental steps toward gradual improvement, reengineering involves a giant leap. **Reengineering** is the complete redesign of a process, with an emphasis on finding creative new ways to accomplish an objective. Reengineering has sometimes been described as taking a blank piece of paper and starting from scratch to redesign a business process. Rather than searching continually for minute improvements, reengineering involves a radical shift in thinking about how an objective should be met. In the words of one reengineering consultant: "Reengineering has captured the attention of U.S. business. Reengineering prescribes radical, quick and significant change. Admittedly, this can entail high risks, but it can also bring big rewards. These benefits are most dramatic when new models are discovered for conducting business."[16]

Theory of Constraints

The theory of constraints (or TOC) is another contemporary management tool that supports continuous improvement and cost management programs. The **theory of constraints** is a management approach that seeks to maximize long-run profit through proper management of organizational bottlenecks or constrained resources.[17] The key idea in TOC is to identify the constraints in a system that are preventing the organization from achieving a higher level of success, then to seek to relieve or relax those constraints. Moreover, TOC recommends subordinating all other management goals to the objective of solving the constraint problems. For example, if limited capacity in a particular machining operation is increasing cycle time, reducing throughput, and reducing profits, then management would concentrate much of its efforts on expanding the capacity of that bottleneck operation.

---

[15]Takao Tanaka, "Kaizen Budgeting: Toyota's Cost Control System under TQC," *Journal of Cost Management* 8, no. 3 (Fall 1994), p. 62.

[16]C. Kevin Cherry, "Re-engineering: Harnessing Creativity and Innovation," *Journal of Cost Management* 8, no. 2 (Summer 1994), p. 49.

[17]John B. MacArthur, "Theory of Constraints and Activity-Based Costing: Friends or Foes?" *Journal of Cost Management* 7, no. 2 (Summer 1993), p. 51.

Focus on Ethics

ETHICAL ISSUES SURROUNDING ABM AND COST-REDUCTION INITIATIVES

We have seen in this chapter how Aerotech Corporation used the insights from its ABC analysis as a catalyst for dramatic changes in the company. Aerotech built a new plant in Bakersfield, which employs a cellular, flexible manufacturing system, JIT production and purchasing, and an automated material-handling system. The company expanded its ABC approach into activity-based management, which led to initiatives to eliminate non-value-added activities, reduce costs, and better understand customer profitability. Kaizen costing for further cost reduction is under active consideration. Such major changes in a company produce great stress and can lead to ethical questions as well. Consider the following hypothetical meeting at Aerotech's Bakersfield plant, which includes Kristin Scott, Aerotech's president (P), Chuck Dickens, the controller (C), and John Stone, vice president for manufacturing (VP).

Scott (P): "Gentlemen, tomorrow's the one-year anniversary of our opening the doors here in Bakersfield. Congratulations on a job well done."

Dickens (C): "Thanks, Kristin. It's amazing to think of the changes that were ushered in by our ABC analysis and subsequent ABM approach. A lot of our success is due to your efforts, John."

Stone (VP): "Thanks, but I wish I was feeling better about it!"

Scott (P): "What do you mean, John? What's bothering you?"

Stone (VP): "It's hard to put my finger on it, Kristin. Everything we've done seemed right at the time. The ABC study, the new plant, JIT, the cost-reduction initiatives, customer-profitability analysis—all of it. But I can't help but feel that we may have hurt a lot of good people and even whole companies by what we've done."

Scott (P): "I can sympathize with your feelings, John, but you have to remember that our job, first and foremost, is to look after the interests of the shareholders who own Aerotech. We have to try to maximize the value of the company."

Stone (VP): "So they say, Kristin. So they say. But I'm just not convinced. Take the move to Bakersfield, for example. I realize that we wanted to operate a state-of-the-art plant and be closer to our suppliers, but what about our employees in Phoenix? What happens to them when we eventually close that plant?"

Scott (P): "You know that we'll accommodate as many of them as we can here in Bakersfield, John."

Stone (VP): "But that won't be more than half at best. Many of them won't have the skill set that we need here, and others just won't want to move. Family reasons, kids in school. You know the story."

Dickens (C): "We'll offer retraining to those who can qualify and are willing to move."

Stone (VP): "It's still a huge disruption in people's lives, Chuck."

Scott (P): "That's true, John, but we still have to do what's right for the company."

Stone (VP): "But the company *is* our people, Kristin. Do we look out for their interests, or those of a bunch of nameless pension fund managers? And it's not even just *our* employees, Kristin. We're in the process of reducing our vendor base to a tenth of what it was. I know that will cut our procurement costs, but what about the companies who've been reliable suppliers that we're just abandoning? And what about their employees? Cost cuts and layoffs and all may help the bottom line, but they put a lot of folks in a tough spot!"

Dickens (C): "No one can deny the truth of what you're saying, John. But people adapt. One company closes its doors, and another one opens theirs. That's just business, John."

Stone (VP): "This business of eliminating non-value-added activities bugs me, too. How do you tell someone who's worked for Aerotech 20 years that what they do doesn't add value anymore?"

Scott (P): "You don't tell them that, John. You know that. When we eliminate an activity as NVA, we almost always can offer the employee retraining and a new job doing something that *does* add value."

Dickens (C): "Don't you think, John, that employees would rather know that they're adding value than be wondering if they really are? People aren't dumb. They know if what they're doing still contributes."

Stone (VP): "Yeah, I suppose you're right. It's just been bothering me, that's all."

Scott (P): "We're all human, John. It's only natural to have these concerns. I have them, too. But in the long run, these kinds of productivity improvements are good for the economy, good for Aerotech, and ultimately they're good even for the people who have to make the changes."

Stone (VP): "I guess so. But you know what else worries me? This customer-profitability analysis stuff. I grew up working in my grandfather's book store, and his philosophy was that 'the customer is always right.'"

Dickens (C): "On that one, John, I have less sympathy with your concerns. It's not a question of whether the customer's right or not. Our customers can have anything they want. If they want their Mode I boards gift wrapped and delivered by pony express, we'll oblige. But we need to make sure that each customer is paying for the special services they demand. Otherwise, it's not fair to the other customers who make fewer demands on us."

Scott (P): "I agree with Chuck on this one, John. Our customer-profitability analysis has enabled us to explain to customers that their demands cost us money, and they need to pay for them. Many of our customers have seen this approach as helping them as much as us."

Stone (VP): "Okay, you've convinced me about that. But all the other stuff, logical as your arguments are, still makes me queasy. Thanks for hearing me out. It's important for us all to keep the human side of what we do squarely in front of us."

Scott (P): "You won't get any argument from me there, John."

Dickens (C): "Ditto."

What do you make of this meandering discussion among these three top Aerotech executives? Are there ethical issues here that need to be addressed? How would you resolve them?

Chapter Summary

To achieve and maintain a competitive advantage in today's global marketplace, many companies are investing heavily in new technology. To reduce cycle time, make operations more efficient, and eliminate non-value-added costs, many companies are adopting a just-in-time inventory and production management philosophy. Under this production system, no raw materials are purchased and no products are manufactured until they are needed. Along with JIT production systems, many companies are modernizing their production processes with computer-assisted manufacturing systems. Although these systems are extremely expensive, the cost savings and strategic benefits they facilitate often justify their acquisition.

In addition to new technology, many organizations are implementing new cost management systems to better meet the needs of management in an economy that continually grows more competitive. One such cost management system is activity-based management, which is the use of activity-based costing information to improve operations and eliminate non-value-added costs. One way of depicting ABM is the two-dimensional ABC model. This model combines the cost assignment role of ABC with the process and evaluation view of an ABC system.

In today's competitive environment, a company must continually improve in order to remain successful. A continuous improvement program is a constant effort to eliminate waste, reduce response time, simplify the design of both products and processes, and improve quality and customer service. Consistent with continuous improvement are the concepts of target costing and kaizen costing. Both of these methods seek to improve a product and its production process and, in so doing, reduce costs. Target costing focuses on the design phase, while kaizen costing concentrates on the manufacturing phase. Other management tools that are consistent with continuous improvement efforts include value engineering, benchmarking, reengineering, and the theory of constraints.

Key Terms

For each term's definition refer to the indicated page, or turn to the glossary at the end of the text.

activity analysis, 224
activity-based management (ABM), 224
automated material-handling system (AMHS), 221
benchmarking (or competitive benchmarking), 236
best practices, 236
capital-intensive, 224
cellular manufacturing, 221
computer-integrated manufacturing (CIM) system, 221
continuous improvement, 232
customer-profitability analysis, 226
customer profitability profile, 226
empowerment, 236
flexible manufacturing system (FMS), 221
FMS cell, 221
just-in-time (JIT) inventory and production management system, 218
just-in-time (JIT) purchasing, 220
kaizen costing, 234
labor-intensive, 224
non-value-added activities, 224
non-value-added costs, 224
off-line quality control, 222
process, 226
process value analysis (PVA), 226
production Kanban, 219
pull method, 219
reengineering, 236
target costing, 233
theory of constraints, 236
total quality control (TQC), 219
two-dimensional ABC model, 224
value engineering (or value analysis), 234
withdrawal Kanban, 219

Review Questions

6–1. Briefly describe the JIT approach to production and inventory management.

6–2. List eight key features of a just-in-time inventory and production management system.

6–3. What is meant by *TQC*? Explain the importance of TQC in a JIT system.

6–4. Explain in words and then draw a diagram depicting the pull method of coordinating steps in a JIT system. (Refer to the JIT discussion in Chapter 6 and to the JIT exhibit in Chapter 1.)

6–5. List five features of JIT purchasing.

6–6. Define the following terms: *CMS, JIT, AMHS, FMS,* and *CIM*.

6–7. Briefly describe the key differences in plant layout between Aerotech's Phoenix and Bakersfield facilities.

6–8. How is a firm's cost structure likely to change if an FMS is installed?

6–9. Explain what is meant by *off-line quality control, cellular manufacturing,* and *activity-based management*.

6–10. Explain the concept of *two-dimensional ABC*. Support your explanation with a diagram.

6–11. What is meant by the term *activity analysis*? Give three criteria for determining whether an activity adds value.

6–12. Distinguish between an activity's *trigger* and its *root cause*. Give an example of each.

6–13. List four techniques for reducing or eliminating non-value-added costs.

6–14. Give an example of activity sharing.

6–15. What is meant by *customer-profitability analysis?* Give an example of an activity that might be performed more commonly for one customer than for another.

6–16. Explain the relationship between customer profitability analysis and activity-based costing.

6–17. What is a customer profitability profile?

6–18. Evaluate the following statement: "A company should stop selling products to a customer that has been identified as unprofitable."

6–19. How can trend analysis of customer-related costs be helpful to management in a customer-profitability analysis?

6–20. What is meant by the following terms: *continuous improvement, price down/cost down* concept, *target costing, target price, target cost, target profit, value engineering,* and *kaizen costing*?

6–21. Which of the following terms is most consistent with the old saying, "Slow and steady wins the race": flexible manufacturing, advanced manufacturing system, product innovation, target costing, kaizen costing, or investment in high technology? Explain.

6–22. What is meant by *employee empowerment, benchmarking, best practices, and reengineering?*

6–23. Explain how the concepts of *continuous improvement* and the *theory of constraints* are related.

6–24. Elimination of production bottleneck activities is an example of what management concept?

6–25. What behavioral problems can you think of that a company such as Aerotech might encounter in modifying its managerial-accounting system to fit today's manufacturing environment?

Exercises

Exercise 6–26
Direct and Indirect Costs; Traditional versus JIT Manufacturing Environment
(LO 1, 2)

The following costs were incurred in each of two automobile-parts factories in June.

Raw materials	Depreciation, plant	Direct labor
Electricity, machines	Depreciation, equipment	Supervisory salaries
Electricity, lighting, and air-conditioning	Insurance	Property taxes
Engineering salaries	Machine repair, wages	Factory supplies
Custodial wages	Machine repair, parts	Inspection

Required: For every cost listed above, indicate whether it is more likely to be treated as a direct cost or an indirect cost in each of the following. Explain your choice for each cost item in each manufacturing environment.

1. A traditional factory with a traditional cost-accounting system.
2. A JIT/FMS factory with an activity-based costing system.

Exercise 6–27
Non-Value-Added Costs
(LO 5)

Non-value-added costs occur in nonmanufacturing firms also.

Required: Identify four potential non-value-added costs in (1) an airline, (2) a bank, and (3) a hotel.

Exercise 6–28
Design Your Own Production Process Using Advanced Manufacturing Systems; Non-Value-Added Costs
(LO 1, 5)

Since you have always wanted to be an industrial baron, invent your own product and describe at least five steps used in its production.

Required: Design a plant layout using the latest in advanced manufacturing technology to manufacture your product. Explain how your plant will eliminate non-value-added costs.

Exercise 6–29
Performance Measures in Two-Dimensional ABC; ABM
(LO 3, 4)

List five activities performed by the employees of an airline *on the ground*. For each of these activities, suggest a performance measure that could be used in activity-based management.

Exercise 6–30
Activity Analysis; Non-Value-Added Activities
(LO 3, 5)

Visit a restaurant for a meal or think carefully about a recent visit to a restaurant. List as many activities as you can think of that would be performed by the restaurant's employees for its customers.

Required: For each activity on your list, indicate the following:

1. Value-added or non-value-added.
2. The trigger of the activity.
3. The possible root causes of the activity.

Exercise 6–31
College Registration; Reengineering
(LO 5, 9)

Think carefully about the various activities and steps involved in the course registration process at your college or university.

Required:

1. List the steps in the registration process in the sequence in which they occur.
2. Prepare an activity analysis of the registration process. Discuss the activity linkages, triggers, and root causes.
3. Reengineer your institution's course registration process with these goals in mind:
   a. Improve the convenience and effectiveness of the process for the student registering.
   b. Improve the effectiveness and cost efficiency of the process from the standpoint of the institution.

Exercise 6–32
Target Costing
(LO 7)

Suppose you have just started a business to manufacture your newest invention, the photon gismo. Let's say you believe that after a few years on the market, photon gismos will sell for about $130. This allows for the introduction of similar devices by your competitors. Furthermore, let's say you want to make a profit of $35 on each gismo sold.

Required:

1. What is the target cost for the photon gismo?
2. What is the target profit?
3. What is the target price?
4. Suppose your engineers and cost accountants conclude that your design of the photon gismo will result in a unit cost of $115. How can you use the concept of target costing to help achieve your objective?
5. How could value engineering help in this process? Suggest an example.
6. How could two-dimensional activity-based costing help? Suggest an example.

Exercise 6–33
Customer-Profitability Analysis; Trend Analysis
(LO 6)

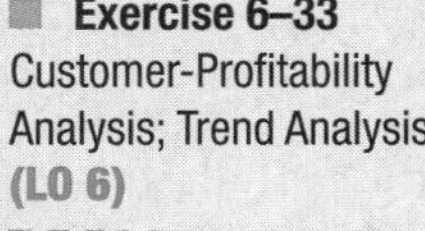

Analysis shows that Zodiac Corporation incurred the following five-year gross margin and cost histories in serving customer number 128.

	Year 1	Year 2	Year 3	Year 4	Year 5
Gross margin	$602,000	$638,000	$636,000	$652,000	$670,000
Cost of engineering changes	6,600	12,120	7,000	7,200	80,250
Special packaging	66,200	73,360	82,600	78,100	80,400

Required:

1. Prepare a trend analysis (in terms of percentage of gross margin) for these two customer-related costs.
2. What different conclusions might management draw about the behavior of these two costs?

Exercise 6–34
Customer-Profitability Analysis; Use of Internet
(LO 6)

Use the Internet to visit FedEx's website (www.fedex.com).

Required: Read about the express delivery services provided by the company. Then discuss how FedEx could use customer profitability analysis.

Exercise 6–35
Customer Profitability Analysis; Customers Ranked by Sales Revenue
(LO 6)

The customer-profitability analysis for Aerotech Corporation, which is displayed in Exhibit 6–7, ranks customers by operating income. An alternative, often-used approach is to rank customers by sales revenue.

Required:

1. List the customer numbers in the left-hand column of Exhibit 6–7 by sales revenue, from highest to lowest. Is the ranking different from that in Exhibit 6–7?
2. Aerotech's smallest customers, in terms of sales revenue, are last in the listing done for requirement (1). Are these customers Aerotech's least profitable?
3. Would the customer-profitability profile in Exhibit 6–8 be different if the customers were ranked by sales revenue instead of operating income? Explain.
4. What factors could cause a larger customer (in terms of sales revenue) to be less profitable than a smaller customer?

Exercise 6–36
Customer-Profitability Graph
(LO 6)

Windy City Design Company specializes in designing commercial office space in Chicago. Suppose the firm's president reviewed the following income statement and noticed that operating profits were below her expectations. She had a hunch that certain customers were not profitable for the company and asked the controller to perform a customer-profitability analysis showing profitability by customer for the month of October.

WINDY CITY DESIGN COMPANY
Income Statement
For the Month Ended October 31

Sales revenue	$300,000
Cost of services billed	255,000
Gross margin	$ 45,000
Marketing and administrative costs	30,000
Operating profit	$ 15,000

The controller provided the following customer-profitability graph:

Windy City Design Company
Customer-Profitability Graph
For the Month Ended October 31

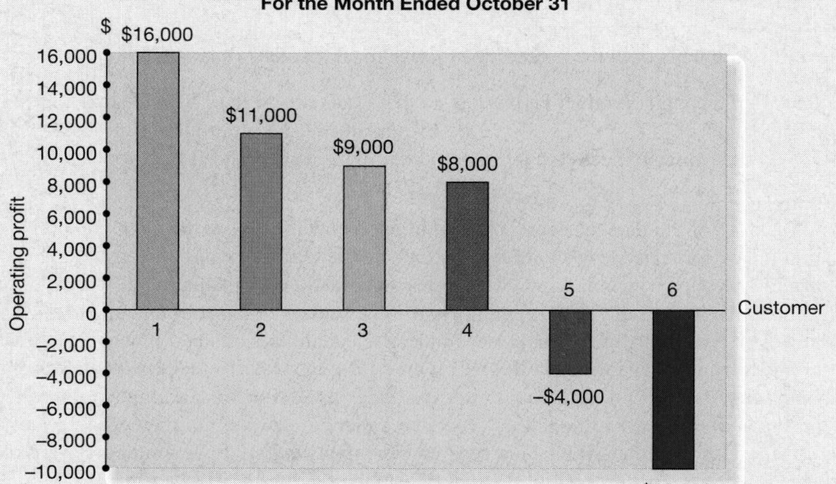

Required: Put yourself in the position of Windy City Design's controller and write a memo to the president to accompany the customer-profitability graph. Comment on the implications of the customer-profitability analysis and raise four or more issues that should be addressed by the firm's management team.

Exercise 6–37
Basic Elements of a Production Process; Non-Value-Added Costs
(LO 3, 5)

Bodacious Bagels, Inc. manufactures a variety of bagels, which are frozen and sold in grocery stores. The production process consists of the following steps.

1. Ingredients, such as flour and raisins, are received and inspected. Then they are stored until needed.
2. Ingredients are carried on hand carts to the mixing room.
3. Dough is mixed in 40-pound batches in four heavy-duty mixers.
4. Dough is stored on large boards in the mixing room until a bagel machine is free.
5. A board of dough is carried into the bagel room. The board is tipped, and the dough slides into the hopper of a bagel machine. This machine pulls off a small piece of dough, rolls it into a cylindrical shape, and then squeezes it into a doughnut shape. The bagel machines can be adjusted in a setup procedure to accommodate different sizes and styles of bagels. Workers remove the uncooked bagels and place them on a tray, where they are kept until a boiling vat is free.
6. Next the trays of uncooked bagels are carried into an adjoining room, which houses three 50-gallon vats of boiling water. The bagels are boiled for approximately one minute.
7. Bagels are removed from the vats with a long-handled strainer and placed on a wooden board. The boards full of bagels are carried to the oven room, where they are kept until an oven rack is free. The two ovens contain eight racks which rotate but remain upright, much like the seats on a Ferris wheel. A rack full of bagels is finished baking after one complete revolution in the oven. When a rack full of bagels is removed from the oven, a fresh rack replaces it. The oven door is opened and closed as each rack completes a revolution in the oven.
8. After the bagels are removed from the oven, they are placed in baskets for cooling.
9. While the bagels are cooling, they are inspected. Misshapen bagels are removed and set aside. (Most are eaten by the staff.)
10. After the bagels are cool, the wire baskets are carried to the packaging department. Here the bagels are dumped into the hopper on a bagging machine. This machine packages a half-dozen bagels in each bag and seals the bag with a twist tie.
11. Then the packaged bagels are placed in cardboard boxes, each holding 24 bags. The boxes are placed on a forklift and are driven to the freezer, where the bagels are frozen and stored for shipment.

Required:

1. Identify the steps in the bagel-production process that fall into each of the following categories: process time, inspection time, move time, waiting time, storage time.
2. List the steps in the production process that could be candidates for non-value-added activities.

Exercise 6–38
Key Features of JIT Production Systems
(LO 1, 2)

Refer to the information given in the preceding exercise for Bodacious Bagels, Inc.

Required: Redesign the bagel production process so that it adheres to the JIT philosophy. Explain how the eight key features of JIT systems would be present in the new production process. What new equipment would the company need to purchase in order to implement the JIT approach fully?

Exercise 6–39
Benchmarking
(LO 9)

The continual search for the most effective method of accomplishing a task through comparison of existing methods and performance levels with those of other organizations or with other subunits within the same organization is called benchmarking. Sometimes organizations benchmark their operations against similar organizations, including their competitors. In other cases, organizations benchmark against a completely different type of organization. For example, a telecommunications company benchmarked its customer service operations against a NASCAR pit crew. The idea was to see how the telecommunications company's customer service unit could improve its response time by learning from the NASCAR crew. The pit crew, of course, had honed its procedures meticulously to get the necessary service accomplished in the least time possible. This type of benchmarking study is sometimes referred to as benchmarking "outside the box."

Required:

1. How could your college or university benefit from benchmarking against a similar institution of higher education? What departments, operations, or procedures might be appropriate for the focus of such a benchmarking study?
2. How could your college or university benefit from benchmarking outside the box? What departments, operations, or procedures might benefit from such a study? What noneducational organizations might be chosen for the benchmarking study?

Problems

Problem 6–40
Just-in-Time Production
(LO 2)

ElectroMobile Company (EMC) manufactures electric golf carts, electric all-terrain vehicles, and electric senior-citizen mobility scooters. Each of the three products has two or three models. Because of the somewhat erratic product demand and the lead-time needed for the setup for a model changeover, EMC has been increasing its raw-material and finished-goods inventories. Work-in-process inventories are relatively low and have consistent costs from one month to the next.

During the last five years, EMC has experienced increased inventory costs, decreasing profit margins, and customer complaints concerning the long lead-time to fill sales orders. EMC's president, Lou Watts, has been concerned about these problems and has been discussing ways to change these deteriorating conditions with his production, marketing, and accounting staff.

For the past few months, this top management group has been looking at how a just-in-time (JIT) manufacturing system utilizing a "Kanban" concept could be used in their company. The team has assembled data that indicates that EMC could change their production process from one of "production push" to "demand pull" by rearranging their production floor into manufacturing cells that would be dedicated to one of the three products produced. Slight modifications to the equipment in the cell would be needed for a changeover from one model to another. Cell production teams would be responsible for cell performance, maintenance on machines and equipment, solving their production problems, and training.

The management team has reached a point where it needs an outside consultant and has hired Grant Withers. EMC wants Withers to explain the procedures and issues involved in changing from a "production push" to a "demand pull" production process.

Required:

1. Discuss the effects on EMC's planning and operating processes if EMC implements a "demand pull" production system.
2. Identify and describe at least five benefits to EMC that should result from the "demand pull" production operating approach.
3. Discuss the behavioral effects of the proposed change at EMC on team participation in planning and production.

(CMA, adapted)

Problem 6–41
Plant Layouts; Traditional and Flexible Manufacturing System
(LO 1, 2)

Borealis, Inc. manufactures special heavy bolts used in spacecraft. The production process consists of the following operations: (1) metal rods are cut to the proper length in a cutting machine; (2) a heading machine flattens the end of the cut rod to form a head; (3) a slotting machine cuts a slot in the bolt's head; (4) the bolt is run through a threading machine, which cuts the bolt's threads; (5) the bolt is washed to remove metal shavings and other foreign particles; (6) the bolt is heat-treated for hardness in a salt bath; (7) the bolt is inspected; (8) the bolt is wrapped and packaged.

The salt bath is a very expensive operation because of the electricity requirements. Another expensive operation is the central oil-filtration system, which is used to provide oil to all of the cutting and threading machines. The oil acts as a lubricant and coolant. After passing through a cutting machine, the oil is pumped back to a central oil-filtration station, which filters foreign particles from the oil.

Required:

1. Draw a factory-layout diagram showing how a traditional layout of Borealis's production process might appear. (Refer to Exhibit 5–1 for guidance.)
2. Repeat requirement (1), assuming that Borealis has adopted a JIT production system and purchased an FMS and an AMHS. Assume that only one central salt bath will be used, and that the company will keep its centralized oil-filtration system. (Refer to Exhibit 6–1 for guidance.)

Problem 6–42
Non-Value-Added Costs
(LO 3, 5)

Refer to the information given in the preceding problem for Borealis, Inc.

Required: Identify the non-value-added costs that might be present in Borealis' traditional plant layout and production process. Write a memo to the company president pointing these costs out and advocating an FMS.

Problem 6–43
Just-in-Time Purchasing; Supplier Focus
(LO 1, 2)

Pacific Rim Enterprises' management recently decided to adopt a just-in-time inventory policy to curb steadily rising costs and free up cash for purposes of investment. The company anticipates that inventory will decrease from $7,200,000 to $1,200,000, with the released funds to be invested at a 12 percent return for the firm. Additional data follow:

- Reduced inventories should produce savings in insurance and property taxes of $54,000.
- The company will lease 75 percent of an existing warehouse to another firm for $4 per square foot. The warehouse has 30,000 square feet.
- Because of the need to handle an increased number of small shipments from suppliers, Pacific Rim Enterprises will remodel production and receiving-dock facilities at a cost of $1,200,000. The construction costs will be depreciated over a 10-year life.
- A shift in suppliers is expected to result in the purchase and use of more expensive raw materials. However, these materials should give rise to fewer warranty and repair problems after Pacific Rim Enterprises' finished product is sold, resulting in a net savings of $50,000.
- Three employees who currently earn $60,000 each will be directly affected by the just-in-time adoption decision. Two employees will be transferred to other positions with Pacific Rim Enterprises; one will be terminated.
- Reduced raw material inventory levels and accompanying stockouts will cost the firm $140,000.

Required:

1. Compute the annual financial impact of the decision to adopt a just-in-time inventory system.
2. If the just-in-time system is implemented in proper fashion, what is the likelihood of excessive raw material stockouts? Briefly explain.
3. Adoption of a just-in-time purchasing system will often result in less need for the inspection of incoming materials and parts. Why?
4. In comparison with a traditional purchasing system, why does a just-in-time system give rise to an increased number of small shipments to the buying firm?

Problem 6–44
Activity Analysis; Non-Value-Added Activities; Reengineering
(LO 5, 9)

Go shopping for groceries; then visit your bank and complete a relatively routine transaction. (Or, if that is inconvenient, think carefully about the last time you performed these errands.)

Required: For each of the errands mentioned above, list the activities you performed as you completed the errand.

1. On your list show the activity sequence and linkages.
2. Indicate whether each specific activity was value-added or non-value-added. Explain how the non-value-added activities could be eliminated (or at least improved).
3. How have banks and grocery stores reengineered their processes in recent years to improve efficiency both for the employees and for the customers?

Problem 6–45
Non-Value-Added Costs; Changeover to a JIT Production System
(LO 2, 3, 5)

Pickwick Paper Company's Richmond plant manufactures paperboard. Its production process involves the following operations.

1. Harvested trees arrive by rail in the wood yard and are stored outside.
2. Logs are moved by a flume into the plant where they pass through a debarker and are cut up into chips.
3. The chips are stored in large bins near the chipping machines.
4. The chips then are transported by small trucks to another building and are placed in a digester, a large pressure cooker where heat, steam, and chemicals convert the chips into moist fibers.
5. The fibers are stored near the digester.

6. In the next step, the fibers are loaded by workers onto a conveyor belt, which carries the fibers to a depressurized blow tank. This operation separates the fibers.
7. The separated fibers are placed on wooden pallets and stored next to the blow tank.
8. Forklifts are used to carry the separated fibers to the refining area, where the fibers are washed, refined, and treated with chemicals and caustic substances until they become pulp.
9. The wood pulp then enters the paper machines through a headbox, which distributes pulp evenly across a porous belt of forming fabric.
10. Water is removed from the pulp by passing it over a wire screen.
11. Additional water is removed from the pulp in a series of presses.
12. Dryers then remove any remaining water from the pulp.
13. The thin, dry sheets of pulp are then smoothed and polished by large rollers called calenders.
14. Then the paperboard is wound into large rolls, and workers place the rolls on wooden pallets.
15. Forklifts are used to move the rolls of paperboard to the labeling building.
16. There the rolls are labeled and stored for shipment.
17. The rolls of paperboard are shipped to customers from the loading dock in the labeling building.

The partially processed product sometimes is stored between production operations for two to three days. This delay can be caused either by a faster production rate in the earlier processes than in the later processes or by breakdowns in the production machinery. The Richmond plant's average cycle time is about 15 days.

Required: Your consulting firm has been hired to advise Pickwick Paper's management on how to improve its production process.

1. Diagram the current production process.
2. Point out areas that you believe to be candidates for non-value-added activities.
3. Prepare a plan for Pickwick to change its production process to a JIT process. Include a diagram of your suggested process. The company is not in a position to buy new production machinery, but management will consider purchasing an AMHS. The plant currently operates in three buildings, which are not far apart. Management is willing to consider minor construction to connect the buildings.

Problem 6–46
Two-Dimensional Activity-Based Costing; Activity Analysis; ABM
(LO 3, 4, 5)

Contemporary Kitchen Furnishings, Inc. (CKF) manufactures a variety of housewares for the consumer market in the midwest. The company's three major product lines are cooking utensils, tableware, and flatware. CKF implemented activity-based costing four years ago and now has a well-developed ABC system in place for determining product costs. Only recently, however, has the ABC system been systematically used for the purposes of activity-based management. As a pilot project, CKF's controller asked the ABC project team to do a detailed activity analysis of the purchasing activity. The following specific activities were identified.

1. Receipt of parts specifications from the Design Engineering Department.
2. Follow-up with design engineers to answer any questions.
3. Vendor (supplier) identification.
4. Vendor consultations (by phone or in person).
5. Price negotiation.
6. Vendor selection.
7. Ordering (by phone or mail).
8. Order follow-up.
9. Expediting (attempting to speed up delivery).
10. Order receiving.
11. Inspection of parts.
12. Return of parts not meeting specifications.
13. Consultation with design engineers and production personnel if parts do not satisfy intended purpose.
14. Further consultation and/or negotiation with vendor if necessary.
15. Ship parts back to vendor if necessary.
16. If satisfactory, move parts to storage.

Required:

1. Draw a diagram to depict CKF's two-dimensional activity-based costing efforts. The diagram should include the following:
   a. The cost assignment role of ABC, with the cost pools, activities, and product lines represented.
   b. The process view of ABC, with the purchasing activities displayed. Also indicated here will be the linkages among the activities. (To save space, indicate the activities by their numbers.)
   c. The activity evaluation phase of two-dimensional ABC.
2. Identify the triggers for each of the following activities in CKF's purchasing activity analysis:
   Follow-up with design engineers (activity 2)
   Expediting (activity 9)
   Inspection of parts (activity 11)
   Return of parts (activity 12)
   Consultation with design engineers and production personnel (activity 13)
3. For each of the activities listed in requirement (2), identify the possible root causes.
4. Choose four activities in CKF's purchasing function, and suggest a performance measure for each of these activities.

Problem 6–47
Activity-Based Management; Cost Cutting
(LO 3, 4, 5)

ReadersNet.Com sells books and software over the Internet. A recent article in a trade journal has caught the attention of management, given that the company has experienced soaring inventory handling costs. The article noted that similar firms have purchasing, warehousing, and distribution costs that average 13 percent of sales, which is attractive when compared against ReadersNet.Com's results for the past year.

The following information is available:

Activity (Cost)	Cost Driver	Cost Driver Quantity	Percent of Cost Driver Activity for Books	Percent of Cost Driver Activity for Software
Incoming receipts ($600,000)	Number of purchase orders	2,000	70%	30%
Warehousing ($720,000)	Number of inventory moves	9,000	80	20
Outgoing shipments ($450,000)	Number of shipments	15,000	25	75

Book sales totaled $7,800,000 and software sales totaled $5,200,000. A review of the company's activities found various inefficiencies with respect to the warehousing of books and outgoing shipments of software. These inefficiencies resulted in an extra 550 moves and 250 shipments, respectively.

Required:

1. What is activity-based management? What is a non-value-added activity?
2. How much did non-value-added activities cost ReadersNet.Com this past year?
3. Cite several examples of situations that may have given rise to non-value-added activities for ReadersNet.Com.
4. Will the elimination of non-value-added activities allow ReadersNet.Com to achieve a 13 percent cost percentage for each of the product lines? Show calculations.
5. Do either of the two product lines require additional cost cutting to achieve the target percentage? If so, how much additional cost cutting is needed, and what tools (i.e., methods) might the company use to achieve the cuts? Briefly describe.

Problem 6–48
JIT Cost Savings
(LO 2)

AutoTech, Inc. is an automotive supplier that uses automatic screw machines to manufacture precision parts from steel bars. AutoTech's inventory of raw steel averages $1,800,000 with a turnover rate of four times per year. John Mercedes, president of AutoTech, is concerned about the costs of carrying inventory. He is considering the adoption of just-in-time inventory procedures in order to eliminate the need to carry any raw steel inventory. Mercedes has asked Katrina Gorman, AutoTech's controller, to evaluate the feasibility of JIT for the corporation. Gorman has identified the following effects of adopting JIT.

- Without scheduling any overtime, lost sales due to stockouts would increase by 35,000 units per year. However, by incurring overtime premiums of $120,000 per year, the increase in lost sales could be reduced to 20,000 units. This would be the maximum amount of overtime that would be feasible for AutoTech.
- Two warehouses presently used for steel bar storage would no longer be needed. AutoTech rents one warehouse from another company at an annual cost of $180,000. The other warehouse is owned by AutoTech and contains 12,000 square feet. Three-fourths of the space in the owned warehouse could be rented out for $4.50 per square foot per year.
- Insurance totaling $42,000 per year would be eliminated.

AutoTech's projected operating results for 20x5 are as follows. Long-term capital investments by AutoTech are expected to produce a rate of return of 20 percent before taxes.

AUTOTECH, INC.
Budgeted Income Statement
For the Year Ended December 31, 20x5
(in thousands)

Sales (900,000 units)		$32,400
Cost of goods sold:		
Variable	$12,150	
Fixed	4,350	16,500
Gross margin		$15,900
Selling and administrative expenses:		
Variable	$ 2,700	
Fixed	4,500	7,200
Income before interest and income taxes		$ 8,700
Interest expense		2,700
Income before taxes		$ 6,000

Required:

1. Calculate the estimated savings or loss for AutoTech, Inc. that would result in 20x5 from the adoption of just-in-time inventory methods. Ignore income taxes. (*Hint*: Try to estimate the costs and benefits associated with the JIT decision. Begin by computing the forgone contribution margin on the lost sales. The contribution margin is the sales revenue minus the variable cost.)
2. Identify and explain the conditions that should exist in order for a company to successfully install JIT.

(CMA, adapted)

Problem 6–49
Cost Drivers; Direct and Indirect Costs; Non-Value-Added Costs; JIT and FMS
(LO 1, 2, 5)

Northern Lights Company manufactures a variety of small parts for the automotive industry. The company's manufacturing overhead cost budget for the current year is as follows:

Electrical power	$22,500	Purchasing	40,000
Supervision	88,000	Waste collection	2,000
Machine maintenance—labor	45,500	Custodial labor	20,000
Machine maintenance—materials	11,500	Telephone service	3,500
Natural gas (for heating)	17,500	Engineering design	34,000
Factory supplies	20,000	Inspection of raw materials	10,000
Setup labor	15,000	Receiving	10,000
Lubricants	5,000	Inspection of finished goods	15,000
Property taxes	12,500	Packaging	31,000
Insurance	17,500	Shipping	15,000
Depreciation on manufacturing equipment	52,500	Wages of parts clerks (find parts for production departments)	30,000
Depreciation on trucks and forklifts	35,000	Wages of material handlers	35,000
Depreciation on material conveyors	7,500	Fuel for trucks and forklifts	35,000
Building depreciation	80,000	Depreciation on raw-material warehouse	25,000
Grinding wheels	2,500	Depreciation on finished-goods warehouse	29,000
Drill bits	1,000		

These budgeted overhead costs total $768,000, and the budgeted amount of direct-labor for the year is 40,000 hours.

Required:

1. Compute the predetermined overhead rate based on direct-labor hours.
2. Management has decided to implement an activity-based costing system. The cost drivers under consideration are the following:
   Production (in units)
   Raw-material cost
   Factory space
   Machine hours
   Number of production runs
   Number of shipments of finished goods
   Number of shipments of raw materials
   Number of different raw materials and parts used in a product
   Engineering specifications and change orders
   Divide Northern Lights' manufacturing-overhead costs into separate cost pools, and identify a cost driver for each cost pool.
3. For each overhead cost, indicate which of the five types of production activity (process time, inspection time, move time, waiting time, and storage time) is involved.
4. Which of the overhead costs are candidates for elimination as non-value-added costs?
5. How would activity accounting help Northern Lights' management reduce or eliminate some of the company's overhead costs? Be specific.
6. Suppose that the firm adopted a JIT production approach and purchased an FMS. Which overhead costs are likely to be treated as direct costs of an FMS cell?
7. For those costs that are not likely to be traceable to an FMS cell, how would you assign them to the company's products?
8. Suppose inspection of raw materials and receiving were combined to form an activity cost pool with the number of shipments of raw materials identified as the cost driver. Compute a pool rate for this cost pool, assuming that 400 shipments are anticipated.

Problem 6–50
JIT Implementation; Cost Savings
(LO 2, 9)

Michael McKenna, manager of FarmCo's Service Division, dialed the division controller's number on his phone: "Janice, this is Mike McKenna. How's that JIT program doing? Has it saved us any money? I've got to report to the president next week, and I'd like to know how our inventory efforts are going."

"Give me a day or two, Mike, and I'll have some figures for you," responded Janice Grady, the division controller.

FarmCo is a manufacturer of farm equipment sold by a network of distributors throughout North America. A majority of the distributors are also repair centers for FarmCo Service Division to provide timely support of spare parts. In an effort to reduce the inventory costs incurred by the Service Division, McKenna implemented a just-in-time inventory program on January 2, 20x4. JIT has now been in place for a year. Grady has been able to document the following results of JIT implementation.

- The Service Division's average inventory declined from $1,100,000 to $300,000.
- Projected annual insurance costs of $160,000 declined by 60 percent due to the lower average inventory.
- A leased, 8,000-square-foot warehouse, previously used for raw-material storage, was not used at all during the year. The division paid $22,400 annual rent for the warehouse and was able to sublet three-quarters of the building to several tenants at $5.00 per square foot. The balance of the space remained idle.
- Two warehouse employees whose services were no longer needed were transferred on January 2, 20x4, to the Purchasing Department to assist in the coordination of the JIT program. The annual salary expense for these two employees totaled $76,000 and continued to be charged to the indirect-labor portion of fixed overhead.
- Despite the use of overtime to manufacture 7,500 spare parts, lost sales due to stockouts totaled 3,800 spare parts. The overtime premium incurred amounted to $11.20 per part manufactured. The use of overtime to fill spare parts orders was immaterial prior to January 1, 20x4.

Prior to the decision to implement the JIT inventory program, FarmCo's Service Division had completed its 20x4 budget. The division's budgeted income statement, without any adjustments for just-in-time inventory, follows. FarmCo's incremental borrowing rate for inventory is 15 percent. (Ignore income taxes in this problem.)

FARMCO SERVICE DIVISION
Budgeted Income Statement
For the Year Ended December 31, 20x4
(in thousands)

Sales (280,000 spare parts)		$12,320
Cost of goods sold:		
Variable	$5,320	
Fixed	2,240	7,560
Gross margin		$4,760
Selling and administrative expenses:		
Variable	$1,400	
Fixed	1,110	2,510
Operating income		$2,250
Other income		150
Income before interest and income taxes		$2,400
Interest expense		300
Income before income taxes		$2,100

Required:

1. Calculate the cash savings (loss) for FarmCo's Service Division that resulted during 20x4 from the adoption of the JIT inventory program. (*Hint*: One of the costs associated with the JIT decision is the forgone contribution margin on lost sales. The contribution margin is the sales revenue minus the variable cost.)
2. Discuss any factors that should be considered before a company implements a JIT program.

(CMA, adapted)

Problem 6–51
Ethical Standards; Lack of Quality Control; Disclosure of Product Quality Information
(LO 9)

Worldwide Electronics Corporation (WEC) is a seven-year-old company that developed a process to produce reliable electronic components at a cost below that of the competition. In seeking to expand its overall components business, WEC decided to enter the facsimile equipment business, because there was a niche for lower-priced facsimile machines in a growing marketplace. The market WEC pursued consisted of small businesses not yet approached by the larger vendors. WEC sells its machines with a one-year warranty and has established a maintenance force to handle machine breakdowns.

As WEC customers learned of the benefits of fax transmissions, some increased their usage significantly. After six months, larger volume users began experiencing breakdowns, and the field technicians' portable test equipment was not sophisticated enough to detect hairline breaks in the electronic circuitry caused by the heavier-than-expected usage. Consequently, field technicians were required to replace the damaged components.

This situation caused an increase in maintenance costs, which added to the cost of the product. Unfortunately, there was no way to determine how many of the businesses would become heavy users and be subject to breakdowns. Some of the heavier-volume users began switching to the more expensive machines available from the larger competitors. Although new sales orders masked the loss of heavier volume customers, the increased maintenance costs had an unfavorable impact on earnings. Andrew Fulton, WEC's assistant controller, summarized this situation in his report prepared for the quarterly meeting of the board of directors.

Jack March, vice president of manufacturing, was concerned that the report did not provide any solutions to the problem. He asked Marie Waters, the controller, to have the matter deferred so that his engineering staff could work on the problem. He believed that the electronic component could be redesigned. This redesigned model, while more costly, could be an appropriate solution for heavier-volume users who should not expect a low-cost model to service their increased needs. March was concerned that the board could decide to discontinue the product line if no immediate solution became available and that the company could miss a potentially profitable opportunity. March further believed that the tone of the report placed his organization in an unfavorable light.

The controller called Fulton into her office and asked him to suppress the part of his formal report related to the component failures. Waters asked Fulton just to cover it orally at the meeting, noting that engineering was working with marketing on the situation to reach a satisfactory solution. Fulton felt strongly that the board would be misinformed about a potentially serious impact on earnings if he followed Waters's advice.

Required:

1. Referring to the specific ethical standards for management accountants of competence, confidentiality, integrity, and objectivity, explain why Marie Waters's request to Andrew Fulton is unethical. Cite not only the concept of each standard but also Waters's action or nonaction that results in an unethical situation.
2. How can Andrew Fulton resolve the situation? What are some of his alternatives?

(CMA, adapted)

Problem 6–52
Customer-Profitability Analysis; Activity-Based Costing
(LO 6)

FiberCom, Inc. manufactures fiber optic cables for the computer and telecommunications industries. At the request of the company vice president of marketing, the cost management staff has recently completed a customer-profitability study. The following activity-based costing information was the basis for the analysis.

Customer-Related Activities	Cost Driver Base	Cost Driver Rate
Sales activity	Sales visits	$2,000
Order taking	Purchase orders	400
Special handling	Units handled	100
Special shipping	Shipments	1,000

Cost-driver data for two of FiberCom's customers for the most recent year are:

Customer-Related Activities	Caltex Computer	Trace Telecom
Sales activity	8 visits	6 visits
Order taking	15 orders	20 orders
Special handling	800 units handled	600 units handled
Special shipping	18 shipments	20 shipments

The following additional information has been compiled for FiberCom for two of its customers, Caltex Computer and Trace Telecom, for the most recent year:

	Caltex Computer	Trace Telecom
Sales revenue	$380,000	$247,600
Cost of goods sold	160,000	124,000
General selling costs	48,000	36,000
General administrative costs	38,000	32,000

Required:

1. Prepare a customer-profitability analysis for Caltex Computer and Trace Telecom. (Hint: Refer to Exhibit 6–3 for guidance.)
2. Prepare a customer-profitability graph, similar to the one in Exhibit 6–4, for Caltex Computer and Trace Telecom.

Problem 6–53
Customer-Profitability Profile; Continuation of Preceding Problem
(LO 6)

Refer to the information given in the preceding problem for FiberCom, Inc. and two of its customers, Caltex Computer and Trace Telecom. Additional information for six of FiberCom's other customers for the most recent year follows:

Customer	Operating Income
Network-All, Inc.	$186,000
The California Group	12,000
Golden Gate Service Associates	142,000
Tele-Install, Inc.	(36,000)
Graydon Computer Company	120,000
Mid-State Computing Company	84,000

Required:

1. Prepare FiberCom's customer-profitability profile for the most recent year.
2. As FiberCom's director of cost management, write a memo to the company's vice president of marketing which will accompany the customer-profitability profile. Include a brief explanation of the methodology used and comment on the results.

Problem 6–54
Kaizen Costing Chart
(LO 8, 9)

New South Wales Television Corporation manufactures TV sets in Australia, largely for the domestic market. Management has recently implemented a kaizen costing program, with the goal of reducing the manufacturing cost per television set by 10 percent during 20x5, the first year of the kaizen effort. The cost per TV set at the end of 20x4 was $500. The following table shows the average cost per television set during each month of 20x5. (The day this problem was written, the Australian dollar was valued at $.53 in U.S. dollars.)

Month	Cost per Set	Month	Cost per Set
January	$500	July	$485
February	500	August	470
March	495	September	460
April	492	October	460
May	490	November	450
June	485	December	440

Required: Prepare a kaizen costing chart for 20x5 to show the results of the company's first year of kaizen costing. In developing the chart, use the following steps.

1. Draw and label the axes of the kaizen costing chart.
2. Indicate the current year cost base and the kaizen goal (cost reduction rate) on the chart.
3. Label the horizontal axis with the months of 20x5. Label the vertical axis with dollar amounts in the appropriate range.
4. Plot the 12 monthly average cost amounts per TV set. Then draw a line connecting the cost points that were plotted.
5. Complete the chart with any further labeling necessary.
6. Briefly explain the purpose of kaizen costing. How could a continuous quality-improvement program, coupled with the kaizen costing effort implemented by New South Wales Television Corporation, help the firm begin competing in the worldwide market?

Cases

Case 6–55
Using an Activity-Based Costing System to Modify Behavior[18]
(LO 3, 4, 9)

The Hospital Instruments Division of MedLife Technology Corporation manufactures a variety of electronic medical equipment. The principal product of the Hospital Instruments Division is a sophisticated instrument for measuring and graphically displaying a variety of medical phenomena, such as heart and respiration rates. The culture throughout the division was primarily engineering-oriented. One result of this culture was that the company's design engineers generally designed new products from scratch, rather than relying on modification of a current design. While this approach usually resulted in an "elegant" design from an engineering standpoint, it often resulted in the use of new or unique parts that were not already being used in the company's other products. The strategy of the Hospital Instruments Division's management was to position the division as a product differentiator and price leader, not as the industry's low-cost producer. This means that the division generally led the medical instruments market with new products that exhibited greater functionality than competing products and that the products were priced at a premium. The company's competitors then would emulate a new product, produce it at a lower cost, and undercut the MedLife Technology price. However, by then MedLife Technology had moved on to a new product with even greater functionality. This strategy had been quite successful until

[18]This case draws on a scenario described in the following sources: Peter B. B. Turney, *Common Cents: The ABC Performance Breakthrough* (Hillsboro, OR: Cost Technology, 1991), pp. 34, 106, 139, 150, 156, 164, 182, 213, 214, 217, and 220; and Peter B. B. Turney and Bruce Anderson, "Accounting for Continuous Improvement," *Sloan Management Review* 30, no. 2 (1991), pp. 37–48.

the Japanese entered the medical instruments market in a major way. MedLife Technology's new competitors were able to set product prices some 25 percent below those of MedLife Technology, while maintaining close to the same level of functionality. In order to compete, the Hospital Instruments Division had to lower its prices below its reported product costs. This resulted in significant losses for the division.

To remedy the situation, the Hospital Instruments Division's management began an extensive continuous improvement program. The division changed its production and inventory management system to a JIT system, ideas of total quality control were aggressively pursued, and management attempted to develop an empowered workforce. All of these efforts paid off dramatically. However, production costs were still relatively high for the industry, and cycle times were considered too long by management. The general feeling was that in order to remain competitive in the long run, the division would have to further lower its production costs and shorten its production cycle times. As management contemplated the high production costs, one problem that kept coming up was the division's part number proliferation. As the engineering-dominated company continued to introduce new products, the number of different parts and components that had to be stocked in inventory continued to increase. Some members of management felt that the division's cost-reduction goals could be achieved (at least partially) by solving the problem of part number proliferation.

As management was pondering the division's cost-reduction goal, the controller was contemplating the introduction of a new cost-accounting system. The controller was thinking about introducing activity-based costing and activity-based management in the Hospital Instruments Division.

Required:

1. Explain why the problem of part number proliferation could increase the division's production costs.
2. Explain how long production cycle times could increase the division's production costs.
3. How could an ABC system be used to help reduce costs by attacking the problem of part number proliferation? Allow yourself to contemplate an entirely new role for ABC that is quite different from the objective of more accurate product costs. The following specific questions may help in completing this requirement.
   a. What is the division's strategy in the marketplace?
   b. How are prices currently being determined?
   c. Does management really need more accurate product costs, given its strategy and the reality of market-driven prices?
   d. What is the current goal of management?
   e. What is (at least partially) to blame for high production costs?
   f. Who is (at least partially) to blame for high production costs?
   g. How could an ABC system help solve the problem and reduce production costs?
4. Following up your answer to requirement (3), what cost drivers could be employed to help solve the problem of part number proliferation? Which cost driver would work best? Explain.
5. How could an ABC system help highlight and solve the problem of production cycle times that are too long?
6. As succinctly as you can, state how the fundamental role of the ABC system differs here from the role described in the Aerotech illustration used in Chapters 5 and 6.

Current Issues in Managerial Accounting

Issue 6–56
Flexible Manufacturing

"Ford: Europe Has a Better Idea," ***Business Week,*** **April 22, 2002, pp. 84, 85, Christine Tierney and Kathleen Kerwin; "Ford Looks to Cost-Cutter Thursfield,"** ***The Wall Street Journal,*** **May 10, 2002, p. A3, Norihiko Shirouzu and Scott Miller; "Honda Goes Its Own Way,"** ***Fortune,*** **July 22, 2002, pp. 148–152, Alex Taylor III.**

Overview

Honda has installed a new flexible manufacturing system dubbed Ultimate Flex. Ford's European operations are also out ahead with flexible manufacturing operations.

Suggested Discussion Question

How does flexible manufacturing help in cost management?

"Germany's Commerzbank Aims to Shun Unprofitable Relationships," ***The Wall Street Journal,*** **March 28, 2002, p. A15, Erik Portanger; "In Search of the Operator,"** ***The Wall Street Journal,*** **May 8, 2002, Jane Spencer.**

Issue 6–57
Customer-Profitability Analysis

Overview

Commerzbank's chairman "says he is putting his customers on notice: 'Either pay a reasonable price for loans and financial services, or be cut off.'" Wells Fargo, KeyCorp, and BMW are also among the many companies using customer-profitability analysis.

Suggested Discussion Question

How do companies use customer-profitability analysis, which is an application of ABM, to cut costs and increase profits?

"Crunch Time for Parts Makers," ***Business Week,*** **January 8, 2001, Jeff Green.**

Issue 6–58
Cost Cutting; Supply Chain; Outsourcing

Overview

The U.S. business unit of DaimlerChrysler ordered all of its suppliers to begin the new year with a 5 percent price cut. "Amid the strongest auto boom in years, suppliers have been getting hammered as auto makers press them for cost cuts to keep vehicle prices low."

Suggested Discussion Questions

Do you think it is a sound strategy to demand a 5 percent price cut from suppliers across the board? What are the potential risks in such an approach to cost cutting?

"As More and More Companies End Little Perks, Critics Call Moves Petty, Pointless," ***The Wall Street Journal,*** **January 4, 2001, Joann S. Lublin.**

Issue 6–59
Cost Cutting; Effects on Employee Morale

Overview

"The frills are gone." Companies are digging deeper and deeper to cut costs in an increasingly competitive marketplace. Aetna notified employees that they would have to start paying for coffee, which was formerly provided by the company. Lucent Technologies reminded employees to stay in budget hotels and fly coach class except on very long business trips. Some Xerox divisions have stopped stocking water coolers. Some critics say that such cost-cutting moves are counterproductive.

Suggested Discussion Questions

As a group, discuss the cost-cutting approaches cited in the article, and then discuss whether you think these measures make sense. Are such cost-cutting moves in the companies' best interests?

"Manufacturing Masters Its ABCs," ***Business Week,*** **August 7, 2000, Hugh Filman.**

Issue 6–60
Activity-Based Costing

Overview

Activity-based costing, a cost-assessment system, is compared to splitting the bill at a restaurant. "Where traditional accounting divides the bill evenly between all diners, ABC determines who had the T-bone and who had the burger," states Anthony Atkinson of Canada's University of Waterloo.

Suggested Discussion Question

How did Alcoa Inc. use activity-based costing?

Chapter Seven

Activity Analysis, Cost Behavior, and Cost Estimation

After completing this chapter, you should be able to:

1. Explain the relationships between cost estimation, cost behavior, and cost prediction.
2. Define and describe the behavior of the following types of costs: variable, step-variable, fixed, step-fixed, semivariable (or mixed), and curvilinear.
3. Explain the importance of the relevant range in using a cost behavior pattern for cost prediction.
4. Define and give examples of engineered costs, committed costs, and discretionary costs.
5. Describe and use the following cost-estimation methods: account classification, visual fit, high-low, and least-squares regression.
6. Describe the multiple regression, engineering, and learning-curve approaches to cost estimation.
7. Describe some problems often encountered in collecting data for cost estimation.
8. After completing the appendix, perform and interpret a least-squares regression analysis with a single independent variable.

Tasty Donuts Takes a Big Bite out of the Donut Business

Toronto, Ontario—Tasty Donuts, Inc. has announced that it will soon open two new donut shops. One shop will be located near the entrance to Ontario Place, a popular tourist attraction on Toronto's waterfront. The second shop will be located near the stadium. "We want to be in position to catch the crowds attending the Blue Jays games," said Will Andrews, company president. "These two new shops will be our 11th and 12th. I'm very pleased with the way the business is growing."

Andrews should be pleased. He started the company a short seven years ago after graduating from college with a degree in hospitality management. A native of Toronto, Andrews says he had his sights set on a restaurant chain from the beginning. "My parents were in the restaurant business, so I sort of grew up with it," said Andrews. "I knew the operational side pretty well from working in my parents' restaurant, so I concentrated on learning the financial and managerial aspects when I was in college." Andrews went on to explain that he started the business by getting what he termed "a hefty bank loan," and then buying two run-down donut shops in the suburbs.

"Now we have 10 restaurants, and we do all of the production of donuts and baked goods in our central bakery. We figured out early on that we could produce donuts centrally and transport them to the shops at a lower cost than we could produce goods in each shop. That was not obvious at first, though, and it took some careful cost analysis to reach that conclusion. We had to project how our costs would behave as we expanded the business over time. When you sell twice as many donuts, some costs, like ingredients for example, will pretty much double. But other costs, like property taxes and depreciation on the bakery building, stay more or less flat. It's tricky, projecting costs, but it's important to do it well if you're trying to stay profitable while growing your business."

Andrews sees a bright future for Tasty Donuts. "Toronto's a wonderful city, and the tourist trade is growing every year. We get a lot of people coming up from the states, as well as our own people from Ontario and Quebec. I'm hoping to have 20 restaurants and two bakeries within five more years. Then we're probably going to go after the pizza business."

Managers in almost any organization want to know how costs will be affected by changes in the organization's activity. The relationship between cost and activity, called **cost behavior,** is relevant to the management functions of planning, control, and decision making. In order to *plan* operations and prepare a budget, managers at Nabisco need to predict the costs that will be incurred at different levels of production and sales. To *control* the costs of providing commercial-loan services at Chase Manhattan Bank, executives need to have a feel for the costs that the bank should incur at various levels of commercial-loan activity. In *deciding* whether to add a new intensive care unit, a hospital's administrators need to predict the cost of operating the new unit at various levels of patient demand. In each of these situations, knowledge of *cost behavior* will help the manager to make the desired cost prediction. A **cost prediction** is a forecast of cost at a particular level of activity. In the first half of this chapter, we will study cost behavior patterns and their use in making cost predictions.

LO 1

Explain the relationships between cost estimation, cost behavior, and cost prediction.

How does a managerial accountant determine the cost behavior pattern for a particular cost item? The determination of cost behavior, which is often called **cost estimation,** can be accomplished in a number of ways. One way is to analyze historical data concerning costs and activity levels. Cost estimation is covered in the second half of this chapter.

The following diagram summarizes the key points in the preceding discussion.

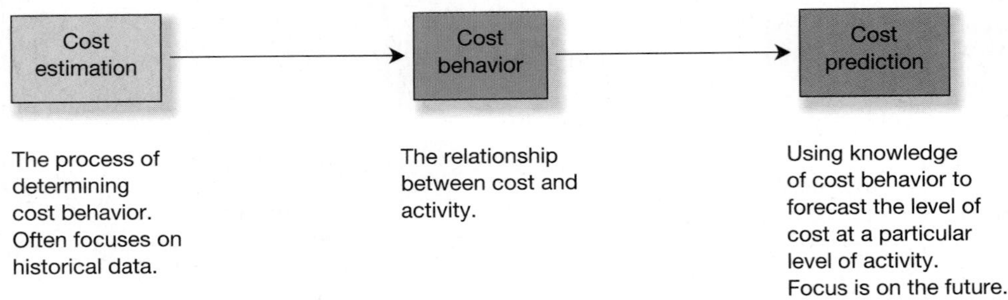
Cost estimation
Cost behavior
Cost prediction
The process of determining cost behavior. Often focuses on historical data.
The relationship between cost and activity.
Using knowledge of cost behavior to forecast the level of cost at a particular level of activity. Focus is on the future.

Cost Behavior Patterns

TASTY
DONUTS

Topic 7–1

Our discussion of cost behavior patterns, also called *cost functions*, will be set in the context of a restaurant business. Tasty Donuts, Inc. operates a chain of 10 donut shops in the city of Toronto, Ontario. Each shop sells a variety of donuts, muffins, and sweet rolls as well as various beverages. Beverages, such as coffee and fruit juices, are prepared in each donut shop, but all of the company's donuts and baked products are made in a centrally located bakery. The company leases several small delivery trucks to transport the bakery items to its restaurants. Use of a central bakery is more cost-efficient. Moreover, this approach allows the firm to smooth out fluctuations in demand for each type of product. For example, the demand for glazed donuts may change from day to day in each donut shop, but these fluctuations tend to cancel each other out when the total demand is aggregated across all 10 shops.

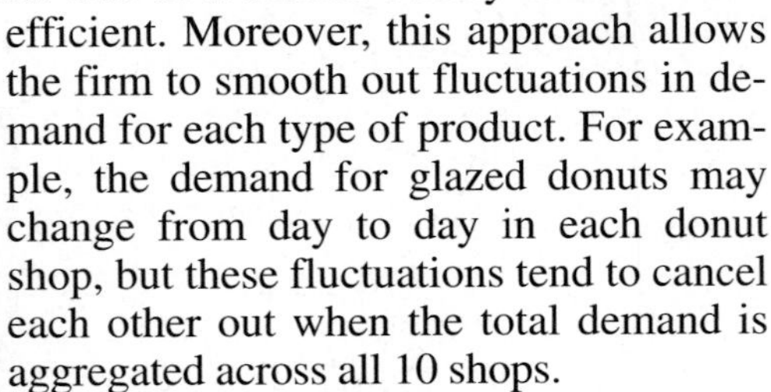

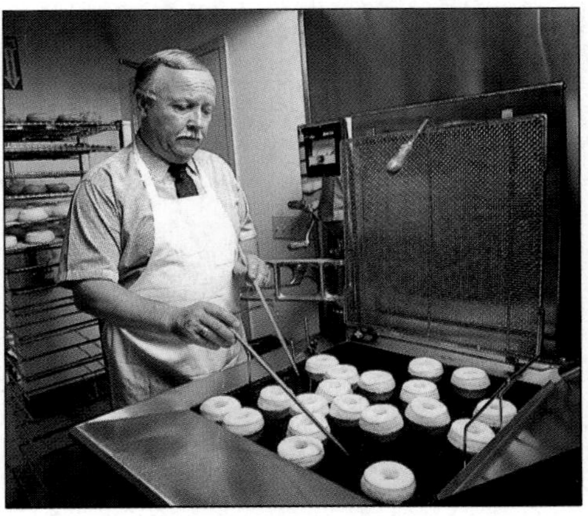

Among the costs incurred to produce these donuts are the ingredients (direct material); the wages of the kitchen employees (direct labor); and the facilities, including the building, cooking equipment, and utilities (overhead).

The corporate controller for Tasty Donuts has recently completed a study of the company's cost behavior to use in preparing the firm's budget for the coming year. The controller studied the following costs.

Direct material: ingredients for donuts, muffins, and sweet rolls; beverages; paper products, such as napkins and disposable cups

Direct labor: wages and fringe benefits of bakers, restaurant sales personnel, and delivery-truck drivers

Overhead:

Facilities costs: property taxes; depreciation on bakery building, donut shops, and equipment; salaries and fringe benefits of maintenance personnel

Indirect labor: salaries and fringe benefits of managers and assistant managers for bakery and restaurants

Delivery trucks: rental payments under lease contract; costs of gasoline, oil, tires, and maintenance

Utilities: electricity, telephone, and trash collection

"Failure to understand costs would have left Portugal Telecom vulnerable to competition. Understanding the company's costs became essential to cost reduction efforts and to the company's long-term viability." (7a)

Accenture (formerly Andersen Consulting), regarding its client Portugal Telecom

In studying the behavior of each of these costs, the controller measured company *activity* in terms of *dozens of bakery items sold.* Thus, dozens of bakery items sold is the *cost driver* for each of the costs studied. A bakery item is one donut, muffin, or sweet roll. The costs to make each of these products are nearly identical. The number of bakery items sold each day is roughly the same as the number produced, since bakery goods are produced to keep pace with demand as reported by the company's restaurant managers.

Variable Costs

LO 2

Define and describe the behavior of the following types of costs: variable, step-variable, fixed, step-fixed, semivariable (or mixed), and curvilinear.

Variable costs were discussed briefly in Chapter 2. We will summarize that discussion here in the context of the Tasty Donuts illustration. A **variable cost** changes *in total* in direct proportion to a change in the activity level (or cost driver). Tasty Donuts' direct-material cost is a variable cost. As the company sells more donuts, muffins, and sweet rolls, the total cost of the ingredients for these goods increases in direct proportion to the number of items sold. Moreover, the quantities of beverages sold and paper products used by customers also increase in direct proportion to the number of bakery items sold. As a result, the costs of beverages and paper products are also variable costs.

Panel A of Exhibit 7–1 displays a graph of Tasty Donuts' direct-material cost. As the graph shows, *total* variable cost increases in proportion to the activity level (or cost driver). When activity triples, for example, from 50,000 dozen items to 150,000 dozen items, total direct-material costs triple, from $55,000 to $165,000. However, the variable cost *per unit* remains the same as activity changes. The total direct-material cost incurred *per dozen* items sold is constant at $1.10 per dozen. The table in panel B of Exhibit 7–1 illustrates this point. The variable cost per unit also is represented in the graph in panel A of Exhibit 7–1 as the slope of the cost line.

To summarize, as activity changes, total variable cost increases in direct proportion to the change in activity level, but the variable cost per unit remains constant.

Step-Variable Costs

Some costs are nearly variable, but they increase in small steps instead of continuously. Such costs, called **step-variable costs,** usually include inputs that are purchased and used in relatively small increments. At Tasty Donuts, Inc. the direct-labor cost of bakers, restaurant counter-service personnel, and delivery-truck drivers is a step-variable cost. Many of these employees are part-time workers, called upon for relatively small increments of time, such as a few hours. On a typical day, for example, Tasty Donuts may have 35 employees at work in the bakery and the donut shops. If activity increases slightly, these employees can handle the extra work. However, if activity increases substantially, the bakery manager or various restaurant managers may call on additional help. Exhibit 7–2, a graph of Tasty Donuts' monthly direct-labor cost, shows that this

Exhibit 7–1
Variable Cost: Direct-Material Cost, Tasty Donuts, Inc.

A. Graph of Total Direct-Material Cost

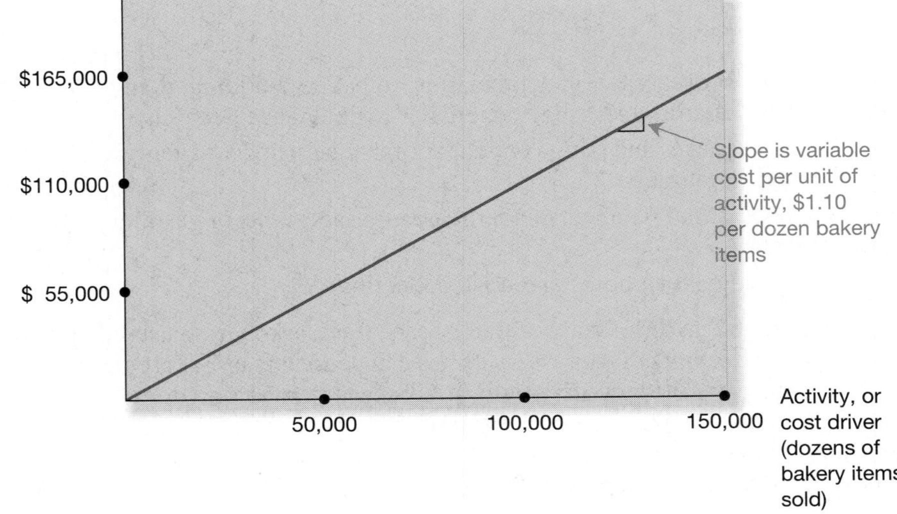

B. Tabulation of Direct-Material Cost

Activity (or cost driver)	Direct-Material Cost per Dozen Bakery Items Sold	Total Direct-Material Cost
50,000	$1.10	$ 55,000
100,000	1.10	110,000
150,000	1.10	165,000

cost remains constant within an activity range of about 5,000 dozen bakery items per month. When monthly activity increases beyond this narrow range, direct-labor costs increase.

Approximating a Step-Variable Cost If the steps in a step-variable cost behavior pattern are small, the step-variable cost function may be approximated by a variable cost function without much loss in accuracy. Exhibit 7–3 shows such an approximation for Tasty Donuts' direct-labor cost.

Fixed Costs

Fixed costs were covered briefly in Chapter 2. We will summarize that discussion here, using the Tasty Donuts illustration. A **fixed cost** remains unchanged *in total* as the activity level (or cost driver) varies. Facilities costs, which include property taxes, depreciation on buildings and equipment, and the salaries of maintenance personnel, are fixed costs for Tasty Donuts, Inc. These fixed costs are graphed in panel A of Exhibit 7–4. This graph shows that the *total* monthly cost of property taxes, depreciation, and maintenance personnel is $200,000 regardless of how many dozen bakery items are produced and sold during the month.

The fixed cost *per unit* does change as activity varies. Exhibit 7–4 (panel B) shows that the company's facilities cost per dozen bakery items is $4.00 when 50,000 dozen items are produced and sold. However, this unit cost declines to $2.00 when 100,000 dozen items are produced and sold. If activity increases to 150,000 dozen items, unit fixed cost will decline further, to about $1.33.

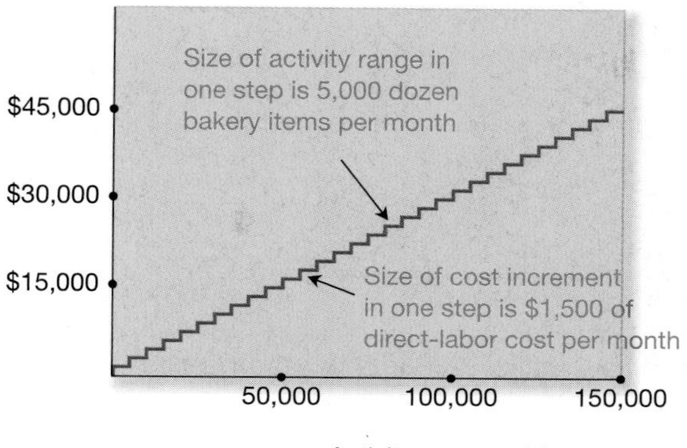

Exhibit 7–2
Step-Variable Cost: Direct-Labor Cost, Tasty Donuts

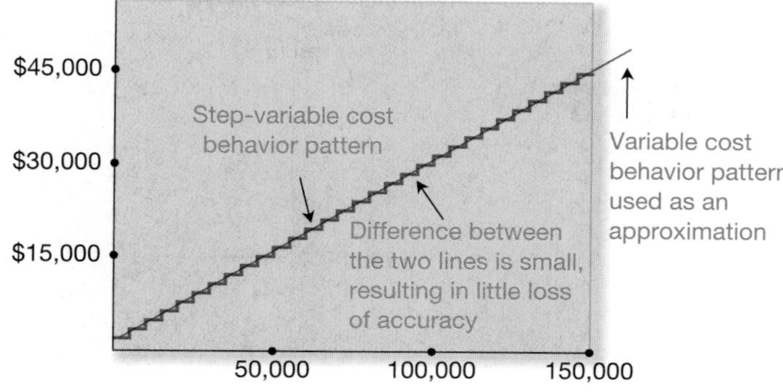

Exhibit 7–3
Approximating a Step-Variable Cost, Tasty Donuts

A graph provides another way of viewing the change in unit fixed cost as activity changes. Panel C of Exhibit 7–4 displays a graph of Tasty Donuts' cost of property taxes, depreciation, and maintenance personnel *per dozen bakery items.* As the graph shows, the fixed cost per dozen bakery items declines steadily as activity increases.

To summarize, as the activity level increases, total fixed cost does not change, but unit fixed cost declines. For this reason, it is preferable in any cost analysis to work with total fixed cost rather than fixed cost per unit.

> "By understanding the costs and workload associated with the real business activities we undertake . . . we are better positioned to understand where value is created. . . . From this information, we can then make better decisions as to the management and direction of the business." (7b)
>
> **Transco**

Step-Fixed Costs

Some costs remain fixed over a wide range of activity but jump to a different amount for activity levels outside that range. Such costs are called **step-fixed costs.** Tasty Donuts' cost of indirect labor is a step-fixed cost. Indirect-labor cost consists of the salaries and fringe benefits for the managers and assistant managers of the company's bakery and restaurants. Tasty Donuts' monthly indirect-labor cost is graphed in Exhibit 7–5.

As Exhibit 7–5 shows, for activity in the range of 50,000 to 100,000 dozen bakery items per month, Tasty Donuts' monthly indirect-labor cost is $35,000. For this range of activity, the company employs a full-time manager and a full-time assistant manager in the bakery and in each restaurant. When monthly activity exceeds this range during the summer tourist season, the company employs additional part-time assistant managers in the bakery and in its busiest donut shops. The company hires college students who are majoring in restaurant management for these summer positions. Their salaries boost the monthly indirect-labor cost to $45,000. Tasty Donuts has not experienced demand of less than 50,000 dozen bakery items per month. However, the controller anticipates that if such a decrease in demand were to occur, the company would reduce the daily operating hours for its donut shops. This would allow the firm to operate each restaurant with only a full-time manager and no assistant manager. As the graph in Exhibit 7–5 indicates, such a decrease in managerial personnel would reduce monthly indirect-labor cost to $25,000.

Exhibit 7–4
Fixed Cost: Facilities Costs, Tasty Donuts, Inc.

A. Graph of Total Monthly Fixed Costs: Facilities Costs

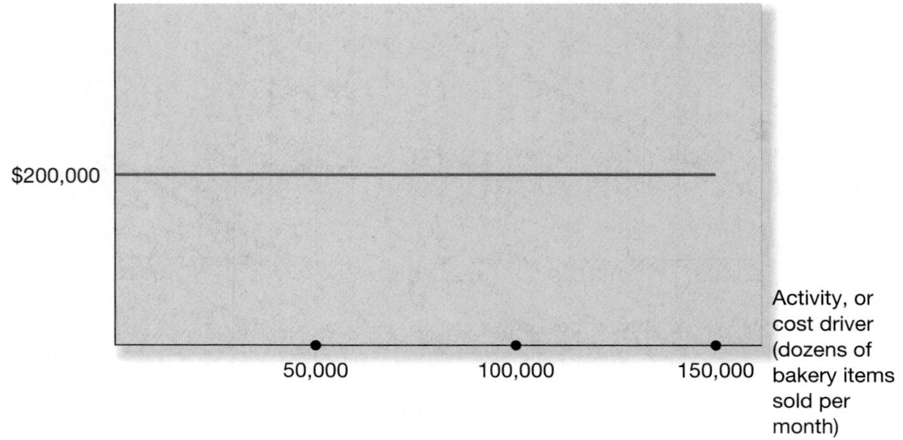

B. Tabulation of Monthly Fixed Costs: Facilities Costs

Activity (or cost driver)	Cost of Facilities per Dozen Bakery Items Sold	Total Monthly Cost of Facilities
50,000	$4.00	$200,000
100,000	2.00	200,000
150,000	1.33*	200,000

* Rounded.

C. Graph of Unit Fixed Cost: Cost of Facilities per Dozen Bakery Items Sold

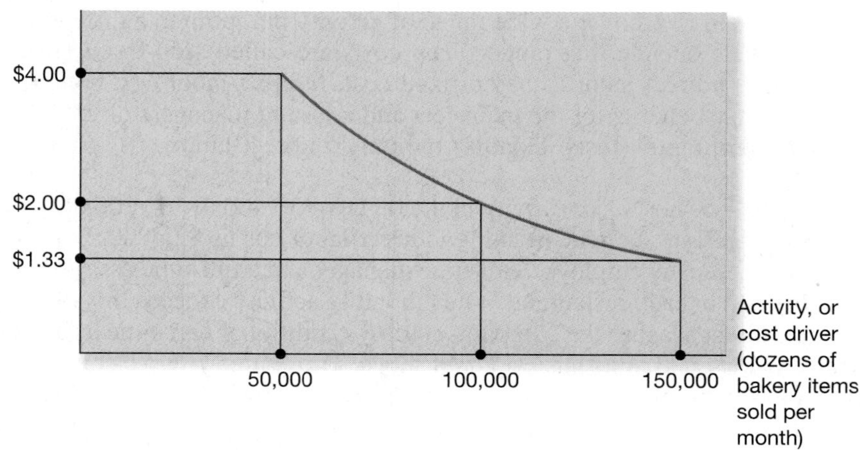

Semivariable Cost

A **semivariable** (or **mixed**) **cost** has both a fixed and a variable component. The cost of operating delivery trucks is a semivariable cost for Tasty Donuts, Inc. These costs are

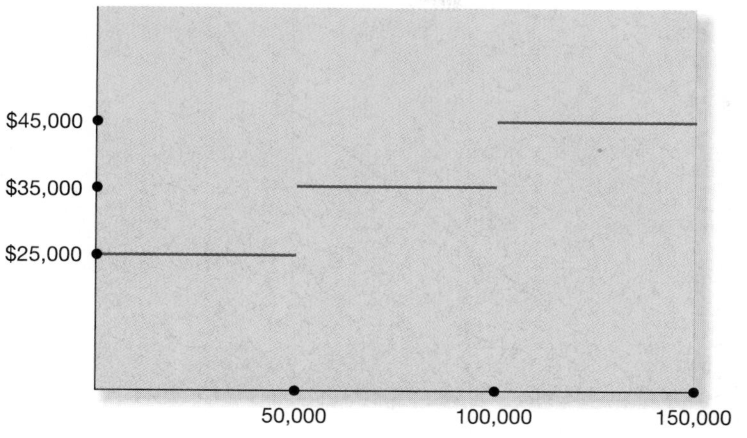

Exhibit 7–5

Step-Fixed Cost: Indirect-Labor Cost, Tasty Donuts, Inc.

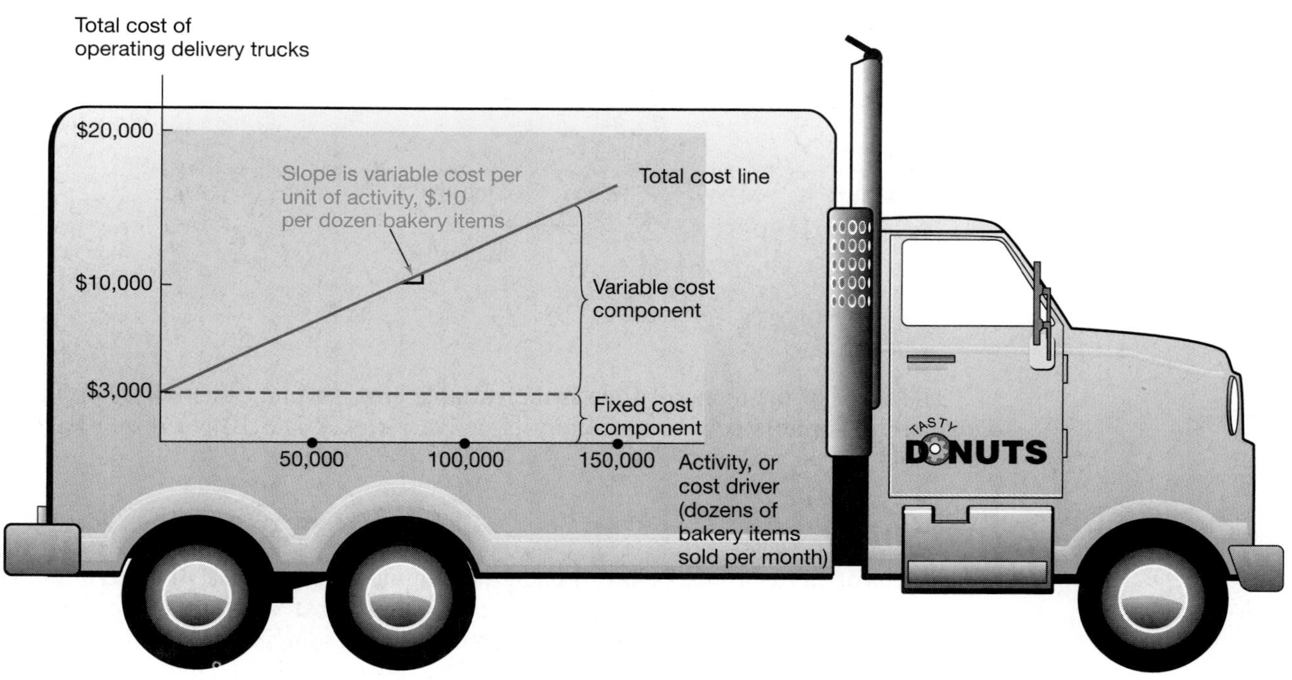

Exhibit 7–6

Semivariable Cost: Cost of Operating Delivery Trucks, Tasty Donuts, Inc.

graphed in Exhibit 7–6. As the graph shows, the company's delivery-truck costs have two components. The fixed-cost component is $3,000 per month, which is the monthly rental payment paid under the lease contract for the delivery trucks. The monthly rental payment is constant, regardless of the level of activity (or cost driver). The variable-cost component consists of the costs of gasoline, oil, routine maintenance, and tires. These costs vary with activity, since greater activity levels result in more deliveries. The distance between the fixed-cost line (dashed line) and the total-cost line in Exhibit 7–6 is the amount of variable cost. For example, at an activity level of 100,000 dozen bakery items, the total variable-cost component is $10,000.

Exhibit 7–7
Curvilinear Cost: Utilities Cost, Tasty Donuts, Inc.

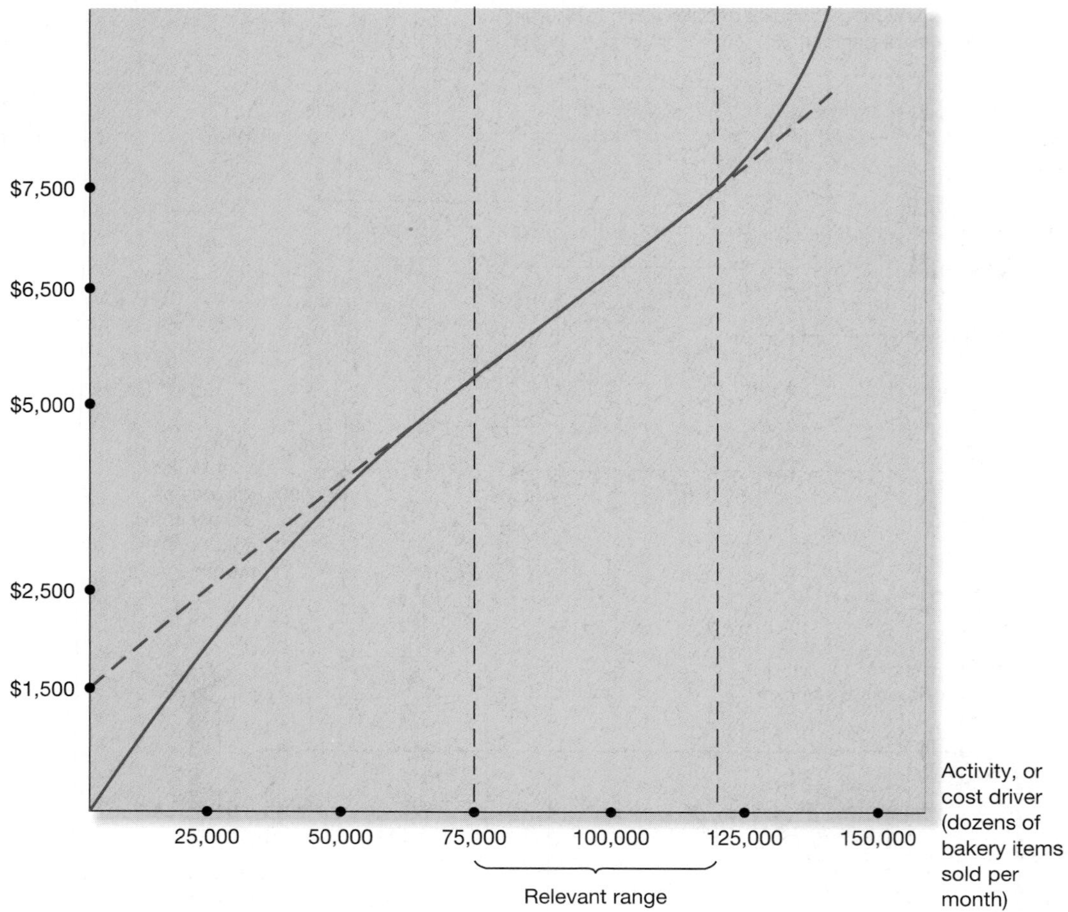

The slope of the total-cost line is the variable cost per unit of activity. For Tasty Donuts, the variable cost of operating its delivery trucks is $.10 per dozen bakery items sold.

Curvilinear Cost

The graphs of all of the cost behavior patterns examined so far consist of either straight lines or several straight-line sections. A **curvilinear cost** behavior pattern has a curved graph. Tasty Donuts' utilities cost, depicted as the *solid curve* in Exhibit 7–7, is a curvilinear cost. For low levels of activity, this cost exhibits *decreasing marginal costs*. As the discussion in Chapter 2 indicated, a marginal cost is the cost of producing the next unit, in this case the next dozen bakery items. As the graph in Exhibit 7–7 shows, the marginal utilities cost of producing the next dozen bakery items declines as activity increases in the range zero to 100,000 dozen items per month. For activity greater than 100,000 dozen bakery items per month, the graph in Exhibit 7–7 exhibits *increasing marginal costs*.

Tasty Donuts' utilities cost includes electricity, telephone, and trash-collection costs. The utilities cost is curvilinear as a result of the company's pattern of electricity usage in the bakery. If the demand in a particular month is less than 100,000 dozen bakery items, the goods can be produced entirely in the modernized section of the bakery. This section uses recently purchased deep-fat fryers and ovens that are very energy-efficient. As long as the bakery operates only the modernized section, the utilities cost per dozen items declines as production increases.

During the summer tourist months, when Tasty Donuts' sales exceed 100,000 dozen items per month, the older section of the bakery also must be used. This section uses much older cooking equipment that is less energy-efficient. As a result, the marginal utilities cost per dozen bakery items rises as monthly activity increases in the range above 100,000 dozen items per month.

Relevant Range The cost behavior graphed in Exhibit 7–7 is very different at low activity levels (below 50,000) than it is at high activity levels (above 125,000). However, management need not concern itself with these extreme levels of activity if it is unlikely that Tasty Donuts, Inc. will operate at those activity levels. Management is interested in cost behavior within the company's **relevant range,** the range of activity within which management expects the company to operate. Tasty Donuts' management believes the firm's relevant range to be 75,000 to 120,000 dozen bakery items per month. Based on past experience and sales projections, management does not expect the firm to operate outside that range of monthly activity. Tasty Donuts' relevant range is shown in Exhibit 7–7 as the section of the graph between the dashed lines.

Explain the importance of the relevant range in using a cost behavior pattern for cost prediction.

Approximating a Curvilinear Cost within the Relevant Range The straight, dashed line in Exhibit 7–7 may be used to approximate Tasty Donuts' utilities cost. Notice that the approximation is quite accurate for activity levels within the relevant range. However, as the activity level gets further away from the boundary of the relevant range, the approximation declines in accuracy. For monthly activity levels of 25,000 or 150,000, for example, the approximation is very poor.

"Cost estimation is a critical part of our job." (7c)
Ford Motor Company

The straight, dashed line used to approximate Tasty Donuts' utilities cost *within the relevant range* represents a semivariable cost behavior pattern. This straight-line graph has a slope of \$.05, which represents a unit variable-cost component of \$.05 per dozen bakery items. The line intersects the vertical axis of the graph at \$1,500, which represents a fixed-cost component of \$1,500 per month. Managerial accountants often use a semivariable-cost behavior pattern to approximate a curvilinear cost. However, it is important to limit this approximation to the range of activity in which its accuracy is acceptable.

Using Cost Behavior Patterns to Predict Costs

How can Tasty Donuts' corporate controller use the cost behavior patterns identified in the cost study to help in the budgeting process? First, a sales forecast is made for each month during the budget year. Suppose management expects Tasty Donuts' activity level to be 110,000 dozen bakery items during the month of June. Second, a *cost prediction* is made for each of the firm's cost items. The following cost predictions are based on the cost behavior patterns discussed earlier. (Try to verify these cost predictions by referring to the graphs in Exhibits 7–1 through 7–7.)

Cost Item	**Cost Prediction for June (110,000 dozen bakery items per month)**
Direct material	\$121,000
Direct labor	33,000
Overhead:	
Facilities costs	200,000
Indirect labor	45,000
Delivery trucks	14,000
Utilities	7,000

Management Accounting Practice

Nestlé, Lincoln Electric, and Hilton Hotels

IS DIRECT LABOR A VARIABLE OR A FIXED COST?

Are direct-labor costs variable or fixed? The answer, as with many questions, is "it depends." What it depends on is the ability and willingness of a company's management to continually fine-tune the size of its workforce. If labor contracts make it difficult to lay off workers during an economic downturn, or if top management adopts a policy of maintaining a stable workforce, direct-labor costs will tend to be largely fixed (or step-fixed). However, if management can *and is willing to* reduce the labor force when activity declines, then labor cost will be a variable (or step-variable) cost.

The current trend in many companies seems to be toward adjusting the workforce to conform to current needs. Here are several cases in point.

Nestlé "Nestlé's prepared foods unit has built an in-house roster of part-time workers in Cherokee County, South Carolina, who stick by the telephone to hear if they should report on a given day to assemble frozen chicken dinners. The county job-placement office sends Nestlé lists of 'call-ins': people available to work when Nestlé phones them. The workers usually get a day's notice. Some agree to stay by the phone in the morning, in case the company is short for the afternoon shift. They typically work two to six days a week and earn slightly more than $11 an hour, which is considered good part-time pay in the area."

The head of human resources for the prepared-foods division, says demand for its Lean Cuisine glazed-chicken entrees and Stouffers creamed-spinach side dishes is fairly steady. The company still hires some people full time. But the Nestlé executive says it is still hard to predict labor needs, because schedules for producing certain meals vary, and each product requires a different number of people to make. "'We don't need the same number of people every day,' he says. 'They work as we need them.'"[1]

Lincoln Electric "In Cleveland, Lincoln Electric Co. shifts salaried workers to hourly clerical jobs, paying them a different wage for each assignment. The Cleveland-based manufacturer of welding and cutting parts says that, for nearly 60 years, it has guaranteed long-term employment for all of its workers who have worked steadily for three years in its U.S. operations. The flip side is that employees have to be willing to change their job assignments, depending on the type and volume of orders Lincoln receives. Increasingly, manufacturers are adopting elements of Lincoln Electric's approach of continual cross-training and moving workers wherever they are needed."[2]

Hilton Hotels "Many employers, wary of losing valued workers altogether, are reducing the workweek rather than the workforce. Officials of Hilton Hotels Corp. in Beverly Hills, California, boast that they have laid off relatively few workers. However, Hilton says workweek reductions are widespread among its 77,000 workers."[3]

By relying more on part-time workers and daily call-ins, cross-training and frequently moving employees to new jobs, and shortening the workweek, Nestlé, Lincoln Electric, and Hilton Hotels are moving toward direct-labor costs that are much more variable than in the past. Other companies trending toward a "just-in-time workforce" are Wal-Mart, Taco Bell, Starbucks, and U-Haul, among others. This is "all part of the larger development in corporate America of transforming labor from a fixed to a more flexible cost."[4]

---

[1]Clare Ansberry, "In the New Workplace, Jobs Morph to Suit Rapid Change of Pace," *The Wall Street Journal,* March 3, 2002, pp. A1, A7.

[2]Ibid., pp. A1, A7.

[3]Jonathan Eig, "Do Part-Time Workers Hold Key to When the Recession Breaks?" *The Wall Street Journal,* January 3, 2002, p. A1.

[4]Michelle Conlin, "The Big Squeeze on Workers," *Business Week,* May 13, 2002, pp. 96–98; and Michelle Conlin, "The Software Says You're Just Average," *Business Week,* February 25, 2002, p. 126.

The preparation of a complete budget involves much more analysis and detailed planning than is shown here.[5] The point is that cost prediction is an important part of the planning process. The cost behavior patterns discussed in this chapter make those cost predictions possible.

Engineered, Committed, and Discretionary Costs

LO 4

Define and give examples of engineered costs, committed costs, and discretionary costs.

In the process of budgeting costs, it is often useful for management to make a distinction between engineered, committed, and discretionary costs. An **engineered cost** bears a definitive physical relationship to the activity measure. Tasty Donuts' direct-material cost is an engineered cost. It is impossible to produce more donuts without incurring greater material cost for food ingredients.

A **committed cost** results from an organization's ownership or use of facilities and its basic organization structure. Property taxes, depreciation on buildings and equipment, costs of renting facilities or equipment, and the salaries of management personnel are examples of committed fixed costs. Tasty Donuts' facilities cost is a committed fixed cost.

A **discretionary cost** arises as a result of a *management decision* to spend a particular amount of money for some purpose. Examples of discretionary costs include amounts spent on research and development, advertising and promotion, management development programs, and contributions to charitable organizations. For example, suppose Tasty Donuts' management decided to spend $12,400 each month on promotion and advertising.

The distinction between committed and discretionary costs is an important one. Management can change committed costs only through relatively major decisions that have long-term implications. Decisions to build a new production facility, lease a fleet of vehicles, or add more management personnel to oversee a new division are examples of such decisions. These decisions will generally influence costs incurred over a long period of time. In contrast, discretionary costs can be changed in the short run much more easily. Management can be flexible about expenditures for advertising, promotion, employee training, or research and development. This does not imply that such programs are unimportant, but simply that management can alter them over time. For example, the management of a manufacturing firm may decide to spend $100,000 on research and development in the current year, but cut back to $60,000 in the next year because of an anticipated economic downturn.

Whether a particular type of cost is committed or discretionary sometimes differs between organizations. For example, one company's board of directors may view the salaries of top management as a committed cost. Even in an economic downturn, it is important for a firm to keep its basic organization structure intact and retain its key executives. In contrast,

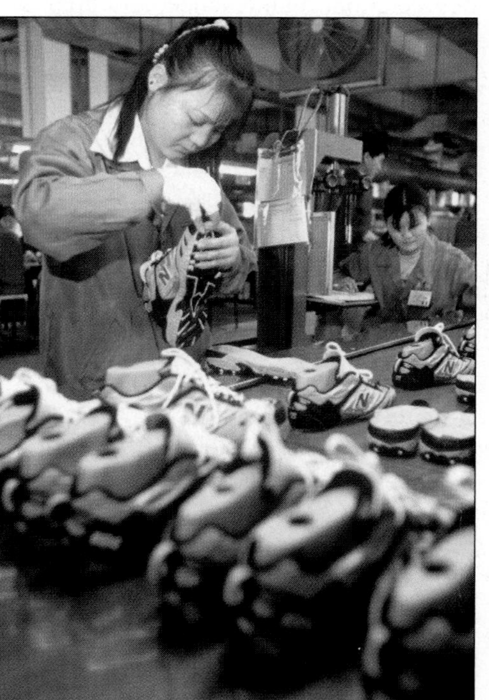

The raw material in these shoes represents an engineered cost. In contrast, the depreciation and property taxes on this manufacturing facility are examples of committed costs. Expenditures on employee development or retraining for these assembly workers are discretionary costs.

[5]The budgeting process is covered in Chapter 9.

"Cost information about activities provides a benchmark to assess how we are doing against best-in-class and competitors." (7d)
BlueCross BlueShield of North Carolina

the tradition in another firm might be to ask its top-management personnel to accept a salary cut during difficult economic times, in order to cut expenses and set an example for other employees.

Shifting Cost Structure in the Contemporary Manufacturing Environment

Fixed costs are becoming more prevalent in many industries. This is due to two factors. First, automation is replacing labor to an increasing extent. Second, labor unions have been increasingly successful in negotiating agreements that result in a relatively stable workforce. This makes management less flexible in adjusting a firm's workforce to the desired level of production.

In the advanced manufacturing environment that is emerging, many costs that once were largely variable have become fixed, most becoming *committed* fixed costs. Take the electronics industry, for example. Years ago, small electronic components were placed onto circuit boards, wired, and soldered by hand. Hundreds of employees performed these operations in "white rooms," which are sterile environments, in order to prevent the electronic units from being contaminated with dust or other foreign particles. Now much of the electronic industry is highly automated. Pick-and-place robots and auto-insertion machines place electronic components on circuit boards with incredible speed and precision. Wash and dry machines eliminate any contaminants, and wave-solder machines solder the connections. A large part of the manufacturing process is computerized. In the past, a major portion of the cost of electronics manufacturing was variable. The workforce could be adjusted as the economy grew rapidly or more slowly. In contrast, companies now spend hundreds of millions of dollars on computer-integrated manufacturing (CIM) systems and flexible manufacturing systems (FMS). Much of the manufacturing labor force consists of computer programmers and highly skilled operators of sophisticated production equipment. The depreciation, maintenance, and upgrades for the CIM systems constitute very large committed fixed costs. Moreover, the compensation costs for the highly skilled computer experts and equipment operators are largely committed fixed costs. Firms often cannot risk losing such highly trained personnel even during an economic downturn. Thus, the shifting cost structure we are observing in today's manufacturing environment has had a major impact on the nature of the cost behavior to be estimated in CIM and FMS settings.

Companies in the food-service industry, like Starbucks, have both volume-based and operations-based cost drivers. The number of customers (customer traffic) is an important volume-based cost driver. Product-line diversity is an example of an operations-based cost driver.

Operations-Based versus Volume-Based Cost Drivers Much of the discussion of cost behavior in this chapter focuses on production volume as the cost driver. As Chapter 5 pointed out, however, production costs are affected by operations-based cost drivers as well. Product complexity, the configuration of the manufacturing process, and the number of production runs are among the many operational cost drivers that have been identified. In today's highly competitive environment, it is crucial that managers thoroughly understand the effects of both operations-based and volume-based cost drivers on the costs incurred in their organizations. For example, it will cost more to produce 10,000 radios in 10 production runs of 1,000 units than in 4 runs of 2,500 units. Increasing the number of production runs will drive setup costs up, even though the other costs of producing each radio may not vary.

Cost Behavior in Other Industries

We have illustrated a variety of cost behavior patterns for Tasty Donuts' restaurant business. The same cost behavior patterns are used in other industries. The cost behavior pattern appropriate for a particular cost item depends on the organization and the activity base (or cost driver). In manufacturing firms, production quantity, direct-labor hours, and machine hours are common cost drivers. Direct-material and direct-labor costs are usually considered variable costs. Other variable costs include some manufacturing-overhead costs, such as indirect material and indirect labor. Fixed manufacturing costs are generally the costs of creating production capacity. Examples include depreciation on plant and equipment, property taxes, and the plant manager's salary. Such overhead costs as utilities and equipment maintenance are usually semivariable or curvilinear costs. A semivariable-cost behavior pattern is generally used to approximate a curvilinear cost within the relevant range. Supervisory salaries are usually step-fixed costs, since one person can supervise production over a range of activity. When activity increases beyond that range, such as when a new shift is added, an additional supervisor is added.

> "In the management of a university, just like any other organization, you have to know your cost structure. We think very carefully about how student enrollment will affect faculty salary costs, computing costs, and lots of other costs students don't necessarily tend to think about." (7e)
>
> **Cornell University**

In merchandising firms, the activity base (or cost driver) usually is sales revenue. The cost of merchandise sold is a variable cost. Most labor costs are fixed or step-fixed costs, since a particular number of sales and stock personnel can generally handle sales activity over a fairly wide range of sales. Store facility costs, such as rent, depreciation on buildings and furnishings, and property taxes, are fixed costs.

In some industries, the choice of the cost driver is not obvious, and the cost behavior pattern can depend on the cost driver selected. In an airline, for instance, the cost driver could be air miles flown, passengers flown, or passenger miles flown. A passenger mile is the transportation of one passenger for one mile. Fuel costs are variable with respect to air miles traveled, but are not necessarily variable with respect to passenger miles flown. An airplane uses more fuel in flying from New York to San Francisco than from New York to Chicago. However, a plane does not require significantly more fuel to fly 200 people from one city to another than to fly 190 people the same distance. In contrast, an airport landing fee is a fixed cost for a particular number of aircraft arrivals, regardless of how far the planes have flown or how many people were transported. The point of this discussion is that both the organization and the cost driver are crucial determinants of the cost behavior for each cost item. Conclusions drawn about cost behavior in one industry are not necessarily transferable to another industry.

Cost Estimation

Topic 7–2

As the preceding discussion indicates, different costs exhibit a variety of cost behavior patterns. **Cost estimation** is the process of determining how a particular cost behaves. Several methods are commonly used to estimate the relationship between cost and activity. Some of these methods are simple, while some are quite sophisticated. In some firms, managers use more than one method of cost estimation. The results of the different methods are then combined by the cost analyst on the basis of experience and

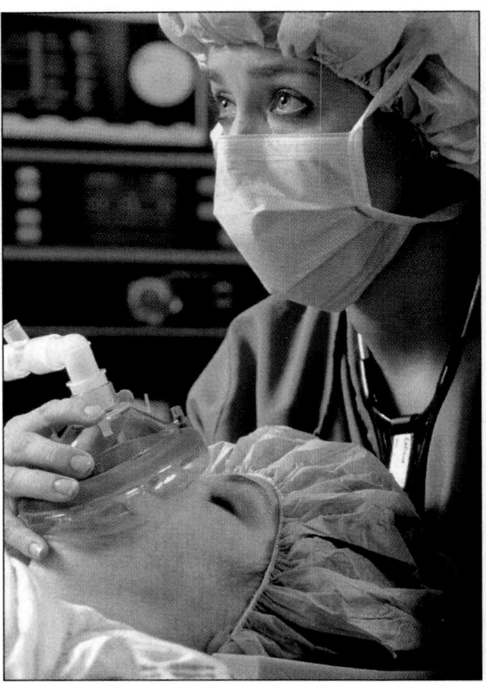

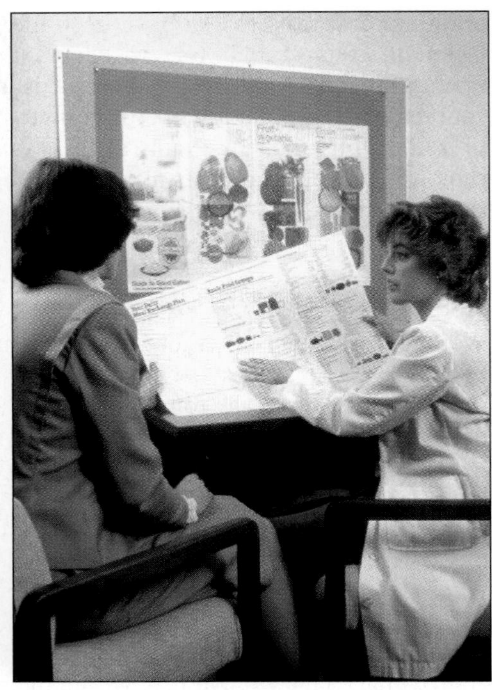

Different types of labor in the same organization can exhibit different cost behavior. The cost of anesthesiology in a hospital, for example, could be a step-fixed cost, while the cost of outsourcing the dietitian's work becomes a fixed cost.

LO 5

Describe and use the following cost-estimation methods: account classification, visual fit, high-low, and least-squares regression.

judgment. We will examine five methods of cost estimation in the context of the Tasty Donuts illustration.

Account-Classification Method

The **account-classification method** of cost estimation, also called **account analysis,** involves a careful examination of the organization's ledger accounts. The cost analyst classifies each cost item in the ledger as a variable, fixed, or semivariable cost. The classification is based on the analyst's knowledge of the organization's activities and experience with the organization's costs. For example, it may be obvious to the analyst going through the ledger that direct-material cost is variable, building depreciation is fixed, and utility costs are semivariable.

Once the costs have been classified, the cost analyst estimates cost amounts by examining job-cost records, paid bills, labor time cards, or other source documents. A property-tax bill, for example, will provide the cost analyst with the information needed to estimate this fixed cost. This examination of historical source documents is combined with other knowledge that may affect costs in the future. For example, the municipal government may have recently enacted a 10 percent property-tax increase, which takes effect the following year.

For some costs, particularly those classified as semivariable, the cost analyst may use one of several more systematic methods of incorporating historical data in the cost estimate. These methods are discussed next.

Visual-Fit Method

When a cost has been classified as semivariable, or when the analyst has no clear idea about the behavior of a cost item, it is helpful to use the **visual-fit method** to plot recent observations of the cost at various activity levels. The resulting **scatter diagram** helps the analyst to visualize the relationship between cost and the level of activity (or

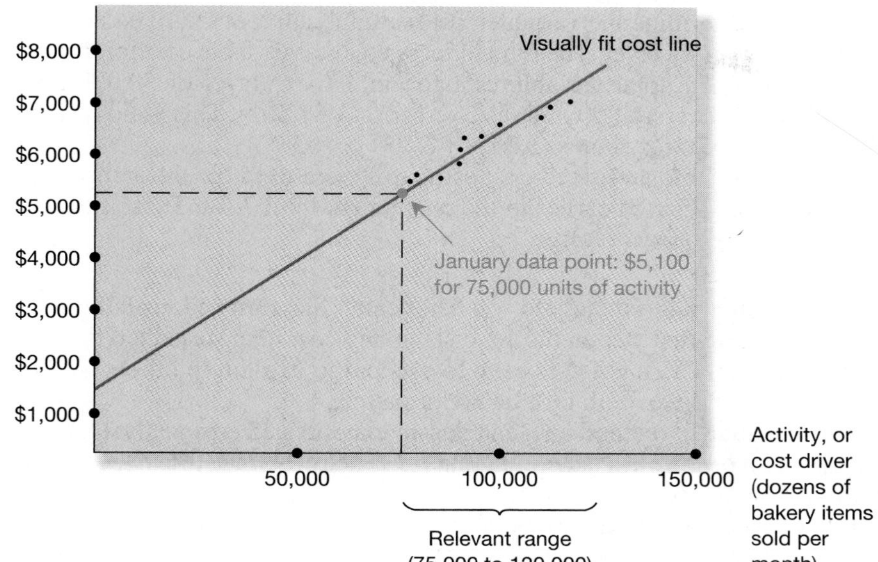

Exhibit 7–8
Scatter Diagram of Cost Data with Visually Fit Cost Line, Tasty Donuts, Inc.

cost driver). To illustrate, suppose Tasty Donuts' controller has compiled the following historical data for the company's utility costs.

Month	Utility Cost for Month	Activity or Cost Driver (dozens of bakery items sold per month)
January	$5,100	75,000
February	5,300	78,000
March	5,650	80,000
April	6,300	92,000
May	6,400	98,000
June	6,700	108,000
July	7,035	118,000
August	7,000	112,000
September	6,200	95,000
October	6,100	90,000
November	5,600	85,000
December	5,900	90,000

The scatter diagram of these data is shown in Exhibit 7–8. The cost analyst can *visually fit a line* to these data by laying a ruler on the plotted points. The line is positioned so that a roughly equal number of plotted points lie above and below the line. Using this method, Tasty Donuts' controller visually fit the line shown in Exhibit 7–8.

Just a glance at the visually fit cost line reveals that Tasty Donuts' utilities cost is a semivariable cost *within the relevant range*. The scatter diagram provides little or no information about the cost relationship outside the relevant range. Recall from the discussion of Tasty Donuts' utilities cost (see Exhibit 7–7) that the controller believes the cost behavior pattern to be curvilinear over the *entire range* of activity. This judgment is based on the controller's knowledge of the firm's facilities and an understanding of electricity usage by the modern bakery equipment and the older bakery equipment. As Exhibit 7–7 shows, however, the curvilinear utilities cost can be approximated closely by a semivariable cost *within the relevant range*. The data plotted in the scatter diagram lie within the relevant range. Consequently, the data provide a sound basis for the semivariable approximation that the controller has chosen to use.

The visually fit cost line in Exhibit 7–8 intercepts the vertical axis at $1,500. Thus, $1,500 is the estimate of the fixed-cost component in the semivariable-cost approximation. To determine the variable cost per unit, subtract the fixed cost from the total cost at any activity level. The remainder is the total variable cost for that activity level. For example, the total variable cost for an activity level of 50,000 dozen items is $2,500 (total cost of $4,000 minus fixed cost of $1,500). This yields a variable cost of $.05 per dozen bakery items ($.05 = $2,500 ÷ 50,000).

These variable and fixed cost estimates were used for the semivariable-cost approximation discussed earlier in the chapter (Exhibit 7–7). These estimates are valid only *within the relevant range.*

Evaluation of Visual-Fit Method The scatter diagram and visually fit cost line provide a valuable first step in the analysis of any cost item suspected to be semivariable or curvilinear. The method is easy to use and to explain to others, and it provides a useful view of the overall cost behavior pattern.

The visual-fit method also enables an experienced cost analyst to spot *outliers* in the data. An **outlier** is a data point that falls far away from the other points in the scatter diagram and is not representative of the data. Suppose, for example, that the data point for January had been $6,000 for 75,000 units of activity. Exhibit 7–8 reveals that such a data point would be way out of line with the rest of the data. The cost analyst would follow up on such a cost observation to discover the reasons behind it. It could be that the data point is in error. Perhaps a utility bill was misread when the data were compiled, or possibly the billing itself was in error. Another possibility is that the cost observation is correct but due to unusual circumstances. Perhaps Toronto experienced a record cold wave during January that required the company's donut shops to use unusually high amounts of electric heat. Perhaps an oven in the bakery had a broken thermostat during January that caused the oven to overheat consistently until discovered and repaired. An outlier can result from many causes. If the outlier is due to an error or very unusual circumstances, the data point should be ignored in the cost analysis.

The primary drawback of the visual-fit method is its lack of objectivity. Two cost analysts may draw two different visually fit cost lines. This is not usually a serious problem, however, particularly if the visual-fit method is combined with other, more objective methods.

High-Low Method

In the **high-low method** the semivariable-cost approximation is computed using exactly two data points. The high and low *activity levels* are chosen from the available data set. These activity levels, together with their associated cost levels, are used to compute the variable and fixed cost components as follows:

$$\text{Variable cost per dozen bakery items} = \frac{\text{Difference between the } \textit{costs} \text{ corresponding to the highest and lowest activity levels}}{\text{Difference between the highest and lowest } \textit{activity} \text{ levels}}$$

$$= \frac{\$7{,}035 - \$5{,}100}{118{,}000 - 75{,}000} = \frac{\$1{,}935}{43{,}000}$$

$$= \$.045 \text{ per dozen items}$$

Now we can compute the total variable cost at either the high or low activity level. At the low activity of 75,000 dozen items, the total variable cost is $3,375 ($.045 × 75,000). Subtracting the total variable cost from the total cost at the 75,000 dozen activity level, we obtain the fixed-cost estimate of $1,725 ($5,100 − $3,375). Notice that the high and low *activity* levels are used to choose the two data points. In general,

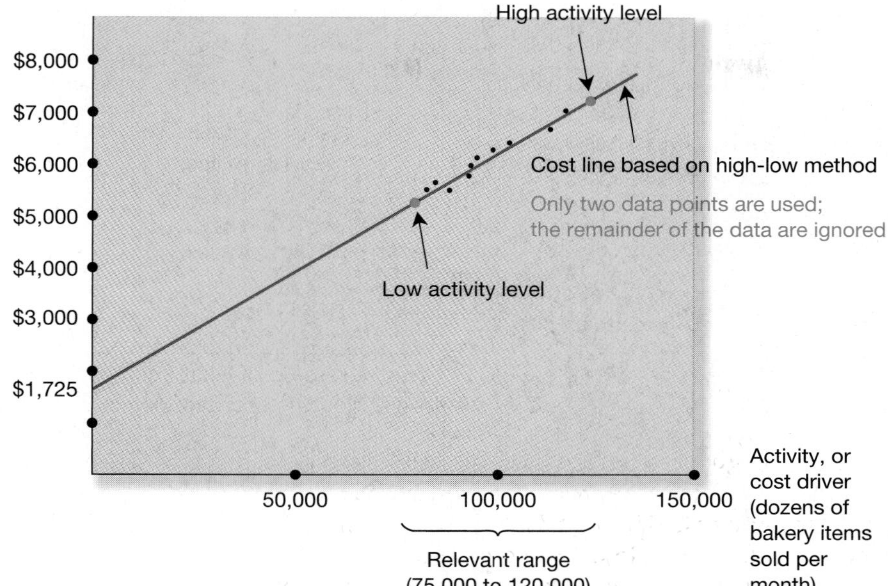

Exhibit 7–9
Graph of Utilities Cost Using High-Low Method, Tasty Donuts, Inc.

these two points need not necessarily coincide with the high and low cost levels in the data set.

Exhibit 7–9 presents a graph of Tasty Donuts' utilities cost, which is based on the high-low method of cost estimation. As in any cost-estimation method, this estimate of the cost behavior pattern should be *restricted to the relevant range*.

Evaluation of High-Low Method The high-low method is more objective than the visual-fit method, since it leaves no room for the cost analyst's judgment. However, the high-low method suffers from a major weakness. Only two data points are used to estimate the cost behavior pattern; the remainder of the data points are ignored. In this regard, the visual-fit method is superior to the high-low method, since the former approach uses all of the available data.

Least-Squares Regression Method

Statistical techniques may be used to estimate objectively a cost behavior pattern using all of the available data. The most common of these methods is called *least-squares regression*. To understand this method, examine Exhibit 7–10, which repeats the scatter diagram of Tasty Donuts' utilities cost data. The exhibit also includes a cost line that has been drawn through the plotted data points. Since the data points do not lie along a perfectly straight line, any cost line drawn through this scatter diagram will miss some or most of the data points. The objective is to draw the cost line so as to make the deviations between the cost line and the data points as small as possible.

In the **least-squares regression method,** the cost line is positioned so as to *minimize* the sum of the *squared deviations* between the cost line and the data points. The inset to Exhibit 7–10 depicts this technique graphically. Note that the deviations between the cost line and the data points are measured vertically on the graph rather than perpendicular to the line. The cost line fit to the data using least-squares regression is called a *least-squares regression line* (or simply a **regression line**).

Why is the regression method based on minimizing the *squares* of the deviations between the cost line and the data points? A complete answer to this question lies in the

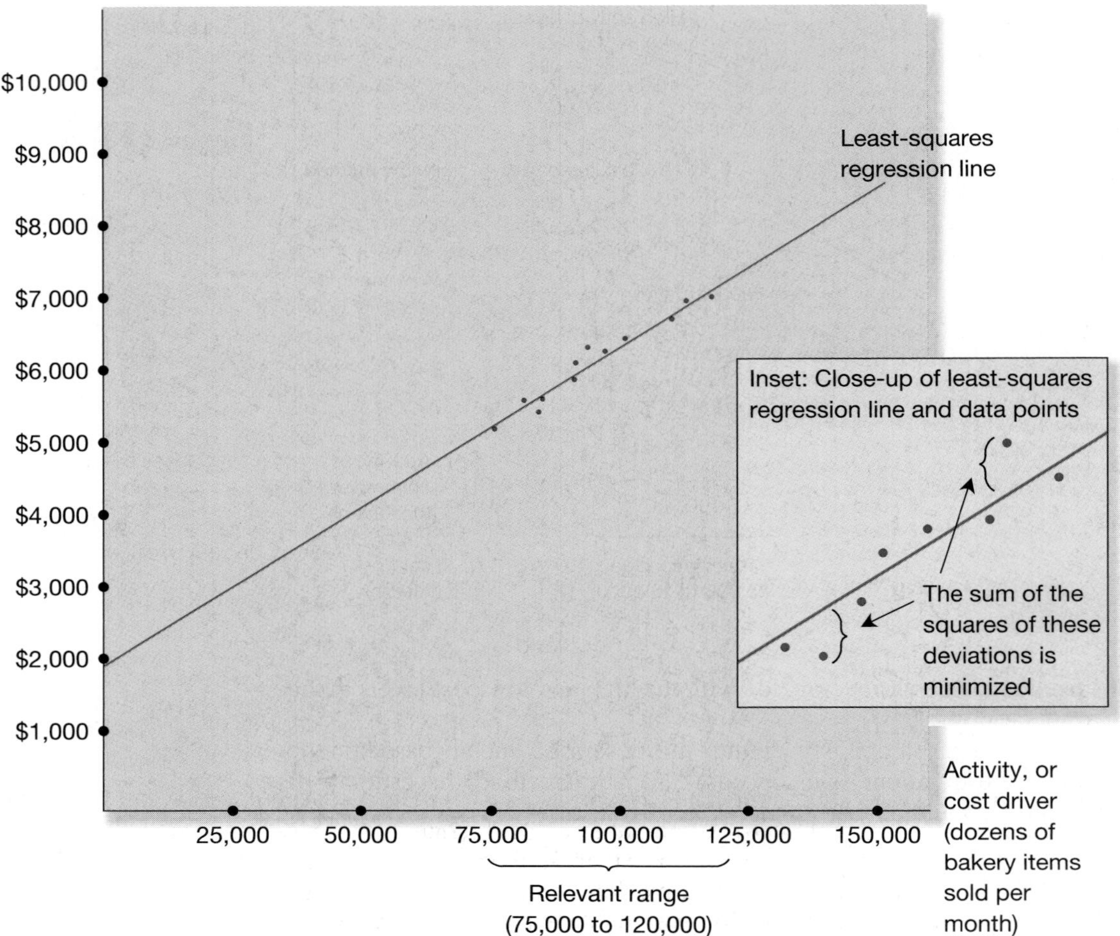

Exhibit 7–10
Graph of Utilities Cost Using Least-Squares Regression Method, Tasty Donuts, Inc.

theory of statistics. In short, statistical theorists have proven that a least-squares regression line possesses some very desirable properties for making cost predictions and drawing inferences about the estimated relationship between cost and activity. As always, the least-squares regression estimate of the cost behavior pattern should be restricted to the relevant range.

Equation Form of Least-Squares Regression Line The least-squares regression line shown in Exhibit 7–10 may be represented by the equation of a straight line. In the following equation, X denotes Tasty Donuts' activity level for a month, and Y denotes the estimated utilities cost for that level of activity. The intercept of the line on the vertical axis is denoted by a, and the slope of the line is denoted by b. *Within the relevant range,* a is interpreted as an estimate of the fixed-cost component, and b is interpreted as an estimate of the variable cost per unit of activity.

$$Y = a + bX \tag{1}$$

In regression analysis, X is referred to as the **independent variable,** since it is the variable upon which the estimate is based. Y is called the **dependent variable,** since its estimate depends on the independent variable.

The least-squares regression line for Tasty Donuts' utilities cost is shown below in equation form.

$$Y = 1{,}920 + .0448X$$

Y: Estimated utilities cost for one month

X: Activity level for one month

Within the relevant range of activity, the regression estimate of the fixed-cost component is $1,920 per month, and the regression estimate of the variable-cost component is $.0448 per dozen bakery items. These estimates are derived in the appendix at the end of this chapter, which you may want to read now.

Evaluation of Least-Squares Regression Method We have seen that least-squares regression is an objective method of cost estimation that makes use of all available data. Moreover, the regression line has desirable statistical properties for making cost predictions and drawing inferences about the relationship between cost and activity. The method does require considerably more computation than either the visual-fit or high-low method. However, computer programs are readily available to perform least-squares regression.

Evaluating a Particular Least-Squares Regression Line We have seen the benefits of least-squares regression *in general.* How does a cost analyst evaluate a *particular* regression line based on a specific set of data? A number of criteria may be used, including *economic plausibility* and *goodness of fit.*

The cost analyst should always evaluate a regression line from the perspective of *economic plausibility.* Does the regression line make economic sense? Is it intuitively plausible to the cost analyst? If not, the analyst should reconsider using the regression line to make cost predictions. It may be that the chosen independent variable is not a good predictor of the cost behavior being analyzed. Perhaps another independent variable should be considered. Alternatively, there may be errors in the data upon which the regression is based. Rechecking the data will resolve this issue. It could be that fundamental assumptions that underlie the regression method have been violated. In this case, the analyst may have to resort to some other method of cost estimation.

Another criterion commonly used to evaluate a particular regression line is to assess its **goodness of fit.** Statistical methods can be used to determine objectively how well a regression line fits the data upon which it is based. If a regression line fits the data well, a large proportion of the variation in the dependent variable will be explained by the variation in the independent variable. One frequently used measure of goodness of fit is described in the appendix at the end of this chapter.[6]

Multiple Regression

Describe the multiple regression, engineering, and learning-curve approaches to cost estimation.

In each of the cost-estimation methods discussed so far, we have based the estimate on a single independent variable. Moreover, all of Tasty Donuts' cost behavior patterns were specified with respect to a single activity (or cost driver), dozens of bakery items produced and sold. However, there may be two or more independent variables that are important predictors of cost behavior.

To illustrate, we will continue our analysis of Tasty Donuts' utilities costs. The company uses electricity for two primary purposes: operating cooking equipment, such as deep-fat fryers and ovens, and heating the bakery and donut shops. The cost of electricity for food production is a function of the firm's activity, as measured in dozens of bakery items produced and sold. However, the cost of electricity for restaurant heating

---

[6]We have only scratched the surface of regression analysis as a tool for cost estimation. For an expanded discussion of the least-squares regression method, see any statistics text.

is related more closely to the number of customers than to the number of bakery items sold. A restaurant's heating costs go up each time the restaurant door is opened, resulting in loss of heat. Two customers purchasing half a dozen donuts each result in greater heating cost than one customer buying a dozen donuts.

Suppose Tasty Donuts' controller wants to estimate a cost behavior pattern for utilities cost that is based on both units of sales and number of customers. The method of *multiple regression* may be used for this purpose. **Multiple regression** is a statistical method that estimates a linear (straight-line) relationship between one dependent variable and two or more independent variables. In Tasty Donuts' case, the following regression equation would be estimated.

$$Y = a + b_1X_1 + b_2X_2 \tag{2}$$

where Y denotes the dependent variable, utilities cost
X_1 denotes the first independent variable, dozens of bakery items sold
X_2 denotes the second independent variable, number of customers served

In regression equation (2), a denotes the regression estimate of the fixed-cost component, b_1 denotes the regression estimate of the variable utilities cost per dozen bakery items, and b_2 denotes the regression estimate of the variable utilities cost per customer served. The multiple-regression equation will likely enable Tasty Donuts' controller to make more accurate cost predictions than could be made with the *simple regression* discussed previously. A **simple regression** is based on a single independent variable. Multiple regression is covered more extensively in cost-accounting and statistics texts.

Data Collection Problems

LO 7

Describe some problems often encountered in collecting data for cost estimation.

Regardless of the method used, the resulting cost estimation will be only as good as the data upon which it is based. The collection of data appropriate for cost estimation requires a skilled and experienced cost analyst. Six problems frequently complicate the process of data collection:

1. *Missing data.* Misplaced source documents or failure to record a transaction can result in missing data.
2. *Outliers.* We have discussed these extreme observations of cost-activity relationships. If outliers are determined to represent errors or highly unusual circumstances, they should be eliminated from the data set.
3. *Mismatched time periods.* The units of time for which the dependent and independent variables are measured may not match. For example, production activity may be recorded daily, but costs may be recorded monthly. A common solution is to aggregate the production data to get monthly totals.
4. *Trade-offs in choosing the time period.* In choosing the length of the time period for which data are collected, there are conflicting objectives. One objective is to obtain as many data points as possible, which implies a short time period. Another objective is to choose a long enough time period to ensure that the accounting system has accurately associated costs with time periods. If, for example, a cost that resulted from production activity in one period is recorded in a later period, the cost and activity data will not be matched properly. Longer time periods result in fewer recording lags in the data.
5. *Allocated and discretionary costs.* Fixed costs are often *allocated* on a per-unit-of-activity basis. For example, fixed manufacturing-overhead costs such as depreciation are allocated to units of production. As a result, such costs may appear to be variable in the cost records. *Discretionary* costs often are budgeted in a manner that makes them appear variable. A cost such as advertising, for example, may be fixed once management decides on the level

of advertising. If management's policy is to budget advertising on the basis of sales dollars, however, the cost will appear to be variable to the cost analyst. An experienced analyst will be wary of such costs and take steps to learn how their amounts are determined.

Advertising costs, which are so vividly depicted in this view of New York City's Times Square, often are discretionary fixed costs. Once management determines the level of advertising expenditure, the cost will remain fixed across a range of activity.

6. *Inflation.* During periods of inflation, historical cost data may not reflect future cost behavior. One solution is to choose historical data from a period of low inflation and then factor in the current inflation rate. Other, more sophisticated approaches are also available, and they are covered in cost-accounting texts.

Engineering Method of Cost Estimation

LO 6

Describe the multiple regression, engineering, and learning-curve approaches to cost estimation.

All of the methods of cost estimation examined so far are based on historical data. Each method estimates the relationship between cost and activity by studying the relationship observed in the past. A completely different method of cost estimation is to study the process that results in cost incurrence. This approach is called the **engineering method** of cost estimation. In a manufacturing firm, for example, a detailed study is made of the production technology, materials, and labor used in the manufacturing process. Rather than asking what the cost of material was last period, the engineering approach is to ask how much material should be needed and how much it should cost. Industrial engineers sometimes perform *time and motion studies*, which determine the steps required for people to perform the manual tasks that are part of the production process. Cost behavior patterns for various types of costs are then estimated on the basis of the engineering analysis. Engineering cost studies are time-consuming and expensive, but they often provide highly accurate estimates of cost behavior. Moreover, in rapidly evolving, high-technology industries, there may not be any historical data on which to base cost estimates. Such industries as genetic engineering, superconductivity, and electronics are evolving so rapidly that historical data are often irrelevant in estimating costs.

Effect of Learning on Cost Behavior

In many production processes, production efficiency increases with experience. As cumulative production output increases, the average labor time required per unit declines. A graphical expression of this phenomenon is called a **learning curve.** An example is shown in panel A of Exhibit 7–11. On this learning curve, when cumulative output doubles, the average labor time per unit declines by 20 percent. Panel B of Exhibit 7–11 displays the total labor time and average labor time per unit for various levels of cumulative output. As cumulative output doubles from 5 to 10 units, for example, the average labor time per unit declines by 20 percent, from 100 hours per unit to 80 hours per unit. As a manufacturer gains experience with a product, estimates of the cost of direct labor should be adjusted downward to take this learning effect into account.

Sometimes the learning-curve concept is applied to a broader set of costs than just labor costs. Then the phenomenon is referred to as an **experience curve.** Suppose, for example, that all labor and variable overhead costs are observed to decline by 20 percent every time cumulative output doubles. Then we would change the vertical axis of

Exhibit 7–11
Learning Curve

A. Graphical Presentation of Learning Curve

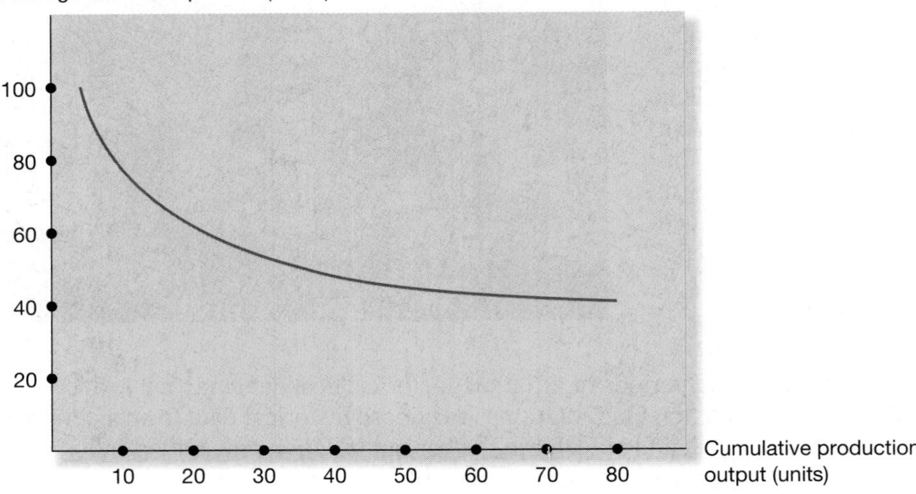

B. Tabular Presentation of Learning Curve

Cumulative Output (in units)	Average Labor Time per Unit (hours)	Total Labor Time (hours)
5	100.00	500.0
10	80.00	800.0
20	64.00	1,280.0
40	51.20	2,048.0
80	40.96	3,276.8

> "We've got to be an integrated, expert business advisor to whoever the equivalent of the CEO is." (7f)
> **Boeing**

Exhibit 7–11 to *labor and variable overhead costs*. The graph would then be called an *experience curve*.

Learning curves have been used extensively in such industries as aircraft production, shipbuilding, and electronics to assist cost analysts in predicting labor costs. These cost predictions are then used in scheduling production, budgeting, setting product prices, and other managerial decisions.

Costs and Benefits of Information

We have discussed a variety of cost-estimation methods ranging from the simple visual-fit approach to sophisticated techniques involving regression or learning curves. Which of these methods is best? In general, the more sophisticated methods will yield more accurate cost estimates than the simpler methods. However, even a sophisticated method still yields only an imperfect estimate of an unknown cost behavior pattern.

All cost-estimation methods are based on simplifying assumptions. The two most important assumptions are as follows:

1. Except for the multiple-regression technique, all of the methods assume that cost behavior depends on *one activity variable*. Even multiple regression uses only a small number of independent variables. In reality, however, costs are affected by a host of factors including the weather, the mood of the employees, and the quality of the raw materials used.
2. Another simplifying assumption usually made in cost estimation is that cost behavior patterns are linear (straight lines) within the relevant range.

The cost analyst must consider on a case-by-case basis whether these assumptions are reasonable. The analyst also must decide when it is important to use a more sophisticated, and more costly, cost-estimation method and when it is acceptable to use a simpler approach. As in any choice among managerial accounting methods, the costs and benefits of the various cost-estimation techniques must be weighed.

Focus on Ethics

CISCO SYSTEMS, WAL-MART, TACO BELL, STARBUCKS, U-HAUL, GENERAL DYNAMICS, AND FARMER'S INSURANCE: IS DIRECT LABOR A VARIABLE COST?

The question as to whether direct labor is a variable cost is interesting from a cost-estimation perspective, but it also presents an interesting ethical issue.

Direct material is always a variable cost. At the other extreme, depreciation on fixed facilities and infrastructure typically is not. What about direct labor? Here it depends on the ability and willingness of management to adjust the labor force to current needs. If management is able *and willing* to hire workers as needed and lay them off when activity declines, direct labor would be a variable cost. The contemporary trend at many companies seems to be in this direction. "Companies are looking first to bring in contract workers that they can quickly *tap and zap* without paying any benefits or severance."[7] In fact, the temps have recently been the fastest-growing sector of employment. "And they aren't accounted for as regular employees. This helps companies that use a lot of them, like Cisco Systems Inc., to drive up revenue per employee."

"The growing use of the *just-in-time workforce* is not the only means by which companies are priming the productivity pump. Workers complain that many employers are taking advantage of outdated labor laws by misclassifying them as salaried-exempt so they can skirt overtime pay. Wal-Mart, Taco Bell, Starbucks, and U-Haul, among others, have been slapped with class actions. In the case of General Dynamics Corp., this resulted in a $100 million award that is now on appeal. At Farmer's Insurance, employees got $90 million. Some employers are so worried about the issue that they are now doing wage-and-hour audits."

Is it ethical to "tap and zap" employees? What do you think? (For more on this issue, see the Management Accounting Practice inset on page 264.)

Chapter Summary

Understanding an organization's cost behavior enables managers to anticipate changes in cost when the organization's level of activity (or cost driver) changes. Cost predictions, which are based on cost behavior patterns, facilitate planning, cost management, and decision making throughout the organization. These cost predictions should be confined to the relevant range, which is the range of activity expected for the organization.

A variety of cost behavior patterns exist, ranging from simple variable and fixed costs to more complicated semivariable and curvilinear costs. Several cost-estimation methods are used to determine which cost behavior pattern is appropriate for a particular cost. The account-classification, visual-fit, high-low, and regression methods are all based on an analysis of historical cost data observed at a variety of activity levels. The engineering method of cost estimation is based on a detailed analysis of the process in which the costs are incurred. These methods are frequently used in combination to provide a more accurate cost estimate.

As in selecting any managerial-accounting technique, the choice of a cost-estimation method involves a trade-off of costs and benefits. More accurate estimation methods provide the benefits of better information, but they are often more costly to apply.

Review Problems on Cost Behavior and Estimation

Problem 1

Erie Hardware, Inc. operates a chain of four retail stores. Data on the company's maintenance costs for its store buildings and furnishings are as follows:

[7]The information and quotations in this inset are from Michelle Conlin, "The Big Squeeze on Workers," *Business Week,* May 13, 2002, pp. 96, 97.

Month	Maintenance Cost	Sales
January	$53,000	$600,000
February	55,000	700,000
March	47,000	550,000
April	51,000	650,000
May	45,000	500,000
June	49,000	610,000

Using the high-low method, estimate and graph the cost behavior for the firm's maintenance costs.

Problem 2

The *Keystone Sentinel* is a weekly newspaper sold throughout Pennsylvania. The following costs were incurred by its publisher during a week when circulation was 100,000 newspapers: total variable costs, $40,000; total fixed costs, $66,000. Fill in your predictions for the following cost amounts.

	Circulation	
	110,000 Newspapers	**120,000 Newspapers**
Total variable cost	______	______
Variable cost per unit	______	______
Total fixed cost	______	______
Fixed cost per unit	______	______

Solutions to Review Problems

Problem 1

	Sales	Cost
At high activity	$700,000	$55,000
At low activity	500,000	45,000
Difference	$200,000	$10,000

$$\text{Variable cost per sales dollar} = \frac{\$10{,}000}{200{,}000} = \$.05 \text{ per sales dollar}$$

Total cost at $700,000 of sales	$55,000
Total variable cost at $700,000 of sales (700,000 × $.05)	35,000
Difference is total fixed cost	$20,000

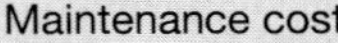

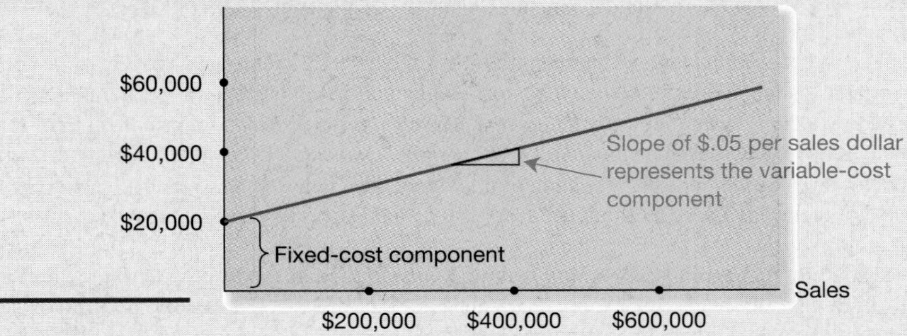

Problem 2

	Circulation	
	110,000 Newspapers	**120,000 Newspapers**
Total variable cost	$\$40{,}000 \times \left(\frac{110{,}000}{100{,}000}\right) = \$44{,}000$	$\$40{,}000 \times \left(\frac{120{,}000}{100{,}000}\right) = \$48{,}000$
Variable cost per unit	$44,000 ÷ 110,000 = $.40	$48,000 ÷ 120,000 = $.40
Total fixed cost	$66,000	$66,000
Fixed cost per unit	$66,000 ÷ 110,000 = $.60	$66,000 ÷ 120,000 = $.55

Key Terms

For each term's definition refer to the indicated page, or turn to the glossary at the end of the text.

account-classification method (also called account analysis), 268
coefficient of determination,* 280
committed cost, 265
cost behavior, 256
cost estimation, 256
cost prediction, 256
curvilinear cost, 262
dependent variable, 272
discretionary cost, 265
engineered cost, 265
engineering method, 275
experience curve, 275
fixed cost, 258
goodness of fit, 273
high-low method, 270
independent variable, 272
learning curve, 275
least-squares regression method, 271
multiple regression, 274
outlier, 270
regression line, 271
relevant range, 263
scatter diagram, 268
semivariable (or mixed) cost, 260
simple regression, 274
step-fixed costs, 259
step-variable costs, 257
variable cost, 257
visual-fit method, 268

*Term appears in the appendix.

Appendix to Chapter 7

Finding the Least-Squares Regression Estimates

LO 8

After completing the appendix, perform and interpret a least-squares regression analysis with a single independent variable.

The least-squares regression line, which is shown below in equation form, includes two estimates. These estimates, which are called *parameters*, are the *intercept* (denoted by a) and the *slope coefficient* (denoted by b).

$$Y = a + bX \tag{3}$$

where X denotes the independent variable (activity level for one month)
Y denotes the dependent variable (cost for one month)

Statistical theorists have shown that these parameters are defined by the following two equations.[8]

$$a = \frac{(\Sigma Y)(\Sigma X^2) - (\Sigma X)(\Sigma XY)}{n(\Sigma X^2) - (\Sigma X)(\Sigma X)} \tag{4}$$

$$b = \frac{n(\Sigma XY) - (\Sigma X)(\Sigma Y)}{n(\Sigma X^2) - (\Sigma X)(\Sigma X)} \tag{5}$$

where n denotes the number of data points
Σ denotes summation; for example, ΣY denotes the sum of the Y (cost) values in the data

The spreadsheet in Exhibit 7–12 (Panel A) shows the numbers used to compute the regression parameters, a and b, for Tasty Donuts' utilities cost. Notice that the X values (activity levels) are expressed in thousands to make the numbers more convenient to handle. Substituting these numbers into equations (4) and (5) yields the following estimates for a and b.

$$a = \frac{(73{,}285)(106{,}759) - (1{,}121)(6{,}937{,}430)}{(12)(106{,}759) - (1{,}121)(1{,}121)} = 1{,}920^* \tag{6}$$

$$b = \frac{(12)(6{,}937{,}430) - (1{,}121)(73{,}285)}{(12)(106{,}759) - (1{,}121)(1{,}121)} = 44.82^* \tag{7}$$

*Rounded.

[8]The derivation of these equations, which requires calculus, is covered in any introductory statistics text.

Exhibit 7–12
Computation of Least-Squares Regression Estimates

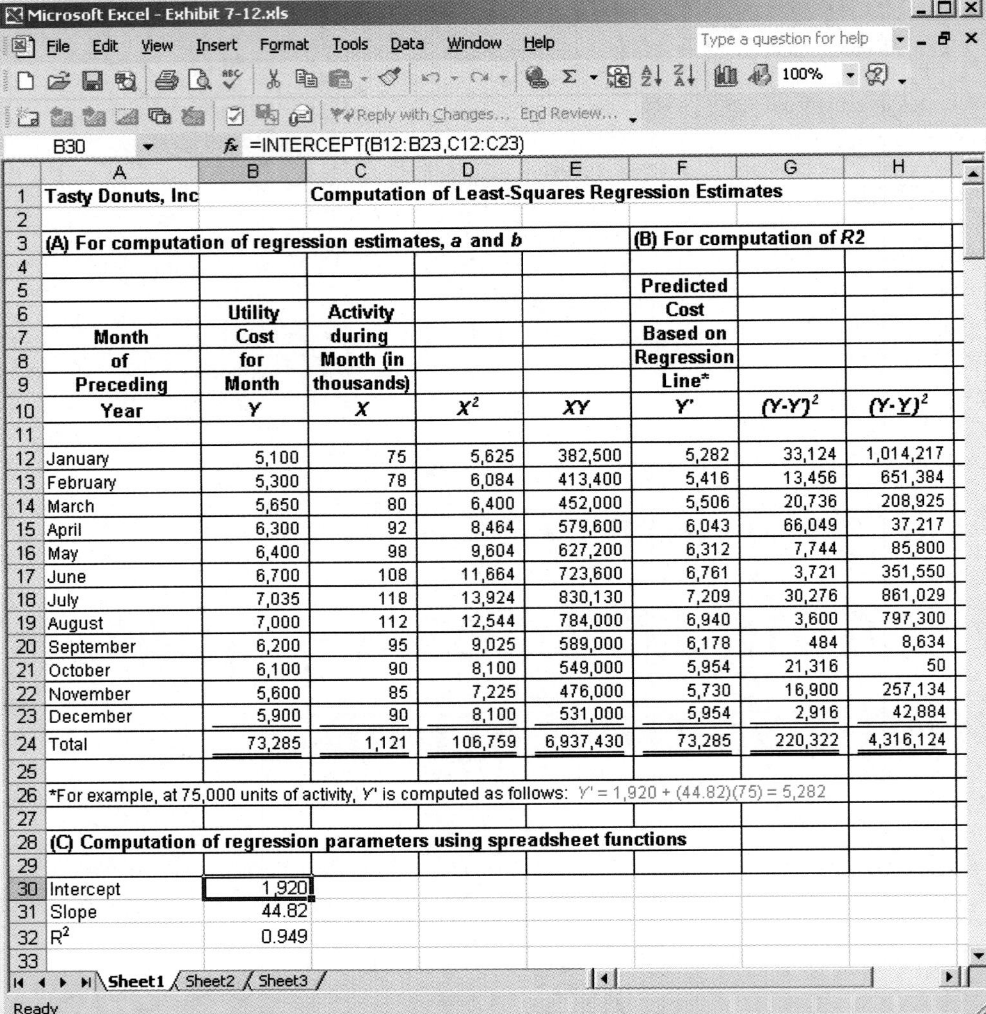

	A	B	C	D	E	F	G	H
1	Tasty Donuts, Inc		Computation of Least-Squares Regression Estimates					
2								
3	(A) For computation of regression estimates, *a* and *b*					(B) For computation of *R2*		
4–10	Month of Preceding Year	Utility Cost for Month *Y*	Activity during Month (in thousands) *X*	X^2	*XY*	Predicted Cost Based on Regression Line* *Y'*	$(Y-Y')^2$	$(Y-\underline{Y})^2$
11								
12	January	5,100	75	5,625	382,500	5,282	33,124	1,014,217
13	February	5,300	78	6,084	413,400	5,416	13,456	651,384
14	March	5,650	80	6,400	452,000	5,506	20,736	208,925
15	April	6,300	92	8,464	579,600	6,043	66,049	37,217
16	May	6,400	98	9,604	627,200	6,312	7,744	85,800
17	June	6,700	108	11,664	723,600	6,761	3,721	351,550
18	July	7,035	118	13,924	830,130	7,209	30,276	861,029
19	August	7,000	112	12,544	784,000	6,940	3,600	797,300
20	September	6,200	95	9,025	589,000	6,178	484	8,634
21	October	6,100	90	8,100	549,000	5,954	21,316	50
22	November	5,600	85	7,225	476,000	5,730	16,900	257,134
23	December	5,900	90	8,100	531,000	5,954	2,916	42,884
24	Total	73,285	1,121	106,759	6,937,430	73,285	220,322	4,316,124
25								
26	*For example, at 75,000 units of activity, *Y'* is computed as follows: *Y'* = 1,920 + (44.82)(75) = 5,282							
27								
28	(C) Computation of regression parameters using spreadsheet functions							
29								
30	Intercept	1,920						
31	Slope	44.82						
32	R^2	0.949						
33								

The intercept of the regression line on the vertical axis is \$1,920. The slope of the line, as solved in equation (7) above, is \$44.82. However, the *X* (activity) values were rescaled in Exhibit 7–12 to be expressed in thousands. Thus, the *b* value computed above represents a variable cost of \$44.82 *per thousand* dozen bakery items. Dividing this number by 1,000 yields the variable cost per dozen bakery items, \$.0448 (rounded to the nearest hundredth of a cent). This is the regression estimate of the variable cost per dozen bakery items reported earlier in the chapter.

Goodness of Fit The goodness of fit for Tasty Donuts' regression line may be measured by the **coefficient of determination,** commonly denoted by R^2. This measure is defined as the percentage of the variability of the dependent variable about its mean that is explained by the variability of the independent variable about its mean. The higher the R^2, the better the regression line fits the data. The interpretation for a high R^2 is that the independent variable is a good predictor of the behavior of the dependent variable. In cost estimation, a high R^2 means that the cost analyst can be relatively confident in the cost predictions based on the estimated cost behavior pattern.

Statistical theorists have shown that R^2 can be computed using the following formula:

$$R^2 = 1 - \frac{\Sigma\,(Y - Y')^2}{\Sigma\,(Y - \overline{Y})^2} \qquad (8)$$

where Y denotes the observed value of the dependent variable (cost) at a particular activity level

Y' denotes the predicted value of the dependent variable (cost), based on the regression line, at a particular activity level

$\overline{Y}$ denotes the mean (average) observation of the dependent variable (cost)

The numbers needed for the R^2 formula are displayed in the spreadsheet in Exhibit 7–12 (Panel B) for the Tasty Donuts illustration.[9] Substituting these numbers in equation (8) yields the following value for R^2:

$$R^2 = 1 - \frac{220,322}{4,316,124} = .949 \qquad (9)$$

This is a high value for R^2, and Tasty Donuts' controller may be quite confident in the resulting cost predictions. As always, these predictions should be confined to the relevant range.

Using Microsoft® Excel to Calculate the Parameters The calculation of the intercept (a), slope coefficient (b), and R^2 is laborious when done manually using the formulas in the preceding section. Fortunately, there are numerous software programs that perform these calculations. All the analyst needs to do is input the data, that is, the values of the dependent and independent variables (columns B and C, respectively, in the spreadsheet in Exhibit 7–12).

Alternatively, the analyst can use commands in Microsoft® Excel to easily calculate the parameters and R^2. Once again, the analyst enters the data into the Excel spreadsheet, as shown in columns B and C in Exhibit 7–12. Then the Excel functions INTERCEPT, SLOPE, and RSQ are used to compute the parameters. To use each command, the analyst specifies the range of cells in the spreadsheet in which the values of the dependent variable and independent variable reside. This is illustrated in Panel (C) of Exhibit 7–12. In the Excel worksheet:

Cell B30 contains the formula =INTERCEPT(B12:B23,C12:C23)

Cell B31 contains the formula =SLOPE(B12:B23,C12:C23)

Cell B32 contains the formula =RSQ(B12:B23,C12:C23)

In these formulas, B12:B23 specifies the range of cells where the values of the dependent variable reside, and C12:C23 specifies the range of cells where the values of the independent variable reside.

[9] In the Excel spreadsheet in Exhibit 7–12, the mean of the observations is denoted by $\underline{Y}$ instead of the usual $\overline{Y}$

Review Questions

7–1. Describe the importance of cost behavior patterns in planning, control, and decision making.

7–2. Define the following terms, and explain the relationship between them: (*a*) cost estimation, (*b*) cost behavior, and (*c*) cost prediction.

7–3. Suggest an appropriate activity base (or cost driver) for each of the following organizations: (*a*) hotel, (*b*) hospital, (*c*) computer manufacturer, (*d*) computer sales store, (*e*) computer repair service, and (*f*) public accounting firm.

7–4. Draw a simple graph of each of the following types of cost behavior patterns: (*a*) variable, (*b*) step-variable, (*c*) fixed, (*d*) step-fixed, (*e*) semivariable, and (*f*) curvilinear.

7–5. Explain the impact of an increase in the level of activity (or cost driver) on (*a*) total fixed cost and (*b*) fixed cost per unit of activity.

7–6. Explain why a manufacturer's cost of supervising production might be a step-fixed cost.

7–7. Explain the impact of an increase in the level of activity (or cost driver) on (*a*) total variable cost and (*b*) variable cost per unit.

7–8. Using graphs, show how a semivariable (or mixed) cost behavior pattern can be used to approximate (*a*) a step-variable cost and (*b*) a curvilinear cost.

7–9. Indicate which of the following descriptions is most likely to describe each cost listed below.

Description	Costs
Engineered cost	Annual cost of maintaining an interstate highway
Committed cost	Cost of ingredients in a breakfast cereal
Discretionary cost	Cost of advertising for a credit card company
	Depreciation on an insurance company's computer
	Cost of charitable donations that are budgeted as 1 percent of sales revenue
	Research and development costs, which have been budgeted at $45,000 per year

7–10. A cost analyst showed the company president a graph that portrayed the firm's utility cost as semivariable. The president criticized the graph by saying, "This fixed-cost component doesn't look right to me. If we shut down the plant for six months, we wouldn't incur half of these costs." How should the cost analyst respond?

7–11. What is meant by a *learning curve*? Explain its role in cost estimation.

7–12. Suggest an appropriate independent variable to use in predicting the costs of the following tasks.

a. Handling materials at a loading dock.

b. Registering vehicles at a county motor vehicle office.

c. Picking oranges.

d. Inspecting computer components in an electronics firm.

7–13. What is an *outlier*? List some possible causes of outliers. How should outliers be handled in cost estimation?

7–14. Explain the cost-estimation problem caused by allocated and discretionary costs.

7–15. Describe the visual-fit method of cost estimation. What are the main strengths and weaknesses of this method?

7–16. What is the chief drawback of the high-low method of cost estimation? What problem could an outlier cause if the high-low method were used?

7–17. Explain the meaning of the term *least squares* in the least-squares regression method of cost estimation.

7–18. Use an equation to express a least-squares regression line. Interpret each term in the equation.

7–19. Distinguish between *simple regression* and *multiple regression*.

7–20. What impact have advances in manufacturing technology had on the problem of cost estimation?

7–21. Briefly describe two methods that can be used to evaluate a particular least-squares regression line.

Exercises

Exercise 7–22
Behavior of Fixed and Variable Costs; Television Station
(LO 1, 2)

WMTB is an independent television station run by a major state university. The station's broadcast hours vary during the year depending on whether the university is in session. The station's production-crew and supervisory costs are as follows for August and October.

Cost Item	Cost Behavior	Cost Amount	Broadcast Hours during Month
Production Crew	Variable		
August		$5,330	410
October		8,840	680
Supervisory employees	Fixed		
August		6,000	410
October		6,000	680

Required:

1. Compute the cost per broadcast hour during August and October for each of these cost items.
2. What will be the total amount incurred for each of these costs during December, when the station's activity will be 440 broadcast hours?
3. What will be the cost per broadcast hour in December for each of the cost items?

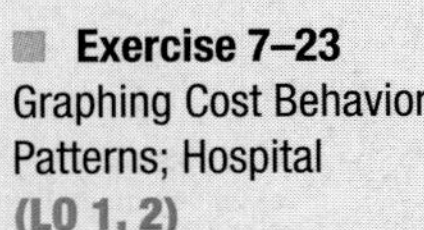

Exercise 7–23
Graphing Cost Behavior Patterns; Hospital
(LO 1, 2)

Draw a graph of the cost behavior for each of the following costs incurred by the Valley View Hospital. The hospital measures monthly activity in patient days. Label both axes and the cost line in each graph.

1. The cost of food varies in proportion to the number of patient days of activity. In January, the hospital provided 2,800 patient days of care, and food costs amounted to $22,400.
2. The cost of salaries and fringe benefits for the administrative staff totals $13,000 per month.
3. The hospital's laboratory costs include two components: (*a*) $40,000 per month for compensation of personnel and depreciation on equipment, and (*b*) $10 per patient day for chemicals and other materials used in performing the tests.
4. The cost of utilities depends on how many wards the hospital needs to use during a particular month. During months with activity under 2,000 patient days of care, two wards are used, resulting in utility costs of $9,000. During months with greater than 2,000 patient days of care, three wards are used, and utility costs total $14,000.
5. Many of the hospital's nurses are part-time employees. As a result, the hours of nursing care provided can be easily adjusted to the amount required at any particular time. The cost of wages and fringe benefits for nurses is approximately $2,500 for each block of 200 patient days of care provided during a month. For example, nursing costs total $2,500 for 1 to 200 patient days, $5,000 for 201 to 400 patient days, $7,500 for 401 to 600 patient days, and so forth.

Exercise 7–24
Account-Classification Method; Food Processing
(LO 1, 2, 5)

Lancaster Meat Company produces one of the best sausage products in southeastern Pennsylvania. The company's controller used the account-classification method to compile the following information.

a. Depreciation schedules revealed that monthly depreciation on buildings and equipment is $21,000.

b. Inspection of several invoices from meat packers indicated that meat costs the company $1.20 per pound of sausage produced.

c. Wage records showed that compensation for production employees costs $.85 per pound of sausage produced.

d. Payroll records showed that supervisory salaries total $11,000 per month.

e. Utility bills revealed that the company incurs utility costs of $5,000 per month plus $.25 per pound of sausage produced.

Required:

1. Classify each cost item as variable, fixed, or semivariable.
2. Write a cost formula to express the cost behavior of the firm's production costs. (Use the form $Y = a + bX$, where Y denotes production cost and X denotes quantity of sausage produced.)

Exercise 7–25
High-Low Method; Tour Company
(LO 1, 2, 5)

Brazilia Bus Tours has incurred the following bus maintenance costs during the recent tourist season. (The *real* is Brazil's national monetary unit. On the day this exercise was written, the *real* was equivalent in value to .3426 U.S. dollar.)

Month	Miles Traveled by Tour Buses	Maintenance Cost
November	12,750	17,100 *real*
December	15,900	17,400
January	19,050	17,550
February	22,500	18,000
March	30,000	18,750
April	12,000	16,500

Required:

1. Use the high-low method to estimate the variable cost per tour mile traveled and the fixed cost per month.
2. Develop a formula to express the cost behavior exhibited by the company's maintenance cost.
3. Predict the level of maintenance cost that would be incurred during a month when 34,000 tour miles are driven. (Remember to express your answer in terms of the *real*.)

Exercise 7–26
Approximating a Curvilinear Cost; Public School District
(LO 1, 2, 3)

The behavior of the annual maintenance and repair cost in the Grounds Department of the Allegheny Public School District is shown by the solid line in the following graph. The dashed line depicts a semivariable-cost approximation of the department's repair and maintenance cost.

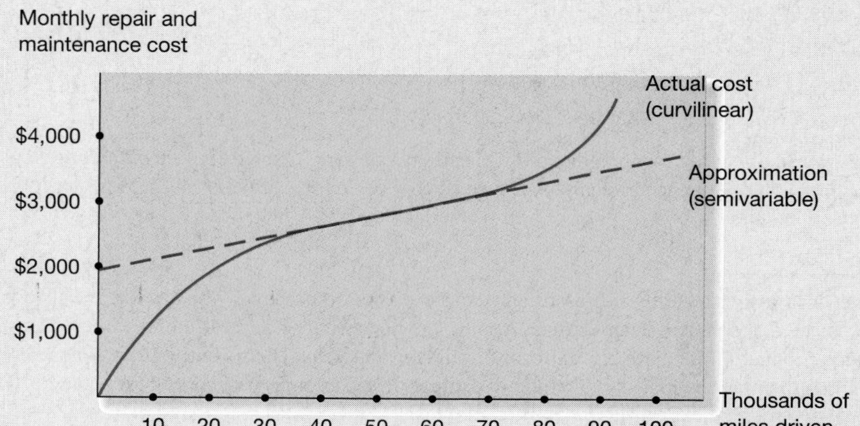

Required:

1. What is the actual (curvilinear) and estimated (semivariable) cost shown by the graph for each of the following activity levels?

	Actual	Estimated
a. 20,000 miles		
b. 40,000 miles		
c. 60,000 miles		
d. 90,000 miles		

2. How good an approximation does the semivariable-cost pattern provide if the department's relevant range is 40,000 to 60,000 miles per month? What if the relevant range is 20,000 to 90,000 miles per month?

Exercise 7–27
Visual-Fit Method; Veterinary Laboratory
(LO 1, 2, 5)

The Kansas City Veterinary Laboratory performs a variety of diagnostic tests on commercial and domestic animals. The lab has incurred the following costs over the past year.

Month	Diagnostic Tests Completed	Cost
January	1,525	$30,100
February	2,250	36,500
March	3,550	50,000
April	3,100	47,800
May	2,350	37,400
June	2,950	44,000
July	3,000	45,500
August	3,050	45,000
September	2,650	43,500
October	2,450	38,300
November	2,400	39,050
December	2,525	40,100

Required:

1. Plot the data above in a scatter diagram. Assign cost to the vertical axis and the number of diagnostic tests to the horizontal axis. Visually fit a line to the plotted data.
2. *Using the visually fit line,* estimate the monthly fixed cost and the variable cost per diagnostic test.

Exercise 7–28
Cost Behavior: Use of Internet
(LO 2)

Visit the website of one of the following companies, or a different company of your choosing.

Levi Strauss	www.levi.com
Dell Computer	www.dell.com
General Electric	www.ge.com
Boeing	www.boeing.com
Ford	www.ford.com/us
Honeywell	www.honeywell.com

Required: Read about the company's products and operations. Then list five manufacturing costs that the company would incur and explain what type of cost behavior you believe would be appropriate for each of these cost items.

Exercise 7–29
Estimating Cost Behavior; High-Low Method
(LO 1, 2, 5)

Jonathan Macintosh is a highly successful upstate New York orchardman who has formed his own company to produce and package applesauce. Apples can be stored for several months in cold storage, so applesauce production is relatively uniform throughout the year. The recently hired controller for the firm is about to apply the high-low method in estimating the company's energy cost behavior. The following costs were incurred during the past 12 months:

Month	Pints of Applesauce Produced	Energy Cost
January	105,000	$70,200
February	63,000	66,300
March	66,000	66,000
April	72,000	67,350
May	90,000	68,700
June	96,000	70,050
July	120,000	84,000
August	90,000	68,400
September	90,000	69,000
October	84,000	68,100
November	123,000	72,300
December	117,000	74,850

Required:

1. Use the high-low method to estimate the company's energy cost behavior and express it in equation form.
2. Predict the energy cost for a month in which 78,000 pints of applesauce are produced.

Exercise 7–30
Estimating Cost Behavior; Visual-Fit Method
(LO 1, 2, 5)

Refer to the data in the preceding exercise.

Required:

1. Draw a scatter diagram and graph the company's energy cost behavior using the visual-fit method.
2. Predict the energy cost for a month in which 78,000 pints of applesauce are produced.
3. What peculiarity is apparent from the scatter diagram? What should the cost analyst do?

Exercise 7–31
Learning Curve; High Technology
(LO 1, 6)

Weathereye, Inc. manufactures weather satellites. The final assembly and testing of the satellites is a largely manual operation involving dozens of highly trained electronics technicians. The following learning curve has been estimated for the firm's newest satellite model, which is about to enter production.

Assembly and Testing

Average labor time per unit (hours)

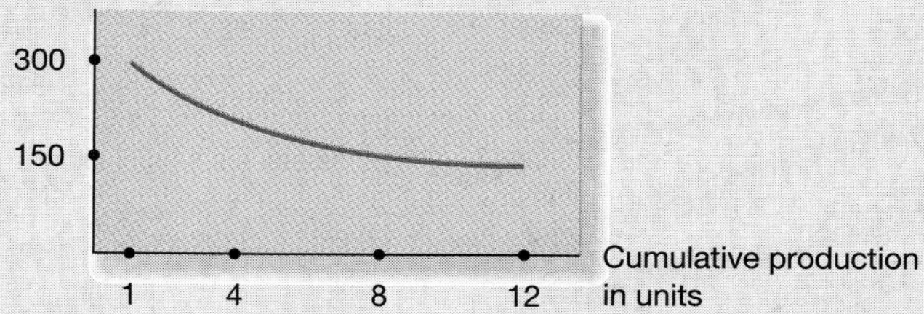

Required:

1. What will be the average labor time required to assemble and test each satellite when the company has produced four satellites? Eight satellites?
2. What will be the total labor time required to assemble and test all satellites produced if the firm manufactures only four satellites? Eight satellites?
3. How can the learning curve be used in the company's budgeting process? In setting cost standards?

Exercise 7–32
Cost Estimation; Government Agency
(LO 2, 6)

The State Department of Taxation processes and audits income-tax returns for state residents. The state tax commissioner has recently begun a program to estimate the costs of running the department. The independent variable used in the program is the number of returns processed. The analysis revealed that the following variable costs are incurred in auditing a typical tax return.

Time spent by tax professional, 20 hours at $25 per hour
Time spent by clerical employees, 10 hours at $12 per hour
Telephone charges, $10 per audit
Computer time, $50 per audit
Postage, $2 per audit

In addition, the department incurs $10,000 of fixed costs each month that are associated with the process of auditing returns.

Required: Draw a graph depicting the monthly costs of auditing state tax returns. Label the horizontal axis, "Tax returns audited."

Exercise 7–33
Estimating Cost Behavior by Multiple Methods (Appendix)
(LO 1, 2, 5, 8)

Gator Beach Marts, a chain of convenience grocery stores in the Fort Lauderdale area, has store hours that fluctuate from month to month as the tourist trade in the community varies. The utility costs for one of the company's stores are listed below for the past six months.

Month	Total Hours of Operation	Total Utility Cost
January	550	$3,240
February	600	3,400
March	700	3,800
April	500	3,200
May	450	2,700
June	400	2,600

Required:

1. Use the high-low method to estimate the cost behavior for the store's utility costs. Express the cost behavior in formula form ($Y = a + bX$). What is the variable utility cost per hour of operation?
2. Draw a scatter diagram of the store's utility costs. Visually fit a cost line to the plotted data. Estimate the variable utility cost per hour of operation.
3. Use least-squares regression to estimate the cost behavior for the store's utility cost. Express the cost behavior in formula form. What is the variable utility cost per hour of operation?
4. During July, the store will be open 300 hours. Predict the store's total utility cost for July using each of the cost-estimation methods employed in requirements (1), (2), and (3).

Exercise 7–34
Airline; Least-Squares Regression (Appendix)
(LO 1, 2, 5, 8)

Recent monthly costs of providing on-board flight service incurred by New England Airlines are shown in the following table.

Month	Thousands of Passengers	Cost of On-Board Flight Service (in thousands)
July	16	$54
August	17	54
September	16	57
October	18	60
November	15	54
December	17	57

Required:

1. Use least-squares regression to estimate the cost behavior of the airline's on-board flight service. Express the cost behavior in equation form. (*Hint*: When interpreting the regression, remember that the data are given in thousands.)
2. Calculate and interpret the R^2 value for the regression line.

Problems

Problem 7–35
Cost Behavior Patterns in a Variety of Settings; International Issues.
(LO 1, 2)

For each of the following cost items (1 through 11), choose the graph (a through l) that best represents it.

1. The cost of utilities at a university. For low student enrollments, utility costs increase with enrollment, but at a decreasing rate. For large student enrollments, utility costs increase at an increasing rate.
2. The cost of telephone service, which is based on the number of message units per month. The charge is $.79 per message unit, for up to 650 message units. Additional message units (above 650) are free.

3. The cost of outsourcing diagnostic blood testing by a hospital. The hospital pays an independent lab a fee of $1,000 per month plus $3 for each test done.
4. The salary costs of the shift supervisors at a truck depot. Each shift is eight hours. The depot operates with one, two, or three shifts at various times of the year.
5. The salaries of the security personnel at a factory. The security guards are on duty around the clock.
6. The wages of table-service personnel in a restaurant. The employees are part-time workers, who can be called upon for as little as two hours at a time.
7. The cost of electricity during peak-demand periods is based on the following schedule.

Up to 10,000 kilowatt-hours (kWh)	$.09 per kWh
Above 10,000 kilowatt-hours	$.12 per kWh

The price schedule is designed to discourage overuse of electricity during periods of peak demand.

8. The cost of sheet metal used to manufacture automobiles.
9. The cost of chartering a private airplane. The cost is $410 per hour for the first three hours of a flight. Then the charge drops to $305 per hour.
10. Under a licensing agreement with a South American import/export company, your firm has begun shipping machine tools to several countries. The terms of the agreement call for an annual licensing fee of $95,000 to be paid to the South American import company if total exports are under $4,500,000. For sales in excess of $4,500,000, an additional licensing fee of 9 percent of sales is due.
11. Your winery exports wine to several Pacific Rim countries. In one nation, you must pay a tariff for every case of wine brought into the country. The tariff schedule is the following:

0 to 6,000 cases per year	$11 per case
6,001 to 12,000 cases per year	$14 per case
Above 12,000 cases per year	$19 per case

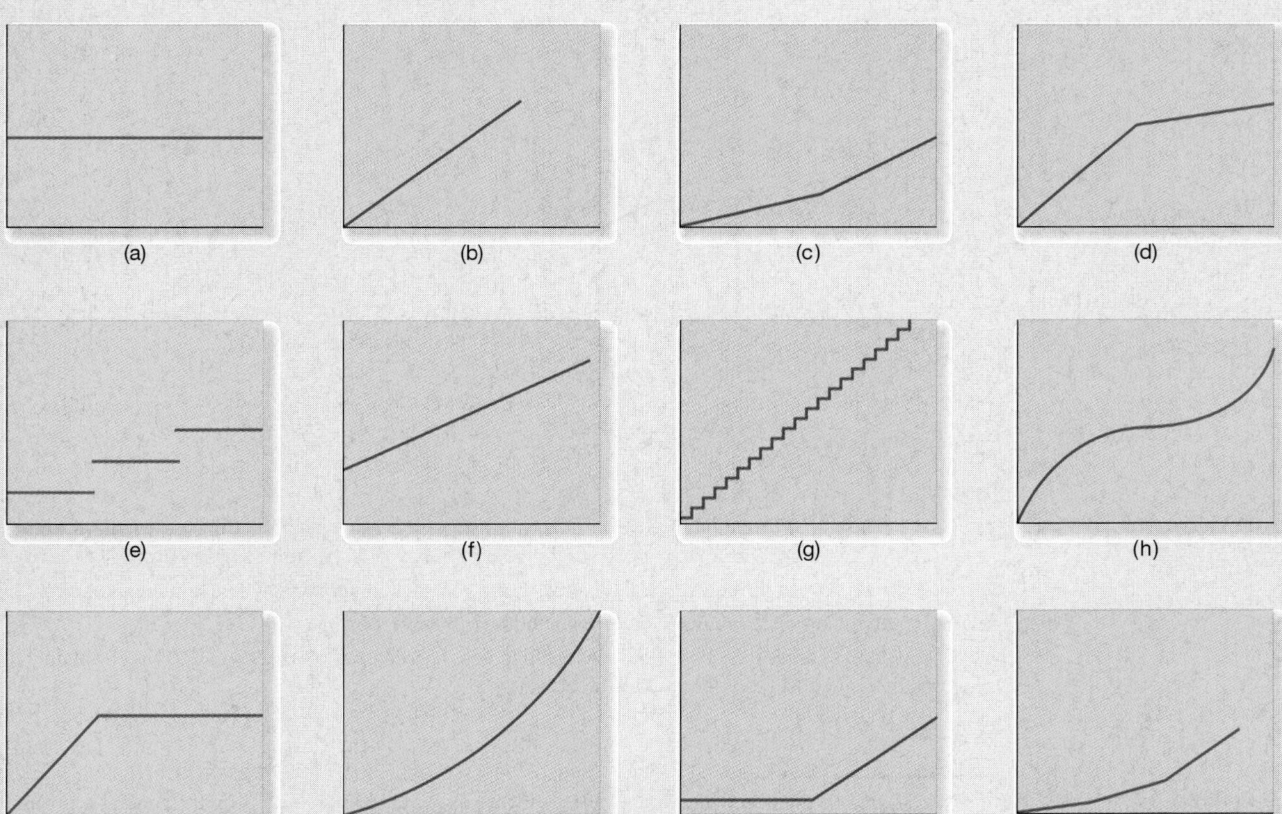

Problem 7–36
Account-Classification Method; Private School
(LO 1, 2, 5)

The Piedmont School of Music has hired you as a consultant to help in analyzing the behavior of the school's costs. Use the account-classification method of cost estimation to classify each of the following costs as variable, fixed, or semivariable. Before classifying the costs, choose an appropriate measure for the school's activity.

1. Cost of buying books, sheet music, and other academic materials that are supplied to the students by the school.
2. Repairs on musical instruments. The school employs a full-time repair technician. Repair jobs that are beyond the technician's capability are taken to a local musical-instrument dealer for repairs.
3. Fee charged by a local public accounting firm to audit the school's accounting records.
4. Salaries and fringe benefits of the school's full-time teachers.
5. Salaries and fringe benefits of the school's full-time administrative staff.
6. Wages of the school's part-time assistant recital instructors. These employees are hired on a temporary basis. For each student enrolled in the school's music programs, four hours of assistant instructor time are needed per week.
7. Depreciation on the school's musical instruments.
8. Rent for the building in which the school operates.
9. Electricity for the school. The school pays a fixed monthly charge plus $.10 per kilowatt-hour of electricity.

Problem 7–37
High-Low Method; Fitness Centers
(LO 1, 2, 5)

Liberty Bell Fitness, Inc. operates a chain of fitness centers in Philadelphia. The firm's controller is accumulating data to be used in preparing its annual profit plan for the coming year. The cost behavior pattern of the firm's equipment maintenance costs must be determined. The accounting staff has suggested the use of an equation, in the form of $Y = a + bX$, for maintenance costs. Data regarding the maintenance hours and costs for last year are as follows:

Month	Hours of Maintenance Service	Maintenance Costs
January	525	$4,710
February	505	4,310
March	310	2,990
April	495	4,200
May	315	3,000
June	485	4,215
July	315	2,950
August	405	3,680
September	475	4,100
October	345	3,250
November	350	3,260
December	335	3,015
Total	4,860	$43,680
Average	405	$3,640

Required:

1. Using the high-low method of cost estimation, estimate the behavior of the maintenance costs incurred by Liberty Bell Fitness, Inc. Express the cost behavior pattern in equation form.
2. Using your answer to requirement (1), what is the variable component of the maintenance cost?
3. Compute the predicted maintenance cost at 600 hours of activity.
4. Compute the variable cost per hour and the fixed cost per hour at 610 hours of activity. Explain why the fixed cost per hour could be misleading.

(CMA, adapted)

Problem 7–38
Cost Behavior and Analysis; High-Low Method
(LO 2, 4, 5)

Lone Mountain Extraction, which mines ore in Idaho, uses a calendar year for both financial-reporting and tax purposes. The following selected costs were incurred in December, the low point of activity, when 1,400 tons of ore were extracted:

Straight-line depreciation	$30,000	Royalties	$140,000
Charitable contributions*	12,000	Trucking and hauling	280,000
Mining labor/fringe benefits	315,000		

*Incurred only in December.

Peak activity of 2,700 tons occurred in June, resulting in mining labor/fringe benefit costs of $607,500, royalties of $224,500, and trucking and hauling outlays of $360,000. The trucking and hauling outlays exhibit the following behavior:

Less than 1,400 tons	$240,000
From 1,400–1,899 tons	280,000
From 1,900–2,399 tons	320,000
From 2,400–2,899 tons	360,000

Lone Mountain Extraction uses the high-low method to analyze costs.

Required:

1. Classify the five costs listed in terms of their behavior: variable, step-variable, committed fixed, discretionary fixed, step-fixed, or semivariable. Show calculations to support your answers for mining labor/fringe benefits and royalties.
2. Calculate the total cost for next February when 1,700 tons are expected to be extracted.
3. Comment on the cost-effectiveness of hauling 1,400 tons with respect to Lone Mountain's trucking/hauling cost behavior. Can the company's effectiveness be improved? How?
4. Distinguish between committed and discretionary fixed costs. If the company were to experience severe economic difficulties, which of the two types of fixed costs should management try to cut? Why?
5. Speculate as to why the company's charitable contribution cost arises only in December.

Problem 7–39
Cost Behavior and Analysis; High-Low Method
(LO 2, 5)

The following selected data were taken from the accounting records of Manitoba Manufacturing Company. The company uses direct-labor hours as its cost driver for overhead costs.

Month	Direct-Labor Hours	Manufacturing Overhead
January	26,000	$749,250
February	25,000	720,000
March	28,000	772,500
April	23,000	681,000
May	30,000	775,500
June	34,000	879,000

June's costs consisted of machine supplies ($153,000), depreciation ($22,500), and plant maintenance ($703,500). These costs exhibit the following respective behavior: variable, fixed, and semivariable.

The manufacturing overhead figures presented in the preceding table do not include supervisory labor cost, which is step-fixed in nature. For volume levels of less than 15,000 hours, supervisory labor amounts to $67,500. The cost is $135,000 from 15,000–29,999 hours and $202,500 when activity reaches 30,000 hours or more.

Required:

1. Determine the machine supplies cost and depreciation for April.
2. Using the high-low method, analyze Manitoba Manufacturing Company's plant maintenance cost and calculate the monthly fixed portion and the variable cost per direct-labor hour.
3. Assume that present cost behavior patterns continue into the latter half of the year. Estimate the *total* amount of manufacturing overhead the company can expect in October if 29,500 direct-labor hours are worked.
4. Briefly explain the difference between a fixed cost and a step-fixed cost.
5. Assume that a company has a step-fixed cost. Generally speaking, where on a step should the firm attempt to operate if it desires to achieve a maximum return on its investment?

Problem 7–40
Cost Estimation with Different Methods; Wholesaler
(LO 1, 2, 5, 6)

(*Note*: Instructors who wish to cover all three cost-estimation methods with the same data set may assign this problem in conjunction with the next one.) Nantucket Marine Supply is a wholesaler for a large variety of boating and fishing equipment. The company's controller, Alan Denney, has recently completed a cost study of the firm's material-handling department. The activity measure (independent variable) used in the study was hundreds of pounds of equipment loaded or unloaded at the company's loading dock. Denney compiled the following data.

Month	Units of Activity (hundreds of pounds of equipment loaded or unloaded)	Material-Handling Department Costs
January	1,800	$11,700
February	1,600	11,300
March	1,300	11,250
April	1,000	10,200
May	2,200	11,100
June	2,400	12,550
July	2,000	12,000
August	1,800	11,400
September	2,600	12,120
October	1,100	11,050
November	1,200	11,350
December	1,400	11,350

Required:

1. Draw a scatter diagram of the cost data for the material-handling department.
2. Visually fit a cost line to the scatter diagram.
3. Estimate the variable and fixed components of the department's cost behavior pattern using the visually fit cost line.
4. Using your estimate from requirement (3), specify an equation to express the department's cost behavior.
5. Estimate the material-handling department's cost behavior using the high-low method. Use an equation to express the results of this estimation method.
6. Write a brief memo to the company's president explaining why the cost estimates developed in requirements (4) and (5) differ.
7. Predict the company's material-handling costs for a month when 2,250 units of activity are recorded. Use each of your cost equations to make the prediction. Which prediction would you prefer to use? Why?

Problem 7–41
Continuation of Preceding Problem; Computing Least-Squares Regression Estimates; Comparing Multiple Methods (Appendix)
(LO 1, 2, 5, 6, 8)

Refer to the data in the preceding problem for Nantucket Marine Supply.

Required:

1. Compute the least-squares regression estimate of the variable- and fixed-cost components in the company's material-handling department costs. Use the formulas given in the appendix to the chapter. (*Hint*: It is helpful to transform both columns of data to thousands. For example, the January observation will be 1.8 units of activity and a cost of $11.70. Be careful, however, how you interpret your results.)
2. Write the least-squares regression equation for the department's costs.
3. Predict the firm's material-handling department's costs for a month when 2,250 units of activity are recorded.
4. Why do the three cost predictions computed in this and the preceding problem differ? Which method do you recommend? Why?

Problem 7–42
Approximating a Step-Variable Cost; Visual-Fit Method; Golf Course
(LO 1, 2, 5)

Shenandoah Valley Golf Association is a nonprofit, private organization that operates three 18-hole golf courses in Virginia. The organization's financial director has just analyzed the course maintenance costs incurred by the golf association during recent summers. The courses are maintained by a full-time crew of four people, who are assisted by part-time employees. These employees are typically college students on their summer vacations. The course maintenance costs vary with the number of people using the course. Since a large part of the maintenance work is done by part-time employees, the maintenance crew size can easily be adjusted to reflect current needs. The financial director's analysis revealed that the course maintenance cost includes two components:

- A fixed component of $13,000 per month (when the courses are open).
- A step-variable cost component. For each additional 1 to 10 people teeing off in one day, $10 in costs are incurred. Thus if 101 to 110 people tee off, $110 of additional cost will be incurred. If 111 to 120 people tee off, $120 of additional cost will be incurred.

Required:

1. Draw a graph of Shenandoah Valley Golf Association's course maintenance costs. Show on the graph the fixed-cost component and the step-variable cost component. Label each clearly.
2. Use a semivariable-cost behavior pattern to approximate the golf association's course maintenance cost behavior. Visually fit the semivariable cost line to your graph.
3. Using your graph, estimate the variable- and fixed-cost component included in your semivariable approximation. Express this approximate cost behavior pattern in equation form.
4. Fill in the following table of cost predictions.

	Predicted Course Maintenance Costs	
	Using Fixed Cost Coupled with Step-Variable Cost Behavior Pattern	**Using Semivariable Cost Approximation**
150 people tee off	?	?
158 people tee off	?	?

Problem 7–43
Comparing Regression and High-Low Estimates; Manufacturer
(LO 1, 2, 5)

The controller of Saratoga Auto Cylinder Company believes that the identification of the variable and fixed components of the firm's costs will enable the firm to make better planning and control decisions. Among the costs the controller is concerned about is the behavior of indirect-materials cost. She believes there is a correlation between machine hours and the amount of indirect materials used.

A member of the controller's staff has suggested that least-squares regression be used to determine the cost behavior of indirect materials. The regression equation shown below was developed from 40 pairs of observations.

$$S = \$190 + \$5H$$

where S = total monthly cost of indirect materials
H = machine hours per month

Required:

1. Explain the meaning of *190* and *5* in the regression equation $S = \$190 + \$5H$.
2. Calculate the estimated cost of indirect materials if 850 machine hours are to be used during a month. (Assume that 850 falls within the relevant range for this cost equation.)
3. To determine the validity of the cost estimate computed in requirement (2), what question would you ask the controller about the data used for the regression?
4. The high and low activity levels during the past four years, as measured by machine hours, occurred during April and August, respectively. Data concerning machine hours and indirect-material usage follow.

	April	**August**
Machine hours	1,000	700
Indirect supplies:		
Beginning inventory	$1,300	$1,000
Ending inventory	1,350	3,000
Purchases	5,900	6,200

   Determine the cost of indirect materials used during April and August.
5. Use the high-low method to estimate the behavior of the company's indirect-material cost. Express the cost behavior pattern in equation form.
6. Which cost estimate would you recommend to the controller, the regression estimate or the high-low estimate? Why?

(CMA, adapted)

Problem 7–44
Cost Estimation Methods; Cost Analysis; E-Commerce
(LO 2, 5)

Shortly after being hired as an analyst with Florida International Airlines, Kim Williams was asked to prepare a report that focused on passenger ticketing cost. The airline writes most of its own tickets, makes little use of travel agents, and has seen an increased passenger interest in e-ticketing.

After some discussion, Williams thought it would be beneficial to begin her report with an overview of three different cost estimation tools: scatter diagrams, least-squares regression, and the high-low method. She would then present the results of her analysis of the past year's monthly ticketing cost, which was driven largely by the number of tickets written. These results would be presented in the form of algebraic equations that were derived by the three tools just cited. The equations follow. (C denotes ticketing cost, and PT denotes number of passenger tickets written.)

Least-squares regression: C = $300,000 + $2.25 PT
Scatter diagram: C = $295,000 + $2.20 PT
High-low method: C = $301,000 + $2.40 PT

Williams had analyzed data over the past 12 months and built equations on these data, purposely including the slowest month of the year (February) and the busiest month (November) so that things would tend to average out. She observed that November was especially busy because of Thanksgiving, passengers purchasing tickets for upcoming holiday travel in December, and the effects of a strike by Southeastern Airlines, Florida International's chief competitor. The lengthy strike resulted in many of Southeastern's passengers being rerouted on Florida International flights.

Required:

1. Prepare a bullet-point list suitable for use in Williams's report that describes the features of scatter diagrams, least-squares regression, and the high-low method. Determine which of the three tools will typically produce the most accurate results.
2. Will the three cost estimation tools normally result in different equations? Why?
3. Assuming the use of least-squares regression, explain what the $300,000 and $2.25 figures represent.
4. Assuming the use of a scatter diagram, predict the cost of an upcoming month when Florida International expects to write 570,000 tickets.
5. Did Williams err in constructing the equations on data of the past 12 months? Briefly explain.
6. Assume that over the next few years, more of Florida International's passengers will take advantage of e-ticketing over the Internet. What will likely happen to the airline's cost structure in terms of variable and fixed cost incurred?

Problem 7–45
Interpreting Regression Analysis in Cost Estimation
(LO 2, 5)

Randolph Dana owns a catering company that prepares banquets and parties for business functions throughout the year. Dana's business is seasonal, with a heavy schedule during the summer months and the year-end holidays. During peak periods there are extra costs; however, even during nonpeak periods Dana must work more to cover his expenses.

One of the major events Dana's customers request is a cocktail party. He offers a standard cocktail party and has developed the following cost structure on a per-person basis.

Food and beverages	$14.00
Labor (.6 hr. @ $11 per hour)	6.60
Overhead (.6 hr. @ $14 per hour)	8.40
Total cost per person	$29.00

When bidding on cocktail parties, Dana adds a 15 percent markup to this cost structure as a profit margin. Dana is quite certain about his estimates of the prime costs but is not as comfortable with the overhead estimate. This estimate was based on the actual data for the past 12 months presented in the following table. These data indicate that overhead expenses vary with the direct-labor hours expended. The $14 per hour overhead estimate was determined by dividing total overhead expended for the 12 months ($805,000) by total labor hours (57,600) and rounding to the nearest dollar.

Month	Labor Hours	Overhead Expenses
January	2,800	$59,000
February	2,500	55,000
March	3,000	60,000
April	4,500	67,000
May	4,200	64,000
June	6,500	74,000
July	5,500	71,000
August	7,000	75,000
September	7,500	77,000
October	4,500	68,000
November	3,100	62,000
December	6,500	73,000

Dana recently attended a meeting of the local chamber of commerce and heard a business consultant discuss regression analysis and its business applications. After the meeting, Dana decided to do a regression analysis of the overhead data he had collected. The following results were obtained.

Intercept (*a*)	48,000
Coefficient (*b*)	4

Required:

1. Explain the difference between the overhead rate originally estimated by Dana and the overhead rate developed from the regression method.
2. Using data from the regression analysis, develop the following cost estimates per person for a cocktail party.
   a. Variable cost per person
   b. Absorption (full) cost per person (includes both variable and fixed cost per person)
   Assume that the level of activity remains within the relevant range.
3. Dana has been asked to prepare a bid for a 250-person cocktail party to be given next month. Determine the minimum bid price that Dana should be willing to submit.
4. What other factors should Dana consider in developing the bid price for the cocktail party?

(CMA adapted)

Problem 7–46
Computing Least-Squares Regression Estimates; Airport Costs (Appendix)
(LO 1, 2, 5, 8)

Jefferson County Airport handles several daily commuter flights and many private flights. The county budget officer has compiled the following data regarding airport costs and activity over the past year.

Month	Airport Costs (in thousands)	Flights Originating at Jefferson County Airport (in hundreds)
January	$20	12
February	19	10
March	18	9
April	19	14
May	17	8
June	20	11
July	21	15
August	17	9
September	21	12
October	19	10
November	24	14
December	18	11

Required:

1. Draw a scatter diagram of the airport costs shown above.
2. Compute the least-squares regression estimates of the variable- and fixed-cost components in the airport's cost behavior pattern. Use the formulas given in the appendix to the chapter. (Use the data as they are presented in the problem: flights measured in hundreds and costs measured in thousands of dollars. Be careful how you interpret the results.)

3. Write the least-squares regression equation for the airport's costs.
4. Predict the airport's costs during a month when 1,500 flights originate at the airport.
5. Compute the coefficient of determination (R^2) for the regression equation. Briefly interpret R^2.

Problem 7–47
Missing Data; Multiple Cost Estimation Methods (Appendix)
(LO 1, 2, 5, 8)

You have been hired recently as a part-time cost analyst for your college's admissions office. Your first task is to estimate the relationship between the cost of operating the admissions office and the number of applications received. After painstakingly collecting six months worth of data, you analyzed the cost behavior using three different methods. You wrote up a brief report and headed for the admissions director's office. However, a gust of wind caught the papers in your hand and blew them out the window, where they were torn to bits by the hockey coach's dog. You and your roommate managed to piece together the following bits and pieces of information from your shredded report.

Month	Applications Received (in thousands) ?	Cost of Operating the Admissions Office (in thousands) ?	X^2	?
August	?	10.0	?	?
September	?	8.9	?	178.0
October	?	9.1	?	200.2
November	25	?	?	240.0
December	10	?	?	?
January	?	8.7	225	?
Total	?	?	2,734	?

a. Least-squares regression:

$$? = \frac{(54.3)(?) - (?)(1{,}128.7)}{(?)(?) - (?)(?)} \qquad ? = \frac{(6)(?) - (122)(?)}{(?)(?) - (?)(?)}$$

Total monthly admissions department costs = ? + ?*X*, where *X* denotes the number of applications in thousands.

b. High-low method:

Variable cost *per application* $= \frac{? - ?}{30 - ?} = \frac{?}{?}$

$=$? per application

Total cost at ? *thousand* applications	?
Total variable cost at ? *thousand* applications	?
Fixed cost per month	?

Total monthly admissions department costs = ? + ?*X*
where X denotes the number of applications in thousands

c. Visual-fit method:

Total monthly admissions department costs = \$7,100 + \$95*X*
where X denotes the number of applications in thousands

Required:

1. Complete the cost analysis and report by finding the missing amounts.
2. Under each cost estimation method, predict the total cost of operating the admissions office during a month when 18,000 applications are received.

Cases

Case 7–48
Interpreting Least-Squares Regression; Landscaping Service; Activity-Based Costing
(LO 1, 2, 5)

Outside Environment, Inc. provides commercial landscaping services in San Diego. Sasha Cairns, the firm's owner, wants to develop cost estimates that she can use to prepare bids on jobs. After analyzing the firm's costs, Cairns has developed the following preliminary cost estimates for each 1,000 square feet of landscaping.

Direct material	$390
Direct labor (5 direct-labor hours at $11 per hour)	55
Overhead (at $18 per direct-labor hour)	90
Total cost per 1,000 square feet	$535

Cairns is quite certain about the estimates for direct material and direct labor. However, she is not as comfortable with the overhead estimate. The estimate for overhead is based on the overhead costs that were incurred during the past 12 months as presented in the following schedule. The estimate of $18 per direct-labor hour was determined by dividing the total overhead costs for the 12-month period ($1,296,000) by the total direct-labor hours (72,000).

	Total Overhead	Regular Direct-Labor Hours	Overtime Direct-Labor Hours*	Total Direct-Labor Hours
January	$108,000	5,820	380	6,200
February	94,000	4,760	40	4,800
March	96,000	4,420	80	4,500
April	112,000	5,180	420	5,600
May	114,000	6,060	940	7,000
June	130,000	6,480	1,520	8,000
July	128,000	6,760	1,240	8,000
August	112,000	6,100	700	6,800
September	106,000	5,520	80	5,600
October	94,000	5,540	60	5,600
November	94,000	4,240	60	4,300
December	108,000	5,120	480	5,600
Total	$1,296,000	66,000	6,000	72,000

*The overtime premium is 50 percent of the direct-labor wage rate.

Cairns believes that overhead is affected by total monthly direct-labor hours. Cairns decided to perform a least-squares regression of overhead (OH) on total direct-labor hours (DLH). The following regression formula was obtained.

$$OH = \$52,400 + \$9.25\ DLH$$

Required:

1. The overhead rate developed from the least-squares regression is different from Cairns' preliminary estimate of $18 per direct-labor hour. Explain the difference in the two overhead rates.
2. Using the overhead formula that was derived from the least-squares regression, determine a total variable-cost estimate for each 1,000 square feet of landscaping.
3. Cairns has been asked to submit a bid on a landscaping project for the city government consisting of 50,000 square feet. Cairns estimates that 30 percent of the direct-labor hours required for the project will be on overtime. Calculate the incremental costs that should be included in any bid that Cairns would submit on this project. Use the overhead formula derived from the least-squares regression.
4. Should management rely on the overhead formula derived from the least-squares regression as the basis for the variable overhead component of its cost estimate? Explain your answer.
5. After attending a seminar on activity-based costing, Cairns decided to further analyze the company's activities and costs. She discovered that a more accurate portrayal of the firm's cost behavior could be achieved by dividing overhead into three separate pools, each with its own cost driver. Separate regression equations were estimated for each of the cost pools, with the following results.

   $OH_1 = \$20,000 + \$4.15DLH,$

   where *DLH* denotes direct-labor hours

   $OH_2 = \$18,200 + \$13.60SFS,$

   where *SFS* denotes the number of square feet of turf seeded (in thousands)

   $OH_3 = \$16,000 + \$5.90PL,$

   where *PL* denotes the number of individual plantings (e.g., trees and shrubs)

Assume that five direct-labor hours will be needed to landscape each 1,000 square feet, regardless of the specific planting material used.

a. Suppose the landscaping project for the city will involve seeding all 50,000 square feet of turf and planting 70 trees and shrubs. Calculate the incremental *variable overhead* cost that Cairns should include in the bid.

b. Recompute the incremental variable overhead cost for the city's landscaping project assuming half of the 50,000 square-foot landscaping area will be seeded and there will be 230 individual plantings. The plantings will cover the entire 50,000 square-foot area.

c. Briefly explain, using concepts from activity-based costing, why the incremental costs differ in requirements (*a*) and (*b*).

(CMA, adapted)

Case 7–49
Approximating a Curvilinear Cost; Visual-Fit Method; Pediatrics Clinic
(LO 1, 2, 5)

(*Note*: Instructors who wish to cover all three cost-estimation methods with the same data set may assign this case in conjunction with the following case.) "I don't understand this cost report at all," exclaimed Jeff Mahoney, the newly appointed administrator of Valley General Hospital. "Our administrative costs in the new pediatrics clinic are all over the map. One month the report shows $7,000, and the next month it's $13,900. What's going on?"

Mahoney's question was posed to Megan McDonough, the hospital's director of cost management. "The main problem is that the clinic has experienced some widely varying patient loads in its first year of operation. There seems to be some confusion in the public's mind about what services we offer in the clinic. When do they come to the clinic? When do they go to the emergency room? That sort of thing. As the patient load has varied, we've frequently changed our clinic administrative staffing."

Mahoney continued to puzzle over the report. "Could you pull some data together, Megan, so we can see how this cost behaves over a range of patient loads?"

"You'll have it this afternoon," McDonough responded. Later that morning, she gathered the following data:

Month	Patient Load	Administrative Cost
January	400	$6,000
February	500	7,000
March	1,400	13,900
April	900	9,200
May	1,300	11,900
June	1,000	10,000
July	700	9,400
August	300	4,100
September	1,100	10,200
October	1,500	16,100
November	600	8,300
December	1,200	11,100

McDonough does not believe the first year's widely fluctuating patient load will be experienced again in the future. She has estimated that the clinic's relevant range of monthly activity in the future will be 600 to 1,200 patients.

Required:

1. Draw a scatter diagram of the clinic's administrative costs during its first year of operation.
2. Visually fit a curvilinear cost line to the plotted data.
3. Mark the clinic's relevant range of activity on the scatter diagram by drawing vertical lines at each end of the relevant range.
4. Visually fit a semivariable-cost line to approximate the curvilinear cost behavior pattern within the clinic's relevant range.
5. Estimate the fixed -and variable-cost components of the visually fit semivariable-cost line.
6. Use an equation to express the semivariable-cost approximation of the clinic's administrative costs.
7. What is your prediction of the clinic's administrative cost during a month when 750 patients visit the clinic? When 350 patients visit? Which one of your visually fit cost lines did you use to make each of these predictions? Why?

■ **Case 7–50**
Comparing Multiple Cost Estimation Methods; Ethics (Appendix)
(LO 1, 2, 5, 8)

Refer to the data and accompanying information in the preceding case.

Required:

1. Use the high-low method to estimate the cost behavior for the clinic's administrative costs. Express the cost behavior in formula form ($Y = a + bX$). What is the variable cost per patient?
2. Use least-squares regression to estimate the administrative cost behavior. Express the cost behavior in formula form. What is the variable cost per patient? (*Hint*: First, convert both columns of data to hundreds. For example, the January observation becomes a patient load of 4 and a cost of $60. Be careful how you interpret your analysis.) If you are familiar with Microsoft® Excel, you can use the Excel functions to estimate the regression parameters, as explained in the chapter's appendix.
3. Write a memo to the hospital administrator comparing the cost estimates using (*a*) least-squares regression, (*b*) the high-low method, and (*c*) the scatter diagram and visually fit semivariable-cost line from the preceding case [requirements (4) and (5)]. Make a recommendation as to which estimate should be used, and support your recommendation. Make any other suggestions you feel are appropriate.
4. After receiving the memo comparing the three cost estimates, Mahoney called McDonough to discuss the matter. The following exchange occurred.

   Mahoney: "As you know, Megan, I was never in favor of this clinic. It's going to be a drag on our administrative staff, and we'd have been far better off keeping the pediatrics operation here in the hospital."

   McDonough: "I was aware that you felt the clinic was a mistake. Of course, the board of trustees had other issues to consider. I believe the board felt the clinic should be built to make pediatric care more accessible to the economically depressed area on the other side of the city."

   Mahoney: "That's true, but the board doesn't realize how difficult it's going to make life for us here in the hospital. In any case, I called to tell you that when you and I report to the board next week, I'm going to recommend that the clinic be shut down. I want you to support my recommendation with one of your cost estimates showing that administrative costs will soar at high activity levels."

   McDonough: "But that estimate was based on the high-low method. It's not an appropriate method for this situation."

   Mahoney: "It *is* an estimate, Megan, and it's based on a well-known estimation method. This is just the ammunition I need to make the board see things my way."

   McDonough: "I don't know, Jeff. I just don't think I can go along with that."

   Mahoney: "Be a team player, Megan. I've got a meeting now. Got to run."

That night McDonough called to discuss the matter with her best friend, you. What would you advise her?

Current Issues in Managerial Accounting

■ **Issue 7–51**
Direct Labor: Variable or Fixed Cost?

"The Software Says You're Just Average," ***Business Week*, February 25, 2002, p. 126, Michelle Conlin.**

Overview

Throughout the corporate world, businesses are transforming labor into a more flexible (and variable) cost. Among such companies are Hewlett-Packard, General Electric, DuPont, Sun Microsystems, and British Airways.

Suggested Discussion Questions

As a group, discuss whether direct labor is a fixed or a variable cost. What are the pros and cons of management treating direct labor as a variable cost? Are there ethical issues to be considered here?

■ **Issue 7–52**
Role of Cost Analysts

"Taking Cues from GE, Mattel's CEO Wants Toy Maker to Grow Up," ***The Wall Street Journal*, November 14, 2001.**

Overview

Mattel has "moved some of its product-development teams—the engineers and cost analyzers who come into play after a toy design has been approved—from California to Hong Kong, to work side by side with the manufacturing teams. In the past, U.S. design and marketing teams would sometimes work on a toy project for as long as three months before sending it to Hong Kong, where it could ultimately be killed as too expensive."

Suggested Discussion Question

What are the benefits of having the cost analysts and design engineers work side by side with the toy maker's manufacturing teams?

Chapter Eight

Cost-Volume-Profit Analysis

After completing this chapter, you should be able to:

1. Compute a break-even point using the contribution-margin approach and the equation approach.
2. Compute the contribution-margin ratio and use it to find the break-even point in sales dollars.
3. Prepare a cost-volume-profit (CVP) graph and explain how it is used.
4. Apply CVP analysis to determine the effect on profit of changes in fixed expenses, variable expenses, sales prices, and sales volume.
5. Compute the break-even point and prepare a profit-volume graph for a multiproduct enterprise.
6. List and discuss the key assumptions of CVP analysis.
7. Prepare and interpret a contribution income statement.
8. Explain the role of cost structure and operating leverage in CVP relationships.
9. Understand the implications of activity-based costing for CVP analysis.
10. Be aware of the effects of advanced manufacturing technology on CVP relationships.
11. After completing the appendix, understand the effect of income taxes on CVP analysis.

Shakespearean Spoof Leads Off the Season for Seattle Contemporary Theater

Seattle, WA—Seattle Contemporary Theater has announced its schedule of productions for the coming year. According to Megan Joseph, the theater's managing director, the first play of the new season will be *The Compleat Works of Wllm Shkspr (Abridged)*. "People are going to love this play," said Joseph. "It's really hilarious. It has all the most famous one-liners from Shakespeare's best-loved plays. It's great fun to watch the players attempt to present 37 plays and 154 sonnets, all in just under two hours. All your favorites are in there. 'To be or not to be?' 'A horse! A horse! My kingdom for a horse!' 'Double, double, toil and trouble.'"

Joseph said she expects this to be the theater's best year yet, with around 8,000 tickets sold per month. "Keep in mind," she pointed out, "that a good year for us does not mean a large profit, because Seattle Contemporary Theater is a nonprofit organization. For us, a good year means lots of people seeing our plays, and serving up the best contemporary theater art that we can."

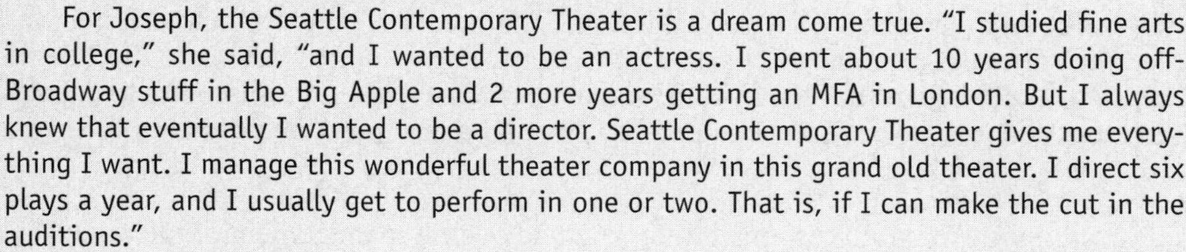

For Joseph, the Seattle Contemporary Theater is a dream come true. "I studied fine arts in college," she said, "and I wanted to be an actress. I spent about 10 years doing off-Broadway stuff in the Big Apple and 2 more years getting an MFA in London. But I always knew that eventually I wanted to be a director. Seattle Contemporary Theater gives me everything I want. I manage this wonderful theater company in this grand old theater. I direct six plays a year, and I usually get to perform in one or two. That is, if I can make the cut in the auditions."

Joseph explained that the theater company got a big boost from the city of Seattle, when its council agreed to allow use of the historic downtown theater owned by the city. "The city gets a monthly rental charge plus a share of the price of each ticket sold. We try to keep the ticket prices quite reasonable because our goal is to bring theater into the lives of as many people as possible. Financially, of course, our goal is to just break even each year. We don't want to make a profit, but we can't operate at a loss either. We still have to pay for royalties for use of the plays, salaries for our actors and other employees, insurance, utilities, and so forth. It's easy to get caught up in the sheer fun of being in theater, but it's an important part of my job to pay attention to the business side of things, too. Sometimes it's tricky to project where our break-even point will be. We have to project what our costs will be, decide on our ticket prices, and estimate how much we'll receive in charitable donations from our many friends and supporters. It's crucial that we keep our act together financially as well as artistically. We want to be bringing great theater to the people of Seattle for many years to come."

In the meantime, be sure to catch *The Compleat Works of Wllm Shkspr (Abridged)* which opens soon.

What effect on profit can United Airlines expect if it adds a flight on the Chicago to New York route? How will NBC's profit change if the ratings increase for its evening news program? How many patient days of care must Massachusetts General Hospital provide to break even for the year? What happens to this break-even patient load if the hospital leases a new computerized system for patient records?

Each of these questions concerns the effects on costs and revenues when the organization's activity changes. The analytical technique used by managerial accountants to address these questions is called **cost-volume-profit analysis.** Often called **CVP analysis** for short, this technique summarizes the effects of changes in an organization's *volume* of activity on its *costs*, revenue, and *profit*. Cost-volume-profit analysis can be extended to cover the effects on profit of changes in selling prices, service fees, costs, income-tax rates, and the organization's mix of products or services. What will happen to profit, for example, if the New York Yankees raise ticket prices for stadium seats? In short, CVP analysis provides management with a comprehensive overview of the effects on revenue and costs of all kinds of short-run financial changes.

Although the word *profit* appears in the term, cost-volume-profit analysis is not confined to profit-seeking enterprises. Managers in nonprofit organizations also routinely use CVP analysis to examine the effects of activity and other short-run changes on revenue and costs. For example, as the State of Florida gains nearly 1,000 people a day in population, the state's political leaders must analyze the effects of this change on sales-tax revenues and the cost of providing services, such as education, transportation, and police protection. Managers at such diverse nonprofit institutions as Massachusetts General Hospital, Stanford University, and the United Way all use CVP analysis as a routine operational tool.

Illustration of Cost-Volume-Profit Analysis

To illustrate the various analytical techniques used in cost-volume-profit analysis, we will focus on a performing arts organization. The Seattle Contemporary Theater was recently formed as a nonprofit enterprise to bring contemporary drama to the Seattle area. The organization has a part-time, unpaid board of trustees comprising local professional people who are avid theater fans. The board has hired the following full-time employees.

Managing director: Responsibilities include overall management of the organization; direction of six plays per year.

Artistic director: Responsibilities include hiring of actors and production crews for each play; direction of six plays per year.

Business manager and producer: Responsibilities include managing the organization's business functions and ticket sales; direction of the production crews, who handle staging, lighting, costuming, and makeup.

> "Accounting is changing. You're no longer sitting behind a desk just working on a computer, just crunching the numbers. You're actually getting to be a part of the day-to-day functions of the business." (8a)
> **Abbott Laboratories**

The board of trustees has negotiated an agreement with the city of Seattle to hold performances in a historic theater owned by the city. The theater has not been used for 30 years, but the city has agreed to refurbish it and to provide lighting and sound equipment. In return, the city will receive a rental charge of $10,000 per month plus $8 for each theater ticket sold.

Projected Expenses and Revenue

The theater's business manager and producer, Andrew Lloyd, has made the following projections for the first few years of operation.

Fixed expenses per month:	
Theater rental	$10,000
Employees' salaries and fringe benefits	8,000
Actors' wages	15,000
(to be supplemented with local volunteer talent)	
Production crew's wages	5,600
(to be supplemented with local volunteers)	
Playwrights' royalties for use of plays	5,000
Insurance	1,000
Utilities—fixed portion	1,400
Advertising and promotion	800
Administrative expenses	1,200
Total fixed expenses per month	$48,000
Variable expenses per ticket sold:	
City's charge per ticket for use of theater	$ 8
Other miscellaneous expenses (for example, printing of playbills and tickets, variable portion of utilities)	2
Total variable cost per ticket sold	$10
Revenue:	
Price per ticket	$16

Importance of Cost Behavior Notice that the theater's expenses have been categorized according to their cost behavior: fixed or variable. Analyzing an organization's cost behavior, the topic of Chapter 7, is a necessary first step in any cost-volume-profit analysis. As we proceed through this chapter, the data pertaining to Seattle Contemporary Theater will be an important part of our cost-volume-profit analysis.

The Break-Even Point

LO 1

Compute a break-even point using the contribution-margin approach and the equation approach.

Topic 8–1

As the first step in the CVP analysis for Seattle Contemporary Theater, we will find the **break-even point**. The break-even point is the volume of activity where the organization's revenues and expenses are equal. At this amount of sales, the organization has no profit or loss; it *breaks even*.

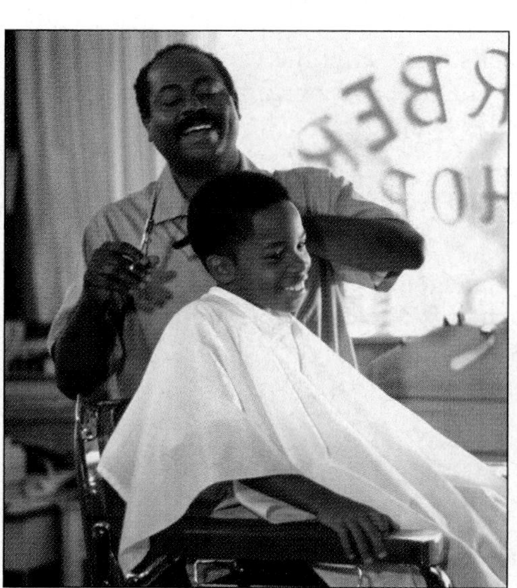

Whether running a small business or a worldwide enterprise, understanding cost-volume-profit relationships is crucial in managing any organization.

"Break-even analyses figure prominently in any discussion of new programs. Although we have programs that operate at a loss because of their importance educationally, overall our cash inflows have to be sufficient to support our total program." (8b)
Cornell University

Suppose Seattle Contemporary Theater sells 8,000 tickets during a play's one-month run. The following income statement shows that the profit for the month will be zero; thus, the theater will break even.

Sales revenue (8,000 × \$16)	\$128,000
Less variable expenses (8,000 × \$10)	80,000
Total contribution margin	\$ 48,000
Less fixed expenses	48,000
Profit	\$ 0

Notice that this income statement highlights the distinction between variable and fixed expenses. The statement also shows the **total contribution margin,** which is defined as total sales revenue minus total variable expenses. This is the amount of revenue that is available to *contribute* to covering fixed expenses after all variable expenses have been covered. The contribution income statement will be covered in more depth later in the chapter. At this juncture, it provides a useful way to think about the meaning of breaking even.

How could we compute Seattle Contemporary Theater's break-even point if we did not already know it is 8,000 tickets per month? This is the question to which we turn our attention next.

Contribution-Margin Approach

Seattle Contemporary Theater will break even when the organization's revenue from ticket sales is equal to its expenses. How many tickets must be sold during one month (one play's run) for the organization to break even?

Each ticket sells for \$16, but \$10 of this is used to cover the variable expense per ticket. This leaves \$6 per ticket to *contribute* to covering the fixed expenses of \$48,000. When enough tickets have been sold in one month so that these \$6 contributions per ticket add up to \$48,000, the organization will break even for the month. Thus, we may compute the break-even volume of tickets as follows:

$$\frac{\text{Fixed expenses}}{\text{Contribution of each ticket toward covering fixed expenses}} = \frac{\$48{,}000}{\$6} = 8{,}000$$

Seattle Contemporary Theater must sell 8,000 tickets during a play's one-month run to break even for the month.

The \$6 amount that remains of each ticket's price, after the variable expenses are covered, is called the **unit contribution margin**. The general formula for computing the break-even sales volume in units is given below.

$$\frac{\text{Fixed expenses}}{\text{Unit contribution margin}} = \text{Break-even point (in units)} \qquad (1)$$

LO 2

Compute the contribution-margin ratio and use it to find the break-even point in sales dollars.

Contribution-Margin Ratio Sometimes management prefers that the break-even point be expressed in sales *dollars* rather than *units*. Seattle Contemporary Theater's break-even point in sales dollars is computed as follows.

Break-even point in units (tickets)	8,000
Sales price per unit	× \$16
Break-even point in sales dollars	\$128,000

The following computation provides an alternative way to determine the break-even point in sales dollars.

$$\frac{\text{Fixed expenses}}{\dfrac{\text{Unit contribution margin}}{\text{Unit sales price}}} = \frac{\$48{,}000}{\dfrac{\$6}{\$16}} = \frac{\$48{,}000}{.375} = \$128{,}000$$

The unit contribution margin divided by the unit sales price is called the **contribution-margin ratio.** This ratio can also be expressed as a percentage, in which case it is called the *contribution-margin percentage*. Seattle Contemporary Theater's contribution-margin ratio is .375 (in percentage form, 37.5%). Thus, the organization's break-even point in sales dollars may be found by dividing its fixed expenses by its contribution-margin ratio. The logic behind this approach is that 37.5 percent of each sales dollar is available to make a contribution toward covering fixed expenses. The general formula is given below.

$$\frac{\text{Fixed expenses}}{\text{Contribution-margin ratio}} = \text{Break-even point in sales dollars} \qquad (2)$$

"Delta Air Lines computes a break-even load factor, which is the average percentage of available passenger seats that need to be occupied on our flights in order for the company to break even." (8c)

Delta Air Lines

Equation Approach

LO 1

Compute a break-even point using the contribution-margin approach and the equation approach.

An alternative approach to finding the break-even point is based on the profit equation. Income (or profit) is equal to sales revenue minus expenses. If expenses are separated into variable and fixed expenses, the essence of the income (profit) statement is captured by the following equation.

$$\text{Sales revenue} - \text{Variable expenses} - \text{Fixed expenses} = \text{Profit}$$

This equation can be restated as follows:

$$\left[\begin{pmatrix}\text{Unit}\\ \text{sales}\\ \text{price}\end{pmatrix} \times \begin{pmatrix}\text{Sales}\\ \text{volume}\\ \text{in units}\end{pmatrix}\right] - \left[\begin{pmatrix}\text{Unit}\\ \text{variable}\\ \text{expense}\end{pmatrix} \times \begin{pmatrix}\text{Sales}\\ \text{volume}\\ \text{in units}\end{pmatrix}\right] - \begin{pmatrix}\text{Fixed}\\ \text{expenses}\end{pmatrix} = \text{Profit} \qquad (3)$$

To find Seattle Contemporary Theater's break-even volume of ticket sales per month, we define profit in equation (3) to be zero.

$$(\$16 \times X) - (\$10 \times X) - \$48{,}000 = 0$$

$$\left[\begin{pmatrix}\text{Unit}\\ \text{sales}\\ \text{price}\end{pmatrix} \times \begin{pmatrix}\text{Sales}\\ \text{volume}\\ \text{in units}\end{pmatrix}\right] - \left[\begin{pmatrix}\text{Unit}\\ \text{variable}\\ \text{expense}\end{pmatrix} \times \begin{pmatrix}\text{Sales}\\ \text{volume}\\ \text{in units}\end{pmatrix}\right] - \begin{pmatrix}\text{Fixed}\\ \text{expenses}\end{pmatrix} = \begin{matrix}\text{Break-even}\\ \text{profit (zero)}\end{matrix} \qquad (4)$$

where

X denotes the number of sales units (tickets) required to break even.

Equation (4) can be solved for X as shown below.

$$\$16X - \$10X - \$48{,}000 = 0$$

$$\$6X = \$48{,}000$$

$$X = \frac{\$48{,}000}{\$6} = 8{,}000$$

Using the equation approach, we have arrived at the same general formula for computing the break-even sales volume (formula 1).

The contribution-margin and equation approaches are two equivalent techniques for finding the break-even point. Both methods reach the same conclusion, and so personal preference dictates which approach should be used.

Graphing Cost-Volume-Profit Relationships

Prepare a cost-volume-profit (CVP) graph and explain how it is used.

While the break-even point conveys useful information to management, it does not show how profit changes as activity changes. To capture the relationship between profit and volume of activity, a **cost-volume-profit (CVP) graph** is commonly used. The following steps are used to prepare a CVP graph for Seattle Contemporary Theater. The graph is displayed in Exhibit 8–1. Notice that the graph shows the *relevant range*, which is the range of activity within which management expects the theater to operate.

Step 1: Draw the axes of the graph. Label the vertical axis in dollars and the horizontal axis in units of sales (tickets).

Step 2: Draw the fixed-expense line. It is parallel to the horizontal axis, since fixed expenses do not change with activity.

Step 3: Compute *total* expense at any convenient volume. For example, select a volume of 6,000 tickets.

Variable expenses (6,000 × $10 per ticket)	$ 60,000
Fixed expenses	48,000
Total expenses (at 6,000 tickets)	$108,000

Plot this point ($108,000 at 6,000 tickets) on the graph. See point *A* on the graph in Exhibit 8–1.

Step 4: Draw the total-expense line. This line passes through the point plotted in step 3 (point *A*) and the intercept of the fixed-expense line on the vertical axis ($48,000).

Step 5: Compute total sales revenue at any convenient volume. We will choose 6,000 tickets again. Total revenue is $96,000 (6,000 × $16 per ticket). Plot this point ($96,000 at 6,000 tickets) on the graph. See point *B* on the graph in Exhibit 8–1.

Step 6: Draw the total revenue line. This line passes through the point plotted in step 5 (point *B*) and the origin.

Step 7: Label the graph as shown in Exhibit 8–1.

Interpreting the CVP Graph

Several conclusions can be drawn from the CVP graph in Exhibit 8–1.

LO 3

Prepare a cost-volume-profit (CVP) graph and explain how it is used.

Break-Even Point The break-even point is determined by the intersection of the total-revenue line and the total-expense line. Seattle Contemporary Theater breaks even for the month at 8,000 tickets, or $128,000 of ticket sales. This agrees with our calculations in the preceding section.

Profit and Loss Areas The CVP graph discloses more information than the break-even calculation. From the graph, a manager can see the effects on profit of changes in volume. The vertical distance between the lines on the graph represents the profit or loss at a particular sales volume. If Seattle Contemporary Theater sells fewer than 8,000 tickets in a month, the organization will suffer a loss. The magnitude of the loss increases as ticket sales decline. The theater organization will have a profit if sales exceed 8,000 tickets in a month.

Implications of the Break-Even Point The position of the break-even point within an organization's relevant range of activity provides important information to

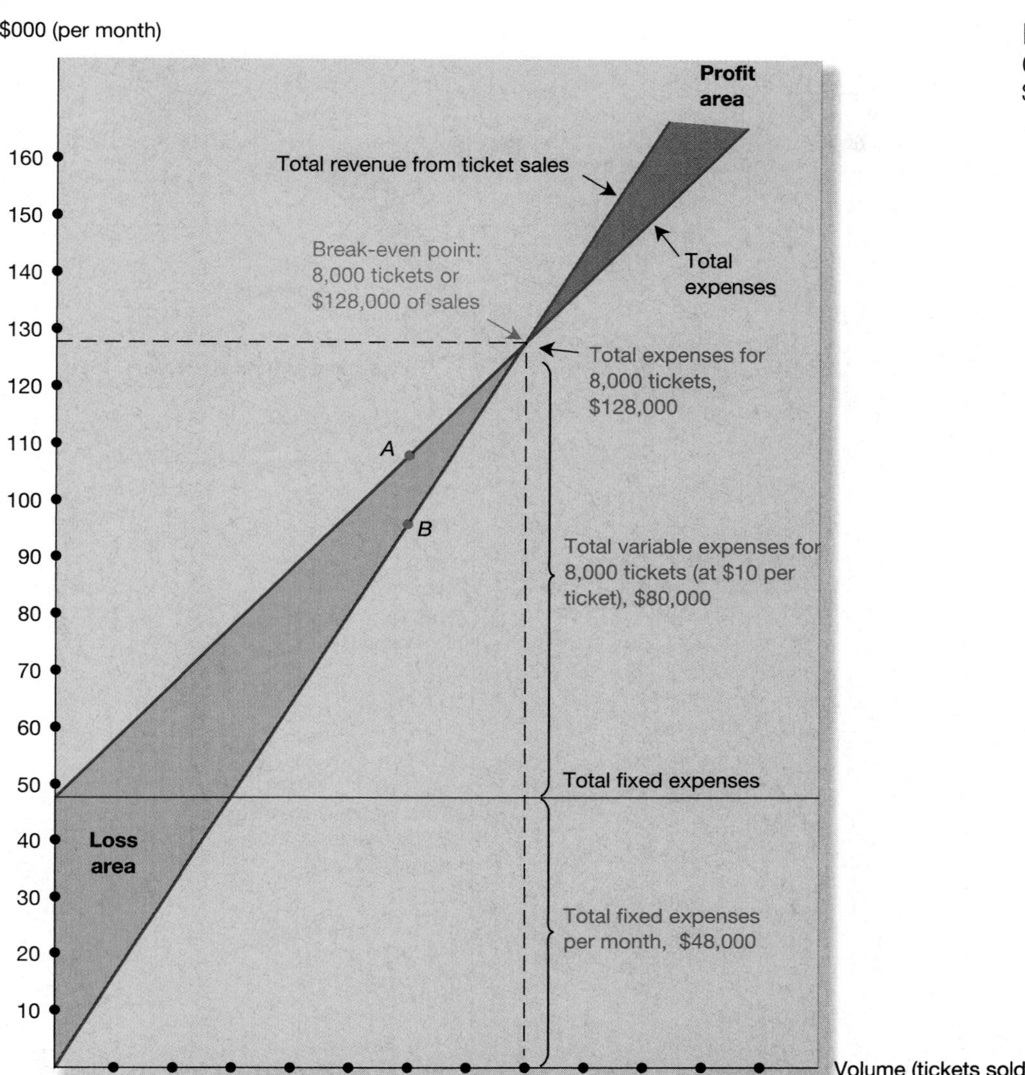

Exhibit 8–1

Cost-Volume-Profit Graph: Seattle Contemporary Theater

management. The Seattle Contemporary Theater building seats 450 people. The agreement with the city of Seattle calls for 20 performances during each play's one-month run. Thus, the maximum number of tickets that can be sold each month is 9,000 (450 seats × 20 performances). The organization's break-even point is quite close to the maximum possible sales volume. This could be cause for concern in a nonprofit organization operating on limited resources.

What could management do to improve this situation? One possibility is to renegotiate with the city to schedule additional performances. However, this might not be feasible, because the actors need some rest each week. Also, additional performances would likely entail additional costs, such as increased theater-rental expenses and increased compensation for the actors and production crew. Other possible solutions are to raise ticket prices or reduce costs. These kinds of issues will be explored later in the chapter.

Exhibit 8–2
Alternate Format for CVP Graph: Seattle Contemporary Theater

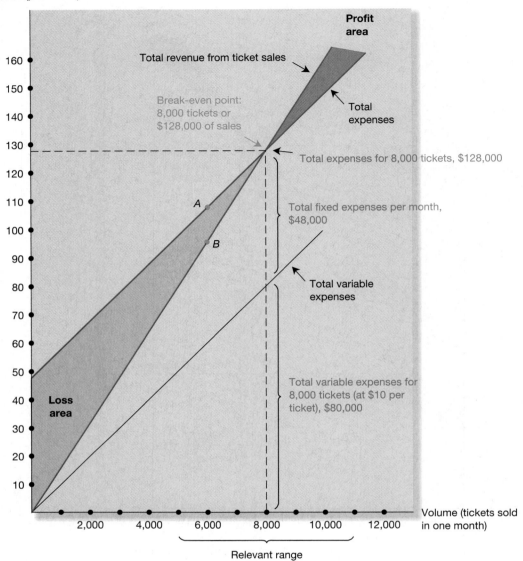

The CVP graph will not resolve this potential problem for the management of Seattle Contemporary Theater. However, the graph will *direct management's attention* to the situation.

Alternative Format for the CVP Graph

An alternative format for the CVP graph, preferred by some managers, is displayed in Exhibit 8–2. The key difference is that fixed expenses are graphed above variable expenses, instead of the reverse as they were in Exhibit 8–1.

Profit-Volume Graph

Yet another approach to graphing cost-volume-profit relationships is displayed in Exhibit 8–3. This format is called a **profit-volume graph,** since it highlights the amount of profit or loss. Notice that the graph intercepts the vertical axis at the amount equal to fixed expenses at the zero activity level. The graph crosses the horizontal axis at the break-even point. The vertical distance between the horizontal axis and the profit line, at a particular level of sales volume, is the profit or loss at that volume.

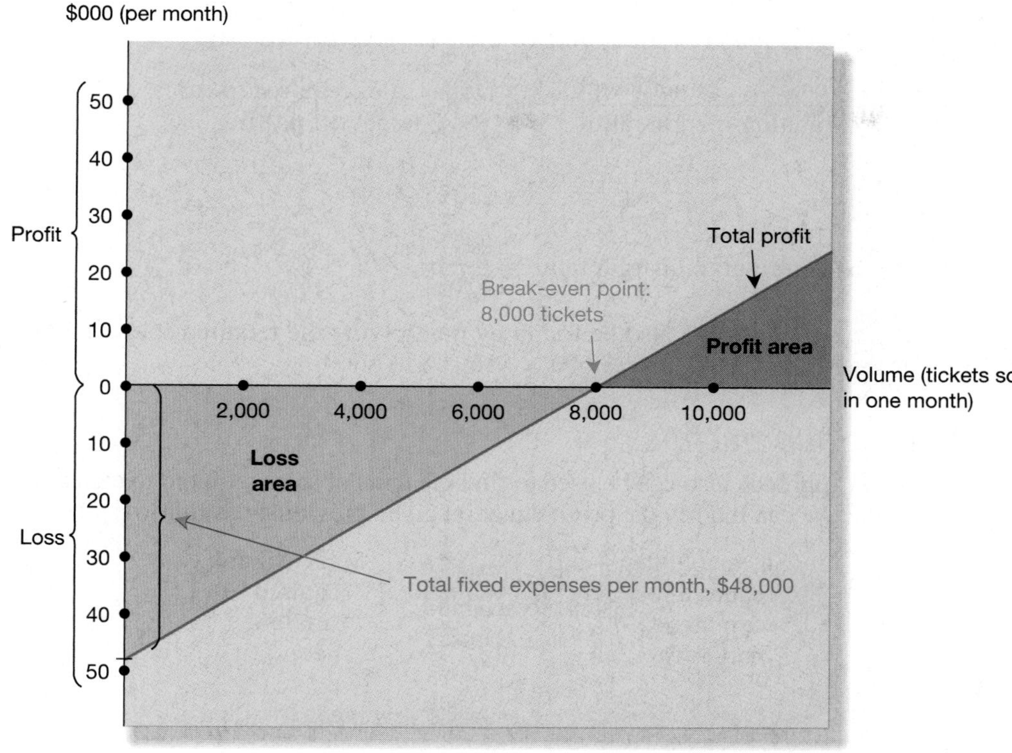

Exhibit 8–3
Profit-Volume Graph: Seattle Contemporary Theater

Target Net Profit

Apply CVP analysis to determine the effect on profit of changes in fixed expenses, variable expenses, sales prices, and sales volume.

The board of trustees for Seattle Contemporary Theater would like to run free workshops and classes for young actors and aspiring playwrights. This program would cost $3,600 per month in fixed expenses, including teachers' salaries and rental of space at a local college. No variable expenses would be incurred. If Seattle Contemporary Theater could make a profit of $3,600 per month on its performances, the Seattle Drama Workshop could be opened. The board has asked Andrew Lloyd, the organization's business manager and producer, to determine how many theater tickets must be sold during each play's one-month run to make a profit of $3,600.

The desired profit level of $3,600 is called a **target net profit** (or **income**). The problem of computing the volume of sales required to earn a particular target net profit is very similar to the problem of finding the break-even point. After all, the break-even point is the number of units of sales required to earn a target net profit of zero.

Contribution-Margin Approach

Each ticket sold by Seattle Contemporary Theater has a unit contribution margin of $6 (sales price of $16 minus unit variable expense of $10). Eight thousand of these $6 contributions will contribute just enough to cover fixed expenses of $48,000. *Each additional ticket sold will contribute $6 toward profit.* Thus, we can modify formula (1) given earlier in the chapter as follows:

$$\frac{\text{Fixed expenses} + \text{Target net profit}}{\text{Unit contribution margin}} = \begin{array}{c}\text{Number of sales units required}\\ \text{to earn target net profit}\end{array} \qquad (5)$$

$$\frac{\$48{,}000 + \$3{,}600}{\$6} = 8{,}600 \text{ tickets}$$

If Seattle Contemporary Theater sells 8,600 tickets during each play's one-month run, the organization will make a monthly profit of $3,600 on its performances. This profit can be used to fund the Seattle Drama Workshop. The total dollar sales required to earn a target net profit is found by modifying formula (2) given previously.

$$\frac{\text{Fixed expenses} + \text{Target net profit}}{\text{Contribution-margin ratio}} = \text{Dollar sales required to earn target net profit} \quad (6)$$

$$\frac{\$48{,}000 + \$3{,}600}{.375} = \$137{,}600$$

$$\text{where the contribution margin ratio} = \frac{\$6}{\$16} = .375$$

This dollar sales figure can also be found by multiplying the required sales of 8,600 tickets by the ticket price of $16 (8,600 × $16 = $137,600).

Equation Approach

The equation approach also can be used to find the units of sales required to earn a target net profit. We can modify the profit equation given previously as follows:

$$\left[\begin{pmatrix}\text{Unit}\\ \text{sales}\\ \text{price}\end{pmatrix} \times \begin{pmatrix}\text{Sales volume}\\ \text{required to}\\ \text{earn target}\\ \text{net profit}\end{pmatrix}\right] - \left[\begin{pmatrix}\text{Unit}\\ \text{variable}\\ \text{expense}\end{pmatrix} \times \begin{pmatrix}\text{Sales volume}\\ \text{required to}\\ \text{earn target}\\ \text{net profit}\end{pmatrix}\right] - \begin{pmatrix}\text{Fixed}\\ \text{expenses}\end{pmatrix} = \text{Target net profit}$$

Filling in the values for Seattle Contemporary Theater, we have the following equation.

$$(\$16 \times X) - (\$10 \times X) - \$48{,}000 = \$3{,}600 \quad (7)$$

where X denotes the sales volume required to earn the target net profit.

Equation (7) can be solved for X as follows:

$$\$16X - \$10X - \$48{,}000 = \$3{,}600$$
$$\$6X = \$51{,}600$$
$$X = \frac{\$51{,}600}{\$6} = 8{,}600$$

Graphical Approach

The profit-volume graph in Exhibit 8–3 can also be used to find the sales volume required to earn a target net profit. First, locate Seattle Contemporary Theater's target net profit of $3,600 on the vertical axis. Then move horizontally until the profit line is reached. Finally, move down from the profit line to the horizontal axis to determine the required sales volume.

Applying CVP Analysis

Apply CVP analysis to determine the effect on profit of changes in fixed expenses, variable expenses, sales prices, and sales volume.

The cost-volume-profit relationships that underlie break-even calculations and CVP graphs have wide-ranging applications in management. We will look at several common applications illustrated by Seattle Contemporary Theater.

Safety Margin

The **safety margin** of an enterprise is the difference between the budgeted sales revenue and the break-even sales revenue. Suppose Seattle Contemporary Theater's business manager expects every performance of each play to be sold out. Then budgeted monthly sales revenue is $144,000 (450 seats × 20 performances of each play × $16 per ticket). Since break-even sales revenue is $128,000, the organization's safety margin is $16,000 ($144,000 − $128,000). The safety margin gives management a feel for how close projected operations are to the organization's break-even point. We will further discuss the safety margin concept later in the chapter.

> "Basically the role of the [accountant] on the team [is] analyzing the financial impact of the business decision and providing advice. Does this make sense financially or not?" (8d)
> **Abbott Laboratories**

Changes in Fixed Expenses

What would happen to Seattle Contemporary Theater's break-even point if fixed expenses change? Suppose the business manager is concerned that the estimate for fixed utilities expenses, $1,400 per month, is too low. What would happen to the break-even point if fixed utilities expenses prove to be $2,600 instead? The break-even calculations for both the original and the new estimate of fixed utilities expenses are as follows:

Topic 8–2

	Original Estimate	**New Estimate**
Fixed utilities expenses	$ 1,400	$ 2,600
Total fixed expenses	$48,000	$49,200
Break-even calculation	$48,000	$49,200
(Fixed expenses ÷ Unit contribution margin)	$6	$6
Break-even point (units)	8,000 tickets	8,200 tickets
Break-even point (dollars)	$128,000	$131,200

The estimate of fixed expenses has increased by 2.5 percent, since $1,200 is 2.5 percent of $48,000. Notice that the break-even point also increased by 2.5 percent (200 tickets is 2.5 percent of 8,000 tickets). This relationship will always exist.

$$\frac{\text{Fixed expenses}}{\text{Unit contribution margin}} = \text{Break-even point (in units)}$$

$$\frac{\text{Fixed expenses} \times 1.025}{\text{Unit contribution margin}} = (\text{Break-even point in units}) \times 1.025$$

Donations to Offset Fixed Expenses Nonprofit organizations often receive cash donations from people or organizations desiring to support a worthy cause. A donation is equivalent to a reduction in fixed expenses, and it reduces the organization's break-even point. In our original set of data, Seattle Contemporary Theater's monthly fixed expenses total $48,000. Suppose that various people pledge donations amounting to $6,000 per month. The new break-even point is computed as follows:

$$\frac{\text{Fixed expenses} - \text{Donations}}{\text{Unit contribution margin}} = \text{Break-even point (in units)}$$

$$\frac{\$48{,}000 - \$6{,}000}{\$6} = 7{,}000 \text{ tickets}$$

Changes in the Unit Contribution Margin

What would happen to Seattle Contemporary Theater's break-even point if miscellaneous variable expenses were $3 per ticket instead of $2? Alternatively, what would be the effect of raising the ticket price to $18?

Change in Unit Variable Expenses If the theater organization's miscellaneous variable expenses increase from $2 to $3 per ticket, the unit contribution margin will fall from $6 to $5. The original and new break-even points are computed as follows:

SEATTLE

TICKETS TICKETS

	Original Estimate	New Estimate
Miscellaneous variable expenses	$2 per ticket	$3 per ticket
Unit contribution margin	$6	$5
Break-even calculation (Fixed expenses ÷ unit contribution margin)	$\frac{\$48{,}000}{\$6}$	$\frac{\$48{,}000}{\$5}$
Break-even point (units)	8,000 tickets	9,600 tickets
Break-even point (dollars)	$128,000	$153,600

If this change in unit variable expenses actually occurs, it will no longer be possible for the organization to break even. Only 9,000 tickets are available for each play's one-month run (450 seats × 20 performances), but 9,600 tickets would have to be sold to break even. Once again, CVP analysis will not solve this problem for management, but it will direct management's attention to potentially serious difficulties.

Cost-volume-profit analysis for a professional sports team must account for the huge impact of TV revenue, as well as ticket sales, players' salaries, and operating costs.

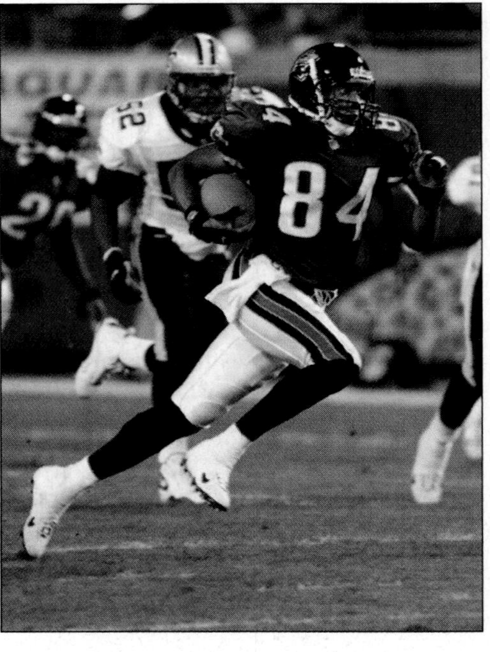

Change in Sales Price Changing the unit sales price will also alter the unit contribution margin. Suppose the ticket price is raised from $16 to $18. This change will raise the unit contribution margin from $6 to $8. The new break-even point will be 6,000 tickets ($48,000 ÷ $8).

A $2 increase in the ticket price will lower the break-even point from 8,000 tickets to 6,000 tickets. Is this change desirable? A lower break-even point decreases the risk of operating with a loss if sales are sluggish. However, the organization may be more likely to at least break even with a $16 ticket price than with an $18 ticket price. The reason is that the lower ticket price encourages more people to attend the theater's performances. It could be that break-even sales of 8,000 tickets at $16 are more likely than break-even sales of 6,000 tickets at $18. Ultimately, the desirability of the ticket-price increase depends on management's assessment of the likely reaction by theater patrons.

Management's decision about the ticket price increase also will reflect the fundamental goals of Seattle Contemporary Theater. This nonprofit drama organization was formed to bring contemporary drama to the people of Seattle. The lower the ticket price, the more accessible the theater's productions will be to people of all income levels.

The point of this discussion is that CVP analysis provides valuable information, but it is only one of several elements that influence management's decisions.

Predicting Profit Given Expected Volume

So far, we have focused on finding the required sales volume to break even or achieve a particular target net profit. Thus, we have asked the following question.

$$\text{Given: } \left\{ \begin{array}{l} \text{Fixed expenses} \\ \text{Unit contribution margin} \\ \text{Target net profit} \end{array} \right\}, \text{ Find: } \{\text{required sales volume}\}$$

We can also use CVP analysis to turn this question around and make the following query.

$$\text{Given: } \left\{ \begin{array}{l} \text{Fixed expenses} \\ \text{Unit contribution margin} \\ \text{Expected sales volume} \end{array} \right\}, \text{ Find: } \{\text{expected profit}\}$$

Suppose the management of Seattle Contemporary Theater expects fixed monthly expenses of $48,000 and unit variable expenses of $10 per ticket. The organization's board of trustees is considering two different ticket prices, and the business manager has forecast monthly demand at each price.

Ticket Price	Forecast Monthly Demand
$16	9,000
$20	6,000

Expected profit may be calculated at each price as shown in the following table. In these profit calculations, the **total contribution margin** is the difference between *total* sales revenue and *total* variable expenses. This use of the term *contribution margin* is a "total" concept rather than the "per unit" concept used earlier in the chapter. The *total contribution margin* is the *total* amount left to contribute to covering fixed expenses after *total* variable expenses have been covered.

	Ticket Price	
	$16	**$20**
Sales revenue:		
9,000 × $16	$144,000	
6,000 × $20		$120,000
Less variable expenses:		
9,000 × $10	90,000	
6,000 × $10		60,000
Total contribution margin	$ 54,000	$ 60,000
Less fixed expenses	48,000	48,000
Profit	$ 6,000	$ 12,000

The difference in expected profit at the two ticket prices is due to two factors:

1. A different *unit* contribution margin, defined previously as *unit* sales price minus *unit* variable expenses
2. A different sales volume

Incremental Approach Rather than presenting the entire income statement under each ticket price alternative, we can use a simpler incremental approach. This analysis focuses only on the difference in the total contribution margin under the two prices. Thus, the combined effect of the change in unit contribution margin and the change in sales volume is as follows:

Expected *total* contribution margin at $20 ticket price:	
6,000 × ($20 − $10)	$60,000
Expected *total* contribution margin at $16 ticket price:	
9,000 × ($16 − $10)	54,000
Difference in *total* contribution margin	$ 6,000

The $6,000 difference in expected profit, at the two ticket prices, is due to a $6,000 difference in the total contribution margin. The board of trustees will consider these projected profits as it decides which ticket price is best. Even though Seattle Contemporary Theater is a nonprofit organization, it may still have legitimate reasons for attempting to make a profit on its theater performances. For example, the board might use these profits to fund a free drama workshop, provide scholarships for local young people to study drama in college, or produce a free outdoor play for Seattle's residents.

Interdependent Changes in Key Variables

Sometimes a change in one key variable will cause a change in another key variable. Suppose the board of trustees is choosing between ticket prices of $16 and $20, and the business manager has projected demand as shown in the preceding section. A famous retired actress who lives in Seattle has offered to donate $10,000 per month to Seattle Contemporary Theater if the board will set the ticket price at $16. The actress is interested in making the theater's performances affordable by as many people as possible. The facts are now as follows:

Ticket Price	Unit Contribution Margin	Forecast Monthly Demand	Net Fixed Expenses (after subtracting donation)
$16	$ 6	9,000	$38,000 ($48,000 − $10,000)
20	10	6,000	48,000

The organization's expected profit at each price is computed as follows:

	Ticket Price	
	$16	**$20**
Sales revenue:		
9,000 × $16	$144,000	
6,000 × $20		$120,000
Less variable expenses:		
9,000 × $10	$90,000	
6,000 × $10		60,000
Total contribution margin	$ 54,000	$ 60,000
Less net fixed expenses (net of donation)	38,000	48,000
Profit	$ 16,000	$ 12,000

Now the difference in expected profit at the two ticket prices is due to three factors:

1. A different *unit* contribution margin.
2. A different sales volume.
3. A difference in the *net* fixed expenses, after deducting the donation.

Incremental Approach The combined effect of these factors is shown in the following analysis, which focuses on the effects of the price alternatives on the total contribution margin and the net fixed expenses.

Expected *total* contribution margin at $20 ticket price:	
6,000 × ($20 − $10)	$60,000
Expected *total* contribution margin at $16 ticket price:	
9,000 × ($16 − $10)	54,000
Difference in *total* contribution margin (higher with $20 ticket price)	$ 6,000
Net fixed expenses at $20 ticket price	$48,000
Net fixed expenses at $16 ticket price	38,000
Difference in net fixed expenses (higher with $20 ticket price)	$10,000

The expected total contribution margin is $6,000 higher with the $20 ticket price, but net fixed expenses are $10,000 higher. Thus, Seattle Contemporary Theater will make $4,000 more in profit at the $16 price ($10,000 − $6,000).

CVP Information in Published Annual Reports

Cost-volume-profit relationships are so important to understanding an organization's operations that some companies disclose CVP information in their published annual reports. The following illustration is from the airline industry.

Management Accounting Practice

Air France, Sabena, British Airways, and JetBlue

AIRLINES KEEP A CLOSE EYE ON BREAK-EVEN LOAD FACTORS

"Air France has been able to make up for cutting Dallas and Miami flights with more flights and larger planes to African cities. The airline has also recently expanded its service to many French-speaking former destinations in the Caribbean and the Indian Ocean. Together with Africa, the former colonies should account for almost the same amount of Air France's revenue this year as North America, analysts say. Still, the operating costs of flying to Africa are 50 percent higher for Air France than flying to the U.S., and the logistical problems are much more challenging."

In recent years, "Sabena lost at least 8 percent on its flights to the U.S., but had margins above 10 percent on routes to its former colonies Congo, Rwanda, and Burundi, according to an internal Sabena study. That kind of difference in profit margins is common. Across the busy North Atlantic, where competition and seasonal variation forces heavy discounting, all airlines are lucky to break even with a plane 75 percent full. For Kinshasa and other parts of Africa, where traffic is steadier, European carriers can break even with their planes barely 60 percent full, and planes often fly 85 percent full."[1]

Airlines generally disclose their systemwide break-even load factors in their annual reports. British Airways, for example, listed its break-even load factor as 64 percent in a recent annual report. The large airlines, like British Airways, usually fill a smaller percentage of their seats than do the upstart, discount airlines. JetBlue is a good example. "The low-fare, low-cost carrier . . . now operates more than 100 flights a day to 18 cities in nine states. Its load factor, or percentage of seats filled, was an industry-leading 78 percent last year."[2]

CVP Analysis with Multiple Products

Our CVP illustration for Seattle Contemporary Theater has assumed that the organization has only one product, a theater seat at a dramatic performance. Most firms have a

LO 5

Compute the break-even point and prepare a profit-volume graph for a multiproduct enterprise.

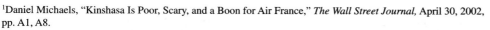

[1]Daniel Michaels, "Kinshasa Is Poor, Scary, and a Boon for Air France," *The Wall Street Journal,* April 30, 2002, pp. A1, A8.

[2]Susan Carey, "JetBlue, One of the Few U.S. Airlines to Buck the Downturn, Files for $125 Million IPO," *The Wall Street Journal,* February 13, 2002, p. B4.

Major airlines keep a close watch on the break-even passenger load factor.

sales mix consisting of more than one product, and this adds some complexity to their CVP analyses.

As we have seen, Seattle Contemporary Theater's monthly fixed expenses total $48,000, and the unit variable expense per ticket is $10. Now suppose that the city of Seattle has agreed to refurbish 10 theater boxes in the historic theater building. Each box has five seats, which are more comfortable and afford a better view of the stage than the theater's general seating. The board of trustees has decided to charge $16 per ticket for general seating and $20 per ticket for box seats. These facts are summarized as follows:

Seat Type	Ticket Price	Unit Variable Expense	Unit Contribution Margin	Seats in Theater	Seats Available per Month (20 performances)
Regular	$16	$10	$ 6	450	9,000
Box	20	10	10	50	1,000

Notice that 90 percent of the available seats are regular seats, and 10 percent are box seats. The business manager estimates that tickets for each type of seat will be sold in the same proportion as the number of seats available. If, for example, 5,000 tickets are sold during a month, sales will be as follows:

Regular seats:	90% × 5,000	4,500
Box seats:	10% × 5,000	500
Total		5,000

For any organization selling multiple products, the relative proportion of each type of product *sold* is called the **sales mix.** The business manager's estimate of Seattle Contemporary Theater's *sales mix* is 90 percent regular seats and 10 percent box seats.

The sales mix is an important assumption in multiproduct CVP analysis. The sales mix is used to compute a **weighted-average unit contribution margin.** This is the *average* of the several products' *unit contribution margins, weighted* by the relative sales proportion of each product. Seattle Contemporary Theater's weighted-average unit contribution margin is computed below.

$$\text{Weighted-average unit contribution margin} = (\$6 \times 90\%) + (\$10 \times 10\%) = \$6.40$$

The organization's break-even point in units is computed using the following formula.

$$\text{Break-even point} = \frac{\text{Fixed expenses}}{\text{Weighted-average unit contribution margin}} \qquad (8)$$

$$= \frac{\$48{,}000}{\$6.40} = 7{,}500 \text{ tickets}$$

The break-even point of 7,500 tickets must be interpreted in light of the sales mix. Seattle Contemporary Theater will break even for the month if it sells 7,500 tickets as follows:

Break-even sales in units	Regular seats:	7,500 × 90%	6,750 tickets
	Box seats:	7,500 × 10%	750 tickets
	Total		7,500 tickets

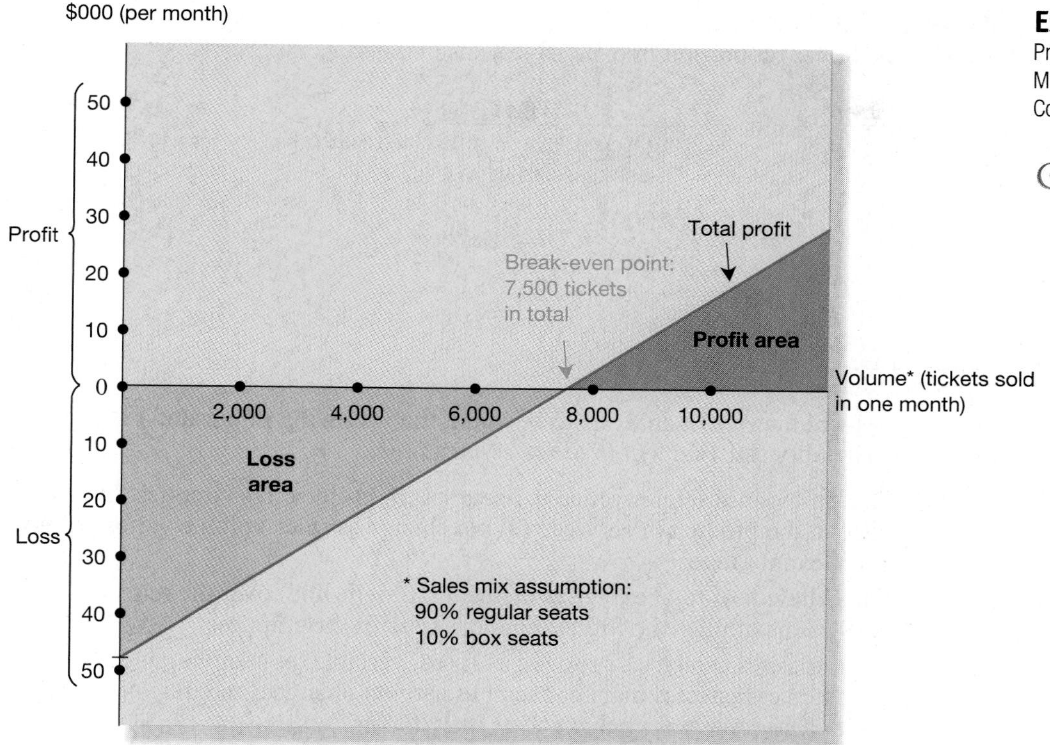

Exhibit 8–4
Profit-Volume Graph with Multiple Products: Seattle Contemporary Theater

The following income calculation verifies the break-even point.

Sales revenue:	
Regular seats: 6,750 × $16	$108,000
Box seats: 750 × $20	15,000
Total revenue: 7,500 seats in total	$123,000
Less variable expenses: 7,500 × $10	75,000
Total contribution margin	$ 48,000
Less fixed expenses	48,000
Profit	$ 0

The break-even point of 7,500 tickets per month is *valid only for the sales mix assumed* in computing the weighted-average unit contribution margin. If 7,500 tickets are sold in any other mix of regular and box seats, the organization will not break even.

Notice that break-even formula (8) is a modification of formula (1) given earlier in the chapter. The only difference is that formula (8) uses the *weighted-average* unit contribution margin.

Seattle Contemporary Theater's business manager has constructed the profit-volume graph in Exhibit 8–4. The PV graph shows the organization's profit at any level of total monthly sales, assuming the sales mix of 90 percent regular seats and 10 percent box seats. For example, if 9,000 tickets are sold in total, at the assumed sales mix, the PV graph indicates that profit will be $9,600.

With multiproduct CVP analysis, a managerial accountant can investigate the impact on profit of changes in sales volume, prices, variable costs, fixed costs, or the sales mix itself. For example, what would be the effect on Seattle Contemporary Theater's break-even point if the sales mix were 95 percent regular seats and 5 percent box seats? With this sales mix, the weighted-average unit contribution margin is computed as follows:

$$\text{Weighted-average unit contribution margin} = (\$6 \times 95\%) + (\$10 \times 5\%) = \$6.20$$

The break-even point increases from 7,500 tickets to approximately 7,742 tickets as a result of the lower proportion of expensive seats in the sales mix.

$$\text{Break-even point} = \frac{\text{Fixed expenses}}{\text{Weighted-average unit contribution margin}}$$

$$= \frac{\$48,000}{\$6.20} = 7,742 \text{ tickets*}$$

*Rounded

Assumptions Underlying CVP Analysis

List and discuss the key assumptions of CVP analysis.

For any cost-volume-profit analysis to be valid, the following important assumptions must be reasonably satisfied *within the relevant range*.

1. The behavior of total revenue is linear (straight-line). This implies that the price of the product or service will not change as sales volume varies within the relevant range.
2. The behavior of total expenses is linear (straight-line) over the relevant range. This implies the following more specific assumptions.
   a. Expenses can be categorized as fixed, variable, or semivariable. *Total* fixed expenses remain constant as activity changes, and the *unit* variable expense remains unchanged as activity varies.
   b. The efficiency and productivity of the production process and workers remain constant.
3. In multiproduct organizations, the sales mix remains constant over the relevant range.
4. In manufacturing firms, the inventory levels at the beginning and end of the period are the same. This implies that the number of units produced during the period equals the number of units sold.

Role of Computerized Planning Models and Electronic Spreadsheets

Cost-volume-profit analysis is based on the four general assumptions listed above as well as specific estimates of all the variables used in the analysis. Since these variables are rarely known with certainty, it is helpful to run a CVP analysis many times with different combinations of estimates. For example, Seattle Contemporary Theater's business manager might do the CVP analysis using different estimates for the ticket prices, sales mix for regular and box seats, unit variable expenses, and fixed expenses. This approach is called **sensitivity analysis,** since it provides the analyst with a feel for how sensitive the analysis is to the estimates upon which it is based. The widespread availability of personal computers and electronic spreadsheet software has made sensitivity analysis relatively easy to do.

CVP Relationships and the Income Statement

The management functions of planning, control, and decision making all are facilitated by an understanding of cost-volume-profit relationships. These relationships are important enough to operating managers that some businesses prepare income statements in a way that highlights CVP issues. Before we examine this new income-statement format, we will review the more traditional income statement used in the preceding chapters.

Exhibit 8–5
Income Statement: Traditional and Contribution Formats

A. Traditional Format

ACCUTIME COMPANY
Income Statement
For the Year Ended December 31, 20x1

Sales		$500,000
Less: Cost of goods sold		380,000
Gross margin		$120,000
Less: Operating expenses:		
Selling expenses	$35,000	
Administrative expenses	35,000	70,000
Net income		$ 50,000

B. Contribution Format

ACCUTIME COMPANY
Income Statement
For the Year Ended December 31, 20x1

Sales		$500,000
Less: Variable expenses:		
Variable manufacturing	$280,000	
Variable selling	15,000	
Variable administrative	5,000	300,000
Contribution margin		$200,000
Less: Fixed expenses:		
Fixed manufacturing	$100,000	
Fixed selling	20,000	
Fixed administrative	30,000	150,000
Net income		$ 50,000

Traditional Income Statement

An income statement for AccuTime Company, a manufacturer of digital clocks, is shown in Exhibit 8–5 (panel A). During 20x1 the firm manufactured and sold 20,000 clocks at a price of $25 each. This income statement is prepared in the traditional manner. *Cost of goods sold* includes both variable and fixed manufacturing costs, as measured by the firm's product-costing system. The *gross margin* is computed by subtracting cost of goods sold from sales. Selling and administrative expenses are then subtracted; each expense includes both variable and fixed costs. *The traditional income statement does not disclose the breakdown of each expense into its variable and fixed components.*

Contribution Income Statement

Prepare and interpret a contribution income statement.

Many operating managers find the traditional income-statement format difficult to use, because it does not separate variable and fixed expenses. Instead they prefer the **contribution income statement.** A contribution income statement for AccuTime is shown in Exhibit 8–5 (panel B). *The contribution format highlights the distinction between variable and fixed expenses.* The variable manufacturing cost of each clock is $14, and the total fixed manufacturing cost is $100,000. On the contribution income statement, all variable expenses are subtracted from sales to obtain the *contribution margin*. For AccuTime, $200,000 remains from total sales revenue, after all variable costs have been covered, to contribute to covering fixed costs and making a profit. All fixed costs are then subtracted from the contribution margin to obtain net income.

Comparison of Traditional and Contribution Income Statements

Operating managers frequently prefer the contribution income statement, because its separation of fixed and variable expenses highlights cost-volume-profit relationships. It is readily apparent from the contribution-format statement how income will be affected when sales volume changes by a given percentage. Suppose management projects that sales volume in 20x2 will be 20 percent greater than in 20x1. No changes are anticipated in the sales price, variable cost per unit, or fixed costs. Examination of the contribution income statement shows that if sales volume increases by 20 percent, the following changes will occur. (Our discussion ignores income taxes, which are covered in the appendix at the end of this chapter.)

Income Statement Item	20x1 Amount	Change	20x2 Amount
Sales	$500,000	$100,000 (20% × $500,000)	$600,000
Total variable expenses	$300,000	$60,000 (20% × $300,000)	$360,000
Contribution margin	$200,000	$40,000 (20% × $200,000)	$240,000
Total fixed expenses	$150,000	–0– (no change in fixed expenses when volume changes)	$150,000
Net income	$50,000	$40,000 (income changes by the amount of the contribution-margin change)	$90,000

Notice that net income increases by the same amount as the increase in the contribution margin. Moreover, the contribution margin changes in direct proportion to the change in sales volume. These two facts enable us to calculate the increase in net income using the following shortcut. Recall that the *contribution-margin ratio* is the percentage of contribution margin to sales.

$$\begin{pmatrix}\text{Increase in}\\ \text{sales revenue}\end{pmatrix} \times \begin{pmatrix}\text{Contribution-margin}\\ \text{ratio}\end{pmatrix} = \begin{pmatrix}\text{Increase in}\\ \text{net income}\end{pmatrix}$$

$$\$100{,}000 \times .40 = \$40{,}000$$

where

$$\begin{pmatrix}\text{Contribution-margin}\\ \text{ratio}\end{pmatrix} = \frac{\text{Contribution margin}}{\text{Sales revenue}}$$

$$.40 = \frac{\$200{,}000}{\$500{,}000}$$

The analysis above makes use of cost-volume-profit relationships that are disclosed in the contribution income statement. Such an analysis cannot be made with the information presented in the traditional income statement.

Cost Structure and Operating Leverage

LO 8

Explain the role of cost structure and operating leverage in CVP relationships.

The **cost structure** of an organization is the relative proportion of its fixed and variable costs. Cost structures differ widely among industries and among firms within an industry. A company using a computer-integrated manufacturing system has a large investment in plant and equipment, which results in a cost structure dominated by fixed costs. In contrast, a public accounting firm's cost structure has a much higher proportion of variable costs. The highly automated manufacturing firm is capital-intensive, whereas the accounting firm is labor-intensive.

Exhibit 8–6
Comparison of Cost Structures

Microsoft Excel - Exhibit 8-6

B10 =B8-B9

	A	B	C	D	E	F	G
1		Company A		Company B		Company C	
2		(AccuTime Company)		(Manual System)		(Automated System)	
3							
4		Amount	%	Amount	%	Amount	%
5							
6	Sales	$ 500,000	100	$ 500,000	100	$ 500,000	100
7	Variable expenses	300,000	60	400,000	80	50,000	10
8	Contribution margin	$ 200,000	40	$ 100,000	20	$ 450,000	90
9	Fixed expenses	150,000	30	50,000	10	400,000	80
10	Net income	$ 50,000	10	$ 50,000	10	$ 50,000	10

Sheet1 / Sheet2 / Sheet3

Ready

Exhibit 8–7
Effect on Profit of Increase in Sales Revenue

	(Increase in Sales Revenue)	×	(Contribution Margin Ratio)	=	(Increase in Net Income)	Percentage Increase in Net Income
Company A (AccuTime)	$50,000	×	40%	=	$20,000	40% ($20,000 ÷ $50,000)
Company B (high variable expenses)	$50,000	×	20%	=	$10,000	20% ($10,000 ÷ $50,000)
Company C (high fixed expenses)	$50,000	×	90%	=	$45,000	90% ($45,000 ÷ $50,000)

An organization's cost structure has a significant effect on the sensitivity of its profit to changes in volume. A convenient way to portray a firm's cost structure is shown in the Excel spreadsheet in Exhibit 8–6.[3] The data for AccuTime Company (company A) comes from the firm's 20x1 contribution income statement in Exhibit 8–5. For comparison purposes, two other firms' cost structures are also shown. Although these three firms have the same sales revenue ($500,000) and net income ($50,000), they have very different cost structures. Company B's production process is largely manual, and its cost structure is dominated by variable costs. It has a low contribution-margin ratio of only 20 percent. In contrast, company C employs a highly automated production process, and its cost structure is dominated by fixed costs. The firm's contribution-margin ratio is 90 percent. Company A falls between these two extremes with a contribution-margin ratio of 40 percent.

Suppose sales revenue increases by 10 percent, or $50,000, in each company. The resulting increase in each company's profit is calculated in Exhibit 8–7.

Notice that company B, with its high variable expenses and low contribution-margin ratio, shows a relatively low *percentage* increase in profit. In contrast, the high fixed expenses and large contribution-margin ratio of company C result in a relatively high *percentage* increase in profit. Company A falls in between these two extremes.

To summarize, the greater the proportion of fixed costs in a firm's cost structure, the greater the impact on profit will be from a given percentage change in sales revenue.

Operating Leverage

The extent to which an organization uses fixed costs in its cost structure is called **operating leverage.** The operating leverage is greatest in firms with a large proportion of

[3]This form of income statement, in which each item on the statement is expressed as a percentage of sales revenue, is often called a *common-size income statement.*

fixed costs, low proportion of variable costs, and the resulting high contribution-margin ratio. Exhibit 8–6 shows that company B has low operating leverage, company C has high operating leverage, and company A falls in between. To a physical scientist, *leverage* refers to the ability of a small force to move a heavy weight. To the managerial accountant, *operating leverage* refers to the ability of the firm to generate an increase in net income when sales revenue increases.

Measuring Operating Leverage The managerial accountant can measure a firm's operating leverage, *at a particular sales volume*, using the **operating leverage factor:**

$$\text{Operating leverage factor} = \frac{\text{Contribution margin}}{\text{Net income}}$$

Using the data in Exhibit 8–6, the operating leverage factors of companies A, B, and C, are computed as follows:

	(Contribution Margin)	÷	(Net Income)	=	(Operating Leverage Factor)
Company A (AccuTime)	$200,000	÷	$50,000	=	4
Company B (high variable expenses)	$100,000	÷	$50,000	=	2
Company C (high fixed expenses)	$450,000	÷	$50,000	=	9

The operating leverage factor is a measure, at a particular level of sales, of the *percentage* impact on net income of a given *percentage* change in sales revenue. Multiplying the *percentage* change in sales revenue by the operating leverage factor yields the *percentage* change in net income.

	(Percentage Increase in Sales Revenue)	×	(Operating Leverage Factor)	=	(Percentage Change in Net Income)
Company A (AccuTime)	10%	×	4	=	40%
Company B (high variable expenses)	10%	×	2	=	20%
Company C (high fixed expenses)	10%	×	9	=	90%

The percentage change in net income shown above for each company may be verified by re-examining Exhibit 8–7.

Break-Even Point and Safety Margin A firm's operating leverage also affects its break-even point. Since a firm with relatively high operating leverage has proportionally high fixed expenses, the firm's break-even point will be relatively high. This fact is illustrated using the data from Exhibit 8–6.

	(Fixed Expenses)	÷	(Contribution Margin Ratio)	=	(Break-Even Sales Revenue)
Company A (AccuTime)	$150,000	÷	40%	=	$375,000
Company B (high variable expenses)	$ 50,000	÷	20%	=	$250,000
Company C (high fixed expenses)	$400,000	÷	90%	=	$444,444*

*Rounded

The safety margin also is affected by a firm's operating leverage. Suppose the budgeted sales revenue for each of the three companies is $500,000. Then the safety margin, defined as budgeted sales revenue minus break-even sales revenue, is calculated as follows:

	Budgeted Sales Revenue	Break-Even Sales Revenue	Safety Margin
Company A (AccuTime)	$500,000	$375,000	$125,000
Company B (high variable expenses)	500,000	250,000	250,000
Company C (high fixed expenses)	500,000	444,444	55,556

To summarize, company C's high fixed expenses result in a high break-even point and low safety margin. Company B displays the opposite characteristics, and company A falls in between the two extremes.

Management Accounting Practice

Expedia, Hotels.com, eBay, and Overture Services

OPERATING LEVERAGE HELPS THESE WEB COMPANIES BECOME PROFITABLE

"Four Web companies made this year's ranking of the Info Tech One Hundred: search engine Overture Services, auctioneer eBay, discount-hotel broker Hotels.com, and travel site Expedia." That's up from only one last year, and all of them are profitable. "The leaders of the Web pack are starting to show that once they turn profitable, they can quickly become big moneymakers. The reason is operating leverage. That's accounting-speak for a simple concept: Once you invest enough to build a Web site and your basic operations, you don't need to spend much money as sales rise. After you cover your fixed costs, the expense of processing each sale is so little that profits grow faster than revenues. That philosophy made for big Internet losses early on." The payoff, however, is at hand.

"Online travel agency Expedia Inc. is a textbook example of leverage in action. In 2002's first quarter, Expedia doubled its sales, to $116 million. Yet its overhead, including administrative and marketing costs, rose only 8 percent, to $63 million. One big reason is that the company already had paid for the computing gear it needed to handle the higher volume of ticket sales."

Just a few years after the boom in e-commerce IPOs, "a clear pecking order of profitability has emerged. The biggest moneymakers: online travel, software, and financial-services firms." Why did these online companies turn profitable first? "Because software, financial services, and travel reservations are pure information products, without a physical widget to store or ship. Once overhead costs are covered, the expense in providing the service to one more customer is close to zero. Online retailers are making slower, yet tangible, progress toward profitability. What's holding Amazon.com Inc. and other e-tailers back is simple: Every time someone buys a book on Amazon, the company has to buy a new copy from the publisher. The upshot is that Amazon's gross margins are around 26 percent, compared with 70 percent at Expedia."

Every year, Web business writes a different story, "but now it's past the point where predictions of profitability are written in sand. Some Web businesses do work. The proof is in the black ink."[4]

Labor-Intensive Production Processes versus Advanced Manufacturing Systems The effects of labor-intensive (manual) production processes and highly automated, advanced manufacturing systems illustrated by companies A, B, and C are typical. As Exhibit 8–8 shows, a movement toward an advanced manufacturing environment often results in a higher break-even point, lower safety margin, and higher operating leverage. However, high-technology manufacturing systems generally have greater throughput, thus allowing greater potential for profitability. Along with the increased potential for profitability comes increased risk. In an economic recession, for example, a highly automated company with high fixed costs will be less able to adapt to lower consumer demand than will a firm with a more labor-intensive production process.

Cost Structure and Operating Leverage: A Cost-Benefit Issue

An organization's cost structure plays an important role in determining its cost-volume-profit relationships. A firm with proportionately high fixed costs has relatively high operating leverage. The result of high operating leverage is that the firm can generate a large percentage increase in net income from a relatively small percentage

[4]Timothy J. Mullaney and Robert D. Hof, "Finally, the Pot of Gold," *Business Week,* June 24, 2002, p. 106.

Exhibit 8–8
Labor-Intensive Production Processes versus Advanced Manufacturing Systems

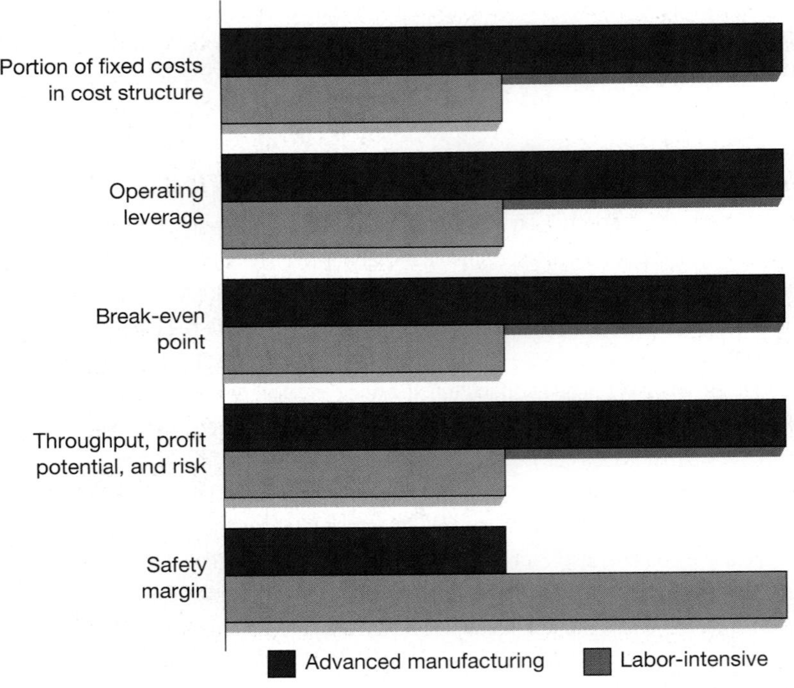

increase in sales revenue. On the other hand, a firm with high operating leverage has a relatively high break-even point. This entails some risk to the firm.

Management Accounting Practice
Kaiser Permanente

COST STRUCTURE AND OPERATING LEVERAGE

Kaiser Permanente was founded in 1945 to provide health care for workers at Henry F. Kaiser's West Coast shipyards and steel mills. It led the U.S. HMOs by building its own hospitals, marketing its own health insurance, and working with doctors in the Permanente Medical Group, who practice exclusively for Kaiser. Such a vertical integration allows Kaiser to control costs better than HMOs that contract with independent doctors and hospitals. This strategy results in Kaiser's cost structure being dominated by fixed costs. Kaiser has to focus on maintaining membership growth because of its high operating leverage.[5]

The optimal cost structure for an organization involves a trade-off. Management must weigh the benefits of high operating leverage against the risks of large committed fixed costs and the associated high break-even point.

CVP Analysis, Activity-Based Costing, and Advanced Manufacturing Systems

LO 9

Understand the implications of activity-based costing for CVP analysis.

Traditional cost-volume-profit analysis focuses on the number of units sold as the only cost and revenue driver. Sales revenue is assumed to be linear in units sold. Moreover, costs are categorized as fixed or variable, with respect to the number of units sold, within the relevant range. This approach is consistent with traditional product-costing systems, in which cost assignment is based on a single, volume-related cost driver. In CVP analysis, as in product costing, the traditional approach can be misleading or

[5]Based on the author's research.

provide less than adequate information for various management purposes. An activity-based costing system can provide a much more complete picture of cost-volume-profit relationships and thus provide better information to managers.

To illustrate the potential impact of activity-based costing on CVP analysis, we will continue our discussion of AccuTime Company. The basic data underlying the contribution income statement shown in Exhibit 8–5 are as follows:

Sales volume	20,000 units
Sales price	$25
Unit variable costs:	
Variable manufacturing	$14
Variable selling and administrative	1
Total unit variable cost	$15
Unit contribution margin	$10
Fixed costs:	
Fixed manufacturing	$100,000
Fixed selling and administrative	50,000
Total fixed costs	$150,000

These data are adequate for a traditional CVP analysis of various questions management may ask. For example, the break-even point is easily calculated as 15,000 units, as the following analysis shows:

$$\text{Break-even point} = \frac{\text{Fixed costs}}{\text{Unit contribution margin}} = \frac{\$150,000}{\$10} = 15,000 \text{ units}$$

Alternatively, management may determine how many clocks must be sold to earn a target net profit of $200,000, as the following calculation demonstrates:

$$\begin{aligned}\text{Sales volume required to earn target net profit of \$200,000} &= \frac{\text{Fixed costs} + \text{Target net profit}}{\text{Unit contribution margin}}\\ &= \frac{\$150,000 + \$200,000}{\$10} = 35,000 \text{ units}\end{aligned}$$

"ABC was critical to the organization in helping us gain a better understanding of our costs. . . . It provided us with a foundation for managing expenses better." (8e)
BlueCross BlueShield of North Carolina

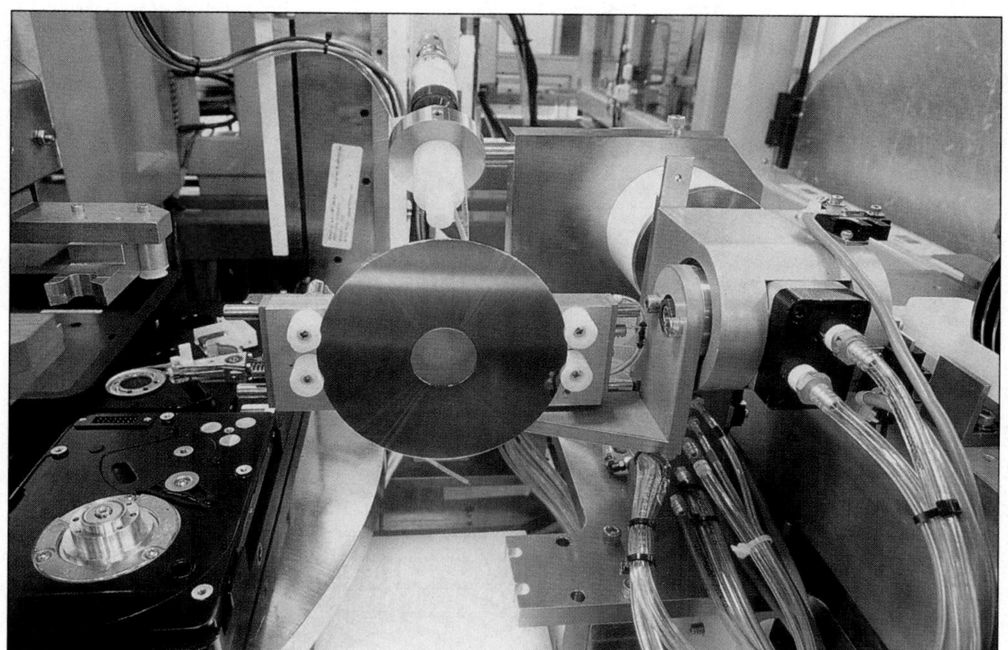

Pictured here is a production cell in a flexible manufacturing system engaged in the production of disks for computer hard disk drives. In such a high-tech manufacturing environment, setups are quicker and more frequent, and production runs are smaller. An activity-based costing CVP analysis will give management a better understanding of cost-volume-profit relationships.

What do these questions have in common? They both focus on *sales volume* as the sole revenue and cost driver. The CVP analysis depends on a distinction between costs that are fixed and costs that are variable *with respect to sales volume*.

A Move Toward JIT and Flexible Manufacturing

LO 10

Be aware of the effects of advanced manufacturing technology on CVP relationships.

Now let's examine another question AccuTime's management could face. Suppose management is considering the installation of a flexible manufacturing system and a move toward just-in-time (JIT) production. In the new production process, setups would be quicker and more frequent and production runs would be smaller. Fewer inspections would be required, due to the total quality control (TQC) philosophy that often accompanies JIT. Variable manufacturing costs would be lower, due to savings in direct labor. Finally, general factory overhead costs would increase, due to the greater depreciation charges on the new production equipment.

Suppose management wants to answer the same two questions addressed previously, under the assumption that the production process changes are adopted. To properly address this issue, we need a much more detailed understanding of the impact of other, *non-volume-based cost drivers* on AccuTime's costs. This type of detail is the hallmark of an activity-based costing system. Suppose AccuTime's controller completes an ABC analysis of the company's 20x1 activity before the new equipment is installed. The results are shown in Exhibit 8–9.

There is a subtle but important point to realize about the cost behavior depicted in Exhibit 8–9. Setup, inspection, and material handling are listed as fixed costs. *They are fixed with respect to sales volume*. However, they are *not* fixed with respect to *other cost drivers*, such as the number of setups, inspections, and hours of material handling. This is the fundamental distinction between a traditional CVP analysis and an activity-based costing CVP analysis. The traditional CVP analysis recognizes a single, volume-based cost driver, namely, sales volume. The activity-based costing CVP analysis recognizes multiple cost drivers. As a result, some costs viewed as fixed under the traditional analysis are considered variable (with respect to the appropriate cost drivers) under the ABC approach.

Now let's return to management's decision regarding the installation of a flexible manufacturing system and the adoption of the JIT and TQC philosophies. The activity-based costing analysis of the proposed production technology is displayed in

Exhibit 8–9
Activity-Based Costing Data under Current Production Process (20x1)

Sales price	$25
Unit variable costs:	
Variable manufacturing	$14
Variable selling and administrative	1
Total unit variable costs	$15
Unit contribution margin	$10
Fixed costs (fixed with respect to sales volume):	
General factory overhead (including depreciation on plant and equipment)	$ 60,000
Setup (52 setups at $100 per setup)*	5,200
Inspection [(52)(21) inspections at $20 per inspection]†	21,840
Material handling (1,080 hours at $12 per hour)	12,960
Total fixed manufacturing costs	$100,000
Fixed selling and administrative costs	50,000
Total fixed costs	$150,000

*One setup per week
†Three inspections per day, seven days a week (52 weeks per year).

Sales price	$25
Unit variable costs:	
Variable manufacturing	$ 9
Variable selling and administrative	1
Total unit variable costs	$10
Unit contribution margin	$15
Fixed costs (fixed with respect to sales volume):	
General factory overhead (including depreciation on plant and equipment)	$184,000
Setup (365 setups at $30 per setup)	10,950
Inspection (365 inspections at $10 per inspection)	3,650
Material handling (100 hours at $14 per hour)	1,400
Total fixed manufacturing costs	$200,000
Fixed selling and administrative costs	50,000
Total fixed costs	$250,000

Exhibit 8–10
Activity-Based Costing Data under Proposed Production Technology

Exhibit 8–10. Due to the decreased use of direct labor, the unit variable manufacturing cost has declined from $14 to $9, thus bringing the total unit variable cost down to $10. This results in an increase in the unit contribution margin to $15. The installation of sophisticated new manufacturing equipment has more than tripled general factory overhead, from $60,000 to $184,000. Under the proposed JIT approach, setups will be daily instead of weekly; each setup will be quicker and less expensive. As a result of the emphasis on total quality control, only one inspection per day will be necessary, instead of three as before. Moreover, each inspection will be less expensive. Finally, the amount of material-handling activity will decline dramatically, although there will be a slight increase in the cost per hour. This is due to the higher skill grade of labor required to operate the new automated material-handling system.

Using the ABC data in Exhibit 8–10, we can answer the two CVP questions posed by management. If the new production technology is adopted, the following CVP computations will be appropriate.

$$\text{Break-even point} = \frac{\text{Fixed costs}}{\text{Unit contribution margin}} = \frac{\$250{,}000}{\$15} = \begin{matrix}\text{16,667 units}\\ \text{(rounded)}\end{matrix}$$

$$\begin{matrix}\text{Sales volume required to earn}\\ \text{target net profit of \$200,000}\end{matrix} = \frac{\text{Fixed costs} + \text{Target net profit}}{\text{Unit contribution margin}}$$

$$= \frac{\$250{,}000 + \$200{,}000}{\$15} = \text{30,000 units}$$

Notice that AccuTime's break-even point increased with the introduction of the advanced manufacturing system (from 15,000 to 16,667 units). However, the number of sales units required to earn a target net profit of $200,000 declined (from 35,000 to 30,000 units). These kinds of CVP changes are typical when firms install an advanced manufacturing system. Typically the cost structure of an advanced manufacturing environment is characterized by a lower proportion of variable costs and a larger proportion of costs that are fixed (with respect to sales volume).

ABC Provides a Richer Understanding of Cost Behavior and CVP Relationships The important point in this section is that activity-based costing provides a richer description of a company's cost behavior. AccuTime's traditional costing system treated setup, inspection, and material handling as fixed costs. However, the ABC analysis showed that while these costs are largely fixed with respect to sales volume, they are not fixed with respect to other appropriate cost drivers. In analyzing the cost-volume-profit implications of the proposed changes in manufacturing technology, it was crucial to have an understanding of how these costs would change with respect to such cost drivers as the number of setups, number of inspections, and amount of material-handling activity.

Just as ABC can improve an organization's product-costing system, it also can facilitate a deeper understanding of cost behavior and CVP relationships.

Chapter Summary

An understanding of cost-volume-profit relationships is necessary for the successful management of any enterprise. CVP analysis provides a sweeping overview of the effects on profit of all kinds of changes in sales volume, expenses, product mix, and sales prices. Calculation of the sales volume required to break even or earn a target net profit provides an organization's management with valuable information for planning and decision making.

Cost-volume-profit relationships are important enough to operating managers that some firms prepare a contribution income statement. This income-statement format separates fixed and variable expenses and helps managers discern the effects on profit from changes in volume. The contribution income statement also discloses an organization's cost structure, which is the relative proportion of its fixed and variable costs. An organization's cost structure has an important impact on its CVP relationships. The cost structure of an organization defines its operating leverage, which determines the impact on profit of changes in sales volume.

Activity-based costing can provide a richer description of an organization's cost behavior and CVP relationships than is provided by a traditional costing system. An ABC cost-volume-profit analysis recognizes that some costs that are fixed with respect to sales volume may not be fixed with respect to other important cost drivers. In many cases, management can benefit substantially from such an improved understanding of cost behavior and relationships.

Review Problem on Cost-Volume-Profit Analysis

Overlook Inn is a small bed-and-breakfast inn located in the Great Smoky Mountains of Tennessee. The charge is $50 per person for one night's lodging and a full breakfast in the morning. The retired couple who own and manage the inn estimate that the variable expense per person is $20. This includes such expenses as food, maid service, and utilities. The inn's fixed expenses total $42,000 per year. The inn can accommodate 10 guests each night.

Required: Compute the following:

1. Contribution margin per unit of service. (A unit of service is one night's lodging for one guest.)
2. Contribution-margin ratio.
3. Annual break-even point in units of service and in dollars of service revenue.
4. The number of units of service required to earn a target net profit of $60,000 for the year. (Ignore income taxes.)

Solution to Review Problem

1. Contribution margin per unit of service = Nightly room charge − Variable expense per person

$$\$30 = \$50 - \$20$$

2. $$\text{Contribution-margin ratio} = \frac{\text{Contribution margin per unit}}{\text{Nightly room charge}}$$

$$.60 = \frac{\$30}{\$50}$$

3. $$\text{Break-even point in units of service} = \frac{\text{Fixed expenses}}{\text{Contribution margin per unit}}$$

$$1{,}400 = \frac{\$42{,}000}{\$30}$$

$$\text{Break-even point in dollars of revenue} = \frac{\text{Fixed expenses}}{\text{Contribution-margin ratio}}$$

$$\$70{,}000 = \frac{\$42{,}000}{.60}$$

4.
$$\text{Number of units of service required to earn target net profit} = \frac{\text{Fixed expenses} + \text{Target net profit}}{\text{Contribution margin per unit of service}}$$

$$3{,}400 = \frac{\$42{,}000 + \$60{,}000}{\$30}$$

Key Terms

For each term's definition refer to the indicated page, or turn to the glossary at the end of the text.

after-tax net income,* 327
before-tax income,* 327
break-even point, 301
contribution income statement, 317
contribution-margin ratio, 303
cost structure, 318
cost-volume-profit (CVP) analysis, 300
cost-volume-profit (CVP) graph, 304
operating leverage, 319
operating leverage factor, 320
profit-volume graph, 306
safety margin, 308
sales mix, 314
sensitivity analysis, 316
target net profit (or income), 307
total contribution margin, 302
unit contribution margin, 302
weighted-average unit contribution margin, 314

*Term appears in the appendix.

Appendix to Chapter 8

Effect of Income Taxes

Profit-seeking enterprises must pay income taxes on their profits. A firm's **after-tax net income,** the amount of income remaining after subtracting the firm's income-tax expense, is less than its **before-tax income.** This fact is expressed in the following formula.

LO11

After completing the appendix, understand the effect of income taxes on CVP analysis.

(After-tax net income) = (Before-tax income) − t(Before-tax income)

where t denotes the income-tax rate.

Rearranging this equation yields the following formula.

(After-tax net income) = (Before-tax income) (1 − t) (9)

To illustrate this formula, suppose AccuTime Company must pay income taxes of 40 percent of its before-tax income. The company's contribution income statement for 20x1 appears below.

Sales, 20,000 units at $25 each	$500,000
Variable expenses, 20,000 units at $15 each*	300,000
Contribution margin	$200,000
Fixed expenses	150,000
Income before taxes	$ 50,000
Income-tax expense, .40 × $50,000	20,000
Net income, $50,000 × (1 − .40)	$ 30,000

*Variable cost per unit is $15: variable manufacturing cost of $14 plus variable selling and administrative costs of $1.

The requirement that companies pay income taxes affects their cost-volume-profit relationships. To earn a particular after-tax net income will require greater before-tax income than if there were no tax. For example, if AccuTime's target after-tax net income were $30,000, the company would have to earn before-tax income of $50,000. AccuTime's income statement shows this relationship.

How much before-tax income must be earned in order to achieve a particular target after-tax net income? Rearranging equation (9) above yields the following formula.

$$\begin{matrix}\text{Target}\\ \text{after-tax}\\ \text{net income}\end{matrix} = \left(\begin{matrix}\text{Target}\\ \text{before-tax}\\ \text{income}\end{matrix}\right)(1 - t)$$

Divide both sides by $(1 - t)$

$$\frac{\begin{matrix}\text{Target}\\ \text{after-tax}\\ \text{net income}\end{matrix}}{1 - t} = \left(\begin{matrix}\text{Target}\\ \text{before-tax}\\ \text{income}\end{matrix}\right)\frac{1 - t}{1 - t}$$

$$\frac{\begin{matrix}\text{Target}\\ \text{after-tax}\\ \text{net income}\end{matrix}}{1 - t} = \begin{matrix}\text{Target}\\ \text{before-tax}\\ \text{income}\end{matrix}$$

If AccuTime Company's target after-tax net income is $30,000, its target before-tax income is calculated as follows:

$$\frac{\begin{matrix}\text{Target after-tax}\\ \text{net income}\end{matrix}}{1 - t} = \frac{\$30{,}000}{1 - .40} = \$50{,}000 = \text{Target before-tax income}$$

Now we are in a position to compute the number of digital clocks that AccuTime must sell in order to achieve a particular after-tax net income. We begin with the following before-tax income equation.

$$\text{Sales} - \text{Variable expenses} - \text{Fixed expenses} = \text{Before-tax income}$$

Now we use our formula for before-tax income.

$$\text{Sales} - \text{Variable expenses} - \text{Fixed expenses} = \frac{\text{After-tax net income}}{1 - t}$$

$$\left[\left(\begin{matrix}\text{Unit}\\ \text{sales}\\ \text{price}\end{matrix}\right) \times \left(\begin{matrix}\text{Sales}\\ \text{volume}\\ \text{in units}\end{matrix}\right)\right] - \left[\left(\begin{matrix}\text{Unit}\\ \text{variable}\\ \text{expense}\end{matrix}\right) \times \left(\begin{matrix}\text{Sales}\\ \text{volume}\\ \text{in units}\end{matrix}\right)\right] - \left(\begin{matrix}\text{Fixed}\\ \text{expenses}\end{matrix}\right) = \frac{\begin{matrix}\text{After-tax}\\ \text{net income}\end{matrix}}{1 - t}$$

Using the data for AccuTime Company, and assuming target after-tax net income of $30,000:

$$(\$25 \times X) - (\$15 \times X) - \$150{,}000 = \frac{\$30{,}000}{1 - .40}$$

where X denotes the number of units that must be sold to achieve the target after-tax net income.

Now we solve for X as follows:

$$\underbrace{(\$25 - \$15)} \times X = \$150{,}000 + \frac{\$30{,}000}{1 - .40}$$

$$\$10 \quad \times X = \$150{,}000 + \frac{\$30{,}000}{1 - .40}$$

$$X = \frac{\$150{,}000 + \dfrac{\$30{,}000}{1 - .40}}{\$10}$$

$$= 20{,}000 \text{ units}$$

In terms of sales revenue, AccuTime must achieve a sales volume of $500,000 (20,000 units × $25 sales price). We can verify these calculations by examining AccuTime's income statement given previously.

Notice in the calculations above that $10 is the unit contribution margin ($25 sales price minus $15 variable expense). Thus, the general formula illustrated above is the following:

$$\text{Number of units of sales required to earn target after-tax net income} = \frac{\text{Fixed expenses} + \dfrac{\text{Target after-tax net income}}{1 - t}}{\text{Unit contribution margin}}$$

where t denotes the income tax rate.

A cost-volume-profit graph for AccuTime Company is displayed in Exhibit 8–11. As the graph shows, 20,000 units must be sold to achieve $30,000 in after-tax net income. The company's break-even point is 15,000 units. The break-even point is not affected by income taxes, because at the break-even point, there is no income.

Notice that AccuTime Company must sell 5,000 units *beyond the break-even point* in order to achieve after-tax net income of $30,000. Each unit sold beyond the break-even point contributes $10 toward *before-tax* income. However, of that $10 contribution margin, $4 will have to be paid in income taxes. This leaves an *after-tax contribution* of $6 toward after-tax net income. Thus, selling 5,000 units beyond the break-even point results in after-tax net income of $30,000 (5,000 units × $6 after-tax contribution per unit).

Exhibit 8–11
Cost-Volume-Profit Graph (with income taxes)

AccuTime Company

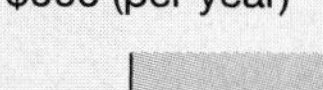

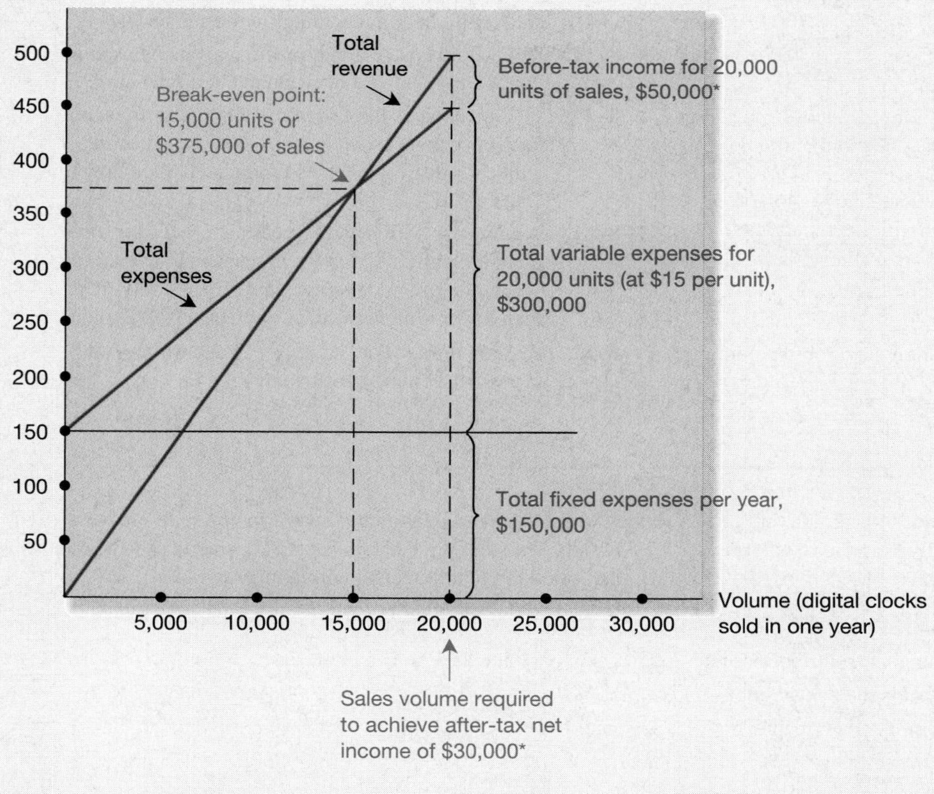

* (Before-tax income) × (1 – Tax rate) = After-tax income

$50,000 × (1 – .40) = $30,000

Review Questions

8–1. Briefly explain each of the following methods of computing a break-even point in units: (*a*) contribution-margin approach, (*b*) equation approach, and (*c*) graphical approach.

8–2. What is the meaning of the term *unit contribution margin?* Contribution to what?

8–3. What information is conveyed by a cost-volume-profit graph in addition to a company's break-even point?

8–4. What does the term *safety margin* mean?

8–5. Suppose the fixed expenses of a travel agency increase. What will happen to its break-even point, measured in number of clients served? Why?

8–6. Delmarva Oyster Company has been able to decrease its variable expenses per pound of oysters harvested. How will this affect the firm's break-even sales volume?

8–7. In a strategy meeting, a manufacturing company's president said, "If we raise the price of our product, the company's break-even point will be lower." The financial vice president responded by saying, "Then we should raise our price. The company will be less likely to incur a loss." Do you agree with the president? Why? Do you agree with the financial vice president? Why?

8–8. What will happen to a company's break-even point if the sales price and unit variable cost of its only product increase by the same dollar amount?

8–9. An art museum covers its operating expenses by charging a small admission fee. The objective of the nonprofit organization is to break even. A local arts enthusiast has just pledged an annual donation of $10,000 to the museum. How will the donation affect the museum's break-even attendance level?

8–10. How can a profit-volume graph be used to predict a company's profit for a particular sales volume?

8–11. List the most important assumptions of cost-volume-profit analysis.

8–12. Why do many operating managers prefer a contribution income statement instead of a traditional income statement?

8–13. What is the difference between a manufacturing company's *gross margin* and its total *contribution margin*?

8–14. East Company manufactures VCRs using a completely automated production process. West Company also manufactures VCRs, but its products are assembled manually. How will these two firms' cost structures differ? Which company will have a higher operating leverage factor?

8–15. When sales volume increases, which company will experience a larger percentage increase in profit: company X, which has mostly fixed expenses, or company Y, which has mostly variable expenses?

8–16. What does the term *sales mix* mean? How is a *weighted-average unit contribution margin* computed?

8–17. A car rental agency rents subcompact, compact, and full-size automobiles. What assumptions would be made about the agency's sales mix for the purpose of a cost-volume-profit analysis?

8–18. How can a hotel's management use cost-volume-profit analysis to help in deciding on room rates?

8–19. How could cost-volume-profit analysis be used in budgeting? In making a decision about advertising?

8–20. Two companies have identical fixed expenses, unit variable expenses, and profits. Yet one company has set a much lower price for its product. Explain how this can happen.

8–21. A company with an advanced manufacturing environment typically will have a higher break-even point, greater operating leverage, and larger safety margin than a labor-intensive firm. True or false? Explain.

8–22. Explain briefly how activity-based costing (ABC) affects cost-volume-profit analysis.

Exercises

Exercise 8–23
Basic CVP Analysis; Pizza Delivery Business
(LO 1, 2, 4)

University Pizza delivers pizzas to the dormitories and apartments near a major state university. The company's annual fixed expenses are $54,000. The sales price of a pizza is $10, and it costs the company $6 to make and deliver each pizza. (In the following requirements, ignore income taxes.)

Required:

1. Using the contribution-margin approach, compute the company's break-even point in units (pizzas).
2. What is the contribution-margin ratio?
3. Compute the break-even sales revenue. Use the contribution-margin ratio in your calculation.
4. How many pizzas must the company sell to earn a target net profit of $60,000? Use the equation method.

Exercise 8–24
Fill in Blanks; Basic CVP Relationships
(LO 1)

Fill in the missing data for each of the following independent cases. (Ignore income taxes.)

	Sales Revenue	Variable Expenses	Total Contribution Margin	Fixed Expenses	Net Income	Break-Even Sales Revenue
1.	?	$120,000	$240,000	?	$150,000	?
2.	$ 55,000	$ 11,000	?	?	19,000	?

(continues)

3.	?	80,000	?	$60,000	?	$ 80,000
4.	160,000	?	30,000	?	?	160,000

Exercise 8–25
CVP Graph; Sports Franchise
(LO 3, 4)

The Dallas Armadillos, a minor-league baseball team, play their weekly games in a small stadium just outside Dallas. The stadium holds 6,000 people and tickets sell for $20 each. The franchise owner estimates that the team's annual fixed expenses are $360,000, and the variable expense per ticket sold is $2. (In the following requirements, ignore income taxes.)

Required:

1. Draw a cost-volume-profit graph for the sports franchise. Label the axes, break-even point, profit and loss areas, fixed expenses, variable expenses, total-expense line, and total-revenue line.
2. If the stadium is two-thirds full for each game, how many games must the team play to break even?

Exercise 8–26
Continuation of Preceding Exercise; Profit-Volume Graph; Safety Margin
(LO 3, 4)

Refer to the data given in the preceding exercise. (Ignore income taxes.)

Required:

1. Prepare a fully labeled profit-volume graph for the Dallas Armadillos.
2. What is the safety margin for the baseball franchise if the team plays a 10-game season and the team owner expects the stadium to be 45 percent full for each game?
3. If the team plays a 10-game season and the stadium is 40 percent full for each game, what ticket price would the team have to charge in order to break even?

Exercise 8–27
Using CVP Analysis; Manufacturing
(LO 1, 4)

Rosario Company, which is located in Buenos Aires, Argentina, manufactures a component used in farm machinery. The firm's fixed costs are 2,000,000 *p* per year. The variable cost of each component is 1,000 *p*, and the components are sold for 1,500 *p* each. The company sold 7,000 components during the prior year. (*p* denotes the peso, Argentina's national currency. Several countries use the peso as their monetary unit. On the day this exercise was written, Argentina's peso was worth 1.003 U.S. dollars. In the following requirements, ignore income taxes.)

Required: Answer requirements (1) through (4) independently.

1. Compute the break-even point in units.
2. What will the new break-even point be if fixed costs increase by 5 percent?
3. What was the company's net income for the prior year?
4. The sales manager believes that a reduction in the sales price to 1,400 *p* will result in orders for 1,000 more components each year. What will the break-even point be if the price is changed?
5. Should the price change discussed in requirement (4) be made? Explain.

Exercise 8–28
Contribution Income Statement; Publishing
(LO 7, 8)

Pacific Rim Publications, Inc. specializes in reference books that keep abreast of political and economic issues in the Pacific Rim countries. The results of the company's operations during the prior year are given in the following table. All units produced during the year were sold. (Ignore income taxes.)

Sales revenue	$1,000,000
Manufacturing costs:	
Fixed	250,000
Variable	500,000
Selling costs:	
Fixed	25,000
Variable	50,000
Administrative costs:	
Fixed	60,000
Variable	15,000

Required:

1. Prepare a traditional income statement and a contribution income statement for the company.
2. What is the firm's operating leverage for the sales volume generated during the prior year?
3. Suppose sales revenue increases by 12 percent. What will be the percentage increase in net income?
4. Which income statement would an operating manager use to answer requirement (3)? Why?

Exercise 8–29
Cost-Volume-Profit Analysis in an Airline; Use of Internet
(LO 4)

Use the Internet to access the website of one of these airlines, or a different airline of your choosing.

American Airlines	www.americanair.com
British Airways	www.british-airways.com
Delta Air Lines	www.delta-air.com
Northwest Airlines	www.nwa.com
Southwest Airlines	www.southwestair.com

Required: Find the company's most recent annual report. Does the management discussion in the report disclose the airline's break-even load factor? If so, what is it for the most recent year reported?

Exercise 8–30
CVP Analysis with Multiple Products; Retail
(LO 1, 5)

Brad's Bicycle Shop sells 21-speed bicycles. For purposes of a cost-volume-profit analysis, the shop owner has divided sales into two categories, as follows:

Product Type	Sales Price	Invoice Cost	Sales Commission
High-quality	$1,000	$550	$50
Medium-quality	600	270	30

Seventy percent of the shop's sales are medium-quality bikes. The shop's annual fixed expenses are $148,500. (In the following requirements, ignore income taxes.)

Required:

1. Compute the unit contribution margin for each product type.
2. What is the shop's sales mix?
3. Compute the weighted-average unit contribution margin, assuming a constant sales mix.
4. What is the shop's break-even sales volume in dollars? Assume a constant sales mix.
5. How many bicycles of each type must be sold to earn a target net income of $99,000? Assume a constant sales mix.

Exercise 8–31
Cost Structure and Operating Leverage; Hotel and Restaurant
(LO 8)

A contribution income statement for the La Jolla Inn is shown below. (Ignore income taxes.)

Revenue	$1,500,000
Less: Variable expenses	900,000
Contribution margin	$ 600,000
Less: Fixed expenses	450,000
Net income	$ 150,000

Required:

1. Show the hotel's cost structure by indicating the percentage of the hotel's revenue represented by each item on the income statement.
2. Suppose the hotel's revenue declines by 20 percent. Use the contribution-margin percentage to calculate the resulting decrease in net income.
3. What is the hotel's operating leverage factor when revenue is $1,500,000?
4. Use the operating leverage factor to calculate the increase in net income resulting from a 25 percent increase in sales revenue.

Exercise 8–32
Continuation of Preceding Exercise
(LO 7)

Refer to the income statement given in the preceding exercise. Prepare a new contribution income statement for the La Jolla Inn in each of the following independent situations. (Ignore income taxes.)

1. The hotel's volume of activity increases by 25 percent, and fixed expenses increase by 50 percent.
2. The ratio of variable expenses to revenue doubles. There is no change in the hotel's volume of activity. Fixed expenses decline by $100,000.

Exercise 8–33
CVP Analysis with Income Taxes; Consulting Firm (Appendix)
(LO 1, 4, 11)

Power Grid Engineering Associates, Inc. provides consulting services to commercial electric utilities. The consulting firm's contribution-margin ratio is 25 percent, and its annual fixed expenses are $200,000. The firm's income-tax rate is 40 percent.

Required:

1. Calculate the firm's break-even volume of service revenue.
2. How much before-tax income must the firm earn to make an after-tax net income of $120,000?
3. What level of revenue for consulting services must the firm generate to earn an after-tax net income of $120,000?
4. Suppose the firm's income-tax rate declines to 35 percent. What will happen to the break-even level of consulting service revenue?

Problems

Problem 8–34
Basic CVP Computations
(LO 1, 2, 4)

ScholarPak Company produced and sold 70,000 backpacks during the year just ended at an average price of $30 per unit. Variable manufacturing costs were $12 per unit, and variable marketing costs were $6 per unit sold. Fixed costs amounted to $540,000 for manufacturing and $216,000 for marketing. There was no year-end work-in-process inventory. (Ignore income taxes.)

Required:

1. Compute ScholarPak's break-even point in sales dollars for the year.
2. Compute the number of sales units required to earn a net income of $540,000 during the year.
3. ScholarPak's variable manufacturing costs are expected to increase by 10 percent in the coming year. Compute the firm's break-even point in sales dollars for the coming year.
4. If ScholarPak's variable manufacturing costs do increase by 10 percent, compute the selling price that would yield the same contribution-margin ratio in the coming year.

(CMA, adapted)

Problem 8–35
Basic CVP Relationships
(LO 1, 2, 4)

Surreal Sound, Inc. manufactures and sells compact disks. Price and cost data are as follows:

Selling price per unit (package of two CDs)	$25.00
Variable costs per unit:	
Direct material	$8.20
Direct labor	4.00
Manufacturing overhead	6.00
Selling expenses	1.60
Total variable costs per unit	$19.80
Annual fixed costs:	
Manufacturing overhead	$ 288,000
Selling and administrative	414,000
Total fixed costs	$ 702,000
Forecasted annual sales volume (140,000 units)	$3,500,000

In the following requirements, ignore income taxes.

Required:

1. What is Surreal Sound's break-even point in units?
2. What is the company's break-even point in sales dollars?
3. How many units would Surreal Sound have to sell in order to earn $390,000?
4. What is the firm's margin of safety?
5. Management estimates that direct-labor costs will increase by 10 percent next year. How many units will the company have to sell next year to reach its break-even point?
6. If the company's direct-labor costs do increase by 10 percent, what selling price per unit of product must it charge to maintain the same contribution-margin ratio?

(CMA, adapted)

Problem 8–36
Basic CVP Relationships; Retailer
(LO 1, 2, 4)

Detroit Disk, Inc. is a retailer for digital video disks. The projected net income for the current year is $600,000 based on a sales volume of 400,000 video disks. Detroit Disk has been selling the disks for $24 each. The variable costs consist of the $15 unit purchase price of the disks and a handling cost of $3 per disk. Detroit Disk's annual fixed costs are $1,800,000.

Management is planning for the coming year, when it expects that the unit purchase price of the video disks will increase 30 percent. (Ignore income taxes.)

Required:

1. Calculate Detroit Disk's break-even point for the *current year* in number of video disks.
2. What will be the company's net income for the *current year* if there is a 10 percent increase in projected unit sales volume?
3. What volume of sales (in dollars) must Detroit Disk achieve in the *coming year* to maintain the same net income as projected for the current year if the unit selling price remains at $24, but the unit purchase price of the disks increases by 30 percent as expected?
4. In order to cover a 30 percent increase in the disk's purchase price for the *coming year* and still maintain the current contribution-margin ratio, what selling price per disk must Detroit Disk establish for the coming year?

(CMA, adapted)

Problem 8–37
CVP Relationships; Indifference Point
(LO 1, 4)

Korosa and Delancey, Ltd. is studying the acquisition of two electrical component insertion systems for producing its sole product, the universal gismo. Data relevant to the systems follow.

Model A:
- Variable costs, $8.00 per unit
- Annual fixed costs, $1,971,200

Model B:
- Variable costs, $6.40 per unit
- Annual fixed costs, $2,227,200

Korosa and Delancey's selling price is $32 per unit for the universal gismo, which is subject to a 5 percent sales commission. (In the following requirements, ignore income taxes.)

Required:

1. How many units must the company sell to break even if Model A is selected?
2. Which of the two systems would be more profitable if sales and production are expected to average 184,000 units per year?
3. Assume Model B requires the purchase of additional equipment that is not reflected in the preceding figures. The equipment will cost $900,000 and will be depreciated over a five-year life by the straight-line method. How many units must the company sell to earn $1,912,800 of income if Model B is selected?
4. Ignoring the information presented in requirement (3), at what volume level will management be indifferent between the acquisition of Model A and Model B? In other words, at what volume level will the annual total cost of each system be equal?

Problem 8–38
CVP Relationships; Retail
(LO 1, 4)

Boundaries, a chain of retail stores, sells books and music CDs. Condensed monthly income data are presented in the following table for November 20x4. (Ignore income taxes.)

	Downtown Store	Mall Store	Total
Sales	$240,000	$360,000	$600,000
Less: Variable expenses	96,000	252,000	348,000
Contribution margin	$144,000	$108,000	$252,000
Less: Fixed expenses	60,000	120,000	180,000
Operating income	$ 84,000	$(12,000)	$ 72,000

Additional information:

- Management estimates that closing the mall store would result in a 10 percent decrease in downtown store sales, while closing the downtown store would not affect mall store sales.

- One-fourth of each store's fixed expenses would continue through December 31, 20x5, if either store were closed.
- The operating results for November 20x4 are representative of all months.

Required:

1. Calculate the increase or decrease in Boundaries' monthly operating income during 20x5 if the mall store is closed.
2. The management of Boundaries is considering a promotional campaign at the mall store that would not affect the downtown store. Annual promotional expenses at the mall store would be increased by $180,000 in order to increase mall store sales by 10 percent. What would be the effect of this promotional campaign on the company's monthly operating income during 20x5?
3. One-half of the mall store's dollar sales are from items sold at their variable cost to attract customers to the store. Boundaries' management is considering the deletion of these items, a move that would reduce the mall store's direct fixed expenses by 15 percent and result in the loss of 20 percent of the remaining mall store's sales volume. This change would not affect the downtown store. What would be the effect on Boundaries' monthly operating income if the items sold at their variable cost are eliminated?

(CMA, adapted)

Problem 8–39
Sales Mix and Employee Compensation; Operating Changes
(LO 4, 5, 7)

Premier Corporation sells two models of home ice cream makers, Mister Ice Cream and Cold King. Current sales total 60,000 units, consisting of 21,000 Mister Ice Cream units and 39,000 Cold King units. Selling price and variable cost information follows.

	Mister Ice Cream	Cold King
Selling price	$37.00	$43.00
Variable cost	20.50	32.50

Salespeople currently receive flat salaries that total $200,000. Management is contemplating a change to a compensation plan that is based on commissions in an effort to boost the company's presence in the marketplace. Two plans are under consideration:

Plan A: 10% commission computed on gross dollar sales. Mister Ice Cream sales are anticipated to be 19,500 units. Cold King sales are expected to total 45,500 units.

Plan B: 30% commission computed on the basis of production contribution margins. Mister Ice Cream sales are expected to total 39,000 units. Cold King sales are anticipated to be 26,000 units.

Required:

1. Define the term *sales mix.*
2. Comparing Plan A to the current compensation arrangement:
   a. Will Plan A achieve management's objective of an increased presence in the marketplace? Briefly explain.
   b. From a sales-mix perspective, will the salespeople be promoting the product that one would logically expect? Briefly discuss.
   c. Will the sales force likely be satisfied with the results of Plan A? Why?
   d. Will Premier likely be satisfied with the resulting impact of Plan A on company profitability? Why?
3. Assume that Plan B is under consideration.
   a. Compare Plan A and Plan B with respect to total units sold and the sales mix. Comment on the results.
   b. In comparison with flat salaries, is Plan B more attractive to the sales force? To the company? Show calculations to support your answers.

Problem 8–40
CVP Analysis; Impact of Operating Changes
(LO 1, 4)

Phoenix-based CompTronics manufactures audio speakers for desktop computers. The following data relate to the period just ended when the company produced and sold 42,000 speaker sets:

Sales	$4,032,000
Variable costs	1,008,000
Fixed costs	2,736,000

Management is considering relocating its manufacturing facilities to northern Mexico to reduce costs. Variable costs are expected to average $21.60 per set; annual fixed costs are anticipated to be $2,380,800. (In the following requirements, ignore income taxes.)

Required:

1. Calculate the company's current income and determine the level of dollar sales needed to double that figure, assuming that manufacturing operations remain in the United States.
2. Determine the break-even point in speaker sets if operations are shifted to Mexico.
3. Assume that management desires to achieve the Mexican break-even point; however, operations will remain in the United States.
   a. If variable costs remain constant, what must management do to fixed costs? By how much must fixed costs change?
   b. If fixed costs remain constant, what must management do to the variable cost per unit? By how much must unit variable cost change?
4. Determine the impact (increase, decrease, or no effect) of the following operating changes.
   a. Effect of an increase in direct material costs on the break-even point.
   b. Effect of an increase in fixed administrative costs on the unit contribution margin.
   c. Effect of an increase in the unit contribution margin on net income.
   d. Effect of a decrease in the number of units sold on the break-even point.

Problem 8–41
Break-Even Analysis; Profit-Volume Graph; Movie Theaters
(LO 1, 3, 4)

Hollywood Stars, Inc. owns and operates a nationwide chain of movie theaters. The chain's 450 properties vary from low-volume, small-town, single-screen theaters to high-volume, urban, multiscreen theaters. The firm's management is considering installing popcorn machines, which would allow the theaters to sell freshly popped corn rather than prepopped corn. The fresh popcorn will be sold for $3.50 per tub. The annual rental costs and the operating costs vary with the size of the popcorn machines. The machine capacities and costs are shown below. (Ignore income taxes.)

	Popper Model		
	Standard	**Super**	**Giant**
Annual capacity	40,000 tubs	80,000 tubs	120,000 tubs
Costs:			
Annual machine rental	$16,000.00	$22,000.00	$40,000.00
Popcorn cost per tub	.26	.26	.26
Other costs per tub	2.44	2.28	2.10
Cost of each tub	.16	.16	.16

Required:

1. Calculate a theater's break-even sales volume (measured in tubs of popcorn) for each model of popcorn popper.
2. Prepare a profit-volume graph for one theater's popcorn sales, assuming that the Giant Popper is purchased.
3. Calculate the volume (in tubs) at which the Standard Popper and the Super Popper earn the same profit or loss in each movie theater.

(CMA, adapted)

Problem 8–42
CVP Graph; Cost Structure; Operating Leverage
(LO 3, 4, 8)

SkiCo, Inc. manufactures ski boots. The company's projected income for the coming year, based on sales of 160,000 units, is as follows:

Sales		$16,000,000
Operating expenses:		
Variable expenses	$4,000,000	
Fixed expenses	6,000,000	
Total expenses		10,000,000
Net income		$ 6,000,000

Required: In completing the following requirements, ignore income taxes.

1. Prepare a CVP graph for SkiCo, Inc. for the coming year.
2. Calculate the firm's break-even point for the year in sales dollars.
3. What is the company's margin of safety for the year?
4. Compute SkiCo's operating leverage factor, based on the budgeted sales volume for the year.
5. Compute SkiCo's required sales in dollars in order to earn income of $9,000,000 in the coming year.
6. Describe the firm's cost structure. Calculate the percentage relationships between variable and fixed expenses and sales revenue.

(CMA, adapted)

Problem 8–43
Leverage; Analysis of Operating Change
(LO 4, 8)

PneumoTech, Inc. is studying the addition of a new valve to its product line. The valve would be used by manufacturers of pneumatic equipment. The company anticipates starting with a relatively low sales volume and then boosting demand over the next several years. A new salesperson must be hired because PneumoTech's current sales force is working at capacity. Two compensation plans are under consideration:

Plan A: An annual salary of $33,000 plus a 10% commission based on gross dollar sales.

Plan B: An annual salary of $99,000 and no commission.

PneumoTech, Inc. will purchase the valve for $75 and sell it for $120. Anticipated demand during the first year is 6,000 units. (In the following requirements, ignore income taxes.)

Required:

1. Compute PneumoTech's break-even point for Plan A and Plan B.
2. What is meant by the term "operating leverage"?
3. Analyze the cost structures of both plans at the anticipated demand of 6,000 units. Which of the two plans is more highly leveraged? Why?
4. Assume that a general economic downturn occurred during year 2, with product demand falling from 6,000 to 5,000 units. Determine the percentage decrease in company net income if PneumoTech had adopted Plan A.
5. Repeat requirement (4) for Plan B. Compare Plan A and Plan B, and explain a major factor that underlies any resulting differences.
6. Briefly discuss the likely profitability impact of an economic recession for highly automated manufacturers. What can you say about the risk associated with these firms?

Problem 8–44
Break-Even Analysis; Operating Leverage; New Manufacturing Environment
(LO 1, 8, 10)

Zodiac Company has decided to introduce a new product, which can be manufactured by either a computer-assisted manufacturing system or a labor-intensive production system. The manufacturing method will not affect the quality of the product. The estimated manufacturing costs by the two methods are as follows:

	Labor-Intensive Production System		Computer-Assisted Manufacturing System	
Direct material		$8.40		$7.50
Direct labor	.8DLH @ $13.50	10.80	.5DLH @ $18.00	9.00
Variable overhead	.8DLH @ $9.00	7.20	.5DLH @ $9.00	4.50
Fixed overhead*		$1,980,000		$3,660,000

*These costs are directly traceable to the new product line. They would not be incurred if the new product were not produced.

The company's marketing research department has recommended an introductory unit sales price of $45. Selling expenses are estimated to be $750,000 annually plus $3 for each unit sold. (Ignore income taxes.)

Required:

1. Calculate Zodiac's estimated break-even point in annual unit sales of the new product if the company uses the (*a*) labor-intensive production system; (*b*) computer-assisted manufacturing system.
2. Determine the annual unit sales volume at which the firm would be indifferent between the two manufacturing methods.
3. Management must decide which manufacturing method to employ. One factor it should consider is operating leverage. Explain the concept of operating leverage. How is this concept related to Zodiac's decision?

4. Describe the circumstances under which the firm should employ each of the two manufacturing methods.
5. Identify some business factors other than operating leverage that management should consider before selecting the manufacturing method.

(CMA, adapted)

Problem 8–45
Break-Even Point; Safety Margin; Law Firm
(LO 1, 4)

Steven Clark and two of his colleagues are considering opening a law office in a large metropolitan area that would make inexpensive legal services available to those who could not otherwise afford services. The intent is to provide easy access for their clients by having the office open 360 days per year, 16 hours each day from 7:00 A.M. to 11:00 P.M. The office would be staffed by a lawyer, paralegal, legal secretary, and clerk-receptionist for each of the two eight-hour shifts.

In order to determine the feasibility of the project, Clark hired a marketing consultant to assist with market projections. The results of this study show that if the firm spends $980,000 on advertising the first year, the number of new clients expected each day will be 50. Clark and his associates believe this number is reasonable and are prepared to spend the $980,000 on advertising. Other pertinent information about the operation of the office follows:

- The only charge to each new client would be $60 for the initial consultation. All cases that warrant further legal work will be accepted on a contingency basis with the firm earning 30 percent of any favorable settlements or judgments. Clark estimates that 20 percent of new client consultations will result in favorable settlements or judgments averaging $4,000 each. It is not expected that there will be repeat clients during the first year of operations.
- The hourly wages of the staff are projected to be $50 for the lawyer, $40 for the paralegal, $30 for the legal secretary, and $20 for the clerk-receptionist. Fringe benefit expense will be 40 percent of the wages paid. A total of 400 hours of overtime is expected for the year; this will be divided equally between the legal secretary and the clerk-receptionist positions. Overtime will be paid at one and one-half times the regular wage, and the fringe benefit expense will apply to the full wage.
- Clark has located 6,000 square feet of suitable office space which rents for $56 per square foot annually. Associated expenses will be $54,000 for property insurance and $74,000 for utilities.
- It will be necessary for the group to purchase malpractice insurance, which is expected to cost $360,000 annually.
- The initial investment in the office equipment will be $120,000. This equipment has an estimated useful life of four years.
- The cost of office supplies has been estimated to be $8 per expected new client consultation.

Required:

1. Determine how many new clients must visit the law office being considered by Steven Clark and his colleagues in order for the venture to break even during its first year of operations.
2. Compute the law firm's safety margin.

(CMA, adapted)

Problem 8–46
CVP Analysis of Changes in Sales Prices and Costs
(LO 1, 4)

Saturn Game Company manufactures computer games. Last year Saturn sold 25,000 games at $50 each. Total costs amounted to $1,050,000 of which $300,000 were considered fixed.

In an attempt to improve its product, the company is considering replacing a component part that has a cost of $5 with a new and better part costing $9 per unit in the coming year. A new machine would also be needed to increase plant capacity. The machine would cost $36,000 with a useful life of six years and no salvage value. The company uses straight-line depreciation on all plant assets. (Ignore income taxes.)

Required:

1. What was Saturn Game Company's break-even point in number of units last year?
2. How many units of product would the company have had to sell in the last year to earn $280,000?
3. If management holds the sales price constant and makes the suggested changes, how many units of product must be sold in the coming year to break even?

4. If the firm holds the sales price constant and makes the suggested changes, how many units of product will the company have to sell to make the same net income as last year?
5. If Saturn Game Company wishes to maintain the same contribution-margin ratio, what selling price per unit of product must it charge next year to cover the increased direct-material cost?

(CMA, adapted)

Problem 8–47
Continuation of Preceding Problem; Activity-Based Costing; Advanced Manufacturing Systems; Ethical Issues
(LO 1, 4, 9, 10)

Refer to the original data given for Saturn Game Company in the preceding problem. An activity-based costing study has revealed that Saturn's $300,000 of fixed costs include the following components:

Setup (40 setups at $800 per setup)	$ 32,000
Engineering (500 hours at $50 per hour)	25,000
Inspection (1,000 inspections at $60 per inspection)	60,000
General factory overhead	123,000
Total	$240,000
Fixed selling and administrative costs	60,000
Total fixed costs	$300,000

Management is considering the installation of new, highly automated manufacturing equipment that would significantly alter the production process. In addition, management plans a move toward just-in-time inventory and production management. If the new equipment is installed, setups will be quicker and less expensive. Under the proposed JIT approach, there would be 300 setups per year at $100 per setup. Since a total quality control program would accompany the move toward JIT, only 100 inspections would be anticipated annually, at a cost of $90 each. After the installation of the new production system, 800 hours of engineering would be required at a cost of $56 per hour. General factory overhead would increase to $332,200. However, the automated equipment would allow Saturn to cut its unit variable cost by 20 percent. Moreover, the more consistent product quality anticipated would allow management to raise the price of computer games to $52 per unit. (Ignore income taxes.)

Required:

1. Upon seeing the ABC analysis given in the problem, Saturn Game Company's vice president for manufacturing exclaimed to the controller, "I thought you told me this $300,000 cost was fixed. These don't look like fixed costs at all. What you're telling me now is that setup costs us $800 every time we set up a production run. What gives?"
   As Saturn's controller, write a short memo explaining to the vice president what is going on.
2. Compute Saturn's new break-even point if the proposed automated equipment is installed.
3. Determine how many units Saturn will have to sell to show a profit of $280,000, assuming the new technology is adopted.
4. If Saturn adopts the new manufacturing technology, will its break-even point be higher or lower? Will the number of sales units required to earn a profit of $280,000 be higher or lower? (Refer to your answers for the first two requirements of the preceding problem.) Are the results in this case consistent with what you would typically expect to find? Explain.
5. The decision as to whether to purchase the automated manufacturing equipment will be made by Saturn's board of directors. In order to support the proposed acquisition, the vice president for manufacturing asked the controller to prepare a report on the financial implications of the decision. As part of the report, the vice president asked the controller to compute the new break-even point, assuming the installation of the equipment. The controller complied, as in requirement (2) of this problem.
   When the vice president for manufacturing saw that the break-even point would increase, he asked the controller to delete the break-even analysis from the report. What should the controller do? Which ethical standards for managerial accountants are involved here?

Problem 8–48
CVP Relationships; International Business; Automation
(LO 1, 4, 10)

Central Pennsylvania Limestone Company produces thin limestone sheets used for cosmetic facing on buildings. The following income statement represents the operating results for the year just ended. The company had sales of 1,800 tons during the year. The manufacturing capacity of the firm's facilities is 3,000 tons per year. (Ignore income taxes.)

CENTRAL PENNSYLVANIA LIMESTONE COMPANY
Income Statement
For the Year Ended December 31, 20x4

Sales	$1,800,000
Variable costs:	
Manufacturing	$ 630,000
Selling costs	360,000
Total variable costs	$ 990,000
Contribution margin	$ 810,000
Fixed costs:	
Manufacturing	$ 200,000
Selling	215,000
Administrative	80,000
Total fixed costs	$ 495,000
Net income	$ 315,000

Required:

1. Calculate the company's break-even volume in tons for 20x4.
2. If the sales volume is estimated to be 2,100 tons in the next year, and if the prices and costs stay at the same levels and amounts, what is the net income that management can expect for 20x5?
3. Central Pennsylvania Limestone has been trying to get a foothold in the European market. The company has a potential German customer that has offered to buy 1,500 tons at $900 per ton. Assume that all of the firm's costs would be at the same levels and rates as in 20x4. What net income would the firm earn if it took this order and rejected some business from regular customers so as not to exceed capacity?
4. Central Pennsylvania Limestone plans to market its product in a new territory. Management estimates that an advertising and promotion program costing $123,000 annually would be needed for the next two or three years. In addition, a $50 per ton sales commission to the sales force in the new territory, over and above the current commission, would be required. How many tons would have to be sold in the new territory to maintain the firm's current net income? Assume that sales and costs will continue as in 20x4 in the firm's established territories.
5. Management is considering replacing its labor-intensive process with an automated production system. This would result in an increase of $117,000 annually in fixed manufacturing costs. The variable manufacturing costs would decrease by $50 per ton. Compute the new break-even volume in tons and in sales dollars.
6. Ignore the facts presented in requirement (5). Assume that management estimates that the selling price per ton would decline by 10 percent next year. Variable costs would increase by $80 per ton, and fixed costs would not change. What sales volume in dollars would be required to earn a net income of $189,000 next year?

(CMA, adapted)

Problem 8–49
CVP; Multiple Products; Changes in Costs and Sales Mix
(LO 4, 5)

Toledo Tool Company (TTC) manufactures a line of electric garden tools that are sold in general hardware stores. The company's controller, Will Fulton, has just received the sales forecast for the coming year for TTC's three products: hedge clippers, line trimmers, and leaf blowers. TTC has experienced considerable variations in sales volumes and variable costs over the past two years, and Fulton believes the forecast should be carefully evaluated from a cost-volume-profit viewpoint. The preliminary budget information for 20x4 follows:

	Hedge Clippers	Line Trimmers	Leaf Blowers
Unit sales	50,000	50,000	100,000
Unit selling price	$84	$108	$144
Variable manufacturing cost per unit	39	36	75
Variable selling cost per unit	15	12	18

For 20x4, TTC's fixed manufacturing overhead is budgeted at $6,000,000, and the company's fixed selling and administrative expenses are forecasted to be $1,800,000. TTC has a tax rate of 40 percent.

Required:

1. Determine TTC Company's budgeted net income for 20x4.
2. Assuming the sales mix remains as budgeted, determine how many units of each product TTC must sell in order to break even in 20x4.
3. After preparing the original estimates, management determined that its variable manufacturing cost of leaf blowers would increase by 20 percent, and the variable selling cost of line trimmers could be expected to increase by $3 per unit. However, management has decided not to change the selling price of either product. In addition, management has learned that its leaf blower has been perceived as the best value on the market, and it can expect to sell three times as many leaf blowers as each of its other products. Under these circumstances, determine how many units of each product TTC would have to sell in order to break even in 20x4.

(CMA, adapted)

Problem 8–50
Break-Even Point; After-Tax Net Income; Profit-Volume Graph; International Issues (Appendix)
(LO 1, 2, 3, 4, 11)

The Asian Division of Worldwide Reference Corporation produces a pocket dictionary containing popular phrases in six Asian languages. Annual budget data for the coming year follow. Projected sales are 100,000 books.

	Variable	Fixed	
Sales			$2,000,000
Costs:			
Direct material	$ 600,000	$ –0–	
Direct labor	400,000	–0–	
Manufacturing overhead	300,000	200,000	
Selling and administrative	100,000	220,000	
Total costs	$1,400,000	$420,000	1,820,000
Budgeted operating income			$ 180,000

Required:

1. Calculate the break-even point in units and in sales dollars.
2. If the Asian Division is subject to an income-tax rate of 40 percent, compute the number of units the division would have to sell to earn an after-tax profit of $180,000.
3. If fixed costs increased $63,000 with no other cost or revenue factor changing, compute the division's break-even sales in units.
4. Assuming the original data, prepare a profit-volume graph for the Asian Division.
5. Due to an unstable political situation in the country in which the Asian Division is located, management believes the country may split into two independent nations. If this happens, the tax rate could rise to 50 percent. Assuming all other data as in the original problem, how many pocket dictionaries must be sold to earn $180,000 after taxes?

(CMA, adapted)

Problem 8–51
Cost-Volume-Profit Analysis with Income Taxes and Multiple Products (Appendix)
(LO 1, 2, 4, 5, 11)

Great Northern Ski Company recently expanded its manufacturing capacity. The firm will now be able to produce up to 15,000 pairs of cross-country skis of either the mountaineering model or the touring model. The sales department assures management that it can sell between 9,000 and 13,000 units of either product this year. Because the models are very similar, the company will produce only one of the two models.

The following information was compiled by the accounting department.

	Model	
	Touring	Mountaineering
Selling price per unit	$132.00	$120.00
Variable costs per unit	79.20	79.20

Fixed costs will total $554,400 if the touring model is produced but will be only $475,200 if the mountaineering model is produced. Great Northern Ski Company is subject to a 40 percent income tax rate. (Round each answer to the nearest whole number.)

Required:

1. Compute the contribution-margin ratio for the mountaineering model.

2. If Great Northern Ski Company desires an after-tax net income of $33,120, how many pairs of mountaineering skis will the company have to sell?
3. How much would the variable cost per unit of the mountaineering model have to change before it had the same break-even point in units as the touring model?
4. Suppose the variable cost per unit of mountaineering skis decreases by 10 percent, and the total fixed cost of mountaineering skis increases by 10 percent. Compute the new break-even point.
5. Suppose management decided to produce both products. If the two models are sold in equal proportions, and total fixed costs amount to $514,800, what is the firm's break-even point in units?

(CMA, adapted)

Problem 8–52
CVP Analysis; Marketing Decisions; Income Taxes (Appendix)
(LO 1, 4, 11)

Seattle Telecom, Inc. manufactures telecommunications equipment. The company has always been production oriented and sells its products through agents. Agents are paid a commission of 15 percent of the selling price. Seattle Telecom's budgeted income statement for 20x5 follows:

SEATTLE TELECOM, INC.
Budgeted Income Statement
For the Year Ended December 31, 20x5
(in thousands)

Sales		$24,000
Manufacturing costs:		
Variable	$10,800	
Fixed overhead	3,510	14,310
Gross margin		$ 9,690
Selling and administrative expenses:		
Commissions	$ 3,600	
Fixed marketing expenses	210	
Fixed administrative expenses	2,670	6,480
Net operating income		$ 3,210
Less fixed interest expense		810
Income before income taxes		$ 2,400
Less income taxes (30%)		720
Net income		$ 1,680

After the profit plan was completed for the coming year, Seattle Telecom's sales agents demanded that the commissions be increased to 22 ½ percent of the selling price. This demand was the latest in a series of actions that Vinnie McGraw, the company's president, believed had gone too far. He asked Maureen Elliott, the most sales-oriented officer in his production-oriented company, to estimate the cost to Seattle Telecom of employing its own sales force. Elliott's estimate of the additional annual cost of employing its own sales force, exclusive of commissions, follows. Sales personnel would receive a commission of 10 percent of the selling price in addition to their salary.

Estimated Annual Cost of
Employing a Company Sales Force
(in thousands)

Salaries:	
Sales manager	$ 150
Sales personnel	1,500
Travel and entertainment	600
Fixed marketing costs	1,350
Total	$3,600

Required:

1. Calculate Seattle Telecom's estimated break-even point in sales dollars for 20x5.
   a. If the events that are represented in the budgeted income statement take place.
   b. If the company employs its own sales force.
2. If Seattle Telecom continues to sell through agents and pays the increased commission of 22 ½ percent of the selling price, determine the estimated volume in sales dollars for 20x5 that would be required to generate the same net income as projected in the budgeted income statement.

3. Determine the estimated volume in sales dollars that would result in equal net income for 20x5 regardless of whether the company continues to sell through agents and pays a commission of 22 ½ percent of the selling price or employs its own sales force.

(CMA, adapted)

Problem 8–53
CVP Analysis with Production and Marketing Decisions; Taxes (Appendix)
(LO 1, 4, 11)

Columbus Canopy Company (CCC) manufactures and sells adjustable canopies that attach to motor homes and trailers. The market covers both new units as well as replacement canopies. CCC developed its 20x4 business plan based on the assumption that canopies would sell at a price of $800 each. The variable cost of each canopy is projected at $400, and the annual fixed costs are budgeted at $200,000. CCC's after-tax profit objective is $480,000; the company's tax rate is 40 percent.

While CCC's sales usually rise during the second quarter, the May financial statements reported that sales were not meeting expectations. For the first five months of the year, only 350 units had been sold at the established price, with variable costs as planned. It was clear the 20x4 after-tax profit projection would not be reached unless some actions were taken. CCC's president, Melanie Grand, assigned a management committee to analyze the situation and develop several alternative courses of action. The following mutually exclusive alternatives were presented to the president.

- Reduce the sales price by $80. The sales organization forecasts that with the significantly reduced sales price, 2,700 units can be sold during the remainder of the year. Total fixed and variable unit costs will stay as budgeted.
- Lower variable costs per unit by $50 through the use of less expensive raw materials and slightly modified manufacturing techniques. The sales price would also be reduced by $60, and sales of 2,200 units for the remainder of the year are forecast.
- Cut fixed costs by $20,000 and lower the sales price by 5 percent. Variable costs per unit will be unchanged. Sales of 2,000 units are expected for the remainder of the year.

Required:

1. If no changes are made to the selling price or cost structure, determine the number of units that Columbus Canopy Company must sell:
   a. In order to break even.
   b. To achieve its after-tax profit objective.
2. Determine which one of the alternatives management should select to achieve its annual after-tax profit objective.

(CMA, adapted)

Cases

Case 8–54
Break-Even Analysis; Hospital CVP Relationships
(LO 1, 4)

Susquehanna Medical Center operates a general hospital in northern Pennsylvania. The medical center also rents space and beds to separately owned entities rendering specialized services, such as Pediatrics and Psychiatric Care. Susquehanna charges each separate entity for common services, such as patients' meals and laundry, and for administrative services, such as billings and collections. Space and bed rentals are fixed charges for the year, based on bed capacity rented to each entity. Susquehanna Medical Center charged the following costs to Pediatrics for the year ended June 30, 20x5:

	Patient Days (variable)	Bed Capacity (fixed)
Dietary	$720,000	—
Janitorial	—	$ 84,000
Laundry	360,000	—
Laboratory	540,000	—
Pharmacy	420,000	—
Repairs and maintenance	—	36,000
General and administrative	—	1,560,000
Rent	—	1,800,000
Billings and collections	360,000	—
Total	$2,400,000	$3,480,000

During the year ended June 30, 20x5, Pediatrics charged each patient an average of $360 per day, had a capacity of 60 beds, and had revenue of $7.2 million for 365 days. In addition, Pediatrics directly employed personnel with the following annual salary costs per employee: supervising nurses, $30,000; nurses, $24,000; and aides, $10,800.

Susquehanna Medical Center has the following minimum departmental personnel requirements, based on total annual budgeted patient days:

Annual Patient Days	Supervising Nurses	Nurses	Aides
Up to 22,000	4	10	20
22,001 to 26,000	5	14	25
26,001 to 29,200	5	16	31

Pediatrics always employs only the minimum number of required personnel. Salaries of supervising nurses, nurses, and aides are therefore fixed within ranges of annual patient days.

Pediatrics operated at 100 percent capacity on 90 days during the year ended June 30, 20x5. Administrators estimate that on these 90 days, Pediatrics could have filled another 20 beds above capacity. Susquehanna Medical Center has an additional 20 beds available for rent for the year ending June 30, 20x6. Such additional rental would increase Pediatrics' fixed charges based on bed capacity. (In the following requirements, ignore income taxes.)

Required:

1. Calculate the minimum number of patient days required for Pediatrics to break even for the year ending June 30, 20x6, if the additional 20 beds are not rented. Patient demand is unknown, but assume that revenue per patient day, cost per patient day, cost per bed, and salary rates will remain the same as for the year ended June 30, 20x5.
2. Assume that patient demand, revenue per patient day, cost per patient day, cost per bed, and salary rates for the year ending June 30, 20x6 remain the same as for the year ended June 30, 20x5. Prepare a schedule of Pediatrics' increase in revenue and increase in costs for the year ending June 30, 20x6. Determine the net increase or decrease in Pediatrics' earnings from the additional 20 beds if Pediatrics rents this extra capacity from Susquehanna Medical Center.

(CPA, adapted)

Case 8–55
Sales Commissions in a Wholesale Firm; Income Taxes (Appendix)
(LO 1, 2, 4, 11)

Lake Champlain Sporting Goods Company, a wholesale supply company, engages independent sales agents to market the company's products throughout New York and Ontario. These agents currently receive a commission of 20 percent of sales, but they are demanding an increase to 25 percent of sales made during the year ending December 31, 20x4. The controller already prepared the 20x4 budget before learning of the agents' demand for an increase in commissions. The budgeted 20x4 income statement is shown below. Assume that cost of goods sold is 100 percent variable cost.

LAKE CHAMPLAIN SPORTING GOODS COMPANY
Budgeted Income Statement
For the Year Ended December 31, 20x4

Sales		$15,000,000
Cost of goods sold		9,000,000
Gross margin		$6,000,000
Selling and administrative expenses:		
Commissions	$3,000,000	
All other expenses (fixed)	150,000	3,150,000
Income before taxes		$2,850,000
Income tax (30%)		855,000
Net income		$1,995,000

The company's management is considering the possibility of employing full-time sales personnel. Three individuals would be required, at an estimated annual salary of $45,000 each, plus commissions of 5 percent of sales. In addition, two sales managers would be employed at fixed annual salaries of $120,000 each. All other fixed costs, as well as the variable cost percentages, would remain the same as the estimates in the 20x4 budgeted income statement.

Required:

1. Compute Lake Champlain Sporting Goods' estimated break-even point in sales dollars for the year ending December 31, 20x4, based on the budgeted income statement prepared by the controller.

2. Compute the estimated break-even point in sales dollars for the year ending December 31, 20x4, if the company employs its own sales personnel.
3. Compute the estimated volume in sales dollars that would be required for the year ending December 31, 20x4, to yield the same net income as projected in the budgeted income statement, if management continues to use the independent sales agents and agrees to their demand for a 25 percent sales commission.
4. Compute the estimated volume in sales dollars that would generate an identical net income for the year ending December 31, 20x4, regardless of whether Lake Champlain Sporting Goods Company employs its own sales personnel or continues to use the independent sales agents and pays them a 25 percent commission.

(CPA, adapted)

Current Issues in Managerial Accounting

Issue 8–56
Break Even

"Planes, Trains and Politicians," ***Business Week,*** **October 7, 2002, Allan Sloan.**

Overview

Amtrak has been criticized for not breaking even, but the airlines, which were in considerable difficulty even before the terrorist attacks of September 11, 2001, have been treated differently.

Suggested Discussion Questions

Discuss these questions as a group. Is the break-even concept being used appropriately by the politicians? Should the government subsidize Amtrak or the major airlines if they don't break even?

Issue 8–57
Cost Structure; Airline Industry

"To Redress Industry Blues, Delta Turns to Song," ***The Wall Street Journal,*** **January 29, 2003, p. A3, Nicole Harris; "Costly Race in the Sky: Same Route, Same Plane, Yet United's Flight Costs More to Operate than JetBlue's,"** ***The Wall Street Journal,*** **September 9, 2002, p. B1, Susan Carey.**

Overview

Big airlines like USAirways, United, and Delta struggle to compete with smaller carriers like JetBlue. Delta answers by introducing its own low-fare airline, Song.

Suggested Discussion Question

How do an airline's cost structure and its basic business model affect its ability to manage costs and charge competitive rates?

Issue 8–58
Impact of Cost Structure; High Fixed Costs

"It's Time to Cash In Some Chips, Big Blue," ***Business Week,*** **June 3, 2002, p. 43, Spencer E. Ante.**

Overview

As the article states, "the high fixed costs of IBM's chip manufacturing mean any revenue slide pummels profits."

Suggested Discussion Question

Using the concept of cost structure, explain the phenomenon mentioned above.

Issue 8–59
Operating Leverage

"Reliance Group May See Shield from Creditors," ***The Wall Street Journal,*** **August 15, 2000, Devon Spurgeon, Gregory Zuckerman, and Francine L. Pope.**

Overview

Reliance Group Holdings, Inc., an insurance company, reported a second quarter loss of over $500 million and stated that it may be forced to seek bankruptcy protection. A. M. Best downgraded the rating of Reliance Insurance Company, pointing to its high operating leverage as a potential source of danger.

Suggested Discussion Question

What is operating leverage and how does high operating leverage affect a company?

Issue 8–60
Outsourcing and Cost Structure

"Levi Will Cut 20% of Work Force, Shut Six Plants in Restructuring," ***The Wall Street Journal,*** **April 9, 2002, Teri Agins.**

Overview

Levi Strauss turn to outsourcing its production, which the company's CEO says "supports a more variable cost structure, helps us maintain strong margins, and enables us to invest more resources in product marketing and retail initiatives."

Suggested Discussion Question

Why would outsourcing result in a "more variable cost structure" for Levi Strauss?

Chapter Nine

Profit Planning, Activity-Based Budgeting, and e-Budgeting

After completing this chapter, you should be able to:

1 List and explain five purposes of budgeting systems.

2 Describe the similarities and differences in the operational budgets prepared by manufacturers, service industry firms, merchandisers, and nonprofit organizations.

3 Explain the concept of activity-based budgeting and the benefits it brings to the budgeting process.

4 Prepare each of the budget schedules that make up the master budget.

5 Discuss the role of assumptions and predictions in budgeting.

6 Describe a typical organization's process of budget administration.

7 Understand the importance of budgeting product life-cycle costs.

8 Discuss the behavioral implications of budgetary slack and participative budgeting.

9 After completing the appendix, understand the differences between the economic-order-quantity and just-in-time approaches to inventory management.

Local Company Goes to the Net as Web-Based Sales Soar

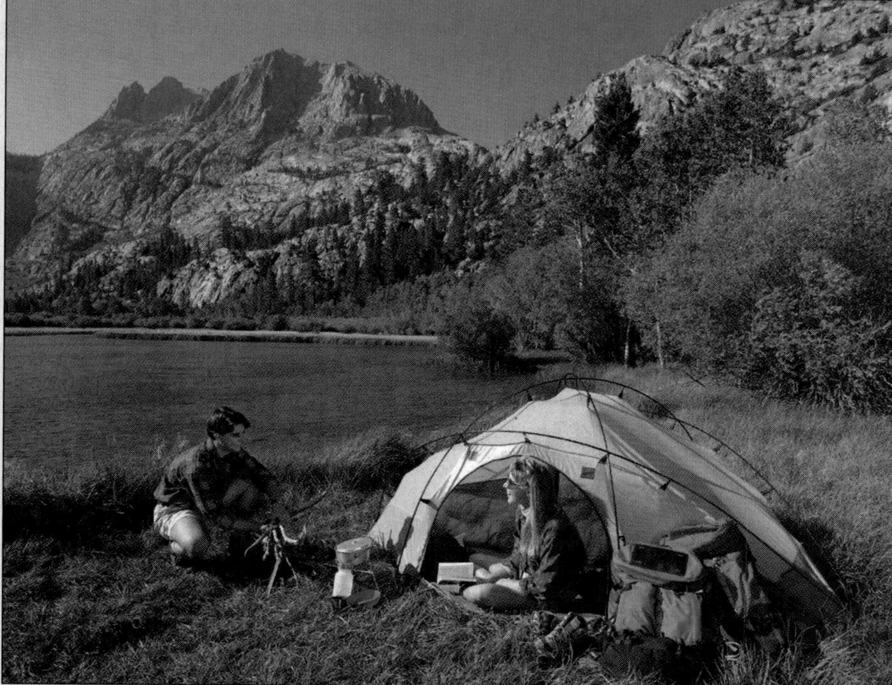

Denver, CO—One of the finest camping tents made in the northern hemisphere is only a mouse click away, as CozyCamp goes dot-com. Originally founded as CozyCamp Company, the company changed its name three years ago to Cozycamp.com. "We changed the name to emphasize that we were really embracing Internet sales," says company founder and owner, Mary Edwards. "In three short years, we've replaced 75 percent of our traditional retail sales with website orders." Edwards says the company can operate more efficiently this way as well as provide better customer service. "I'm not looking back," says Edwards. "We're on the Web to stay."

Things weren't always so cozy for this small manufacturer of camping tents and related equipment, though. "Like most entrepreneurial efforts," admits Edwards, "we had a few lean years at the beginning." According to Edwards, Cozycamp's success lies in two areas: a world-class product and a top-notch management team. "We're a small outfit," says Edwards, "but we run things tightly. We spend a lot of time on planning, and it really pays off. We rarely get those nasty surprises that are promised by Murphy's Law. We take great pains to prepare a master budget each year that takes us from the sales forecast, through the acquisition of resources, and on through each step in the production process. The culmination of the budgeting process is a set of budgeted financial statements." Edwards insists that she manages the business week to week, day to day, by the budget. "I've got to be confident that the profit is going to be there when all's said and done," says Edwards, "or I don't eat very well. Or sleep very well for that matter!" According to Edwards, Cozycamp's sound budgeting process has enabled her to grow the company, while at the same time not overextending herself or her company's financial underpinning. "The proof of the pudding for our strategic planning program," says Edwards, "is that in next year's budget we have a $1 million loan which has been approved for a major plant expansion. And we'll pay that loan off out of the cash flow from operations in one year flat."

Cozycamp is here to stay—in Denver, on the Web, and in campsites around the world.

Developing a budget is a critical step in planning any economic activity. This is true for businesses, for governmental agencies, and for individuals. We must all budget our money to meet day-to-day expenses and to plan for major expenditures, such as buying a car or paying for college tuition. Similarly, businesses of all types and governmental units at every level must make financial plans to carry out routine operations, to plan for major expenditures, and to help in making financial decisions.

Purposes of Budgeting Systems

LO 1

List and explain five purposes of budgeting systems.

A **budget** is a detailed plan, expressed in quantitative terms, that specifies how resources will be acquired and used during a specified period of time. The procedures used to develop a budget constitute a **budgeting system.** Budgeting systems have five primary purposes.

Planning The most obvious purpose of a budget is to quantify a plan of action. The budgeting process forces the individuals who make up an organization to plan ahead. The development of a quarterly budget for a Sheraton Hotel, for example, forces the hotel manager, the reservation manager, and the food and beverage manager to plan for the staffing and supplies needed to meet anticipated demand for the hotel's services.

Facilitating Communication and Coordination For any organization to be effective, each manager throughout the organization must be aware of the plans made by other managers. In order to plan reservations and ticket sales effectively, the reservations manager for Delta Air Lines must know the flight schedules developed by the airline's route manager. The budgeting process pulls together the plans of each manager in an organization.

Allocating Resources Generally, an organization's resources are limited, and budgets provide one means of allocating resources among competing uses. The city of Chicago, for example, must allocate its revenue among basic life services (such as police and fire protection), maintenance of property and equipment (such as city streets, parks, and vehicles), and other community services (such as child-care services and programs to prevent alcohol and drug abuse).

"Budgeting is used extensively for cost control. Each plant manager develops a plant budget, and then each department supervisor is responsible for his or her own cost center . . . . There are budgets for every department in the company." (9a)
Best Foods (recently purchased by Unilever)

Controlling Profit and Operations A budget is a plan, and plans are subject to change. Nevertheless, a budget serves as a useful benchmark with which actual results can be compared. For example, Prudential Insurance Company can compare its actual sales of insurance policies for a year against its budgeted sales. Such a comparison can help managers evaluate the firm's effectiveness in selling insurance. The next two chapters examine the control purpose of budgets in more depth.

Evaluating Performance and Providing Incentives Comparing actual results with budgeted results also helps managers to evaluate the performance of individuals, departments, divisions, or entire companies. Since budgets are used to evaluate performance, they can also be used to provide incentives for people to perform well. For example, General Motors Corporation, like many other companies, provides incentives for managers to improve profits by awarding bonuses to managers who meet or exceed their budgeted profit goals.

Types of Budgets

Different types of budgets serve different purposes. A **master budget,** or **profit plan,** is a comprehensive set of budgets covering all phases of an organization's operations for a specified period of time. We will examine a master budget in detail later in this chapter.

Budgeted financial statements, often called **pro forma financial statements,** show how the organization's financial statements will appear at a specified time if operations proceed according to plan. Budgeted financial statements include a *budgeted income statement, a budgeted balance sheet,* and *a budgeted statement of cash flows.*

Diverse organizations use budgets for a variety of reasons. Theme parks, such as Disney's Magic Kingdom, use budgets to plan for meeting the payroll and operating expenses, and to coordinate operations by matching staffing with projected attendance. Disney also uses its budgeting process to allocate capital improvement funds among competing projects, such as proposed new rides and attractions.

A **capital budget** is a plan for the acquisition of capital assets, such as buildings and equipment. Capital budgeting is covered in depth later in the text. A **financial budget** is a plan that shows how the organization will acquire its financial resources, such as through the issuance of stock or incurrence of debt.

Budgets are developed for specific time periods. *Short-range budgets* cover a year, a quarter, or a month, whereas *long-range budgets* cover periods longer than a year. **Rolling budgets** are continually updated by periodically adding a new incremental time period, such as a quarter, and dropping the period just completed. Rolling budgets are also called **revolving budgets** or **continuous budgets.**

The Master Budget: A Planning Tool

Topic 9–1

The master budget, the principal output of a budgeting system, is a comprehensive profit plan that ties together all phases of an organization's operations. The master budget comprises many separate budgets, or schedules, that are interdependent. Exhibit 9–1 portrays these interrelationships in a flowchart.

Sales of Services or Goods

The starting point for any master budget is a sales revenue budget based on a sales forecast for services or goods. Airlines forecast the number of passengers on each of their routes. Banks forecast the number and dollar amount of consumer loans and home mortgages to be provided. Hotels forecast the number of rooms that will be occupied during various seasons. Manufacturing and merchandising companies forecast sales of their goods. Some companies sell both goods and services. For example, Penney's is a large merchandising company, but its automotive-service branch provides the firm with substantial service revenue.

Sales Forecasting

All companies have two things in common when it comes to forecasting sales of services or goods. **Sales forecasting** is a critical step in the budgeting process, and it is very difficult to do accurately.

Various procedures are used in sales forecasting, and the final forecast usually combines information from many different sources. Many firms have a top-management-level market research staff whose job is to coordinate the company's sales forecasting

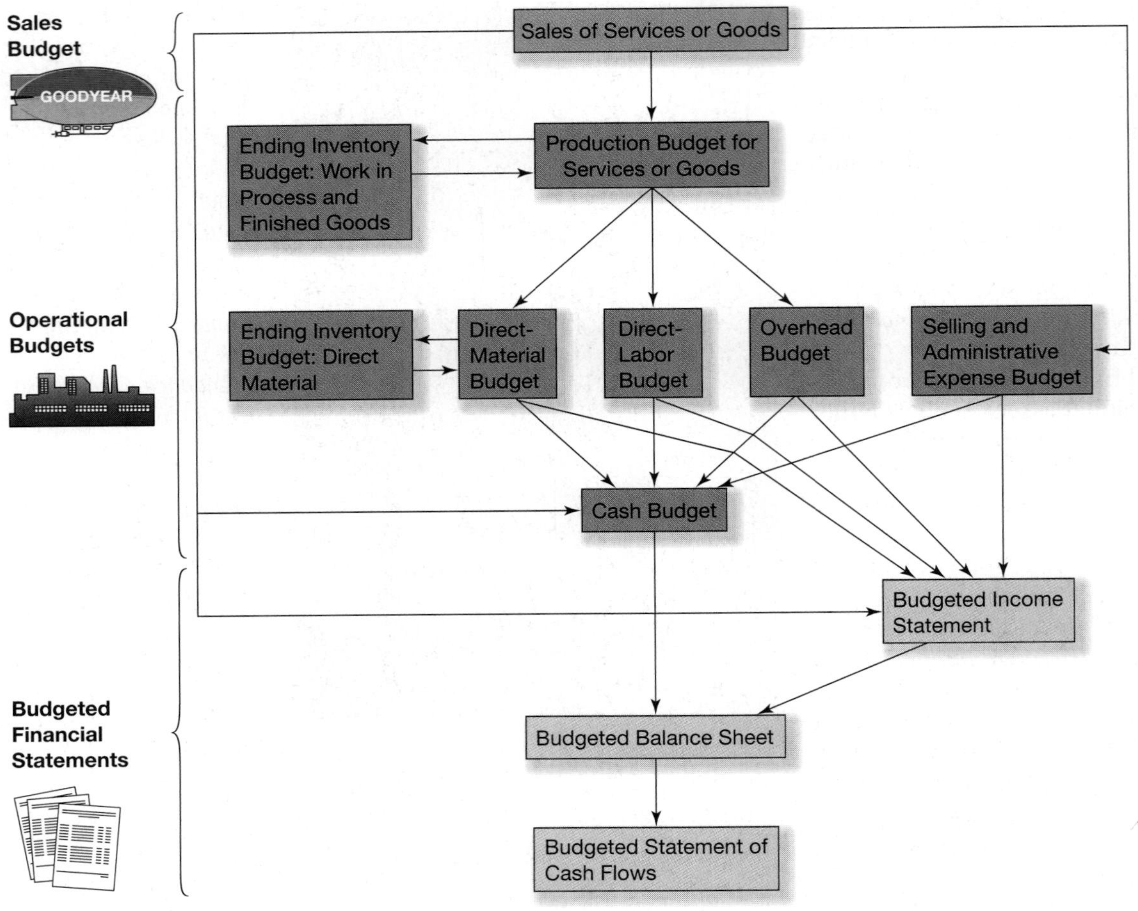

Exhibit 9–1
Components of a Master Budget

efforts. Typically, everyone from key executives to the firm's sales personnel will be asked to contribute sales projections.

Major factors considered when forecasting sales include the following:

> "Sales forecasting is difficult in every industry, but it's especially difficult in a highly competitive industry such as ours. Sales forecasting relies on several areas for input—market research, sales and marketing. We forecast the size of the market for each product, and then we forecast our share of that market." (9b)
>
> **Best Foods** (recently purchased by Unilever)

1. Past sales levels and trends:
   a. For the firm developing the forecast (for example, Exxon).
   b. For the entire industry (for example, the petroleum industry).
2. General economic trends. (Is the economy growing? How fast? Is a recession or economic slowdown expected?)
3. Economic trends in the company's industry. (In the petroleum industry, for example, is personal travel likely to increase, thereby implying increased demand for gasoline?)
4. Other factors expected to affect sales in the industry. (Is an unusually cold winter expected, which would result in increased demand for home heating oil in northern climates?)
5. Political and legal events. (For example, is any legislation pending in Congress that would affect the demand for petroleum, such as tax incentives to use alternative energy sources?)
6. The intended pricing policy of the company.
7. Planned advertising and product promotion.
8. Expected actions of competitors.

9. New products contemplated by the company or other firms. (For example, has an automobile firm announced the development of a new vehicle that runs on battery power, thereby reducing the demand for gasoline?)
10. Market research studies.

The starting point in the sales forecasting process is generally the sales level of the prior year. Then the market research staff considers the information discussed above along with input from key executives and sales personnel. In many firms, elaborate *econometric models* are built to incorporate all the available information systematically. (*Econometric* means economic measurement.) Statistical methods, such as regression analysis and probability distributions for sales, are often used. All in all, a great deal of effort generally goes into the sales forecast, since it is such a critical step in the budgeting process. Making a sales forecast is like shooting an arrow. If the archer's aim is off by only a fraction of an inch, the arrow will go further and further astray and miss the bull's-eye by a wide margin. Similarly, a slightly inaccurate sales forecast, coming at the very beginning of the budgeting process, will throw off all of the other schedules comprising the master budget.

"I see more and more forecasting and less time spent on what has happened." (9c)
Caterpillar

Operational Budgets

Based on the sales budget, a company develops a set of **operational budgets** that specify how its operations will be carried out to meet the demand for its goods or services. The budgets constituting this operational portion of the master budget are depicted in the middle portion of Exhibit 9–1.

Describe the similarities and differences in the operational budgets prepared by manufacturers, service industry firms, merchandisers, and nonprofit organizations.

Manufacturing Firms A manufacturing company develops a production budget, which shows the number of product units to be manufactured. Coupled with the production budget are ending-inventory budgets for both work in process and finished goods. Manufacturers plan to have some inventory on hand at all times to meet peak demand while keeping production at a stable level. From the production budget, a manufacturer develops budgets for the direct materials, direct labor, and overhead that will be required in the production process. A budget for selling and administrative expenses is also prepared.

Merchandising Firms The operational portion of the master budget is similar in a merchandising firm, but instead of a production budget for goods, a merchandiser develops a budget for merchandise purchases. A merchandising firm will not have a budget for direct material, because it does not engage in production. However, the merchandiser will develop budgets for labor (or personnel), overhead, and selling and administrative expenses.

Service Industry Firms Based on the sales budget for its services, a service industry firm develops a set of budgets that show how the demand for those services will be met. An airline, for example, prepares the following operational budgets: a budget of planned air miles to be flown; material budgets for spare aircraft parts, aircraft fuel, and in-flight food; labor budgets for flight crews and maintenance personnel; and an overhead budget.

Cash Budget Every business prepares a cash budget. This budget shows expected cash receipts, as a result of selling goods or services, and planned cash disbursements, to pay the bills incurred by the firm.

Summary of Operational Budgets Operational budgets differ since they are adapted to the operations of individual companies in various industries. However, operational budgets are also similar in important ways. In each firm they encompass a detailed plan for using the basic factors of production—material, labor, and overhead—to produce a product or provide a service.

Budgeted Financial Statements

The final portion of the master budget, depicted in Exhibit 9–1, includes a budgeted income statement, a budgeted balance sheet, and a budgeted statement of cash flows. These budgeted financial statements show the overall financial results of the organization's planned operations for the budget period.

Nonprofit Organizations

The master budget for a nonprofit organization includes many of the components shown in Exhibit 9–1. However, there are some important differences. Many nonprofit organizations provide services free of charge. Hence, there is no sales budget as shown in Exhibit 9–1. However, such organizations do begin their budgeting process with a budget that shows the level of services to be provided. For example, the budget for the city of Houston would show the planned levels of various public services.

Nonprofit organizations must plan carefully in order to achieve their objectives. This Habitat for Humanity project in upstate New York would not have been possible without careful financial planning.

Nonprofit organizations also prepare budgets showing their anticipated funding. The city of Houston budgets for such revenue sources as city taxes, state and federal revenue sharing, and sale of municipal bonds.

In summary, all organizations begin the budgeting process with plans for (1) the goods or services to be provided and (2) the revenue to be available, whether from sales or from other funding sources.

Activity-Based Budgeting

LO 3

Explain the concept of activity-based budgeting and the benefits it brings to the budgeting process.

Topic 9–2

The process of constructing a master budget can be significantly enhanced if the concepts of activity-based costing are applied.[1] Activity-based costing uses a two-stage cost-assignment process. In stage I, overhead costs are assigned to cost pools that represent the most significant *activities* constituting the production process. The activities identified vary across manufacturers, but such activities as engineering design, material handling, machine setup, production scheduling, inspection, quality control, and purchasing provide examples.

After assigning costs to the activity cost pools in stage I, cost drivers are identified that are appropriate for each cost pool. Then in stage II the overhead costs are allocated from each activity cost pool to cost objects (e.g., products, services, and customers) in proportion to the amount of activity consumed.

Exhibit 9–2 portrays the two-stage allocation process used in activity-based costing systems.

[1]Activity-based costing (ABC) was introduced conceptually in Chapter 3, and it is covered in depth in Chapter 5.

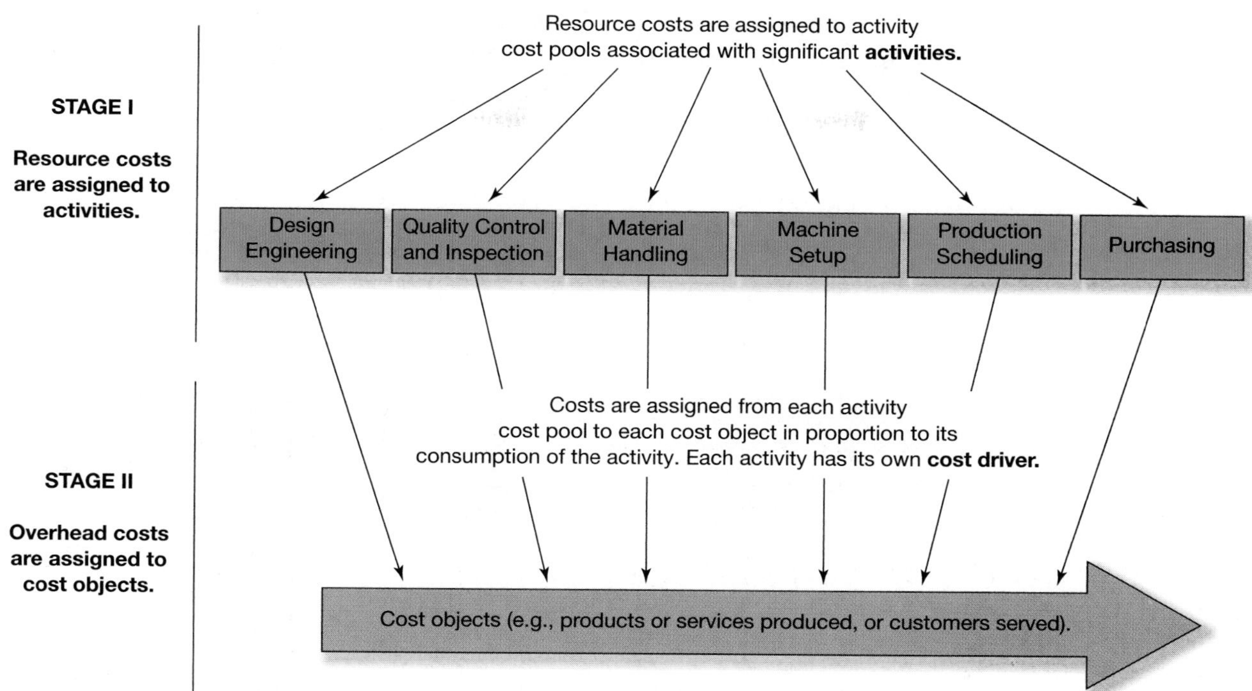
Resource costs are assigned to activity cost pools associated with significant **activities.**
STAGE I
Resource costs are assigned to activities.
Design Engineering
Quality Control and Inspection
Material Handling
Machine Setup
Production Scheduling
Purchasing
Costs are assigned from each activity cost pool to each cost object in proportion to its consumption of the activity. Each activity has its own **cost driver.**
STAGE II
Overhead costs are assigned to cost objects.
Cost objects (e.g., products or services produced, or customers served).

Exhibit 9–2
Activity-Based Costing System

Management Accounting Practice

American Express, AT&T Paradyne

ACTIVITY-BASED BUDGETING (ABB) AT AMERICAN EXPRESS AND AT&T PARADYNE

American Express has successfully used ABB for its travel-related services in its New York operations. This relatively new system has been used to identify and implement cost reduction and process improvement initiatives. Then, an activity-by-activity analysis of each department has allowed process improvement savings to be factored into the forecasted costs for each department in the next budget cycle.[2]

AT&T Paradyne designs and produces medium- and high-speed data communications equipment, which provides an interface between telephone networks and computers. The company's activity-based costing project ultimately led to activity-based budgeting. As ABM and ABB matured at AT&T Paradyne, the company began to experience a culture change. A key lesson learned in this case was that linking activity-based costing to the budgeting process and performance evaluation led to the integration of ABC into the management of the company.[3]

Applying ABC concepts to the budgeting process yields **activity-based budgeting (ABB).**[4] Under ABB, the first step is to specify the products or services to be produced

---

[2]David M. Aldea and David E. Bullinger, "Using ABC for Shared Services, Charge-Outs, Activity-Based Budgeting, and Benchmarking," in *Activity-Based Management: Arthur Andersen's Lessons from the ABM Battlefield,* Steve Player and David E. Keys, eds. (New York: John Wiley & Sons, 1999), pp. 138–145.

[3]Jay Collins, "Advanced Use of ABM: Using ABC for Target Costing, Activity-Based Budgeting, and Benchmarking," in *Activity-Based Management: Arthur Andersen's Lessons from the ABM Battlefield,* Steve Player and David E. Keys, eds. (New York: John Wiley & Sons, 1999), pp. 152–58.

[4]This section is based on the following references: James A. Brimson and John Antos, *Driving Value Using Activity-Based Budgeting* (New York: John Wiley & Sons, 1999); Sofia Börjesson, "A Case Study on Activity-Based Budgeting," *Journal of Cost Management* 10, no. 4, (Winter 1997), pp. 7–18; and Robert S. Kaplan and Robin Cooper, *Cost and Effect* (Boston: Harvard Business School Press, 1998), pp. 301–15.

Exhibit 9–3
Activity-Based Costing versus Activity-Based Budgeting*

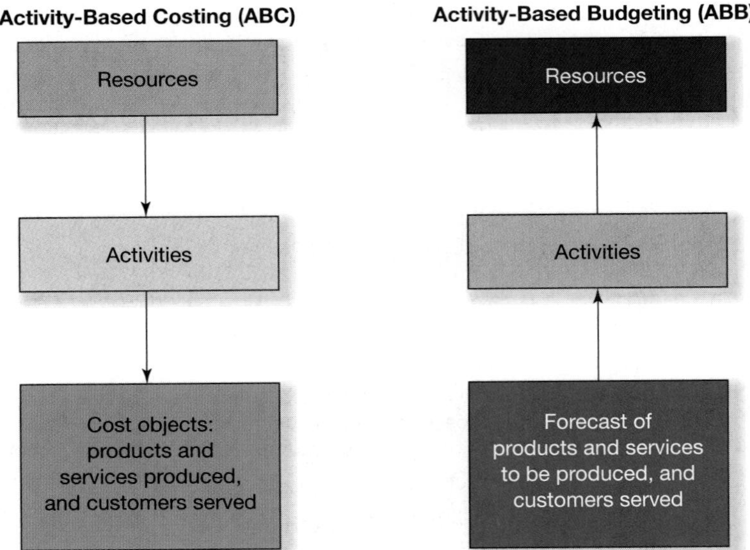

*Source: Robert S. Kaplan and Robin Cooper, *Cost and Effect* (Boston: Harvard Business School Press, 1998), pp. 303.

> Commenting on how the company's ABC and ABM initiatives led to activity-based budgeting: "We are using ABM as a means to execute our strategic management process." (9d)
>
> **AT&T Paradyne Corporation**

and the customers to be served. Then the activities that are necessary to produce these products and services are determined. Finally, the resources necessary to perform the specified activities are quantified. Conceptually, ABB takes the ABC model and reverses the flow of the analysis, as depicted in Exhibit 9–3. As portrayed in the diagram, ABC assigns resource costs to activities, and then it assigns activity costs to products and services produced and customers served. ABB, on the other hand, begins by forecasting the demand for products and services as well as the customers to be served. These forecasts then are used to plan the activities for the budget period and budget the resources necessary to carry out the activities.

In the next section of the chapter, we will illustrate the process of constructing a master budget. Notice how the conceptual activity-based budgeting model is employed in the budgeting process. In the context of the master-budget illustration, we will explore the benefits and implications of the ABB approach.

Using Activity-Based Budgeting to Prepare the Master Budget

LO 4

Prepare each of the budget schedules that make up the master budget.

cozycamp.com

To illustrate the steps in developing a master budget, or profit plan, we will focus on Cozycamp.com, a manufacturer of backpacking tents based in Denver, Colorado. The company is wholly owned by Mary Edwards, who started the company in her basement 15 years ago. After a difficult two to three years, success came quickly for the company, and Edwards eventually built a production facility outside Denver. The manufacturing process is highly automated, using several machines to cut out pieces of tent fabric and sew them together to form a lightweight but durable backpacking tent. Production of the aluminum tent poles are outsourced to a company in Kansas City, and the poles are purchased on a just-in-time basis so they can be packaged with the finished tents just before they are shipped. Initially, Edwards called her firm CozyCamp Company, and its sales were made to regional retailers in the mountain states using a traditional sales approach. Three years ago, however, Edwards changed the company's name to Cozycamp.com and made a major foray into the world of Internet sales. Now almost 75 percent of Cozycamp.com's sales are made through the company's website. Although Cozycamp.com retained several of its sales personnel to handle the traditional sales to area retailers, new personnel had to be hired to handle the company's Internet sales environment. Tents are shipped to Internet customers via UPS, FedEx, and other express delivery services.

The 20x2 master budget for Cozycamp.com has just been completed. It contains the following schedules, which are displayed and explained in the following pages.

Schedule	Title of Schedule
1	Sales Budget
2	Production Budget
3	Direct-Material Budget
4	Direct-Labor Budget
5	Manufacturing Overhead Budget
6	Selling, General, and Administrative Expense Budget
7	Cash Receipts Budget
8	Cash Disbursements Budget
9	Cash Budget
10	Budgeted Schedule of Cost of Goods Manufactured and Sold
11	Budgeted Income Statement
12	Budgeted Statement of Cash Flows
13	Budgeted Balance Sheet

Sales Budget

The first step in developing Cozycamp.com's 20x2 master budget is to prepare the **sales budget,** which is displayed as schedule 1. This budget displays the projected sales in units for each quarter and then multiplies the unit sales by the sales price to determine sales revenue. Notice that there is a significant seasonal pattern in the sales forecast, with the bulk of the sales coming in the spring and summer.

Schedule 1

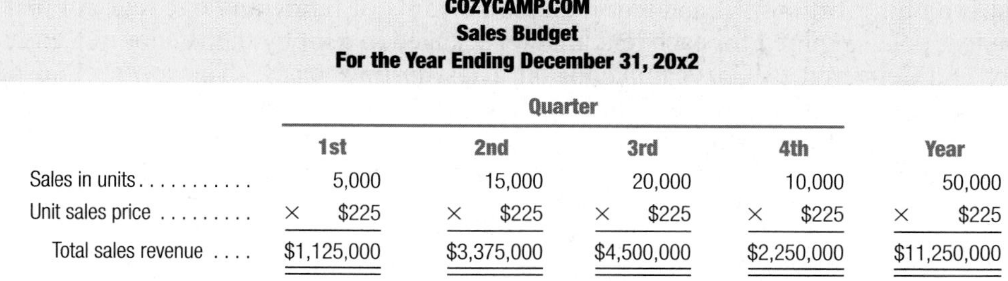

COZYCAMP.COM
Sales Budget
For the Year Ending December 31, 20x2

	Quarter				
	1st	2nd	3rd	4th	Year
Sales in units	5,000	15,000	20,000	10,000	50,000
Unit sales price	× $225	× $225	× $225	× $225	× $225
Total sales revenue	$1,125,000	$3,375,000	$4,500,000	$2,250,000	$11,250,000

Production Budget

The **production budget** shows the number of units of services or goods that are to be produced during a budget period. Cozycamp.com's production budget, displayed as schedule 2, determines the number of tents to be produced each quarter based on the quarterly sales projections in the sales budget. Schedule 2 is based on the following formula.

Sales in units + Desired ending inventory of finished goods = Total units required

Total units required − Expected beginning inventory of finished goods = Units to be produced

Focus on the second-quarter column in schedule 2, which is shaded. Expected sales are 15,000 tents, and Edwards desires to have 2,000 finished units on hand at the end of the quarter. This is 10 percent of the expected sales for the third quarter. However, 1,500 tents are expected to be in inventory at the beginning of the second quarter. Thus, only 15,500 tents need to be produced.

Schedule 2

COZYCAMP.COM
Production Budget
For the Year Ending December 31, 20x2

	Quarter				
	1st	2nd	3rd	4th	Year
Sales in units (from schedule 1)	5,000	15,000	20,000	10,000	50,000
Add desired ending inventory of finished goods*	1,500	2,000	1,000	500†	500
Total units required	6,500	17,000	21,000	10,500	50,500
Less expected beginning inventory of finished goods	500	1,500	2,000	1,000	500
Units to be produced	6,000	15,500	19,000	9,500	50,000

*Ten percent of the next quarter's expected sales.

†Ten percent of the expected sales for the 1st quarter of the next year, 20x3, which is predicted to be 5,000 units.

Direct-Material Budget

The **direct-material budget** shows the number of units and the cost of material to be purchased and used during a budget period. Cozycamp.com's direct-material budget, which is displayed as schedule 3, has two sections: one for tent fabric and one for tent poles. As is true for almost all manufacturers, Cozycamp.com's direct-material cost is a unit-level cost.[5] Each tent requires 12 yards of fabric and one tent pole kit. The tent poles required for each tent are prepackaged in a kit by the vendor in Kansas City and delivered to Cozycamp.com on a just-in-time basis.[6] The top section of Cozycamp.com's direct-material budget shows the total amount of tent fabric needed to make tents during each quarter. The shaded portion of schedule 3 computes the amount of tent fabric to be purchased each quarter. This part of the schedule is based on the following formula.

$$\text{Raw material required for production} + \text{Desired ending inventory of raw material} = \text{Total raw material required}$$

$$\text{Total raw material required} - \text{Expected beginning inventory of raw material} = \text{Raw material to be purchased}$$

The shaded portion of schedule 3 also computes the cost of each quarter's tent fabric purchases. (This information also will be needed later in the budgeting process, in schedule 10.)

The lower unshaded section of schedule 3 calculates the quantity and cost of tent pole kits to be purchased each quarter.

Finally, the last row of schedule 3 totals the cost of tent fabric and tent pole kits to yield the total cost of raw material to be purchased each quarter.

[5]A unit-level cost is one that must be incurred each time a unit is produced.

[6]Just-in-time production and inventory control systems are covered in Chapter 6.

Schedule 3

COZYCAMP.COM
Direct-Material Budget
For the Year Ending December 31, 20x2

	Quarter				
	1st	**2nd**	**3rd**	**4th**	**Year**
Tent fabric:					
Tents to be produced (from schedule 2)	6,000	15,500	19,000	9,500	50,000
Raw material required per unit (yards of fabric)	× 12	× 12	× 12	× 12	× 12
Raw material required for production (yards)	72,000	186,000	228,000	114,000	600,000
Add desired ending inventory of raw material (yards)*	18,600	22,800	11,400	7,200†	7,200
Total raw material required	90,600	208,800	239,400	121,200	607,200
Less expected beginning inventory of raw material (yards)	7,200	18,600	22,800	11,400	7,200
Raw material to be purchased (yards)	83,400	190,200	216,600	109,800	600,000
Cost per yard	× $9	× $9	× $9	× $9	× $9
Total cost of tent fabric purchases	$750,600	$1,711,800	$1,949,400	$ 988,200	$5,400,000
Tent poles:					
Tents to be produced (from schedule 2)	6,000	15,500	19,000	9,500	50,000
Tent pole kits required per tent	× 1	× 1	× 1	× 1	× 1
Tent pole kits to be purchased‡	6,000	15,500	19,000	9,500	50,000
Cost per tent pole kit	× $20	× $20	× $20	× $20	× $20
Total cost of tent pole kit purchases	$120,000	$ 310,000	$ 380,000	$ 190,000	$1,000,000
Total cost of raw material purchases (fabric and poles)	$870,600	$2,021,800	$2,329,400	$1,178,200	$6,400,000

*Ten percent of the next quarter's expected raw material requirements.

†Ten percent of the expected raw material requirements for the 1st quarter of the next year, 20x3, which is assumed to be 72,000 yards. (Sales, and therefore production, is predicted to be the same in each quarter of 20x3 as in the corresponding quarter of 20x2.)

‡Since the tent pole kits are prepackaged by the vendor and delivered on a just-in-time basis, there is no need for buffer inventory stocks. Thus, the number of tent pole kits purchased each quarter is the same as the number needed each quarter.

Production and Purchasing: An Important Link Notice the important link between planned production and purchases of raw material. This link is apparent in schedule 3, and it is also emphasized in the formula preceding the schedule. Let's focus on the second quarter. Since 15,500 tents are to be produced, 186,000 yards of tent material will be needed (15,500 tents times 12 yards per unit). In addition, Edwards desires to have 22,800 yards of material in inventory at the end of the quarter.[7] Thus, total needs are 208,800 yards. Does Cozycamp.com need to purchase this much raw material? No it does not, because 18,600 yards will be in inventory at the beginning of the quarter. Therefore, the firm needs to purchase only 190,200 yards of material during the quarter (208,800 yards less 18,600 yards in the beginning inventory).

Inventory Management The linkage between planned production and raw material purchases is a particularly critical linkage in manufacturing firms. Thus, considerable effort is devoted to careful inventory planning and management. How did Edwards

[7]It often is desirable to have a buffer inventory just before a bottleneck manufacturing operation.

decide how much raw material to have in inventory at the end of each quarter? Examination of schedule 3 reveals that each quarter's desired ending inventory of raw material is 10 percent of the *material needed for production* in the next quarter. For example, 22,800 yards of raw material will be in inventory at the end of the second quarter, because 228,000 yards will be needed for production in the third quarter (22,800 = 10% × 228,000). The effect of this approach is to have a larger ending inventory when the next quarter's planned production is greater. Inventories are drawn down when the subsequent quarter's planned production is lower.

Direct-Labor Budget

The **direct-labor budget** shows the number of hours and the cost of the direct labor to be used during the budget period. Cozycamp.com's direct-labor budget is displayed as schedule 4. Based on each quarter's planned production, this schedule computes the amount of direct labor needed each quarter and the cost of the required labor. Cozycamp.com is a relatively small company, and owner Mary Edwards hires all of her direct-labor production employees on a part-time basis only. This allows Cozycamp.com to meet the labor demands of a given time period, which vary significantly with the seasonal pattern of demand and production. Thus, Cozycamp.com's direct labor may be adjusted up or down to meet short-term needs. As a result, direct labor for this company is a unit-level cost. As schedule 4 shows, each tent manufactured requires half an hour of direct labor.

A Note on Direct Labor and the Cost Hierarchy It is important to note that where direct labor belongs in the cost hierarchy depends on management's ability to adjust the organization's labor force to match short-term requirements, as well as management's attitude about making such adjustments.[8] For either strategic business reasons, or due to ethical concerns, many companies strive to maintain a relatively stable labor force. If production employees are retained when production declines, then direct labor will not be a unit-level cost. In the extreme case, where employees are virtually never laid off, direct labor becomes a facility, or general-operations, level cost. Cozycamp.com's ability to easily adjust the total hours of its part-time work force results in a unit-level designation for direct-labor cost in this situation.

Schedule 4

cozycamp.com

COZYCAMP.COM
Direct-Labor Budget
For the Year Ending December 31, 20x2

	Quarter				
	1st	**2nd**	**3rd**	**4th**	**Year**
Units to be produced (from schedule 2)	6,000	15,500	19,000	9,500	50,000
Direct-labor required per unit (hours)	× .5	× .5	× .5	× .5	× .5
Total direct-labor hours required	3,000	7,750	9,500	4,750	25,000
Direct-labor cost per hour	× $15	× $15	× $15	× $15	× $15
Total direct-labor cost	$45,000	$116,250	$142,500	$71,250	$375,000

[8]A typical cost hierarchy includes costs incurred at the unit level, batch level, product-sustaining level, customer level, and facility or general-operations level. Cost hierarchies are discussed in detail in Chapter 5.

Manufacturing-Overhead Budget

The **manufacturing-overhead budget** shows the cost of overhead expected to be incurred in the production process during the budget period. Cozycamp.com's manufacturing overhead budget, displayed as schedule 5, lists the expected cost of each overhead item by quarter. At the bottom of the schedule, the total budgeted overhead for each quarter is shown. Then each quarter's depreciation is subtracted to determine the total cash disbursements to be expected for overhead during each quarter. This cash disbursement information will be needed later in the budgeting process when the cash disbursements budget is constructed (schedule 8).

Activity-Based Budgeting and the Cost Hierarchy Cozycamp.com uses an activity-based budgeting (ABB) approach in the construction of the manufacturing-overhead budget. This budget explicitly uses activity-based costing information in that the budgeted costs for various overhead items are based on the expected quantity of the appropriate cost driver. For example, the cost driver used to budget setup costs is the number of production runs.

In Cozycamp.com's cost hierarchy, unit-level costs include indirect material and electricity used to run the production machinery.[9] Batch-level costs include machine setup, purchasing and material handling, and quality control and inspection. The cost driver for these costs is the number of production runs. A run typically produces 500 tents. Cozycamp.com's only product-level cost is design engineering. The company typically develops one new tent design each quarter. Each new design costs $1,200. The remaining overhead costs in schedule 5 are costs incurred at the facility, or general-operations, level.

LO 3

Explain the concept of activity-based budgeting and the benefits it brings to the budgeting process.

Benefits of ABB Proponents of ABB believe that real, sustainable payoffs from activity-based costing and activity-based management will not be forthcoming until an organization's budgeting process embraces the ABM approach. Utilizing ABC information in the budgeting process provides solid reasoning for budgeting costs at particular levels, since the underlying ABC information is based explicitly on the relationships among cost drivers, activities, and resources consumed. Moreover, the resulting budget is more useful to management, because it reveals how cost levels will change if the predicted quantities of the cost drivers change. For example, what will happen to Cozycamp.com's setup costs in the 1st quarter if the quantity produced is 6,000 units as reflected in the budget (see schedule 5), but 15 production runs are used to produce these 6,000 units instead of 12 runs as specified in the budget? According to schedule 5, setup cost is $400 per production run ($4,800/12 runs). Therefore, 15 runs would result in $6,000 of setup cost in the 1st quarter, instead of $4,800 as forecast in the budget. This will be true even if 6,000 units are produced as forecast in the budget.

Traditional budgeting processes, which did not embrace the ABB approach, often classified such costs as setup, purchasing and material handling, quality control and inspection, or design engineering as *fixed* costs, since they do not vary with the number of units produced. The ABB approach, however, recognizes that these costs are really *variable* if the budget analyst is careful to identify the appropriate cost driver with which each of these costs varies.

"Activity-based budgets are more actionable and understandable." (9e)
James A. Brimson and John Antos (both presidents of management consulting firms)[10]

[9]A typical cost hierarchy includes costs incurred at the unit level, batch level, product-sustaining level, customer level, and facility or general-operations level. Cost hierarchies are discussed in detail in Chapter 5.

[10]These management consulting firms specialize in ABC, ABM, ABB, and cost management systems.

Schedule 5

COZYCAMP.COM
Manufacturing Overhead Budget
For the Year Ending December 31, 20x2

	Quarter				
	1st	2nd	3rd	4th	Year
Unit-level costs:					
Units	*6,000*	*15,500*	*19,000*	*9,500*	*50,000*
Indirect material	$ 18,000	$ 46,500	$ 57,000	$ 28,500	$ 150,000
Electricity (for machinery)	6,000	15,500	19,000	9,500	50,000
Total unit-level costs	$ 24,000	$ 62,000	$ 76,000	$ 38,000	$ 200,000
Batch-level costs:					
Production runs	*12*	*31*	*38*	*19*	*100*
Setup	$ 4,800	$ 12,400	$ 15,200	$ 7,600	$ 40,000
Purchasing and material handling	7,200	18,600	22,800	11,400	60,000
Quality control and inspection	6,000	15,500	19,000	9,500	50,000
Total batch-level costs	$ 18,000	$ 46,500	$ 57,000	$ 28,500	$ 150,000
Product-level costs:					
New tent designs	*1*	*1*	*1*	*1*	*4*
Design engineering	$ 1,200	$ 1,200	$ 1,200	$ 1,200	$ 4,800
Total product-level costs	$ 1,200	$ 1,200	$ 1,200	$ 1,200	$ 4,800
Facility and general operations-level costs:					
Supervisory salaries	$ 52,500	$ 52,500	$ 52,500	$ 52,500	$ 210,000
Insurance and property taxes	11,300	11,300	11,300	11,300	45,200
Maintenance	47,500	47,500	47,500	47,500	190,000
Utilities	40,000	40,000	40,000	40,000	160,000
Depreciation	110,000	110,000	110,000	110,000	440,000
Total facility and general operations-level costs	$261,300	$261,300	$261,300	$261,300	$1,045,200
Total overhead	$304,500	$371,000	$395,500	$329,000	$1,400,000
Less depreciation	110,000	110,000	110,000	110,000	440,000
Total cash disbursements for overhead	$194,500	$261,000	$285,500	$219,000	$ 960,000

Selling, General, and Administrative (SG&A) Expense Budget

The **selling, general, and administrative (SG&A) budget** shows the planned amounts of expenditures for selling, general, and administrative expenses during the budget period. Cozycamp.com's selling, general, and administrative expense budget is displayed as schedule 6. This budget lists the expenses of administering the firm and selling its product.

Activity-Based Budgeting and the Cost Hierarchy Similar to the manufacturing-overhead budget, Cozycamp.com's SG&A expense budget reflects the activity-based budgeting (ABB) approach. Activity-based costing information was used to develop this budget. For example, the cost driver used to budget sales commissions (for sales in the firm's traditional market) is the number of units sold.

In Cozycamp.com's cost hierarchy, the only unit-level marketing expenses consist of sales commissions.[11] For Cozycamp's traditional sales through regional retail out-

[11]A typical cost hierarchy includes costs incurred at the unit level, batch level, product-sustaining level, customer level, and facility, or general-operations, level. Cost hierarchies are discussed in detail in Chapter 5.

lets, sales personnel are paid commissions based on the number of units sold. The SG&A budget reflects a $5 commission paid on each tent sold through traditional outlets, which account for 25 percent of Cozycamp.com's sales. In the second quarter, for example, sales commissions are predicted to be $18,750 (15,000 tents × 25% traditional sales × $5).

The customer-level expenses incurred by Cozycamp.com are the sales personnel salaries, which differ depending on whether the customers are traditional regional retailers or Web shoppers. In order to sell its tents in the traditional marketplace, Cozycamp.com employs sales personnel who travel to the retailers in the area and personally take orders. These sales personnel receive both a salary and sales commissions. (The sales commissions are unit-level expenses, as noted above.) To serve its Internet customers, Cozycamp.com employs computer operators to update the company's website and a couple of telephone operators to provide customer service over the phone. For example, some Internet customers are hesitant to give their credit card numbers to Cozycamp.com online, so they place their orders online and then phone in to an authorized telephone number to submit their credit card information.

The remainder of Cozycamp.com's selling, general, and administrative expenses are incurred at the facility or general operations level.

Schedule 6

COZYCAMP.COM
Selling, General, and Administrative Expense Budget
For the Year Ending December 31, 20x2

	Quarter				
	1st	**2nd**	**3rd**	**4th**	**Year**
Unit-level expenses:					
Units	*5,000*	*15,000*	*20,000*	*10,000*	*50,000*
Sales commissions (traditional market)	$ 6,250	$ 18,750	$ 25,000	$ 12,500	$ 62,500
Total unit-level expenses	$ 6,250	$ 18,750	$ 25,000	$ 12,500	$ 62,500
Customer-level expenses:					
Sales personnel salaries (traditional market)	$ 16,000	$ 16,000	$ 16,000	$ 16,000	$64,000
Computer operator salaries	18,000	18,000	18,000	18,000	72,000
Telephone operator salaries	6,000	6,000	6,000	6,000	24,000
Total customer-level expenses	$ 40,000	$ 40,000	$ 40,000	$ 40,000	$ 160,000
Facility and general operations-level expenses:					
Sales manager's salary	$ 15,000	$ 15,000	$ 15,000	$ 15,000	$ 60,000
Media advertising	61,000	61,000	61,000	61,000	244,000
Administrative salaries	220,000	220,000	220,000	220,000	880,000
Total facility and general operations-level expenses	$296,000	$296,000	$296,000	$296,000	$1,184,000
Total expenses	$342,250	$354,750	$361,000	$348,500	$1,406,500

Cash Receipts Budget

The **cash receipts budget** details the expected cash collections during a budget period. Cozycamp.com's cash receipts budget is displayed as schedule 7. The firm collects 80 percent of its billings during the same quarter in which the sale is made, and another 18 percent in the following quarter. Two percent of each quarter's sales are expected to be uncollectible accounts.

Schedule 7

COZYCAMP.COM
Cash Receipts Budget
For the Year Ending December 31, 20x2

	Quarter				
	1st	2nd	3rd	4th	Year
Sales revenue (from schedule 1)	$1,125,000	$3,375,000	$4,500,000	$2,250,000	$11,250,000
Collections in quarter of sale (80% of revenue)	$ 900,000	$2,700,000	$3,600,000	$1,800,000	$ 9,000,000
Collections in quarter following sale (18% of prior quarter's revenue)*	405,000†	202,500	607,500	810,000	2,025,000
Total cash receipts	$1,305,000	$2,902,500	$4,207,500	$2,610,000	$11,025,000

*Two percent of each quarter's sales are expected to be uncollectible, as follows:

	Quarter				
	1st	2nd	3rd	4th	Year
Uncollectible accounts	$22,500	$67,500	$90,000	$45,000	$225,000

†The revenue in the prior quarter (i.e., the 4th quarter of 20x1) is assumed to be $2,250,000. Therefore, the $405,000 is 18% of $2,250,000.

How to Budget Cash Receipts To understand how the cash receipts budget is prepared, let's focus again on the second quarter column, which is shaded. The $3,375,000 of total revenue comes directly from schedule 1, the sales budget (second column, last row). Since most of Cozycamp.com's sales are on account, not all of the second quarter's revenue will be collected during the second quarter. The cash that the firm will collect during the second quarter comprises two components, as depicted in the following diagram.

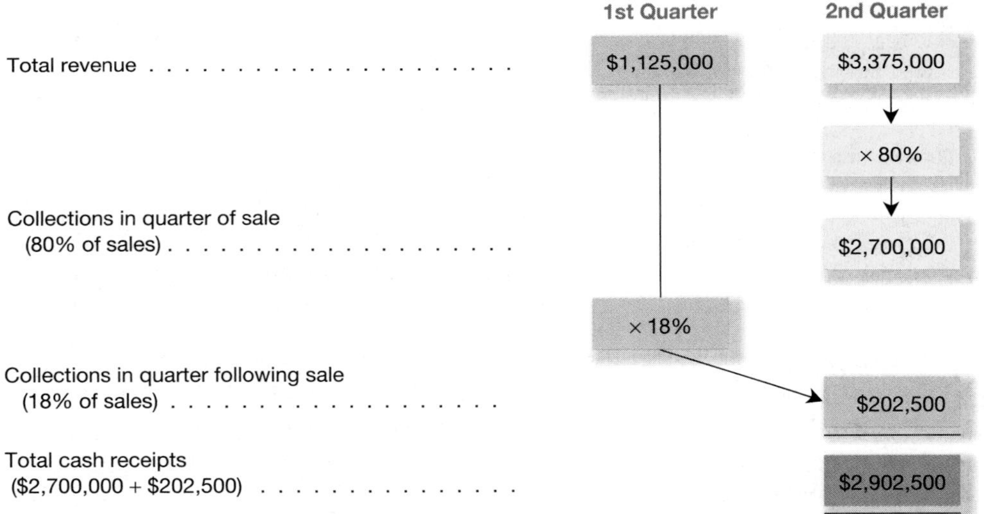

The second quarter's total cash receipts are the sum of $2,700,000 (80 percent of second quarter sales) and $202,500 (18 percent of first quarter sales).

One final point to notice is that 2 percent of each quarter's sales are not expected to be collected. Thus, the $67,500 of second quarter uncollectible accounts amounts to 2 percent of the second quarter's revenue ($67,500 = 2% × $3,375,000). Almost all of Cozycamp.com's uncollectible accounts relate to the company's traditional sales.

Cash Disbursements Budget

The **cash disbursements budget** details the expected cash payments during a budget period. Schedule 8 displays Cozycamp.com's cash disbursements budget. The shaded top portion shows the schedule of cash payments for raw material purchases, which are made on account. The company pays for 60 percent of its purchases on account during the quarter in which the purchase is made. The remaining 40 percent of each quarter's purchases are paid for during the quarter following the purchase.

The unshaded lower portion of schedule 8 shows all of Cozycamp.com's direct-labor, manufacturing overhead, and selling, general, and administrative expenditures.

Schedule 8

COZYCAMP.COM
Cash Disbursements Budget
For the Year Ending December 31, 20x2

	Quarter				
	1st	**2nd**	**3rd**	**4th**	**Year**
Cost of raw material purchases (from schedule 3)	$ 870,600	$2,021,800	$2,329,400	$1,178,200	$6,400,000
Cash payments for purchases made during the quarter (60% of current quarter's purchases)	$ 522,360	$1,213,080	$1,397,640	$ 706,920	$3,840,000
Cash payments for prior quarter's purchases (40% of prior quarter's purchases)	471,280*	348,240	808,720	931,760	2,560,000
Total cash payments for raw material purchases	$ 993,640	$1,561,320	$2,206,360	$1,638,680	$6,400,000
Other cash disbursements					
Direct labor (schedule 4)	$ 45,000	$ 116,250	$ 142,500	$ 71,250	$ 375,000
Indirect material (schedule 5)	18,000	46,500	57,000	28,500	150,000
Electricity (schedule 5)	6,000	15,500	19,000	9,500	50,000
Setup (schedule 5)	4,800	12,400	15,200	7,600	40,000
Purchasing and material handling (schedule 5)	7,200	18,600	22,800	11,400	60,000
Quality control and inspection (schedule 5)	6,000	15,500	19,000	9,500	50,000
Design engineering (schedule 5)	1,200	1,200	1,200	1,200	4,800
Supervisory salaries (schedule 5)	52,500	52,500	52,500	52,500	210,000
Insurance and property taxes (schedule 5)	11,300	11,300	11,300	11,300	45,200
Maintenance (schedule 5)	47,500	47,500	47,500	47,500	190,000
Utilities (schedule 5)	40,000	40,000	40,000	40,000	160,000
Sales commissions (schedule 6)	6,250	18,750	25,000	12,500	62,500
Sales personnel (schedule 6)	16,000	16,000	16,000	16,000	64,000
Computer operators (schedule 6)	18,000	18,000	18,000	18,000	72,000
Telephone operators (schedule 6)	6,000	6,000	6,000	6,000	24,000
Sales manager (schedule 6)	15,000	15,000	15,000	15,000	60,000
Media advertising (schedule 6)	61,000	61,000	61,000	61,000	244,000
Administration (schedule 6)	220,000	220,000	220,000	220,000	880,000
Total of other cash disbursements	$ 581,750	$ 732,000	$ 789,000	$ 638,750	$2,741,500
Total cash disbursements	$1,575,390	$2,293,320	$2,995,360	$2,277,430	$9,141,500

*Forty percent of the purchases in the 4th quarter of the prior year, 20x1, which is assumed to be $1,178,200.

How to Budget Cash Disbursements Cozycamp.com purchases raw material, direct labor, and various services. The raw material purchases are made on account, which means payment is not made in cash at the time of the purchase. The shaded top portion of schedule 8 shows the purchases on account. Let's focus on the second quarter column. The second quarter's raw material purchases on account amount to

$2,021,800. Does the company pay for all of the $2,021,800 purchases on account during the same quarter? No, it does not. As the following diagram shows, the second quarter's actual cash payment for purchases made on account comprises two components.

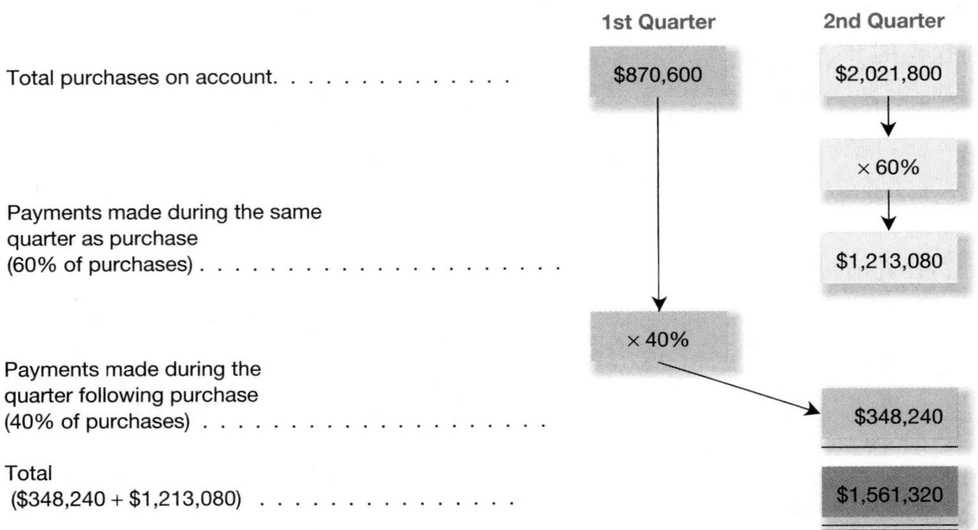

The second quarter's total cash payments *for purchases made on account* are the sum of $1,213,080 (which relates to second quarter purchases on account) and $348,240 (which relates to first quarter purchases on account).

We are not finished with the second quarter's cash disbursements yet, because Cozycamp.com *also pays for some of its purchases in cash at the time of purchase.* These cash expenditures are detailed in the unshaded lower portion of schedule 8. The amounts are drawn from schedules 4, 5, and 6, which detail expenditures for direct-labor, manufacturing-overhead, and selling, general, and administrative expenses, respectively. For example, schedule 4 lists $116,250 for direct labor in the second quarter; schedule 5 lists $261,000 for cash expenditures on manufacturing-overhead costs; and schedule 6 lists $354,750 for selling, general, and administrative expenditures.

Finally, the last row in the cash disbursements budget (schedule 8) shows the total cash disbursements during each quarter. Thus, the $2,293,320 total payment in the second quarter is the sum of $1,561,320 (for raw material purchases on account) and $732,000 for other purchases made in cash.

Cash Budget: Combining Receipts and Disbursements

The **cash budget** details the expected cash receipts and disbursements during a budget period. Cozycamp.com's completed cash budget is displayed as schedule 9. The shaded top portion pulls together the cash receipts and cash disbursements detailed in schedules 7 and 8. The lower portion of schedule 9 discloses the company's plans to take out a short-term bank loan on January 2, 20x2, for the purpose of building an addition to its production facility. The pattern of construction payments reflects high outlays early in the year as the major construction takes place. The high payment in the fourth quarter is due to the costs of reconfiguring the production line after the addition is finished. The company will repay the loan (with interest) in four equal installments on the last day of each quarter in 20x2. The funds for this repayment will come from excess cash generated from operations during 20x2.

Also shown in schedule 9 are the interest payments on the short-term bank loan.

Schedule 9

COZYCAMP.COM
Cash Budget
For the Year Ending December 31, 20x2

	Quarter				
	1st	**2nd**	**3rd**	**4th**	**Year**
Cash receipts (from schedule 7)	$1,305,000	$2,902,500	$4,207,500	$2,610,000	$11,025,000
Less cash disbursements (from schedule 8)	(1,575,390)	(2,293,320)	(2,995,360)	(2,277,430)	(9,141,500)
Change in cash balance during quarter due to operations	$ (270,390)	$ 609,180	$1,212,140	$ 332,570	$ 1,883,500
Proceeds from bank loan (1/2/x2)	1,000,000				1,000,000
Payments for construction of plant addition	(500,000)	(120,000)	(80,000)	(300,000)	(1,000,000)
Repayment of principal on bank loan (at the end of each quarter)	(250,000)	(250,000)	(250,000)	(250,000)	(1,000,000)
Interest on bank loan (at 10% per year)*	(25,000)	(18,750)	(12,500)	(6,250)	(62,500)
Change in cash balance during the year					$ 821,000
Cash balance 1/1/x2					10,000
Cash balance 12/31/x2					$ 831,000

*Interest computations:

Quarter	Unpaid Principal during the Quarter	Annual Interest Rate	Portion of Year	Interest Payment†
1st	$1,000,000	10%	1/4	$25,000‡
2nd	750,000	10%	1/4	18,750
3rd	500,000	10%	1/4	12,500
4th	250,000	10%	1/4	6,250

†Unpaid principal × Annual interest rate × 1/4.

‡$1,000,000 × .10 × 1/4 = $25,000.

Budgeted Schedule of Cost of Goods Manufactured and Sold

The **budgeted schedule of cost of goods manufactured and sold** details the direct material, direct-labor, and manufacturing-overhead costs to be incurred, and shows the cost of the goods to be sold during the budget period. Schedule 10 shows Cozycamp.com's budgeted schedule of cost of goods manufactured and sold. The following Excel spreadsheet shows how the cost of the beginning and ending inventories of finished goods in schedule 10 are determined. From schedule 2, we see that the expected beginning and ending inventories of finished goods for 20x2 consist of 500 units. The absorption manufacturing cost for one unit of product is $163.50. The direct-material cost per unit is $128.00 ($108.00 + $20.00) (schedule 3), and the unit direct-labor cost is $7.50 (schedule 4). Recall that the *absorption* cost includes the direct-material and direct-labor costs and an allocation of all manufacturing overhead costs (i.e., overhead at the unit, batch, product, and facility, or general-operations, levels). The overhead cost data come from schedule 5.

Microsoft Excel - Aborption cost per unit

File Edit View Insert Format Tools Data Window Help

G9 =SUM(G1:G7)

	A–F	G
1	Direct material, tent fabric (12 yards x $9 per yard)	$108.000
2	Direct material, tent poles (1 tent pole kit x $20 per kit)	20.000
3	Direct labor (.5 hour x $15 per hour)	7.500
4	Unit-level manufacturing overhead ($200,000/50,000 units)	4.000
5	Batch-level manufacturing overhead ($150,000/50,000 units)	3.000
6	Product-level manufacturing overhead ($4,800/50,000 units)	0.096
7	Facility-level manufacturing overhead ($1,045,200/50,000 units)	20.904
8		
9	Total absorption cost per unit	$163.500

Sheet1 / Sheet2 / Sheet3

Ready

Schedule 10

COZYCAMP.COM
Budgeted Schedule of Cost of Goods Manufactured and Sold
For the Year Ending December 31, 20x2

Direct material (see schedule 3 for details):		
Raw-material inventory, January 1	$ 64,800[a]	
Add: Purchases of raw material	6,400,000[b]	
Raw material available for use	$6,464,800[b]	
Deduct: Raw-material inventory, December 31	64,800[a]	
Direct material used		$6,400,000[b]
Direct labor (see schedule 4 for details)		375,000
Manufacturing overhead (see schedule 5 for details)		1,400,000
Total manufacturing costs		$8,175,000
Add: Work-in-process inventory, January 1		0[c]
Subtotal		$8,175,000
Deduct: Work-in-process inventory, December 31		0[c]
Cost of goods manufactured		$8,175,000
Add: Finished-goods inventory, January 1		81,750[d]
Cost of goods available for sale		$8,256,750
Deduct: Finished-goods inventory, December 31		81,750[d]
Cost of goods sold		$8,175,000

[a]From schedule 3: 7,200 yards of tent fabric × $9 per yard, and zero inventory of tent pole kits.
[b]From schedule 3: $5,400,000 for tent fabric + $1,000,000 for tent pole kits.
[c]The company's production cycle is short enough that there is no work-in-process inventory at any time.
[d]From schedule 2: 500 units × $163.50 per unit, which is the absorption manufacturing cost per unit.

Budgeted Income Statement

The **budgeted income statement** shows the expected revenue and expenses for the budget period, assuming that planned operations are carried out. Cozycamp.com's budgeted income statement is displayed as schedule 11.

Schedule 11

COZYCAMP.COM
Budgeted Income Statement
For the Year Ending December 31, 20x2

Sales revenue (from schedule 1)		$11,250,000
Less: Cost of goods sold (from schedule 10)		8,175,000
Gross margin		$ 3,075,000
Other expenses:		
Selling, general, and administrative expenses (from schedule 6)	$1,406,500	
Uncollectible accounts expense (from schedule 7: 2% × $11,250,000)*	225,000	
Interest expense (from schedule 9)*	62,500	
Total other expenses		1,694,000
Net income		$ 1,381,000

*Usually these two expenses would be included in selling, general, and administrative expenses. They are listed separately in our illustration because they were determined after the selling, general, and administrative expense budget had already been explained.

Budgeted Statement of Cash Flows

The **budgeted statement of cash flows** provides information about the expected sources and uses of cash for operating activities, investing activities, and financing activities during a particular period of time. Cozycamp.com's budgeted statement of cash flows for 20x2 is displayed as schedule 12. Notice that the format used in the budgeted statement of cash flows follows that specified under the *direct method* of preparing the statement, which is recommended by the Financial Accounting Standards Board (FASB).[12] The format used in the statement of cash flows, which is a statement prepared by companies for *external* reporting purposes, generally differs from the format used in the cash receipts and cash disbursements budgets, which are prepared for *internal* use by management. Notice the differences in the format of schedule 11 when compared with schedules 7, 8, and 9. Notice also the greater detail in schedules 7, 8, and 9, which are designed for internal managerial use.

Schedule 12

COZYCAMP.COM
Budgeted Statement of Cash Flows
For the Year Ending December 31, 20x2

cozycamp.com

Cash flows from operating activities:		
Cash receipts from customers[a]		$11,025,000
Cash payments:		
To suppliers of raw material[b]	$6,400,000	
For direct labor[c]	375,000	
For manufacturing-overhead expenditures[d]	960,000	
For selling, general, and administrative expenses[e]	1,406,500	
For interest[f]	62,500	
Total cash payments		9,204,000
Net cash flow from operating activities		$ 1,821,000
Cash flows from investing activities:		
Construction of building addition[g]	(1,000,000)	
Net cash used by investing activities		(1,000,000)
Cash flows from financing activities:		
Principle of bank loan[f]	$1,000,000	
Repayment of bank loan[f]	(1,000,000)	
Net cash provided by financing activities		0
Net increase in cash and cash equivalents		$ 821,000
Balance in cash and cash equivalents, beginning of year		10,000
Balance in cash and cash equivalents, end of year		$ 831,000

[a]From Schedule 7.
[b]From Schedule 8.
[c]From Schedule 4.
[d]From Schedule 5.
[e]From Schedule 6.
[f]From Schedule 9.
[g]From Schedule 9.

[12]The direct and indirect methods of preparing the statement of cash flows are covered in financial accounting texts. They are also covered in the supplement to this text entitled *The Statement of Cash Flows and Financial Statement Analysis,* which is available from the publisher. This supplement is *not* needed in order to understand the preparation of the budget, as explained in this chapter.

Exhibit 9–4
Balance Sheet for December 31, 20x1

cozycamp.com

COZYCAMP.COM
Balance Sheet
December 31, 20x1

Assets		
Current assets:		
Cash		$ 10,000
Accounts receivable (net of allowance for uncollectible accounts)		405,000
Inventory:		
Raw material	$ 64,800	
Finished goods	81,750	
Supplies	42,000	
Total inventory		188,550
Total current assets		$ 603,550
Long-lived assets:		
Building	$8,200,000	
Equipment	2,280,000	
Less accumulated depreciation on building and equipment	(1,883,550)	
Building and equipment, net of accumulated depreciation		8,596,450
Total assets		$9,200,000
Liabilities and Owner's Equity		
Current liabilities:		
Accounts payable		$ 471,280
Total current liabilities		$ 471,280
Long-term liabilities:		
Note payable (non-interest bearing; due on December 31, 20x4)		4,100,000
Total liabilities		$4,571,280
Owner's equity		4,628,720
Total liabilities and owner's equity		$9,200,000

Budgeted Balance Sheet

The **budgeted balance sheet** shows the expected end-of-period balances for the company's assets, liabilities, and owner's equity, assuming that planned operations are carried out. Cozycamp.com's budgeted balance sheet for December 31, 20x2, is displayed as schedule 13. To construct this budgeted balance sheet, we start with the firm's balance sheet projected for the *beginning* of the budget year (Exhibit 9–4) and adjust each account balance for the changes expected during 20x2. These expected changes are reflected in the various 20x2 budget schedules.

Balance sheet December 31, 20x1 (Exhibit 9–4) → Expected changes in account balances during 20x2 → Balance sheet December 31, 20x2 (schedule 13)

Explanations for the account balances on the budgeted balance sheet for December 31, 20x2, are given in the second half of schedule 13. Examine these explanations carefully. Notice how the budgeted balance sheet pulls together information from most of the schedules constituting the master budget.

Schedule 13

COZYCAMP.COM
Budgeted Balance Sheet
December 31, 20x2

Assets		
Current assets:		
Cash (from schedule 9)		$ 831,000
Accounts receivable (net of allowance for uncollectible accounts)		405,000[a]
Inventory:		
Raw material (from schedule 10)	$ 64,800	
Finished goods (from schedule 10)	81,750	
Supplies	42,000	
Total inventory		188,550
Total current assets		$ 1,424,550
Long-lived assets:		
Building	$9,200,000[b]	
Equipment	2,280,000	
Less accumulated depreciation on building and equipment	(2,323,550)[c]	
Building and equipment, net of accumulated depreciation		9,156,450
Total assets		$10,581,000
Liabilities and Owner's Equity		
Current liabilities:		
Accounts payable		$ 471,280[d]
Total current liabilities		$ 471,280
Long-term liabilities:		
Note payable (non-interest-bearing; due on December 31, 20x4)		4,100,000
Total liabilities		4,571,280
Owner's equity		6,009,720[e]
Total liabilities and owner's equity		$10,581,000

[a]From schedule 7: 4th quarter sales of $2,250,000 times 18% amounts to $405,000.

[b]Balance in the Building account on the December 31, 20x1, balance sheet, plus the $1,000,000 cost of the building construction project in 20x2 (schedule 9).

[c]Balance in the Accumulated Depreciation account on the December 31, 20x1, balance sheet, plus the $440,000 in depreciation during 20x2 (schedule 5).

[d]From schedule 8: 4th quarter raw-material purchases of $1,178,200 times 40% amounts to $471,280.

[e]Balance in Owner's Equity on the December 31, 20x1, balance sheet, plus the 20x2 budgeted net income of $1,381,000 (schedule 11).

Assumptions and Predictions Underlying the Master Budget

LO 5 Discuss the role of assumptions and predictions in budgeting.

A master budget is based on many assumptions and estimates of unknown parameters. What are some of the assumptions and estimates used in Cozycamp.com's master budget? The professional sales budget was built on an assumption about the seasonal nature of demand for backpacking tents. The direct-material budget uses an estimate of the tent fabric price ($9.00 per yard), and the quantity of fabric required per tent (12 yards). An estimate of the direct labor required to make a tent was used in the direct-labor budget.

These are only a few of the many assumptions and estimates used in Cozycamp.com's master budget. Some of these estimates are much more likely to be accurate than others. For example, the amount of tent fabric required to make a tent is not likely to differ from past experience unless the type of material or production process is changed. In contrast, estimates such as the price of material, the cost of utilities, and sales demand are much more difficult to predict.

Financial Planning Models

Managers must make assumptions and predictions in preparing budgets because organizations operate in a world of uncertainty. One way of coping with that uncertainty is to supplement the budgeting process with a *financial planning model.* A **financial planning model** is a set of mathematical relationships that express the interactions among the various operational, financial, and environmental events that determine the overall results of an organization's activities. A financial planning model is a mathematical expression of all the relationships expressed in the flowchart of Exhibit 9–1.

To illustrate this concept, focus on the following equation, which was used to budget uncollectible accounts expense in schedule 7.

$$(\text{Uncollectible accounts expense}) = .02 \times (\text{Sales revenue})$$

Suppose Cozycamp.com's management is uncertain about this 2 percent estimate. A financial planning model might include the following equation instead.

$$(\text{Uncollectible accounts expense}) = p \times (\text{Sales revenue})$$

where $0 \leq p \leq 1.0$.

The budget staff can run the financial planning model as many times as desired on a computer, using a different value for p each time. Perhaps the following values would be tried: .04, .045, .05, .055, and .06. Now management can answer the question, What if 4 percent of sales prove to be uncollectible? In a fully developed financial planning model, all of the key estimates and assumptions are expressed as general mathematical relationships. Then the model is run on a computer many times to determine the impact of different combinations of these unknown variables. "What if" questions can be answered about such unknown variables as inflation, interest rates, the value of the dollar, demand, competitors' actions, production efficiency, union demands in forthcoming wage negotiations, and a host of other factors. The widespread availability of personal computers and electronic-spreadsheet software has made financial planning models a more and more common management tool.

Budget Administration

LO 6

Describe a typical organization's process of budget administration.

In small organizations, the procedures used to gather information and construct a master budget are usually informal. In the early days of Cozycamp, for example, when the company was still quite small, the budgeting process was coordinated by the business manager in consultation with the firm's owner. In contrast, larger organizations use a formal process to collect data and prepare the master budget. Such organizations usually designate a **budget director** or **chief budget officer.** This is often the organization's controller. The budget director specifies the process by which budget data will be gathered, collects the information, and prepares the master budget. To communicate budget procedures and deadlines to employees throughout the organization, the budget director often develops and disseminates a **budget manual.** The budget manual states who is responsible for providing various types of information, when the information is required, and what form the information is to take. For example, the budget manual for a manufacturing firm might specify that each regional sales director is to send an estimate of the following year's sales, by product line, to the budget director by September 1. The budget manual also states who should receive each schedule when the master budget is complete.

A **budget committee,** consisting of key senior executives, is often appointed to advise the budget director during the preparation of the budget. The authority to give final approval to the master budget usually belongs to the board of directors, or a board of trustees in many nonprofit organizations. Usually the board has a subcommittee whose task is to examine the proposed budget carefully and recommend approval or any changes deemed necessary. By exercising its authority to make changes in the budget and grant final approval, the board of directors, or trustees, can wield considerable influence on the overall direction the organization takes.

Management Accounting Practice

Cornell University

BUDGET ADMINISTRATION AT CORNELL UNIVERSITY

Cornell University's annual budget covers the period from July 1 through the following June 30. The budgeting process begins in October, when the deans and senior vice presidents have meetings to discuss the programs the university will conduct during the following budget year. The university's priorities in educational, research, and public service programs are established during these meetings. In early January, the university's budget director, together with other members of the Operating Plans Committee, settles on a set of assumptions to be used during the remainder of the budgeting process. These assumptions include such key forecasts as the next year's inflation rate, interest rates, and tuition levels. Based on these assumptions, the dean of each of Cornell's colleges or professional schools must develop a detailed budget for salaries and general expenses. These detailed budgets are prepared during January and February by the financial staff in each college or professional school. In March, the university president and provost review these budgets with the deans. After any needed revisions have been made, the budgets for the various colleges and professional schools are consolidated by the university controller's staff into a master budget. This budget is presented to the university's board of trustees in May for their final approval.

e-Budgeting

As more and more companies operate globally, the Internet is playing an ever-greater role in the budgeting process. E-budgeting is an increasingly popular, Internet-based budgeting tool that can help streamline and speed up an organization's budgeting process. The *e* in **e-budgeting** stands for both *electronic* and *enterprise-wide;* employees throughout an organization, at all levels and around the globe, can submit and retrieve budget information electronically via the Internet. Budgeting software is utilized and made available on the Web, so that budget information electronically submitted from any location is in a consistent companywide format. Managers in organizations using e-budgeting have found that it greatly streamlines the entire budgeting process. In the past these organizations have compiled their master budgets on hundreds of spreadsheets, which had to be collected and integrated by the corporate controller's office. One result of this cumbersome approach was that a disproportionate amount of time was spent compiling and verifying data from multiple sources. Under e-budgeting, both the submission of budget information and its compilation are accomplished electronically by the Web-based budgeting software. Thus e-budgeting is just one more area where the Internet has transformed how the workplace operates in the era of e-business.[13]

"Implementing a Web-based, enterprise-wide budgeting solution will help us develop business plans and allow our analysts to be proactive in monitoring quarterly results." (9f)
Toronto Dominion Bank

Firewalls and Information Security

Since most companies' budget information is extremely sensitive and confidential, it is absolutely critical that adequate network security provisions are in place to keep unauthorized people from hacking into an organization's budget database. Unauthorized individuals include competitors, all other outsiders to the organization, and even the organization's own employees who are not permitted access to particular budget

[13]Steve Hornyak, "Budgeting Made Easy," *Management Accounting* 80, no. 4 (October 1998), pp. 18–23.

information. A **firewall** is a computer or information router placed between a company's internal network and the Internet to control and monitor all information between the outside world and the company's local network. "Typically, the firewall device allows the organization's insiders to have full access to Internet services on the outside while granting access from the outside only selectively, based on a log-on name, password, IP (Internet protocol) address, or other identifiers."[14]

Management Accounting Practice

Lockheed Martin

LOCKHEED MARTIN

Lockheed Martin's IBS business unit (Integrated Business Solutions) selected SRC Software's Advisor Series for budgeting and financial reporting. "IBS needed a multidimensional budgeting and long-term forecasting system that would integrate with several data sources and easily distribute budgets to managers at remote sites." Before implementing SRC's enterprise-wide budgeting software, Lockheed Martin's IBS unit "was utilizing a combination of spreadsheet and database programs for budgeting and reporting. This was time-consuming and labor intensive, and it did not provide the required standardization and consolidation capabilities. What IBS wanted was an easy-to-use system that would serve as a 'data mart' for all the information it required, allow full multidimensional consolidation capabilities and ad hoc reporting and provide an automated method for distributing the information throughout the organization." Now when an IBS manager needs to create and distribute a budget-related document, the manager simply logs on to the Advisor software application, automatically imports the data, creates the desired report, and distributes it to the appropriate recipient list via an automated e-mail utility. The SRC Advisor software application has greatly facilitated Lockheed Martin's IBS business unit's companywide access to financial information.[15]

Zero-Base Budgeting

Zero-base budgeting is used in a wide variety of organizations, including Southern California Edison, Texas Instruments, and the state of Georgia. Under zero-base budgeting, the budget for virtually every activity in the organization is initially set to zero. To receive funding during the budgeting process, each activity must be justified in terms of its continued usefulness. The zero-base-budgeting approach forces management to rethink each phase of an organization's operations before allocating resources.

Base Budgeting Some organizations use a **base-budgeting** approach without going to the extreme of zero-base budgeting. Under this approach, the initial budget for each of the organization's departments is set in accordance with a **base package,** which includes the minimal resources required for the subunit to exist at an absolute minimal level. Below this level of funding, the subunit would not be a viable entity. Any increases above the base package would result from a decision to fund an **incremental package,** which describes the resources needed to add various activities to the base package. The decision to approve such an incremental budget package would

---

[14]Ravi Kalakota and Andrew B. Whinston, *Frontiers of Electronic Commerce* (Reading, MA: Addison-Wesley, 1996), pp. 185–92; and Marilyn Greenstein and Todd M. Feinman, *Electronic Commerce: Security, Risk Management and Control* (Burr Ridge, IL: McGraw-Hill/Irwin, 2000), pp. 267–91.

[15]"SRC Software Provides Enterprise-Wide Budgeting and Reporting Solution to Lockheed Martin Business Unit," *Financial Software Supplement to Management Accounting,* August 1998, p. 24.

have to be justified on the basis of the costs and benefits of the activities included. Base budgeting has been effective in many organizations because it forces managers to take an evaluative, questioning attitude toward each of the organization's programs.

International Aspects of Budgeting

As this photo from Tokyo, Japan, shows, McDonald's operates restaurants throughout the world. Multinational companies like McDonald's face special challenges in preparing their budgets.

As the economies and cultures of countries throughout the world become intertwined, more and more companies are becoming multinational in their operations. Firms with international operations face a variety of additional challenges in preparing their budgets. First, a multinational firm's budget must reflect the translation of foreign currencies into U.S. dollars. Since almost all the world's currencies fluctuate in their values relative to the dollar, this makes budgeting for those translations difficult. Although multinationals have sophisticated financial ways of hedging against such currency fluctuations, the budgeting task is still more challenging. Second, it is difficult to prepare budgets when inflation is high or unpredictable. While the United States has experienced periods of high inflation, some foreign countries have experienced hyperinflation, sometimes with annual inflation rates well over 100 percent. Predicting such high inflation rates is difficult and further complicates a multinational's budgeting process. Finally, the economies of all countries fluctuate in terms of consumer demand, availability of skilled labor, laws affecting commerce, and so forth. Companies with off-shore operations face the task of anticipating such changing conditions in their budgeting processes.

Budgeting Product Life-Cycle Costs

LO 7

Understand the importance of budgeting product life-cycle costs.

A relatively recent focus of the budgeting process is to plan for all of the costs that will be incurred throughout a product's life cycle, before a commitment is made to the product.[16] Product life-cycle costs encompass the following five phases in a product's life cycle:

- Product planning and concept design.
- Preliminary design.
- Detailed design and testing.
- Production.
- Distribution and customer service.

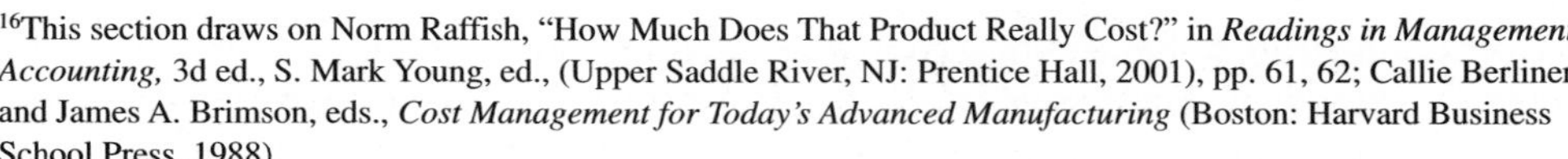

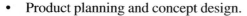

[16]This section draws on Norm Raffish, "How Much Does That Product Really Cost?" in *Readings in Management Accounting,* 3d ed., S. Mark Young, ed., (Upper Saddle River, NJ: Prentice Hall, 2001), pp. 61, 62; Callie Berliner and James A. Brimson, eds., *Cost Management for Today's Advanced Manufacturing* (Boston: Harvard Business School Press, 1988).

Exhibit 9–5
Product Life-Cycle Costs and Cost Commitment for a Typical Product

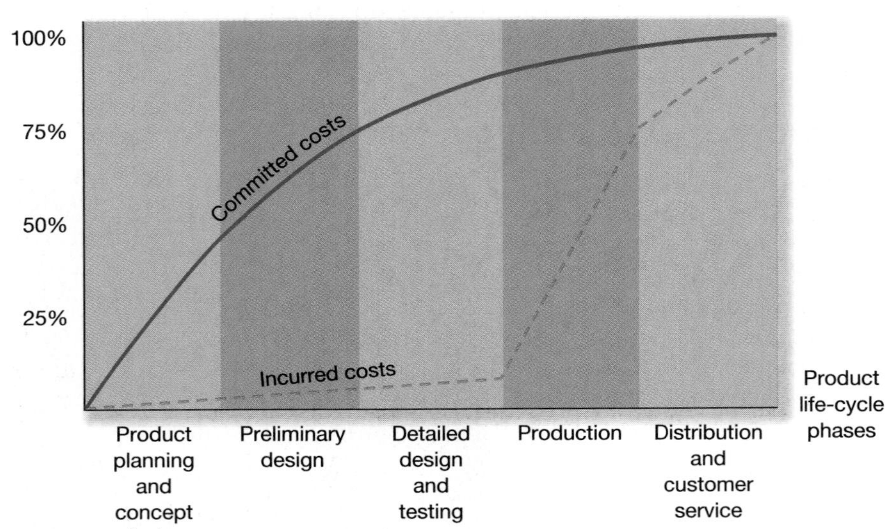

Exhibit 9–6
Product Life-Cycle Cost Budget

	Year				
Life-Cycle Phase	**20x0**	**20x1**	**20x2**	**20x3**	**20x4**
Product planning and concept design	$300,000				
Preliminary design	100,000				
Detail design and testing		$600,000			
Production		300,000	$2,000,000	$2,700,000	$1,200,000
Distribution and customer service		50,000	750,000	1,000,000	1,000,000

In order to justify a product's introduction, the sales revenues it will generate over its life must be sufficient to cover all of these costs. Thus planning these life-cycle costs is a crucial step in making a decision about the introduction of a new product. This is particularly true for firms with very short product life cycles, such as some products in the computer and electronics industries. When product life cycles are as short as a year or two, the firm does not have time to adjust its pricing strategy or production methods to ensure that the product turns a profit. Management must be fairly certain before a commitment is made to the product that its life-cycle costs will be covered. As Exhibit 9–5 shows, most of a product's life-cycle costs are committed rather early in the product's life. By the time the planning, design, and testing phases are complete, roughly 85 percent of this product's life-cycle costs have been committed, while only about 5 percent actually have been incurred.

Given the early commitment that must be made to significant downstream costs in a product's life cycle, it is crucial to budget these costs as early as possible. Exhibit 9–6 displays a product life-cycle cost budget for an ancillary computer device with an anticipated five-year life cycle.

Behavioral Impact of Budgets

LO 8
Discuss the behavioral implications of budgetary slack and participative budgeting.

One of the underlying themes stressed in this text is the behavioral impact of managerial accounting practices. There is no other area where the behavioral implications are more important than in the budgeting area. A budget affects virtually everyone in an organization: those who prepare the budget, those who use the budget to facilitate decision mak-

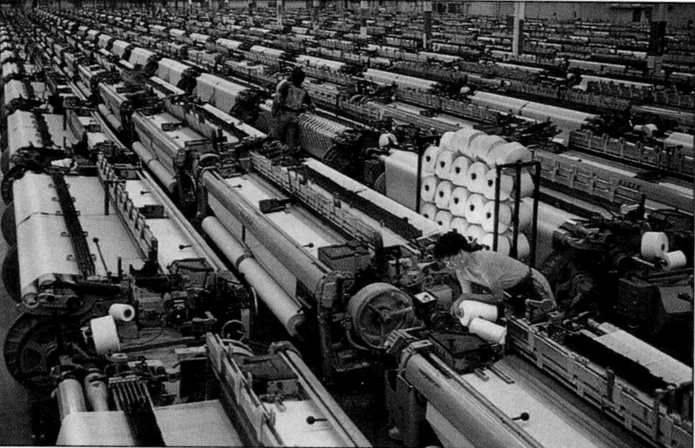

Product life-cycle costing plans for the costs to be incurred throughout a product's life cycle. Pictured here are the design and production of fabric by a textile manufacturer.

ing, and those who are evaluated using the budget. The human reactions to the budgeting process can have considerable influence on an organization's overall effectiveness.

A great deal of study has been devoted to the behavioral effects of budgets. Here we will barely scratch the surface by briefly considering two issues: budgetary slack and participative budgeting.

Budgetary Slack: Padding the Budget

The information upon which a budget is based comes largely from people throughout an organization. For example, the sales forecast relies on market research and analysis by a market research staff but also incorporates the projections of sales personnel. If a territorial sales manager's performance is evaluated on the basis of whether the sales budget for the territory is exceeded, what is the incentive for the sales manager in projecting sales? The incentive is to give a conservative, or cautiously low sales estimate. The sales manager's performance will look much better in the eyes of top management when a conservative estimate is exceeded than when an ambitious estimate is not met. At least that is the *perception* of many sales managers, and in the behavioral area perceptions are what count most.

When a supervisor provides a departmental cost projection for budgetary purposes, there is an incentive to overestimate costs. When the actual cost incurred in the department proves to be less than the inflated cost projection, the supervisor appears to have managed in a cost-effective way.

These illustrations are examples of **padding the budget.** Budget padding means underestimating revenue or overestimating costs. The difference between the revenue or cost projection that a person provides and a realistic estimate of the revenue or cost is called **budgetary slack.** For example, if one of Cozycamp.com's department managers believes the annual utilities cost will be $18,000, but gives a budgetary projection of $20,000, the manager has built $2,000 of slack into the budget.

Why do people pad budgets with budgetary slack? There are three primary reasons. First, people often *perceive* that their performance will look better in their superiors' eyes if they can "beat the budget." Second, budgetary slack often is used to cope with uncertainty. A departmental supervisor may feel confident in the cost projections for 10 cost items. However, the supervisor also may feel that some unforeseen event during the budgetary period could result in unanticipated costs. For example, an unexpected machine breakdown could occur. One way of dealing with that unforeseen event is to pad the budget. If nothing goes wrong, the supervisor can beat the cost budget. If some negative event does occur, the supervisor can use the budgetary slack to absorb the impact of the event and still meet the cost budget.

The third reason why cost budgets are padded is that budgetary cost projections are often cut in the resource-allocation process. Thus, we have a vicious circle. Budgetary projections are padded because they will likely be cut, and they are cut because they are likely to have been padded.

How does an organization solve the problem of budgetary slack? First, it can avoid relying on the budget as a negative evaluation tool. If a departmental supervisor is harassed by the budget director or some other top manager every time a budgetary cost projection is exceeded, the likely behavioral response will be to pad the budget. In contrast, if the supervisor is allowed some managerial discretion to exceed the budget when necessary, there will be less tendency toward budgetary padding. Second, managers can be given incentives not only to achieve budgetary projections but also to *provide accurate projections.* This can be accomplished by asking managers to justify all or some of their projections and by rewarding managers who consistently provide accurate estimates.

Participative Budgeting

Most people will perform better and make greater attempts to achieve a goal if they have been consulted in setting the goal. The idea of **participative budgeting** is to involve employees throughout an organization in the budgetary process. Such participation can give employees the feeling that "this is our budget," rather than the all-too-common feeling that "this is the budget you imposed on us."

While participative budgeting can be very effective, it can also have shortcomings. Too much participation and discussion can lead to vacillation and delay. Also, when those involved in the budgeting process disagree in significant and irreconcilable ways, the process of participation can accentuate those differences. Finally, the problem of budget padding can be severe unless incentives for accurate projections are provided.

Focus on Ethics

IS PADDING THE BUDGET UNETHICAL?

A departmental or divisional budget often is used as the basis for evaluating a manager's performance. Actual results are compared with budgeted performance levels, and those who outperform the budget often are rewarded with promotions or salary increases. In many cases, bonuses are tied explicitly to performance relative to a budget. For example, the top-management personnel of a division may receive a bonus if divisional profit exceeds budgeted profit by a certain percentage.

Serious ethical issues can arise in situations where a budget is the basis for rewarding managers. For example, suppose a division's top-management personnel will split a bonus equal to 10 percent of the amount by which actual divisional profit exceeds the budget. This may create an incentive for the divisional budget officer, or other managers supplying data, to pad the divisional profit budget. Such padding would make the budget easier to achieve, thus increasing the chance of a bonus. Alternatively, there may be an incentive to manipulate the actual divisional results in order to maximize management's bonus. For example, year-end sales could be shifted between years to increase reported revenue in a particular year. Budget personnel could have such incentives for either of two reasons: (1) they might share in the bonus, or (2) they might feel pressure from the managers who would share in the bonus.

Put yourself in the position of the division controller. Your bonus, and that of your boss, the division vice president, will be determined in part by the division's income in comparison to the budget. When your division has submitted budgets in the past, the corporate management has usually cut your budgeted expenses, thereby increasing the division's budgeted profit. This, of course, makes it more difficult for your division to achieve the budgeted profit. Moreover, it makes it less likely that you and your divisional colleagues will earn a bonus.

Now your boss is pressuring you to pad the expense budget, because "the budgeted expenses will just be cut anyway at the corporate level." Is padding the budget ethical under these circumstances? What do you think?

Chapter Summary

The budget is a key tool for planning, control, and decision making in virtually every organization. Budgeting systems are used to force planning, to facilitate communication and coordination, to allocate resources, to control profit and operations, and to evaluate performance and provide incentives. Various types of budgets are used to accomplish these objectives.

The comprehensive set of budgets that covers all phases of an organization's operations is called a master budget. The first step in preparing a master budget is to forecast sales of the organization's services or goods. Based on the sales forecast, operational budgets are prepared to plan production of services or goods and to outline the acquisition and use of material, labor, and other resources. Finally, a set of budgeted financial statements is prepared to show what the organization's overall financial condition will be if planned operations are carried out.

The application of activity-based costing (ABC) concepts to the budgeting process yields activity-based budgeting (ABB). Utilizing ABC information in the budgeting process through activity-based budgeting provides sound information for budgeting costs, because the underlying ABC information is based explicitly on the relationships among cost drivers, activities, and resources consumed.

E-budgeting means electronic and enterprise-wide budgeting by making use of the Internet. Employees throughout an organization, at all levels and around the world, can submit and retrieve budget information via the Internet.

Since budgets affect almost everyone in an organization, they can have significant behavioral implications and can raise difficult ethical issues. One common problem in budgeting is the tendency of people to pad budgets. The resulting budgetary slack makes the budget less useful because the padded budget does not present an accurate picture of expected revenue and expenses.

Participative budgeting is the process of allowing employees throughout the organization to have a significant role in developing the budget. Participative budgeting can result in greater commitment to meet the budget by those who participated in the process.

A relatively recent focus of the budgeting process is to plan for product life-cycle costs. A large portion of these costs often are committed early in a product's life cycle. It is important for management to be fairly certain that the revenue to be generated by a product will cover all of its life-cycle costs.[17]

[17]For an extensive treatment of budgeting issues, see Glenn Welsch, Ronald Hilton, and Paul Gordon, *Budgeting: Profit Planning and Control,* 5th ed. (Englewood Cliffs, NJ: Prentice Hall, 1988).

Key Terms

For each term's definition refer to the indicated page, or turn to the glossary at the end of the text.

*Term appears in the appendix.

Appendix to Chapter 9

Inventory Management

LO 9

After completing the appendix, understand the differences between the economic-order-quantity and just-in-time approaches to inventory management.

cozycamp.com

A key decision in manufacturing, retail, and some service industry firms is how much inventory to keep on hand. Once inventory levels are established, they become an important input to the budgeting system. Inventory decisions involve a delicate balance between three classes of costs: ordering costs, holding costs, and shortage costs. Examples of costs in each of these categories are given in Exhibit 9–7.

The following illustration emphasizes the benefits of a sound inventory policy.

Economic Order Quantity

Cozycamp.com has expanded its product line into winter sports equipment. The company's newest product is a fiberglass snowboard. One of the raw materials is a special resin used to bind the fiberglass in the molding phase of production. The production manager, Hi Mogul, uses an **economic order quantity (EOQ)** decision model to determine the size and frequency with which resin is ordered. The EOQ model is a mathematical tool for determining the order quantity that minimizes the costs of ordering and holding inventory.

Resin is purchased in 50-gallon drums, and 9,600 drums are used each year. Each drum costs $400. The controller estimates that the cost of placing and receiving a typical resin order is $225. The controller's estimate of the annual cost of carrying resin in inventory is $3 per drum.

Tabular Approach Suppose Mogul orders 800 drums of resin in each order placed during the year. The total annual cost of ordering and holding resin in inventory is calculated as follows:

$$\frac{\text{Annual requirement}}{\text{Quantity per order}} = \frac{9{,}600}{800} = 12 = \text{Number of orders}$$

$$\text{Annual ordering cost} = 12 \text{ orders} \times \$225 \text{ per order} = \$2{,}700$$

$$\text{Average quantity in inventory} = \frac{\text{Quantity per order}}{2} = \frac{800}{2} = 400 \text{ drums}$$

Exhibit 9–7
Inventory Ordering, Holding, and Shortage Costs

Ordering Costs
- Clerical costs of preparing purchase orders
- Time spent finding suppliers and expediting orders
- Transportation costs
- Receiving costs (e.g., unloading and inspection)

Holding Costs
- Costs of storage space (e.g., warehouse depreciation)
- Security
- Insurance
- Forgone interest on working capital tied up in inventory
- Deterioration, theft, spoilage, or obsolescence

Shortage Costs
- Disrupted production when raw materials are unavailable:
  - Idle workers
  - Extra machinery setups
- Lost sales resulting in dissatisfied customers
- Loss of quantity discounts on purchases

Exhibit 9–8
Tabulation of Inventory Ordering and Holding Costs

Order size	800	960	1,200	1,600	2,400
Number of orders (9,600 ÷ order size)	12	10	8	6	4
Ordering costs ($225 × number of orders)	$2,700	$2,250	$1,800	$1,350	$ 900
Average inventory (order size ÷ 2)	400	480	600	800	1,200
Holding costs ($3 × average inventory)	$1,200	$1,440	$1,800	$2,400	$3,600
Total annual cost (ordering cost + holding cost)	$3,900	$3,690	$3,600	$3,750	$4,500
			↑ Minimum		

$$\text{Annual holding cost} = (\text{Average quantity in inventory}) \times (\text{Annual carrying cost per drum})$$
$$= 400 \times \$3 = \$1{,}200$$

$$\begin{matrix}\text{Total annual cost}\\ \text{of inventory policy}\end{matrix} = \text{Ordering cost} + \text{Holding cost} = \$2{,}700 + \$1{,}200 = \$3{,}900$$

Notice that the $3,900 cost does not include the purchase cost of the resin at $400 per drum. We are focusing only on the costs of *ordering* and *holding* resin inventory.

Can Mogul do any better than $3,900 for the annual cost of his resin inventory policy? Exhibit 9–8, which tabulates the inventory costs for various order quantities, indicates that Mogul can lower the costs of ordering and holding resin inventory. Of the five order quantities listed, the 1,200 drum order quantity yields the lowest total annual cost. Unfortunately, this tabular method for finding the least-cost order quantity is cumbersome. Moreover, it does not necessarily result in the optimal order quantity. It is possible that some order quantity other than those listed in Exhibit 9–8 is the least-cost order quantity.

Equation Approach The total annual cost of ordering and holding inventory is given by the following equation.

$$\text{Total annual cost} = \left(\frac{\text{Annual requirement}}{\text{Order quantity}}\right)\left(\frac{\text{Cost per}}{\text{order}}\right) + \left(\frac{\text{Order quantity}}{2}\right)\left(\frac{\text{Annual holding}}{\text{cost per unit}}\right)$$

The following formula for the least-cost order quantity, called the economic order quantity (or EOQ), has been developed using calculus.

$$\text{Economic order quantity} = \sqrt{\frac{(2)(\text{Annual requirement})(\text{Cost per order})}{(\text{Annual holding cost per unit})}}$$

Applying the EOQ formula in Cozycamp.com's problem yields the following EOQ for resin.

$$\text{EOQ} = \sqrt{\frac{(2)(9{,}600)(225)}{3}} = 1{,}200$$

Graphical Approach Another method for solving the EOQ problem is the graphical method, which is presented in Exhibit 9–9. Notice that the ordering-cost line slants down to the right. This indicates a decline in these costs as the order size increases and the order frequency decreases. However, as the order size increases, so does the average inventory on hand. This results in an increase in holding costs, as indicated by the positive slope of the holding-cost line. The EOQ falls at 1,200 units, where the best balance is struck between these two costs. Total costs are minimized at $3,600.

Timing of Orders

The EOQ model helps management decide how much to order at a time. Another important decision is when to order. This decision depends on the **lead time,** which is the length of time it takes for the material to be received after an order is placed. Suppose the lead time for resin is one month. Since Cozycamp.com uses 9,600 drums of resin per year, and the production rate is constant throughout the year, this implies that 800 drums are used each month. Production manager Mogul should order resin, in the economic order quantity of 1,200 drums, when the inventory falls to 800 drums. By the time the new

Exhibit 9–9
Graphical Solution to Economic Order Quantity Decision

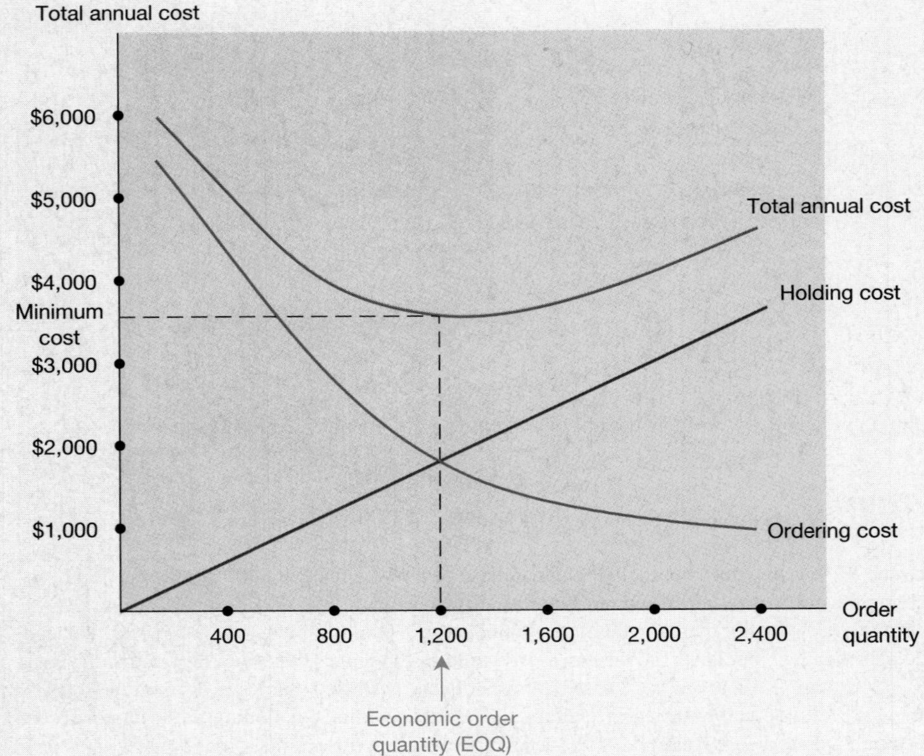

Exhibit 9–10
Ordering, Lead Time, and Usage of Inventory

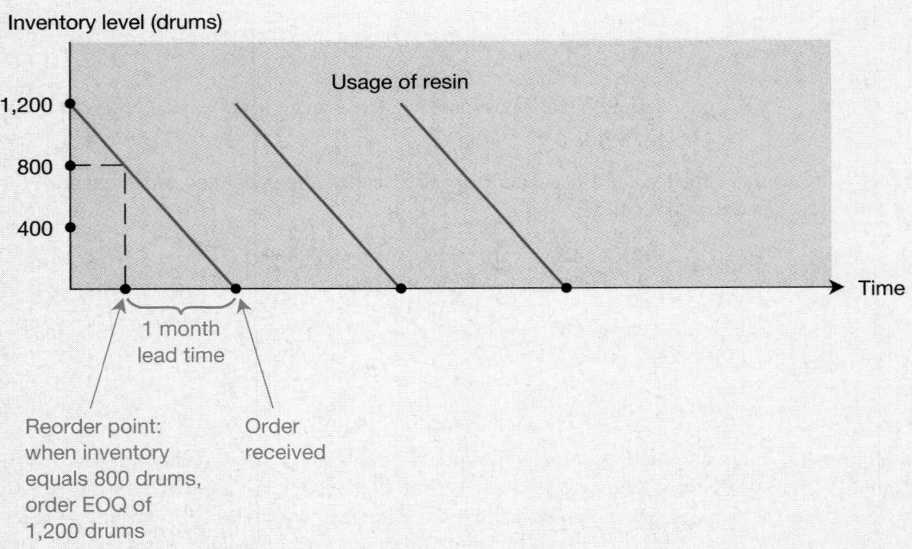

order arrives, one month later, the 800 drums in inventory will have been used in production. Exhibit 9–10 depicts this pattern of ordering and using inventory. By placing an order early enough to avoid a stockout, management takes into account the potential costs of shortages.

Safety Stock Our example assumed that the usage of resin is constant at 800 drums per month. Suppose instead that monthly usage fluctuates between 600 and 1,000 drums. Although average monthly usage still is 800 drums, there is the potential for an excess usage of 200 drums in any particular month. In light of this uncertainty, management may wish to keep a safety stock of resin equal to the potential excess monthly usage of 200 drums. With a safety stock of 200 drums, the reorder point is 1,000 drums.

Holding Costs per Unit	Ordering Costs per Order				
	$225	$150	$100	$50	
$3	1,200*	980	800	566	EOQ declines
4	1,039	849	693	490	
5	930	759	620	438	
6	849	693	566	400	
	EOQ declines				

Exhibit 9–11
Economic Order Quantity with Different Ordering and Holding Costs

cozycamp.com

*The annual requirement is assumed to be 9,600 units for each case in this table. This was the annual requirement for drums of resin in the Cozycamp.com illustration. (Several of the EOQs in the table are rounded.)

Thus, Mogul should order the EOQ of 1,200 drums whenever resin inventory falls to 1,000 drums. During the one-month lead time, another 600 to 1,000 drums of resin will be consumed in production. Although a safety stock will increase inventory holding costs, it will minimize the potential costs caused by shortages.

JIT Inventory Management: Implications for EOQ

The EOQ model minimizes the total cost of ordering and holding purchased inventory. Thus, this inventory management approach seeks to balance the cost of ordering against the cost of storing inventory. Under the JIT philosophy, the goal is to keep *all* inventories as low as possible. *Any* inventory holding costs are seen as inefficient and wasteful. Moreover, under JIT purchasing, ordering costs are minimized by reducing the number of vendors, negotiating long-term supply agreements, making less frequent payments, and eliminating inspections. The implication of the JIT philosophy is that inventories should be minimized by more frequent deliveries in smaller quantities. This result can be demonstrated using the EOQ formula, as shown in Exhibit 9–11. As the cost of holding inventory increases, the EOQ decreases. Moreover, as the cost of placing an order declines, the EOQ decreases.

The economics underlying the EOQ model support the JIT viewpoint that inventory should be purchased or produced in small quantities, and inventories should be kept to the absolute minimum. However, the basic philosophies of JIT and EOQ are quite different. The EOQ approach takes the view that some inventory is necessary, and the goal is to optimize the order quantity in order to balance the cost of ordering against the cost of holding inventory. In contrast, the JIT philosophy argues that holding costs tend to be higher than may be apparent because of the inefficiency and waste of storing inventory. Thus, inventory should be minimized, or even eliminated completely if possible. Moreover, under the JIT approach, orders typically will vary in size, depending on needs. The EOQ model, in contrast, results in a constant order quantity.

Review Questions

9–1. Explain how a budget facilitates communication and coordination.

9–2. Use an example to explain how a budget could be used to allocate resources in a university.

9–3. Explain what a *master budget* is, and list five of its parts.

9–4. Draw a flowchart similar to the one in Exhibit 9–1 for a service station. The service station provides automotive maintenance services in addition to selling gasoline and related products.

9–5. Give an example of how general economic trends would affect sales forecasting in the airline industry.

9–6. What is meant by the term *operational budgets?* List three operational budgets that would be prepared by a hospital.

9–7. How does activity-based budgeting differ from more traditional budgeting methods?

9–8. How does e-budgeting make use of the Internet?

9–9. Give three examples of how the city of Boston could use a budget for planning purposes.

9–10. Describe the role of a *budget director.*

9–11. What is the purpose of a *budget manual?*

9–12. How can a company's board of directors use the budget to influence the future direction of the firm?

9–13. Explain the concept of *zero-base budgeting.*

9–14. Discuss the importance of predictions and assumptions in the budgeting process.

9–15. Define the term *budgetary slack,* and briefly describe a problem it can cause.

9–16. How can an organization help to reduce the problems caused by budgetary slack?

9–17. Why is participative budgeting often an effective management tool?

9–18. Discuss this comment by a small-town bank president: "Budgeting is a waste of time. I've been running this business for 40 years. I don't need to plan."

9–19. List the steps you would go through in developing a budget to meet your college expenses.

9–20. Briefly describe three issues that create special challenges for multinational firms in preparing their budgets.

9–21. List five phases in a product's *life cycle,* and explain why it is important to budget the costs in each of these phases.

9–22. (Appendix) Define and give examples of *inventory ordering, holding,* and *shortage costs.*

9–23. (Appendix) Explain the differences in the basic philosophies underlying the JIT and EOQ approaches to inventory management.

Exercises

Exercise 9–24
Budgeting Production and Raw-Material Purchases
(LO 2, 4)

San Fernando Fertilizer Company plans to sell 40,000 units of finished product in July and anticipates a growth rate in sales of 5 percent per month. The desired monthly ending inventory in units of finished product is 80 percent of the next month's estimated sales. There are 32,000 finished units in inventory on June 30. Each unit of finished product requires four pounds of raw material at a cost of $1.40 per pound. There are 140,000 pounds of raw material in inventory on June 30.

Required:

1. Compute the company's total required production in units of finished product for the entire three-month period ending September 30.
2. Independent of your answer to requirement (1), assume the company plans to produce 120,000 units of finished product in the three-month period ending September 30, and to have raw-material inventory on hand at the end of the three-month period equal to 25 percent of the use in that period. Compute the total estimated cost of raw-material purchases for the entire three-month period ending September 30.

(CMA, adapted)

Exercise 9–25
Cash Collections
(LO 2, 4)

Coyote Loco, Inc., a manufacturer of salsa, has the following historical collection pattern for its credit sales.

70 percent collected in the month of sale.
15 percent collected in the first month after sale.
10 percent collected in the second month after sale.
4 percent collected in the third month after sale.
1 percent uncollectible.

The sales on account have been budgeted for the last seven months as follows:

Month	Sales
June	$122,500
July	150,000
August	175,000
September	200,000
October	225,000
November	250,000
December	212,500

Required:

1. Compute the estimated total cash collections during October from credit sales.
2. Compute the estimated total cash collections during the fourth quarter from sales made on account during the fourth quarter.

(CMA, adapted)

Exercise 9–26
Missing Amounts; Various Types of Budgets
(LO 2, 4)

Fill in the missing amounts in the following schedules.

	July	August	September
1. Sales*	$240,000	$180,000	$?
Cash receipts:			
From cash sales	$?	$?	$135,000
From sales on account†	?	102,000	?
Total cash receipts	$?	$?	$?

2. Accounts payable, 12/31/x0	600,000 *Euros*‡
Purchase of goods and services on account during 20x1	2,400,000
Payments of accounts payable during 20x1	?
Accounts payable, 12/31/x1	800,000
3. Accounts receivable, 12/31/x0	1,700,000 *yen*§
Sales on account during 20x1	4,500,000
Collections of accounts receivable during 20x1	3,900,000
Accounts receivable, 12/31/x1	?
4. Accumulated depreciation, 12/31/x0	$ 405,000
Depreciation expense during 20x1	75,000
Accumulated depreciation, 12/31/x1	?
5. Retained earnings, 12/31/x0	$1,537,500
Net income for 20x1	300,000
Dividends paid in 20x1	–0–
Retained earnings, 12/31/x1	?

*Half of each month's sales are on account. June sales amounted to $180,000.

†60% of credit sales is collected in the month of sale; 40% is collected in the following month.

‡The new monetary unit, the *Euro*, has now been introduced in most European markets.

§*Yen* is the Japanese national currency.

Exercise 9–27
Budgeting Production and Direct-Material Purchases
(LO 2, 4)

Adler Company budgets on an annual basis. The following beginning and ending inventory levels (in units) are planned for the next year. Two units of raw material are required to produce each unit of finished product.

	January 1	December 31
Raw material	245,000	315,000
Work in process	84,000	84,000
Finished goods	560,000	350,000

Required:

1. If Alder Company plans to sell 3,360,000 units during the year, compute the number of units the firm would have to manufacture during the year.
2. If 3,500,000 finished units were to be manufactured by Adler Company during the year, determine the amount of raw material to be purchased.

(CMA, adapted)

Exercise 9–28
Cash Budgeting
(LO 2, 4)

The following information is from White Mountain Furniture Company's financial records.

Month	Sales	Purchases
July	$180,000	$105,000
August	165,000	120,000
September	150,000	90,000
October	195,000	135,000

Collections from customers are normally 70 percent in the month of sale, 20 percent in the month following the sale, and 9 percent in the second month following the sale. The balance is expected to be uncollectible. All purchases are on account. Management takes full advantage of the 2 percent discount allowed on purchases paid for by the tenth of the following month. Purchases for November are budgeted at $150,000, and sales for November are forecasted at $165,000. Cash disbursements for expenses are expected to be $36,000 for the month of November. The company's cash balance on November 1 was $55,000.

Required: Prepare the following schedules.

1. Expected cash collections during November.
2. Expected cash disbursements during November.
3. Expected cash balance on November 30.

(CPA, adapted)

Exercise 9–29
City or State Budget; Use of Internet
(LO 1, 2)

Choose a city or state in the United States (or a Canadian city or province), and use the Internet to explore the annual budget of the governmental unit you selected. For example, you could check out the budget for Los Angeles at www.losangeles.com. Alternatively, take a look at the U.S. federal budget at www.fms.treas.gov/annualreport/index.html.

Required: List three items in the budget that you found surprising or particularly interesting, and explain why.

Exercise 9–30
Budgeted Financial Statements; Retailer
(LO 2, 4)

Village Hardware is a retail hardware store. Information about the store's operations follows.

- November 20x4 sales amounted to $400,000.
- Sales are budgeted at $440,000 for December 20x4 and $400,000 for January 20x5.
- Collections are expected to be 60 percent in the month of sale and 38 percent in the month following the sale. Two percent of sales are expected to be uncollectible. Bad debts expense is recognized monthly.
- The store's gross margin is 25 percent of its sales revenue.
- A total of 80 percent of the merchandise for resale is purchased in the month prior to the month of sale, and 20 percent is purchased in the month of sale. Payment for merchandise is made in the month following the purchase.
- Other monthly expenses paid in cash amount to $45,200.
- Annual depreciation is $432,000.

The company's balance sheet as of November 30, 20x4, is as follows:

VILLAGE HARDWARE, INC.
Balance Sheet
November 30, 20x4

Assets	
Cash	$ 44,000
Accounts receivable (net of $7,000 allowance for uncollectible accounts)	152,000
Inventory	280,000
Property, plant, and equipment (net of $1,180,000 accumulated depreciation)	1,724,000
Total assets	$2,200,000
Liabilities and Stockholders' Equity	
Accounts payable	$ 324,000
Common stock	1,590,000
Retained earnings	286,000
Total liabilities and stockholders' equity	$2,200,000

Required: Compute the following amounts.

1. The budgeted cash collections for December 20x4.
2. The budgeted income (loss) before income taxes for December 20x4.
3. The projected balance in accounts payable on December 31, 20x4.

(CMA, adapted)

Exercise 9–31
Budgetary Slack; Bank
(LO 8)

Tanya Williams is the new accounts manager at East Bank of Mississippi. She has just been asked to project how many new bank accounts she will generate during 20x5. The economy of the county in which the bank operates has been growing, and the bank has experienced a 10 percent increase in its number of bank accounts over each of the past five years. In 20x4, the bank had 10,000 accounts.

The new accounts manager is paid a salary plus a bonus of $45 for every new account she generates above the budgeted amount. Thus, if the annual budget calls for 500 new accounts, and 540 new accounts are obtained, Williams's bonus will be $1,800 (40 × $45).

Williams believes the economy of the county will continue to grow at the same rate in 20x5 as it has in recent years. She has decided to submit a budgetary projection of 800 new accounts for 20x5.

Required: Your consulting firm has been hired by the bank president to make recommendations for improving its operations. Write a memorandum to the president defining and explaining the negative consequences of budgetary slack. Also discuss the bank's bonus system for the new accounts manager and how the bonus program tends to encourage budgetary slack.

Exercise 9–32
Using Budgets for Financial Planning
(LO 1, 4, 5)

Splendid Stereo, Inc. is a large retailer of stereo equipment. The controller is about to prepare the budget for the first quarter of 20x5. Past experience has indicated that 75 percent of the store's sales are cash sales. The collection experience for the sales on account is as follows:

80 percent during month of sale
15 percent during month following sale
5 percent uncollectible

The total sales for December 20x4 are expected to be $380,000. The controller feels that sales in January 20x5 could range from $200,000 to $320,000.

Required:

1. Demonstrate how financial planning can be used to project cash receipts in January of 20x5 for three different levels of January sales. Use the following columnar format.

	Total Sales in January, 20x5		
	$200,000	**$260,000**	**$320,000**
Cash receipts in January 20x5:			
From December sales on account	$	$	$
From January cash sales.			
From January sales on account			
Total cash receipts	$	$	$

2. How could the controller of Splendid Stereo, Inc. use this financial planning approach to help in planning operations for January?

Exercise 9–33
Professional Services Budget; Dental Practice; Activity-Based Budgeting
(LO 2, 3, 4)

Three Rivers Dental Associates is a large dental practice in Pittsburgh. The firm's controller is preparing the budget for the next year. The controller projects a total of 48,000 office visits, to be evenly distributed throughout the year. Eighty percent of the visits will be half-hour appointments, and the remainder will be one-hour visits. The average rates for professional dental services are $60 for half-hour appointments and $105 for one-hour office visits. Ninety percent of each month's professional service revenue is collected during the month when services are rendered, and the remainder is collected the month following service. Uncollectible billings are negligible. Metropolitan's dental associates earn $90 per hour.

Metropolitan uses activity-based budgeting to budget office overhead and administrative expenses. Two cost drivers are used: office visits and direct professional labor. The cost-driver rates are as follows:

Patient registration and records	$3.00 per office visit (of any length)
All other overhead and administrative expenses.	$7.50 per direct professional labor hour

Required: Prepare the following budget schedules.

1. Direct-professional-labor budget for the month of June.
2. Cash collections during June for professional services rendered during May and June.
3. Overhead and administrative expense budget for the month of June.

Exercise 9–34
Economic Order Quantity (Appendix)
(LO 9)

For each of the following independent cases, use the equation method to compute the economic order quantity.

	Case A	Case B	Case C
Annual requirement (in units)	7,290	4,563	150
Cost per order	$500	$10	$100
Annual holding cost per unit	$ 9	$15	$ 12

Exercise 9–35
Lead Time and Safety Stock (Appendix)
(LO 9)

Andrew and Fulton, Inc. uses 840 tons of a chemical bonding agent each year. Monthly demand fluctuates between 55 and 85 tons. The lead time for each order is one month, and the economic order quantity is 130 tons.

Required:

1. Determine the safety stock appropriate for the chemical bonding agent.
2. At what order point, in terms of tons remaining in inventory, should Andrew and Fulton, Inc. order the bonding agent?

Problems

Problem 9–36
Cash budgeting
(LO 2, 4)

Sophisticates, Inc., a distributor of jewelry throughout California, is in the process of assembling a cash budget for the first quarter of 20x1. The following information has been extracted from the company's accounting records:

- All sales are on account. Sixty percent of customer accounts are collected in the month of sale; 35 percent are collected in the following month. Uncollectibles amounting to 5 percent of sales are anticipated, and management believes that only 20 percent of the accounts outstanding on December 31, 20x0, will be recovered and that the recovery will be in January 20x1.
- Seventy percent of the merchandise purchases are paid for in the month of purchase; the remaining 30 percent are paid for in the month after acquisition.
- The December 31, 20x0, balance sheet disclosed the following selected figures: cash, $60,000; accounts receivable, $165,000; and accounts payable, $66,000.
- Sophisticates, Inc. maintains a $60,000 minimum cash balance at all times. Financing is available (and retired) in $1,000 multiples at an 8 percent interest rate, with borrowings taking place at the beginning of the month and repayments occurring at the end of the month. Interest is paid at the time of repaying principal and computed on the portion of principal repaid at that time.
- Additional data:

	January	February	March
Sales revenue	$450,000	$540,000	$555,000
Merchandise purchases	270,000	300,000	420,000
Cash operating costs	93,000	72,000	135,000
Proceeds from sale of equipment	—	—	15,000

Required:

1. Prepare a schedule that discloses the firm's total cash collections for January through March.
2. Prepare a schedule that discloses the firm's total cash disbursements for January through March.
3. Prepare a schedule that discloses the firm's cash needs, if any, for January through March. The schedule should present the following information in the order cited: Beginning cash balance, total receipts (from requirement 1), total payments (from requirement 2), the cash excess (deficiency) before financing, borrowing needed to maintain minimum balance, loan principal repaid, loan interest paid, and ending cash balance

Problem 9–37
Production and Direct-Labor Budgets; Activity-Based Overhead Budget
(LO 2, 3, 4)

Shady Shades, Inc. manufactures artistic frames for sunglasses. Talia Demarest, controller, is responsible for preparing the company's master budget. In compiling the budget data for 20x1, Demarest has learned that new automated production equipment will be installed on March 1. This will reduce the direct labor per frame from 1 hour to .75 hours.

Labor-related costs include pension contributions of $.50 per hour, workers' compensation insurance of $.20 per hour, employee medical insurance of $.80 per hour, and employer contributions to

Social Security equal to 7 percent of direct-labor wages. The cost of employee benefits paid by the company on its employees is treated as a direct-labor cost. Shady Shades, Inc. has a labor contract that calls for a wage increase to $18.00 per hour on April 1, 20x1. Management expects to have 32,000 frames on hand at December 31, 20x0, and has a policy of carrying an end-of-month inventory of 100 percent of the following month's sales plus 50 percent of the second following month's sales.

These and other data compiled by Demarest are summarized in the following table.

	January	February	March	April	May
Direct-labor hours per unit	1.0	1.0	.75	.75	.75
Wage per direct-labor hour	$16.00	$16.00	$16.00	$18.00	$18.00
Estimated unit sales	20,000	24,000	16,000	18,000	18,000
Sales price per unit	$50.00	$47.50	$47.50	$47.50	$47.50
Manufacturing overhead:					
Shipping and handling (per unit sold)	$3.00	$3.00	$3.00	$3.00	$3.00
Purchasing, material handling, and inspection (per unit produced)	$4.50	$4.50	$4.50	$4.50	$4.50
Other manufacturing overhead (per direct-labor hour)	$10.50	$10.50	$10.50	$10.50	$10.50

Required:

1. Prepare a production budget and a direct-labor budget for Shady Shades, Inc. by month and for the first quarter of 20x1. Both budgets may be combined in one schedule. The direct-labor budget should include direct-labor hours and show the detail for each direct-labor cost category.
2. For each item used in the firm's production budget and direct-labor budget, identify the other components of the master budget that also would use these data.
3. Prepare a manufacturing-overhead budget for each month and for the first quarter.

(CMA, adapted)

Problem 9–38
Production and Materials Budgets
(LO 2, 4)

Niagra Chemical Company produces three products using three different continuous processes. The products are Yarex, Darol, and Norex. Projected sales in gallons for the three products for the years 20x2 and 20x3 are as follows:

	20x2	20x3
Yarex	120,000	130,000
Darol	80,000	70,000
Norex	50,000	60,000

- Because of the continuous nature of Niagra's processes, work-in-process inventory for each of the products remains constant throughout the year.
- Inventories are planned for each product so that the projected finished-goods inventory at the beginning of each year is equal to 8 percent of that year's projected sales.
- The conversion requirements in hours per gallon for the three products are Yarex, .07 hours; Darol, .10 hours; and Norex, .16 hours. The conversion cost of $20 per hour is considered 100 percent variable.
- The raw-material requirements of the three products are shown in the following chart.

Raw Material	Units	Unit Price	Yarex	Darol	Norex
Gamma	pounds	$ 8.00	.2	.4	—
Murad	pounds	6.00	.4	—	.5
Islin	gallons	5.00	1.0	.7	.5
Tarden	gallons	10.00	—	.3	.5

- Raw-material inventories are planned so that each raw material's projected inventory at the beginning of a year is equal to 10 percent of the previous year's usage of that raw material.

Required:

1. Determine Niagra Chemical Company's production budget (in gallons) for the three products for 20x2.

2. Determine Niagra Chemical Company's conversion cost budget for 20x2.
3. Assuming the 20x1 usage of Islin is 200,000 gallons, determine the company's raw-material purchases budget (in dollars) for Islin for 20x2.
4. Assume that for 20x2 production, Niagra Chemical Company could replace the raw material Islin with the raw material Philin. The usage of Philin would be the same as the usage of Islin. However, Philin would cost 20 percent more than Islin and would cut production times on all three products by 10 percent. Determine whether management should use Philin or Islin for the 20x2 production, supporting your decision with appropriate calculations. For this requirement, ignore any impact of beginning and ending inventory balances.

(CMA, adapted)

Problem 9–39
Revenue and Labor Budgeting for a University; Budget Linkages
(LO 4, 6)

Eastern State University (ESU) is preparing its master budget for the upcoming academic year. Currently, 12,000 students are enrolled on campus; however, the admissions office is forecasting a 5 percent growth in the student body despite a tuition hike to $75 per credit hour. The following additional information has been gathered from an examination of university records and conversations with university officials:

- ESU is planning to award 180 tuition-free scholarships.
- The average class has 25 students, and the typical student takes 15 credit hours each semester. Each class is three credit hours. ESU operates two semesters per year and has no summer term.
- ESU's faculty members are evaluated on the basis of teaching, research, and university and community service. Each faculty member teaches fives classes during the academic year.

Required:

1. Prepare a tuition revenue budget for the upcoming academic year.
2. Determine the number of faculty members needed to cover classes.
3. Assume there is a shortage of full-time faculty members. List at least five actions that ESU might take to accommodate the growing student body.
4. You have been requested by the university's administrative vice president (AVP) to construct budgets for other areas of operation (e.g., the library, grounds, dormitories, and maintenance). The AVP noted: "The most important resource of the university is its faculty. Now that you know the number of faculty needed, you can prepare the other budgets. Faculty members are indeed the key driver—without them we don't operate." Does the administrative vice president really understand the linkages within the budgeting process? Explain.

Problem 9–40
Completion of Budget Schedules
(LO 2, 4)

School Days Furniture, Inc. manufactures a variety of desks, chairs, tables, and shelf units which are sold to public school systems throughout the midwest. The controller of the company's Desk Division is currently preparing a budget for the third quarter of the year. The following sales forecast has been made by the division's sales manager.

July	5,000 desk-and-chair sets
August	6,000 desk-and-chair sets
September	7,500 desk-and-chair sets

Each desk-and-chair set requires 10 board feet of pine planks and 1.5 hours of direct labor. Each set sells for $60. Pine planks cost $.60 per board foot, and the division ends each month with enough wood to cover 10 percent of the next month's production requirements. The division incurs a cost of $21.00 per hour for direct-labor wages and fringe benefits. The division ends each month with enough finished-goods inventory to cover 20 percent of the next month's sales.

Required: Complete the following budget schedules.

1. Sales budget:

	July	August	September
Sales (in sets)	5,000		
Sales price per set	× $60		
Sales revenue	$300,000		

2. Production budget (in sets):

	July	August	September
Sales	5,000		
Add: Desired ending inventory	1,200		1,500
Total requirements	6,200		
Less: Projected beginning inventory	1,000		
Planned production	5,200		

3. Raw material purchases:

	July	August	September
Planned production (sets)	5,200		
Raw material required per set (board feet)	× 10		
Raw material required for production (board feet)	52,000		
Add: Desired ending inventory of raw material, in board feet (10% of next month's requirement)	6,300		8,000
Total requirements	58,300		
Less: Projected beginning inventory of raw material, in board feet (10% of current month's requirement)	5,200		
Planned purchases of raw material (board feet)	53,100		
Cost per board foot	× $.60		
Planned purchases of raw material (dollars)	$ 31,860		

4. Direct-labor budget:

	July	August	September
Planned production (sets)	5,200		
Direct-labor hours per set	× 1.5		
Direct-labor hours required	7,800		
Cost per hour	× $21		
Planned direct-labor cost	$163,800		

Problem 9–41
Relationships of the Master-Budget Components
(LO 2, 4)

Dakota Fan, Inc. manufactures an inexpensive household fan that it sells to retailers for $20 per unit. All sales are on account, with 40 percent of sales collected in the month of sale and 60 percent collected in the following month. The data that follow were extracted from the company's accounting records.

- Dakota Fan maintains a minimum cash balance of $15,000. Total payments in January 20x1 are budgeted at $195,000.
- A schedule of cash collections for January and February of 20x1 revealed the following receipts for the period:

	Cash Receipts	
	January	February
From December 31 accounts receivable	$108,000	
From January sales	76,000	$114,000
From February sales		78,400

- March 20x1 sales are expected to total 10,000 units.
- Finished-goods inventories are maintained at 20 percent of the following month's sales.
- The December 31, 20x0, balance sheet revealed the following selected figures: cash, $22,500; accounts receivable, $108,000; and finished goods, $22,350.

Required:

1. Determine the number of units that Dakota Fan sold in December 20x0.
2. Compute the sales revenue for March 20x1.
3. Compute the total sales revenue to be reported on Dakota Fan's budgeted income statement for the first quarter of 20x1.

4. Determine the accounts receivable balance to be reported on the March 31, 20x1, budgeted balance sheet.
5. Calculate the number of units in the December 31, 20x0, finished-goods inventory.
6. Calculate the number of units of finished goods to be manufactured in January 20x1.
7. Calculate the financing required in January, if any, to maintain the firm's minimum cash balance.

Problem 9–42
Interrelationships between Components of Master Budget
(LO 1, 2, 4, 6)

Continental Security Systems, Inc. (CSSI) manufactures and sells security systems. The company started by installing photoelectric security systems in offices and has expanded into the private-home market. CSSI has a basic security system that has been developed into three standard products, each of which can be adapted to meet the specific needs of customers. The manufacturing operation is moderate in size, as the bulk of the component manufacturing is completed by independent contractors. The security systems are approximately 75 percent complete when received from contractors and require only final assembly in the CSSI plant. Each product passes through at least one of three assembly operations.

CSSI operates in a rapidly growing community. There is evidence that a great deal of new commercial construction will take place in the near future, and management has decided to pursue this new market. In order to be competitive, the firm will have to expand its operations.

In view of the expected increase in business, Sandra Feldman, the controller, believes that CSSI should implement a complete budgeting system. Feldman has decided to make a formal presentation to the company's president explaining the benefits of a budgeting system and outlining the budget schedules and reports that would be necessary.

Required:

1. Explain the benefits that CSSI would gain from implementing a budgeting system.
2. If Sandra Feldman develops a master budget:
   a. Identify, in order, the schedules that will have to be prepared.
   b. Identify the subsequent schedules that would be based on the schedules identified above.
   Use the following format for your answer.

Schedule	Subsequent Schedule

(CMA, adapted)

Problem 9–43
Sales, Production, and Purchases Budgets; Activity-Based Overhead Budget
(LO 2, 3, 4)

Condor Corporation manufactures two different types of coils used in electric motors. In the fall of the current year, the controller compiled the following data.

- Sales forecast for 20x3 (all units to be shipped in 20x3):

Product	Units	Price
Light coil	60,000	$130
Heavy coil	40,000	190

- Raw-material prices and inventory levels:

Raw Material	Expected Inventories January 1, 20x3	Desired Inventories, December 31, 20x3	Anticipated Purchase Price
Sheet metal	32,000 lb.	36,000 lb.	$16
Copper wire	29,000 lb.	32,000 lb.	10
Platform	6,000 units	7,000 units	6

- Use of raw material:

	Amount Used per Unit	
Raw Material	Light Coil	Heavy Coil
Sheet metal	4 lb.	5 lb.
Copper wire	2 lb.	3 lb.
Platform		1 unit

- Direct-labor requirements and rates:

Product	Hours per Unit	Rate per Hour
Light coil	4	$15
Heavy coil	6	20

- Finished-goods inventories (in units):

Product	Expected January 1, 20x3	Desired December 31, 20x3
Light coil	20,000	25,000
Heavy coil	8,000	9,000

- Manufacturing overhead:

Overhead Cost Item	Activity-Based Budget Rate
Purchasing and material handling	$.50 per pound of sheet metal and copper wire purchased
Depreciation, utilities and inspection	$8.00 per coil produced (either type)
Shipping	$2.00 per coil shipped (either type)
General manufacturing overhead	$6.00 per direct-labor hour

Required: Prepare the following budgets for 20x3.

1. Sales budget (in dollars).
2. Production budget (in units).
3. Raw-material purchases budget (in quantities).
4. Raw-material purchases budget (in dollars).
5. Direct-labor budget (in dollars).
6. Manufacturing-overhead budget (in dollars).

(CPA, adapted)

Problem 9–44
Preparation of Master Budget
(LO 2, 3, 4)

Edgeworth Box Corporation manufactures two types of cardboard boxes used in shipping canned food, fruit, and vegetables. The canned food box (type C) and the perishable food box (type P) have the following material and labor requirements.

	Type of Box C	Type of Box P
Direct material required per 100 boxes:		
Corrugating medium ($.15 per pound)	20 pounds	30 pounds
Paperboard ($.30 per pound)	30 pounds	70 pounds
Direct labor required per 100 boxes ($18.00 per hour)	.25 hour	.50 hour

The following manufacturing-overhead costs are anticipated for the next year. The predetermined overhead rate is based on a production volume of 495,000 units for each type of box. Manufacturing overhead is applied on the basis of direct-labor hours.

Indirect material	$ 15,750
Indirect labor	75,000
Utilities	37,500
Property taxes	27,000
Insurance	24,000
Depreciation	43,500
Total	$222,750

The following selling and administrative expenses are anticipated for the next year.

Salaries and fringe benefits of sales personnel	$112,500
Advertising	22,500
Management salaries and fringe benefits	135,000
Clerical wages and fringe benefits	39,000
Miscellaneous administrative expenses	6,000
Total	$315,000

The sales forecast for the next year is as follows:

	Sales Volume	Sales Price
Box type C	500,000 boxes	$135 per hundred boxes
Box type P	500,000 boxes	195 per hundred boxes

The following inventory information is available for the next year.

	Expected Inventory January 1	Desired Ending Inventory December 31
Finished goods:		
Box type C	10,000 boxes	5,000 boxes
Box type P	20,000 boxes	15,000 boxes
Raw material:		
Corrugating medium	5,000 pounds	10,000 pounds
Paperboard	15,000 pounds	5,000 pounds

Required: Prepare a master budget for Edgeworth Box Corporation for the next year. Assume an income tax rate of 35 percent. Include the following schedules.

1. Sales budget.
2. Production budget.
3. Direct-material budget.
4. Direct-labor budget.
5. Manufacturing-overhead budget.
6. Selling and administrative expense budget.
7. Budgeted income statement. (*Hint:* To determine cost of goods sold, first compute the manufacturing cost per unit for each type of box. Include applied manufacturing overhead in the cost. Carry these calculations to three decimal places.)

Problem 9–45
Revised Operating Budget; Consulting Firm
(LO 1, 4)

Vancouver Consulting Associates, a division of Maple Leaf Services Corporation, offers management and computer consulting services to clients throughout Canada and the northwestern United States. The division specializes in website development and other Internet applications. The corporate management at Maple Leaf Services is pleased with the performance of Vancouver Consulting Associates for the first nine months of the current year and has recommended that the division manager, Richard Howell, submit a revised forecast for the remaining quarter, as the division has exceeded the annual plan year-to-date by 20 percent of operating income. An unexpected increase in billed hour volume over the original plan is the main reason for this increase in income. The original operating budget for the first three quarters for Vancouver Consulting Associates follows.

VANCOUVER CONSULTING ASSOCIATES
20x4 Operating Budget

	1st Quarter	2nd Quarter	3rd Quarter	Total for First Three Quarters
Revenue:				
Consulting fees:				
Computer system consulting	$ 843,750	$ 843,750	$ 843,750	$2,531,250
Management consulting	630,000	630,000	630,000	1,890,000
Total consulting fees	$1,473,750	$1,473,750	$1,473,750	$4,421,250
Other revenue	20,000	20,000	20,000	60,000
Total revenue	$1,493,750	$1,493,750	$1,493,750	$4,481,250
Expenses:				
Consultant salary expenses	$ 773,500	$ 773,500	$ 773,500	$2,320,500
Travel and related expenses	91,250	91,250	91,250	273,750
General and administrative expenses	200,000	200,000	200,000	600,000
Depreciation expense	80,000	80,000	80,000	240,000
Corporate expense allocation	100,000	100,000	100,000	300,000
Total expenses	$1,244,750	$1,244,750	$1,244,750	$3,734,250
Operating income	$ 249,000	$ 249,000	$ 249,000	$ 747,000

Howell will reflect the following information in his revised forecast for the fourth quarter.

- Vancouver Consulting Associates currently has 25 consultants on staff, 10 for management consulting and 15 for computer systems consulting. Three additional management consultants have been hired to start work at the beginning of the fourth quarter in order to meet the increased client demand.
- The hourly billing rate for consulting revenue will remain at $180 per hour for each management consultant and $150 per hour for each computer consultant. However, due to the favorable increase in billing hour volume when compared to the plan, the hours for each consultant will be increased by 50 hours per quarter.
- The budgeted annual salaries and actual annual salaries, paid monthly, are the same: $100,000 for a management consultant and $92,000 for a computer consultant. Corporate management has approved a merit increase of 10 percent at the beginning of the fourth quarter for all 25 existing consultants, while the new consultants will be compensated at the planned rate.
- The planned salary expense includes a provision for employee fringe benefits amounting to 30 percent of the annual salaries. However, the improvement of some corporatewide employee programs will increase the fringe benefits to 40 percent.
- The original plan assumes a fixed hourly rate for travel and other related expenses for each billing hour of consulting. These are expenses that are not reimbursed by the client, and the previously determined hourly rate has proven to be adequate to cover these costs.
- Other revenue is derived from temporary rentals and interest income and remains unchanged for the fourth quarter.
- General and administrative expenses have been favorable at 7 percent below the plan; this 7 percent savings on fourth quarter expenses will be reflected in the revised plan.
- Depreciation of office equipment and personal computers will stay constant at the projected straight-line rate.
- Due to the favorable experience for the first three quarters and the division's increased ability to absorb costs, the corporate management at Maple Leaf Services has increased the corporate expense allocation by 50 percent.

Required:

1. Prepare a revised operating budget for the fourth quarter for Vancouver Consulting Associates that Richard Howell will present to corporate management.
2. Discuss the reasons why an organization would prepare a revised operating budget.

(CMA, adapted)

Problem 9–46
Budgeting; Financial Objectives; Ethics
(LO 1, 2, 4)

Fit-for-Life Foods Inc., a manufacturer of breakfast cereals and snack bars, has experienced several years of steady growth in sales, profits, and dividends while maintaining a relatively low level of debt. The board of directors has adopted a long-run strategy to maximize the value of the shareholders' investment. In order to achieve this goal, the board of directors established the following five-year financial objectives.

- Increase sales by 12 percent per year.
- Increase income before taxes by 15 percent per year.
- Maintain long-term debt at a maximum of 16 percent of assets.

These financial objectives have been attained for the past three years. At the beginning of last year, the president of Fit-for-Life Foods, Andrea Donis, added a fourth financial objective of maintaining cost of goods sold at a maximum of 70 percent of sales. This goal also was attained last year.

The company's budgeting process is to be directed toward attaining these goals for the forthcoming year, a difficult task with the economy in a prolonged recession. In addition, the increased emphasis on eating healthful foods has driven up the price of ingredients used by the company significantly faster than the expected rate of inflation. John Winslow, cost accountant at Fit-for-Life Foods, has responsibility for preparation of the profit plan for next year. Winslow assured Donis that he could present a budget that achieved all of the financial objectives. Winslow believed that he could overestimate the ending inventory and reclassify fruit and grain inspection costs as administrative rather than manufacturing costs to attain the desired objective. The actual statements for 20x4 and the budgeted statements for 20x5 that Winslow prepared are as follows:

FIT-FOR-LIFE FOODS INC.
Income Statement

	20x4 Actual	20x5 Budgeted
Sales	$1,700,000	$1,895,500
Less: Variable costs:		
Cost of goods sold	1,020,000	1,149,450
Selling and administrative	180,000	175,000
Contribution margin	$ 500,000	$ 571,050
Less: Fixed costs:		
Manufacturing	170,000	189,550
Selling and administrative	120,000	140,000
Income before taxes	$ 210,000	$ 241,500

FIT-FOR-LIFE FOODS INC.
Balance Sheet

	20x4 Actual	20x5 Budgeted
Assets:		
Cash	$ 20,000	$ 34,000
Accounts receivable	120,000	136,000
Inventory	600,000	730,000
Plant and equipment (net of accumulated depreciation)	3,260,000	3,200,000
Total	$4,000,000	$4,100,000
Liabilities:		
Accounts payable	$ 220,000	$ 244,000
Long-term debt	640,000	616,000
Stockholders' equity:		
Common stock	800,000	800,000
Retained earnings	2,340,000	2,440,000
Total	$4,000,000	$4,100,000

The company paid dividends of $55,440 in 20x4, and the expected tax rate for 20x5 is 34 percent.

Required:

1. Describe the role of budgeting in a firm's strategic planning.
2. For each of the financial objectives established by the board of directors and the president of Fit-for-Life Foods Inc. determine whether John Winslow's budget attains these objectives. Support your conclusion in each case by presenting appropriate calculations, and use the following format for your answer.

   Objective **Attained/Not Attained** **Calculations**
3. Explain why the adjustments contemplated by John Winslow are unethical, citing specific standards of ethical conduct for management accountants.

(CMA, adapted)

Problem 9–47
Comprehensive Master Budget; Borrowing; Acquisition of Automated Material-Handling System
(LO 1, 2, 4)

"We really need to get this new material-handling equipment in operation just after the new year begins. I hope we can finance it largely with cash and marketable securities, but if necessary we can get a short-term loan down at MetroBank." This statement by Beth Davies-Lowry, president of Global Electronics Company, concluded a meeting she had called with the firm's top management. Global is a small, rapidly growing wholesaler of consumer electronic products. The firm's main product lines are small kitchen appliances and power tools. Marcia Wilcox, Global Electronics' general manager of marketing, has recently completed a sales forecast. She believes the company's sales during the first quarter of 20x1 will increase by 10 percent each month over the previous month's sales. Then Wilcox expects sales to remain constant for several months. Global's projected balance sheet as of December 31, 20x0 is as follows:

Cash	$ 70,000
Accounts receivable	540,000
Marketable securities	30,000
Inventory	308,000
Buildings and equipment (net of accumulated depreciation)	1,252,000
Total assets	$2,200,000
Accounts payable	$ 352,800
Bond interest payable	25,000
Property taxes payable	7,200
Bonds payable (10%; due in 20x6)	600,000
Common stock	1,000,000
Retained earnings	215,000
Total liabilities and stockholders' equity	$2,200,000

Jack Hanson, the assistant controller, is now preparing a monthly budget for the first quarter of 20x1. In the process, the following information has been accumulated:

1. Projected sales for December of 20x0 are $800,000. Credit sales typically are 75 percent of total sales. Global's credit experience indicates that 10 percent of the credit sales are collected during the month of sale, and the remainder are collected during the following month.
2. Global Electronics' cost of goods sold generally runs at 70 percent of sales. Inventory is purchased on account, and 40 percent of each month's purchases are paid during the month of purchase. The remainder is paid during the following month. In order to have adequate stocks of inventory on hand, the firm attempts to have inventory at the end of each month equal to half of the next month's projected cost of goods sold.
3. Hanson has estimated that Global's other monthly expenses will be as follows:

Sales salaries	$42,000
Advertising and promotion	32,000
Administrative salaries	42,000
Depreciation	50,000
Interest on bonds	5,000
Property taxes	1,800

In addition, sales commissions run at the rate of 1 percent of sales.

4. Global Electronics' president, Davies-Lowry, has indicated that the firm should invest $250,000 in an automated inventory-handling system to control the movement of inventory in the firm's warehouse just after the new year begins. These equipment purchases will be financed primarily from the firm's cash and marketable securities. However, Davies-Lowry believes that the company needs to keep a minimum cash balance of $50,000. If necessary, the remainder of the equipment purchases will be financed using short-term credit from a local bank. The minimum period for such a loan is three months. Hanson believes short-term interest rates will be 10 percent per year at the time of the equipment purchases. If a loan is necessary, Davies-Lowry has decided it should be paid off by the end of the first quarter if possible.
5. Global Electronics' board of directors has indicated an intention to declare and pay dividends of $100,000 on the last day of each quarter.
6. The interest on any short-term borrowing will be paid when the loan is repaid. Interest on Global Electronics' bonds is paid semiannually on January 31 and July 31 for the preceding six-month period.
7. Property taxes are paid semiannually on February 28 and August 31 for the preceding six-month period.

Required: Prepare Global Electronics Company's master budget for the first quarter of 20x1 by completing the following schedules and statements.

1. Sales budget:

	20x0	20x1			
	December	**January**	**February**	**March**	**1st Quarter**
Total sales					
Cash sales					
Sales on account					

2. Cash receipts budget:

	20x1			
	January	**February**	**March**	**1st Quarter**
Cash sales				
Cash collections from credit sales made during current month				
Cash collections from credit sales made during preceding month				
Total cash receipts				

3. Purchases budget:

	20x0	20x1			
	December	**January**	**February**	**March**	**1st Quarter**
Budgeted cost of goods sold					
Add: Desired ending inventory					
Total goods needed					
Less: Expected beginning inventory . . .					
Purchases					

4. Cash disbursements budget:

	20x1			
	January	**February**	**March**	**1st Quarter**
Inventory purchases:				
Cash payments for purchases during the current month*				
Cash payments for purchases during the preceding month†				
Total cash payments for inventory purchases				
Other expenses:				
Sales salaries				
Advertising and promotion				
Administrative salaries				
Interest on bonds‡				
Property taxes‡				
Sales commissions				
Total cash payments for other expenses				
Total cash disbursements				

*40% of the current month's purchases (schedule 3).

†60% of the prior month's purchases (schedule 3).

‡Bond interest is paid every six months, on January 31 and July 31. Property taxes also are paid every six months, on February 28 and August 31.

5. Complete the first three lines of the summary cash budget. Then do the analysis of short-term financing needs in requirement (6). Then finish requirement (5).

Summary cash budget:

	20x1			
	January	**February**	**March**	**1st Quarter**
Cash receipts (from schedule 2)				
Less: Cash disbursements (from schedule 4)				
Change in cash balance during period due to operations				
Sale of marketable securities (1/2/x1)				
Proceeds from bank loan (1/2/x1)				
Purchase of equipment				
Repayment of bank loan (3/31/x1)				
Interest on bank loan				
Payment of dividends				
Change in cash balance during first quarter . . .				
Cash balance, 1/1/x1				
Cash balance, 3/31/x1				

6. Analysis of short-term financing needs:

Projected cash balance as of December 31, 20x0	$
Less: Minimum cash balance	
Cash available for equipment purchases	$
Projected proceeds from sale of marketable securities	
Cash available	$
Less: Cost of investment in equipment	
Required short-term borrowing	$

7. Prepare Global Electronics' budgeted income statement for the first quarter of 20x1. (Ignore income taxes.)
8. Prepare Global Electronics' budgeted statement of retained earnings for the first quarter of 20x1.
9. Prepare Global Electronics' budgeted balance sheet as of March 31, 20x1. (*Hint:* On March 31, 20x1, Bond Interest Payable is $10,000 and Property Taxes Payable is $1,800.)

Problem 9–48
Economic Order Quantity; Equation Approach; JIT Purchasing (Appendix)
(LO 9)

Fiber Technology, Inc. manufactures glass fibers used in the communications industry. The company's materials and parts manager is currently revising the inventory policy for XL-20, one of the chemicals used in the production process. The chemical is purchased in 10-pound canisters for $95 each. The firm uses 4,800 canisters per year. The controller estimates that it costs $150 to place and receive a typical order of XL-20. The annual cost of storing XL-20 is $4 per canister.

Required:

1. Write the formula for the total annual cost of ordering and storing XL-20.
2. Use the EOQ formula to determine the optimal order quantity.
3. What is the total annual cost of ordering and storing XL-20 at the economic order quantity?
4. How many orders will be placed per year?
5. Fiber Technology's controller, Jay Turnbull, recently attended a seminar on JIT purchasing. Afterward he analyzed the cost of storing XL-20, including the costs of wasted space and inefficiency. He was shocked when he concluded that the real annual holding cost was $19.20 per canister. Turnbull then met with Doug Kaplan, Fiber Technology's purchasing manager. Together they contacted Reno Industries, the supplier of XL-20, about a JIT purchasing arrangement. After some discussion and negotiation, Kaplan concluded that the cost of placing an order for XL-20 could be reduced to just $20. Using these new cost estimates, Turnbull computed the new EOQ for XL-20.
   a. Use the equation approach to compute the new EOQ.
   b. How many orders will be placed per year?

Problem 9–49
Economic Order Quantity; Tabular Approach (Appendix)
(LO 9)

Refer to the *original* data given in the preceding problem for Fiber Technology, Inc.

Required:

1. Prepare a table showing the total annual cost of ordering and storing XL-20 for each of the following order quantities: 400, 600, and 800 canisters.
2. What are the weaknesses in the tabular approach?

Problem 9–50
Economic Order Quantity; Graphical Approach (Appendix)
(LO 9)

Refer to the *original* data given in Problem 9–48 for Fiber Technology, Inc.

Required: Prepare a graphical analysis of the economic order quantity decision for XL-20.

Problem 9–51
Economic Order Quantity; Lead Time and Safety Stock (Appendix)
(LO 9)

Refer to the *original* data given in Problem 9–48 for Fiber Technology, Inc. The lead time required to receive an order of XL-20 is one month.

Required:

1. Assuming stable usage of XL-20 each month, determine the reorder point for XL-20.
2. Draw a graph showing the usage, lead time, and reorder point for XL-20.
3. Suppose that monthly usage of XL-20 fluctuates between 300 and 500 canisters, although annual demand remains constant at 4,800 canisters. What level of safety stock should the materials and parts manager keep on hand for XL-20? What is the new reorder point for the chemical?

Problem 9–52
Economic Order Quantity; JIT Purchasing; International (Appendix)
(LO 9)

Dallas Auto Glass is a regional distributor of automobile window glass. The windshields are manufactured in Mexico and shipped to Dallas. Management is expecting an annual demand of 10,800 windshields. The purchase price per windshield is $415. Other costs associated with ordering and maintaining an inventory of these windshields are as follows:

- The historical ordering costs incurred in the Purchase Order Department for placing and processing orders are shown below.

Year	Orders Placed and Processed	Total Processing Costs
20x0	17	$12,000
20x1	48	12,010
20x2	97	12,400

Management expects the ordering costs to increase 16 percent over the amounts and rates experienced the last three years.

- Dallas Auto Glass operates on a six-day workweek for 50 weeks each year. The firm is closed two weeks each year.
- Each order is inspected by both Mexican and U.S. officials at the border. A $47 fee is charged.
- A clerk in the Receiving Department receives, inspects, and secures the windshields as they arrive from the manufacturer. This activity requires eight hours per order received. This clerk has no other responsibilities and is paid at the rate of $12 per hour. Related variable overhead costs in this department are applied at the rate of $3 per hour.
- Additional warehouse space will have to be rented to store the new windshields. Space can be rented as needed in a warehouse at an estimated cost of $2,500 per year plus $4.25 per windshield.
- Breakage cost is estimated to average $4.00 per windshield.
- Taxes and fire insurance on the inventory are $1.25 per windshield.
- Other storage costs amount to $10.50 per windshield.

Six working days are required from the time the order is placed with the manufacturer until it is received.

Required: Calculate the following values for Dallas Auto Glass Company.

1. The value of the ordering cost that should be used in the EOQ formula. (*Hint:* Use the high-low method, discussed in Chapter 7, to estimate the variable portion of the processing cost per order.)
2. The value of the storage cost that should be used in the EOQ formula.
3. The economic order quantity.

4. The minimum annual relevant cost of ordering and storage at the economic order quantity.
5. The reorder point in units.
6. Management has been able to negotiate a JIT purchasing agreement with the Mexican manufacturer, and the inspection fee has been renegotiated with the border officials. The purchasing manager has determined that JIT purchasing would enable the company to reduce the cost per order to $32.40. Moreover, she has analyzed the cost of storing windshields, taking care to include the cost of wasted space and inefficiency. She estimates that the real annual cost of holding inventory is $60 per windshield.
   a. Calculate the new EOQ, given the purchasing manager's new cost estimates.
   b. How many orders would now be placed each year?
   c. Compute the new minimum annual relevant cost of ordering and storage.

(CMA, adapted)

Cases

Case 9–53
Participative Budgeting
(LO 1, 2, 8)

Jack Riley, controller in the division of social services for the state, recognizes the importance of the budgetary process for planning, control, and motivational purposes. He believes that a properly implemented participative budgetary process for planning purposes and an evaluation procedure will motivate the managers to improve productivity within their particular departments. Based upon this philosophy, Riley has implemented the following budgetary procedures.

- An appropriation target figure is given to each department manager. This amount is the maximum funding that each department can expect to receive in the next year.
- Department managers develop their individual budgets within the following spending constraints as directed by the controller's staff.
  - Expenditure requests cannot exceed the appropriation target.
  - All fixed expenditures should be included in the budget. Fixed expenditures would include such items as contracts and salaries at current levels.
  - All government projects directed by higher authority should be included in the budget in their entirety.
- The controller's staff consolidates the budget requests from the various departments into a master budget submission for the entire division.
- Upon final budget approval by the legislature, the controller's staff allocates the appropriation to the various departments on instructions from the division manager. However, a specified percentage of each department's appropriation is held back in anticipation of budget cuts and special funding needs. The amount and use of this contingency fund is left to the discretion of the division manager.
- Each department is allowed to adjust its budget when necessary to operate within the reduced appropriation level. However, as stated in the original directive, specific projects authorized by higher authority must remain intact.
- The final budget is used as the basis of control. Excessive expenditures by account for each department are highlighted on a monthly basis. Department managers are expected to account for all expenditures over budget. Fiscal responsibility is an important factor in the overall performance evaluation of department managers.

Riley believes his policy of allowing the department managers to participate in the budgetary process and then holding them accountable for their performance is essential, especially during times of limited resources. He further believes that the department managers will be positively motivated to increase the efficiency and effectiveness of their departments because they have provided input into the initial budgetary process and are required to justify any unfavorable performances.

Required:

1. Describe several operational and behavioral benefits that are generally attributed to a participative budgetary process.
2. Identify at least four deficiencies in Jack Riley's participative policy for planning and performance evaluation purposes. For each deficiency identified, recommend how it can be corrected.

(CMA, adapted)

Case 9–54
Using Budgets to Evaluate Business Decisions
(LO 1, 2)

Triple-F Health Club (Family, Fitness, and Fun) offers tennis, swimming, and other physical fitness facilities to its members. There are four of these clubs in the metropolitan area. Each club has between 1,700 and 2,500 members. Revenue is derived from annual membership fees and hourly court fees. The annual membership fees are as follows:

Individual	$ 45
Student	30
Family	100

The hourly court fees vary from $8 to $12 depending upon the season and the time of day (prime versus non-prime time).

The peak racquetball season is considered to run from September through April. During this period court usage averages 90 to 100 percent of capacity during prime time (5:00–9:00 P.M.) and 50 to 60 percent of capacity during the remaining hours. Daily court usage during the off-season (i.e., summer) averages only 20 to 40 percent of capacity.

Most of Triple-F's memberships have September expirations. A substantial amount of the cash receipts are collected during the early part of the racquetball season due to the renewal of the annual membership fees and heavy court usage. However, cash receipts are not as large in the spring and drop significantly in the summer months.

Triple-F is considering changing its membership and fee structure in an attempt to change its cash receipts. Under the new membership plan, only an annual membership fee would be charged, rather than a membership fee plus hourly court fees. There would be two classes of membership

Individual	$300
Family	500

The annual fee would be collected in advance at the time the membership application is completed. Members would be allowed to use the racquetball courts as often as they wish during the year under the new plan.

All future memberships would be sold under these new terms. Current memberships would be honored on the old basis until they expire. However, a special promotional campaign would be instituted to attract new members and to encourage current members to convert to the new membership plan immediately.

The annual fees for individual and family memberships would be reduced to $250 and $450, respectively, during the two-month promotional campaign. In addition, all memberships sold or renewed during this period would be for 15 months rather than the normal one-year period. Current members also would be given a credit toward the annual fee for the unexpired portion of their membership fee, and for all prepaid hourly court fees for league play which have not yet been used.

Triple-F's management estimates that 60 to 70 percent of the present membership would continue with the club. The most active members (45 percent of the present membership) would convert immediately to the new plan, while the remaining members who continue would wait until their current memberships expire. Those members who would not continue are not considered active (i.e., they play five or less times during the year). Management estimates that the loss of members would be offset fully by new members within six months of instituting the new plan. Furthermore, many of the new members would be individuals who would play during non-prime time. Management estimates that adequate court time will be available for all members under the new plan.

If the new membership plan is adopted, it would be instituted on February 1, well before the summer season. The special promotional campaign would be conducted during March and April. Once the plan is implemented, annual renewal of memberships and payment of fees would take place as each individual or family membership expires.

Required: Your consulting firm has been hired to help Triple-F Health Club evaluate its new fee structure. Write a letter to the club's president answering the following questions.

1. Will Triple-F Health Club's new membership plan and fee structure improve its ability to plan its cash receipts? Explain your answer.
2. Triple-F Health Club should evaluate the new membership plan and fee structure completely before it decides to adopt or reject it.
   a. Identify the key factors that Triple-F should consider in its evaluation.
   b. Explain what type of financial analyses Triple-F should prepare in order to make a complete evaluation.

3. Explain how Triple-F Health Club's cash management would differ from the present if the new membership plan and fee structure were adopted.

(CMA, adapted)

Case 9–55
Comprehensive Master Budget; Short-Term Financing; Acquisition of Robotic Equipment
(LO 1, 2, 4)

Jay Rexford, president of Photo Artistry Company, was just concluding a budget meeting with his senior staff. It was November of 20x4, and the group was discussing preparation of the firm's master budget for 20x5. "I've decided to go ahead and purchase the industrial robot we've been talking about. We'll make the acquisition on January 2 of next year, and I expect it will take most of the year to train the personnel and reorganize the production process to take full advantage of the new equipment."

In response to a question about financing the acquisition, Rexford replied as follows: "The robot will cost $950,000. There will also be an additional $50,000 in ancillary equipment to be purchased. We'll finance these purchases with a one-year $1,000,000 loan from Shark Bank and Trust Company. I've negotiated a repayment schedule of four equal installments on the last day of each quarter. The interest rate will be 10 percent, and interest payments will be quarterly as well." With that the meeting broke up, and the budget process was on.

Photo Artistry Company is a manufacturer of metal picture frames. The firm's two product lines are designated as S (small frames; 5 × 7 inches) and L (large frames; 8 × 10 inches). The primary raw materials are flexible metal strips and 9-inch by 24-inch glass sheets. Each S frame requires a 2-foot metal strip; an L frame requires a 3-foot strip. Allowing for normal breakage and scrap glass, the company can get either four S frames or two L frames out of a glass sheet. Other raw materials, such as cardboard backing, are insignificant in cost and are treated as indirect materials. Emily Jackson, Photo Artistry's controller, is in charge of preparing the master budget for 20x5. She has gathered the following information:

1. Sales in the fourth quarter of 20x4 are expected to be 50,000 S frames and 40,000 L frames. The sales manager predicts that over the next two years, sales in each product line will grow by 5,000 units each quarter over the previous quarter. For example, S frame sales in the first quarter of 20x5 are expected to be 55,000 units.
2. Photo Artistry's sales history indicates that 60 percent of all sales are on credit, with the remainder of the sales in cash. The company's collection experience shows that 80 percent of the credit sales are collected during the quarter in which the sale is made, while the remaining 20 percent is collected in the following quarter. (For simplicity, assume the company is able to collect 100 percent of its accounts receivable.)
3. The S frame sells for $10, and the L frame sells for $15. These prices are expected to hold constant throughout 20x5.
4. The production manager attempts to end each quarter with enough finished-goods inventory in each product line to cover 20 percent of the following quarter's sales. Moreover, an attempt is made to end each quarter with 20 percent of the glass sheets needed for the following quarter's production. Since metal strips are purchased locally, the company buys them on a just-in-time basis; inventory is negligible.
5. All direct-material purchases are made on account, and 80 percent of each quarter's purchases are paid in cash during the same quarter as the purchase. The other 20 percent is paid in the next quarter.
6. Indirect materials are purchased with cash as needed. Work-in-process is negligible.
7. Projected manufacturing costs in 20x5 are as follows:

	S Frame	L Frame
Direct material:		
Metal strips:		
S: 2 ft. @ $1 per foot	$2	
L: 3 ft. @ $1 per foot		$3
Glass sheets:		
S: ¼ sheet @ $8 per sheet	2	
L: ½ sheet @ $8 per sheet		4
Direct labor:		
.1 hour @ $20	2	2
Manufacturing overhead:		
.1 direct-labor hour × $10 per hour	1	1
Total manufacturing cost per unit	$7	$10

8. The predetermined overhead rate is $10 per direct-labor hour. The following manufacturing-overhead costs are budgeted for 20x5.

	1st Quarter	2nd Quarter	3rd Quarter	4th Quarter	Entire Year
Indirect material	$ 10,200	$ 11,200	$ 12,200	$ 13,200	$ 46,800
Indirect labor	40,800	44,800	48,800	52,800	187,200
Other overhead	31,000	36,000	41,000	46,000	154,000
Depreciation	20,000	20,000	20,000	20,000	80,000
Total overhead	$102,000	$112,000	$122,000	$132,000	$468,000

All of these costs will be paid in cash during the quarter incurred except for depreciation.

9. Photo Artistry's quarterly selling and administrative expenses are $100,000, paid in cash.
10. Jackson anticipates that dividends of $50,000 will be declared and paid in cash each quarter.
11. Photo Artistry's projected balance sheet as of December 31, 20x4, follows:

Cash	$ 95,000
Accounts receivable	132,000
Inventory:	
Raw material	59,200
Finished goods	167,000
Plant and equipment (net of accumulated depreciation)	8,000,000
Total assets	$8,453,200
Accounts payable	$ 99,400
Common stock	5,000,000
Retained earnings	3,353,800
Total liabilities and stockholders' equity	$8,453,200

Required: Prepare Photo Artistry Company's master budget for 20x5 by completing the following schedules and statements.

1. Sales budget:

	20x4	20x5				
	4th Quarter	1st Quarter	2nd Quarter	3rd Quarter	4th Quarter	Entire Year
S frame unit sales						
× S sales price						
S frame sales revenue						
L frame unit sales						
× L sales price						
L frame sales revenue						
Total sales revenue						
Cash sales*						
Sales on account†						

*40% of total sales.

†60% of total sales.

2. Cash receipts budget:

	20x5				
	1st Quarter	2nd Quarter	3rd Quarter	4th Quarter	Entire Year
Cash sales					
Cash collections from credit sales made during current quarter*					
Cash collections from credit sales made during previous quarter†					
Total cash receipts					

*80% of current quarter's credit sales.

†20% of previous quarter's credit sales.

3. Production budget:

	20x4	20x5				
	4th Quarter	1st Quarter	2nd Quarter	3rd Quarter	4th Quarter	Entire Year
S frames:						
Sales (in units)						
Add: Desired ending inventory . . .						
Total units needed.						
Less: Expected beginning inventory.						
Units to be produced						
L frames:						
Sales (in units)						
Add: Desired ending inventory . . .						
Total units needed.						
Less: Expected beginning inventory.						
Units to be produced						

4. Direct-material budget:

	20x4	20x5				
	4th Quarter	1st Quarter	2nd Quarter	3rd Quarter	4th Quarter	Entire Year
Metal strips:						
S frames to be produced						
× Metal quantity per unit (ft.) . . .						
Needed for S frame production . .						
L frames to be produced						
× Metal quantity per unit (ft.) . . .						
Needed for L frame production . .						
Total metal needed for production; to be purchased (ft.)						
× Price per foot						
Cost of metal strips to be purchased						
Glass sheets:						
S frames to be produced						
× Glass quantity per unit (sheets)						
Needed for S frame production . .						
L frames to be produced						
× Glass quantity per unit (sheets)						
Needed for L frame production . .						
Total glass needed for production (sheets)						
Add: Desired ending inventory					10,400	10,400
Total glass needs						
Less: Expected beginning inventory.						
Glass to be purchased.						
× Price per glass sheet						
Cost of glass to be purchased						
Total raw-material purchases (metal and glass)						

5. Cash disbursements budget:

	20x5				
	1st Quarter	2nd Quarter	3rd Quarter	4th Quarter	Entire Year
Raw-material purchases:					
Cash payments for purchases during the current quarter					
Cash payments for purchases during the preceding quarter					
Total cash payments for raw-material purchases					
Direct labor:					
Frames produced (S and L)					
× Direct-labor hours per frame					
Direct-labor hours to be used					
× Rate per direct-labor hour					
Total cash payments for direct labor					
Manufacturing overhead:					
Indirect material					
Indirect labor					
Other					
Total cash payments for manufacturing overhead					
Cash payments for selling and administrative expenses					
Total cash disbursements					

6. Summary cash budget:

	20x5				
	1st Quarter	2nd Quarter	3rd Quarter	4th Quarter	Entire Year
Cash receipts (from schedule 2)					
Less: Cash disbursements (from schedule 5)					
Change in cash balance due to operations					
Payment of dividends					
Proceeds from bank loan (1/2/x5)					
Purchase of equipment					
Quarterly installment on loan principal					
Quarterly interest payment					
Change in cash balance during the period					
Cash balance, beginning of period					
Cash balance, end of period					

7. Prepare a budgeted schedule of cost of goods manufactured and sold for the year 20x5. (*Hint:* In the budget, actual and applied overhead will be equal.)
8. Prepare Photo Artistry's budgeted income statement for 20x5. (Ignore income taxes.)
9. Prepare Photo Artistry's budgeted statement of retained earnings for 20x5.
10. Prepare Photo Artistry's budgeted balance sheet as of December 31, 20x5.

Current Issues in Managerial Accounting

Issue 9–56
Budgeting in the Film Industry

"At Disney, String of Weak Cartoons Leads to Cost Cuts: Disney Puts Lilo and Stitch on a Tight Budget," ***The Wall Street Journal,*** **June 18, 2002, pp. Al, A6, Bruce Orwall.**

Overview

Disney has emphasized meeting release dates for films, to the detriment of keeping them within budget.

Suggested Discussion Question

How did Disney change its approach with the production of *Lilo and Stitch*?

"Facing Computer Slowdown, Intel Boosts Focus on Consumer Devices," ***The Wall Street Journal,*** **January 2, 2001, p. A9, Molly Williams.**

Issue 9–57
Sales Forecasting in Budgeting

Overview

Intel bets that increased demand for its chips will come from consumer products, more than the PC market. The company introduces new products, such as ChatPad and WebTablet.

Suggested Discussion Question

What are the implications of this phenomenon for sales forecasting in the process of preparing Intel's master budget?

"U.S. Airlines Consider Impact of Higher Fuel Bill," ***The Wall Street Journal,*** **October 13, 2000; see also "American's Net Soars, but High Oil Prices Sting U.S. Airways,"** ***The Wall Street Journal,*** **October 19, 2000, Melanie Trottman and Susan Carey.**

Issue 9–58
Impact of Higher Oil Prices on the Airlines' Budgeting Processes

Overview

Rising oil prices have caused increases in the airlines' fuel costs.

Suggested Discussion Questions

How will rising fuel costs affect the budgeting process for airlines like American and US Airways? Would there be other effects on the airlines' budgets from generally higher oil prices, besides their effect on fuel costs?

Chapter Ten

Standard Costing, Operational Performance Measures, and the Balanced Scorecard

After completing this chapter, you should be able to:

1. Explain how standard costing is used to help manage costs.
2. Describe two ways to set standards, and distinguish between perfection and practical standards.
3. Compute and interpret the direct-material price and quantity variances and the direct-labor rate and efficiency variances.
4. Explain several methods for determining the significance of cost variances.
5. Describe some behavioral effects of standard costing.
6. Explain how standard costs are used in product costing.
7. Summarize some advantages of standard costing.
8. Describe the changing role of standard-costing systems in today's manufacturing environment.
9. Describe the operational performance measures appropriate for today's manufacturing environment.
10. Describe the balanced scorecard concept and explain the reasoning behind it.
11. After completing the appendix, prepare journal entries to record and close out cost variances.

Cyber Desserts from DCdesserts.com

Washington, DC—People living here in the nation's capital are often surprised to learn that many of the city's sweet tooths are being served by a Web-based company called DCdesserts.com. An innovative purveyor of fancy desserts, DCdesserts.com operates its business almost entirely over the Internet. "We supply fancy desserts to some of Washington's best restaurants, caterers, and gourmet food stores," says Tyler Martin, DCdesserts.com's founder and owner. "We've supplied desserts for the U.S. Senate dining room, and we've even had a president or two sample our wares."

The interesting thing about this company, though, is that almost all of its business dealings are done via the Internet. "We post our menu on our website, say on a Monday," explains Martin. "Then we accept orders up until midnight on Tuesday, for delivery on Friday. On Wednesday, we order ingredients, again mostly over the Web, and accept delivery on Thursday. We bake the desserts throughout the day on Friday and deliver them Friday afternoon. Of course, we do all this on a rolling basis, so we're starting a new sequence every day."

A tour of DCdesserts.com's production facilities and a talk with the company's director of cost management, however, demonstrated that there is much more to the company's success than its innovative Web-based strategy. "We have an incredibly tight cost control system here," says Maria Gonzales. "We set standards for everything, including the quantity and price of ingredients and the expected time and hourly rate for labor. When we have deviations from our standard cost to produce a batch of desserts, we investigate. If something's going wrong, we want to correct it. And if someone's discovered a more efficient way to do something, which results in a favorable cost variance, we want to know that, too."

Gonzales was quick to add, though, that the standard-costing system was not used punitively. "We never use it to beat people over the head. It's a diagnostic tool, that's all. It helps us keep tabs on the financial dimensions of our production process."

"We collect a lot of nonfinancial data as well," explained Gonzales. "We measure all kinds of things, like machine downtime, time for raw-material delivery, and a host of others. We're doing a lot with these nonfinancial, operational performance measures now."

DCdesserts.com is thriving by supplying some of the best desserts in Washington, and doing so in a cost-efficient manner.

A budget provides a plan for managers to follow in making decisions and directing an organization's activities. At the end of a budget period, the budget serves another useful purpose. At that time, managers use the budget as a benchmark against which to compare the results of actual operations. Did the company make as much profit as anticipated in the budget? Were costs greater or less than expected? These questions involve issues of cost management and control. In this chapter, we will study one of the tools used by managerial accountants to assist managers in controlling an organization's operations and costs.

Managing Costs

LO 1

Explain how standard costing is used to help manage costs.

How can managers use a control system as a cost management tool? Any control system has three basic parts: a predetermined or *standard* performance level, a measure of *actual* performance, and a *comparison* between standard and actual performance. A thermostat is a control system with which we are all familiar. First, a thermostat has a predetermined or standard temperature, which can be set at any desired level. If you want the temperature in a room to be 68 degrees, you set the thermostat at the *standard* of 68 degrees. Second, the thermostat has a thermometer, which measures the *actual* temperature in the room. Third, the thermostat *compares* the preset or standard temperature with the actual room temperature. If the actual temperature falls below the preset or standard temperature, the thermostat activates a heating device. The three features of a control system are depicted in Exhibit 10–1.

A managerial accountant's budgetary-control system works like a thermostat. First, a predetermined or **standard cost** is set. In essence, a standard cost is a budget for the production of one unit of product or service. It is the cost chosen by the managerial accountant to serve as the benchmark in the budgetary-control system. When the firm produces many units, the managerial accountant uses the standard unit cost to determine the total standard or budgeted cost of production. For example, suppose the standard direct-material cost for one unit of product is \$5 and 100 units are manufactured. The total standard or budgeted direct-material cost, given an actual output of 100 units, is \$500 (\$5 × 100).

Second, the managerial accountant measures the actual cost incurred in the production process.

Third, the managerial accountant compares the actual cost with the budgeted or standard cost. Any difference between the two is called a **cost variance.** Cost variances then are used in controlling costs.

Management by Exception

Managers are busy people. They do not have time to look into the causes of every variance between actual and standard costs. However, they do take the time to investigate

Exhibit 10–1
Control System: A Thermostat

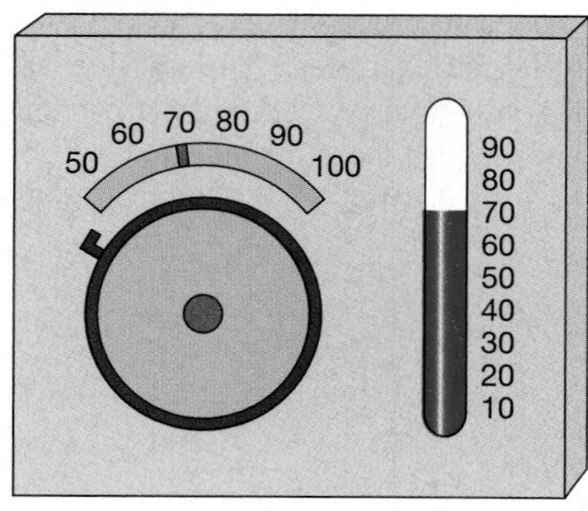

1. Predetermined or standard performance (The thermostat is set to a standard temperature.)

2. Measure of actual performance (The thermometer measures the actual room temperature.)

3. Comparison of actual and standard performance (The thermostat compares the preset or standard temperature with the actual temperature.)

the causes of significant cost variances. This process of following up on only significant cost variances is called **management by exception.** When operations are going along as planned, actual costs and profit will typically be close to the budgeted amounts. However, if there are significant departures from planned operations, such effects will show up as significant cost variances. Managers investigate these variances to determine their causes, if possible, and take corrective action when indicated.

What constitutes a significant variance? No precise answer can be given to this question, since it depends on the size and type of the organization and its production process. We will consider this issue later in the chapter when we discuss common methods for determining the significance of cost variances. First, however, we will turn our attention to the process of setting standards.

Setting Standards

Methods for Setting Standards

Managerial accountants typically use two methods for setting cost standards: analysis of historical data and task analysis.

LO 2

Describe two ways to set standards, and distinguish between perfection and practical standards.

Analysis of Historical Data One indicator of future costs is historical cost data. In a mature production process, where the firm has a lot of production experience, historical costs can provide a good basis for predicting future costs. The methods for analyzing cost behavior that we studied in Chapter 7 are used in making cost predictions. The managerial accountant often will need to adjust these predictions to reflect movements in price levels or technological changes in the production process. For example, the amount of rubber required to manufacture a particular type of tire will likely be the same this year as last year, unless there has been a significant change in the process used to manufacture tires. However, the price of rubber is likely to be different this year than last, and this fact must be reflected in the new standard cost of a tire.

Despite the relevance of historical cost data in setting cost standards, managerial accountants must guard against relying on them excessively. Even a seemingly minor change in the way a product is manufactured may make historical data almost totally irrelevant. Moreover, new products also require new cost standards. For new products, such as genetically engineered medicines, there are no historical cost data upon which to base standards. In such cases, the managerial accountant must turn to another approach.

Task Analysis Another way to set cost standards is to analyze the process of manufacturing a product to determine what it *should* cost. The emphasis shifts from what the product *did* cost in the past to what it *should* cost in the future. In using **task analysis,** the managerial accountant typically works with engineers who are intimately familiar with the production process. Together they conduct studies to determine exactly how much direct material should be required and how machinery should be used in the production process. Time and motion studies are conducted to determine how long each step performed by direct laborers should take.

A Combined Approach Managerial accountants often apply both historical cost analysis and task analysis in setting cost standards. It may be, for example, that the technology has changed for only one step in the production process. In such a case, the managerial accountant would work with engineers to set cost standards for the technologically changed part of the production process. However, the accountant would likely rely on the less expensive method of analyzing historical cost data to update the cost standards for the remainder of the production process.

Participation in Setting Standards

Standards should not be determined by the managerial accountant alone. People generally will be more committed to meeting standards if they are allowed to participate in setting them. For example, production supervisors should have a role in setting production cost standards, and sales managers should be involved in setting targets for sales prices and volume. In addition, knowledgeable staff personnel should participate in the standard-setting process. For example, task analysis should be carried out by a team consisting of production engineers, production supervisors, and managerial accountants.

Perfection versus Practical Standards: A Behavioral Issue

How difficult should it be to attain standard costs? Should standards be set so that actual costs rarely exceed standard costs? Or should it be so hard to attain standards that actual costs frequently exceed them? The answers to these questions depend on the purpose for which standards will be used and how standards affect behavior.

Perfection Standards A **perfection** (or **ideal**) **standard** is one that can be attained only under nearly perfect operating conditions. Such standards assume peak efficiency, the lowest possible input prices, the best-quality materials obtainable, and no disruptions in production due to such causes as machine breakdowns or power failures. Some managers believe that perfection standards motivate employees to achieve the lowest cost possible. They claim that since the standard is theoretically attainable, employees will have an incentive to come as close as possible to achieving it.

Other managers and many behavioral scientists disagree. They feel that perfection standards discourage employees, since they are so unlikely to be attained. Moreover, setting unrealistically difficult standards may encourage employees to sacrifice product quality to achieve lower costs. By skimping on raw-material quality or the attention given manual production tasks, employees may be able to lower the production cost. However, this lower cost may come at the expense of a higher rate of defective units. Thus, the firm ultimately may incur higher costs than necessary as defective products are returned by customers or scrapped upon inspection.

Practical Standards Standards that are as tight as practical, but still are expected to be attained, are called **practical** (or **attainable**) **standards.** Such standards assume a production process that is as efficient as practical under normal operating conditions. Practical standards allow for such occurrences as occasional machine breakdowns and normal amounts of raw-material waste. Attaining a practical standard keeps employees on their toes, without demanding miracles. Most behavioral theorists believe that practical standards encourage more positive and productive employee attitudes than do perfection standards.

Use of Standards by Nonmanufacturing Organizations

"At Best Foods, standard costs are set at attainable levels." (10a)
Best Foods (recently purchased by Unilever)

Many service industry firms, nonprofit organizations, and governmental units make use of standard costs. For example, airlines set standards for fuel and maintenance costs. A county motor vehicle office may have a standard for the number of days required to process and return an application for vehicle registration. These and similar organizations use standards in budgeting and cost control in much the same way that manufacturers use standards.

Cost Variance Analysis

To illustrate the use of standards in managing costs, we will focus on a producer of fancy desserts located in the Washington, DC, area. DCdesserts.com supplies fresh and frozen desserts to a variety of restaurants, caterers, and upscale food stores. The company's order-taking system is entirely Web-based. DCdesserts.com posts its menu of fresh fancy dessert products for each day on its website fours days in advance of the delivery date. Orders are accepted via the Internet three days in advance of delivery. For example, the menu of desserts to be available for delivery on Friday afternoon is posted to DCdesserts.com's website on Monday, and orders are accepted up to midnight on Tuesday. The company places orders for ingredients on Wednesday and accepts delivery on Thursday. DCdesserts.com's ordering is also done largely via the Internet. Production then takes place throughout the day on Friday, and the desserts are delivered Friday afternoon. DCdesserts.com uses three independent delivery services to deliver its dessert products: Capital Couriers, Potomac Door-to-Door, and Washington Delivery Service.

LO 3

Compute and interpret the direct-material price and quantity variances and the direct-labor rate and efficiency variances.

DCdesserts.com also produces frozen dessert products for upscale grocery stores. Unlike the fresh desserts, which vary daily, the frozen desserts are stock items that are varied less frequently. Like the fresh desserts, however, the frozen dessert menu is posted to DCdesserts.com's website, and orders are accepted entirely via the Internet. DCdesserts.com produces its fresh fancy desserts and frozen desserts in two different production facilities, both located near the Washington beltway.

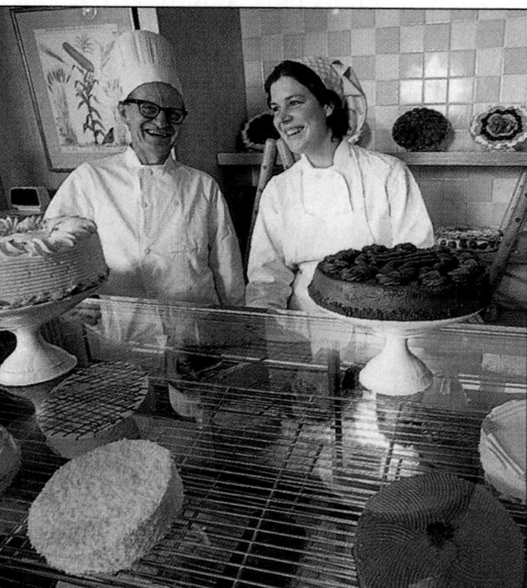

Fancy desserts such as these require considerable skilled direct labor.

The production process for the fresh fancy desserts involves a combination of semiautomated equipment and manual labor. Even in this era of widespread automation, making fancy desserts still involves considerable direct labor. In the words of DCdesserts.com's founder and owner, "making a Black Forest cake or a linzer torte to be served in the U.S. Senate dining room is not the same as making your basic pumpkin pie. There's a lot of touch labor by skilled people in doing these fancy desserts." The basic steps in the production process are much as you might expect. These steps include selecting ingredients, mixing, baking, cooling, and finishing. The finishing work, of course, involves the most skilled direct labor. In making a six-layer chocolate raspberry cake, for example, each individual cake layer must be sliced into two pieces, and then fillings and icings are applied to each layer. The cake's top is finished artistically, and any additional toppings are carefully applied.

DCdesserts.com's director of cost management has set standards for direct material and direct labor as follows for a category of dessert products generically referred to as multilayer fancy cakes.

Direct-Material Standards

The standard quantity and price of ingredients for one multilayer fancy cake, such as a Black Forest cake, are shown in the following table:

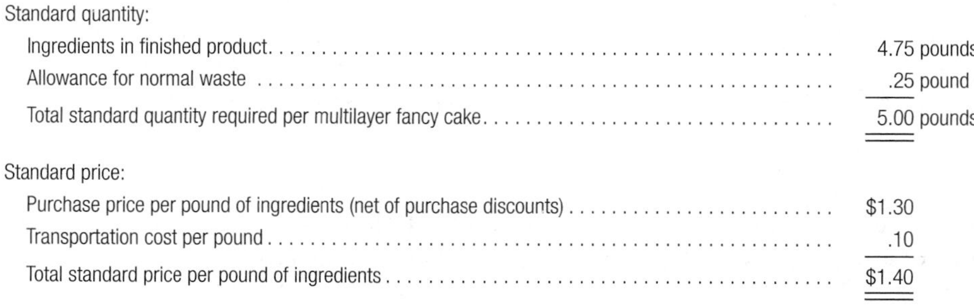

Standard quantity:	
Ingredients in finished product	4.75 pounds
Allowance for normal waste	.25 pound
Total standard quantity required per multilayer fancy cake	5.00 pounds
Standard price:	
Purchase price per pound of ingredients (net of purchase discounts)	$1.30
Transportation cost per pound	.10
Total standard price per pound of ingredients	$1.40

The standard quantity of ingredients needed to produce one cake is 5 pounds, even though only 4.75 pounds actually remain in the finished product. One-quarter pound of ingredients is wasted as a normal result of the production process. Therefore, the entire amount of ingredients needed to produce a fancy cake is included in the standard quantity of material.

The standard price of ingredients reflects all of the costs incurred to acquire the material and transport it to the plant. Notice that the cost of transportation is added to the purchase price. Any purchase discounts would be subtracted out from the purchase price to obtain a net price.

To summarize, the **standard direct-material quantity** is the total amount of direct material normally required to produce a finished product, including allowances for normal waste or inefficiency. The **standard direct-material price** is the total delivered cost, after subtracting any purchase discounts.

Direct-Labor Standards

The standard quantity and rate for direct labor for the production of one multilayer fancy cake are:

Standard quantity:		
Direct labor required per multilayer fancy cake		.5 hours
Standard rate:		
Hourly wage rate	$16	
Fringe benefits (25% of wages)	4	
Total standard rate per hour	$20	

The **standard direct-labor quantity** is the number of direct-labor hours normally needed to manufacture one unit of product. The **standard direct-labor rate** is the total hourly cost of compensation, including fringe benefits.

Standard Costs Given Actual Output

During September DCdesserts.com produced 2,000 multilayer fancy cakes. The total standard or budgeted costs for direct material and direct labor are computed as follows:

Direct material:	
Standard direct-material cost per cake (5 pounds × $1.40 per pound)	$ 7
Actual output	× 2,000
Total standard direct-material cost	$14,000
Direct labor:	
Direct-labor cost per cake (.5 hours × $20.00 per hour)	$ 10
Actual output	× 2,000
Total standard direct-labor cost	$20,000

Notice that the total standard cost for the direct-material and direct-labor inputs is based on DCdesserts.com's actual *output.* The company should incur costs of $34,000 for direct material and direct labor, *given that it produced 2,000 multilayer fancy cakes.* The total standard costs for direct material and direct labor serve as the managerial accountant's benchmarks against which to compare actual costs. This comparison then serves as the basis for controlling direct-material and direct-labor costs.

Analysis of Cost Variances

During September, DCdesserts.com incurred the following actual costs for direct material and direct labor in the production of multilayer fancy cakes.

Exhibit 10–2
Direct-Material Price and Quantity Variances

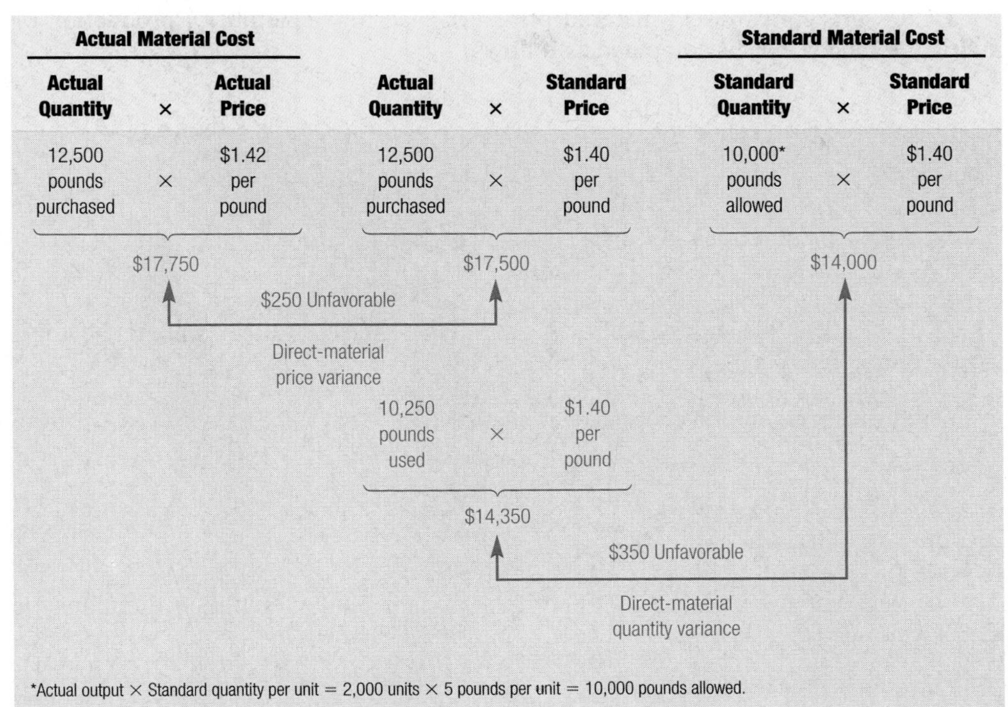

Direct material purchased: actual cost 12,500 pounds at $1.42 per pound	$17,750
Direct material used: actual cost 10,250 pounds at $1.42 per pound	$14,555
Direct labor: actual cost 980 hours at $21 per hour	$20,580

Compare these actual expenditures with the total standard costs for the production of 2,000 multilayer fancy cakes. DCdesserts.com spent more than the budgeted amount for both direct material and direct labor. But why were these excess costs incurred? Is there any further analysis the managerial accountant can provide to help answer this question?

Direct-Material Variances

Topic 10–1

What caused DCdesserts.com to spend more than the anticipated amount on direct material? First, the company purchased ingredients at a higher price ($1.42 per pound) than the standard price ($1.40 per pound). Second, the company used more ingredients than the standard amount. The amount actually used was 10,250 pounds instead of the standard amount of 10,000 pounds, which is based on actual output of 2,000 multilayer fancy cakes. The managerial accountant can show both of these deviations from standards by computing a **direct-material price variance** (or **purchase price variance**) and a **direct-material quantity variance.** The computation of these variances is depicted in Exhibit 10–2.

The formula for the direct-material price variance is as follows:

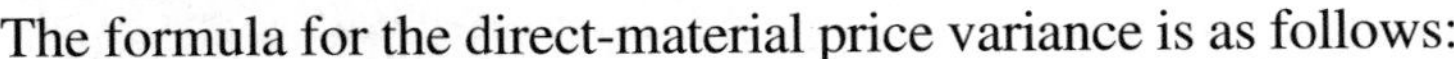

$$\text{Direct-material price variance} = (PQ \times AP) - (PQ \times SP) = PQ(AP - SP)$$

where

PQ = Quantity purchased
AP = Actual price
SP = Standard price

DCdesserts.com's direct-material price variance for September's production of multilayer fancy cakes is computed as follows:

$$\begin{aligned}\text{Direct-material price variance} &= \text{PQ}(\text{AP} - \text{SP})\\ &= 12{,}500(\$1.42 - \$1.40)\\ &= \$250 \text{ Unfavorable}\end{aligned}$$

This variance is unfavorable, because the actual purchase price exceeded the standard price. Notice that the price variance is based on the quantity of material *purchased* (PQ), not the quantity actually used in production.

As Exhibit 10–2 shows, the following formula defines the direct-material quantity variance.

$$\text{Direct-material quantity variance} = (\text{AQ} \times \text{SP}) - (\text{SQ} \times \text{SP}) = \text{SP}(\text{AQ} - \text{SQ})$$

where

AQ = Actual quantity used
SQ = Standard quantity allowed

DCdesserts.com's direct-material quantity variance for September's production of multilayer fancy cakes is computed as follows:

$$\begin{aligned}\text{Direct-material quantity variance} &= \text{SP}(\text{AQ} - \text{SQ})\\ &= \$1.40(10{,}250 - 10{,}000)\\ &= \$350 \text{ Unfavorable}\end{aligned}$$

This variance is unfavorable, because the actual quantity of direct material used in September exceeded the standard quantity allowed, *given actual September output* of 2,000 multilayer fancy cakes. The quantity variance is based on the quantity of material actually *used* in production (AQ).

> "The folks that have had the opportunity in the last eight months to engage as a real business partner are really excited by it, and we are doing some exciting things about our material [purchasing] organization, and finance, what we call vendor cost analysis folks." (10b)
>
> **Boeing**

Quantity Purchased versus Quantity Used As stated above, the direct-material price variance is based on the quantity purchased (PQ). This makes sense, because deviations between the actual and standard price, which are highlighted by the price variance, relate to the *purchasing* function in the firm. Timely action to follow up a significant price variance will be facilitated by calculating this variance as soon as possible after the material is *purchased.*

In contrast, the direct-material quantity variance is based on the amount of material *used* in production (AQ). The quantity variance highlights deviations between the quantity of material actually used (AQ) and the standard quantity allowed (SQ). Thus, it makes sense to compute this variance at the time the material is *used* in production.

Basing the Quantity Variance on Actual Output Notice that the standard quantity of material must be based on the actual production output in order for the quantity variance to be meaningful. It would not make any sense to compare standard or budgeted material usage at one level of output (say, 1,000 multilayer fancy cakes) with the actual material usage at a *different* level of output (say, 2,000 multilayer fancy cakes). Everyone would expect more direct material to be used in the production of 2,000 cakes than in the production of 1,000 cakes. For the direct-material quantity variance to provide helpful information for management, the standard or budgeted quantity must be based on *actual output.* Then the quantity variance compares the following two quantities.

Standard quantity allowed, given *actual output*	**Actual quantity** used in the production of *actual output*

Comparison of these quantities is the basis of the **direct-material quantity variance**

Direct-Labor Variances

Topic 10–2

Why did DCdesserts.com spend more than the anticipated amount on direct labor during September? First, the division incurred a cost of \$21 per hour for direct labor instead of the standard amount of \$20 per hour. Second, the division used only 980 hours of direct labor, which is less than the standard quantity of 1,000 hours, given actual output of 2,000 multilayer fancy cakes. The managerial accountant analyzes direct-labor costs by computing a **direct-labor rate variance** and a **direct-labor efficiency variance.** Exhibit 10–3 depicts the computation of these variances.

The formula for the direct-labor rate variance is shown below.

$$\text{Direct-labor rate variance} = (AH \times AR) - (AH \times SR) = AH(AR - SR)$$

where

AH = Actual hours used
AR = Actual rate per hour
SR = Standard rate per hour

DCdesserts.com's direct-labor rate variance for September's production of multilayer fancy cakes is computed as follows:

$$\text{Direct-labor rate variance} = AH(AR - SR)$$
$$= 980(\$21 - \$20) = \$980 \text{ Unfavorable}$$

Exhibit 10–3
Direct-Labor Rate and Efficiency Variances

Actual Labor Cost						Standard Labor Cost		
Actual Hours	×	**Actual Rate**	**Actual Hours**	×	**Standard Rate**	**Standard Hours**	×	**Standard Rate**
980 hours used	×	\$21 per hour	980 hours used	×	\$20 per hour	1,000* hours allowed	×	\$20 per hour
\$20,580			\$19,600			\$20,000		

\$980 Unfavorable — Direct-labor rate variance

\$400 Favorable — Direct-labor efficiency variance

\$580 Unfavorable — Direct-labor variance

*Actual output × Standard hours per unit = 2,000 units × .5 hours per unit = 1,000 hours allowed.

This variance is unfavorable because the actual rate exceeded the standard rate during September.

As Exhibit 10–3 shows, the formula for the direct-labor efficiency variance is as follows:

$$\text{Direct-labor efficiency variance} = (\text{AH} \times \text{SR}) - (\text{SH} \times \text{SR}) = \text{SR}(\text{AH} - \text{SH})$$

where

SH = Standard hours allowed

DCdesserts.com's direct-labor efficiency variance for September is computed as follows:

$$\begin{aligned}\text{Direct-labor efficiency variance} &= \text{SR}(\text{AH} - \text{SH}) \\ &= \$20(980 - 1{,}000) \\ &= \$400 \text{ Favorable}\end{aligned}$$

This variance is favorable, because the actual direct-labor hours used in September were less than the standard hours allowed, *given actual September output* of 2,000 multilayer fancy cakes.

Management Accounting Practice

Parker Hannifin

PARKER HANNIFIN CORPORATION'S BRASS PRODUCTS DIVISION

Parker Hannifin's Brass Products Division, a world-class manufacturer of brass fittings, valves, and tubing, is a standard-costing success story.[1] "Parker Brass uses its standard-costing system and variance analyses as important business tools to target problem areas so it can develop solutions for continuous improvement. Variances are reported for each product line, and if any production variance exceeds 5 percent of product-line sales, the product-line manager is required to provide an explanation. Also required is a plan to correct the problems underlying any unfavorable variances. Variance reports, which are generated within one day of the completion of a job order, are distributed to managers and production schedulers. A variance database is kept, which can be accessed by product-line managers, to provide variance data by part number, by job-order number, or by dollar amount."

From the perspective of Parker Brass's management, the division has modified its standard-costing system to provide disaggregated and timely cost information to enable timely corrective action in a rapidly changing business environment.

Notice that the direct-labor rate and efficiency variances add up to the total direct-labor variance. However, the rate and efficiency variances have opposite signs, since one variance is unfavorable and the other is favorable.

Direct-labor rate variance	$980 Unfavorable	Different signs of variances cancel just as plus and minus signs cancel in arithmetic.
Direct-labor efficiency variance	400 Favorable	
Direct-labor variance	$580 Unfavorable	

Basing the Efficiency Variance on Actual Output The number of standard hours of direct labor allowed is based on the *actual* production output. It would not be meaningful to compare standard or budgeted labor usage at one level of output with the actual hours used at a different level of output.

[1]David Johnsen and Parvez Sopariwala, "Standard Costing Is Alive and Well at Parker Brass," *Management Accounting Quarterly* 1, no. 2 (Winter 2000), pp. 12–20.

Multiple Types of Direct Material or Direct Labor

Manufacturing processes usually involve several types of direct material. In such cases, direct-material price and quantity variances are computed for each type of material. Then these variances are added to obtain a total price variance and a total quantity variance, as follows:

	Price Variance	Quantity Variance
Direct material A	$1,000 F	$1,600 U
Direct material B	2,500 U	200 U
Direct material C	800 U	500 F
Total variance	$2,300 U	$1,300 U

Similarly, if a production process involves several types of direct labor, rate and efficiency variances are computed for each labor type. Then they are added to obtain a total rate variance and a total efficiency variance.

Allowing for Spoilage or Defects

In some manufacturing processes, a certain amount of spoilage or defective production is normal. This must be taken into account when the standard quantity of material is computed. To illustrate, suppose that 100 gallons of chemicals are normally required in a chemical process in order to obtain 80 gallons of good output. If total good output in January is 500 gallons, what is the standard allowed quantity of input?

$$\text{Good output quantity} = 80\% \times \text{Input quantity}$$

Dividing both sides of the equation by 80%

$$\frac{\text{Good output quantity}}{80\%} = \text{Input quantity allowed}$$

Using the numbers in the illustration

$$\frac{\text{500 gallons of good output}}{80\%} = \text{625 gallons of input allowed}$$

The total standard allowed input is 625 gallons, given 500 gallons of good output.

Significance of Cost Variances

LO 4

Explain several methods for determining the significance of cost variances.

Managers do not have time to investigate the causes of every cost variance. Management by exception enables managers to look into the causes of only significant variances. But what constitutes an exception? How does the manager know when to follow up on a cost variance and when to ignore it?

These questions are difficult to answer, because to some extent the answers are part of the art of management. A manager applies judgment and experience in making guesses, pursuing hunches, and relying on intuition to determine when a variance should be investigated. Nevertheless, there are guidelines and rules of thumb that managers often apply.

Size of Variances The absolute size of a variance is one consideration. Managers are more likely to follow up on large variances than on small ones. The relative size of the variance is probably even more important. A manager is more likely to investigate a $20,000 material quantity variance that is 20 percent of the standard direct-material cost of $100,000, than a $50,000 labor efficiency variance that is only 2 percent of the standard direct-labor cost of $2,500,000. The *relative* magnitude of the $20,000 material quantity variance (20 percent) is greater than the *relative* magnitude of the $50,000 labor efficiency variance (2 percent). For this reason, managerial accountants often show the relative magnitude of variances in their cost-variance reports. For example,

Exhibit 10–4
Cost Variance Report for September: DCdesserts.com

	Amount		Percentage of Standard Cost
Direct material			
Standard cost, given actual output	$14,000		
Direct-material price variance	250	Unfavorable	1.79%
Direct-material quantity variance	350	Unfavorable	2.50%
Direct labor			
Standard cost, given actual output	$20,000		
Direct-labor rate variance	980	Unfavorable	4.9%
Direct-labor efficiency variance	400	Favorable	(2.0%)

the September cost-variance report for DCdesserts.com's production of multilayer fancy cakes is shown in Exhibit 10–4.

Managers often apply a rule of thumb that takes into account both the absolute and the relative magnitudes of a variance. An example of such a rule is the following: Investigate variances that are either greater than $10,000 or greater than 10 percent of standard cost.

Recurring Variances Another consideration in deciding when to investigate a variance is whether the variance occurs repeatedly or only infrequently. Suppose a manager uses the rule of thumb stated above and direct-material quantity variances occur as shown in the following Excel spreadsheet.

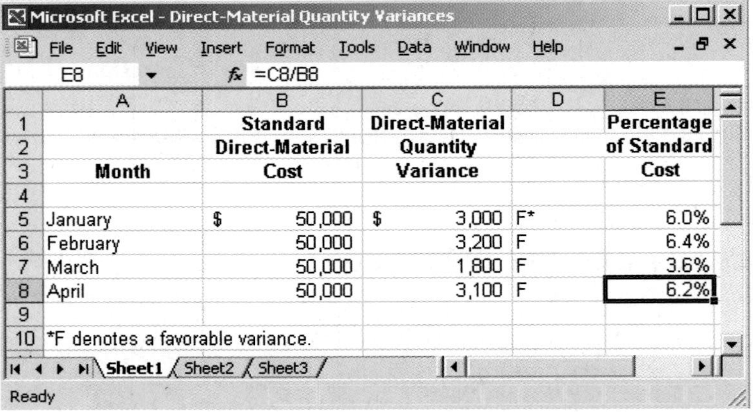
Microsoft Excel - Direct-Material Quantity Variances

File Edit View Insert Format Tools Data Window Help

E8 =C8/B8

	A	B	C	D	E
1		**Standard**	**Direct-Material**		**Percentage**
2		**Direct-Material**	**Quantity**		**of Standard**
3	**Month**	**Cost**	**Variance**		**Cost**
4					
5	January	$ 50,000	$ 3,000	F*	6.0%
6	February	50,000	3,200	F	6.4%
7	March	50,000	1,800	F	3.6%
8	April	50,000	3,100	F	6.2%
9					
10	*F denotes a favorable variance.				

Sheet1 Sheet2 Sheet3

Ready

A strict adherence to the rule of thumb indicates no investigation, since none of the monthly variances is greater than $10,000 or 10 percent of standard cost. Nevertheless, the manager might investigate this variance in April, since it has *recurred* at a reasonably high level for several consecutive months. In this case, the consistency of the variance triggers an investigation, not its absolute or relative magnitude.

Trends A trend in a variance may also call for investigation. Suppose a manager observes the direct-labor efficiency variances shown in the following Excel spreadsheet.

None of these variances is large enough to trigger an investigation if the manager uses the "$10,000 or 10 percent" rule of thumb. However, the four-month *trend* is worrisome. An alert manager will likely follow up on this unfavorable trend to determine its causes before costs get out of hand.

Microsoft Excel - Direct-Labor Efficiency Variances

File Edit View Insert Format Tools Data Window Help

E8 fx =C8/B8

	A	B	C	D	E
1		Standard	Direct-Labor		Percentage
2		Direct-Labor	Efficiency		of Standard
3	Month	Cost	Variance		Cost
4					
5	January	$ 100,000	$ 100	U*	0.10%
6	February	100,000	550	U	0.55%
7	March	100,000	3,000	U	3.00%
8	April	100,000	9,100	U	9.10%
9					
10	*U denotes an unfavorable variance.				

Sheet1 / Sheet2 / Sheet3

Ready

Controllability Another important consideration in deciding when to look into the causes of a variance is the manager's view of the **controllability** of the cost item. A manager is more likely to investigate the variance for a cost that is controllable by someone in the organization than one that is not. For example, there may be little point to investigating a material price variance if the organization has no control over the price. This could happen, for example, if the firm has a long-term contract with a supplier of the material at a price determined on the international market. In contrast, the manager is likely to follow up on a variance that should be controllable, such as a direct-labor efficiency variance or a direct-material quantity variance.

Favorable Variances It is just as important to investigate significant favorable variances as significant unfavorable variances. For example, a favorable direct-labor efficiency variance may indicate that employees have developed a more efficient way of performing a production task. By investigating the variance, management can learn about the improved method. It may be possible to use a similar approach elsewhere in the organization.

Costs and Benefits of Investigation The decision whether to investigate a cost variance is a cost-benefit decision. The costs of investigation include the time spent by the investigating manager and the employees in the department where the investigation occurs. Other potential costs include disruption of the production process as the investigation is conducted, and corrective actions taken to eliminate the cause of a variance. The benefits of a variance investigation include reduced future production costs if the cause of an unfavorable variance is eliminated. Another potential benefit is the cost saving associated with the lowering of cost standards when the cause of a favorable variance is discovered.

Weighing these considerations takes the judgment of skillful and experienced managers. Key to this judgment is an intimate understanding of the organization's production process and day-to-day contact with its operations.

A Statistical Approach

There are many reasons for cost variances. For example, a direct-labor efficiency variance could be caused by inexperienced employees, employee inefficiency, poor-quality raw materials, poorly maintained machinery, an intentional work slowdown due to employee grievances, or many other factors. In addition to these substantive reasons, there are purely random causes of variances. People are not robots, and they are not

Exhibit 10–5
Statistical Control Chart

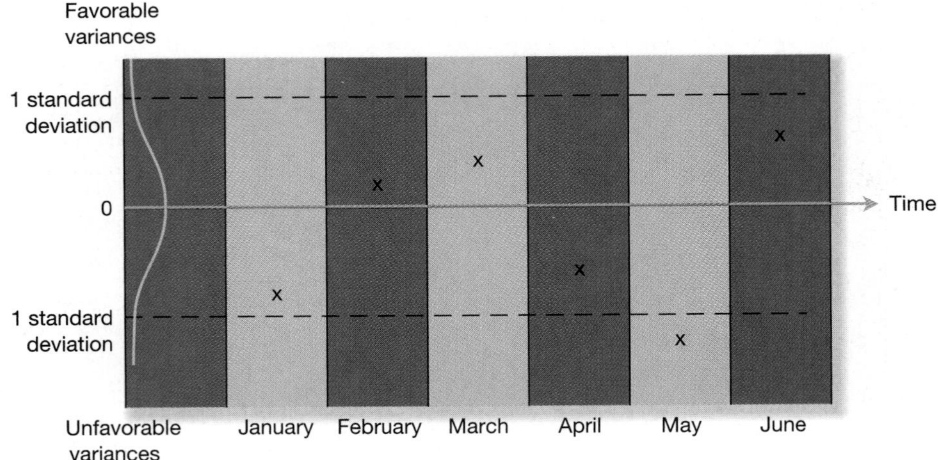

perfectly consistent in their work habits. Random fluctuations in direct-labor efficiency variances can be caused by such factors as employee illnesses, workers experimenting with different production methods, or simply random fatigue. Ideally, managers would be able to sort out the randomly caused variances from those with substantive and controllable underlying causes. It is impossible to accomplish this with 100 percent accuracy, but a **statistical control chart** can help.

A statistical control chart plots cost variances across time and compares them with a statistically determined *critical value* that triggers an investigation. This critical value is usually determined by assuming that cost variances have a normal probability distribution with a mean of zero. The critical value is set at some multiple of the distribution's standard deviation. Variances greater than the critical value are investigated.

Exhibit 10–5 shows a statistical control chart with a critical value of 1 standard deviation. The manager would investigate the variance observed in May, since it falls further than 1 standard deviation from the mean (zero). The variances for the remaining five months would not be investigated. The presumption is that these minor variances are due to random causes and are not worth investigating.

Behavioral Impact of Standard Costing

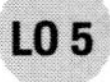
LO 5

Describe some behavioral effects of standard costing.

Standard costs and variance analysis are useful in diagnosing organizational performance. These tools help managers discern "the story behind the story"—the details of operations that underlie reported cost and profit numbers. Standard costs, budgets, and variances are also used to evaluate the performance of individuals and departments. The performance of individuals, relative to standards or budgets, often is used to help determine salary increases, bonuses, and promotions. When standards and variances affect employee reward structures, they can profoundly influence behavior.

For example, suppose the manager of a hotel's Food and Beverage Department earns a bonus when food and beverage costs are below the budgeted amount, given actual sales. This reward structure will provide a concrete incentive for the manager to keep food and beverage costs under control. But such an incentive can have either positive or negative effects. The bonus may induce the manager to seek the most economical food suppliers and to watch more carefully for employee theft and waste. However, the bonus could also persuade the manager to buy cheaper but less tender steaks for the restaurant. This could ultimately result in lost patronage for the restaurant and the hotel.

One aspect of skillful management is knowing how to use standards, budgets, and variances to get the most out of an organization's employees. Unfortunately, there are no simple answers or formulas for success in this area. Despite such difficulties, standards, budgets, and variances are used in the executive compensation schemes of many well-known companies.

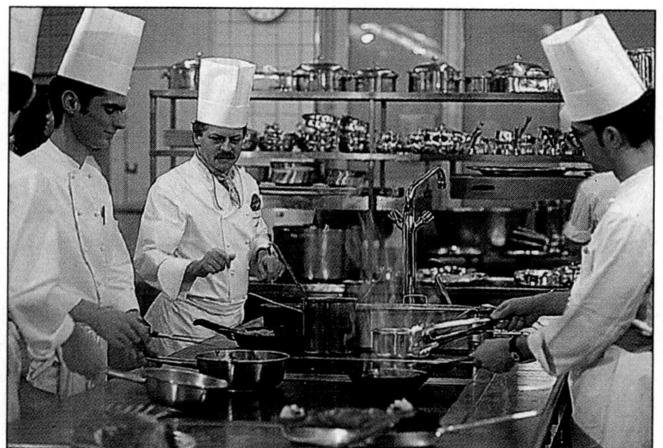

Incentive systems should be carefully designed so that employees try to carefully manage costs without allowing a deterioration in product or service quality. The head chef in this hotel's restaurant is evaluated both on his ability to control costs and on the satisfaction level of the restaurant's customers.

Controllability of Variances

Cost control is accomplished through the efforts of individual managers in an organization. By determining which managers are in the best position to influence each cost variance, the managerial accountant can assist managers in deriving the greatest benefit from cost variance analysis.

Who is responsible for the direct-material price and quantity variances? The direct-labor rate and efficiency variances? Answering these questions is often difficult, because it is rare that any one person completely controls any event. Nevertheless, it is often possible to identify the manager who is *most able to influence* a particular variance, even if he or she does not exercise complete control over the outcome.

Direct-Material Price Variance The purchasing manager is generally in the best position to influence material price variances. Through skillful purchasing practices, an expert purchasing manager can get the best prices available for purchased goods and services. To achieve this goal, the purchasing manager uses such practices as buying in quantity, negotiating purchase contracts, comparing prices among vendors, and global sourcing.

Despite these purchasing skills, the purchasing manager is not in complete control of prices. The need to purchase component parts with precise engineering specifications, the all-too-frequent rush requests from the production department, and worldwide shortages of critical materials all contribute to the challenges faced by the purchasing manager.

"We designate variances as controllable or uncontrollable. Plant managers are held accountable for the controllable variances." (10c)

Best Foods (recently purchased by Unilever)

Direct-Material Quantity Variance The production supervisor is usually in the best position to influence material quantity variances. Skillful supervision and motivation of production employees, coupled with the careful use and handling of materials, contribute to minimal waste. Production engineers are also partially responsible for material quantity variances, since they determine the grade and technical specifications of materials and component parts. In some cases, using a low-grade material may result in greater waste than using a high-grade material.

Direct-Labor Rate Variance Direct-labor rate variances generally result from using a different mix of employees than that anticipated when the standards were set. Wage rates differ among employees due to their skill levels and their seniority with the organization. Using a higher proportion of more senior or more highly skilled employees than a task requires can result in unfavorable direct-labor rate variances. The production supervisor is generally in the best position to influence the work schedules of employees.

Direct-Labor Efficiency Variance Once again, the production supervisor is usually most responsible for the efficient use of employee time. Through motivation toward production goals and effective work schedules, the efficiency of employees can be maximized.

Interaction among Variances

Interactions among variances often occur, making it even more difficult to determine the responsibility for a particular variance. To illustrate, consider the following anecdote from a manufacturer of brass musical instruments. The purchasing manager obtained a special price on brass alloy from a new supplier. When the material was placed into production, it turned out to be a lower grade of material than the production employees were used to. The alloy was of a slightly different composition, which made the material bend less easily during the formation of brass instruments. The company could have returned the material to the supplier, but that would have interrupted production and kept the division from filling its orders on time. Since using the off-standard material would not affect the quality of the company's finished products, the division manager decided to keep the material and make the best of the situation.

The ultimate result was that the company incurred four interrelated variances during May. The material was less expensive than normal, so the direct-material price variance was favorable. However, the employees had difficulty using the material, which resulted in more waste than expected. Hence, the division incurred an unfavorable direct-material quantity variance.

What were the labor implications of the off-standard material? Due to the difficulty in working with the metal alloy, the employees required more than the standard amount of time to form the instruments. This resulted in an unfavorable direct-labor efficiency variance. Finally, the production supervisor had to use his most senior employees to work with the off-standard material. Since these people earned relatively high wages, the direct-labor rate variance was also unfavorable.

To summarize, the purchase of off-standard material resulted in the following interrelated variances.

Purchase of off-standard material => { Favorable direct-material price variance; Unfavorable direct-material quantity variance; Unfavorable direct-labor rate variance; Unfavorable direct-labor efficiency variance }

Such interactions of variances make it more difficult to assign responsibility for any particular variance.

Trade-Offs among Variances Does the incident described above mean that the decision to buy and use the off-standard material was a poor one? Not necessarily. Perhaps these variances were anticipated, and a conscious decision was made to buy the material anyway. How could this be a wise decision? Suppose the amounts of the variances were as follows:

$(8,500)	Favorable direct-material price variance
1,000	Unfavorable direct-material quantity variance
2,000	Unfavorable direct-labor rate variance
1,500	Unfavorable direct-labor efficiency variance
$(4,000)	Favorable net overall variance

The company saved money overall on the decision to use a different grade of brass alloy. Given that the quality of the final product was not affected, the company's management acted wisely.

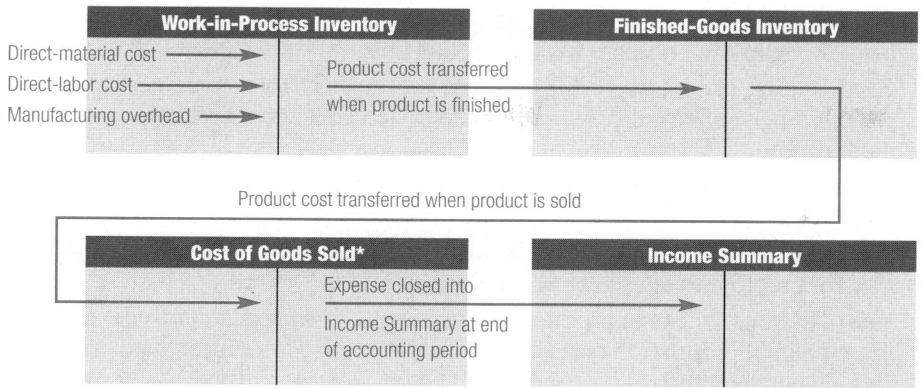

Exhibit 10–6
Flow of Product Costs through Manufacturing Accounts

*Cost of Goods Sold is an expense. Although it is more descriptive, the term *cost-of-goods-sold expense* is not used as much in practice as the simpler term *cost of goods sold.*

Standard Costs and Product Costing

LO 6 Explain how standard costs are used in product costing.

Our discussion of standard costing has focused on its use in controlling costs. But firms that use standard costs for control also use them for product costing. Recall from Chapter 3 that *product costing* is the process of accumulating the costs of a production process and assigning them to the completed products. Product costs are used for various purposes in both financial and managerial accounting.

As production takes place, product costs are added to the Work-in-Process Inventory account. The flow of product costs through a firm's manufacturing accounts is depicted in Exhibit 10–6.

Different types of product-costing systems are distinguished by the type of costs that are entered into Work-in-Process Inventory. In Chapter 3, we studied *actual-* and *normal*-costing systems. In these product-costing systems, the *actual* costs of direct material and direct labor are charged to Work-in-Process Inventory. In a **standard-costing system** the *standard* costs of direct material and direct labor are entered into Work-in-Process Inventory.

Further explanation of the use of standard costs for product-costing purposes is provided in the appendix at the end of this chapter, which can be studied now if desired.

Advantages of Standard Costing

LO 7 Summarize some advantages of standard costing.

Standard costing has been the predominant accounting system in manufacturing companies, for both cost control and product-costing purposes, for several decades. This remains true today, and the use of standard costing is spreading to nonmanufacturing firms as well. The widespread use of standard costing over such a long time period suggests that it has traditionally been perceived as offering several advantages. However, today's manufacturing environment is changing dramatically. Some managers are calling into question the usefulness of the traditional standard-costing approach. They argue that the role of standard-costing systems must change.

In this section, we will list some of the advantages traditionally attributed to standard-costing systems. In the next section, we will discuss some of the contemporary criticisms of the standard-costing approach, and suggest several ways in which the role of standard costing is beginning to change.

Some advantages traditionally attributed to standard costing include the following:

1. Standard costs provide a basis for *sensible cost comparisons.* As we discussed earlier, it would make no sense to compare budgeted costs at one (planned) activity level with actual costs incurred at a different (actual) activity level. Standard costs enable the managerial accountant to compute

the standard allowed cost, given actual output, which then serves as a sensible benchmark to compare with the actual cost.

2. Computation of standard costs and cost variances enables managers to employ *management by exception.* This approach conserves valuable management time.
3. Variances provide a means of *performance evaluation* and rewards for employees.
4. Since the variances are used in performance evaluation, they provide *motivation* for employees to adhere to standards.
5. Use of standard costs in product costing results in *more stable product costs* than if actual production costs are used. Actual costs often fluctuate erratically, whereas standard costs are changed only periodically.
6. A standard-costing system is usually *less expensive* than an actual or normal product-costing system.

Like any tool, a standard-costing system can be misused. When employees are criticized for every cost variance, the positive motivational effects will quickly vanish. Moreover, if standards are not revised often enough, they will become outdated. Then the benefits of cost benchmarks and product costing will disappear.

Changing Role of Standard-Costing Systems in Today's Manufacturing Environment

Describe the changing role of standard-costing systems in today's manufacturing environment.

The rise of global competition, the introduction of JIT production methods and flexible manufacturing systems, the goal of continuous process improvement, and the emphasis on product quality are dramatically changing the manufacturing environment. What are the implications of these changes for the role of standard-costing systems? We will begin by listing some contemporary criticisms of standard costing.

Criticisms of Standard Costing in Today's Manufacturing Environment

Listed below are several drawbacks attributed to standard costing in an advanced manufacturing setting.[2]

1. The variances calculated under standard costing are at too aggregate a level and come too late to be useful. Some managerial accountants argue that traditional standard costing is out of step with the philosophy of *cost management systems* and *activity-based management.* A production process comprises many activities. These activities result in costs. By focusing on the activities that cause costs to be incurred, by eliminating non-value-added activities, and by continually improving performance in value-added activities, costs will be minimized and profit maximized.[3] What is needed are performance measures that focus directly on performance in the activities that management wants to improve. For example, such activities could

[2]The sources for this material are Robert S. Kaplan, "Limitations of Cost Accounting in Advanced Manufacturing Environments," in *Measures for Manufacturing Excellence,* Robert S. Kaplan, ed. (Boston: Harvard Business School Press, 1990), pp. 1–14; H. Thomas Johnson, "Performance Measurement for Competitive Excellence," in *Measures for Manufacturing Excellence,* Robert S. Kaplan, ed. (Boston: Harvard Business School Press, 1990), pp. 63–90; Robert A. Bonsack, "Does Activity-Based Costing Replace Standard Costing?" *Journal of Cost Management* 4, no. 4 (Winter 1991), pp. 46, 47; and Michiharu Sukurai, "The Influence of Factory Automation on Management Accounting Practices: A Study of Japanese Companies," in *Measures for Manufacturing Excellence,* Robert S. Kaplan, ed. (Boston: Harvard Business School Press, 1990), pp. 39–62.

[3]Cost management systems and activity-based management are covered in Chapters 5 and 6. Elimination of non-value-added costs is covered in Chapter 6.

include product quality, processing time, and delivery performance. (We will explore such measures later in this chapter.)

2. Traditional cost variances are also too aggregate in the sense that they are not tied to specific product lines, production batches, or FMS cells. The aggregate nature of the variances makes it difficult for managers to determine their cause.
3. Traditional standard-costing systems focus too much on the cost and efficiency of direct labor, which is rapidly becoming a relatively unimportant factor of production.
4. One of the most important conditions for the successful use of standard costing is a stable production process. Yet the introduction of flexible manufacturing systems has reduced this stability, with frequent switching among a variety of products on the same production line.
5. Shorter product life cycles mean that standards are relevant for only a short time. When new products are introduced, new standards must be developed.
6. Traditional standard costs are not defined broadly enough to capture various important aspects of performance. For example, the standard direct-material price does not capture all of the *costs of ownership.* In addition to the purchase price and transportation costs, the *cost of ownership* includes the costs of ordering, paying bills, scheduling delivery, receiving, inspecting, handling and storing, and any production-line disruptions resulting from untimely or incorrect delivery.[4]

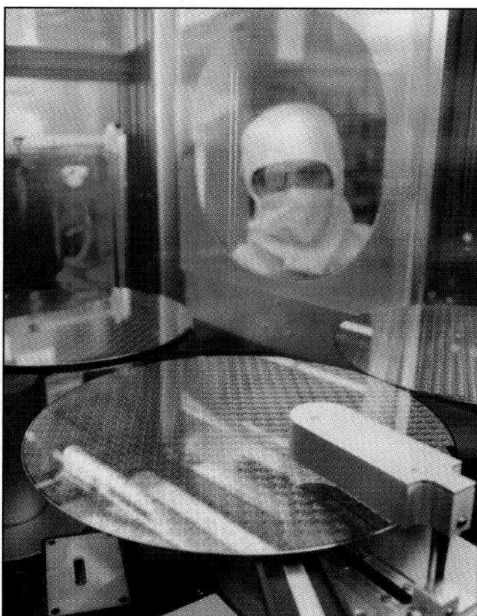

This Texas Instruments manufacturing facility relies on its suppliers for high-quality raw materials delivered on a timely basis. Texas Instruments, like many other companies, employs a sophisticated supplier rating system to measure the performance of its vendors.

Management Accounting Practice

Texas Instruments, Northrup, and Black & Decker

COST OF OWNERSHIP

Texas Instruments has developed a supplier rating system referred to as CETRAQ, which stands for cost, environmental responsibility, technology, responsiveness, assurance of supply, and quality. The company's vendors are regularly measured on these six criteria.

Northrop Aircraft Division tracks various elements of the total cost of ownership (TCO)* through its cost-based Supplier Performance Rating System (SPRS). Among the cost factors measured by the SPRS are the costs Northrop incurs due to suppliers' hardware, paperwork, or delivery deficiencies. Any "nonconformance event is assigned a standard cost based on industrial engineering studies of the hours required to resolve the problem."

At a Spennymore, England, plant owned by Black & Decker, the company "has integrated the cost-of-ownership concept into its activity-based costing system." Among the TCO issues included are quality, delivery, flexibility, and customer service. Also considered is a supplier's billing reliability. "As one Spennymore manager noted, 'You can be dealing with the best company in the world in terms of quality, but if they can't get their invoices right, you're going to have trouble doing business with them.'"

*The *total cost of ownership* includes all costs incurred in order to have materials in place and ready for use in production, including the purchase price; transportation cost; and costs of ordering, receiving, inspecting, and storing the materials."[5]

[4]Some companies are developing cost of ownership reporting systems. Among them are Northrop Aircraft Division, Texas Instruments, and Black & Decker. See L. Carr and C. Ittner, "Measuring the Cost of Ownership," *Journal of Cost Management* 6, no. 3 (Fall 1992), pp. 42–51. The information about Texas Instruments is based on the author's research.

[5]Carr, L., and C. Ittner. "Measuring the Cost of Ownership," *Journal of Cost Management* 6, no. 3 (Fall 1992), pp. 42–51.

7. Traditional standard-costing systems tend to focus too much on cost minimization, rather than increasing product quality or customer service. Indeed, standard-costing systems can cause dysfunctional behavior in a JIT/FMS environment. For example, buying the least expensive materials of a given quality, in order to avoid a material price variance, may result in using a vendor whose delivery capabilities are not consistent with JIT requirements.
8. Automated manufacturing processes tend to be more consistent in meeting production specifications. As a result, variances from standards tend to be very small or nonexistent.

Adapting Standard-Costing Systems

As a result of these criticisms, some highly automated manufacturers are deemphasizing standard costing in their control systems. Yet most manufacturing firms continue to use standard costing to some extent even after adopting advanced manufacturing methods.[6] However, such firms do make changes in their use of standard costing to reflect various features of the advanced manufacturing environment.

Reduced Importance of Labor Standards and Variances As direct labor occupies a diminished role in the new manufacturing environment, the standards and variances used to control labor costs also decline in importance. The heavy emphasis of traditional standard-costing systems on labor efficiency variances must give way to variances that focus on the more critical inputs to the production process. Machine hours, material and overhead costs, product quality, and manufacturing cycle times take on greater importance as the objects of managerial control.

Emphasis on Material and Overhead Costs As labor diminishes in importance, material and overhead costs take on greater significance. Controlling material costs and quality, and controlling overhead costs through cost-driver analysis, become key aspects of the cost management system (CMS).

"Many people have condemned standard costing, saying it is irrelevant to the current just-in-time, fast-paced business environment. Yet surveys consistently show that most industrial companies in the U.S. and abroad still use it. Apparently, these companies have successfully adapted their standard-costing system to their particular business environments." (10d)
Brass Products Division, Parker Hannifin Corporation

Cost Drivers Identification of the factors that drive production costs takes on greater importance in the CMS. Such cost drivers as machine hours, number of parts, engineering change orders, and production runs become the focus of the CMS and activity-based costing system.

Shifting Cost Structures Advanced manufacturing systems require large outlays for production equipment, which entail a shift in the cost structure from variable costs toward fixed costs. Overhead cost control becomes especially critical. Chapter 11 explores the role of standard-costing systems in controlling overhead costs.

High Quality and Zero Defects Total quality control (TQC) programs that typically accompany a JIT approach strive for very high quality levels for both raw materials and finished products. One result should be very low material price and quantity variances and low costs of rework.

---

[6]For example, see Jonathan B. Schiff, "ABC at Lederle," *Management Accounting* 75, no. 2 (August 1993), p. 58; and Robert A. Bonsack, "Does Activity-Based Costing Replace Standard Costing?" *Journal of Cost Management* 4, no. 4 (Winter 1991), pp. 46–47.

Non-Value-Added Costs A key objective of a CMS is the elimination of non-value-added costs. As these costs are reduced or eliminated, standards must be revised frequently to provide accurate benchmarks for cost control.

Shorter Product Life Cycles As product life cycles shorten, standards must be developed and revised more frequently.

Real-Time Information Systems A computer-integrated manufacturing (CIM) system enables the managerial accountant to collect operating data as production takes place and to report relevant performance measures to management on a real-time basis. This enables managers to eliminate the causes of unfavorable variances more quickly.

Nonfinancial Measures for Operational Control Managerial accountants traditionally have focused on financial measures of performance, such as deviations from budgeted costs. Financial measures are still very important, but to an ever-greater extent financial performance criteria are being augmented by nonfinancial measures. In the new manufacturing environment, operational measures are being developed to control key aspects of the production process. In the next section we will discuss some of these measures.

Benchmarking One widely used method to control costs and improve operational efficiency is **benchmarking.** This is the continual search for the most effective method of accomplishing a task, by comparing existing methods and performance levels with those of other organizations, or with other subunits within the same organization. For example, hospitals routinely benchmark their costs of patient care by diagnostic-related groups (such as circulatory disorders), with the costs of other hospitals.

Operational Performance Measures in Today's Manufacturing Environment

Describe the operational performance measures appropriate for today's manufacturing environment.

In today's advanced manufacturing environment, operational performance measures are taking on ever-greater importance.[7] Under the philosophy of *activity-based management,* the goal is to focus on continually improving each activity. As a result, the emerging operational control measures focus on the key *activities* in which the organization engages. Exhibit 10–7 lists some commonly used operational performance measures. The measures listed in Exhibit 10–7 are representative, but not exhaustive, of those used in practice. In using these measures to control operations, management emphasizes trends over time. The goal is to continually improve all aspects of the plant's operations.

Raw Material and Scrap Raw material continues to be a significant cost element in any manufacturing process, whether labor-intensive or highly automated. Worldwide material sourcing and international competition have resulted in the purchasing

[7]This section draws on Howard M. Armitage and Anthony A. Atkinson, "The Choice of Productivity Measures in Organizations," in Robert S. Kaplan, ed., *Measures for Manufacturing Excellence* (Boston: Harvard Business School Press, 1990), pp. 91–128; and Robert S. Kaplan and David P. Norton, *The Strategy-Focused Organization: How Balanced-Scorecard Companies Thrive in the New Business Environment* (Boston: Harvard Business School Press, 2001).

Raw Material and Scrap
Number of vendors
Number of unique parts
Number of common parts
Raw material as a percentage of total cost
Lead time for material delivery
Percentage of orders received on time
Total raw-material cost
Deviations between actual and budgeted raw-material prices
Scrap as a percentage of raw-material cost
Cost of scrap
Quality of raw material

Inventory
Average value of inventory
Average amount of time various inventory items are held
Ratio of inventory value to sales revenue
Number of inventoried parts

Machinery
Hours of machine downtime
Percentage of machine downtime
Percentage of machine availability
Bottleneck machine downtime
Percentage of bottleneck machine downtime
Percentage of bottleneck machine availability
Detailed maintenance records
Percentage of on-time routine maintenance procedures
Setup time
Machine flexibility:
- Product switchover times in an FMS cell
- Number of different products manufactured in an FMS cell

Product Quality
Customer acceptance measures:
- Number of customer complaints
- Number of warranty claims
- Number of products returned
- Cost of repairing returned products

In-process quality measures:
- Number of defects found
- Cost of rework

Quality costs

Production and Delivery
Manufacturing cycle time
Velocity
Manufacturing cycle efficiency
Percentage of on-time deliveries
Percentage of orders filled
Delivery cycle time

Productivity
Financial measures:
- Aggregate or total productivity (output in dollars ÷ total input in dollars)
- Partial or component productivity (output in dollars ÷ a particular input in dollars)

Operational (physical) measures:
- Partial or component productivity measures. These measures express relationships between inputs and outputs, in physical terms. For example:
  - Finished products produced per day per employee
  - Square feet of floor space required per finished product per day
  - Electricity required per finished product

Innovation and Learning
New products:
- Percentage of sales from new products
- New products introduced by this firm versus introductions by competitors

Process improvements:
- Number of process improvements made
- Cost savings from process improvements

Exhibit 10–7
Operational Performance Measures for an Advanced Manufacturing Environment

function taking on greater importance in many firms. As a result, purchasing performance has become an important area of measurement; criteria include total raw-material cost, deviations between actual and budgeted material prices, the quality of raw materials, and the delivery performance of vendors.

The cost of scrap is highlighted as a separate item, rather than being included in the standard direct-material cost as a normal production cost. The objective is to reduce scrap to the absolute minimal level possible.

Inventory The essence of the just-in-time production environment is low inventories at every stage of production. Thus, inventory control is of paramount importance in achieving the benefits of the JIT philosophy. Inventory control measures include the average value of inventory, the average amount of time various inventory items are held, and other inventory turnover measures, such as the ratio of inventory value to sales revenue.

Machinery If inventories are to be kept low, as the JIT philosophy demands, then the production process must be capable of producing goods quickly. This goal requires that production machinery must work when it is needed, which means that routine maintenance schedules must be adhered to scrupulously. Performance controls in this area include measures of machine downtime and machine availability, and detailed maintenance records. Some manufacturers make a distinction between *bottleneck machinery* and nonbottleneck machinery. A bottleneck operation is one that limits the production capacity of the entire facility. It is vital that the machinery in bottleneck operations be available 100 percent of the time, excluding time for routine required maintenance. In an advanced manufacturing environment, based on JIT and FMS, the investment in machinery is extremely large. To obtain the anticipated return from this investment, through the benefits of JIT and FMS, the machinery has to be kept running. This emphasis on bottleneck operations is consistent with the management philosophy known as the *theory of constraints.* This approach stresses the importance of identifying and easing the organization's constraints, which are the phenomena that limit the organization's productive capacity.[8]

Setup time also is highlighted as a machinery performance measure, and the objective in a JIT/FMS setting is to minimize this non-value-added activity. Machine flexibility measures emphasize the value of producing many different products in the same FMS cell.

Product Quality A JIT philosophy demands adherence to strict quality standards for raw materials, manufactured components, and finished products. Various nonfinancial data are vital for assessing a manufacturer's effectiveness in maintaining product quality. **Customer-acceptance measures** focus on the extent to which a firm's customers perceive its product to be of high quality. Typical performance measures include the number of customer complaints, the number of warranty claims, the number of products returned, and the cost of repairing returned products. **In-process quality controls** refer to procedures designed to assess product quality before production is completed. For example, in a *quality audit program,* partially completed products are randomly inspected at various stages of production. Defect rates are measured, and corrective actions are suggested. A third area of quality measurement relates to *raw-material quality.* Suppliers are rated on the basis of the quality of their materials as well as customer service.

Some companies routinely prepare a *quality cost report,* which details the costs incurred in assuring product quality. We will discuss quality costs in Chapter 12.

Production and Delivery A company will achieve little success if it manufactures a great product but delivers it to the customer a week late. World-class manufacturers are striving toward a goal of filling 100 percent of their orders on time. Common measures of product delivery performance include the percentage of on-time deliveries and the percentage of orders filled. Another measure is **delivery cycle time,** the average time between the receipt of a customer order and delivery of the goods.

Delivering goods on time requires that they be produced on time. Various operational performance measures have been developed to assess the timeliness of the production process. **Manufacturing cycle time** is the total amount of production time (or throughput time) required per unit. It can be computed by dividing the total time required to produce a batch by the number of units in the batch. **Velocity** is defined as the number of units produced in a given time period. Perhaps an even more important operational measure is the **manufacturing cycle efficiency (MCE),** defined as follows:

[8]Eliyahu M. Goldratt, *Theory of Constraints* (Croton-on-Hudson, New York: North River Press, 1990).

$$\text{Manufacturing cycle efficiency} = \frac{\text{Processing time}}{\text{Processing time} + \text{Inspection time} + \text{Waiting time} + \text{Move time}}$$

The value of the MCE measure lies in its comparison between value-added time (processing) and non-value-added time (inspection, waiting, and moving). In many manufacturing companies, MCE is less than 10 percent. Firms with advanced manufacturing systems strive for as high an MCE measure as possible.

Productivity Global competitiveness has forced virtually all manufacturers to strive for greater productivity. One *financial* productivity measure is **aggregate** (or **total**) **productivity,** defined as total output divided by total input. A firm's total output is measured as the sum, across all of the goods and services produced, of those products and services times their sales prices. Total input is the sum of the direct-material, direct-labor, and overhead costs incurred in production. Another financial measure is a **partial** (or **component**) **productivity** measure, in which total output (in dollars) is divided by the cost of a particular input.

A preferable approach to productivity measurement is to record multiple physical measures that capture the most important determinants of a company's productivity. These *operational* (or *physical*) measures are also partial productivity measures, since each one focuses on a particular input. For example, a large automobile manufacturer routinely records the following data for one of its plants: the number of engines produced per day per employee, and the number of square feet of floor space required per engine produced in a day. A large chemical company keeps track of the amount of energy (in British thermal units, BTU) required to convert a kilogram of raw chemicals into a kilogram of finished product. Data such as these convey more information to management than a summary financial measure such as aggregate productivity.

"We have to be the best in cost throughout the world. And cycle time is also very important." (10e)

MiCRUS (joint venture of IBM and Cirrus Logic)

Innovation and Learning Global competition requires that companies continually improve and innovate. New products must be developed and introduced to replace those that become obsolete. New processes must continually be developed to make production more efficient. In a world-class manufacturer or service firm, the one thing that is most constant is change.

Although most large manufacturers continue to use standard-costing systems as aids in cost control and product costing, they are also placing greater emphasis on operational (nonfinancial) performance measures. A leader among such companies is Harley-Davidson, pictured here.

To summarize, nonfinancial measures are being used increasingly to augment standard-costing systems. These operational performance measures assist management in its goal of continuous process improvement. To be most effective, operational controls should be tied to the strategic objectives of the organization. Specific improvement targets can be set for various measures to provide motivation for improvement in the areas deemed most important by management.

Gain-Sharing Plans

One widely used method of providing incentives to employees to improve their performance on various operational control measures is gain sharing. A **gain-sharing plan** is an incentive system that specifies a formula by which cost or productivity gains achieved by a company are shared with the workers who helped accomplish the improvements. For example, suppose an electronics manufacturer reduced its defect rate in the Manual Insertion Department by 2 percent for a savings of $100,000. A gain-sharing formula might call for 25 percent of the savings to be shared with the employees in that department.

The Balanced Scorecard

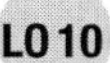

LO10

Describe the balanced scorecard concept and explain the reasoning behind it.

Managers of the most successful organizations do not rely on either financial or nonfinancial performance measures alone. They recognize that financial performance measures summarize the results of past actions. These measures are important to a firm's owners, creditors, employees, and so forth. Thus, they must be watched carefully by management as well.

Nonfinancial performance measures concentrate on *current* activities, which will be the drivers of *future* financial performance. Thus, effective management requires a balanced perspective on performance measurement, a viewpoint that some call the *balanced scorecard* perspective. Exhibit 10–8 depicts ExxonMobil's balanced scorecard for its North American Marketing and Refining business segment,[9] which integrates performance measures in four key areas: financial, internal operations, customer, and learning and growth.

"When you buy into [the balanced scorecard] you've got to be willing to put the time and energy and commitment into it. At the end of the day, the rewards and benefits you can reap from this are tremendous." (10f)
FMC Corporation

So, what is the rationale behind the ExxonMobil balanced scorecard in Exhibit 10–8? The company's overarching, *long-term* goal is financial growth, which will be assessed by several, mostly financial, measures. This begs the question, though, as to what the company must be doing right now to ensure that its long-term financial goal will be met. The company's management has decided on several key goals that must be achieved in the near term, in order for the company's long-term goal of financial growth to be met.

Let's first look at the customer perspective in the balanced scorecard. Although ExxonMobil ultimately sells its gasoline and other products to customers like you, it does so through dealers. Many of the gas stations and convenience store/gas stations are owned and operated by an independent company or individual. Thus, in order to sell its products, ExxonMobil must satisfy not only its end customers, but also its dealers. Otherwise, a dissatisfied dealer could turn to another supplier of gasoline. To assess its current success in this area, ExxonMobil measures its share of selected key markets (e.g., gasoline sales in New England) as well as its dealers' profit growth. ExxonMobil's management figures that satisfied dealers and customers now will translate into financial growth for the company in the long term.

What about ExxonMobil's internal operations? In what activities must the company excel now in order to achieve its long-term financial-growth goal? ExxonMobil's management has decided on several key goals in this area, which include building its business through new products, maintaining safety, being a competitive supplier, providing a high-quality product, and being a good neighbor. The measures shown in the internal operations perspective of the scorecard detail how management will assess its current performance on each of these key internal-operations goals. For example, the company will track the number of environmental incidents in which it is involved as an indicator of its success in being a good neighbor.

Finally, ExxonMobil's management figures that it needs a motivated and prepared work force in order to meet its current goals in the learning and growth perspective of the scorecard. A key performance measure used in this area will come from employee surveys covering such issues as morale, training programs attended, and absenteeism.

[9]This balanced scorecard, which is slightly abridged, was developed for Mobil's NAM&R (North American Marketing and Refining) business segment shortly before Mobil's acquisition by Exxon. It is touted as one of the best examples of using the balanced scorecard to develop a strategy-focused organization. Robert S. Kaplan and David D. Norton, *The Strategy-Focused Organization: How Balanced Scorecard Companies Thrive in the New Business Environment* (Boston: Harvard Business School Press, 2001), pp. 29–43.

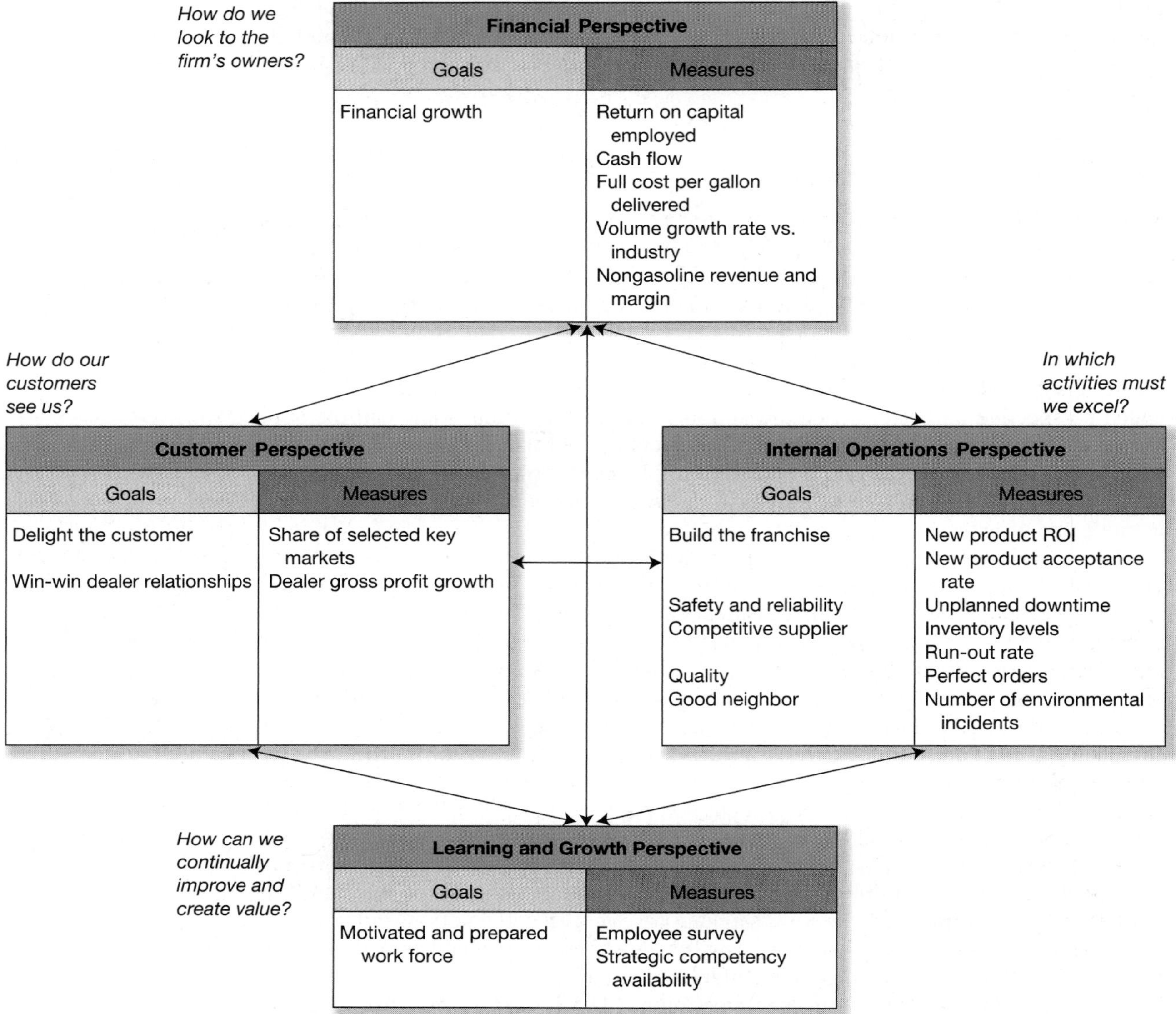

Exhibit 10–8
Balanced Scorecard Developed for ExxonMobil's North American Marketing and Refining Business Segment

All in all, ExxonMobil's management team believes that if the company meets its current goals for its customer, internal operations, and learning and growth perspectives, the company will ultimately be successful in achieving its long-term goal of financial growth.

Lead and Lag Measures: The Key to the Balanced Scorecard

Key to understanding the balanced scorecard is the distinction between lead and lag indicators of performance. *Lead indicators* of performance are measures of nonfinancial and financial outcomes that guide management in making current decisions that will result in desirable results in the future. In other words, lead indicators guide management to take actions *now* that will have positive effects on enterprise performance *later.* For example, ExxonMobil's scorecard includes the company's share of selected key markets as an indicator of future sales growth, which will ultimately translate into

Rockwater, which is now owned by Haliburton, is a global, undersea oil field construction company headquartered in Aberdeen, Scotland. Doing the undersea engineering and construction for drilling rigs such as the one pictured here requires diverse technical operations, both on- and offshore. Rockwater's management found the balanced scorecard to be an invaluable tool in clarifying the company's goals and communicating them to the employees. Among the measures in Rockwater's balanced scorecard are the following: cash flow and project profitability (financial); safety index and hours spent with customers on new work (internal); project pricing and customer satisfaction (customer); percentage of revenue from new services and number of employee suggestions (innovation and learning).[10]

Exhibit 10–9
Selected Performance Measures Used in Balanced Scorecards

Financial Perspective	
Earnings	Cash flow
Earnings per share	Cash flow from operations
Customer Perspective	
Customer contacts	Customer satisfaction (surveyed)
Repeat customers	Customer complaints
New customers	Market share
Learning and Growth Perspective	
Employee training hours	New processes
Employee promotion rate	Employee suggestions
New products	Employee retention
Internal Operations Perspective	
Product quality/defect rates	Finished products per day per employee
Number of vendors	Floor space per finished product
Cycle time	Cost of inventories held
Throughput	Number of common parts
Machine downtime	Number of part numbers

growth of the company's profitability. By including this key lead indicator in its scorecard, management is directed to take actions now that will increase the company's share of important geographic markets for its products.

Lag indicators are measures of the final outcomes of earlier management decisions. Examples of lag indicators are a company's profit and cash flow. These key financial measures, while important, only improve in later time periods, well after management has taken important actions to affect key operational results.

The whole idea of the balanced scorecard is to *use lead indicators to communicate with, motivate, and evaluate individuals* with the expectation that their current actions will result in improvements in the company's important lag measures (e.g., profitability) in the future. Exhibit 10–9 gives examples of several key lead and lag measures used in a variety of organizations' balanced scorecards. In addition, note that most of the operational performance measures listed in Exhibit 10–7 could be (and are) used in balanced scorecards.

"Because of the balanced scorecard, the nature of the monthly financial meetings changed from a focus on the things Pitney Bowes is doing well to the three things we need to improve, with the emphasis on an appropriate action plan." (10g)
Pitney Bowes

[10]Robert S. Kaplan and David P. Norton, *The Strategy-Focused Organization: How Balanced Scorecard Companies Thrive in the New Business Environment* (Boston: Harvard Business School Press, 2001).

Exhibit 10–10
Linkage between the Balanced Scorecard and Organizational Strategy

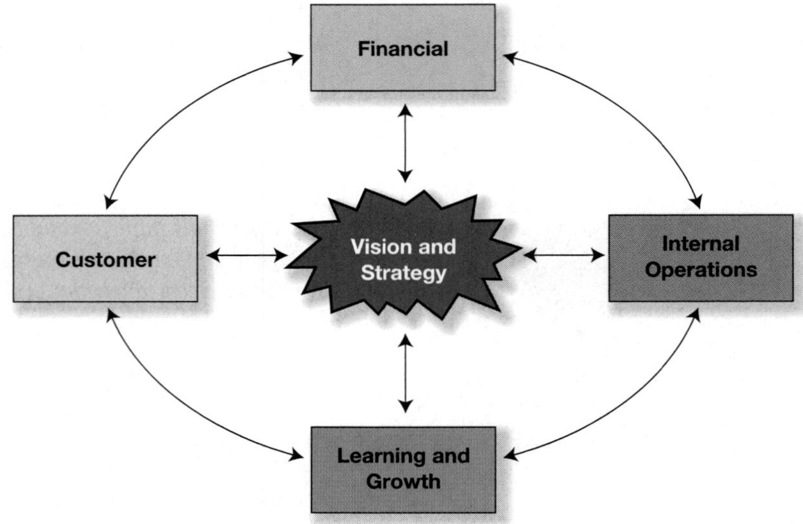

Linking the Balanced Scorecard to Organizational Strategy

A key to making successful use of the balanced scorecard is linking the scorecard's lead and lag measures to the organization's strategy. As depicted in the diagram in Exhibit 10–10, the organization's vision and strategy drive the specification of both goals and metrics in the scorecard's financial, customer, internal operations, and learning and growth perspectives.[11]

The precise form of the linkage between strategy and the goals and measures in the balanced scorecard will, of course, depend on the nature of the organization and its strategy. The following case in point explores this linkage for Dell Computer Corporation, which is arguably one of the most successful companies of our time. (See also the Management Accounting Practice inset on page 42 in Chapter 2.)

Management Accounting Practice
Dell Computer

LINKING THE BALANCED SCORECARD TO ORGANIZATIONAL STRATEGY

Key to successfully using the balanced scorecard is linking the scorecard's lead and lag measures to the organization's strategy. According to Dell Computer's website, the company's strategy is "to be the most successful computer company in the world at delivering the best customer experience in markets we serve."[12]

As the following diagram shows, Dell's strategy of using its direct-sales model to provide unparalleled customer service drives through each of the perspectives that comprise a balanced scorecard.

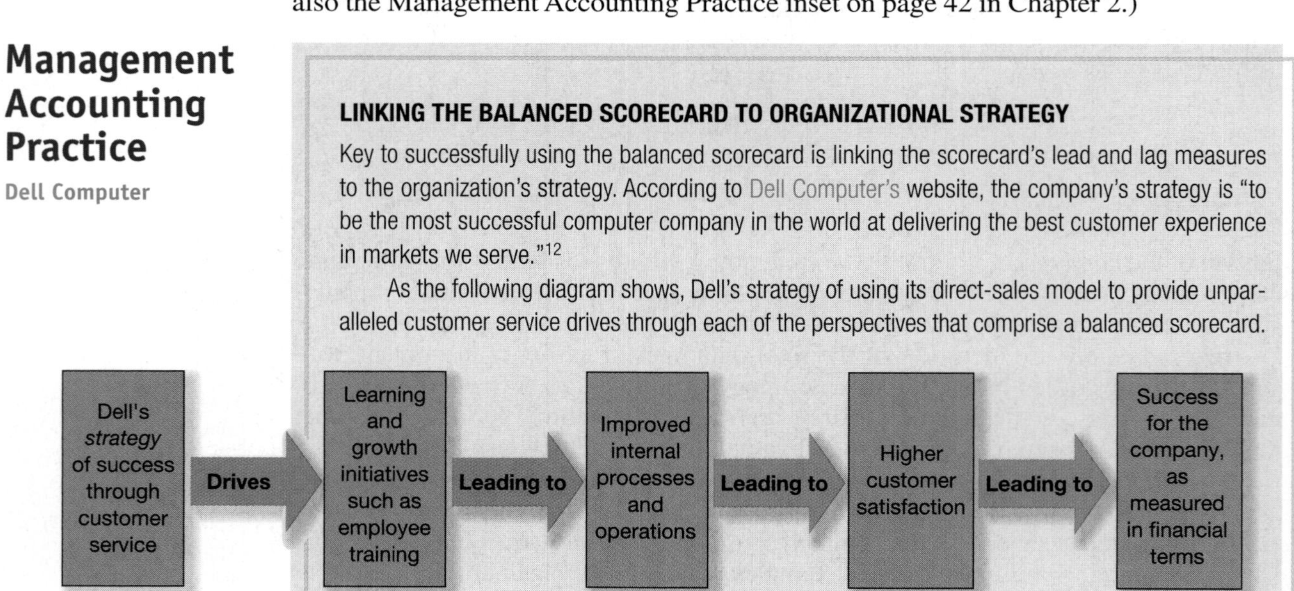

[11]Robert S. Kaplan and David P. Norton, *The Strategy-Focused Organization: How Balanced Scorecard Companies Thrive in the New Business Environment* (Boston: Harvard Business School Press, 2001).

[12]This material is based on "Putting Strategy into the Balanced Scorecard," *Strategic Finance* 83, no. 7 (January 2002), pp. 44–52, and Robert S. Kaplan and David P. Norton, *The Strategy-Focused Organization: How Balanced Scorecard Companies Thrive in the New Business Environment* (Boston: Harvard Business School Press, 2001).

The following selected balanced scorecard measures are among those relevant for Dell Computer to successfully implement its strategy. Notice the frequency of the words *customer* or *sales* in these measures. Dell's strategy and its relevant balanced scorecard measures are dominated by its customer-focused direct-sales business model.

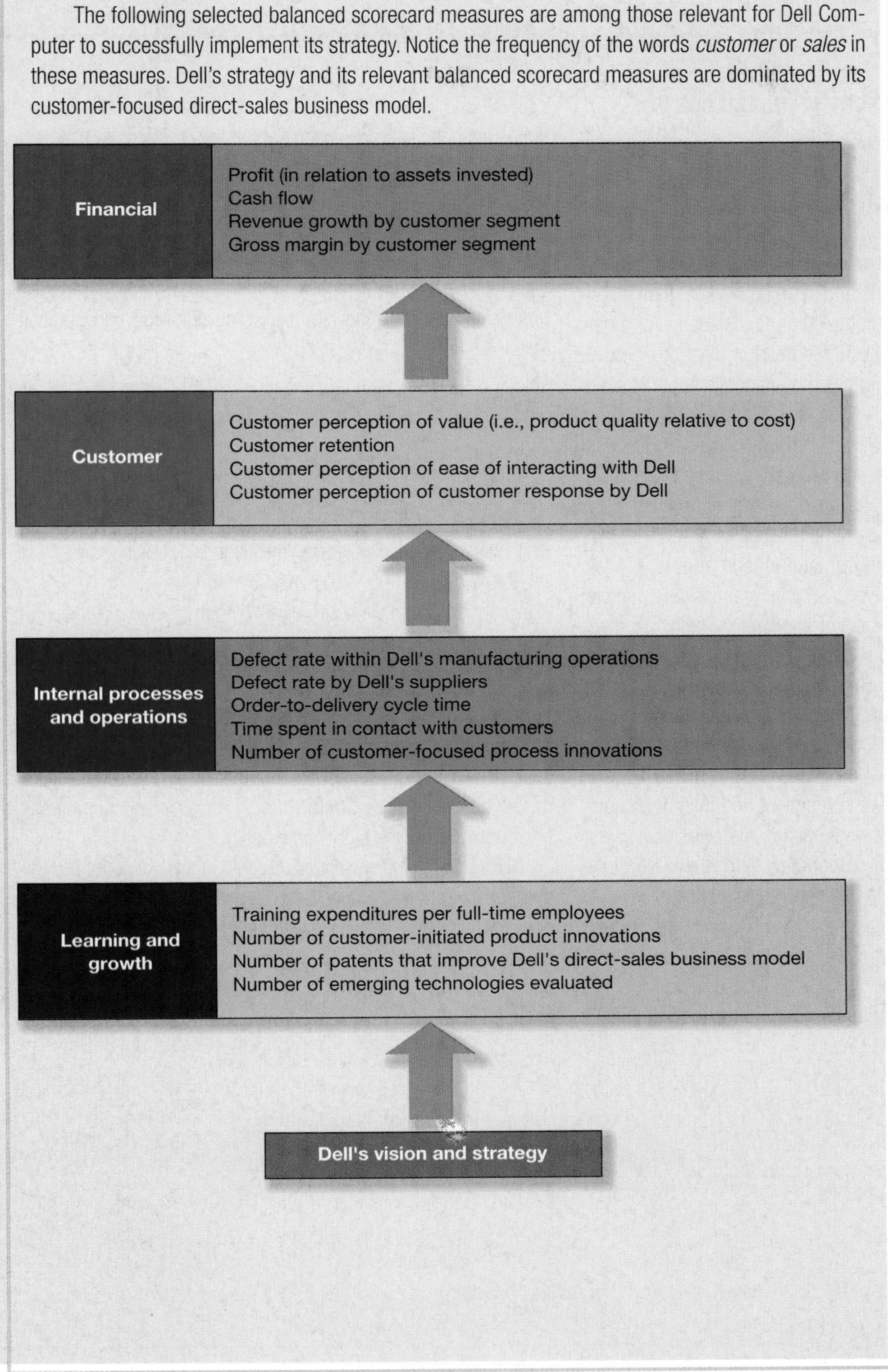

Financial
Profit (in relation to assets invested)
Cash flow
Revenue growth by customer segment
Gross margin by customer segment
Customer
Customer perception of value (i.e., product quality relative to cost)
Customer retention
Customer perception of ease of interacting with Dell
Customer perception of customer response by Dell
Internal processes and operations
Defect rate within Dell's manufacturing operations
Defect rate by Dell's suppliers
Order-to-delivery cycle time
Time spent in contact with customers
Number of customer-focused process innovations
Learning and growth
Training expenditures per full-time employees
Number of customer-initiated product innovations
Number of patents that improve Dell's direct-sales business model
Number of emerging technologies evaluated
Dell's vision and strategy

Focus on Ethics

SACRIFICING QUALITY TO CUT STANDARD COSTS

Pressures to control costs, coupled with bonus systems based on adherence to standards, can present the opportunity to engage in ethical lapses. The following hypothetical scenario describes such a situation.

Keystone Company manufactures small wooden household items, such as cutting boards and knife racks. Keystone's controller, Marc Rigas, recently completed the installation of a new standard-costing system, which has been in place now for six months. Jack Smith, the purchasing manager, is about to place an order for wood to be used in Keystone's cutting boards. Smith has found a supplier that will furnish the necessary wood at $2.00 per board foot, rather than the standard cost of $3.00. This is very appealing to Smith, since his annual bonus is influenced by any favorable price variances he is able to obtain. Smith is due to be transferred at the end of the year to Keystone's Allentown Division, which manufactures metal kitchen utensils. The transfer is a promotion for Smith.

After further discussions with the potential supplier, Smith realized that the wood being offered would not be well-suited for use in cutting boards. Although the wood would seem fine in the manufacturing process, and it would result in an attractive product, it would not hold up well over time. This particular type of wood, after repeated cycles of getting wet and then drying out, would tend to crack. Smith figured that it would take about a year for the cutting boards to deteriorate, and then Keystone Company would be beset with customer complaints.

Smith mulled over the situation for a while and then decided to accept the new supplier's offer. The $2.00 price would help him get a nice annual bonus, which he could use to help with the down payment on a new home. By the time the cutting boards cracked and customers started to complain, he would be long gone. Someone else could worry about the problem then, he reasoned. After all, he thought, people shouldn't expect a cutting board to last forever.

Several weeks later, when the invoice for the first shipment of wood came through, Rigas noticed the large, favorable price variance. When he ran into Smith on the golf course, Rigas congratulated Smith on the purchase. The following conversation resulted.

Rigas (C): "That was quite a price break on that wood, Jack. How'd you swing it?"

Smith (PM): "Hard-ball negotiating, Marc. It's as simple as that."

Rigas(C): "Is it good wood? And how about the supplier, Jack? Will they deliver on time?"

Smith (PM): "This supplier is very timely in their deliveries. I made sure of that."

Rigas (C): "How about the quality, Jack? Did you check into that?"

Smith (PM): "Sure I did, Marc. Hey, what is this? An interrogation? I thought we were here to play golf."

Rigas was left feeling puzzled and disconcerted by Smith's evasiveness. The next day Rigas talked to the production manager, Amy Wilcox, about his concerns. Later that day, Wilcox raised the issue with Smith. After a lengthy and sometimes heated exchange, the story came out.

Discuss the ethical issues involved in this scenario. Did the purchasing manager, Jack Smith, act ethically? Did the controller, Marc Rigas, act ethically when he asked Smith about the quality of the wood? Did Rigas act ethically when he went to the production manager with his concerns? What should the controller do now?

Chapter Summary

A standard-costing system serves two purposes: cost control and product costing. The managerial accountant works with others in the organization to set standard costs for direct material, direct labor, and manufacturing overhead through either historical cost analysis or task analysis. The accountant then uses the standard cost as a benchmark against which to compare actual costs incurred. Managers use management by exception to determine the causes of significant cost variances. This control purpose of the standard-costing system is accomplished by computing a direct-material price variance, a direct-material quantity variance, a direct-labor rate variance, and a direct-labor efficiency variance.

Managers determine the significance of cost variances through judgment and rules of thumb. The absolute and relative sizes of variances, recurrence of variances, variance trends, and controllability of variances are all considered in deciding whether variances warrant investigation. The managerial accountant achieves the product-costing purpose of the standard-costing system by entering the standard cost of production into Work-in-Process Inventory as a product cost. Standard-costing systems offer an organization many benefits. However, these benefits will be obtained only if the standard-costing system is used properly.

Today's manufacturing environment is rapidly changing, due to the influences of worldwide competition, JIT, FMS, and an emphasis on product quality and customer service. As a result, many manufacturers are adapting their standard-costing systems to reflect these aspects of the new manufacturing environment. Moreover, nonfinancial measures of operational performance are widely used to augment the control information provided by standard costing. These measures typically focus on raw material and scrap, inventory, machinery, product quality, production and delivery, productivity, and innovation and learning.

The balanced scorecard is an important tool designed to focus management's attention on key current goals, which, if achieved, will facilitate the attainment of the organization's long-term goals. By achieving current goals in the customer, internal operations, and learning and growth perspectives, the company will ultimately achieve its long-term financial goals.

Review Problems on Standard Costing and Operational Performance Measures

Problem 1

In November DCdesserts.com produced 3,000 multilayer fancy cakes and incurred the following actual costs for direct material and direct labor.

Purchased 16,500 pounds of ingredients at $1.44 per pound.

Used 15,500 pounds of ingredients at $1.44 per pound.

Used 1,520 hours of direct labor at $22 per hour.

The standard costs for production of multilayer fancy cakes were the same in November as those given earlier in the chapter for September.

Compute DCdesserts.com's direct-material and direct-labor variances for November using the format shown in Exhibits 10–2 and 10–3.

Problem 2

Tuscarora Door Company manufactures high-quality wooden doors used in home construction. The following information pertains to operations during April.

Processing time (average per batch)	6 hours
Inspection time (average per batch)	1 hour
Waiting time (average per batch)	4 hours
Move time (average per batch)	5 hours
Units per batch	40 units

Compute the following operational measures: (1) average value-added time per batch; (2) average non-value-added time per batch; (3) manufacturing cycle efficiency; (4) manufacturing cycle time; (5) velocity.

Solution to Review Problem 1

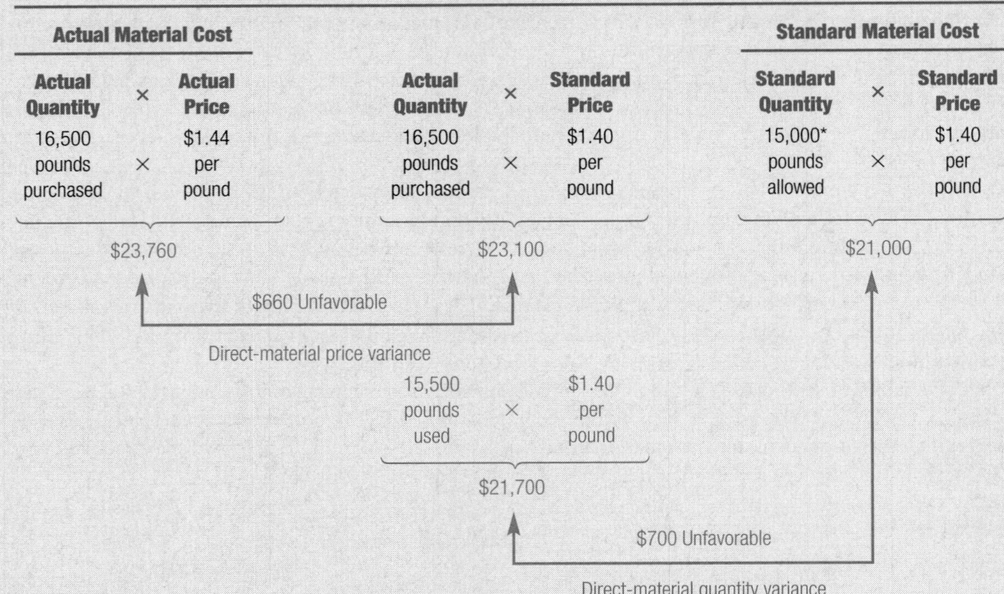

*Actual output × Standard quantity per unit = 3,000 units × 5 pounds per unit = 15,000 pounds allowed.

Using Formulas

$$\begin{aligned}\text{Direct-material price variance} &= PQ(AP - SP)\\ &= 16{,}500(\$1.44 - \$1.40)\\ &= \$660 \text{ Unfavorable}\\ \text{Direct-material quantity variance} &= SP(AQ - SQ)\\ &= \$1.40(15{,}500 - 15{,}000)\\ &= \$700 \text{ Unfavorable}\end{aligned}$$

Direct-Labor Rate and Efficiency Variances

Actual Labor Cost				Standard Labor Cost
Actual Hours × Actual Rate		**Actual Hours × Standard Rate**		**Standard Hours × Standard Rate**
1,520 hours used × $22 per hour		1,520 hours used × $20 per hour		1,500* hours allowed × $20 per hour
$33,440		$30,400		$30,000
	$3,040 Unfavorable		$400 Unfavorable	
	Direct-labor rate variance		Direct-labor efficiency variance	

*Actual output × Standard hours per unit = 3,000 units × .5 hours per unit = 1,500 hours allowed.

Using Formulas

$$\begin{aligned}\text{Direct-labor rate variance} &= AH(AR - SR)\\ &= 1{,}520(\$22 - \$20)\\ &= \$3{,}040 \text{ Unfavorable}\\ \text{Direct-labor efficiency variance} &= SR(AH - SH)\\ &= \$20(1{,}520 - 1{,}500)\\ &= \$400 \text{ Unfavorable}\end{aligned}$$

Solution to Review Problem 2

1. Average value-added time per batch = Processing time = 6 hours
2. Average non-value-added time per batch = Inspection time + Waiting time + Move time = 10 hours
3. $$\text{Manufacturing cycle efficiency} = \frac{\text{Processing time}}{\text{Processing time} + \text{Inspection time} + \text{Waiting time} + \text{Move time}}$$
$$= \frac{6 \text{ hours}}{6 \text{ hours} + 1 \text{ hour} + 4 \text{ hours} + 5 \text{ hours}} = 37.5\%$$
4. $$\text{Manufacturing cycle time} = \frac{\text{Total production time per batch}}{\text{Units per batch}}$$
$$= \frac{16 \text{ hours}}{40 \text{ units per batch}} = .4 \text{ hours (or 24 minutes) per unit}$$
5. $$\text{Velocity} = \frac{\text{Units per batch}}{\text{Total production time per batch}}$$
$$= \frac{40 \text{ units}}{16 \text{ hours}} = 2.5 \text{ units per hour}$$

Key Terms

For each term's definition refer to the indicated page, or turn to the glossary at the end of the text.

aggregate (or total) productivity, 430
benchmarking, 427
controllability, 419
cost variance, 408
customer-acceptance measures, 429
delivery cycle time, 429
direct-labor efficiency variance, 415
direct-labor rate variance, 415
direct-material price variance (or purchase price variance), 413
direct-material quantity variance, 413
gain-sharing plan, 430
in-process quality controls, 429
management by exception, 409
manufacturing cycle efficiency (MCE), 429
manufacturing cycle time, 429
partial (or component) productivity, 430
perfection (or ideal) standard, 410
practical (or attainable) standard, 410
standard cost, 408
standard-costing system, 423
standard direct-labor quantity, 412
standard direct-labor rate, 412
standard direct-material price, 412
standard direct-material quantity, 412
statistical control chart, 420
task analysis, 409
velocity, 429

Appendix to Chapter 10

Use of Standard Costs for Product Costing

In addition to providing a tool for *cost management,* standard-costing systems also provide the necessary information to be used in *product costing.* As shown in Exhibit 10–6, under standard costing, it is the *standard costs* that are entered into Work-in-Process Inventory as a product cost.

LO 11

After completing the appendix, prepare journal entries to record and close out cost variances.

Journal Entries under Standard Costing To illustrate the use of standard costs in product costing, we will continue our illustration of DCdesserts.com. For September's production of multilayer fancy cakes, the company purchased 12,500 pounds of direct material for $17,750. The actual quantity of material used in production was 10,250 pounds. However, the standard cost of direct material, given September's actual output of 2,000 multilayer fancy cakes, was only $14,000. The following journal entries record these facts and isolate the direct-material price and quantity variances.

Raw-Material Inventory	17,500	
Direct-Material Price Variance	250	
Accounts Payable		17,750
To record the purchase of raw material and the incurrence of an unfavorable price variance.		

Work-in-Process Inventory	14,000	
Direct-Material Quantity Variance	350	
Raw-Material Inventory		14,350
To record the use of direct material in production and the incurrence of an unfavorable quantity variance.		

Notice that the material purchase is recorded in the Raw-Material Inventory account at its standard price ($17,500 = 12,500 pounds purchased × $1.40 per pound). The $14,000 debit entry to Work-in-Process Inventory adds only the standard cost of the material to Work-in-Process Inventory as a product cost ($14,000 = 10,000 pounds allowed × $1.40 per pound). The two variances are isolated in their own variance accounts. Since they are both unfavorable, they are represented by debit entries.

The following journal entry records the actual September cost of direct labor, as an addition to Wages Payable. The entry also adds the standard cost of direct labor to Work-in-Process Inventory and isolates the direct-labor variances.

Work-in-Process Inventory	20,000	
Direct-Labor Rate Variance	980	
Direct-Labor Efficiency Variance		400
Wages Payable		20,580
To record the usage of direct labor and the direct-labor variances for September.		

Since the direct-labor efficiency variance is favorable, it is recorded as a credit entry.

Disposition of Variances Variances are temporary accounts, like revenue and expense accounts, and they are closed out at the end of each accounting period. Most companies close their variance accounts directly into Cost of Goods Sold. The journal entry required to close out the September variances incurred in the production of multilayer fancy cakes is as follows:

Cost of Goods Sold	1,180	
Direct-Labor Efficiency Variance	400	
Direct-Labor Rate Variance		980
Direct-Material Price Variance		250
Direct-Material Quantity Variance		350

The increase of $1,180 in Cost of Goods Sold is explained as follows:

	Unfavorable Variances Increase Cost of Goods Sold		Favorable Variance Decreases Cost of Goods Sold		Net Increase in Cost of Goods Sold
Direct-labor efficiency variance			$400		
Direct-labor rate variance	$ 980				
Direct-material price variance	250				
Direct-material quantity variance	350				
Total	$1,580	−	$400	=	$1,180

The unfavorable variances represent costs of operating inefficiently, relative to the standards, and thus cause Cost of Goods Sold to be higher. The opposite is true for favorable variances.

An alternative method of variance disposition is to apportion all variances among Work-in-Process Inventory, Finished-Goods Inventory, and Cost of Goods Sold. This accounting treatment reflects the effects of unusual inefficiency or efficiency in all of the accounts through which the manufacturing costs flow. This method, called *variance proration,* is covered more fully in cost accounting texts.

Cost Flow under Standard Costing In a standard-costing system, since standard costs are entered into Work-in-Process Inventory, standard costs flow through all of the manufacturing accounts. Thus, as depicted in Exhibit 10–6, all of the product costs flowing through the accounts are standard costs. To illustrate, suppose DCdesserts.com produced 2,000 multilayer fancy cakes in September and sold all 2,000 of them. The journal entries to record the flow of standard direct-material and direct-labor costs are shown below.

Finished-Goods Inventory	34,000*	
Work-in-Process Inventory		34,000

*Total standard cost of direct material and direct labor: $34,000 = $14,000 + $20,000.

Cost of Goods Sold	34,000*	
Finished-Goods Inventory		34,000

*All 2,000 multilayer fancy cakes were sold.

A Note on Perishable Products and JIT Production Management Systems Traditional manufacturing systems typically exhibit the cost flows explained in this section. Direct-material, direct-labor and manufacturing-overhead costs are entered in Work-in-Process Inventory, from which they flow into Finished-Goods Inventory when the goods are finished, and then on into Cost of Goods Sold. Since DCdesserts.com produces perishable goods, which are produced and sold on the same day, a simpler procedure could be used. In DCdesserts.com's case, the *standard* costs of direct material, direct labor, and manufacturing overhead could be entered directly into Cost of Goods Sold as they are incurred. This simplified procedure could be used, because the production process is very short and the goods are sold immediately. Thus, there is never any work-in-process inventory or finished-goods inventory on hand. Such situations are common with producers of perishable goods.

An analogous situation occurs in manufacturers that employ a just-in-time (JIT) production and inventory control system. In a JIT environment, raw materials are delivered just in time to be entered into production, and parts or components are manufactured in each stage of the production process just in time for the next production stage. Thus, like the case of perishable goods, there is little or no work-in-process or finished-goods inventory at any given time in a JIT environment. For this reason, many manufacturers that employ the JIT approach make use of highly simplified cost accounting procedures similar to those explained in the preceding paragraph for DCdesserts.com.

Our illustration is not really complete yet, because we have not discussed manufacturing-overhead costs. This topic is covered in the next chapter. The important point at this juncture is that in a standard-costing system, *standard costs rather than actual costs flow through the manufacturing accounts.*

Review Questions

10–1. List the three parts of a control system, and explain how such a system works.

10–2. What is meant by the phrase *management by exception?*

10–3. Describe two methods of setting standards.

10–4. Distinguish between *perfection* and *practical* standards. Which type of standard is likely to produce the best motivational effects?

10–5. Describe how a bank might use standards.

10–6. Explain how standard material prices and quantities are set.

10–7. What is the interpretation of the *direct-material price variance?*

10–8. What manager is usually in the best position to influence the direct-material price variance?

10–9. What is the interpretation of the *direct-material quantity variance?*

10–10. What manager is usually in the best position to influence the direct-material quantity variance?

10–11. Explain why the quantity purchased (PQ) is used in computing the direct-material price variance, but the actual quantity consumed (AQ) is used in computing the direct-material quantity variance.

10–12. What is the interpretation of the *direct-labor rate variance?* What are some possible causes?

10–13. What manager is generally in the best position to influence the direct-labor rate variance?

10–14. What is the interpretation of the *direct-labor efficiency variance?*

10–15. What manager is generally in the best position to influence the direct-labor efficiency variance?

10–16. Refer to Review Question 10–11. Why does an analogous question *not* arise in the context of the direct-labor variances?

10–17. Describe five factors that managers often consider when determining the significance of a variance.

10–18. Discuss several ways in which standard-costing systems should be adapted in today's manufacturing environment.

10–19. Describe how standard costs are used for product costing.

10–20. List six advantages of a standard-costing system.

10–21. List seven areas in which nonfinancial, operational performance measures are receiving increased emphasis in today's manufacturing environment.

10–22. Define the term *manufacturing cycle efficiency.*

10–23. List four examples of customer acceptance measures.

10–24. What is meant by *aggregate productivity,* and what are its limitations?

10–25. List eight criticisms of standard costing in an advanced manufacturing environment.

10–26. Suggest two performance measures in each of the four balanced scorecard categories for a service industry firm of your choosing. Using these measures as examples, explain the difference between lead and lag measures.

10–27. Give an example of a gain-sharing plan that could be implemented by an airline.

Exercises

Exercise 10–28
Straightforward Calculation of Variances
(LO 1, 3)

During April, Dryden Company's material purchases amounted to 6,500 pounds at a price of $7.40 per pound. Actual costs incurred in the production of 2,000 units were as follows:

Direct labor:	$118,035 ($18.30 per hour)
Direct material:	$31,820 ($7.40 per pound)

The standards for one unit of Dryden Company's product are as follows:

Direct labor:	Direct material:
Quantity, 3 hours per unit	Quantity, 2 pounds per unit
Rate, $18.00 per hour	Price, $7.20 per pound

Required: Compute the direct-material price and quantity variances and the direct-labor rate and efficiency variances. Indicate whether each variance is favorable or unfavorable.

Exercise 10–29
Diagramming Direct-Material and Direct-Labor Variances
(LO 3)

Refer to the data in the preceding exercise. Draw diagrams depicting the direct-material and direct-labor variances similar to the diagrams in Exhibits 10–2 and 10–3.

Exercise 10–30
Computing Standard Direct-Material Cost
(LO 2)

Seneca Hardwoods produces handcrafted jewelry boxes. A standard-size box requires 7 board feet of hardwood in the finished product. In addition, 1.5 board feet of scrap lumber is normally left from the production of one box. Hardwood costs $5.00 per board foot, plus $1.20 in transportation charges per board foot.

Required: Compute the standard direct-material cost of a jewelry box.

Exercise 10–31
Straightforward Computation of Variances
(LO 1, 3)

Canandaigua Container Company manufactures recyclable soft-drink cans. A unit of production is a case of 12 dozen cans. The following standards have been set by the production-engineering staff and the controller.

Direct labor:	Direct material:
Quantity, .25 hour	Quantity, 4 kilograms
Rate, $12 per hour	Price, $.60 per kilogram

Actual material purchases amounted to 240,000 kilograms at $.62 per kilogram. Actual costs incurred in the production of 50,000 units were as follows:

Direct labor:	$158,600 for 13,000 hours
Direct material:	$130,200 for 210,000 kilograms

Required: Use the variance formulas to compute the direct-material price and quantity variances and the direct-labor rate and efficiency variances. Indicate whether each variance is favorable or unfavorable.

Exercise 10–32
Determination of Variances Using Diagrams
(LO 3)

Refer to the data in the preceding exercise. Use diagrams similar to those in Exhibits 10–2 and 10–3 to determine the direct-material and direct-labor variances. Indicate whether each variance is favorable or unfavorable.

Exercise 10–33
Developing Standards for New Products; Use of Internet
(LO 2)

Choose one of the following manufacturers (or any manufacturer of your choosing), and use the Internet to gather information about any new products the company has recently introduced or plans to introduce.

Boeing	www.boeing.com	Kodak	www.kodak.com
Caterpillar	www.caterpillar.com	Pfizer	www.pfizer.com
Ford	www.ford.com/us	Xerox	www.xerox.com

Required: Discuss the steps you think the company would go through in establishing standard costs for its new product.

Exercise 10–34
Standard Allowed Input
(LO 2)

Due to evaporation during production, Plasto Company requires 4 pounds of material input for every 3 pounds of good plastic sheets manufactured. During May, the company produced 6,000 pounds of good sheets.

Required: Compute the total standard allowed input quantity, given the good output produced.

Exercise 10–35
Reconstructing Standard-Cost Information from Partial Data
(LO 1, 3)

Part of your company's accounting database was destroyed when Godzilla attacked the city. You have been able to gather the following data from your files. Reconstruct the remaining information using the available data. All of the raw material purchased during the period was used in production. (*Hint:* It is helpful to solve for the unknowns in the order indicated by the letters in the following table.)

	Direct Material	Direct Labor
Standard price or rate per unit of input	$16 per pound	e
Standard quantity per unit of output	c	f
Actual quantity used per unit of output	a	3.5 hours
Actual price or rate per unit of input	$14 per pound	$21 per hour
Actual output	20,000 units	20,000 units
Direct-material price variance	$120,000 F	—
Direct-material quantity variance	b	—
Total of direct-material variances	$40,000 F	—
Direct-labor rate variance	—	d
Direct-labor efficiency variance	—	$200,000 F
Total of direct-labor variances	—	$130,000 F

Exercise 10–36
Cost Variance Investigation
(LO 4)

The director of cost management for Odessa Company uses a statistical control chart to help management determine when to investigate variances. The critical value is 1 standard deviation. The company incurred the following direct-labor efficiency variances during the first six months of the current year.

January	$ 500 F	April	$1,800 U
February	1,600 U	May	2,100 U
March	1,400 U	June	2,400 U

The standard direct-labor cost during each of these months was $38,000. The controller has estimated that the firm's monthly direct-labor variances have a standard deviation of $1,900.

Required:

1. Draw a statistical control chart and plot the variance data given above. Which variances will be investigated?
2. Suppose the controller's rule of thumb is to investigate all variances equal to or greater than 6 percent of standard cost. Then which variances will be investigated?
3. Would you investigate any of the variances listed above other than those indicated by the rules discussed in requirements (1) and (2)? Why?

Exercise 10–37
Productivity Measurement
(LO 9)

Managerial accounting procedures developed for the manufacturing industry often are applied in nonmanufacturing settings also. Ontario Bank and Trust Company's total output of financial services during the year just ended was valued at $11 million. The total cost of the firm's inputs, primarily direct labor and overhead, was $10 million.

Required:

1. Compute Ontario's aggregate (or total) productivity for the year.
2. Do you believe this is a useful measure? Why? Suggest an alternative approach that Ontario Bank and Trust might use to measure productivity.

Exercise 10–38
Performance Measures for Production and Delivery
(LO 9)

Data Screen Corporation is a highly automated manufacturing firm. The vice president of finance has decided that traditional standards are inappropriate for performance measures in an automated environment. Labor is insignificant in terms of the total cost of production and tends to be fixed, material quality is considered more important than minimizing material cost, and customer satisfaction is the number one priority. As a result, production and delivery performance measures have been chosen to evaluate performance. The following information is considered typical of the time involved to complete and ship orders.

Waiting time:	
From order being placed to start of production	16 days
From start of production to completion	14 days
Inspection time	3 days
Processing time	6 days
Move time	5 days

Required:

1. Calculate the manufacturing cycle efficiency.
2. Calculate the delivery cycle time.

(CMA, adapted)

Exercise 10–39
Operational Performance Measures; JIT/FMS Setting
(LO 9)

Hiawatha Hydrant Company manufactures fire hydrants in Oswego, New York. The following information pertains to operations during May.

Processing time (average per batch)	4.25 hours
Inspection time (average per batch)	.25 hour
Waiting time (average per batch)	.25 hour
Move time (average per batch)	.25 hour
Units per batch	20 units

Required: Compute the following operational measures: (1) manufacturing cycle efficiency; (2) manufacturing cycle time; (3) velocity.

Exercise 10–40
Balanced Scorecard; Higher Education
(LO 10)

Think carefully about the overall mission and goals of your college or university.

Required:

1. How does the task of building a balanced scorecard for an educational institution differ from that for a profit-seeking enterprise?
2. Design a simple balanced scorecard for your institution, with a minimum of two measures in each of the scorecard's perspectives.

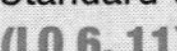

Exercise 10–41
Journal Entries under Standard Costing (Appendix)
(LO 6, 11)

Refer to the data in Exercise 10–31, regarding Canandaigua Container Company. Prepare journal entries to:

1. Record the purchase of direct material on account.
2. Add direct-material and direct-labor cost to Work-in-Process Inventory.
3. Record the direct-material and direct-labor variances.
4. Close these variances into Cost of Goods Sold.

Exercise 10–42
Posting Journal Entries for Variances (Appendix)
(LO 6, 11)

Refer to your answer for Exercise 10–41. Set up T-accounts, and post the journal entries to the general ledger.

Problems

Problem 10–43
Direct-Material and Direct-Labor Variances
(LO 1, 3)

During March Manhattan Fabrics Corporation manufactured 1,000 units of a special multilayer fabric with the trade name Stylex. The following information from the Stylex production department also pertains to March.

Direct material purchased: 36,000 yards at $1.38 per yard	$49,680
Direct material used: 19,000 yards at $1.38 per yard	26,220
Direct labor: 4,200 hours at $9.15 per hour	38,430

The standard prime costs for one unit of Stylex are as follows:

Direct material: 20 yards at $1.35 per yard	$27
Direct labor: 4 hours at $9.00 per hour	36
Total standard prime cost per unit of output	$63

Required: Compute the following variances for the month of March, indicating whether each variance is favorable or unfavorable.

1. Direct-material price variance.
2. Direct-material quantity variance.
3. Direct-labor rate variance.
4. Direct-labor efficiency variance.

(CPA, adapted)

Problem 10–44
Direct-Material and Direct-Labor Variances
(LO 1, 3)

Gandolph Game Company has established the following standards for the prime costs of one unit of its chief product, dartboards.

	Standard Cost	Standard Quantity	Standard Price or Rate
Direct material	$14.00	8 kilograms	$1.75 per kilogram
Direct labor	2.00	.25 hour	$8.00 per hour
Total	$16.00		

During September, Gandolph purchased 320,000 kilograms of direct material at a total cost of $608,000. The total wages for September were $84,000, 90 percent of which were for direct labor. Gandolph manufactured 38,000 dartboards during September, using 285,000 kilograms of direct material and 10,000 direct-labor hours.

Required: Compute the following variances for September, and indicate whether each is favorable or unfavorable.

1. The direct-material price variance.
2. The direct-material quantity variance.
3. The direct-labor rate variance.
4. The direct-labor efficiency variance.

(CMA, adapted)

Problem 10–45
Determining Standard Material Cost
(LO 2)

South Atlantic Chemical Company manufactures industrial chemicals in Rio de Janeiro, Brazil. The company plans to introduce a new chemical solution and needs to develop a standard product cost. The new chemical solution is made by combining a chemical compound (nyclyn) and a solution (salex), heating the mixture, adding a second compound (protet), and bottling the resulting solution in 10-liter containers. The initial mix, which is 11 liters in volume, consists of 12 kilograms of nyclyn and 9.6 liters of salex. A 1-liter reduction in volume occurs during the boiling process. The solution is cooled slightly before 5 kilograms of protet are added. The addition of protet does not affect the total liquid volume.

The purchase price of the direct materials used in the manufacture of this new chemical solution are given below. (The *real* is Brazil's national currency. On the day this problem was written, the *real* was equivalent to .345 U.S. dollar.)

Nyclyn	4.35 *real* per kilogram
Salex	5.40 *real* per liter
Protet	7.20 *real* per kilogram

Required: Determine the standard material cost of a 10-liter container of the new product. (Remember to express your answer in terms of the *real*, the Brazilian national currency.)

(CMA, adapted)

Problem 10–46
Variance Calculation; Analysis; Service Business
(LO 1, 3)

Harrison Wolfe operates a residential landscaping business in an affluent suburb of Atlanta. In an effort to provide quality service, he has concentrated solely on the design and installation of upscale landscaping plans (e.g., trees, shrubs, fountains, and lighting). With his clients continually requesting additional services, Wolfe recently expanded into lawn maintenance, including fertilization.

The following data relate to his first year's experience with 55 fertilization clients. Each client required six applications throughout the year and was billed $40 per application.

- Two applications involved Type I fertilizer, which contains a special ingredient for weed control. The remaining four applications involved Type II fertilizer.
- Wolfe purchased 5,000 pounds of Type I fertilizer at $.53 per pound and 10,000 pounds of Type II fertilizer at $.40 per pound. Actual usage amounted to 3,700 pounds of Type I and 7,800 pounds of Type II.
- A new, part-time employee was hired to spread the fertilizer. Wolfe had to pay premium wages of $11.50 per hour because of a very tight labor market; the employee logged a total of 165 hours at client residences.
- Based on previous knowledge of the operation, articles in trade journals, and conversations with other landscapers, Wolfe established the following standards:

  Typical hourly wage rate of landscape personnel: $9
  Labor time per application: 40 minutes
  Fertilizer purchase price per pound: Type I, $.50; Type II, $.42
  Fertilizer usage: 40 pounds per application

Unfortunately, Wolfe's new lawn fertilization service did not go as smoothly as planned, with customer complaints being much higher than expected.

Required:

1. Compute Wolfe's direct-material variances for each type of fertilizer.
2. Compute the direct-labor variances.
3. Compute the actual cost of the client applications. (*Note:* Exclude any fertilizer in inventory, as remaining fertilizer can be used next year.) Was the new service a financial success? Explain.
4. Analyze the variances that you computed in requirements (1) and (2).
   a. Was the new service a success from an overall cost-control perspective? Briefly discuss.
   b. What seems to have happened that would give rise to customer complaints?
5. In view of the complaints, should the fertilizer service be continued next year? Why?

Problem 10–47
Direct-Labor Variances at Colgate Palmolive[13] Company; Cost Variance Investigation
(LO 4)

The following data pertain to Colgate Palmolive's liquid filling line during the first 10 months of a particular year. The standard ratio of direct-labor hours to machine hours is 4:1. The standard direct-labor rate is $15.08.

Colgate Palmolive: Direct-Labor Efficiency Variance Data

	Units Produced	Machine Hours	Standard Direct-Labor Hours	Actual Direct-Labor Hours	Direct-Labor Efficiency Variance
January	50,478	165.5	662.00	374.00	$ 4,343
February	31,943	100.3	401.20	214.00	2,823
March	185,179	552.0	2,208.00	1,068.00	17,191
April	212,274	713.8	2,855.20	1,495.75	20,501
May	48,390	160.0	640.00	364.00	4,162
June	82,436	232.0	928.00	536.50	5,904

(continues)

[13]Source of data: Alan S. Levitan and Sidney J. Baxendale, "Analyzing the Labor Efficiency Variance to Signal Process Engineering Problems," *Journal of Cost Management* 6, no. 2 (Summer 1992), p. 70.

July	36,208	104.0	416.00	283.00	$2,006
August	33,483	96.0	384.00	317.50	1,003
September	31,560	96.0	384.00	328.50	837
October	28,191	72.0	288.00	158.00	1,960

Required:

1. Show how the following amounts were calculated for the month of January:
   a. Standard direct-labor hours.
   b. Direct-labor efficiency variance.
2. Calculate the following amounts.
   a. The standard direct-labor cost for each of the 10 months.
   b. For each month, 20 percent of the standard direct-labor cost.
3. Suppose management investigates all variances in excess of 20 percent of standard cost. Which variances will be investigated?
4. Suppose the standard deviation for the direct-labor efficiency variance is $5,000. Draw a statistical control chart, and plot the variance data.
5. Using the chart developed in requirement (4), which variances will be investigated?
6. The variances for March, April, and June are much larger than the others. Suggest at least one reason for this.

Problem 10–48
Direct-Material and Direct-Labor Variances
(LO 1, 3)

Valport Valve Company manufactured 15,600 units during March of a control valve used by milk processors in its Shreveport plant. Records indicated the following:

Direct labor	80,200 hr. at $10.95
Direct material purchased	50,000 lb. at $5.20
Direct material used	46,200 lb.

The control valve has the following standard prime costs.

Direct material:	3 lb. at $5.00 per lb.	$15.00
Direct labor:	5 hr. at $11.25 per hr.	56.25
Standard prime cost per unit		$71.25

Required:

1. Prepare a schedule of standard production costs for March, based on actual production of 15,600 units.
2. For the month of March, compute the following variances, indicating whether each is favorable or unfavorable.
   a. Direct-material price variance.
   b. Direct-material quantity variance.
   c. Direct-labor rate variance.
   d. Direct-labor efficiency variance.

(CPA, adapted)

Problem 10–49
Analyzing Performance and Responsibility; Computing Variances
(LO 1, 3)

SolarPrime, Inc. uses a standard-costing system to assist in the evaluation of operations. The company has had considerable trouble in recent months with suppliers and employees, so much so that management hired a new production supervisor, Marc Hoctor. The new supervisor has been on the job for five months and has seemingly brought order to an otherwise chaotic situation.

The vice president of manufacturing recently commented that ". . . Hoctor has really done the trick. The change to a new direct-material supplier and Hoctor's team-building/morale-boosting training exercises have truly brought things under control." The VP's comments were based on both a plant tour, where he observed a contented work force, and a review of a performance report. Included in the report were the following variances: direct material, $4,620 favorable; and direct labor, $6,175 favorable. These variances are especially outstanding, given that the amounts are favorable and small. (SolarPrime's budgeted material and labor costs generally each average about $350,000 for similar periods.) Additional data follow:

- The company purchased and consumed 45,000 pounds of direct material at $7.70 per pound, and paid $16.25 per hour for 20,900 direct-labor hours of activity. Total completed production amounted to 9,500 units.
- A review of the firm's standard cost records found that each completed unit requires 4.2 pounds of direct material at $8.80 per pound and 2.6 direct-labor hours at $14 per hour.

Required:

1. On the basis of the information contained in the performance report, should SolarPrime's management be concerned about its variances? Why?
2. Calculate the company's direct-material variances and direct-labor variances.
3. On the basis of your answers to requirement (2), should SolarPrime's management be concerned about its variances? Why?
4. Are things going as smoothly as the vice president believes? Evaluate the company's variances and determine whether the change to a new supplier and Hoctor's team-building/morale-boosting training exercises appear to be working. Explain.
5. Is it possible that some of the company's current problems lie outside Hoctor's area of responsibility? Explain.

Problem 10–50
Direct-Labor Variances
(LO 1, 3)

The director of cost management for Peoria Instrument Corporation compares each month's actual results with a monthly plan. The standard direct-labor rates for the year just ended and the standard hours allowed, given the actual output in April, are shown in the following schedule.

	Standard Direct-Labor Rate per Hour	Standard Direct-Labor Hours Allowed, Given April Output
Labor class III	$24.00	1,000
Labor class II	21.00	1,000
Labor class I	15.00	1,000

A new union contract negotiated in March resulted in actual wage rates that differed from the standard rates. The actual direct-labor hours worked and the actual direct-labor rates per hour experienced for the month of April were as follows:

	Actual Direct-Labor Rate per Hour	Actual Direct-Labor Hours
Labor class III	$25.80	1,100
Labor class II	22.50	1,300
Labor class I	16.20	750

Required:

1. Compute the following variances for April. Indicate whether each is favorable or unfavorable.
   a. Direct-labor rate variance for *each* labor class.
   b. Direct-labor efficiency variance for *each* labor class.
2. Discuss the advantages and disadvantages of a standard-costing system in which the standard direct-labor rates are not changed during the year to reflect such events as a new labor contract.

(CMA, adapted)

Problem 10–51
Setting Standards;
Responsibility for Variances
(LO 2)

Instructional Resources International (IRI) is a rapidly expanding company involved in the mass reproduction of instructional materials. Ralph Boston, owner and manager of IRI, has made a concentrated effort to provide a quality product at a fair price, with delivery on the promised date. Boston is finding it increasingly difficult to personally supervise the operations of IRI, and he is beginning to institute an organizational structure that would facilitate management control.

One change recently made was the transfer of control over departmental operations from Boston to each departmental manager. However, the Quality Control Department still reports directly to Boston, as do the Finance and Accounting Departments. A materials manager was hired to purchase all raw materials and to oversee the material-handling (receiving, storage, etc.) and recordkeeping functions. The materials manager also is responsible for maintaining an adequate inventory based on planned production levels.

The loss of personal control over the operations of IRI caused Boston to look for a method of efficiently evaluating performance. Dave Cress, a new managerial accountant, proposed the use of a standard-costing system. Variances for material and labor could then be calculated and reported directly to Boston.

Required:

1. Assume that IRI's management is going to implement a standard-costing system and establish standards for materials and labor. Identify and discuss for each of these cost components:
   a. Who should be involved in setting the standards?
   b. What factors should be considered in establishing the standards?
2. Describe the basis for assignment of responsibility for variances under a standard-costing system.

(CMA, adapted)

Problem 10–52
Determining Standard Costs; Ethics
(LO 1, 2)

Concord Farms produces items made from local farm products that are distributed to supermarkets. For many years, Concord's products have had strong regional sales on the basis of brand recognition; however, other companies have begun marketing similar products in the area, and price competition has become increasingly important. Doug Gilbert, the company's controller, is planning to implement a standard cost system for Concord and has gathered considerable information from his co-workers on production and material requirements for Concord's products. Gilbert believes that the use of standard costing will allow Concord to improve cost control and make better pricing decisions.

Concord's most popular product is strawberry jam. The jam is produced in 10-gallon batches, and each batch requires six quarts of good strawberries. The fresh strawberries are sorted by hand before entering the production process. Because of imperfections in the strawberries and normal spoilage, one quart of berries is discarded for every four quarts of acceptable berries. Three minutes is the standard direct-labor time for sorting required to obtain one quart of acceptable strawberries. The acceptable strawberries are then blended with the other ingredients. Blending requires 12 minutes of direct-labor time per batch. After blending, the jam is packaged in quart containers. Gilbert has gathered the following information from Joe Adams, Concord's cost accountant.

- Concord purchases strawberries at a cost of $1.60 per quart. All other ingredients cost a total of $.90 per gallon.
- Direct labor is paid at the rate of $18.00 per hour.
- The total cost of material and labor required to package the jam is $.76 per quart.

Adams has a friend who owns a strawberry farm that has been losing money in recent years. Because of good crops, there has been an oversupply of strawberries, and prices have dropped to $1.00 per quart. Adams has arranged for Concord to purchase strawberries from his friend and hopes that $1.60 per quart will help his friend's farm become profitable again.

Required:

1. Develop the standard cost for the direct-cost components of a 10-gallon batch of strawberry jam. The standard cost should identify the following amounts for each direct-cost component of a batch of strawberry jam: (*a*) standard quantity, (*b*) standard price or rate, and (*c*) standard cost per batch.
2. Citing the specific ethical standards of competence, confidentiality, integrity, and objectivity for management accountants, explain why Joe Adams's behavior regarding the cost information provided to Doug Gilbert is unethical.
3. As part of the implementation of a standard-costing system at Concord Farms, Doug Gilbert plans to train those responsible for maintaining the standards in the use of variance analysis. Gilbert is particularly concerned with the causes of unfavorable variances. Discuss the possible causes of the following unfavorable variances and identify the individual(s) who should be held responsible: (*a*) direct-material price variance and (*b*) direct-labor efficiency variance.

(CMA, adapted)

Problem 10–53
Investigating Cost Variances
(LO 4)

McKeag Corporation manufactures agricultural machinery. At a recent staff meeting, the following direct-labor variance report for the year just ended was presented by the controller.

MCKEAG CORPORATION
Direct-Labor Variance Report

	Direct-Labor Rate Variance		Direct-Labor Efficiency Variance	
	Amount	Standard Cost, %	Amount	Standard Cost, %
January	$ 1,600 F	.16%	$ 10,000 U	1.00%
February	9,800 F	.98%	15,000 U	1.50%
March	200 U	.02%	19,400 U	1.94%
April	4,000 U	.40%	25,600 U	2.56%
May	7,600 F	.76%	40,200 U	4.02%
June	7,800 F	.78%	34,000 U	3.40%
July	8,400 F	.84%	57,000 U	5.70%
August	10,200 F	1.02%	76,000 U	7.60%
September	9,600 F	.96%	74,000 U	7.40%
October	11,400 F	1.14%	84,000 U	8.40%
November	8,400 F	.84%	120,000 U	12.00%
December	8,600 F	.86%	104,000 U	10.40%

McKeag's controller uses the following rule of thumb: Investigate all variances equal to or greater than $60,000, which is 6 percent of standard cost.

Required:

1. Which variances would have been investigated during the year? (Indicate month and type of variance.)
2. What characteristics of the variance pattern shown in the report should draw the controller's attention, regardless of the usual investigation rule? Explain. Given these considerations, which variances would you have investigated? Why?
3. Is it important to follow up on favorable variances, such as those shown in the report? Why?
4. The controller believes that the firm's direct-labor rate variance has a normal probability distribution with a mean of zero and a standard deviation of $10,000. Prepare a statistical control chart, and plot the company's direct-labor rate variances for each month. The critical value is 1 standard deviation. Which variances would have been investigated under this approach?

Problem 10–54
Development of Standard Costs; Ethics
(LO 2, 5)

California Housewares' Merced Division is a small manufacturer of wooden household items. Al Rivkin, divisional controller, plans to implement a standard-costing system. Rivkin has collected information from several co-workers that will assist him in developing standards. One of the Merced Division's products is a wooden cutting board. Each cutting board requires 1.25 board feet of lumber and 12 minutes of direct-labor time to prepare and cut the lumber. The cutting boards are inspected after they are cut. Because the cutting boards are made of a natural material that has imperfections, one board is normally rejected for each five that are accepted. Four rubber foot pads are attached to each good cutting board. A total of 15 minutes of direct-labor time is required to attach all four foot pads and finish each cutting board. The lumber for the cutting boards cost $4.00 per board foot, and each foot pad costs $.10. Direct labor is paid at the rate of $8.00 per hour.

Required:

1. Develop the standard cost for direct material and direct labor of a cutting board.
2. Explain the role of each of the following people in developing standards.
   a. Purchasing manager.
   b. Industrial engineer.
   c. Managerial accountant.
3. The production manager complained that the standards are unrealistic, stifle motivation by concentrating only on unfavorable variances, and are out of date too quickly. He noted that his recent switch to cherry for the cutting boards has resulted in higher material costs but decreased labor hours. The net result was no increase in the total cost to produce the product. The monthly reports continue to show an unfavorable material variance and a favorable labor variance despite indications that the workers are slowing down.
   a. Explain why a standard-costing system can strengthen cost management.

b. Give at least two reasons to explain why a standard-costing system could negatively impact the motivation of production employees.

(CMA, adapted)

Problem 10–55
Manufacturing Performance Measurement
(LO 9)

Diagnostic Technology, Inc. manufactures diagnostic testing equipment used in hospitals. The company practices JIT production management and has a state-of-the-art manufacturing system, including an FMS and an AMHS. The following nonfinancial data were collected biweekly in the Albany plant during the first quarter of the current year.

	Biweekly Measurement Period					
	1	**2**	**3**	**4**	**5**	**6**
Cycle time (days)	1.7	1.5	1.5	1.4	1.4	1.3
Number of defective finished products	3	3	2	3	2	2
Manufacturing-cycle efficiency	95%	94%	96%	96%	97%	96%
Customer complaints	5	6	5	4	6	7
Unresolved complaints	2	1	0	0	0	0
Products returned	3	3	2	2	1	1
Warranty claims	2	2	2	0	1	0
In-process products rejected	5	5	7	9	10	10
Aggregate productivity	1.5	1.5	1.5	1.5	1.4	1.5
Number of units produced per day per employee	410	405	412	415	415	420
Percentage of on-time deliveries	94%	95%	95%	97%	100%	100%
Percentage of orders filled	100%	100%	100%	98%	100%	100%
Inventory value/sales revenue	2%	2%	2%	1.5%	2%	1.5%
Machine downtime (minutes)	80	80	120	80	70	75
Bottleneck machine downtime (minutes)	25	20	15	0	60	10
Overtime (minutes) per employee	20	0	0	10	20	10
Average setup time (minutes)	119	119	114	111	107	100

Required:

1. For each nonfinancial performance measure, indicate which of the following areas of manufacturing performance is involved: (*a*) production processing, (*b*) product quality, (*c*) customer acceptance, (*d*) in-process quality control, (*e*) productivity, (*f*) delivery performance, (*g*) raw material and scrap, (*h*) inventory, (*i*) machine maintenance. Some measures may relate to more than one area.
2. Write a memo to management commenting on the performance data collected for the Albany plant. Be sure to note any trends or other important results you see in the data. Evaluate the Albany plant in each of the areas listed in requirement (1).

Problem 10–56
Production Efficiency Report; Operational Performance Measures
(LO 9)

Southern Plastics Corporation manufactures a range of molded plastic products, such as kitchen utensils and desk accessories. The production process in the Baton Rouge plant is a JIT system, which operates in four FMS cells. An AMHS is used to transport products between production operations. Each month the controller prepares a production efficiency report, which is sent to corporate headquarters. The data compiled in these reports, for the first six months of the year, are as follows:

PRODUCTION EFFICIENCY REPORT
Southern Plastics Corporation
Baton Rouge Plant
January through June

	Jan.	**Feb.**	**Mar.**	**Apr.**	**May**	**June**	**Average**
Overtime hours	59	69	74	79	84	104	78.2
Total setup time	69	69	64	63	61	61	64.5
Cycle time (average in hours)	19	19	18	17	18	16	17.8
Manufacturing-cycle efficiency	95%	94%	96%	90%	89%	90%	92.3%
Percentage of orders filled	100%	100%	100%	100%	100%	100%	100%
Percentage of on-time deliveries	99%	98%	99%	100%	96%	94%	97.7%
Inventory value/sales revenue	5%	5%	5%	4%	5%	5%	4.8%
Number of defective units, finished goods	80	82	75	40	25	22	54

(continues)

(concluded)	Jan.	Feb.	Mar.	Apr.	May	June	Average
Number of defective units, in process	9	29	34	39	59	59	38.2
Number of raw-material shipments with defective materials	3	3	2	0	0	0	1.3
Number of products returned	0	0	0	0	0	0	0
Aggregate productivity	1.3	1.3	1.2	1.25	1.2	1.15	1.23
Power consumption (thousands of kilowatt-hours)	800	795	802	801	800	800	799.7
Machine downtime (hours)	30	25	25	20	20	10	21.7
Bottleneck machine downtime	0	0	2	0	15	2	3.2
Number of unscheduled machine maintenance calls	0	0	1	0	2	3	1

Required:

1. Write a memo to the company president evaluating the Baton Rouge plant's performance. Structure your report by dividing it into the following parts: (*a*) production processing and productivity, (*b*) product quality and customer acceptance, (*c*) delivery performance, (*d*) raw material, scrap, and inventory, and (*e*) machine maintenance.
2. If you identify any areas of concern in your memo, indicate an appropriate action for management.

Problem 10–57
Gain-Sharing; Operational Performance Measures; Cost Reduction
(LO 6, 9)

CommLine Equipment Corporation specializes in the manufacture of communications equipment, a field that has become increasingly competitive. Approximately two years ago, Ben Harrington, president of CommLine, became concerned that the company's bonus plan, which focused on division profitability, was not helping CommLine remain competitive. Harrington decided to implement a gain-sharing plan that would encourage employees to focus on operational areas that were important to customers and that added value without increasing cost. In addition to a profitability incentive, the revised plan also includes incentives for reduced rework costs, reduced sales returns, and on-time deliveries. Bonuses are calculated and awarded semiannually on the following basis. The bonuses are distributed among the relevant employees according to a formula developed by the division manager.

- Profitability: Two percent of operating income.
- Rework: Costs in excess of 2 percent of operating income are deducted from the bonus amount.
- On-time delivery: $10,000 if over 98 percent of deliveries are on time, $4,000 if 96 to 98 percent of deliveries are on time, and no increment if on-time deliveries are below 96 percent.
- Sales returns: $6,000 if returns are less than 1.5 percent of sales. Fifty percent of any amount in excess of 1.5 percent of sales is deducted from the bonus amount.
- *Note:* If the calculation of the bonus results in a negative amount for a particular period, there is no bonus, and the negative amount is not carried forward to the next period.

The revised bonus plan was implemented on January 1, 20x1. Presented in the following table are the results for two of CommLine's divisions, Charter and Mesa Divisions, for the first year under the new bonus plan. Both of these divisions had similar sales and operating income results for the prior year, when the old bonus plan was in effect. Based on the 20x0 results, the employees of the Charter Division earned a bonus of $54,120 while the employees of the Mesa Division earned $44,880.

	Charter Division		Mesa Division	
	January 20x1–June 20x1	July 20x1–December 20x1	January 20x1–June 20x1	July 20x1–December 20x1
Sales	$8,400,000	$8,800,000	$5,700,000	$5,800,000
Operating income	$924,000	$880,000	$684,000	$812,000
On-time delivery	95.4%	97.3%	98.2%	94.6%
Rework costs	$23,000	$22,000	$12,000	$16,000
Sales returns	$168,000	$140,000	$89,500	$85,000

Required:

1. For the Charter Division:
   a. Compute the semiannual installments and total bonus awarded for 20x1.
   b. Discuss the likely behavior of the Charter Division employees under the revised bonus plan.

2. For the Mesa Division:
   a. Compute the semiannual installments and total bonus awarded for 20x1.
   b. Discuss the likely behavior of the Mesa Division employees under the revised bonus plan.
3. Citing specific examples, evaluate whether or not Harrington's revisions to the bonus plan at CommLine Equipment Corporation have achieved the desired results, and recommend any changes that might improve the plan.

(CMA, adapted)

Problem 10–58
Balanced Scorecard; Banking; Use of Internet
(LO 10)

Visit the website of a major bank, e.g., Citibank at www.citibank.com. Explore the website to learn about the bank's services and operations.

Required:

1. What do you think the bank's overall, long-term goals are?
2. Develop a balanced scorecard for the bank. Include two to five measures in each of the scorecard's perspectives.
3. How would the balanced scorecard affect the way managers develop the bank's strategy?
4. Explain the concept of lead and lag measures in the context of the scorecard you have developed.

Problem 10–59
Direct-Material Variances; Journal Entries (Appendix)
(LO 1, 3, 11)

Ozarks Camping Equipment, Inc. has established the following direct-material standards for its two products.

	Standard Quantity	Standard Price
Standard camping tent.	12 yards	$6 per yard
Deluxe backpacking tent	6 yards	$8 per yard

During May, the company purchased 4,200 yards of tent fabric for its standard model at a cost of $26,880. The actual May production of the standard tent was 200 tents, and 2,500 yards of fabric were used. Also during May, the company purchased 1,600 yards of tent fabric for its deluxe backpacking tent at a cost of $12,640. The firm used 1,440 yards of the fabric during May in the production of 240 deluxe tents.

Required:

1. Compute the direct-material price variance and quantity variance for May.
2. Prepare journal entries to record the purchase of material, use of material, and incurrence of variances in May.

Problem 10–60
Variances; Journal Entries; Missing Data (Appendix)
(LO 3, 6, 11)

Execucraft, Inc. manufactures upholstered office chairs. The standard cost for material and labor is $89.20 per chair. This includes 8 kilograms of direct material at a standard cost of $5.00 per kilogram, and 6 hours of direct labor at $8.20 per hour. The following data pertain to September.

- Units completed: 5,600 chairs.
- Purchases of materials: 50,000 kilograms for $249,250.
- Total actual labor costs: $300,760.
- Actual hours of labor: 36,500 hours.
- Direct-material quantity variance: $1,500 unfavorable.
- Work-in-process inventory on September 1: none.
- Work-in-process inventory on September 30: 800 chairs (75 percent complete as to labor; material is issued at the beginning of processing).

Required:

1. Compute the following amounts. Indicate whether each variance is favorable or unfavorable.
   a. Direct-labor rate variance for September.
   b. Direct-labor efficiency variance for September.
   c. Actual kilograms of material used in the production process during September.
   d. Actual price paid per kilogram of direct material in September.
   e. Total amounts of direct-material and direct-labor cost transferred to Finished-Goods Inventory during September.

f. The total amount of direct-material and direct-labor cost in the ending balance of Work-in-Process Inventory at the end of September.

2. Prepare journal entries to record the following:
   a. Purchase of raw material.
   b. Adding direct material to Work-in-Process Inventory.
   c. Adding direct labor to Work-in-Process Inventory.
   d. Recording of variances.

(CMA, adapted)

Problem 10–61
Comprehensive Problem on Variance Analysis
(LO 1, 3)

McCartney Company manufactures guitars. The company uses a standard, job-order cost-accounting system in two production departments. In the Construction Department the wooden guitars are built by highly skilled craftspeople and coated with several layers of lacquer. Then the units are transferred to the Finishing Department, where the bridge of the guitar is attached and the strings are installed. The guitars also are tuned and inspected in the Finishing Department. The diagram below depicts the production process.

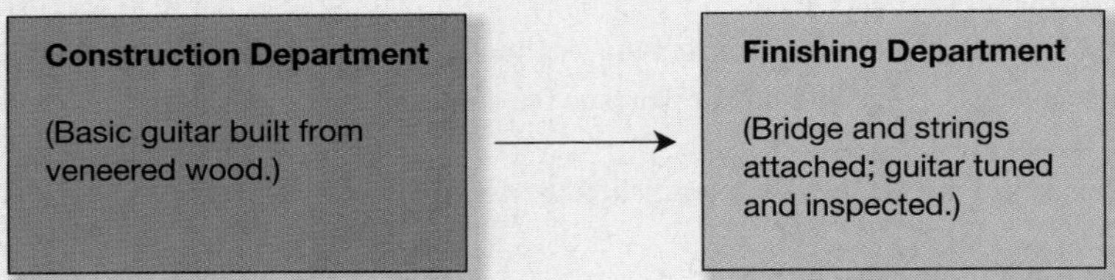

Each finished guitar contains seven pounds of veneered wood. In addition, one pound of wood is typically wasted in the production process. The veneered wood used in the guitars has a standard price of $12 per pound. The other parts needed to complete each guitar, such as the bridge and strings, cost $15 per guitar. The labor standards for McCartney's two production departments are as follows:

Construction Department: 6 hours of direct labor at $20 per hour
Finishing Department: 3 hours of direct labor at $15 per hour

The following pertains to the month of July.

1. There were no beginning or ending work-in-process inventories in either production department.
2. There was no beginning finished-goods inventory.
3. Actual production was 750 guitars, and 450 guitars were sold on account for $390 each.
4. The company purchased 9,000 pounds of veneered wood at a price of $12.50 per pound.
5. Actual usage of veneered wood was 6,750 pounds.
6. Enough parts (bridges and strings) to finish 900 guitars were purchased at a cost of $13,500.
7. The Construction Department used 4,275 direct-labor hours. The total direct-labor cost in the Construction Department was $81,225.
8. The Finishing Department used 2,355 direct-labor hours. The total direct-labor cost in that department was $37,680.
9. There were no direct-material variances in the Finishing Department.

Required:

1. Prepare a schedule that computes the standard costs of direct material and direct labor in each production department and in total for the month of July.
2. Prepare three exhibits which compute the July direct-material and direct-labor variances in the Construction Department and the July direct-labor variances in the Finishing Department. (Refer to Exhibits 10–2 and 10–3 for guidance.)
3. Prepare a cost variance report for July similar to that shown in Exhibit 10–4.

Problem 10–62
Journal Entries under Standard Costing; Continuation of Preceding Problem (Appendix)
(LO 6, 11)

Refer to your solution for the preceding problem regarding McCartney Company.

Required:

1. Prepare journal entries to record all of the events listed for McCartney Company during July. Specifically, these journal entries should reflect the following events.

   a. Purchase of direct material.
   b. Use of direct material.
   c. Incurrence of direct-labor costs.
   d. Addition of production costs to the Work-in-Process Inventory account for each department.
   e. Incurrence of all variances.
   f. Completion of 750 guitars.
   g. Sale of 450 guitars.
   h. Closing of all variance accounts into Cost of Goods Sold.
2. Draw T-accounts, and post the journal entries prepared in requirement (1). Assume the beginning balance in all accounts is zero.

Cases

Case 10–63
Direct-Material and Direct-Labor Variances; Job-Order Costing; Journal Entries (Appendix)
(LO 1, 3, 6, 11)

Metro Fashions, Inc. manufactures women's blouses of one quality, which are produced in lots to fill each special order. Its customers are department stores in various cities. Metro Fashions sews the particular stores' labels on the blouses. During November the company worked on three orders, for which the month's job-cost records disclose the following data.

Lot Number	Boxes in Lot	Material Used (yards)	Hours Worked
N42	2,000	48,200	5,960
N43	3,400	80,880	10,260
N44	2,400	57,650	5,780

The following additional information is available:

1. The firm purchased 190,000 yards of material during November at a cost of $212,800.
2. Direct labor during November amounted to $330,000. According to payroll records, production employees were paid $15 per hour.
3. There was no work in process on November 1. During November, lots N42 and N43 were completed. All material was issued for lot N44, which was 80 percent completed as to conversion (i.e., direct labor and overhead).
4. The standard costs for a box of six blouses are as follows:

Direct material	24 yards at $1.10	$ 26.40
Direct labor	3 hours at $14.70	44.10
Manufacturing overhead	3 hours at $12.00	36.00
Standard cost per box		$106.50

Required:

1. Prepare a schedule computing the standard cost of lots N42, N43, and N44 for November.
2. Prepare a schedule showing, for each lot produced during November:
   a. Direct-material price variance. (*Hint:* Must be computed in total, across all three production lots.)
   b. Direct-material quantity variance.
   c. Direct-labor efficiency variance.
   d. Direct-labor rate variance.
   Indicate whether each variance is favorable or unfavorable.
3. Prepare journal entries to record each of the following events.
   a. Purchase of material.
   b. Incurrence of direct-labor cost.
   c. Addition of direct-material and direct-labor cost to Work-in-Process Inventory.
   d. Recording of direct-material and direct-labor variances.

(CPA, adapted)

Case 10–64
Missing Data; Variances, Ledger Accounts (Appendix)
(LO 1, 3, 11)

MacGyver Corporation manufactures a product called Miracle Goo, which comes in handy for just about anything. The thick tarry substance is sold in six-gallon drums. Two raw materials are used; these are referred to by people in the business as A and B. Two types of labor are required also. These are mixers (labor class I) and packers (labor class II). You were recently hired by the company president, Pete Thorn, to be the controller. You soon learned that MacGyver uses a standard-costing system. Variances are computed and closed into Cost of Goods Sold monthly. After your first month on the job, you gathered the necessary data to compute the month's variances for direct material and direct labor. You finished everything up by 5:00 P.M. on the 31st, including the credit to Cost of Goods Sold for the sum of the variances. You decided to take all your notes home to review them prior to your formal presentation to Thorn first thing in the morning. As an afterthought, you grabbed a drum of Miracle Goo as well, thinking it could prove useful in some unanticipated way.

You spent the evening boning up on the data for your report and were ready to call it a night. As luck would have it though, you knocked over the Miracle Goo as you rose from the kitchen table. The stuff splattered everywhere, and, most unfortunately, obliterated most of your notes. All that remained legible is the following information.

Direct Material A: Quantity Variance	
3,750	

Direct Material B: Price Variance	
1,800	

Direct Labor I: Rate Variance	
900	

Direct Labor II: Efficiency Variance	
1,800	

Cost of Goods Sold	
214,500	
	2,265

Accounts Payable	
	2,250 Beg. bal.
105,000	109,800
	7,050 End. bal.

Other assorted data gleaned from your notes:

- The standards for each drum of Miracle Goo include 10 pounds of material A at a standard price of $5 per pound.
- The standard cost of material B is $15 for each drum of Miracle Goo.
- Purchases of material A were 18,000 pounds at $4.50 per pound.
- Given the actual output for the month, the standard allowed quantity of material A was 15,000 pounds. The standard allowed quantity of material B was 7,500 gallons.
- Although 9,000 gallons of B were purchased, only 7,200 gallons were used.
- The standard wage rate for mixers is $15 per hour. The standard labor cost per drum of product for mixers is $30 per drum.
- The standards allow 4 hours of direct labor II (packers) per drum of Miracle Goo. The standard labor cost per drum of product for packers is $48 per drum.
- Packers were paid $11.90 per hour during the month.

You happened to remember two additional facts. There were no beginning or ending inventories of either work in process or finished goods for the month. The increase in accounts payable relates to direct-material purchases only.

Required: Now you've got a major problem. Somehow you've got to reconstruct all the missing data in order to be ready for your meeting with the president. You start by making the following list of the facts you want to use in your presentation. Before getting down to business, you need a brief walk to clear your head. Out to the trash you go, and toss the remaining Miracle Goo.

Fill in the missing amounts in the following list, using the available facts.

1. Actual output (in drums): ________

2. Direct material:

	A	B
a. Standard quantity per drum:	________	________
b. Standard price:	________	________
c. Standard cost per drum:	________	________
d. Standard quantity allowed, given actual output:	________	________
e. Actual quantity purchased:	________	________
f. Actual price:	________	________

g. Actual quantity used:	_______	_______
h. Price variance:	_______	_______
i. Quantity variance:	_______	_______
3. Direct labor:	**I (mixers)**	**II (packers)**
a. Standard hours per drum:	_______	_______
b. Standard rate per hour:	_______	_______
c. Standard cost per drum:	_______	_______
d. Standard quantity allowed, given actual output:	_______	_______
e. Actual rate per hour:	_______	_______
f. Actual hours:	_______	_______
g. Rate variance:	_______	_______
h. Efficiency variance:	_______	_______

4. Total of all variances for the month: _______

Current Issues in Managerial Accounting

Issue 10–65
Setting Standard Costs for Radical New Products

"When Hybrid Cars Collide," *The Wall Street Journal,* February 6, 2003, p. B1, Norihiko Shirouzu.

Overview

Automakers Toyota, Honda, Ford, and General Motors are jockeying to determine the format for the new hybrid gas-electric vehicles. The situation is reminiscent of the VHS vs. Betamax wars.

Suggested Discussion Questions

As a group, discuss how companies developing new, high-tech products would set standard costs for them. What special challenges does the "format" issue present in standard setting for the new hybrid automobiles?

Issue 10–66
Quality and Cost Management; Balanced Scorecard

"Hotel Cost Cutting Produces a General Decline in Services," *The Wall Street Journal,* January 27, 2003, p. B2, Christina Binkley.

Overview

As major hotel companies like Marriott International and Hilton Hotels cut costs, the break-even occupancy level has come down to 47.4 percent, the lowest ever. But some executives worry about the effect on service.

Suggested Discussion Question

How could a balanced scorecard help hotel companies make the trade-offs between cost cuts and service?

Issue 10–67
Balanced Scorecard; Innovation

"Can Yahoo! Thrive in a Harsh Climate?" *The Wall Street Journal,* October 16, 2000.

Overview

Many of Yahoo!'s employees have been with the company since its founding. The article raises concerns about whether Yahoo! "has enough new blood with enough new ideas to be vital in the next phase of Internet business."

Suggested Discussion Questions

Describe Yahoo!'s business. What services does the company provide? How could Yahoo!'s management employ concepts from the balanced scorecard?

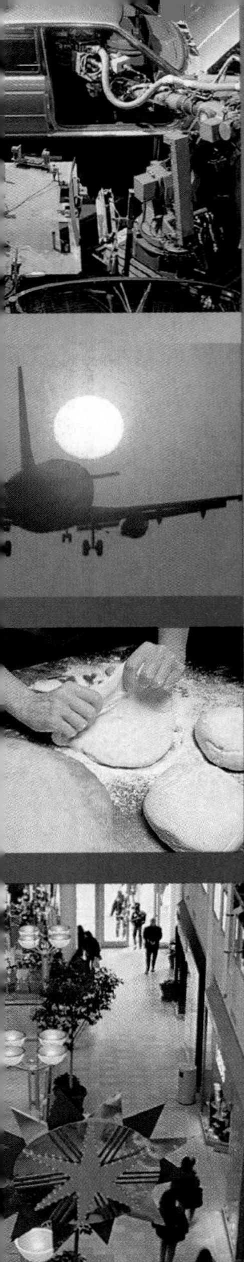

Chapter Eleven

Flexible Budgeting and the Management of Overhead and Support Activity Costs

After completing this chapter, you should be able to:

1. Distinguish between static and flexible budgets and explain the advantages of a flexible overhead budget.
2. Prepare a flexible overhead budget, using both a formula and a columnar format.
3. Explain how overhead is applied to Work-in-Process Inventory under standard costing.
4. Explain some important issues in choosing an activity measure for overhead budgeting and application.
5. Compute and interpret the variable-overhead spending and efficiency variances and the fixed-overhead budget and volume variances.
6. Prepare an overhead cost performance report.
7. Explain how an activity-based flexible budget differs from a conventional flexible budget.
8. After completing Appendix A, prepare journal entries to record manufacturing overhead under standard costing.
9. After completing Appendix B, compute and interpret the sales-price and sales-volume variances.

DCdesserts.com Inks Contract to Supply Desserts for State Dinners

Washington, DC—A spokesman for DCdesserts.com announced today that it has signed a contract to supply desserts for all state dinners to be held at the White House for the next two years. "We're really excited about this," said Tyler Martin, the company's founder. "It shows that we really are the best producer of fancy desserts in the Washington area. It's a little daunting, though, to realize that heads of state from all over the world will be eating our chocolate cheese cake and raspberry chocolate layer cake."

DCdesserts.com is an innovative purveyor of fine desserts, which conducts virtually all of its business on the Internet. Customers place orders for desserts on the company's website, ingredients are ordered via the Web, and the delivery services that deliver the products for DCdesserts.com are notified of delivery schedules online. DCdesserts.com's products appear in virtually all of Washington's finest restaurants and gourmet food stores.

Martin was asked if the projected increase in production would strain capacity in the company's two beltway production facilities. "We're looking closely at that now," said Martin. "I know we can get the product out the door in both places, but the question is what the increase in output will do to our costs. We employ a flexible budgeting system here at DCdesserts.com, and our director of cost management is using it to project our overhead costs at various levels of activity. We express our activity in terms of process hours. We can predict pretty accurately what our costs will be at various levels of process hours, for utilities, or inspection, or setup, or what have you. With this kind of planning, I'm sure we'll be able to meet our contract and keep the lid on our costs, too."

DCdesserts.com will be producing desserts for its first state dinner, when the British prime minister comes next month.

How do manufacturing firms, such as General Motors Corporation and Hewlett-Packard Company, control the many overhead costs incurred in their production processes? Unlike direct material and direct labor, manufacturing-overhead costs are not traceable to individual products. Moreover, manufacturing overhead is a pool of many different kinds of costs. Indirect material, indirect labor, and other indirect production costs often exhibit different relationships to productive activity. Some overhead costs are variable, and some are fixed. Moreover, different individuals in an organization are responsible for different types of overhead costs. Considering all of these issues together, controlling manufacturing overhead presents a challenge for managerial accountants. In this chapter, we will study an accounting system that is widely used to control overhead costs.

Overhead Budgets

LO 1

Distinguish between static and flexible budgets and explain the advantages of a flexible overhead budget.

Since direct material and direct labor are traceable to products, it is straightforward to determine standard costs for these inputs. If a table requires 20 board feet of oak lumber at $4 per board foot, the standard direct-material cost for the table is $80. But how much electricity does it take to produce a table? How much supervisory time, equipment depreciation, or machinery repair services does the table require? Since all of these overhead costs are indirect costs of production, we cannot set overhead cost standards for the oak table. If standard costs do not provide the answer to controlling overhead, what does?

Flexible Budgets

Topic 11–1

The tool used by most companies to control overhead costs is called a **flexible budget.** A flexible budget resembles the budgets we studied in Chapter 9, with one important difference: *A flexible budget is not based on only one level of activity.* Instead, a flexible budget covers a range of activity within which the firm may operate. A *flexible overhead budget* is defined as a detailed plan for controlling overhead costs that is valid in the firm's relevant range of activity. In contrast, a **static budget** is based on a particular planned level of activity.

At DCdesserts.com, the measure of activity used for flexible budgeting purposes is process time. The process time for a dessert is the total amount of time the product is in process, including selecting ingredients, mixing, baking, cooling, assembly and finishing, and packaging. DCdesserts.com's director of cost management estimates that the average process time required for fancy desserts is three hours.

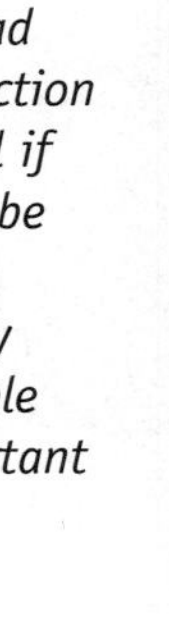

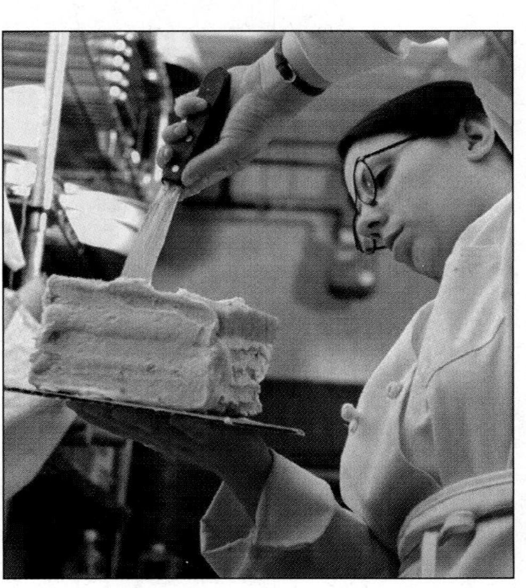

Controlling overhead costs in this production operation is crucial if the company is to be profitable in its production of fancy desserts. The flexible budget is an important tool in cost management.

To illustrate the flexible budgeting concept, suppose DCdesserts.com's director of cost management has determined that electricity is a variable cost, incurred at the rate of $.50 per hour of process time. Two different budgets for electricity cost are shown in Exhibit 11–1. The static budget is based on management's predicted level of activity for September—7,500 hours of process time. This estimate is based on planned production of 2,500 multilayer fancy cakes, where each cake requires three hours of total process time. The flexible budget includes three different production activity levels within the relevant range: 6,000, 7,500, and 9,000 hours of process time.

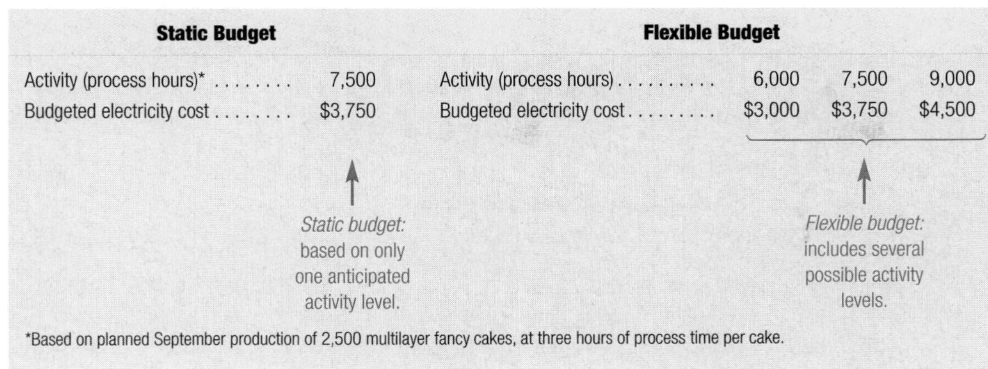

Static Budget		Flexible Budget			
Activity (process hours)*	7,500	Activity (process hours)	6,000	7,500	9,000
Budgeted electricity cost	$3,750	Budgeted electricity cost	$3,000	$3,750	$4,500

Static budget: based on only one anticipated activity level.

Flexible budget: includes several possible activity levels.

*Based on planned September production of 2,500 multilayer fancy cakes, at three hours of process time per cake.

Exhibit 11–1
Static Budget versus Flexible Budget

Advantages of Flexible Budgets

Why is the distinction between static and flexible budgets so important? Suppose DCdesserts.com produced 2,000 multilayer fancy cakes during September, used 6,000 hours of process time, and incurred electricity costs of $3,200. Does this constitute good control or poor control of electricity costs? Which budget in Exhibit 11–1 is more useful in answering this question?

A manager using the static budget makes the following comparison.

Actual Electricity Cost	Budgeted Electricity Cost (static budget)	Cost Variance
$3,200	$3,750	$550 Favorable

This comparison suggests that operating personnel maintained excellent control over electricity costs during September, generating a favorable variance of $550. Is this a valid analysis and conclusion?

The fault with this analysis is that the manager is comparing the electricity cost incurred at the *actual* activity level, 2,000 multilayer fancy cakes, with the budgeted electricity cost at the *planned* activity level, 2,500 multilayer fancy cakes. Since these activity levels are different, we should expect the electricity cost to be different.

A more sensible approach is to compare the actual electricity cost incurred with the cost that should be incurred when 2,000 multilayer fancy cakes are produced. At this production level, 6,000 process hours should be used (3 per cake). The flexible budget in Exhibit 11–1 shows that the manager should expect $3,000 of electricity cost at the 6,000 process-hour level of activity. Therefore, an analysis based on the flexible budget gives the following comparison.

Actual Electricity Cost	Budgeted Electricity Cost (flexible budget)	Cost Variance
$3,200	$3,000	$200 Unfavorable

Now the manager's conclusion is different; the revised analysis indicates an unfavorable variance. Electricity cost was greater than it should have been, given the actual level of output. The flexible budget provides the correct basis for comparison between actual and expected costs, given actual activity.

The Activity Measure

Notice that the flexible budget for electricity cost in Exhibit 11–1 is based on hours of process time, which is an input in the production process. The process-hour activity levels shown in the flexible budget are the standard allowed process hours given various levels of output. If 2,000 multilayer fancy cakes are produced, and the standard allowance per cake is 3 process hours, then the standard allowed number of process hours is 6,000.

Exhibit 11–2
Flexible Budgets: Input versus Output

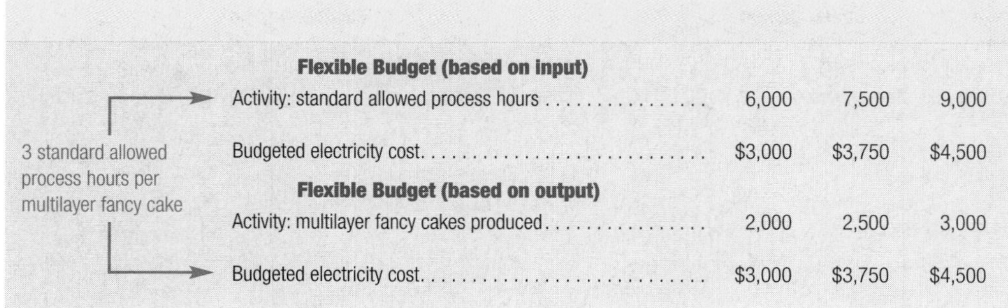

3 standard allowed process hours per multilayer fancy cake

Flexible Budget (based on input)			
Activity: standard allowed process hours	6,000	7,500	9,000
Budgeted electricity cost	$3,000	$3,750	$4,500
Flexible Budget (based on output)			
Activity: multilayer fancy cakes produced	2,000	2,500	3,000
Budgeted electricity cost	$3,000	$3,750	$4,500

Why are the activity levels in the flexible budget based on process hours, an *input* measure, instead of the number of multilayer fancy cakes produced, an *output* measure? When only a single product is manufactured, it makes no difference whether the flexible budget is based on input or output. In our illustration, either of the flexible budgets shown in Exhibit 11–2 could be used.

Now suppose that during August, DCdesserts.com produced three different products: 1,000 multilayer fancy cakes, 1,500 single-layer sheet cakes, and 600 specialty cakes (such as wedding cakes). The following standards have been assigned to these products.

Product	**Standard Process Hours per Unit**
Multilayer fancy cakes	3
Single-layer sheet cakes	2
Specialty cakes	6

"I will give you an example of when we were supporting budgets. We would have to go out to the person and say, 'What is going on in your budget? I don't understand why you are overspending or underspending.' Now a person looks at their budget and comes to accounting and will say, 'Can you help me with this problem?' " (11a)
Abbott Laboratories

During August, the company's production output was 3,100 cakes. Is 3,100 cakes a meaningful output measure? Adding numbers of multilayer fancy cakes, sheet cakes, and specialty cakes, which require different amounts of productive inputs, is like adding apples and oranges. It would not make sense to base a flexible budget for electricity cost on units of output when the output consists of different products with different electricity requirements. In this case, the flexible budget must be based on an *input* measure. The standard allowed number of process hours for the August production is computed as follows:

Product	**Units Produced**	**Standard Process Hours per Unit**	**Total Standard Allowed Process Hours**
Multilayer fancy cakes	1,000	3	3,000
Single-layer sheet cakes	1,500	2	3,000
Specialty cakes	600	6	3,600
Total			9,600

Recall that the controller estimates electricity cost at $.50 per process hour. Thus, the flexible-budget cost of electricity during August is computed as follows:

Standard allowed process hours given August output	9,600
Electricity cost per process hour	× $.50
Flexible budget for electricity cost	$4,800

The important point is that *units of output* usually is not a meaningful measure in a multiproduct firm, because it would require us to add numbers of unlike products. To avoid this problem, output is measured in terms of the *standard allowed input, given actual output.* The flexible overhead budget is then based on this standard input measure.

Exhibit 11–3
Flexible Overhead Budget

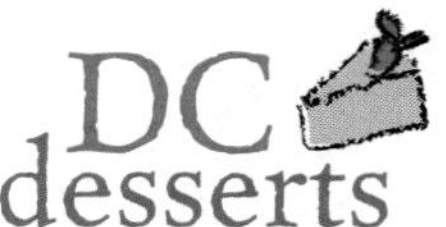

	A	E	F	G
1	**DCdesserts.com**			
2	**Monthly Flexible Overhead Budget**			
3			**Process Hours**	
4		**6,000**	**7,500**	**9,000**
5	**Budgeted costs:**			
6				
7	**Variable costs:**			
8	Indirect material:			
9	Nonstick cooking spray	$ 12,000	$ 15,000	$ 18,000
10	Waxed paper	2,000	2,500	3,000
11	Other paper products	2,000	2,500	3,000
12	Miscellaneous supplies	6,000	7,500	9,000
13	Indirect labor: maintenance	4,000	5,000	6,000
14	Utilities			
15	Electricity	3,000	3,750	4,500
16	Natural gas	1,000	1,250	1,500
17	Total variable cost	$ 30,000	$ 37,500	$ 45,000
18				
19				
20	**Fixed costs:**			
21	Indirect labor:			
22	Inspection	$ 2,200	$ 2,200	$ 2,200
23	Production supervisors	6,000	6,000	6,000
24	Setup	3,000	3,000	3,000
25	Material handling	2,000	2,000	2,000
26	Depreciation: plant and equipment	500	500	500
27	Insurance and property taxes	100	100	100
28	Test kitchen	1,200	1,200	1,200
29	Total fixed cost	$ 15,000	$ 15,000	$ 15,000
30	**Total overhead cost**	$ 45,000	$ 52,500	$ 60,000

Flexible Overhead Budget Illustrated

LO 2

Prepare a flexible overhead budget, using both a formula and a columnar format.

DCdesserts.com's monthly flexible overhead budget is shown in the Excel spreadsheet in Exhibit 11–3. The overhead costs on the flexible budget are divided into variable and fixed costs. The total budgeted variable cost increases proportionately with increases in the activity. Thus, when the number of process hours increases by 50 percent, from 6,000 hours to 9,000 hours, the total budgeted variable overhead cost also increases by 50 percent, from $30,000 to $45,000. In contrast, the total budgeted fixed overhead does not change with increases in activity; it remains constant at $15,000 per month.

Formula Flexible Budget When overhead costs can be divided into variable and fixed categories, we can express the flexible overhead budget differently. The format used in Exhibit 11–3 is called a *columnar flexible budget.* The budgeted overhead cost for each overhead item is listed in a column under a particular activity level. Notice that the columnar format allows for only a limited number of activity levels. DCdesserts.com's flexible budget shows only three.

A more general format for expressing a flexible budget is called a *formula flexible budget.* In this format, the managerial accountant expresses the relationship between activity and total budgeted overhead cost by the following formula.

$$\begin{array}{c}\text{Total budgeted}\\\text{monthly overhead}\\\text{cost}\end{array} = \left(\begin{array}{c}\text{Budgeted variable-}\\\text{overhead cost per}\\\text{activity unit}\end{array} \times \begin{array}{c}\text{Total}\\\text{activity}\\\text{units}\end{array}\right) + \begin{array}{c}\text{Budgeted fixed-}\\\text{overhead cost}\\\text{per month}\end{array}$$

To use this formula for DCdesserts.com, we first need to compute the budgeted variable-overhead cost per process hour. Dividing total budgeted variable-overhead cost by the associated activity level yields a budgeted variable-overhead rate of $5 per process hour. Notice that we can use any activity level in Exhibit 11–3 to compute this rate.

$$\frac{\$30{,}000}{6{,}000} = \frac{\$37{,}500}{7{,}500} = \frac{\$45{,}000}{9{,}000} = \$5 \text{ per process hour}$$

DCdesserts.com's formula flexible overhead budget is shown below.

$$\begin{matrix}\text{Total budgeted}\\ \text{monthly overhead cost}\end{matrix} = (\$5 \times \text{Total process hours}) + \$15{,}000$$

To check the accuracy of the formula, compute the total budgeted overhead cost at each of the activity levels shown in Exhibit 11–3.

Activity (process hours)	Formula Flexible Overhead Budget		Budgeted Monthly Overhead Cost
6,000	$5 × 6,000 + $15,000	=	$45,000
7,500	$5 × 7,500 + $15,000	=	$52,500
9,000	$5 × 9,000 + $15,000	=	$60,000

"It's critical to understand variable and fixed overhead costs. When activity levels change, what costs will change and how?" (11b)
A.T. Kearney

The budgeted monthly overhead cost computed above is the same as that shown in Exhibit 11–3 for each activity level.

The formula flexible budget is more general than the columnar flexible budget, because the formula allows the managerial accountant to compute budgeted overhead costs at any activity level. Then the flexible-budgeted overhead cost can be used at the end of the period as a benchmark against which to compare the actual overhead costs incurred.

Overhead Application in a Standard-Costing System

LO 3

Explain how overhead is applied to Work-in-Process Inventory under standard costing.

Recall that *overhead application* refers to the addition of overhead cost to the Work-in-Process Inventory account as a product cost. In the normal-costing system, described in Chapter 3, overhead is applied as shown in the top panel of Exhibit 11–4. Overhead application is based on *actual* hours. In a standard-costing system, overhead application is based on standard hours allowed, given actual output. This system is depicted in the bottom panel of Exhibit 11–4. Notice that the difference between normal costing and standard costing, insofar as overhead is concerned, lies in the quantity of hours used.

Both normal- and standard-costing systems use a predetermined overhead rate. In a standard-costing system, the predetermined overhead rate also is referred to as the standard overhead rate. DCdesserts.com calculates its predetermined or standard overhead rate annually. The rate for the current year, computed in Exhibit 11–5, is based on *planned* activity of 7,500 process hours per month. Notice that DCdesserts.com breaks its predetermined overhead rate into a variable rate and a fixed rate. We will discuss further the use of standard costs for product costing in Appendix A at the end of this chapter.

Choice of Activity Measure

LO 4

Explain some important issues in choosing an activity measure for overhead budgeting and application.

DCdesserts.com's flexible overhead budget is based on process hours. A variety of activity measures are used in practice. Machine hours, direct-labor hours, direct-labor cost, total process time, and direct-material cost are among the most common measures. Choosing the appropriate activity measure for the flexible overhead budget is important, because the flexible budget is the chief tool for managing overhead costs.

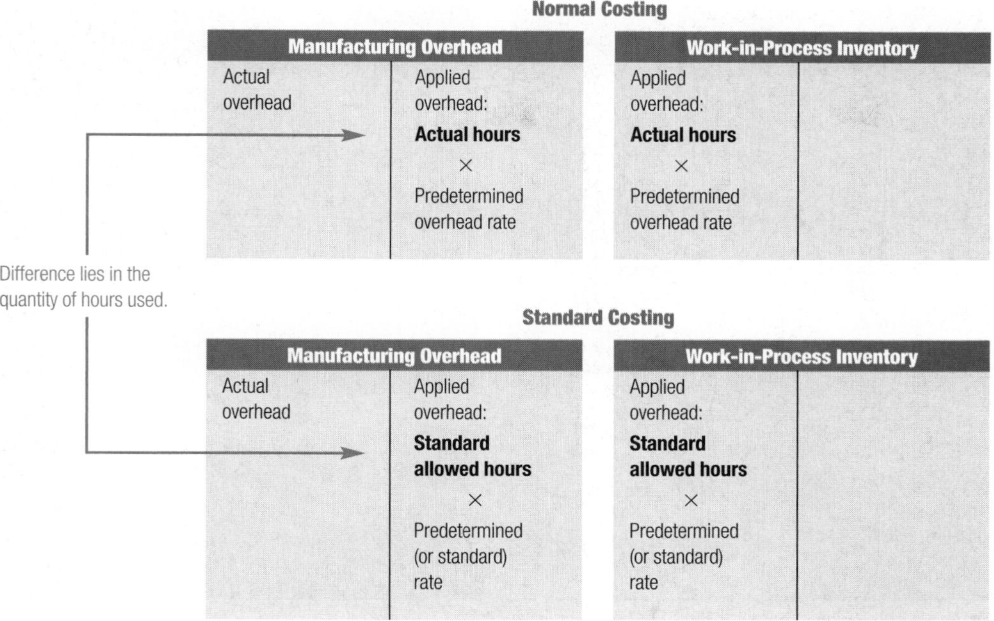

Exhibit 11–4
Overhead Application

Exhibit 11–5
Predetermined Overhead Rate: DCdesserts.com

	Budgeted Overhead	Planned Monthly Activity	Predetermined Overhead Rate
Variable	$37,500*	7,500 process hours	$5.00 per process hour
Fixed	15,000*	7,500 process hours	2.00 per process hour
Total	$52,500	7,500 process hours	$7.00 per process hour

*From the flexible budget (Exhibit 11–3) for planned monthly activity of 7,500 process hours.

Criteria for Choosing the Activity Measure

How should the managerial accountant select the activity measure for the flexible budget? The activity measure should be one that varies in a similar pattern to the way that variable overhead varies. As productive activity increases, both variable-overhead cost and the activity measure should increase in roughly the same proportion. As productive activity declines, both variable-overhead cost and the activity measure should decline in roughly the same proportion. In short, variable-overhead cost and the activity measure should *move together* as overall productive activity changes.

Changing Manufacturing Technology: Computer-Integrated Manufacturing Direct-labor time has traditionally been the most popular activity measure in manufacturing firms. However, as automation increases, more and more firms are switching to such measures as machine hours or process time for their flexible overhead budgets. Machine hours and process time are linked more closely than direct-labor hours to the robotic technology and computer-integrated manufacturing (CIM) systems common in today's manufacturing environment.

Cost Drivers As we discussed in Chapter 5, some companies have refined their cost management systems even further. *Cost drivers* are identified as the most significant factors affecting overhead costs. Then multiple overhead rates based on these cost drivers are used to compute product costs and control overhead expenditures. A

As manufacturing has become increasingly automated, direct labor is becoming less appropriate as an activity measure in flexible budgeting. Moreover, computer-integrated manufacturing entails a shift in the cost structure away from direct-labor costs and toward greater overhead costs. Left, putting the finishing touches on these violins is a labor-intensive process. Right, automated equipment like that used in this Kellogg's assembly line is commonplace in manufacturing.

relentless search for *non-value-added* costs is an integral part of such a cost management system. We will discuss the role of *activity-based costing* in flexible budgeting later in the chapter.

Beware of Dollar Measures Dollar measures, such as direct-labor or raw-material costs, often are used as the basis for flexible overhead budgeting. However, such measures have significant drawbacks, and they should be avoided. Dollar measures are subject to price-level changes and fluctuate more than physical measures. For example, the direct-labor *hours* required to produce a fancy dessert will be relatively stable over time. However, the direct-labor *cost* will vary as wage levels and fringe-benefit costs change with inflation and conditions in the labor market.

The choice of an activity measure upon which to base the flexible budget for variable overhead is really a cost-estimation problem, which is the topic addressed in Chapter 7.

Cost Management Using Overhead Cost Variances

LO 5

Compute and interpret the variable-overhead spending and efficiency variances and the fixed-overhead budget and volume variances.

The flexible overhead budget is one of the managerial accountant's primary tools for the control of manufacturing-overhead costs. At the end of each accounting period, the managerial accountant uses the flexible overhead budget to determine the level of overhead cost that should have been incurred, given the actual level of activity. Then the accountant compares the overhead cost in the flexible budget with the actual overhead cost incurred. The managerial accountant then computes four separate overhead variances, each of which conveys information useful in controlling overhead costs.

To illustrate overhead variance analysis, we will continue our illustration for DCdesserts.com.

Flexible Budget DCdesserts.com's monthly flexible overhead budget, displayed in Exhibit 11–3, shows budgeted variable and fixed manufacturing-overhead costs at three levels of production activity. During September, DCdesserts.com produced 2,000 multilayered fancy cakes. Since production standards allow three process hours per cake, the total standard allowed number of process hours is 6,000 hours.

Actual production output	2,000 multilayered fancy cakes
Standard allowed process hours per multilayered fancy cake	× 3
Total standard allowed process hours	6,000 process hours

From the 6,000 process-hour column in Exhibit 11–3, the budgeted overhead cost for September is as follows:

	Budgeted Overhead Cost for September
Variable overhead	$30,000
Fixed overhead	15,000

From the cost-accounting records, DCdesserts.com's director of cost management determined that the following overhead costs were actually incurred during September.

	Actual Cost for September
Variable overhead	$34,650
Fixed overhead	16,100
Total overhead	$50,750

The production supervisor's records indicate that the actual total process time in September was as follows:

Actual process hours for September	6,300

Notice that the actual number of process hours used (6,300) exceeds the standard allowed number of process hours, given actual production output (6,000).

We now have assembled all of the information necessary to compute DCdesserts.com's overhead variances for September.

Variable Overhead

DCdesserts.com's total variable-overhead variance for September is computed below.

Actual variable overhead	$34,650
Budgeted variable overhead	30,000
Total variable-overhead variance	$ 4,650 Unfavorable

Topic 11–2

What caused the company to spend $4,650 more than the budgeted amount on variable overhead? To discover the reasons behind this performance, the managerial accountant computes a **variable-overhead spending variance** and a **variable-overhead efficiency variance.** The computation of these variances is depicted in Exhibit 11–6.

Two equivalent formulas for the variable-overhead spending variance are shown below.

1. $\text{Variable-overhead spending variance} = \text{Actual variable overhead} - (AH \times SVR)$, or

2. $\text{Variable-overhead spending variance} = (AH \times AVR) - (AH \times SVR)$

where AH denotes actual process hours
AVR denotes actual variable-overhead rate (actual variable overhead ÷ AH)
SVR denotes standard variable-overhead rate

These two formulas are equivalent because actual variable overhead is equal to actual hours times the actual variable overhead rate (AH × AVR). Formula 2 above can be simplified:

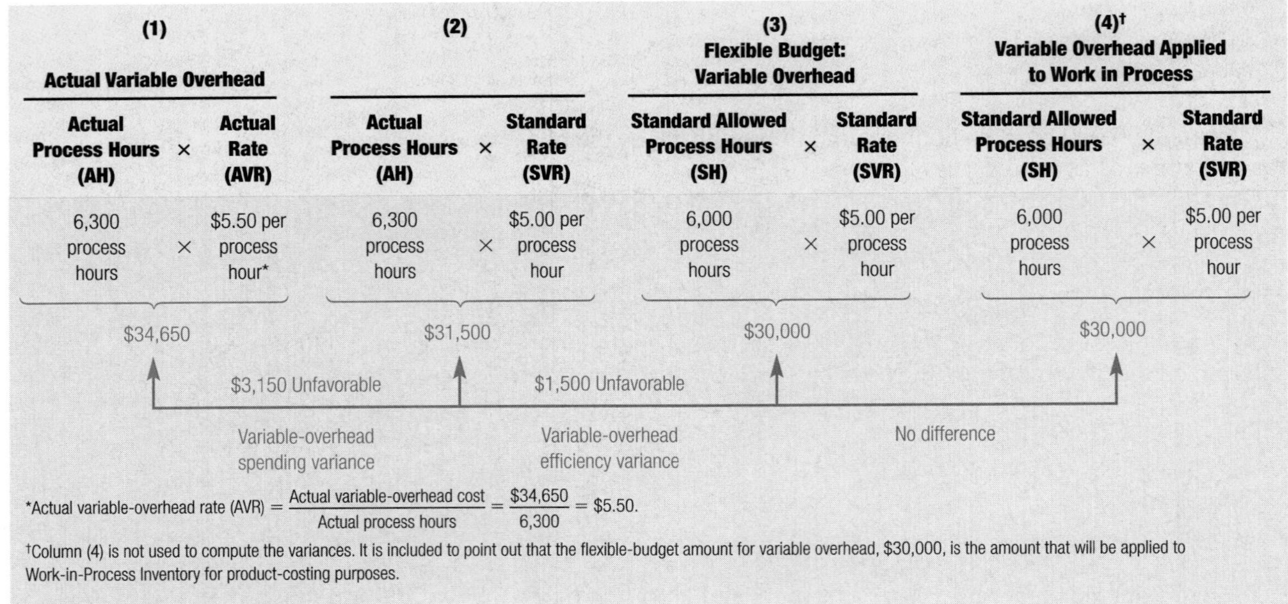

Exhibit 11–6
Variable-Overhead Spending and Efficiency Variances

3. Variable-overhead spending variance = AH(AVR − SVR)

DCdesserts.com's variable-overhead spending variance for September is computed as follows (using formula 1):

$$\text{Variable-overhead spending variance} = \text{Actual variable overhead} - (\text{AH} \times \text{SVR})$$
$$= \$34{,}650 - (6{,}300 \times \$5.00)$$
$$= \$3{,}150 \text{ Unfavorable}$$

This variance is unfavorable because the actual variable-overhead cost exceeded the expected amount, after adjusting that expectation for the actual number of process hours used.

As Exhibit 11–6 shows, the following formula defines the variable-overhead efficiency variance.

$$\text{Variable-overhead efficiency variance} = (\text{AH} \times \text{SVR}) - (\text{SH} \times \text{SVR})$$

where SH denotes standard process hours

Writing this formula more simply, we have the following expression.

$$\text{Variable-overhead efficiency variance} = \text{SVR}(\text{AH} - \text{SH})$$

DCdesserts.com's variable-overhead efficiency variance for September is computed as follows:

$$\text{Variable-overhead efficiency variance} = \text{SVR}(\text{AH} - \text{SH})$$
$$= \$5.00(6{,}300 - 6{,}000)$$
$$= \$1{,}500 \text{ Unfavorable}$$

This variance is unfavorable because actual process hours exceeded standard allowed process hours, given actual output.

Product Costing versus Cost Management Columns (1), (2), and (3) in Exhibit 11–6 are used to compute the variances for *cost-management purposes.* Column (4) in the exhibit shows the variable overhead applied to work in process for the *product-*

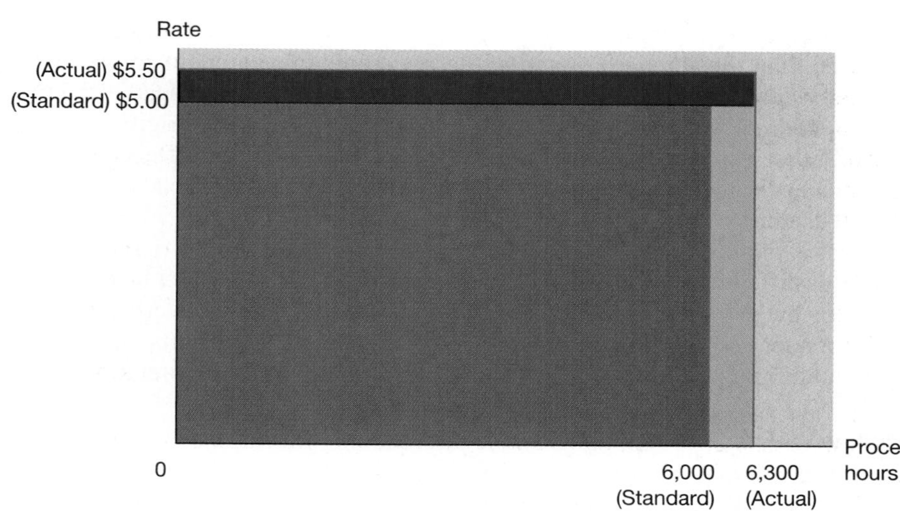

Exhibit 11–7
Graphical Analysis of Variable-Overhead Variances

costing purpose. Notice that the variable-overhead cost on the flexible budget, $30,000, is the same as the amount applied to work in process.

Graphing Variable-Overhead Variances Exhibit 11–7 provides a graphical analysis of DCdesserts.com's variable-overhead variances for September. The graph shows the variable-overhead rate per process hour on the vertical axis. The standard rate is $5.00 per process hour, while the actual rate is $5.50 per process hour (actual variable-overhead cost of $34,650 divided by actual process hours of 6,300). Process hours are shown on the horizontal axis.

The blue area on the graph represents the flexible-budget amount for variable overhead, given actual September output of 2,000 multilayered fancy cakes. The large area on the graph enclosed by colored lines on the top and right sides represents actual variable-overhead cost. The colored area in between, representing the total variable-overhead variance, is divided into the spending and efficiency variances.

Managerial Interpretation of Variable-Overhead Variances What do the variable-overhead variances mean? What information do they convey to management? The formulas for computing the variable-overhead variances resemble those used to compute the direct-labor variances. To see this, compare Exhibit 11–6 (variable overhead) with Exhibit 10–3 (direct labor).

Despite the similar formulas, the interpretation of the variable-overhead variances is quite different from that applicable to the direct-labor variances.

Efficiency Variance Recall that an unfavorable direct-labor efficiency variance results when more direct labor is used than the standard allowed quantity. Thus, direct labor has been used inefficiently, relative to the standard. However, that is not the proper interpretation of an unfavorable variable-overhead efficiency variance. DCdesserts.com's variable-overhead efficiency variance did *not* result from using more of the variable-overhead items, such as electricity and indirect material, than the standard allowed amount. Instead, this variance resulted when the division used *more process hours* than the standard quantity, given actual output. Recall that the company's director of cost management has found that variable-overhead cost varies in a pattern similar to that with which process hours vary. Since 300 more process hours were used than the standard quantity, the division's management should expect that variable-overhead costs will be greater. Thus, the variable-overhead efficiency variance has nothing to do with efficient or inefficient usage of electricity, indirect material, and other variable-overhead items. This variance simply reflects an adjustment in the managerial accountant's expectation about variable-overhead cost, because the division used more than the standard quantity of process hours.

What is the important difference between direct labor and variable overhead that causes this different interpretation of the efficiency variance? Direct labor is a traceable cost and is budgeted on the basis of direct-labor hours. Variable overhead, on the other hand, is a pool of *indirect* costs that are budgeted on the basis of *process hours*. The indirect nature of variable-overhead costs causes the different interpretation.

Spending Variance An unfavorable direct-labor rate variance is straightforward to interpret; the actual labor rate *per hour* exceeds the standard rate. Although the formula for computing the variable-overhead spending variance is similar to that for the direct-labor rate variance, its interpretation is quite different.

An unfavorable spending variance simply means that the total actual cost of variable overhead is greater than expected, after adjusting for the actual quantity of process hours used. An unfavorable spending variance could result from paying a higher than expected price per unit for variable-overhead items. Or, the variance could result from using more of the variable-overhead items than expected.

Suppose, for example, that electricity were the only variable-overhead cost item. An unfavorable variable-overhead spending variance could result from paying a higher than expected price per kilowatt-hour for electricity, from using more than the expected amount of electricity, or from both.

Management of Variable Overhead Costs Since the variable-overhead efficiency variance says nothing about efficient or inefficient usage of variable overhead, the spending variance is the real control variance for variable overhead. Managers can use the spending variance to alert them if variable-overhead costs are out of line with expectations.

Fixed Overhead

To analyze performance with regard to fixed overhead, the managerial accountant calculates two fixed-overhead variances.

Fixed-Overhead Budget Variance The variance used by managers to control fixed overhead is called the **fixed-overhead budget variance.** It is defined as follows:

$$\text{Fixed-overhead budget variance} = \text{Actual fixed overhead} - \text{Budgeted fixed overhead}$$

DCdesserts.com's fixed-overhead budget variance for September is as follows:

$$\begin{aligned}\text{Fixed-overhead budget variance} &= \text{Actual fixed overhead} - \text{Budgeted fixed overhead}\\ &= \$16{,}100 - \$15{,}000^{*}\\ &= \$1{,}100 \text{ Unfavorable}\end{aligned}$$

*From the flexible budget (Exhibit 11–3).

The fixed-overhead budget variance is unfavorable, because the company spent more than the budgeted amount on fixed overhead. Notice that we need not specify an activity level to determine budgeted fixed overhead. All three columns in the flexible budget (Exhibit 11–3) specify $15,000 as budgeted fixed overhead.

Fixed-Overhead Volume Variance The **fixed-overhead volume variance** is defined as follows:

$$\text{Fixed-overhead volume variance} = \text{Budgeted fixed overhead} - \text{Applied fixed overhead}$$

DCdesserts.com's applied fixed overhead for September is $12,000:

$$\begin{aligned}\text{Applied fixed overhead} &= \text{Predetermined fixed overhead rate} \times \text{Standard allowed hours} \\ &= \$2.00 \text{ per process hour} \times 6{,}000 \text{ process hours} \\ &= \$12{,}000\end{aligned}$$

The $2.00 predetermined fixed-overhead rate was calculated in Exhibit 11–5. The 6,000 standard allowed process hours is based on actual September production of 2,000 multilayered fancy cakes, each with a standard allowance of three process hours.

DCdesserts.com's fixed-overhead volume variance is calculated below.

$$\begin{aligned}\text{Fixed-overhead volume variance} &= \text{Budgeted fixed overhead} - \text{Applied fixed overhead} \\ &= \$15{,}000 - \$12{,}000 \\ &= \$3{,}000 \text{ Unfavorable}\end{aligned}$$

Managerial Interpretation of Fixed-Overhead Variances Exhibit 11–8 shows DCdesserts. com's two fixed-overhead variances for September. The budget variance is the real control variance for fixed overhead, because it compares actual expenditures with budgeted fixed-overhead costs.

The volume variance provides a way of reconciling two different purposes of the cost management system. For the *control purpose,* the system recognizes that fixed overhead does not change as production activity varies. Hence, budgeted fixed overhead is the same at all activity levels in the flexible budget. (Review Exhibit 11–3 to verify this.) Budgeted fixed overhead is the basis for controlling fixed overhead, because it provides the benchmark against which actual expenditures are compared.

For the *product-costing purpose* of the system, budgeted fixed overhead is divided by planned activity to obtain a predetermined (or standard) fixed-overhead rate. For

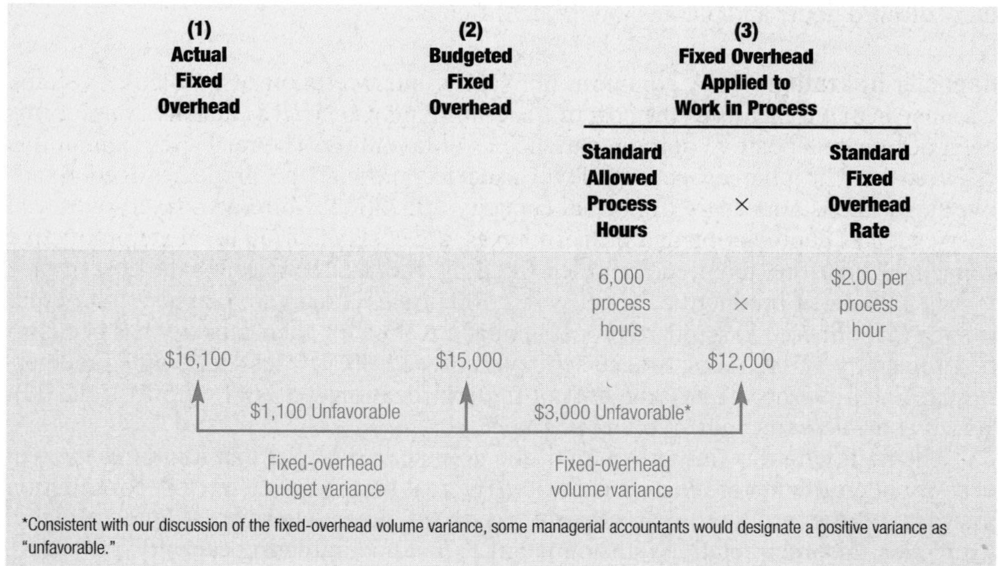

Exhibit 11–8
Fixed-Overhead Budget and Volume Variances

Exhibit 11–9
Budgeted versus Applied Fixed Overhead

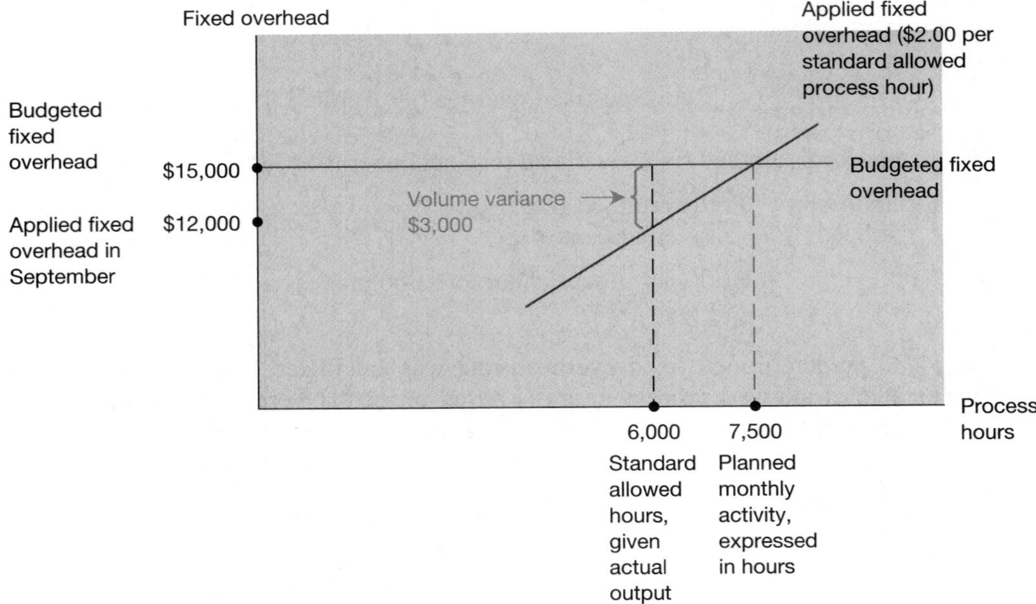

DCdesserts.com, this rate is $2.00 per process hour (budgeted fixed overhead of $15,000 divided by planned activity of 7,500 process hours). This predetermined rate is then used to apply fixed overhead to Work-in-Process Inventory. During any period in which the standard allowed number of process hours, given actual output, differs from the planned level of process hours, the budgeted fixed overhead differs from applied fixed overhead.

Exhibit 11–9 illustrates this point graphically. Budgeted fixed overhead is constant at $15,000 for all levels of activity. However, applied fixed overhead increases with activity, since fixed overhead is applied to Work-in-Process Inventory at the rate of $2.00 per standard allowed process hour. Notice that budgeted and applied fixed overhead are equal *only* if the number of standard allowed hours equals the planned activity level of 7,500 process hours. When this happens, there is no fixed-overhead volume variance. DCdesserts.com has a $3,000 volume variance in September because the standard allowed hours and planned hours are different.

Capacity Utilization A common, but faulty, interpretation of a positive volume variance is that it measures the cost of underutilizing productive capacity. Some firms even designate a positive volume variance as unfavorable. The reasoning behind this view is that the planned activity level used to compute the predetermined fixed-overhead rate is a measure of normal capacity utilization. Moreover, fixed-overhead costs, such as depreciation and property taxes, are costs incurred to create productive capacity. Therefore, the predetermined fixed-overhead rate measures the cost of providing an hour of productive capacity. If 7,500 process hours are planned, but output is such that only 6,000 standard process hours are allowed, then capacity has been underutilized by 1,500 hours. Since each hour costs $2.00 (DCdesserts.com's predetermined fixed-overhead rate), the cost of underutilization is $3,000 (1,500 × $2.00), which is DCdesserts.com's volume variance.

The fault with this interpretation of the volume variance is that it ignores the real cost of underutilizing productive capacity. The real cost is due to the lost contribution margins of the products that are not produced when capacity is underutilized. Moreover, this interpretation fails to recognize that underutilizing capacity and reducing inventory may be a wise managerial response to slackening demand.

For this reason, many managerial accountants interpret the volume variance merely as a way of reconciling the two purposes of the cost management system. Moreover, these managerial accountants would choose not to designate the volume variance as either favorable or unfavorable. However, some accountants designate a positive volume variance as *unfavorable.* Their reasoning is that when the volume variance is closed into Cost of Goods Sold expense at the end of the accounting period (as explained in Appendix A), the effect is to increase Cost of Goods Sold, which in turn has an *unfavorable* effect on income. In contrast, other accountants argue that no sign (favorable or unfavorable) should be assigned to the fixed-overhead volume variance.

Overhead Cost Performance Report

Prepare an overhead cost performance report.

The variable-overhead spending and efficiency variances and the fixed-overhead budget variance can be computed for each overhead cost item in the flexible budget. When these itemized variances are presented along with actual and budgeted costs for each overhead item, the result is an **overhead cost performance report.** DCdesserts.com's performance report is displayed in Exhibit 11–10. This report would be used by management to exercise control over each of the division's overhead costs.

Notice that the performance report includes only spending and efficiency variances for the variable items, and only a budget variance for the fixed items. Upon receiving this report, a manager might investigate the relatively large variances for indirect maintenance labor, electricity, and production supervisory labor.

Management Accounting Practice

COST MANAGEMENT SYSTEMS IN GERMANY

Throughout the world, flexible budgeting is found in cost management systems as a means of controlling overhead costs. In Germany, for example, *grenzplankostenrechnung* (or "flexible standard costing") exhibits many of the features illustrated in this chapter. Under the German approach "each cost center distinguishes between variable costs (e.g., energy) and fixed costs (e.g., a manager's salary)." The number of machine hours is a common activity measure. "For purposes of cost planning and control, companies budget each cost center's expenses and then distribute the expenses to each month of the budget year. The budgeted costs are standards for efficient resource consumption. . . ." The cost and performance information "allows for effective discussions about productivity improvement" among department managers, management accountants, and plant managers.[1]

Activity-Based Flexible Budget

Explain how an activity-based flexible budget differs from a conventional flexible budget.

The flexible budget shown in Exhibit 11–3, which underlies our variance analysis for DCdesserts.com, is based on a single cost driver. Overhead costs that vary with respect to *process hours* are categorized as variable; all other overhead costs are treated as fixed. This approach is consistent with traditional, volume-based product-costing systems.

Under the more accurate product-costing method called activity-based costing, several cost drivers are identified.[2] Costs that may appear fixed with respect to a single volume-based cost driver, such as process hours, may be variable with respect to some other cost driver. The activity-based costing approach can also be used as the basis for a

[1]Gaiser, Bernd, "German Cost Management Systems," *Journal of Cost Management* 11, no. 5 (September/October 1997), pp. 35–41.

[2]Activity-based costing, introduced conceptually in Chapter 3, is explored in detail in Chapter 5.

	(1) Flexible Budget (for 6,000 process hr.)	(2) Standard Rate per Process Hr. [variable costs only; col. (1) ÷ 6,000 process hr.]	(3) 6,300 Actual Process Hr. × Standard Rate	(4) Actual Cost	(5) Spending Variance [col. (4) – col. (3)]	(6) Efficiency Variance [col. (3) – col. (1)]	(7) Budget Variance [col. (4) – col. (1)]
Variable costs:							
Indirect material:							
Nonstick cooking spray	$12,000	$2.00	$12,600	$12,700	$100 U	$600 U	
Waxed paper	2,000	.33	2,079	2,090	11 U	79 U	
Other paper products	2,000	.33	2,079	2,000	(79) F	79 U	
Miscellaneous supplies	6,000	1.00	6,300	6,500	200 U	300 U	
Indirect labor:							
Maintenance	4,000	.67	4,221	6,400	2,179 U	221 U	
Utilities:							
Electricity	3,000	.50	3,150	4,050	900 U	150 U	
Natural gas	1,000	.17	1,071	910	(161) F	71 U	
Total variable cost	$30,000	$5.00	$31,500	$34,650	$3,150 U	$1,500 U	
Fixed costs:							
Indirect labor:							
Inspection	$ 2,200			$ 2,210			$ 10 U
Production supervisors	6,000			7,000			1,000 U
Setup	3,000			3,000			–0–
Material handling	2,000			2,000			–0–
Depreciation:							
Plant and equipment	500			500			–0–
Insurance and property taxes	100			100			–0–
Test kitchen	1,200			1,290			90 U
Total fixed cost	$15,000			$16,100			$1,100 U
Total overhead cost	$45,000			$50,750			$1,100 U
Total variance between actual overhead cost and flexible budget		$5,750 U		Sum of spending, efficiency, and budget variances →		$5,750 U	

Exhibit 11–10
Overhead Cost Performance Report: DCdesserts.com

"ABC provides a methodology for tracking costs by product and establishing more appropriate linkages of resources to products through the use of activity analysis." (11c)
BlueCross BlueShield of North Carolina

flexible budget for planning and cost management purposes. Exhibit 11–11 displays an **activity-based flexible budget** for DCdesserts.com, using the same data as Exhibit 11–3.

Compare the conventional flexible budget (Exhibit 11–3) and the activity-based flexible budget (Exhibit 11–11). The key difference lies in the costs that were categorized as fixed on the conventional flexible budget. These costs are fixed with respect to process hours but are not fixed with respect to other more appropriate cost drivers. For example, cost pool II includes inspection and setup costs, which vary with respect to the number of production runs.

Effect on Performance Reporting The activity-based flexible budget provides a more accurate prediction (and benchmark) of overhead costs. For example, suppose that activity in December is as follows:

December Activity	Process hours	6,000
	Production runs	12
	New products tested	40
	Direct material handled (pounds)	30,000

Exhibit 11–11
Activity-Based Flexible Budget

DCDESSERTS.COM
Monthly Flexible Overhead Budget

Budgeted Cost		**Level of Activity**	
Cost Pool I (cost driver: process hours)	**6,000**	**7,500**	**9,000**
Indirect material:			
Nonstick cooking spray	$12,000	$15,000	$18,000
Waxed paper	2,000	2,500	3,000
Other paper products	2,000	2,500	3,000
Miscellaneous supplies	6,000	7,500	9,000
Indirect labor: maintenance	4,000	5,000	6,000
Utilities:			
Electricity	3,000	3,750	4,500
Natural gas	1,000	1,250	1,500
Total of cost pool I	$30,000	$37,500	$45,000
Cost Pool II (cost driver: production runs)	**8**	**12**	**16**
Indirect labor:			
Inspection	$ 2,200	$ 3,300	$ 4,400
Setup	3,000	4,500	6,000
Total of cost pool II	$ 5,200	$ 7,800	$10,400
Cost Pool III (cost driver: new products tested)	**20**	**30**	**40**
Test kitchen	$ 1,200	$ 1,800	$ 2,400
Total of cost pool III	$ 1,200	$ 1,800	$ 2,400
Cost Pool IV (cost driver: pounds of material handled)	**20,000**	**30,000**	**40,000**
Material handling	$ 2,000	$ 3,000	$ 4,000
Total of cost pool IV	$ 2,000	$ 3,000	$ 4,000
Cost Pool V (facility level costs)			
Indirect labor: production supervisors	$ 6,000	$ 6,000	$ 6,000
Depreciation: plant and equipment	500	500	500
Insurance and property taxes	100	100	100
Total of cost pool V	$ 6,600	$ 6,600	$ 6,600
Total overhead cost	**$45,000**	**$56,700**	**$68,400**

The following table compares the budgeted cost levels for several overhead items on the conventional and activity-based flexible budgets.

Overhead Cost Item	**Conventional Flexible Budget**	**Activity-Based Flexible Budget**
Electricity	$3,000	$3,000
Inspection	2,200	3,300
Setup	3,000	4,500
Test kitchen	1,200	2,400
Material handling	2,000	3,000
Insurance and property taxes	100	100

The budgeted electricity cost is the same on both budgets, because both use the same cost driver (process hours). Insurance and property taxes are also the same, because both budgets recognize these as facility-level fixed costs. However, the other overhead costs are budgeted at different levels, because the conventional and activity-based flexible budgets use *different cost drivers* for these items. While the conventional budget

"In the past decade, Whirlpool has faced increasing competition, higher overhead, and greater product diversity. Managers initiated and supported ABC to obtain accurate information for dealing with these challenges." (11d)

Whirlpool

"ABC has enhanced our clients' ability to manage overhead costs through flexible budgeting systems." (11e)

A. T. Kearney

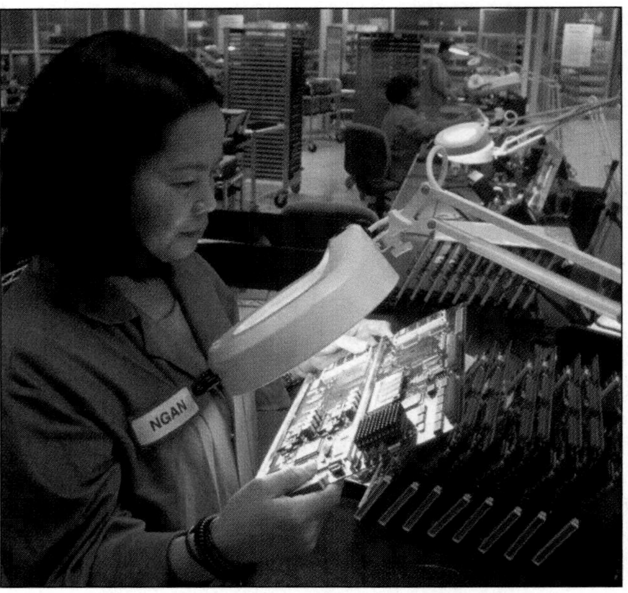

An activity-based flexible budget is based on several cost drivers. For example, the cost driver for equipment maintenance costs might be process hours, while the cost driver for inspection costs could be production runs. An appropriate cost driver for material handling often is the number of setups. Pictured here is the inspection of circuit boards in Lake Forest, California.

treats inspection, setup, test kitchen, and material-handling costs as fixed, the activity-based flexible budget shows that they are all variable with respect to the appropriate cost driver.

These differences are important for performance reporting. The activity-based flexible budget provides a more accurate benchmark against which to compare actual costs. Suppose the actual inspection cost in December is $3,000. Using the conventional flexible budget would result in an unfavorable variance of $800 ($3,000 − $2,200). However, the activity-based flexible budget yields a favorable variance of $300 ($3,000 − $3,300).

To summarize, activity-based flexible budgeting provides a richer view of cost behavior and the underlying cost drivers, and it provides a valuable tool for cost management.[3]

Focus on Ethics

MISSTATED STANDARDS AFFECT ACCURACY OF REPORTS

The scenario described here, while placed in the context of a fictitious enterprise, is based on an actual situation that occurred at NuTone Housing Group, which at the time was a subsidiary of Scoville, Inc.[4]

To set the stage, consider these facts about the standard-costing system in place at Shrood Division, a subsidiary of Gigantic Enterprises, Inc. Shrood Division manufactures a wide range of electric household products, such as lighting, fans, water pumps, and security systems. The division manufactures approximately 10,000 products, made from over 70,000 components. Tom Cleverly has run the division in what he calls a hands-on manner for over a quarter century. When Shrood Division was acquired by Gigantic Enterprises a decade ago, Cleverly was at first unhappy with the merger, but it soon became apparent that Gigantic's top management would let him run the business the way he was used to running it. Three aspects of Cleverly's management style are noteworthy. First, he insists on being involved in all major pricing decisions; he's not a delegator. Second, he has developed a second-level management that is loyal and supportive of his approach. Third, he has refused to lower the direct-labor time standards for years, even though many productivity improvements have been made. At present, the actual direct-labor times are on average only about a third of the standard times. Moreover, since manufacturing overhead is applied on the basis of direct labor, both the standard direct-labor and the standard overhead costs are inflated relative to actual costs.

The implications of this practice are that huge favorable variances are experienced all year long in both direct labor and overhead. Cleverly has used these favorable variances to "manage the quarterly earnings" reported by Shrood Division to corporate. Cleverly has instructed his manager of accounting, Evan

[3]For further reading on this topic, see Robert E. Malcolm, "Overhead Control Implications of Activity Costing," *Accounting Horizons* 5, no. 4, pp. 69–78; Y. T. Mak and Melvin L. Roush, "Flexible Budgeting and Variance Analysis in an Activity-Based Costing Environment," *Accounting Horizons* 8, no. 2 (June 1994), pp. 93–103; and Robert S. Kaplan, "Flexible Budgeting in an Activity-Based Costing Framework," *Accounting Horizons* 8, no. 2 (June 1994), pp. 104–9.

[4]"Scoville: NuTone Housing Group," a management accounting case, published by Harvard Business School.

Twixt, to release just enough of the favorable variances into Cost of Goods Sold (CGS) on a quarterly basis to ensure that Shrood Division just meets its earnings target in the budget. Then at the end of the year, the remainder of this large favorable variance is released into CGS, with the result that Shrood Division ends each year with fourth-quarter earnings far in excess of the target. Like a knight in shining white armor, Shrood Division saves the day for Gigantic Enterprises year after year. Shrood has come to be known in corporate circles as "the jewel in the crown of Gigantic Enterprises."

Now for the conflict. Gigantic has hired a new corporate controller, Jeffrey Fixit, whose charge is to introduce more consistency in the reporting methods of Gigantic's various divisions. When Fixit visited Shrood Division and discovered what was going on, he tried to get Tom Cleverly to instruct Evan Twixt to correct the direct-labor standards to reflect attainable results (i.e., reality). Cleverly has refused, though, and Fixit doesn't have the power to force him to do so. Meanwhile, poor Twixt is caught in the middle.

Here is what each of them had to say about the situation.

Cleverly (division manager): "I've been running this business for 25 years. And you know what? We've been profitable for 25 years! The high labor standards help me make sure that neither I nor my salespeople shave prices too much. It's like setting the clock 10 minutes ahead to make sure you're not late. We always make budget. We always report the highest profits in the company. And we are, in fact, the 'jewel in the crown.'"

Fixit (corporate controller): "This is a really bad situation. Shrood is reporting fictitious numbers to corporate on a quarterly basis, which then get rolled up into Gigantic's quarterly results. Then these numbers get published to the shareholders. We're misleading them. I don't have the authority to get Tom Cleverly to fix the problem. I can, however, go to the board of directors and explain to them that they need to get Cleverly to do what needs to be done."

Twixt (Shrood's accounting manager): "I'm caught in the middle. We basically have two sets of books: the ones based on Mr. Cleverly's labor standards, and the ones based on the more accurate results that Mr. Fixit wants. I can report either set of results. I feel like I'm serving two gods—and so far I'm getting away with it."

What do you make of this situation? Can a company that keeps two sets of books be well managed? What ethical issues do you see here? What actions should Cleverly, Twixt, and Fixit take?

Chapter Summary

Overhead is a heterogeneous pool of indirect costs. Since overhead costs cannot be traced easily to products or services, a flexible budget is used to budget overhead costs at various levels of activity. A columnar flexible budget is based on several distinct activity levels, while a formula flexible budget is valid for a continuous range of activity. The flexible overhead budget is based on some activity measure that varies in a pattern similar to that of variable overhead. Machine hours, process time, and direct-labor hours are common activity bases.

In a standard-costing system, the flexible budget is used to control overhead costs. The managerial accountant uses the amount of overhead cost specified by the flexible budget as a benchmark against which to compare actual overhead costs. The accountant computes four overhead variances: the variable-overhead spending and efficiency variances and the fixed-overhead budget and volume variances. These variances help management to control overhead costs.

The managerial accountant also uses the standard or predetermined overhead rate as the basis for product costing in a standard-costing system. The amount of overhead cost entered into Work-in-Process Inventory is equal to the standard overhead rate multiplied by the standard allowed amount of the activity base, given actual output.

When an activity-based costing system is in use, an activity-based flexible budget may be developed. Such a flexible budget is more accurate than conventional budgets, because multiple cost drivers are identified to explain the behavior of overhead costs.

Review Problem on Overhead Variances

In November DCdesserts.com produced 3,000 multilayered fancy cakes, used 9,100 hours of process time, and incurred the following manufacturing-overhead costs.

Variable overhead	$45,955
Fixed overhead	$15,800

DCdesserts.com's monthly flexible overhead budget for November is the same as that given in Exhibit 11–3.

Compute DCdesserts.com's variable-overhead variances using the format shown in Exhibit 11–6. Compute the company's fixed-overhead variances using the format shown in Exhibit 11–8.

Solution to Review Problem

The solution to the review problem is given in Exhibits 11–12 and 11–13.

Exhibit 11–12
Variable-Overhead Spending and Efficiency Variances: Review Problem

(1) Actual Variable Overhead			(2)			(3) Flexible Budget: Variable Overhead			(4)† Variable Overhead Applied to Work in Process		
Actual Process Hours (AH)	×	Actual Rate (AVR)	Actual Process Hours (AH)	×	Standard Rate (SVR)	Standard Allowed Process Hours (SH)	×	Standard Rate (SVR)	Standard Allowed Process Hours (SH)	×	Standard Rate (SVR)
9,100 process hours	×	$5.05 per process hour*	9,100 process hours	×	$5.00 per process hour	9,000 process hours	×	$5.00 per process hour	9,000 process hours	×	$5.00 per process hour
$45,955			$45,500			$45,000			$45,000		

(1) → (2): $455 Unfavorable — Variable-overhead spending variance

(2) → (3): $500 Unfavorable — Variable-overhead efficiency variance

(3) → (4): No difference

*Actual variable-overhead rate (AVR) $= \frac{\text{Actual variable-overhead cost}}{\text{Actual process hours}} = \frac{\$45,955}{9,100} = \$5.05$

†Column (4) is not used to compute the variances. It is included to point out that the flexible-budget amount for variable overhead, $45,000, is the amount that will be applied to Work-in-Process Inventory for product-costing purposes.

Exhibit 11–13
Fixed-Overhead Budget and Volume Variances: Review Problem

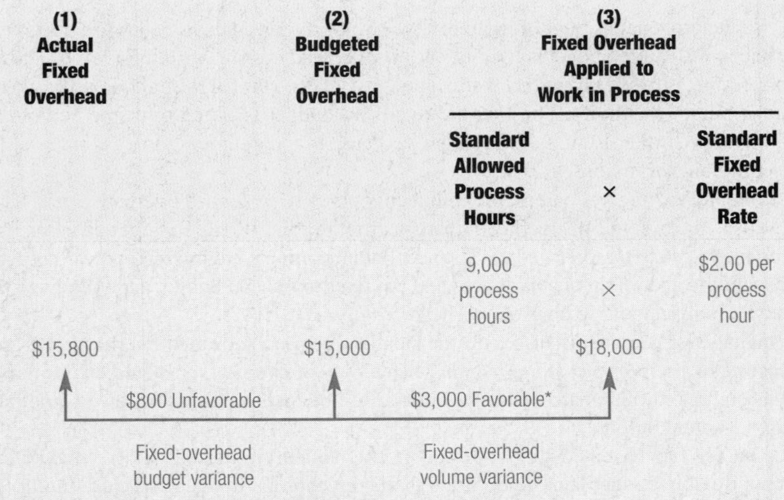

*Some managerial accountants would designate a negative fixed-overhead volume variance as "favorable."

Key Terms

For each term's definition refer to the indicated page, or turn to the glossary at the end of the text.

activity-based flexible budget, 474
fixed-overhead budget variance, 470
fixed-overhead volume variance, 471
flexible budget, 460
overhead cost performance report, 473
sales-price variance,* 481
sales-volume variance,* 481
static budget, 460
total contribution margin,* 481
unit contribution margin,* 481
variable-overhead efficiency variance, 467
variable-overhead spending variance, 467

*Term appears in Appendix B.

Appendix A to Chapter 11

Standard Costs and Product Costing

In a standard-costing system, the standard costs are used for product costing as well as for cost control. The costs of direct material, direct labor, and manufacturing overhead are all entered into Work-in-Process Inventory at their standard costs. (Review Exhibit 11–4.)

LO 8

After completing Appendix A, prepare journal entries to record manufacturing overhead under standard costing.

Journal Entries under Standard Costing During September, DCdesserts.com incurred actual manufacturing-overhead costs of $50,750, which includes $34,650 of variable overhead and $16,100 of fixed overhead. A summary journal entry to record these actual expenditures follows.

Manufacturing Overhead	50,750	
Indirect-Material Inventory		23,290*
Wages Payable		20,610*
Utilities Payable		4,960
Accumulated Depreciation		500
Prepaid Insurance and Property Taxes		100
Test Kitchen Salaries Payable		1,290

*The credit amounts can be verified in column (4) of Exhibit 11–10. For example, indirect-material costs amounted to $23,290 ($12,700 + $2,090 + $2,000 + $6,500). The credit to Wages Payable is for indirect-labor costs, which amounted to $20,610 ($6,400 + $2,210 + $7,000 + $3,000 + $2,000).

The application of manufacturing overhead to Work-in-Process Inventory is based on a predetermined overhead rate of $7.00 per process hour (the total of the variable and the fixed rates) and 6,000 standard allowed process hours, given an actual output of 2,000 multilayered fancy cakes. The summary journal entry is as follows:

Work-in-Process Inventory	42,000	
Manufacturing Overhead		42,000*

*Applied overhead = $7.00 × 6,000 = $42,000

Now the Manufacturing Overhead account appears as follows:

Manufacturing Overhead			
Actual	$50,750	$42,000	Applied

The *underapplied overhead* for September is $8,750 ($50,750 − $42,000). This means that the overhead applied to Work-in-Process Inventory in September was $8,750 less than the actual overhead cost incurred. Notice that the underapplied overhead is equal to the sum of the four overhead variances for September. The total of the four overhead variances will always be equal to the overapplied or underapplied overhead for the accounting period.[5]

Disposition of Variances As explained in the preceding chapter, variances are temporary accounts, and most companies close them directly into Cost of Goods Sold at the end of each accounting period. The journal entry required to close out DCdesserts.com's underapplied overhead for September is as follows:

Cost of Goods Sold	8,750	
Manufacturing Overhead		8,750

The journal entry to close out underapplied or overapplied overhead typically is made only annually, rather than monthly.

An alternative accounting treatment is to prorate underapplied or overapplied overhead among Work-in-Process Inventory, Finished-Goods Inventory, and Cost of Goods Sold, as explained in Chapter 3.

A Note on Perishable Products and JIT Production Management Systems As noted in the preceding chapter, traditional manufacturing systems typically exhibit the cost flows explained in this section. Direct-material, direct-labor, and manufacturing-overhead costs are entered in Work-in-Process Inventory, from which they flow into Finished-Goods Inventory when the goods are finished, and then on into Cost of Goods Sold. Since DCdesserts.com produces perishable goods, which are produced and sold on the same day, a simpler procedure could be used. In DCdesserts.com's case, the *standard* costs of direct material, direct labor, and manufacturing overhead could be entered directly into Cost of Goods Sold as they are incurred. This simplified procedure could be used, because the production process is very short and the goods are sold immediately. Thus, there is never any work-in-process inventory or finished-goods inventory on hand. Such situations are common with producers of perishable goods.

An analogous situation occurs in manufacturers that employ a just-in-time (JIT) production and inventory control system. In a JIT environment, raw materials are delivered just in time to be entered into production, and parts or components are manufactured in each stage of the production process just in time for the next production stage. Thus, like the case of perishable goods, there is little or no work-in-process or finished-goods inventory at any given time in a JIT environment. For this reason, many manufacturers that employ the JIT approach make use of highly simplified cost accounting procedures similar to those explained in the preceding paragraph for DCdesserts.com.

Appendix B to Chapter 11

Sales Variances

LO 9

After completing Appendix B, compute and interpret the sales-price and sales-volume variances.

The variances discussed in Chapters 10 and 11 focus on production costs. Managerial accountants also compute variances to help management analyze the firm's sales performance. To illustrate two commonly used sales variances, we will continue our discussion of DCdesserts.com. The expected sales price and standard variable cost for a multilayered fancy cake are as follows:

[5]Overapplied and underapplied manufacturing overhead are discussed in Chapter 3.

Expected sales price	$38
Standard variable costs:	
Direct material	$ 7
Direct labor	10
Variable overhead (3 process hours at $5 per hour)	15
Total unit variable cost	$32

The difference between the sales price and the unit variable cost is called the **unit contribution margin.** DCdesserts.com's unit contribution margin is $6 per multilayered fancy cake ($38 − $32). This is the amount that the sale of one multilayered fancy cake contributes toward covering the company's fixed costs and making a profit.

During October, DCdesserts.com's management expects to sell 1,500 multilayered fancy cakes. Based on this sales forecast, the controller computed the following budgeted **total contribution margin.**

Budgeted sales revenue (1,500 multilayered fancy cakes × $38)	$57,000
Budgeted variable costs (1,500 multilayered fancy cakes × $32)	48,000
Budgeted total contribution margin (1,500 multilayered fancy cakes × $6)	$ 9,000

The *actual* results for October were as follows:

Actual sales volume	1,600 cakes
Actual sales price	$37
Actual unit variable cost	$32

Using these actual results, DCdesserts.com's actual total contribution margin for October is:

Actual sales revenue (1,600 multilayered fancy cakes × $37)	$59,200
Actual variable costs (1,600 multilayered fancy cakes × $32)	51,200
Actual total contribution margin (1,600 multilayered fancy cakes × $5)	$ 8,000

DCdesserts.com's actual total contribution margin was $1,000 less in October than the budgeted amount. What caused this variance?

Two partially offsetting effects are present. First, the division sold more multilayered fancy cakes than expected. This will cause the total contribution margin to increase. Second, the sales price was lower than expected, and this will cause the total contribution margin to decline. The managerial accountant computes two sales variances to reflect these facts. These variances are defined and computed for DCdesserts.com as follows:

$$\text{Sales-price variance} = \begin{pmatrix} \text{Actual} & & \text{Expected} \\ \text{sales} & - & \text{sales} \\ \text{price} & & \text{price} \end{pmatrix} \times \text{Actual sales volume}$$

$$= (\$37 - \$38) \times 1{,}600$$

$$= \$1{,}600 \text{ Unfavorable}$$

$$\text{Sales-volume variance} = \begin{pmatrix} \text{Actual} & & \text{Budgeted} \\ \text{sales} & - & \text{sales} \\ \text{volume} & & \text{volume} \end{pmatrix} \times \begin{matrix} \text{Budgeted unit} \\ \text{contribution} \\ \text{margin} \end{matrix}$$

$$= (1{,}600 - 1{,}500) \times \$6$$

$$= \$600 \text{ Favorable}$$

Together, the **sales-price** and **sales-volume variances** explain the $1,000 variance between actual and budgeted total contribution margin. (Note that in this example, actual and budgeted variable cost is the same.)

Sales-price variance	$1,600 Unfavorable
Sales-volume variance	600 Favorable
Variance between actual and budgeted total contribution margin	$1,000 Unfavorable

Review Questions

11–1. Distinguish between static and flexible budgets.

11–2. Explain the advantage of using a flexible budget.

11–3. Why are flexible overhead budgets based on an activity measure, such as hours of process time, machine time, or direct-labor hours?

11–4. Distinguish between a columnar and a formula flexible budget.

11–5. Show, using T-accounts, how manufacturing overhead is added to Work-in-Process Inventory when standard costing is used.

11–6. How has computer-integrated-manufacturing (CIM) technology affected overhead application?

11–7. What is the interpretation of the variable-overhead spending variance?

11–8. Jeffries Company's only variable-overhead cost is electricity. Does an unfavorable variable-overhead spending variance imply that the company paid more than the anticipated rate per kilowatt-hour?

11–9. What is the interpretation of the variable-overhead efficiency variance?

11–10. Distinguish between the interpretations of the direct-labor and variable-overhead efficiency variances.

11–11. What is the fixed-overhead budget variance?

11–12. What is the correct interpretation of the fixed-overhead volume variance?

11–13. Describe a common but misleading interpretation of the fixed-overhead volume variance. Why is this interpretation misleading?

11–14. Draw a graph showing budgeted and applied fixed overhead, and show a positive volume variance on the graph.

11–15. What types of organizations use flexible budgets?

11–16. What is the conceptual problem of applying fixed manufacturing overhead as a product cost?

11–17. Distinguish between the control purpose and the product-costing purpose of standard costing and flexible budgeting.

11–18. Why are fixed-overhead costs sometimes called capacity-producing costs?

11–19. Draw a graph showing both budgeted and applied variable overhead. Explain why the graph appears as it does.

11–20. Give one example of a plausible activity base to use in flexible budgeting for each of the following organizations: an insurance company, an express delivery service, a restaurant, and a state tax-collection agency.

11–21. Explain how an activity-based flexible budget differs from a conventional flexible budget.

Exercises

Exercise 11–22
Straightforward Computation of Overhead Variances
(LO 5)

The following data are the actual results for Marvelous Marshmallow Company for August.

Actual output	13,500 cases
Actual variable overhead	$607,500
Actual fixed overhead	$183,000
Actual machine time	60,750 machine hours

Standard cost and budget information for Marvelous Marshmallow Company follows:

Standard variable-overhead rate	$9.00 per machine hour
Standard quantity of machine hours	4 hours per case of marshmallows
Budgeted fixed overhead	$180,000 per month
Budgeted output	15,000 cases per month

Required: Use any of the methods explained in the chapter to compute the following variances. Indicate whether each variance is favorable or unfavorable, where appropriate.

1. Variable-overhead spending variance.
2. Variable-overhead efficiency variance.
3. Fixed-overhead budget variance.
4. Fixed-overhead volume variance.

Exercise 11–23
Overhead Variances
(LO 5)

Mankato Control Company, which manufactures electrical switches, uses a standard-costing system. The standard manufacturing overhead costs per switch are based on direct-labor hours and are as follows:

Variable overhead (5 hours @ $12.00 per hour)	$ 60
Fixed overhead (5 hours @ $18.00 per hour)*	90
Total overhead	$150

*Based on capacity of 300,000 direct-labor hours per month.

The following information is available for the month of October.

- Variable overhead costs were $3,510,000.
- Fixed overhead costs were $5,625,000.
- 56,000 switches were produced, although 60,000 switches were scheduled to be produced.
- 275,000 direct-labor hours were worked at a total cost of $3,825,000.

Required: Compute the variable-overhead spending and efficiency variances and the fixed-overhead budget and volume variances for October. Indicate whether a variance is favorable or unfavorable where appropriate.

(CMA, adapted)

Exercise 11–24
Standard Hours Allowed; Flexible Budgeting; Multiple Products
(LO 1, 2)

Outdoor Optics Company produces binoculars of two quality levels: field and professional. The field model requires four direct-labor hours, while the professional binoculars require six hours. The firm uses direct-labor hours for flexible budgeting.

Required:

1. How many standard hours are allowed in May, when 300 field models and 400 professional binoculars are manufactured?
2. Suppose the company based its flexible overhead budget for May on the number of binoculars manufactured, which is 700. What difficulties would this approach cause?

Exercise 11–25
Straightforward Computation of Overhead Variances
(LO 5)

Starlight Glassware Company has the following standards and flexible-budget data.

Standard variable-overhead rate	$18.00 per direct-labor hour
Standard quantity of direct labor	2 hours per unit of output
Budgeted fixed overhead	$300,000
Budgeted output	25,000 units

Actual results for February are as follows:

Actual output	20,000 units
Actual variable overhead	$960,000
Actual fixed overhead	$291,000
Actual direct labor	50,000 hours

Required: Use the variance formulas to compute the following variances. Indicate whether each variance is favorable or unfavorable, where appropriate.

1. Variable-overhead spending variance.
2. Variable-overhead efficiency variance.
3. Fixed-overhead budget variance.
4. Fixed-overhead volume variance.

Exercise 11-26
Diagram of Overhead Variances
(LO 5)

Refer to the data in the preceding exercise. Use diagrams similar to those in Exhibits 11–6 and 11–8 to compute the variable-overhead spending and efficiency variances, and the fixed-overhead budget and volume variances.

Exercise 11–27
Graphing Overhead Variances
(LO 5)

Refer to the data in Exercise 11–25 for Starlight Glassware Company. Draw graphs similar to those in Exhibit 11–7 (variable overhead) and Exhibit 11–9 (fixed overhead) to depict the overhead variances.

Exercise 11–28
Interpretation of Variable-Overhead Efficiency Variance
(LO 5)

You recently received the following note from the production supervisor of the company where you serve as controller. "I don't understand these crazy variable-overhead efficiency variances. My employees are very careful in their use of electricity and manufacturing supplies, and we use very little indirect labor. What are we supposed to do?" Write a brief memo responding to the production supervisor's concern.

Exercise 11–29
City or State Budget; Activity-Based Flexible Budget; Cost Drivers; Use of Internet
(LO 4, 7)

Choose a city or state in the United States (or a Canadian city or province), and use the Internet to explore the annual budget for the governmental unit you selected. For example, you could check out the annual budget for Los Angeles at www.losangeles.com, or the state of Florida at www.ebudget.state.fl.us.

Required:

1. Select three items in the budget and explain how these items would be treated if the budget were converted to an activity-based flexible budget.
2. What would be appropriate cost drivers for the budgetary items you selected?

Exercise 11–30
Activity-Based Flexible Budget
(LO 7)

Refer to DCdesserts.com's activity-based flexible budget in Exhibit 11–11. Suppose that the company's activity in June is described as follows:

Process hours	9,000
Production runs	12
New products tested	40
Direct material handled (pounds)	30,000

Required:

1. Determine the flexible budgeted cost for each of the following:
   a. Indirect material
   b. Utilities
   c. Inspection
   d. Test kitchen
   e. Material handling
   f. Total overhead cost
2. Compute the variance for setup cost during the month, assuming that the actual setup cost was $3,500:
   a. Using the activity-based flexible budget.
   b. Using DCdesserts.com's conventional flexible budget (Exhibit 11–3).

Exercise 11–31
Reconstruct Missing Information from Partial Data
(LO 2, 5)

You brought your work home one evening, and your nephew spilled his chocolate milk shake on the variance report you were preparing. Fortunately, you were able to reconstruct the obliterated information from the remaining data. Fill in the missing numbers below. (*Hint:* It is helpful to solve for the unknowns in the order indicated by the letters in the following table.)

Budgeted fixed overhead	$ 25,000
Actual fixed overhead	a
Budgeted production in units	12,500
Actual production in units	c
Standard machine hours per unit of output	4 hours
Standard variable-overhead rate per machine hour	$8.00
Actual variable-overhead rate per machine hour	b
Actual machine hours per unit of output	d
Variable-overhead spending variance	$ 36,000 U
Variable-overhead efficiency variance	$ 96,000 F
Fixed-overhead budget variance	$ 7,500 U
Fixed-overhead volume variance	g
Total actual overhead	$356,500
Total budgeted overhead (flexible budget)	e
Total budgeted overhead (static budget)	f
Total applied overhead	$408,000

Exercise 11–32
Construct a Flexible Overhead Budget; Hospital
(LO 1, 2)

The controller for Rainbow Children's Hospital, located in Munich, Germany, estimates that the hospital uses 25 kilowatt-hours of electricity per patient-day, and that the electric rate will be .13 *euro* per kilowatt-hour. The hospital also pays a fixed monthly charge of 2,000 *euros* to the electric utility to rent emergency backup electric generators.*

Required: Construct a flexible budget for the hospital's electricity costs using each of the following techniques.

1. Formula flexible budget.
2. Columnar flexible budget for 30,000, 40,000 and 50,000 patient-days of activity. List variable and fixed electricity costs separately.

*The European monetary unit, the *Euro,* has been introduced in most European markets.

Exercise 11–33
Journal Entries for Overhead (Appendix A)
(LO 8)

Refer to the data in Exercise 11–25 for Starlight Glassware Company. Prepare journal entries to:

- Record the incurrence of actual variable overhead and actual fixed overhead.
- Add variable and fixed overhead to Work-in-Process Inventory.
- Close underapplied or overapplied overhead into Cost of Goods Sold.

Exercise 11–34
Sales Variances (Appendix B)
(LO 9)

The following data pertain to Alexis Electronics for the month of April.

	Static Budget	Actual
Units sold	15,000	13,500
Sales revenue	$180,000	$155,250
Variable manufacturing cost	60,000	54,000
Fixed manufacturing cost	30,000	30,000
Variable selling and administrative cost	15,000	13,500
Fixed selling and administrative cost	15,000	15,000

Required: Compute the sales-price and sales-volume variances for April.

Problems

Problem 11–35
Straightforward Overhead Variances
(LO 5)

Manitoba Paper Company packages paper for photocopiers. The company has developed standard overhead rates based on a monthly capacity of 180,000 direct-labor hours as follows:

Standard costs per unit (one box of paper):	
Variable overhead (2 hours @ $6)	$12
Fixed overhead (2 hours @ $10)	20
Total	$32

During June, 45,000 units were scheduled for production; however, only 40,000 units were actually produced. The following data relate to June.

1. Actual overhead incurred totaled $1,371,500, of which $511,500 was variable and $860,000 was fixed.
2. Actual direct-labor cost incurred was $1,567,500 for 82,500 actual hours of work.

Required: Prepare two exhibits similar to Exhibits 11–6 and 11–8 in the chapter, which show the following variances. State whether each variance is favorable or unfavorable, where appropriate.

1. Variable-overhead spending variance.
2. Variable-overhead efficiency variance.
3. Fixed-overhead budget variance.
4. Fixed-overhead volume variance.

(CMA, adapted)

Problem 11–36
Graphing Budgeted and Applied Overhead; Recording Studio
(LO 1, 2, 3)

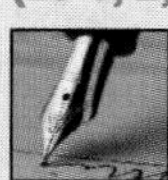

Countrytime Studios is a recording studio in Nashville. The studio budgets and applies overhead costs on the basis of production time. Countrytime's controller anticipates 10,000 hours of production time to be available during the year. The following overhead amounts have been budgeted for the year.

Variable overhead	$80,000
Fixed overhead	90,000

Required:

1. Draw two graphs, one for variable overhead and one for fixed overhead. The variable on the horizontal axis of each graph should be production time in hours, ranging from 5,000 to 15,000 hours.

The variable on the vertical axis of each graph should be overhead cost (variable or fixed). Each graph should include lines representing the flexible-budget amount of overhead and applied overhead.

2. Write a brief memo to Countrytime Studio's general manager, explaining the graphs so that she will understand the concepts of budgeted and applied overhead.

Problem 11–37
Overhead Variances
(LO 5)

Wilmington Composites, Inc. developed its overhead application rate from the annual budget. The budget is based on an expected total output of 720,000 units requiring 3,600,000 machine hours. The company is able to schedule production uniformly throughout the year.

A total of 66,000 units requiring 315,000 machine hours were produced during March. Actual overhead costs for March amounted to $750,000. The actual costs, as compared to the annual budget and to one-twelfth of the annual budget, are as follows:

WILMINGTON COMPOSITES, INC.
Annual Budget

	Total Amount	Per Unit	Per Machine Hour	Monthly Budget	Actual Costs for March
Variable overhead:					
Indirect material	$2,448,000	$ 3.40	$ .68	$204,000	$222,000
Indirect labor.	1,800,000	2.50	.50	150,000	150,000
Fixed overhead:					
Supervision.	1,296,000	1.80	.36	108,000	102,000
Utilities	1,080,000	1.50	.30	90,000	108,000
Depreciation	2,016,000	2.80	.56	168,000	168,000
Total.	$8,640,000	$12.00	$2.40	$720,000	$750,000

Required:

1. Prepare a schedule showing the following amounts for Wilmington Composites, Inc. for March.
   a. Applied overhead costs.
   b. Variable-overhead spending variance.
   c. Fixed-overhead budget variance.
   d. Variable-overhead efficiency variance.
   e. Fixed-overhead volume variance.

   Where appropriate, be sure to indicate whether each variance is favorable or unfavorable.
2. Draw a graph similar to Exhibit 11–7 to depict the variable-overhead variances.
3. Why does your graph differ from Exhibit 11–7, other than the fact that the numbers differ?

(CMA, adapted)

Problem 11–38
Standard Hours Allowed; Flexible Budget; Multiple Products; Insurance Company
(LO 1, 2, 4)

Rock Solid Insurance Company uses a flexible overhead budget for its application-processing department. The firm offers five types of policies, with the following standard hours allowed for clerical processing.

Automobile	1 hour
Renter's	1.5 hours
Homeowner's	2 hours
Health.	2 hours
Life.	5 hours

The following numbers of insurance applications were processed during May.

Automobile	375
Renter's	300
Homeowner's	150
Health.	600
Life.	300

The controller estimates that the variable-overhead rate in the application-processing department is $5.00 per hour, and that fixed-overhead costs will amount to $3,000 per month.

Required:

1. How many standard clerical hours are allowed in May, given actual application activity?
2. Why would it not be sensible to base the company's flexible budget on the number of applications processed instead of the number of clerical hours allowed?
3. Construct a formula flexible-overhead budget for the company.
4. What is the flexible budget for total overhead cost in May?

Problem 11–39
Overhead Calculations; Variance Interpretation
(LO 5)

Lackawanna Licorice Company uses a standard cost accounting system and applies manufacturing overhead to products on the basis of machine hours. The following information is available for the year just ended:

Actual variable overhead: $166,320
Actual total overhead: $467,700
Actual machine hours worked: 23,100
Standard variable-overhead rate per hour: $7.50
Standard fixed-overhead rate per hour: $12.00
Planned activity during the period: 20,000 machine hours
Actual production: 10,700 finished units
Machine-hour standard: Two completed units per machine hour

Required:

1. Calculate the budgeted fixed overhead for the year.
2. Compute the variable-overhead spending variance.
3. Calculate the company's fixed-overhead volume variance.
4. Did the company spend more or less than anticipated for fixed overhead? How much?
5. Was variable overhead underapplied or overapplied during the year? By how much?
6. On the basis of the data presented, does it appear that the company suffered a lengthy strike during the year by its production workers? Briefly explain.

Problem 11–40
Budgets and Performance Evaluation
(LO 1, 6)

Midwest Ventilation, Inc. produces industrial ventilation fans. The company plans to manufacture 72,000 fans evenly over the next quarter at the following costs: direct material, $2,880,000; direct labor, $720,000; variable manufacturing overhead, $900,000; and fixed manufacturing overhead, $1,800,000. The last amount includes $144,000 of straight-line depreciation and $216,000 of supervisory salaries.

Shortly after the conclusion of the quarter's first month, Midwest reported the following costs:

Direct material	$ 865,000
Direct labor	221,200
Variable manufacturing overhead	304,000
Depreciation	48,000
Supervisory salaries	75,600
Other fixed manufacturing overhead	478,000
Total	$1,991,800

Dave Kellerman and his crews turned out 20,000 fans during the month—a remarkable feat given that the firm's manufacturing plant was closed for several days because of storm damage and flooding. Kellerman was especially pleased with the fact that overall financial performance for the period was favorable when compared with the budget. His pleasure, however, was very short-lived, as Midwest's general manager issued a stern warning that performance must improve, and improve quickly, if Kellerman had any hopes of keeping his job.

Required:

1. Explain the difference between a static budget and a flexible budget.
2. Which of the two budgets would be more useful when planning the company's cash needs over a range of activity?

3. Prepare a performance report that compares budgeted and actual costs for the period just ended (i.e., the report that Kellerman likely used when assessing his performance).
4. Prepare a performance report that compares budgeted and actual costs for the period just ended (i.e., the report that the general manager likely used when assessing Kellerman's performance).
5. Which of the two reports is preferred? Should Kellerman be praised for outstanding performance or is the general manager's warning appropriate? Explain, citing any apparent problems for the firm.

Problem 11–41
Linkages between the Flexible Budget and Variances
(LO 1, 2, 5)

Valley View Hospital has an outpatient clinic. Jeffrey Harper, the hospital's chief administrator, is very concerned about cost control and has asked that performance reports be prepared that compare budgeted and actual amounts for medical assistants, clinic supplies, and lab tests. Past financial studies have shown that the cost of clinic supplies used is driven by the number of medical assistant labor hours worked, whereas lab tests are highly correlated with the number of patients served.

The following information is available for June:

- *Lab tests:* Actual lab tests for June cost $159,027 and averaged 3.3 per patient. Each patient is anticipated to have three lab tests, at an average budgeted cost of $65 per test.
- *Medical assistants:* Valley View's standard wage rate is $14 per hour, and each assistant is expected to spend 30 minutes with a patient. Assistants totaled 420 hours in helping the 790 patients seen, at an average pay rate of $15.50 per hour.
- *Clinic supplies:* The cost of clinic supplies used is budgeted at $12 per labor hour, and the actual cost of supplies used was $4,575.

Required:

1. Prepare a report that shows budgeted and actual costs for the 790 patients served during June. Compute the differences (variances) between these amounts and label them as favorable or unfavorable.
2. On the basis of your answer to requirement (1), determine whether Valley View Hospital has any significant problems with respect to clinic supplies and lab tests. Briefly discuss your findings.
3. By performing a detailed analysis, determine the spending and efficiency variances for lab tests. Does it appear that Valley View Hospital has any significant problems with the cost of its lab tests? Briefly explain. (*Hint:* In applying the overhead variance formulas, think of the number of tests as analogous to the number of hours, and think of the cost per test as analogous to the variable overhead rate.)
4. Compare the lab test variance computed in requirement (1), a flexible-budget variance, with the sum of the variances in requirement (3). Discuss your findings and explain the relationship of flexible-budget variances and standard cost variances for variable overhead.

Problem 11–42
Flexible Budgeting; Variances; Impact on Behavior
(LO 1, 2, 5)

LakeMaster Company manufactures outboard motors that are sold throughout the United States and Canada. The company uses a comprehensive budgeting process and compares actual results to budgeted amounts on a monthly basis. Each month, LakeMaster's accounting department prepares a variance analysis and distributes the report to all responsible parties. Al Richmond, production manager, is upset about the results for June. Richmond, who is responsible for the cost of goods manufactured, has implemented several cost-cutting measures in the manufacturing area and is discouraged by the unfavorable variance in variable costs.

LAKEMASTER COMPANY
Operating Results
For the Month of June

	Budget	Actual	Variance
Units sold	5,000	4,800	200 U
Revenue	$1,800,000	$1,728,000	$ 72,000 U
Variable cost	1,140,000	1,170,000	30,000 U
Contribution margin	$ 660,000	$ 558,000	$102,000 U
Fixed overhead	270,000	270,000	—
Fixed general and administrative cost	180,000	172,500	7,500 F
Operating income	$ 210,000	$ 115,500	$ 94,500 U

When the master budget was prepared, LakeMaster's cost accountant, Joan Ballard, supplied the following unit costs: direct material, $90; direct labor, $66; variable overhead, $54; and variable selling, $18.

The total variable costs of $1,170,000 for June include $480,000 for direct material, $288,000 for direct labor, $264,000 for variable overhead, and $138,000 for variable selling expenses. Ballard believes that monthly reports would be more meaningful to everyone if the company adopted flexible budgeting and prepared more detailed analyses.

Required:

1. Prepare a flexible budget for LakeMaster Company for the month of June that includes separate variable-cost budgets for each type of cost (direct material, etc.).
2. Determine the variance between the flexible budget and actual cost for each cost item.
3. Discuss how the revised budget and variance data are likely to impact the behavior of Al Richmond, the production manager.

(CMA, adapted)

Problem 11–43
Preparing and Using a Columnar Flexible Budget; Tour Company; Ethical Issues
(LO 1, 2, 6)

Vermont Sky Tours is a small sightseeing tour company based in Burlington, Vermont. The firm specializes in aerial tours of the New England countryside during September and October, when the fall color is at its peak. Until recently, the company had not had an accounting department. Routine bookkeeping tasks, such as billing, had been handled by an individual who had little formal training in accounting. As the business began to grow, however, the owner recognized the need for more formal accounting procedures. Jacqueline Frost has recently been hired as the new controller, and she will have the authority to hire an assistant.

During her first week on the job, Frost was given the following performance report. The report was prepared by Red Leif, the company's manager of aircraft operations, who was planning to present it to the owner the next morning. "Look at these favorable variances for fuel and so forth," Leif pointed out, as he showed the report to Frost. "My operations people are really doing a great job." Later that day, Frost looked at the performance report more carefully. She immediately realized that it was improperly prepared and would be misleading to the company's owner.

VERMONT SKY TOURS
Performance Report
For the Month of September

	Formula Flexible Budget (per air mile)	Actual (32,000 air miles)	Static Budget (35,000 air miles)	Variance
Passenger revenue	$10.50	$336,000	$367,500	$31,500 U
Less: Variable expenses:				
Fuel	1.50	$ 51,000	$ 52,500	$ 1,500 F
Aircraft maintenance	2.25	70,500	78,750	8,250 F
Flight crew salaries	1.20	39,300	42,000	2,700 F
Selling and administrative	2.40	74,700	84,000	9,300 F
Total variable expenses	$ 7.35	$235,500	$257,250	$21,750 F
Contribution margin	$ 3.15	$100,500	$110,250	9,750 U
	Per Month			
Less: Fixed expenses:				
Depreciation on aircraft	$ 8,700	$ 8,700	$ 8,700	$ 0
Landing fees	2,700	3,000	2,700	300 U
Supervisory salaries	27,000	25,800	27,000	1,200 F
Selling and administrative	33,000	37,200	33,000	4,200 U
Total fixed expenses	$71,400	$ 74,700	$ 71,400	$ 3,300 U
Net income		$ 25,800	$ 38,850	$13,050 U

Required:

1. Prepare a columnar flexible budget for Vermont Sky Tours' expenses, based on the following activity levels: 32,000 air miles, 35,000 air miles, and 38,000 air miles.

2. In spite of several favorable expense variances shown on the report above, the company's September net income was only about two-thirds of the expected level. Why?
3. Write a brief memo to the manager of aircraft operations explaining why the original variance report is misleading.
4. Prepare a revised expense variance report for September, which is based on the flexible budget prepared in requirement (1).
5. Jacqueline Frost presented the revised expense report to Leif along with the memo explaining why the original performance report was misleading. Leif did not take it well. He complained of Frost's "interference" and pointed out that the company had been doing just fine without her. "I'm taking my report to the owner tomorrow," Leif insisted. "Yours just makes us look bad." What are Frost's ethical obligations in this matter? What should she do?

Problem 11–44
Flexible Budget;
Performance Report
(LO 1, 6)

EduSoft Corporation's president, Mark Fletcher, was looking forward to seeing the performance reports for October because he knew the company's sales for the month had exceeded budget by a considerable margin. EduSoft, a distributor of educational software packages, had been growing steadily for approximately two years. Fletcher's biggest challenge at this point was to ensure that the company did not lose control of expenses during this growth period. When Fletcher received the October reports, he was dismayed to see the large unfavorable variance in the company's Monthly Selling Expense Report that follows.

EDUSOFT CORPORATION
Monthly Selling Expense Report
For the Month of October

	Annual Budget	October Budget	October Actual	October Variance
Dollar sales	$160,000,000	$22,400,000	$24,800,000	$2,400,000
Unit sales	2,000,000	280,000	310,000	30,000
Orders processed	54,000	6,500	5,800	(700)
Sales personnel per month	90	90	96	(6)
Advertising	$ 39,600,000	$ 3,300,000	$ 3,320,000	$ 20,000 U
Staff salaries	3,000,000	250,000	250,000	—
Sales salaries	2,592,000	216,000	230,800	14,800 U
Commissions	6,400,000	896,000	992,000	96,000 U
Per diem expense	3,564,000	297,000	325,200	28,200 U
Office expenses	8,160,000	760,000	716,800	43,200 F
Shipping expenses	13,500,000	1,805,000	1,953,000	148,000 U
Total expenses	$ 76,816,000	$ 7,524,000	$ 7,787,800	$ 263,800 U

Fletcher called in the company's new controller, Susan Porter, to discuss the implications of the variances reported for October and to plan a strategy for improving performance. Porter suggested that the company's reporting format might not be giving Fletcher a true picture of the company's operations. She proposed that EduSoft implement flexible budgeting. Porter offered to redo the Monthly Selling Expense Report for October using flexible budgeting so that Fletcher could compare the two reports and see the advantages of flexible budgeting.

Porter discovered the following information about the behavior of EduSoft's selling expenses.

- The total compensation paid to the sales force consists of a monthly base salary and a commission; the commission varies with sales dollars.
- Sales office expense is a semivariable cost with the variable portion related to the number of orders processed. The fixed portion of office expense is $6,000,000 annually and is incurred uniformly throughout the year.
- Subsequent to the adoption of the annual budget for the current year, EduSoft decided to open a new sales territory. As a consequence, approval was given to hire six additional salespeople effective October 1. Porter decided that these additional six people should be recognized in her revised October report.
- Per diem reimbursement to the sales force, while a fixed amount per day, is variable with the number of sales personnel and the number of days spent traveling. The original budget was based on an average sales force of 90 people throughout the year with each salesperson traveling 15 days per month.

- The company's shipping expense is a semivariable cost with the variable portion, $6.00 per unit, dependent on the number of units sold. The fixed portion is incurred uniformly throughout the year.

Required:

1. Citing the benefits of flexible budgeting, explain why Susan Porter would propose that EduSoft use flexible budgeting in this situation.
2. Prepare a revised Monthly Selling Expense Report for October that would permit Mark Fletcher to more clearly evaluate EduSoft's control over selling expenses. The report should have a line for each selling expense item showing the appropriate budgeted amount, the actual selling expense, and the monthly dollar variance.

(CMA, adapted)

Problem 11–45
Finding Missing Data; Overhead Accounting
(LO 1, 5)

For each of the following independent cases, fill in the missing information. The company budgets and applies manufacturing-overhead costs on the basis of direct-labor hours. (U denotes *unfavorable variance;* F denotes *favorable variance.*)

	Case A	Case B
1. Standard variable-overhead rate	$7.50 per hour	? per hour
2. Standard fixed-overhead rate	? per hour	? per hour
3. Total standard overhead rate	? per hour	$13.00 per hour
4. Flexible budget for variable overhead	$270,000	?
5. Flexible budget for fixed overhead	$630,000	?
6. Actual variable overhead	?	?
7. Actual fixed overhead	$621,000	?
8. Variable-overhead spending variance	$16,650 U	$8,000 U
9. Variable-overhead efficiency variance	?	$1,600 F
10. Fixed-overhead budget variance	?	$4,320 U
11. Fixed-overhead volume variance	?	$14,400 U (positive sign)
12. Under- (or over-) applied variable overhead	?	?
13. Under- (or over-) applied fixed overhead	?	?
14. Budgeted production (in units)	5,000 units	?
15. Standard direct-labor hours per unit	6 hours per unit	8 hours per unit
16. Actual production (in units)	?	?
17. Standard direct-labor hours allowed, given actual production	36,000 hours	6,400 hours
18. Actual direct-labor hours	37,000 hours	6,000 hours
19. Applied variable overhead	?	?
20. Applied fixed overhead	?	?

Problem 11–46
Interactions between Variances; Flexible Manufacturing System
(LO 5)

Western Auto Parts Company manufactures replacement parts for automobile repair. The company recently installed a flexible manufacturing system, which has significantly changed the production process. The installation of the new FMS was not anticipated when the current year's budget and cost structure were developed. The installation of the new equipment was hastened by several major breakdowns in the company's old production machinery.

The new equipment was very expensive, but management expects it to cut the labor time required by a substantial amount. Management also expects the new equipment to allow a reduction in direct-material waste. On the negative side, the FMS requires a more highly skilled labor force to operate it than the company's old equipment.

The following cost variance report was prepared for the month of May, the first full month after the equipment was installed.

WESTERN AUTO PARTS COMPANY
Cost Variance Report
For the Month of May

Direct material:	
Standard cost	$301,225
Actual cost	299,350
Direct-material price variance	75 U*

(continues)

(concluded)

Direct-material quantity variance	$ 1,950 F
Direct labor:	
Standard cost	196,500
Actual cost	191,900
Direct-labor rate variance	2,400 U
Direct-labor efficiency variance	7,000 F
Manufacturing overhead:	
Applied to work in process	200,000
Actual cost	204,000
Variable-overhead spending variance	4,000 U
Variable-overhead efficiency variance	5,000 F
Fixed-overhead budget variance	15,000 U
Fixed-overhead volume variance	(10,000)†

*F denotes favorable variance; U denotes unfavorable variance.

†The sign of the volume variance is negative, applied fixed overhead exceeded budgeted fixed overhead.

Required: Comment on the possible interactions between the variances listed in the report. Which ones are likely to have been caused by the purchase of the new production equipment? The company budgets and applies manufacturing overhead on the basis of direct-labor hours. (You may find it helpful to review the discussion of variance interactions in Chapter 10.)

Problem 11–47
Using a Flexible Budget
(LO 1, 2, 5)

Williamsport Wheel and Axle, Inc. has an automated production process, and production activity is quantified in terms of process hours. The company uses a standard-costing system. The annual static budget for 20x4 called for 6,000 units to be produced, requiring 30,000 machine hours. The standard overhead rate for the year was computed using this planned level of production. The 20x4 manufacturing cost report follows.

WILLIAMSPORT WHEEL AND AXLE, INC.
Manufacturing Cost Report
For 20x4
(in thousands of dollars)

	Static Budget	Flexible Budget		
Cost Item	**30,000 Machine Hours**	**31,000 Machine Hours**	**32,000 Machine Hours**	**Actual Cost**
Direct material:				
A42 aluminum	$ 504.0	$ 520.8	$ 537.6	$ 540.0
S18 steel alloy	156.0	161.2	166.4	166.0
Direct labor:				
Assembler	546.0	564.2	582.4	574.0
Grinder	468.0	483.6	499.2	500.0
Manufacturing overhead:				
Maintenance	48.0	49.6	51.2	50.0
Supplies	258.0	266.6	275.2	260.0
Supervision	160.0	164.0	168.0	162.0
Inspection	288.0	294.0	300.0	294.0
Insurance	100.0	100.0	100.0	100.0
Depreciation	400.0	400.0	400.0	400.0
Total cost	$2,928.0	$3,004.0	$3,080.0	$3,046.0

The company's controller develops flexible budgets for different levels of activity for use in evaluating performance. A total of 6,200 units was produced during 20x4, requiring 32,000 machine hours. The preceding manufacturing cost report compares the company's actual cost for the year with the static budget and the flexible budget for two different activity levels.

Required: Compute the following amounts. For variances, indicate whether favorable or unfavorable where appropriate. Answers should be rounded to two decimal places when necessary.

1. The standard number of machine hours allowed to produce one unit of product.
2. The actual cost of direct material used in one unit of product.
3. The cost of material that should be processed per machine hour.

4. The standard direct-labor cost for each unit produced.
5. The variable-overhead rate per machine hour in a flexible-budget formula. (*Hint:* Separate the overhead costs from direct material and direct labor, and then use the high-low method to estimate cost behavior.)
6. The standard fixed-overhead rate per machine hour used for product costing.
7. The variable-overhead spending variance. (Assume management has determined that the actual fixed overhead cost in 20x4 amounted to $648,000.)
8. The variable-overhead efficiency variance.
9. The fixed-overhead budget variance.
10. The fixed-overhead volume variance. [Make the same assumption as in requirement (7).]
11. The total budgeted manufacturing cost (in thousands of dollars) for an output of 6,050 units. (*Hint:* Use the flexible-budget formula.)

(CMA, adapted)

Problem 11–48
Flexible Budget; Improved Performance Report; Behavioral Issues
(LO 1, 6)

Albuquerque Wood Crafts, Inc. is a manufacturer of furniture for specialty shops throughout the southwest and has an annual sales volume of $24 million. The company has four major product lines: bookcases, magazine racks, end tables, and bar stools. Each line is managed by a production manager. Since production is spread fairly evenly over the 12 months of operation, Sara McKinley, the controller, has prepared an annual budget divided into 12 periods for monthly reporting purposes.

Albuquerque Wood Crafts uses a standard-costing system and applies variable overhead on the basis of process hours. Fixed production cost is allocated on the basis of square footage occupied using a predetermined plantwide rate; the size of the space occupied varies considerably among the product lines. All other costs are assigned on the basis of revenue dollars earned. At the monthly meeting to review November performance, Steve Clark, manager of the bookcase line, received the following report.

ALBUQUERQUE WOOD CRAFTS, INC.
Bookcase Production Performance Report
For the Month of November

	Actual	Budget	Variance
Units	3,000	2,500	500 F
Revenue	$483,000	$412,500	$70,500 F
Variable production costs:			
Direct material	$ 69,300	$ 60,000	$ 9,300 U
Direct labor	54,900	45,000	9,900 U
Machine time	57,600	48,750	8,850 U
Manufacturing overhead	123,000	105,000	18,000 U
Fixed production costs:			
Indirect labor	28,200	18,000	10,200 U
Depreciation	16,500	16,500	—
Property taxes	7,200	6,900	300 U
Insurance	13,500	13,500	—
Administrative expenses	36,000	27,000	9,000 U
Marketing expenses	24,900	21,000	3,900 U
Research and development	18,000	13,500	4,500 U
Total expenses	$449,100	$375,150	$73,950 U
Operating income	$ 33,900	$ 37,350	$ 3,450 U

While distributing the monthly reports at the meeting, McKinley remarked to Clark, "We need to talk about getting your division back on track. Be sure to see me after the meeting."

Clark had been so convinced that his division did well in November that McKinley's remark was a real surprise. He spent the balance of the meeting avoiding the looks of his fellow managers and trying to figure out what could have gone wrong. The monthly performance report was no help.

Required:

1. a. Identify three weaknesses in Albuquerque Wood Crafts, Inc.'s monthly Bookcase Production Performance Report.

b. Discuss the behavioral implications of Sara McKinley's remarks to Steve Clark during the meeting.

2. The company could do a better job of reporting monthly performance to the production managers.

a. Recommend how the report could be improved to eliminate weaknesses, and revise it accordingly.

b. Discuss how the recommended changes in reporting are likely to affect Steve Clark's behavior.

(CMA, adapted)

Problem 11–49
Complete Analysis of Cost Variances; Review of Chapters 10 and 11
(LO 5)

Ice Box Gourmet, Inc. produces containers of frozen food. During April, The company produced 725 cases of food and incurred the following actual costs.

Variable overhead	$ 5,500
Fixed overhead	13,000
Actual labor cost (4,000 direct-labor hours)	75,600
Actual material cost (15,000 pounds purchased and used)	33,000

Standard cost and annual budget information are as follows:

Standard Costs per Case

Direct labor (5 hours at $18)	$ 90.00
Direct material (20 pounds at $2)	40.00
Variable overhead (5 hours at $1.50)	7.50
Fixed overhead (5 hours at $3)	15.00
Total	$152.50

Annual Budget Information

Variable overhead	$ 75,000
Fixed overhead	$150,000
Planned activity for year	50,000 direct-labor hours

Required: Prepare as complete an analysis of cost variances as is possible from the available data.

Problem 11–50
Overhead Variances; Journal Entries (Appendix A)
(LO 5, 8)

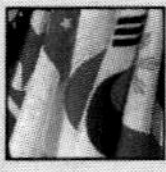

Vancouver Scholastic Supply Company uses a standard-costing system. The firm estimates that it will operate its manufacturing facilities at 600,000 machine hours for the year. The estimate for total budgeted overhead is $1,500,000. The standard variable-overhead rate is estimated to be $2 per machine hour or $6 per unit. The actual data for the year are presented below.

Actual finished units	187,500
Actual machine hours	573,000
Actual variable overhead	$1,275,750
Actual fixed overhead	$ 294,000

Required:

1. Compute the following variances. Indicate whether each is favorable or unfavorable, where appropriate.

a. Variable-overhead spending variance.

b. Variable-overhead efficiency variance.

c. Fixed-overhead budget variance.

d. Fixed-overhead volume variance.

2. Prepare journal entries to:

a. Record the incurrence of actual variable overhead and actual fixed overhead.

b. Add variable and fixed overhead to Work-In-Process Inventory.

c. Close underapplied or overapplied overhead into Cost of Goods Sold.

(CMA, adapted)

Problem 11–51
Comprehensive Problem on Overhead Accounting under Standard Costing; Journal Entries (Appendix A)
(LO 2, 5, 8)

EuroGuide, Inc. publishes European Tour Guide Books in New York City. A monthly flexible overhead budget for the firm follows.

EUROGUIDE, INC.
Monthly Flexible Overhead Budget

	Direct-Labor Hours		
Budgeted Cost	**1,500**	**1,750**	**2,000**
Variable costs:			
Indirect material:			
Glue	$ 1,500	$ 1,750	$ 2,000
Tape	600	700	800
Miscellaneous supplies	6,000	7,000	8,000
Indirect labor	15,000	17,500	20,000
Utilities:			
Electricity	3,000	3,500	4,000
Natural gas	900	1,050	1,200
Total variable cost	$27,000	$31,500	$36,000
Fixed costs:			
Supervisory labor	25,000	25,000	25,000
Depreciation	6,800	6,800	6,800
Property taxes and insurance	8,200	8,200	8,200
Total fixed cost	$40,000	$40,000	$40,000
Total overhead cost	$67,000	$71,500	$76,000

The planned monthly production is 6,400 yearbooks. The standard direct-labor allowance is .25 hours per book. During February, EuroGuide, Inc. produced 8,000 yearbooks and actually used 2,100 direct-labor hours. The actual overhead costs for the month were as follows:

Actual variable overhead	$39,060
Actual fixed overhead	75,200

Required:

1. Determine the formula flexible overhead budget for EuroGuide, Inc.
2. Prepare a display similar to Exhibit 11–6, which shows the variable-overhead variances for February. Indicate whether each variance is favorable or unfavorable.
3. Draw a graph similar to Exhibit 11–7, which shows the variable-overhead variances for February.
4. Explain how to interpret each of the variances computed in requirement (2).
5. Prepare a display similar to Exhibit 11–8, which shows the fixed-overhead variances for February.
6. Draw a graph similar to Exhibit 11–9, which depicts the company's applied and budgeted fixed overhead for February. Show the February volume variance on the graph.
7. Explain the interpretation of the variances computed in requirement (5).
8. Prepare journal entries to record each of the following:
   a. Incurrence of February's actual overhead cost.
   b. Application of February's overhead cost to Work-in-Process Inventory.
   c. Close underapplied or overapplied overhead into Cost of Goods Sold.
9. Draw T-accounts for all of the accounts used in the journal entries of requirement (8). Then post the journal entries to the T-accounts.

Problem 11–52
Sales Variances (Appendix B)
(LO 9)

Bear Mountain Sled Company manufactures children's snow sleds. The company's performance report for December is as follows.

	Actual	Budget
Sleds sold	7,500	9,000
Sales	$360,000	$450,000
Variable costs	225,000	270,000
Contribution margin	$135,000	$180,000
Fixed costs	126,000	120,000
Operating income	$ 9,000	$ 60,000

The company uses a flexible budget to analyze its performance and to measure the effect on operating income of the factors affecting the difference between budgeted and actual operating income.

Required: Compute the following variances and indicate whether each is favorable or unfavorable.

1. December sales-price variance.
2. December sales-volume variance.

(CMA, adapted)

Problem 11–53
Analyzing Sales Variances (Appendix B)
(LO 9)

Kalamazoo Computer Accessory Company (KCAC) distributes keyboard trays to computer stores. The keyboard trays can be attached to the underside of a desk, effectively turning it into a computer table. The keyboard trays are purchased from a manufacturer that attaches KCAC's private label to the trays. The wholesale selling prices to the computer stores are $120 for the business grade keyboard tray and $60 for the residential grade product. The 20x5 budget and actual results are as follows. The budget was adopted in late 20x4 and was based on KCAC's estimated share of the market for the two types of keyboard trays.

KALAMAZOO COMPUTER ACCESSORY COMPANY
Income Statement
For the Year Ending December 31, 20x5
(in thousands)

	Business Grade		Residential Grade		Total		
	Budget	Actual	Budget	Actual	Budget	Actual	Variance
Sales in units	40	37	60	43	100	80	20
Revenue	$4,800	$4,255	$3,600	$2,537	$8,400	$6,792	$(1,608)
Cost of goods sold	3,200	3,034	3,000	2,150	6,200	5,184	1,016
Gross margin	$1,600	$1,221	$ 600	$ 387	$2,200	$1,608	$ (592)
Unallocated costs:							
Selling					$ 500	$ 500	$ —
Advertising					500	530	(30)
Administrative					200	203	(3)
Income taxes (45%)					450	169	281
Total unallocated costs					$1,650	$1,402	$ 248
Net income					$ 550	$ 206	$ (344)

During the first quarter of 20x5, management estimated that the total market for these products actually would be 10 percent below the original estimates. In an attempt to prevent unit sales from declining as much as industry projections, management implemented a marketing program. Included in the program were dealer discounts and increased direct advertising. The business grade line was emphasized in this program.

Required:

1. Compute the sales-price and sales-volume variances for each product line. Indicate whether each variance is favorable or unfavorable.
2. Discuss the apparent effect of KCAC's special marketing program (i.e., dealer discounts and additional advertising) on the 20x5 operating results.

(CMA, adapted)

Cases

Case 11–54
Integrative Case on Chapters 10 and 11; Drawing Conclusions from Missing Data
(LO 1, 3, 5)

Your next-door neighbor recently began a new job as assistant controller for Conundrum Corporation. As her first assignment, she prepared a performance report for March. She was scheduled to present the report to management the next morning, so she brought it home to review. As the two of you chatted in the backyard, she decided to show you the report she had prepared. Unfortunately, your dog thought the report was an object to be fetched. The pup made a flying leap and got a firm grip on the report. After chasing the dog around the block you managed to wrest the report from its teeth. Needless to say, it was torn to bits. Only certain data are legible on the report. This information follows:

CONUNDRUM CORPORATION
Performance Report for the Month of March

	Direct Material	Direct Labor	Variable Overhead	Fixed Overhead
Standard allowed cost given actual output	?	?		
	(? kilograms at $18 per kilogram)	(2 hours at $21 per hour)		
Flexible overhead budget			?	$60,000
Actual cost	$283,500	?	?	?
	(14,000 kilograms at $20.25 per kilogram)	(8,800 hours at ? per hour)		
Direct-material price variance	?			
Direct-material quantity variance	$9,000 U			
Direct-labor rate variance		$13,200 U		
Direct-labor efficiency variance		4,200 F		
Variable-overhead spending variance			$3,960 U	
Variable-overhead efficiency variance			1,800 F	
Fixed-overhead budget variance				$4,875 U
Fixed-overhead volume variance				?

In addition to the fragmentary data still legible on the performance report, your neighbor happened to remember the following facts.

- Planned production of Conundrum's sole product was 500 units more than the actual production.
- All of the direct material purchased in March was used in production.
- There were no beginning or ending inventories.
- Variable and fixed overhead are applied on the basis of direct-labor hours. The fixed overhead rate is $6.00 per hour.

Required: Feeling guilty, you have agreed to help your neighbor reconstruct the following facts, which will be necessary for her presentation.

1. Planned production (in units).
2. Actual production (in units).
3. Actual fixed overhead.
4. Total standard allowed direct-labor hours.
5. Actual direct-labor rate.
6. Standard variable-overhead rate.
7. Actual variable-overhead rate.
8. Standard direct-material quantity per unit.
9. Direct-material price variance.

10. Applied fixed overhead.
11. Fixed-overhead volume variance.

Case 11–55
Comprehensive Variance Analysis Used to Explain Operational Results; Review of Chapters 10 and 11; Activity-Based Costing (Appendix B)
(LO 4, 5, 7, 9)

Colonial Cookies, Inc. bakes cookies for retail stores. The company's best-selling cookie is chocolate nut supreme which is marketed as a gourmet cookie and regularly sells for $8.00 per pound. The standard cost per pound of chocolate nut supreme, based on Colonial's normal monthly production of 200,000 pounds, is as follows:

Cost Item	Quantity	Standard Unit Cost	Total Cost
Direct material:			
Cookie mix	10 oz.	$.02 per oz.	$ .20
Milk chocolate	5 oz.	.15 per oz.	.75
Almonds	1 oz.	.50 per oz.	.50
			$1.45
Direct labor:*			
Mixing	1 min.	14.40 per hr.	$ .24
Baking	2 min.	18.00 per hr.	.60
			$ .84
Variable overhead†	3 min.	32.40 per hr.	$1.62
Total standard cost per pound			$3.91

*Direct-labor rates include employee benefits.
†Applied on the basis of direct-labor hours.

Colonial's management accountant, Karen Blair, prepares monthly budget reports based on these standard costs. February's contribution report, which compares budgeted and actual performance, is shown in the following schedule.

Contribution Report for February

	Budget	Actual	Variance
Units (in pounds)	200,000	225,000	25,000 F
Revenue	$1,600,000	$1,777,500	$177,500 F
Direct material	$ 290,000	$ 432,500	$142,500 U
Direct labor	168,000	174,000	6,000 U
Variable overhead	324,000	375,000	51,000 U
Total variable costs	$ 782,000	$ 981,500	$199,500 U
Contribution margin	$ 818,000	$ 796,000	$ 22,000 U

Justine Madison, president of the company, is disappointed with the results. Despite a sizable increase in the number of cookies sold, the product's expected contribution to the overall profitability of the firm decreased. Madison has asked Blair to identify the reason why the contribution margin decreased. Blair has gathered the following information to help in her analysis of the decrease.

Usage Report for February

Cost Item	Quantity	Actual Cost
Direct materials:		
Cookie mix	2,325,000 oz.	$ 46,500
Milk chocolate	1,330,000 oz.	266,000
Almonds	240,000 oz.	120,000
Direct labor:		
Mixing	225,000 min.	54,000
Baking	400,000 min.	120,000
Variable overhead		375,000
Total variable costs		$981,500

Required:

1. Prepare an explanation of the $22,000 unfavorable variance between the budgeted and actual contribution margin for the chocolate nut supreme cookie product line during February by calculating the following variances. Assume that all materials are used in the month of purchase.
   a. Direct-material price variance.
   b. Direct-material quantity variance.
   c. Direct-labor rate variance.
   d. Direct-labor efficiency variance.
   e. Variable-overhead spending variance.
   f. Variable-overhead efficiency variance.
   g. Sales-price variance.
   h. Sales-volume variance.
2. a. Explain the problems that might arise in using direct-labor hours as the basis for applying overhead.
   b. How might activity-based costing (ABC) solve the problems described in requirement (2a)?

(CMA, adapted)

Current Issues in Managerial Accounting

Issue 11–56
Sharing Cost-Saving Ideas

"On Factory Floors, Top Workers Hide Secrets to Success," ***The Wall Street Journal,*** **July 1, 2002, pp. A1, A10, Timothy Aeppel.**

Overview

Experienced factory workers are reluctant to share their best cost-saving ideas.

Suggested Discussion Questions

As a group, discuss the phenomenon described in the article. Why does it occur? What can be done to mitigate against this behavior? How could standard costs be affected? Is this behavior ethical?

Issue 11–57
Cost-Cutting Programs

"Xerox Pledges to Cut $1 Billion in Costs, Reports a Quarterly Loss of $167 Million," ***The Wall Street Journal,*** **October 25, 2000, John Hechinger and Laura Johannes. See also "GE Says Earnings Rose 20% in 3rd Period: Results Reflect Net Growth in Every Major Unit, the Fruit of Cost Cuts,"** ***The Wall Street Journal,*** **October 12, 2000, Matt Murray.**

Overview

Xerox and GE both reported major cost-cutting programs to bolster the companies' profits.

Suggested Discussion Questions

How did each of these companies implement its cost-cutting program? Could standard costing have an important role to play in cutting costs?

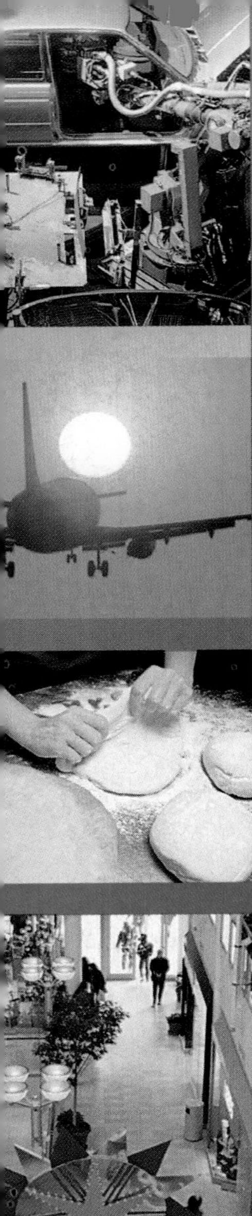

Chapter Twelve

Responsibility Accounting, Quality Control, and Environmental Cost Management

After completing this chapter, you should be able to:

1. Explain the role of responsibility accounting in fostering goal congruence.
2. Define and give an example of a cost center, a revenue center, a profit center, and an investment center.
3. Prepare a performance report and explain the relationships between the performance reports for various responsibility centers.
4. Use a cost allocation base to allocate costs.
5. Prepare a segmented income statement.
6. Prepare a quality cost report.
7. Discuss the traditional and contemporary views of the optimal level of product quality.
8. Understand the different types of environmental costs and discuss environmental cost management.

Construction Begins on Luxury Tower at Waikiki Sands Hotel

Honolulu, HI—Construction began today on the $50 million luxury tower at the Waikiki Sands Hotel. Located on world-famous Waikiki Beach, the hotel has undergone a major face-lift over the past two years since it was purchased by Aloha Hotels and Resorts. The new 20-story luxury tower will be the final step in the hotel chain's bid to make the Waikiki Sands the premier resort hotel on Oahu. According to a company officer, who wished to remain anonymous, the president of Aloha Hotels and Resorts made the final decision on the luxury tower. "It's lonely at the top, and the president felt she would have to take some big risks to separate the Waikiki Sands from the rest of the pack." And a big risk it was to give the go-ahead on the new tower. Aloha Hotels and Resorts will have to achieve a higher than average occupancy rate at the Waikiki Sands in order to make the kind of profit such a huge investment will require. "That's what the president gets paid for," said our source. "She makes the call. And then she accepts the praise—or takes the heat—whichever way it goes."

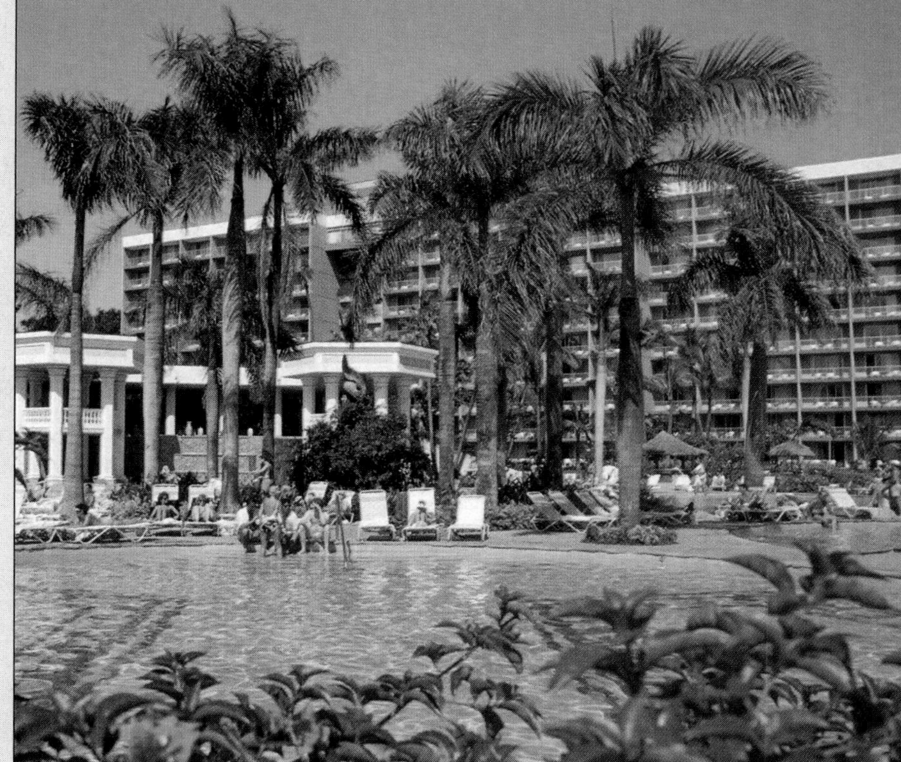

Thomas Boudreau, vice president of Aloha's Oahu Division, was contacted for comment on the construction at the Waikiki Sands. "It was a gutsy move by our president," said Boudreau, "but I think she made the right decision. Tourism is still increasing by leaps and bounds in Hawaii. Just yesterday Japan Airlines announced two additional daily flights into Honolulu. I have no doubt the luxury tower will earn its keep. But keep in mind that's not all we're doing at the Waikiki Sands. Just yesterday, I approved construction of a new multilevel, free-form swimming pool at the hotel. And last year I approved a new fitness center for the Waikiki Sands."

Boudreau went on to explain that upon acquiring the Waikiki Sands Hotel, Aloha had put in its own management team. "We have really experienced people at all management levels in the hotel," said Boudreau. "And we let them make significant decisions appropriate to their spheres of responsibility. For example, the hotel's general manager has authorized a lot of guest room redecorating without any divisional interference at all. We've got a great director of the Food and Beverage Department at the hotel, too. I've been told she's really changing the menu, entertainment, and special events schedule. We're really serious about making the Waikiki Sands the top hotel on the island."

Except for the new luxury tower, all of the projects contemplated for the Waikiki Sands Hotel are scheduled to be completed by October 31, in time for the high tourist season. The new tower is scheduled to be finished in 18 months.

Explain the role of responsibility accounting in fostering goal congruence.

Most organizations are divided into smaller units, each of which is assigned particular responsibilities. These units are called by various names, including divisions, segments, business units, and departments. Each department is comprised of individuals who are responsible for particular tasks or managerial functions. The managers of an organization should ensure that the people in each department are striving toward the same overall goals. **Goal congruence** results when the managers of subunits throughout an organization strive to achieve the goals set by top management.

How can an organization's managerial-accounting system promote goal congruence? **Responsibility accounting** refers to the various concepts and tools used by managerial accountants to measure the performance of people and departments in order to foster goal congruence.

Responsibility Centers

Define and give an example of a cost center, a revenue center, a profit center, and an investment center.

Topic 12–1

The basis of a responsibility-accounting system is the designation of each subunit in the organization as a particular type of *responsibility center.* A **responsibility center** is a subunit in an organization whose manager is held accountable for specified financial results of the subunit's activities. There are four common types of responsibility centers.

Cost Center A **cost center** is an organizational subunit, such as a department or division, whose manager is held accountable for the costs incurred in the subunit. The Painting Department in an automobile plant is an example of a cost center.

Revenue Center The manager of a **revenue center** is held accountable for the revenue attributed to the subunit. For example, the Reservations Department of an airline and the Sales Department of a manufacturer are revenue centers.

Exhibit 12–1
Organization Chart: Aloha Hotels and Resorts

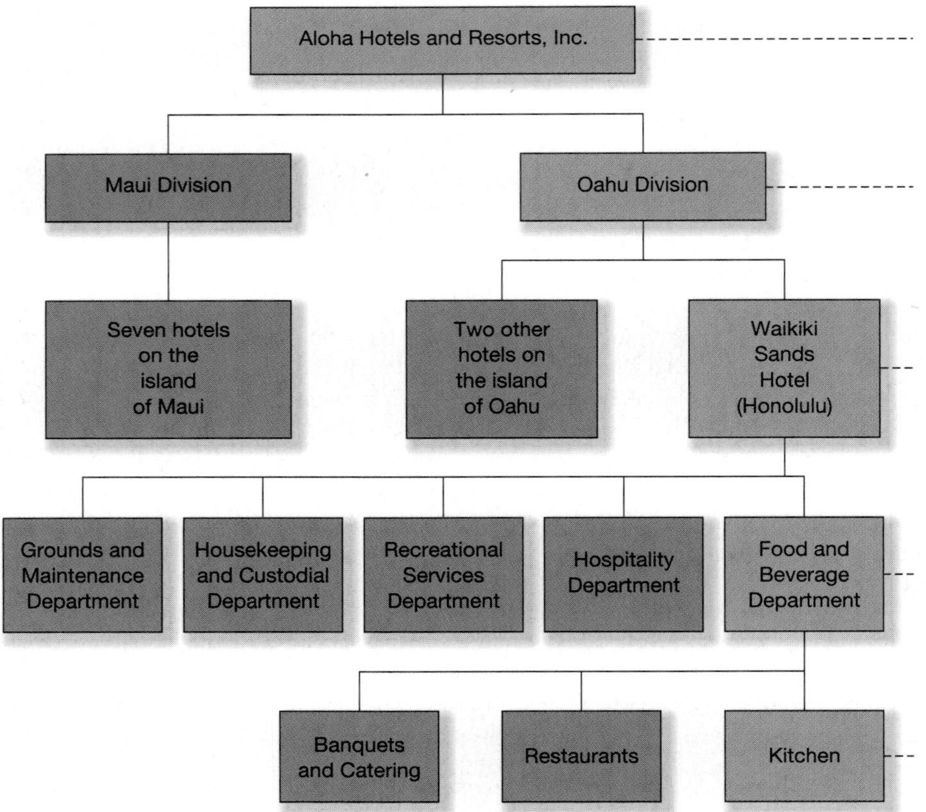

Profit Center A **profit center** is an organizational subunit whose manager is held accountable for profit. Since profit is equal to revenue minus expense, profit-center managers are held accountable for both the revenue and expenses attributed to their subunits. An example of a profit center is a company-owned restaurant in a fast-food chain.

Investment Center The manager of an **investment center** is held accountable for the subunit's profit *and the invested capital* used by the subunit to generate its profit. A division of a large corporation is typically designated as an investment center.[1]

Illustration of Responsibility Accounting

To illustrate the concepts used in responsibility accounting, we will focus on a hotel chain. Aloha Hotels and Resorts operates 10 luxury hotels in the state of Hawaii. The company is divided into the Maui Division, which operates seven hotels on the island of Maui, and the Oahu Division, with three properties on the island of Oahu. Exhibit 12–1 shows the company's organization chart, and Exhibit 12–2 depicts the responsibility-accounting system.

[1]Although there is an important conceptual difference between profit centers and investment centers, the latter term is not always used in practice. Some managers use the term *profit center* to refer to both types of responsibility centers. Hence, when businesspeople use the term *profit center,* they may be referring to a true profit center (as defined in this chapter) or to an investment center.

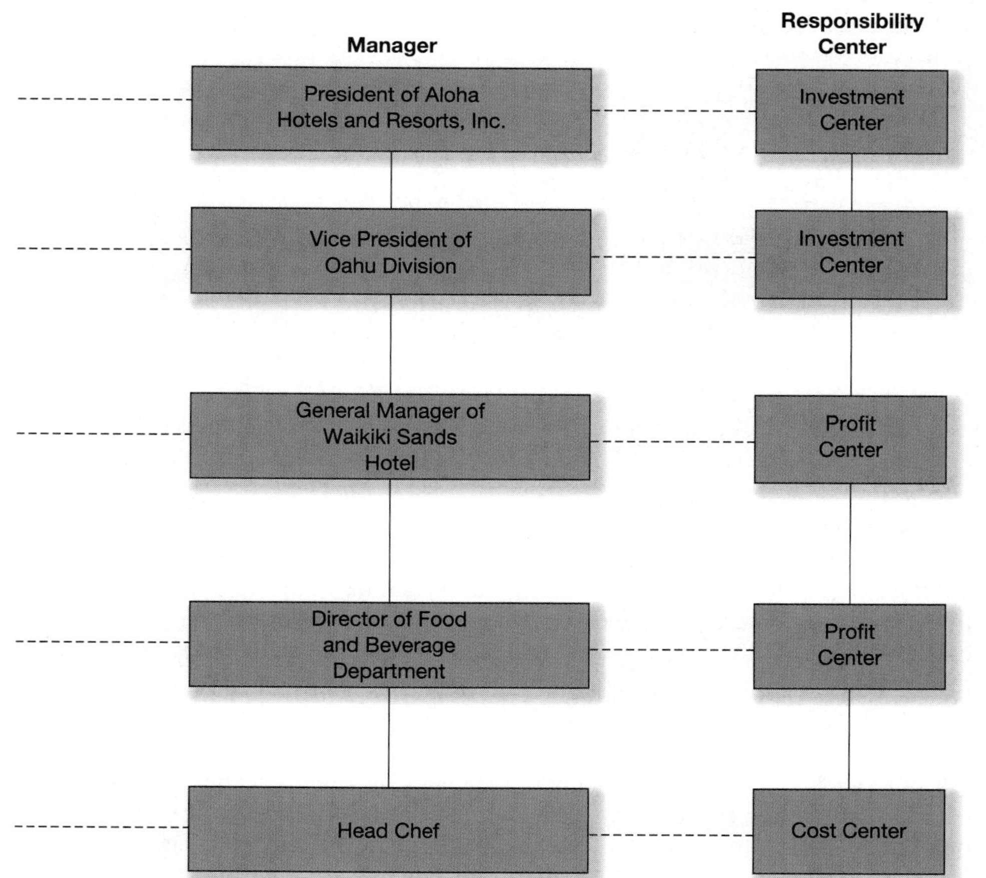

Exhibit 12–2
Responsibility Accounting System: Aloha Hotels and Resorts

This world globe assembly department is a cost center. The telemarketing operation shown here is a revenue center. These fast-food restaurants in Pittsburgh are profit centers. The power plant pictured here is an investment center. What sort of responsibility center designation would be appropriate for your local car wash, hair salon, and laundromat?

Corporate Level The chief executive officer of Aloha Hotels and Resorts, Inc. is the company's president. The president, who is responsible to the company's stockholders, is accountable for corporate profit in relation to the capital (assets) invested in the company. Therefore, the entire company is an *investment center*. The president has the autonomy to make significant decisions that affect the company's profit and invested capital. For example, the final decision to add a new luxury tower to any of the company's resort properties would be made by the president.

> "Responsibility accounting is an integral part of our reporting process in this company. Always has been. Always will." (12a)
>
> **DaimlerChrysler**

Division Level The vice president of the Oahu Division is accountable for the profit earned by the three resort hotels on Oahu in relation to the capital invested in those properties. Hence, the Oahu Division is also an *investment center*. The vice president has the authority to make major investment decisions regarding the properties on

Oahu, up to a limit of $300,000. For example, the vice president could decide to install a new swimming pool at one of the Oahu resort hotels, but could not decide to add a new wing.

Hotel Level The Waikiki Sands Hotel, in Honolulu, is one of the properties in the Oahu Division. The general manager of the Waikiki Sands Hotel is accountable for the profit earned by the hotel. The general manager does not have the authority to make major investment decisions, but is responsible for operational decisions. For example, the general manager hires all of the hotel's departmental managers, sets wage rates, determines procedures and standards for operations, approves decorating decisions, and generally oversees the hotel's operation. Since the hotel's general manager has no authority to make major investment decisions, she is held accountable only for the hotel's profit, not the capital invested in the property. Thus, the Waikiki Sands Hotel is a *profit center.*

Departmental Level The Waikiki Sands Hotel has five departments, as shown in Exhibit 12–1. The Grounds and Maintenance Department includes landscaping, building and equipment maintenance, and hotel security. The Housekeeping and Custodial Services Department covers laundry and janitorial services. These two departments are called service departments, since they provide services to the hotel's other departments but do not deal directly with hotel guests. The Recreational Services Department operates the hotel's swimming pools, saunas, video arcade, and tennis courts. The Hospitality Department includes the hotel's reservations desk, rooms, bell staff, and shopping facilities. Finally, the Food and Beverage Department operates the resort's restaurants, coffee shop, lounges, poolside snack bar, banquet operations, and catering service.

The director of the Food and Beverage Department is accountable for the profit earned on all food and beverage operations. Therefore, this department is a *profit center.* The director has the authority to approve the menu, set food and beverage prices, hire the wait staff, schedule entertainers, and generally oversee all food and beverage operations.

"But you have to wear the hat of the management team you are on to help them achieve the goals. You also have to wear the corporate finance hat to recognize that you have a duty, to the corporate finance function, to do things right and do them correctly, to stand up for what has to be done, and to say no when no is the appropriate thing to say." (12b)
Abbott Laboratories

Kitchen Level The Food and Beverage Department is divided further into subunits responsible for Banquets and Catering, Restaurants, and the Kitchen.

The head chef manages the kitchen and is accountable for the costs incurred there. Thus, the Kitchen is a *cost center.* The head chef hires the kitchen staff, orders food supplies, and oversees all food preparation. The head chef is responsible for providing high-quality food at the lowest possible cost.

Performance Reports

LO 3 Prepare a performance report and explain the relationships between the performance reports for various responsibility centers.

The performance of each responsibility center is summarized periodically on a *performance report.* A **performance report** shows the budgeted and actual amounts, and the variances between these amounts, of key financial results appropriate for the type of responsibility center involved. For example, a cost center's performance report concentrates on budgeted and actual amounts for various cost items attributable to the cost center. Performance reports also typically show the variance between budgeted and actual amounts for the financial results conveyed in the report. The data in a performance report help managers use *management by exception* to control an organization's operations effectively.

The performance report for the kitchen of the Waikiki Sands Hotel for February is shown in the Excel spreadsheet in Exhibit 12–3.

As the organization chart in Exhibit 12–1 shows, Aloha Hotels and Resorts is a *hierarchy.* Each subunit manager reports to one higher-level manager, from the head chef all the way up to the president. In such an organization, there is also a hierarchy of

Microsoft Excel - Exhibit 12-3

F9 =B9-D9

	A	B	C	D	E	F	G	H	I
1		**Flexible Budget**		**Actual Results**		**Variance***			
2		**February**	**Year to Date**	**February**	**Year to Date**	**February**		**Year to Date**	
3									
4	Kitchen staff wages	$ 80,000	$ 168,000	$ 78,000	$ 169,000	$ 2,000	F	$ 1,000	U
5	Food	675,000	1,420,000	678,000	1,421,000	3,000	U	1,000	U
6	Paper products	120,000	250,000	115,000	248,000	5,000	F	2,000	F
7	Variable overhead	70,000	150,000	71,000	154,000	1,000	U	4,000	U
8	Fixed overhead	85,000	180,000	83,000	181,000	2,000	F	1,000	U
9	Total expense	$ 1,030,000	$ 2,168,000	$ 1,025,000	$ 2,173,000	$ 5,000	F	$ 5,000	U
10									
11	*F denotes favorable variance, U denotes unfavorable variance.								

Sheet1 Sheet2 Sheet3

Ready

Exhibit 12–3
Performance Report for February: Kitchen, Waikiki Sands Hotel

performance reports, since the performance of each subunit constitutes part of the performance of the next higher-level subunit. For example, the cost performance in the kitchen of the Waikiki Sands Hotel constitutes part of the profit performance of the hotel's Food and Beverage Department.

Exhibit 12–4 shows the relationships between the February performance reports for several subunits of Aloha Hotels and Resorts. Notice that the numbers for the Grounds and Maintenance Department, the Housekeeping and Custodial Department, and the Kitchen are in parentheses. These subunits are cost centers, so the numbers shown are expenses. All of the other subunits shown in Exhibit 12–4 are either profit centers or investment centers. The numbers shown for these subunits are profits, so they are not enclosed in parentheses. In addition to the profit figures shown, the performance reports for the investment centers should include data about invested capital. The Maui Division, the Oahu Division, and the company as a whole are investment centers. Performance evaluation in investment centers is covered in the next chapter.

Notice the relationships between the performance reports in Exhibit 12–4. The kitchen is the lowest-level subunit shown, and its performance report is the same as that displayed in Exhibit 12–3. The *total expense* line from the kitchen performance report is included as one line in the performance report for the Food and Beverage Department. Also included are the total profit figures for the department's other two subunits: Banquets and Catering, and Restaurants. How is the *total profit* line for the Food and Beverage Department used in the performance report for the Waikiki Sands Hotel? Follow the relationships emphasized with arrows in Exhibit 12–4.

"It is real important that accountants or finance people, when you get into the numbers, to be able to take a spreadsheet that has a zillion numbers on it and then turn around and present that to somebody at a high enough level in a meaningful manner that they can understand. I think probably in the last five years that is what I spend most of my time on—working on communications." (12c)
Caterpillar

The hierarchy of performance reports starts at the bottom and builds toward the top, just like the organization structure depicted in Exhibit 12–1 builds from the bottom upward. Each manager in the organization receives the performance report for his or her own subunit in addition to the performance reports for the major subunits in the next lower level. For example, the general manager of the Waikiki Sands Hotel receives the reports for the hotel, and each of its departments: Grounds and Maintenance, Housekeeping and Custodial, Recreational Services, Hospitality, and Food and Beverage. With these reports, the hotel's general manager can evaluate her subordinates as well as her own performance. This will help the general manager in improving the hotel's performance, motivating employees, and planning future operations.

Budgets, Variance Analysis, and Responsibility Accounting

Notice that the performance reports in Exhibit 12–4 make heavy use of budgets and variance analysis. Thus, the topics of budgeting, variance analysis, and responsibility

	Flexible Budget*		Actual Results*		Variance†	
	February	Year to Date	February	Year to Date	February	Year to Date
Company	$30,660	$64,567	$30,716	$64,570	$56 F	$ 3 F
Maui Division	$18,400	$38,620	$18,470	$38,630	$70 F	$10 F
Oahu Division	12,260	25,947	12,246	25,940	14 U	7 U
Total profit	$30,660	$64,567	$30,716	$64,570	$56 F	$ 3 F
Oahu Division						
Waimea Beach Resort	$ 6,050	$12,700	$ 6,060	$12,740	$10 F	$40 F
Diamond Head Lodge	2,100	4,500	2,050	4,430	50 U	70 U
Waikiki Sands Hotel	4,110	8,747	4,136	8,770	26 F	23 F
Total profit	$12,260	$25,947	$12,246	$25,940	$14 U	$ 7 U
Waikiki Sands Hotel						
Grounds and Maintenance	$ (45)	$ (90)	$ (44)	$ (90)	$ 1 F	—
Housekeeping and Custodial	(40)	(90)	(41)	(90)	1 U	—
Recreational Services	40	85	41	88	1 F	$ 3 F
Hospitality	2,800	6,000	2,840	6,030	40 F	30 F
Food and Beverage	1,355	2,842	1,340	2,832	15 U	10 U
Total profit	$ 4,110	$ 8,747	$ 4,136	$ 8,770	$26 F	$23 F
Food and Beverage Department						
Banquets and Catering	$ 600	$ 1,260	$ 605	$ 1,265	$ 5 F	$ 5 F
Restaurants	1,785	3,750	1,760	3,740	25 U	10 U
Kitchen	(1,030)	(2,168)	(1,025)	(2,173)	5 F	5 U
Total profit	$ 1,355	$ 2,842	$ 1,340	$ 2,832	$15 U	$10 U
Kitchen						
Kitchen staff wages	$ (80)	$ (168)	$ (78)	$ (169)	$ 2 F	$ 1 U
Food	(675)	(1,420)	(678)	(1,421)	3 U	1 U
Paper products	(120)	(250)	(115)	(248)	5 F	2 F
Variable overhead	(70)	(150)	(71)	(154)	1 U	4 U
Fixed overhead	(85)	(180)	(83)	(181)	2 F	1 U
Total expense	$ (1,030)	$ (2,168)	$ (1,025)	$(2,173)	$ 5 F	$ 5 U

*Numbers without parentheses denote profit; numbers with parentheses denote expenses; numbers in thousands.

†F denotes favorable variance; U denotes unfavorable variance.

Exhibit 12–4

Performance Reports for February: Selected Subunits of Aloha Hotels and Resorts

accounting are closely interrelated. The flexible budget provides the benchmark against which actual revenues, expenses, and profits are compared. As you saw in Chapter 11, it is important to use a flexible budget so that appropriate comparisons can be made. It would make no sense, for example, to compare the actual costs incurred in the kitchen at Waikiki Sands Hotel with budgeted costs established for a different level of hotel occupancy.

The performance reports in Exhibit 12–4 also show variances between budgeted and actual performance. These variances often are broken down into smaller components to help management pinpoint responsibility and diagnose performance. Variance analysis, which was discussed in detail in Chapters 10 and 11, is an important tool in a responsibility-accounting system.

Cost Allocation

LO 4

Use a cost allocation base to allocate costs.

Many costs incurred by an organization are the joint result of several subunits' activities. For example, the property taxes and utility costs incurred by Aloha Hotels and Resorts for the Waikiki Sands Hotel are the joint result of all of the hotel's activities.

Cost Pool	Responsibility Center	Allocation Base	Percentage of Total	Costs Distributed
Administration	Grounds and Maintenance	12 employees	10.0%	$ 2,500
	Housekeeping and Custodial	24 employees	20.0	5,000
	Recreational Services	12 employees	10.0	2,500
	Hospitality	36 employees	30.0	7,500
	Food and Beverage	36 employees	30.0	7,500
	Total	120 employees	100.0%	$25,000
Facilities	Grounds and Maintenance	2,000 sq. ft.	1.0%	$ 300
	Housekeeping and Custodial	2,000 sq. ft.	1.0	300
	Recreational Services	5,000 sq. ft.	2.5	750
	Hospitality	175,000 sq. ft.	87.5	26,250
	Food and Beverage	16,000 sq. ft.	8.0	2,400
	Total	200,000 sq. ft.	100.0%	$30,000
Marketing	Grounds and Maintenance	—	—	—
	Housekeeping and Custodial	—	—	—
	Recreational Services	$ 20,000 of sales	4.0%	$ 2,000
	Hospitality	400,000 of sales	80.0	40,000
	Food and Beverage	80,000 of sales	16.0	8,000
	Total	$500,000 of sales	100.0%	$50,000

Exhibit 12–5
Cost Distribution to Responsibility Centers: Waikiki Sands Hotel

One function of a responsibility-accounting system is to assign all of an organization's costs to the subunits that cause them to be incurred.

A collection of costs to be assigned is called a **cost pool.** At the Waikiki Sands Hotel, for example, all utility costs are combined into a *utility cost pool,* which includes the costs of electricity, water, sewer, trash collection, television cable, and telephone. The responsibility centers, products, or services to which costs are to be assigned are called **cost objects.** The Waikiki Sands' cost objects are its major departments. (See the organization chart in Exhibit 12–1.) The process of assigning the costs in the *cost pool* to the *cost objects* is called **cost allocation** or **cost distribution.**

Cost Allocation Bases

To distribute (or allocate) costs to responsibility centers, the managerial accountant chooses an *allocation base* for each cost pool. An **allocation base** is a measure of activity, physical characteristic, or economic characteristic that is associated with the responsibility centers, which are the cost objects in the allocation process. The allocation base chosen for a cost pool should reflect some characteristic of the various responsibility centers that is related to the incurrence of costs. An allocation base also may be referred to as a *cost driver.*

Exhibit 12–5 shows the Waikiki Sands Hotel's February cost distribution for selected cost pools. Each cost pool is distributed to each responsibility center in proportion to that center's relative amount of the allocation base. For example, the Food and Beverage Department receives 30 percent of the total administrative costs, $25,000, because that department's 36 employees constitute 30 percent of the hotel's employees. Notice that no marketing costs are allocated to either the Grounds and Maintenance Department or the Housekeeping and Custodial Department. Neither of these responsibility centers generates any sales revenue.

Responsibility Center	Budgeted Sales Revenue	Actual Sales Revenue	Marketing Cost Distribution: Based on Budget	Marketing Cost Distribution: Based on Actual
Recreational Services	$ 20,000 (4%)*	$ 4,500 (1%)*	$ 2,000	$ 500
Hospitality	400,000 (80%)	405,000 (90%)	40,000	45,000
Food and Beverage	80,000 (16%)	40,500 (9%)	8,000	4,500
Total	$500,000	$450,000	$50,000	$50,000

*Percentage of column total.

Exhibit 12–6
Cost Distribution: Budgeted versus Actual Allocation Bases

Allocation Bases Based on Budgets

At the Waikiki Sands Hotel, administrative and marketing costs are distributed on the basis of *budgeted* amounts of the relevant allocation bases, rather than *actual* amounts. The managerial accountant should design an allocation procedure so that the behavior of one responsibility center does not affect the costs allocated to other responsibility centers.

Suppose, for example, that the budgeted and actual February sales revenues for the hotel were as shown in Exhibit 12–6. Notice that the Hospitality Department's actual sales revenue is close to the budget. However, the actual sales of the Recreational Services Department and the Food and Beverage Department are substantially below the budget. If the distribution of marketing costs is based on actual sales, instead of budgeted sales, then the cost distributed to the Hospitality Department jumps from $40,000 to $45,000, an increase of 12.5 percent. Why does this happen? As a result of a sales performance substantially below the budget for the *other two departments,* the Hospitality Department is penalized with a hefty increase in its cost distribution. This is misleading and unfair to the Hospitality Department manager. A preferable cost distribution procedure is to use budgeted sales revenue as the allocation base, rather than actual sales revenue. Then the marketing costs distributed to each department do not depend on the performance in the other two departments.

Activity-Based Responsibility Accounting

Traditional responsibility-accounting systems tend to focus on the financial performance measures of cost, revenue, and profit for the *subunits* of an organization. Contemporary cost management systems, however, are beginning to focus more and more on *activities.* Costs are incurred in organizations and their subunits because of activities. *Activity-based costing (ABC)* systems associate costs with the activities that drive those costs. The database created by an ABC system, coupled with nonfinancial measures of operational performance for each activity, enables management to employ **activity-based responsibility accounting.** Under this approach management's attention is directed not only to the cost incurred in an activity but also to the activity itself. Is the activity necessary? Does it add value to the organization's product or service? Can the activity be improved? By seeking answers to these questions, managers can eliminate non-value-added activities and increase the cost-effectiveness of the activities that do add value.[2]

[2]Activity-based costing, introduced conceptually in Chapter 3, is covered in detail in Chapter 5. Activity analysis and the elimination of non-value-added activities are covered in Chapters 5 and 6.

Behavioral Effects of Responsibility Accounting

Responsibility-accounting systems can influence behavior significantly. Whether the behavioral effects are positive or negative, however, depends on how responsibility accounting is implemented.

Information versus Blame

The proper focus of a responsibility-accounting system is *information.* The system should identify the individual in the organization who is in the best position to explain each particular event or financial result. The emphasis should be on providing that individual and higher-level managers with information to help them understand the reasons behind the organization's performance. When properly used, a responsibility-accounting system *does not emphasize blame.* If managers feel they are beaten over the head with criticism and rebukes when unfavorable variances occur, they are unlikely to respond in a positive way. Instead, they will tend to undermine the system and view it with skepticism. But when the responsibility-accounting system emphasizes its informational role, managers tend to react constructively, and strive for improved performance.

Controllability

Some organizations use performance reports that distinguish between controllable and uncontrollable costs or revenues. For example, the head chef at the Waikiki Sands Hotel can influence the hours and efficiency of the kitchen staff, but he probably cannot change the wage rates. A performance report that distinguishes between the financial results influenced by the head chef and those he does not influence has the advantage of providing complete information to the head chef. Yet the report recognizes that certain results are beyond his control.

Identifying costs as controllable or uncontrollable is not always easy. Many cost items are influenced by more than one person. The time frame also may be important in determining controllability. Some costs are controllable over a long time frame, but not within a short time period. To illustrate, suppose the Waikiki Sands' head chef has signed a one-year contract with a local seafood supplier. The cost of seafood can be influenced by the head chef if the time period is a year or more, but the cost cannot be controlled on a weekly basis.

Motivating Desired Behavior

"Distinguishing between controllable and uncontrollable costs can increase the effectiveness of a cost management system, if it's done from the perspective of helping a client department understand where the opportunities for cost reduction are." (12d)
American Management Systems

Managerial accountants often use the responsibility-accounting system to motivate actions considered desirable by upper-level management. Sometimes the responsibility-accounting system can solve behavioral problems as well. As a case in point, consider the problem of rush orders. To accept or reject a rush order is a cost-benefit decision:

Costs of Accepting Rush Order	Benefits of Accepting Rush Order
Disrupted production	Satisfied customers
More setups	Greater future sales
Higher costs	

The following real-world example involving rush orders provides a case in point.

The production scheduler in a manufacturing firm was frequently asked to interrupt production of one product with a rush order for another product. Rush orders typically resulted in greater costs because more product setups were required. Since the production scheduler was evaluated on the basis of costs, he was reluctant to accept rush orders. The sales manager, on the other hand, was evaluated on the basis of sales revenue. By agreeing to customers' demands for rush orders, the sales manager satisfied his customers. This resulted in more future sales and favorable performance ratings for the sales manager.

As the rush orders became more and more frequent, the production manager began to object. The sales manager responded by asking if the production scheduler wanted to take the responsibility for losing a customer by refusing a rush order. The production scheduler did not want to be blamed for lost sales, so he grudgingly accepted the rush orders. However, considerable ill will developed between the sales manager and production scheduler.

The company's managerial accountant came to the rescue by redesigning the responsibility-accounting system. The system was modified to accumulate the extra costs associated with rush orders and charge them to the sales manager's responsibility center, rather than the production scheduler's center. The ultimate result was that the sales manager chose more carefully which rush-order requests to make, and the production manager accepted them gracefully.

The problem described in the preceding illustration developed because two different managers were considering the costs and benefits of the rush-order decision. The production manager was looking only at the costs, while the sales manager was looking only at the benefits. The modified responsibility-accounting system made the sales manager look at *both the costs and the benefits* associated with each rush order. Then the sales manager could make the necessary trade-off between costs and benefits in considering each rush order. Some rush orders were rejected, because the sales manager decided the costs exceeded the benefits. Other rush orders were accepted, when the importance of the customer and potential future sales justified it.

This example illustrates how a well-designed responsibility-accounting system can make an organization run more smoothly and achieve higher performance.

Segmented Reporting

LO 5

Prepare a segmented income statement.

Subunits of an organization are often called *segments. Segmented reporting* refers to the preparation of accounting reports by segment and for the organization as a whole. Many organizations prepare **segmented income statements,** which show the income for major segments and for the entire enterprise.

In preparing segmented income statements, the managerial accountant must decide how to treat costs that are incurred to benefit more than one segment. Such costs are called **common costs.** The salary of the president of Aloha Hotels and Resorts is a common cost. The president manages the entire company. Some of her time is spent on matters related specifically to the Maui Division or the Oahu Division, but much of it is spent on tasks that are not traced easily to either division. The president works with the company's board of directors, develops strategic plans for the company, and helps set policy and goals for the entire enterprise. Thus, the president's compensation is a common cost, which is not related easily to any segment's activities.

Many managerial accountants believe that it is misleading to allocate common costs to an organization's segments. Since these costs are not traceable to the activities of segments, they can be allocated to segments only on the basis of some highly arbitrary allocation base. Consider the salary of Aloha Hotels and Resorts' president. What allocation base would you choose to reflect the contribution of the president's managerial efforts to the company's two divisions? The possible allocation bases include budgeted divisional sales revenue, the number of hotels or employees in each division, or some measure of divisional size, such as total assets. However, all of these allocation bases would yield arbitrary cost allocations and possibly misleading segment profit information. For this reason, many organizations choose not to allocate common costs on segmented income statements.

> "Senior management wants to know yesterday. So the pace has quickened and there's more pressure to get information much sooner and at the same time there is so much more information there." (12e)
>
> **Qwest** (formerly US West)

Exhibit 12–7 shows February's segmented income statement (on a budgeted basis) for Aloha Hotels and Resorts. Each segment's income statement is presented in the

	Segment of Company			Segment of Oahu Division			
	Aloha Hotels and Resorts	**Maui Division**	**Oahu Division**	**Waimea Beach Resort**	**Diamond Head Lodge**	**Waikiki Sands Hotel**	**Not Allocated**
Sales revenue	$2,500,000	$1,600,000	$900,000	$450,000	$150,000	$300,000	—
Variable operating expenses:							
Personnel	$820,900	$ 510,400	$310,500	$155,500	$ 50,000	$105,000	—
Food, beverages, and supplies	738,000	458,600	279,400	139,700	46,400	93,300	—
Other	83,000	58,000	25,000	12,500	4,000	8,500	—
Total	$1,641,900	$1,027,000	$614,900	$307,700	$100,400	$206,800	—
Segment contribution margin	$ 858,100	$ 573,000	$285,100	$142,300	$ 49,600	$ 93,200	—
Less: Fixed expenses controllable by segment manager	30,000	21,000	9,000	4,000	1,000	3,000	$ 1,000
Profit margin controllable by segment manager	$ 828,100	$ 552,000	$276,100	$138,300	$ 48,600	$ 90,200	$ (1,000)
Less: Fixed expenses, traceable to segment, but controllable by others	750,000	500,000	250,000	26,000	8,000	16,000	200,000
Segment profit margin	$ 78,100	$ 52,000	$ 26,100	$112,300	$ 40,600	$ 74,200	$(201,000)
Less: Common fixed expenses	10,000						
Income before taxes	$ 68,100						
Less: Income tax expense	37,440						
Net income	$ 30,660						

Exhibit 12–7
Segmented Income Statements: Aloha Hotels and Resorts (in thousands)

contribution format discussed in Chapter 8. Notice that Exhibit 12–7 shows income statements for the following segments.

Aloha Hotels and Resorts	Maui Division	
	Oahu Division	Waimea Beach Resort Diamond Head Lodge Waikiki Sands Hotel

Three numbers in Exhibit 12–7 require special emphasis. First, the $10,000,000 of common fixed expenses in the left-hand column is not allocated to the company's two divisions. Included in this figure are such costs as the company president's salary. These costs cannot be allocated to the divisions, except in some arbitrary manner.

Second, $1,000,000 of controllable fixed expense in the right-hand column constitutes part of the Oahu Division's $9,000,000 of controllable fixed expense. All $9,000,000 of expense is controllable by the vice president of the Oahu Division. However, $1,000,000 of these expenses cannot be traced to the division's three hotels, except on an arbitrary basis. For example, this $1,000,000 of expense includes the salary of the Oahu Division's vice president. Therefore, the $1,000,000 of expense is *not allocated* among the division's three hotels. This procedure illustrates an important point. Costs that are traceable to segments at one level in an organization may become common costs at a lower level in the organization. The vice president's salary is traceable to the Oahu Division, but it cannot be allocated among the division's three hotels except arbitrarily. Thus, the vice president's salary is a traceable cost at the divisional level, but it becomes a common cost at the hotel level.

Third, the $200,000,000 of fixed expenses controllable by others in the right-hand column constitutes part of the Oahu Division's $250,000,000 of fixed expenses controllable by others. However, the $200,000,000 portion cannot be allocated among the division's three hotels, except arbitrarily.

Segments versus Segment Managers

One advantage of segmented reports like the one in Exhibit 12–7 is that they make a distinction between segments and segment managers. Some costs that are traceable to a segment may be completely beyond the influence of the segment manager. Property taxes on the Waikiki Sands Hotel, for example, are traceable to the hotel, but the hotel's general manager cannot influence them. To properly evaluate the *Waikiki Sands Hotel as an investment* of the company's resources, the property taxes should be included in the hotel's costs. However, in evaluating the general manager's performance, the property-tax cost should be *excluded,* since the manager has no control over it.

Key Features of Segmented Reporting

To summarize, Exhibit 12–7 illustrates three important characteristics of segmented reporting:

1. ***Contribution format.*** These income statements use the contribution format. The statements subtract variable expenses from sales revenue to obtain the *contribution margin.*
2. ***Controllable versus uncontrollable expenses.*** The income statements in Exhibit 12–7 highlight the costs that can be controlled, or heavily influenced, by each segment manager. This approach is consistent with *responsibility accounting.*
3. ***Segmented income statement.*** *Segmented reporting* shows income statements for the company as a whole and for its major segments.

Customer Profitability Analysis and Activity-Based Costing

Analyzing profitability by segments of the company can help managers gain insight into the factors that are driving the company's performance. In addition to focusing on the major organizational subunits in the company, profitability analysis can focus on major market segments, geographical regions, distribution channels, or customers.

Customer profitability analysis uses the concept of activity-based costing to determine how serving particular customers causes activities to be performed and costs to be incurred. Suppose, for example, that customer A frequently changes its orders after they are placed, but customer B typically does not. Then the costs incurred in updating sales orders for changes should be recorded in a manner that reflects the fact that customer A is more responsible for those activities and costs than is customer B.

Many factors can result in some customers being more profitable than others. Customers that order in small quantities, order frequently, often change their orders, require special packaging or handling, demand faster delivery, or need special parts or engineering design generally are less profitable than customers who demand less in terms of customized services. If managers have a good understanding of which customers are generating the greatest profit, they can make more-informed decisions about customer service. Moreover, customers can be educated as to the costs they are causing by demanding special services. In many cases, customers' behavior can be changed in a way that reduces costs to the supplier. Then these cost savings can be shared by the supplier and the customer. (Customer-profitability analysis is covered more extensively in Chapter 6.)

Total Quality Management

Traditional responsibility-accounting systems focus primarily on the financial performance of an organization's subunits. However, nowadays it is crucial for organizations to monitor performance in many nonfinancial areas as well. For many companies, quality is at the forefront of the areas in which nonfinancial performance is critically important. The quality of the product or service that an organization provides can spell the difference between future profitability and disaster. Quality is equally important in the service and manufacturing industries. For Aloha Hotels and Resorts, the quality of service includes the comfort of the guest rooms, the amenities provided to guests, the friendliness of the staff, the quality of food served in the restaurant, and so forth. Hotel guests are ever more discriminating as they assess the overall quality of service and then select their accommodations accordingly. Similar comments apply to the airlines, long-distance telecommunications companies, banks, car rental firms, and financial investment firms.

In the manufacturing industry, product quality has become a key factor in determining a firm's success or failure in the global marketplace. Advanced, highly reliable manufacturing methods have made it possible to achieve very high standards of product quality. As a result, more and more firms are making product quality a keystone of their competitive strategy.

Measuring and Reporting Quality Costs

Recognizing the importance of maintaining high product quality, companies often measure and report the costs of doing so. Before we examine the costs that companies incur to maintain high product quality, let's consider what product quality means.

Product Quality What is meant by a high-quality product? There are two concepts of quality that determine a product's degree of excellence or the product's ultimate fitness for its intended use. A product's **grade** refers to the extent of its capability in performing its intended purpose, in relation to other products with the same functional use. For example, a computer monitor that displays 65,536 colors is of a higher grade than a monitor that displays only 256 colors. A product's **quality of design** refers to how well it is conceived or designed for its intended use. For example, a coffee mug designed with a handle that is too small for the user's fingers is a poorly designed mug. The **quality of conformance** refers to the extent to which a product meets the specifications of its design. A coffee mug with an appropriately sized handle could be well designed, but if the handle breaks off due to shoddy manufacturing, it will be useless. This mug fails to conform to its design specifications. Both quality of design and quality of conformance are required in order to achieve a high-quality finished product.

LO 6 Prepare a quality cost report.

Costs of Quality Due to the increasing importance of maintaining high product quality, many companies routinely measure and report the costs of ensuring high quality. Four types of costs are monitored.

First are **prevention costs,** the costs of preventing defects. Second are **appraisal costs,** the costs of determining whether defects exist. The third type of costs are **internal failure costs,** those costs of repairing defects found prior to product sale. The last type of costs are **external failure costs,** those costs incurred when defective products have been sold.

Exhibit 12–8 shows a quality-cost report prepared by Handico, Inc., a manufacturer of cordless telephones.[3] As is always true in cost monitoring, quality-cost report-

[3]For further information on cost of quality, see Zafar U. Khan, "Cost of Quality," in Barry J. Brinker, ed. *Guide to Cost Management* (New York: John Wiley & Sons, 2000), pp. 319–44. For examples of quality cost reporting, see Lawrence Carr, "Cost of Quality: Making It Work," *Journal of Cost Management* 9, no. 1 (Spring 1995), pp. 61–65, and S. Brinkman and M. Applebaum, "The Quality Cost Report: It's Alive and Well," *Management Accounting* 76, no. 3 (September 1994), pp. 61–65.

	Current Month's Cost	Percent of Total
Prevention costs		
Quality training	$ 2,000	1.3
Reliability engineering	10,000	6.5
Pilot studies	5,000	3.3
Systems development	8,000	5.2
Total prevention costs	$ 25,000	16.3
Appraisal costs		
Materials inspection	$ 6,000	3.9
Supplies inspection	3,000	2.0
Reliability testing	5,000	3.3
Metallurgical laboratory	25,000	16.3
Total appraisal costs	$ 39,000	25.5
Internal failure costs		
Scrap	$ 15,000	9.8
Repair	18,000	11.8
Rework	12,000	7.8
Downtime	6,000	3.9
Total internal failure costs	$ 51,000	33.3
External failure costs		
Warranty costs	$ 14,000	9.2
Out-of-warranty repairs and replacement	6,000	3.9
Customer complaints	3,000	2.0
Product liability	10,000	6.5
Transportation losses	5,000	3.3
Total external failure costs	$ 38,000	24.9
Total quality costs	$153,000	100.00

Exhibit 12–8

Quality-Cost Report: Handico

Handico

ing is most useful when cost trends are examined over a period of time. Through trend analysis, management can see where improvement is occurring and where difficulties exist. Goals can be set to achieve a particular cost target in an area of concern. For example, Handico's management might strive to reduce warranty costs to zero by a certain date.

Observable versus Hidden Quality Costs The quality costs discussed in the preceding section are *observable.* They can be measured and reported, often on the basis of information in the accounting records. In addition to these observable quality costs, however, companies incur *hidden* quality costs. When products of inferior quality make it to market, customers are dissatisfied. Their dissatisfaction can result in decreased sales and a tarnished reputation for the company. Not only does the company experience lost sales for the inferior products but it will also likely experience lost sales in its other product lines. The opportunity cost of these lost sales and decreased market share can represent a significant hidden cost. Such hidden costs are difficult to estimate or report.

Exhibit 12–9
Quality Costs and the Optimal Level of Product Quality

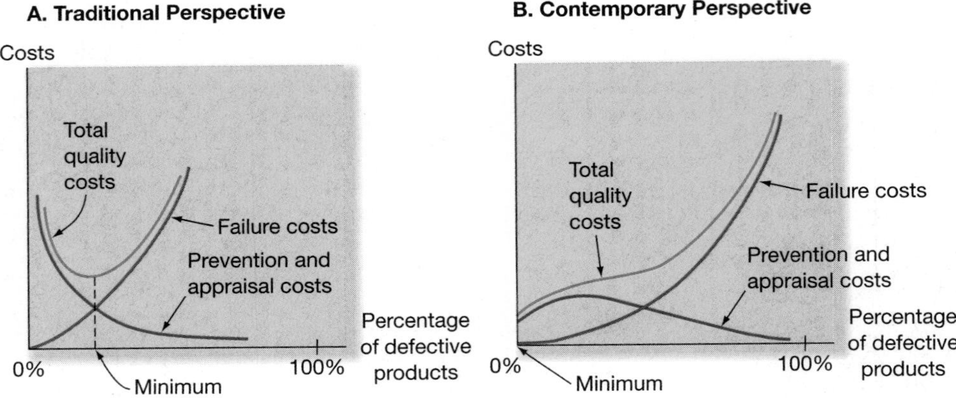

Changing Views of Optimal Product Quality

LO 7

Discuss the traditional and contemporary views of the optimal level of product quality.

One way to express product quality is in the percentage of products that fail to conform to their specifications, that is, the percentage of defects. Given this perspective, what is the optimal level of product quality?[4]

Traditional Perspective The traditional viewpoint holds that finding the optimal level of product quality is a balancing act between incurring costs of prevention and appraisal on one hand and incurring costs of failure on the other. Panel A of Exhibit 12–9 depicts this trade-off. As the percentage of defective products decreases, the costs of prevention and appraisal increase. However, the costs of internal and external failure decrease. Adding the costs of prevention, appraisal, internal and external failure yields total quality costs. The optimal product quality level is the point that minimizes total quality costs.

Contemporary Perspective Due largely to the influence of Japanese product quality expert Genichi Taguchi, the contemporary viewpoint of optimal product quality differs from the traditional perspective. The contemporary view is that if both observable and hidden costs of quality are considered, *any* deviation from a product's target specifications results in the incurrence of increasing quality costs. Under the contemporary viewpoint, as depicted in Panel B of Exhibit 12–9, the optimal level of product quality occurs at the *zero defect level.* As Panel B shows, the observable and hidden costs of internal and external failure increase as the percentage of defective products increases. The observable and hidden costs of prevention and appraisal increase slightly and then decrease as the percentage of defects increases. The most important point, though, is that the total costs of quality are minimized at the zero defect level.

Whether the traditional or contemporary view of optimal product quality is most accurate is still being debated by quality control experts. Moreover, the exact shape of the cost functions in Exhibit 12–9 is largely an empirical question, and the cost functions probably differ among industries and product types. One thing is certain, though. To compete successfully in today's global market, any company must pay very close attention to achieving a very high level of product quality.

---

[4]This discussion is based on the following sources: Wayne J. Morse, Harold P. Roth, and Kay M. Poston, *Measuring, Planning and Controlling Quality Costs* (Montvale, NJ: National Association of Accountants, 1987); Jack Campanella, ed., *Principles of Quality Costs* (Milwaukee, WI: ASQC Quality Press, 1990); and Alahassane Diallo, Zafar V. Kahn, and Curtis F. Vail, "Cost of Quality in the New Manufacturing Environment," *Management Accounting* 77, no. 2 (August 1993), pp. 20–25.

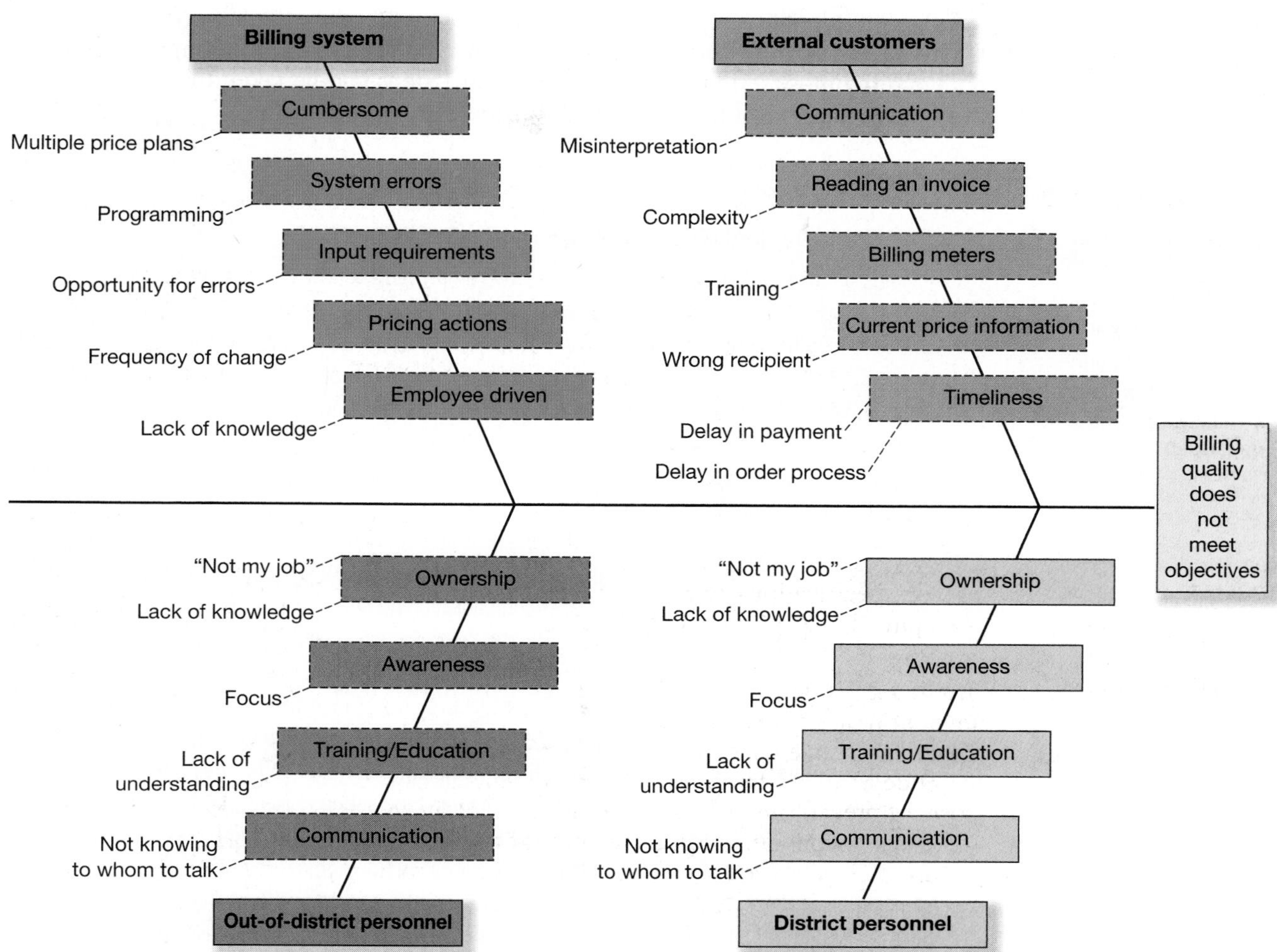

Source: David M. Buehlman and Donald Stover, "How Xerox Solves Quality Problems," *Management Accounting* 75, no. 3 (September 1993), pp. 33–36.

Exhibit 12–10
Cause and Effect Diagram: Billing Quality at Xerox Corporation

Total Quality Management Monitoring product quality coupled with measuring and reporting quality costs helps companies maintain programs of **total quality management, or TQM.** This refers to the broad set of management and control processes designed to focus the entire organization and all of its employees on providing products or services that do the best possible job of satisfying the customer. Among the tools used in total quality management is the **Six Sigma** program, an analytical method that aims at achieving near-perfect results in a production process. (See the Management Accounting Practice illustration on p. 518 for details.)

Identifying Quality Control Problems An effective TQM program includes methods for identifying quality control problems. One method of identifying quality problems is the cause and effect diagram (also called an Ishikawa diagram or a fishbone diagram). Exhibit 12–10 displays a cause and effect diagram used by Xerox Corporation to identify the causes of errors in its customer billing process. As the diagram shows, the quality improvement team has identified a wide range of possible causes for billing errors. After identifying possible causes for billing errors, the Xerox team, nicknamed the Billing Bloopers Team, could take systematic steps to eliminate the root causes of the errors.

"Six Sigma might be the maturation of everything we've learned over the past 100 years about quality." (12f)
President, American Society for Quality

Another helpful tool in quality improvement programs is the Pareto diagram. Depicted in Exhibit 12–11, the Pareto diagram shows graphically the frequency with which various quality control problems are observed for a particular model of cordless telephone. The Pareto diagram helps the TQM team visualize and communicate to others what the most serious types of defects are. Steps can be taken then to attack the most serious and most frequent problems first.

Management Accounting Practice

Motorola, General Electric, Dell Computer, Wal-Mart, Dow Chemical, Allied Signal, and Honeywell

SIX SIGMA FOR QUALITY MANAGEMENT AND COST REDUCTION

"Originally conceived by Motorola Inc. as a quality-improvement device" two decades ago, "Six Sigma soon morphed into a cost-cutting utensil for manufacturers of all stripes. Now, it's fast becoming the Swiss army knife of the business world. Goods producers still make up the bulk of users, who typically rely on statistics to uncover and then reduce product variance in order to boost quality and efficiency. But increasingly, manufacturers are applying Six Sigma to functions as varied as accounts receivable, sales, and research and development. And their success in these nonfactory domains has inspired Six Sigma projects at financial institutions, retailers, health-care concerns, and in other areas of the service sector."

Six Sigma is "an analytical method aimed at achieving *near-perfect results* in a production process. In statistics, the Greek letter *sigma* denotes variation in a standard bell curve. One sigma equals 690,000 defects per 1 million. Most companies do no better than three sigma, or 66,000 errors per million. Six Sigma reduces that count to *3.4 defects per million.* That saves money by preventing waste."

Six Sigma "achieves results by reducing subjective errors in the assessment of problems. First, auditors *define* a process where results are subpar. Then they *measure* the process to determine current performance, *analyze* this information to pinpoint where things are going wrong, and *improve* the process and eliminate the error. Last, *controls* are set up to prevent future bugs."

"In the world of manufacturing, Six Sigma has become something akin to a religion." When General Electric's former chairman Jack Welch embraced Six Sigma, for example, "he quickly assembled an unprecedented army of employees to pinpoint and fix problems throughout GE" using their Six Sigma training. "The results were awesome: In three years alone, these troops saved the company $8 billion, according to GE." Now "GE is sending out its Six Sigma squads to customers such as Dell Computer and Wal-Mart stores to help them root out what GE estimates to be more than $1 billion in inefficiencies and waste—and help GE win more business."[5]

Dow Chemical has initiated several Six Sigma projects, each of which has saved an average of a half million dollars in its first year alone.[6] Allied Signal, which uses activity-based costing in conjunction with its Six Sigma program, saved over $500 million in the program's first year.[7] Honeywell is using the Six Sigma approach, in conjunction with other productivity improvements, with a goal of over a billion dollars in cost savings.[8]

"Employees charged with Six Sigma duties generally have what's called a *black belt."* At Allied Signal, for example, "it's awarded to those employees who complete four separate weeks of classroom study. In between those weeks of class, black-belt candidates must use what they've learned to focus on a project within the company and show some cost savings achieved by using Six Sigma."[9]

---

[5]Michael Arndt, "Quality Isn't Just for Widgets," *Business Week,* July 22, 2002, pp. 72, 73.

[6]Ibid., p. 73.

[7]Tad Leahy, "In Search of Perfection with Six Sigma," *Business Finance* 5, no. 1 (January 2000), pp. 73–76.

[8]Amy Barrett and Diane Brady, "At Honeywell, It's Larry the Knife," *Business Week,* November 26, 2001, pp. 98–100.

[9]Leahy, op. cit. See also, Gregory T. Lucier and Sridhar Seshadri, "GE Takes Six Sigma beyond the Bottom Line," *Strategic Finance* 82, no. 11 (May 2001), pp. 41–46.

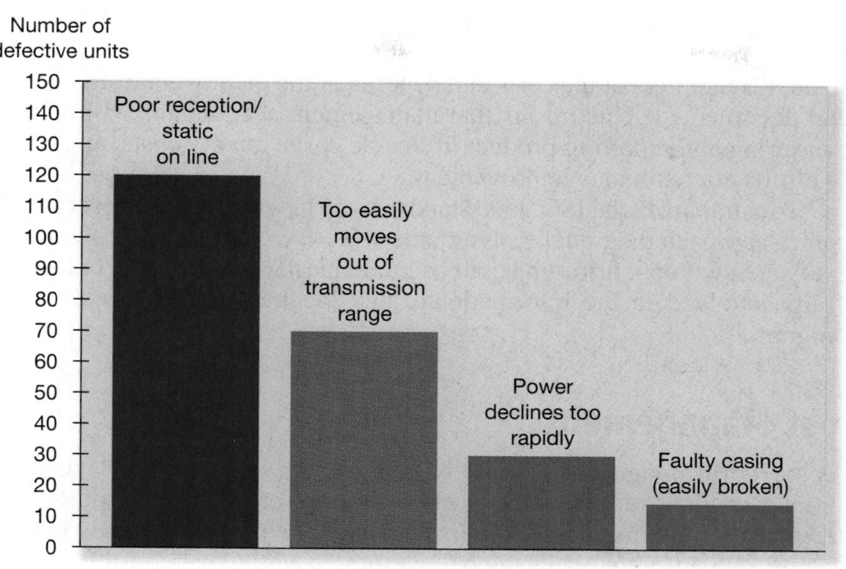

Exhibit 12–11

Pareto Diagram: Frequency of Defect Types for Cordless Telephone (Handico)

Handico

ISO 9000 Standards

A key factor in determining the quality of a company's products is its quality control system. The organizational structure, personnel, procedures, and policies that are in place to monitor product quality will greatly affect a firm's ability to achieve high-quality standards. In 1987, the International Standards Organization (ISO), based in Geneva, Switzerland, issued a set of quality control standards for companies selling products in Europe. The ISO 9000 standards, as they have come to be known, focus on a manufacturer's quality control system. The ISO 9000 standards basically require that a manufacturer have a well-defined quality control system in place, and that the target level of product quality be maintained consistently. Moreover, the ISO 9000 standards require a manufacturer to prepare extensive documentation of all aspects of the quality control system. The first standard, ISO 9000, lists three objectives:

- The company should sustain the quality of its product or service at a level that continually meets the purchaser's stated or implied needs.
- The quality control system should be sufficient to give the supplier's own management confidence that the intended quality is being maintained.
- The supplying company should give the purchaser confidence that the intended quality is consistently achieved in the delivered product or service.

The ISO 9000 standards are now being adopted in the United States as well. The U.S. government and many large companies are more and more inclined to require adherence to the standards by their suppliers.

The ISO 9000 standards consist of five major parts. ISO 9000 states the objectives of the standards, defines a quality-related vocabulary, and provides a guide to the other standards in the series. ISO 9001 provides a model for quality assurance in design, development, production, installation, and servicing. ISO 9002 focuses more narrowly on quality assurance in production and installation. ISO 9003 addresses quality assurance in final inspection and testing. Finally, ISO 9004 provides guidelines for the design of a quality management system.

Implications for Managerial Accounting The ISO 9000 standards have several implications for managerial accountants. First, the standards require extensive documentation of the quality control system. This task often falls to the controller's office.

In fact, several of the largest public accounting firms are offering assurance services in helping companies meet the ISO documentation requirements. Second, the ISO standards require that the costs and benefits of the quality control system be measured and documented. This means that management accountants will be responsible for measuring and reporting product life-cycle costs, quality costs, and the effectiveness of efforts at continuous improvement.

To summarize, the ISO 9000 standards are having a global impact on the way companies approach their quality assurance objectives. The standards will affect virtually every area within a firm subject to its guidelines. Managerial accountants will be integrally involved in the informational and documentation aspects of the ISO 9000 program.[10]

Environmental Cost Management

Understand the different types of environmental costs and discuss environmental cost management.

Topic 12–2

As the world's population grows, business activity expands, and the globe seemingly shrinks, millions of people the world over are ever-more aware of the critical need to preserve our environment for ourselves and our posterity. Issues like air and water quality, hidden carcinogens, global warming, and the overconsumption of nonrenewable energy sources are in the headlines every day. Business leaders have come to talk of the desirability of **sustainable development,** which means business activity that produces the goods and services needed in the present without limiting the ability of future generations to meet their needs. Many companies are striving for greater *ecoefficiency,* which means increasing their production of goods and services while at the same time decreasing the deleterious effects on the environment of that production. Unfortunately, not all companies are striving equally hard toward these desirable goals. To force companies to pay attention to environmental issues, in the United States we have environmental laws, such as the *U.S. Clean Air Act* and the U.S. *Superfund Act,* as well as the federal watchdog agency, the Environmental Protection Agency (EPA). On a global scale, there are environmental initiatives as well, such as the *Kyoto Protocol,* which seeks to reduce emissions of greenhouse gases that many scientists believe contribute to global warming.

So, besides being a very important issue to all of us due to the clear health and quality-of-life implications, what does any of this have to do with managerial accounting? The answer is that the *costs* of dealing with environmental issues in one way or another are enormous. These **environmental costs** take many forms, such as installing scrubbers on a smokestack to comply with EPA regulations, improving a production process to reduce or eliminate certain pollutants, or cleaning up a contaminated river. In the next section, we will systematically explore these costs with the goal of having a better understanding of how to manage them.

Classifying Environmental Costs

There are many types of environmental costs.

Private versus Social Environmental Costs One important distinction is between private costs and social (or public) costs. *Private environmental costs* are those borne by a company or individual. Examples would be costs incurred by a company to comply with EPA regulations or to clean up a polluted lake. *Social environmental costs* are those borne by the public at large. Examples of these include costs borne by the taxpayers to staff the EPA, costs borne by the taxpayers to clean up a polluted lake or river, costs borne by individuals, insurance companies and Medicare due to health

[10]The ISO standards are available from the American National Standards Institute, 105–111 South State Street, Hackensack, NJ 07601.

problems caused by pollutants, and the unquantifiable quality-of-life costs we all bear from a degraded environment. While these social environmental costs are of great importance to all of us, we will focus our attention here on **environmental cost management,** which is the systematic attempt to measure and control or reduce the private environmental costs borne by a company or other organization.[11]

Visible versus Hidden Environmental Costs Both social and private environmental costs can be *visible* or *hidden. Visible social environmental costs* are those that are known and clearly identified as tied to environmental issues, such as the taxpayers' costs of staffing the EPA or cleaning up a polluted lake. *Hidden social environmental costs* include those that are caused by environmental issues but have not been so identified, such as the costs borne by individuals, insurance companies, or Medicare due to cancers caused by pollutants but not clearly identified as such. For example, is melanoma (a serious type of skin cancer) caused by a familial tendency, failure to use sun block, or a thinning of the ozone layer resulting from industrial emissions of chlorofluorocarbons? No one knows for sure.

Managing Private Environmental Costs

Let's focus our attention now on environmental cost management, or the measuring and control or reduction of private environmental costs.

Visible versus Hidden Private Environmental Costs Once again, we need to distinguish between visible and hidden costs. *Visible private environmental costs* are those that are measurable and have been clearly identified as tied to environmental issues. *Hidden private environmental costs* are those that are caused by environmental issues but have not been so identified by the accounting system.[12] Exhibit 12–12 provides examples of both visible and hidden private environmental costs.[13] Notice that the visible and the hidden costs listed in Exhibit 12–12 are further classified as follows:

- *Monitoring costs.* Costs of monitoring the production process to determine if pollution is being generated (e.g., costs of testing wastewater for contaminants).
- *Abatement costs.* Costs incurred to reduce or eliminate pollution (e.g., changing a product's design to use more expensive materials that do not result in environmental contamination).
- *Remediation costs* (i.e., clean-up costs).
  - *On-site remediation.* Costs of reducing or preventing the discharge into the environment of pollutants that have been generated in the production process (e.g., cost of installing scrubbers on a smokestack to remove certain air pollutants in the smoke).
  - *Off-site remediation.* Costs of reducing or eliminating pollutants from the environment after they have been discharged (e.g., cost of cleaning up a river polluted by a company's operations).

The distinction between the visible and hidden costs listed in Exhibit 12–12 is an important but subtle one. Consider, for example, the incremental cost of using a more expensive material because it causes less (or no) negative environmental impact. Is this a visible or a hidden cost? The answer is *it depends* on whether the accounting system

---

[11]Based on the discussion in German Böer, Margaret Curtin, and Louis Hoyt, "Environmental Cost Management," *Management Accounting* 80, no. 3 (September 1998), pp. 28–38.

[12]Based on Satish Joshi, Ranjani Krishnan, and Lester Lave, "Estimating the Hidden Costs of Environmental Regulation," *The Accounting Review* 76, no. 2 (April 2001), pp. 171–98.

[13]Joshi et al., Ibid.

Exhibit 12–12
Private Environmental Costs

	Visible Costs	Hidden Costs*
Monitoring	Inspecting products for contamination Measuring contamination of processes or machinery Verifying vendor compliance with environmental standards	Inspection of products Incremental costs of procurement staff to ensure vendor compliance with environmental standards
Abatement	Qualifying vendors for environmental compliance Recycling materials, containers, or water Designing products and processes to reduce or eliminate negative environmental impacts Doing environmental impact analyses	Incremental material costs incurred to use less-polluting materials Incremental direct-labor costs incurred to perform duties related to reducing pollution Incremental costs of more expensive processes installed all or in part to reduce pollution Incremental costs of purchasing hybrid (electric and gasoline powered) vehicles to reduce air pollution
Remediation		
On-site	Installing pollution reduction or elimination devices Disposing of toxic waste in an environmentally sound manner Treating toxic waste	Incremental direct-labor costs incurred to maintain remediation equipment Incremental energy or other overhead costs incurred to operate remediation equipment
Off-site	Cleaning up polluted sites (e.g., water, soil, or buildings) Defending or settling environmental lawsuits Paying EPA fines	Incremental direct-labor costs for workers used to perform environmental clean-up tasks Forgone contribution margins on lost sales due to an unfavorable environmental record or reputation

*Each of the costs listed in the *hidden costs* column is included under the assumption that although these costs are caused by environmental concerns, the accounting system has not identified them as such. A study by Joshi et al. provides evidence for the plausibility of this assumption. See Satish Joshi, Ranjani Krishnan, and Lester Lave, "Estimating the Hidden Costs of Environmental Regulation," *The Accounting Review* 76, no. 2 (April 2001) pp. 171–98.

has measured this cost and identified it as an environmental cost. Studies show that many environmental costs are hidden, because the accounting system does not measure and identify them as environmental costs. "Most accounting systems accumulate visible costs into environmental cost pools, separate from other overhead cost pools. . . . For example, many steel mills compile separate cost pools for wastewater treatment, remediation, hazardous waste disposal, pollution-abatement capital expenditures, and depreciation on pollution abatement equipment."[14] However, a steel mill's incremental material costs caused by changing from sinters to less-polluting pellets in response to more stringent environmental regulations, is typically not separately reported by the accounting system as an environmental cost.[15] Hence, it remains a *hidden* environmental cost.

Why is this point about visible versus hidden costs so important? Because many observers believe that the visible costs reported by most accounting systems may be only a small proportion of the hidden costs. A steel-industry study, for example, concluded that the hidden costs were nearly 10 times the visible costs!

[14]Joshi et al., Ibid.

[15]Joshi et al., Ibid.

Environmental Cost Strategies

We have only scratched the surface in our discussion of environmental costs, and it is an area certain to receive much greater attention in the future—both in practice and in academia. Let's conclude our discussion with a brief mention of three strategies for managing environmental costs.[16]

1. *End-of-pipe strategy.* Under this approach, companies produce the waste or pollutant, and then clean it up before it is discharged into the environment. Smokestack scrubbers, wastewater treatment, and carbon air filters are examples of end-of-pipe strategies.
2. *Process improvement strategy.* Under this approach, companies modify products and production processes to produce little or no pollutants, or find ways to recycle wastes internally.
3. *Prevention strategy.* "The ultimate strategy for maximizing the value of pollution-related activities involves . . . not producing any pollutants in the first place. With this strategy, companies avoid all problems with regulatory authorities and, in many cases, generate significant profit improvements."[17]

Tie-In to the Responsibility-Accounting System

As a concluding thought, consider why our discussion of environmental costs—and in the preceding section, quality costs—is located in the chapter covering responsibility accounting. For any type of cost, an important key to managing or controlling the cost is to make it someone's responsibility. "Line managers make the decisions that cause waste and environmental costs, and these managers should see the financial consequences of their decisions. Without a tight link between decision makers and environmental costs, any cost-control efforts will be difficult and prone to failure."[18]

Focus on Ethics

SHORT-SIGHTED VIEW OF COST CUTTING

The hypothetical scenario described here is based on a compilation of anecdotes taken from the literature on responsibility accounting, quality management, and environmental cost accounting. Jamie Ericsson, the controller for Handico, has just compiled a cost report for the second quarter. The report is prepared each quarter for corporate headquarters. She has taken particular notice of several major cost categories that show significant reductions in expenditures when compared to the first quarter. She made the following list of the major cost cuts:

Cost Item	Cost Reduction ($)	Cost Reduction (%)
General employee training	$12,000	25%
Routine machine maintenance	13,500	20
Process improvement	12,000	12
Quality training*	18,000	8
Raw-material inspection*	$ 6,500	9%
Product redesign for compliance with environmental policies†	7,100	13
Random testing of materials for environmental contaminants†	11,200	10

*Categorized as quality costs.
†Categorized as environmental costs.

Concerned that there may have been errors in compiling the data, Ericsson scheduled an appointment with the divisional vice president, Les Winters. At the meeting, the conversation went like this.

Ericsson (C): "Les, I'm concerned about these cost cuts. Are these mistakes, or are we really making such substantial cuts in these areas?"

Winters (VP): "Your numbers look right, Jamie. I ordered these cutbacks myself. I think there's a lot of fat in this operation that can be cut, and I'm just getting started."

[16]Böer et al., op. cit.
[17]Böer et al., op. cit.
[18]Böer et al., op. cit.

Ericsson (C): "But these are all important areas to invest in, Les. I see the invoices for these costs every month, and I don't think it's wasted money at all."

Winters (VP): "Corporate wants a lean company, Jamie. I'm just trying to give them one."

Ericsson (C): "Have you thought through the implications, Les? Cutting general employee training will eventually take a toll on our productivity gains. Same thing for the cuts in process improvements. And cutting routine machine maintenance could mean breakdowns later on. Maybe not for a year or so, but eventually it'll take its toll."

Winters (VP): Becoming annoyed, "Those are my concerns, Ms. Ericsson, not yours."

Ericsson (C): "Look, Les, we're all on the same team. I'm just concerned, that's all. I'm especially worried about these cuts in quality and environmental costs. These quality costs are in the areas of prevention and appraisal. If we make these cuts now, we'll likely have higher costs for internal, or even external, failure down the road. And the same goes for these environmental cost cuts. If we scrimp on monitoring and abatement costs, we're just going to be shelling out more for remediation costs in the future."

Winters (VP): "Those are all hypotheticals. You don't know any of that for sure."

Ericsson (C): "Les, I feel as though I need to highlight these cost cuts in my report to corporate. They should at least be made aware of these issues. I'll need your authorization for that."

Winters (VP): "No can do, Jamie. You are instructed to make your usual quarterly report using the standard format."

After the meeting, Ericsson was commiserating with her close friend, Amy Ling, the chief of engineering.

Ericsson (C): "Amy, I just had a very unsatisfactory meeting with Les Winters. I shouldn't go into the details, but I'm concerned about some things."

Ling (E): "Well, I have good news for you then. The grapevine has it that Les is on the very short list for taking over as president of our Japanese subsidiary. That would be a huge promotion for him. Word is that all he's got to do is turn in a good performance for the year here. If he does that, the job's his."

Ericsson (C): "That explains a lot, Amy. Thanks for the heads up. I've got some thinking to do."

What do you think is going on here? What is the VP, Les Winters, up to? Is he acting ethically? What steps should the controller, Jamie Ericsson, take? Also, how could a balanced scorecard help mitigate against the problems apparent in this scenario?[19]

Chapter Summary

Responsibility-accounting systems are designed to foster goal congruence among the managers in decentralized organizations. Each subunit in an organization is designated as a cost center, revenue center, profit center, or investment center. The managerial accountant prepares a performance report for each responsibility center. These reports show the performance of the responsibility center and its manager for a specified time period.

To use responsibility accounting effectively, the emphasis must be on information rather than blame. The intent should be to provide managers with information to help them better manage their subunits. Responsibility-accounting systems can bring about desired behavior, such as reducing the number of rush orders in a manufacturing company.

Segmented income statements often are included in a responsibility-accounting system, to show the performance of the organization and its various segments. To be most effective, such reports should distinguish between the performance of segments and segment managers. Customer profitability analysis is an increasingly used tool that helps managers to better understand which customers are providing the greatest profit.

Product and service quality has become a key factor in determining a firm's success or failure in the global marketplace. As product quality becomes ever more important, many firms are beginning to carefully monitor the costs of maintaining product quality. Quality costs often are categorized as follows: prevention costs, appraisal costs, internal failure costs, and external failure costs. In addition to observable quality costs, companies experience hidden quality costs, such as the opportunity cost associated with lost

[19]The balanced scorecard was introduced in Chapter 1 and covered extensively in Chapter 10.

market share. The contemporary perspective on product quality holds that if both observable and hidden costs of product quality are considered, the optimal level of product quality occurs at the zero defect level.

Monitoring product quality coupled with measuring and reporting quality costs helps companies maintain programs of total quality management, or TQM. This refers to the broad set of management and control processes designed to focus the entire organization and all of its employees on providing products or services that do the best possible job of satisfying the customer.

Environmental issues have come to the forefront in many ways. Companies incur a variety of environmental costs, some visible and some hidden, in dealing with environmental issues. Companies are pursuing several different strategies to manage these environmental costs.

Review Problem on Responsibility Accounting

James Madison National Bank has a division for each of the two counties in which it operates, Cayuga and Oneida. Each divisional vice president is held accountable for both profit and invested capital. Each division consists of two branch banks, East and West. Each branch manager is responsible for that bank's profit. The Cayuga Division's East Branch has a Deposit Department, a Loan Department, and an Administrative Services Department. The department supervisors of the Loan and Deposit Departments are accountable for departmental revenues; the Administrative Services Department supervisor is accountable for costs.

All of James Madison National Bank's advertising and promotion is done centrally. The advertising and promotion cost pool for the year just ended, which amounted to $40,000, is allocated across the four branch banks on the basis of budgeted branch revenue. Budgeted revenue for the year is shown below.

Cayuga Division:	West Branch	$400,000
	East Branch	200,000
Oneida Division:	West Branch	250,000
	East Branch	150,000

Required:

1. Draw an organization chart for James Madison National Bank, which shows each subunit described above, its manager's title, and its designation as a responsibility center.
2. Distribute (allocate) the bank's advertising cost pool to the four branch banks.

Solution to Review Problem

1. Organization chart (subunits, managers, responsibility center designation) is shown below.

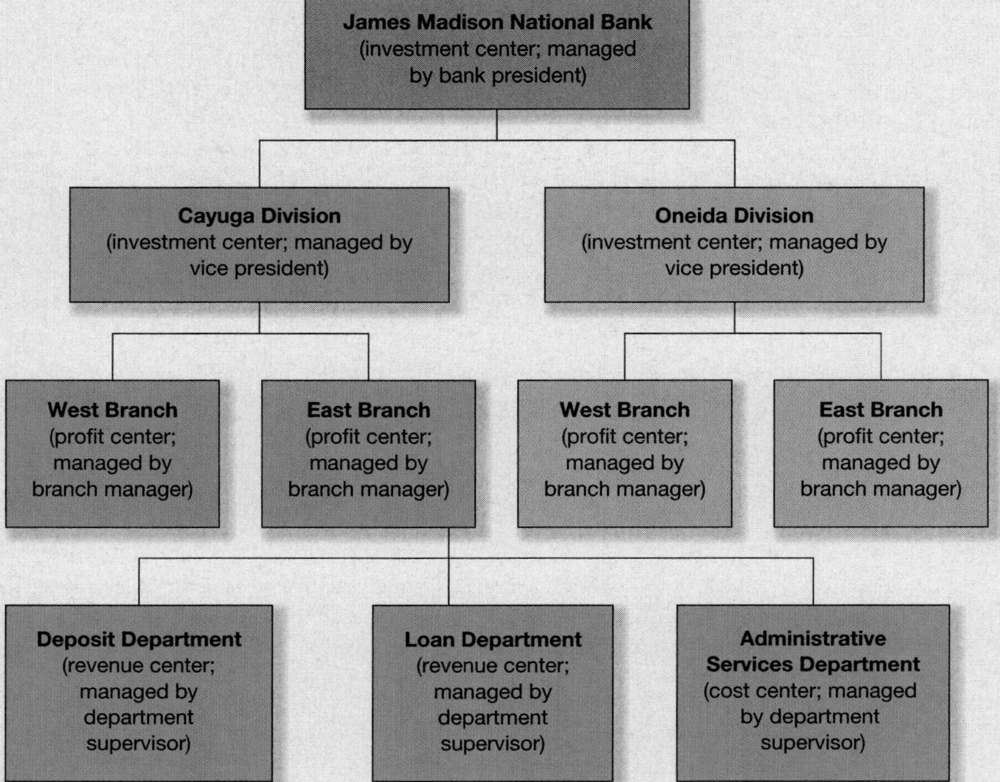

2. Cost distribution (or allocation):

Cost Pool	Responsibility Center	Allocation Base: Revenue	Percentage of Total*	Costs Distributed
Advertising	Cayuga, West Branch	$ 400,000	40%	$16,000
and	Cayuga, East Branch	200,000	20	8,000
promotion	Oneida, West Branch	250,000	25	10,000
costs	Oneida, East Branch	150,000	15	6,000
	Total	$1,000,000	100%	$40,000

*Branch revenue as a percentage of total revenue, $1,000,000.

Key Terms

For each term's definition refer to the indicated page, or turn to the glossary at the end of the text.

activity-based responsibility accounting, 509
allocation base, 508
appraisal costs, 514
common costs, 511
cost allocation (or distribution), 508
cost center, 502
cost objects, 508
cost pool, 508
customer profitability analysis, 513
environmental cost management, 521
environmental costs, 520
external failure costs, 514
goal congruence, 502
grade, 514
internal failure costs, 514
investment center, 503
performance report, 505
prevention costs, 514
profit center, 503
quality of conformance, 514
quality of design, 514
responsibility accounting, 502
responsibility center, 502
revenue center, 502
segmented income statement, 511
Six Sigma, 517
sustainable development, 520
total quality management (TQM), 517

Review Questions

12–1. Why is goal congruence important to an organization's success?

12–2. How does a responsibility-accounting system foster goal congruence?

12–3. Define and give examples of the following terms: *cost center, revenue center, profit center, and investment center.*

12–4. Under what circumstances would it be appropriate to change the Waikiki Sands Hotel from a profit center to an investment center?

12–5. Explain the relationship between performance reports and flexible budgeting.

12–6. What is the key feature of activity-based responsibility accounting? Briefly explain.

12–7. Explain how to get positive behavioral effects from a responsibility-accounting system.

12–8. "Performance reports based on controllability are impossible. Nobody really *controls* anything in an organization!" Do you agree or disagree? Explain your answer.

12–9. Define and give examples of the following terms: *cost pool* and *cost object.*

12–10. Define and give an example of *cost allocation* (or *distribution*).

12–11. Give an example of a common resource in an organization. List some of the opportunity costs associated with using the resource. Why might allocation of the cost of the common resource to its users be useful?

12–12. Explain how and why cost allocation might be used to assign the costs of a mainframe computer system used for research purposes in a university.

12–13. Define the term *cost allocation base.* What would be a sensible allocation base for assigning advertising costs to the various components of a large theme park?

12–14. Referring to Exhibit 12–5, why are marketing costs distributed to the Waikiki Sands Hotel's departments on the basis of *budgeted* sales dollars?

12–15. Explain what is meant by a *segmented income statement.*

12–16. Why do some managerial accountants choose not to allocate common costs in segmented reports?

12–17. Why is it important in responsibility accounting to distinguish between segments and segment managers?

12–18. List and explain three key features of the segmented income statement shown in Exhibit 12–7.

12–19. Can a common cost for one segment be a traceable cost for another segment? Explain your answer.

12–20. What is meant by *customer profitability analysis?* Give an example of an activity that might be performed more commonly for one customer than for another.

12–21. List and define four types of product quality costs.

12–22. Explain the difference between observable and hidden quality costs.

12–23. Distinguish between a product's quality of design and its quality of conformance.

12–24. What is meant by a product's *grade,* as a characteristic of quality? Give an example in the service industry.

12–25. "An ounce of prevention is worth a pound of cure." Interpret this old adage in light of Exhibit 12–8.

12–26. Briefly explain the purpose of a cause and effect (or fishbone) diagram.

12–27. Define the following types of environmental costs: private, social, visible, hidden, monitoring, abatement, and both on-site and off-site remediation.

12–28. Explain three strategies of environmental cost management.

Exercises

Exercise 12–29
Assigning Responsibility for Skilled Employees' Wages
(LO 1)

Oradell Electronics Company manufactures complex circuit boards for the aerospace industry. Demand for the company's products has fallen in recent months, and the firm has cut its production significantly. Many unskilled workers have been temporarily laid off. Top management has made a decision, however, not to lay off any highly skilled employees, such as inspectors and machinery operators. Management was concerned that these highly skilled employees would easily find new jobs elsewhere and not return when production returned to normal levels.

To occupy the skilled employees during the production cutback, they have been reassigned temporarily to the Maintenance Department. Here they are performing general maintenance tasks, such as repainting the interior of the factory, repairing the loading dock, and building wooden storage racks for the warehouse. The skilled employees continued to receive their normal wages, which average $19 per hour. However, the normal wages for Maintenance Department employees average $11 per hour.

The supervisor of the Maintenance Department recently received the March performance report, which indicated that his department's labor cost exceeded the budget by $21,230. The department's actual labor cost was approximately 85 percent over the budget. The department supervisor complained to the controller.

Required: As the controller, how would you respond? Would you make any modification in Oradell's responsibility-accounting system? If so, list the changes you would make. Explain your reasoning.

Exercise 12–30
Designating Responsibility Centers.
(LO 2)

For each of the following organizational subunits, indicate the type of responsibility center that is most appropriate.

1. An orange juice factory operated by a large orange grower.
2. The College of Engineering at a large state university.
3. The European Division of a multinational manufacturing company.
4. The outpatient clinic in a profit-oriented hospital.
5. The Mayor's Office in a large city.
6. A movie theater in a company that operates a chain of theaters.
7. A radio station owned by a large broadcasting network.
8. The claims department in an insurance company.
9. The ticket sales division of a major airline.
10. A bottling plant of a soft drink company.

Exercise 12–31
Performance Report; Hotel
(LO 3)

The following data pertain to the Waikiki Sands Hotel for the month of March.

	Flexible Budget March (in thousands)*	Actual Results March (in thousands)*
Banquets and Catering	$ 650	$ 658
Restaurants	1,800	1,794
Kitchen staff wages	(85)	(86)
Food	(690)	(690)
Paper products	(125)	(122)
Variable overhead	(75)	(78)
Fixed overhead	(90)	(93)

*Numbers without parentheses denote profit; numbers with parentheses denote expenses.

Required: Prepare a March performance report similar to the lower portion of Exhibit 12–4. The report should have six numerical columns with headings analogous to those in Exhibit 12–4. Your performance report should cover only the Food and Beverage Department and the Kitchen. Draw arrows to show the relationships between the numbers in the report. Refer to Exhibit 12–4 for guidance. For the year-to-date columns in your report, use the data given in Exhibit 12–4. You will need to update those figures using the March data given above.

Exercise 12–32
Responsibility Accounting; Equipment Breakdown
(LO 1, 2)

How should a responsibility-accounting system handle each of the following scenarios?

1. Department A manufactures a component, which is then used by Department B. Department A recently experienced a machine breakdown which held up production of the component. As a result, Department B was forced to curtail its own production, thereby incurring large costs of idle time. An investigation revealed that Department A's machinery had not been properly maintained.
2. Refer to the scenario above, but suppose the investigation revealed the machinery in Department A had been properly maintained.

Exercise 12–33
Responsibility-Accounting Centers; Xerox Corporation
(LO 1, 2)

Xerox Corporation has been an innovator in its responsibility-accounting system. In one initiative, management changed the responsibility-center orientation of its Logistics and Distribution Department from a cost center to a profit center. The department manages the inventories and provides other logistical services to the company's Business Systems Group. Formerly, the manager of the Logistics and Distribution Department was held accountable for adherence to an operating expense budget. Now the department "sells" its services to the company's other segments, and the department's manager is evaluated partially on the basis of the department's profit. Xerox Corporation's management feels that the change has been beneficial. The change has resulted in more innovative thinking in the department and has moved decision making down to lower levels in the company.

Required: Comment on the new responsibility-center designation for the Logistics and Distribution Department.

Exercise 12–34
Cost Allocation in a College
(LO 4)

Wyoming Community College has three divisions: Liberal Arts, Sciences, and Business Administration. The college's comptroller is trying to decide how to allocate the costs of the Admissions Department, the Registrar's Department, and the Computer Services Department. The comptroller has compiled the following data for the year just ended.

Department	Annual Cost
Admissions	$117,000
Registrar	195,000
Computer Services	416,000

Division	Budgeted Enrollment	Budgeted Credit Hours	Planned Courses Requiring Computer Work
Liberal Arts	1,000	30,000	12
Sciences	800	28,000	24
Business Administration	700	22,000	24

Required:

1. For each department, choose an allocation base and distribute the departmental costs to the college's three divisions. Justify your choice of an allocation base.
2. Would you have preferred a different allocation base than those available using the data compiled by the comptroller? Why?

Exercise 12–35
Segmented Income Statement; TV Cable Company
(LO 5)

Tri-County Cable Services, Inc. is organized with three segments: Metro, Suburban, and Outlying. Data for these segments for the year just ended follow.

	Metro	Suburban	Outlying
Service revenue	$950,000	$750,000	$350,000
Variable expenses	150,000	100,000	50,000
Controllable fixed expenses	350,000	270,000	100,000
Fixed expenses controllable by others	180,000	150,000	40,000

In addition to the expenses listed above, the company has $45,000 of common fixed expenses. Income-tax expense for the year is $245,000.

Required: Prepare a segmented income statement for Tri-County Cable Services, Inc. Use the contribution format.

Exercise 12–36
Costs of Quality; Airline
(LO 6)

List three observable and three hidden quality costs that could occur in the airline industry related to the quality of service provided.

Exercise 12–37
Responsibility Accounting; Use of Internet
(LO 1, 2)

Visit the website for one of the following companies, or a different company of your choosing.

Marriott Hotels	www.marriott.com	Pizza Hut	www.pizzahut.com
McDonald's	www.mcdonalds.com	Ramada Inn	www.ramada.com
NationsBank	www.nationsbank.com	Xerox	www.xerox.com

Required: Read about the company's activities and operations. Then do as good a job as you can in preparing an organization chart for the firm. For each subunit in the organization chart, indicate what type of responsibility accounting center designation you believe would be most appropriate. (Refer to Exhibits 12–1 and 12–2 for guidance.)

Exercise 12–38
Quality Costs
(LO 6)

The following costs were incurred by Akasaka Metals Company to maintain the quality of its products. (*yen* is the national currency of Japan.)

1. Operating an X-ray machine to detect faulty welds, 99,000 *yen*
2. Repairs of products sold last year, 103,000 *yen*
3. Cost of rewelding faulty joints, 19,000 *yen*
4. Cost of sending machine operators to a three-week training program so they could learn to use new production equipment with a lower defect rate, 17,900 *yen*

Required: Classify each of these costs as a prevention, appraisal, internal failure, or external failure cost.

Exercise 12–39
Quality-Cost Report
(LO 6)

Cerritos Circuitry manufactures electrical instruments for a variety of purposes. The following costs related to maintaining product quality were incurred in May.

Training of quality-control inspectors	$31,500
Tests of instruments before sale	45,000
Inspection of electrical components purchased from outside suppliers	18,000
Costs of rework on faulty instruments	13,500
Replacement of instruments already sold, which were still covered by warranty	24,750
Costs of defective parts that cannot be salvaged	9,150

Required: Prepare a quality-cost report similar to the report shown in Exhibit 12–8.

Exercise 12–40
Environmental Cost Management; Internet
(LO 8)

Visit the website of Interface, Inc. at http://www.ifsia.com. Then go to the part of the company's website about its efforts toward sustainable development at www.ifsia.com/us/company/sustainability.

Required: What is Interface's product? Describe the company's efforts toward sustainable development.

Problems

Problem 12–41
Create an Organization
(LO 1, 2)

Here is your chance to be a tycoon. Create your own company. You will be the president and chief executive officer. It could be a manufacturer, retailer, or service industry firm, but *not* a hotel or bank. Draw an organization chart for your company, similar to the one in Exhibit 12–1. Identify divisions and departments at all levels in the organization. Then prepare a companion chart similar to the one in Exhibit 12–2. This chart should designate the title of the manager of a subunit at each level in the organization. It also should designate the type of responsibility center appropriate for each of these subunits. Finally, write a letter to your company's stockholders summarizing the major responsibilities of each of the managers you identified in your chart. For guidance, refer to the discussion of Exhibits 12–1 and 12–2 in the chapter. (Have some fun, and be creative.)

Problem 12–42
Design Performance Reports; Continuation of Preceding Problem
(LO 3)

After designing your company, design a set of performance reports for the subunits you identified in your chart. Make up numbers for the performance reports, and show the relationship between the reports. Refer to Exhibit 12–4 for guidance.

Problem 12–43
Designating Responsibility Centers; Hotel
(LO 2)

The following partial organization chart is an extension of Exhibit 12–1 for Aloha Hotels and Resorts.

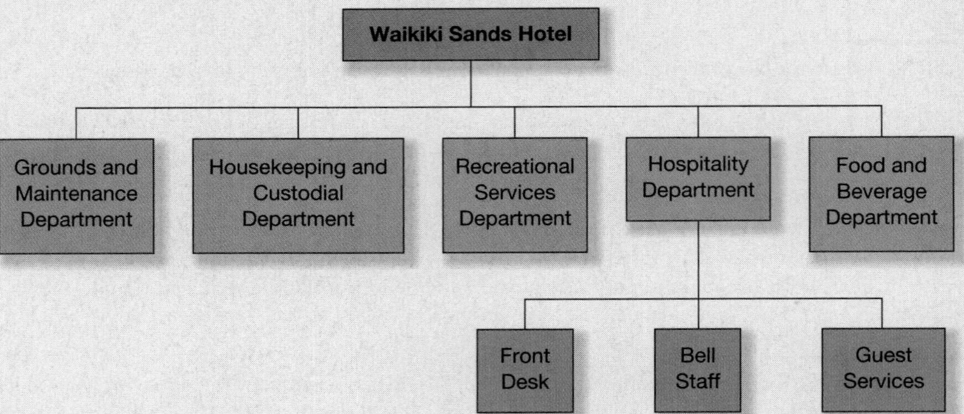

Each of the hotel's five main departments is managed by a director (e.g., director of hospitality). The Front Desk subunit, which is supervised by the front desk manager, handles the hotel's reservations, room assignments, guest payments, and key control. The Bell Staff, managed by the bell captain, is responsible for greeting guests, front door service, assisting guests with their luggage, and delivering room-service orders. The Guest Services subunit, supervised by the manager of Guest Services, is responsible for assisting guests with local transportation arrangements, advising guests on tourist attractions, and such conveniences as valet and floral services.

Required: As an outside consultant, write a memo to the hotel's general manager suggesting a responsibility-center designation for each of the subunits shown in the organization chart above. Justify your choices.

Problem 12–44
Preparation of Performance Reports; Hospital.
(LO 3)

Mount Ranier General Hospital serves three counties in the state of Washington. The hospital is a nonprofit organization, which is supported by patient billings, county and state funds, and private donations. The hospital's organization chart follows.

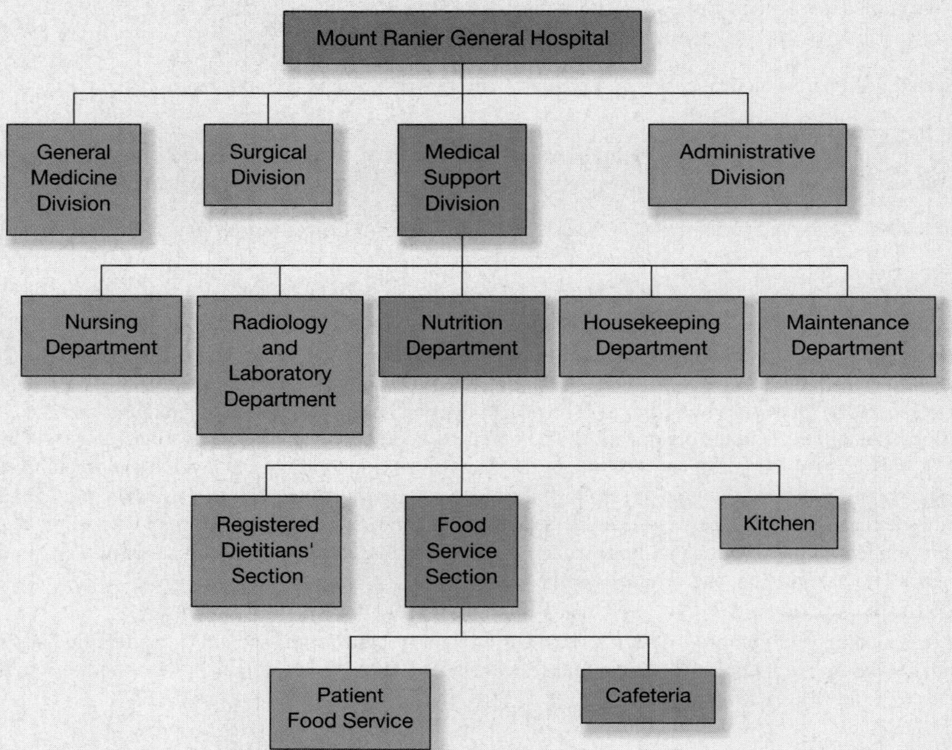

The following cost information has been compiled for August.

	Budget		Actual	
	August	**Year to Date**	**August**	**Year to Date**
Cafeteria:				
Food servers' wages	$ 16,000	$ 128,000	$ 18,000	$ 144,000
Paper products	9,000	72,000	8,800	72,400
Utilities	2,000	16,000	2,100	16,200
Maintenance	800	6,400	200	2,200
Custodial	2,200	17,600	2,200	17,200
Supplies	2,400	19,200	1,800	19,200
Patient Food Service	34,000	272,000	37,000	274,000
Registered Dietitians' Section	15,000	120,000	15,000	120,000
Kitchen	62,000	496,000	58,800	492,000
Nursing Department	140,000	1,120,000	150,000	1,160,000
Radiology and Laboratory Department	36,000	288,000	36,200	288,000
Housekeeping Department	20,000	160,000	23,200	172,000
Maintenance Department	26,000	208,000	12,000	154,000
General Medicine Division	420,000	3,360,000	408,000	3,341,800
Surgical Division	280,000	2,240,000	282,000	2,231,600
Administrative Division	100,000	800,000	107,000	812,000

Required:

1. Prepare a set of cost performance reports similar to Exhibit 12–4. The report should have six columns, as in Exhibit 12–4. The first four columns will have the same headings as those used above. The last two columns will have the following headings: Variance—August, and Variance—Year to Date.

   Since all of the information in the performance reports for Mount Ranier General Hospital is cost information, you do not need to show these data in parentheses. Use F or U to denote whether each variance in the reports is favorable or unfavorable.
2. Using arrows, show the relationships between the numbers in your performance reports for Mount Ranier General Hospital. Refer to Exhibit 12–4 for guidance.
3. Put yourself in the place of the hospital's administrator. Which variances in the performance reports would you want to investigate further? Why?

Problem 12–45
Cost Distribution Using Allocation Bases; Hospital
(LO 4)

Refer to the organization chart for Mount Ranier General Hospital given in the preceding problem. Ignore the rest of the data in that problem. The following table shows the cost allocation bases used to distribute various costs among the hospital's divisions.

Cost Pool	Cost Allocation Base	Annual Cost
Facilities:		
Building depreciation	Square feet of space	$380,000
Equipment depreciation		
Insurance		
Utilities:		
Electricity	Cubic feet of space	48,000
Waste disposal		
Water and sewer		
Cable TV and phone		
Heat		
General administration:		
Administrator	Budgeted number of employees	440,000
Administrative staff		
Office supplies		
Community outreach:		
Public education	Budgeted dollars of patient billings	80,000
School physical exams		

Shown below are the amounts of each cost allocation base associated with each division.

	Square Feet	Cubic Feet	Number of Employees	Patient Billings
General Medicine Division	15,000	135,000	30	$4,000,000
Surgical Division	8,000	100,000	20	2,500,000
Medical Support Division	9,000	90,000	20	1,500,000
Administrative Division	8,000	75,000	30	0
Total	40,000	400,000	100	$8,000,000

Required:

1. Prepare a table similar to Exhibit 12–5 which distributes each of the costs listed in the preceding table to the hospital's divisions.
2. Comment on the appropriateness of patient billings as the basis for distributing community outreach costs to the hospital's divisions. Can you suggest a better allocation base?
3. Is there any use in allocating utilities costs to the divisions? What purposes could such an allocation process serve?

Problem 12–46
Prepare Segmented Income Statement; Contribution-Margin Format; Retail
(LO 5)

Buckeye Department Stores, Inc. operates a chain of department stores in Ohio. The company's organization chart appears below. Operating data for 20x5 follow.

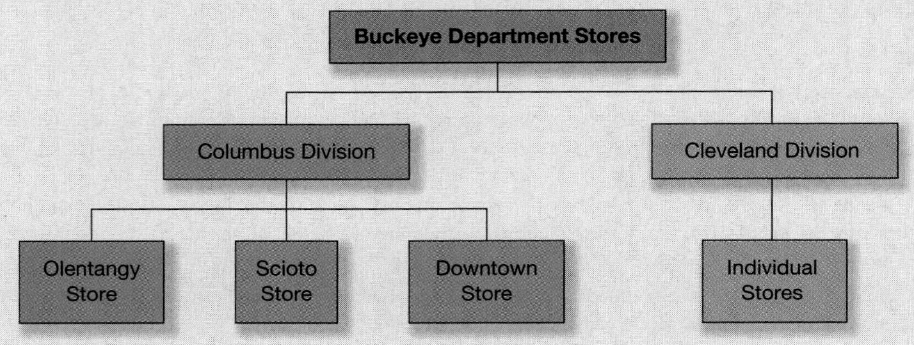

BUCKEYE DEPARTMENT STORES, INC.
Operating Data for 20x5
(in thousands)

	Columbus Division			
	Olentangy Store	Scioto Store	Downtown Store	Cleveland Division (total for all stores)
Sales revenue	$15,000	$7,200	$33,000	$63,000
Variable expenses:				
Cost of merchandise sold	9,000	6,000	18,000	36,000
Sales personnel—salaries	1,200	900	2,250	4,800
Sales commissions	150	120	270	600
Utilities	240	180	450	900
Other	180	105	360	750
Fixed expenses:				
Depreciation—buildings	360	270	750	1,410
Depreciation—furnishings	240	150	420	870
Computing and billing	120	90	225	480
Warehouse	210	180	600	1,350
Insurance	120	75	270	600
Property taxes	105	60	240	510
Supervisory salaries	450	300	1,200	2,700
Security	90	90	240	630

The following fixed expenses are controllable at the divisional level: depreciation—furnishings, computing and billing, warehouse, insurance, and security. In addition to these expenses, each division annually incurs $150,000 of computing costs, which are not allocated to individual stores.

The following fixed expenses are controllable only at the company level: depreciation—building, property taxes, and supervisory salaries. In addition to these expenses, each division incurs costs for supervisory salaries of $300,000, which are not allocated to individual stores.

Buckeye Department Stores incurs common fixed expenses of $360,000, which are not allocated to the two divisions. Income-tax expense for 20x5 is $5,850,000.

Required:

1. Prepare a segmented income statement similar to Exhibit 12–7 for Buckeye Department Stores, Inc. The statement should have the following columns:

	Segments of Company		Segments of Columbus Division			
Buckeye Department Stores, Inc.	**Cleveland Division**	**Columbus Division**	**Olentangy Store**	**Scioto Store**	**Downtown Store**	**Not Allocated**

   Prepare the statement in the contribution format, and indicate the controllability of expenses. Subtract all variable expenses, including cost of merchandise sold, from sales revenue to obtain the contribution margin.

2. How would the segmented income statement help the president of Buckeye Department Stores manage the company?

Problem 12–47
Responsibility Accounting; Participation; Behavioral Issues
(LO 1, 2, 3)

RELY Cleaning Services, Inc. was started a number of years ago by Rick Ely to provide cleaning services to both large and small businesses in their home city. Over the years, as local businesses reduced underutilized building maintenance staffs, more and more cleaning services were subcontracted to RELY. RELY also expanded into other building services such as painting and local moving.

RELY maintains a pool of skilled workers who are contracted to perform the noncleaning services because these services do not recur on a day-to-day basis for the individual buildings. Many of RELY's full-time employees have been with the firm for a number of years. Five zone managers are each responsible for furnishing recurring nightly cleaning services to several businesses. In addition, the zone manager sells and schedules noncleaning service jobs for the company's central pool of skilled employees. Informal meetings are held periodically to discuss RELY's performance, personnel allocations, and scheduling problems. RELY's budgeting and planning have been done by Ely, who also manages variations from budgets.

Ely recently decided to retire and sold the business to Commercial Maintenance, Inc. (CMI), which provides similar services in a number of metropolitan locations that surround RELY's business area. After news of the sale, several of RELY's long-term employees appeared resentful of the change in ownership and did not know what to expect.

CMI's senior management met with RELY's managers and announced that George Fowler would become president of RELY and that RELY would continue to operate as a separate subsidiary of CMI. Furthermore, in accordance with CMI's management philosophy, a responsibility-accounting system is to be implemented at RELY. Also, in line with other CMI subsidiaries, a participatory budgeting process is being considered. However, no decision will be made until an evaluation of RELY's existing policies, operational culture, and management is completed. In view of the significant change in management philosophy, CMI has taken considerable time in explaining how each system operates and assuring RELY's managers that they are expected and encouraged to participate in both the planning and implementation of any of the systems that are to be adopted.

Required: Two new initiatives are being considered at RELY Cleaning Services, Inc.

- Responsibility-accounting system
- Participatory budgeting system

For each of these new approaches:

1. Identify at least two behavioral advantages that could arise.
2. Identify at least two potential problems that could arise.
3. Discuss the likelihood that the new approach will contribute to the alignment of organizational and personal goals.

(CMA, adapted)

Problem 12–48
Segmented Income Statement; Responsibility Accounting
(LO 3, 5)

Piedmont Novelties, Inc. sells merchandise through three retail outlets—in Raleigh, Charlotte, and Savannah—and operates a general corporate headquarters in Charlotte. A review of the company's income statement indicates a record year in terms of sales and profits. Management, though, desires additional insights about the individual stores and has asked that Judson Wyatt, a newly hired intern, prepare a segmented income statement. The following information has been extracted from Piedmont's accounting records:

- Sales volume, sales price, and purchase price data:

	Raleigh	Charlotte	Savannah
Sales volume	37,000 units	41,000 units	46,000 units
Unit selling price	$18.00	$16.50	$14.25
Unit purchase price	8.25	8.25	9.00

- The following expenses were incurred for sales commissions, local advertising, property taxes, management salaries, and other noncontrollable (but traceable) costs:

	Raleigh	Charlotte	Savannah
Sales commissions	6%	6%	6%
Local advertising	$16,500	$33,000	$72,000
Local property taxes	6,750	3,000	9,000
Sales manager salary	—	—	48,000
Store manager salaries	46,500	58,500	57,000
Other noncontrollable costs	8,700	6,900	26,700

Local advertising decisions are made at the store manager level. The sales manager's salary in Savannah is determined by the Savannah store manager; in contrast, store manager salaries are set by Piedmont Novelties's vice president.

- Nontraceable fixed corporate expenses total $288,450.
- The company uses a responsibility accounting system.

Required:

1. Assume the role of Judson Wyatt and prepare a segmented income statement for Piedmont.
2. Determine the weakest-performing store and present an analysis of the probable causes of poor performance.
3. Assume that an opening has arisen at the Charlotte corporate headquarters and the company's chief executive officer (CEO) desires to promote one of the three existing store managers. In evaluating the store managers' performance, should the CEO use a store's segment contribution margin, the profit margin controllable by the store manager, or a store's segment profit margin? Justify your answer.

Problem 12–49
Designing a Responsibility-Accounting System
(LO 1, 2)

Ujvari Equipment Company, which is located in Stutgardt, Germany, manufactures heavy construction equipment. The company's primary product, an especially powerful bulldozer, is among the best produced in Europe. The company operates in a very price-competitive industry, so it has little control over the price of its products. It must meet the market price. To do so, the firm has to keep production costs in check by operating as efficiently as possible. Mathew Basler, the company's president, has stated that to be successful, the company must provide a very high-quality product and meet its delivery commitments to customers on time. Ujvari Equipment Company is organized as shown below.

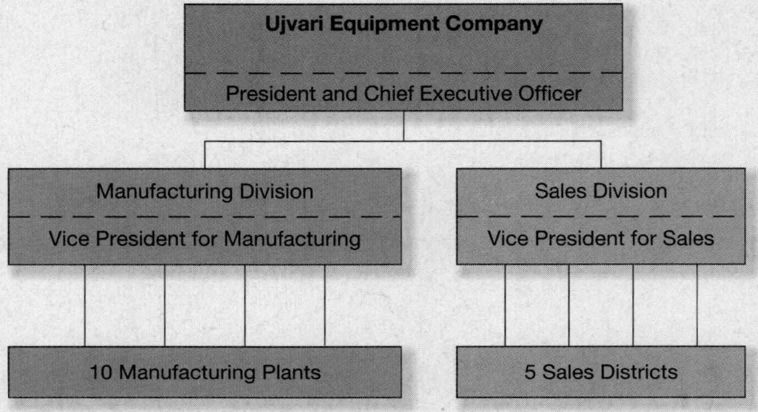

There is currently a disagreement between the company's two vice presidents regarding the responsibility-accounting system. The vice president for manufacturing claims that the 10 plants should be cost centers. He recently expressed the following sentiment: "The plants should be cost centers because the plant managers do not control the sales of our products. Designating the plants as profit centers would result in holding the plant managers responsible for something they can't control." A contrary view is held by the vice president for marketing. He recently made the following remarks: "The plants should be profit centers. The plant managers are in the best position to affect the company's overall profit."

Required: As the company's new controller, you have been asked to make a recommendation to Mathew Basler, the company president, regarding the responsibility center issue. Write a memo to the president making a recommendation and explaining the reasoning behind it. In your memo address the following points.

1. Assuming that Ujvari Equipment Company's overall goal is profitability, what are the company's critical success factors? A *critical success factor* is a variable that meets these two criteria: It is largely under the company's control, and the company must succeed in this area in order to reach its overall goal of profitability.
2. Which responsibility-accounting arrangement is most consistent with achieving success on the company's critical success factors?
3. What responsibility-center designation is most appropriate for the company's sales districts?
4. As a specific example, consider the rush-order problem illustrated in the chapter. Suppose that Ujvari Equipment Company often experiences rush orders from its customers. Which of the two proposed responsibility-accounting arrangements is best suited to making good decisions about accepting or rejecting rush orders? Specifically, should the plants be cost centers or profit centers?

Problem 12–50
Quality Costs: Identification and Analysis
(LO 6)

Industrial Technologies, Inc. (ITI) produces two compression machines that are popular with manufacturers of plastics: no. 165 and no. 172. Machine no. 165 has an average selling price of $30,000, whereas no. 172 typically sells for approximately $27,500. The company is very concerned about quality and has provided the following information:

	No. 165	**No. 172**
Number of machines produced and sold	160	200
Warranty costs:		
Average repair cost per unit	$900	$350
Percentage of units needing repair	70%	10%
Reliability engineering at $150 per hour	1,600 hours	2,000 hours
Rework at ITI's manufacturing plant:		
Average rework cost per unit	$1,900	$1,600
Percentage of units needing rework	35%	25%
Manufacturing inspection at $50 per hour	300 hours	500 hours
Transportation costs to customer sites to fix problems	$29,500	$15,000
Quality training for employees	$35,000	$50,000

Required:

1. Classify the preceding costs as prevention, appraisal, internal failure, or external failure.
2. Using the classifications in requirement (1), compute ITI's quality costs for machine no. 165 in dollars and as a percentage of sales revenues. Also calculate prevention, appraisal, internal failure, and external failure costs as a percentage of total quality costs.
3. Repeat requirement (2) for machine no. 172.
4. Comment on your findings, noting whether the company is "investing" its quality expenditures differently for the two machines.
5. Quality costs can be classified as observable or hidden. What are hidden quality costs, and how do these costs differ from observable costs?

Problem 12–51
Quality-Improvement Programs and Quality Costs
(LO 6)

News Technology, Inc. manufactures computerized laser printing equipment used by newspaper publishers throughout North America. In recent years, the company's market share has been eroded by stiff competition from Asian and European competitors. Price and product quality are the two key areas in which companies compete in this market.

Ben McDonough, News Technology's president, decided to devote more resources to the improvement of product quality after learning that his company's products had been ranked fourth in product quality in a recent survey of newspaper publishers. He believed that the company could no longer afford to ignore the importance of product quality. McDonough set up a task force which he headed to implement a formal quality-improvement program. Included on the task force were representatives from engineering, sales, customer service, production, and accounting, because McDonough believed this was a companywide program and all employees should share the responsibility for its success.

After the first meeting of the task force, Sheila Hayes, manager of sales, asked Tony Reese, the production manager, what he thought of the proposed program. Reese replied, "I have reservations. Quality is too abstract to be attaching costs to it and then to be holding you and me responsible for cost improvements. I like to work with goals that I can see and count! I don't like my annual income to be based on a decrease in quality costs; there are too many variables that we have no control over!"

News Technology's quality-improvement program has now been in operation for 18 months, and the following quality cost report has recently been issued. As they were reviewing the report, Hayes asked Reese what he thought of the quality program now. "The work is really moving through the Production Department," replied Reese. "We used to spend time helping the Customer Service Department solve their problems, but they are leaving us alone these days. I have no complaints so far. I'll be anxious to see how much the program increases our bonuses."

NEWS TECHNOLOGY, INC.
Cost of Quality Report
(in thousands)

	Quarter Ended					
	6/30/x3	9/30/x3	12/31/x3	3/31/x4	6/30/x4	9/30/x4
Prevention costs:						
Design review	$ 19	$ 101	$ 110	$ 99	$ 103	$ 94
Machine maintenance	215	215	202	190	170	160
Training suppliers	6	46	26	21	21	16
Total	$ 240	$ 362	$ 338	$ 310	$ 294	$ 270
Appraisal costs:						
Incoming inspection	$ 45	$ 53	$ 57	$ 36	$ 34	$ 22
Final testing	160	160	154	140	115	94
Total	$ 205	$ 213	$ 211	$ 176	$ 149	$ 116
Internal failure costs:						
Rework	$ 120	$ 106	$ 114	$ 88	$ 78	$ 62
Scrap	68	64	53	42	40	40
Total	$ 188	$ 170	$ 167	$ 130	$ 118	$ 102
External failure costs:						
Warranty repairs	$ 69	$ 31	$ 24	$ 25	$ 23	$ 23
Customer returns	262	251	122	116	87	80
Total	$ 331	$ 282	$ 146	$ 141	$ 110	$ 103
Total quality cost	$ 964	$1,027	$ 862	$ 757	$ 671	$ 591
Total production cost	$4,120	$4,540	$4,380	$4,650	$4,580	$4,510

Required:

1. Identify at least three factors that should be present for an organization to successfully implement a quality-improvement program.
2. By analyzing the cost of quality report presented, determine if News Technology's quality-improvement program has been successful. List specific evidence to support your answer.
3. Discuss why Tony Reese's current reaction to the quality-improvement program is more favorable than his initial reaction.

4. News Technology's president believed that the quality-improvement program was essential and that the firm could no longer afford to ignore the importance of product quality. Discuss how the company could measure the opportunity cost of not implementing the quality-improvement program.

(CMA, adapted)

Problem 12–52
Environmental Cost Management
(LO 8)

As a group, take a walking tour of your campus and the surrounding community. Make a list of all of the environmental costs of which you see evidence.

Required: Make a presentation to the class about your findings. List and categorize the environmental costs you noted for either your college or for businesses in the community. (You might consider writing a letter to your campus newspaper regarding these environmental issues and their costs.)

Cases

Case 12–53
Segmented Income Statement; International Operations
(LO 1, 5)

North American Industries is a diversified company whose products are marketed both domestically and internationally. The company's major product lines are furniture, sports equipment, and household appliances. At a recent meeting of the board of directors, there was a lengthy discussion on ways to improve overall corporate profitability. The members of the board decided that they required additional financial information about individual corporate operations in order to target areas for improvement.

Danielle Murphy, the controller, has been asked to provide additional data that would assist the board in its investigation. Murphy believes that income statements, prepared along both product lines and geographic areas, would provide the directors with the required insight into corporate operations. Murphy had several discussions with the division managers for each product line and compiled the following information from these meetings.

	Product Lines			
	Furniture	**Sports**	**Housewares**	**Total**
Production and sales in units	80,000	90,000	80,000	250,000
Average selling price per unit	$16.00	$40.00	$30.00	
Average variable manufacturing cost per unit	$8.00	$19.00	$16.50	
Average variable selling expense per unit	$4.00	$5.00	$4.50	
Fixed manufacturing overhead, excluding depreciation				$ 500,000
Depreciation of plant and equipment				$ 400,000
Administrative and selling expense				$1,160,000

1. The division managers concluded that Murphy should allocate fixed manufacturing overhead to both product lines and geographic areas on the basis of the ratio of the variable costs expended to total variable costs.
2. Each of the division managers agreed that a reasonable basis for the allocation of depreciation on plant and equipment would be the ratio of units produced per product line (or per geographical area) to the total number of units produced.
3. There was little agreement on the allocation of administrative and selling expenses, so Murphy decided to allocate only those expenses that were traceable directly to a segment. For example, manufacturing staff salaries would be allocated to product lines, and sales staff salaries would be allocated to geographical areas. Murphy used the following data for this allocation.

Manufacturing Staff		Sales Staff	
Furniture	$120,000	United States	$ 60,000
Sports	140,000	Canada	100,000
Housewares	80,000	Mexico	250,000

4. The division managers were able to provide reliable sales percentages for their product lines by geographical area.

	Percentage of Unit Sales		
	United States	**Canada**	**Mexico**
Furniture	40%	10%	50%
Sports	40%	40%	20%
Housewares	20%	20%	60%

Murphy prepared the following product-line income statement based on the data presented above.

NORTH AMERICAN INDUSTRIES
Segmented Income Statement by Product Lines
For the Fiscal Year Ended April 30, 20x4

	Product Lines				
	Furniture	**Sports**	**Housewares**	**Unallocated**	**Total**
Sales in units	80,000	90,000	80,000		
Sales	$1,280,000	$3,600,000	$2,400,000	—	$7,280,000
Variable manufacturing and selling costs	960,000	2,160,000	1,680,000	—	4,800,000
Contribution margin	$ 320,000	$1,440,000	$ 720,000	—	$2,480,000
Fixed costs:					
Fixed manufacturing overhead	$ 100,000	$ 225,000	$ 175,000	$ —	$ 500,000
Depreciation	128,000	144,000	128,000	—	400,000
Administrative and selling expenses	120,000	140,000	80,000	820,000	1,160,000
Total fixed costs	$ 348,000	$ 509,000	$ 383,000	$ 820,000	$2,060,000
Operating income (loss)	$ (28,000)	$ 931,000	$ 337,000	$(820,000)	$ 420,000

Required:

1. Prepare a segmented income statement for North American Industries based on the company's geographical areas. The statement should show the operating income for each segment.
2. As a result of the information disclosed by both segmented income statements (by product line and by geographical area), recommend areas where North American Industries should focus its attention in order to improve corporate profitability.

(CMA, adapted)

Case 12–54
Segmented Income Statement; Responsibility Accounting; Bonuses; Motivation; Ethics
(LO 1, 2, 5)

Elite Classic Clothes is a retailer that sells to professional women in the northeast. The firm leases space for stores in upscale shopping centers, and the organizational structure consists of regions, districts, and stores. Each region consists of two or more districts; each district consists of three or more stores. Each store, district, and region has been established as a profit center. At all levels, the company uses a responsibility-accounting system focusing on information and knowledge rather than blame and control. Each year, managers, in consultation with their supervisors, establish financial and nonfinancial goals, and these goals are integrated into the budget. Actual performance is measured each month.

The New England Region consists of the Coastal District and the Inland District. The Coastal District includes the New Haven, Boston, and Portland stores. The Coastal District's performance has not been up to expectations in the past. For the month of May, the district manager has set performance goals with the managers of the New Haven and Boston stores, who will receive bonuses if certain performance measures are exceeded. The manager in Portland decided not to participate in the bonus scheme. Since the district manager is unsure what type of bonus will encourage better performance, the New Haven manager will receive a bonus based on sales in excess of budgeted sales of $1,140,000, while the Boston manager will receive a bonus based on net income in excess of budgeted net income. The company's net income goal for each store is 12 percent of sales. The budgeted sales revenue for the Boston store is $1,060,000.

Other pertinent data for May are as follows:

- Coastal District sales revenue was $3,000,000, and its cost of goods sold amounted to $1,267,500.
- The Coastal District spent $150,000 on advertising.
- General and administrative expenses for the Coastal District amounted to $360,000.
- At the New Haven store, sales were 40 percent of Coastal District sales, while sales at the Boston store were 35 percent of district sales. The cost of goods sold in both New Haven and Boston was 42 percent of sales.

- Variable selling expenses (sales commissions) were 6 percent of sales for all stores, districts, and regions.
- Variable administrative expenses were 2.5 percent of sales for all stores, districts, and regions.
- Maintenance cost includes janitorial and repair services and is a direct cost for each store. The store manager has complete control over this outlay. Maintenance costs were incurred as follows: New Haven, $15,000; Boston, $1,200; and Portland, $9,000.
- Advertising is considered a direct cost for each store and is completely under the control of the store manager. The New Haven store spent two-thirds of the Coastal District total outlay for advertising, which was 10 times the amount spent in Boston on advertising.
- Coastal District rental expense amounted to $300,000.
- The rental expenses at the New Haven store were 40 percent of the Coastal District's total, while the Boston store incurred 30 percent of the district total.
- District expenses were allocated to the stores based on sales.
- New England Region general and administrative expenses of $330,000 were allocated to the Coastal District. These expenses were, in turn, allocated equally to the district's three stores.

Required:

1. Prepare the May segmented income statement for the Coastal District and for the New Haven and Boston stores.
2. Compute the Portland store's net income for May.
3. Discuss the impact of the responsibility-accounting system and bonus structure on the managers' behavior and the effect of their behavior on the financial results for the New Haven store and the Boston store.
4. The assistant controller for the New England Region, Jack Isner, has been a close friend of the New Haven store manager for over 20 years. When Isner saw the segmented income statement [as prepared in requirement (1)], he realized that the New Haven store manager had really gone overboard on advertising expenditures. To make his friend look better to the regional management, he reclassified $50,000 of the advertising expenditures as miscellaneous expenses, and buried them in rent and other costs. Comment on the ethical issues in the assistant controller's actions. (Refer to specific ethical standards, which were given in Chapter 1.)

(CMA, adapted)

Current Issues in Managerial Accounting

"Honda Will Introduce Fuel-Cell Cars," ***The Wall Street Journal,*** **July 25, 2002, p. D4, Joseph B. White; "California Clean-Air Czar's Shift Is New Boost for Diesel Engines,"** ***The Wall Street Journal,*** **October 24, 2002, pp. A1, A8, Jeffrey Ball; "The 99-mpg Wonder,"** ***Fortune,*** **January 21, 2002, p. 92, Stuart F. Brown.**

Issue 12–55
Environmental Cost Management

Overview

Honda and Toyota race to get new clean-burning fuel-cell-powered vehicles onto the road. Environmentally friendly diesel cars also are becoming more popular, especially in Europe.

Suggested Discussion Questions

What categories of environmental costs would these automakers incur in making the switch to fuel-cell or diesel-fuel cars? Are these costs likely to be visible or hidden environmental costs?

"How Ford, Firestone Let the Warnings Slide by as Debacle Developed: Their Separate Goals, Gaps in Communication Gave Rise to Risky Situation," ***The Wall Street Journal,*** **September 6, 2000.**

Issue 12–56
Managing Quality; the Value Chain

Overview

The problem with certain Firestone tire models experiencing tread separation, especially when used on the Ford Explorer, is well-documented in this and many other articles in the popular press.

Suggested Discussion Questions

As a group, discuss the following questions and present your conclusions to the class. What steps should Firestone and Ford have taken to remedy this problem before it became such a public relations disaster? How does the concept of the value chain fit into this scenario?

Chapter Thirteen

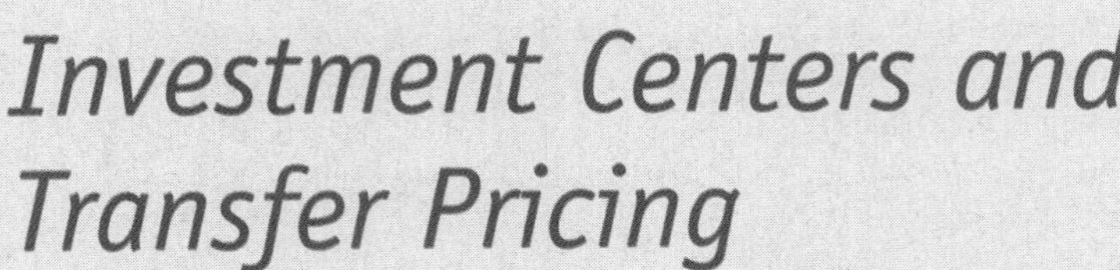

Investment Centers and Transfer Pricing

After completing this chapter, you should be able to:

1. Explain the role of managerial accounting in achieving goal congruence.
2. Compute an investment center's return on investment (ROI), residual income (RI), and economic value added (EVA).
3. Explain how a manager can improve ROI by increasing either the sales margin or capital turnover.
4. Describe some advantages and disadvantages of both ROI and residual income as divisional performance measures.
5. Explain how to measure a division's income and invested capital.
6. Use the general economic rule to set an optimal transfer price.
7. Explain how to base a transfer price on market prices, costs, or negotiations.

Suncoast Food Centers to Expand Operations in Several Coastal Cities

Miami, FL—A spokesman for Suncoast Food Centers announced today that the company will be expanding its retail grocery operations in Miami, Daytona Beach, and Jacksonville. The Florida-based company will add up to a dozen new stores over the next five years in these three cities. All of the new stores will be part of Suncoast's Atlantic Division, headquartered in Miami.

During a brief news conference, Atlantic Division Manager Katherine James explained Suncoast's rationale. "Florida is gaining over a thousand people a day in population," said James. "And many of these people are still moving into the coastal areas where Suncoast's strength is. Our Atlantic Division has been doing very well, and we're convinced we can continue to grow our business. Last year we had sales of $135 million in the Atlantic Division, and the division's income was just under $7 million.

"Of course, income alone isn't enough. What top management and our investors need to see is a return on the dollars they've invested in the division. Before our new stores are added, the Atlantic Division has around $45 million in invested capital. So we're pulling down a very respectable return on investment in the division. When our top management compares our division's return with industrywide numbers, they can see we're doing a good job."

James said most of Suncoast's new stores would be built from the ground up, but the company is also considering the acquisition of a couple of existing stores from other grocery chains.

How do the top managers of large companies such as DaimlerChrysler Corporation and General Electric Company evaluate their divisions and other major subunits? The largest subunits within these and similar organizations usually are designated as **investment centers.** The manager of this type of *responsibility center* is held accountable not only for the investment center's *profit* but also for the *capital invested* to earn that profit. Invested capital refers to assets, such as buildings and equipment, used in a subunit's operations. In this chapter we will study the methods that managerial accountants use to evaluate investment centers and the performance of their managers.[1]

In many organizations, one subunit manufactures a product or produces a service which is then transferred to another subunit in the same organization. For example, automobile parts manufactured in one division of General Motors are then transferred to another GM division that assembles vehicles.

The price at which products or services are transferred between two subunits in an organization is called a **transfer price.** Since a transfer price affects the profit of both the buying and selling divisions, the transfer price affects the performance evaluation of these responsibility centers. Later in this chapter, we will study the methods that managerial accountants use to determine transfer prices.

Delegation of Decision Making

Explain the role of managerial accounting in achieving goal congruence.

Most large organizations are decentralized. Managers throughout these organizations are given autonomy to make decisions for their subunits. Decentralization takes advantage of the specialized knowledge and skills of managers, permits an organization to respond quickly to events, and relieves top management of the need to direct the organization's day-to-day activities. The biggest challenge in making a decentralized organization function effectively is to obtain *goal congruence* among the organization's autonomous managers.

Obtaining Goal Congruence: A Behavioral Challenge

Goal congruence is obtained when the managers of subunits throughout an organization strive to achieve the goals set by top management. This desirable state of affairs is difficult to achieve for a variety of reasons. Managers often are unaware of the effects of their decisions on the organization's other subunits. Also, it is only human for people to be more concerned with the performance of their own subunit than with the effectiveness of the entire organization. The behavioral challenge in designing any management control system is to come as close as possible to obtaining goal congruence.

To obtain goal congruence, the behavior of managers throughout an organization must be directed toward top management's goals. Successful managers not only have their sights set on these organizational goals, but also have been given positive incentives to achieve them. *The managerial accountant's objective* in designing a responsibility-accounting system is to provide these incentives to the organization's subunit managers. *The key factor in deciding how well the responsibility-accounting system works is the extent to which it directs managers' efforts toward organizational goals.* Thus, the accounting measures used to evaluate investment-center managers should provide them with incentives to act in the interests of the overall organization.

Management by Objectives (MBO) An emphasis on obtaining goal congruence is consistent with a broad managerial approach called **management by objectives,** or **MBO.** Under the MBO philosophy, managers participate in setting goals which they

[1]Recall from Chapter 12 that in practice the term *profit center* sometimes is used interchangeably with the term *investment center.* To be precise, however, the term *profit center* should be reserved for a subunit whose manager is held accountable for profit but not for invested capital.

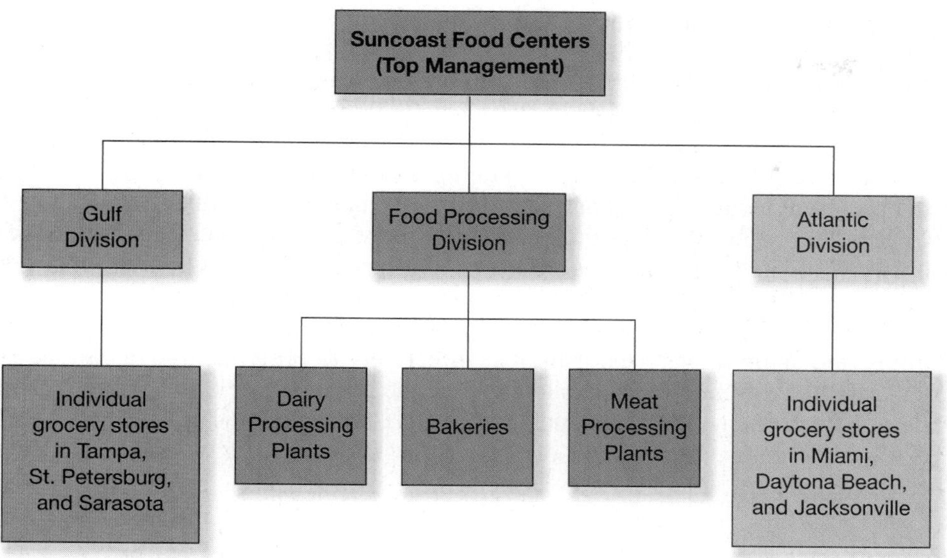

Exhibit 13–1
Organization Chart: Suncoast Food Centers

then strive to achieve. The goals usually are expressed in financial or other quantitative terms, and the responsibility-accounting system is used to evaluate performance in achieving them.

Adaptation of Management Control Systems

When an organization begins its operations, it is usually small and decision making generally is centralized. The chief executive can control operations without a formal responsibility-accounting system. It is relatively easy in a small organization for managers to keep in touch with routine operations through face-to-face contact with employees.

As an organization grows, however, its managers need more formal information systems, including managerial-accounting information, in order to maintain control. Accounting systems are established to record events and provide the framework for internal and external financial reports. Budgets become necessary to plan the organization's activity. As the organization gains experience in producing its goods or services, cost standards and flexible budgets often are established to help control operations. As the organization continues to grow, some delegation of decision making becomes necessary. Decentralization is often the result of this tendency toward delegation. Ultimately, a fully developed responsibility-accounting system emerges. Managerial accountants designate cost centers, revenue centers, profit centers, and investment centers, and develop appropriate performance measures for each subunit.

Thus, an organization's accounting and managerial control systems usually adapt and become more complex as the organization grows and changes.

Measuring Performance in Investment Centers

In our study of investment-center performance evaluation, we will focus on Suncoast Food Centers. This Florida chain of retail grocery stores has three divisions, as depicted by the organization chart in Exhibit 13–1.

Topic 13–1

The Gulf and Atlantic divisions consist of individual grocery stores located in six coastal cities. The company's Food Processing Division operates dairy plants, bakeries, and meat processing plants in Miami, Orlando, and Jacksonville. These facilities provide all Suncoast Food Centers with milk, ice cream, yogurt, cheese, breads and desserts, and packaged meat. These Suncoast brand food products are transferred to the

> "Accounting is changing. You're no longer sitting behind a desk just working on a computer, just crunching the numbers. You're actually getting to be a part of the day to day functions of the business." (13a)
> **Abbott Laboratories**

company's Gulf and Atlantic divisions at transfer prices established by the corporate controller's office.

Suncoast Food Centers' three divisions are investment centers. This responsibility-center designation is appropriate, because each division manager has the authority to make decisions that affect both profit and invested capital. For example, the Gulf Division manager approves the overall pricing policies in the Gulf Division's stores, and also has the autonomy to sign contracts to buy food and other products for resale. These actions influence the division's profit. In addition, the Gulf Division manager has the authority to build new Suncoast Food Centers, rent space in shopping centers, or close existing stores. These decisions affect the amount of capital invested in the division.

The primary goals of any profit-making enterprise include maximizing its profitability and using its invested capital as effectively as possible. Managerial accountants use three different measures to evaluate the performance of investment centers: return on investment (ROI), residual income (RI), and economic value added (EVA®). (EVA® is a registered trademark of Stern Stewart & Co.) We will illustrate each of these measures for Suncoast Food Centers.

Return on Investment

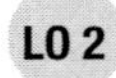

LO 2 Compute an investment center's return on investment (ROI), residual income (RI), and economic value added (EVA).

The most common investment-center performance measure is **return on investment,** or **ROI,** which is defined as follows:

$$\text{Return on investment (ROI)} = \frac{\text{Income}}{\text{Invested capital}}$$

The most recent year's ROI calculations for Suncoast Food Centers' three divisions are:

	$\frac{\text{Income}}{\text{Invested capital}}$	=	Return on investment (ROI)
Gulf Division	$\frac{\$3{,}000{,}000}{\$20{,}000{,}000}$	=	15%
Food Processing Division	$\frac{\$3{,}600{,}000}{\$18{,}000{,}000}$	=	20%
Atlantic Division	$\frac{\$6{,}750{,}000}{\$45{,}000{,}000}$	=	15%

Notice how the ROI calculation for each division takes into account *both divisional income and the capital invested* in the division. Why is this important? Suppose each division were evaluated only on the basis of its divisional profit. The Atlantic Division reported a higher divisional profit than the Gulf Division. Does this mean the Atlantic Division performed better than the Gulf Division? The answer is no. Although the Atlantic Division's profit exceeded the Gulf Division's profit, the Atlantic Division used a much larger amount of invested capital to earn its profit. The Atlantic Division's assets are more than two times the assets of the Gulf Division.

Considering the relative size of the two divisions, we should expect the Atlantic Division to earn a larger profit than the Gulf Division. The important question is not how much profit each division earned, but rather how effectively each division used its invested capital to earn a profit.

Factors Underlying ROI We can rewrite the ROI formula as follows:

$$\text{Return on investment} = \frac{\text{Income}}{\text{Invested capital}} = \frac{\text{Income}}{\text{Sales revenue}} \times \frac{\text{Sales revenue}}{\text{Invested capital}}$$

Notice that the *sales revenue* term cancels out in the denominator and numerator when the two right-hand fractions are multiplied.

Writing the ROI formula in this way highlights the factors that determine a division's return on investment. Income divided by sales revenue is called the **sales margin.** This term measures the percentage of each sales dollar that remains as profit after all expenses are covered. Sales revenue divided by invested capital is called the **capital turnover.** This term focuses on the number of sales dollars generated by every dollar of invested capital. The sales margin and capital turnover for Suncoast Food Centers' three divisions are calculated below for the most recent year.

"The ROI of pollution prevention rises radically when 'hidden' environmental management costs are revealed." (13b)
Kestrel Management Services (an environmental consulting firm)

$$\text{Sales margin} \times \text{Capital turnover} = \text{ROI}$$

$$\frac{\text{Income}}{\text{Sales revenue}} \times \frac{\text{Sales revenue}}{\text{Invested capital}} = \text{ROI}$$

	Sales margin		Capital turnover		ROI
Gulf Division	$\frac{\$3{,}000{,}000}{\$60{,}000{,}000}$	×	$\frac{\$60{,}000{,}000}{\$20{,}000{,}000}$	=	15%
Food Processing Division	$\frac{\$3{,}600{,}000}{\$9{,}000{,}000}$	×	$\frac{\$9{,}000{,}000}{\$18{,}000{,}000}$	=	20%
Atlantic Division	$\frac{\$6{,}750{,}000}{\$135{,}000{,}000}$	×	$\frac{\$135{,}000{,}000}{\$45{,}000{,}000}$	=	15%

The Gulf Division's sales margin is 5 percent ($3,000,000 of profit ÷ $60,000,000 of sales revenue). Thus, each dollar of divisional sales resulted in a five-cent profit. The division's capital turnover was 3 ($60,000,000 of sales revenue ÷ $20,000,000 of invested capital). Thus, three dollars of sales revenue were generated by each dollar of capital invested in the division's assets, such as store buildings, display shelves, checkout equipment, and inventory.

LO 3 Explain how a manager can improve ROI by increasing either the sales margin or capital turnover.

Improving ROI How could the Gulf Division manager improve the division's return on investment? Since ROI is the product of the sales margin and the capital turnover, ROI can be improved by increasing either or both of its components. For example, if the Gulf Division manager increased the division's sales margin to 6 percent while holding the capital turnover constant at 3, the division's ROI would climb from 15 percent to 18 percent, as follows:

$$\begin{array}{c} \text{Gulf Division's} \\ \text{improved ROI} \end{array} = \begin{array}{c} \text{Improved} \\ \text{sales margin} \end{array} \times \begin{array}{c} \text{Same} \\ \text{capital turnover} \end{array}$$

$$= \quad 6\% \quad \times \quad 3 \quad = 18\%$$

To bring about the improved sales margin, the Gulf Division manager would need to increase divisional profit to $3,600,000 on sales of $60,000,000 ($3,600,000 ÷ $60,000,000 = 6%). How could profit be increased without changing total sales revenue? There are two possibilities: increase sales prices while selling less quantity, or decrease expenses. Neither of these is necessarily easy to do. In increasing sales prices, the division manager must be careful not to lose sales to the extent that total sales revenue declines. Similarly, reducing the expenses must not diminish product quality, customer service, or overall store atmosphere. Any of these changes could also result in lost sales revenue.

An alternative way of increasing the Gulf Division's ROI would be to increase its capital turnover. Suppose the Gulf Division manager increased the division's capital turnover to 4 while holding the sales margin constant at 5 percent. The division's ROI would climb from 15 percent to 20 percent:

$$\begin{array}{c} \text{Gulf Division's} \\ \text{improved ROI} \end{array} = \begin{array}{c} \text{Same} \\ \text{sales margin} \end{array} \times \begin{array}{c} \text{Improved} \\ \text{capital turnover} \end{array}$$

$$= \quad 5\% \quad \times \quad 4 \quad = 20\%$$

To obtain the improved capital turnover, the Gulf Division manager would need to either increase sales revenue or reduce the division's invested capital. For example, the improved ROI could be achieved by reducing invested capital to $15,000,000 while maintaining sales revenue of $60,000,000. This would be a very tall order. The division manager can lower invested capital somewhat by reducing inventories and can increase sales revenue by using store space more effectively. But reducing inventories may lead to stockouts and lost sales, and crowded aisles may drive customers away.

Improving ROI is a balancing act that requires all the skills of an effective manager. The ROI analysis above merely shows the arena in which the balancing act is performed.

Residual Income

LO 2

Compute an investment center's return on investment (ROI), residual income (RI), and economic value added (EVA).

Although ROI is the most popular investment-center performance measure, it has one major drawback. To illustrate, suppose Suncoast's Food Processing Division manager can buy a new food processing machine for $500,000, which will save $80,000 in operating expenses and thereby raise divisional profit by $80,000. The return on this investment in new equipment is 16 percent:

$$\frac{\text{Return on investment}}{\text{in new equipment}} = \frac{\text{Increase in divisional profit}}{\text{Increase in invested capital}} = \frac{\$80{,}000}{\$500{,}000} = 16\%$$

Now suppose it costs Suncoast Food Centers 12 cents for each dollar of capital to invest in operational assets. What is the optimal decision for the Food Processing Division manager to make, *viewed from the perspective of the company as a whole?* Since it costs Suncoast Food Centers 12 percent for every dollar of capital, and the return on investment in new equipment is 16 percent, the equipment should be purchased. For goal congruence, the autonomous division manager should decide to buy the new equipment.

Now consider what is likely to happen. The Food Processing Division manager's performance is evaluated on the basis of his division's ROI. Without the new equipment, the divisional ROI is 20 percent ($3,600,000 of divisional profit ÷ $18,000,000 of invested capital). If he purchases the new equipment, his divisional ROI will decline:

Food Processing Division's Return on Investment

Without Investment in New Equipment	With Investment in New Equipment
$\frac{\$3{,}600{,}000}{\$18{,}000{,}000} = 20\%$	$\frac{\$3{,}600{,}000 + \$80{,}000}{\$18{,}000{,}000 + \$500{,}000} < 20\%$

Why did this happen? Even though the investment in new equipment earns a return of 16 percent, which is greater than the company's cost of raising capital (12 percent), the return is less than the division's ROI without the equipment (20 percent). Averaging the new investment with those already in place in the Food Processing Division merely reduces the division's ROI. Since the division manager is evaluated using ROI, he will be reluctant to decide in favor of acquiring the new equipment.

The problem is that the ROI measure leaves out an important piece of information: it ignores the firm's cost of raising investment capital. For this reason, many managers prefer to use a different investment-center performance measure instead of ROI.

Computing Residual Income An investment center's **residual income** is defined as follows:

$$\frac{\text{Residual}}{\text{income}} = \frac{\text{Investment center's}}{\text{profit}} - \left(\frac{\text{Investment center's}}{\text{invested capital}} \times \frac{\text{Imputed}}{\text{interest rate}}\right)$$

where the imputed interest rate is the firm's cost of acquiring investment capital.

ROI and residual income are common performance measures for investment centers. Both measures relate the profit earned from selling the final product to the capital required to carry out production operations.

Residual income is a dollar amount, not a ratio like ROI. It is the amount of an investment center's profit that remains (as a residual) after subtracting an imputed interest charge. The term *imputed* means that the interest charge is estimated by the managerial accountant. This charge reflects the firm's minimum required rate of return on invested capital. In some firms, the imputed interest rate depends on the riskiness of the investment for which the funds will be used. Thus, divisions that have different levels of risk sometimes are assigned different imputed interest rates.

LO 4

Describe some advantages and disadvantages of both ROI and residual income as divisional performance measures.

The residual income of Suncoast's Food Processing Division is computed below, both with and without the investment in the new equipment. The imputed interest rate is 12 percent.

Food Processing Division's Residual Income

	Without Investment in New Equipment		With Investment in New Equipment	
Divisional profit		$3,600,000		$3,680,000
Less imputed interest charge:				
Invested capital	$18,000,000		$18,500,000	
× Imputed interest rate	× .12		× .12	
Imputed interest charge	→	2,160,000	→	2,220,000
Residual income		$1,440,000		$1,460,000

Investment in new equipment raises residual income by $20,000.

Notice that the Food Processing Division's residual income will *increase* if the new equipment is purchased. What will be the division manager's incentive if he is evaluated on the basis of residual income instead of ROI? He will want to make the investment because that decision will increase his division's residual income. Thus, goal congruence is achieved when the managerial accountant uses residual income to measure divisional performance.

Why does residual income facilitate goal congruence while ROI does not? Because the residual-income formula incorporates an important piece of data that is excluded from the ROI formula: the firm's minimum required rate of return on invested capital. To summarize, ROI and residual income are compared as follows:

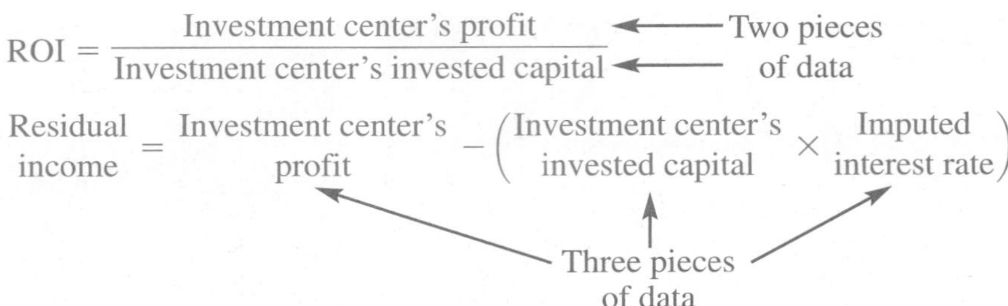

ROI = Investment center's profit / Investment center's invested capital
Two pieces of data
Residual income = Investment center's profit − (Investment center's invested capital × Imputed interest rate)
Three pieces of data

Unfortunately, residual income also has a serious drawback: It should not be used to compare the performance of different-sized investment centers because it incorporates a bias in favor of the larger investment center. To illustrate, the following table compares the residual income of Suncoast Food Centers' Gulf and Atlantic divisions. Notice that the Atlantic Division's residual income is considerably higher than the Gulf Division's. This is entirely due to the much greater size of the Atlantic Division, as evidenced by its far greater invested capital.

Comparison of Residual Income: Two Divisions

	Gulf Division		**Atlantic Division**	
Divisional profit		$3,000,000		$6,750,000
Less imputed interest charge:				
Invested capital	$20,000,000		$45,000,000	
× Imputed interest rate	× .12		× .12	
Imputed interest charge	→	2,400,000	→	5,400,000
Residual income		$ 600,000		$1,350,000

The Atlantic Division's residual income is much higher simply because it is larger than the Gulf Division.

In short, neither ROI nor residual income provides a perfect measure of investment-center performance. ROI can undermine goal congruence. Residual income distorts comparisons between investment centers of different sizes. As a result, some companies routinely use both measures for divisional performance evaluation.

Shareholder Value Analysis Some companies apply the residual income concept to individual product lines. **Shareholder value analysis** calculates the residual income for a major product line, with the objective of determining how the product line affects the firm's value to the shareholders. Suppose, for example, that Suncoast Food Centers offers in-store, one-hour film development in selected stores. Let's say that the company's investment in this service is $200,000 and the annual profit is $40,000. Then the residual income on one-hour film development is $16,000 [$40,000 − ($200,000 × 12%)].

Economic Value Added

LO 2

Compute an investment center's return on investment (ROI), residual income (RI), and economic value added (EVA).

The most contemporary measure of investment center performance is **economic value added (EVA),** which is defined as follows:

$$\text{Economic value added} = \text{Investment center's after-tax operating income} - \left[\left(\text{Investment center's total assets} - \text{Investment center's current liabilities}\right) \times \text{Weighted-average cost of capital}\right]$$

Like residual income, the economic value added is a dollar amount. However, it differs from residual income in two important ways. First, an investment center's current liabilities are subtracted from its total assets. Second, the weighted-average cost of capital is used in the calculation.

Weighted-Average Cost of Capital Suncoast Food Centers has two sources of long-term capital: debt and equity. The cost to Suncoast of issuing debt is the after-tax cost of the interest payments on the debt, taking account of the fact that the interest payments are tax deductible. The cost of Suncoast's equity capital is the investment opportunity rate of Suncoast Food Centers' investors, that is, the rate they could earn on investments of similar risk to that of investing in Suncoast Food Centers. The **weighted-average cost of capital (WACC)** is defined as follows:

$$\text{Weighted-average cost of capital} = \frac{\begin{pmatrix}\text{After-tax cost}\\\text{of debt}\\\text{capital}\end{pmatrix}\begin{pmatrix}\text{Market}\\\text{value}\\\text{of debt}\end{pmatrix} + \begin{pmatrix}\text{Cost of}\\\text{equity}\\\text{capital}\end{pmatrix}\begin{pmatrix}\text{Market}\\\text{value}\\\text{of equity}\end{pmatrix}}{\text{Market value of debt} + \text{Market value of equity}}$$

The interest rate on Suncoast Food Centers' $40 million of debt is 9 percent, and the company's tax rate is 30 percent. Therefore, Suncoast's after-tax cost of debt is 6.3 percent [9% × (1 − 30%)]. Let's assume that the cost of Suncoast's equity capital is 12 percent. Moreover, the market value of the company's equity is $60 million.[2] The following calculation shows that Suncoast Food Centers' WACC is 9.72 percent.

$$\text{Weighted-average cost of capital} = \frac{(.063)(\$40{,}000{,}000) + (.12)(\$60{,}000{,}000)}{\$40{,}000{,}000 + \$60{,}000{,}000} = .0972$$

Finally, Suncoast Food Centers had an average balance of $2 million in current liabilities, distributed as follows:

Division	Current Liabilities
Gulf Division	$ 400,000
Food Processing Division	1,000,000
Atlantic Division	600,000

Now we can compute the economic value added (or EVA) for each of Suncoast's three divisions.

Division	After-tax operating income (in millions)	−	[(Total assets (in millions)	−	Current liabilities (in millions))	× WACC]	=	Economic value added
Gulf	$3.00 × (1 − .30)	−	[($20	−	$ .4)	× .0972]	=	$194,880
Food Processing	$3.60 × (1 − .30)	−	[($18	−	$1.0)	× .0972]	=	867,600
Atlantic	$6.75 × (1 − .30)	−	[($45	−	$ .6)	× .0972]	=	409,320

The EVA analysis reveals that all three of Suncoast Food Centers' divisions are contributing substantially to the company's economic value.

What does an EVA analysis tell us? EVA indicates how much shareholder wealth is being created, as Roberto Goizueta, Coca-Cola's former CEO, explained: "We raise capital to make concentrate and sell it at an operating profit. Then we pay the cost of that capital. Shareholders pocket the difference (EVA amount)."

[2]The *book value* of Suncoast Food Centers' equity is $41 million, but that amount does not reflect the current value of the company's assets or the value of intangible assets such as the Suncoast Food Centers name.

Management Accounting Practice

Siemens and Royal Bank of Canada

PAY FOR PERFORMANCE BASED ON EVA

In the wake of the excesses in top management compensation over the past few years, at many companies pay for performance is back in vogue. Top executives earn hefty bonuses when times are good, but are expected to share in the pain during a decline in business.

Siemens, a global electronics firm, links the compensation of its top 500 managers to their business units' economic value added (EVA) measure. Similarly, the Royal Bank of Canada, upon observing that its lower-level managers were not acting in accordance with the bank's overall strategy, began linking their compensation to the bank's EVA and revenue growth.[3]

Measuring Income and Invested Capital

LO 5

Explain how to measure a division's income and invested capital.

The ROI, residual-income, and economic value added (EVA) measures of investment-center performance all use profit and invested capital in their formulas. This raises the question of how to measure divisional profit and invested capital. This section will illustrate various approaches to resolving these measurement issues.

Invested Capital

We will focus on Suncoast Food Centers' Food Processing Division to illustrate several alternative approaches to measuring an investment center's capital. Exhibit 13–2 lists the assets and liabilities associated with the Food Processing Division. Notice that Exhibit 13–2 does not constitute a complete balance sheet. First, there are no long-term liabilities, such as bonds payable, associated with the Food Processing Division. Although Suncoast Food Centers may have such long-term debt, it would not be meaningful to assign portions of that debt to the company's individual divisions. Second, there is no stockholders' equity associated with the Food Processing Division. The owners of the company own stock in Suncoast Food Centers, not in its individual divisions.

Average Balances ROI, residual income, and EVA are computed for a period of time, such as a year or a month. Asset balances, on the other hand, are measured at a point in time, such as December 31. Since divisional asset balances generally will

Exhibit 13–2

Assets and Liabilities Associated with Food Processing Division

Assets*		
Current assets (cash, accounts receivable, inventories, etc.)		$ 2,000,000
Long-lived assets (land, buildings, equipment, vehicles, etc.):		
Gross book value (acquisition cost)	$19,000,000	
Less: Accumulated depreciation	4,000,000	
Net book value		15,000,000
Plant under construction		1,000,000
Total assets		$18,000,000
Liabilities		
Current liabilities (accounts payable, salaries payable, etc.)		$ 1,000,000

*This is not a balance sheet, but rather a listing of certain assets and liabilities associated with the Food Processing Division.

[3] Louis Lavelle, "The Gravy Train Just Got Derailed—'Pay for Performance' Is Back in Vogue," *Business Week,* November 19, 2001; and Tad Leahy, "All the Right Moves," *Business Finance* 6, no. 1 (April 2000), p. 32.

change over time, we use average balances in calculating ROI, residual income, and EVA. For example, if the Food Processing Division's balance in invested capital was $19,000,000 on January 1, and $17,000,000 on December 31, we would use the year's average invested capital of $18,000,000 in the ROI, residual income, and EVA calculations.

Should Total Assets Be Used? Exhibit 13–2 shows that the Food Processing Division had average balances during the year of $2,000,000 in current assets, $15,000,000 in long-lived assets, and $1,000,000 tied up in a plant under construction. (Suncoast Food Centers is building a new high-tech dairy plant in Orlando to produce its innovative zero-calorie ice cream.) In addition, Exhibit 13–2 discloses that the Food Processing Division's average balance of current liabilities was $1,000,000.

What is the division's invested capital? Several possibilities exist.

1. ***Total assets.*** The management of Suncoast Food Centers has decided to use *average total assets* for the year in measuring each division's invested capital. Thus, $18,000,000 is the amount used in the ROI, residual-income, and EVA calculations discussed earlier in this chapter. This measure of invested capital is appropriate if the division manager has considerable authority in making decisions about *all* of the division's assets, *including nonproductive assets.* In this case, the Food Processing Division's partially completed dairy plant is a nonproductive asset. Since the division manager had considerable influence in deciding to build the new plant and he is responsible for overseeing the project, average total assets provides an appropriate measure.
2. ***Total productive assets.*** In other companies, division managers are directed by top management to keep nonproductive assets, such as vacant land or construction in progress. In such cases, it is appropriate to exclude nonproductive assets from the measure of invested capital. Then *average total productive assets* is used to measure invested capital. If Suncoast Food Centers had chosen this alternative, $17,000,000 would have been used in the ROI, residual-income, and EVA calculations (total assets of $18,000,000 less $1,000,000 for the plant under construction).
3. ***Total assets less current liabilities.*** Some companies allow division managers to secure short-term bank loans and other short-term credit. In such cases, invested capital often is measured by *average total assets less average current liabilities.* This approach encourages investment-center managers to minimize resources tied up in assets and maximize the use of short-term credit to finance operations. If this approach had been used by Suncoast Food Centers, the Food Processing Division's invested capital would have been $17,000,000, total assets of $18,000,000 less current liabilities of $1,000,000. (Note that current liabilities are always subtracted from total assets for the measure of invested capital used in the EVA measure.)

Gross or Net Book Value Another decision to make in choosing a measure of invested capital is whether to use the *gross book value (acquisition cost)* or the *net book value* of long-lived assets. (Net book value is the acquisition cost less accumulated depreciation.) Suncoast Food Centers' management has decided to use the average net book value of $15,000,000 to value the Food Processing Division's long-lived assets. If gross book value had been used instead, the division's measure of invested capital would have been $22,000,000 as the following calculation shows.

Current assets	$ 2,000,000
Long-lived assets (at gross book value)	19,000,000
Plant under construction	1,000,000
Total assets (at gross book value)	$22,000,000

There are advantages and disadvantages associated with both gross and net book value as a measure of invested capital.

Advantages of Net Book Value; Disadvantages of Gross Book Value

1. Using net book value maintains consistency with the balance sheet prepared for external reporting purposes. This allows for more meaningful comparisons of return-on-investment measures across different companies.
2. Using net book value to measure invested capital is also more consistent with the definition of income, which is the numerator in ROI calculations. In computing income, the current period's depreciation on long-lived assets is deducted as an expense.

Advantages of Gross Book Value; Disadvantages of Net Book Value

1. The usual methods of computing depreciation, such as the straight-line and the declining-balance methods, are arbitrary. Hence, they should not be allowed to affect ROI, residual-income, or EVA calculations.
2. When long-lived assets are depreciated, their net book value declines over time. This results in a misleading increase in ROI, residual income, and EVA across time. Exhibit 13–3 provides an illustration of this phenomenon for the ROI calculated on an equipment purchase under consideration by the Food Processing Division manager. Notice that the ROI rises steadily across the five-year horizon if invested capital is measured by net book value. However, using gross book value eliminates this problem. If an accelerated depreciation method were used instead of the straight-line method, the increasing trend in ROI would be even more pronounced.

A Behavioral Problem The tendency for net book value to produce a misleading increase in ROI over time can have a serious effect on the incentives of investment-center managers. Investment centers with old assets will show much higher ROIs than investment centers with relatively new assets. This can discourage investment-center managers from investing in new equipment. If this behavioral tendency persists, a division's assets can become obsolete, making the division uncompetitive.

Allocating Assets to Investment Centers Some companies control certain assets centrally, although these assets are needed to carry on operations in the divisions.

Exhibit 13–3
Increase in ROI over Time (when net book value is used)

Acquisition cost of equipment	$500,000
Useful life	5 years
Salvage value at end of useful life	0
Annual straight-line depreciation	$100,000
Annual income generated by asset (before deducting depreciation)	$150,000

Year	Income before Depreciation	Annual Depreciation	Income Net of Depreciation	Average Net Book Value*	ROI Based on Net Book Value†	Average Gross Book Value	ROI Based on Gross Book Value
1	$150,000	$100,000	$50,000	$450,000	11.1%	$500,000	10%
2	150,000	100,000	50,000	350,000	14.3	500,000	10
3	150,000	100,000	50,000	250,000	20.0	500,000	10
4	150,000	100,000	50,000	150,000	33.3	500,000	10
5	150,000	100,000	50,000	50,000	100.0	500,000	10

*Average net book value is the average of the beginning and ending balances for the year in net book value. In year 1, for example, the average net book value is:

$$\frac{\$500{,}000 + \$400{,}000}{2}$$

†ROI rounded to nearest tenth of 1 percent.

Common examples are cash and accounts receivable. Divisions need cash in order to operate, but many companies control cash balances centrally in order to minimize their total cash holdings. Some large retail firms manage accounts receivable centrally. A credit customer of some national department-store chains can make a payment either at the local store or by mailing the payment to corporate headquarters.

When certain assets are controlled centrally, some allocation basis generally is chosen to allocate these asset balances to investment centers, for the purpose of measuring invested capital. For example, cash may be allocated based on the budgeted cash needs in each division or on the basis of divisional sales. Accounts receivable usually are allocated on the basis of divisional sales. Divisions with less stringent credit terms are allocated proportionately larger balances of accounts receivable.

Measuring Investment-Center Income

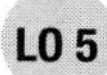

Explain how to measure a division's income and invested capital.

In addition to choosing a measure of investment-center capital, an accountant must also decide how to measure a center's income. The key issue is controllability; the choice involves the extent to which uncontrollable items are allowed to influence the income measure. The Excel spreadsheet in Exhibit 13–4 illustrates several different possibilities for measuring the income of Suncoast Food Centers' Food Processing Division.

Suncoast Food Centers' top management uses the *profit margin controllable by division manager,* $3,600,000, to evaluate the Food Processing Division manager. This profit measure is used in calculating ROI, residual income, or EVA. Some fixed costs traceable to the division have not been deducted from this $3,600,000 amount, but the division manager cannot control or significantly influence these costs. Hence they are excluded from the ROI calculation in evaluating the division manager. In calculating EVA, the $3,600,000 profit-margin amount is converted to an after-tax basis by multiplying by 1 minus the tax rate of 30 percent.

Pay for Performance Some companies reward investment-center managers with **cash bonuses** if they meet a predetermined target on a specified performance criterion, such as residual income, ROI, or EVA. Such payments often are referred to as **pay for performance, merit pay,** or **incentive compensation.** These cash bonuses generally are single payments, independent of a manager's base salary.

Exhibit 13–4

Divisional Income Statement: Food Processing Division

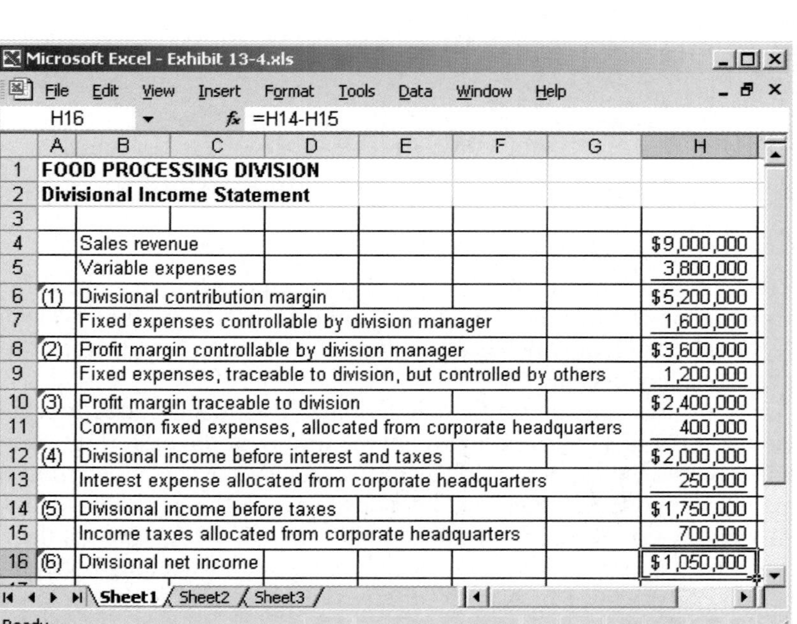

	A	B	H
1	**FOOD PROCESSING DIVISION**		
2	**Divisional Income Statement**		
3			
4		Sales revenue	$9,000,000
5		Variable expenses	3,800,000
6	(1)	Divisional contribution margin	$5,200,000
7		Fixed expenses controllable by division manager	1,600,000
8	(2)	Profit margin controllable by division manager	$3,600,000
9		Fixed expenses, traceable to division, but controlled by others	1,200,000
10	(3)	Profit margin traceable to division	$2,400,000
11		Common fixed expenses, allocated from corporate headquarters	400,000
12	(4)	Divisional income before interest and taxes	$2,000,000
13		Interest expense allocated from corporate headquarters	250,000
14	(5)	Divisional income before taxes	$1,750,000
15		Income taxes allocated from corporate headquarters	700,000
16	(6)	Divisional net income	$1,050,000

Managers versus Investment Centers It is important to make a distinction between an investment center and its manager. In evaluating the *manager's* performance, only revenues and costs that the manager can control or significantly influence should be included in the profit measure. Remember that the overall objective of the performance measure is to provide incentives for goal-congruent behavior. No performance measure can motivate a manager to make decisions about costs he or she cannot control. This explains why Suncoast Food Centers' top management relies on the profit margin controllable by division manager to compute the manager's ROI performance measure.

Evaluating the Food Processing Division as a viable economic investment is a different matter altogether. In this evaluation, traceability of costs, rather than controllability, is the issue. For this purpose, Suncoast Food Centers' top management uses the profit margin traceable to division to compute the divisional ROI, residual income, or EVA. As Exhibit 13–4 shows, this amount is $2,400,000.

Other Profit Measures The other measures of divisional profit shown in Exhibit 13–4 (lines 4, 5, and 6) are also used by some companies. The rationale behind these divisional income measures is that all corporate costs have to be covered by the operations of the divisions. Allocating corporate costs, interest, and income taxes to the divisions makes division managers aware of these costs.

Inflation: Historical-Cost versus Current-Value Accounting

Whether measuring investment-center income or invested capital, the impact of price-level changes should not be forgotten. During periods of inflation, historical-cost asset values soon cease to reflect the cost of replacing those assets. Therefore, some accountants argue that investment-center performance measures based on historical-cost accounting are misleading. Yet surveys of corporate managers indicate that an accounting system based on current values would not alter their decisions. Most managers believe that measures based on historical-cost accounting are adequate when used in conjunction with budgets and performance targets. As managers prepare those budgets, they build their expectations about inflation into the budgets and performance targets.

Another reason for using historical-cost accounting for internal purposes is that it is required for external reporting. Thus, historical-cost data already are available, while installing current-value accounting would add substantial incremental costs to the organization's information system.

Other Issues in Segment Performance Evaluation

Alternatives to ROI, Residual Income, and Economic Value Added (EVA)

ROI, residual income, and EVA are short-run performance measures. They focus on only one period of time. Yet an investment center is really a collection of assets (investments), each of which has a multiperiod life. Exhibit 13–5 portrays this perspective of an investment center.

To evaluate any one of these individual investments correctly requires a multiperiod viewpoint, which takes into account the timing of the cash flows from the investment. For example, investment E in Exhibit 13–5 may start out slowly in years 4 and 5, but it may be economically justified by its expected high performance in years 8, 9, and 10. Any evaluation of the investment center in year 5 that ignores the long-term performance of its various investments can result in a misleading conclusion. Thus, single-period performance measures suffer from myopia. They focus on only a short time segment that slices across the division's investments as portrayed in Exhibit 13–5.

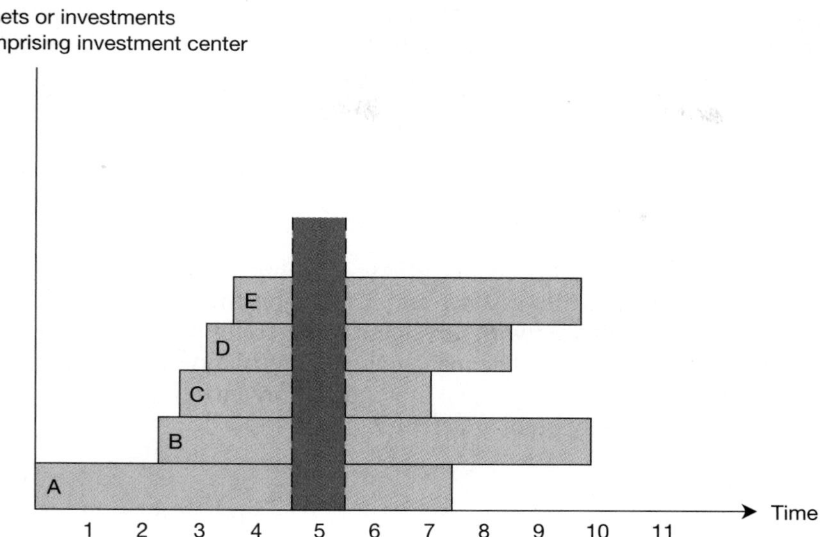

Exhibit 13–5
Investment Center Viewed as a Collection of Investments

To avoid this short-term focus, some organizations downplay ROI, residual income, and EVA in favor of an alternative approach. Instead of relating profit to invested capital in a single measure, these characteristics of investment-center performance are evaluated separately. Actual divisional profit for a time period is compared to a flexible budget, and variances are used to analyze performance. The division's major investments are evaluated through a *postaudit* of the investment decisions. For example, investment E may have been undertaken because of expected high performance in years 8, 9, and 10. When that time comes, a review will determine whether the project lived up to expectations.

Evaluating periodic profit through flexible budgeting and variance analysis, coupled with postaudits of major investment decisions, is a more complicated approach to evaluating investment centers. However, it does help management avoid the myopia of single-period measures such as ROI, residual income, and EVA.

Importance of Nonfinancial Information

Although financial measures such as segment profit, ROI, residual income, and EVA are widely used in performance evaluation, nonfinancial measures are important also. Manufacturers collect data on rates of defective products, airlines record information on lost bags and aircraft delays, and hotels keep track of occupancy rates. The proper evaluation of an organization and its segments requires that multiple performance measures be defined and used. The *balanced scorecard,* with its *lead* and *lag measures* of performance is one tool that is more and more widely used as a means of introducing nonfinancial measures into performance evaluation. See Chapter 10 for a discussion of the balanced scorecard.

Measuring Performance in Nonprofit Organizations

Management control in a nonprofit organization presents a special challenge. Such organizations often are managed by professionals, such as physicians in a hospital. Moreover, many people participate in a nonprofit organization at some personal sacrifice, motivated by humanitarian or public service ideals. Often, such people are less receptive to formal control procedures than their counterparts in business.

The goals of nonprofit organizations often are less clear-cut than those of businesses. Public service objectives may be difficult to specify with precision and even more difficult to measure in terms of achievement. For example, one community health center was established in an economically depressed area with three stated goals:

1. To reduce costs in a nearby hospital by providing a clinic for people to use instead of the hospital emergency room.
2. To provide preventive as well as therapeutic care, and establish outreach programs in the community.
3. To become financially self-sufficient.

There is some conflict between these objectives, since goal 2 does not provide revenue to the center, while goals 1 and 3 focus on financial efficiency. Moreover, the health center was staffed with physicians who could have achieved much greater incomes in private practice. The management control tools described in this and the preceding three chapters can be used in nonprofit organizations. However, the challenges in doing so effectively often are greater.

Transfer Pricing

The problem of measuring performance in profit centers or investment centers is made more complicated by transfers of goods or services between responsibility centers. The amount charged when one division sells goods or services to another division is called a **transfer price.** This price affects the profit measurement for both the selling division and the buying division. A high transfer price results in high profit for the selling division and low profit for the buying division. A low transfer price has the opposite effect. Consequently, the transfer-pricing policy *can* affect the *incentives* of autonomous division managers as they decide whether to make the transfer. Exhibit 13–6 depicts this scenario.

Transfer pricing is widely used in the manufacturing industry. When the chassis for this Ford Mustang was transferred from the manufacturing division to the assembly division, a transfer price was specified.

Goal Congruence

What should be management's goal in setting transfer prices for internally transferred goods or services? In a decentralized organization, the managers of profit centers and investment centers often have considerable autonomy in deciding whether to accept or reject orders and whether to buy inputs from inside the organization or from outside. For example, a large manufacturer of farm equipment allows its Assembly Division managers to buy parts either from another division of the company or from independent manufacturers. The goal in setting transfer prices is to establish incentives for autonomous division managers to make decisions that support the overall goals of the organization.

Suppose it is in the best interests of Suncoast Food Centers for the baked goods produced by the Food Processing Division's Orlando Bakery to be transferred to the Gulf Division's stores in the Tampa Bay area. Thus, if the firm were centralized, bakery products would be transferred from the Food Processing Division to the Gulf Division. However, Suncoast Food Centers is a decentralized company, and the Gulf Division manager is free to buy baked goods either from the Food Processing Division or from an outside bakery company. Similarly, the Food Processing Division manager is free to accept or reject an order for baked goods, at any given price, from the Gulf Division. The goal of the company's controller in setting the transfer price is to provide incentives for each of these division managers to act in the company's best interests.

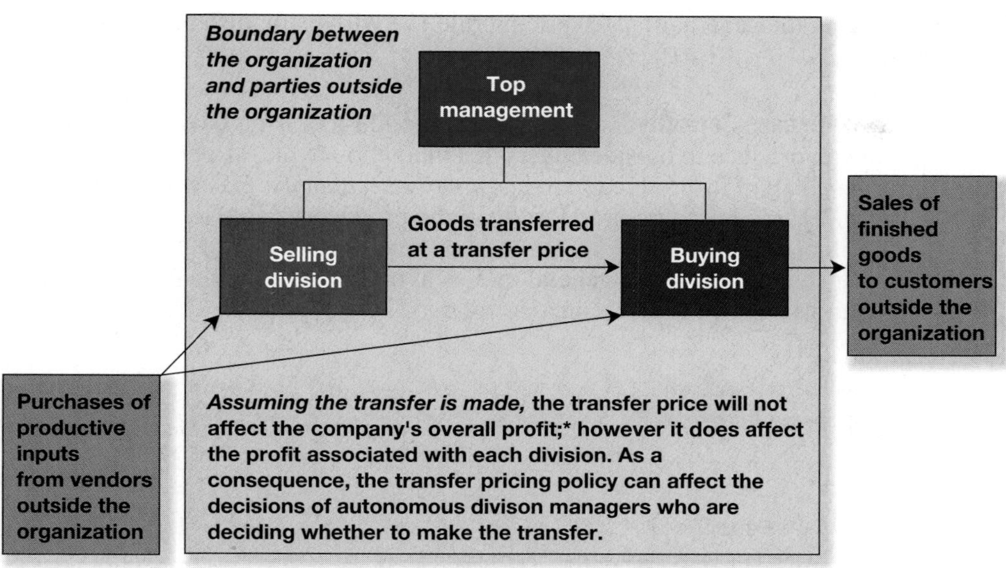

Exhibit 13–6
The Transfer-Pricing Scenario

The transfer price should be chosen so that each division manager, when striving to maximize his or her own division's profit, makes the decision that maximizes the company's profit.

General Transfer-Pricing Rule

Use the general economic rule to set an optimal transfer price.

Management's objective in setting a transfer price is to encourage goal congruence among the division managers involved in the transfer. A general rule that will ensure goal congruence is given below.

$$\text{Transfer price} = \begin{array}{c}\text{Additional } \textit{outlay cost}\\ \text{per unit incurred because}\\ \text{goods are transferred}\end{array} + \begin{array}{c}\textit{Opportunity cost} \text{ per unit}\\ \text{to the organization}\\ \text{because of the transfer}\end{array}$$

Topic 13–2

The general rule specifies the transfer price as the sum of two cost components. The first component is the outlay cost incurred by the division that produces the goods or services to be transferred. Outlay costs will include the direct variable costs of the product or service and any other outlay costs that are incurred only as a result of the transfer. The second component in the general transfer-pricing rule is the opportunity cost incurred by the organization as a whole because of the transfer. Recall from Chapter 2 that an *opportunity cost* is a benefit that is forgone as a result of taking a particular action.

We will illustrate the general transfer-pricing rule for Suncoast Food Centers. The company's Food Processing Division produces bread in its Orlando Bakery. The division transfers some of its products to the company's Gulf and Atlantic divisions, and sells some of its products to other companies in the *external market* under different labels.

"Transfer pricing is a business issue as well as a tax issue that should be considered in the board room." (13c)
Ernst & Young

Bread is transported to stores in racks containing one dozen loaves of packaged bread. In the Orlando bakery, the following variable costs are incurred to produce bread and transport it to a buyer.

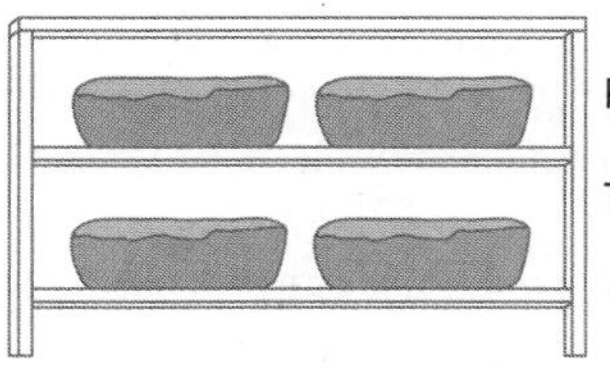

Production:
Standard variable cost per rack (including packaging) $7.00
Transportation:
Standard variable cost per rack to transport bread . . . . $ .25

In applying the general transfer-pricing rule, we will distinguish between two different scenarios.

Scenario I: No Excess Capacity Suppose the Food Processing Division can sell all the bread it can produce to outside buyers at a market price of $11 per rack. Since the division can sell all of its production, it has *no excess capacity. Excess capacity* exists only when more goods can be produced than the producer is able to sell, due to low demand for the product.

What transfer price does the general rule yield under this scenario of no excess capacity? The transfer price is determined as follows:

Outlay cost:		
Standard variable cost of production	$ 7.00	per rack
Standard variable cost of transportation	.25	per rack
Total outlay cost	$ 7.25	per rack
Opportunity cost:		
Selling price per unit in external market	$11.00	per rack
Less: Variable cost of production and transportation	7.25	per rack
Opportunity cost (forgone contribution margin)	$ 3.75	per rack

General transfer-pricing rule:

Transfer price = Outlay cost + Opportunity cost

$11.00 = $7.25 + $3.75

The *outlay cost* incurred by the Food Processing Division in order to transfer a rack of bread includes the standard variable production cost of $7.00 and the standard variable transportation cost of $.25. The *opportunity cost* incurred by Suncoast Food Centers when its Food Processing Division transfers a rack of bread to the Gulf Division *instead* of selling it in the external market is the forgone contribution margin from the lost sale, equal to $3.75. Why does the company lose a sale in the external market for every rack of bread transferred to the Gulf Division? The sale is lost because there is *no excess capacity* in the Food Processing Division. Every rack of bread transferred to another company division results in one less rack of bread sold in the external market.

Goal Congruence How does the general transfer-pricing rule promote goal congruence? Suppose the Gulf Division's grocery stores can sell a loaf of bread for $1.50, or $18 for a rack of 12 loaves ($18 = 12 × $1.50). What is the best way for Suncoast Food Centers to use the limited production capacity in the Food Processing Division's Orlando bakery? The answer is determined as follows:

Contribution to Suncoast Food Centers from Sale in External Market		Contribution to Suncoast Food Centers from Transfer to Gulf Division	
Wholesale selling price per rack	$11.00	Retail selling price per rack	$18.00
Less: Variable costs	7.25	Less: Variable costs	7.25
Contribution margin	$ 3.75	Contribution margin	$10.75

The best use of the bakery's limited production capacity is to produce bread for transfer to the Gulf Division. If the transfer price is set at $11.00, as the general rule specifies, goal congruence is maintained. The Food Processing Division manager is willing to transfer bread to the Gulf Division, because the transfer price of $11.00 is equal to the external market price. The Gulf Division manager is willing to buy the bread, because her division will have a contribution margin of $7.00 on each rack of bread transferred ($18.00 sales price minus the $11.00 transfer price).

Now consider a different situation. Suppose a local organization makes a special offer to the Gulf Division manager to buy several hundred loaves of bread to sell in a promotional campaign. The organization offers to pay \$.80 per loaf, which is \$9.60 per rack of a dozen loaves. What will the Gulf Division manager do? She must pay a transfer price of \$11.00 per rack, so the Gulf Division would lose \$1.40 per rack if the special offer were accepted (\$1.40 = \$11.00 − \$9.60). The Gulf Division manager will decline the special offer. Is this decision in the best interests of Suncoast Food Centers as a whole? If the offer were accepted, the company as a whole would make a positive contribution of \$2.35 per rack, as shown below.

Contribution to Suncoast Food Centers If Special Offer Is Accepted

Special price per rack	\$9.60	per rack
Less: Variable cost to company	7.25	per rack
Contribution to company, per rack	\$2.35	per rack

However, the company can make even more if its Food Processing Division sells bread directly in its external market. Then the contribution to the company is \$3.75, as we have just seen. (The external market price of \$11.00 per rack minus a variable cost of \$7.25 per rack equals \$3.75 per rack.) Thus, Suncoast Food Centers is better off, as a whole, if the Gulf Division's special offer is rejected. Once again, the general transfer-pricing rule results in goal-congruent decision making.

Scenario II: Excess Capacity Now let's change our basic assumption, and suppose the Food Processing Division's Orlando bakery has excess production capacity. This means that the total demand for its bread from all sources, including the Gulf and Atlantic divisions and the external market, is less than the bakery's production capacity. Under this scenario of excess capacity, what does the general rule specify for a transfer price?

$$\text{Transfer price} = \text{Outlay cost} + \text{Opportunity cost}$$
$$\$7.25 = \$7.25 + 0$$

The *outlay cost* in the Food Processing Division's Orlando bakery is still \$7.25, since it does not depend on whether there is idle capacity or not. The *opportunity cost,* however, is now zero. There is no opportunity cost to the company when a rack of bread is transferred to the Gulf Division, because the Food Processing Division can still satisfy all of its external demand for bread. Thus, the general rule specifies a transfer price of \$7.25, the total standard variable cost of production and transportation.

> "It is difficult for people 'doing the business' to stop and consult about the transfer pricing implications of their moves, but they have to." (13d)
>
> **Respondent, Ernst & Young survey**

Goal Congruence Let's reconsider what will happen when the Gulf Division manager receives the local organization's special offer to buy bread at \$9.60 per rack. The Gulf Division will now show a positive contribution of \$2.35 per rack on the special order.

Special price per rack	\$9.60	per rack
Less: Transfer price paid by Gulf Division	7.25	per rack
Contribution to Gulf Division	\$2.35	per rack

The Gulf Division manager will accept the special offer. This decision is also in the best interests of Suncoast Food Centers. The company, as a whole, will also make a contribution of \$2.35 per rack on every rack transferred to the Gulf Division to satisfy the special order. Once again, the general transfer-pricing rule maintains goal-congruent decision-making behavior.

Notice that the general rule yields a transfer price that leaves the Food Processing Division manager indifferent as to whether the transfer will be made. At a transfer price of \$7.25, the contribution to the Food Processing Division will be zero (transfer price of \$7.25 less variable cost of \$7.25). To avoid this problem, we can view the general rule as providing a lower bound on the transfer price. Some companies allow the producing division to add a markup to this lower bound in order to provide a positive contribution margin. This in turn provides a positive incentive to make the transfer.

Difficulty in Implementing the General Rule The general transfer-pricing rule will always promote goal-congruent decision making *if the rule can be implemented.* However, the rule is often difficult or impossible to implement due to the difficulty of measuring opportunity costs. Such a cost-measurement problem can arise for a number of reasons. One reason is that the external market may not be perfectly competitive. Under **perfect competition,** the market price does not depend on the quantity sold by any one producer. Under **imperfect competition,** a single producer or group of producers can affect the market price by varying the amount of product available in the market. In such cases, the external market price depends on the production decisions of the producer. This in turn means that the opportunity cost incurred by the company as a result of internal transfers depends on the quantity sold externally. These interactions may make it impossible to measure accurately the opportunity cost caused by a product transfer.

Other reasons for difficulty in measuring the opportunity cost associated with a product transfer include uniqueness of the transferred goods or services, a need for the producing division to invest in special equipment in order to produce the transferred goods, and interdependencies among several transferred products or services. For example, the producing division may provide design services as well as production of the goods for a buying division. What is the opportunity cost associated with each of these related outputs of the producing division? In many such cases it is difficult to sort out the opportunity costs.

The general transfer-pricing rule provides a good conceptual model for the managerial accountant to use in setting transfer prices. Moreover, in many cases it can be implemented. When the general rule cannot be implemented, organizations turn to other transfer-pricing methods, as we shall see next.

Transfers Based on the External Market Price

LO 7

Explain how to base a transfer price on market prices, costs, or negotiations.

A common approach is to set the transfer price equal to the price in the external market. In the Suncoast Food Centers illustration, the Food Processing Division would set the transfer price for bread at $11.00 per rack, since that is the price the division can obtain in its external market. When the producing division has no excess capacity and perfect competition prevails, where no single producer can affect the market price, the general transfer-pricing rule and the external market price yield the same transfer price. This fact is illustrated for Suncoast Food Centers as follows:

General Transfer-Pricing Rule

Transfer price	=	Outlay cost	+	Opportunity cost	
	=	Variable cost of production and transportation	+	Forgone contribution margin of an external sale	
	=	\$7.25	+	(\$11.00 − \$7.25)	= \$11.00

Market Price

Transfer price = External market price = \$11.00

If the producing division has excess capacity or the external market is imperfectly competitive, the general rule and the external market price will not yield the same transfer price.

If the transfer price is set at the market price, the producing division should have the option of either producing goods for internal transfer or selling in the external market. The buying division should be required to purchase goods from inside its organization if the producing division's goods meet the product specifications. Otherwise, the buying division should have the autonomy to buy from a supplier outside its own organization. To handle pricing disputes that may arise, an arbitration process should be established.

Transfer prices based on market prices are consistent with the responsibility-accounting concepts of profit centers and investment centers. In addition to encouraging division managers to focus on divisional profitability, market-based transfer prices help to show the contribution of each division to overall company profit. Suppose the Food Processing Division of Suncoast Food Centers transfers bread to the Gulf Division at a market-based transfer price of $11.00 per rack. The following contribution margins will be earned by the two divisions and the company as a whole.

Food Processing Division		**Gulf Division**	
Transfer price	$11.00 per rack	Retail sales price	$18.00 per rack
Less: Variable costs	7.25 per rack	Less: Transfer price	11.00 per rack
Contribution margin	$ 3.75 per rack	Contribution margin	$ 7.00 per rack

Suncoast Food Centers		
Retail sales price	$18.00	per rack
Less: Variable costs	7.25	per rack
Contribution margin	$10.75	per rack

When aggregate divisional profits are determined for the year, and ROI and residual income are computed, the use of a market-based transfer price helps to assess the contributions of each division to overall corporate profits.

Distress Market Prices Occasionally an industry will experience a period of significant excess capacity and extremely low prices. For example, when gasoline prices soared due to a foreign oil embargo, the market prices for recreational vehicles and power boats fell temporarily to very low levels.

Under such extreme conditions, basing transfer prices on market prices can lead to decisions that are not in the best interests of the overall company. Basing transfer prices on artificially *low distress market prices* could lead the producing division to sell or close the productive resources devoted to producing the product for transfer. Under distress market prices, the producing division manager might prefer to move the division into a more profitable product line. While such a decision might improve the division's profit in the short run, it could be contrary to the best interests of the company overall. It might be better for the company as a whole to avoid divesting itself of any productive resources and to ride out the period of market distress. To encourage an autonomous division manager to act in this fashion, some companies set the transfer price equal to the long-run average external market price, rather than the current (possibly depressed) market price.

Negotiated Transfer Prices

Many companies use negotiated transfer prices. Division managers or their representatives actually negotiate the price at which transfers will be made. Sometimes they start with the external market price and then make adjustments for various reasons. For example, the producing division may enjoy some cost savings on internal transfers that are not obtained on external sales. Commissions may not have to be paid to sales personnel on internally transferred products. In such cases, a negotiated transfer price may split the cost savings between the producing and buying divisions.

In other instances, a negotiated transfer price may be used because no external market exists for the transferred product.

Two drawbacks sometimes characterize negotiated transfer prices. First, negotiations can lead to divisiveness and competition between participating division managers. This can undermine the spirit of cooperation and unity that is desirable throughout an organization. Second, although negotiating skill is a valuable managerial talent, it should not be the sole or dominant factor in evaluating a division manager. If, for example, the producing division's manager is a better negotiator than the buying division's manager, then the producing division's profit may look better than it should, simply because of its manager's superior negotiating ability.

Cost-Based Transfer Prices

Organizations that do not base prices on market prices or negotiations often turn to a cost-based transfer-pricing approach.

Variable Cost One approach is to set the transfer price equal to the standard variable cost. The problem with this approach is that even when the producing division has excess capacity, it is not allowed to show any contribution margin on the transferred products or services. To illustrate, suppose the Food Processing Division has excess capacity and the transfer price is set at the standard variable cost of $7.25 per rack of bread. There is no positive incentive for the division to produce and transfer bread to the Gulf Division. The Food Processing Division's contribution margin from a transfer will be zero (transfer price of $7.25 minus variable costs of $7.25 equals zero). Some companies avoid this problem by setting the transfer price at standard variable cost plus a markup to allow the producing division a positive contribution margin.

Full Cost An alternative is to set the transfer price equal to the *full cost* of the transferred product or service. **Full** (or **absorption**) **cost** is equal to the product's variable cost plus an allocated portion of fixed overhead.

Suppose the Food Processing Division's Orlando bakery has budgeted annual fixed overhead of $500,000 and budgeted annual production of 200,000 racks of bread. The full cost of the bakery's product is computed as follows:

$$
\begin{aligned}
\text{Full cost} &= \text{Variable cost} + \text{Allocated fixed overhead} \\
&= \$7.25 \text{ per rack} + \frac{\$500{,}000 \text{ budgeted fixed overhead}}{200{,}000 \text{ budgeted racks of bread}} \\
&= \$7.25 + \$2.50 \\
&= \$9.75 \text{ per rack}
\end{aligned}
$$

Under this approach, the transfer price is set at $9.75 per rack of bread.

Dysfunctional Decision-Making Behavior Basing transfer prices on full cost entails a serious risk of causing dysfunctional decision-making behavior. Full-cost-based transfer prices lead the buying division to view costs that are fixed for the company as a whole as variable costs to the buying division. This can cause faulty decision making.

To illustrate, suppose the Food Processing Division has excess capacity, and the transfer price of bread is equal to the full cost of $9.75 per rack. What will happen if the Gulf Division receives the special offer discussed previously, where it can sell bread to a local organization at a special price of $9.60 per rack? The Gulf Division manager will reject the special order, since otherwise her division would incur a loss of $.15 per rack.

Special price per rack	$9.60	per rack
Less: Transfer price based on full cost	9.75	per rack
Loss	$ .15	per rack

What is in the best interests of the company as a whole? Suncoast Food Centers would make a positive contribution of $2.35 per rack on the bread sold in the special order.

Special price per rack	$9.60	per rack
Less: Variable cost in Food Processing Division	7.25	per rack
Contribution to company as a whole	$2.35	per rack

What has happened here? Setting the transfer price equal to the full cost of $9.75 has turned a cost that is fixed in the Food Processing Division, and hence is fixed for the company as a whole, into a variable cost from the viewpoint of the Gulf Division manager. The manager would tend to reject the special offer, even though accepting it would benefit the company as a whole.

Although the practice is common, transfer prices should not be based on full cost. The risk is too great that the cost behavior in the producing division will be obscured. This can all too easily result in poor decisions in the buying division.

Standard versus Actual Costs

Throughout our discussion of transfer prices, we have used standard costs rather than actual costs. This was true in our discussion of the general transfer-pricing rule as well as for cost-based transfer prices. Transfer prices should not be based on actual costs, because such a practice would allow an inefficient producing division to pass its excess production costs on to the buying division in the transfer price. When standard costs are used in transfer-pricing formulas, the buying division is not forced to pick up the tab for the producer's inefficiency. Moreover, the producing division is given an incentive to control its costs, since any costs of inefficiency cannot be passed on.

Undermining Divisional Autonomy

Suppose the manager of Suncoast Food Centers' Food Processing Division has excess capacity but insists on a transfer price of $9.75, based on full cost. The Gulf Division manager is faced with the special offer for bread at $9.60 per rack. She regrets that she will have to decline the offer because it would cause her division's profit to decline, even though the company's interests would be best served by accepting the special order. The Gulf Division manager calls the company president and explains the situation. She asks the president to intervene and force the Food Processing Division manager to lower his transfer price.

As the company president, what would you do? If you stay out of the controversy, your company will lose the contribution on the special order. If you intervene, you will run the risk of undermining the autonomy of your division managers. You established a decentralized organization structure for Suncoast Centers and hired competent managers because you believed in the benefits of decentralized decision making.

There is no obvious answer to this dilemma. In practice, central managers are reluctant to intervene in such disputes unless the negative financial consequences to the organization are quite large. Most managers believe the benefits of decentralized decision making are important to protect, even if it means an occasional dysfunctional decision.

> "[Transfer pricing] affects nearly every aspect of multinational operations—R&D, manufacturing, marketing and distribution, after-sale services." (13e)
>
> **Ernst & Young**

An International Perspective

Two international issues arise in the case of multinational firms setting transfer prices between divisions in different countries.

Income-Tax Rates Multinational companies often consider domestic and foreign income-tax rates when setting transfer prices. For example, suppose a company based in Europe also has a division in Asia. A European division produces a subassembly, which is transferred to the Asian division for assembly and sale of the final product. Suppose also that the income-tax rate for the company's European division is higher than the rate in the Asian division's country. How would these different tax rates affect the transfer price for the subassembly?

The company's management has an incentive to set a low transfer price for the subassembly. This will result in relatively low profits for the company's European division and a relatively high income for the Asian division. Since the tax rate is lower in the Asian country, the overall company will save on income tax. By setting a low transfer price, the company will shift a portion of its income to a country with a lower tax rate. Tax laws vary among countries with regard to flexibility in setting transfer prices. Some countries' tax laws prohibit the behavior described in our example, while other countries' laws permit it.

Import Duties Another international issue that can affect a firm's transfer pricing policy is the imposition of import duties, or tariffs. These are fees charged to an importer, generally on the basis of the reported value of the goods being imported. Consider again the example of a firm with divisions in Europe and Asia. If the Asian country imposes an import duty on goods transferred in from the European division, the company has an incentive to set a relatively low transfer price on the transferred goods. This will minimize the duty to be paid and maximize the overall profit for the company as a whole. As in the case of taxation, countries sometimes pass laws to limit a multinational firm's flexibility in setting transfer prices for the purpose of minimizing import duties.

Management Accounting Practice

Ernst & Young, IRS

TRANSFER PRICING AND TAX ISSUES

According to a survey by Ernst & Young LLP, "transfer pricing is the top tax issue facing multinational corporations. Of the international tax directors at 582 multinational organizations polled in the survey, 75 percent expect their company to face a transfer-pricing audit within the next two years. Respondents cited related-party transactions (including the intercompany transfer of goods, services, properties, loans, and leases) involving administrative and management services as the most likely to be audited.[4]

"The Internal Revenue Service (IRS) is concerned that companies could use transfer prices to shift profits between related entities through cost of goods sold. Thus, transfer pricing manipulation could be used by taxpayers to shift income from high tax jurisdictions like the U.S. to low tax jurisdictions. The right price from the IRS's perspective is the market value price. Because it's difficult to prove that the transfer price was equal to the market price, companies often find themselves in disputes with the IRS. But now there's help. The IRS's Advanced Pricing Agreement Program provides companies an opportunity to avoid costly audits and litigation by allowing them to negotiate a prospective agreement with the IRS regarding the facts, the transfer pricing methodology, and an acceptable range of results. The program is aimed at multinational corporations interested in avoiding penalties, managing risk, and determining their tax liability with certainty."[5]

> "Transfer pricing has become the most difficult area of international taxation." (13f)
>
> Ernst & Young

[4]Eric Krell, "Scrutiny of Transfer Pricing Grows," *Business Finance* 6, no. 4 (August 2000), p. 12.

[5]Steven C. Wrappe, Ken Milani, and Julie Joy, "The Transfer Price Is Right," *Strategic Finance* 81, no. 1 (July 1999), p. 40.

Transfer Pricing in the Service Industry

Service industry firms and nonprofit organizations also use transfer pricing when services are transferred between responsibility centers. In banks, for example, the interest rate at which depositors' funds are transferred to the loan department is a form of transfer price. At Cornell University, if a student in the law school takes a course in the business school, a transfer price is charged to the law school for the credit hours of instruction provided to the law student. Since the transfer price is based on tuition charges, it is a market-price-based transfer price.

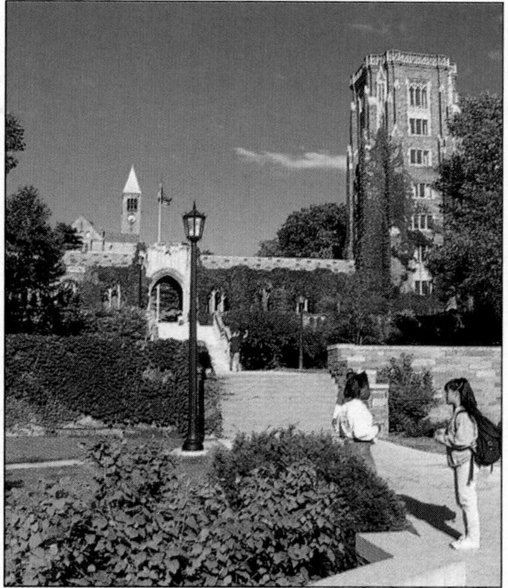

Transfer prices are used in the service industry as well as in manufacturing. Cornell University, for example, charges an accessory instruction fee to a campus unit when one of its students enrolls in a course offered in a different unit.

Behavioral Issues: Risk Aversion and Incentives

The designer of a performance-evaluation system for responsibility-center managers must consider many factors. Trade-offs often must be made between competing objectives. The overall objective is to achieve goal congruence by providing *incentives* for managers to act in the best interests of the organization as a whole. Financial performance measures such as divisional income, ROI, and residual income go a long way toward achieving this objective. However, these measures do have the disadvantage of imposing *risk* on a manager, because the measures also are affected by factors beyond the manager's control. For example, the income of an orange-growing division of an agricultural company will be affected not only by the manager's diligence and ability, but also by the weather and insect infestations.

Since most people exhibit *risk aversion,* managers must be compensated for the risk they must bear. This compensation comes in the form of higher salaries or bonuses. Thus, the design of a managerial performance evaluation and reward system involves a trade-off between the following two factors:

Evaluation of a manager on the basis of financial performance measures, which provide incentives for the manager to act in the organization's interests.	Imposition of risk on a manager who exhibits risk aversion, because financial performance measures are controllable only partially by the manager.

Trade-offs in designing managerial performance evaluation and reward system.

Achieving the optimal trade-off between risk and incentives is a delicate balancing act that requires the skill and experience of top management.

Goal Congruence and Internal Control Systems

Although most business professionals have high ethical standards, there are unfortunately those who will cut corners. An **internal control system** comprises the set of procedures designed to ensure that an organization's employees act in a legal, ethical, and responsible manner. Internal control procedures are designed to prevent the major lapses in responsible behavior described below.

Fraud Theft or misuse of an organization's resources constitutes *fraud.* To prevent and detect fraud, organizations establish well-defined procedures that prescribe how valuable resources will be handled. For example, many organizations require all checks above a particular amount to be authorized by two people.

Corruption Activities such as bribery, deceit, illegal political campaign contributions, and kickbacks constitute *corruption.* Most organizations have internal control procedures and codes of conduct to prevent and detect corrupt practices. For example, many organizations forbid their purchasing personnel from accepting gifts or gratuities from the sales personnel with whom they conduct business. The Foreign Corrupt Practices Act, passed by the U.S. Congress in 1977, prohibits a variety of corrupt practices in foreign business operations. For example, the law prohibits a company's management from bribing officials of a foreign government in return for favorable treatment of their company.

Financial Misrepresentation Internal control systems also are designed to prevent managers from intentionally (or accidentally) misstating an organization's financial records. Most companies have an *internal audit* staff, which reviews financial records throughout the organization to ensure their accuracy.

Unauthorized Action Sometimes a well-meaning employee is tempted to take an action that is not illegal or even unethical, but it is contrary to the organization's policies. Internal control procedures also are designed to detect and prevent unauthorized actions by an organization's employees, when those actions could reflect unfavorably on the organization. For example, a company may prohibit its employees from using company facilities for a rally in support of a controversial social cause.

An internal control system constitutes an integral part of an organization's efforts to achieve its goals. To be effective, internal control procedures require top management's full support and intolerance of intentional violations.

Chapter Summary

An important objective of any organization's managerial accounting system is to promote goal congruence among its employees. Thus, the primary criterion for judging the effectiveness of performance measures for responsibility-center managers is the extent to which the measures promote goal congruence.

The three most common measures of investment-center performance are return on investment (ROI), residual income (RI), and economic value added (EVA). Each of these performance measures relates an investment center's income to the capital invested to earn it. Residual income and EVA have the additional advantage of incorporating the organization's cost of acquiring capital in the performance measure. An investment center's ROI may be improved by increasing either the sales margin or capital turnover. ROI, residual income, and EVA all require the measurement of a division's income and invested capital, and the methods for making the measurements vary in practice.

When products or services are transferred between divisions in the same organization, divisional performance is affected by the transfer price. A general rule states that the transfer price should be equal to the outlay cost incurred to make the transfer plus the organization's opportunity cost associated with the transfer. Due to difficulties in implementing the rule, most companies base transfer prices on external market prices, costs, or negotiations. In some cases, these practical transfer-pricing methods may result in dysfunctional decisions. Top management then must weigh the benefits of intervening to prevent suboptimal decisions against the costs of undermining divisional autonomy.

Review Problems on Investment Centers and Transfer Pricing

Problem 1

Stellar Systems Company manufactures guidance systems for rockets used to launch commercial satellites. The company's Software Division reported the following results for 20x1.

Income	$ 300,000
Sales revenue	2,000,000
Invested capital (total assets)	3,000,000
Average balance in current liabilities	20,000

Stellar Systems' weighted-average cost of capital (WACC) is 9 percent, and the company's tax rate is 40 percent. Moreover, the company's required rate of return on invested capital is 9 percent.

Required:

1. Compute the Software Division's sales margin, capital turnover, return on investment (ROI), residual income, and economic value added (EVA) for 20x1.
2. If income and sales remain the same in 20x2, but the division's capital turnover improves to 80 percent, compute the following for 20x2: (*a*) invested capital and (*b*) ROI.

Problem 2

Stellar Systems Company's Microprocessor Division sells a computer module to the company's Guidance Assembly Division, which assembles completed guidance systems. The Microprocessor Division has no excess capacity. The computer module costs $10,000 to manufacture, and it can be sold in the external market to companies in the computer industry for $13,500.

Required: Compute the transfer price for the computer module using the general transfer-pricing rule.

Solutions to Review Problems

Problem 1

1. $$\text{Sales margin} = \frac{\text{Income}}{\text{Sales revenues}} = \frac{\$300{,}000}{\$2{,}000{,}000} = 15\%$$

$$\text{Capital turnover} = \frac{\text{Sales revenue}}{\text{Invested capital}} = \frac{\$2{,}000{,}000}{\$3{,}000{,}000} = 67\%$$

$$\text{Return on investment} = \frac{\text{Income}}{\text{Invested capital}} = \frac{\$300{,}000}{\$3{,}000{,}000} = 10\%$$

Residual income:

Divisional income		$300,000
Less: Imputed interest charge:		
Invested capital	$3,000,000	
× Imputed interest rate	× .09	
Imputed interest charge		270,000
Residual income		$ 30,000

Economic value added (EVA):

$$\text{EVA} = \begin{matrix}\text{Investment center's}\\ \text{after-tax}\\ \text{operating income}\end{matrix} - \left[\left(\begin{matrix}\text{Investment center's}\\ \text{total assets}\end{matrix} - \begin{matrix}\text{Investment center's}\\ \text{current liabilities}\end{matrix}\right) \times \begin{matrix}\text{Weighted-average}\\ \text{cost of capital}\end{matrix}\right]$$

$$= \$300{,}000\,(1 - .40) - [(\$3{,}000{,}000 - \$20{,}000) \times .09]$$

$$= \$(88{,}200)$$

2. a. $$\text{Capital turnover} = \frac{\text{Sales revenue}}{\text{Invested capital}} = \frac{\$2{,}000{,}000}{?} = 80\%$$

$$\text{Therefore, invested capital} = \frac{\$2{,}000{,}000}{.80} = \$2{,}500{,}000$$

b. New ROI = 15% × 80% = 12%

Problem 2

$$\begin{aligned}\text{Transfer price} &= \text{Outlay cost} + \text{Opportunity cost}\\ &= \$10{,}000 + (\$13{,}500 - \$10{,}000)\\ &= \$13{,}500\end{aligned}$$

The $3,500 opportunity cost of a transfer is the contribution margin that will be forgone if a computer module is transferred instead of sold in the external market.

Key Terms

For each term's definition refer to the indicated page, or turn to the glossary at the end of the text.

capital turnover, 545
cash bonus, 553
economic value added (EVA), 548
full (or absorption) cost, 562
goal congruence, 542
imperfect competition, 560
incentive compensation, 553
internal control system, 565
investment center, 542
management by objectives (MBO), 542
merit pay, 553
pay for performance, 553
perfect competition, 560
residual income, 546
return on investment (ROI), 544
sales margin, 545
shareholder value analysis, 548
transfer price, 542
weighted-average cost of capital (WACC), 549

Review Questions

13–1. What is the managerial accountant's primary objective in designing a responsibility-accounting system?

13–2. Define *goal congruence,* and explain why it is important to an organization's success.

13–3. Describe the managerial approach known as *management by objectives* or *MBO.*

13–4. Define and give three examples of an *investment center.*

13–5. Write the formula for ROI, showing sales margin and capital turnover as its components.

13–6. Explain how the manager of the Automobile Division of an insurance company could improve her division's ROI.

13–7. Make up an example showing how residual income is calculated. What information is used in computing residual income that is not used in computing ROI?

13–8. What is the chief disadvantage of ROI as an investment-center performance measure? How does the residual-income measure eliminate this disadvantage?

13–9. Why is there typically a rise in ROI or residual income across time in a division? What undesirable behavioral implications could this phenomenon have?

13–10. Define the term *economic value added.* How does it differ from residual income?

13–11. Distinguish between the following measures of invested capital, and briefly explain when each should be used: (*a*) total assets, (*b*) total productive assets, and (*c*) total assets less current liabilities.

13–12. Why do some companies use gross book value instead of net book value to measure a division's invested capital?

13–13. Explain why it is important in performance evaluation to distinguish between investment centers and their managers.

13–14. How do organizations use pay for performance to motivate managers?

13–15. Describe an alternative to using ROI or residual income to measure investment-center performance.

13–16. How does inflation affect investment-center performance measures?

13–17. List three nonfinancial measures that could be used to evaluate a division of an insurance company.

13–18. Discuss the importance of nonfinancial information in measuring investment-center performance.

13–19. Identify and explain the managerial accountant's primary objective in choosing a transfer-pricing policy.

13–20. Describe four methods by which transfer prices may be set.

13–21. Explain the significance of excess capacity in the transferring division when transfer prices are set using the general transfer-pricing rule.

13–22. Why might income-tax laws affect the transfer-pricing policies of multinational companies?

13–23. Explain the role of import duties, or tariffs, in affecting the transfer-pricing policies of multinational companies.

Exercises

Exercise 13–24
Components of ROI
(LO 2)

The following data pertain to Pensacola Division's most recent year of operations.

Income	$ 10,000,000
Sales revenue	125,000,000
Average invested capital	50,000,000

Required: Compute Pensacola Division's sales margin, capital turnover, and return on investment for the year.

Exercise 13–25
Improving ROI
(LO 3)

Refer to the preceding exercise.

Required: Demonstrate two ways Pensacola Division's manager could improve the division's ROI to 25 percent.

Exercise 13–26
Residual Income
(LO 2)

Refer to the data for Exercise 13–24. Assume that the company's minimum desired rate of return on invested capital is 11 percent.

Required: Compute Pensacola Division's residual income for the year.

Exercise 13–27
Improving ROI
(LO 2, 3)

The following data pertain to British Isles Aggregates Company, a producer of sand, gravel, and cement, for the year just ended.

Sales revenue	£6,000,000
Cost of goods sold	3,300,000
Operating expenses	2,400,000
Average invested capital	3,000,000

£ denotes the British pound sterling, the national monetary unit of the United Kingdom. Although the new monetary unit, the *euro*, has been introduced in most European markets, the U.K. continues to use pounds sterling for its national currency.

Required:

1. Compute the company's sales margin, capital turnover, and ROI.
2. If the sales and average invested capital remain the same during the next year, to what level would total expenses have to be reduced in order to improve the firm's ROI to 15 percent?
3. Assume expenses are reduced, as calculated in requirement (2). Compute the firm's new sales margin. Show how the new sales margin and the old capital turnover together result in a new ROI of 15 percent.

Exercise 13–28
ROI and Residual Income; Annual Reports; Use of Internet
(LO 2)

Select one of the following companies (or any company of your choosing) and use the Internet to explore the company's most recent annual report.

American Airlines	(www.americanair.com)
Deere and Company	(www.deere.com)
Firestone	www.firestone.com
IBM	www.ibm.com
Pizza Hut	www.pizzahut.com
Ramada Inn	www.ramada.com
Wal-Mart	www.wal-mart.com

Required:

1. Calculate the company's overall return on investment (ROI). Also, calculate the company's overall residual income. (Assume an imputed interest rate of 10 percent.) List and explain any assumptions you make.
2. Does the company include a calculation of ROI in its on-line annual report? If it does, do your calculations agree with those of the company? If not, what would be some possible explanations?

Exercise 13–29
ROI; Residual Income
(LO 1, 2)

Suburban Lifestyles, Inc. has manufactured prefabricated houses for over 20 years. The houses are constructed in sections to be assembled on customers' lots. Suburban Lifestyles expanded into the precut housing market when it acquired Fairmont Company, one of its suppliers. In this market, various types of lumber are precut into the appropriate lengths, banded into packages, and shipped to customers' lots for assembly. Suburban Lifestyles' management designated the Fairmont Division as an investment center. Suburban uses return on investment (ROI) as a performance measure with investment defined as average productive assets. Management bonuses are based in part on ROI. All investments are expected to earn a minimum return of 15 percent before income taxes. Fairmont's ROI has ranged from 19.3 to 22.1 percent since it was acquired. Fairmont had an investment opportunity in 20x1 that had an estimated ROI of 18 percent. Fairmont's management decided against the investment because it believed the investment would decrease the division's overall ROI. The 20x1 income statement for Fairmont Division follows. The division's productive assets were $25,200,000 at the end of 20x1, a 5 percent increase over the balance at the beginning of the year.

FAIRMONT DIVISION
Income Statement
For the Year Ended December 31, 20x1
(in thousands)

Sales revenue		$48,000
Cost of goods sold		31,600
Gross margin		$16,400
Operating expenses:		
Administrative	$4,280	
Selling	7,200	11,480
Income from operations before income taxes		$ 4,920

Required:

1. Calculate the following performance measures for 20x1 for the Fairmont Division.
   a. Return on investment (ROI).
   b. Residual income.
2. Would the management of Fairmont Division have been more likely to accept the investment opportunity it had in 20x1 if residual income were used as a performance measure instead of ROI? Explain your answer.

(CMA, adapted)

Exercise 13–30
Increasing ROI over Time
(LO 2, 4, 5)

Refer to Exhibit 13–3. Assume that you are a consultant who has been hired by Suncoast Food Centers.

Required: Write a memorandum to the company president explaining why the ROI based on net book value (in Exhibit 13–3) behaves as it does over the five-year time horizon.

Exercise 13–31
Internal Control
(LO 1)

Galviston Supply Company is an auto parts supplier. At the end of each month, the employee who maintains all of the inventory records takes a physical inventory of the firm's stock. When discrepancies occur between the recorded inventory and the physical count, the employee changes the physical count to agree with the records.

Required:

1. What problems could arise as a result of Galviston Supply Company's inventory procedures?
2. How could the internal control system be strengthened to eliminate the potential problems?

Exercise 13–32
Calculate Weighted-Average Cost of Capital for EVA
(LO 2)

Golden Gate Construction Associates, a real estate developer and building contractor in San Francisco, has two sources of long-term capital: debt and equity. The cost to Golden Gate of issuing debt is the after-tax cost of the interest payments on the debt, taking into account the fact that the interest payments are tax deductible. The cost of Golden Gate's equity capital is the investment opportunity rate of Golden Gate's investors, that is, the rate they could earn on investments of similar risk to that of investing in Golden Gate Construction Associates. The interest rate on Golden Gate's $90 million of long-term debt is 10 percent, and the company's tax rate is 40 percent. The cost of Golden Gate's equity capital is 15 percent. Moreover, the market value (and book value) of Golden Gate's equity is $135 million.

Required: Calculate Golden Gate Construction Associates' weighted-average cost of capital.

Exercise 13–33
Economic Value Added (EVA); Continuation of Preceding Exercise
(LO 2)

Refer to the data in the preceding exercise for Golden Gate Construction Associates. The company has two divisions: the real estate division and the construction division. The divisions' total assets, current liabilities, and before-tax operating income for the most recent year are as follows:

Division	Total Assets	Current Liabilities	Before-Tax Operating Income
Real estate	$150,000,000	$9,000,000	$30,000,000
Construction	90,000,000	6,000,000	27,000,000

Required: Calculate the economic value added (EVA) for each of Golden Gate Construction Associates' divisions. (You will need to use the weighted-average cost of capital, which was computed in the preceding exercise.)

Exercise 13–34
General Transfer-Pricing Rule
(LO 6)

Milwaukee Metallurgy Corporation (MMC) has two divisions. The Fabrication Division transfers partially completed components to the Assembly Division at a predetermined transfer price. The Fabrication Division's standard variable production cost per unit is $450. The division has no excess capacity, and it could sell all of its components to outside buyers at $570 per unit in a perfectly competitive market.

Required:

1. Determine a transfer price for MMC using the general rule.
2. How would the transfer price change if the Fabrication Division had excess capacity?

Exercise 13–35
Cost-Based Transfer Pricing
(LO 7)

Refer to the preceding exercise. The Fabrication Division's full (absorption) cost of a component is $510, which includes $60 of applied fixed-overhead costs. The transfer price has been set at $561, which is the Fabrication Division's full cost plus a 10 percent markup.

The Assembly Division has a special offer for its product of $700. The Assembly Division incurs variable costs of $150 in addition to the transfer price for the Fabrication Division's components. Both divisions currently have excess production capacity.

Required:

1. What is the Assembly Division's manager likely to do regarding acceptance or rejection of the special offer? Why?
2. Is this decision in the best interests of the company as a whole? Why?
3. How could the situation be remedied using the transfer price?

Problems

Problem 13–36
Comparing the Performance of Two Divisions
(LO 2, 4)

Omaha Grain Company has two divisions, which reported the following results for the most recent year.

	Division I	Division II
Income	$ 2,700,000	$ 600,000
Average invested capital	$18,000,000	$3,000,000
ROI	15%	20%

Required: Which was the most successful division during the year? Think carefully about this, and explain your answer.

Problem 13–37
ROI and Residual Income; Missing Data
(LO 2, 3)

The following data pertain to three divisions of Calrisian Enterprises. The company's required rate of return on invested capital is 8 percent.

	Division I	Division II	Division III
Sales revenue	$40,000,000	?	?
Income	$8,000,000	$1,600,000	?
Average investment	$10,000,000	?	?
Sales margin	?	20%	25%
Capital turnover	?	1	?
ROI	?	?	20%
Residual income	?	?	$480,000

Required: Fill in the blanks above.

Problem 13–38
Improving ROI
(LO 3)

Refer to the preceding problem about Calrisian Enterprises.

Required:

1. Explain three ways the Division I manager could improve her division's ROI. Use numbers to illustrate these possibilities.
2. Suppose Division II's sales margin increased to 25 percent, while its capital turnover remained constant. Compute the division's new ROI.

Problem 13–39
Residual Income
(LO 2, 4)

Refer to the data for problem 13–36 regarding Omaha Grain Company.

Required: Compute each division's residual income for the year under each of the following assumptions about the firm's cost of acquiring capital.

1. 12 percent.
2. 15 percent.
3. 18 percent.

Which division was most successful? Explain your answer.

Problem 13–40
ROI and Residual Income; Investment Evaluation
(LO 2, 4)

Megatronics Corporation, a massive retailer of electronic products, is organized in four separate divisions. The four divisional managers are evaluated at year-end, and bonuses are awarded based on ROI. Last year, the company as a whole produced a 13 percent return on its investment.

During the past week, management of the company's Western Division was approached about the possibility of buying a competitor that had decided to redirect its retail activities. The data that follow relate to recent performance of the Western Division and the competitor:

	Western Division	Competitor
Sales	$4,200,000	$2,600,000
Variable costs	70% of sales	65% of sales
Fixed costs	$1,075,000	$835,000
Invested capital	$925,000	$312,500

Management has determined that in order to upgrade the competitor to Megatronics' standards, an additional $187,500 of invested capital would be needed.

Required:

1. Compute the current ROI of the Western Division and the division's ROI if the competitor is acquired.
2. What is the likely reaction of divisional management toward the acquisition? Why?
3. What is the likely reaction of Megatronics' corporate management toward the acquisition? Why?
4. Would the division be better off if it didn't upgrade the competitor to Megatronics' standards? Show computations to support your answer.
5. Assume that Megatronics uses residual income to evaluate performance and desires a 12 percent minimum return on invested capital. Compute the current residual income of the Western Division and the division's residual income if the competitor is acquired. Will divisional management be likely to change its attitude toward the acquisition? Why?

Problem 13–41
Increasing ROI over Time; Accelerated Depreciation
(LO 2, 4, 5)

Refer to Exhibit 13–3. Prepare a similar table of the changing ROI assuming the following accelerated depreciation schedule. Assume the same income before depreciation as shown in Exhibit 13–3. (If there is a loss, leave the ROI column blank.)

Year	Depreciation
1	$200,000
2	120,000
3	72,000
4	54,000
5	54,000
Total	$500,000

Required:

1. How does your table differ from the one in Exhibit 13–3? Why?
2. What are the implications of the ROI pattern in your table?

Problem 13–42
Increasing Residual Income over Time
(LO 2, 4, 5)

Prepare a table similar to Exhibit 13–3, which focuses on residual income. Use a 10 percent rate to compute the imputed interest charge. The table should show the residual income on the investment during each year in its five-year life. Assume the same income before depreciation and the same depreciation schedule as shown in Exhibit 13–3.

Problem 13–43
ROI and Performance Evaluations
(LO 2, 4)

Hoosier Industries manufactures a variety of household products. Roy Washburn, head of the company's Hardware Division, has just completed a miserable nine months. "If it could have gone wrong, it did. Sales are down, income is down, inventories are bloated, and quite frankly, I'm beginning to worry about my job," he moaned. Washburn is evaluated on the basis of ROI. Selected figures for the Hardware Division for the past nine months follow.

Sales	$7,200,000
Operating income	540,000
Invested capital	9,000,000

In an effort to make something out of nothing and to salvage the current year's performance, Washburn was contemplating implementation of some or all of the following four strategies:

a. Write off and discard $90,000 of obsolete inventory. The company will take a loss on the disposal.

b. Accelerate the collection of $120,000 of overdue customer accounts receivable.

c. Stop advertising through year-end and drastically reduce outlays for repairs and maintenance. These actions are expected to save the division $225,000 of expenses and will conserve cash resources.

d. Acquire two competitors that are expected to have the following financial characteristics:

	Projected Sales	Projected Operating Expenses	Projected Invested Capital
Anderson Manufacturing	$4,500,000	$3,600,000	$7,500,000
Palm Beach Enterprises	6,750,000	6,180,000	7,125,000

Required:

1. Briefly define sales margin, capital turnover, and return on investment and then compute these amounts for the Hardware Division over the past nine months.
2. Evaluate each of the first two strategies listed, with respect to its effect on the division's last nine months' performance, and make a recommendation to Washburn regarding which, if any, to adopt.
3. Are there possible long-term problems associated with strategy (c)? Briefly explain.
4. Determine the ROI of the investment in Anderson Manufacturing and do the same for the investment in Palm Beach Enterprises. Should Washburn reject both acquisitions, acquire one company, or acquire both companies? Assume that sufficient capital is available to fund investments in both organizations.

Problem 13–44
Weighted-Average Cost of Capital; Economic Value Added (EVA)
(LO 2)

Maple Leaf Industries, headquartered in Toronto, is a multiproduct company with three divisions: Pacific Division, Plains Division, and Atlantic Division. The company has two sources of long-term capital: debt and equity. The interest rate on Maple Leaf's $400 million debt is 9 percent, and the company's tax rate is 30 percent. The cost of Maple Leaf's equity capital is 12 percent. Moreover, the market value of the company's equity is $600 million. (The *book value* of Maple Leaf's equity is $430 million, but that amount does not reflect the current value of the company's assets or the value of intangible assets.)

The following data (in millions) pertains to Maple Leaf's three divisions.

Division	Before-Tax Operating Income	Current Liabilities	Total Assets
Pacific	$14	$6	$ 70
Plains	45	5	300
Atlantic	48	9	480

Required:

1. Compute Maple Leaf's weighted-average cost of capital (WACC).
2. Compute the economic value added (or EVA) for each of the company's three divisions.
3. What conclusions can you draw from the EVA analysis?

Problem 13–45
Weighted-Average Cost of Capital; Economic Value Added (EVA)
(LO 2)

Cape Cod Lobster Shacks, Inc. (CCLS) is a seafood restaurant chain operating throughout the northeast. The company has two sources of long-term capital: debt and equity. The cost to CCLS of issuing debt is the after-tax cost of the interest payments on the debt, taking into account the fact that the interest payments are tax deductible. The cost of CCLS's equity capital is the investment opportunity rate of CCLS's investors, that is, the rate they could earn on investments of similar risk to that of investing in Cape Cod Lobster Shacks, Inc. The interest rate on CCLS's $120 million of long-term debt is 9 percent, and the company's tax rate is 40 percent. The cost of CCLS's equity capital is 14 percent. Moreover, the market value (and book value) of CCLS's equity is $180 million.

Cape Cod Lobster Shacks, Inc., consists of two divisions, the properties division and the food service division. The divisions' total assets, current liabilities, and before-tax operating income for the most recent year are as follows:

Division	Total Assets	Current Liabilities	Before-Tax Operating Income
Properties	$217,500,000	$4,500,000	$43,500,000
Food Service	96,000,000	9,000,000	22,500,000

Required:

1. Calculate the weighted-average cost of capital for Cape Cod Lobster Shacks, Inc.
2. Calculate the economic value added (EVA) for each of CCLS's divisions.

Problem 13–46
Transfer Pricing; Negotiation
(LO 7)

Mitachlordion Technology, Inc. (MTI) has two divisions: Birmingham and Tampa. Birmingham currently sells a diode reducer to manufacturers of aircraft navigation systems for $1,550 per unit. Variable costs amount to $1,000, and demand for this product currently exceeds the division's ability to supply the marketplace.

Despite this situation, MTI is considering another use for the diode reducer, namely, integration into a satellite positioning system that would be made by Tampa. The positioning system has an anticipated selling price of $2,800 and requires an additional $1,340 of variable manufacturing costs. A transfer price of $1,500 has been established for the diode reducer.

Top management is anxious to introduce the positioning system; however, unless the transfer is made, an introduction will not be possible because of the difficulty of obtaining needed diode reducers. Birmingham and Tampa are in the process of recovering from previous financial problems, and neither division can afford any future losses. The company uses responsibility accounting and ROI in measuring divisional performance, and awards bonuses to divisional management.

Required:

1. How would Birmingham's divisional manager likely react to the decision to transfer diode reducers to Tampa? Show computations to support your answer.
2. How would Tampa's divisional management likely react to the $1,500 transfer price? Show computations to support your answer.
3. Assume that a lower transfer price is desired. Should top management lower the price or should the price be lowered by another means? Explain.
4. From a contribution margin perspective, does MTI benefit more if it sells the diode reducers externally or transfers the reducers to Tampa? By how much?

Problem 13–47
Comprehensive Transfer-Pricing Problem; Ethics
(LO 6, 7)

Weathermaster Window Company manufactures windows for the home-building industry. The window frames are produced in the Frame Division. The frames are then transferred to the Glass Division, where the glass and hardware are installed. The company's best-selling product is a three-by-four-foot, double-paned operable window.

The Frame Division can also sell frames directly to custom home builders, who install the glass and hardware. The sales price for a frame is $160. The Glass Division sells its finished windows for $380. The markets for both frames and finished windows exhibit perfect competition.

The standard cost of the window is detailed as follows:

	Frame Division	Glass Division
Direct material	$ 30	$60*
Direct labor	40	30
Variable overhead	60	60
Total	$130	$150

*Not including the transfer price for the frame.

Required:

1. Assume that there is no excess capacity in the Frame Division.
   a. Use the general rule to compute the transfer price for window frames.
   b. Calculate the transfer price if it is based on standard variable cost with a 10 percent markup.
2. Assume that there is excess capacity in the Frame Division.
   a. Use the general rule to compute the transfer price for window frames.
   b. Explain why your answers to requirements (1*a*) and (2*a*) differ.
   c. Suppose the predetermined fixed-overhead rate in the Frame Division is 125 percent of direct-labor cost. Calculate the transfer price if it is based on standard full cost plus a 10 percent markup.
   d. Assume the transfer price established in requirement (2*c*) is used. The Glass Division has been approached by the U.S. Army with a special order for 1,000 windows at $310. From the perspective of Weathermaster Window Company as a whole, should the special order be accepted or rejected? Why?
   e. Assume the same facts as in requirement (2*d*). Will an autonomous Glass Division manager accept or reject the special order? Why?
   f. Comment on any ethical issues you see in the questions raised in requirements (2*d*) and (2*e*).
3. Comment on the use of full cost as the basis for setting transfer prices.

Problem 13–48
Transfer Pricing; Management Behavior
(LO 6, 7)

Redstone Industrial Resources Company (RIRC) has several divisions. However, only two divisions transfer products to other divisions. The Mining Division refines toldine, which is then transferred to the Metals Division. The toldine is processed into an alloy by the Metals Division, and the alloy is sold to customers at a price of $450 per unit. The Mining Division is currently required by RIRC to transfer its total yearly output of 400,000 units of toldine to the Metals Division at total actual manufacturing cost plus 10 percent. Unlimited quantities of toldine can be purchased and sold on the open market at $270 per unit. While the Mining Division could sell all the toldine it produces at $270 per unit on the open market, it would incur a variable selling cost of $15 per unit.

Brian Jones, manager of the Mining Division, is unhappy with having to transfer the entire output of toldine to the Metals Division at 110 percent of cost. In a meeting with the management of RIRC, he said, "Why should my division be required to sell toldine to the Metals Division at less than market price? For the year just ended in May, Metals' contribution margin was over $57 million on sales of 400,000 units, while Mining's contribution was just over $15 million on the transfer of the same number of units. My division is subsidizing the profitability of the Metals Division. We should be allowed to charge the market price for toldine when transferring to the Metals Division."

The following table shows the detailed unit cost structure for both the Mining and Metals divisions during the most recent year.

	Mining Division	Metals Division
Transfer price from Mining Division	—	$198
Direct material	$ 36	18
Direct labor	48	60
Manufacturing overhead	96*	75†
Total cost per unit	$180	$351

*Manufacturing-overhead cost in the Mining Division is 25 percent fixed and 75 percent variable.
†Manufacturing-overhead cost in the Metals Division is 60 percent fixed and 40 percent variable.

Required:

1. Explain why transfer prices based on total actual costs are not appropriate as the basis for divisional performance measurement.

2. Using the market price as the transfer price, determine the contribution margin for both the Mining Division and the Metals Division.
3. If Redstone Industrial Resources Company were to institute the use of negotiated transfer prices and allow divisions to buy and sell on the open market, determine the price range for toldine that would be acceptable to both the Mining Division and the Metals Division. Explain your answer.
4. Use the general transfer-pricing rule to compute the lowest transfer price that would be acceptable to the Mining Division. Is your answer consistent with your conclusion in requirement (3)? Explain.
5. Identify which one of the three types of transfer prices (cost-based, market-based, or negotiated) is most likely to elicit desirable management behavior at RIRC. Explain your answer.

(CMA, adapted)

Problem 13–49
Setting a Transfer Price; International Setting; Differential Tax Rates
(LO 6, 7)

Delta Telecom, Inc., which produces telecommunications equipment in the United States, has a very strong local market for its circuit board. The variable production cost is $390, and the company can sell its entire supply domestically for $510. The U.S. tax rate is 40 percent.

Alternatively, Delta Telecom can ship the circuit board to its division in Germany, to be used in a product that the German division will distribute throughout Europe. Information about the German product and the division's operating environment follows.

Selling price of final product: $1,080
Shipping fees to import circuit board: $60
Labor, overhead, and additional material costs of final product: $345
Import duties levied on circuit board (to be paid by the German division): 10% of transfer price
German tax rate: 60%

Assume that U.S. and German tax authorities allow a transfer price for the circuit board set at either U.S. variable manufacturing cost or the U.S. market price. Delta Telecom's management is in the process of exploring which transfer price is best for the firm as a whole.

Required:

1. Compute overall company profitability per unit if all units are transferred and U.S. variable manufacturing cost is used as the transfer price. Show separate calculations for the U.S. operation and the German division.
2. Repeat requirement (1), assuming the use of the U.S. market price as the transfer price. Which of the two transfer prices is best for the firm?
3. Assume that the German division can obtain the circuit board in Germany for $465.
   a. If you were the head of the German division, would you rather do business with your U.S. division or buy the circuit board locally? Why?
   b. Rather than proceed with the transfer, is it in the best interest of Delta Telecom to sell its goods domestically and allow the German division to acquire the circuit board in Germany? Why? Show computations to support your answer.
4. Generally speaking, when tax rates differ between countries, what strategy should a company use in setting its transfer prices?

Cases

Case 13–50
ROI versus Residual Income; Incentive Effects
(LO 1, 2, 4)

Fun Times Entertainment Corporation (FTEC), a subsidiary of New Age Industries, manufactures go-carts and other recreational vehicles. Family recreational centers that feature not only go-cart tracks but miniature golf, batting cages, and arcade games as well have increased in popularity. As a result, FTEC has been receiving some pressure from New Age's management to diversify into some of these other recreational areas. Recreational Leasing, Inc. (RLI), one of the largest firms that leases arcade games to family recreational centers, is looking for a friendly buyer. New Age's top management believes that RLI's assets could be acquired for an investment of $1.6 million and has strongly urged Bill Grieco, division manager of FTEC, to consider acquiring RLI.

Grieco has reviewed RLI's financial statements with his controller, Marie Donnelly, and they believe the acquisition may not be in the best interest of FTEC. "If we decide not to do this, the New Age people are not going to be happy," said Grieco. "If we could convince them to base our bonuses on something other than return on investment, maybe this acquisition would look more attractive. How would we do if the bonuses were based on residual income, using the company's 15 percent cost of capital?"

New Age Industries traditionally has evaluated all of its divisions on the basis of return on investment. The desired rate of return for each division is 20 percent. The management team of any division reporting an annual increase in the ROI is automatically eligible for a bonus. The management of divisions reporting a decline in the ROI must provide convincing explanations for the decline in order to be eligible for a bonus. Moreover, this bonus is limited to 50 percent of the bonus paid to divisions reporting an increase in ROI.

In the following table are condensed financial statements for both FTEC and RLI for the most recent year.

	RLI	FTEC
Sales revenue	—	$4,750,000
Leasing revenue	$1,550,000	—
Variable expenses	(650,000)	(3,000,000)
Fixed expenses	(600,000)	(750,000)
Operating income	$ 300,000	$1,000,000
Current assets	$ 950,000	$1,150,000
Long-lived assets	550,000	2,850,000
Total assets	$1,500,000	$4,000,000
Current liabilities	$ 425,000	$ 700,000
Long-term liabilities	600,000	1,900,000
Stockholders' equity	475,000	1,400,000
Total liabilities and stockholders' equity	$1,500,000	$4,000,000

Required:

1. If New Age Industries continues to use ROI as the sole measure of divisional performance, explain why FTEC would be reluctant to acquire Recreational Leasing, Inc.
2. If New Age Industries could be persuaded to use residual income to measure the performance of FTEC, explain why FTEC would be more willing to acquire RLI.
3. Discuss how the behavior of division managers is likely to be affected by the use of the following performance measures: (*a*) return on investment and (*b*) residual income.

(CMA, adapted)

Case 13–51
Minimum and Maximum Acceptable Transfer Prices; Multinational
(LO 6, 7)

General Instrumentation Corporation manufactures dashboard instruments for heavy construction equipment. The firm is based in Baltimore, but operates several divisions in the United States, Canada, and Europe. The Hudson Bay Division manufactures complex electrical panels that are used in a variety of the firm's instruments. There are two basic types of panels. The high-density panel (HDP) is capable of many functions and is used in the most sophisticated instruments, such as tachometers and pressure gauges. The low-density panel (LDP) is much simpler and is used in less complicated instruments. Although there are minor differences among the different high-density panels, the basic manufacturing process and production costs are the same. The high-density panels require considerably more skilled labor than the low-density panels, but the unskilled labor needs are about the same. Moreover, the direct materials in the high-density panel run substantially more than the cost of materials in the low-density panels. Production costs are summarized as follows:

	LDP	HDP
Unskilled labor (.5 hour @ $10)	$ 5	$ 5
Skilled labor:		
LDP (.25 hour @ $20)	5	
HDP (1.5 hours @ $20)		30
Raw material	3	8
Purchased components	5	15
Variable overhead	4	12
Total variable cost	$22	$70

The annual fixed overhead in the Hudson Bay Division is $1,000,000. There is a limited supply of skilled labor available in the area, and the division must constrain its production to 40,000 hours of skilled labor each year. This has been a troublesome problem for Jacqueline Ducharme, the division manager. Ducharme has successfully increased demand for the LDP line to the point where it is essentially unlimited. Each LDP sells for $28. Business also has increased in recent years for the HDP, and Ducharme estimates the division could now sell anywhere up to 6,000 units per year at a price of $115.

On the other side of the Atlantic, General Instrumentation operates its Volkmar Tachometer Division in Berlin. A recent acquisition of General Instrumentation, the division was formerly a German company known as Volkmar Construction Instruments. The division's main product is a sophisticated tachometer used in heavy-duty cranes, bulldozers, and backhoes. The instrument, designated as a TCH–320, has the following production costs.

TCH–320	
Unskilled labor (.5 hour @ $9)	$ 4.50
Skilled labor (3 hours @ $17)	51.00
Raw material	10.50
Purchased components	150.00
Variable overhead	12.00
Total variable cost	$228.00

The cost of purchased components includes a $145 control pack currently imported from Japan. Fixed overhead in the Volkmar Tachometer Division runs about $800,000 per year. Both skilled and unskilled labor are in abundant supply. The TCH–320 sells for $275.

Bertram Mueller, the division manager of the Volkmar Tachometer Division, recently attended a high-level corporate meeting in Baltimore. In a conversation with Jacqueline Ducharme, it was apparent that Hudson Bay's high-density panel might be a viable substitute for the control pack currently imported from Japan and used in Volkmar's TCH–320. Upon returning to Berlin, Mueller asked his chief engineer to look into the matter. Hans Schmidt obtained several HDP units from Hudson Bay, and a minor R&D project was mounted to determine if the HDP could replace the Japanese control pack. Several weeks later, the following conversation occurred in Mueller's office:

Schmidt: There's no question that Hudson Bay's HDP unit will work in our TCH–320. In fact, it could save us some money.

Mueller: That's good news. If we can buy our components within the company, we'll help Baltimore's bottom line without hurting ours. Also, it will look good to the brass at corporate if they see us working hard to integrate our division into General Instrumentation's overall production program.

Schmidt: I've also been worried about the reliability of supply of the control pack. I don't like being dependent on such a critical supplier that way.

Mueller: I agree. Let's look at your figures on the HDP replacement.

Schmidt: I got together with the controller's people, and we worked up some numbers. If we replace the control pack with the HDP from Canada, we'll avoid the $145 control pack cost we're now incurring. In addition, I figure we'll save $5.50 on the basic raw materials. There is one catch, though. The HDP will require some adjustments in order to use it in the TCH–320. We can make the adjustments here in Berlin. I'm guessing it will require an additional two hours of skilled labor to make the necessary modifications. I don't think variable overhead would be any different. Then there is the cost of transporting the HDPs to Berlin. Let's figure on $4.50 per unit.

Mueller: Sounds good. I'll give Jacqueline Ducharme a call and talk this over. We can use up to 10,000 of the HDP units per year given the demand for the TCH–320. I wonder what kind of a transfer price Hudson Bay will want.

Required:

1. Draw a simple diagram depicting the two divisions and their products. Also show the two alternatives that the Volkmar Tachometer Division has in the production of its TCH–320.

2. From the perspective of General Instrumentation's top management, should any of the TCH–320 units be produced using the high-density panel? If so, how many?
3. Suppose Hudson Bay transfers 10,000 HDP units per year to Volkmar. From the perspective of General Instrumentation's top management, what effect will the transfer price have on the company's income?
4. What is the minimum transfer price that the Hudson Bay Division would find acceptable for the HDP?
5. What is the maximum transfer price that the Volkmar Tachometer Division would find acceptable for the HDP?
6. As the corporate controller for General Instrumentation, recommend a transfer price.

Case 13–52
Interdivisional Transfers; Pricing the Final Product
(LO 6, 7)

Continental Industries is a diversified corporation with separate operating divisions. Each division's performance is evaluated on the basis of profit and return on investment. The Air Comfort Division manufactures and sells air-conditioner units. The coming year's budgeted income statement, which follows, is based upon a sales volume of 15,000 units.

AIR COMFORT DIVISION
Budgeted Income Statement
(In thousands)

	Total	Per Unit
Sales revenue	$12,000	$800
Manufacturing costs:		
Compressor	$ 2,100	$140
Other direct material	1,110	74
Direct labor	900	60
Variable overhead	1,350	90
Fixed overhead	960	64
Total manufacturing costs	$ 6,420	$428
Gross margin	$ 5,580	$372
Operating expenses:		
Variable selling	$ 540	$ 36
Fixed selling	570	38
Fixed administrative	1,140	76
Total operating expenses	$ 2,250	$150
Net income before taxes	$ 3,330	$222

Air Comfort's division manager believes sales can be increased if the price of the air-conditioners is reduced. A market research study by an independent firm indicates that a 5 percent reduction in the selling price would increase sales volume 16 percent or 2,400 units. The division has sufficient production capacity to manage this increased volume with no increase in fixed costs.

The Air Comfort Division uses a compressor in its units, which it purchases from an outside supplier at a cost of $140 per compressor. The Air Comfort Division manager has asked the manager of the Compressor Division about selling compressor units to Air Comfort. The Compressor Division currently manufactures and sells a unit to outside firms which is similar to the unit used by the Air Comfort Division. The specifications of the Air Comfort Division compressor are slightly different, which would reduce the Compressor Division's direct material cost by $3 per unit. In addition, the Compressor Division would not incur any variable selling costs in the units sold to the Air Comfort Division. The manager of the Air Comfort Division wants all of the compressors it uses to come from one supplier and has offered to pay $100 for each compressor unit.

The Compressor Division has the capacity to produce 75,000 units. Its budgeted income statement for the coming year, which follows, is based on a sales volume of 64,000 units without considering Air Comfort's proposal.

COMPRESSOR DIVISION
Budgeted Income Statement
(In thousands)

	Total	Per Unit
Sales revenue	$12,800	$200
Manufacturing costs:		
Direct material	$ 1,536	$ 24
Direct labor	1,024	16
Variable overhead	1,280	20
Fixed overhead	1,408	22
Total manufacturing costs	$ 5,248	$ 82
Gross margin	$ 7,552	$118
Operating expenses:		
Variable selling	$ 768	$ 12
Fixed selling	512	8
Fixed administrative	896	14
Total operating expenses	$ 2,176	$ 34
Net income before taxes	$ 5,376	$ 84

Required:

1. Should the Air Comfort Division institute the 5 percent price reduction on its air-conditioner units even if it cannot acquire the compressors internally for $100 each? Support your conclusion with appropriate calculations.
2. Independently of your answer to requirement (1), assume the Air Comfort Division needs 17,400 units. Should the Compressor Division be willing to supply the compressor units for $100 each? Support your conclusions with appropriate calculations.
3. Independently of your answer to requirement (1), assume Air Comfort needs 17,400 units. Suppose Continental's top management has specified a transfer price of $100. Would it be in the best interest of *Continental Industries* for the Compressor Division to supply the compressor units at $100 each to the Air Comfort Division? Support your conclusions with appropriate calculations.
4. Is $100 a goal-congruent transfer price? [Refer to your answers for requirements (2) and (3).]

(CMA, adapted)

Current Issues in Managerial Accounting

Issue 13–53
Tariffs; Cost Management

"Is Wolverine Human? A Judge Answers No; Fans Howl in Protest," ***The Wall Street Journal,*** **January 20, 2003, pp. A1, A5, Neil King, Jr.**

Overview

A U.S. Court of International Trade judge rules whether Marvel Comics' subsidiary Toy Biz, Inc. should classify X-Men figures as toys or dolls.

Suggested Discussion Question

What implications does this seemingly innocuous question have for tariffs and cost management at Toy Biz, Inc.?

Issue 13–54
Investment in Technology; ROI

"7-Eleven, Amid Pressures, Makes Big Bets," ***The Wall Street Journal,*** **April 25, 2002, Ann Zimmerman.**

Overview

7-Eleven's "investment in technological systems that help keep the stores in stock on the best-selling items has lowered costs while contributing to sales increases."

Suggested Discussion Question

Referring to the chapter's discussion of how to increase ROI, how will 7-Eleven's investment likely impact the company's ROI?

"Well-Hidden Perk Means Big Money for Top Executives," ***The Wall Street Journal,*** **October 11, 2002, pp. A1, A9, Ellen E. Shultz and Theo Francis.**

Issue 13–55
Executive Compensation; Ethics

Overview

Companies such as Wyeth, Xerox, Walgreen, and Lucent Technologies use deferred-compensation plans to reward top executives.

Suggested Discussion Questions

Discuss as a group. According to the article, these "plans add to company liabilities, but are poorly disclosed." Are these types of executive compensation effective in getting the best performance out of executives? Are they ethical?

"What's a New Economy without Research?" ***Fortune,*** **May 15, 2000, Stewart Alsop.**

Issue 13–56
Return on Investment

Overview

The author reviews corporate projects that have given rise to such items as the laser printer, graphical word processor, the mouse, and the main protocol for the World Wide Web. Much research was done under conditions that did not demand an intermediate return on investment. Corporations today are interested in development of new products where technology is already understood. The corporate interest in research has waned.

Suggested Discussion Question

Why would capital investment on research and development activities tend to provide a lower return on investment than would other activities?

Chapter Fourteen

Decision Making: Relevant Costs and Benefits

After completing this chapter, you should be able to:

1. Describe six steps in the decision-making process and the managerial accountant's role in that process.
2. Explain the relationship between quantitative and qualitative analyses in decision making.
3. List and explain two criteria that must be satisfied by relevant information.
4. Identify relevant costs and benefits, giving proper treatment to sunk costs, opportunity costs, and unit costs.
5. Prepare analyses of various special decisions, properly identifying the relevant costs and benefits.
6. Analyze manufacturing decisions involving joint products and limited resources.
7. Explain the impact of an advanced manufacturing environment and activity-based costing on a relevant-cost analysis.
8. After completing the appendix, formulate a linear program to solve a product-mix problem with multiple constraints.

Worldwide Airways Rejects "Sweet Deal" with Local Bakery

Atlanta, GA—Worldwide Airways' Vice President for Media Relations, Elizabeth Williams, announced today that the airline will continue to make its own desserts for its in-flight food-service operations. The announcement follows months of speculation that the airline would outsource its desserts to Southern Sweets, Inc., a large Atlanta bakery. Had Worldwide Airways decided to sign the dessert contract with Southern Sweets, it could have meant layoffs at the airline's huge Atlanta flight kitchen. The flight kitchen prepares a million full-course meals each month for Worldwide Airways' flights that pass through Atlanta.

According to Williams, the decision was a complex one. "This was not an easy call for us," said Williams. "Southern Sweets produces a first-class product, and they made us a very aggressive pricing offer on their desserts. At first blush, it looked as though we should go with the outsourcing arrangement. But we wanted to make sure we got this one right. We're talking about costs of around a quarter of a million dollars per month here, as well as the jobs of several of our loyal employees. After a careful analysis, we concluded that we would not save enough of our current costs to justify paying the price Southern Sweets was asking. They didn't feel they could go any lower, so we decided to keep the operation in-house. Personally, I'm glad it worked out that way. Signing an outsourcing deal, although it might be financially sound, often has a negative impact on employee morale."

Decision making is a fundamental part of management. Decisions about the acquisition of equipment, mix of products, methods of production, and pricing of products and services confront managers in all types of organizations. This chapter covers the role of managerial accounting information in a variety of common decisions. The next chapter examines pricing decisions.

The Managerial Accountant's Role in Decision Making

Managerial accountants are increasingly playing important roles as full-fledged members of cross-functional management teams. These management teams face a broad array of decisions, including production, marketing, financial, and other decisions. All managers and management teams need information pertinent to their decisions. In support of the decision-making process, managerial accountants play a specific role in providing relevant information. Thus, the managerial accountant must have a good understanding of the decisions faced by managers throughout the organization.

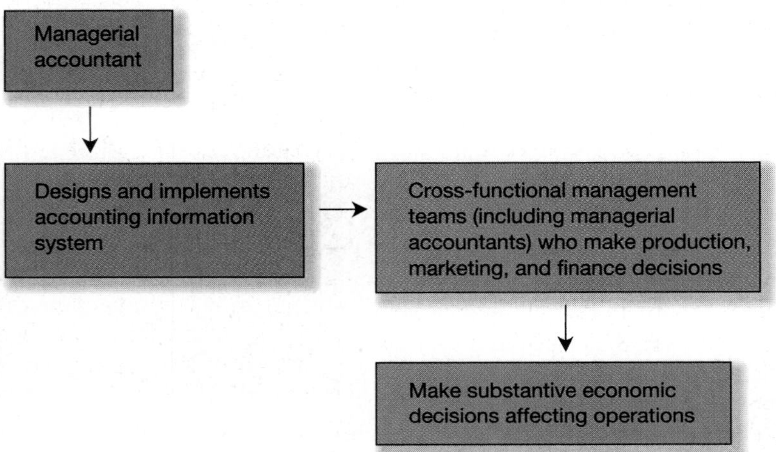

Steps in the Decision-Making Process

LO 1

Describe six steps in the decision-making process and the managerial accountant's role in that process.

Six steps characterize the decision-making process:

1. ***Clarify the decision problem.*** Sometimes the decision to be made is clear. For example, if a company receives a special order for its product at a price below the usual price, the decision problem is to accept or reject the order. But the decision problem is seldom so clear and unambiguous. Perhaps demand for a company's most popular product is declining. What exactly is causing this problem? Increasing competition? Declining quality control? A new alternative product on the market? Before a decision can be made, the problem needs to be clarified and defined in more specific terms. Considerable managerial skill is required to define a decision problem in terms that can be addressed effectively.
2. ***Specify the criterion.*** Once a decision problem has been clarified, the manager should specify the criterion upon which a decision will be made. Is the objective to maximize profit, increase market share, minimize cost, or improve public service? Sometimes the objectives are in conflict, as in a decision problem where production cost is to be minimized but product quality must be maintained. In such cases, one objective is specified as the decision criterion—for example, cost minimization. The other objective is established as a constraint—for example, product quality must not fall below one defective part in 1,000 manufactured units.

"We are looked upon as more business advisors than just accountants, and that has a lot to do with the additional analysis and the forward looking goals we are setting." (14a)
Caterpillar

3. ***Identify the alternatives.*** A decision involves selecting between two or more alternatives. If a machine breaks down, what are the alternative courses of action? The machine can be repaired or replaced, or a replacement can be leased. But perhaps repair will turn out to be more costly than replacement. Determining the possible alternatives is a critical step in the decision process.
4. ***Develop a decision model.*** A *decision model* is a simplified representation of the choice problem. Unnecessary details are stripped away, and the most important elements of the problem are highlighted. Thus, the decision model brings together the elements listed above: the criterion, the constraints, and the alternatives.
5. ***Collect the data.*** Although the managerial accountant often is involved in steps 1 through 4, he or she is chiefly responsible for step 5. Selecting data pertinent to decisions is one of the managerial accountant's most important roles in an organization.
6. ***Select an alternative.*** Once the decision model is formulated and the pertinent data are collected, the appropriate manager makes a decision.

Quantitative versus Qualitative Analysis

Explain the relationship between quantitative and qualitative analyses in decision making.

Decision problems involving accounting data typically are specified in quantitative terms. The criteria in such problems usually include objectives such as profit maximization or cost minimization. When a manager makes a final decision, however, the qualitative characteristics of the alternatives can be just as important as the quantitative measures. **Qualitative characteristics** are the factors in a decision problem that cannot be expressed effectively in numerical terms. To illustrate, suppose Worldwide Airways' top management is considering the elimination of its hub operation in London. Airlines establish hubs at airports where many of their routes intersect. Hub operations include facilities for in-flight food preparation, aircraft maintenance and storage, and administrative offices. A careful quantitative analysis indicates that Worldwide Airway's profit-maximizing alternative is to eliminate the London hub. In making its decision, however, the company's managers will consider such qualitative issues as the effect of the closing on its London employees and on the morale of its remaining employees in the airline's Paris, Atlanta, and Tokyo hubs.

To clarify what is at stake in such qualitative analyses, quantitative analysis can allow the decision maker to put a "price" on the sum total of the qualitative characteristics. For example, suppose Worldwide Airways' controller gives top management a quantitative analysis showing that elimination of the London hub will increase annual profits by $2,000,000. However, the qualitative considerations favor the option of continuing the London operation. How important are these qualitative considerations to the top managers? If they decide to continue the London operation, the qualitative considerations must be worth at least $2,000,000 to them. Weighing the quantitative and qualitative considerations in making decisions is the essence of management. The skill, experience, judgment, and ethical standards of managers all come to bear on such difficult choices.

Exhibit 14–1 depicts the six steps in the decision process, and the relationship between quantitative and qualitative analysis.

Obtaining Information: Relevance, Accuracy, and Timeliness

What criteria should the managerial accountant use in designing the accounting information system that supplies data for decision making? Three characteristics of information determine its usefulness.

Topic 14–1

Exhibit 14–1
The Decision-Making Process

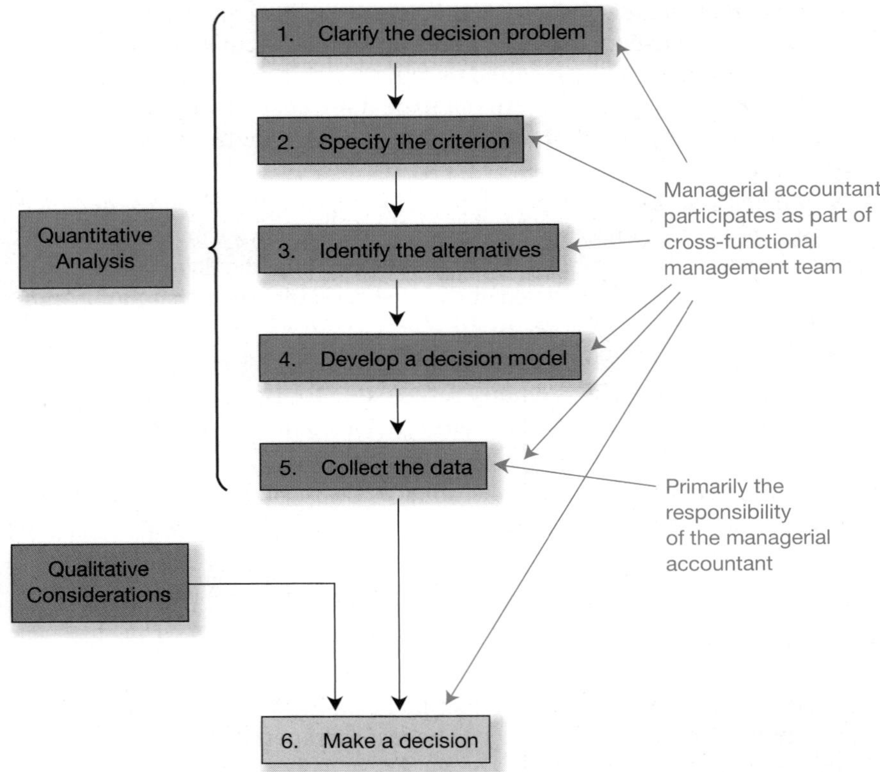

Relevance Information is **relevant** if it is *pertinent* to a decision problem. Different decisions typically will require different data. The primary theme of this chapter is how to decide what information is relevant to various common decision problems.

Accuracy Information that is pertinent to a decision problem must also be **accurate,** or it will be of little use. This means the information must be precise. For example, the cost incurred by Worldwide Airways to rent facilities at London's Heathrow Airport is relevant to a decision about eliminating the airline's London hub. However, if the rental cost data are imprecise, due to incomplete or misplaced records, the usefulness of the information will be diminished.

Conversely, highly accurate but irrelevant data are of no value to a decision maker. Suppose Worldwide Airways will continue its daily round-trip flight between New York and London regardless of its decision about eliminating the London hub. Precise data about fuel consumption on the New York–London route are irrelevant to the decision about closing down the London hub.

Timeliness Relevant and accurate data are of value only if they are **timely,** that is, available in time for a decision. Thus, timeliness is the third important criterion for determining the usefulness of information. Some situations involve a trade-off between the accuracy and the timeliness of information. More accurate information may take longer to produce. Therefore, as accuracy improves, timeliness suffers, and vice versa. For example, a company may test-market a potential new product in a particular city. The longer the test-marketing program runs, the more accurate will be the marketing data generated. However, a long wait for the accurate marketing report may unduly delay management's decision to launch the new product nationally.

To summarize, the managerial accountant's primary role in the decision-making process is twofold:

1. Decide what information is *relevant* to each decision problem.
2. Provide *accurate* and *timely* data, keeping in mind the proper balance between these often conflicting criteria.

Relevant Information

What makes information relevant to a decision problem? Two criteria are important.

LO 3

List and explain two criteria that must be satisfied by relevant information.

Bearing on the Future The consequences of decisions are borne in the future, not the past. To be relevant to a decision, cost or benefit information must involve a future event. The cost information relevant to Worldwide Airways' decision concerning its London operations involves the costs that *will be incurred in the future* under the airline's two alternatives. Costs incurred in the past in the airline's London operations will not change regardless of management's decision, and they are irrelevant to the decision at hand.

Since relevant information involves future events, the managerial accountant must predict the amounts of the relevant costs and benefits. In making these predictions, the accountant often will use estimates of cost behavior based on historical data. There is an important and subtle issue here. *Relevant* information must involve costs and benefits to be realized in the *future.* However, the accountant's *predictions* of those costs and benefits often are based on data from the *past.*

Different under Competing Alternatives Relevant information must involve costs or benefits that *differ among the alternatives.* Costs or benefits that are the same across all the available alternatives have no bearing on the decision. For example, suppose Worldwide Airways' management decides to keep its reservations and ticketing office in London regardless of whether its London hub is eliminated. Then the costs of the reservations and ticketing office will not differ between the two alternatives regarding elimination of the London hub. Hence, those costs are irrelevant to that decision.

"You have to try to summarize numbers. You can't just give numbers. People in marketing are going to make decisions based on your numbers. They have to understand what those numbers mean." (14b)
Abbott Laboratories

Unique versus Repetitive Decisions

Unique decisions arise infrequently or only once. Worldwide Airways' decision regarding its London hub is an example. Compiling data for unique decisions usually requires a special analysis by the managerial accountant. The relevant information often will be found in many diverse places in the organization's overall information system.

In contrast, *repetitive decisions* are made over and over again, at either regular or irregular intervals. For example, Worldwide Airways makes route-scheduling decisions every six months. Such a routine decision makes it worthwhile for the managerial accountant to keep a special file of the information relevant to the scheduling decision.

Cost predictions relevant to repetitive decisions typically can draw on a large amount of historical data. Since the decisions have been made repeatedly in the past, the data from those decisions should be readily available. Information relevant to unique decisions is harder to generate. The managerial accountant typically will have to give more thought to deciding which data are relevant, and will have less historical data available upon which to base predictions.

Importance of Identifying Relevant Costs and Benefits

Why is it important for the managerial accountant to isolate the relevant costs and benefits in a decision analysis? The reasons are twofold. First, generating information is a costly process. The relevant data must be sought, and this requires time and effort. By focusing on only the relevant information, the managerial accountant can simplify and shorten the data-gathering process.

Second, people can effectively use only a limited amount of information. Beyond this, they experience **information overload,** and their decision-making effectiveness declines. By routinely providing only information about relevant costs and benefits, the managerial accountant can reduce the likelihood of information overload.

Identifying Relevant Costs and Benefits

LO 4

Identify relevant costs and benefits, giving proper treatment to sunk costs, opportunity costs, and unit costs.

To illustrate how managerial accountants determine relevant costs and benefits, we will consider several decisions faced by the management of Worldwide Airways. Based in Atlanta, the airline flies routes between the United States and Europe, between various cities in Europe, and between the United States and several Asian cities.

Sunk Costs

Sunk costs are costs that have already been incurred. They do not affect any future cost and cannot be changed by any current or future action. Sunk costs are irrelevant to decisions, as the following two examples show.

Book Value of Equipment At Charles de Gaulle Airport in Paris, Worldwide Airways has a three-year-old loader truck used to load in-flight meals onto airplanes. The box on the truck can be lifted hydraulically to the level of a jumbo jet's side doors. The *book value* of this loader, defined as the asset's acquisition cost less the accumulated depreciation to date, is computed as follows:

Acquisition cost of old loader	$100,000
Less: Accumulated depreciation	75,000
Book value	$ 25,000

Most major airlines have a frequent flyer program, in which customers can receive free flights or upgrades by accumulating miles flown with a particular airline. These programs require recurring decisions by airline management about the terms of the frequent flyer awards. Accurate, relevant, and timely information is needed for such decisions. Also, predictions need to be made about passenger response to various frequent flyer provisions.

The loader has one year of useful life remaining, after which its salvage value will be zero. However, it could be sold now for $5,000. In addition to the annual depreciation of $25,000, Worldwide Airways annually incurs $80,000 in variable costs to operate the loader. These include the costs of operator labor, gasoline, and maintenance.

John Orville, Worldwide Airways' ramp manager at Charles de Gaulle Airport, faces a decision about replacement of the loader. A new kind of loader uses a conveyor belt to move meals into an airplane. The new loader is much cheaper than the old hydraulic loader and costs less to operate. However, the new loader would be operable for only one year before it would need to be replaced. Pertinent data about the new loader are as follows:

Acquisition cost of new loader	$15,000
Useful life	1 year

Salvage value after one year	0
Annual depreciation	$15,000
Annual operating costs	$45,000

Orville's initial inclination is to continue using the old loader for another year. He exclaims, "We can't dump that equipment now. We paid $100,000 for it, and we've only used it three years. If we get rid of that loader now, we'll lose $20,000 on the disposal." Orville reasons that the old loader's book value of $25,000, less its current salvage value of $5,000, amounts to a loss of $20,000.

Fortunately, Orville's comment is overheard by Joan Wilbur, the managerial accountant in the company's Charles de Gaulle Airport administrative offices. Wilbur points out to Orville that the book value of the old loader is a *sunk cost.* It cannot affect any future cost the company might incur. To convince Orville that she is right, Wilbur prepares the analysis shown in Exhibit 14–2.

Regardless of which alternative is selected, the $25,000 book value of the old loader will be an expense or loss in the next year. If the old loader is kept in service, the $25,000 will be recognized as depreciation expense; otherwise, the $25,000 cost will be incurred by the company as a write-off of the asset's book value. Thus, the current book value of the old loader is a *sunk cost* and irrelevant to the replacement decision.

Notice that the *relevant* data in the equipment replacement decision are items (3), (4), and (5). Each of these items meets the two tests of relevant information:

1. The costs or benefits relate to the future.
2. The costs or benefits differ between the alternatives.

"[We are continually moving] from being the scorekeeper to being an active, involved participant in crafting business solutions." (14c)

Boeing

The proceeds from selling the old loader, item (3), will be received in the future only under the "replace" alternative. Similarly, the acquisition cost (depreciation) of the new loader, item (4), is a future cost incurred only under the "replace" alternative. The operating cost, item (5), is also a future cost that differs between the two alternatives.

Differential Costs Exhibit 14–2 includes a column entitled *Differential Cost.* A **differential cost** is the difference in a cost item under two decision alternatives. The computation of differential costs is a convenient way of summarizing the relative advantage of one alternative over the other. John Orville can make a correct equipment-replacement decision in either of two ways: (1) by comparing the total cost of the two alternatives, shown in columns (a) and (b); or (2) by focusing on the total differential cost, shown in column (c), which favors the "replacement" option.

Cost of Inventory on Hand Never having taken a managerial accounting course in college, John Orville is slow to learn how to identify sunk costs. The next week he goofs again.

Exhibit 14–2
Equipment Replacement Decision: Worldwide Airways

		Costs of Two Alternatives		
		(a) Do Not Replace Old Loader	**(b) Replace Old Loader**	**(c) Differential Cost**
Sunk cost	(1) Depreciation of old loader	$ 25,000		
	OR			–0–
	(2) Write-off of old loader's book value		$25,000	
Relevant data	(3) Proceeds from disposal of old loader	–0–	(5,000)	$ 5,000
	(4) Depreciation (cost) of new loader	–0–	15,000	(15,000)
	(5) Operating costs	80,000	45,000	35,000
	Total cost	$105,000	$80,000	$25,000

Exhibit 14–3
Obsolete Inventory Decision: Worldwide Airways

		Costs of Two Alternatives		
		(a) Modify and Use Parts	(b) Dispose of Parts	(c) Differential Cost
Sunk cost	Book value of parts inventory: asset value written off whether parts are used or not	$20,000	$20,000	$ –0–
Relevant data	Proceeds from disposal of parts	–0–	(17,000)	17,000
	Cost to modify parts	12,000	–0–	12,000
	Cost incurred to buy new parts for current aircraft fleet	–0–	26,000	(26,000)
	Total cost	$32,000	$29,000	$ 3,000

The inventory of spare aircraft parts held by Worldwide Airways at Charles de Gaulle includes some obsolete parts originally costing $20,000. The company no longer uses the planes for which the parts were purchased. The obsolete parts include spare passenger seats, luggage racks, and galley equipment. The spare parts could be sold to another airline for $17,000. However, with some modifications, the obsolete parts could still be used in the company's current fleet of aircraft. Using the modified parts would save Worldwide Airways the cost of purchasing new parts for its airplanes.

John Orville decides not to dispose of the obsolete parts, because doing so would entail a loss of $3,000. Orville reasons that the $20,000 book value of the parts, less the $17,000 proceeds from disposal, would result in a $3,000 loss on disposal. Joan Wilbur, the managerial accountant, comes to the rescue again, demonstrating that the right decision is to dispose of the parts. Wilbur's analysis is shown in Exhibit 14–3.

Notice that the book value of the obsolete inventory is a sunk cost. If the parts are modified, the $20,000 book value will be an expense during the period when the parts are used. Otherwise, the $20,000 book value of the asset will be written off when the parts are sold. As a sunk cost, the book value of the obsolete inventory will not affect any future cash flow of the company.

As the managerial accountant's analysis reveals, the relevant data include the $17,000 proceeds from disposal, the $12,000 cost to modify the parts, and the $26,000 cost to buy new parts. All of these data meet the two tests of relevance: they affect future cash flows and they differ between the two alternatives. As Joan Wilbur's analysis shows, Worldwide Airways' cost will be $3,000 less if the obsolete parts are sold and new parts are purchased.

Irrelevant Future Costs and Benefits

At Worldwide Airways' headquarters in Atlanta, Amy Earhart, manager of flight scheduling, is in the midst of making a decision about the Atlanta to Honolulu route. The flight is currently nonstop, but she is considering a stop in San Francisco. She feels that the route would attract additional passengers if the stop is made, but there would also be additional variable costs. Her analysis appears in Exhibit 14–4.

The analysis indicates that the preferable alternative is the route that includes a stop in San Francisco. Notice that the cargo revenue [item (2)] and the aircraft maintenance cost [item (8)] are irrelevant to the flight-route decision. Although these data do affect future cash flows, they *do not differ between the two alternatives.* All of the other data in Exhibit 14–4 are relevant to the decision, because they do differ between the two alternatives. The analysis in Exhibit 14–4 could have ignored the irrelevant data; the same decision would have been reached. (Exercise 14–30, at the end of the chapter, will ask you to prove this assertion by redoing the analysis without the irrelevant data.)

Exhibit 14–4
Flight-Route Decision: Worldwide Airways

			Revenues and Costs under Two Alternatives		
Relevant or Irrelevant			**(a) Nonstop Route***	**(b) With Stop in San Francisco***	**(c) Differential Amount†**
Relevant		(1) Passenger revenue	$240,000	$258,000	$(18,000)
	Irrelevant	(2) Cargo revenue	80,000	80,000	–0–
Relevant		(3) Landing fee in San Francisco	–0–	(5,000)	5,000
Relevant		(4) Use of airport gate facilities	–0–	(3,000)	3,000
Relevant		(5) Flight crew cost	(2,000)	(2,500)	500
Relevant		(6) Fuel	(21,000)	(24,000)	3,000
Relevant		(7) Meals and services	(4,000)	(4,600)	600
	Irrelevant	(8) Aircraft maintenance	(1,000)	(1,000)	–0–
		Total revenue less costs	$292,000	$297,900	$ (5,900)

*In columns (a) and (b), parentheses denote costs and numbers without parentheses are revenues.
†In column (c), parentheses denote differential items favoring option (b).

Exhibit 14–5
Decision to Add Flights: Worldwide Airways

	(a) Add Flights	**(b) Do Not Add Flights**	**(c) Differential Amount**
Additional revenue from new flights less additional costs	$30,000	–0–	$ 30,000
Rental of excess hangar space	–0–	$40,000	(40,000)*
Total	$30,000	$40,000	$(10,000)

*Parentheses denote that differential benefit favors option (b).

Opportunity Costs

Another decision confronting Amy Earhart is whether to add two daily round-trip flights between Atlanta and Montreal. Her initial analysis of the relevant costs and benefits indicates that the additional revenue from the flights will exceed their costs by $30,000 per month. Hence, she is ready to add the flights to the schedule. However, Chuck Lindbergh, Worldwide Airways' hangar manager in Atlanta, points out that Earhart has overlooked an important consideration.

Worldwide Airways currently has excess space in its hangar. A commuter airline has offered to rent the hangar space for $40,000 per month. However, if the Atlanta-to-Montreal flights are added to the schedule, the additional aircraft needed in Atlanta will require the excess hangar space.

If Worldwide Airways adds the Atlanta-to-Montreal flights, it will forgo the opportunity to rent the excess hangar space for $40,000 per month. Thus, the $40,000 in rent forgone is an *opportunity cost* of the alternative to add the new flights. An **opportunity cost** is the potential benefit given up when the choice of one action precludes a different action. Although people tend to overlook or underestimate the importance of opportunity costs, they are just as relevant as out-of-pocket costs in evaluating decision alternatives. In Worldwide Airways' case, the best action is to rent the excess warehouse space to the commuter airline, rather than adding the new flights. The analysis in Exhibit 14–5 supports this conclusion.

It is a common mistake for people to overlook or underweigh opportunity costs. The $40,000 hangar rental, which will be forgone if the new flights are added, is an *opportunity cost* of the option to add the flights. It is a *relevant cost* of the decision, and it is just as important as any out-of-pocket expenditure.

Summary

Relevant costs and benefits satisfy the following two criteria:

1. They affect the future.
2. They differ between alternatives.

"I would say that they [line managers] view us as business partners." (14d)

Boeing

Sunk costs are *not* relevant costs, because they do not affect the future. An example of a sunk cost is the book value of an asset, either equipment or inventory. *Future costs or benefits that are identical across all decision alternatives are not relevant.* They can be ignored when making a decision. *Opportunity costs are relevant costs.* Such costs deserve particular attention because many people tend to overlook them when making decisions.

Analysis of Special Decisions

LO 5

Prepare analyses of various special decisions, properly identifying the relevant costs and benefits.

Topic 14–2

What are the relevant costs and benefits when a manager must decide whether to add or drop a product or service? What data are relevant when deciding whether to produce or buy a service or component? These decisions and certain other nonroutine decisions merit special attention in our discussion of relevant costs and benefits.

Accept or Reject a Special Offer

Jim Wright, Worldwide Airways' vice president for operations, has been approached by a Japanese tourist agency about flying chartered tourist flights from Japan to Hawaii. The tourist agency has offered Worldwide Airways $150,000 per round-trip flight on a jumbo jet. Given the airline's usual occupancy rate and air fares, a round-trip jumbo-jet flight between Japan and Hawaii typically brings in revenue of $250,000. Thus, the tourist agency's specially priced offer requires a special analysis by Jim Wright.

Wright knows that Worldwide Airways has two jumbo jets that are not currently being used. The airline has just eliminated several unprofitable routes, freeing these aircraft for other uses. The airline was not currently planning to add any new routes, and therefore the two jets were idle. To help in making his decision, Wright asks for cost data from the controller's office. The controller provides the information in Exhibit 14–6, which pertains to a typical round-trip jumbo-jet flight between Japan and Hawaii.

The variable costs cover aircraft fuel and maintenance, flight-crew costs, in-flight meals and services, and landing fees. The fixed costs allocated to each flight cover Worldwide Airways' fixed costs, such as aircraft depreciation, maintenance and depreciation of facilities, and fixed administrative costs.

Exhibit 14–6

Data for Typical Flight Between Japan and Hawaii: Worldwide Airways

Revenue:		
Passenger	$250,000	
Cargo	30,000	
Total revenue		$280,000
Expenses:		
Variable expenses of flight	$ 90,000	
Fixed expenses allocated to each flight	100,000	
Total expenses		190,000
Profit		$ 90,000

If Jim Wright had not understood managerial accounting, he might have done the following *incorrect analysis.*

Special price for charter	$150,000
Total cost per flight	190,000
Loss on charter flight	$ (40,000)

This calculation suggests that the special charter offer should be declined. What is the error in this analysis? The mistake is the inclusion of allocated fixed costs in the cost per flight. This is an error, because the *fixed costs will not increase in total* if the charter flight is added. Since the fixed costs will not change under either of the alternate choices, they are irrelevant.

Fortunately, Jim Wright does not make this mistake. He knows that only the variable costs of the proposed charter are relevant. Moreover, Wright determines that the variable cost of the charter would be lower than that of a typical flight, because Worldwide Airways would not incur the variable costs of reservations and ticketing. These variable expenses amount to $5,000 for a scheduled flight. Thus, Wright's analysis of the charter offer is as shown below.

Assumes excess capacity (idle aircraft)

Special price for charter		$150,000
Variable cost per routine flight	$90,000	
Less: Savings on reservations and ticketing	5,000	
Variable cost of charter		85,000
Contribution from charter		$ 65,000

Wright's analysis shows that the special charter flight will contribute $65,000 toward covering the airline's fixed costs and profit. Since the airline has excess flight capacity, due to the existence of idle aircraft, the optimal decision is to accept the special charter offer.

"I've seen it (managerial accounting) evolve to become more of a team player and being involved in major projects and being looked to as a business advisor or consultant to help leverage our expertise on profitability of certain products or sourcing decisions." (14e)

Caterpillar

No Excess Capacity Now let's consider how Wright's analysis would appear if Worldwide Airways had no idle aircraft. Suppose that in order to fly the charter between Japan and Hawaii, the airline would have to cancel its least profitable route, which is between Japan and Hong Kong. This route contributes $80,000 toward covering the airline's fixed costs and profit. Thus, if the charter offer is accepted, the airline will incur an opportunity cost of $80,000 from the forgone contribution of the Japan–Hong Kong route. Now Wright's analysis should appear as shown below.

Assumes no excess capacity (no idle aircraft)

Special price for charter		$150,000
Variable cost per routine flight	$90,000	
Less: Savings on reservations and ticketing	5,000	
Variable cost of charter	$85,000	
Add: Opportunity cost, forgone contribution on canceled Japan–Hong Kong route	80,000	165,000
Loss from charter		$ (15,000)

Thus, if Worldwide Airways has no excess flight capacity, Jim Wright should reject the special charter offer.

Summary The decision to accept or reject a specially priced order is common in both service industry and manufacturing firms. Manufacturers often are faced with decisions about selling products in a special order at less than full price. The correct analysis of such decisions focuses on the relevant costs and benefits. Fixed costs, which often are allocated to individual units of product or service, are usually irrelevant. Fixed costs typically will not change in total, whether the order is accepted or rejected.

When excess capacity exists, the only relevant costs usually will be the variable costs associated with the special order. When there is no excess capacity, the opportunity cost of using the firm's facilities for the special order are also relevant to the decision.

Outsource a Product or Service

Ellie Rickenbacker is Worldwide Airways' manager of in-flight services. She supervises the airline's flight attendants and all of the firm's food and beverage operations. Rickenbacker currently faces a decision regarding the preparation of in-flight dinners at the airline's Atlanta hub. In the Atlanta flight kitchen, full-course dinners are prepared and packaged for long flights that pass through Atlanta. In the past, all of the desserts were baked and packaged in the flight kitchen. However, Rickenbacker has received an offer from an Atlanta bakery to bake the airline's desserts. Thus, her decision is whether to *outsource* the dessert portion of the in-flight dinners. An **outsourcing decision,** also called a **make-or-buy decision,** entails a choice between producing a product or service in-house or purchasing it from an outside supplier. To help guide her decision, Rickenbacker has assembled the cost information in Exhibit 14–7, which shows a total cost per dessert of 25 cents.

The Atlanta bakery has offered to supply the desserts for 21 cents each. Rickenbacker's initial inclination is to accept the bakery's offer, since it appears that the airline would save 4 cents per dessert. However, the controller reminds Rickenbacker that not all of the costs listed in Exhibit 14–7 are relevant to the outsourcing decision. The controller modifies Rickenbacker's analysis as shown in Exhibit 14–8.

Management Accounting Practice

LoanCity.com

OUTSOURCING

The Internet has provided new opportunities for outsourcing, as explained in an article in *The Wall Street Journal:* "Why spend millions on in-house technology, when you can grab it off the Web for a fraction of the cost?"[1] As a case in point, consider the decision by LoanCity.com, as reported in *The Wall Street Journal.*

LoanCity.com, an online mortgage company in San Jose, California, was formed to arrange residential mortgages via its website. The company was starting out with no revenue, but its plans were to serve more than a million customers within a few years. "Any online operation of that scale would require a sprawling computing center, which in turn would require a sprawling set of resources: a few million dollars of hardware, several hundred thousand dollars more for software licenses, a staff of as many as 20 engineers and an endless list of headaches." Unless, of course, LoanCity.com's management could get someone else to worry about the problem. So the company's chief technology officer decided to outsource the operation. "He hired an *application service provider,* or ASP, to set up and run the various *enterprise resource planning,* or ERP, business-software packages that LoanCity.com would need to handle such areas as sales, accounting and human resources. So instead of making a huge technology investment upfront," LoanCity.com uses the Internet to connect to the applications it needs on machines located at the company's ASP. According to LoanCity.com's chief technology officer, "I had six months to go from a mom-and-pop start-up to a world-class system," he says. "I don't think I could have done that myself."

If Worldwide Airways stops making desserts, it will save all of the variable costs but only 1 cent of fixed costs. The 1-cent saving in supervisory salaries would result because the airline could get along with two fewer kitchen supervisors. The remainder

[1]"Somebody Else's Problem," *The Wall Street Journal,* November 15, 1999, p. R8.

	Cost per Dessert
Variable costs:	
Direct material (food and packaging)	$.06
Direct labor	.04
Variable overhead	.04
Fixed costs (allocated to products):	
Supervisory salaries	.04
Depreciation of flight-kitchen equipment	.07
Total cost per dessert	$.25

Exhibit 14–7
Cost of In-Flight Desserts: Worldwide Airways

of the fixed costs would be incurred even if the desserts were purchased. These remaining fixed costs of supervision and depreciation would have to be reallocated to the flight kitchen's other products. In light of the controller's revised analysis, Rickenbacker realizes that the airline should continue to make its own desserts. To outsource the desserts would require an expenditure of 21 cents per dessert, but only 15 cents per dessert would be saved.

To clarify her decision further, Rickenbacker asks the controller to prepare an analysis of the *total costs* per month of making or buying desserts. The controller's report, displayed in Exhibit 14–9, shows the total cost of producing 1,000,000 desserts, the flight kitchen's average monthly volume.

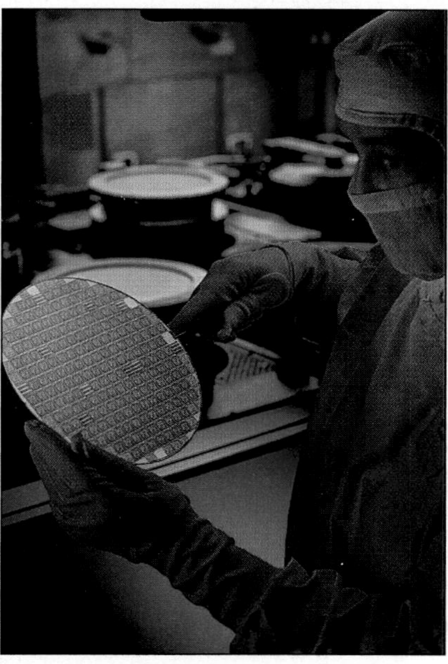

In today's global economy, more and more companies are outsourcing significant products and services. Gallo Winery, for example, buys a significant portion of its grapes from other vintners. Kodak outsources its entire data processing operation. Cummins Engine outsources many of its pistons, and Intel Corporation buys microchips. Continental Bank outsources its cafeteria and legal services. Many pharmaceutical companies, such as Japan's Yamanouchi Pharmaceutical, have outsourced much of their production to cut costs.[2]

[2]Peter Landers, "Japan's Local Drug Makers to Outsource to Suppliers," *The Wall Street Journal,* March 26, 2002, p. A20.

Exhibit 14–8
Cost Savings from Buying In-Flight Desserts: Worldwide Airways

	Cost per Dessert	Costs Saved by Purchasing Desserts
Variable costs:		
Direct material	$.06	$.06
Direct labor	.04	.04
Variable overhead	.04	.04
Fixed costs (allocated to products):		
Supervisory salaries	.04	.01
Depreciation of flight-kitchen equipment	.07	–0–
Total cost per dessert	$.25	$.15
Cost of purchasing desserts (per dessert)		$.21
Loss per dessert if desserts are purchased (savings per dessert minus purchase cost per dessert, or $.15 – $.21)		$(.06)

Exhibit 14–9
Total-Cost Analysis of Outsourcing Decision: Worldwide Airways

	Cost per Month	Costs Saved by Purchasing Desserts
Variable costs:		
Direct material	$ 60,000	$ 60,000
Direct labor	40,000	40,000
Variable overhead	40,000	40,000
Fixed costs (allocated to products):		
Supervisory salaries	40,000	10,000*
Depreciation of flight-kitchen equipment	70,000	–0–
Total cost per month	$250,000	$150,000
Cost of purchasing desserts (per month)		$210,000
Total loss if desserts are purchased (total savings minus total cost of purchasing, or $150,000 – $210,000)		$ (60,000)

*Cost of monthly compensation for two kitchen supervisors, who will not be needed if desserts are purchased.

The total-cost analysis confirmed Rickenbacker's decision to continue making desserts in the airline's flight kitchen.

Beware of Unit-Cost Data Fixed costs often are allocated to individual units of product or service for product-costing purposes. For decision-making purposes, however, unitized fixed costs can be misleading. As the total-cost analysis above shows, only $10,000 in fixed monthly cost will be saved if the desserts are purchased. The remaining $100,000 in monthly fixed cost will continue whether the desserts are made or purchased. Rickenbacker's initial cost analysis in Exhibit 14–7 implies that each dessert costs the airline 25 cents, but that 25-cent cost includes 11 cents of unitized fixed costs. Most of these costs will remain unchanged regardless of the outsourcing decision. By allocating fixed costs to individual products or services, they are made to appear variable even though they are not.

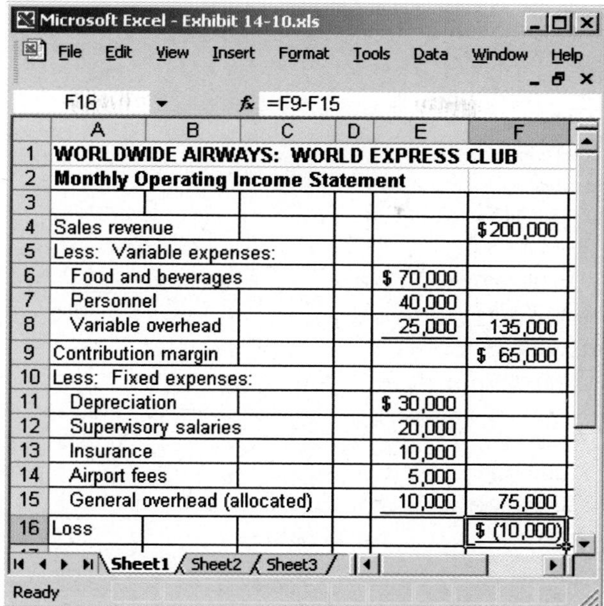

Microsoft Excel - Exhibit 14-10.xls

F16 =F9-F15

	A	B	C	D	E	F
1	**WORLDWIDE AIRWAYS: WORLD EXPRESS CLUB**					
2	**Monthly Operating Income Statement**					
3						
4	Sales revenue					$200,000
5	Less: Variable expenses:					
6	Food and beverages				$ 70,000	
7	Personnel				40,000	
8	Variable overhead				25,000	135,000
9	Contribution margin					$ 65,000
10	Less: Fixed expenses:					
11	Depreciation				$ 30,000	
12	Supervisory salaries				20,000	
13	Insurance				10,000	
14	Airport fees				5,000	
15	General overhead (allocated)				10,000	75,000
16	Loss					$ (10,000)

Sheet1 / Sheet2 / Sheet3

Ready

Exhibit 14–10

World Express Club Monthly Operating Income Statement: Worldwide Airways

Add or Drop a Service, Product, or Department

Worldwide Airways offers its passengers the opportunity to join its World Express Club. Club membership entitles a traveler to use the club facilities at the airport in Atlanta. Club privileges include a private lounge and restaurant, discounts on meals and beverages, and use of a small health spa.

Jayne Wing, the president of Worldwide Airways, is worried that the World Express Club might not be profitable. Her concern is caused by the statement of monthly operating income shown in the Excel spreadsheet in Exhibit 14–10.

In her weekly staff meeting, Wing states her concern about the World Express Club's profitability. The controller responds by pointing out that not all of the costs on the club's income statement would be eliminated if the club were discontinued. The vice president for sales adds that the club helps Worldwide Airways attract passengers whom it might otherwise lose to a competitor. As the meeting adjourns, Wing asks the controller to prepare an analysis of the relevant costs and benefits associated with the World Express Club. The controller's analysis is displayed in Exhibit 14–11.

The controller's report contains two parts. Part I focuses on the relevant costs and benefits of the World Express Club only, while ignoring any impact of the club on other airline operations. In column (a), the controller has listed the club's revenues and expenses from the income statement given previously (Exhibit 14–10). Column (b) lists the expenses that will continue if the club is eliminated. These expenses are called **unavoidable expenses.** In contrast, the expenses appearing in column (a) but not column (b) are **avoidable expenses.** The airline will no longer incur these expenses if the club is eliminated.

Notice that all of the club's variable expenses are avoidable. The depreciation expense, $30,000, is an allocated portion of the depreciation on a Worldwide Airways building, part of which is used by the World Express Club. If the Club is discontinued, the airline will continue to own and use the building, and the depreciation expense will continue. Thus, it is an unavoidable expense. The fixed supervisory salaries are avoidable, since these employees will no longer be needed if the club is eliminated. The fixed insurance expense of $10,000 is not avoidable; the $5,000 fee paid to the airport for the privilege of operating the club is avoidable. Finally, the club's allocated portion

Exhibit 14–11
Relevant Costs and Benefits of World Express Club: Worldwide Airways

	(a) Keep Club	(b) Eliminate Club	(c) Differential Amount
Part I:			
Sales revenue	$200,000	–0–	$200,000
Less: Variable expenses:			
Food and beverages	(70,000)	–0–	(70,000)
Personnel	(40,000)	–0–	(40,000)
Variable overhead	(25,000)	–0–	(25,000)
Contribution margin	$ 65,000	–0–	$ 65,000
Less: Fixed expenses:			
Depreciation	$ (30,000)	$(30,000)	$ –0–
Supervisory salaries	(20,000)	–0–	(20,000)
Insurance	(10,000)	(10,000)	–0–
Airport fees	(5,000)	–0–	(5,000)
General overhead (allocated)	(10,000)	(10,000)	–0–
Total fixed expenses	$ (75,000)	$(50,000)	$ (25,000)
Profit (loss)	$ (10,000)	$(50,000)	$ 40,000
		Expenses in the column above are **unavoidable** expenses	Expenses in the column above are **avoidable** expenses
Part II:			
Contribution margin from general airline operations that will be forgone if club is eliminated	$ 60,000	–0–	$ 60,000

of general overhead expenses, $10,000, is not avoidable. Worldwide Airways will incur these expenses regardless of its decision about the World Express Club.

The conclusion shown by Part I of the controller's report is that the club should not be eliminated. If the club is closed, the airline will lose more in contribution margin, $65,000, than it saves in avoidable fixed expenses, $25,000. Thus, the club's $65,000 contribution margin is enough to cover the avoidable fixed expenses of $25,000 and still contribute $40,000 toward covering the overall airline's fixed expenses.

World Express Club's contribution margin	$65,000
Avoidable fixed expenses	25,000
Contribution of club toward covering overall airline's fixed expenses	$40,000

Now consider Part II of the controller's analysis in Exhibit 14–11. As the vice president for sales pointed out, the World Express Club is an attractive feature to many travelers. The controller estimates that if the club were discontinued, the airline would lose $60,000 each month in forgone contribution margin from general airline operations. This loss in contribution margin would result from losing to a competing airline current passengers who are attracted to Worldwide Airways by its World Express Club. This $60,000 in forgone contribution margin is an *opportunity cost* of the option to close down the club.

Considering both Parts I and II of the controller's analysis, Worldwide Airways' monthly profit will be greater by $100,000 if the club is kept open. Recognition of two issues is key to this conclusion:

1. Only the avoidable expenses of the club will be saved if it is discontinued.
2. Closing the club will adversely affect the airline's other operations.

Management Accounting Practice

FedEx

ADDING A SERVICE

Sometimes a business development that threatens the viability of one product line can create an opportunity for another new line of business. As reported in an article in *The Wall Street Journal,* FedEx has found itself in just this situation.[3] "What does Federal Express do now, in a world that may not absolutely, positively need it overnight? Frederick W. Smith foresaw today's fast-cycle economy a quarter century ago when he created Federal Express, a company obsessed with speed and reliability. He leapfrogged the rest of the transportation industry, and FedEx's parent, FDX Corp., became a $17 billion-a-year landmark of the new economy. Now, the need for a fast but pricey delivery service, something that was a brilliant bet not that long ago, isn't so clear. Indeed, the rate of growth in FedEx's delivery volume within the U.S., which accounts for about two-thirds of the company's revenue, has slowed significantly this year."

What has caused this slowdown in FedEx's growth? E-mail delivers documents instantly, and discount air carriers now provide tracking of shipments via the Internet. FDX rivals, such as United Parcel Service and Airborne Freight offer reliable ground and air services that once distinguished FDX from the pack.

However, something else is threatening FedEx. Companies are operating more intelligently than they used to. "A big part of FedEx's business has traditionally come from firms that would suddenly realize they were short of key parts needed for their production, or that they were low on goods demanded by their customers. Because those companies couldn't plan their needs particularly well, they relied on FedEx to make up in speed what they lacked in precision. Now, many businesses are deploying complex new 'supply chain management' systems. Those systems are designed to eliminate much of the unpredictability in their operations—and also much of the need for the kind of expensive, rapid-fire delivery FedEx excels at providing." So the "chairman and CEO of FDX, is making two more big bets. First, he is gambling that his company can remake itself by slowing some things down. The company is improving its delivery services that compete more directly with UPS and the U.S. Postal Service. It has invested $500 million in the past two years to double capacity at its business-to-business delivery network. [This network] transports packages more slowly, more cheaply, and with much higher profit margins."

"Second, and more ambitiously, FDX is trying to recast itself as a major provider of the very management systems that threaten the company." FDX "wants to design a network that can supplant a company's inefficient stream of faxes and phone calls with digital exchanges of information about demand, factory schedules, and the availability of materials."

Special Decisions in Manufacturing Firms

Some types of decisions are more likely to arise in manufacturing companies than in service industry firms. We will examine two of these decisions.

Analyze manufacturing decisions involving joint products and limited resources.

Joint Products: Sell or Process Further

A **joint production process** results in two or more products, called *joint products.* An example is the processing of cocoa beans into cocoa powder and cocoa butter. Cocoa

[3]"Overnight, Everything Changed for FedEx; Can It Reinvent Itself?" *The Wall Street Journal,* November 4, 1999, p. A1.

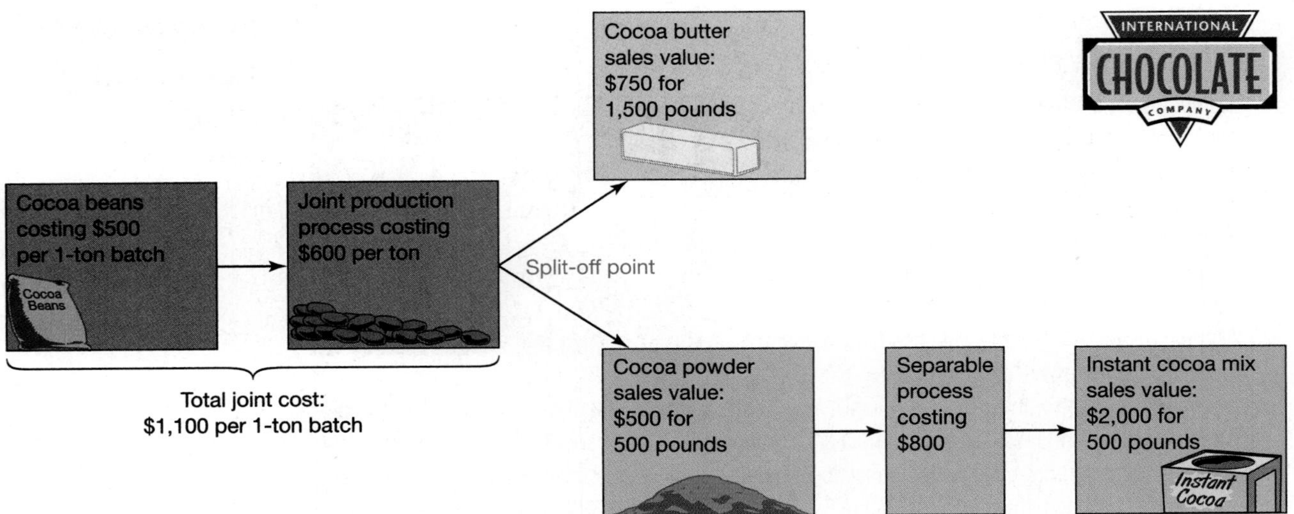

Exhibit 14–12

Joint Processing of Cocoa Beans: International Chocolate Company

beans constitute the input to the joint production process, and the two joint products are cocoa powder and cocoa butter. The point in the production process where the joint products are identifiable as separate products is called the **split-off point.** Other examples of joint production processes include the slaughtering of animals for various cuts of meat and the processing of petroleum into various products, such as kerosene and gasoline.

Manufacturers with joint production processes sometimes must decide whether a joint product should be sold at the split-off point or processed further before being sold. Such a decision recently confronted Bill Candee, the president of International Chocolate Company. Candee's firm imports cocoa beans and processes them into cocoa powder and cocoa butter. Only a portion of the cocoa powder is used by International Chocolate Company in the production of chocolate candy. The remainder of the cocoa powder is sold to an ice cream producer. Candee is considering the possibility of processing his remaining cocoa powder into an instant cocoa mix to be marketed under the brand name ChocoTime. Data pertaining to Candee's decision are displayed in Exhibit 14–12.

Notice from the diagram that cocoa beans are processed in 1-ton batches. The total cost of the cocoa beans and the joint processing is $1,100. This is called the **joint cost.** The output of the joint process is 1,500 pounds of cocoa butter and 500 pounds of cocoa powder.

How should Bill Candee approach the decision about processing the cocoa powder into instant cocoa mix? What are the relevant costs and benefits? First, let's consider the joint cost of $1,100. Is this a relevant cost in the decision at hand? *The joint cost is not a relevant cost,* because it will not change regardless of the decision Candee makes.

Suppose the $1,100 joint cost had been allocated to the two joint products for product-costing purposes. A common method of allocating a joint cost is the **relative-sales-value method,** in which the joint cost is allocated between the joint products in proportion to their sales value at the split-off point.[4] International Chocolate Company would make the following joint cost allocation.

Joint Cost	Joint Products	Sales Value at Split-Off Point	Relative Proportion	Allocation of Joint Cost
$1,100	Cocoa butter	$750	.60	$ 660
	Cocoa powder	500	.40	440
	Total joint cost allocated			$1,100

[4]Other methods of allocating joint costs are covered in Chapter 18.

Relevant or Irrelevant			(a) Sell Cocoa Powder at Split-Off Point	(b) Process Cocoa Powder into Instant Cocoa Mix	(c) Differential Amount (a) − (b)
		Sales revenue:			
	Irrelevant	Cocoa butter	$ 750	$ 750	-0-
Relevant		Cocoa powder	500		$(1,500)
Relevant		Instant cocoa mix		2,000	
		Less: Costs:			
	Irrelevant	Joint cost	(1,100)	(1,100)	-0-
Relevant		Separable cost of processing cocoa powder into instant cocoa mix	-0-	(800)	800
		Total	$ 150	$ 850	$ (700)

Exhibit 14–13
Decision to Sell or Process Further: International Chocolate Company

Does this allocation of the $1,100 joint cost make it relevant to the decision about processing cocoa powder into instant cocoa mix? The answer is no. *The $1,100 joint cost still does not change in total,* whether the cocoa powder is processed further or not. The joint cost is irrelevant to the decision at hand.

The only costs and benefits relevant to Candee's decision are those that differ between the two alternatives. The proper analysis is shown in Exhibit 14–13.

There is a shortcut method that arrives at the same conclusion as Exhibit 14–13. In this approach, the incremental revenue from the further processing of cocoa powder is compared with the **separable processing cost,** which is the cost incurred after the split-off point, as follows:

Sales value of instant cocoa mix	$2,000
Sales value of cocoa powder	500
Incremental revenue from further processing	$1,500
Less: Separable processing cost	800
Net benefit from further processing	$ 700

Both analyses indicate that Bill Candee should process his excess cocoa powder into instant cocoa mix. The same conclusion is reached if the analysis is done on a per-unit basis rather than a total basis:

Sales value of instant cocoa mix ($2,000 ÷ 500 pounds)	$4.00 per pound
Sales value of cocoa powder ($500 ÷ 500 pounds)	1.00 per pound
Incremental revenue from further processing	$3.00 per pound
Less: Separable processing cost ($800 ÷ 500 pounds)	1.60 per pound
Net benefit from further processing	$1.40 per pound

Once again, the analysis shows that Bill Candee should decide to process the cocoa powder into instant cocoa mix.

Decisions Involving Limited Resources

Organizations typically have limited resources. Limitations on floor space, machine time, labor hours, or raw materials are common. Operating with limited resources, a firm often must choose between sales orders, deciding which orders to fill and which ones to decline. In making such decisions, managers must decide which product or service is the most profitable.

Exhibit 14–14
Contribution Margin per Case: International Chocolate Company

	Chewies	Chompo Bars
Sales price	$10.00	$14.00
Less: Variable costs:		
Direct material	$ 3.00	$ 3.75
Direct labor	2.00	2.50
Variable overhead	3.00	3.75
Variable selling and administrative costs	1.00	2.00
Total variable costs	$ 9.00	$12.00
Contribution margin per case	$ 1.00	$ 2.00

Exhibit 14–15
Contribution Margin per Machine Hour: International Chocolate Company

		Chewies	Chompo Bars
(a)	Contribution margin per case	$1.00	$2.00
(b)	Machine hours required per case	.02	.05
(a) ÷ (b)	Contribution margin per machine hour	$50	$40

To illustrate, suppose International Chocolate Company's Phoenix plant makes two candy-bar products, Chewies and Chompo Bars. The contribution margin for a case of each of these products is computed in Exhibit 14–14.

A glance at the contribution-margin data suggests that Chompo Bars are more profitable than Chewies. It is true that a case of Chompo Bars contributes more toward covering the company's fixed cost and profit. However, an important consideration has been ignored in the analysis so far. The Phoenix plant's capacity is limited by its available machine time. Only 700 machine hours are available in the plant each month. International Chocolate Company can sell as many cases of either candy bar as it can produce, so production is limited only by the constraint on machine time.

To maximize the plant's total contribution toward covering fixed cost and profit, management should strive to use each machine hour as effectively as possible. This realization alters the analysis of product profitability. The relevant question is *not,* Which candy bar has the highest contribution margin *per case?* The pertinent question is, Which product has the highest contribution margin *per machine hour?* This question is answered with the calculation in Exhibit 14–15.

A machine hour spent in the production of Chewies will contribute $50 toward covering fixed cost and profit, while a machine hour devoted to Chompo Bars contributes only $40. Hence, the Phoenix plant's most profitable product is Chewies, when the plant's scarce resource is taken into account.

Suppose International Chocolate Company's Phoenix plant manager, Candace Barr, is faced with a choice between two sales orders, only one of which can be accepted. Only 100 hours of unscheduled machine time remains in the month, and it can be used to produce either Chewies or Chompos. The analysis in Exhibit 14–16 shows that Barr should devote the 100-hour block of machine time to filling the order for Chewies.

As Exhibit 14–16 demonstrates, a decision about the best use of a limited resource should be made on the basis of the *contribution margin per unit of the scarce resource.*

Multiple Scarce Resources Suppose the Phoenix plant had a limited amount of *both* machine hours *and* labor hours. Now the analysis of product profitability is more complicated. The choice as to which product is most profitable typically will involve a trade-off between the two scarce resources. Solving such a problem requires a powerful mathematical tool called *linear programming,* which is covered in the appendix to this chapter.

	Chewies	Chompo Bars
Contribution margin per case	$1.00	$2.00
Number of cases produced in 100 hours of machine time	× 5,000*	× 2,000†
Total contribution toward covering fixed cost and profit	$5,000	$4,000

*Chewies: 100 hours ÷ .02 hour per case = 5,000 cases
†Chompo Bars: 100 hours ÷ .05 hour per case = 2,000 cases

Exhibit 14–16
Total Contribution from 100 Machine Hours: International Chocolate Company

Theory of Constraints As the previous analysis suggests, a binding constraint can limit a company's profitability. For example, a manufacturing company may have a *bottleneck operation,* through which every unit of a product must pass before moving on to other operations. The *theory of constraints (TOC)* calls for identifying such limiting constraints and seeking ways to relax them. Also referred to as *managing constraints,* this management approach can significantly improve an organization's level of goal attainment. Among the ways that management can relax a constraint by expanding the capacity of a bottleneck operation are the following:

- *Outsourcing* (subcontracting) all or part of the bottleneck operation.
- Investing in additional production equipment and employing *parallel processing,* in which multiple product units undergo the same production operation simultaneously.
- Working *overtime* at the bottleneck operation.
- *Retraining* employees and shifting them to the bottleneck.
- Eliminating any *non-value-added activities* at the bottleneck operation.

Uncertainty

Our analyses of the decisions in this chapter assumed that all relevant data were known with certainty. In practice, of course, decision makers are rarely so fortunate. One common technique for addressing the impact of uncertainty is *sensitivity analysis.* **Sensitivity analysis** is a technique for determining what would happen in a decision analysis if a key prediction or assumption proved to be wrong.

To illustrate, let's return to Candace Barr's decision about how to use the remaining 100 hours of machine time in International Chocolate Company's Phoenix plant. The calculation in Exhibit 14–15 showed that Chewies have the highest contribution margin per machine hour. Suppose Barr is uncertain about the contribution margin per case of Chewies. A sensitivity analysis shows how sensitive her decision is to the value of this uncertain parameter. As Exhibit 14–17 shows, the Chewies contribution margin could decline to $.80 per case before Barr's decision would change. As long as the contribution margin per case of Chewies exceeds $.80 per case, the 100 hours of available machine time should be devoted to Chewies.

Sensitivity analysis can help the managerial accountant decide which parameters in an analysis are most critical to estimate accurately. In this case, the managerial accountant knows that the contribution margin per case of Chewies could be as much as 20 percent lower than the original $1.00 prediction without changing the outcome of the analysis.

Expected Values Another approach to dealing explicitly with uncertainty is to base the decision on expected values. The **expected value** of a random variable is equal to the sum of the possible values for the variable, each weighted by its probability. To illustrate, suppose the contribution margins per case for Chewies and Chompos are uncertain, as shown in Exhibit 14–18. As the exhibit shows, the choice as to which product to produce with excess machine time may be based on the *expected*

Exhibit 14–17
Sensitivity Analysis: International Chocolate Company

		Chewies	Chompo Bars
Original Analysis			
(a)	Contribution margin per case predicted	$1.00	$2.00
(b)	Machine hours required per case	.02	.05
(a) ÷ (b)	Contribution per machine hour	$50.00	$40.00
Sensitivity Analysis			
(c)	Contribution margin per case hypothesized in sensitivity analysis	$.80	
(d)	Machine hours required per case	.02	same
(c) ÷ (d)	Contribution per machine hour	$40.00	

Exhibit 14–18
Use of Expected Values: International Chocolate Company

Chewies: Possible Values of Contribution Margin	Chewies: Probability	Chompo Bars: Possible Values of Contribution Margin	Chompo Bars: Probability
$ .75	.5	$1.50	.3
1.25	.5	2.00	.4
		2.50	.3
Expected value (.5)($.75) + (.5)($1.25) = $1.00		(.3)($1.50) + (.4)($2.00) + (.3)($2.50) = $2.00	
Machine hours required per case	.02		.05
Expected value of contribution per machine hour	$50	>	$40

value of the contribution per machine hour. Statisticians have developed many other methods for dealing with uncertainty in decision making. These techniques are covered in statistics and decision analysis courses.

Activity-Based Costing and Today's Advanced Manufacturing Environment

LO 7

Explain the impact of an advanced manufacturing environment and activity-based costing on a relevant-cost analysis.

In this chapter we have explored how to identify the relevant costs and benefits in various types of decisions. How will the relevant costing approach change in the new manufacturing environment, characterized by JIT production methods and flexible manufacturing systems? How would a relevant-costing analysis change if a company uses an activity-based costing (ABC) system?[5]

The *concepts* underlying a relevant-costing analysis continue to be completely valid in an advanced manufacturing setting and in a situation where activity-based costing is used. The objective of the decision analysis is to determine the costs and benefits that are relevant to the decision. As we found earlier in this chapter, relevant costs and benefits *have a bearing on the future and differ among the decision alternatives.*

What *will* be different in a setting where activity-based costing is used is the decision maker's ability to determine what costs are relevant to a decision. Under ABC the decision maker typically can associate costs with the activities that drive them much more accurately than under a conventional product-costing system. Let's explore these issues with an illustration.

[5]Activity-based costing (ABC), which was introduced conceptually in Chapter 3, is thoroughly explored in Chapter 5. This section can be studied most effectively after completing Chapter 5.

Exhibit 14–19
Conventional Product-Costing Data and Outsourcing Analysis: International Chocolate Company

A. Manufacturing Overhead Budget for Savannah Plant	
Variable overhead:	
Electricity	$ 700,000
Oil and lubricants	120,000
Equipment maintenance	180,000
Total variable overhead	$1,000,000
Variable overhead rate: $1,000,000 ÷ 100,000 direct-labor hours = $10 per hour	
Fixed overhead:	
Plant depreciation	$1,650,000
Product development	300,000
Supervisory salaries	600,000
Material handling	800,000
Purchasing	250,000
Inspection	300,000
Setup	400,000
Machinery depreciation	200,000
Total fixed overhead	$4,500,000
Fixed overhead rate: $4,500,000 ÷ 100,000 direct-labor hours = $45 per hour	
B. Conventional Product-Costing Data: Gift Boxes	
Direct material	$ 100,000
Direct labor (10,000 hr. at $15 per hr.)	150,000
Variable overhead ($10 per direct-labor hr.)	100,000
Fixed overhead ($45 per direct-labor hr.)	450,000
Total cost	$ 800,000
Unit cost: $800,000 ÷ 1,000,000 boxes = $.80 per box	
C. Conventional Outsourcing Analysis: Gift Boxes	
Relevant costs (costs that will be avoided if the gift boxes are purchased):	
Direct material	$ 100,000
Direct labor	150,000
Variable overhead	100,000
Fixed overhead:	
Supervision	60,000
Machinery depreciation	20,000
Total costs to be avoided by purchasing	$ 430,000
Total cost of purchasing (1,000,000 boxes × $.45 per box)	$ 450,000

Conventional Outsourcing (Make-or-Buy) Analysis

International Chocolate Company makes fine chocolates in its Savannah plant. The chocolates are packaged in two-pound and five-pound gift boxes. The company also manufactures the gift boxes in the Savannah plant. The plant manager, Marsha Mello, was approached recently by a packaging company with an offer to supply the gift boxes at a price of $.45 each. Mello concluded that the offer should be rejected on the basis of the relevant-costing analysis in Exhibit 14–19. International Chocolate Company's traditional, volume-based product-costing system showed a unit product cost of $.80 per box. However, Mello realized that not all of the costs would be avoided. She reasoned that all of the direct material, direct labor, and variable overhead would be avoided, but only a small part of the assigned fixed overhead would be saved.

She concluded that $60,000 of supervisory salaries and $20,000 of machinery depreciation could be traced directly to gift package production. These costs would be avoided, she felt, but the remaining fixed costs would not. Mello concluded that only $430,000 of costs would be avoided by purchasing, while $450,000 would be spent to buy the boxes. The decision was clear; the supplier's offer should be rejected.

Activity-Based Costing Analysis of the Outsourcing Decision

At a staff meeting, Mello mentioned her tentative decision to Dave Mint, the plant controller. Mint then explained to Mello that he was completing a pilot project using activity-based costing. Mint offered to analyze the outsourcing decision using the new ABC database. Mello agreed, and Mint proceeded to do the ABC analysis shown in Exhibit 14–20.

In stage one of the ABC analysis, Mint had designated 11 activity cost pools corresponding to the major items in the Savannah plant's overhead budget. These activity cost pools were categorized as facility-level, product-sustaining level, batch-level, or unit-level activities. In stage two of the ABC project, cost drivers were identified and pool rates were computed. The ABC analysis showed that $243,000 of overhead should be assigned to the gift boxes, rather than $550,000 as the conventional product-costing system had indicated.

Exhibit 14–20
Activity-Based Costing Analysis of Outsourcing Decision: International Chocolate Company

A. Activity Cost Pools and Pool Rates

Activity Cost Pools	Budgeted Cost	Pool Rate and Cost Driver	Cost Assigned to Gift Boxes	
Facility level:				
Plant depreciation	$1,650,000	—		
Product-sustaining level:				
Product development	300,000	$600 per product spec	$600 × 5* =	$ 3,000
Supervisory salaries	600,000	$40 per supervisory hour	$40 × 1,500 =	60,000
Batch level:				
Material handling	800,000	$8 per material-handling hour	$8 × 5,000 =	40,000
Purchasing	250,000	$250 per purchase order	$250 × 40 =	10,000
Inspection	300,000	$300 per inspection	$300 × 20 =	6,000
Setup	400,000	$400 per setup	$400 × 10 =	4,000
Unit level:				
Electricity	700,000	$1.40 per machine hour	$1.40 × 50,000 =	70,000
Oil and lubrication	120,000	$.24 per machine hour	$.24 × 50,000 =	12,000
Equipment maintenance	180,000	$.36 per machine hour	$.36 × 50,000 =	18,000
Machinery depreciation	200,000	$.40 per machine hour	$.40 × 50,000 =	20,000
Total overhead for Savannah plant	$5,500,000			
Total overhead assigned to gift box production				$243,000

*The numbers in this column are the quantities of each cost driver required for gift box production.

B. ABC Outsourcing Analysis: Gift Boxes

Relevant costs (costs that will be avoided if the gift boxes are purchased):	
Direct material	$100,000
Direct labor	150,000
Overhead (from ABC analysis in panel A, above)	243,000
Total costs to be avoided by purchasing	$493,000
Total cost of purchasing (1,000,000 boxes × $.45 per box)	$450,000

Using the ABC database, Mint completed a new relevant-costing analysis of the outsourcing decision. Mint felt that all of the overhead costs assigned to the gift box operation could be avoided if the boxes were purchased. Notice that none of the facility-level costs are relevant to the analysis. They will not be avoided by purchasing the gift boxes. Mint's ABC analysis showed that a total of $493,000 of costs could be avoided by purchasing the boxes at a cost of $450,000. This would result in a net saving of $43,000.

Mint showed the ABC relevant-costing analysis to Mello. After some discussion they agreed that various qualitative issues needed to be explored before a final decision was made. For example, would the new supplier be reliable, and would the gift boxes be of good quality? Nevertheless, Mello and Mint agreed that the ABC data cast an entirely different light on the decision.

The Key Point What has happened here? Why did the conventional and ABC analyses of this decision reach different conclusions? Is the relevant-costing concept faulty?

The answer is no; the relevant-costing idea is alive and well. Both analyses sought to identify the relevant costs as those that would be avoided by purchasing the gift boxes. That approach is valid. The difference in the analyses lies in the superior ability of the ABC data to properly identify what the avoidable costs are. This is the key point. The conventional analysis relied on a traditional, volume-based product-costing system. That system lumps all of the fixed overhead costs together and assigns them using a single, unit-based cost driver (i.e., direct-labor hours). That analysis simply failed to note that many of the so-called fixed costs are *not* really fixed with respect to the appropriate cost driver. The more accurate ABC system correctly showed this fact, and identified additional costs that could be avoided by purchasing.

To summarize, under activity-based costing, the concepts underlying relevant-costing analysis remain valid. However, the ABC system does enable the decision maker to apply the relevant-costing decision model more accurately.

Other Issues in Decision Making

Incentives for Decision Makers

In this chapter we studied how managers should make decisions by focusing on the relevant costs and benefits. In previous chapters we covered accounting procedures for evaluating managerial performance. There is an important link between *decision making* and *managerial performance evaluation.* Managers typically will make decisions that maximize their perceived performance evaluations and rewards. This is human nature. If we want managers to make optimal decisions by properly evaluating the relevant costs and benefits, then the performance evaluation system and reward structure had better be consistent with that perspective.

The proper treatment of sunk costs in decision making illustrates this issue. Earlier in this chapter we saw that sunk costs should be ignored as irrelevant. For example, the book value of an outdated machine is irrelevant in making an equipment-replacement decision. Suppose, however, that a manager correctly ignores an old machine's book value and decides on early replacement of the machine he purchased a few years ago. Now suppose the hapless manager is criticized by his superior for "taking a loss" on the old machine, or for "buying a piece of junk" in the first place. What is our manager likely to do the next time he faces a similar decision? If he is like many people, he will tend to keep the old machine in order to justify his prior decision to purchase it. In so doing, he will be compounding his error. However, he may also be avoiding criticism from a superior who does not understand the importance of goal congruence.

The point is simply that if we want managers to make optimal decisions, we must give them incentives to do so. This requires that managerial performance be judged on the same factors that should be considered in making correct decisions.

Short-Run versus Long-Run Decisions

The decisions we have examined in this chapter were treated as short-run decisions. *Short-run decisions* affect only a short time period, typically a year or less. In reality, many of these decisions would have longer-term implications. For example, managers usually make a decision involving the addition or deletion of a product or service with a relatively long time frame in mind. The process of identifying relevant costs and benefits is largely the same whether the decision is viewed from a short-run or long-run perspective. One important factor that does change in a long-run analysis, however, is the *time value of money.* When several time periods are involved in a decision, the analyst should account for the fact that a $1.00 cash flow today is different from a $1.00 cash flow in five years. A dollar received today can be invested to earn interest, while the dollar received in five years cannot be invested over the intervening time period. The analysis of long-run decisions requires a tool called *capital budgeting,* which is covered in Chapter 16.

Pitfalls to Avoid

Identification of the relevant costs and benefits is an important step in making any economic decision. Nonetheless, analysts often overlook relevant costs or incorrectly include irrelevant data. In this section, we review four common mistakes to avoid in decision making.

1. ***Sunk costs.*** The book value of an asset, defined as its acquisition cost less the accumulated depreciation, is a sunk cost. Sunk costs cannot be changed by any current or future course of action, so they are irrelevant in decision making. Nevertheless, a common behavioral tendency is to give undue importance to book values in decisions that involve replacing an asset or disposing of obsolete inventory. People often seek to justify their past decisions by refusing to dispose of an asset, even if a better alternative has been identified. *The moral: Ignore sunk costs.*
2. ***Unitized fixed costs.*** For product-costing purposes, fixed costs often are divided by some activity measure and assigned to individual units of product. The result is to make a fixed cost appear variable. While there are legitimate reasons for this practice, from a *product-costing* perspective, it can create havoc in *decision making.* Therefore, in a decision analysis it is usually wise to include a fixed cost in its total amount, rather than as a per-unit cost. *The moral: Beware of unitized fixed costs in decision making.*
3. ***Allocated fixed costs.*** It is also common to allocate fixed costs across divisions, departments, or product lines. A possible result is that a product or department may appear unprofitable when in reality it does make a contribution toward covering fixed costs and profit. Before deciding to eliminate a department, be sure to ask which costs will be *avoided* if a particular alternative is selected. A fixed cost that has been allocated to a department may continue, in total or in part, even after the department has been eliminated. *The moral: Beware of allocated fixed costs; identify the avoidable costs.*
4. ***Opportunity costs.*** People tend to overlook opportunity costs, or to treat such costs as less important than out-of-pocket costs. Yet opportunity costs are just as real and important to making a correct decision as are out-of-pocket costs. *The moral: Pay special attention to identifying and including opportunity costs in a decision analysis.*

Focus on Ethics

EFFECTS OF DECISION TO CLOSE A DEPARTMENT AND OUTSOURCE

Outsourcing has become a common way of reducing costs in many organizations. Such decisions, though, often have repercussions that may not be captured "by the numbers." Employee morale, product quality, and vendor reliability are some of the issues that should be considered. Let's revisit the scenario described earlier at the International Chocolate Company. Recall that the Savannah plant manager, Marsha Mello (M), was considering outsourcing the production of gift boxes for the company's fine chocolates. A conventional analysis of the decision pointed toward keeping the production operation in-house. Now let's change the scenario a bit, and consider the following conversation between Dave Mint, plant controller (C), and Jack Edgeworth, supervisor of the gift box production department (SG). The conversation takes place after the two friends' weekly tennis game.

Mint (C): "Well you took me again, Jack. I'm starting to feel old."

Edgeworth (SG): "It was a close match, Dave. Always is. Fortunately, it looks like we'll be able to keep our matches up, too."

Mint (C): "What do you mean?"

Edgeworth (SG): "I'm talking about the outsourcing decision Marsha was considering. Fortunately, the analysis showed her that we should keep making our own gift boxes. So my department stays in business. And I won't have to consider a transfer. My wife's very happy about that, with the twins in middle school and all."

Mint (C): "Uh, Jack, I think there's something you need to know about."

Edgeworth (SG): "What's that?"

Mint (C): "I've been doing some preliminary studies using a technique called activity-based costing. I think it could improve our decision making in a lot of areas."

Edgeworth (SG): "So?"

Mint (C): "That outsourcing decision is one of the areas where I tried out the new ABC approach. I just finished the analysis yesterday. I was going to schedule an appointment with Marsha and you next week to discuss it."

Edgeworth (SG): "I'm getting queasy about where this is going, Jack. What did your analysis show?"

Mint (C): "It changes the conclusion—pretty dramatically, in fact. The ABC study shows that we'd save over $40,000 each year by outsourcing."

Edgeworth (SG): "Is that really all that much, Dave? Among friends, I mean?"

Mint (C): "It's not a trivial amount, Jack."

Edgeworth (SG): "Look, Dave, I don't think I've ever asked anything of you before. But can't you bury this one for me? Our family really doesn't need another move. And I've got people working for me who will probably lose their jobs. We've done a good job for the company. Our product is top notch. Nobody's ever complained about a thing."

Mint (C): "I don't see how I can withhold the analysis from Marsha, Jack. She has a right to all the information I have."

Edgeworth (SG): "But you said you were just doing preliminary studies, Dave. Marsha doesn't know anything about this one does she?"

Mint (C): "Not yet, Jack, but I've got a professional obligation to show it to her."

Edgeworth (SG): "You're opening a pandora's box, Dave. What about employee morale if you close my department? And what about product quality, and reliability of the supply?"

Mint (C): "Those are valid issues, Jack. But they need to be addressed on their own merits, in a full and open discussion."

Edgeworth (SG): "Could you at least share this so-called ABC study with me before you show it to Marsha? Maybe I'll see something you've missed."

Mint (C): "I don't see why not, Jack. Come by my office tomorrow morning—say about 10:00."

Identify any ethical issues you see in this scenario. How would you resolve them? What should the controller do?

Chapter Summary

The managerial accountant's key role in the decision-making process is to provide data relevant to the decision. Managers can then use these data in preparing a quantitative analysis of the decision. Qualitative factors are considered also in making the final decision.

In order to be relevant to a decision, a cost or benefit must: (1) bear on the future, and (2) differ under the various decision alternatives. Sunk costs, such as the book value of equipment or inventory, are not relevant in decisions. Such costs do not have any bearing on the future. Opportunity costs frequently are relevant to decisions, but they often are overlooked by decision makers. To analyze any special decision, the proper approach is to determine all of the costs and benefits that will differ among the alternatives.

Since decisions often are made under uncertainty, sensitivity analysis should be used to determine if the decision will change if various predictions prove to be wrong.

The concepts underlying a relevant-cost analysis remain valid in an advanced manufacturing environment and in situations where activity-based costing is used. However, an ABC system typically enables a decision maker to estimate the relevant costs in a decision problem more accurately.

Review Problem on Relevant Costs

Lansing Camera Company has received a special order for photographic equipment it does not normally produce. The company has excess capacity, and the order could be manufactured without reducing production of the firm's regular products. Discuss the relevance of each of the following items in computing the cost of the special order.

1. Equipment to be used in producing the order has a book value of $2,000. The equipment has no other use for Lansing Camera Company. If the order is not accepted, the equipment will be sold for $1,500. If the equipment is used in producing the order, it can be sold in three months for $800.
2. If the special order is accepted, the operation will require some of the storage space in the company's plant. If the space is used for this purpose, the company will rent storage space temporarily in a nearby warehouse at a cost of $18,000. The building depreciation allocated to the storage space to be used in producing the special order is $12,000.
3. If the special order is accepted, it will require a subassembly. Lansing Camera can purchase the subassembly for $24.00 per unit from an outside supplier or make it for $30.00 per unit. The $30.00 cost per unit was determined as follows:

Direct material	$10.00
Direct labor	6.00
Variable overhead	6.00
Allocated fixed overhead	8.00
Total unit cost of subassembly	$30.00

Solution to Review Problem

1. The book value of the equipment is a sunk cost, irrelevant to the decision. The relevant cost of the equipment is $700, determined as follows:

Sales value of equipment now	$1,500
Sales value after producing special order	800
Differential cost	$ 700

2. The $12,000 portion of building depreciation allocated to the storage space to be used for the special order is irrelevant. First, it is a sunk cost. Second, any costs relating to the company's factory building will continue whether the special order is accepted or not. The relevant cost is the $18,000 rent that will be incurred only if the special order is accepted.
3. Lansing Camera should make the subassembly. The subassembly's relevant cost is $22.00 per unit.

Relevant Cost of Making Subassembly (per unit)		Relevant Cost of Purchasing Subassembly (per unit)	
Direct material	$10.00	Purchase price	$24.00
Direct labor	6.00		
Variable overhead	6.00		
Total	$22.00		

Notice that the unitized fixed overhead, $8.00, is not a relevant cost of the subassembly. Lansing Camera Company's *total* fixed cost will not change, whether the special order is accepted or not.

Key Terms

For each term's definition refer to the indicated page, or turn to the glossary at the end of the text.

*Term appears in the appendix.

Appendix to Chapter 14

Linear Programming

LO 8

After completing the appendix, formulate a linear program to solve a product-mix problem with multiple constraints.

When a firm produces multiple products, management must decide how much of each output to produce. In most cases, the firm is limited in the total amount it can produce, due to constraints on resources such as machine time, direct labor, or raw materials. This situation is known as a *product-mix problem.*

To illustrate, we will use International Chocolate Company's Phoenix plant, which produces Chewies and Chompo Bars. Exhibit 14–21 provides data pertinent to the problem.

Linear programming is a powerful mathematical tool, well suited to solving International Chocolate Company's product-mix problem. The steps in constructing the linear program are as follows:

1. Identify the **decision variables,** which are the variables about which a decision must be made. International Chocolate's decision variables are as follows:

   Decision variables: X = Number of cases of Chewies to produce each month
   Y = Number of cases of Chompo Bars to produce each month

2. Write the **objective function,** which is an algebraic expression of the firm's goal. International Chocolate's goal is to *maximize its total contribution margin.* Since Chewies bring a contribution margin of $1 per case, and Chompos result in a contribution margin of $2 per case, the firm's objective function is the following:

   Objective function: Maximize $Z = X + 2Y$

	Chewies	Chompo Bars
Contribution margin per case	$1.00	$2.00
Machine hours per case	.02	.05
Direct-labor hours per case	.20	.25
	Machine Hours	**Direct-Labor Hours**
Limited resources: hours available per month	700	5,000

Exhibit 14–21
Data for Product-Mix Problem: International Chocolate Company

3. Write the **constraints,** which are algebraic expressions of the limitations faced by the firm, such as those limiting its productive resources. International Chocolate has a constraint for machine time and a constraint for direct labor.

Machine-time constraint	$.02X + .05Y \leq 700$
Labor-time constraint	$.20X + .25Y \leq 5{,}000$

Suppose, for example, that management decided to produce 20,000 cases of Chewies and 6,000 cases of Chompos. The machine-time constraint would appear as follows:

$$(.02)(20{,}000) + (.05)(6{,}000) = 700$$

Thus, at these production levels, the machine-time constraint would just be satisfied, with no machine hours to spare.

Graphical Solution

To understand how the linear program described above will help International Chocolate's management solve its product-mix problem, examine the graphs in Exhibit 14–22. The two colored lines in panel A represent the constraints. The colored arrows indicate that the production quantities, X and Y, must lie on or below these lines. Since the production quantities must be nonnegative, colored arrows also appear on the graphs' axes. Together, the axes and constraints form an area called the **feasible region,** in which the solution to the linear program must lie.

The black slanted line in panel A represents the objective function. Rearrange the objective function equation as follows:

$$Z = X + 2Y \longrightarrow Y = \frac{Z}{2} - \frac{1}{2}X$$

This form of the objective function shows that the slope of the equation is $-\frac{1}{2}$, which is the slope of the objective-function line in the exhibit. Management's goal is to maximize total contribution margin, denoted by Z. To achieve the maximum, the objective-function line must be moved as far outward and upward in the feasible region as possible, while maintaining the same slope. This goal is represented in panel A by the arrow which points outward from the objective-function line.

Solution The result of moving the objective-function line as far as possible in the indicated direction is shown in panel B of the exhibit. The objective-function line intersects the feasible region at exactly one point, where X equals 15,000 and Y equals 8,000. Thus, International Chocolate's optimal product mix is 15,000 cases of Chewies and 8,000 cases of Chompos per month. The total contribution margin is calculated as shown below.

$$\text{Total contribution margin} = (15{,}000)(\$1) + (8{,}000)(\$2) = \$31{,}000$$

Simplex Method and Sensitivity Analysis Although the graphical method is instructive, it is a cumbersome technique for solving a linear program. Fortunately, mathematicians have developed a more efficient solution method called the *simplex algorithm.* A computer can apply the algorithm to a complex linear program and determine the solution in seconds. In addition, most linear programming computer packages provide a sensitivity analysis of the problem. This analysis shows the decision maker the extent to which the estimates used in the objective function and constraints can change without changing the solution.

Managerial Accountant's Role

What is the managerial accountant's role in International Chocolate's product-mix decision? The production manager in the company's Phoenix plant makes this decision, with the help of a linear program. However, the linear program uses *information supplied by the managerial accountant.* The coefficients of X and Y in the objective function are unit contribution margins. Exhibit 14–14 shows that calculating these contribution margins requires estimates of direct-material, direct-labor, variable-overhead, and variable selling and administrative costs. These estimates were provided by a managerial accountant, along with estimates of the machine time and direct-labor time required to produce a case of Chewies or Chompos. All of these estimates were obtained from the standard-costing system, upon which the Phoenix plant's product costs are based. Thus, the managerial accountant makes the product-mix decision possible by providing the relevant cost data.

Exhibit 14–22
Product-Mix Problem Expressed as Linear Program: International Chocolate Company

A. Constraints, Feasible Region, and Objective Function

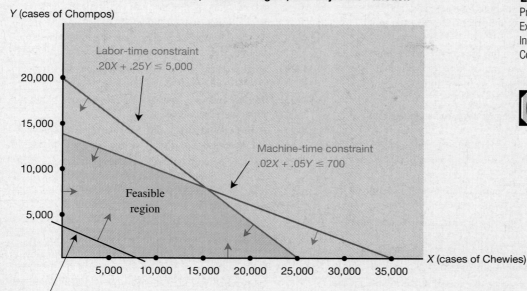

Y (cases of Chompos)
Labor-time constraint
$.20X + .25Y \leq 5{,}000$
Machine-time constraint
$.02X + .05Y \leq 700$
Feasible region
20,000
15,000
10,000
5,000
5,000 10,000 15,000 20,000 25,000 30,000 35,000
X (cases of Chewies)
Objective function:
$Z = X + 2Y$

B. Solution of Linear Program

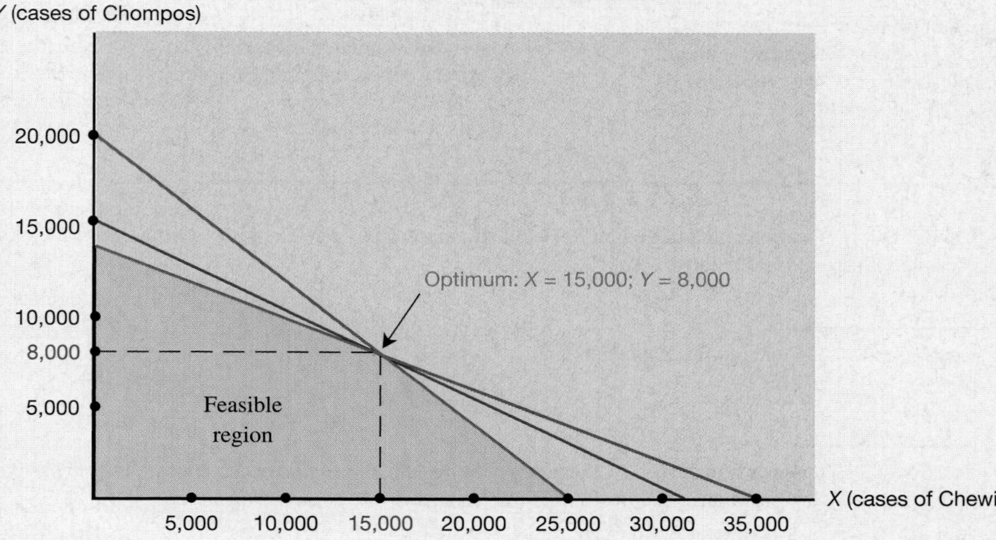

Linear programming is widely used in business decision making. Among the applications are blending in the petroleum and chemical industries, scheduling of personnel, railroad cars, and aircraft, and the mixing of ingredients in the food industry. In all of these applications, managerial accountants provide information crucial to the analysis.

Review Questions

14–1. List the six steps in the decision-making process.

14–2. Describe the managerial accountant's role in the decision-making process.

14–3. Distinguish between qualitative and quantitative decision analyses.

14–4. Explain what is meant by the term *decision model.*

14–5. A quantitative analysis enables a decision maker to put a "price" on the sum total of the qualitative characteristics in a decision situation. Explain this statement, and give an example.

14–6. What is meant by each of the following potential characteristics of information: relevant, accurate, and timely? Is objective information always relevant? Accurate?

14–7. List and explain two important criteria that must be satisfied in order for information to be relevant.

14–8. Explain why the book value of equipment is not a relevant cost.

14–9. Is the book value of inventory on hand a relevant cost? Why?

14–10. Why might a manager exhibit a behavioral tendency to inappropriately consider sunk costs in making a decision?

14–11. Give an example of an irrelevant future cost. Why is it irrelevant?

14–12. Define the term *opportunity cost,* and give an example of one.

14–13. What behavioral tendency do people often exhibit with regard to opportunity costs?

14–14. How does the existence of excess production capacity affect the decision to accept or reject a special order?

14–15. What is meant by the term *differential cost analysis?*

14–16. Briefly describe the proper approach for making a decision about adding or dropping a product line.

14–17. What is a *joint production process?* Describe a special decision that commonly arises in the context of a joint production process. Briefly describe the proper approach for making this type of decision.

14–18. Are allocated joint processing costs relevant when making a decision to sell a joint product at the split-off point or process it further? Why?

14–19. Briefly describe the proper approach to making a production decision when limited resources are involved.

14–20. What is meant by the term *contribution margin per unit of scarce resource?*

14–21. How is sensitivity analysis used to cope with uncertainty in decision making?

14–22. There is an important link between *decision making* and *managerial performance evaluation.* Explain.

14–23. List four potential pitfalls in decision making, which represent common errors.

14–24. Why can unitized fixed costs cause errors in decision making?

14–25. Give two examples of sunk costs, and explain why they are irrelevant in decision making.

14–26. "Accounting systems should produce only relevant data and forget about the irrelevant data. Then I'd know what was relevant and what wasn't!" Comment on this remark by a company president.

14–27. Are the concepts underlying a relevant-cost analysis still valid in an advanced manufacturing environment? Are these concepts valid when activity-based costing is used? Explain.

14–28. List five ways that management can seek to relax a constraint by expanding the capacity of a bottleneck operation.

Exercises

Exercise 14–29
Steps in Decision-Making Process
(LO 1)

Choose an organization and a particular decision situation. Then give examples, using that context, of each step illustrated in Exhibit 14–1.

Exercise 14–30
Irrelevant Future Costs and Benefits
(LO 3, 4)

Redo Exhibit 14–4 without the irrelevant data.

Exercise 14–31
Drop Product Line
(LO 4, 5)

Day Street Deli's owner is disturbed by the poor profit performance of his ice cream counter. He has prepared the following profit analysis for the year just ended.

Sales		$67,500
Less: Cost of food		30,000
Gross profit		$37,500
Less: Operating expenses:		
Wages of counter personnel	$18,000	
Paper products (e.g., napkins)	6,000	
Utilities (allocated)	4,350	
Depreciation of counter equipment and furnishings	3,750	
Depreciation of building (allocated)	6,000	
Deli manager's salary (allocated)	4,500	
Total		42,600
Loss on ice cream counter		$ (5,100)

Required: Criticize and correct the owner's analysis.

Exercise 14–32
Closing a Department
(LO 4, 5)

Toon Town Toy Company is considering the elimination of its Packaging Department. Management has received an offer from an outside firm to supply all Toon Town's packaging needs. To help her in making the decision, Toon Town's president has asked the controller for an analysis of the cost of running Toon Town's Packaging Department. Included in that analysis is $11,100 of rent, which represents the Packaging Department's allocation of the rent on Toon Town's factory building. If the Packaging Department is eliminated, the space it used will be converted to storage space. Currently Toon Town rents storage space in a nearby warehouse for $13,000 per year. The warehouse rental would no longer be necessary if the Packaging Department were eliminated.

Required:

1. Discuss each of the figures given in the exercise with regard to its relevance in the department-closing decision.
2. What type of cost is the $13,000 warehouse rental, from the viewpoint of the costs of the Packaging Department?

Exercise 14–33
Continuation of Preceding Exercise
(LO 4, 5)

If Toon Town Toy Company closes its Packaging Department, the department manager will be appointed manager of the Cutting Department. The Packaging Department manager makes $51,000 per year. To hire a new Cutting Department manager will cost Toon Town $66,000 per year.

Required: Discuss the relevance of each of these salary figures to the department-closing decision.

Exercise 14–34
Machine Replacement
(LO 4, 5)

College Town Pizza's owner bought his current pizza oven two years ago for $10,500, and it has one more year of life remaining. He is using straight-line depreciation for the oven. He could purchase a new oven for $2,200, but it would last only one year. The owner figures the new oven would save him $3,000 in annual operating expenses compared to operating the old one. Consequently, he has decided against buying the new oven, since doing so would result in a "loss" of $500 over the next year.

Required:

1. How do you suppose the owner came up with $500 as the loss for the next year if the new pizza oven were purchased? Explain.
2. Criticize the owner's analysis and decision.
3. Prepare a correct analysis of the owner's decision.

Exercise 14–35
Outsourcing Decision; Use of Internet
(LO 1, 2, 5)

Visit the website of one of the following companies, or a different company of your choosing.

Burger King	www.burgerking.com
Compaq	www.compaq.com
Corning	www.corning.com
Kmart	www.kmart.com
Kodak	www.kodak.com
NBC	www.nbc.com

Required: Read about the company's activities and operations. Choose an activity that is necessary for the company's operations, and then discuss the pros and cons of outsourcing that activity.

Exercise 14–36
Obsolete Inventory
(LO 4, 5)

Armstrong Corporation manufactures bicycle parts. The company currently has a $19,500 inventory of parts that have become obsolete due to changes in design specifications. The parts could be sold for $7,000, or modified for $10,000 and sold for $20,300.

Required:

1. Which of the data above are relevant to the decision about the obsolete parts?
2. Prepare an analysis of the decision.

Exercise 14–37
Joint Products
(LO 4, 6)

Thorpe Industries produces chemicals for the swimming pool industry. In one joint process, 10,000 gallons of GSX are processed into 7,000 gallons of xenolite and 3,000 gallons of banolide. The cost of the joint process, including the GSX, is $17,500. The firm allocates $11,800 of the joint cost to the xenolite and $5,700 of the cost to the banolide. The 3,000 gallons of banolide can be sold at the split-off point for

$3,500, or be processed further into a product called kitrocide. The sales value of 3,000 gallons of kitrocide is $11,000, and the additional processing cost is $7,900.

Required: Thorpe's president has asked your consulting firm to make a recommendation as to whether the banolide should be sold at the split-off point or processed further. Write a letter providing an analysis and a recommendation.

Exercise 14–38
Joint Products; Relevant Costs; Cost-Volume-Profit Analysis
(LO 4, 6)

Juarez Corporation produces cleaning compounds and solutions for industrial and household use. While most of its products are processed independently, a few are related. Grit 337, a coarse cleaning powder with many industrial uses, costs $3.20 a pound to make and sells for $4.00 a pound. A small portion of the annual production of this product is retained for further processing in the Mixing Department, where it is combined with several other ingredients to form a paste, which is marketed as a silver polish selling for $8.00 per jar. This further processing requires ¼ pound of Grit 337 per jar. Costs of other ingredients, labor, and variable overhead associated with this further processing amount to $5.00 per jar. Variable selling costs are $.60 per jar. If the decision were made to cease production of the silver polish, $11,200 of Mixing Department fixed costs could be avoided. Juarez has limited production capacity for Grit 337, but unlimited demand for the cleaning powder.

Required: Calculate the minimum number of jars of silver polish that would have to be sold to justify further processing of Grit 337.

(CMA, adapted)

Exercise 14–39
Special Order
(LO 4, 5)

Global Chemical Company, located in Buenos Aires, Argentina, recently received an order for a product it does not normally produce. Since the company has excess production capacity, management is considering accepting the order. In analyzing the decision, the assistant controller is compiling the relevant costs of producing the order. Production of the special order would require 8,000 kilograms of theolite. Global does not use theolite for its regular product, but the firm has 8,000 kilograms of the chemical on hand from the days when it used theolite regularly. The theolite could be sold to a chemical wholesaler for 21,750 *p*. The book value of the theolite is 3.00 *p* per kilogram. Global could buy theolite for 3.60 *p* per kilogram. (*p* denotes the peso, Argentina's national monetary unit. Many countries use the peso as their unit of currency. On the day this exercise was written, Argentina's peso was worth 1.0004 U.S. dollars.)

Required:

1. What is the relevant cost of theolite for the purpose of analyzing the special-order decision? (Remember to express your answer in terms of Argentina's peso.)
2. Discuss each of the numbers given in the exercise with regard to its relevance in making the decision.

Exercise 14–40
Continuation of Preceding Exercise
(LO 4, 5)

Global's special order also requires 1,000 kilograms of genatope, a solid chemical regularly used in the company's products. The current stock of genatope is 8,000 kilograms at a book value of 12.15 *p* per kilogram. If the special order is accepted, the firm will be forced to restock genatope earlier than expected, at a predicted cost of 13.05 *p* per kilogram. Without the special order, the purchasing manager predicts that the price will be 12.45 *p*, when normal restocking takes place. Any order of genatope must be in the amount of 5,000 kilograms.

Required:

1. What is the relevant cost of genatope?
2. Discuss each of the figures in the exercise in terms of its relevance to the decision.

Exercise 14–41
Limited Resource
(LO 6)

Plato Corporation manufactures two products, Alpha and Beta. Contribution margin data follow.

	Alpha	Beta
Unit sales price	$39.00	$93.00
Less variable cost:		
Direct material	$21.00	$15.00
Direct labor	3.00	18.00
Variable overhead	3.75	22.50
Variable selling and administrative cost	2.25	1.50

(continues)

Total variable cost	$30.00	$57.00
Unit contribution margin	$ 9.00	$36.00

Plato Corporation's production process uses highly skilled labor, which is in short supply. The same employees work on both products and earn the same wage rate.

Required: Which of Plato Corporation's products is most profitable? Explain.

Exercise 14–42
Linear Programming (Appendix)
(LO 6, 8)

Refer to the data given in the preceding exercise for Plato Corporation. Assume that the direct-labor rate is $12 per hour, and 11,000 labor hours are available per year. In addition, the company has a short supply of machine time. Only 9,000 hours are available each year. Alpha requires one machine hour per unit, and Beta requires two machine hours per unit.

Required: Formulate the production planning problem as a linear program. Specifically identify (1) the decision variables, (2) the objective function, and (3) the constraints.

Exercise 14–43
Linear Programming; Formulate and Solve Graphically (Appendix)
(LO 8)

New Jersey Chemical Company manufactures two industrial chemical products, called zanide and kreolite. Two machines are used in the process, and each machine has 24 hours of capacity per day. The following data are available:

	Zanide	Kreolite
Selling price per drum	$108	$126
Variable cost per drum	$ 84	$ 84
Hours required per drum on machine I	2 hr.	2 hr.
Hours required per drum on machine II	1 hr.	3 hr.

The company can produce and sell partially full drums of each chemical. For example, a half drum of zanide sells for $54.

Required:

1. Formulate the product-mix problem as a linear program.
2. Solve the problem graphically.
3. What is the value of the objective function at the optimal solution?

Problems

Problem 14–44
Closing an Unprofitable Department
(LO 4, 5)

Contemporary Trends sells paint and paint supplies, carpet, and wallpaper at a single-store location in suburban Baltimore. Although the company has been very profitable over the years, management has seen a significant decline in wallpaper sales and earnings. Much of this decline is attributable to the Internet and to companies that advertise deeply discounted prices in magazines and offer customers free shipping and toll-free telephone numbers. Recent figures follow.

	Paint and Supplies	Carpeting	Wallpaper
Sales	$190,000	$230,000	$70,000
Variable costs	$114,000	$161,000	$56,000
Fixed costs	28,000	37,500	22,500
Total costs	$142,000	$198,500	$78,500
Operating income (loss)	$ 48,000	$ 31,500	$ (8,500)

Management is studying whether to drop wallpaper because of the changing market and accompanying loss. If the line is dropped, the following changes are expected to occur:

- The vacated space will be remodeled at a cost of $6,200 and will be devoted to an expanded line of high-end carpet. Sales of carpet are expected to increase by $60,000, and the line's overall contribution margin ratio will rise by five percentage points.
- Contemporary Trends can cut wallpaper's fixed costs by 40 percent. Remaining fixed costs will continue to be incurred.

- Customers who purchased wallpaper often bought paint and paint supplies. Sales of paint and paint supplies are expected to fall by 20 percent.
- The firm will increase advertising expenditures by $12,500 to promote the expanded carpet line.

Required:

1. Should Contemporary Trends close its wallpaper operation? Show your computations.
2. Assume that Contemporary Trends' wallpaper inventory at the time of the closure decision amounted to $11,850. How would you have treated this additional information in making the decision?
3. What advantages might Internet- and magazine-based firms have over Contemporary Trends that would allow these organizations to offer deeply discounted prices—prices far below what Contemporary Trends can offer?

Problem 14–45
Add a Product Line
(LO 4, 5)

Golden Gate Fashions, Inc. a high-fashion dress manufacturer, is planning to market a new cocktail dress for the coming season. Golden Gate Fashions supplies retailers primarily on the west coast.

Four yards of material are required to lay out the dress pattern. Some material remains after cutting, which can be sold as remnants. The leftover material also could be used to manufacture a matching handbag and an accessory cape to be worn about the shoulders. However, if the leftover material is to be used for the cape and handbag, more care will be required in the cutting operation, which will increase the cutting costs.

The company expects to sell 1,250 dresses. Market research reveals that dress sales will be 20 percent higher if a matching cape and handbag are available. The market research indicates that the cape and handbag will be salable only as accessories with the dress. The combination of dresses, capes, and handbags expected to be sold by retailers are as follows:

	Percent of Total
Complete sets of dress, handbag, and accessory cape	70%
Dress and accessory cape	6
Dress and handbag	15
Dress only	9
Total	100%

The material used in the dress costs $20.00 a yard or $80.00 for each dress. The cost of cutting the dress if the accessory cape and handbag are not manufactured is estimated at $32.00 a dress, and the resulting remnants can be sold for $8.00 per dress. If the accessory cape and handbag are manufactured, the cutting costs will be increased by $14.40 per dress and there will be no salable remnants. The selling prices and the costs to complete the three items once they are cut are as follows:

	Selling Price per Unit	Unit Cost to Complete (excludes costs of material and cutting operation)
Dress	$320.00	$128.00
Accessory cape	44.00	31.20
Handbag	15.20	10.40

Required:

1. Calculate Golden Gate Fashions' incremental profit or loss from manufacturing the accessory capes and handbags in conjunction with the dresses.
2. Identify any qualitative factors that could influence the company's management in its decision to manufacture accessory capes and handbags to match the dresses.

(CMA, adapted)

Problem 14–46
Production Decisions; Limited Capacity
(LO 5, 6)

Chef Gourmet, Inc. has assembled the following data pertaining to its two most popular products.

	Blender	Food Processor
Direct material	$18	$ 33
Direct labor	12	27

(continues)

Manufacturing overhead @ $48 per machine hour	48	96
Cost if purchased from an outside supplier	60	114
Annual demand (units)	20,000	28,000

Past experience has shown that the fixed manufacturing overhead component included in the cost per machine hour averages $30. Management has a policy of filling all sales orders, even if it means purchasing units from outside suppliers.

Required:

1. If 50,000 machine hours are available, and management desires to follow an optimal strategy, how many units of each product should the firm manufacture? How many units of each product should be purchased?
2. With all other things constant, if management is able to reduce the direct material for a food processor to $18 per unit, how many units of each product should be manufactured? Purchased?

(CMA, adapted)

Problem 14–47
Outsource a Component; Relevant Costs, Opportunity Costs, and Quality Control
(LO 3, 4, 5)

Dentech, Inc. uses 10 units of part RM67 each month in the production of dentistry equipment. The cost of manufacturing one unit of RM67 is the following:

Direct material	$ 3,000
Material handling (20% of direct-material cost)	600
Direct labor	24,000
Manufacturing overhead (150% of direct labor)	36,000
Total manufacturing cost	$63,600

Material handling represents the direct variable costs of the Receiving Department that are applied to direct materials and purchased components on the basis of their cost. This is a separate charge in addition to manufacturing overhead. Dentech's annual manufacturing overhead budget is one-third variable and two-thirds fixed. Scott Supply, one of Dentech's reliable vendors, has offered to supply part number RM67 at a unit price of $45,000.

Required:

1. If Dentech purchases the RM67 units from Scott, the capacity Dentech used to manufacture these parts would be idle. Should Dentech decide to purchase the parts from Scott, the unit cost of RM67 would increase (or decrease) by what amount?
2. Assume Dentech is able to rent out all its idle capacity for $75,000 per month. If Dentech decides to purchase the 10 units from Scott Supply, Dentech's monthly cost for RM67 would increase (or decrease) by what amount?
3. Assume that Dentech does not wish to commit to a rental agreement but could use its idle capacity to manufacture another product that would contribute $156,000 per month. If Dentech's management elects to manufacture RM67 in order to maintain quality control, what is the net amount of Dentech's cost from using the space to manufacture part RM67?

(CMA, adapted)

Problem 14–48
Make or Buy
(LO 4, 5)

Cincinnati Flow Technology (CFT) has purchased 10,000 pumps annually from Kobec, Inc. Because the price keeps increasing and reached $102.00 per unit last year, CFT's management has asked for an estimate of the cost of manufacturing the pump in CFT's facilities. CFT makes stampings and castings and has little experience with products requiring assembly.

The engineering, manufacturing, and accounting departments have prepared a report for management which includes the following estimate for an assembly run of 10,000 pumps. Additional production employees would be hired to manufacture the pumps but no additional equipment, space, or supervision would be needed.

The report states that total costs for 10,000 units are estimated at $1,435,500 or $143.55 per unit. The current purchase price is $102.00 per unit, so the report recommends continued purchase of the product.

Components (outside purchases)	$ 180,000
Assembly labor*	450,000

(continues)

(concluded)

Manufacturing overhead†	675,000
General and administrative overhead‡	130,500
Total costs	$1,435,500

*Assembly labor consists of hourly production workers.

†Manufacturing overhead is applied to products on a direct-labor-dollar basis. Variable-overhead costs vary closely with direct-labor dollars.

Fixed overhead	50% of direct-labor dollars
Variable overhead	100% of direct-labor dollars
Manufacturing-overhead rate	150% of direct-labor dollars

‡General and administrative overhead is applied at 10 percent of the total cost of material (or components), assembly labor, and manufacturing overhead.

Required: Was the analysis prepared by Cincinnati Flow Technology's engineering, manufacturing, and accounting departments and their recommendation to continue purchasing the pumps correct? Explain your answer and include any supporting calculations you consider necessary.

(CMA, adapted)

Problem 14–49
Introducing a New Product
(LO 4, 5)

Martinez, Inc. is a small firm involved in the production and sale of electronic business products. The company is well known for its attention to quality and innovation.

During the past 15 months, a new product has been under development that allows users handheld access to e-mail and video images. Martinez named the product the Wireless Wizard and has been quietly designing two models: Standard and Enhanced. Development costs have amounted to $181,500 and $262,500, respectively. The total market demand for each model is expected to be 40,000 units, and management anticipates being able to obtain the following market shares: Standard, 25 percent; Enhanced, 20 percent. Forecasted data follow.

	Standard	Enhanced
Projected selling price	$375.00	$495.00
Production costs per unit:		
Direct material	42.00	67.50
Direct labor	22.50	30.00
Variable overhead	36.00	48.00
Fixed overhead	54.00	72.00
Marketing and advertising per product line	195,000	300,000
Sales salaries per product line	85,500	85,500
Sales commissions*	10%	10%

*Computed on the basis of sales dollars.

Since the start of development work on the Wireless Wizard, advances in technology have altered the market somewhat, and management now believes that the company can introduce only one of the two models. Consultants confirmed this fact not too long ago, with Martinez paying $34,500 for an in-depth market study.

Required:

1. Compute the per-unit contribution margin for both models.
2. Which of the data above should be ignored in making the product-introduction decision? For what reason?
3. Prepare a financial analysis and determine which of the two models should be introduced.
4. What other factors should Martinez consider before a final decision is made?

Problem 14–50
Excess Production Capacity
(LO 5, 6)

Handy Dandy Tools Company manufactures electric carpentry tools. The Production Department has met all production requirements for the current month and has an opportunity to produce additional units of product with its excess capacity. Unit selling prices and unit costs for three different saw models are as follows:

	Basic Model	Deluxe Model	Pro Model
Selling price	$116	$130	$160
Direct material	32	40	38

(continues)

Direct labor ($20 per hour)	20	30	40
Variable overhead	16	24	32
Fixed overhead	32	10	30

Variable overhead is applied on the basis of direct-labor dollars, while fixed overhead is applied on the basis of machine hours. There is sufficient demand for the additional production of any model in the product line.

Required:

1. If the company has excess machine capacity and can add more labor as needed (i.e., neither machine capacity nor labor is a constraint), the excess production capacity should be devoted to producing which product? (Assume that the excess capacity will be used for a single product line.)
2. If the company has excess machine capacity but a limited amount of labor time, the excess production capacity should be devoted to producing which product or products?

(CMA, adapted)

Problem 14–51
Special Order; Financial and Production Considerations
(LO 4, 5)

Mercury Skateboard Company manufactures skateboards. Several weeks ago, the firm received a special-order inquiry from Venus, Inc. Venus desires to market a skateboard similar to one of Mercury's and has offered to purchase 11,000 units if the order can be completed in three months. The cost data for Mercury's Champion model skateboard follow.

Direct material	$16.40
Direct labor: .25 hours at $18.00	4.50
Total manufacturing overhead:	
.5 machine hours at $40.00	20.00
Total	$40.90

The following additional information is available.

- The normal selling price of the Champion model is $53.00; however, Venus has offered Mercury only $31.50 because of the large quantity it is willing to purchase.
- Venus requires a modification of the design that will allow a $4.20 reduction in direct-material cost.
- Mercury's production supervisor notes that the company will incur $7,400 in additional setup costs and will have to purchase a $4,800 special device to manufacture these units. The device will be discarded once the special order is completed.
- Total manufacturing overhead costs are applied to production at the rate of $40 per machine hour. This figure is based, in part, on budgeted yearly fixed overhead of $1,500,000 and planned production activity of 60,000 machine hours (5,000 per month).
- Mercury will allocate $3,600 of existing fixed administrative costs to the order as ". . . part of the cost of doing business."

Required:

1. Assume that present sales will not be affected. Should the order be accepted from a financial point of view (i.e., is it profitable)? Why? Show calculations.
2. Assume that Mercury's current production activity consumes 70 percent of planned machine-hour activity. Can the company accept the order and meet Venus' deadline?
3. What options might Mercury consider if management truly wanted to do business with Venus in hopes of building a long-term relationship with the firm?

Problem 14–52
Special Order; Ethics
(LO 3, 5)

Treasure Island Beach Equipment, Inc. manufactures deluxe beach cabanas in Tampa, Florida. Its manufacturing plant has the capacity to produce 2,500 cabanas each month. Current monthly production is 1,875 cabanas. The company normally charges $525 per cabana. Variable costs and fixed costs for the current activity level of 75 percent of capacity are shown in the table on the next page.

Management has just received a special one-time order for 625 cabanas at $300 per cabana. For this particular order, no variable marketing costs will be incurred. Samantha Peters, the assistant controller, has been assigned the task of analyzing this order and recommending whether the company should accept or reject it. After examining the costs Peters suggested to her supervisor, Katie Maas, who is the controller, that they request competitive bids from vendors for the raw material as the current quote seems high. Maas insisted that the prices are in line with other vendors and told her that she was not to discuss her observations with anyone else. Peters later discovered that Maas is a sister-in-law of the owner of the current raw-material supply vendor.

Current Product Costs (at 75% of Capacity)

Variable costs:	
Manufacturing:	
Direct labor	$281,250
Direct material	196,875
Marketing	140,625
Total variable costs	$618,750
Fixed costs:	
Manufacturing	$206,250
Marketing	131,250
Total fixed costs	$337,500
Total costs	$956,250
Variable cost per unit	$330
Fixed cost per unit	180
Average unit cost	$510

Required:

1. Identify and explain the costs that will be relevant to Peters' analysis of the special order being considered by Treasure Island Beach Equipment, Inc.
2. Determine if management should accept the special order. In explaining your answer, compute the new average unit cost for (*a*) current monthly production alone; (*b*) the special order alone; and (*c*) total combined production.
3. Discuss any other considerations that Peters should include in her analysis of the special order.
4. What steps could Peters take to resolve the ethical conflict arising out of the controller's insistence that the company avoid competitive bidding.

(CMA, adapted)

Problem 14–53
Outsourcing Decision; Relevant Costs; Ethics
(LO 3, 4, 5)

Palisades Corporation's Midwest Division manufactures subassemblies that are used in the corporation's final products. Lynn Hardt of Midwest's Profit Planning Department has been assigned the task of determining whether a component, JY–65, should continue to be manufactured by Midwest or purchased from Marley Company, an outside supplier. JY–65 is part of a subassembly manufactured by Midwest.

Marley has submitted a bid to manufacture and supply the 32,000 units of JY–65 that Palisades will need for 20x1 at a unit price of $8.65. Marley has assured Palisades that the units will be delivered according to Palisades' production specifications and needs. While the contract price of $8.65 is only applicable in 20x1, Marley is interested in entering into a long-term arrangement beyond 20x1.

Hardt has gathered the following information regarding Midwest's cost to manufacture JY–65 in 20x0. These annual costs will be incurred to manufacture 30,000 units.

Direct material	$ 97,500
Direct labor	60,000
Factory space rental	42,000
Equipment leasing costs	18,000
Other manufacturing overhead	112,500
Total manufacturing costs	$330,000

Hardt has collected the following additional information related to manufacturing JY–65.

- Direct materials used in the production of JY–65 are expected to increase 8 percent in 20x1.
- Midwest's direct-labor contract calls for a 5 percent increase in 20x1.
- The facilities used to manufacture JY–65 are rented under a month-to-month rental agreement. Thus, Midwest can withdraw from the rental agreement without any penalty. Midwest will have no need for this space if JY–65 is not manufactured.

- Equipment leasing costs represent special equipment that is used in the manufacture of JY–65. This lease can be terminated by paying the equivalent of one month's lease payment for each year left on the lease agreement. Midwest has two years left on the lease agreement, through the end of the year 20x2.
- Forty percent of the other manufacturing overhead is considered variable. Variable overhead changes with the number of units produced, and this rate per unit is not expected to change in 20x1. The fixed manufacturing overhead costs are not expected to change regardless of whether JY–65 is manufactured. Equipment other than the leased equipment can be used in Midwest's other manufacturing operations.

John Porter, divisional manager of Midwest, stopped by Hardt's office to voice his concern regarding the outsourcing of JY–65. Porter commented, "I am really concerned about outsourcing JY–65. I have a son-in-law and a nephew, not to mention a member of our bowling team, who work on JY–65. They could lose their jobs if we buy that component from Marley. I really would appreciate anything you can do to make sure the cost analysis comes out right to show we should continue making JY–65. Corporate is not aware of the material increases and maybe you can leave out some of those fixed costs. I just think we should continue making JY–65!"

Required:

1. **a.** Prepare an analysis of relevant costs that shows whether or not the Midwest Division of Palisades Corporation should make JY–65 or purchase it from Marley Company for 20x1.
   b. Based solely on the financial results, recommend whether the 32,000 units of JY–65 for 20x1 should be made by Midwest or purchased from Marley.
2. Identify and briefly discuss three qualitative factors that the Midwest Division and Palisades Corporation should consider before agreeing to purchase JY–65 from Marley Company.
3. By referring to the standards of ethical conduct for managerial accountants given in Chapter 1, explain why Lynn Hardt would consider the request of John Porter to be unethical.

(CMA, adapted)

Problem 14–54
Outsourcing Decision
(LO 4, 5)

PennTech Corporation has been producing two precision bearings, components T79 and B81, for use in production in its central Pennsylvania plant. Data regarding these two components follow.

	T79	B81
Machine hours required per unit	2.5	3.0
Standard cost per unit:		
Direct material	$ 6.75	$11.25
Direct labor	12.00	13.50
Manufacturing overhead		
Variable*	6.00	6.75
Fixed†	11.25	13.50
Total	$36.00	$45.00

*Variable manufacturing overhead is applied on the basis of direct-labor hours.
†Fixed manufacturing overhead is applied on the basis of machine hours.

PennTech's annual requirement for these components is 8,000 units of T79 and 11,000 units of B81. Recently, management decided to devote additional machine time to other product lines, leaving only 41,000 machine hours per year for producing the bearings. An outside company has offered to sell PennTech its annual supply of bearings at prices of $33.75 for T79 and $40.50 for B81. Management wants to schedule the otherwise idle 41,000 machine hours to produce bearings so that the firm can minimize costs (maximize net benefits).

Required:

1. Compute the net benefit (loss) per machine hour that would result if PennTech Corporation accepts the supplier's offer of $40.50 per unit for component B81.
2. Choose the correct answer. PennTech Corporation will maximize its net benefits by:
   a. Purchasing 4,800 units of T79 and manufacturing the remaining bearings.
   b. Purchasing 8,000 units of T79 and manufacturing 11,000 units of B81.

c. Purchasing 11,000 units of B81 and manufacturing 8,000 units of T79.

d. Purchasing 4,000 units of B81 and manufacturing the remaining bearings.

e. Purchasing and manufacturing some amounts other than those given above.

3. Suppose management has decided to drop product T79. Independently of requirements (1) and (2), assume that the company's idle capacity of 41,000 machine hours has a traceable, avoidable annual fixed cost of $132,000, which will be incurred only if the capacity is used. Calculate the maximum price PennTech Corporation should pay a supplier for component B81.

(CMA, adapted)

Problem 14–55
Joint Products; Sell or Process Further
(LO 6)

Milwaukee Specialty Chemical Company (MSCC) is a diversified chemical processing company. The firm manufactures swimming pool chemicals, chemicals for metal processing, specialized chemical compounds, and pesticides.

Currently, the Noorwood plant is producing two derivatives, RNA–1 and RNA–2, from the chemical compound VDB developed by the company's research labs. Each week 1,200,000 pounds of VDB are processed at a cost of $393,600 into 800,000 pounds of RNA–1 and 400,000 pounds of RNA–2. The proportion of these two outputs cannot be altered, because this is a joint process. RNA–1 has no market value until it is converted into a pesticide with the trade name Fastkil. Processing RNA–1 into Fastkil costs $384,000. Fastkil wholesales at $80 per 100 pounds.

RNA–2 is sold as is for $128 per hundred pounds. However, management has discovered that RNA–2 can be converted into two new products by adding 400,000 pounds of compound LST to the 400,000 pounds of RNA–2. This joint process would yield 400,000 pounds each of DMZ–3 and Pestrol, the two new products. The additional direct-material and related processing costs of this joint process would be $192,000. DMZ–3 and Pestrol would each be sold for $92.00 per 100 pounds. The company's management has decided not to process RNA–2 further based on the analysis presented in the following schedule.

		Process Further		
	RNA–2	**DMZ–3**	**Pestrol**	**Total**
Production in pounds	400,000	400,000	400,000	
Revenue	$512,000	$368,000	$368,000	$736,000
Costs:				
VDB costs	$131,200*	$ 98,400	$ 98,400	$196,800†
Additional direct materials (LST) and processing of RNA–2	—	96,000	96,000	192,000
Total costs	$131,200	$194,400	$194,400	$388,800
Weekly gross profit	$380,800	$173,600	$173,600	$347,200

*$131,200 is one-third of the $393,600 cost of processing VDB. When RNA–2 is not processed further, one-third of the final output is RNA–2 (400,000 out of a total of 1,200,000 pounds).

†$196,800 is one-half of the $393,600 cost of processing VDB. When RNA–2 is processed further, one-half of the final output consists of DMZ–3 and Pestrol. The final products then are: 800,000 pounds of RNA–1; 400,000 pounds of DMZ–3; and 400,000 pounds of Pestrol.

Required: Evaluate MSCC's management's analysis, and make any revisions that are necessary. Your critique and analysis should indicate:

a. Whether management made the correct decision.

b. The gross savings or loss per week resulting from the decision not to process RNA–2 further, if different from management's analysis.

(CMA, adapted)

Problem 14–56
Conventional versus Activity-Based-Costing Analyses; Relevant Costs
(LO 5, 7)

In addition to fine chocolate, International Chocolate Company also produces chocolate-covered pretzels in its Savannah plant. This product is sold in five-pound metal canisters, which also are manufactured at the Savannah facility. The plant manager, Marsha Mello, was recently approached by Catawba Canister Company with an offer to supply the canisters at a price of $.95 each. International Chocolate's traditional product-costing system assigns the following costs to canister production.

Direct material	$ 288,000
Direct labor (12,000 hr. at $16 per hr.)	192,000
Variable overhead ($10 per direct-labor hr.)	120,000

(continues)

Fixed overhead ($45 per direct-labor hr.)	540,000
Total cost	$1,140,000

Unit costs: $1,140,000 ÷ 760,000 canisters = $1.50 per canister

Mello's conventional make-or-buy analysis indicated that Catawba's offer should be rejected, since only $708,000 of costs would be avoided (including $80,000 of supervisory salaries and $28,000 of machinery depreciation). In contrast, the firm would spend $722,000 buying the canisters. The controller, Dave Mint, came to the rescue with an activity-based costing analysis of the decision. Mint concluded that the cost-driver levels associated with canister production are as follows:

10 product specs	30 inspections
2,000 supervisory hours	15 setups
6,000 material-handling hours	70,000 machine hours
55 purchase orders	

Additional conventional and ABC data from the Savannah plant are given in Exhibits 14–19 and 14–20 on pages 605 and 606.

Required:

1. Show how Mello arrived at the $708,000 of cost savings in her conventional make-or-buy analysis.
2. Determine the costs that will be saved by purchasing canisters, using Mint's ABC data.
3. Complete the ABC relevant-costing analysis of the make-or-buy decision. Should the firm buy from Catawba?
4. If the conventional and ABC analyses yield different conclusions, briefly explain why.

Problem 14–57
Analysis of Special Order
(LO 4, 5)

Excalibur, Inc. received an order for a piece of special machinery from Rex Company. Just as Excalibur completed the machine, Rex Company declared bankruptcy, defaulted on the order, and forfeited the 10 percent deposit paid on the selling price of $217,500.

Excalibur's manufacturing manager identified the costs already incurred in the production of the special machinery for Rex Company as follows:

Direct material		$ 49,800
Direct labor		64,200
Manufacturing overhead applied:		
Variable	$32,100	
Fixed	16,050	48,150
Fixed selling and administrative costs		16,215
Total		$178,365

Another company, Kaytell Corporation, will buy the special machinery if it is reworked to Kaytell's specifications. Excalibur, Inc. offered to sell the reworked machinery to Kaytell as a special order for $205,200. Kaytell agreed to pay the price when it takes delivery in two months. The additional identifiable costs to rework the machinery to Kaytell's specifications are as follows:

Direct materials	$18,600
Direct labor	12,600
Total	$31,200

A second alternative available to Excalibur's management is to convert the special machinery to the standard model, which sells for $187,500. The additional identifiable costs for this conversion are as follows:

Direct materials	$ 8,550
Direct labor	9,900
Total	$18,450

A third alternative for Excalibur, Inc. is to sell the machine as is for a price of $156,000. However, the potential buyer of the unmodified machine does not want it for 60 days. This buyer has offered a $21,000 down payment, with the remainder due upon delivery.

The following additional information is available regarding Excalibur's operations.

- The allocation rates for manufacturing overhead and fixed selling and administrative costs are:

Manufacturing costs:	
Variable	50% of direct-labor cost
Fixed	25% of direct-labor cost
Fixed selling and administrative costs	10% of the total of direct-material, direct-labor, and manufacturing-overhead costs

- The sales commission rate on sales of standard models is 2 percent, while the rate on special orders is 3 percent.
- Normal credit terms for sales of standard models are 2/10, net/30. This means that a customer receives a 2 percent discount if payment is made within 10 days, and payment is due no later than 30 days after billing. Most customers take the 2 percent discount. Credit terms for a special order are negotiated with the customer.
- Normal time required for rework is one month.

Required:

1. Determine the dollar contribution each of the three alternatives will add to Excalibur's before-tax profit.
2. If Kaytell makes Excalibur a counteroffer, what is the lowest price Excalibur should accept for the reworked machinery from Kaytell? Explain your answer.
3. Discuss the influence fixed manufacturing-overhead cost should have on the sales price quoted by Excalibur, Inc. for special orders.

(CMA, adapted)

Problem 14–58
Production Planning
(LO 5, 6)

Oceana Corporation manufactures and sells three products, which are manufactured in a factory with four departments. Both labor and machine time are applied to the products as they pass through each department. The machines and labor skills required in each department are so specialized that neither machines nor labor can be switched from one department to another.

Inventory levels are satisfactory and need not be increased or decreased during the next six months. Unit price and cost data that will be valid for the next six months are as follows:

	Product		
	M50	T79	B81
Unit costs:			
Direct material	$ 28	$ 52	$ 68
Direct labor:			
Department 1	48	24	48
Department 2	84	56	56
Department 3	96	—	64
Department 4	36	72	36
Variable overhead	108	80	100
Fixed overhead	60	40	128
Variable selling expenses	12	8	16
Unit selling price	784	492	668

Oceana Corporation's management is planning its production schedule for the next few months. The planning is complicated, because there are labor shortages in the community and some machines will be down several months for repairs.

The sales department believes that the monthly demand for the next six months will be as follows:

Product	Monthly Unit Sales
M50	500
T79	400
B81	1,000

Management has assembled the following information regarding available machine and labor time by department and the machine hours and direct-labor hours required per unit of product. These data should be valid for the next six months.

		Department			
Monthly Capacity Availability		**1**	**2**	**3**	**4**
Normal machine capacity in machine hours		3,500	3,500	3,000	3,500
Capacity of machines being repaired in machine hours		(500)	(400)	(300)	(200)
Available machine capacity in machine hours		3,000	3,100	2,700	3,300
Available labor in direct-labor hours		3,700	4,500	2,750	2,600
Labor and Machine Specifications per Unit of Product					
Product	**Labor and Machine Time**				
M50	Direct-labor hours	2	3	3	1
	Machine hours	1	1	2	2
T79	Direct-labor hours	1	2	—	2
	Machine hours	1	1	—	2
B81	Direct-labor hours	2	2	2	1
	Machine hours	2	2	1	1

Required:

1. Calculate the monthly requirement for machine hours and direct-labor hours for the production of products M50, T79, and B81 to determine whether the monthly sales demand for the three products can be met by the factory.
2. What monthly production schedule should Oceana's management select in order to maximize its dollar profits? Explain how you selected this production schedule, and present a schedule of the contribution to profit that would be generated by your production schedule.
3. Identify the alternatives management might consider so it can supply its customers with all the product they demand.

(CMA, adapted)

Problem 14–59
Linear Programming (Appendix)
(LO 8)

Time Saver Meals, Inc. offers monthly service plans providing prepared meals that are delivered to the customers' homes. The target market for these meal plans includes double-income families with no children and retired couples in upper income brackets. The firm offers two monthly plans: Premier Cuisine and Haute Cuisine. The Premier Cuisine plan provides frozen meals that are delivered twice each month; this plan generates a contribution margin of $60 for each monthly plan sold. The Haute Cuisine plan provides freshly prepared meals delivered on a daily basis and generates a contribution margin of $45 for each monthly plan sold. The company's reputation provides a market that will purchase all the meals that can be prepared. All meals go through food preparation and cooking steps in the company's kitchens. After these steps, the Premier Cuisine meals are flash frozen. The time requirements per monthly meal plan and hours available per month are as follows:

	Preparation	Cooking	Freezing
Hours required:			
Premier Cuisine	2	2	1
Haute Cuisine	1	3	0
Hours available	60	120	45

For planning purposes, management uses linear programming to determine the most profitable number of Premier Cuisine and Haute Cuisine monthly meal plans to produce.

Required:

1. Using the notation P for Premier Cuisine and H for Haute Cuisine, state the objective function and the constraints that management should use to maximize the total contribution margin generated by the monthly meal plans.
2. Graph the constraints on the meal preparation process. Be sure to clearly label the graph.
3. Using the graph prepared in requirement (2), determine the optimal solution to the company's production planning problem in terms of the number of each type of meal plan to produce.
4. Calculate the value of the objective function at the optimal solution.
5. If the constraint on preparation time could be eliminated, determine the revised optimal solution.

(CMA, adapted)

Problem 14–60
Linear Programming; Formulate and Solve Graphically (Appendix)
(LO 8)

Galaxy Candy Company manufactures two popular candy bars, the Eclipse bar and the Nova bar. Both candy bars go through a mixing operation where the various ingredients are combined, and the Coating Department where the bars from the Mixing Department are coated with chocolate. The Eclipse bar is coated with both white and dark chocolate to produce a swirled effect. A material shortage of an ingredient in the Nova bar limits production to 300 batches per day. Production and sales data are presented in the following table. Both candy bars are produced in batches of 200 bars.

		Use of Capacity in Hours per Batch of Product	
Department	**Available Daily Capacity in Hours**	**Eclipse**	**Nova**
Mixing	525	1.5	1.5
Coating	500	2.0	1.0

Management believes that Galaxy can sell all of its daily production of both the Eclipse and Nova bars. Other data follow.

	Eclipse	Nova
Selling price per batch	$ 600	$ 700
Variable cost per batch	200	450
Monthly fixed costs (allocated evenly between both products)	750,000	750,000

Required:

1. Formulate the objective function and all of the constraints in order to maximize contribution margin. Be sure to define the variables.
2. How many batches of each type of candy bar (Eclipse and Nova) should be produced to maximize the total contribution margin?
3. Calculate the contribution margin at the optimal solution

(CMA, adapted)

Problem 14–61
Linear Programming; Formulate and Discuss (Appendix)
(LO 8)

CoffeeTime, Inc. manufactures two types of electric coffeemakers, Regular and Deluxe. The major difference between the two appliances is capacity. Both are considered top-quality units and sell for premium prices. Both coffeemakers pass through two manufacturing departments: Plating and Assembly. The company has two assembly operations, one automated and one manual. The Automated Assembly Department has been in operation for one year and was intended to replace the Labor Assembly Department. However, business has expanded rapidly in recent months, and both assembly operations are still being used. Workers have been trained for both operations and can be used in either department. The only difference between the two departments is the proportion of machine time versus direct labor used. Data regarding the two coffeemakers are presented in the following schedules.

Machine-Hour Data

	Plating	Labor Assembly	Automated Assembly
Machine hours required per unit	.15	.02	.05
Machine hours available per month	25,000	1,500	5,000
Annual machine hours available	300,000	18,000	60,000

Unit Variable Manufacturing Costs

	Plating Department		Labor Assembly	Automated Assembly
	Regular	**Deluxe**		
Raw material:				
Casing	$15.50	$29.00	—	—
Heating element	12.00	12.00	—	—
Other	16.50	16.50	—	—
Direct labor:				
At $20 per hour	4.00	4.00	—	—
At $24 per hour	—	—	$6.00	$1.20
Manufacturing overhead:				
Supplies	2.50	2.50	3.00	3.00
Power	2.40	2.40	1.50	3.60

Sales Data

	Regular Model	Deluxe Model
Selling price per unit	$ 90.00	$ 120.00
Variable selling cost per unit	6.00	6.00
Annual allocated fixed overhead	1,800,000	1,800,000

CoffeeTime produced and sold 600,000 Deluxe coffeemakers and 900,000 Regular coffeemakers last year. Management estimates that total unit sales could increase by 20 percent or more if the units can be produced. CoffeeTime already has contracts to produce and sell 35,000 units of each model each month. CoffeeTime has a monthly maximum labor capacity of 30,000 direct-labor hours in the Plating Department and 40,000 direct-labor hours for the assembly operation (Automated Assembly and Labor Assembly, combined). Sales, production, and costs occur uniformly throughout the year.

Required:

1. CoffeeTime's management believes that linear programming could be used to determine the optimum mix of Regular and Deluxe coffeemakers to produce and sell. Explain why linear programming is appropriate to use in this situation.
2. Management has decided to use linear programming to determine the optimal product mix. Formulate and label the:
   a. Objective function
   b. Constraints

   Be sure to define your variables.

(CMA, adapted)

Cases

Case 14–62
Drop a Product Line
(LO 4, 5)

Ontario Pump Company, a small manufacturing company in Toronto, Ontario, manufactures three types of pumps used in a variety of applications. For many years the company has been profitable and has operated at capacity. However, in the last two years prices on all pumps were reduced and selling expenses increased to meet competition and keep the plant operating at capacity. Second-quarter results for the current year, which follow, typify recent experience.

ONTARIO PUMP COMPANY
Income Statement
Second Quarter
(in thousands)

	R-Pump	F-Pump	S-Pump	Total
Sales	$4,800	$2,700	$2,700	$10,200
Cost of goods sold	3,144	2,310	2,850	8,304
Gross margin	$1,656	$ 390	$ (150)	$ 1,896
Selling and administrative expenses	1,110	555	405	2,070
Income before taxes	$ 546	$ (165)	$ (555)	$ (174)

Maria Carlo, the company's president, is concerned about the results of the pricing, selling, and production prices. After reviewing the second-quarter results she asked her management staff to consider the following three suggestions:

- Discontinue the S-Pump line immediately. S-Pumps would not be returned to the product line unless the problems with the pump can be identified and resolved.
- Increase quarterly sales promotion by $300,000 on the R-Pump product line in order to increase sales volume by 15 percent.
- Cut production on the F-Pump line by 50 percent, and cut the traceable advertising and promotion for this line to $60,000 each quarter.

Justin Sperry, the controller, suggested a more careful study of the financial relationships to determine the possible effects on the company's operating results of the president's proposed course of action. The president agreed and assigned JoAnn Brower, the assistant controller, to prepare an analysis. Brower has gathered the following information.

- The unit sales prices for the three pumps are as follows:

R-Pump	$600
F-Pump	270
S-Pump	540

- The company is manufacturing at capacity and is selling all the pumps it produces.
- All three pumps are manufactured with common equipment and facilities.
- The selling and administrative expense is allocated to the three pump lines based on average sales volume over the past three years.
- Special selling expenses (primarily advertising, promotion, and shipping) are incurred for each pump as follows:

	Quarterly Advertising and Promotion	Shipping Expenses
R-Pump	$630,000	$30 per unit
F-Pump	300,000	12 per unit
S-Pump	120,000	30 per unit

- The unit manufacturing costs for the three pumps are as follows:

	R-Pump	F-Pump	S-Pump
Direct material	$ 93	$ 51	$150
Direct labor	120	60	180
Variable manufacturing overhead	135	90	180
Fixed manufacturing overhead	45	30	60
Total	$393	$231	$570

Required:

1. JoAnn Brower says that Ontario Pump Company's product-line income statement for the second quarter is not suitable for analyzing proposals and making decisions such as the ones suggested by Maria Carlo. Write a memo to Ontario Pump's president that addresses the following points.
   a. Explain why the product-line income statement as presented is not suitable for analysis and decision making.
   b. Describe an alternative income-statement format that would be more suitable for analysis and decision making, and explain why it is better.
2. Use the operating data presented for Ontario Pump Company and assume that the president's proposed course of action had been implemented at the beginning of the second quarter. Then evaluate the president's proposal by specifically responding to the following points.
   a. Are each of the three suggestions cost-effective? Support your discussion with an analysis that shows the net impact on income before taxes for each of the three suggestions.
   b. Was the president correct in proposing that the S-Pump line be eliminated? Explain your answer.
   c. Was the president correct in promoting the R-Pump line rather than the F-Pump line? Explain your answer.
   d. Does the proposed course of action make effective use of the company's capacity? Explain your answer.
3. Are there any qualitative factors that Ontario Pump Company's management should consider before it drops the S-Pump line? Explain your answer.

(CMA, adapted)

Case 14–63
Adding a Product Line
(LO 4, 5)

All Sports Company's production manager Chris Adler had requested to have lunch with the company president. Adler wanted to put forward his suggestion to add a new product line. As they finished lunch, Meg Thomas, the company president, said, "I'll give your proposal some serious thought, Chris. I think you're right about the increasing demand for skateboards. What I'm not sure about is whether the skateboard line will be better for us than our tackle boxes. Those have been our bread and butter the past few years."

Adler responded with, "Let me get together with one of the controller's people. We'll run a few numbers on this skateboard idea that I think will demonstrate the line's potential."

All Sports is a wholesale distributor supplying a wide range of moderately priced sports equipment to large chain stores. About 60 percent of All Sports' products are purchased from other companies while the remainder of the products are manufactured by All Sports. The company has a Plastics Department that is currently manufacturing molded fishing tackle boxes. All Sports is able to manufacture and sell

8,000 tackle boxes annually, making full use of its direct-labor capacity at available work stations. The selling price and costs associated with All Sports' tackle boxes are as follows:

Selling price per box		$91.00
Costs per box:		
Molded plastic	$13.00	
Hinges, latches, handle	9.00	
Direct labor ($15.00 per hour)	18.75	
Manufacturing overhead	12.50	
Selling and administrative cost	17.00	70.25
Profit per box		$20.75

Because All Sports' sales manager believes the firm could sell 12,000 tackle boxes if it had sufficient manufacturing capacity, the company has looked into the possibility of purchasing the tackle boxes for distribution. Maple Products, a steady supplier of quality products, would be able to provide up to 9,000 tackle boxes per year at a price of $73.00 per box delivered to All Sports' facility.

All Sports' production manager has come to the conclusion that the company could make better use of its Plastics Department by manufacturing skateboards. Adler has a market study that indicates an expanding market for skateboards and a need for additional suppliers. Adler believes that All Sports could expect to sell 17,500 skateboards annually at a price of $50.00 per skateboard.

After his lunch with the company president, Adler worked out the following estimates with the assistant controller.

Selling price per skateboard		$50.00
Costs per skateboard:		
Molded plastic	$10.50	
Wheels, hardware	7.00	
Direct labor ($15.00 per hour)	7.50	
Manufacturing overhead	5.00	
Selling and administrative cost	9.00	39.00
Profit per skateboard		$11.00

In the Plastics Department, All Sports uses direct-labor hours as the application base for manufacturing overhead. Included in the manufacturing overhead for the current year is $50,000 of factorywide, fixed manufacturing overhead that has been allocated to the Plastics Department. For each unit of product that All Sports sells, regardless of whether the product has been purchased or is manufactured by All Sports, there is an allocated $6.00 fixed overhead cost per unit for distribution that is included in the selling and administrative cost for all products. Total selling and administrative costs for the purchased tackle boxes would be $10.00 per unit.

Required: In order to maximize the company's profitability, prepare an analysis that will show which product or products All Sports Company should manufacture or purchase.

1. First determine which of All Sports' options makes the best use of its scarce resources. How many skateboards and tackle boxes should be manufactured? How many tackle boxes should be purchased?
2. Calculate the improvement in All Sports' total contribution margin if it adopts the optimal strategy rather than continuing with the status quo.

(CMA, adapted)

Current Issues in Managerial Accounting

"Is Your Job Next?" and "A World of Outsourcing," ***Business Week,*** **February 3, 2003, pp. 50–60, Pete Engardio, Aaron Bernstein, and Manjeet Kripalani.**

Issue 14–64
Outsourcing

Overview

"A new round of globalization is sending upscale jobs offshore. They include chip design, engineering, basic research—even financial analysis. Affected are a wide range of companies from service companies like Bank of America to tech companies like Texas Instruments."

Suggested Discussion Question

What are the trade-offs companies face in making major outsourcing decisions?

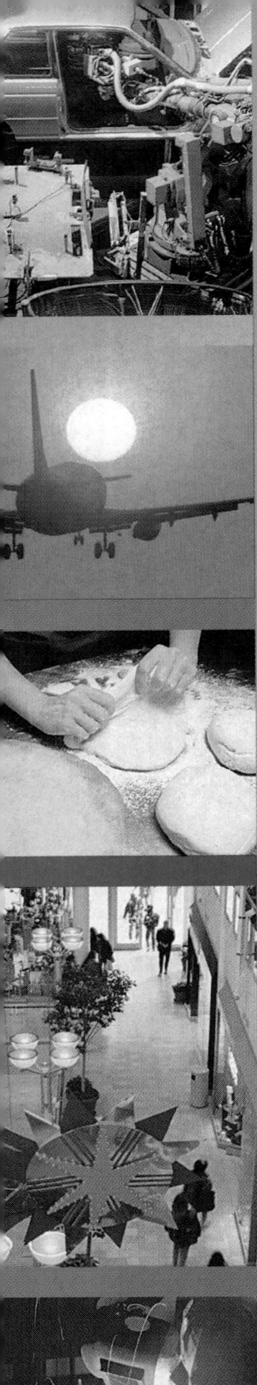

Chapter Fifteen

Target Costing and Cost Analysis for Pricing Decisions

After completing this chapter, you should be able to:

1. List and describe the four major influences on pricing decisions.
2. Explain and use the economic, profit-maximizing pricing model.
3. Set prices using cost-plus pricing formulas.
4. Discuss the issues involved in the strategic pricing of new products.
5. List and discuss the key principles of target costing.
6. Explain the role of activity-based costing in setting a target cost.
7. Explain how product-cost distortion can undermine a firm's pricing strategy.
8. Explain the process of value engineering and its role in target costing.
9. Determine prices using the time and material pricing approach.
10. Set prices in special-order or competitive-bidding situations by analyzing the relevant costs.
11. Describe the legal restrictions on setting prices.

Local Sailboat Manufacturer Sails to Record Profits

Sydney, Australia—Sydney Sailing Supplies yesterday announced record earnings for the fiscal year just ended. Despite ups and downs in the Australian economy, Sydney Sailing continues to show solid financial performance year in and year out. Headquartered in Sydney, the company manufactures a range of sailboats, sailing supplies, and related equipment. The company also has a Marine Construction Division specializing in building and refurbishing marinas, docks, and seawalls.

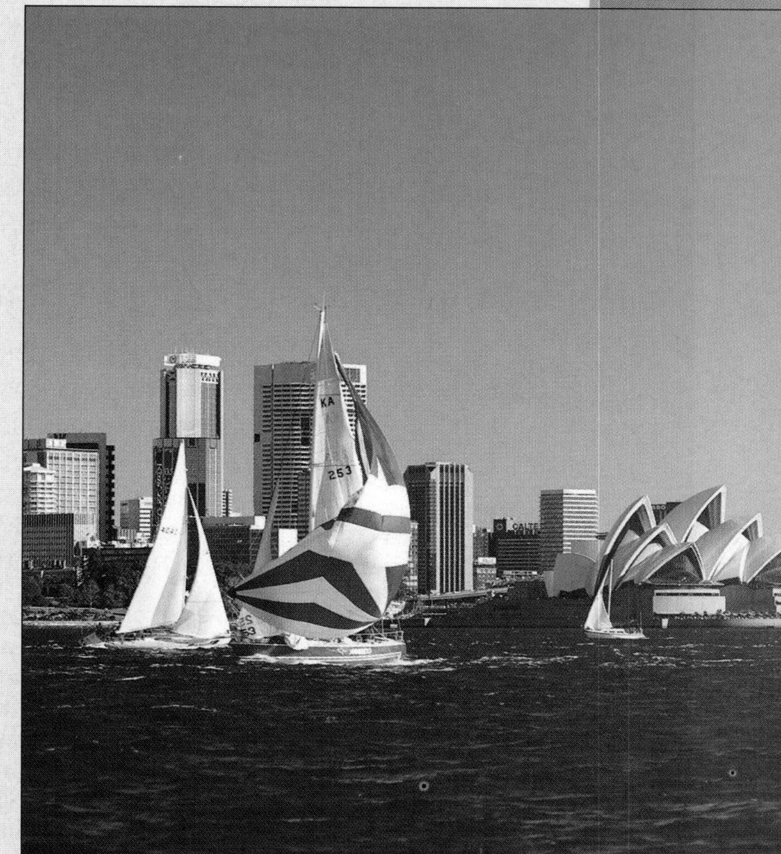

In his annual media interview, President Winston Darrough III praised the firm's managerial staff and rank-and-file workers for continuing the company's string of profitable years. "We've been blessed with top-notch people here at Sydney Sailing," said Mr. Darrough. "I believe we've set a very sensible course for the company. We have very carefully developed our product mix, so that we're in just the right markets. Some recreational marine markets—like personal watercraft—are tough as nails. We've steered clear of those. And as for the markets we are in, we produce a quality product, which is priced just right to maximize profitability. Pricing is a sticky wicket, you know. You've got to keep an eye on your costs as well as your competitors. The competition will always be driving your price down, you see, and you've got to respond. You can't sell the same product for more than the other bloke does. But at the same time, you've got to cover your costs. Nobody can indefinitely sell their products at less than their costs. Just doesn't work that way. And new markets are the trickiest of all.

"For new products, we use a target costing approach. We estimate what we think consumers will pay for a new product, and then we back out the cost that we have to hit in order to sell at that price. That's where our design engineers come into play, and we've got some good ones."

Asked if Sydney Sailing would be introducing any new products this year, Darrough was evasive. "Can't tip our hand just yet, good fellow. Now, if you'll excuse me, I've got a business to run. G'day."

Setting the price for an organization's product or service is one of the most important decisions a manager faces. It is also one of the most difficult, due to the number and variety of factors that must be considered. The pricing decision arises in virtually all types of organizations. Manufacturers set prices for the products they manufacture; merchandising companies set prices for their goods; service firms set prices for such services as insurance policies, train tickets, theme park admissions, and bank loans. Nonprofit organizations often set prices also. For example, governmental units price vehicle registrations, park-use fees, and utility services. The optimal approach to pricing often depends on the situation. Pricing a mature product or service which a firm has sold for a long time may be quite different from pricing a new product or service. Public utilities and TV cable companies face political considerations in pricing their products and services, since their prices often must be approved by a governmental commission.

In this chapter, we will study pricing decisions, with an emphasis on the role of managerial accounting information. The setting for our discussion is Sydney Sailing Supplies, a manufacturer of sailing supplies and equipment located in Sydney, Australia.

Major Influences on Pricing Decisions

Four major influences govern the prices set by Sydney Sailing Supplies:

1. Customer demand.
2. Actions of competitors.
3. Costs.
4. Political, legal, and image-related issues.

Customer Demand

List and describe the four major influences on pricing decisions.

The demands of customers are of paramount importance in all phases of business operations, from the design of a product to the setting of its price. Product-design issues and pricing considerations are interrelated, so they must be examined simultaneously. For example, if customers want a high-quality sailboat, this will entail greater production time and more expensive raw materials. The result almost certainly will be a higher price. On the other hand, management must be careful not to price its product out of the market. Discerning customer demand is a critically important and continuous process. Companies routinely obtain information from market research, such as customer surveys and test-marketing campaigns, and through feedback from sales personnel. To be successful, Sydney Sailing Supplies must provide the products its customers want at a price they perceive to be appropriate.

Actions of Competitors

Although Sydney Sailing Supplies' managers would like the company to have the sailing market to itself, they are not so fortunate. Domestic and foreign competitors are striving to sell their products to the same customers. Thus, as Sydney Sailing Supplies' management designs products and sets prices, it must keep a watchful eye on the firm's competitors. If a competitor reduces its price on sailboats of a particular type, Sydney Sailing Supplies may have to follow suit to avoid losing its market share. Yet the company cannot follow its competitors blindly either. Predicting competitive reactions to its product-design and pricing strategy is a difficult but important task for Sydney Sailing Supplies' management.

In considering the reactions of customers and competitors, management must be careful to properly define its product. Should Sydney Sailing Supplies' management define its product narrowly as sailing supplies, or more broadly as boating supplies?

For example, if the company raises the price of its two-person sailboat, will this encourage potential customers to switch to canoes, rowboats, and small motorboats? Or will most potential sailboat customers react to a price increase only by price-shopping among competing sailboat manufacturers? The way in which Sydney Sailing Supplies' management answers these questions can profoundly affect its marketing and pricing strategies.

Costs

The role of costs in price setting varies widely among industries. In some industries, prices are determined almost entirely by market forces. An example is the agricultural industry, where grain and meat prices are market-driven. Farmers must meet the market price. To make a profit, they must produce at a cost below the market price. This is not always possible, so some periods of loss inevitably result. In other industries, managers set prices at least partially on the basis of production costs. For example, cost-based pricing is used in the aircraft, household appliance, and gasoline industries. Prices are set by adding a markup to production costs. Managers have some latitude in determining the markup, so market forces influence prices as well. In public utilities, such as electricity and natural gas companies, prices generally are set by a regulatory agency of the state government. Production costs are of prime importance in justifying utility rates. Typically, a public utility will make a request to the Public Utility Commission for a rate increase on the basis of its current and projected production costs.

Balance of Market Forces and Cost-Based Pricing In most industries, both market forces and cost considerations heavily influence prices. No organization or industry can price its products below their production costs indefinitely. And no company's management can set prices blindly at cost plus a markup without keeping an eye on the market. In most cases, pricing can be viewed in either of the following ways.

How Are Prices Set?

Prices are determined by the market, subject to the constraint that costs must be covered in the long run.

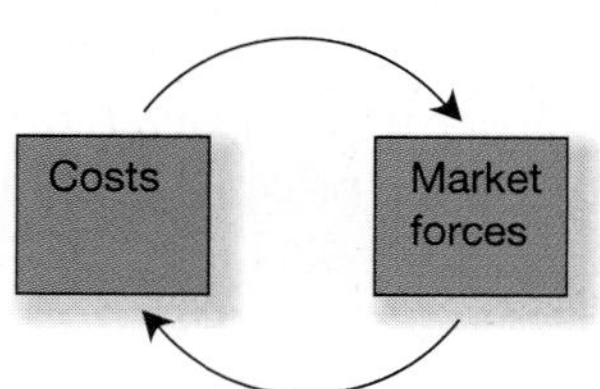

Prices are based on costs, subject to the constraint that the reactions of customers and competitors must be heeded.

In our illustration of Sydney Sailing Supplies' pricing policies, we will assume the company responds to both market forces and costs.

Political, Legal, and Image-Related Issues

Beyond the important effects on prices of market forces and costs are a range of environmental considerations. In the *legal* area, managers must adhere to certain laws. The law generally prohibits companies from discriminating among their customers in setting prices. Also prohibited is collusion in price setting, where the major firms in an industry all agree to set their prices at high levels.

Political considerations also can be relevant. For example, if the firms in an industry are *perceived* by the public as reaping unfairly large profits, there may be political pressure on legislators to tax those profits differentially or to intervene in some way to regulate prices.

Companies also consider their *public image* in the price-setting process. A firm with a reputation for very high-quality products may set the price of a new product

> "You're looked to for business expertise. You're looked to also [for] business perspective, pricing strategies, manufacturing strategies, to see if they make sense financially." (15a)
>
> **Caterpillar**

Setting prices requires a balance between cost considerations and market forces. A good example is provided by the airlines, which keep a close eye on the fares of their competitors, while striving to cover operating costs. The large airlines, like American, Delta, and United, are increasingly finding it necessary to cut fares to compete with discounters like Southwest.[1]

high to be consistent with its image. As we have all discovered, the same brand-name product may be available in a discount store at half the price charged in a more exclusive store.

Economic Profit-Maximizing Pricing

LO 2

Explain and use the economic, profit-maximizing pricing model.

Companies are sometimes **price takers,** which means their products' prices are determined totally by the market. Some agricultural commodities and precious metals are examples of such products. In most cases, however, firms have some flexibility in setting prices. Generally speaking, as the price of a product or service is increased, the quantity demanded declines, and vice versa.

Total Revenue, Demand, and Marginal Revenue Curves

The trade-off between a higher price and a higher sales quantity can be shown in the shape of the firm's **total revenue curve,** which graphs the relationship between total sales revenue and quantity sold. Sydney Sailing Supplies' total revenue curve for its two-person sailboat, the Wave Darter, is displayed in Exhibit 15–1, panel A. The total revenue curve increases throughout its range, but the rate of increase declines as monthly sales quantity increases. To see this, notice that the increase in total revenue when the sales quantity increases from zero to *a* units is greater than the increase in total revenue when the sales quantity increases from *a* units to *b* units.

Closely related to the total revenue curve are two other curves, which are graphed in panel B of Exhibit 15–1. The **demand curve** shows the relationship between the sales price and the quantity of units demanded. The demand curve decreases throughout its range, because any decrease in the sale price brings about an increase in the

[1]Martha Brannigan, "Delta Air Lines Plans a Fare War with Discounters," *The Wall Street Journal,* July 26, 2002, p. 32.

Exhibit 15–1
Total Revenue, Demand, and Marginal Revenue Curves

A. Total Revenue Curve

Dollars

Total revenue

Curve is increasing throughout its range, but at a declining rate

0 a b

Quantity sold per month

B. Demand (or Average Revenue) Curve and Marginal Revenue Curve

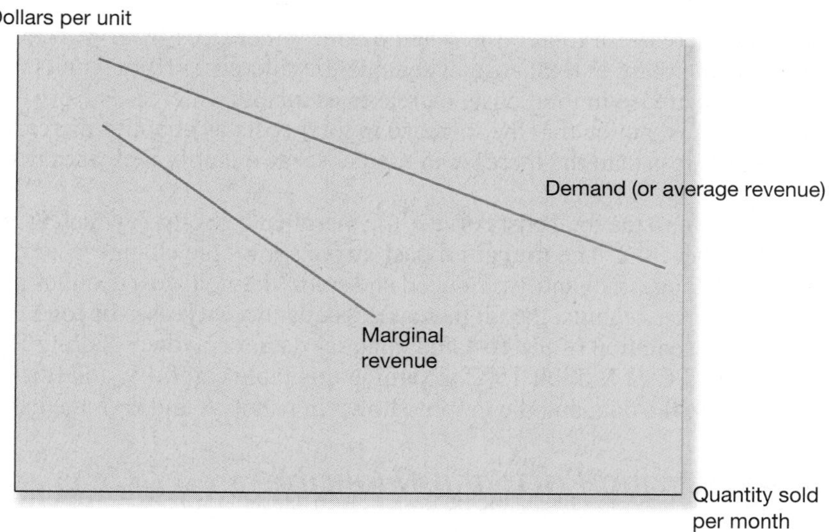

C. Tabulated Price, Quantity, and Revenue Data

Quantity Sold per Month	Unit Sales Price	Total Revenue per Month	Changes in Total Revenue
10	$1,000	$10,000	
			$9,500
20	975	19,500	
			9,000
30	950	28,500	
			8,500
40	925	37,000	
			8,000
50	900	45,000	
			7,500
60	875	52,500	

Related to demand curve — Related to total revenue curve — Related to marginal revenue curve monthly sales quantity. The demand curve is also called the **average revenue curve,** since it shows the average price at which any particular quantity can be sold.

The **marginal revenue curve** shows the *change* in total revenue that accompanies a *change* in the quantity sold. The marginal revenue curve is decreasing throughout its range to show that total revenue increases at a declining rate as monthly sales quantity increases.

A tabular presentation of the price, quantity, and revenue data for Sydney Sailing Supplies is displayed in panel C of Exhibit 15–1. Study this table carefully to see how the data relate to the graphs shown in panels A and B of the exhibit. No matter what approach a manager takes to the pricing decision, a good understanding of the relationships shown in Exhibit 15–1 will lead to better decisions. Before we can fully use the revenue data, however, we must examine the cost side of Sydney Sailing Supplies' business.

Total Cost and Marginal Cost Curves

Understanding cost behavior is important in many business decisions, and pricing is no exception. How does total cost behave as the number of Wave Darters produced and sold by Sydney Sailing Supplies changes? Panel A of Exhibit 15–2 displays the firm's **total cost curve,** which graphs the relationship between total cost and the quantity produced and sold each month.[2] Total cost increases throughout its range. The rate of increase in total cost declines as quantity increases from zero to *c* units. To verify this, notice that the increase in total costs when quantity increases from zero to *a* units is greater than the increase in total costs when quantity increases from *a* units to *b* units.

The rate of increase in total costs increases as quantity increases from *c* units upward. To verify this, notice that the increase in total costs as quantity increases from *c* units to *d* units is less than the increase in total costs as quantity increases from *d* units to *e* units.

Closely related to the total cost curve is the marginal cost curve, which is graphed in panel B of Exhibit 15–2. The **marginal cost curve** shows the change in total cost that accompanies a change in quantity produced and sold. Marginal cost declines as quantity increases from zero to *c* units; then it increases as quantity increases beyond *c* units.

A tabular presentation of the cost and quantity data for Sydney Sailing Supplies is displayed in panel C of Exhibit 15–2. Examine this table carefully, and trace the relationships between the data and the graphs shown in panels A and B of the exhibit.

Profit-Maximizing Price and Quantity

Now we have the tools we need to determine the profit-maximizing price and quantity. In Exhibit 15–3, we combine the revenue and cost data presented in Exhibits 15–1 and 15–2. Sydney Sailing Supplies' profit-maximizing sales quantity for the Wave Darter is determined by the intersection of the marginal cost and marginal revenue curves. (See panel B of Exhibit 15–3.) This optimal quantity is denoted by q^* on the graph. The profit-maximizing price, denoted by p^*, is determined from the demand curve for the quantity, q^*.

Examine the total revenue and total cost curves in panel A of Exhibit 15–3. At the profit-maximizing quantity (and price), the distance between these curves, which is equal to total profit, is maximized.

A tabular presentation of the revenue, cost, and profit data is shown in panel C of Exhibit 15–3. Notice that monthly profit is maximized when the price is set at $925 and 40 Wave Darters are produced and sold each month.

---

[2]Notice that the demand and revenue curves are based on the quantity sold, while the cost curves are based on the quantity produced. We will assume for simplicity that Sydney Sailing Supplies' monthly sales and production quantities are the same. This assumption tends to be true in the pleasure boat industry.

Exhibit 15–2
Total Cost and Marginal Cost Curves

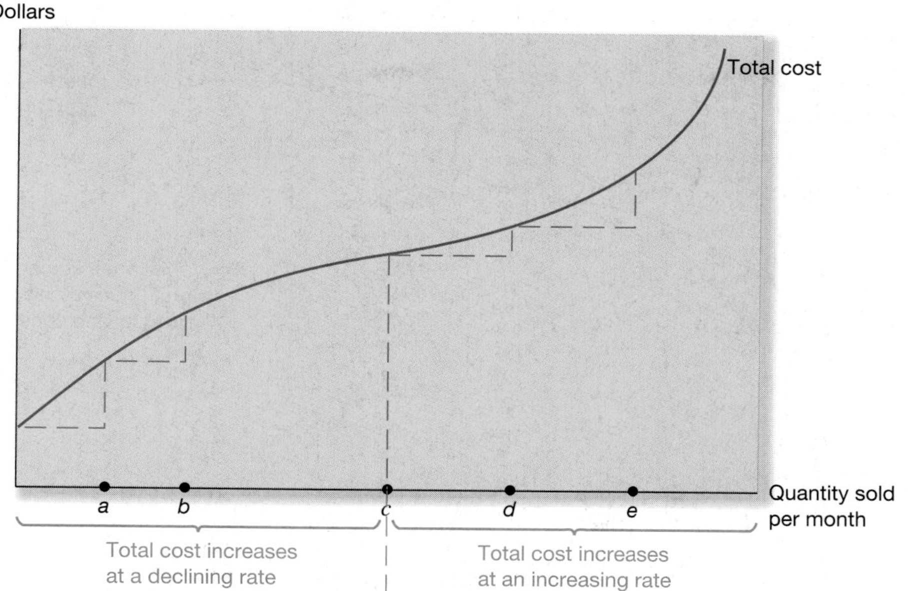

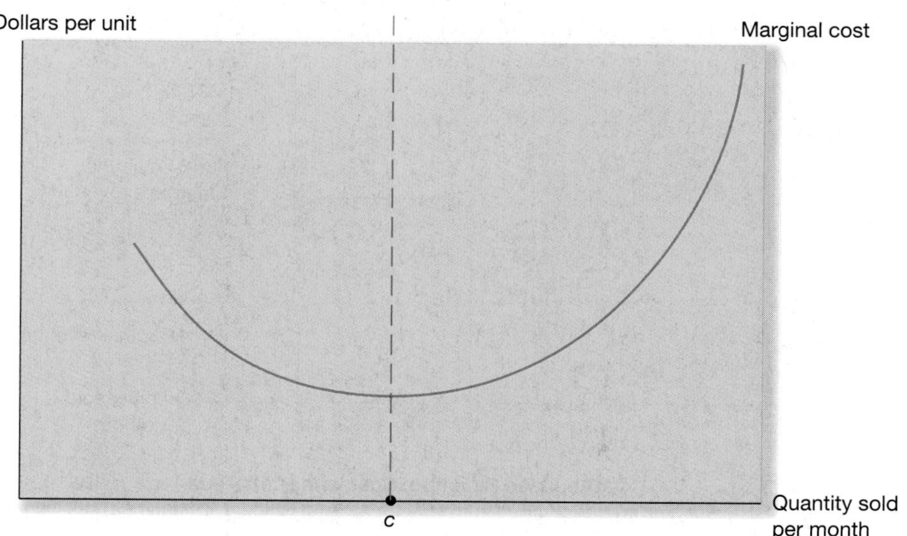

C. Tabulated Cost and Quantity Data

Quantity Produced and Sold per Month	Average Cost per Unit	Total Cost per Month	Changes in Total Cost
10	$1,920	$19,200	
			$ 5,600
20	1,240	24,800	
			4,300
30	970	29,100	
			2,900
40	800	32,000	
			9,000
50	820	41,000	
			15,400
60	940	56,400	

Related to total cost curve | Related to marginal cost curve

Exhibit 15–3
Determining the Profit-Maximizing Price and Quantity

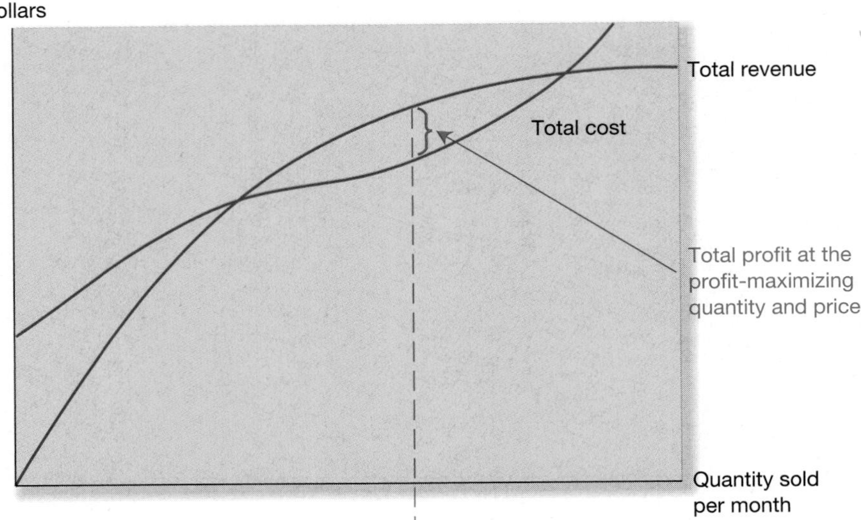

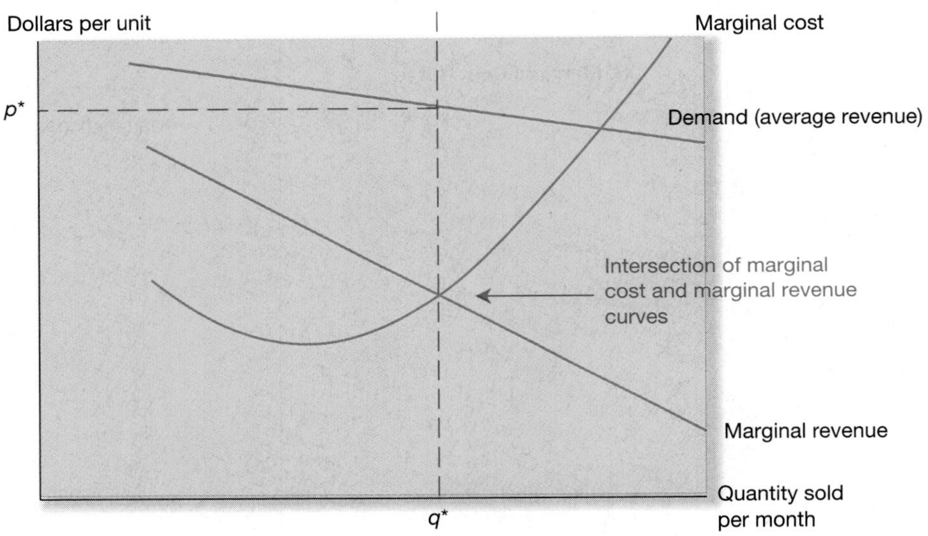

C. Tabulated Revenue, Cost, and Profit Data

	Quantity Produced and Sold per Month	Unit Sales Price	Total Revenue per Month	Total Cost per Month	Profit (Loss) per Month
	10	$1,000	$10,000	$19,200	$(9,200)
	20	975	19,500	24,800	(5,300)
	30	950	28,500	29,100	(600)
Profit-maximizing quantity and price	40	925	37,000	32,000	5,000
	50	900	45,000	41,000	4,000
	60	875	52,500	56,400	(3,900)

Price Elasticity

The impact of price changes on sales volume is called the **price elasticity.** Demand is *elastic* if a price increase has a large negative impact on sales volume, and vice versa.

Demand is *inelastic* if price changes have little or no impact on sales quantity. **Cross-elasticity** refers to the extent to which a change in a product's price affects the demand for other *substitute products.* For example, if Sydney Sailing Supplies raises the price of its two-person sailboat, there may be an increase in demand for substitute recreational craft, such as small powerboats, canoes, or windsurfers.

Measuring price elasticity and cross-elasticity is an important objective of market research. Having a good understanding of these economic concepts helps managers to determine the profit-maximizing price.

Limitations of the Profit-Maximizing Model

The economic model of the pricing decision serves as a useful framework for approaching a pricing problem. However, it does have several limitations. First, the firm's demand and marginal revenue curves are difficult to discern with precision. Although market research is designed to gather data about product demand, it rarely enables management to predict completely the effects of price changes on the quantity demanded. Many other factors affect product demand in addition to price. Product design and quality, advertising and promotion, and company reputation also significantly influence consumer demand for a product.

Second, the marginal-revenue, marginal-cost paradigm is not valid for all forms of market organization. In an **oligopolistic market,** where a small number of sellers compete among themselves, the simple economic pricing model is no longer appropriate. In an *oligopoly,* such as the automobile industry, the reactions of competitors to a firm's pricing policies must be taken into account. While economists have studied oligopolistic pricing, the state of the theory is not sufficient to provide a thorough understanding of the impact of prices on demand.

The third limitation of the economic pricing model involves the difficulty of measuring marginal cost. Cost-accounting systems are not designed to measure the marginal changes in cost incurred as production and sales increase unit by unit. To measure marginal costs would entail a very costly information system. Most managers believe that any improvements in pricing decisions made possible by marginal-cost data would not be sufficient to defray the cost of obtaining the information.

Costs and Benefits of Information

Managerial accountants always face a cost-benefit trade-off in the production of cost information for pricing and other decisions. As Exhibit 15–4 shows, only a sophisticated information system can collect marginal-cost data. However, such information is

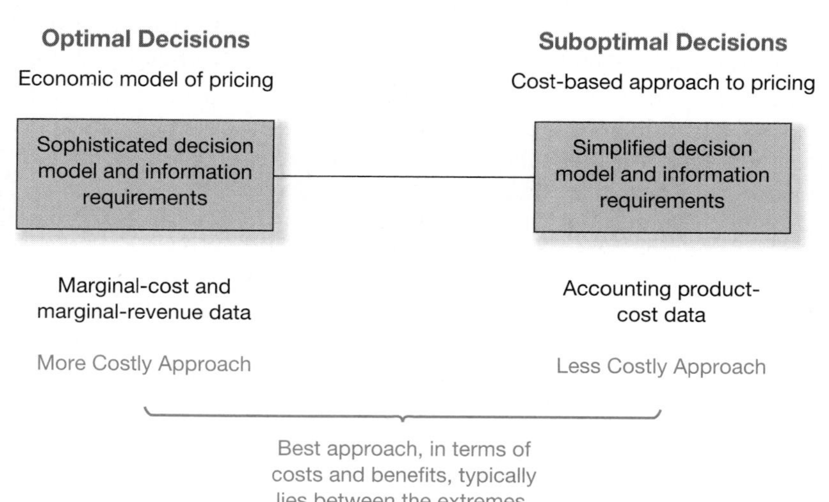

Exhibit 15–4
Cost-Benefit Trade-Off in Information Production

more costly to obtain. The result is that the optimal approach to pricing and other decisions is likely to lie in between the extremes shown in Exhibit 15–4. For this reason, most managers make pricing decisions based on a combination of economic considerations and accounting product-cost information.

In spite of its limitations, the marginal-revenue, marginal-cost paradigm of pricing serves as a useful conceptual framework for the pricing decision. Within this overall framework, managers typically rely heavily on a cost-based pricing approach, as we shall see next.

Role of Accounting Product Costs in Pricing

"Today we spend more of our time analyzing and understanding . . . our margins, understanding our prices, understanding the markets in which we do business." (15b)
Caterpillar

Most managers base prices on accounting product costs, at least to some extent. There are several reasons for this. First, most companies sell many products or services. There simply is not time enough to do a thorough demand and marginal-cost analysis for every product or service. Managers must rely on a quick and straightforward method for setting prices, and cost-based pricing formulas provide it. Second, even though market considerations ultimately may determine the final product price, a cost-based pricing formula gives the manager a place to start. Finally, and most importantly, the cost of a product or service provides a floor below which the price cannot be set in the long run. Although a product may be "given away" initially, at a price below cost, a product's price ultimately must cover its costs in order for the firm to remain in business. Even a nonprofit organization, unless it is heavily subsidized, cannot forever price products or services below their costs.

Cost-Plus Pricing

Set prices using cost-plus pricing formulas.

Topic 15–1

Cost-based pricing formulas typically have the following general form.

Price = Cost + (Markup percentage × Cost)

Such a pricing approach often is called **cost-plus pricing,** because the price is equal to *cost plus a markup.* Depending on how cost is defined, the markup percentage may differ. Several different definitions of cost, each combined with a different markup percentage, can result in the same price for a product or service.

Exhibit 15–5 illustrates how Sydney Sailing Supplies' management could use several different cost-plus pricing formulas and arrive at a price of $925 for the Wave Darter. Cost-plus formula (1) is based on variable manufacturing cost. Formula (2) is based on absorption (or full) manufacturing cost, which includes an allocated portion of fixed manufacturing costs. Formula (3) is based on all costs: both variable and fixed costs of the manufacturing, selling, and administrative functions. Formula (4) is based on all variable costs, including variable manufacturing, selling, and administrative costs. Notice that all four pricing formulas are based on a linear representation of the cost function, in which all costs are categorized as fixed or variable.

As Sydney Sailing Supplies includes more costs in the cost base of the pricing formula, the required markup percentage declines. This reflects the fact that, one way or another, the price must cover all costs as well as a normal profit margin. If only variable manufacturing costs are included explicitly in the cost base, as in formula (1), then all of the other costs (and the firm's profit) must be covered by the markup. However, if the cost base used in the pricing formula includes all costs, as in formula (3), the markup can be much lower, since it need cover only the firm's normal profit margin.

A company typically uses only one of the four cost-plus pricing formulas illustrated in Exhibit 15–5. Which formula is best? Let's examine the advantages and disadvantages of each approach.

Each of the following cost-plus pricing formulas yields the same $925 price for the Wave Darter.

Price and Cost Data			Cost-Plus Pricing Formulas
Variable manufacturing cost	$400	1	$\$925 = \$400 + (131.25\% \times \$400) = \text{Variable manufacturing cost} + \left(\text{Markup percentage} \times \text{Variable manufacturing cost}\right)$
Applied fixed manufacturing cost	250*		
Absorption manufacturing cost	650	2	$\$925 = \$650 + (42.3\%^{\dagger} \times \$650) = \text{Absorption manufacturing cost} + \left(\text{Markup percentage} \times \text{Absorption manufacturing cost}\right)$
Variable selling and administrative cost	50		
Allocated fixed selling and administrative cost	100*		
Total cost	$800	3	$\$925 = \$800 + (15.63\%^{\dagger} \times \$800) = \text{Total cost} + \left(\text{Markup percentage} \times \text{Total cost}\right)$
Variable manufacturing cost	$400		
Variable selling and administrative cost	50		
Total variable cost	$450	4	$\$925 = \$450 + (105.56\%^{\dagger} \times \$450) = \text{Total variable cost} + \left(\text{Markup percentage} \times \text{Total variable cost}\right)$

*Based on planned monthly production of 40 units (or 480 units per year).

†Rounded.

Exhibit 15–5
Alternative Cost-Plus Pricing Formulas

Absorption-Cost Pricing Formulas

Most companies that use cost-plus pricing use either absorption manufacturing cost or total cost as the basis for pricing products or services. [See formulas (2) and (3) in Exhibit 15–5.] The reasons generally given for this tendency are as follows:

1. In the long run, the price must cover *all* costs and a normal profit margin. Basing the cost-plus formula on only variable costs could encourage managers to set too low a price in order to boost sales. This will not happen if managers understand that a variable cost-plus pricing formula requires a higher markup to cover fixed costs and profit. Nevertheless, many managers argue that people tend to view the cost base in a cost-plus pricing formula as the floor for setting prices. If prices are set too close to variable manufacturing cost, the firm will fail to cover its fixed costs. Ultimately, such a practice could result in the failure of the business.
2. Absorption-cost or total-cost pricing formulas provide a justifiable price that tends to be perceived as equitable by all parties. Consumers generally understand that a company must make a profit on its product or service in order to remain in business. Justifying a price as the total cost of production, sales, and administrative activities, plus a reasonable profit margin, seems reasonable to buyers.
3. When a company's competitors have similar operations and cost structures, cost-plus pricing based on full costs gives management an idea of how competitors may set prices.
4. Absorption-cost information is provided by a firm's cost-accounting system, because it is required for external financial reporting under generally accepted accounting principles. Since absorption-cost information already exists, it is cost-effective to use it for pricing. The alternative would involve preparing special product-cost data specifically for the pricing decision. In a firm with hundreds of products, such data could be expensive to produce.

"An indemnity [insurance] company prices products by looking at existing costs and at what the trends have been. The company then predicts, or forecasts, costs for the next year and uses this information to set the price." (15c)
BlueCross BlueShield of North Carolina

The primary disadvantage of absorption-cost or total-cost pricing formulas is that they obscure the cost behavior pattern of the firm. Since absorption-cost and total-cost data include allocated fixed costs, it is not clear from these data how the firm's total costs will change as volume changes. Another way of stating this criticism is that absorption-cost data are not consistent with cost-volume-profit analysis. CVP analysis emphasizes the distinction between fixed and variable costs. This approach enables managers to predict the effects of changes in prices and sales volume on profit. Absorption-cost and total-cost information obscures the distinction between variable and fixed costs.

Variable-Cost Pricing Formulas

To avoid blurring the effects of cost behavior on profit, some managers prefer to use cost-plus pricing formulas based on either variable manufacturing costs or total variable costs. [See formulas (1) and (4) in Exhibit 15–5.] Three advantages are attributed to this pricing approach:

1. Variable-cost data do not obscure the cost behavior pattern by unitizing fixed costs and making them appear variable. Thus, variable-cost information is more consistent with cost-volume-profit analysis often used by managers to see the profit implications of changes in price and volume.
2. Variable-cost data do not require allocation of common fixed costs to individual product lines. For example, the annual salary of Sydney Sailing Supplies' vice president of sales is a cost that must be borne by all of the company's product lines. Arbitrarily allocating a portion of her salary to the Wave Darter product line is not meaningful.
3. Variable-cost data are exactly the type of information managers need when facing certain decisions, such as whether to accept a special order. This decision, examined in detail in the preceding chapter, often requires an analysis that separates fixed and variable costs.

The primary disadvantage of the variable-cost pricing formula was described earlier. If managers perceive the variable cost of a product or service as the floor for the price, they may tend to set the price too low for the firm to cover its fixed costs. Eventually this can spell disaster. Therefore, if variable-cost data are used as the basis for cost-plus pricing, managers must understand the need for higher markups to ensure that all costs are covered.

Determining the Markup

Regardless of which cost-plus formula is used, Sydney Sailing Supplies must determine its markup on the Wave Darter. If management uses a variable-cost pricing formula, the markup must cover all fixed costs and a reasonable profit. If management uses an absorption-costing formula, the markup still must be sufficient to cover the firm's profit on the Wave Darter product line. What constitutes a reasonable or normal profit margin?

Return-on-Investment Pricing A common approach to determining the profit margin in cost-plus pricing is to base profit on the firm's target return on investment (ROI). To illustrate **return-on-investment pricing,** suppose Sydney Sailing Supplies' production plan calls for 480 Wave Darters to be manufactured during the year. Based on the cost data shown in Exhibit 15–5, this production plan will result in the following total costs.

Variable costs:		
Manufacturing	$192,000	
Selling and administrative	24,000	
Total variable costs		$216,000

(continues)

Fixed costs:		
Manufacturing	$120,000	
Selling and administrative	48,000	
Total fixed costs		168,000
Total costs		$384,000

Suppose the year's average amount of capital invested in the Wave Darter product line is $300,000. If Sydney Sailing Supplies' target return on investment for the Wave Darter line is 20 percent, the required annual profit is computed as follows:

$$\text{Average invested capital} \times \text{Target ROI} = \text{Target profit}$$
$$\$300{,}000 \times 20\% = \$60{,}000$$

The markup percentage required to earn Sydney Sailing Supplies a $60,000 profit on the Wave Darter line depends on the cost-plus formula used. We will compute the markup percentage for two cost-plus formulas.

1. ***Cost-plus pricing based on total costs.*** The total cost of a Wave Darter is $800 per unit (Exhibit 15–5). To earn a profit of $60,000 on annual sales of 480 sailboats, the company must make a profit of $125 per boat ($125 = $60,000 ÷ 480). This entails a markup percentage of 15.63 percent *above* total cost of $800.

$$15.63\% = \frac{\$925}{\$800} - 100\%$$

A shortcut to the same conclusion uses the following formula.

$$\text{Markup percentage on total cost} = \frac{\text{Target profit}}{\text{Annual volume} \times \text{Total cost per unit}}$$

$$15.63\% = \frac{\$60{,}000}{480 \times \$800}$$

2. ***Cost-plus pricing based on total variable costs.*** The total variable cost of a Wave Darter is $450 per unit (Exhibit 15–5). The markup percentage applied to variable cost must be sufficient to cover *both* annual profit of $60,000 *and* total annual fixed costs of $168,000. The required markup percentage is computed as follows:

$$\text{Markup percentage on total variable cost} = \frac{\text{Target profit} + \text{Total annual fixed cost}}{\text{Annual volume} \times \text{Total variable cost per unit}}$$

$$105.56\% = \frac{\$60{,}000 + \$168{,}000}{480 \times \$450}$$

General Formula The general formula for computing the markup percentage in cost-plus pricing to achieve a target ROI is as follows:

$$\text{Markup percentage applied to cost base in cost-plus pricing formula} = \frac{\text{Profit required to achieve target ROI} + \text{Total annual costs } \textit{not} \text{ included in cost base}}{\text{Annual volume} \times \text{Cost base per unit used in cost-plus pricing formula}}$$

Exercise 15–35 at the end of the chapter gives you an opportunity to employ this formula to compute the markup percentage for the other two cost-plus pricing formulas in Exhibit 15–5.

Cost-Plus Pricing: Summary and Evaluation

We have examined two different approaches to setting prices: (1) the economic, profit-maximizing approach and (2) cost-plus pricing. Although the techniques involved in these methods are quite different, the methods complement each other. In setting prices, managers cannot ignore the market, nor can they ignore costs. Cost-plus pricing is used widely in practice to establish a starting point in the process of determining a price. Cost-plus formulas are simple; they can be applied mechanically without taking the time of top management. They make it possible for a company with hundreds of products or services to cope with the tasks of updating prices for existing products and setting initial prices for new products.

Cost-plus pricing formulas can be used effectively with a variety of cost definitions, but the markup percentage must be appropriate for the type of cost used. It is imperative that price-setting managers understand that ultimately the price must cover all costs and a normal profit margin. Absorption-cost-plus or total-cost-plus pricing has the advantage of keeping the manager's attention focused on covering total costs. The variable-cost-plus formulas have the advantage of not obscuring important information about cost behavior.

Cost-plus pricing formulas establish a starting point in setting prices. Then the price setter must weigh market conditions, likely actions of competitors, and general business conditions. Thus, effective price setting requires a constant interplay of market considerations and cost awareness.

Strategic Pricing of New Products

LO 4

Discuss the issues involved in the strategic pricing of new products.

Pricing a new product is an especially challenging decision problem. The newer the concept of the product, the more difficult the pricing decision is. For example, if Sydney Sailing Supplies comes out with a new two-person sailboat, its pricing problem is far easier than the pricing problem of a company that first markets products using a radically new technology. Genetic engineering, superconductivity, artificial hearts, and space-grown crystals are all examples of such frontier technologies.

Pricing a new product is harder than pricing a mature product because of the magnitude of the uncertainties involved. New products entail many uncertainties. For example, what obstacles will be encountered in manufacturing the product, and what will be the costs of production? Moreover, after the product is available, will anyone want to buy it, and at what price? If Sydney Sailing Supplies decides to market a new two-person sailboat, management can make a good estimate of both the production costs and the potential market for the product. The uncertainties here are far smaller than the uncertainties facing a company developing artificial hearts.

In addition to the production and demand uncertainties, new products pose another sort of challenge. There are two widely differing strategies that a manufacturer of a new product can adopt. One strategy is called **skimming pricing,** in which the initial product price is set high, and short-term profits are reaped on the new product. The initial market will be small, due in part to the high initial price. This pricing approach often is used for unique products, where there are people who "must have it" whatever the price. As the product gains acceptance and its appeal broadens, the price is lowered gradually. Eventually the product is priced in a range that appeals to several kinds of buyers. An example of a product for which skimming pricing was used is the home video game. Initially these games were priced quite high and were affordable by only a few buyers. Eventually the price was lowered, and the games were purchased by a wide range of consumers.

An alternative initial pricing strategy is called **penetration pricing,** in which the initial price is set relatively low. By setting a low price for a new product, management hopes to penetrate a new market deeply, quickly gaining a large market share. This pricing approach often is used for products that are of good quality, but do not stand out as vastly better than competing products.

The decision between skimming and penetration pricing depends on the type of product and involves trade-offs of price versus volume. Skimming pricing results in much slower acceptance of a new product, but higher unit profits. Penetration pricing results in greater initial sales volume, but lower unit profits.

The following illustration points out the importance of cost reduction in enabling a firm to maintain price competitiveness.

Management Accounting Practice

Ford Motor Company

COST CUTTING TO MAINTAIN PRICES

"Ford Motor Co., pressured by industry price wars, is sharply stepping up efforts to cut the cost of [materials] used in its vehicles, while taking care not to reduce the quality of its products or their appeal to the customer. The number-two automaker had set a goal to slash $700 in costs from each of its North American vehicles by 2005 in an effort to regain healthy profitability. That level of cost cutting could potentially add $2.8 billion a year to Ford's profits.

In order "to identify new areas to cut costs, Ford is more than tripling to 1,000 engineers the size of a team assigned to work directly with the company's suppliers. Ford launched the cost-cutting team with 300 engineers assigned to collaborate with counterparts at suppliers to come up with cost-saving ideas. A Ford product executive said that the team, as it worked with suppliers, discovered some 'huge opportunities' to cut costs without sacrificing vehicle appeal. One example of Ford's new approach involves its popular Explorer sport-utility vehicle. The team that redesigned the vehicle last year chose to use a nylon insert for its platform for better crash protection, which was 'very expensive.' The engineering team found an alternative way that offered 'better functionality' and a relatively hefty cost saving of about $125 per vehicle."[3]

Ford is also focusing on its big Expedition sport-utility vehicle. The company will hold price increases on the redesigned version "to a fraction of a percent, despite adding lots of new features. The new Expedition, as well as its cousin the Lincoln Navigator, are among Ford's most profitable vehicles and critical to Ford's financial results. But the new models were developed before the current intense focus on costs and are packed with expensive features." However, Ford is counting on reducing costs of parts in order to boost profits. Ford is also expecting a major reduction in marketing costs for the Expedition.[4]

Ford is also planning to alter its product mix to boost profits. "Ford is returning to a revenue system it pioneered in the '90s. Simply put, Ford tries to push its most profitable models by reducing prices enough to nudge consumers into choosing high-margin options."[5]

Target Costing

List and discuss the key principles of target costing.

Topic 15–2

Earlier in this chapter, we described product pricing as a process whereby the cost of the product is determined, and then an appropriate price is chosen. Increasingly, the opposite approach is being taken. The company first uses market research to determine the price at which a new product can be sold. Given the likely sales price, management computes the cost for which the product must be manufactured in order to provide the firm with an acceptable profit margin. Finally, engineers and cost analysts work together to design a product that can be manufactured for the allowable cost. This process, called **target costing,** is used widely by companies in the development stages of new products. A new product's **target cost** is the projected long-run cost that will

[3]Norihiko Shirouzu, "Ford Intensifies Its Plans to Cut Costs," *The Wall Street Journal,* May 8, 2002.

[4]Norihiko Shirouzu, "Ford Keeps Ceiling on Expedition Price," *The Wall Street Journal,* March 26, 2002.

[5]Kathleen Kerwin, "Where Are the Hot Cars?" *Business Week,* June 24, 2002, p. 68.

enable a firm to enter and remain in the market for the product and compete successfully with the firm's competitors.

Management Accounting Practice

Amazon.com

PRICING ON THE INTERNET BY "E-TAILERS"

One of the most difficult issues in building an online retail business has proven to be pricing. "Many Internet merchants are still struggling to find ways to set prices to attract as many customers as possible, while fattening up their razor-thin profit margins. What these retailers do know is what *hasn't* worked."

As the dot-com industry continues to implode, flawed pricing strategies have taken much of the blame. "Too many merchants raced for the bottom with deep discounts that made profits all but impossible to achieve—especially when the stock market bottomed out and funding for dot-coms froze. Others have felt the consumer backlash to so-called price discrimination, as the Internet has given shoppers the ability to better detect price discrepancies and bargains. The survivors must now figure out if it is even possible to take advantage of the Internet's unique capabilities to set dynamic prices, which would better reflect a customer's willingness to pay more under different circumstances. 'Before the Internet existed, retail was a very competitive, difficult, low-margin business,' says economist Austan Goolsbee. 'With the advent of Internet retailers, there was a brief moment in which they and others believed they had broken the iron chain of low margins and high competition in retail by introducing the Internet. Now, retail online is starting to look like retail offline—very competitive, with squeezed profit margins. In all, a very tough place to be.' "

Pricing on the Internet, "was expected to offer retailers a number of advantages." First, "it would be far easier to raise or lower prices in response to demand, without the need of a clerk running through a store with a pricing gun. Online prices could be changed in far smaller increments—even by just a penny or two—as frequently as a merchant desired, making it possible to fine-tune pricing strategies."

The real payoff, though, "was supposed to be better information on exactly how price-conscious customers are. For instance, knowing that customer A doesn't care whether the 'Gladiator' DVD in her shopping basket costs $21.95 or $25.95 would leave an enterprising merchant free to charge the higher price on the spot. By contrast, knowing that customer B is going to put author John Le Carre's latest thriller back on the shelf unless it's priced at $20, instead of $28, would open an opportunity for a bookseller to make the sale by cutting the price in real time." However, putting this concept "into practice online has turned out to be exceptionally difficult, in part because the Internet also has empowered consumers to compare prices to find out if other merchants are offering a better deal or if other consumers are getting a bigger break." It has also made it easier for consumers to register a complaint. For example, "Amazon.com raised a furor . . . when customers learned they were paying different prices for the same DVD movies, the result of a marketing test in which the retailer varied prices to gauge the effect on demand." After receiving many complaints from irate consumers, "Amazon announced it would refund the difference between the highest and lowest prices in the test."[6]

A Strategic Profit and Cost Management Process

Target costing can be a critical tool for management as it seeks to strategically manage the company's costs and profits. By ensuring that products are designed so that they

[6]David P. Hamilton, "The Price Isn't Right: Internet Pricing Has Turned Out to Be a Lot Trickier than Retailers Expected," *The Wall Street Journal,* February 12, 2001, p. R8.

can be produced at a low enough cost to be priced competitively, management can achieve and maintain a sustainable competitive position in the market.

Key Principles of Target Costing Target costing involves seven key principles.[7]

- *Price-led costing.* Target costing sets the target cost by *first* determining the price at which a product can be sold in the marketplace. Subtracting the *target profit margin* from this *target price* yields the *target cost,* that is, the cost at which the product must be manufactured. This simple, but strategically important, relationship can be expressed in the following equation.

  Target cost = Target price − Target profit

  Notice that in a target costing approach, the price is set *first,* and *then* the target product cost is determined. This is opposite from the order in which the product cost and selling price are determined under traditional cost-plus pricing.
- *Focus on the customer.* To be successful at target costing, management must listen to the company's customers. What products do they want? What features are important? How much are they willing to pay for a certain level of product quality? Management needs to aggressively seek customer feedback, and then products must be designed to satisfy customer demand and be sold at a price they are willing to pay. In short, the target costing approach is market driven.
- *Focus on product design.* Design engineering is a key element in target costing. Engineers must design a product from the ground up so that it can be produced at its target cost. This design activity includes specifying the raw materials and components to be used as well as the labor, machinery, and other elements of the production process. In short, a product must be designed for manufacturability.
- *Focus on process design.* As indicated in the preceding point, every aspect of the production *process* must be examined to make sure that the product is produced as efficiently as possible. The use of touch labor, technology, global sourcing in procurement, and every aspect of the production process must be designed with the product's target cost in mind.
- *Cross-functional teams.* Manufacturing a product at or below its target cost requires the involvement of people from many different functions in an organization: market research, sales, design engineering, procurement, production engineering, production scheduling, material handling, and cost management. Individuals from all these diverse areas of expertise can make key contributions to the target costing process. Moreover, "a cross-functional team is not a set of specialists who contribute their expertise and then leave; they are responsible for the entire product."[8]
- *Life-cycle costs.* In specifying a product's target cost, analysts must be careful to incorporate all of the product's *life-cycle costs.* These include the costs of product planning and concept design, preliminary design, detailed design and testing, production, distribution, and customer service. Traditional cost-accounting systems have tended to focus only on the production phase and have not paid enough attention to the product's other life-cycle costs.[9]

"HMOs go to the marketplace and ask what is the competitive market rate to sell business. Through market pricing, they determine what the rate has to be and then manage their costs accordingly." (15d)
BlueCross BlueShield of North Carolina

"Target costing is neither easily nor quickly done." (15e)
U.S. Navy Acquisition Center

[7]This section is based on Shahid L. Ansari, Jan E. Bell, and the CAM-I Target Cost Core Group, *Target Costing: The Next Frontier in Strategic Cost Management* (Burr Ridge, IL: Irwin, 1997).

[8]Ibid., p. 15.

[9]See Chapter 9 for further discussion of product life-cycle costing.

"Target costing with suppliers involves developing detailed cost models of both existing products and those in development. This necessitates the open sharing of cost information in an ethical and professional manner." (15f)
Eastman Kodak Company

- *Value-chain orientation.* Sometimes the projected cost of a new product is above the target cost. Then efforts are made to eliminate *non-value-added costs* to bring the projected cost down.[10] In some cases, a close look at the company's entire *value chain* can help managers identify opportunities for cost reduction. For example, Procter & Gamble placed order-entry computers in Wal-Mart stores. This resulted in substantial savings in order-processing costs for both companies.[11]

Activity-Based Costing and Target Costing

LO 6

Explain the role of activity-based costing in setting a target cost.

An activity-based costing (ABC) system can be particularly helpful as product design engineers try to achieve a product's target cost. ABC enables designers to break down the production process for a new product into its component activities. Then designers can attempt cost improvement in particular activities to bring a new product's projected cost in line with its target cost.

To illustrate, Sydney Sailing Supplies' Marine Instruments Division, located in Perth, Australia, wants to introduce a new depth finder. Target costing studies indicate that a target cost of $340 must be met in order to successfully compete in this market. Exhibit 15–6 shows how ABC was used to bring the depth finder's initial cost estimate of $399 down to $337, just below the target cost. The company's design engineers were able to focus on key activities in the production process, such as material handling and inspection, and reduce the projected costs.

"A key Honda philosophy is that 'cost is a result.' To get better results, you must manage the cost drivers." (15g)
Honda of America Manufacturing, Inc.

Computer-Integrated Manufacturing When a computer-integrated manufacturing (CIM) system is used, the process of target costing sometimes is computerized. A manufacturer's computer-aided design and cost-accounting software are interconnected. An engineer can try out many different design features and immediately see the product-cost implications, without ever leaving the computer terminal.

[10]The elimination of non-value-added costs is covered in Chapter 6 as part of the discussion of activity-based management.

[11]J. Shank and V. Govindarajan, "Strategic Cost Management and the Value Chain," *Journal of Cost Management* 5, no. 4 (Winter 1992), p. 10. See also T. Tanaka, "Target Costing at Toyota," *Journal of Cost Management* 7, no. 1 (Spring 1993), pp. 4–12.

Exhibit 15–6
Target Costing and Cost Improvement for a New Product

A. Activity-Based Costing System

Activity Cost Pool	Cost Driver	Pool Rate
Purchasing	Number of parts	$1 per part
Material handling	Dollar value of parts	$.20 per direct-material dollar
Inspection	Inspection hours	$28 per inspection hour

This is a highly simplified example of activity-based costing. ABC systems, which were introduced conceptually in Chapter 3, are covered in detail in Chapter 5.

B. Cost Projections for a New Product: Depth Finder

	Original Cost Projection		Improved Cost Projection
Direct material	$200		$190
Direct labor	100		70
Purchasing:			
$1 per part (45 parts)	45		
$1 per part (32 parts)			32
Material handling:			
$.20 per direct-material dollar ($200)	40		
$.20 per direct-material dollar ($190)			38
Inspection:			
$28 per inspection hour (.5 hour)	14		
$28 per inspection hour (.25 hour)			7
Total projected cost	$399		$337
Target cost		$340	

Product-Cost Distortion and Pricing: The Role of Activity-Based Costing

LO 7 Explain how product-cost distortion can undermine a firm's pricing strategy.

Use of a traditional, volume-based product-costing system may result in significant cost distortion among product lines. In many cases, high-volume and relatively simple products are overcosted while low-volume and complex products are undercosted. This results from the fact that high-volume and relatively simple products require proportionately less activity per unit for various manufacturing-support activities than do low-volume and complex products. Yet a traditional product-costing system, in which all overhead is assigned on the basis of a single unit-level activity like direct-labor hours, fails to capture the cost implications of product diversity. In contrast, an activity-based costing (ABC) system does measure the extent to which each product line drives costs in the key production-support activities.

Managers should be aware that cost distortion can result in overpricing high-volume and relatively simple products, while low-volume and complex products are undercosted. This can undermine any effort to set prices competitively, even under the target-costing approach. The competitive implications of such strategic pricing errors can be disastrous.[12]

LO 8 Explain the process of value engineering and its role in target costing.

Value Engineering and Target Costing

Target costing is an outgrowth of the concept of **value engineering,** which is a cost-reduction and process-improvement technique that utilizes information collected about

[12]This whole issue of cost distortion and the role of ABC in product pricing is covered extensively in Chapter 5.

a product's design and production processes and then examines various attributes of the design and processes to identify candidates for improvement efforts.

Much of the historical development of the target-costing approach has taken place in Japanese industry, where now "more than 80 percent of all assembly industries in Japan use target costing. Some of the best practitioners of target costing are leading Japanese companies."[13] In recent years, however, many other companies, including Caterpillar, DaimlerChrysler, Boeing, and Kodak, have made significant contributions to target costing theory and practice.

Isuzu Motors, Ltd. is a leading Japanese manufacturer of automobiles, buses, and both light and heavy-duty trucks. "At Isuzu, value engineering (VE) has been developed to cover all stages of product design and manufacture. Indeed, three different stages of VE—zeroth, first, and second 'looks'—are used in the design phase to increase the functionality of new products."[14]

- *Zeroth look VE* is applied at the earliest stages of new product design—"the concept proposal stage, when the basic concept of the product is developed and its preliminary quality, cost, and investment targets are established."
- *First look VE* is applied during the last half of the concept proposal stage and throughout the product planning phase. During this stage, a product's quality, functionality, and selling price are determined, a design plan is submitted, and target costs are determined for each of the new vehicle's major functions (e.g., engine and transmission). Also, the degree of component commonality is set. "First look VE is used at this stage to increase the value of the product by increasing its functionality without increasing its cost."
- *Second look VE* is applied during the last half of the product planning stage and the first half of the product development and preparation stage. "The components of the vehicle's major functions are identified, and hand-made prototypes are assembled. At this stage, VE works to improve the value and functionality of existing components, not to create new ones."

In addition, various *tear-down methods* are used by Isuzu, and many other companies, "to analyze competitive products in terms of materials they contain, parts they use, ways they function, and ways they are manufactured." At Isuzu, for example, *dynamic tear-down* focuses on reducing the number of vehicle assembly operations or the time required to perform them. *Cost tear-down* examines ways to reduce the cost of the components used in a vehicle. *Material tear-down* compares the materials and surface treatments of the components used by Isuzu with those of its competitors. *Static tear-down* disassembles a competitor's product into its components to enable Isuzu's engineers to compare Isuzu's components with those used in the competitor's product.

> "An old Japanese saying states that 'there are many ways to the top of a mountain.' Analogously, there is no one right way to do target costing." (15h)
> **Honda of America Manufacturing, Inc.**

Although the Isuzu approach is illustrative of target costing methods, many different approaches are used by the hundreds of companies now engaged in target costing programs. However, the Isuzu target costing and value-engineering process is indicative of the seriousness with which companies approach the problem of reducing costs in order to meet a product's target cost and remain competitive in an ever more difficult market.

---

[13]Shahid L. Ausari, Jan E. Bell, and the CAM-I Target Cost Core Group, *Target Costing: The Next Frontier in Strategic Cost Management* (Burr Ridge, IL: Irwin, 1997). See also Y. Kato, "Target Costing Support Systems: Lessons from Leading Japanese Companies," *Management Accounting Research* 4 (1992), pp. 33–47; and T. Tani, H. Okano, N. Shimizu, Y. Iwabuchi, J. Fukuda, and S. Cooray, "Target Cost Management in Japanese Companies: Current State of the Art," *Management Accounting Research* 6 (1994), pp. 67–81.

[14]This description of Isuzu's target costing and value-engineering methods is drawn from Robin Cooper, *When Lean Enterprises Collide* (Boston, MA: Harvard Business School Press, 1995), pp. 165–83.

Time and Material Pricing

LO9 Determine prices using the time and material pricing approach.

Another cost-based approach to pricing is called **time and material pricing.** Under this approach, the company determines one charge for the labor used on a job and another charge for the materials. The labor typically includes the direct cost of the employee's time and a charge to cover various overhead costs. The material charge generally includes the direct cost of the materials used in a job plus a charge for material handling and storage. Time and material pricing is used widely by construction companies, printers, repair shops, and professional firms, such as engineering, law, and public accounting firms.

To illustrate, we will examine a special job undertaken by Sydney Sailing Supplies. The company's vice president for sales, Richard Moby, was approached by a successful local physician about refurbishing her yacht. She wanted an engine overhaul, complete refurbishment and redecoration of the cabin facilities, and stripping and repainting of the hull and deck. The work would be done in the Repair Department of the company's Yacht Division, located in Melbourne, Australia.

Data regarding the operations of the Repair Department are as follows:

Labor rate, including fringe benefits	$18.00 per hour
Hourly charge to cover profit margin	$7.00 per hour
Annual labor hours	10,000 hours
Annual overhead costs:	
Material handling and storage	$40,000
Other overhead costs (supervision, utilities, insurance, and depreciation)	$200,000
Annual cost of materials used in Repair Department	$1,000,000

Based on this data, the Repair Department computed its time and material prices as follows:

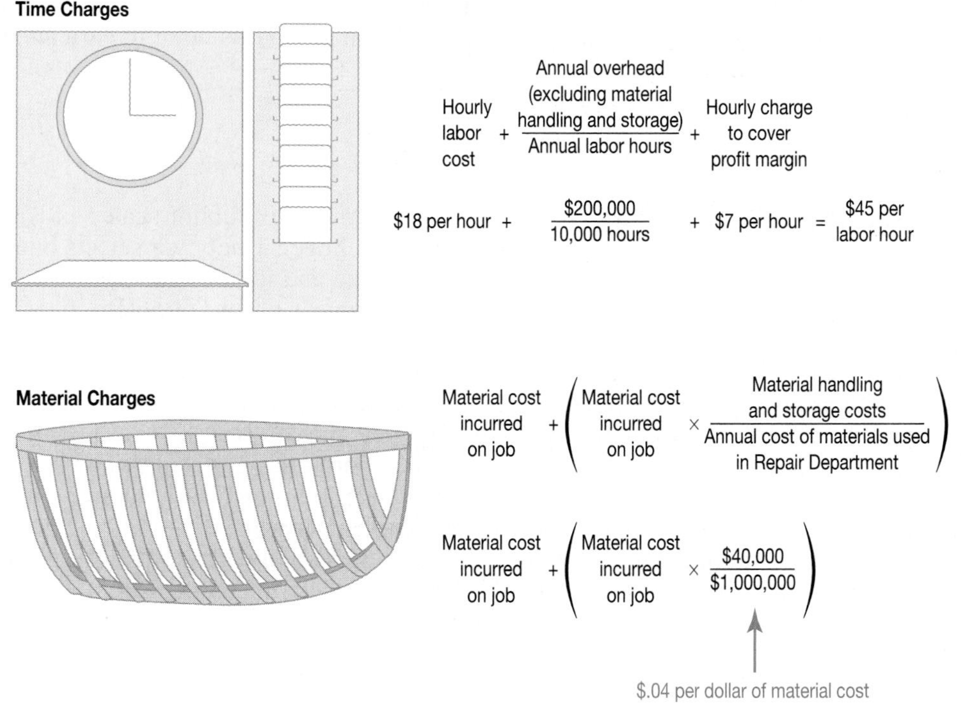

The effect of the material-charge formula is to include a charge for the costs incurred in the handling and storage of materials.

Exhibit 15–7
Time and Material Pricing

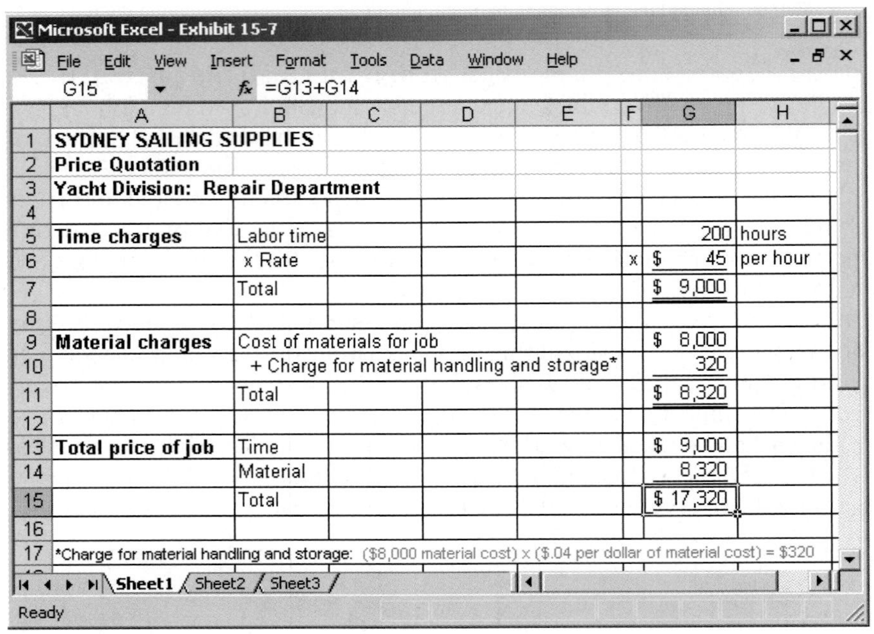

	A	B	C	D	E	F	G	H
1	SYDNEY SAILING SUPPLIES							
2	Price Quotation							
3	Yacht Division: Repair Department							
4								
5	Time charges	Labor time					200	hours
6		x Rate				x	$ 45	per hour
7		Total					$ 9,000	
8								
9	Material charges	Cost of materials for job					$ 8,000	
10		+ Charge for material handling and storage*					320	
11		Total					$ 8,320	
12								
13	Total price of job	Time					$ 9,000	
14		Material					8,320	
15		Total					$ 17,320	
16								
17	*Charge for material handling and storage: ($8,000 material cost) x ($.04 per dollar of material cost) = $320							

Richard Moby estimates that the yacht refurbishment job will require 200 hours of labor and $8,000 in materials. Moby's price quotation for the job is shown in the Excel spreadsheet in Exhibit 15–7.

Included in the $17,320 price quotation for the yacht refurbishment are charges for labor costs, overhead, material costs, material handling and storage costs, and a normal profit margin. Some companies also charge an additional markup on the materials used in a job in order to earn a profit on that component of their services. Sydney Sailing Supplies' practice is to charge a high enough profit charge on its labor to earn an appropriate profit for the Repair Department.

Competitive Bidding

Set prices in special-order or competitive-bidding situations by analyzing the relevant costs.

In a **competitive bidding** situation, two or more companies submit sealed bids (or prices) for a product, service, or project to a potential buyer. The buyer selects one of the companies for the job on the basis of the bid price and the design specifications for the job. Competitive bidding complicates a manager's pricing problem, because now the manager is in direct competition with one or more competitors. If all of the companies submitting bids offer a roughly equivalent product or service, the bid price becomes the sole criterion for selecting the contractor. The higher the price that is bid, the greater will be the profit on the job, *if* the firm gets the contract. However, a higher price also lowers the probability of obtaining the contract to perform the job. Thus, there is a trade-off between bidding high, to make a good profit, and bidding low, to land the contract. Some say there is a "winner's curse" in competitive bidding, meaning that the company bidding low enough to beat out its competitors probably bid too low to make an acceptable profit on the job. Despite the winner's curse, competitive bidding is a common form of selecting contractors in many types of business.

Richard Moby was approached recently by the city of Sydney about building a new marina for moderate-sized sailing vessels. Moby decided that his company's Marine Construction Division should submit a bid on the job. The city announced that three other firms would also be submitting bids. Since all four companies were equally capable of building the marina to the city's specifications, Moby assumed that the bid price would be the deciding factor in selecting the contractor.

Moby consulted with the controller and chief engineer of the Marine Construction Division, and the following data were compiled.

Estimated direct-labor requirements, 1,500 hours at $12.00 per hour	$18,000
Estimated direct-material requirements	30,000
Estimated variable overhead (allocated on the basis of direct labor), 1,500 direct-labor hours at $5.00 per hour	7,500
Total estimated variable costs	$55,500
Estimated fixed overhead (allocated on the basis of direct labor), 1,500 direct-labor hours at $8.00 per hour	12,000
Estimated total cost	$67,500

The Marine Construction Division allocates variable-overhead costs to jobs on the basis of direct-labor hours. These costs consist of indirect-labor costs, such as the wages of equipment-repair personnel, gasoline and lubricants, and incidental supplies such as rope, chains, and drill bits. Fixed-overhead costs, also allocated to jobs on the basis of direct-labor hours, include such costs as workers' compensation insurance, depreciation on vehicles and construction equipment, depreciation of the division's buildings, and supervisory salaries.

It was up to Richard Moby to decide on the bid price for the marina. In his meeting with the divisional controller and the chief engineer, Moby argued that the marina job was important to the company for two reasons. First, the Marine Construction Division had been operating well below capacity for several months. The marina job would not preclude the firm from taking on any other construction work, so it would not entail an opportunity cost. Second, the marina job would be good advertising for Sydney Sailing Supplies. City residents would see the firm's name on the project, and this would promote sales of the company's boats and sailing supplies.

Based on these arguments, Moby pressed for a bid price that just covered the firm's variable costs and allowed for a modest contribution margin. The chief engineer was obstinate, however, and argued for a higher bid price that would give the division a good profit on the job. "My employees work hard to do an outstanding job, and their work is worth a premium to the city," was the engineer's final comment on the issue. After the threesome tossed the problem around all morning, the controller agreed with Moby. A bid price of $60,000 was finally agreed upon.

This is a typical approach to setting prices for special jobs and competitively bid contracts. When a firm has excess capacity, a price that covers the incremental costs incurred because of the job will contribute toward covering the company's fixed cost and profit. None of the Marine Construction Division's fixed costs will increase as a result of taking on the marina job. Thus, a bid price of $60,000 will cover the $55,500 of variable costs on the job and contribute $4,500 toward covering the division's fixed costs.

Bid price	$60,000
Variable costs of marina job (incremental costs incurred only if job is done)	55,500
Contribution from marina job (contribution to covering the division's fixed costs)	$ 4,500

Naturally, Sydney Sailing Supplies' management would like to make a larger profit on the marina job, but bidding a higher price means running a substantial risk of losing the job to a competitor.

No Excess Capacity What if the Marine Construction Division has no excess capacity? If management expects to have enough work to fully occupy the division, a different approach is appropriate in setting the bid price. The fixed costs of the division are capacity-producing costs, which are costs incurred in order to create productive capacity. Depreciation of buildings and equipment, supervisory salaries, insurance, and property taxes are examples of fixed costs incurred to give a company the capacity to carry on its operations. When such costs are allocated to individual jobs, the cost of each job reflects an estimate of the opportunity cost of using limited capacity to do that particular job. For this reasoning to be valid, however, the organization must be at full capacity. If there is excess capacity, there is no opportunity cost in using that excess capacity.

If the Marine Construction Division has no excess capacity, it would be appropriate to focus on the estimated full cost of the marina job, $67,500, which includes an allocation of the division's fixed capacity-producing costs. Now Richard Moby might legitimately argue for a bid price in excess of $67,500. If the division is awarded the marina contract by the city, a price above $67,500 will cover all the costs of the job and make a contribution toward the division's profit.

However, as Richard Moby pointed out, there will be valuable promotional benefits to Sydney Sailing Supplies if its Marine Construction Division builds the marina. This is a qualitative factor, because these potential benefits are difficult to quantify. Moby will have to make a judgment regarding just how important the marina job is to the company. The greater the perceived qualitative benefits, the lower the bid price should be set to maximize the likelihood that the company will be awarded the contract.

Summary of Competitive-Bidding Analysis The Marine Construction Division's pricing problem is summarized in Exhibit 15–8. As you can see, the final pricing decision requires managerial judgment to fully consider the quantitative cost data, the qualitative promotional benefits, and the trade-off between a higher profit and a greater likelihood of getting the marina contract.

Accept or Reject a Special Order In the preceding chapter, we examined in detail the decision as to whether a special order should be accepted or rejected. The analysis focused on identifying the relevant costs of the special order. The existence of excess capacity was an important factor in that analysis. Accepting a special order when excess capacity exists entails no opportunity cost. But when there is no excess capacity, one relevant cost of accepting a special order is the opportunity cost incurred by using the firm's limited capacity for the special order instead of some other job. After all relevant costs of the order have been identified, the decision maker compares the total relevant cost of the order with the price offered. If the price exceeds the relevant cost, the order generally should be accepted.

The decision is conceptually very similar to the bid-pricing problem discussed in this chapter. Setting a price for a special order or competitive bid also entails an analysis of the relevant costs of the job. Whether the decision maker is setting a price or has been offered a price, he or she must identify the relevant costs of providing the product or service requested.

Effect of Antitrust Laws on Pricing

LO 11

Describe the legal restrictions on setting prices.

Businesses are not free to set any price they wish for their products or services. American antitrust laws, including the Robinson-Patman Act, the Clayton Act, and the Sherman Act, restrict certain types of pricing behavior. These laws prohibit **price discrimination,** which means quoting different prices to different customers for the same product or service. Such price differences are unlawful unless they can be clearly justified by differences in the costs incurred to produce, sell, or deliver the product or service. Managers should keep careful records justifying such cost differences when they exist, because the records may be vital to a legal defense if price differences are challenged in court.

Another pricing practice prohibited by law is **predatory pricing.** This practice involves temporarily cutting a price to broaden demand for a product with the intention

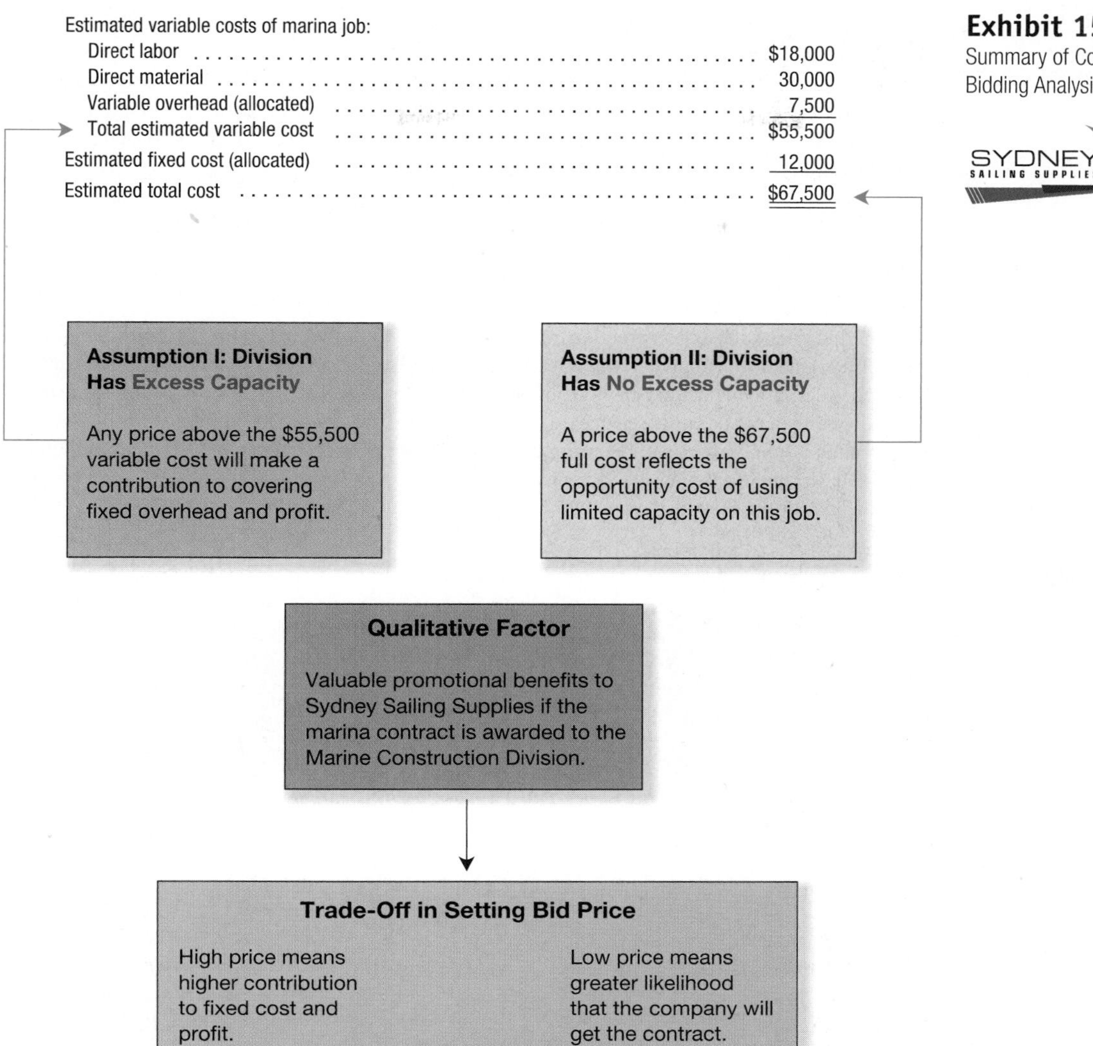

Estimated variable costs of marina job:
Direct labor $18,000
Direct material 30,000
Variable overhead (allocated) 7,500
Total estimated variable cost $55,500
Estimated fixed cost (allocated) 12,000
Estimated total cost $67,500
Assumption I: Division Has Excess Capacity
Any price above the $55,500 variable cost will make a contribution to covering fixed overhead and profit.
Assumption II: Division Has No Excess Capacity
A price above the $67,500 full cost reflects the opportunity cost of using limited capacity on this job.
Qualitative Factor
Valuable promotional benefits to Sydney Sailing Supplies if the marina contract is awarded to the Marine Construction Division.
Trade-Off in Setting Bid Price
High price means higher contribution to fixed cost and profit.
Low price means greater likelihood that the company will get the contract.

Exhibit 15–8
Summary of Competitive-Bidding Analysis

SYDNEY SAILING SUPPLIES

of later restricting the supply and raising the price again. In determining whether a price is predatory, the courts examine a business's cost records. If the product is sold below cost, the pricing is deemed to be predatory. The laws and court cases are ambiguous as to the appropriate definition of cost. However, various court decisions make it harder to prove predatory pricing. Nevertheless, this is one area where a price-setting decision maker is well advised to have an accountant on the left and a lawyer on the right before setting prices that could be deemed predatory.

Chapter Summary

Pricing of products and services is one of the most challenging decisions faced by management. Many influences affect pricing decisions. Chief among these are customer demand, the actions of competitors, and the costs of the products or services. Other factors such as political, legal, and image-related issues also affect pricing decisions.

Economic theory shows that under certain assumptions, the profit-maximizing price and quantity are determined by the intersection of the marginal-revenue and marginal-cost curves. While the economic model serves as a useful conceptual framework for the pricing decision, it is limited by its assumptions and the informational demands it implies.

Most companies set prices, at least to some extent, on the basis of costs. Cost-plus pricing formulas add a markup to some version of cost, typically either total variable cost or total absorption cost. Markups often are set to earn the company a target profit on its products, based on a target rate of return on investment.

Strategic pricing of new products is an especially challenging problem for management. Various pricing approaches, such as skimming pricing or penetration pricing, may be appropriate depending on the product. Target costing often is used to design a new product that can be produced at a cost that will enable the firm to sell it at a competitive price. Value engineering and activity-based costing are valuable tools used in the target costing process.

In industries such as construction, repair, printing, and professional services, time and material pricing is used. Under this approach the price is determined as the sum of a labor-cost component and a material-cost component. Either or both of these components may include a markup to ensure that the company earns a profit on its services.

Pricing special orders and determining competitive bid prices entail an analysis of the relevant costs to be incurred in completing the job. The relevant-cost analysis should incorporate the existence of excess capacity or the lack of it.

Review Problem on Cost-Plus Pricing

Kitchenware Corporation manufactures high-quality copper pots and pans. Greta Cooke, one of the company's price analysts, is involved in setting a price for the company's new Starter Set. This set consists of seven of the most commonly used pots and pans. During the next year, the company plans to produce 10,000 Starter Sets, and the controller has provided Cooke with the following cost data.

Predicted Costs of 10,000 Starter Sets	
Direct material per set	$60
Direct labor per set, 2 hours at $10.00 per hr.	20
Variable selling cost per set	5
Total	$85
Variable-overhead rate	$ 8.00 per direct-labor hour
Fixed-overhead rate	$12.00 per direct-labor hour

In addition, the controller indicated that the Accounting Department would allocate $20,000 of fixed administrative expenses to the Starter Set product line.

Required:

1. Compute the cost of a Starter Set using each of the four cost definitions commonly used in cost-plus pricing formulas.
2. Determine the markup percentage required for the Starter Set product line to earn a target profit of $317,500 before taxes during the next year. Use the total cost as the cost definition in the cost-plus formula.

Solution to Review Problem

1.

Variable manufacturing cost*	$ 96	1
Applied fixed-overhead cost†	24	
Absorption manufacturing cost	$120	2
Variable selling cost	5	
Allocated fixed administrative cost‡	2	
Total cost	$127	3
Variable manufacturing cost	$ 96	
Variable selling cost	5	
Total variable cost	$101	4

(continues)

*Direct material	$60	
Direct labor	20	
Variable overhead	16	(2 × $8.00 per hour)
Total variable manufacturing cost	$96	
†Applied fixed overhead cost	$24	(2 × $12 per hour)
‡Allocated fixed administrative cost	$ 2	($20,000 ÷ 10,000 sets)

2. Markup percentage on total cost $= \dfrac{\$317{,}500}{10{,}000 \times \$127} = 25\%$

Proof: Price = Total cost + (.25 × Total cost) = $127 + (.25)($127) = $158.75

Income Statement

Sales revenue (10,000 × $158.75)		$1,587,500
Less: Variable costs:		
Direct material	$600,000	
Direct labor	200,000	
Variable overhead	160,000	
Variable selling cost	50,000	
Total variable costs		1,010,000
Contribution margin		$ 577,500
Less: Fixed costs:		
Manufacturing overhead	$240,000	
Administrative cost	20,000	
Total fixed costs		260,000
Profit		$ 317,500

Key Terms

For each term's definition refer to the indicated page, or turn to the glossary at the end of the text.

competitive bidding, 654
cost-plus pricing, 642
cross-elasticity, 641
demand curve (average revenue curve), 636
marginal cost curve, 638
marginal revenue curve, 638
oligopolistic market, 641
penetration pricing, 646
predatory pricing, 656
price discrimination, 656
price elasticity, 640
price taker, 636
return-on-investment pricing, 644
skimming pricing, 646
target cost, 647
target costing, 647
time and material pricing, 653
total cost curve, 638
total revenue curve, 636
value engineering, 651

Review Questions

15–1. Comment on the following remark made by a bank president: "The prices of our banking services are determined by the financial-services market. Costs are irrelevant."

15–2. "All this marginal revenue and marginal cost stuff is just theory. Prices are determined by production costs." Evaluate this assertion.

15–3. List and briefly describe four major influences on pricing decisions.

15–4. Explain what is meant by the following statement: "In considering the reactions of competitors, it is crucial to define your product."

15–5. Explain the following assertion: "Price setting generally requires a balance between market forces and cost considerations."

15–6. Briefly explain the concept of *economic, profit-maximizing pricing.* It may be helpful to use graphs in your explanation.

15–7. Define the following terms: *total revenue, marginal revenue, demand curve, price elasticity,* and *cross-elasticity.*

15–8. Briefly define *total cost* and *marginal cost.*

15–9. Describe three limitations of the economic, profit-maximizing model of pricing.

15–10. Determining the best approach to pricing requires a cost-benefit trade-off. Explain.

15–11. Write the general formula for cost-plus pricing, and briefly explain its use.

15–12. List the four common cost bases used in cost-plus pricing. How can they all result in the same price?

15–13. List four reasons often cited for the widespread use of absorption cost as the cost base in cost-plus pricing formulas.

15–14. What is the primary disadvantage of basing the cost-plus pricing formula on absorption cost?

15–15. List three advantages of pricing based on variable cost.

15–16. Explain the behavioral problem that can result when cost-plus prices are based on variable cost.

15–17. Briefly explain the concept of *return-on-investment pricing.*

15–18. Explain the phrase *price-led costing.*

15–19. Why is a focus on the customer such a key principle of target costing?

15–20. Explain the role of value engineering in target costing.

15–21. Could *tear-down* methods be used effectively for target pricing in a service-industry company, such as a hotel or an airline? Explain.

15–22. Briefly describe the *time-and-material pricing approach.*

15–23. Explain the importance of the excess-capacity issue in setting a competitive bid price.

15–24. The decision to accept or reject a special order and the selection of a price for a special order are very similar decisions. Explain.

15–25. Describe the following approaches to pricing new products: skimming pricing, penetration pricing, and target costing.

15–26. Explain what is meant by unlawful price discrimination and predatory pricing.

15–27. Briefly explain the potential negative consequences in pricing decisions from using a traditional, volume-based product-costing system.

Exercises

Exercise 15–28
Marginal Revenue and Marginal Cost Curves
(LO 1, 2)

The marginal cost, marginal revenue, and demand curves for Halifax Home and Garden's deluxe wheelbarrow are shown in the graph below.

Required: Before completing any of the following requirements, read over the entire list.

1. Trace the graph onto a blank piece of paper, and label all parts of the graph.
2. Draw a companion graph directly above the traced graph. Use this graph to draw the firm's total revenue and total cost curves.
3. Show the company's profit-maximizing price on the lower graph and its profit-maximizing quantity on both graphs.

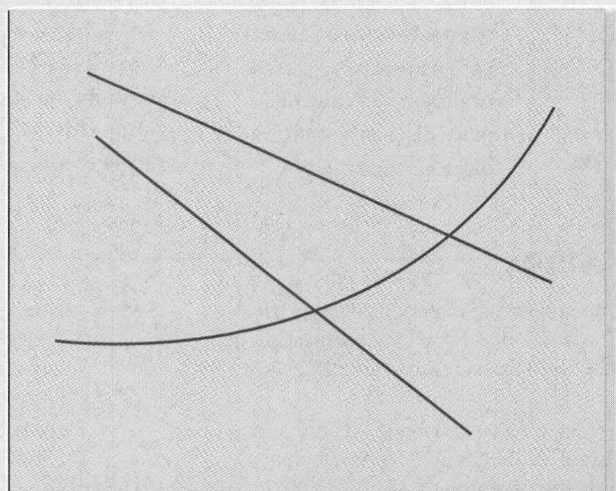

Exercise 15–29
Demand and Revenue Data
(LO 1, 2)

Serendipity Sound, Inc. manufactures compact disk players with unusual features in its Minneapolis Division. The divisional sales manager has estimated the following demand-curve data.

Quantity Sold per Month	Unit Sales Price
20	$500
40	475
60	450

(continues)

80	425
100	400

Required:

1. Prepare a table similar to panel C of Exhibit 15–1 summarizing Serendipity Sound's price, quantity, and revenue data.
2. Draw a graph similar to panel A of Exhibit 15–1 reflecting the data tabulated in requirement (1).

Exercise 15–30
Continuation of Preceding Exercise; Cost Data
(LO 1, 2)

Refer to the preceding exercise. The divisional controller at Serendipity Sound's Minneapolis Division has estimated the following cost data for the division's CD players. (Assume there are no fixed costs.)

Quantity Produced and Sold per Month	Average Cost per Unit
20	$450
40	425
60	410
80	430
100	445

Required:

1. Prepare a table similar to panel C of Exhibit 15–2 summarizing Serendipity Sound's cost relationships.
2. Draw a graph similar to panel A of Exhibit 15–2 reflecting the data tabulated in requirement (1).

Exercise 15–31
Continuation of Preceding Two Exercises; Profit-Maximizing Price
(LO 1, 2)

Refer to the data given in the preceding two exercises.

1. Prepare a table of Serendipity Sound's revenue, cost, and profit relationships. For guidance refer to panel C of Exhibit 15–3.
2. Draw a graph similar to panel A of Exhibit 15–3 reflecting the data tabulated in requirement (1).
3. To narrow down the pricing decision, the Minneapolis Division's sales manager has decided to price the CD player at one of the following prices: $400, $425, $450, or $500. Which price do you recommend? Why?

Exercise 15–32
Cost-Plus Pricing Formulas; Missing Data
(LO 1, 3)

The following data pertain to LawnMate Corporation's top-of-the-line lawn mower.

Variable manufacturing cost	$275
Applied fixed manufacturing cost	55
Variable selling and administrative cost	66
Allocated fixed selling and administrative cost	?

To achieve a target price of $495 per lawn mower, the markup percentage is 12.5 percent on total unit cost.

Required:

1. What is the fixed selling and administrative cost allocated to each unit of LawnMate's top-of-the-line mower?
2. For each of the following cost bases, develop a cost-plus pricing formula that will result in a target price of $495 per mower: (*a*) variable manufacturing cost, (*b*) absorption manufacturing cost, and (*c*) total variable cost.

Exercise 15–33
Pricing, Advertising, and Special-Order Decisions
(LO 10)

Rosario Company produces a single product in its Buenos Aires plant, which currently sells for 7.50 *p* per unit. Fixed costs are expected to amount to 90,000 *p* for the year, and all variable manufacturing and administrative costs are expected to be incurred at a rate of 4.50 *p* per unit. Rosario has two salespeople who are paid strictly on a commission basis. Their commission is 10 percent of the sales dollars they generate. (Ignore income taxes.) (*p* denotes the peso, Argentina's national currency. Many countries use the peso as their national currency. On the day this exercise was written, Argentina's peso was worth 1.0004 U.S. dollars.)

Required:

1. Suppose management alters its current plans by spending an additional amount of 7,500 *p* on advertising and increases the selling price to 9.00 *p* per unit. Calculate the profit on 60,000 units.

2. The Salente Company has just approached Rosario to make a special one-time purchase of 10,000 units. These units would not be sold by the sales personnel, and, therefore, no commission would have to be paid. What is the price Rosario would have to charge per unit on this special order to earn additional profit of 30,000 *p?*

(CMA, adapted)

Exercise 15–34
Cost-Plus Pricing Formulas
(LO 1, 3)

The following data pertain to Legion Lighting Company's oak-clad, contemporary chandelier.

Variable manufacturing cost	$300
Applied fixed manufacturing cost	105
Variable selling and administrative cost	45
Allocated fixed selling and administrative cost	75

Required: For each of the following cost bases, develop a cost-plus pricing formula that will result in a price of $600 for the oak chandelier.

1. Variable manufacturing cost.
2. Absorption manufacturing cost.
3. Total cost.
4. Total variable cost.

Exercise 15–35
Determining Markup Percentage; Target ROI
(LO 1, 3)

Refer to the cost and production data for the Wave Darter in Exhibit 15–5. The target profit is $60,000.

Required: Use the general formula for determining a markup percentage to compute the required markup percentages with the following two cost-plus formulas:

1. Variable manufacturing costs [formula (1) in Exhibit 15–5].
2. Absorption manufacturing cost [formula (2) in Exhibit 15–5].

Exercise 15–36
Time and Material Pricing
(LO 9)

Refer to Exhibit 15–7. Suppose the Repair Department of Sydney Sailing Supplies adds a markup of 5 percent on the material charges of a job (including the cost of material handling and storage).

Required:

1. Rewrite the material component of the time and material pricing formula to reflect the markup on material cost.
2. Compute the new price to be quoted on the yacht refurbishment described in Exhibit 15–7.

Exercise 15–37
Target Costing for a New Product; Use of Internet
(LO 4, 5, 8)

Visit the website of one of the following companies, or a different company of your choosing.

Nintendo	www.nintendo.com
Procter & Gamble	www.pg.com
Carnival Cruise Lines	www.carnival.com
Chase Manhattan Bank	www.chase.com
General Electric Company	www.ge.com
Hewlett-Packard	www.hp.com
Intel Corporation	www.intel.com

Required: Read about a new product or service to be offered by the company. Then explain how the firm could use target costing to price the new product or service.

Problems

Note: Several of the problems and cases in Chapter 5 relate to pricing and may be assigned with Chapter 15 as well. These problems emphasize the impact of cost distortion on pricing decisions. They stress the differences between traditional, volume-based costing systems and activity-based costing systems with respect to their role in pricing. These problems should be assigned only after Chapter 5 has been completed. The following problems are relevant: 5–40, 5–41, 5–45, 5–46, and 5–50.

Problem 15–38
Pricing of Special Order
(LO 10)

Heartland Corporation manufactures flour milling machinery according to customer specifications. The company operated at 75 percent of practical capacity during the year just ended, with the following results (in thousands):

Sales revenue	$12,500
Less: Sales commissions (10%)	1,250
Net sales	$11,250
Expenses:	
Direct material	$ 3,000
Direct labor	3,750
Manufacturing overhead—variable	1,125
Manufacturing overhead—fixed	750
Corporate administration—fixed	375
Total costs	$ 9,000
Income before taxes	$ 2,250
Income taxes (40%)	900
Net income	$ 1,350

Heartland, which expects continued operations at 75 percent of capacity, recently submitted a bid of $82,500 on custom-designed machinery for Premier Foods, Inc. Heartland used a pricing formula in deriving the bid amount, the formula being based on last year's operating results. The formula follows.

Estimated direct material	$14,600
Estimated direct labor	28,000
Estimated manufacturing overhead at 50% of direct labor	14,000
Estimated corporate overhead at 10% of direct labor	2,800
Estimated total costs excluding sales commissions	$59,400
Add 25% for profit and taxes	14,850
Suggested price (with profit) before sales commissions	$74,250
Suggested total price: $74,250 ÷ 0.9 to adjust for 10% commission	$82,500

Required:

1. Calculate the impact the order would have on Heartland's net income if the $82,500 bid were accepted by Premier Foods, Inc.
2. Assume that Premier has rejected Heartland's bid but has stated it is willing to pay $63,500 for the machinery. Should Heartland manufacture the machinery for the counteroffer of $63,500? Explain your answer and show calculations.
3. At what bid price will Heartland break even on the order?
4. Explain how the profit performance in the coming year would be affected if Heartland accepted all of its work at prices similar to Premier's $63,500 counteroffer described in requirement (2).

(CMA, adapted)

Problem 15–39
Time and Material Pricing
(LO 9)

Suburban Heating, Inc. installs heating systems in new homes built in suburban Philadelphia. Jobs are priced using the time and materials method. The following predictions pertain to the company's operations for the next year.

Labor rate, including fringe benefits	$20.00 per hour
Annual labor hours	12,000 hours
Annual overhead costs:	
Material handling and storage	$31,250
Other overhead costs	$135,000
Annual cost of materials used	$312,500

The president of Suburban Heating, B. T. Ewing, is pricing a job involving the heating systems for six houses to be built by a local developer. He has made the following estimates.

Material cost	$75,000
Labor hours	400

Required: Suburban Heating adds a markup of $5.00 per hour on its time charges, but there is no markup on material costs.

1. Develop formulas for the company's (*a*) time charges and (*b*) material charges.
2. Compute the price for the job described above.
3. What would be the price of the job if Suburban Heating also added a markup of 10 percent on all material charges (including material handling and storage costs)?

Problem 15–40
Cost-Plus Pricing; Bidding
(LO 3, 10)

Manhattan Pharmaceuticals, Inc. specializes in packaging bulk drugs in standard dosages for local hospitals. Wyant Memorial Hospital has asked Manhattan Pharmaceuticals to bid on the packaging of one million doses of medication at total cost plus a return on total cost of no more than 15 percent. Wyant defines total cost as including all variable costs of performing the service, a reasonable amount of fixed overhead, and reasonable administrative costs. The hospital will supply all packaging materials and ingredients. Wyant's administrator has indicated that any bid over $.03 per dose will be rejected. The controller for Manhattan Pharmaceuticals has accumulated the following data prior to the preparation of the bid.

Direct labor	$16.00 per direct-labor hour (DLH)
Variable overhead	$12.00 per DLH
Fixed overhead	$20.00 per DLH
Incremental administrative costs	$2,000 for the order
Production rate	2,000 doses per DLH

Required:

1. Calculate the minimum price per dose that Manhattan Pharmaceuticals could bid for the Wyant Memorial Hospital job that would not reduce the pharmaceutical company's income.
2. Calculate the bid price per dose using total cost and the maximum allowable return specified by Wyant Memorial Hospital.
3. Independent of your answer to requirement (2), suppose that the price per dose that Manhattan Pharmaceuticals, Inc. calculated using the cost-plus criterion specified by Wyant Memorial Hospital is greater than the maximum bid of $.03 per dose allowed by Wyant. Discuss the factors that the pharmaceutical company's management should consider before deciding whether or not to submit a bid at the maximum price of $.03 per dose that Wyant allows.

(CMA, adapted)

Problem 15–41
Pricing a Special Order; International
(LO 10)

Wolverine Valve and Fitting Company, located in southern Michigan, manufactures a variety of industrial valves and pipe fittings. Currently, the company is operating at about 70 percent capacity. Management has been approached by Glasgow Industries Ltd. of Scotland with an offer to buy 120,000 units of a pressure valve. Glasgow Industries manufactures a valve that is almost identical to Wolverine's pressure valve; however, a fire in Glasgow Industries' valve plant has shut down its manufacturing operations. Glasgow needs the 120,000 valves over the next four months to meet commitments to its regular customers. Glasgow is prepared to pay $28.50 each for the valves. Wolverine's total product cost for the pressure valve is $30, calculated as follows:

Direct material	$ 7.50
Direct labor	9.00
Manufacturing overhead	13.50
Total product cost	$30.00

Manufacturing overhead is applied to production at the rate of $27 per direct-labor hour. This overhead rate is made up of the following components.

Variable manufacturing overhead	$ 9.00
Fixed manufacturing overhead (traceable)	12.00
Fixed manufacturing overhead (allocated)	6.00
Applied manufacturing overhead rate	$27.00

Additional costs incurred in connection with sales of the pressure valve include sales commissions of 5 percent and freight expense of $1.50 per unit. However, the company does not pay sales commissions on special orders that come directly to management. In determining selling prices, Wolverine adds a 40 percent markup to total product cost. This provides a $42.00 suggested selling price for the pressure valve. The Marketing Department, however, has set the current selling price at $40.50 in order to maintain market share. Production management believes that it can handle the Glasgow Industries order without disrupting its scheduled production. The order would, however, require additional fixed factory overhead of $18,000 per month in the form of supervision and clerical costs. If management accepts the order, 30,000 pressure valves will be manufactured and shipped to Glasgow Industries each month for the next four months. Glasgow's management has agreed to pay the shipping charges for the valves.

Required:

1. Determine how many direct-labor hours would be required each month to fill the Glasgow Industries order.
2. Prepare an analysis showing the impact of accepting the Glasgow Industries order.
3. Calculate the minimum unit price that Wolverine Valve and Fitting Company's management could accept for the Glasgow Industries order without reducing net income.
4. Identify the factors, other than price, that Wolverine's management should consider before accepting the Glasgow Industries order.

(CMA, adapted)

Problem 15–42
Cost-Plus Pricing vs. Target Costing
(LO 3, 5, 6, 8)

For many years, Lehigh Corporation has used a straightforward cost-plus pricing system, marking its goods up approximately 25 percent of total cost. The company has been profitable; however, it has recently lost considerable business to foreign competitors that have become very aggressive in the marketplace. These firms appear to be using target costing. An example of Lehigh's problem is typified by item DC66, which has the following unit-cost characteristics:

Direct material	$ 90
Direct labor	225
Manufacturing overhead	150
Selling and administrative expenses	75

The going market price for an identical product of comparable quality is $585, which is significantly below what Lehigh is charging.

Required:

1. Contrast cost-plus pricing and target costing. Which of the two approaches could be aptly labeled price-led costing? Why?
2. What is Lehigh's current selling price of item DC66?
3. If Lehigh used target costing for item DC66, by how much must costs change if the company desires to meet the market price and maintain its current rate of profit *on sales?*
4. Would the identification of value-added and non-value-added costs assist Lehigh in this situation? Briefly explain.
5. Suppose that by previous cost-cutting drives, costs had already been "pared to the bone" on item DC66. What might Lehigh be forced to do with its markup on cost to remain competitive? By how much must the markup change?
6. Early in this chapter, the text noted that in many industries, prices are the result of an interaction between market forces and costs. Explain what is meant by this statement.

Problem 15–43
Bidding on a Special Order
(LO 10)

Detroit Synthetic Fibers, Inc. specializes in the manufacture of synthetic fibers used in many products such as blankets, coats, and uniforms. The company applies overhead on the basis of direct-labor hours. Management has recently received a request to bid on the manufacture of 800,000 blankets scheduled for delivery to several military bases. The bid must be stated at full cost per unit plus a return on full cost of no more than 15 percent before income taxes. Full cost has been defined as including all variable costs of manufacturing the product, a reasonable amount of fixed overhead, and reasonable incremental administrative costs associated with the manufacture and sale of the product. The contractor has indicated that bids in excess of $50 per blanket are not likely to be considered.

In order to prepare the bid for the 800,000 blankets, Andrea Lightner, director of cost management, has gathered the following information about the costs associated with the production of the blankets.

Direct material	$3.00 per pound of fibers
Direct labor	$14.00 per hour
Direct machine costs*	$20.00 per blanket
Variable overhead	$6.00 per direct-labor hour
Fixed overhead	$16.00 per direct-labor hour
Incremental administrative costs	$5,000 per 1,000 blankets
Special fee†	$1.00 per blanket
Material usage	6 pounds per blanket
Production rate	4 blankets per direct-labor hour

*Direct machine costs consist of items such as special lubricants, replacement of needles used in stitching, and maintenance costs. These costs are not included in the normal overhead rates.

†Detroit Synthetic Fibers recently developed a new blanket fiber at a cost of $1,500,000. In an effort to recover this cost, management has instituted a policy of adding a $1.00 fee to the cost of each blanket using the new fiber. To date, the company has recovered $250,000. Lightner knows that this fee does not fit within the definition of full cost as it is not a cost of manufacturing the product.

Required:

1. Calculate the minimum price per blanket that Detroit Synthetic Fibers, Inc. could bid without reducing the company's net income.
2. Using the full-cost criteria and the maximum allowable return specified, calculate Detroit Synthetic Fibers, Inc.'s bid price per blanket.
3. Independent of your answer to requirement (2), assume that the price per blanket that Detroit Synthetic Fibers, Inc. calculated using the cost-plus criteria specified is greater than the maximum bid of $50 per blanket allowed. Discuss the factors that management should consider before deciding whether to submit a bid at the maximum acceptable price of $50 per blanket.

(CMA, adapted)

Problem 15–44
Target Costing
(LO 5, 6, 8)

Maritime Services Corporation (MSC) will soon enter a very competitive marketplace in which it will have limited influence over the prices that are charged. Management and consultants are currently working to fine-tune the company's sole service, which they hope will generate a 12 percent first-year return (profit) on the firm's $27,000,000 asset investment. Although the normal return in MSC's industry is 14 percent, executives are willing to accept the lower figure because of various start-up inefficiencies. The following information is available for first-year operations:

Hours of service to be provided: 25,000
Anticipated variable cost per service hour: $33
Anticipated fixed cost: $2,850,000 per year

Required:

1. Assume that management is contemplating what price to charge in the first year of operation. The company can take its cost and add a markup to achieve a 12 percent return; alternatively, it can use target costing. Given MSC's marketplace, which approach is probably more appropriate? Why?
2. How much profit must MSC generate in the first year to achieve a 12 percent return?
3. Calculate the revenue per hour that MSC must generate in the first year to achieve a 12 percent return.
4. Assume that prior to the start of business in year 1, management conducted a planning exercise to determine if MSC could attain a 14 percent return in year 2. Can the company achieve this return if (*a*) competitive pressures dictate a maximum selling price of $265 per hour and (*b*) service hours and the variable cost per service hour are the same as the amounts anticipated in year 1? Show calculations.
5. If your answer to requirement (4) is no, suggest and briefly describe a procedure that MSC might use to achieve the desired results.

Problem 15–45
Target Costing; Value Engineering; ABC; JIT
(LO 5, 6, 8)

Portland Electronics Company's (PEC) president, Marsha Kunselman, is concerned about the prospects of one of the firm's major products. The president has been reviewing a marketing report with Jeff Keller, marketing product manager, for their top-of-the-line stereo amplifier. The report indicates another price reduction is needed to meet anticipated competitors' reductions in sales prices. The current selling price for PEC's amplifier is $700 per unit. It is expected that within three months PEC's two major competitors will be selling their comparable amplifiers for $600 per unit. This concerns Kunselman because PEC's current cost of producing the amplifiers is $630, which yields a $70 profit on each unit sold.

The situation is especially disturbing because PEC had implemented an activity-based costing (ABC) system about two years ago. The ABC system helped them better identify costs, cost pools, cost drivers, and cost reduction opportunities. Changes made when adopting ABC reduced costs on this product by approximately 15 percent during the last two years. Now it appears that costs will need to be reduced considerably more to remain competitive and to earn a profit on the amplifier. Total costs to produce, sell, and service the amplifiers are as follows:

Amplifiers

	Cost Item	Per Unit
Material	Purchased components	$215
	All other material	85
Labor	Manufacturing, direct	130
	Setups	18
	Material handling	36
	Inspection	46
Machining	Cutting, shaping, and drilling	42
	Bending and finishing	28
Other	Finished-goods warehousing	10
	Warranty	20
	Total unit cost	$630

Kunselman has decided to hire Donald Collins, a consultant, to help decide how to proceed. After a value-engineering analysis, Collins suggested that PEC adopt a just-in-time (JIT) cell manufacturing process to help reduce costs. He also suggested that using target costing would help in meeting the new target price. By changing to a JIT cell manufacturing system, PEC expects that manufacturing direct labor will increase by $30 per finished unit. However, setup, material handling, inspection, and finished goods warehousing will all be eliminated. Machine costs will be reduced from $70 to $60 per unit, and warranty costs are expected to be reduced by 40 percent.

Required:

1. Define *target costing*.
2. Define *value engineering*.
3. Determine Portland Electronics Company's unit target cost at the $600 competitive sales price while maintaining the same percentage of profit on sales as is earned on the current $700 sales price.
4. If the just-in-time cell manufacturing process is implemented with the changes in costs noted, will PEC meet the unit target cost you determined in requirement (3)? Prepare a schedule detailing cost reductions and the unit cost under the proposed JIT cell manufacturing process.

(CMA, adapted)

Problem 15–46
Product Cost Distortion and Product Pricing; Departmental Overhead Rates
(LO 7)

Super Sounds, Inc. manufactures two models of stereo speaker sets. The company uses an absorption (or full) product-costing system, which means that both variable and fixed overhead are included in the product cost. Cost estimates for the two models for the coming year are as follows:

	Standard Model	Deluxe Model
Direct material	$240	$390
Direct labor (10 hours at $21 per hour)	210	210
Manufacturing overhead*	150	150
Total cost per set	$600	$750

*The predetermined overhead rate is $15 per direct-labor hour.

Each stereo speaker set requires 10 hours of direct labor. Each Standard model set requires two hours in Department I and eight hours in Department II. Each set of the Deluxe model requires eight hours in Department I and two hours in Department II. The manufacturing overhead costs expected during the coming year in Departments I and II are as follows:

	Department I	Department II
Variable overhead	$12 per direct-labor hour	$6 per direct-labor hour
Fixed overhead	$225,000	$225,000

The expected operating activity for the coming year is 37,500 direct-labor hours in each department.

Required:

1. Show how Super Sounds, Inc. derived its predetermined overhead rate.
2. What will be the price of each model stereo speaker set if the company prices its products at absorption manufacturing cost plus 15 percent?
3. Suppose Super Sounds, Inc. were to use departmental overhead rates. Compute these rates for Departments I and II for the coming year.
4. Compute the absorption cost of each model stereo speaker set using the departmental overhead rates computed in requirement (3).
5. Suppose management sticks with its policy of setting prices equal to absorption cost plus 15 percent. Compute the new price for each speaker model using the product costs developed in requirement (4).
6. Should Super Sounds, Inc. use plantwide or departmental overhead rates? Explain your answer.

Problem 15–47
Target Costing; Selection of Product Features
(LO 5, 6, 8)

Danish Interiors, Ltd. manufactures easy-to-assemble wooden furniture for home and office. Management is considering modification of a table to make it more attractive to individuals and businesses that buy products through outlets such as Office Max, Office Depot, and Staples stores. The table is small, can be used to hold a computer printer or fax machine, and has several shelves for storage.

The company's marketing department surveyed potential buyers of the table regarding five proposed modifications. The 200 survey participants were asked to evaluate the modifications by using a five-point scale that ranged from 1 (strongly disagree) to 5 (strongly agree). Their responses, along with Danish Interiors' related unit costs for the modifications, follow.

	1 Strongly Disagree	2 Disagree	3 Neutral	4 Agree	5 Strongly Agree
Add cabinet doors in storage area ($18.00)	10	20	30	60	80
Expand storage area ($7.50)	10	40	70	50	30
Add security lock to storage area ($4.95)	30	60	50	40	20
Give table top a more rich, marble appearance ($12.75)	10	20	50	60	60
Extend warranty to five years ($15.30)	40	70	30	35	25

The table currently costs $192 to produce and distribute, and Danish Interiors' selling price for this unit averages $240. An analysis of competitive tables in the marketplace revealed a variety of features, with some models having all of the features that management is considering and other models having only a few. The current manufacturers' selling prices for these tables averages $285.

Required:

1. Why is there a need in target costing to (*a*) focus on the customer and (*b*) have a marketing team become involved with product design?
2. Danish Interiors' marketing team will evaluate the survey responses by computing a weighted-average rating of each of the modifications. This will be accomplished by weighting (multiplying) the point values (1, 2, etc.) by the frequency of responses, summing the results, and dividing by 200. Rank the popularity of the five modifications using this approach.
3. Management desires to earn approximately the same rate of profit on sales that is being earned with the current design.
   a. If Danish Interiors uses target costing and desires to meet the current competitive selling price, what is the maximum cost of the modified table?
   b. Which of the modifications should management consider?
4. Assume that Danish Interiors wanted to add a modification or two that you excluded in your answer to requirement (3*b*). What process might management adopt to allow the company to make its target profit for the table? Briefly explain.

Cases

Case 15–48
Bidding on a Special Order; Ethics
(LO 10)

Bair Company is a manufacturer of standard and custom-designed bottling equipment. Early in December 20x0 Lyan Company asked Bair to quote a price for a custom-designed bottling machine to be delivered in April. Lyan intends to make a decision on the purchase of such a machine by January 1, so Bair would have the entire first quarter of 20x1 to build the equipment.

Bair's pricing policy for custom-designed equipment is 50 percent markup on absorption manufacturing cost. Lyan's specifications for the equipment have been reviewed by Bair's Engineering and Cost Management departments, which made the following estimates for direct material and direct labor.

Direct material	$307,200
Direct labor (11,000 hours at $18)	198,000

Manufacturing overhead is applied on the basis of direct-labor hours. Bair normally plans to run its plant at a level of 15,000 direct-labor hours per month and assigns overhead on the basis of 180,000 direct-labor hours per year. The overhead application rate for 20x1 of $10.80 per hour is based on the following budgeted manufacturing overhead costs for 20x1.

Variable manufacturing overhead	$1,166,400
Fixed manufacturing overhead	777,600
Total manufacturing overhead	$1,944,000

Bair's production schedule calls for 12,000 direct-labor hours per month during the first quarter. If Bair is awarded the contract for the Lyan equipment, production of one of its standard products would have to be reduced. This is necessary because production levels can only be increased to 15,000 direct-labor hours each month on short notice. Furthermore, Bair's employees are unwilling to work overtime.

Sales of the standard product equal to the reduced production would be lost, but there would be no permanent loss of future sales or customers. The standard product for which the production schedule would be reduced has a unit sales price of $14,400 and the following cost structure.

Direct material	$ 3,000
Direct labor (250 hours at $18)	4,500
Manufacturing overhead (250 hours at $10.80)	2,700
Total cost	$10,200

Lyan needs the custom-designed equipment to increase its bottle-making capacity so that it will not have to buy bottles from an outside supplier. Lyan Company requires 5,000,000 bottles annually. Its present equipment has a maximum capacity of 4,500,000 bottles with a directly traceable cash outlay cost of 18 cents per bottle. Thus, Lyan has had to purchase 500,000 bottles from a supplier at 48 cents each. The new equipment would allow Lyan to manufacture its entire annual demand for bottles at a direct-material cost savings of 1.2 cents per bottle. Bair estimates that Lyan's annual bottle demand will continue to be 5,000,000 bottles over the next five years, the estimated life of the special-purpose equipment.

Required: Bair Company's management plans to submit a bid to Lyan Company for the manufacture of the special-purpose bottling equipment.

1. Calculate the bid Bair would submit if it follows its standard pricing policy for special-purpose equipment.
2. Calculate the minimum bid Bair would be willing to submit on the Lyan equipment that would result in the same total contribution margin as planned for the first quarter of 20x1.
3. Suppose Bair has submitted a bid slightly above the minimum calculated in requirement (2). Upon receiving Bair's bid, Lyan's assistant purchasing manager telephoned his friend at Tygar Corporation: "Hey Joe, we just got a bid from Bair on some customized equipment. I think Tygar would stand a good chance of beating it. Stop by the house this evening, and I'll show you the details of Bair's bid and the specifications on the machine."

   Is Lyan Company's assistant purchasing manager acting ethically? Explain.

(CMA, adapted)

Case 15–49
Pricing in a Tight Market; Possible Plant Closing
(LO 10)

Handy Household Products, Inc. is a multiproduct company with several manufacturing plants. The Shreveport Plant manufactures and distributes two household cleaning and polishing compounds, standard and commercial, under the Clean & Bright label. The forecasted operating results for the first six months of the current year, when 100,000 cases of each compound are expected to be manufactured and sold, are presented in the following statement.

CLEAN & BRIGHT COMPOUNDS—SHREVEPORT PLANT
Forecasted Results of Operations
For the Six-Month Period Ending June 30
(in thousands)

	Standard	Commercial	Total
Sales	$4,000	$6,000	$10,000
Cost of goods sold	3,200	3,800	7,000
Gross profit	$ 800	$2,200	$ 3,000
Selling and administrative expenses:			
Variable	$ 800	$1,400	$ 2,200
Fixed*	480	720	1,200
Total selling and administrative expenses	$1,280	$2,120	$ 3,400
Income (loss) before taxes	$ (480)	$ 80	$ (400)

*The fixed selling and administrative expenses are allocated between the two products on the basis of dollar sales volume.

The standard compound sold for $40 a case and the commercial compound sold for $60 a case during the first six months of the year. The manufacturing costs, by case of product, are presented in the schedule below. Each product is manufactured on a separate production line. Annual normal manufacturing capacity is 200,000 cases of each product. However, the plant is capable of producing 250,000 cases of standard compound and 350,000 cases of commercial compound annually.

	Cost per Case	
	Standard	Commercial
Direct material	$14.00	$16.00
Direct labor	8.00	8.00
Variable manufacturing overhead	2.00	4.00
Fixed manufacturing overhead*	8.00	10.00
Total manufacturing cost	$32.00	$38.00
Variable selling and administrative costs	$ 8.00	$14.00

*Depreciation charges are 50 percent of the fixed manufacturing overhead of each line.

The following schedule reflects the consensus of top management regarding the price-volume alternatives for the Clean & Bright products for the last six months of the current year. These are essentially the same alternatives management had during the first six months of the year.

Standard Compound		Commercial Compound	
Alternative Prices (per case)	Sales Volume (in cases)	Alternative Prices (per case)	Sales Volume (in cases)
$38	120,000	$52	175,000
40	100,000	54	140,000
42	90,000	60	100,000
44	80,000	64	55,000
46	50,000	70	35,000

Handy Household Products' top management believes the loss for the first six months reflects a tight profit margin caused by intense competition. Management also believes that many companies will leave this market by next year and profit should improve.

Required:

1. What unit selling price should management select for each of the Clean & Bright compounds for the remaining six months of the year? Support your selection with appropriate calculations.

2. Independently of your answer to requirement (1), assume the optimum alternatives for the last six months were as follows: a selling price of $46 and volume of 50,000 cases for the standard compound, and a selling price of $70 and volume of 35,000 cases for the commercial compound.
   a. Should management consider closing down its operations until January 1 of the next year in order to minimize its losses? Support your answer with appropriate calculations.
   b. Identify and discuss the qualitative factors that should be considered in deciding whether the Shreveport Plant should be closed down during the last six months of the current year.

(CMA, adapted)

Current Issues in Managerial Accounting

"America Online Faces New Threat from Cut-Rate Internet Services," ***The Wall Street Journal,*** **February 3, 2003, pp. A1, A11, Julia Angwin.**

Issue 15–50
Effect of Market Forces and Costs on Pricing

Overview
America Online faces a booming price war with cut-rate service providers.

Suggested Discussion Question
Comment on the interplay of market forces and cost issues in price setting at America Online.

"Airlines' Move to Raise Fares Falls Apart as Northwest Balks," ***The Wall Street Journal,*** **February 18, 2003, p. D5, Scott McCartney and Susan Carey.**

Issue 15–51
Effect of Market Forces and Costs on Pricing

Overview
Northwest Airlines stymied attempts by American Airlines and United Airlines to raise fares by refusing to go along.

Suggested Discussion Question
Comment on the interplay of market forces and cost issues in setting prices in the airline industry.

"High Fuel Prices May Hurt Stores, Not Consumers," ***The Wall Street Journal,*** **September 28, 2000, Daniel Machalaba and Rebecca Quick.**

Issue 15–52
Cost-Based Pricing versus Market-Based Pricing

Overview
Sharply higher oil prices are causing significantly higher shipping costs for retailers, due to higher fuel prices. The article discusses the competitive pressures felt by companies such as Wal-Mart, L.L. Bean, and Lands' End.

Suggested Discussion Questions
Can the retailers pass these increased shipping costs on to their customers or will they have to absorb the costs while keeping prices the same? Discuss this issue in terms of cost-based versus market-based pricing approaches.

"Car Makers May Try to Alter Pricing Practices," ***The Wall Street Journal,*** **January 24, 2000, Joseph B. White and Fara Warner.**

Issue 15–53
Pricing Policies

Overview
Pricing policies are changing for American carmakers. Online car retailers are posting invoice or "street" prices on their websites, rendering the MSRP somewhat irrelevant. Consumers may bargain upward from the wholesale price using information from the Web. James Schroer, Ford's vice president for global marketing, states there will be an increase in cost-plus pricing as a result of online marketing.

Suggested Discussion Question
How are the U.S. automakers changing their pricing policies as a result of the surge in online auto trading?

"Auto Makers Boost Charges for Shipping New Cars Because of Higher Fuel Costs," ***The Wall Street Journal,*** **October 25, 2000, Sholnn Freeman.**

Issue 15–54
Cost-Based Pricing versus Market-Based Pricing

Overview
DaimlerChrysler, Ford, General Motors, and Mitsubishi all have boosted "destination charges," which are the nonnegotiable freight charges that consumers pay on new vehicles, by 5 to 15 percent in order to cover higher fuel costs.

Suggested Discussion Questions
What issues are involved for these automakers in deciding whether to pass on higher fuel costs to consumers in the form of higher destination charges or to simply absorb these costs? Discuss this issue in terms of cost-based versus market-based pricing approaches.

Chapter Sixteen

Capital Expenditure Decisions

After completing this chapter, you should be able to:

1 Use the net-present-value method and the internal-rate-of-return method to evaluate an investment proposal.

2 Compare the net-present-value and internal-rate-of-return methods, and state the assumptions underlying each method.

3 Use both the total-cost approach and the incremental-cost approach to evaluate an investment proposal.

4 Determine the after-tax cash flows in an investment analysis.

5 Use the Modified Accelerated Cost Recovery System to determine an asset's depreciation schedule for tax purposes.

6 Evaluate an investment proposal using a discounted-cash-flow analysis, giving full consideration to income-tax issues.

7 Discuss the difficulty of ranking investment proposals, and use the profitability index.

8 Use the payback method and accounting-rate-of-return method to evaluate capital-investment projects.

9 Describe the impact of activity-based costing and advanced manufacturing technology on capital-budgeting decisions.

10 After completing Appendix B, explain the impact of inflation on a capital-budgeting analysis.

City Council Approves Computer System

Mountainview, NM—Mayor Debby Richards announced in a press conference held earlier today that city council has approved the purchase of a new computer system to serve municipal functions. "The council vote was unanimous," said Richards. "I recommended the new system on the basis of a thorough analysis by the city controller's office. It was a pretty clear decision, and it's nice to have the whole council see things my way, for a change."

The city's new computer system will be a set of networked personal computers. A variety of new software applications will be purchased as well to manage everything from municipal personnel records, to the city tax rolls, to insurance records on the city's vehicles. "The new system will be more powerful, in terms of both speed and memory, and it will be much more convenient in many ways. We expect to save over $200,000 per year in operating costs in

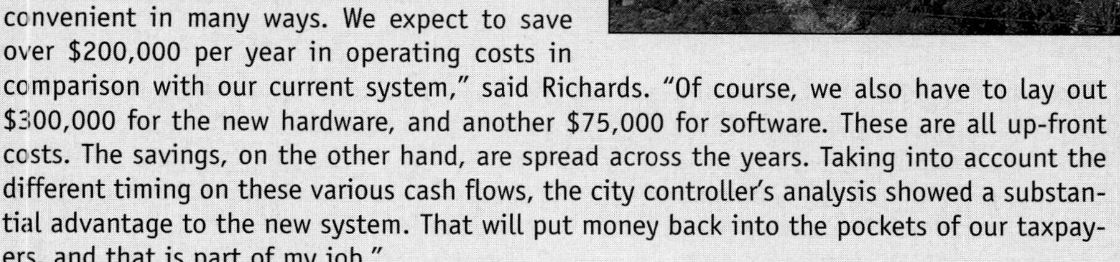

comparison with our current system," said Richards. "Of course, we also have to lay out $300,000 for the new hardware, and another $75,000 for software. These are all up-front costs. The savings, on the other hand, are spread across the years. Taking into account the different timing on these various cash flows, the city controller's analysis showed a substantial advantage to the new system. That will put money back into the pockets of our taxpayers, and that is part of my job."

Mayor Richards also announced that she has been notified by the management of High Country Department Stores, the city's largest retailer, that the company may build two new stores in the area. "High Country's president, Jean Walters, has informed me that the company is still analyzing these projects. They're looking at the cash flows and tax implications, along with other factors." The mayor said that she's doing everything she can to encourage High Country to go forward. "The city of Mountainview will benefit in many ways if High Country continues to invest here," said Mayor Richards.

Managers in all organizations periodically face major decisions that involve cash flows over several years. Decisions involving the acquisition of machinery, vehicles, buildings, or land are examples of such decisions. Other examples include decisions involving significant changes in a production process or adding a major new line of products or services to the organization's activities.

Decisions involving cash inflows and outflows beyond the current year are called **capital-budgeting decisions.** Managers encounter two types of capital-budgeting decisions.

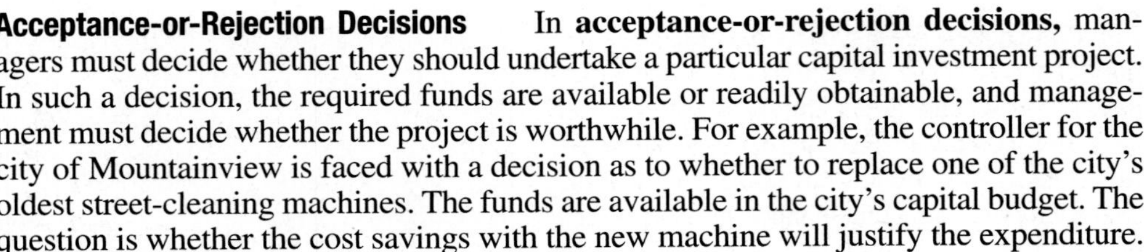

Acceptance-or-Rejection Decisions In **acceptance-or-rejection decisions,** managers must decide whether they should undertake a particular capital investment project. In such a decision, the required funds are available or readily obtainable, and management must decide whether the project is worthwhile. For example, the controller for the city of Mountainview is faced with a decision as to whether to replace one of the city's oldest street-cleaning machines. The funds are available in the city's capital budget. The question is whether the cost savings with the new machine will justify the expenditure.

Capital-Rationing Decisions In **capital-rationing decisions,** managers must decide which of several worthwhile projects makes the best use of limited investment funds. To illustrate, suppose the voters in the city of Mountainview have recently passed a proposition mandating the city government to undertake a cost-reduction program to trim administrative expenses. The voters also passed a bond issue, which enables the city government to raise $100,000 through the sale of bonds, to provide capital to finance the cost-reduction program. The mayor has in mind three cost-reduction programs, each of which would reduce administrative costs significantly over the next five years. However, the city can afford only two of the programs with the $100,000 of investment capital available. The mayor's decision problem is to decide which projects to pursue.

Focus on Projects Capital-budgeting problems tend to focus on specific projects or programs. Is it best for Mountainview to purchase the new street cleaner or not? Which cost-reduction programs will provide the city with the greatest benefits? Should a university buy a new electron microscope? Should a manufacturing firm acquire a computer-integrated manufacturing system?

Over time, as managers make decisions about a variety of specific programs and projects, the organization as a whole becomes the sum total of its individual investments, activities, programs, and projects. The organization's performance in any particular year is the combined result of all the projects under way during that year.

Chapter Organization This chapter is divided into three modular sections, each of which explores a particular aspect of capital expenditure decisions. Section 1 should be studied first, after which either Section 2 or Section 3 may be studied.

- Section 1: Discounted-Cash-Flow Analysis
- Section 2: Income Taxes and Capital Budgeting
- Section 3: Alternative Methods for Making Investment Decisions

Section 1: Discounted-Cash-Flow Analysis

How do managers evaluate capital investment projects? Our discussion will be illustrated by several decisions made by the Mountainview city government. The controller of Mountainview routinely advises the mayor and city council on major capital-investment decisions.

LO 1

Use the net-present-value method and the internal-rate-of-return method to evaluate an investment proposal.

Currently under consideration is the purchase of a new street cleaner. The controller has estimated that the city's old street-cleaning machine would last another five years. A new street cleaner, which also would last for five years, can be purchased for $50,470. It would cost the city $14,000 less each year to operate the new equipment than it costs to operate the old machine. The expected cost savings with the new machine are due to lower expected maintenance costs. Thus, the new street cleaner will cost $50,470 and save $70,000 over its five-year life ($70,000 = 5 × $14,000 savings per year). Since the $70,000 in cost savings exceeds the $50,470 acquisition cost, one might be tempted to conclude that the new machine should be purchased. However, *this analysis is flawed, since it does not account for the time value of money.* The $50,470 acquisition cost will occur now, but the cost savings are spread over a five-year period. It is a mistake to add cash flows occurring at different points in time. The proper approach is to use **discounted-cash-flow analysis,** which takes into account the timing of the cash flows. There are two widely used methods of discounted-cash-flow analysis: the net-present-value method and the internal-rate-of-return method. [Those who wish to review the basic concept of present value should read Appendix I (on pages 776–782) before continuing.]

Net-Present-Value Method

Topic 16–1

The following four steps constitute a net-present-value analysis of an investment proposal:

1. Prepare a table showing the cash flows during each year of the proposed investment.
2. Compute the present value of each cash flow, using a discount rate that reflects the cost of acquiring investment capital. This discount rate is often called the **hurdle rate** or **minimum desired rate of return.**
3. Compute the **net present value,** which is the sum of the present values of the cash flows.
4. If the net present value (NPV) is equal to or greater than zero, accept the investment proposal. Otherwise, reject it.

Exhibit 16–1 displays these four steps for the Mountainview controller's street-cleaner decision. In step (2) the controller used a discount rate of 10 percent. Notice that the cost savings are $14,000 in each of the years 1 through 5. Thus, the cash flows in those years comprise a five-year, $14,000 annuity. The controller used the annuity discount factor to compute the present value of the five years of cost savings. (The discount factors are found in Table IV in Appendix A at the end of this chapter.)

"We're key members of the decision making team when it comes to significant capital expenditure decisions." (16a)
Ford Motor Company

The net-present-value analysis indicates that the city should purchase the new street cleaner. The present value of the cost savings exceeds the new machine's acquisition cost.

Internal-Rate-of-Return Method

Topic 16–2

An alternative discounted-cash-flow method for analyzing investment proposals is the internal-rate-of-return method. An asset's **internal rate of return** (or **time-adjusted rate of return**) is the true economic return earned by the asset over its life. Another way of stating the definition is that an asset's *internal rate of return (IRR)* is the discount rate that would be required in a net-present-value analysis in order for the asset's net present value to be exactly *zero.*

What is the internal rate of return on Mountainview's proposed street-cleaner acquisition? Recall that the asset has a positive net present value, given that the city's cost of acquiring investment capital is 10 percent. Would you expect the asset's IRR to be higher or lower than 10 percent? Think about this question intuitively. The higher the discount rate used in a net-present-value analysis, the lower the present value of all future cash flows will be. This is true because a higher discount rate means that it is

Exhibit 16–1
Net-Present-Value Method

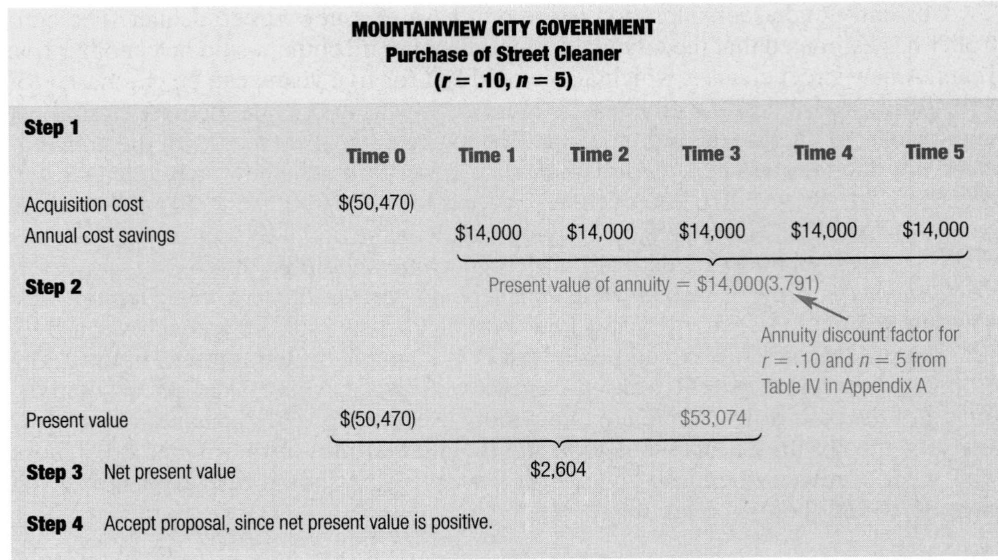

MOUNTAINVIEW CITY GOVERNMENT
Purchase of Street Cleaner
(r = .10, n = 5)

Step 1	**Time 0**	**Time 1**	**Time 2**	**Time 3**	**Time 4**	**Time 5**
Acquisition cost	\$(50,470)					
Annual cost savings		\$14,000	\$14,000	\$14,000	\$14,000	\$14,000

Step 2 Present value of annuity = \$14,000(3.791)

Annuity discount factor for r = .10 and n = 5 from Table IV in Appendix A

Present value \$(50,470) \$53,074

Step 3 Net present value \$2,604

Step 4 Accept proposal, since net present value is positive.

even more important to have the money earlier instead of later. Thus, a discount rate higher than 10 percent would be required to drive the new street cleaner's net present value down to zero.

Finding the Internal Rate of Return How can we find this rate? One way is trial and error. We could experiment with different discount rates until we find the one that yields a zero net present value. We already know that a 10 percent discount rate yields a positive NPV. Let's try 14 percent. Discounting the five-year, \$14,000 cost-savings annuity at 14 percent yields a negative NPV of \$(2,408).

$$(3.433)(\$14{,}000) - \$50{,}470 = \$(2{,}408)$$

↑ Annuity discount factor for r = .14 and n = 5 from Table IV in Appendix A.

What does this negative NPV at a 14 percent discount rate mean? We increased the discount rate too much. Therefore, the street cleaner's internal rate of return must lie between 10 percent and 14 percent. Let's try 12 percent:

$$(3.605)(\$14{,}000) - \$50{,}470 = 0$$

↑ Annuity discount factor for r = .12 and n = 5 from Table IV in Appendix A.

That's it. The new street cleaner's internal rate of return is 12 percent. With a 12 percent discount rate, the investment proposal's net present value is zero, since the street cleaner's acquisition cost is equal to the present value of the cost savings.

We could have found the internal rate of return more easily in this case, because the street cleaner's cash flows exhibit a very special pattern. The cash inflows in years 1 through 5 are identical, as shown below.

When we have this special pattern of cash flows, the internal rate of return is determined in two steps, as follows:

1. Divide the initial cash outflow by the equivalent annual cash inflows:

$$\frac{\$50{,}470}{\$14{,}000} = 3.605 = \text{Annuity discount factor}$$

2. In Table IV, find the discount rate associated with the annuity discount factor computed in step (1), given the appropriate number of years in the annuity.

From Table IV of Appendix A

	r		
	10%	12%	14%
$n = 5$	3.791	3.605	3.433

Decision Rule Now that we have determined the investment proposal's internal rate of return to be 12 percent, how do we use this fact in making a decision? The decision rule in the internal-rate-of-return method is to accept an investment proposal if its internal rate of return is greater than the organization's cost of capital (or hurdle rate). Thus, Mountainview's controller should recommend that the new street cleaner be purchased. The internal rate of return on the proposal, 12 percent, exceeds the city's hurdle rate, 10 percent.

To summarize, the internal-rate-of-return method of discounted-cash-flow analysis includes the following three steps:

1. Prepare a table showing the cash flows during each year of the proposed investment. This table will be identical to the cash-flow table prepared under the net-present-value method. (See Exhibit 16–1.)
2. Compute the internal rate of return (IRR) for the proposed investment. This is accomplished by finding a discount rate that yields a zero net present value for the proposed investment.
3. If the IRR is equal to or greater than the hurdle rate (cost of acquiring investment capital), accept the investment proposal. Otherwise, reject it.

"Our role is to be internal management consultants for the key decisions facing management." (16b)
Hewlett-Packard

Recovery of Investment The reason for purchasing an asset is an expectation that it will provide benefits in the future. Thus, Mountainview may purchase the new street cleaner because of expected future operating-cost savings. For a capital-investment proposal to be accepted, the expected future benefits must be sufficient for the purchaser to recover the investment and earn a return on the investment equal to or greater than the cost of acquiring capital. We can illustrate this point with Mountainview's street-cleaner acquisition.

Exhibit 16–2 examines the investment proposal's cash flows from the perspective of recovering the investment and earning a return on the investment. Focus on the Year 1 column in the exhibit. The street cleaner costs $50,470, so this is the unrecovered investment at the beginning of year 1. The operating-cost savings in year 1 are $14,000. Since the asset's internal rate of return is 12 percent, it must earn $6,056 during the first year (12% × $50,470). Therefore, $6,056 of the $14,000 cost savings represents a *return on* the unrecovered investment. This leaves $7,944 as a *recovery of* the investment during year 1 ($14,000 − $6,056). Subtracting the year 1 recovery of investment from the unrecovered investment at the beginning of the year leaves an unrecovered investment of $42,526 at year-end ($50,470 − $7,944).

Uneven Cash Flows A complication that often arises in finding a project's internal rate of return is an uneven pattern of cash flows. In Mountainview's proposed street-

Exhibit 16–2
Recovery of Investment and Return on Investment

MOUNTAINVIEW CITY GOVERNMENT
Purchase of Street Cleaner
($r = .12, n = 5$)

	Year 1	Year 2	Year 3	Year 4	Year 5
1. Unrecovered investment at beginning of year	$50,470	$42,526	$33,629	$23,664	$12,504
2. Cost savings during year	14,000	14,000	14,000	14,000	14,000
3. Return on unrecovered investment [12% × amount in row (1)]	6,056	5,103	4,035	2,840	1,500
4. Recovery of investment during year [row (2) amount minus row (3) amount]	7,944	8,897	9,965	11,160	12,500
5. Unrecovered investment at end of year [row (1) amount minus row (4) amount]	42,526	33,629	23,664	12,504	4*

*We are left with an unrecovered investment of $4 because of accumulated rounding errors in the table. If we had carried out each number to cents, the table would have finished up with an unrecovered investment of zero.

cleaner acquisition, the cost savings are $14,000 per year for all five years of the machine's life. Suppose, instead, that the pattern of cost savings is as follows:

Such an uneven cost-savings pattern is quite plausible, since the maintenance costs could rise in the machine's latter years. When the cash-flow pattern is uneven, iteration must be used to find the internal rate of return. You can try various discount rates iteratively until you find the one that yields a zero net present value for the investment proposal. This sort of computationally intensive work is the kind of task for which computers are designed. Numerous computer software packages are available to find a project's IRR almost instantaneously.

Comparing the NPV and IRR Methods

Compare the net-present-value and internal-rate-of-return methods, and state the assumptions underlying each method.

The decision to accept or reject an investment proposal can be made using either the net-present-value method or the internal-rate-of-return method. The different approaches used in the methods are summarized as follows:

Net-Present-Value Method

1. Compute the investment proposal's net present value, using the organization's hurdle rate as the discount rate.
2. Accept the investment proposal if its net present value is equal to or greater than zero; otherwise reject it.

Internal-Rate-of-Return Method

1. Compute the investment proposal's internal rate of return, which is the discount rate that yields a zero net present value for the project.
2. Accept the investment proposal if its internal rate of return is equal to or greater than the organization's hurdle rate; otherwise reject it.

Notice that the hurdle rate is used in each of the two methods.

Advantages of Net-Present-Value Method The net-present-value method exhibits two potential advantages over the internal-rate-of-return method. First, if the investment analysis is carried out by hand, it is easier to compute a project's NPV than its IRR. For example, if the cash flows are uneven across time, trial and error must be used to find the IRR. This advantage of the NPV approach is not as important, however, when a computer is used.

A second potential advantage of the NPV method is that the analyst can adjust for risk considerations. For some investment proposals, the further into the future that a cash flow occurs, the less certain the analyst can be about the amount of the cash flow. Thus, the later a projected cash flow occurs, the riskier it may be. It is possible to adjust a net-present-value analysis for such risk factors by using a higher discount rate for later cash flows than earlier cash flows. It is not possible to include such a risk adjustment in the internal-rate-of-return method, because the analysis solves for only a single discount rate, the project's IRR.

Assumptions Underlying Discounted-Cash-Flow Analysis

As is true of any decision model, discounted-cash-flow methods are based on assumptions. Four assumptions underlie the NPV and IRR methods of investment analysis.

1. In the present-value calculations used in the NPV and IRR methods, all cash flows are treated as though they occur at year-end. If the city of Mountainview were to acquire the new street cleaner, the $14,000 in annual operating-cost savings actually would occur uniformly throughout each year. The additional computational complexity that would be required to reflect the exact timing of all cash flows would complicate an investment analysis considerably. The error introduced by the year-end cash-flow assumption generally is not large enough to cause any concern.
2. Discounted-cash-flow analyses treat the cash flows associated with an investment project as though they were known with certainty. Although methods of capital budgeting under uncertainty have been developed, they are not used widely in practice. Most decision makers do not feel that the additional benefits in improved decisions are worth the additional complexity involved. As mentioned above, however, risk adjustments can be made in an NPV analysis to partially account for uncertainty about the cash flows.
3. Both the NPV and IRR methods assume that each cash inflow is immediately reinvested in another project that earns a return for the organization. In the NPV method, each cash inflow is assumed to be reinvested at the same rate used to compute the project's NPV, the organization's hurdle rate. In the IRR method, each cash inflow is assumed to be reinvested at the same rate as the project's internal rate of return.

   What does this reinvestment assumption mean in practice? In the case of Mountainview's proposed new street cleaner, the city must instantly reinvest the money saved each year either in some interest-bearing investment or in some other capital project.
4. A discounted-cash-flow analysis assumes a perfect capital market. This implies that money can be borrowed or lent at an interest rate equal to the hurdle rate used in the analysis.

In practice, these four assumptions rarely are satisfied. Nevertheless, discounted-cash-flow models provide an effective and widely used method of investment analysis. The improved decision making that would result from using more complicated models seldom is worth the additional cost of information and analysis.

Choosing the Hurdle Rate

The choice of a hurdle rate is a complex problem in finance. The hurdle rate is determined by management based on the **investment opportunity rate.** This is the rate of return the organization can earn on its best alternative investments of equivalent risk. In general, the greater a project's risk is, the higher the hurdle rate should be.

Investment versus Financing Decisions In capital-expenditure decisions, the investment decision should be separated from the financing decision. The decision as to whether to invest in a project should be made first using a discounted-cash-flow approach with a hurdle rate based on the investment opportunity rate. If a project is accepted, then a separate analysis should be made as to the best way to finance the project.

Cost of Capital How do organizations generate investment capital? Nonprofit organizations, such as local, city, and state governments and charitable organizations, often acquire capital through special bond issues or borrowing from financial institutions. In such cases, the cost of capital is based on the interest rate paid on the debt.

Another source of capital for both nonprofit and profit-oriented organizations is invested funds, such as a university's endowment fund. In this case, the cost of using the capital for an investment project is the interest rate forgone on the original investment. For example, suppose your university's endowment earns interest at the rate of 10 percent. If the university uses a portion of these funds to buy new laboratory equipment, the cost of capital is the 10 percent interest rate that is no longer earned on the funds removed from the endowment.

Profit-oriented enterprises fund capital projects by borrowing, by issuing stock, or by using invested funds. In most cases, capital projects are funded by all of these sources. Then the cost of capital should be a combination of the costs of obtaining money from each of these sources.

Depreciable Assets

When a long-lived asset is purchased, its acquisition cost is allocated to the time periods in the asset's life through depreciation charges. However, we did not include any depreciation charges in our discounted-cash-flow analysis. Both the NPV and IRR methods focus on cash flows, and *periodic depreciation charges are not cash flows.* Suppose that the controller for the city of Mountainview depreciates assets using the straight-line method. If the city purchases the new street cleaner for $50,470, the depreciation charges will be recorded as follows:

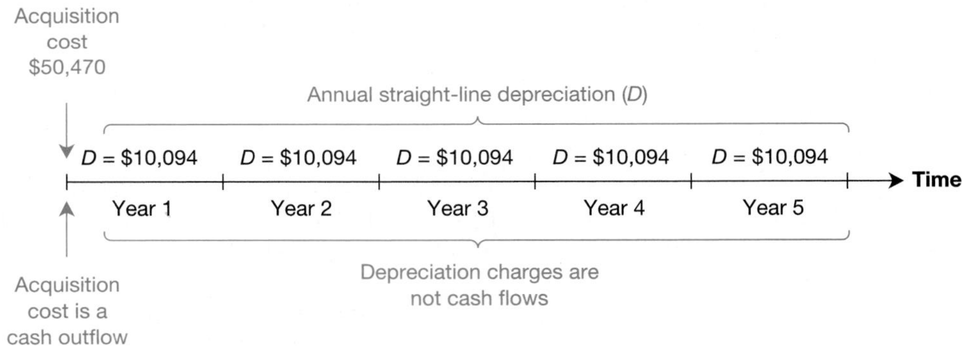

The only cash flow in the diagram above is the $50,470 cash outflow incurred to acquire the street cleaner. The $10,094 annual depreciation charges are not cash flows. Thus, the acquisition cost is recorded as a cash flow in our investment analysis (Exhibit 16–1), but the annual depreciation charges are not.

Nonprofit versus Profit-Oriented Organizations Suppose our illustration had focused on a profit-seeking enterprise instead of the city of Mountainview. For example, if the street-cleaner acquisition is contemplated by a theme-park company, would this change our treatment of the annual depreciation charges for the street cleaner? The depreciation charges still are not cash flows. However, in a profit-seeking enterprise, depreciation expense is deductible for income-tax purposes. Since tax payments *are* cash flows, the reduction in tax due to depreciation expense is a legitimate cash flow that should be included in an investment analysis. In Section 2 of this chapter, we will study the tax implications of depreciable assets in detail. For now, let's return to our focus on the city of Mountainview. As a nonprofit enterprise, the city pays no income tax. Therefore, depreciation is irrelevant in our discounted-cash-flow analysis.

Comparing Two Investment Projects

Use both the total-cost approach and the incremental-cost approach to evaluate an investment proposal.

We have developed all of the tools and concepts required to use discounted-cash-flow analysis in an investment decision. Now we can expand on our discussion using an illustration that combines the net-present-value method of investment analysis with the concepts of relevant costs and benefits studied in Chapter 14. The first step in any investment analysis is to determine the cash flows that are relevant to the analysis.

The computing system used by the city of Mountainview is outdated. The city council has voted to purchase a new computing system to be funded through municipal bonds. The mayor has asked the city's controller to make a recommendation as to which of two computing systems should be purchased. The two systems are equivalent in their ability to meet the city's needs and in their ease of use. The mainframe system consists of one large mainframe computer with remote terminals and printers located throughout the city offices. The personal computer system consists of a much smaller mainframe computer, a few remote terminals, and a dozen personal computers, which will be networked to the small mainframe. Each system would last five years. The controller has decided to use a 12 percent hurdle rate for the analysis.

Exhibit 16–3 presents data pertinent to the decision. Examine these data carefully. Most of the items are self-explanatory. Item (9) is the annual cost of a data-link service.

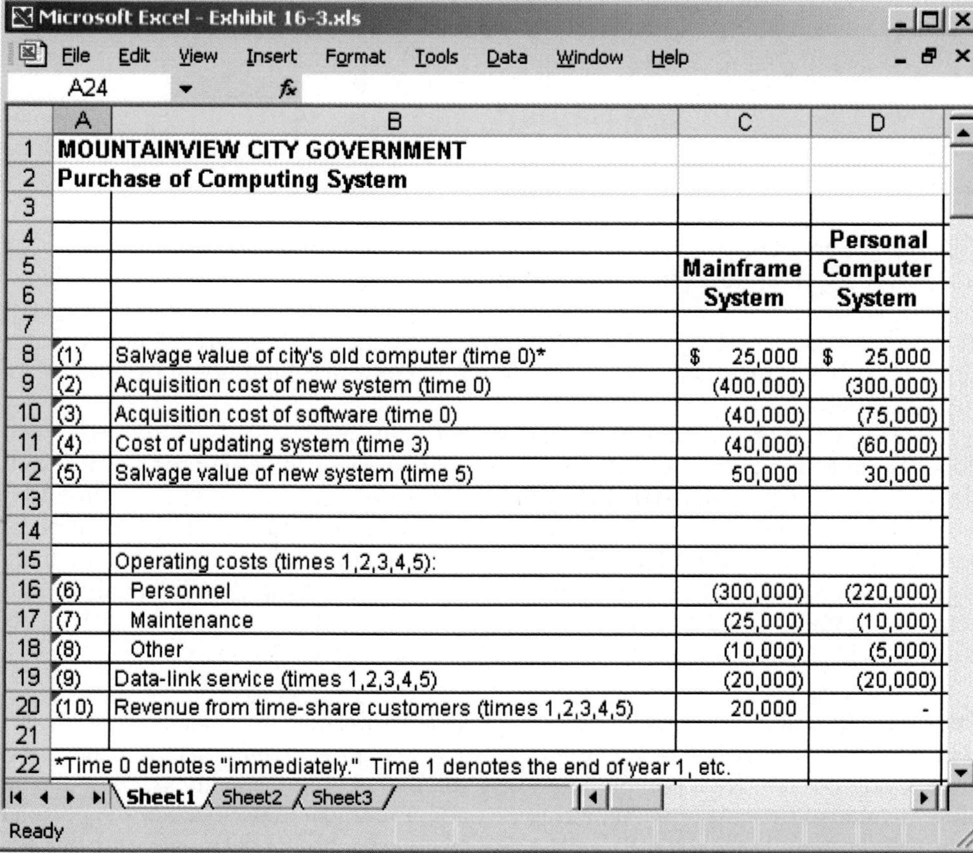

	A	B	C	D
1	**MOUNTAINVIEW CITY GOVERNMENT**			
2	**Purchase of Computing System**			
3				
4				**Personal**
5			**Mainframe**	**Computer**
6			**System**	**System**
7				
8	(1)	Salvage value of city's old computer (time 0)*	$ 25,000	$ 25,000
9	(2)	Acquisition cost of new system (time 0)	(400,000)	(300,000)
10	(3)	Acquisition cost of software (time 0)	(40,000)	(75,000)
11	(4)	Cost of updating system (time 3)	(40,000)	(60,000)
12	(5)	Salvage value of new system (time 5)	50,000	30,000
13				
14				
15		Operating costs (times 1,2,3,4,5):		
16	(6)	Personnel	(300,000)	(220,000)
17	(7)	Maintenance	(25,000)	(10,000)
18	(8)	Other	(10,000)	(5,000)
19	(9)	Data-link service (times 1,2,3,4,5)	(20,000)	(20,000)
20	(10)	Revenue from time-share customers (times 1,2,3,4,5)	20,000	-
21				
22	*Time 0 denotes "immediately." Time 1 denotes the end of year 1, etc.			

Exhibit 16–3
Data for Extended Illustration of Net-Present-Value Analysis

MOUNTAINVIEW CITY GOVERNMENT
Purchase of Computing System
($r = .12$, $n = 5$)

Item Number (from Exhibit 16–3)	Time 0	Time 1	Time 2	Time 3	Time 4	Time 5
Mainframe System						
(2) Acquisition cost: computer	$(400,000)					
(3) Acquisition cost: software	(40,000)					
(4) System update				$ (40,000)		
(5) Salvage value						$ 50,000
(6), (7), (8) Operating costs		$(335,000)	$(335,000)	(335,000)	$(335,000)	(335,000)
(10) Time-sharing revenue		20,000	20,000	20,000	20,000	20,000
Total cash flow	$(440,000)	$(315,000)	$(315,000)	$(355,000)	$(315,000)	$(265,000)
× Discount factor	× 1.000	× .893	× .797	× .712	× .636	× .567
Present value	$(440,000)	$(281,295)	$(251,055)	$(252,760)	$(200,340)	$(150,255)
Net present value of costs			Sum = $(1,575,705)			
Personal Computer System						
(2) Acquisition cost: computer	$(300,000)					
(3) Acquisition cost: software	(75,000)					
(4) System update				$ (60,000)		
(5) Salvage value						$ 30,000
(6), (7), (8) Operating costs		$(235,000)	$(235,000)	(235,000)	$(235,000)	(235,000)
(10) Time-sharing revenue		-0-	-0-	-0-	-0-	-0-
Total cash flow	$(375,000)	$(235,000)	$(235,000)	$(295,000)	$(235,000)	$(205,000)
× Discount factor	× 1.000	× .893	× .797	× .712	× .636	× .567
Present value	$(375,000)	$(209,855)	$(187,295)	$(210,040)	$(149,460)	$(116,235)
Net present value of costs			Sum = $(1,247,885)			
Difference in NPV of costs (favors personal computer system)			$ (327,820)			

Exhibit 16–4
Net-Present-Value Analysis: Total-Cost Approach

> "We make considerable use of discounted-cash-flow analysis when we're considering facility upgrades. We realize that we need to continually invest in our research facilities in order to do the kind of research that is needed." (16c)
> **Cornell University**

This service enables Mountainview to participate in a nationwide computer network, which allows cities to exchange information on such issues as crime rates, demographic data, and economic data. Item (10) is the revenue the city will receive from two time-sharing customers. The Mountainview City School District and the county legislature each have agreed to pay the city in return for a limited amount of time on the city's computer.

Before we begin the steps of the net-present-value method, let's examine the cash-flow data in Exhibit 16–3 to determine if any of the data can be ignored as irrelevant. Notice that items (1) and (9) do not differ between the two alternatives. Regardless of which new computing system is purchased, certain components of the old system can be sold now for $25,000. Moreover, the data-link service will cost $20,000 annually, regardless of which system is acquired. If the only purpose of the NPV analysis is to determine which computer system is the least-cost alternative, items (1) and (9) can be ignored as irrelevant, since they will affect both alternatives' NPVs equally.

Total-Cost Approach Exhibit 16–4 displays a net-present-value analysis of the two alternative computing systems. The exhibit uses the *total-cost approach,* in which all of the relevant costs of each computing system are included in the analysis. Then the net present value of the cost of the mainframe system is compared with that of the personal computer system. Since the NPV of the costs is lower with the personal computer system, that will be the controller's recommendation to the Mountainview City Council.

MOUNTAINVIEW CITY GOVERNMENT
Purchase of Computing System
(r = .12, n = 5)

Item Number (from Exhibit 16–3)	Time 0	Time 1	Time 2	Time 3	Time 4	Time 5
Incremental Cost of Mainframe System Over Personal Computer System						
(2) Acquisition cost: computer	$(100,000)					
(3) Acquisition cost: software	35,000					
(4) System update				$ 20,000		
(5) Salvage value						$ 20,000
(6), (7), (8) Operating costs		$(100,000)	$(100,000)	(100,000)	$(100,000)	(100,000)
(10) Time-sharing revenue		20,000	20,000	20,000	20,000	20,000
Incremental cash flow	$ (65,000)	$ (80,000)	$ (80,000)	$ (60,000)	$ (80,000)	$ (60,000)
× Discount factor	× 1.000	× .893	× .797	× .712	× .636	× .567
Present value	$ (65,000)	$ (71,440)	$ (63,760)	$ (42,720)	$ (50,880)	$ (34,020)
Net present value of incremental costs (favors personal computer system)				Sum = $(327,820)		

Exhibit 16–5
Net-Present-Value Analysis: Incremental-Cost Approach

A decision such as Mountainview's computing-system choice, in which the objective is to select the alternative with the lowest cost, is called a *least-cost decision.* Rather than maximizing the NPV of cash inflows minus cash outflows, the objective is to *minimize the NPV of the costs to be incurred.*

Incremental-Cost Approach Exhibit 16–5 displays a different net-present-value analysis of the city's two alternative computing systems. This exhibit uses the *incremental-cost approach,* in which the difference in the cost of each relevant item under the two alternative systems is included in the analysis. For example, the incremental computer acquisition cost is shown in Exhibit 16–5 as $(100,000). This is the amount by which the acquisition cost of the mainframe system exceeds that of the personal computer system. The result of this analysis is that the NPV of the costs of the mainframe system exceeds that of the personal computer system by $327,820. Notice that this is the same as the difference in NPVs shown at the bottom of Exhibit 16–4.

The total-cost and incremental-cost approaches always will yield equivalent conclusions. Choosing between them is a matter of personal preference.

Managerial Accountant's Role

To use discounted-cash-flow analysis in deciding about investment projects, managers need accurate cash-flow projections. This is where the managerial accountant plays a role. The accountant often is asked to predict cash flows related to operating-cost savings, additional working-capital requirements, or incremental costs and revenues. Such predictions are difficult in a world of uncertainty. The managerial accountant often draws upon historical accounting data to help in making cost predictions. Knowledge of market conditions, economic trends, and the likely reactions of competitors also can be important in projecting cash flows.

Postaudit

The discounted-cash-flow approach to evaluating investment proposals requires cash-flow projections. The desirability of a proposal depends heavily on those projections. If they are highly inaccurate, they may lead the organization to accept undesirable projects or to reject projects that should be pursued. Because of the importance of the

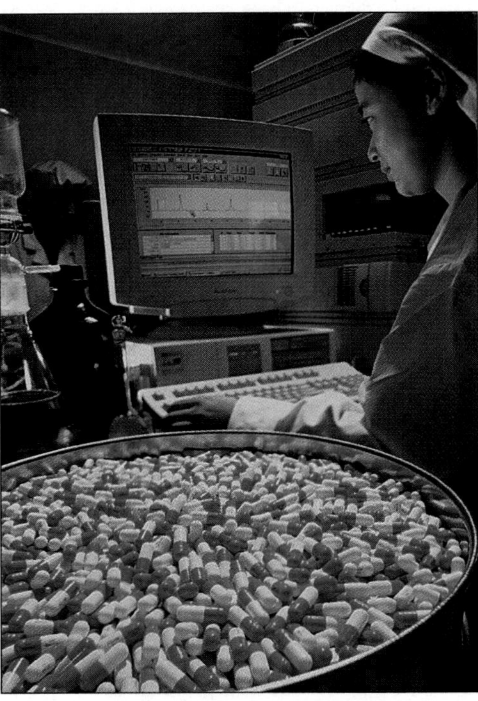

Capital-investment decisions, such as the installation of this automated equipment used in the pharmaceutical industry, go through an elaborate capital-budgeting process. For what types of decisions would capital budgeting be used by the administration of the college you attend?

capital-budgeting process, most organizations systematically follow up on projects to see how they turn out. This procedure is called a **postaudit** (or **reappraisal**).

In a postaudit, the managerial accountant gathers information about the actual cash flows generated by a project. Then the project's actual net present value or internal rate of return is computed. Finally, the projections made for the project are compared with the actual results. If the project has not lived up to expectations, an investigation may be warranted to determine what went awry. Sometimes a postaudit will reveal shortcomings in the cash-flow projection process. In such cases, action may be taken to improve future cash-flow predictions. Two types of errors can occur in discounted-cash-flow analyses: undesirable projects may be accepted, and desirable projects may be rejected. The postaudit is a tool for following up on accepted projects. Thus, a postaudit helps to detect only the first kind of error, not the second.

As in any performance-evaluation process, a postaudit should not be used punitively. The focus of a postaudit should provide information to the capital-budgeting staff, the project manager, and the management team.

Real Option Analysis

One way managerial accountants can assist the management team is by assessing the consequences of changes in an investment decision that may develop after the project has been approved. In long-term projects, there is often considerable uncertainty about the future cash flows, due to uncertainty about future economic, political, or natural events. As a project unfolds, management may decide to alter the course of the project or even postpone it. Suppose, for example, that the city of Mountainview decides to build a new municipal water system that will take 5 years to build and is expected to last 75 years. The project involves collaboration with several private enterprises, other municipalities, and the state and federal governments. As the project develops and various uncertainties are resolved, it may be desirable to make changes in the water system or postpone certain parts of it. A capital-budgeting tool called *real option analysis* can be used to quantify and analyze the merits of such changes. Real option analysis is covered in more advanced cost management and finance courses.

Section 2: Income Taxes and Capital Budgeting

LO 4

Determine the after-tax cash flows in an investment analysis.

When a business makes a profit, it usually must pay income taxes, just as individuals do. Since many of the cash flows associated with an investment proposal affect the company's profit, they also affect the firm's income-tax liability. The following equation shows the four types of items that appear on an income statement.

$$\text{Income} = \text{Revenue} - \text{Expenses} + \text{Gains} - \text{Losses}$$

Any aspect of an investment project that affects any of the items in this equation generally will affect the company's income-tax payments. These income-tax payments are cash flows, and they must be considered in any discounted-cash-flow analysis. In some cases, tax considerations are so crucial in a capital-investment decision that they dominate all other aspects of the analysis.

After-Tax Cash Flows

The first step in a discounted-cash-flow analysis for a profit-seeking enterprise is to determine the after-tax cash flows associated with the investment projects under consideration. An **after-tax cash flow** is the cash flow expected after all tax implications have been taken into account. Each financial aspect of a project must be examined carefully to determine its potential tax impact.

To illustrate the tax implications of various types of financial items, we will focus on a retail business. High Country Department Stores, Inc. operates two department stores in the city of Mountainview. The firm has a large downtown store and a smaller branch store in the suburbs. The company is quite profitable, and management is considering several capital projects that will enhance the firm's future profit potential. Before analyzing these projects, let's pause to consider the tax issues the company is likely to face. For the purposes of our discussion, we will assume that High Country Department Stores' income tax rate is 40 percent. Thus, if the company's net income is \$1,000,000, its income-tax payment will be \$400,000 (\$1,000,000 × 40%).

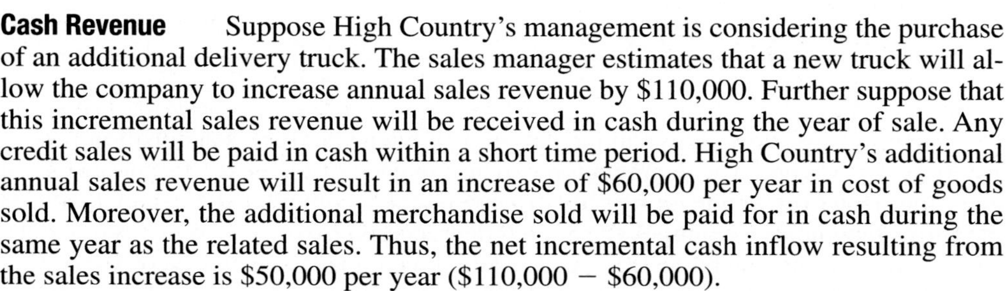

Cash Revenue Suppose High Country's management is considering the purchase of an additional delivery truck. The sales manager estimates that a new truck will allow the company to increase annual sales revenue by \$110,000. Further suppose that this incremental sales revenue will be received in cash during the year of sale. Any credit sales will be paid in cash within a short time period. High Country's additional annual sales revenue will result in an increase of \$60,000 per year in cost of goods sold. Moreover, the additional merchandise sold will be paid for in cash during the same year as the related sales. Thus, the net incremental cash inflow resulting from the sales increase is \$50,000 per year (\$110,000 − \$60,000).

"It's clear that we have an important role to play in the decision making process. We bring a perspective that is different from the other functions." (16d)
Boeing

What is High Country's *after-tax cash flow* from the incremental sales revenue, net of cost of goods sold? As the following calculation shows, the firm's incremental cash inflow from the additional sales is only \$30,000.

Incremental sales revenue, net of cost of goods sold (cash inflow)	\$50,000
Incremental income tax (cash outflow), \$50,000 × 40%	(20,000)
After-tax cash flow (net inflow after taxes)	\$30,000

Although the incremental sales amounted to an additional net cash inflow of \$50,000, the cash outflow for income taxes also increased by \$20,000. Thus, the after-tax cash inflow from the incremental sales, net of cost of goods sold, is \$30,000.

A quick method for computing the after-tax cash inflow from incremental sales is the following:

$$\begin{array}{ccccc} \text{Incremental sales revenue,} \\ \text{net of cost of goods sold} & \times & (1 - \text{Tax rate}) & = & \text{After-tax cash inflow} \\ \$50{,}000 & \times & (1 - .40) & = & \$30{,}000 \end{array}$$

Cash Expenses What are the tax implications of cash expenses? Suppose the addition of the delivery truck under consideration by High Country's management will involve hiring an additional employee, whose annual compensation and fringe benefits will amount to \$30,000. As the following computation shows, the company's incremental cash outflow is only \$18,000.

Incremental expense (cash outflow)	\$(30,000)
Reduction in income tax (reduced cash outflow), \$30,000 × 40%	12,000
After-tax cash flow (net outflow after taxes)	\$(18,000)

Although the incremental employee compensation is $30,000, this expense is tax-deductible. Thus, the firm's income-tax payment will be reduced by $12,000. As a result, the after-tax cash outflow from the additional compensation is $18,000.

A quick method for computing the after-tax cash outflow from an incremental cash expense is shown below.

$$\text{Incremental cash expense} \times (1 - \text{Tax rate}) = \text{After-tax cash outflow}$$

$$\$(30{,}000) \times (1 - .40) = \$(18{,}000)$$

Noncash Expenses Not all expenses represent cash outflows. The most common example of a noncash expense is depreciation expense. Suppose High Country Department Stores' management is considering the purchase of a delivery truck that costs $40,000 and has no salvage value. We will discuss the specific methods of depreciation allowed under the tax law later in the chapter, but for now assume the truck will be depreciated as follows:

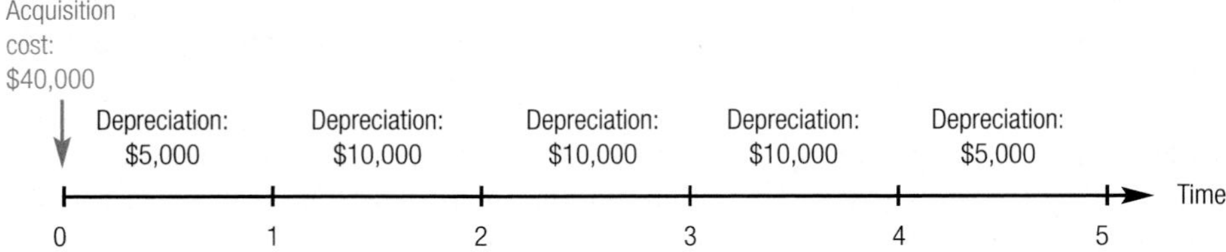

The only cash flow shown in the diagram above is the truck's acquisition cost of $40,000 at time zero. The depreciation expense in each of the next five years is *not a cash flow.* However, *depreciation is an expense* on the income statement, and it reduces the firm's income. For example, the $5,000 depreciation expense in year 1 will reduce High Country's income by $5,000. As a result, the company's year 1 income-tax payment will decline by $2,000 (40% × $5,000).

The annual depreciation expense associated with the truck provides a reduction in income-tax expense equal to the firm's tax rate times the depreciation deduction. This reduction in income taxes is called a **depreciation tax shield.**

To summarize, depreciation is a noncash expense. Although depreciation is not a cash flow, it does cause a reduced cash outflow through the depreciation tax shield.

$$\text{Depreciation or any other noncash expense} \times \text{Tax rate} = \text{Reduced cash outflow for income taxes}$$

$$\text{Year 1 depreciation of } \$5{,}000 \times 40\% = \$2{,}000$$

Year 1 depreciation of $5,000 ↑ Is not a cash flow; $2,000 ↑ Is a cash flow

The following schedule shows High Country Department Stores' depreciation tax shield over the depreciable life of the proposed delivery truck.

Year	Depreciation Expense	Tax Rate	Cash Flow: Reduced Tax Payment	
1	$ 5,000	40%	$2,000	Depreciation tax shield
2	10,000	40	4,000	
3	10,000	40	4,000	
4	10,000	40	4,000	
5	5,000	40	2,000	

HIGH COUNTRY DEPARTMENT STORES, INC. Purchase of Delivery Truck ($r = .10, n = 5$)						
	Time 0	**Time 1**	**Time 2**	**Time 3**	**Time 4**	**Time 5**
Acquisition cost	$(40,000)					
After-tax cash flow from incremental sales revenue, net of cost of goods sold $50,000 × (1 − .40)		$30,000	$30,000	$30,000	$30,000	$30,000
After-tax cash flow from incremental compensation expense, $30,000 × (1 − .40)		(18,000)	(18,000)	(18,000)	(18,000)	(18,000)
After-tax cash flow from depreciation tax shield, depreciation expense × .40		2,000	4,000	4,000	4,000	2,000
Total cash flow	$(40,000)	$14,000	$16,000	$16,000	$16,000	$14,000
× Discount factor	× 1.000	× .909	× .826	× .751	× .683	× .621
Present value	$(40,000)	$12,726	$13,216	$12,016	$10,928	$ 8,694
Net present value	Sum = $17,580					

Exhibit 16–6
Net-Present-Value Analysis with After-Tax Cash Flows

HIGH COUNTRY
DEPARTMENT STORES

The cash flows constituting the depreciation tax shield occur in five different years. Thus, in a discounted-cash-flow analysis, we still must discount these cash flows to find their present value.

Cash Flows Not on the Income Statement Some cash flows do not appear on the income statement. They are not revenues, expenses, gains, or losses. A common example of such a cash flow is the purchase of an asset. If High Country Department Stores purchases the delivery truck, the $40,000 acquisition cost is a cash outflow but not an expense. A purchase is merely the exchange of one asset (cash) for another (a delivery truck). The expense associated with the truck's purchase is recognized through depreciation expense recorded throughout the asset's depreciable life. Thus, the cash flow resulting from the purchase of an asset does not affect income and has no direct tax consequences.

Net-Present-Value Analysis Now let's complete our example by preparing a net-present-value analysis of the proposed delivery-truck acquisition. The company's after-tax hurdle rate is 10 percent. Exhibit 16–6 displays the net-present-value analysis. Since the NPV is positive, the delivery truck should be purchased.

Timing of Tax Deductions We have assumed in our analysis of High Country Department Stores' delivery-truck purchase that the cash flows resulting from income taxes occur during the same year as the related before-tax cash flows. This assumption is realistic, as most businesses must make estimated tax payments throughout the tax year. They generally cannot wait until the following year and pay their prior year's taxes in one lump sum.

Inflation Our discussion of discounted-cash-flow analysis has assumed no inflation. The additional complexity of inflation is discussed in Appendix B at the end of this chapter.

Exhibit 16–7
Present Value of Depreciation Tax Shield: Alternative Depreciation Methods

Depreciation Expense (Double-Declining-Balance*)	Depreciation Tax Shield (Depreciation × 40%)	Depreciation Expense (Sum-of-the-Years'-Digits)	Depreciation Tax Shield (Depreciation × 40%)	Depreciation Expense (Straight-Line)	Depreciation Tax Shield (Depreciation × 40%)
$5,000	$2,000	$4,000	$1,600	$2,500	$1,000
2,500	1,000	3,000	1,200	2,500	1,000
1,250	500	2,000	800	2,500	1,000
1,250	500	1,000	400	2,500	1,000
Present value of depreciation tax shield (10% discount rate)	$3,361		$3,320		$3,170

*Steps in applying the double-declining-balance (DDB) method:

To apply the double-declining-balance depreciation method, use the following steps:

1. Divide 100% by the number of years of depreciation to be taken.
2. Multiply the answer obtained in step (1) by 200%.
3. Compute the asset's depreciation each year by applying the percentage obtained in step (2) to the asset's undepreciated cost at the beginning of the year.
4. Switch to straight-line depreciation during the first year in which the straight-line amount, computed for the asset's remaining life, is greater than the double-declining-balance amount.

Accelerated Depreciation

The main concept underlying discounted-cash-flow analysis is the time value of money. We discount each cash flow to find its present value. Since money has a time value, it is advantageous for a business to take tax deductions as early as allowable under the tax law.

Although federal and state income tax laws are changed periodically by the appropriate governmental legislative bodies, income-tax laws usually permit some form of accelerated depreciation for tax purposes. An *accelerated depreciation method* is any method under which an asset is depreciated more quickly in the early part of its life than it would by using straight-line depreciation. For example, suppose High Country Department Stores purchased a personal computer and peripheral devices for $10,000. The equipment's useful life is four years with no salvage value. Exhibit 16–7 shows the pattern of depreciation deductions, the associated after-tax cash flows, and the present value of the depreciation tax shield under three different depreciation methods. Notice that both the 200%-declining-balance method and the sum-of-the-years'-digits method result in a greater present value for the depreciation tax shield than the straight-line method does. Thus, it usually is desirable for a business to use accelerated depreciation for tax purposes whenever the tax law permits. The current tax law does not require that the same depreciation method be used for both the tax purpose and the external-reporting purpose. Thus, management could use straight-line depreciation when preparing published financial statements but use an accelerated method for tax purposes.

Modified Accelerated Cost Recovery System (MACRS)

LO 5

Use the Modified Accelerated Cost Recovery System to determine an asset's depreciation schedule for tax purposes.

Under U.S. tax laws, most depreciable assets acquired after December 31, 1980, have been depreciated for tax purposes in accordance with the Accelerated Cost Recovery System (ACRS). The Tax Reform Acts of 1986 and 1989 modified the ACRS depreciation program. Under the **Modified Accelerated Cost Recovery System,** or **MACRS,** every asset is placed in one of eight classes, depending on the asset's expected useful life. These eight classes, along with examples of the assets included, are shown in columns (a) and (b) of Exhibit 16–8. For each class, the Internal Revenue Code specifies the number of years over which the asset may be depreciated, and the depreciation

(a) Asset's Useful Life*	(b) Types of Assets in MACRS Class	(c) MACRS Class and Depreciation Method
Up to 4 years	Industrial tools	3-year class; double-declining-balance
Between 4 and 10 years	Automobiles, trucks, office equipment, computers, research equipment	5-year class; double-declining-balance
Between 10 and 16 years	Most industrial equipment and machinery; office furniture	7-year class; double-declining-balance
Between 16 and 20 years	Equipment and machinery for specified purposes	10-year class; double-declining-balance
Between 20 and 25 years	Land improvements; some industrial machinery	15-year class; 150%-declining-balance
25 years or longer	Specified real property, such as farm buildings	20-year class; 150%-declining-balance
—	Residential rental property	27.5-year class; straight-line
—	Nonresidential real property	39-year class; straight-line

*In the tax law, an asset's useful life is referred to as the Asset Depreciation Range (ADR) Midpoint Life.

Exhibit 16–8

Modified Accelerated Cost Recovery System (as modified by the Tax Reform Acts of 1986, 1989, and 1993)

method to be used. These specifications are shown in column (c) of Exhibit 16–8. Notice that the number of years of depreciation specified by the tax code is not the same as an asset's useful life. Thus, each asset's useful life is used only to place the asset in its appropriate MACRS class. Then the tax code specifies the appropriate number of years of depreciation.[1]

Depreciation Methods As Exhibit 16–8 indicates, assets in the 3-year, 5-year, 7-year, and 10-year MACRS property classes are depreciated using the double-declining-balance (DDB) method. Assets in the 15-year and 20-year MACRS property classes are depreciated using the 150%-declining-balance method. To apply this depreciation method, use the same steps as those listed in Exhibit 16–7 for the DDB method, except change 200% in step (2) to 150%. Assets in the 27.5-year and 39-year MACRS property classes are depreciated using the straight-line method.

The utility company that owns this service truck uses an accelerated method of depreciation. The truck is categorized in the five-year property class under the Modified Accelerated Cost Recovery System (MACRS).

Half-Year Convention An asset may be purchased at any time during the tax year. MACRS assumes that, on average, assets will be placed in service halfway through the tax year. Thus, the tax code allows only a half-year's depreciation during the tax year in which an asset is placed in service. The other half of the first year's depreciation is picked up in the second tax year in which the asset is in service. The following diagram shows

"The tax issues can often drive a client's business decision." (16e)

A. T. Kearney

[1]The U.S. tax law changes almost every year. The most recent major change was in 2003. Occasionally, changes are made in the assignment of assets to property classes and in the associated depreciation schedules. Moreover, the terminology frequently changes. The tax act of 1980 established the Accelerated Cost Recovery System, which then was referred to as ACRS. Since the tax act of 1986, the program has been referred to in various publications by a variety of names. Among these are the Modified Accelerated Cost Recovery System (MACRS), the ACRS as modified, the CRS, or simply the ACRS. We will follow the common convention of referring to the current system as MACRS. Our discussion incorporates the latest tax law changes known as this book went to press. Regardless of what minor changes the tax laws may make in terminology or depreciation schedules, it is likely that the tax code will continue to allow depreciation by an accelerated schedule similar to MACRS.

Exhibit 16–9
Selected MACRS Depreciation Percentages as Computed by the IRS (incorporates half-year convention; also incorporates recent modifications in the tax laws)

	MACRS Property Class		
Year	**3-year**	**5-year**	**7-year**
1	33.33%	20.00%	14.29%
2	44.45	32.00	24.49
3	14.81*	19.20	17.49
4	7.41	11.52*	12.49
5		11.52	8.93*
6		5.76	8.92
7			8.93
8			4.46

*Denotes the year during which the depreciation method switches to the straight-line method.
Source: IRS Publication 534, entitled Depreciation.

the pattern with which a five-year asset's depreciation is recorded, for tax purposes, under MACRS.

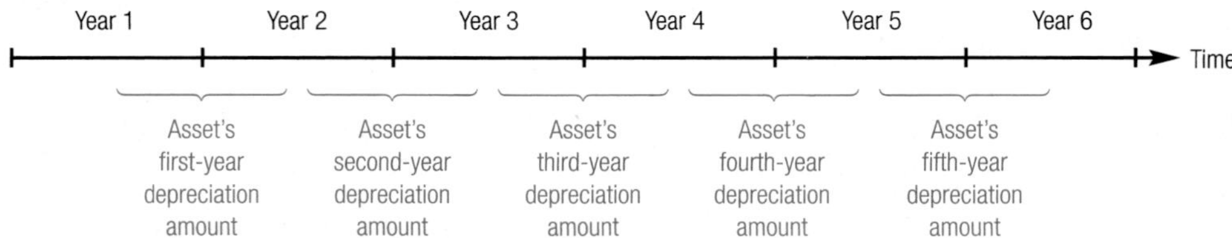

MACRS Depreciation Tables To assist taxpayers, the Internal Revenue Service has published tables of the MACRS depreciation percentages for each MACRS property class. The IRS tables use the depreciation method specified in Exhibit 16–8 and incorporate the half-year convention. Exhibit 16–9 provides a convenient table of the MACRS percentages, as computed by the IRS, for selected property classes. In the 5-year column, we see 20 percent for year 1. This results from the half-year convention, since 20 percent is half of the double-declining balance rate of 40 percent.

No Salvage Values Under MACRS, an asset's estimated salvage value is not subtracted in computing the asset's depreciation basis. Thus, for an asset costing $10,000 with an estimated salvage value of $1,000, the full $10,000 cost is depreciated over the asset's life.

Optional Straight-Line Depreciation The tax law permits a business to depreciate any asset using the straight-line method instead of the method prescribed in Exhibit 16–8. A business with a loss might prefer this approach for tax reasons. If the straight-line method is used, the business may depreciate the asset over either the MACRS life or the asset's estimated useful life. Thus, businesses have considerable flexibility in choosing a depreciation schedule for tax purposes. Regardless of the depreciation method chosen, the half-year convention still must be followed.

Income-Tax Complexities The U.S. tax code is a complex document with a multitude of provisions. It is not possible to cover all of these provisions in this text, so it is wise to consult a tax expert regarding the complexities that may apply in a particular investment decision. Since the tax code is changed frequently by Congress, a tax rule that applied last year may not apply this year. For example, the *investment tax credit* is one important tax-code provision that has been switched on and off repeatedly by Congress. During periods when the investment tax credit has been in effect, a company has been allowed a substantial reduction in its income taxes when particular types of investments are made. The intent of the investment credit was to stimulate the economy by giving businesses an incentive to make new investments. As this text was written, the investment credit was not in effect, but its status is always subject to change. If there is a moral to the changing-tax-code story, it is this: When making an important investment decision, a manager should have a managerial accountant on one side and a tax accountant on the other.

Gains and Losses on Disposal

Evaluate an investment proposal using a discounted-cash-flow analysis, giving full consideration to income-tax issues.

When a business sells an asset, there often is a gain or loss on the sale. Since gains and losses are included in income, the business's income taxes generally are affected. Capital investment decisions frequently involve the disposal of assets, and sometimes gains or losses are recorded on those sales. Thus, the tax effects of gains and losses on disposal of assets can be an important feature of an investment decision.

The *book value* of an asset is defined as the asset's acquisition cost minus the accumulated depreciation on the asset. When an asset is sold for more than its current book value, a *gain on disposal* is recorded. The *gain* is defined as the difference between the sales proceeds and the asset's book value. A *loss on disposal* is recorded when an asset is sold for less than its current book value. The *loss* is equal to the difference between the asset's current book value and the sales proceeds.

To illustrate, suppose High Country Department Stores owns a forklift, which cost \$10,000 and currently has accumulated depreciation of \$6,000. The forklift's book value is computed as follows:

Book value	=	Acquisition cost	−	Accumulated depreciation
\$4,000	=	\$10,000	−	\$6,000

Scenario I: Gain on Disposal Suppose High Country sells the forklift for \$5,000. The gain on the sale is \$1,000 (\$5,000 proceeds minus \$4,000 book value). If High Country's income-tax rate is 40 percent, the following cash flows will occur at the time of the sale.

Cash inflow: proceeds from sale	\$5,000
Cash outflow: incremental income tax due to the gain, \$1,000 × 40%	(400)
Net cash flow	\$4,600

Although High Country sold the forklift for \$5,000, the company's net cash benefit is only \$4,600. The firm will have to pay the other \$400 in increased income taxes on the \$1,000 gain.

Scenario II: Loss on Disposal Now assume instead that High Country Department Stores sells the forklift for \$3,200. The *loss* on the sale is \$800 (\$3,200 proceeds minus \$4,000 book value). If High Country's income-tax rate is 40 percent, the following cash flows will occur at the time of the sale.

Cash inflow: proceeds from sale	\$3,200
Reduced cash outflow: reduction in income tax due to the loss, \$800 × 40%	320
Total cash flow	\$3,520

Although High Country sold the forklift for only \$3,200, the company's total benefit from the sale is \$3,520. The extra \$320 comes in the form of a reduction in income taxes due to the loss on the sale.

Implications for Investment Decisions Why is the analysis above likely to be relevant in an investment decision? Suppose High Country Department Stores has the

Exhibit 16–10
Net-Present-Value Analysis with Loss on Disposal

HIGH COUNTRY DEPARTMENT STORES, INC.
Forklift Replacement Decision

Acquisition cost of new forklift		$(12,000)
Proceeds from sale of old forklift		3,200
Reduced taxes due to loss on sale, 40% × $800		320
Net cash outflow at time 0 (now)		$ (8,480)
Present value of annual cost savings:		
Annual cost savings	$2,500	
× (1 − tax rate)	.60	
After-tax cost savings	$1,500	
× Annuity discount factor (n = 10, r = .10)	× 6.145*	
Present value of after-tax cost savings	→	9,218
Net present value of new forklift		$ 738

*Annuity discount factor from Table IV in Appendix A. Assumes an after-tax hurdle rate of 10%.

opportunity to sell its old forklift for $3,200 and buy a new one for $12,000. The company will save $2,500 in annual operating expenses over the next 10 years if the new forklift is used instead of the old machine. A net-present-value analysis of this machine-replacement decision is presented in Exhibit 16–10. The tax impact of the loss on disposal is a prominent part of the machine-replacement analysis. Without the tax savings associated with the loss, the net present value of the new forklift would have been cut from $738 to only $418 ($738 NPV minus tax effect of $320).

Notice that the presentation format used for the analysis in Exhibit 16–10 is different from the format we used previously. Instead of listing the cash flows for each item by year and then adding the columns, we have computed the present value of each financial item pertinent to the decision. The one-time cash flows at time zero then are added to the present value of the cost-savings annuity to determine the net present value. This alternative presentation format will yield the same conclusion as the year-by-year, columnar approach. The choice of format is a matter of personal preference.

Tax Rates on Gains and Losses Another complexity of the tax code that changes from time to time is that capital gains and losses may be taxed at different rates than ordinary income (i.e., revenue minus expenses). Thus, before preparing an NPV analysis, it is wise to check with a tax expert to obtain the proper income-tax rate to apply to a gain or loss on disposal.

Investment in Working Capital

Evaluate an investment proposal using a discounted-cash-flow analysis, giving full consideration to income-tax issues.

Some investment proposals require additional outlays for working capital. **Working capital,** defined as the excess of current assets over current liabilities, often increases as the result of higher balances in accounts receivable or inventory necessary to support a project. Such increases are uses of cash and should be included in a discounted-cash-flow analysis. To illustrate, suppose the city of Mountainview has offered High Country Department Stores a contract to sell special T-shirts and mementos commemorating the city's bicentennial. The contract covers the three-year period leading up to the bicentennial celebration. The cash flows associated with the proposal are displayed in panel A of Exhibit 16–11. Notice that the sales proposal would require a $2,000 outlay for additional working capital throughout the three-year period. The increased working capital is largely due to a higher balance in merchandise inventory. Panel B of Exhibit 16–11 analyzes the contract proposal. Notice that the time 0 cash investment in working capital is included as a $2,000 cash outflow. Since the increase in working

Exhibit 16–11
Investment In Working Capital

HIGH COUNTRY DEPARTMENT STORES, INC.
Contract Proposal for the City's Bicentennial

A. Data for Illustration

Annual sales revenue from T-shirts and mementos	$25,000
Annual expenses	(12,000)
Annual contract fee to city	(3,000)
Investment in working capital (time 0)	(2,000)
Release of working capital (end of year 3)	2,000
Tax rate	40%
After-tax hurdle rate	10%

B. Discounted-Cash-Flow Analysis

Investment in working capital (time 0)		$ (2,000)
Release of working capital:		
Working capital released (end of year 3)	$2,000	
Discount factor ($n = 3, r = .10$)	× .751*	
Present value of working capital released	⟶	1,502
Annual revenue and expenses:		
Sales revenue	$25,000	
Expenses	(12,000)	
Contract fee	(3,000)	
Before-tax annual income	10,000	
× (1 − tax rate)	× .60	
After-tax annual income	6,000	
× Annuity discount factor	× 2.487†	
Present value of after-tax annual income	⟶	14,922
Net present value of contract proposal		$14,424

*From Table III of Appendix A.
†From Table IV of Appendix A.

capital is not released until the end of year 3, that $2,000 inflow is discounted. The city's proposal has a positive net present value, so it should be accepted.

Extended Illustration of Income-Tax Effects in Capital Budgeting

Evaluate an investment proposal using a discounted-cash-flow analysis, giving full consideration to income-tax issues.

Now we have covered all of the most important concepts for analyzing an investment proposal in a profit-seeking enterprise. A comprehensive illustration will help you solidify your understanding of these concepts. High Country Department Stores' management is considering the installation of a new checkout system for its suburban store. The new computerized system would include new cash registers at each checkout station. In addition, the new checkout system would include an updated bar-code reading system. The new system will be faster and more accurate, and it will minimize the annoyance of the reader failing to recognize a product's bar code. Among the advantages of the new system are accuracy in the checkout process, automatic updating of computerized inventory records, and the ability to gather data about customers' buying patterns and trends.

Exhibit 16–12 presents the data pertinent to the decision. Notice that the old equipment has been fully depreciated already. However, its useful life can be extended to six more years if an overhaul is done in year 2. The new equipment also has an expected useful life of six years, so its MACRS classification is the 5-year property class.

Exhibit 16–12
Data for Extended Illustration

HIGH COUNTRY DEPARTMENT STORES, INC. **Computerized Checkout Equipment Decision**	
Old checkout equipment:	
Remaining useful life, assuming overhaul in year 2	6 years
Cost of overhaul in year 2	$3,500
Current book value (fully depreciated)	–0–
Current salvage value	$1,200
Salvage value in six more years	–0–
New checkout equipment:	
Useful (ADR midpoint) life	6 years
MACRS property classification	5-year class
Acquisition cost of new equipment	$50,000
Update of software required in year 3	$4,000
Salvage value of new equipment in six years	$1,000
Cost to retrain checkout personnel	$5,000
Cost to retag merchandise	$3,000
Annual data:	
Annual operating-cost savings	$15,000
Annual cost of computer-system operator	$30,000
Annual cost of marketing-data analysis	$4,500
Annual incremental sales resulting from marketing analysis, net of cost of goods sold	$40,000
After-tax hurdle rate	10%
Tax rate	40%

Most of the data in Exhibit 16–12 are self-explanatory. The last two items in the exhibit under annual data relate to the new checkout system's ability to gather data about customer demand patterns. The extra data analysis will cost $4,500 annually, but it is expected to generate another $40,000 in annual sales, net of cost of goods sold.

A net-present-value analysis of the checkout equipment proposal is presented in Exhibit 16–13. A total-cost approach is used. The present value of each financial item is computed for both alternatives; then these present values are added to determine each alternative's net present value. An explanation of each line in the exhibit follows.

(1) Line (1) in Exhibit 16–13 records the acquisition cost of the new checkout equipment. This cash flow has no tax impact and does not need to be discounted since it occurs at time 0.

(2), (3) These one-time cash flows are required to retrain checkout personnel and retag merchandise to accommodate the new bar-code readers. Since these costs are expenses, we multiply by (1 − .40).

(4), (5) Since the old equipment has a current book value of zero, there is a $1,200 gain on the sale. The $1,200 proceeds are not taxed [line (4)], but the $1,200 gain on the sale is taxed [line (5)].

(6) The cost of updating the software in year 3 is an expense, so we multiply by (1 − .40).

(7), (8) The new equipment can be sold in year 6 for $1,000. Since it will be fully depreciated, there will be a $1,000 gain. The $1,000 proceeds are not taxed [line (7)], but the $1,000 gain is taxed [line (8)].

(9) The depreciation tax shield on the new equipment is computed using the MACRS depreciation schedule for the 5-year property class. The annual depreciation deductions are not cash flows, but they do cause a reduction in income taxes. Each cash flow is then discounted using the appropriate discount factor from Table III in Appendix A.

HIGH COUNTRY DEPARTMENT STORES, INC.
Computerized Checkout Equipment Decision

	Year	Amount	Income-Tax Impact	After-Tax Cash Flow	Discount Factor (10%)	Present Value of Cash Flow
Purchase New Equipment						
(1) Acquisition cost of new equipment	Time 0	$50,000	None	$(50,000)	1.000	$(50,000)
(2) Cost to retrain checkout personnel	Time 0	5,000	(1 − .40)*	(3,000)	1.000	(3,000)
(3) Cost to retag merchandise	Time 0	3,000	(1 − .40)	(1,800)	1.000	(1,800)
(4) Proceeds from sale of old equipment	Time 0	1,200	None	1,200	1.000	1,200
(5) Gain on sale of old equipment	Time 0	1,200	.40	(480)	1.000	(480)
(6) Update of software	Year 3	4,000	(1 − .40)	(2,400)	.751	(1,802)
(7) Salvage value of new equipment	Year 6	1,000	None	1,000	.564	564
(8) Gain on sale of new equipment	Year 6	1,000	.40	(400)	.564	(226)
(9) Depreciation tax shield:						

Year	Cost	MACRS Percentage (rounded)	Depreciation Expense	Amount	Income-Tax Impact	After-Tax Cash Flow	Discount Factor (10%)	Present Value of Cash Flow
1	$50,000	20.0%	$10,000	10,000	.40	4,000	.909	3,636
2	50,000	32.0%	16,000	16,000	.40	6,400	.826	5,286
3	50,000	19.2%	9,600	9,600	.40	3,840	.751	2,884
4	50,000	11.5%	5,750	5,750	.40	2,300	.683	1,571
5	50,000	11.5%	5,750	5,750	.40	2,300	.621	1,428
6	50,000	5.8%	2,900	2,900	.40	1,160	.564	654
Total			$50,000					

Annual incremental costs and benefits (years 1 through 6):		Year	Amount	Income-Tax Impact	After-Tax Cash Flow	Discount Factor (10%)	Present Value of Cash Flow
(10) Annual operating cost savings	$15,000						
(11) Annual cost of computer operator	(30,000)						
(12) Annual cost of marketing analysis	(4,500)					Annuity discount factor for $n = 6, r = .10$	
(13) Annual incremental sales revenue, net of cost of goods sold	40,000						
Total annual amount	$20,500		$20,500	(1 − .40)	$12,300	4.355	53,567
(14) Net present value							$13,482
Keep Old Equipment†							
(15) Cost of overhaul		Year 2	$3,500	(1 − .40)	$(2,100)	.826	$ (1,735)
(16) Net present value							$ (1,735)

*High Country Department Stores' tax rate is 40%.
†There is no depreciation tax shield if the old equipment is kept, since it has been depreciated fully already.

Exhibit 16–13
Net-Present-Value Analysis for Extended Illustration

(10), (11), (12), (13) These items are annual cash flows. The flows are summed, and then the $20,500 annuity is multiplied by (1 − .40) because each of the cash flows will be on the income statement. The after-tax cash-flow annuity of $12,300 is then discounted using the annuity discount factor for $n = 6$ and $r = .10$.

(14) The net present value of the new equipment is $13,482.

(15) The only specific cash flow related to the alternative of keeping the old equipment is the $3,500 overhaul in year 2. This will be an expense, so we multiply by (1 − .40). Then the after-tax cash flow is discounted.

(16) The net present value of the alternative to keep the old equipment is $(1,735).

Decision Rule The analysis indicates that High Country Department Stores should purchase the new checkout equipment. The NPV of the new equipment exceeds that of the old equipment.

Management Accounting Practice

Pfizer and Merck

CAPITAL BUDGETING AT PHARMACEUTICAL FIRMS

Among the many large companies making extensive use of capital budgeting are the big pharmaceutical companies. It can take 10 years or more to develop a new drug. It takes huge outlays of cash to develop a drug, test it, and then shepherd it through the governmental approval process. Yet much of what the drug companies claim as the cost of a new drug is actually the opportunity cost of tying up these big dollar outlays for many years before any revenue stream begins.

"Overall, the average tab for developing a new drug is $500 million to $880 million, the industry says. But the amount actually spent on any one marketable product is roughly one-quarter of that. To understand why, just look at the drug-development process. In the past, scientists made many variations of existing chemicals and tested them to see which ones had the ability to fight a particular disease." Now, with the advent of genetic engineering and greatly expanded knowledge of biology, "the process has gotten more complicated—and oddly enough, more difficult. Researchers try to identify the best target in a particular disease—for instance, a damaged gene that causes cancer—then they make a drug to hit the target and cure the disease. Since that process can take 10 years or more, that means that about half of the calculated $500 million to $880 million total isn't actually spent at all. Instead, it's the opportunity cost—the measure of what the money tied up in the drug for so many years could have earned with alternative investments." This is where capital budgeting comes into play, since the NPV of a drug development project takes into account the opportunity cost associated with the time value of money.

Pharmaceutical companies "have upped research spending in recent years—Pfizer spends $4.9 billion annually; Merck, about $2.6 billion—but with no big payoff in productivity. Hefty up-front investments in genomics, in particular, have so far failed to yield a big crop of new compounds." The uncertainties big pharmaceutical companies confront are a large part of the problem. First, only a small percentage of drugs under development ever make it as far as human trials. And only 1 in 10 of those makes it through to wide-scale testing. Then there's the pricing uncertainty as well. How much will people pay for a new drug treatment? To take account of these uncertainties, many drug companies use simulation in conjunction with capital budgeting to decide whether to proceed with a drug's development. A discounted-cash-flow analysis is run many times with differing assumptions about the drug's success, its development costs, and its eventual pricing. Then a probability distribution is generated for the drug's NPV. Management can then make a decision about proceeding with development given the likelihood of a profitable drug.[2]

Ranking Investment Projects

LO 7

Discuss the difficulty of ranking investment proposals, and use the profitability index.

Suppose a company has several potential investment projects, all of which have positive net present values. If a project has a positive net present value, this means that the return projected for the project exceeds the company's cost of capital. In this case, every project with a positive NPV should be accepted. In spite of the theoretical validity of this argument, practice often does not reflect this viewpoint. In practice, managers often attempt to rank investment projects with positive net present values. Then only a limited number of the higher-ranking proposals are accepted.

[2]Based on John Carey and Amy Barrett, "Drug Prices: What's Fair," *Business Week,* December 10, 2001, pp. 61–70, and the author's discussions with pharmaceutical company personnel.

The reasons for this common practice are not clear. If a discount rate is used that accurately reflects the firm's cost of capital, then any project with a positive NPV will earn a return greater than the cost of obtaining capital to fund it. One possible explanation for the practice of ranking investment projects is a limited supply of scarce resources, such as managerial talent. Thus, a form of *capital rationing* takes place, not because of a limited supply of investment capital, but because of limitations on other resources. A manager may feel that he or she simply cannot devote sufficient attention to all of the desirable projects. The solution, then, is to select only some of the positive-NPV proposals, which implies a ranking.

Unfortunately, no valid method exists for ranking independent investment projects with positive net present values. To illustrate, suppose the management of High Country Department Stores has the following two investment opportunities:

1. Proposal A: Open a gift shop at the Mountainview Convention Center. High Country's management believes the benefits of this proposal would last only six years. High Country's management expects that after six years, the firm's competitors will move into the Convention Center and eliminate High Country's current advantageous position.
2. Proposal B: Open a small gift shop at the Mountainview Airport. The airport gift concession would belong to High Country Department Stores for 10 years under a contract with the city.

The predicted cash flows for these investment proposals are as follows:

	Cash Outflow	After-Tax Cash Inflows		Present Value of Inflows	Net Present	Internal Rate of
Investment Proposal	Time 0	Years 1–6	Years 7–10	(10% Discount Rate)	Value	Return
A (Convention Center)	$ (54,450)	$14,000	—	$ 60,970	$6,520	14%
B (Airport)	(101,700)	18,000	$18,000	110,610	8,910	12%

Both investment proposals have positive net present values. Suppose, however, that due to limited managerial time, High Country's management has decided to pursue only one of the projects. Which proposal should be ranked higher? This is a difficult question to answer. Proposal B has a higher net present value, but it also requires a much larger initial investment. Proposal A exhibits a higher internal rate of return. However, proposal A's return of 14 percent applies only to its six-year time horizon. If management accepts proposal A, what will happen in years 7 through 10? Will the facilities and equipment remain idle? Or could they be used profitably for some other purpose? These questions are left unanswered by the analysis above.

The main reason that the NPV and IRR methods of analysis yield different rankings for these two proposals is that the projects have different lives. Without making an assumption about what will happen in years 7 through 10 if proposal A is accepted, the NPV and IRR methods simply are not capable of ranking the proposals in any sound manner. The only theoretically correct answer to the problem posed in this illustration is that both projects are desirable, and both should be accepted. Each proposal exhibits a positive NPV and an IRR greater than the hurdle rate of 10 percent.

Profitability Index One criterion that managers sometimes apply in ranking investment proposals is called the **profitability index** (or **excess present value index**), which is defined as follows:

$$\text{Profitability index} = \frac{\begin{array}{c}\text{Present value of cash flows,}\\ \text{exclusive of initial investment}\end{array}}{\text{Initial investment}}$$

The profitability indices for High Country's two investment proposals are computed as follows:

Investment Proposal	Calculation				Profitability Index	Net Present Value	Internal Rate of Return
A	Present value of inflows / Initial investment	=	$60,970 / $54,450	=	1.12	$6,520	14%
					>	<	>
B	Present value of inflows / Initial investment	=	$110,610 / $101,700	=	1.09	$8,910	12%

Although proposal A has a lower NPV than proposal B, proposal A exhibits a higher profitability index. Proposal A's higher profitability index is due to its considerably lower initial investment than that required for proposal B. Is the profitability index a foolproof method for ranking investment proposals? Unfortunately, it too suffers from the same drawbacks as those associated with the NPV or IRR method. Both proposals exhibit a profitability index greater than 1.00, which merely reflects their positive NPVs. Thus, both projects are desirable. The unequal lives of the two proposals prevent the profitability index from indicating a theoretically correct ranking of the proposals. The relative desirability of proposals A and B simply depends on what will happen in years 7 through 10 if proposal A is selected.

In summary, the problem of ranking investment projects with positive NPVs has not been solved in a satisfactory manner. This lack of resolution is due to an inconsistency inherent to the problem. The inconsistency is that if several projects have positive NPVs, they all are desirable. They all will earn a return greater than the cost of capital. If a manager chooses not to accept all projects with positive NPVs, then the required ranking ultimately must be made on the basis of subjective criteria.

Section 3: Alternative Methods for Making Investment Decisions

Use the payback method and accounting-rate-of-return method to evaluate capital-investment projects.

The best way to decide whether to accept an investment project is to use discounted-cash-flow analysis, as described in Sections 1 and 2 of this chapter. Both the net-present-value and the internal-rate-of-return methods will yield the correct accept-or-reject decision. The strength of these methods lies in the fact that they properly account for the time value of money. In spite of the conceptual superiority of discounted-cash-flow decision models, managers sometimes use other methods for making investment decisions. In some cases, these alternative methods are used in conjunction with a discounted-cash-flow analysis. Two of these alternative decision methods are described next.

HIGH COUNTRY
DEPARTMENT STORES

Our discussion is based on decisions faced by the management of High Country Department Stores. The firm operates two department stores in the city of Mountainview.

Payback Method

The **payback period** of an investment proposal is the amount of time it will take for the after-tax cash inflows from the project to accumulate to an amount that covers the original investment. The following formula defines an investment project's payback period.

$$\text{Payback period} = \frac{\text{Initial investment}}{\text{Annual after-tax cash inflow}}$$

There is no adjustment in the payback method for the time value of money. A cash inflow in year 5 is treated the same as a cash inflow in year 1.

To illustrate the payback method, suppose High Country Department Stores' management is considering the purchase of a new conveyor system for its warehouse. The two alternative machines under consideration have the following projected cash flows.

Conveyor System	Initial Investment	After-Tax Cash Flows: Years 1 through 7	After-Tax Cash Flow When System Is Sold
I	$(20,000)	$4,000	-0-
II	(27,000)	4,500	$14,000

The payback period for each conveyor system is computed below. Notice that *after-tax cash flows are used* in the payback method, just as they are in discounted-cash-flow methods of analysis.

Conveyor System	Initial Investment / Annual After-Tax Cash Inflow	Payback Period
I	$20,000 / $4,000	5 years
II	$27,000 / $4,500	6 years

According to the payback method, system I is more desirable than system II. System I will "pay back" its initial investment in five years, while system II requires six years. This conclusion is too simplistic, however, because it ignores the large salvage value associated with system II. Indeed, the NPV of system I is negative, while the NPV of system II is positive, as shown in the following analysis.

	Present Value of Cash Flows (10% Discount Factor)	
After-Tax Cash Flows	**System I**	**System II**
Initial investment	$(20,000) × 1.000 = $(20,000)	$(27,000) × 1.000 = $(27,000)
Years 1–7	4,000 × 4.868 = 19,472	4,500 × 4.868 = 21,906
Cash inflow from sale	-0-	14,000 × .513 = 7,182
Net present value	$ (528)	$ 2,088

The net-present-value analysis demonstrates that only system II can generate cash flows sufficient to cover the company's cost of capital. The payback method makes it appear as though system I "pays back" its initial investment more quickly, but the method fails to consider the time value of money.

Another shortcoming of the payback method is that it fails to consider an investment project's profitability beyond the payback period. Suppose High Country Department Stores' management has a third alternative for its warehouse conveyor system. System III requires an initial investment of only $12,000 and will generate after-tax cash inflows of $6,000 in years 1 and 2. Thus, System III's payback period is two years, as computed below.

$$\text{System III payback period} = \frac{\$12{,}000}{\$6{,}000} = 2 \text{ years}$$

Strict adherence to the payback method would rank system III above systems I and II, due to its shorter payback period. However, suppose we add another piece of information. System III's useful life is only two years, and it has no salvage value after two years. It is true that system III will "pay back" its initial investment in only two years if we ignore the time value of money. But then what? System III provides no further benefits beyond year 2. In spite of system III's short payback period, it is not a desirable investment proposal. The NPV of system III, $(1,584), is negative [$(1,584) = (1.736 × $6,000) − $12,000].

Payback Period with Uneven Cash Flows The simple payback formula given on page 698 will not work if a project exhibits an uneven pattern of cash flows. Instead, the after-tax cash flows must be accumulated on a year-to-year basis until the accumulation equals the initial investment. Suppose High Country Department Stores' management is considering the expansion of the downtown store's parking facilities. Management expects that the additional parking will result in much greater sales initially. However, this benefit will gradually taper off, due to the reactions of competitors. The projected after-tax cash flows are shown in Exhibit 16–14, which also presents the payback calculation for the parking lot proposal. The project's payback period is five years.

Exhibit 16–14
Payback Period with Uneven Cash Flows

HIGH COUNTRY DEPARTMENT STORES, INC.
Parking Lot Expansion

		After-Tax Cash Flows			
Year	**Type of Cash Flow**	**Outflows**	**Inflows**	**Accumulated Cash Flows (excluding initial investment)**	
0	Initial investment	$(200,000)		—	
1	Incremental sales*		$60,000	$ 60,000	
2	Incremental sales*		50,000	110,000	
3	Incremental sales*		45,000	155,000	
4	Incremental sales*		35,000	190,000	
4	Repave parking lot	(20,000)		170,000	Payback
5	Incremental sales*		30,000	200,000	← period:
6	Incremental sales*		30,000	230,000	5 years
7	Incremental sales*		30,000	260,000	
8	Incremental sales*		30,000	290,000	

*Incremental sales, net of cost of goods sold.

Payback: Pro and Con In summary, the payback method of evaluating investment proposals has two serious drawbacks. First, the method fails to consider the time value of money. Second, it does not consider a project's cash flows beyond the payback period. Despite these shortcomings, the payback method is used widely in practice, for two legitimate reasons.

First, the payback method provides a tool for roughly screening investment proposals. If a project does not meet some minimal criterion for the payback period, management may wish to reject the proposal regardless of potential large cash flows predicted well into the future. Second, a young firm may experience a shortage of cash. For such a company, it may be crucial to select investment projects that recoup their initial investment quickly. A cash-poor firm may not be able to wait for the big payoff of a project with a long payback period. Even in these cases, it is wise not to rely on the payback method alone. If the payback method is used, it should be in conjunction with a discounted-cash-flow analysis.

Accounting-Rate-of-Return Method

Discounted-cash-flow methods of investment analysis focus on *cash flows* and incorporate the time value of money. The **accounting-rate-of-return method** focuses on the incremental *accounting income* that results from a project. Accounting income is based on accrual accounting procedures. Revenue is recognized during the period of sale, not necessarily when the cash is received; expenses are recognized during the period they are incurred, not necessarily when they are paid in cash. The following formula is used to compute the accounting rate of return on an investment project.

$$\text{Accounting rate of return} = \frac{\begin{pmatrix}\text{Average}\\\text{incremental}\\\text{revenue}\end{pmatrix} - \begin{pmatrix}\text{Average incremental expenses}\\\text{(including depreciation}\\\text{and income taxes)}\end{pmatrix}}{\text{Initial investment}}$$

To illustrate the accounting-rate-of-return method, suppose High Country Department Stores' management is considering the installation of a small lunch counter in its downtown store. The required equipment and furnishings cost $210,000 and are in the MACRS 7-year property class. The company has elected to use the optional straight-line depreciation method with the half-year convention. The Excel spreadsheet shown in Exhibit 16–15 displays management's revenue and expense projections for the lunch

Microsoft Excel - Exhibit 16-15

File Edit View Insert Format Tools Data Window Help

H8 =F8-G8

	A	B	C	D	E	F	G	H
1	HIGH COUNTRY DEPARTMENT STORES, INC.							
2	Lunch Counter for Downtown Store							
3								
4						Income	Income	
5		Sales	Cost of	Operating	MACRS	Before	Taxes	Net
6	Year	Revenue	Goods Sold	Expenses	Depreciation*	Taxes	40%	Income
7								
8	1	$ 200,000	$ 100,000	$ 50,000	$ 15,000	$ 35,000	$ 14,000	$ 21,000
9	2	200,000	100,000	50,000	30,000	20,000	8,000	12,000
10	3	200,000	100,000	50,000	30,000	20,000	8,000	12,000
11	4	200,000	100,000	50,000	30,000	20,000	8,000	12,000
12	5	200,000	100,000	50,000	30,000	20,000	8,000	12,000
13	6	200,000	100,000	50,000	30,000	20,000	8,000	12,000
14	7	200,000	100,000	50,000	30,000	20,000	8,000	12,000
15	8	200,000	100,000	50,000	15,000	35,000	14,000	21,000
16	9	200,000	100,000	50,000	-	50,000	20,000	30,000
17	10	200,000	100,000	50,000	-	50,000	20,000	30,000
18	Total				$ 210,000			$ 174,000
19								
20	*Annual straight-line depreciation = ($210,000 / 7) = $30,000							
21								
22	Note: In accordance with the half-year convention, only half a year's depreciation is recorded in years 1 & 8							

Sheet1 / Sheet2 / Sheet3

Ready

Exhibit 16–15
Accounting-Rate-of-Return Method

counter. The total income projected over the project's 10-year useful life is $174,000. Thus, the average annual income is $17,400. The accounting rate of return on the lunch-counter proposal is computed as follows:

$$\text{Accounting rate of return} = \frac{\$17{,}400}{\$210{,}000} = 8.3\% \text{ (rounded)}$$

To compute the lunch-counter project's internal rate of return, let's assume that each year's sales revenue, cost of goods sold, operating expenses, and income taxes are cash flows in the same year that they are recorded under accrual accounting. Recall that the depreciation expense is not a cash flow. These assumptions imply the following cash flow pattern for the project.

Net After-Tax Cash Inflows

Year	Amount	Year	Amount
Initial investment	$(210,000)		
1	36,000	6	$42,000
2	42,000	7	42,000
3	42,000	8	36,000
4	42,000	9	30,000
5	42,000	10	30,000

The internal rate of return on the lunch-counter proposal is approximately 13.5 percent. That is, if we compute the present value of the cash flows using a discount rate of 13.5 percent, we obtain approximately a zero NPV.[3] Notice that the project's accounting rate of return, at 8.3 percent, is much lower than its IRR of 13.5 percent.

[3]You can verify the IRR of 13.5% using Table III in Appendix A. You will need to interpolate to find the discount factors for 13.5%, which lie between the 12% and 14% discount factors. For example, .881 is the approximate discount factor for 13.5% and $n = 1$ [$.881 = .877 + (.25)(.893 - .877)$].

Use of the Average Investment Some managers prefer to compute the accounting rate of return using the average amount invested in a project for the denominator, rather than the project's full cost. The formula is modified as follows:

$$\begin{array}{c}\text{Accounting rate of return}\\\text{(using average investment)}\end{array} = \frac{\begin{pmatrix}\text{Average}\\\text{incremental}\\\text{revenue}\end{pmatrix} - \begin{pmatrix}\text{Average incremental expenses}\\\text{(including depreciation}\\\text{and income taxes)}\end{pmatrix}}{\text{Initial investment}}$$

A project's average investment is the average accounting book value over the project's life.

Refer again to High Country Department Stores' lunch-counter data given in Exhibit 16–15. The project's book value at the beginning of each year is tabulated as follows:

Year	(a) Book Value at Beginning of Year	MACRS Depreciation	(b) Book Value at End of Year	$\frac{(a) + (b)}{2}$ Average Book Value During Year
1	$210,000	$15,000	$195,000	$202,500
2	195,000	30,000	165,000	180,000
3	165,000	30,000	135,000	150,000
4	135,000	30,000	105,000	120,000
5	105,000	30,000	75,000	90,000
6	75,000	30,000	45,000	60,000
7	45,000	30,000	15,000	30,000
8	15,000	15,000	–0–	7,500
9	–0–	–0–	–0–	–0–
10	–0–	–0–	–0–	–0–

The average investment over the project's useful life is the average of the amounts in the right-hand column, which is $84,000. Thus, the modified version of the project's accounting rate of return is 20.7 percent. (The average annual income of $17,400 divided by the average investment of $84,000 equals 20.7 percent, rounded.)

Notice that this modified version of the accounting rate of return yields a significantly higher return than the project's internal rate of return, which we computed as 13.5 percent. As a general rule of thumb, the following relationships will be observed.

$$\begin{array}{c}\text{Accounting rate of return}\\\text{(using initial investment)}\end{array} < \begin{array}{c}\text{Internal rate}\\\text{of return}\end{array} < \begin{array}{c}\text{Accounting rate of return}\\\text{(using average investment)}\end{array}$$

Accounting Rate of Return: Pro and Con Like the payback method, the accounting-rate-of-return method is a simple way of screening investment proposals. Some managers use this method because they believe it parallels financial accounting statements, which also are based on accrual accounting. However, like the payback method, the accounting-rate-of-return method does not consider the time value of money.

Inconsistent Terminology Many different terms for the accounting rate of return are used in practice. Among these terms are *simple rate of return, rate of return on assets,* and the *unadjusted rate of return.*

Estimating Cash Flows: The Role of Activity-Based Costing

The validity of any discounted-cash-flow analysis is dependent on the accuracy of the cash-flow estimates. Activity-based-costing (ABC) systems generally improve the ability of an analyst to estimate the cash flows associated with a proposed project. By separating costs into activity cost pools and identifying a cost driver for each pool, the

analyst can more accurately determine the levels of various costs that will be incurred if the project is implemented. Costs that are treated as fixed under a traditional, volume-based costing system often are seen to be variable, with respect to the appropriate cost driver, under an ABC system.[4]

LO 9

Describe the impact of activity-based costing and advanced manufacturing technology on capital-budgeting decisions.

Accuracy in estimating cash flows is particularly important in evaluating a proposed investment in advanced manufacturing equipment. These decisions are complex, involving many peripheral cash flows besides the actual purchase of the equipment. Flexible manufacturing systems (FMSs) generally require cash outlays for software, retraining of employees, realignment of the production line, and engineering. The benefits of such systems often are difficult to quantify also. Intangible benefits such as greater production flexibility are important considerations in making these investment decisions.

In today's manufacturing environment, it is crucial that companies make the best decisions possible regarding huge investments such as those in flexible manufacturing systems. Flawed decisions can spell disaster in today's globally competitive arenas.

Management Accounting Practice

INTERACTIVE TELEVISION—CAPITAL BUDGETING AND ABC

A high-tech company applied the ABC model to a capital-budgeting analysis of new business opportunities in the electronic (broadband) marketplace of interactive television. The ABC analysis provided an understanding of projected business processes, activities, and cost drivers to calculate detailed revenue and resource consumption patterns. The ABC project also compiled key operating statistics for the critical parties in the cybermall value chain—buyers, sellers, networks, and infrastructure.[5]

Justification of Investments in Advanced Manufacturing Systems

LO 9

Describe the impact of activity-based costing and advanced manufacturing technology on capital-budgeting decisions.

The manufacturing industry is changing dramatically as firms adopt the just-in-time (JIT) philosophy and move toward computer-integrated-manufacturing (CIM) systems. In Chapters 5 and 6 we explored many of the managerial accounting issues in the contemporary manufacturing environment. Many firms have found that JIT and CIM, coupled with a revised managerial accounting system, have provided a competitive edge in the marketplace. In many cases, however, managers have been frustrated when an NPV analysis projects a negative net present value for a proposed investment in a CIM system. Managers often believe intuitively that such an investment is justified, but they are stymied when the NPV analysis points to rejection of the proposal.

What is the problem here? Are managers overly optimistic about the advantages of CIM? Or is the NPV approach inappropriate for such an investment decision? Most likely neither of these conjectures is true. Managers often are right when their intuition tells them that the company would benefit from advanced manufacturing technology. And it is difficult to find fault with the NPV investment decision model. It is economically and mathematically sound. The problem lies in the difficulties of applying the NPV approach in a CIM investment decision. Some of these difficulties are:[6]

[4]Activity-based-costing systems, introduced conceptually in Chapter 3, are covered extensively in Chapter 5.

[5]S. Coburn, H. Grove, and T. Cook, "How ABC Was Used in Capital Budgeting," *Management Accounting* 78, no. 11 (May 1996), pp. 38–46.

[6]This section is based on discussions in R. Kaplan, "Must CIM Be Justified by Faith Alone?" *Harvard Business Review* 64, no. 2 (March 1986), pp. 87–95; Callie Berliner and James A. Brimson, eds., *Cost Management for Today's Advanced Manufacturing* (Boston: Harvard Business School Press, 1988), pp. 16–18, 36–38, 150; and Jean L. Noble, "A New Approach for Justifying Computer-Integrated Manufacturing," *Journal of Cost Management* 3, no. 4 (Winter 1990), pp. 14–19.

1. *Hurdle rates that are too high.* Sometimes managers have a tendency to set hurdle rates that are too high in a CIM investment analysis. They tend to forget that the purpose of discounting in the NPV model is to account for the time value of money. The appropriate hurdle rate for any investment decision is the investment opportunity rate for alternative investment projects of equivalent risk. In many cases managers tend to overstate this rate.
2. *Time horizons that are too short.* Another common mistake is to evaluate a CIM investment proposal with too short a time horizon. The acquisition cost of a CIM system can be enormous, and the benefits may be realized over a lengthy period of time.
3. *Bias toward incremental projects.* Most firms require that large investments be authorized by managers at higher levels than are required for smaller investments. One result of this sensible practice is an incentive for lower-level managers to request relatively small, incremental improvements in the manufacturing process rather than a large, comprehensive improvement, such as a move to CIM. In many cases, a series of such incremental improvements will not bring about the benefits that could be attained with a full commitment to advanced manufacturing technology.
4. *Greater uncertainty about operating cash flows.* Managers often have greater uncertainty about the cash flows that will result when an advanced manufacturing system is implemented. This increased uncertainty is due to the complexity of the machinery and the firm's inexperience with such advanced technology.
5. *Exclusion of benefits that are difficult to quantify.* The benefits to the firm from JIT and CIM systems are extensive. Some are easy to estimate, such as lower inventory levels, less floor space, and improved product quality. Others that can be even more significant are often difficult to quantify. Some of these benefits are:
   - *a.* *Greater flexibility in the production process.* A flexible manufacturing system cell often can produce runs of several distinct products in the same day. Flexible manufacturing systems also allow engineering changes to be made more easily as products are adapted to changing customer preferences.
   - *b.* *Shorter cycle times and reduced lead times* are possible with an FMS. This enables the firm to fill customer orders more quickly.
   - *c.* *Reduction of non-value-added costs* often results when JIT and FMS systems are adopted. Part of the philosophy of these systems is to encourage employees to seek out activities that can be made more efficient or eliminated.
   - *d.* *Reduced inventory levels* result in savings on working capital investment, less storage space, and reduced obsolescence.
   - *e.* *Lower floor-space requirements* in a flexible manufacturing system require less space than several stand-alone machines.
   - *f.* *Product quality* becomes higher and more constant because of advanced manufacturing systems.

Although it is difficult to quantify these benefits, few managers doubt their existence. Excluding them from an NPV analysis means they are being valued at zero. In many cases it would be preferable to make some estimate of these benefits, however crude it may be, than to ignore them. If a manager believes it is impossible to make such an estimate, then the investment criteria should be expanded to consider these intangible benefits along with a proposal's NPV.

Focus on Ethics

DYSFUNCTIONAL FOCUS ON EARLY CASH FLOWS

The timing of cash flows in investment decisions can sometimes create behavioral incentives to make dysfunctional decisions. The following hypothetical scenario presents such a situation.

The Institute for Environmental Studies (IES) is a privately funded, nonprofit scientific organization based in Montreal. The organization's director of field research is scheduled to retire in two years, and the assistant director, Marie Fenwar, is hoping to be appointed to the post at that time. In her current position, Fenwar has significant administrative responsibilities, including the approval of research proposals and equipment acquisitions. Fenwar has developed a reputation for carefully scrutinizing every proposed project and keeping the institute's field research branch within its budget. Fenwar has been so successful in her job that she has been quietly assured by several members of the IES board of directors that she is in line for her boss's job. She knows, however, that her prospects depend on her continued success in keeping the field research branch in solid financial shape.

IES recently signed a contract with the U.S. and Canadian governments to do a five-year study of the effects of global warming on the migration of water fowl. The contract fee is $500,000, payable in equal annual installments over the contract term. Fenwar is now considering two alternative proposals for carrying out the study. Each proposal entails the purchase of equipment and the incurrence of various operating costs throughout the term of the contract. Fenwar's normal procedure for project evaluation is to calculate each proposal's NPV, using an 8 percent hurdle rate. The projected costs follow:

Year	Type of Cost	Research Proposal I	Research Proposal II
Time 0	Equipment acquisition*	$ 40,000	$70,000
Year 1	Operating costs	150,000	75,000
Year 2	Operating costs	120,000	75,000
Year 3	Operating costs	75,000	95,000
Year 4	Operating costs	40,000	95,000
Year 5	Operating costs	40,000	95,000

*The equipment will be obsolete at the end of the contract term.

Fenwar calculated an NPV of $1,370 for Proposal I and $(14,375) for Proposal II. After completing her NPV analysis, however, Fenwar was tempted to ignore it. These thoughts ran through her mind as she drove to work: "If I approve Proposal I, the financial picture for the field research branch is going to pieces for the next two years. After a $40,000 initial investment in equipment, I'm going to show losses of $50,000 and $20,000 in the first two years. That's not going to look very good when the board considers my promotion." When she arrived at the office, Fenwar wrote a memo approving Proposal II.

Which research proposal should Fenwar have accepted? Why? Comment on the ethical issues in this scenario.

Chapter Summary

Capital-budgeting decisions involve cash flows occurring over several periods of time. Such decisions tend to focus on specific projects. The most common type of capital-budgeting analysis is concerned with the decision to accept or reject a particular investment proposal. Since capital-budgeting decisions involve cash flows over several time periods, the time value of money is a key feature of the analysis.

Section 1 covers two discounted-cash-flow methods for analyzing capital-investment decisions: the net-present-value and the internal-rate-of-return methods.

Under the net-present-value method, an investment proposal should be accepted if its net present value is zero or positive. A project's net present value is the present value of the project's future cash flows, less its initial acquisition cost. In computing the present value of the cash flows, the discount rate is the organization's cost of acquiring investment capital.

Under the internal-rate-of-return method, an investment proposal should be accepted if its internal rate of return equals or exceeds the organization's hurdle rate. A project's internal rate of return is the discount rate required to make the project's net present value equal to zero.

Both the net-present-value method and the internal-rate-of-return method are based on important assumptions. The net-present-value method is somewhat easier to apply. It also has the advantage of allowing the decision maker to adjust the discount rate upward for highly uncertain cash flows.

Section 2 covers the important role played by income taxes in the capital-budgeting decisions of a profit-seeking enterprise. For any organization subject to income taxes, the first step in a discounted-cash-flow analysis is to determine the after-tax cash flows related to the investment proposal under consideration. Cash flows that are also on the income statement should be multiplied by 1 minus the organization's tax rate. This rule applies to cash expenses and cash revenues. Cash flows that are not on the income statement, such as asset acquisitions, have no direct tax consequences. Expenses that are not cash flows in their own right, such as depreciation expenses, cause a cash flow by reducing the organization's income taxes. Thus, depreciation expenses should be multiplied by the tax rate to determine their tax impact. The resulting reductions in income-tax cash flows comprise a depreciation tax shield on a depreciable asset.

The time value of money makes it advantageous for a company to use an accelerated depreciation method for tax purposes. The current U.S. tax law specifies that the Modified Accelerated Cost Recovery System (MACRS) be used to determine depreciation deductions. When assets are sold for more or less than their current book value, the gain or loss on disposal is taxed. Thus, the tax implications of asset dispositions also should be included in a discounted-cash-flow analysis.

Section 3 covers two alternative methods for making investment decisions: the payback method and the accounting-rate-of-return method. Since these methods do not account for the time value of money, they are conceptually inferior to discounted-cash-flow methods. However, many organizations use these methods in conjunction with the NPV or IRR method.

Key Terms

For each term's definition refer to the indicated page, or turn to the glossary at the end of the text.

acceptance-or-rejection decision, 674
accounting-rate-of-return method, 700
after-tax cash flow, 685
capital-budgeting decision, 674
capital-rationing decision, 674
depreciation tax shield, 686
discounted-cash-flow analysis, 675
hurdle rate (or minimum desired rate of return), 675
internal rate of return (or time-adjusted rate of return), 675
investment opportunity rate, 679
Modified Accelerated Cost Recovery System (MACRS), 688
net present value, 675
nominal dollars,* 709
nominal interest rate,* 709
payback period, 698
postaudit (or reappraisal), 684
profitability index (or excess present value index), 697
real dollars,* 709
real interest rate,* 709
working capital, 692

*Terms appear in Appendix B.

Appendix A to Chapter 16

Future Value and Present Value Tables

Table I
Future Value of $1.00
$(1 + r)^n$

Period	4%	6%	8%	10%	12%	14%	20%
1	1.040	1.060	1.080	1.100	1.120	1.140	1.200
2	1.082	1.124	1.166	1.210	1.254	1.300	1.440
3	1.125	1.191	1.260	1.331	1.405	1.482	1.728
4	1.170	1.263	1.361	1.464	1.574	1.689	2.074
5	1.217	1.338	1.469	1.611	1.762	1.925	2.488
6	1.265	1.419	1.587	1.772	1.974	2.195	2.986
7	1.316	1.504	1.714	1.949	2.211	2.502	3.583
8	1.369	1.594	1.851	2.144	2.476	2.853	4.300
9	1.423	1.690	1.999	2.359	2.773	3.252	5.160
10	1.480	1.791	2.159	2.594	3.106	3.707	6.192
11	1.540	1.898	2.332	2.853	3.479	4.226	7.430
12	1.601	2.012	2.518	3.139	3.896	4.818	8.916
13	1.665	2.133	2.720	3.452	4.364	5.492	10.699
14	1.732	2.261	2.937	3.798	4.887	6.261	12.839
15	1.801	2.397	3.172	4.177	5.474	7.138	15.407
20	2.191	3.207	4.661	6.728	9.646	13.743	38.338
30	3.243	5.744	10.063	17.450	29.960	50.950	237.380
40	4.801	10.286	21.725	45.260	93.051	188.880	1469.800

Table II
Future Value of a Series of $1.00 Cash Flows (Ordinary Annuity)
$\frac{(1 + r)^n - 1}{r}$

Period	4%	6%	8%	10%	12%	14%	20%
1	1.000	1.000	1.000	1.000	1.000	1.000	1.000
2	2.040	2.060	2.080	2.100	2.120	2.140	2.220
3	3.122	3.184	3.246	3.310	3.374	3.440	3.640
4	4.247	4.375	4.506	4.641	4.779	4.921	5.368
5	5.416	5.637	5.867	6.105	6.353	6.610	7.442
6	6.633	6.975	7.336	7.716	8.115	8.536	9.930
7	7.898	8.394	8.923	9.487	10.089	10.730	12.916
8	9.214	9.898	10.637	11.436	12.300	13.233	16.499
9	10.583	11.491	12.488	13.580	14.776	16.085	20.799
10	12.006	13.181	14.487	15.938	17.549	19.337	25.959
11	13.486	14.972	16.646	18.531	20.655	23.045	32.150
12	15.026	16.870	18.977	21.385	24.133	27.271	39.580
13	16.627	18.882	21.495	24.523	28.029	32.089	48.497
14	18.292	21.015	24.215	27.976	32.393	37.581	59.196
15	20.024	23.276	27.152	31.773	37.280	43.842	72.035
20	29.778	36.778	45.762	57.276	75.052	91.025	186.690
30	56.085	79.058	113.283	164.496	241.330	356.790	1181.900
40	95.026	154.762	259.057	442.597	767.090	1342.000	7343.900

Period	4%	6%	8%	10%	12%	14%	16%	18%	20%	22%	24%	26%	28%	30%	32%
1	.962	.943	.926	.909	.893	.877	.862	.847	.833	.820	.806	.794	.781	.769	.758
2	.925	.890	.857	.826	.797	.769	.743	.718	.694	.672	.650	.630	.610	.592	.574
3	.889	.840	.794	.751	.712	.675	.641	.609	.579	.551	.524	.500	.477	.455	.435
4	.855	.792	.735	.683	.636	.592	.552	.516	.482	.451	.423	.397	.373	.350	.329
5	.822	.747	.681	.621	.567	.519	.476	.437	.402	.370	.341	.315	.291	.269	.250
6	.790	.705	.630	.564	.507	.456	.410	.370	.335	.303	.275	.250	.227	.207	.189
7	.760	.665	.583	.513	.452	.400	.354	.314	.279	.249	.222	.198	.178	.159	.143
8	.731	.627	.540	.467	.404	.351	.305	.266	.233	.204	.179	.157	.139	.123	.108
9	.703	.592	.500	.424	.361	.308	.263	.225	.194	.167	.144	.125	.108	.094	.082
10	.676	.558	.463	.386	.322	.270	.227	.191	.162	.137	.116	.099	.085	.073	.062
11	.650	.527	.429	.350	.287	.237	.195	.162	.135	.112	.094	.079	.066	.056	.047
12	.625	.497	.397	.319	.257	.208	.168	.137	.112	.092	.076	.062	.052	.043	.036
13	.601	.469	.368	.290	.229	.182	.145	.116	.093	.075	.061	.050	.040	.033	.027
14	.577	.442	.340	.263	.205	.160	.125	.099	.078	.062	.049	.039	.032	.025	.021
15	.555	.417	.315	.239	.183	.140	.108	.084	.065	.051	.040	.031	.025	.020	.016
20	.456	.312	.215	.149	.104	.073	.051	.037	.026	.019	.014	.010	.007	.005	.004
30	.308	.174	.099	.057	.033	.020	.012	.007	.004	.003	.002	.001	.001	—	—
40	.208	.097	.046	.022	.011	.005	.003	.001	.001	—	—	—	—	—	—

Table III

Present Value of $1.00

$$\frac{1}{(1+r)^n}$$

Period	4%	6%	8%	10%	12%	14%	16%	18%	20%	22%	24%	25%	26%	28%	30%
1	0.962	0.943	0.926	0.909	0.893	0.877	0.862	0.847	0.833	0.820	0.806	0.800	0.794	0.781	0.769
2	1.886	1.833	1.783	1.736	1.690	1.647	1.605	1.566	1.528	1.492	1.457	1.440	1.424	1.392	1.361
3	2.775	2.673	2.577	2.487	2.402	2.322	2.246	2.174	2.106	2.042	1.981	1.952	1.923	1.868	1.816
4	3.630	3.465	3.312	3.170	3.037	2.914	2.798	2.690	2.589	2.494	2.404	2.362	2.320	2.241	2.166
5	4.452	4.212	3.993	3.791	3.605	3.433	3.274	3.127	2.991	2.864	2.745	2.689	2.635	2.532	2.436
6	5.242	4.917	4.623	4.355	4.111	3.889	3.685	3.498	3.326	3.167	3.020	2.951	2.885	2.759	2.643
7	6.002	5.582	5.206	4.868	4.564	4.288	4.039	3.812	3.605	3.416	3.242	3.161	3.083	2.937	2.802
8	6.733	6.210	5.747	5.335	4.968	4.639	4.344	4.078	3.837	3.619	3.421	3.329	3.241	3.076	2.925
9	7.435	6.802	6.247	5.759	5.328	4.946	4.607	4.303	4.031	3.786	3.566	3.463	3.366	3.184	3.019
10	8.111	7.360	6.710	6.145	5.650	5.216	4.833	4.494	4.192	3.923	3.682	3.571	3.465	3.269	3.092
11	8.760	7.887	7.139	6.495	5.938	5.453	5.029	4.656	4.327	4.035	3.776	3.656	3.544	3.335	3.147
12	9.385	8.384	7.536	6.814	6.194	5.660	5.197	4.793	4.439	4.127	3.851	3.725	3.606	3.387	3.190
13	9.986	8.853	7.904	7.103	6.424	5.842	5.342	4.910	4.533	4.203	3.912	3.780	3.656	3.427	3.223
14	10.563	9.295	8.244	7.367	6.628	6.002	5.468	5.008	4.611	4.265	3.962	3.824	3.695	3.459	3.249
15	11.118	9.712	8.559	7.606	6.811	6.142	5.575	5.092	4.675	4.315	4.001	3.859	3.726	3.483	3.268
20	13.590	11.470	9.818	8.514	7.469	6.623	5.929	5.353	4.870	4.460	4.110	3.954	3.808	3.546	3.316
30	17.292	13.765	11.258	9.427	8.055	7.003	6.177	5.517	4.979	4.534	4.160	3.995	3.842	3.569	3.332
40	19.793	15.046	11.925	9.779	8.244	7.105	6.234	5.548	4.997	4.544	4.166	3.999	3.846	3.571	3.333

Table IV

Present Value of Series of $1.00 Cash Flows

$$\frac{1}{r}\left(1-\frac{1}{(1+r)^n}\right)$$

Appendix B to Chapter 16

Impact of Inflation

LO 10

After completing Appendix B, explain the impact of inflation on a capital-budgeting analysis.

Most countries have experienced inflation to some degree over the past 30 years. *Inflation* is defined as a decline in the general purchasing power of a monetary unit, such as a dollar, across time. Since capital-budgeting decisions involve cash flows over several time periods, it is worthwhile to examine the impact of inflation in capital-budgeting analyses.

Inflation can be incorporated in a discounted-cash-flow analysis in either of two ways. Both approaches yield correct results, but the analyst must be careful to be consistent in applying either approach. The two approaches are distinguished by the use of either *nominal* or *real* interest rates and dollars. These terms are defined below.

Interest Rates: Real or Nominal The **real interest rate** is the underlying interest rate, which includes compensation to investors for the *time value of money* and the *risk* of an investment. The **nominal interest rate** includes the real interest rate, plus an additional premium to compensate investors for inflation. Suppose the real interest rate is 10 percent, and inflation of 5 percent is projected. Then the nominal interest rate is determined as follows:[7]

Real interest rate	.10
Inflation rate	.05
Combined effect (.10 × .05)	.005
Nominal interest rate	.155

Dollars: Real or Nominal A cash flow measured in **nominal dollars** is the actual cash flow we observe. For example, a particular model of automobile cost $10,000 in year 1 but it cost $12,155 in year 5. Both the $10,000 cash flow in year 1 and $12,155 cash flow in year 5 are measured in *nominal dollars*. A cash flow measured in **real dollars** reflects an adjustment for the dollar's purchasing power. The following table shows the relationship between nominal and real dollars, assuming an inflation rate of 5 percent.

Year	(a) Cash Flow in Nominal Dollars	(b) Price Index	(c) = (a) ÷ (b) Cash Flow in Real Dollars
Year 1	$10,000	1.0000	$10,000
Year 2	10,500	$(1.05)^1 = 1.0500$	10,000
Year 3	11,025	$(1.05)^2 = 1.1025$	10,000
Year 4	11,576	$(1.05)^3 = 1.1576$	10,000
Year 5	12,155	$(1.05)^4 = 1.2155$	10,000

As the table shows, cash flows in nominal dollars must be deflated, which means dividing by the price index, to convert them to cash flows in real dollars. The real-dollar cash flows are expressed in year 1 dollars.

Two Capital-Budgeting Approaches under Inflation

A correct capital-budgeting analysis may be done using either of the following approaches.

1. Use cash flows measured in *nominal dollars* and a nominal interest rate to determine the *nominal discount rate.*
2. Use cash flows measured in *real dollars* and a real interest rate to determine the *real discount rate.*

[7]An alternative way to compute the nominal interest rate is: (1.10 × 1.05) − 1.00 = .155.

To illustrate these two approaches, we will focus on an equipment-replacement decision faced by the management of High Country Department Stores. The company operates an appliance-repair service for the household appliances it sells. Management is considering the replacement of a sophisticated piece of testing equipment used in repairing TVs and VCRs. The new equipment costs $5,000 and will have no salvage value. Over its four-year life, the new equipment is expected to generate the cost savings and depreciation tax shield shown below. The cash flows in column (f) of the table are the total after-tax cash inflows, measured in *nominal dollars.*

Measured in Nominal Dollars

Year	(a) Acquisition Cost	(b) Cost Savings	(c) After-Tax Cost Savings [(b) × (1 − .40)]	(d) MACRS Depreciation (3-year class)	(e) Depreciation Tax Shield [(d) × .40]	(f) Total After-Tax Cash Flow [(c) + (e)]
Year 1	$(5,000)					
Year 2		$1,900	$1,140	$1,667	$667	$1,807
Year 3		2,000	1,200	2,223	889	2,089
Year 4		2,100	1,260	740	296	1,556
Year 5		2,500	1,500	370	148	1,648

Approach 1: Nominal Dollars and Nominal Discount Rate Under this capital-budgeting approach, we discount the nominal-dollar cash flows in the preceding table using the nominal discount rate of 15.5 percent. The net-present-value analysis is as follows:

Year	(a) Cash Flow in Nominal Dollars	(b) Discount Factor for Nominal Discount Rate of 15.5%	(c) = (a) × (b) Present Value
Year 1	$(5,000)	1.000	$(5,000)
Year 2	1,807	.8658 [1/(1.155)]*	1,564
Year 3	2,089	.7496 [1/(1.155)^2]	1,565
Year 4	1,556	.6490 [1/(1.155)^3]	1,009
Year 5	1,648	.5619 [1/(1.155)^4]	926
Net present value			$ 64

*The 15.5% discount factors are computed using the formula in Table III of Appendix A.

High Country's management should purchase the new testing equipment, since its NPV is positive.

Approach 2: Real Dollars and Real Discount Rate Under this capital-budgeting approach, we first convert the cash flows measured in nominal dollars to cash flows in real dollars, as follows:

Year	(a) After-Tax Cash Flow in Nominal Dollars	(b) Price Index	(c) = (a) ÷ (b) After-Tax Cash Flow in Real Dollars*
Year 1	$(5,000)	1.0000	$(5,000)
Year 2	1,807	1.0500	1,721
Year 3	2,089	1.1025	1,895
Year 4	1,556	1.1576	1,344
Year 5	1,648	1.2155	1,356

*Real-dollar cash flows expressed in terms of year 1 dollars.

Now we discount the after-tax cash flows, measured in real dollars, using the real discount rate of 10 percent. The net-present-value analysis is shown below.

Year	(a) Cash Flow in Real Dollars	(b) Discount Factor for Real Discount Rate of 10%	(c) = (a) × (b) Present Value
Year 1	$(5,000)	1.000	$(5,000)
Year 2	1,721	.909	1,564
Year 3	1,895	.826	1,565

(continues)

Year 4	1,344	.751	1,009
Year 5	1,356	.683	926
Net present value			$ 64

Notice that the new testing equipment's NPV is the same under both capital-budgeting approaches. Under both approaches, we conclude that High Country Department Stores should purchase the new equipment.

Consistency Is the Key Either capital-budgeting approach will provide the correct conclusion, as long as it is applied consistently. Use either nominal dollars and a nominal discount rate or real dollars and a real discount rate. A common error in capital budgeting is to convert the after-tax cash flows to real dollars, but then use the nominal discount rate. This faulty analysis creates a bias against acceptance of worthwhile projects.

To illustrate, suppose High Country's management had made this error in its testing-equipment analysis. The following *incorrect* analysis is the result.

Incorrect Analysis of Testing-Equipment Decision

Inconsistency (between (a) and (b))

Year	(a) Cash Flow in Real Dollars	(b) Discount Factor for Nominal Discount Rate of 15.5%	(c) = (a) × (b) Present Value
Year 1	$(5,000)	1.0000	$(5,000)
Year 2	1,721	.8658	1,490
Year 3	1,895	.7496	1,420
Year 4	1,344	.6490	872
Year 5	1,356	.5619	762
Net present value			$ (456)

This inconsistent and incorrect analysis will lead High Country's management to the wrong conclusion.

Review Questions

Note: Review questions 1 through 10 relate to Section 1 of the chapter. Questions 11 through 18 relate to Section 2, and questions 19 through 22 relate to Section 3. Questions 16–23 relate to Appendix B.

16–1. "Time is money!" is an old saying. Relate this statement to the evaluation of capital-investment projects.

16–2. Distinguish between the following two types of capital-budgeting decisions: acceptance-or-rejection decisions and capital-rationing decisions.

16–3. "The greater the discount rate, the greater the present value of a future cash flow." True or false? Explain your answer.

16–4. Briefly explain the concept of *discounted-cash-flow analysis.* What are the two common methods of discounted-cash-flow analysis?

16–5. State the decision rule used to accept or reject an investment proposal under each of these methods of analysis: (1) net-present-value method and (2) internal-rate-of-return method.

16–6. Explain the following terms: *recovery of investment* versus *return on investment.*

16–7. List and briefly explain two advantages that the net-present-value method has over the internal-rate-of-return method.

16–8. List and briefly explain four assumptions underlying discounted-cash-flow analysis.

16–9. Distinguish between the following approaches to discounted-cash-flow analysis: total-cost approach versus incremental-cost approach.

16–10. What is meant by a *postaudit* of an investment project?

16–11. Give an example of a noncash expense. What impact does such an expense have in a capital-budgeting analysis? Explain how to compute the after-tax impact of a noncash expense.

16–12. Explain how to compute the after-tax amount of a cash revenue or expense.

16–13. What is a *depreciation tax shield?* Explain the effect of a depreciation tax shield in a capital-budgeting analysis.

16–14. Give an example of a cash flow that is not on the income statement. How do you determine the after-tax amount of such a cash flow?

16–15. Why is accelerated depreciation advantageous to a business?

16–16. Explain how a gain or loss on disposal is handled in a capital-budgeting analysis.

16–17. Why may the net-present-value and internal-rate-of-return methods yield different rankings for investments with different lives?

16–18. Define the term *profitability index.* How is it used in ranking investment proposals?

16–19. What is meant by the term *payback period?* How is this criterion sometimes used in capital budgeting?

16–20. What are the two main drawbacks of the payback method?

16–21. How is an investment project's *accounting rate of return* defined? Why do the accounting rate of return and internal rate of return on a capital project generally differ?

16–22. Discuss the pros and cons of the accounting rate of return as an investment criterion.

16–23. (Appendix B) Briefly describe two correct methods of net-present-value analysis in an inflationary period.

Exercises

Note: Several exercises on the basics of compound interest and the concept of present value are included in Appendix I, which appears at the end of the text. See page 782.

Exercise 16–24
Net Present Value (Section 1)
(LO 1)

Jefferson County's Board of Representatives is considering the purchase of a site for a new sanitary landfill. The purchase price for the site is $234,000 and preparatory work will cost $88,080. The landfill would be usable for 10 years. The board hired a consultant, who estimated that the new landfill would cost the county $48,000 per year less to operate than the county's current landfill. The current landfill also will last 10 more years. For a landfill project, Jefferson County can borrow money from the federal government at a subsidized rate. The county's hurdle rate is only 6 percent for this project.

Required: Compute the net present value of the new landfill. Should the board approve the project?

Exercise 16–25
Internal Rate of Return (Section 1)
(LO 1)

Refer to the data given in the preceding exercise.

Required: Calculate the landfill project's internal rate of return. Should the board approve the project?

Exercise 16–26
Recovery of Investment (Section 1)
(LO 2)

Refer to the data given in Exercise 16–24.

Required: Prepare a display similar to Exhibit 16–2 to show the recovery of investment and return on investment for Jefferson County's landfill project.

Exercise 16–27
Internal Rate of Return; Uneven Cash Flows (Section 1)
(LO 1)

The trustees of the Danube School of Art and Music, located in Tuttlingen, Germany, are considering a major overhaul of the school's audio system. With or without the overhaul, the system will be replaced in two years. If an overhaul is done now, the trustees expect to save the following repair costs during the next two years: year 1, 3,000 *euros*; year 2, 5,000 *euros*. The overhaul will cost 6,664 *euros*. (The new monetary unit, the *euro,* has now been introduced in most European markets.)

Required: Use trial and error to compute the internal rate of return on the proposed overhaul. (*Hint:* The NPV of the overhaul is positive if an 8 percent discount rate is used, but the NPV is negative if a 16 percent rate is used.)

Exercise 16–28
Use of Internet; City Government; Capital Projects (Section 1)
(LO 1)

Use the internet to access the home page for the city of Chicago, www.ci.chi.il.us. Use one of the links there to access the home page for one of Chicago's sister organizations, such as the following:

Chicago Park District	www.chicagoparkdistrict.com
Chicago Public Schools	www.cps.k12.il.us
Chicago Transit Authority	www.transitchicago.com
Chicago Housing Authority	www.thecha.org

Each of these linked pages contains information about the organization's budget and its capital projects. Read about one or more of these capital projects, and then discuss how the organization's managers should go about making significant decisions about expenditures for major capital projects like the one you have explored.

Exercise 16–29
New Present Value with Different Discount Rates (Section 1)
(LO 1)

Toronto Shakespearean Theater's board of directors is considering the replacement of the theater's lighting system. The old system requires two people to operate it, but the new system would require only a single operator. The new lighting system will cost $129,750 and save the theater $27,000 annually for the next eight years.

Required: Prepare a table showing the proposed lighting system's net present value for each of the following discount rates: 8 percent, 10 percent, 12 percent, 14 percent, and 16 percent. Use the following headings in your table. Comment on the pattern in the right-hand column.

Discount Rate	Annuity Discount Factor	Annual Savings	Present Value of Annual Savings	Acquisition Cost	Net Present Value

Exercise 16–30
Sensitivity Analysis; NPV (Section 1)
(LO 1)

Refer to the data given in the preceding exercise. Suppose the Toronto Shakespearean Theater's board is uncertain about the cost savings with the new lighting system.

Required: How low could the new lighting system's annual savings be and still justify acceptance of the proposal by the board of directors? Assume the theater's hurdle rate is 12 percent.

Exercise 16–31
After-Tax Cash Flows (Section 2)
(LO 4)

Portsmouth Printing Corporation recently purchased a truck for $36,000. Under MACRS, the first year's depreciation was $7,200. The truck driver's salary in the first year of operation was $38,400.

Required: Show how each of the amounts mentioned above should be converted to an after-tax amount. The company's tax rate is 30 percent.

Exercise 16–32
Using the Modified Accelerated Cost Recovery System (Section 2)
(LO 5)

For each of the following assets, indicate the MACRS property class and depreciation method.

1. A pharmaceutical company bought a new microscope to use in its Research and Development Division.
2. A midwestern farmer constructed a new barn to house beef cattle.
3. A steel fabrication company bought a machine, which is expected to be useful for 18 years.
4. The president of an insurance company authorized the purchase of a new desk for her office.
5. A pizza restaurant purchased a new delivery car.

Exercise 16–33
Depreciation Tax Shield (Section 2)
(LO 5)

Trenton Fabrication Company purchased industrial tools costing $110,000, which fall in the 3-year property class under MACRS.

Required:

1. Prepare a schedule of depreciation deductions assuming:
   a. The firm uses the accelerated depreciation schedule specified by MACRS.
   b. The firm uses the optional straight-line depreciation method and the half-year convention.
2. Calculate the present value of the depreciation tax shield under each depreciation method listed in requirement (1). Trenton Fabrication Company's after-tax hurdle rate is 12 percent, and the firm's tax rate is 30 percent.

Exercise 16–34
Gain or Loss on Disposal; Taxes (Section 2)
(LO 4)

In December of 20x4, Memphis Plastics sold a forklift for $9,255. The machine was purchased in 20x1 for $50,000. Since then $38,845 in depreciation has been recorded on the forklift.

Required:

1. What was the forklift's book value at the time of sale?
2. Compute the gain or loss on the sale.
3. Determine the after-tax cash flow at the time the forklift was sold. The firm's tax rate is 45 percent.

Exercise 16–35
Profitability Index; Taxes (Section 2)
(LO 7)

The owner of Cape Cod Confectionary is considering the purchase of a new semiautomatic candy machine. The machine will cost $30,000 and last 10 years. The machine is expected to have no salvage value at the end of its useful life. The owner projects that the new candy machine will generate $4,800 in after-tax savings each year during its life (including the depreciation tax shield).

Required: Compute the profitability index on the proposed candy machine, assuming an after-tax hurdle rate of: (*a*) 8 percent, (*b*) 10 percent, and (*c*) 12 percent.

Exercise 16–36
Payback Period; Even Cash Flows (Section 3)
(LO 8)

The management of Iroquois National Bank is considering an investment in automatic teller machines. The machines would cost $124,200 and have a useful life of seven years. The bank's controller has estimated that the automatic teller machines will save the bank $27,000 after taxes during each year of their life (including the depreciation tax shield). The machines will have no salvage value.

Required:

1. Compute the payback period for the proposed investment.
2. Compute the net present value of the proposed investment assuming an after-tax hurdle rate of: (*a*) 10 percent, (*b*) 12 percent, and (*c*) 14 percent.
3. What can you conclude from your answers to requirements (1) and (2) about the limitations of the payback method?

Exercise 16–37
Payback, Accounting Rate of Return; Net Present Value; Taxes (Sections 1, 2, and 3)
(LO 8)

Yankay Specialty Metals Corporation is reviewing an investment proposal. The initial cost as well as the estimate of the book value of the investment at the end of each year, the net after-tax cash flows for each year, and the net income for each year are presented in the following schedule. The salvage value of the investment at the end of each year is equal to its book value. There would be no salvage value at the end of the investment's life.

Year	Initial Cost and Book Value	Annual Net After-Tax Cash Flows	Annual Net Income
0	$105,000		
1	70,000	$50,000	$15,000
2	42,000	45,000	17,000
3	21,000	40,000	19,000
4	7,000	35,000	21,000
5	0	30,000	23,000

Management uses a 16 percent after-tax target rate of return for new investment proposals.

Required: For requirement (1) *only* assume that the cash flows in years 1 through 5 occur uniformly throughout each year.

1. Compute the project's payback period.
2. Calculate the accounting rate of return on the investment proposal. Base your calculation on the initial cost of the investment.
3. Compute the proposal's net present value.

(CMA, adapted)

Exercise 16–38
Inflation and Capital Budgeting (Appendix B)
(LO 10)

The state's secretary of education is considering the purchase of a new computer for $150,000. A cost study indicates that the new computer should save the Department of Education $45,000, measured in real dollars, during each of the next eight years.

The real interest rate is 20 percent and the inflation rate is 10 percent. As a governmental agency, the Department of Education pays no taxes.

Required:

1. Prepare a schedule of cash flows measured in real dollars. Include the initial acquisition and the cost savings for each of the next eight years.
2. Using cash flows measured in real dollars, compute the net present value of the proposed computer. Use a real discount rate equal to the real interest rate.

Exercise 16–39
Inflation and Capital Budgeting (Appendix B)
(LO 10)

Refer to the data in the preceding exercise.

Required:

1. Compute the nominal interest rate.
2. Prepare a schedule of cash flows measured in nominal dollars.
3. Using cash flows measured in nominal dollars, compute the net present value of the proposed computer. Use a nominal discount rate equal to the nominal interest rate.

Problems

■ **Problem 16–40**
Net Present Value; Outsourcing (Section 1)
(LO 1, 3)

Community Challenges, a nonprofit organization for physically and mentally challenged people, manufactures a variety of products in four plants located in California. The company is currently purchasing an electronic igniter from an outside supplier for $62 per unit. Because of supplier reliability problems, the company is considering producing the igniters internally in a currently idle manufacturing plant. Annual volume over the next five years is expected to total 400,000 units at variable manufacturing costs of $60 per unit. Management must hire a factory supervisor and assistant for a total annual salary and fringe benefit package of $95,000.

In addition, the company must acquire $60,000 of new equipment. The equipment has a five-year service life and a $12,000 salvage value, and will be depreciated by the straight-line method. Repairs and maintenance are expected to average $4,500 per year in years 3–5, and the equipment will be sold at the end of its life.

Required:

1. Should discounted cash flows be used in this outsourcing decision? Why?
2. Ignoring your answer to requirement (1), use the net-present-value method (total-cost approach) and a 14 percent hurdle rate to determine whether management should manufacture or outsource the igniters.
3. Suppose management is able to negotiate a lower purchase price from its supplier. At what purchase price would management be financially indifferent between manufacturing and outsourcing the igniters.

■ **Problem 16–41**
Net Present Value; Total Cost Approach (Section 1)
(LO 1, 3)

Medical Arts Hospital's board of trustees is considering the addition of a comprehensive medical testing laboratory. In the past, the hospital has sent all blood and tissue specimens to Diagnostic Testing Services, an independent testing service. The hospital's current contract with the testing service is due to expire, and the testing service has offered a new 10-year contract. Under the terms of the new contract, Medical Arts Hospital would pay Diagnostic Testing Services a flat fee of $80,000 per year plus $20 per specimen tested.

Since Medical Arts Hospital does not have its own comprehensive testing lab, the hospital staff is forced to refer some types of cases to a nearby metropolitan hospital. If Medical Arts Hospital had its own lab, these cases could be handled in-house. Medical Arts Hospital's administrator estimates that the hospital loses $100,000 per year in contribution margin on the cases that currently must be referred elsewhere.

The proposed new lab would not require construction of a new building, since it would occupy space currently used by the hospital for storage. However, the hospital then would be forced to rent storage space in a nearby medical building at a cost of $30,000 per year. The equipment for the lab would cost $625,000 initially. Additional equipment costing $300,000 would be purchased after four years. Due to the rapid technological improvement of medical testing equipment, the equipment would have negligible salvage value after 10 years. Staffing the lab would require two supervisors and four technicians. Annual compensation costs would run $40,000 each for the supervisors and $30,000 each for the lab technicians. Fixed operating costs in the lab would be $50,000 per year, and variable costs would amount to $10 per medical test.

Medical Arts Hospital requires 20,000 tests per year. The capacity of the lab would be 25,000 tests per year. Medical Arts Hospital's administrator believes that physicians in private practice would utilize the lab's excess capacity by sending their own tests to Medical Arts Hospital. The administrator has projected a charge of $20 per test for physicians in private practice. Medical Arts Hospital's hurdle rate is 12 percent.

Required: Use the total-cost approach to prepare a net-present-value analysis of the proposed testing laboratory.

■ **Problem 16–42**
Net Present Value; Incremental-Cost Approach (Section 1)
(LO 1, 3)

Refer to the data in the preceding problem regarding Medical Arts Hospital.

Required: Use the incremental-cost approach to prepare a net-present-value analysis of Medical Arts Hospital's proposed new medical testing laboratory.

■ **Problem 16–43**
Net-Present-Value Analysis; Hospital (Section 1)
(LO 1, 3)

San Joaquin Community Hospital is a nonprofit hospital operated by the county. The hospital's administrator is considering a proposal to open a new outpatient clinic in the nearby city of San Marco. The administrator has made the following estimates pertinent to the proposal.

1. Construction of the clinic building will cost $780,000 in two equal installments of $390,000, to be paid at the end of 20x0 and 20x1. The clinic will open on January 2, 20x2. All staffing and operating costs begin in 20x2.
2. Equipment for the clinic will cost $150,000, to be paid in December of 20x1.
3. Staffing of the clinic will cost $800,000 per year.
4. Other operating costs at the clinic will be $200,000 per year.
5. Opening the clinic is expected to increase charitable contributions to the hospital by $250,000 per year.
6. The clinic is expected to reduce costs at San Joaquin Community Hospital. Annual cost savings at the hospital are projected to be $1,000,000.
7. A major refurbishment of the clinic is expected to be necessary toward the end of 20x5. This work will cost $180,000.
8. Due to shifting medical needs in the county, the administrator doubts the clinic will be needed after 20x9.
9. The clinic building and equipment could be sold for $290,000 at the end of 20x9.
10. The hospital's hurdle rate is 12 percent.

Required:

1. Compute the cash flows for each year relevant to the analysis.
2. Prepare a table of cash flows, by year, similar to Exhibit 16–4.
3. Compute the net present value of the proposed outpatient clinic.
4. Should the administrator recommend to the hospital's trustees that the clinic be built? Why?

Problem 16–44
Net Present Value; Qualitative Issues (Section 1)
(LO 1, 3)

Special People Industries (SPI) is a nonprofit organization which employs only people with physical or mental disabilities. One of the organization's activities is to make cookies for its snack food store. Several years ago, Special People Industries purchased a special cookie-cutting machine. As of December 31, 20x0, this machine will have been used for three years. Management is considering the purchase of a newer, more efficient machine. If purchased, the new machine would be acquired on December 31, 20x0. Management expects to sell 300,000 dozen cookies in each of the next six years. The selling price of the cookies is expected to average $1.15 per dozen.

Special People Industries has two options: continue to operate the old machine, or sell the old machine and purchase the new machine. No trade-in was offered by the seller of the new machine. The following information has been assembled to help management decide which option is more desirable.

	Old Machine	New Machine
Original cost of machine at acquisition	$80,000	$120,000
Remaining useful life as of December 31, 20x0	6 years	6 years
Expected annual cash operating expenses:		
Variable cost per dozen	$.38	$.29
Total fixed costs	$21,000	$ 11,000
Estimated cash value of machines:		
December 31, 20x0	$40,000	$120,000
December 31, 20x6	$ 7,000	$ 20,000

Assume that all operating revenues and expenses occur at the end of the year.

Required:

1. Use the net-present-value method to determine whether Special People Industries should retain the old machine or acquire the new machine. The organization's hurdle rate is 16 percent.
2. Independent of your answer to requirement (1), suppose the quantitative differences are so slight between the two alternatives that management is indifferent between the two proposals. Write a memo to the president of SPI, which identifies and discusses any nonquantitative factors that management should consider.

(CMA, adapted)

Problem 16–45
Internal Rate of Return; Even Cash Flows (Section 1)
(LO 1, 3)

Adams County's Board of Representatives is considering the construction of a longer runway at the county airport. Currently, the airport can handle only private aircraft and small commuter jets. A new, long runway would enable the airport to handle the midsize jets used on many domestic flights. Data pertinent to the board's decision appear below.

Cost of acquiring additional land for runway	$ 70,000
Cost of runway construction	200,000
Cost of extending perimeter fence	29,840
Cost of runway lights	39,600
Annual cost of maintaining new runway	28,000
Annual incremental revenue from landing fees	40,000

In addition to the preceding data, two other facts are relevant to the decision. First, a longer runway will require a new snowplow, which will cost $100,000. The old snowplow could be sold now for $10,000. The new, larger plow will cost $12,000 more in annual operating costs. Second, the County Board of Representatives believes that the proposed long runway, and the major jet service it will bring to the county, will increase economic activity in the community. The board projects that the increased economic activity will result in $64,000 per year in additional tax revenue for the county.

In analyzing the runway proposal, the board has decided to use a 10-year time horizon. The county's hurdle rate for capital projects is 12 percent.

Required:

1. Compute the initial cost of the investment in the long runway.
2. Compute the annual net cost or benefit from the runway.
3. Determine the IRR on the proposed long runway. Should it be built?

Problem 16–46
Net Present Value
(Section 1)
(LO 1, 3)

Refer to the data given in the preceding problem.

Required:

1. Prepare a net-present-value analysis of the proposed long runway.
2. Should the County Board of Representatives approve the runway?
3. Which of the data used in the analysis are likely to be most uncertain? Least uncertain? Why?

Problem 16–47
Internal Rate of Return; Sensitivity Analysis
(Section 1)
(LO 1, 3)

Refer to the data given in Problem 16–45. The County Board of Representatives believes that if the county conducts a promotional effort costing $20,000 per year, the proposed long runway will result in substantially greater economic development than was projected originally. However, the board is uncertain about the actual increase in county tax revenue that will result.

Required: Suppose the board builds the long runway and conducts the promotional campaign. What would the increase in the county's annual tax revenue need to be in order for the proposed runway's internal rate of return to equal the county's hurdle rate of 12 percent?

Problem 16–48
MACRS Depreciation; Present Value of Tax Shield
(Section 2)
(LO 4, 5)

Flotilla Beam, the owner of the Bay City Boatyard, recently had a brilliant idea. There is a shortage of boat slips in the harbor during the summer. Beam's idea is to develop a system of "dry slips." A dry slip is a large storage rack in a warehouse on which a boat is stored. When the boat owner requests, a forklift is used to remove the boat from the dry slip and place the boat in the water. The entire operation requires one hour when a launch reservation is made in advance. The boatyard already has a vacant warehouse, which could be used for this purpose. However, Beam's idea will require the following capital investment by the boatyard.

- Storage racks: cost, $200,000; useful life, 18 years; MACRS class, 10-year property.
- Forklift: cost, $120,000; useful life, six years; MACRS class, 5-year property.

Bay City Boatyard's tax rate is 35 percent, and its after-tax hurdle rate is 14 percent.

Required: For each of the boatyard's proposed capital investments:

1. Prepare a schedule of the annual depreciation expenses for tax purposes.
2. Compute the present value of the depreciation tax shield.

Problem 16–49
Net Present Value; Taxes
(Section 2)
(LO 3, 4, 6)

MicroTest Technology, Inc. is a high-technology company that manufactures sophisticated testing instruments for evaluating microcircuits. These instruments sell for $3,500 each and cost $2,450 each to manufacture. An essential component of the company's manufacturing process is a sealed vacuum chamber where the interior approaches a pure vacuum. The technology of the vacuum pumps that the firm uses to prepare its chamber for sealing has been changing rapidly. On January 2, 20x0, MicroTest bought the latest in electronic high-speed vacuum pumps, a machine that allowed the company to evacuate a chamber for sealing in only six hours. The company paid $400,000 for the pump. Recently, the manufacturer of the pump approached MicroTest with a new pump that would reduce the evacuation time to two hours. MicroTest's management is considering the acquisition of this new pump and has asked Melanie Harris, the controller, to evaluate the financial impact of replacing the existing pump with the new model. Harris has gathered the following information prior to preparing her analysis.

- The new pump would be installed on December 31, 20x2, and placed in service on January 1, 20x3. The cost of the pump is $608,000, and the costs for installing, testing, and debugging the new pump will be $12,000. For depreciation purposes, these costs will be considered part of the cost of the equipment. The pump would be assigned to the 3-year MACRS class for depreciation and is expected to have a salvage value of $80,000 when sold at the end of four years.
- The old pump will be fully depreciated at the time the new pump is placed in service. If the new pump is purchased, arrangements will be made to sell the old pump for $50,000, the estimated salvage value on December 31, 20x2.
- At the current rate of production, the new pump's greater efficiency will result in annual cash savings of $125,000.
- MicroTest is able to sell all of the testing instruments it can produce. Because of the increased speed of the new pump, output is expected to be 30 units greater in 20x3 than in 20x2. In 20x4 and 20x5, production will be 50 units greater than in 20x2. The production in 20x6 will exceed 20x2 production by 70 units. For all *additional* units produced, the manufacturing costs would be reduced by $150 per unit.
- MicroTest is subject to a 40 percent tax rate. For evaluating capital investment proposals, MicroTest's management uses a 16 percent after-tax discount rate.

Required:

1. Determine whether or not MicroTest should purchase the new pump by calculating the net present value of the investment.
2. Describe the factors, other than the net present value, that MicroTest should consider before making the pump replacement decision.

(CMA, adapted)

Problem 16–50
After-Tax Cash Flows; NPV
(Section 2)
(LO 3, 4, 6)

LifeLine Corporation manufactures fire extinguishers. One part used in all types of fire extinguishers is a unique pressure fitting that requires specialized machine tools that need to be replaced. LifeLine's production manager has concluded that the only alternative to replacing these machine tools is to buy the pressure fitting from Milwaukee Pipe and Fitting Company. LifeLine could buy the fitting for $20 if a minimum order of 70,000 fittings is placed annually. LifeLine has used an average of 80,000 fittings over the past three years. The production manager believes this volume will remain constant for five more years.

Cost records indicate that unit manufacturing costs for the last several years have been as follows:

Direct material	$ 4.10
Direct labor	3.70
Variable overhead	1.70
Fixed overhead*	4.50
Total unit cost	$14.00

*Depreciation accounts for two-thirds of the fixed overhead. The balance is for other fixed-overhead costs of the factory that require cash expenditures.

If the specialized tools are purchased, they will cost $2,500,000 and will have a disposal value of $100,000 after their expected life of five years. Straight-line depreciation is used for book purposes, but MACRS is used for tax purposes. The specialized tools are considered 3-year property for MACRS purposes. The company has a 40 percent tax rate, and management requires a 12 percent after-tax return on investment.

The sales representative for the manufacturer of the new tools stated, "The new tools will allow direct labor and variable overhead to be reduced by $1.60 per unit." Data from another manufacturer using identical tools and experiencing similar operating conditions, except that annual production generally averages 110,000 units, confirm the direct-labor and variable-overhead savings. However, the manufacturer indicated that it experienced an increase in direct-material cost to $4.50 per unit due to the higher quality of material that had to be used with the new tools.

Required:

1. Prepare a net-present-value analysis covering the life of the new specialized tools to determine whether management should replace the old tools or purchase the pressure fittings. Include all tax implications.
2. Identify any additional factors management should consider before a decision is made to replace the tools or purchase the pressure fittings.

(CMA, adapted)

Problem 16–51
Net Present Value; Internal Rate of Return; Payback; Sensitivity Analysis; Taxes (Sections 2, 3)
(LO 3, 4, 6, 8)

Weisinger Corporation's management is considering the replacement of an old machine. It is fully depreciated but it can be used by the corporation through 20x5. If management decides to replace the old machine, James Company has offered to purchase it for $60,000 on the replacement date. The old machine would have no salvage value in 20x5. If the replacement occurs, a new machine would be acquired from Hillcrest Industries on December 31, 20x1. The purchase price of $1,000,000 for the new machine would be paid in cash at the time of replacement. Due to the increased efficiency of the new machine, estimated annual cash savings of $300,000 would be generated through 20x5, the end of its expected useful life. The new machine is not expected to have any salvage value at the end of 20x5. Weisinger's management requires all investments to earn a 12 percent after-tax return. The company's tax rate is 40 percent. The new machine would be classified as three-year property for MACRS purposes.

Required:

1. Compute the net present value of the machine replacement investment.
2. Between which of the following two percentages is the internal rate of return on the machine replacement: 4 percent, 6 percent, 8 percent, 10 percent, 12 percent, and 14 percent?
3. Between what two whole numbers of years is the machine replacement's payback period?
4. How much would the salvage value of the new machine have to be on December 31, 20x5, in order to turn the machine replacement into an acceptable investment?

(CMA, adapted)

Problem 16–52
Ranking Investment Proposals; NPV versus Profitability Index; Taxes (Section 2)
(LO 4, 6, 7)

The owner of Zivanov's Pancake House is considering an expansion of the business. He has identified two alternatives, as follows:

- Build a new restaurant near the mall.
- Buy and renovate an old building downtown for the new restaurant.

The projected cash flows from these two alternatives are shown below. The owner of the restaurant uses a 10 percent after-tax discount rate.

Investment Proposal	Cash Outflow: Time 0	Net After-Tax Cash Inflows* Years 1–10	Years 11–20
Mall restaurant	$400,000	$50,000	$50,000
Downtown restaurant	200,000	35,800	—

*Includes after-tax cash flows from all sources, including incremental revenue, incremental expenses, and depreciation tax shield.

Required:

1. Compute the net present value of each alternative restaurant site.
2. Compute the profitability index for each alternative.
3. How do the two sites rank in terms of (*a*) NPV and (*b*) the profitability index?
4. Comment on the difficulty of ranking the owner's two options for the new restaurant site.

Problem 16–53
Payback; Accounting Rate of Return (Section 3)
(LO 8)

Refer to the data given in the preceding problem. The owner of Zivanov's Pancake House will consider capital projects only if they have a payback period of six years or less. The owner also favors projects that exhibit an accounting rate of return of at least 15 percent. The owner bases a project's accounting rate of return on the initial investment in the project.

Required:

1. Compute the payback period for each of the proposed restaurant sites.
2. Compute the accounting rate of return for each proposed site. Assume the average annual incremental income is $50,000 for the mall restaurant and $35,800 for the downtown restaurant.
3. If the owner of the restaurant sticks to his criteria, which site will he choose?
4. Comment on the pros and cons of the restaurant owner's investment criteria.

Problem 16–54
Payback; Accounting Rate of Return; Ethics (Section 3)
(LO 8)

The Golden Triangle Theater is a nonprofit enterprise in downtown Pittsburgh. The board of directors is considering an expansion of the theater's seating capacity, which will entail significant renovations to the existing facilities. The board has been promised by the city government that in five years the city will build a new building for the theater, so the proposed expansion is only a temporary solution to the theater's strained seating capacity. The seating expansion project will cost $120,000. The following table lists the incremental ticket revenue, the incremental operating expenses, the depreciation expense, and the incremental operating income over the five-year life of the investment expected as a result of the theater expansion. The theater's revenue and operating expenses are in cash. Thus, depreciation is the only noncash expense. As a nonprofit enterprise, the theater company is not subject to income taxes.

Year	Incremental Revenue	Incremental Operating Expenses	Net Incremental Cash Flow	Annual Straight-Line Depreciation	Incremental Operating Income
1	$70,000	$30,000	$40,000	$24,000	$20,000
2	72,000	32,000	40,000	24,000	20,000
3	74,000	34,000	40,000	24,000	20,000
4	76,000	38,000	38,000	24,000	18,000
5	78,000	41,000	37,000	24,000	17,000

Required:

1. Compute the payback period for the proposed expansion of the theater's seating capacity.
2. Compute the project's accounting rate of return using the project's initial investment.
3. Compute the project's accounting rate of return using the project's average investment.
4. Explain why many managerial accountants believe that discounted-cash-flow methods of evaluating investment proposals are superior to the payback and accounting-rate-of-return methods.
5. Suppose the chairperson of the theater's board, who was formerly a managerial accountant, has calculated the seating expansion project's internal rate of return to be lower than the project's accounting rate of return. Moreover, the theater's cost of acquiring expansion capital is above the expansion project's internal rate of return but below its accounting rate of return. As a champion of the theater, and a strong proponent of the expansion, the board chairperson has decided to present only the project's accounting rate of return to the board for its approval of the project. Is this ethical on the part of the board's chairperson? Explain.

Problem 16–55
Inflation; NPV; Nominal Dollars (Appendix B)
(LO 4, 6, 10)

Vallejo Cablevision Company provides television cable service to two counties in Southern California. The firm's management is considering the construction of a new satellite dish in December of 20x0. The new antenna would improve reception and the service provided to customers. The dish antenna and associated equipment will cost $200,000 to purchase and install. The company's old equipment, which is fully depreciated, can be sold now for $20,000. The company president expects the firm's improved capabilities to result in additional revenue of $80,000 per year during the dish's useful life of seven years. The incremental operating expenses associated with the new equipment are projected to be $10,000 per year. These incremental revenues and expenses are in real dollars.

The new satellite dish will be depreciated under the MACRS depreciation schedule for the 5-year property class. The company's tax rate is 40 percent.

Vallejo Cablevision's president expects the real rate of interest in the economy to remain stable at 10 percent. She expects the inflation rate, currently running at 20 percent, to remain unchanged.

Required:

1. Prepare a schedule of cash flows projected over the next eight years (20x0 through 20x7), measured in nominal dollars. The schedule should include the initial costs of purchase and installation,

the after-tax incremental revenue and expenses, and the depreciation tax shield. Remember to express the incremental revenues and expenses in nominal dollars.

2. Compute the nominal interest rate.
3. Prepare a net-present-value analysis of the proposed new satellite dish. Use cash flows measured in nominal dollars and a nominal discount rate equal to the nominal interest rate.

Problem 16–56
Inflation; NPV; Real Dollars (Appendix B)
(LO 4, 6, 10)

Refer to the data given in the preceding problem for Vallejo Cablevision Company.

Required:

1. Compute the price index for each year from 20x1 through 20x7, using 1.0000 as the index for 20x0.
2. Prepare a schedule of after-tax cash flows measured in real dollars.
3. Compute the net present value of the proposed new satellite dish using cash flows measured in real dollars. Use a real discount rate equal to the real interest rate.

Cases

Case 16–57
Decision Problem with Suboptions; NPV; IRR; Ethics (Section 1)
(LO 1, 2, 3)

The board of education for the Blue Ridge School District is considering the acquisition of several minibuses for use in transporting students to school. Five of the school district's bus routes are underpopulated, with the result that the full-size buses on those routes are not fully utilized. After a careful study, the board has decided that it is not feasible to consolidate these routes into fewer routes served by full-size buses. The area in which the students live is too large for that approach, since some students' bus ride to school would exceed the state maximum of 45 minutes.

The plan under consideration by the board is to replace five full-size buses with eight minibuses, each of which would cover a much shorter route than a full-size bus. The bus drivers in this rural school district are part-time employees whose compensation costs the school district $18,000 per year for each driver. In addition to the drivers' compensation, the annual costs of operating and maintaining a full-size bus amount to $50,000. In contrast, the board projects that a minibus will cost only $20,000 annually to operate and maintain. A minibus driver earns the same wages as a full-size bus driver. The school district controller has estimated that it will cost the district $15,250, initially, to redesign its bus routes, inform the public, install caution signs in certain hazardous locations, and retrain its drivers.

A minibus costs $27,000, whereas a full-size bus costs $90,000. The school district uses straight-line depreciation for all of its long-lived assets. The board has two options regarding the five full-size buses. First, the buses could be sold now for $15,000 each. Second, the buses could be kept in reserve to use for field trips and out-of-town athletic events and to use as backup vehicles when buses break down. Currently, the board charters buses from a private company for these purposes. The annual cost of chartering buses amounts to $30,000. The school district controller has estimated that this cost could be cut to $5,000 per year if the five buses were kept in reserve. The five full-size buses have five years of useful life remaining, either as regularly scheduled buses or as reserve buses. The useful life of a new minibus is projected to be five years also.

Blue Ridge School District uses a hurdle rate of 12 percent on all capital projects.

Required:

1. Think about the decision problem faced by the board of education. What are the board's two main alternatives?
2. One of these main alternatives has two options embedded within it. What are those two options?
3. Before proceeding, check the hint given at the end of the chapter, which explains and diagrams the school board's alternatives. Suppose the board of education chooses to buy the minibuses. Prepare a net-present-value analysis of the two options for the five full-size buses. Should these buses be sold now or kept in reserve?
4. From your answer to requirement (3), you know the best option for the board to choose regarding the full-size buses *if* the minibuses are purchased. Now you can ignore the other option. Prepare a net-present-value analysis of the school board's two *main alternatives: (a)* continue to use the full-size buses on regular routes, or *(b)* purchase the minibuses. Should the minibuses be purchased?
5. Compute the internal rate of return on the proposed minibus acquisition.
6. What information given in this case was irrelevant to the school board's decision problem? Explain why the information was irrelevant.

7. Independent of requirements (1) through (6), suppose the NPV analysis favors keeping the full-size buses. Michael Jeffries, the business manager for the Blue Ridge School District, was prepared to recommend that the board not purchase the minibuses. Before doing so, however, Jeffries ran into a long-time friend at the racquet club. Peter Reynolds was the vice president for sales at a local automobile dealership from which the minibuses would have been purchased. Jeffries broke the bad news about his impending recommendation about the minibuses to his friend. The two talked for some time about the pros and cons of the minibus alternative. Finally, Reynolds said, "Michael, you and I go back a long time. I know you're not paid all that well at the school district. Our top financial person is retiring next year. How would you like to come to work for the dealership?"

   "That's pretty tempting, Peter. Let me think it over," was Jeffries' response.
   "Sure, Michael, take all the time you want. In the meantime, how about rethinking that minibus decision? It's no big deal to you, and I could sure use the business."
   "But Peter, I told you what the figures say about that," responded Jeffries.
   "Come on, Michael. What are friends for?"

   Discuss the ethical issues in this situation. What should Michael Jeffries do?

Case 16–58
Capital-Budgeting Analysis of Automated-Material-Handling System; Taxes; Ethical Issues (Section 2)
(LO 3, 4, 6)

Instant Dinners, Inc. (IDI) is an established manufacturer of microwavable frozen foods. Leland Forrest is a member of the planning and analysis staff. Forrest has been asked by Bill Rolland, chief financial officer of IDI, to prepare a net-present-value analysis for a proposed capital equipment expenditure that should improve the profitability of the western plant. This analysis will be given to the board of directors for approval. Several years ago, as director of planning and analysis at IDI, Rolland was instrumental in convincing the board to open the western plant. However, recent competitive pressures have forced all of IDI's manufacturing divisions to consider alternatives to improve their market position. To Rolland's dismay, the western plant may be sold in the near future unless significant improvement in cost control and production efficiency are achieved.

Western's production manager, an old friend of Rolland, has submitted a proposal for the acquisition of an automated-material-handling system. Rolland is anxious to have this proposal approved as it will ensure the continuation of the western plant and preserve his friend's position. The plan calls for the replacement of a number of forklift trucks and operators with a computer-controlled conveyor belt system that feeds directly into the refrigeration units. This automation would eliminate the need for a number of material handlers and increase the output capacity of the plant. Rolland has given this proposal to Forrest and instructed him to use the following information to prepare his analysis.

Automated-Material-Handling System Projections

Projected useful life	10 years
Purchase and installation of equipment	$4,500,000
Increased working capital needed*	1,000,000
Increased annual operating costs (exclusive of depreciation)	200,000
Equipment repairs to maintain production efficiency (end of year 5)	800,000
Increase in annual sales revenue	700,000
Reduction in annual manufacturing costs	500,000
Reduction in annual maintenance costs	300,000
Estimated salvage value of conveyor belt system	850,000

*The working capital will be released at the end of the 10-year useful life of the conveyor belt system.

The forklift trucks have a net book value of $500,000 with a remaining useful life of five years and no salvage value for depreciation purposes. If the conveyor belt system is purchased now, these trucks will be sold for $100,000. IDI has a 40 percent tax rate, has chosen the straight-line depreciation method for both book and tax purposes, and uses a 12 percent discount rate. For the purpose of analysis, all tax effects and cash flows from the equipment acquisition and disposal are considered to occur at the time of the transaction while those from operations are considered to occur at the end of each year.

When Forrest completed his initial analysis, the proposed project appeared quite healthy. However, after investigating equipment similar to that proposed, Forrest discovered that the estimated salvage value of $850,000 was very optimistic. Information previously provided by several vendors estimates this value to be only $100,000. Forrest also discovered that industry trade publications considered eight years to be the maximum life of similar conveyor belt systems. As a result, Forrest prepared a second analysis based on this new information. When Rolland saw the second analysis, he told Forrest to discard this revised material, warned him not to discuss the new estimates with anyone at IDI, and ordered him not to present any of this information to the board of directors.

Required:

1. Prepare a net-present-value analysis of the purchase and installation of the material-handling system using the revised estimates obtained by Leland Forrest. (For this problem, ignore the half-year convention. Assume annual straight-line depreciation of $562,500, which is $4,500,000 ÷ 8.)
2. Explain how Leland Forrest, a management accountant, should evaluate Bill Rolland's directives to repress the revised analysis. Take into consideration the specific ethical standards of competence, confidentiality, integrity, and objectivity discussed in Chapter 1.
3. Identify some steps Leland Forrest could take to resolve this situation.

(CMA, adapted)

Current Issues in Managerial Accounting

Issue 16–59
IT Spending; Payback Criterion

"IT Spending Is Expected to Rebound," ***The Wall Street Journal,*** **January 14, 2002, p. B4, Donna Fuscaldo.**

Overview

General Electric plans to spend $3 billion on technology during the current year. According to the article, GE's management expects a payback of 12 months on small projects and 24 months on large ones.

Suggested Discussion Question

Comment on GE's use of the payback criterion.

Issue 16–60
Capital Investment in Alternative Energy Sources

"Oil Companies Seek to Develop Energy Options," ***The Wall Street Journal,*** **October 4, 2000, Thaddeus Herrick.**

Overview

Major oil companies, among them BP Amoco and Royal Dutch Shell, are making major investments in renewable energy sources, such as biomass, solar power, and wind power.

Suggested Discussion Questions

How would discounted cash flow analysis be used in analyzing such major investment decisions? What types of cash flows would be the most difficult to project in a DCF analysis of renewable energy sources?

Issue 16–61
Major Acquisition Decisions

"Kellogg to Pay $3.86 Billion for Keebler," ***The Wall Street Journal,*** **October 27, 2000, Scott Kilman and Nikhil Deogun.**

Overview

Kellogg Co. agreed to acquire Keebler Foods Co. for $3.86 billion, or $42 per share.

Suggested Discussion Questions

How would discounted cash flow analysis be used in analyzing such a major acquisition decision? What were Kellogg's objectives in the acquisition? What kinds of qualitative issues could enter into the decision?

Hint for Case 16–57

The school board's two main alternatives are as follows: (1) continue to use the five full-size buses on regular routes, or (2) purchase eight minibuses to cover the regular bus routes. Under alternative (2), the board has two options. The full-size buses could be *(a)* sold now or *(b)* kept in reserve.

Thus, the board's decision problem can be diagrammed as follows:

Chapter Seventeen

Absorption, Variable, and Throughput Costing

After completing this chapter, you should be able to:

1 Explain the accounting treatment of fixed manufacturing overhead under absorption and variable costing.

2 Prepare an income statement under absorption costing.

3 Prepare an income statement under variable costing.

4 Reconcile reported income under absorption and variable costing.

5 Explain the implications of absorption and variable costing for cost-volume-profit analysis.

6 Evaluate absorption and variable costing.

7 Explain the rationale behind throughput costing.

8 Prepare an income statement under throughput costing.

9 After completing the appendix, explain the effect of the volume variance under absorption and variable costing.

Quikmath.com Announces New Product Line

Boston—The president of Quikmath.com announced today that the company will soon introduce a low-cost calculator with a built-in pager. This highly successful Internet-based company specializes in manufacturing and selling calculators and other electronic gadgetry to school-age kids. Virtually all its sales activity is Web-based.

Abby Rivendell, Quikmath's president, said the product will be noteworthy because it will be affordably priced. "There are plenty of high-tech gizmos on the market," Rivendell acknowledged. "You can buy a calculator combined with an electronic address book, pager, and GPS locator. But these high-tech gadgets are high-priced. We intend to bring out a product that parents can afford to get for their school-age kids.

"The school-age population has been our market since we formed Quikmath.com. Kids' lives are busy and complicated these days, and it's a challenge for parents to know where their kids are and what they're doing. The pager built into our calculator will enable a parent, sibling, or friend to page a kid by dialing a certain phone number and then punching in the kid's personal ID number. Then the calculator emits a soft tone and displays the phone number from which the page originated. The paged person then calls the displayed number to check in or whatever."

When asked how Quikmath would be able to price its new product so competitively, Rivendell's answer was interesting. "We're going to price this product aggressively. We'll set the price just high enough to cover our variable costs of manufacturing and marketing the Calc'n'Page. That's what we're calling it, by the way. In other words, we want to ensure that the product price is sufficient to cover the incremental costs we will incur to make each unit—costs such as the direct material and direct labor and so forth.

"We want the product to be accessible to all kids' families, and we want to quickly achieve a broad-based market. This is a real departure from our usual approach to product pricing. Generally we use a full-cost approach, meaning that we price products to cover all costs of production, including fixed costs like the plant manager's salary and the property taxes on the plant. We will continue that pricing approach for our well-established, bread-and-butter products. But the Calc'n'Page is different. Here we need to quickly establish a market presence. The variable-cost approach to pricing, in this instance, will help us accomplish that."

According to Quikmath's VP of sales, Anne Tyler, the new Calc'n'Page will be available from Quikmath's website in about six to eight months.

Income is one of many important measures used to evaluate the performance of companies and segments of companies. There are two, commonly used methods for determining product costs and reporting income in a manufacturing firm, depending on the accounting treatment of fixed manufacturing overhead. In this chapter, we will examine these two income-reporting alternatives, called *absorption costing* and *variable costing*. In addition, we will study a third alternative for product costing and income reporting, which is called *throughput costing*.[1]

Product Costs

In the product-costing systems we have studied so far, manufacturing overhead is applied to Work-in-Process Inventory as a product cost along with direct material and direct labor. When the manufactured goods are finished, these product costs flow from Work-in-Process Inventory into Finished-Goods Inventory. Finally, during the accounting period when the goods are sold, the product costs flow from Finished-Goods Inventory into Cost of Goods Sold, an expense account. The following diagram summarizes this flow of costs.

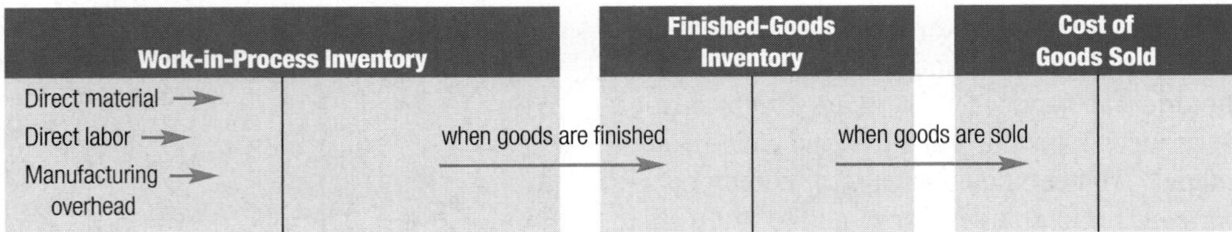

Since the costs of production are stored in inventory accounts until the goods are sold, these costs are said to be *inventoried costs*.

LO 1

Explain the accounting treatment of fixed manufacturing overhead under absorption and variable costing.

Fixed Manufacturing Overhead: The Key In our study of product-costing systems, we have included both variable and fixed manufacturing overhead in the product costs that flow through the manufacturing accounts. This approach to product costing is called **absorption costing** (or **full costing**), because *all* manufacturing-overhead costs are applied to (or absorbed by) manufactured goods. An alternative approach to product costing is called **variable costing** (or **direct costing**), in which *only variable* manufacturing overhead is applied to Work-in-Process Inventory as a product cost.

The distinction between absorption and variable costing is summarized in Exhibit 17–1. Notice that the distinction involves the *timing* with which fixed manufacturing overhead becomes an expense. Eventually, fixed overhead is expensed under both product-costing systems. Under variable costing, however, fixed overhead is expensed *immediately,* as it is incurred. Under absorption costing, fixed overhead is *inventoried* until the accounting period during which the manufactured goods are sold.

Illustration of Absorption and Variable Costing

Quikmath.com

Topic 17–1

Quikmath.com began operations on January 1, 20x0, to manufacture hand-held electronic calculators. The company uses a standard-costing system. Cost, production, and sales data for the first three years of Quikmath's operations are given in Exhibit 17–2. Comparative income statements for 20x0, 20x1, and 20x2 are presented in Exhibit 17–3, using both absorption and variable costing.

[1]This chapter, excluding the appendix, can be studied anytime after Chapter 8 has been completed. The appendix should be studied after Chapter 11 has been completed.

A. Absorption Costing

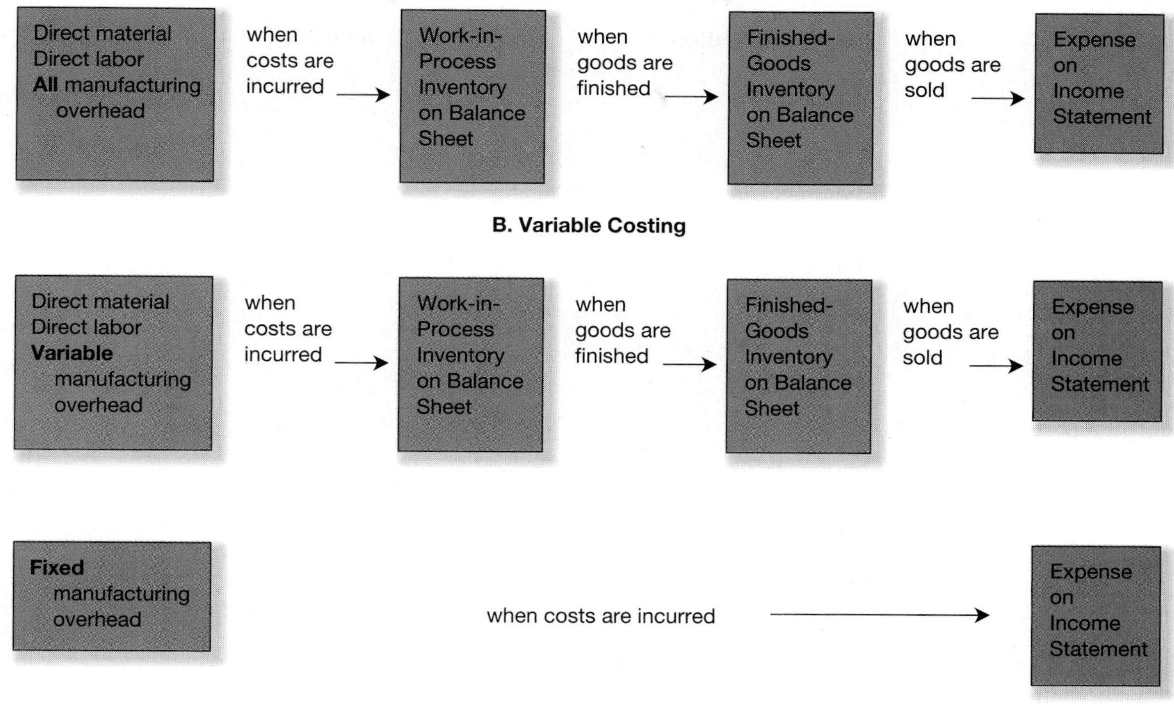

Exhibit 17–1
Absorption versus Variable Costing

Absorption-Costing Income Statements

LO 2
Prepare an income statement under absorption costing.

Examine the absorption-costing income statements in the upper half of Exhibit 17–3. Two features of these income statements are highlighted in the left-hand margin. First, notice that the Cost of Goods Sold expense for each year is determined by multiplying

The fixed costs of operating this Boeing plant in Everett, Washington, include such costs as the depreciation on plant and equipment, property taxes, insurance, and the salary of the plant manager. Fixed manufacturing costs are incurred in order to generate production capacity. Under absorption costing, these costs are treated as product costs and included in the cost of inventory. Under variable costing, they are expensed during the period incurred. Pictured here is the production of Boeing 757s.

Exhibit 17–2
Data for Illustration: Quikmath.com

Quikmath.com

	20x0	20x1	20x2
Production and inventory data:			
Planned production (in units)	50,000	50,000	50,000
Finished-goods inventory (in units), January 1	–0–	–0–	15,000
Actual production (in units)	50,000	50,000	50,000
Sales (in units)	50,000	35,000	65,000
Finished-goods inventory (in units), December 31	–0–	15,000	–0–
Revenue and cost data, all three years:			
Sales price per unit			$12
Standard manufacturing costs per unit:			
Direct material			$ 3
Direct labor			2
Variable manufacturing overhead			1
Total variable standard cost per unit			$ 6
Used only under absorption costing: Fixed manufacturing overhead: Budgeted annual fixed overhead / Planned annual production = $150,000 / 50,000			3
Total absorption standard cost per unit			$ 9
Variable selling and administrative cost per unit			$ 1
Fixed selling and administrative cost per year			$25,000

Variances:
There were no variances during 20x0, 20x1, or 20x2.

Exhibit 17–3
Income Statements under Absorption and Variable Costing

Quikmath.com

QUIKMATH.COM
Absorption-Costing Income Statement

		20x0	20x1	20x2
	Sales revenue (at $12 per unit)	$600,000	$420,000	$780,000
1	Less: Cost of goods sold (at standard absorption cost of $9 per unit)	450,000	315,000	585,000
	Gross margin	$150,000	$105,000	$195,000
	Less: Selling and administrative expenses:			
2 No fixed overhead	Variable (at $1 per unit)	50,000	35,000	65,000
	Fixed	25,000	25,000	25,000
	Net income	$ 75,000	$ 45,000	$105,000

QUIKMATH.COM
Variable-Costing Income Statement

		20x0	20x1	20x2
	Sales revenue (at $12 per unit)	$600,000	$420,000	$780,000
	Less: Variable expenses:			
1	Variable manufacturing costs (at standard variable cost of $6 per unit)	300,000	210,000	390,000
	Variable selling and administrative costs (at $1 per unit)	50,000	35,000	65,000
	Contribution margin	$250,000	$175,000	$325,000
	Less: Fixed expenses:			
2	Fixed manufacturing overhead	150,000	150,000	150,000
	Fixed selling and administrative expenses	25,000	25,000	25,000
	Net income	$ 75,000	$ 0	$150,000

the year's sales by the standard absorption manufacturing cost per unit, $9. Included in the $9 cost per unit is the predetermined fixed manufacturing-overhead cost of $3 per unit. Second, notice that on Quikmath's absorption-costing income statements, the only period expenses are the selling and administrative expenses. There is no deduction of fixed-overhead costs as a lump-sum period expense at the bottom of each income statement. As mentioned above, fixed manufacturing-overhead costs are included in Cost of Goods Sold on these absorption-costing income statements.

Variable-Costing Income Statements

LO 3

Prepare an income statement under variable costing.

Topic 17–2

Now examine the income statements based on variable costing in the lower half of Exhibit 17–3. Notice that the format of the statements is different from the format used in the absorption-costing statements. In the variable-costing statements, the contribution format is used to highlight the separation of variable and fixed costs. Let's focus on the same two aspects of the variable-costing statements that we discussed for the absorption-costing statements. First, the manufacturing expenses subtracted from sales revenue each year include only the variable costs, which amount to $6 per unit. Second, fixed manufacturing overhead is subtracted as a lump-sum period expense at the bottom of each year's income statement.

Reconciling Income under Absorption and Variable Costing

LO 4

Reconcile reported income under absorption and variable costing.

Examination of Exhibit 17–3 reveals that the income reported under absorption and variable costing is sometimes different. Although income is the same for the two product-costing methods in 20x0, it is different in 20x1 and 20x2. Let's figure out why these results occur.

No Change in Inventory In 20x0 there is no change in inventory over the course of the year. Beginning and ending inventory are the same, because actual production and sales are the same. Think about the implications of the stable inventory level for the treatment of fixed manufacturing overhead. On the variable-costing statement, the $150,000 of fixed manufacturing overhead incurred during 20x0 is an expense in 20x0. Under absorption costing, however, fixed manufacturing overhead was applied to production at the predetermined rate of $3 per unit. Since all of the units produced in 20x0 also were sold in 20x0, all of the fixed manufacturing-overhead cost flowed through into Cost of Goods Sold. Thus, $150,000 of fixed manufacturing overhead was expensed in 20x0 under absorption costing also.

The 20x0 column of Exhibit 17–4 reconciles the 20x0 net income reported under absorption and variable costing. The reconciliation focuses on the two places in the income statements where differences occur between absorption and variable costing. The numbers in the left-hand margin of Exhibit 17–4 correspond to the numbers in the left-hand margin of the income statements in Exhibit 17–3.

"The operational managers' bonuses are based on profitability, so they are keenly interested in the financial management reports' results. We constantly receive calls and assist them with ways to manage costs." (17a)

John Deere Health Care, Inc.

Increase in Inventory In 20x1 inventory increased from zero on January 1 to 15,000 units on December 31. The increase in inventory was the result of production exceeding sales. Under variable costing, the $150,000 of fixed overhead cost incurred in 20x1 is expensed, just as it was in 20x0. Under absorption costing, however, only a portion of the 20x1 fixed manufacturing overhead is expensed in 20x1. Since the fixed overhead is inventoried under absorption costing, some of this cost *remains in inventory* at the end of 20x1.

The 20x1 column of Exhibit 17–4 reconciles the 20x1 net income reported under absorption and variable costing. As before, the reconciliation focuses on the two places in the income statements where differences occur between absorption and variable costing.

Exhibit 17–4
Reconciliation of Income under Absorption and Variable Costing: Quikmath.com

Quikmath.com

		20x0	20x1	20x2
1	Cost of goods sold under absorption costing	$450,000	$315,000	$585,000
	Variable manufacturing costs under variable costing	300,000	210,000	390,000
	Subtotal	$150,000	$105,000	$195,000
2	Fixed manufacturing overhead as period expense under variable costing	150,000	150,000	150,000
	Total	$ 0	$ (45,000)	$ 45,000
	Net income under variable costing	$ 75,000	$ 0	$150,000
	Net income under absorption costing	75,000	45,000	105,000
	Difference in net income	$ 0	$ (45,000)	$ 45,000

Decrease in Inventory In 20x2 inventory decreased from 15,000 units to zero. Sales during the year exceeded production. As in 20x0 and 20x1, under variable costing, the $150,000 of fixed manufacturing overhead incurred in 20x2 is expensed in 20x2. Under absorption costing, however, *more than* $150,000 of fixed overhead is expensed in 20x2. Why? Because some of the fixed overhead incurred during the prior year, which was inventoried then, is now expensed in 20x2 as the goods are sold.

The 20x2 column of Exhibit 17–4 reconciles the 20x2 income under absorption and variable costing. Once again, the numbers on the left-hand side of Exhibit 17–4 correspond to those on the left-hand side of the income statements in Exhibit 17–3.

A Shortcut to Reconciling Income When inventory increases or decreases during the year, reported income differs under absorption and variable costing. This results from the fixed overhead that is inventoried under absorption costing but expensed immediately under variable costing. The following formula may be used to compute the difference in the amount of fixed overhead expensed in a given time period under the two product-costing methods.

$$\begin{array}{c}\text{Difference in fixed overhead}\\\text{expensed under absorption}\\\text{and variable costing}\end{array} = \left(\begin{array}{c}\text{Change in}\\\text{inventory,}\\\text{in units}\end{array}\right) \times \left(\begin{array}{c}\text{Predetermined}\\\text{fixed-overhead}\\\text{rate per unit}\end{array}\right)$$

As the following table shows, this difference in the amount of fixed overhead expensed explains the difference in reported income under absorption and variable costing.

Year	Change in Inventory (in units)		Predetermined Fixed-Overhead Rate		Difference in Fixed Overhead Expensed		Absorption-Costing Income Minus Variable-Costing Income
20x0	–0–	×	$3	=	–0–	=	–0–
20x1	15,000 increase	×	$3	=	$45,000	=	$45,000
20x2	15,000 decrease	×	$3	=	$(45,000)	=	$(45,000)

Length of Time Period The discrepancies between absorption-costing and variable-costing income in Exhibit 17–3 occur because of the changes in inventory levels during 20x1 and 20x2. It is common for production and sales to differ over the course of a week, month, or year. Therefore, the income measured for those time periods often will differ between absorption and variable costing. This discrepancy is likely to be smaller over longer time periods. Over the course of a decade, for example, Quikmath.com cannot sell much more or less than it produces. Thus, the income amounts under the two product-costing methods, when added together over a lengthy time period, will be approximately equal under absorption and variable costing.

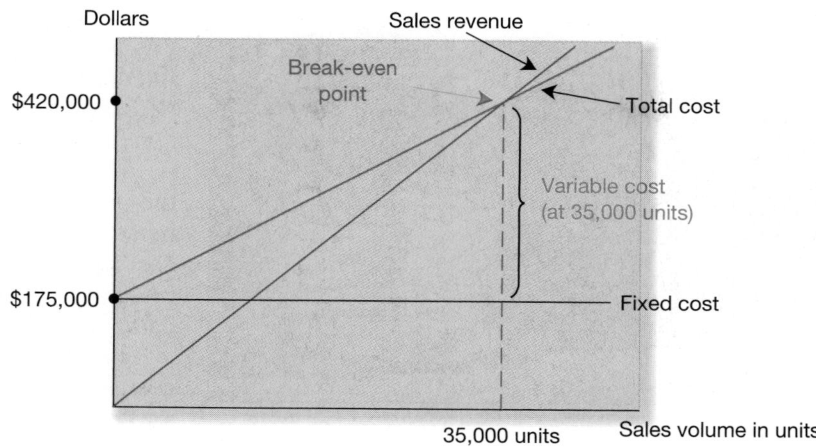

Exhibit 17–5
Break-Even Graph: Quikmath.com

Notice in Exhibit 17–3 that Quikmath.com's total income over the three-year period is $225,000 under *both* absorption and variable costing. This results from the fact that the company produced and sold the same total amount over the three-year period.

Cost-Volume-Profit Analysis

LO 5 Explain the implications of absorption and variable costing for cost-volume-profit analysis.

One of the tools used by managers to plan and control business operations is cost-volume-profit analysis, which we studied in Chapter 8. Quikmath.com's break-even point in units can be computed as follows:

$$\text{Break-even point} = \frac{\text{Fixed costs}}{\text{Unit contribution margin}} = \frac{\$150{,}000 + \$25{,}000}{\$12 - \$6 - \$1}$$

$$= \frac{\$175{,}000}{\$5} = 35{,}000 \text{ units}$$

If Quikmath.com sells 35,000 calculators, net income should be zero, as Exhibit 17–5 confirms.

Now return to Exhibit 17–3 and examine the 20x1 income statements under absorption and variable costing. In 20x1 Quikmath.com sold 35,000 units, the break-even volume. This fact is confirmed on the variable-costing income statement, since net income is zero. On the absorption-costing income statement, however, the 20x1 net income is $45,000. What has happened here?

The answer to this inconsistency lies in the different treatment of fixed manufacturing overhead under absorption and variable costing. Variable costing highlights the separation between fixed and variable costs, as do cost-volume-profit analysis and break-even calculations. Both of these techniques account for fixed manufacturing overhead as a lump sum. In contrast, *absorption costing is inconsistent with CVP analysis,* because fixed overhead is applied to goods as a product cost on a per-unit basis.

Evaluation of Absorption and Variable Costing

LO 6 Evaluate absorption and variable costing.

Some managers find the inconsistency between absorption costing and CVP analysis troubling enough to warrant using variable costing for internal income reporting. Variable costing dovetails much more closely than absorption costing with any operational analyses that require a separation between fixed and variable costs.

Pricing Decisions Many managers prefer to use absorption-costing data in cost-based pricing decisions. They argue that fixed manufacturing overhead is a necessary

Before shipping these new automobiles to the dealership, company executives had to decide on a price for the cars. Most manufacturers, including auto producers, use production costs based on absorption costing as the basis for pricing decisions. Of course the prices set by competitors also heavily influence a company's pricing decisions.

cost incurred in the production process. To exclude this fixed cost from the inventoried cost of a product, as is done under variable costing, is to understate the cost of the product. For this reason, most companies that use cost-based pricing base their prices on absorption-costing data.

Proponents of variable costing argue that a product's variable cost provides a better basis for the pricing decision. They point out that any price above a product's variable cost makes a positive contribution to covering fixed cost and profit.

Definition of an Asset Another controversy about absorption and variable costing hinges on the definition of an asset. An *asset* is a thing of value owned by the organization with future service potential. By accounting convention, assets are valued at their cost. Since fixed costs comprise part of the cost of production, advocates of absorption costing argue that inventory (an asset) should be valued at its full (absorption) cost of production. Moreover, they argue that these costs have future service potential since the inventory can be sold in the future to generate sales revenue.

Proponents of variable costing argue that the fixed-cost component of a product's absorption-costing value has no future service potential. Their reasoning is that the fixed manufacturing-overhead costs during the current period will not prevent these costs from having to be incurred again next period. Fixed-overhead costs will be incurred every period, regardless of production levels. In contrast, the incurrence of variable costs in manufacturing a product does allow the firm to avoid incurring these costs again.

To illustrate, Quikmath.com produced 15,000 more calculators in 20x1 than it sold. These units will be carried in inventory until they are sold in some future year. Quikmath.com will never again have to incur the costs of direct material, direct labor, and variable overhead incurred in 20x1 to produce those calculators. Yet Quikmath.com will have to incur approximately $150,000 of fixed-overhead costs every year, even though the firm has the 15,000 units from 20x1 in inventory.

External Reporting For external reporting purposes, generally accepted accounting principles require that income reporting be based on absorption costing. Federal tax laws also require the use of absorption costing in reporting income for tax purposes.

Why Not Both? In the age of computerized accounting systems, it is straightforward for a company to prepare income statements under both absorption and variable costing. Since absorption-costing statements are required for external reporting, managers will want to keep an eye on the effects of their decisions on financial reports to outsiders. Yet the superiority of variable-costing income reporting as a method for dovetailing with operational analyses cannot be denied. Preparation of both absorption-costing and variable-costing data is perhaps the best solution to the controversy.

JIT Manufacturing Environment In a just-in-time inventory and production management system, all inventories are kept very low. Since finished-goods inventories are minimal, there is little change in inventory from period to period. Thus, in a JIT environment, the income differences under absorption and variable costing generally will be insignificant.

Management Accounting Practice

IRS

IRS: UNIQUE PRODUCT PACKAGING IS AN INVENTORIABLE COST

The Internal Revenue Service (IRS) requires absorption costing for tax purposes. Thus absorption costing must be used in valuing inventory and in determining cost-of-goods-sold expense, which in turn affects taxable income. The IRS defines inventoriable costs (i.e., product costs) that must be included in valuing inventory and cost-of-goods-sold expense to include the following: (1) direct material consumed in the production of the product and (2) direct labor, and all indirect costs deemed to be necessary for the production of the company's product. These necessary indirect costs include fixed-overhead costs. Thus, absorption costing is mandated by the IRS.

One interesting nuance in the IRS interpretation of what constitutes inventoriable costs concerns a company's expenditures on the design of the packaging for the company's products. Packaging design costs can run into hundreds of thousands of dollars for large consumer products companies. The IRS has specified that packaging design costs must be inventoried as product costs if the resulting design is successful—that is, it remains in use for several years. If, however, a package design fails in the marketplace, the company can deduct the package design costs early as an expense. Examples of products with unique packaging designs that would be affected by this IRS ruling include Pringles potato chips (sold in a can), Realemon and Realime (sold in plastic citrus-fruit-shaped containers), and L'eggs pantyhose (sold in the familiar plastic egg-shaped containers).

Fixed-Overhead Volume Variance Our illustration of absorption and variable costing does not include the fixed-overhead volume variance, which was covered in Chapter 11. The impact of the volume variance is explored in the appendix to this chapter.

Throughput Costing

LO 7

Explain the rationale behind throughput costing.

Some managers advocate *throughput costing* as an alternative to either absorption or variable costing for product costing and income reporting. **Throughput costing** assigns *only* the unit-level *spending* for direct costs as the cost of products or services. A unit-level cost is one that is incurred every time a unit of product is manufactured and will *not* be incurred if another unit is not manufactured.[2] Advocates of throughput costing argue that classifying any other past or committed cost as a product cost creates an incentive to drive down the average cost per unit simply by manufacturing more units on nonbottleneck processes.

Throughput-Costing Income Statements

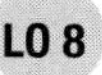
LO 8

Prepare an income statement under throughput costing.

Suppose Quikmath.com's management team decided that only direct material qualified as a throughput cost. This implies that Quikmath.com's management has *committed,* at least for the time being, to provide *all* other resources (i.e., direct labor and all manufacturing support costs included in manufacturing overhead) regardless of how many calculators and other devices Quikmath.com produces. Under throughput costing, then, Quikmath.com's income statements for the three years in our illustration would appear as in the Excel spreadsheet shown in Exhibit 17–6. Notice that all costs other than the throughput cost (only direct material in this hypothetical illustration) are considered to be operating costs of the period.

[2]See Chapter 5 for a thorough discussion of the concept of unit-level costs and cost hierarchies in the context of an activity-based-costing system.

Exhibit 17–6
Income Statements under Throughput Costing

Quikmath.com

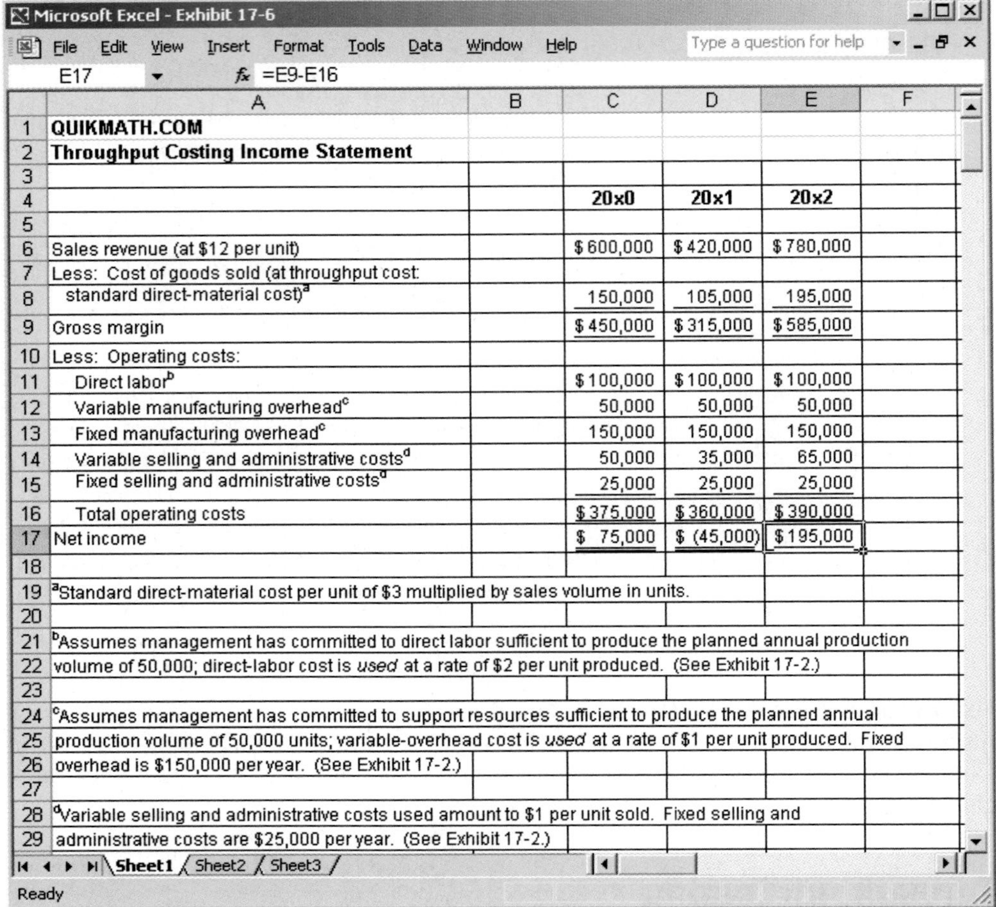

Microsoft Excel - Exhibit 17-6

E17 =E9-E16

	A	B	C	D	E	F
1	**QUIKMATH.COM**					
2	**Throughput Costing Income Statement**					
3						
4			**20x0**	**20x1**	**20x2**	
5						
6	Sales revenue (at $12 per unit)		$600,000	$420,000	$780,000	
7	Less: Cost of goods sold (at throughput cost:					
8	standard direct-material cost)[a]		150,000	105,000	195,000	
9	Gross margin		$450,000	$315,000	$585,000	
10	Less: Operating costs:					
11	Direct labor[b]		$100,000	$100,000	$100,000	
12	Variable manufacturing overhead[c]		50,000	50,000	50,000	
13	Fixed manufacturing overhead[c]		150,000	150,000	150,000	
14	Variable selling and administrative costs[d]		50,000	35,000	65,000	
15	Fixed selling and administrative costs[d]		25,000	25,000	25,000	
16	Total operating costs		$375,000	$360,000	$390,000	
17	Net income		$ 75,000	$ (45,000)	$195,000	
18						
19	[a]Standard direct-material cost per unit of $3 multiplied by sales volume in units.					
20						
21	[b]Assumes management has committed to direct labor sufficient to produce the planned annual production					
22	volume of 50,000; direct-labor cost is *used* at a rate of $2 per unit produced. (See Exhibit 17-2.)					
23						
24	[c]Assumes management has committed to support resources sufficient to produce the planned annual					
25	production volume of 50,000 units; variable-overhead cost is *used* at a rate of $1 per unit produced. Fixed					
26	overhead is $150,000 per year. (See Exhibit 17-2.)					
27						
28	[d]Variable selling and administrative costs used amount to $1 per unit sold. Fixed selling and					
29	administrative costs are $25,000 per year. (See Exhibit 17-2.)					

Sheet1 Sheet2 Sheet3

Ready

A comparison of the reported income under throughput costing (Exhibit 17–6) with the reported income under either variable or absorption costing (Exhibit 17–3) reveals substantial differences in the "bottom line" under the three methods for each year. Proponents of throughput costing argue that this method alone eliminates the incentive to produce excess inventory simply to reduce unit costs by spreading *committed* resource costs (i.e., direct labor and variable and fixed manufacturing overhead) across more units. The incentive for such overproduction disappears under throughput costing, because all nonthroughput costs (direct labor and manufacturing overhead in our illustration) will be expensed as period costs regardless of how many units are produced.

Focus on Ethics

INCENTIVE TO OVERPRODUCE INVENTORY

This classic case is based on an actual company's experience.[3] Brandolino Company uses an actual cost system to apply all production costs to units produced. The plant has a maximum production capacity of 40 million units but produced and sold only 10 million units during year 1. There were no beginning or ending inventories. The company's absorption-costing income statement for year 1 follows:

[3]This scenario is based on the case "I Enjoy Challenges," originally written by Michael W. Maher. It is used here with permission.

BRANDOLINO COMPANY
Income Statement
For Year 1

Sales (10,000,000 units at $6)		$ 60,000,000
Cost of goods sold:		
Direct costs (material and labor) (10,000,000 at $2)	$20,000,000	
Manufacturing overhead	48,000,000	68,000,000
Gross margin		$ (8,000,000)
Selling and administrative costs		10,000,000
Operating profit (loss)		$(18,000,000)

The board of directors is upset about the $18 million loss. A consultant approached the board with the following offer: "I agree to become president for no fixed salary. But I insist on a year-end bonus of 10 percent of operating profit (before considering the bonus)." The board of directors agreed to these terms and hired the consultant as Brandolino's new president. The new president promptly stepped up production to an annual rate of 30 million units. Sales for year 2 remained at 10 million units. The resulting absorption-costing income statement for year 2 is displayed in the right-hand column.

The day after the year 2 statement was verified, the president took his check for $1,400,000 and resigned to take a job with another corporation. He remarked, "I enjoy challenges. Now that Brandolino Company is in the black, I'd prefer tackling another challenging situation." (His contract with his new employer is similar to the one he had with Brandolino Company.)

BRANDOLINO COMPANY
Income Statement
For Year 2

Sales (10,000,000 units at $6)		$60,000,000
Cost of goods sold:		
Costs of goods manufactured:		
Direct costs, material and labor (30,000,000 at $2)	$ 60,000,000	
Manufacturing overhead	48,000,000	
Total cost of goods manufactured	$108,000,000	
Less: Ending inventory:		
Direct costs, material and labor (20,000,000 at $2)	$ 40,000,000	
Manufacturing overhead (20/30 × $48,000,000)	32,000,000	
Total ending inventory costs	$ 72,000,000	
Cost of goods sold		36,000,000
Gross margin		$24,000,000
Selling and administrative costs		10,000,000
Operating profit before bonus		$14,000,000
Bonus		1,400,000
Operating profit after bonus		$12,600,000

What do you think is going on here? How would you evaluate the company's year 2 performance? Using variable costing, what would operating profit be for year 1? For year 2? (Assume that all selling and administrative costs are committed and unchanged.) Compare those results with the absorption-costing statements. Comment on the ethical issues in this scenario.

Chapter Summary

Absorption and variable costing are two alternative product-costing systems that differ in their treatment of fixed manufacturing overhead. Under absorption (or full) costing, fixed overhead is applied to manufactured goods as a product cost. The fixed-overhead cost remains in inventory until the goods are sold. Under variable (or direct) costing, fixed overhead is a period cost expensed during the period when it is incurred. Absorption costing is required for external reporting and tax purposes. However, variable costing is more consistent with operational decision analyses, which require a separation of fixed and variable costs.

One of the tools used by managers to plan and control business operations is cost-volume-profit analysis. Variable costing highlights the separation between fixed and variable costs, as do cost-volume-profit analysis and break-even calculations. Both of these techniques account for fixed manufacturing overhead as a lump sum. In contrast, absorption costing is inconsistent with CVP analysis, because fixed overhead is applied to goods as a product cost on a per-unit basis. Some managers find the inconsistency between absorption costing and CVP analysis troubling enough to warrant using variable costing for internal income reporting. Variable costing dovetails much more closely than absorption costing with any operational analyses that require a separation between fixed and variable costs.

Some accountants and managers advocate throughput costing, in which only throughput costs are inventoried as product costs. They argue that throughput costing reduces the incentive for management to produce excess inventory simply for the purpose of spreading committed (nonthroughput) costs across a larger number of units produced.

Key Terms

For each term's definition refer to the indicated page, or turn to the glossary at the end of the text.

absorption (or full) costing, 726
throughput costing, 733
variable (or direct) costing, 726

Appendix to Chapter 17

Effect of the Volume Variance under Absorption and Variable Costing

LO 9

After completing the appendix, explain the effect of the volume variance under absorption and variable costing.

Quikmath.com

Our illustration of absorption and variable costing did not include a fixed-overhead volume variance.[4] Recall from Chapter 11 that the volume variance is defined as follows:

$$\begin{aligned}\text{Fixed-overhead volume variance} &= \text{Budgeted fixed overhead} - \text{Applied fixed overhead}\\ &= \begin{pmatrix}\text{Predetermined}\\ \text{fixed-}\\ \text{overhead rate}\end{pmatrix}\begin{pmatrix}\text{Planned}\\ \text{production}\\ \text{in units}\end{pmatrix} - \begin{pmatrix}\text{Predetermined}\\ \text{fixed-}\\ \text{overhead rate}\end{pmatrix}\begin{pmatrix}\text{Actual}\\ \text{production}\\ \text{in units}\end{pmatrix}\end{aligned}$$

When planned production equals actual production for the year, the volume variance is zero. This was the case in 20x0, 20x1, and 20x2 for our Quikmath.com illustration.

To show the effect of a volume variance on income reporting under absorption and variable costing, let's extend the data for Quikmath.com through the next three years. Exhibit 17–7 displays the data for 20x3, 20x4, and 20x5; Exhibit 17–8 shows comparative income statements for these three years.

Now there are three key places where the absorption-costing and variable-costing income statements differ. The absorption-costing statements include the fixed-overhead volume variance. But there is no volume variance on the variable-costing statements, because fixed overhead is not applied as a product cost under variable costing. Exhibit 17–9 reconciles Quikmath.com's reported income under the two alternative product-costing systems. The numbers in the left-hand margin correspond to those on the left-hand side of the income statements in Exhibit 17–8.

[4]This appendix should be studied after Chapter 11 has been completed, since it discusses the volume variance for fixed overhead.

Exhibit 17–7
Data for Illustration: Quikmath.com

Quikmath.com

	20x3	20x4	20x5
Production and inventory data:			
Planned production (in units)	50,000	50,000	50,000
Finished-goods inventory (in units), January 1	–0–	–0–	25,000
Actual production (in units)	50,000	60,000	40,000
Sales (in units)	50,000	35,000	55,000
Finished-goods inventory (in units), December 31	–0–	25,000	10,000

Revenue and cost data, all three years:	
Sales price per unit	$12
Standard manufacturing costs per unit:	
Direct material	$ 3
Direct labor	2
Variable manufacturing overhead	1
Total variable standard cost per unit	$ 6
Used only under absorption costing: Fixed manufacturing overhead: $\frac{\text{Budgeted annual fixed overhead}}{\text{Planned annual production}} = \frac{\$150,000}{50,000}$	3
Used only under absorption costing: Total absorption standard cost per unit	$ 9
Variable selling and administrative cost per unit	$ 1
Fixed selling and administrative cost per year	$25,000

Variances, all three years:

There are no direct-material, direct-labor, or variable overhead variances.

Moreover, there is no fixed-overhead budget variance.

Exhibit 17–8
Income Statements under Absorption and Variable Costing

Quikmath.com

QUIKMATH.COM
Absorption-Costing Income Statement

		20x3	20x4	20x5
	Sales revenue (at $12 per unit)	$600,000	$420,000	$660,000
1	Less: Cost of goods sold (at standard absorption cost of $9 per unit)	450,000	315,000	495,000
	Gross margin (at standard)	$150,000	$105,000	$165,000
2	Adjust for: Fixed-overhead volume variance	0*	30,000*	30,000*
	Gross margin (at actual)	$150,000	$135,000	$135,000
	Less: Selling and administrative expenses:			
3 No fixed overhead	Variable (at $1 per unit)	50,000	35,000	55,000
	Fixed	25,000	25,000	25,000
	Net income	$ 75,000	$ 75,000	$ 55,000

*Computation of fixed-overhead volume variance:

$$\text{Fixed-overhead volume variance} = \text{Budgeted fixed overhead} - \text{Applied fixed overhead} = \text{Budgeted fixed overhead} - \left(\text{Predetermined fixed-overhead rate}\right)\left(\text{Actual production}\right)$$

20x3: Volume variance = 0 = $150,000 − ($3)(50,000)

20x4: Volume variance = −$30,000 = $150,000 − ($3)(60,000)

20x5: Volume variance = $30,000 = $150,000 − ($3)(40,000)

(continues)

Exhibit 17–8
(concluded)

Quikmath.com

QUIKMATH.COM
Variable-Costing Income Statement

		20x3	20x4	20x5
	Sales revenue (at $12 per unit)	$600,000	$420,000	$660,000
	Less: Variable expenses:			
1	Variable manufacturing costs (at standard variable cost of $6 per unit)	300,000	210,000	330,000
	Variable selling and administrative costs (at $1 per unit)	50,000	35,000	55,000
2 No volume variance	Contribution margin	$250,000	$175,000	$275,000
	Less: Fixed expenses:			
3	Fixed manufacturing overhead	150,000	150,000	150,000
	Fixed selling and administrative costs	25,000	25,000	25,000
	Net income	$ 75,000	$ 0	$100,000

Exhibit 17–9
Reconciliation of Income under Absorption and Variable Costing: Quikmath.com

Quikmath.com

		20x3	20x4	20x5
1	Cost of goods sold under absorption costing	$450,000	$315,000	$495,000
	Variable manufacturing costs under variable costing	300,000	210,000	330,000
	Subtotal	$150,000	$105,000	$165,000
2	Volume variance under absorption costing	0	30,000*	30,000†
	Subtotal	$150,000	$ 75,000	$195,000
3	Fixed manufacturing overhead as period expense under variable costing	150,000	150,000	150,000
	Total	$ 0	$ (75,000)	$ 45,000
	Net income under variable costing	$ 75,000	$ 0	$100,000
	Net income under absorption costing	75,000	75,000	55,000
	Difference in net income	$ 0	$ (75,000)	$ 45,000

*Negative volume variance. As discussed in Chapter 11, some accountants would classify this variance as *favorable*.

†Positive volume variance. As discussed in Chapter 11, some accountants would classify this variance as *unfavorable*.

Review Questions

17–1. Briefly explain the difference between absorption costing and variable costing.

17–2. Timing is the key in distinguishing between absorption and variable costing. Explain this statement.

17–3. The term *direct costing* is a misnomer. *Variable costing* is a better term for the product-costing method. Do you agree or disagree? Why?

17–4. When inventory increases, will absorption-costing or variable-costing income be greater? Why?

17–5. Why do many managers prefer variable costing over absorption costing?

17–6. Explain how throughput costing differs from absorption and variable costing.

17–7. Explain why some management accountants believe that absorption costing may provide an incentive for managers to overproduce inventory. How does throughput costing avoid this problem?

17–8. Will variable and absorption costing result in significantly different income measures in a JIT setting? Why?

17–9. Why do proponents of absorption costing argue that absorption costing is preferable as the basis for pricing decisions?

17–10. Why do proponents of variable costing prefer variable costing when making pricing decisions?

17–11. Which is more consistent with cost-volume-profit analysis, variable costing or absorption costing? Why?

17–12. Explain how the accounting definition of an asset is related to the choice between absorption and variable costing.

Exercises

Exercise 17–13
Difference in Income under Absorption and Variable Costing
(LO 1, 4)

Dolphin Company manufactures two-person sailboats with a standard variable cost of $1,000. The sailboats sell for $1,750 each. Budgeted fixed manufacturing overhead for the most recent year was $11,000,000. Planned and actual production for the year were the same.

Required: Under each of the following conditions, state (*a*) whether income is higher under variable or absorption costing and (*b*) the amount of the difference in reported income under the two methods. Treat each condition as an independent case.

1.	Production	22,000 units
	Sales	25,000 units
2.	Production	10,600 units
	Sales	10,600 units
3.	Production	11,000 units
	Sales	9,800 units

Exercise 17–14
Variable Costing and Cost-Volume-Profit Analysis.
(LO 5)

Refer to the data given in the preceding exercise for Dolphin Company.

Required:

1. Prepare a cost-volume-profit graph for the company. (Scale the vertical axis in millions of dollars, and draw the CVP graph up through 15,000 units on the horizontal axis.)
2. Calculate Dolphin Company's break-even point in units, and show the break-even point on the CVP graph.
3. Explain why variable costing is more compatible with your CVP graph than absorption costing would be.

Exercise 17–15
Absorption and Variable Costing
(LO 1, 4)

Altoona Valve Company's planned production for the year just ended was 20,000 units. This production level was achieved, and 21,000 units were sold. Other data follow:

Direct material used	$300,000
Direct labor incurred	150,000
Fixed manufacturing overhead	210,000
Variable manufacturing overhead	100,000
Fixed selling and administrative expenses	175,000
Variable selling and administrative expenses	52,500
Finished-goods inventory, January 1	2,000 units

The cost per unit remained the same in the current year as in the previous year. There were no work-in-process inventories at the beginning or end of the year.

Required:

1. What would be Altoona Valve Company's finished-goods inventory cost on December 31 under the variable-costing method?
2. Which costing method, absorption or variable costing, would show a higher operating income for the year? By what amount?

(CMA, adapted)

Exercise 17–16
Difference in Income under Absorption and Variable Costing
(LO 1, 4)

Starfish Company manufactures diving masks with a standard variable cost of $12.50. The masks sell for $17.00. Budgeted fixed manufacturing overhead for the most recent year was $396,000. Actual production was equal to planned production.

Required: Under each of the following conditions, state (*a*) whether income is higher under variable or absorption costing and (*b*) the amount of the difference in reported income under the two methods. Treat each condition as an independent case.

1.	Production	110,000 units
	Sales	107,000 units
2.	Production	88,000 units
	Sales	93,000 units

(continues)

(concluded)

3. Production.	80,100 units
Sales	80,100 units

Exercise 17–17
Absorption versus Variable Costing
(LO 1)

Information taken from Collegiate Sporting Goods Company's records for the most recent year is as follows:

Direct material used	$272,000
Direct labor	128,000
Variable manufacturing overhead	60,000
Fixed manufacturing overhead.	100,000
Variable selling and administrative costs	56,000
Fixed selling and administrative costs	29,600

Required:

1. Assuming the company uses absorption costing, compute the inventoriable costs for the year.
2. Compute the year's inventoriable costs using variable costing.

(CMA, adapted)

Exercise 17–18
Absorption, Variable, and Throughput Costing; Use of Internet
(LO 1, 7)

Visit the website for one of the following companies, or a different company of your choosing.

Coca-Cola	www.cocacola.com
Firestone	www.firestone.com
Motorola	www.motorola.com
Texas Instruments	www.ti.com
Toyota	www.toyota.com
Xerox Corporation	www.xerox.com

Required: Read about the company's products and operations. Discuss the pros and cons of absorption, variable, and throughput costing as the basis for product costing if the firm uses cost-based pricing.

Exercise 17–19
Absorption, Variable, and Throughput Costing
(LO 1, 4, 7)

Pinellas Pillow Company's planned production for the year just ended was 10,000 units. This production level was achieved, but only 9,000 units were sold. Other data follows:

Direct material used	$80,000
Direct labor incurred	40,000
Fixed manufacturing overhead.	50,000
Variable manufacturing overhead	24,000
Fixed selling and administrative expenses	60,000
Variable selling and administrative expenses	9,000
Finished-goods inventory, January 1	None

There were no work-in-process inventories at the beginning or end of the year.

Required:

1. What would be Pinellas Pillow Company's finished-goods inventory cost on December 31 under the variable-costing method?
2. Which costing method, absorption or variable costing, would show a higher operating income for the year? By what amount?
3. Suppose Pinellas Pillow Company uses throughput costing, and direct material is its only unit-level cost. What would be Pinellas' finished-goods inventory on December 31?

(CPA, adapted)

Exercise 17–20
Absorption, Variable, and Throughput Costing
(LO 1, 7)

Information taken from Ticonderoga Paper Company's records for the most recent year is as follows:

Direct material used	$203,000
Direct labor	70,000
Variable manufacturing overhead	35,000
Fixed manufacturing overhead.	56,000

(continues)

Variable selling and administrative costs	28,000
Fixed selling and administrative costs	14,000

Required:

1. Assuming Ticonderoga Paper Company uses variable costing, compute the inventoriable costs for the year.
2. Compute the year's inventoriable costs using absorption costing.
3. Now assume that Ticonderoga Paper Company uses throughput costing, and the company has *committed* to spending for direct labor, variable overhead, and fixed overhead in the amounts given in the problem. Under this scenario, compute the company's inventoriable cost for the year.

(CMA, adapted)

Problems

Problem 17–21
Variable-Costing and Absorption-Costing Income Statement; Reconciling Reported Income
(LO 2, 3, 4)

Chenango Can Company manufactures metal cans used in the food-processing industry. A case of cans sells for $25. The variable standard costs of production for one case of cans are as follows:

Direct material	$ 7.50
Direct labor	2.50
Variable manufacturing overhead	6.00
Total variable manufacturing cost per case	$16.00

Variable selling and administrative costs amount to $.50 per case. Budgeted fixed manufacturing overhead is $400,000 per year, and fixed selling and administrative cost is $37,500 per year. The following data pertain to the company's first three years of operation. (A *unit* refers to one case of cans.)

	Year 1	Year 2	Year 3
Planned production (in units)	80,000	80,000	80,000
Finished-goods inventory (in units), January 1	0	0	20,000
Actual production (in units)	80,000	80,000	80,000
Sales (in units)	80,000	60,000	90,000
Finished-goods inventory (in units), December 31	0	20,000	10,000

There were no variances during Chenango's first three years of operation. Actual costs were the same as the budgeted and standard costs.

Required:

1. Prepare operating income statements for Chenango Can Company for its first three years of operations using:
   a. Absorption costing.
   b. Variable costing.
2. Reconcile Chenango Can Company's operating income reported under absorption and variable costing for each of its first three years of operation. Use the shortcut method.
3. Suppose that during Chenango's fourth year of operation actual production equals planned production, actual costs are equal to budgeted or standard costs, and the company ends the year with no inventory on hand.
   a. What will be the difference between absorption-costing income and variable-costing income in year 4?
   b. What will be the relationship between total operating income for the four-year period as reported under absorption and variable costing? Explain.

Problem 17–22
Throughput Costing
(LO 7, 8)

Refer to the information in the preceding problem for Chenango Can Company. Assume that direct material is the *only unit-level* manufacturing cost.

Required: Prepare income statements for all three years using throughput costing.

Problem 17–23
Absorption and Variable Costing; CVP Analysis
(LO 4, 5, 6)

Cincinnati Cylinder Company began operations on January 1 to produce pneumatic cylinders used in a variety of machines. It used a standard absorption costing system with a planned production volume of

100,000 units. During its first year of operations, no variances were incurred and there were no fixed selling or administrative expenses. Inventory on December 31 was 20,000 units, and net income for the year was $480,000.

Required:

1. If Cincinnati Cylinder Company had used variable costing, its net income would have been $440,000. Compute the break-even point in units under variable costing.
2. Draw a profit-volume graph for Cincinnati Cylinder Company. (Use variable costing.)

Problem 17–24
Straightforward Problem on Absorption versus Variable Costing
(LO 2, 3, 4, 6)

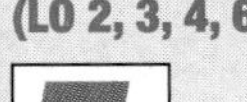

Skinny Dippers, Inc. produces nonfat frozen yogurt which it sells to restaurants and ice cream shops. The product is sold in 10-gallon containers, which have the following price and standard variable costs.

Sales price	$30
Direct material	10
Direct labor	4
Variable overhead	6

Budgeted fixed overhead in 20x4 was $600,000. Actual production was 150,000 10-gallon containers, of which 125,000 were sold. There were no variances recorded in 20x4. Skinny Dippers, Inc. incurred the following selling and administrative expenses.

Fixed	$100,000 for the year
Variable	$2 per container sold

Required:

1. Compute the standard product cost per container of frozen yogurt under (*a*) absorption costing and (*b*) variable costing.
2. Prepare income statements for 20x4 using (*a*) absorption costing and (*b*) variable costing.
3. Reconcile the income reported under the two methods by listing the two key places where the income statements differ.
4. Reconcile the income reported under the two methods using the shortcut method.

Problem 17–25
Straightforward Problem on Throughput Costing
(LO 7, 8)

Refer to the information given in the preceding problem for Skinny Dippers, Inc. Assume that the company has *committed* spending for direct labor and manufacturing overhead; direct material is the only unit-level production cost.

Required:

1. Compute the cost of Skinny Dippers' year-end finished-goods inventory using throughput costing.
2. Prepare an income statement for 20x4 using throughput costing.
3. Briefly explain the difference between gross margin computed under absorption costing and gross margin computed under throughput costing.

Problem 17–26
Variable versus Absorption Costing; JIT
(LO 1, 4)

Outback, Ltd. manufactures rechargeable flashlights in Melbourne, Australia. The firm uses a standard absorption-costing system for internal reporting purposes; however, the company is considering using variable costing. Data regarding planned and actual operations for 20x4 follow:

	Budgeted Costs		
	Per Unit	Total	Actual Costs
Direct material	$ 6.00	$ 840,000	$ 780,000
Direct labor	4.50	630,000	585,000
Variable manufacturing overhead	2.00	280,000	260,000
Fixed manufacturing overhead	2.50	350,000	357,500
Variable selling expenses	4.00	560,000	500,000
Fixed selling expenses	3.50	490,000	490,000
Variable administrative expenses	1.00	140,000	125,000
Fixed administrative expenses	1.50	210,000	212,500
Total	$25.00	$3,500,000	$3,310,000

	Planned Activity	Actual Activity
Sales in units	140,000	125,000
Production in units	140,000	130,000
Beginning finished-goods inventory in units	35,000	35,000

The budgeted per-unit cost figures were based on the company producing and selling 140,000 units in 20x4. Outback uses a predetermined overhead rate for applying manufacturing overhead to its product. A total manufacturing overhead rate of $4.50 per unit was employed for absorption costing purposes in 20x4. Any overapplied or underapplied manufacturing overhead is closed to the Cost of Goods Sold account at the end of the year. The 20x4 beginning finished-goods inventory for absorption costing purposes was valued at the 20x3 budgeted unit manufacturing cost, which was the same as the 20x4 budgeted unit manufacturing cost. There are no work-in-process inventories at either the beginning or the end of the year. The planned and actual unit selling price for 20x4 was $35 per unit.

Required: Was Outback's 20x4 income higher under absorption costing or variable costing? Why? Compute the following amounts.

1. The value of the 20x4 ending finished-goods inventory under absorption costing.
2. The value of the 20x4 ending finished-goods inventory under variable costing.
3. The difference between Outback's 20x4 reported income calculated under absorption costing and calculated under variable costing.
4. Suppose Outback had introduced a JIT production and inventory management system at the beginning of 20x4.
   a. What would likely be different about the scenario as described in the problem?
   b. Would reported income under variable and absorption costing differ by the magnitude you found in requirement (3)? Explain.

(CMA, adapted)

Problem 17–27
Throughput Costing, Absorption Costing, and Variable Costing
(LO 1, 2, 3, 7, 8)

Adelphia Corporation, which uses throughput costing, just completed its first year of operations. Planned and actual production equaled 10,000 units, and sales totaled 9,600 units at $216 per unit. Cost data for the year are as follows:

Direct material (per unit)	$36
Conversion cost:	
Direct labor	135,000
Variable manufacturing overhead	195,000
Fixed manufacturing overhead	660,000
Selling and administrative costs:	
Variable (per unit)	24
Fixed	354,000

The company classifies only direct material as a throughput cost.

Required:

1. Compute the company's total cost for the year assuming that variable manufacturing costs are driven by the number of units produced, and variable selling and administrative costs are driven by the number of units sold.
2. How much of this cost would be held in year-end inventory under (*a*) absorption costing, (*b*) variable costing, and (*c*) throughput costing?
3. How much of the company's total cost for the year would be included as an expense on the period's income statement under (*a*) absorption costing, (*b*) variable costing, and (*c*) throughput costing?
4. Prepare Adelphia's throughput-costing income statement.

Problem 17–28
Comparison of Absorption and Variable Costing; Actual Costing
(LO 2, 3, 4)

Huron Chalk Company manufactures blackboard chalk for educational uses. The company's product is sold by the box at $25 per unit. Huron uses an actual costing system, which means that the actual costs of direct material, direct labor, and manufacturing overhead are entered into work-in-process inventory. The actual application rate for manufacturing overhead is computed each year; actual manufacturing overhead is divided by actual production (in units) to compute the application rate. Information for Huron's first two years of operations is as follows:

	Year 1	Year 2
Sales (in units)	2,500	2,500
Production (in units)	3,000	2,000
Production costs:		
Variable manufacturing costs	$10,500	$ 7,000
Fixed manufacturing overhead	21,000	21,000
Selling and administrative costs:		
Variable	12,500	12,500
Fixed	10,000	10,000

Required: Huron Chalk Company had no beginning or ending work-in-process inventories for either year.

1. Prepare operating income statements for both years based on absorption costing.
2. Prepare operating income statements for both years based on variable costing.
3. Prepare a numerical reconciliation of the difference in income reported under the two costing methods used in requirements (1) and (2).

Problem 17–29
Analysis of Differences in Absorption-Costing and Variable-Costing Income Statements; Continuation of Preceding Problem
(LO 1, 4)

Refer to the information given in the preceding problem for Huron Chalk Company.

Required:

1. Reconcile Huron's income reported under absorption and variable costing, during each year, by comparing the following two amounts on each income statement:
   - Cost of goods sold
   - Fixed cost (expensed as a period expense)
2. What was Huron's total income across both years under absorption costing and under variable costing?
3. What was the total sales revenue across both years under absorption costing and under variable costing?
4. What was the total of all costs expensed on the income statements across both years under absorption costing, and under variable costing?
5. Subtract the total costs expensed across both years [requirement (4)] from the total sales revenue across both years [requirement (3)]: (*a*) under absorption costing and (*b*) under variable costing.
6. Comment on the results obtained in requirements (1), (2), (3), and (4) in light of the following assertion: *Timing is the key in distinguishing between absorption and variable costing.*

Problem 17–30
Absorption and Variable Costing; Effect on the Balance Sheet; Continuation of Preceding Problem
(LO 1, 4)

Refer to the information given in Problem 17–28 for Huron Chalk Company. Selected information from Huron's year-end balance sheets for its first two years of operation is as follows:

HURON CHALK COMPANY
Selected Balance Sheet Information

Based on absorption costing	**End of Year 1**	**End of Year 2**
Finished-goods inventory	$5,250	$ 0
Retained earnings	8,250	12,300
Based on variable costing	**End of Year 1**	**End of Year 2**
Finished-goods inventory	$1,750	$ 0
Retained earnings	4,750	12,300

Required:

1. Why is the year 1 ending balance in finished-goods inventory higher if absorption costing is used than if variable costing is used?
2. Why is the year 2 ending balance in finished-goods inventory the same under absorption and variable costing?
3. Notice that the ending balance of finished-goods inventory under absorption costing is greater than or equal to the ending finished-goods inventory balance under variable costing *for both years 1 and 2.* Will this relationship always hold true at any balance sheet date? Explain.

4. Compute the amount by which the year-end balance in finished-goods inventory declined during year 2 (i.e., between December 31 of year 1 and December 31 of year 2):
   - Using the data from the balance sheet prepared under absorption costing.
   - Using the data from the balance sheet prepared under variable costing.
5. Refer to your calculations from requirement (4). Compute the difference in the amount by which the year-end balances in finished-goods inventory declined under absorption versus variable costing. Then compare the amount of this difference with the difference in the company's reported income for year 2 under absorption versus variable costing. (Refer to the income statements prepared in Problem 17–28.)
6. Notice that the retained earnings balance at the end of both years 1 and 2 on the balance sheet prepared under absorption costing is greater than or equal to the corresponding retained earnings balance on the statement prepared under variable costing. Will this relationship hold true at any balance sheet date? Explain.

Problem 17–31
Variable and Absorption Costing (Appendix)
(LO 4, 9)

Ozarks Lighting Company had net income for the first 10 months of the current year of $300,000. The company used a standard-costing system, and there were no variances through October 31. One hundred thousand units were manufactured during this period, and 100,000 units were sold. Fixed manufacturing overhead was $3,000,000 over the 10-month period (i.e., $300,000 per month). There are no selling and administrative expenses for Ozarks Lighting Company. All variances are disposed of at year-end by an adjustment to cost of goods sold. Both variable and fixed costs are expected to continue at the same rates for the balance of the year (i.e., fixed costs at $300,000 per month and variable costs at the same variable cost per unit). There were 10,000 units in inventory on October 31. Seventeen thousand units are to be produced and 19,000 units are to be sold in total over the last two months of the current year. Assume the standard unit variable cost is the same in the current year as in the previous year. (*Hint:* You cannot calculate revenue or cost of goods sold; you must work directly with contribution margin or gross margin.)

Required:

1. If operations proceed as described, will net income be higher under variable or absorption costing for the current year in total? Why?
2. If operations proceed as described, what will net income for the year *in total* be under (*a*) variable costing and (*b*) absorption costing? (Ignore income taxes.)

Problem 17–32
Variable-Costing and Absorption-Costing Income Statements; FMS; JIT (Appendix)
(LO 2, 3, 4, 6, 9)

Great Outdoze, Inc. manufactures high-quality sleeping bags, which sell for $130 each. The variable standard costs of production are as follows:

Direct material	$40
Direct labor	22
Variable manufacturing overhead	16

Budgeted fixed overhead in 20x4 was $400,000 and budgeted production was 20,000 sleeping bags. The year's actual production was 25,000 units, of which 22,000 were sold. There were no variances during 20x4, except for the fixed-overhead volume variance. Variable selling and administrative costs were $2 per unit sold; fixed selling and administrative costs were $60,000. The firm does not prorate variances.

Required:

1. Calculate the standard product cost per sleeping bag under (*a*) absorption costing and (*b*) variable costing.
2. Compute the fixed-overhead volume variance for 20x4, assuming the company uses absorption costing.
3. Prepare income statements for the year using (*a*) absorption costing and (*b*) variable costing.
4. Reconcile reported income under the two methods using the shortcut method.
5. Suppose that Great Outdoze, Inc. implemented a JIT inventory and production management system at the beginning of 20x4. In addition, the firm installed a flexible manufacturing system. Would you expect reported income under variable and absorption costing to be different by as great a magnitude as you found in requirement (3)? Explain.

Problem 17–33
Throughput Costing
(LO 7, 8)

Refer to the information given in the preceding problem for Great Outdoze, Inc. Assume that direct material is the *only unit-level* manufacturing cost. The company has *committed* its spending for direct labor and overhead (variable and fixed).

Required:

1. Calculate the standard product cost per sleeping bag under throughput costing.
2. Prepare an income statement for the year 20x4 using throughput costing.
3. Give an argument for and against throughput costing.

Case

Case 17–34
Absorption and Variable Costing: Reconciling Reported Income; Balance Sheet Effects; Ethics; Appendix
(LO 4, 6, 9)

Joe Duval was proud of the way he had guided Screen Technology Corporation over the past year since he had accepted the job as the company's president. Under Duval's direction, the privately held company's sales had grown each quarter, and several new sales contacts in Europe looked promising for future business. Duval had taken a personal interest in developing new business, and the company's future looked bright. Duval had also seen to it that the company's costs had remained in check. One of the new president's first moves had been to benchmark several of Screen Technology's performance measures against other high-tech electronics firms. Duval was convinced that the company's production technology and business practices were as efficient as any firm in the business.

Screen Technology Corporation had been formed some five years earlier to manufacture aperture masks, which are an important component in computer monitors and TV picture tubes. Aperture masks direct a beam of electrons to the red, blue, and green phosphor stripes on the inside face of a picture tube. Thus, the aperture mask is a critical component in the creation of a color picture on the computer monitor or TV tube. Ranging in size from 18 to 90 centimeters, Screen Technology's masks are manufactured from nickel alloy. Several patented manufacturing steps are used to produce the aperture masks, including highly accurate photographic and etching processes, chemical coating processes, and cleaning processes. Screen Technology's masks already were being marketed in North America and Asia, and negotiations were proceeding with several potential European customers.

At the beginning of his second year on the job, Duval had been looking forward to the fourth-quarter financial statements. Upon reading the financial reports, though, Duval was dismayed when he saw that Screen Technology's fourth-quarter profit was actually lower than that reported in the third quarter. "What's going on here?" he thought. Duval picked up the phone to call Alison West, Screen Technology's controller, for an explanation.

Shown here are the third- and fourth-quarter income statements that were perplexing Duval.

SCREEN TECHNOLOGY CORPORATION
Income Statements
For the 3rd and 4th Quarters of 20x3

	3rd Quarter	4th Quarter
Sales revenue	$5,040,000	$7,920,000
Less: Cost of goods sold (at standard absorption cost)	3,780,000	5,940,000
Gross margin (at standard)	$1,260,000	$1,980,000
Adjust for: Fixed overhead volume variance*	360,000	360,000
Gross margin (at actual)	$1,620,000	$1,620,000
Less: Selling and administrative expenses	720,000	960,000
Net income	$ 900,000	$ 660,000

*There were no other variances during the 3rd or 4th quarters of 20x3. The 3rd-quarter volume variance is negative (or *favorable*), and the 4th-quarter volume variance is positive (or *unfavorable*).

When Alison West arrived at Joe Duval's office, she could see the president was upset and puzzled. "You're the controller, Alison," began Duval. "I hope you have a good explanation for this. When sales go up from one quarter to the next, and production efficiency and standard costs remain about the same, I would expect profits to increase also. And I can assure you that our owners will expect increased profits, too, when I go to the quarterly meeting next week."

West tried to explain to Duval why Screen Technology's profit had fallen, even though sales had risen substantially. "Our financial statements are prepared using absorption costing," explained West. "This means that all manufacturing costs are treated as product costs. Direct material, direct labor, and all manufacturing overhead costs are stored in inventory until the units are sold. It's true that sales rose during the fourth quarter, but production did not keep pace with sales. In fact, actual fourth-quarter production was somewhat lower even than our planned production for the quarter. When that happens, we end up expensing fixed manufacturing overhead during the current period, even though it was incurred during a previous period."

"Well, I'm no accountant," retorted Duval. "I'm an engineer and I've spent most of my career in marketing. But this just doesn't seem reasonable to me. If sales go up, and production efficiency remains more or less the same, then I still think income ought to go up. I was counting on a bonus this quarter, and I would think you would've been expecting one, too. Can't you produce an income statement where profits increase when sales increase?"

"Yes, I can, Joe," replied the controller. "I can use a method called variable costing instead of absorption costing. Under that method, fixed manufacturing overhead is expensed during the period it's incurred. That effectively eliminates the kind of distortion that's bothering you. Since Screen Tech is a privately held company, we can use either method we want. The owners should be informed if we change methods, though. And they should also be made aware of the effect of the change on executive bonuses."

"I think we should change to the other method, then," responded Duval. "What'd you call it? Variable costing, was it?"

"That's right, Joe. It's called variable costing because only variable manufacturing costs are inventoried."

"Okay, here's what I would like you to do, Alison. Please prepare third-quarter and fourth-quarter income statements for me using variable costing. Then come along with me to next week's meeting and explain to our bosses why the results differ."

"You got it," replied West. "And I'll show you the effect of the accounting method change on the balance sheet also."

"That sounds good," replied Duval. "By the way, is there a down side to variable costing? What do you see as the advantages and disadvantages?"

Before West could respond, Duval got a phone call from an important customer. Before meeting with Duval again to answer his last question, West prepared the following third-quarter and fourth-quarter income statements. She also summarized the effect of the proposed accounting method change on Screen Technology's comparative balance sheets.

SCREEN TECHNOLOGY CORPORATION
Income Statements
For the 3rd and 4th Quarters of 20x3
(prepared using variable costing)

	3rd Quarter	4th Quarter
Sales revenue	$5,040,000	$7,920,000
Less: Variable expenses:		
Variable manufacturing costs (at standard variable cost)*	2,520,000	3,960,000
Variable selling and administrative costs	420,000	660,000
Contribution margin	$2,100,000	$3,300,000
Less: Fixed expenses:		
Fixed manufacturing overhead	1,800,000	1,800,000
Fixed selling and administrative costs	300,000	300,000
Net income	$ 0	$1,200,000

*There were no variances during the 3rd or 4th quarters of 20x3.

SCREEN TECHNOLOGY CORPORATION
Selected Balance Sheet Information
For the Quarters Ending 9/30/x3 and 12/31/x3

Balance sheets prepared using absorption costing	**9/30/x3**	**12/31/x3**
Inventory	$2,700,000	$1,080,000
Retained earnings	3,400,000	4,060,000
Balance sheets prepared using variable costing	**9/30/x3**	**12/31/x3**
Inventory	$1,800,000	$ 720,000
Retained earnings	2,500,000	3,700,000

Required:

1. How would you respond to the president's last question to the controller regarding the pros and cons of variable and absorption costing?

2. Prepare a reconciliation of the reported fourth-quarter income under variable and absorption costing.
3. Explain how and why the balance sheets differ under variable and absorption costing.
4. Would there be differences in reported income under variable and absorption costing if the statements had been annual statements instead of quarterly statements? Explain.
5. Roughly how busy was Screen Technology's production operation during the fourth quarter relative to the expected production volume? Explain.
6. Discuss the following comment made by Duval to West the next afternoon. Citing specific ethical standards for managerial accountants (given in Chapter 1), explain how West should respond.

> "Alison, I've been thinking about this whole issue some more. Why don't we just choose between variable and absorption costing each quarter, depending on which will report the highest profit for the quarter and give us the biggest bonuses?"

Current Issues in Managerial Accounting

Issue 17–35
Excess Capacity; Throughput versus Absorption Costing

"The Economy—The Outlook: Manufacturing Confounds Economists," ***The Wall Street Journal,*** **May 5, 2003, Clare Ansberry.**

Overview

According to the article, many industries have excess capacity. Among them are the airline and telecommunications industries, as well several manufacturing industries, such as steel, aluminum, and aircraft manufacturing.

Suggested Discussion Question

Some management accountants argue that absorption costing provides an incentive to continue producing goods for inventory, even when sales decline. They go on to suggest that this incentive problem is alleviated if throughput costing is used. Discuss this position, making reference to the excess capacity in several manufacturing industries.

Issue 17–36
Absorption Costing

"The Reality of Product Costing," ***Management Accounting,*** **February 2000, Mike Lucas.**

Overview

The author suggests that to gain access to sources of capital, managers had to supply financial information using absorption costing. It was thought by many that to generate separate information for management accounting would not be cost effective.

Suggested Discussion Question

What are some of the arguments against a more efficient system of product costing, which have in turn encouraged the use of an absorption-costing system.

Chapter Eighteen

Allocation of Support Activity Costs and Joint Costs

After completing this chapter, you should be able to:

1. Allocate service department costs using the direct method, step-down method, or reciprocal-services method (appendix).
2. Use the dual approach to service department cost allocation.
3. Explain the difference between two-stage cost allocation with departmental overhead rates and activity-based costing (ABC).
4. Allocate joint costs among joint products using each of the following techniques: physical-units method, relative-sales-value method, and net-realizable-value method.
5. Describe the purposes for which joint cost allocation is useful and those for which it is not.

Riverside Clinic Inks Health Care Deal with Local Colleges

Philadelphia, PA—A spokesperson for Riverside Clinic announced today that the clinic will be providing certain types of outpatient medical care to students in three local colleges. Although the colleges each will continue to operate their own student health services on campus, Riverside Clinic will augment the on-campus clinics with specialized medical services.

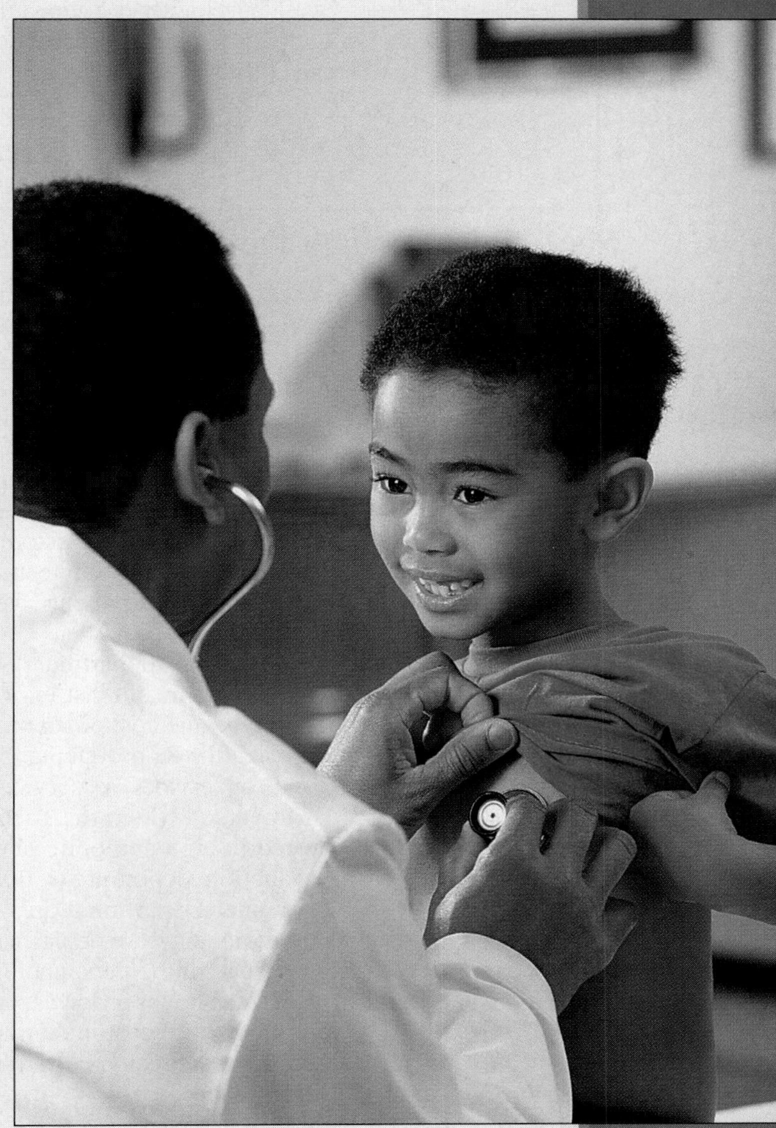

According to Anne Josephson, Riverside's administrator, "Some student health services are specialized enough that it doesn't make sense for each college to cover all those bases individually. That would mean a duplication of effort that would increase costs. On the other hand, it's not necessary to go to an in-patient facility like one of Philly's hospitals for these kinds of services. Riverside Clinic provides just the right answer. It keeps the services on an outpatient basis and avoids expensive duplication on several college campuses." Asked how the student health services would be priced by Riverside, Josephson said, "The pricing details aren't final yet. The agreement we signed with the colleges was an agreement in principle. Now we all need to sit down and figure out a fair fee schedule. We'll approach it the same way we do for the fees we charge the general public here at Riverside. The first thing we have to do is figure out what certain kinds of services cost the clinic. And that's not an easy job. There are a lot of activities behind the scenes in the clinic that are necessary in support of the primary patient care activities. For example, we have patient records, personnel, administration, and accounting departments. All of these service department costs have to be allocated to the Orthopedics and Internal Medicine departments, which actually provide direct patient care. There are different methods for making these allocations. So we'll have to talk with the folks in the college health services to see what seems to be fair to all concerned."

Josephson said Riverside hopes to have the student health services in place for the next academic year.

In earlier chapters we studied cost allocation and explored its role in an organization's overall managerial accounting system. We also examined several purposes of cost allocation. The goal of cost allocation is to ensure that all costs incurred by the organization ultimately are assigned to its products or services. This is important for several purposes, including cost-based pricing and bidding, cost reimbursements from outside parties such as insurance companies, valuation of inventory, and determination of cost of goods sold. In addition, the allocation of all costs to departments serves to make departmental managers aware of the costs incurred to produce services their departments use.

This chapter is divided into two sections, each of which explores a particular cost-allocation topic in greater detail. The two sections, which may be studied separately, cover the following topics:

- Service department cost allocation[1]
- Joint product cost allocation[2]

Section 1: Service Department Cost Allocation

LO 1

Allocate service department costs using the direct method, step-down method, or reciprocal-services method (appendix).

Topic 18–1

A **service department** is a unit in an organization that is not involved *directly* in producing the organization's goods or services. However, a service department does provide a service that enables the organization's production process to take place. For example, the Maintenance Department in an automobile plant does not make automobiles, but if it did not exist, the production process would stop when the manufacturing machines broke down. Thus, the Maintenance Department is crucial to the production operation even though the repair personnel do not work directly on the plant's products.

Service departments are important in nonmanufacturing organizations also. For example, a hospital's Personnel Department is responsible for staffing the hospital with physicians, nurses, lab technicians, and other employees. The Personnel Department never serves the patients, yet without it the hospital would have no staff to provide medical care.

A service department such as the Maintenance Department or the Personnel Department must exist in order for an organization to carry out its primary function. Therefore, the cost of running a service department is part of the cost incurred by the organization in producing goods or services. In order to determine the cost of those goods or services, all service department costs must be allocated to the production departments in which the goods or services are produced. For this reason, the costs incurred in an automobile plant's Maintenance Department are allocated to all of the production departments that have machinery. The costs incurred in a hospital's Personnel Department are allocated to all of the departments that have personnel. Direct-patient-care departments, such as Surgery and Physical Therapy, are allocated their share of the Personnel Department's costs.

To see how service department cost allocation fits into the overall picture of product and service costing, it may be helpful to review Exhibit 3–12 on page 101. The exhibit shows three types of allocation processes, as follows:

1. *Cost distribution.* Costs in various cost pools are distributed to all departments, including both service and production departments.
2. *Service department cost allocation.* Service department costs are allocated to production departments.

[1]The section on service department cost allocation is written as a module, which can be studied separately from the rest of the chapter. This material may be studied after the completion of Chapter 12, which covers basic issues in cost allocation.

[2]The section on joint cost allocation is written as a module, which can be studied separately from the rest of the chapter. This material may be studied after the completion of Chapter 14.

The cost of operating service departments, such as maintenance or inspection, are allocated to the departments that directly manufacture products or provide services to customers. Pictured here is Universal Studios' Florida theme park. How would you allocate the cost of the maintenance department to the theme park's various attractions?

3. *Cost application.* Costs are assigned to the goods or services produced by the organization.

It is the second type of allocation process listed above that we are focusing on now. The context for our discussion is Riverside Clinic, an outpatient medical facility in Philadelphia.

RIVERSIDE CLINIC

The clinic is organized into three service departments and two direct-patient-care departments. Exhibit 18–1 displays a simple organization chart for Riverside Clinic. Since the clinic is not a manufacturing organization, we refer to *direct-patient-care departments* instead of *production departments.* These two departments, Orthopedics and Internal Medicine, directly provide the health care that is the clinic's primary objective. Thus, the clinic's direct-patient-care departments are like the production departments in a manufacturing firm.

"Support, or service, department costs are becoming a greater and greater percentage of our cost structure." (18a)
DaimlerChrysler

Notice that the Personnel Department and the Administration and Accounting Department provide services to each other. When this situation occurs, the two service departments exhibit *reciprocal services.*

Exhibit 18–2 provides some of the details for our illustration of service department cost allocation. Panel A shows the proportion of each service department's output that is consumed by each of the departments using its services. Panel B shows the allocation

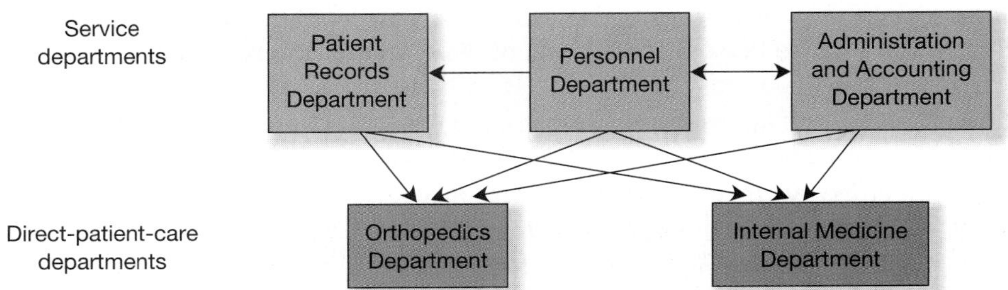

Exhibit 18–1
Organization Chart for Riverside Clinic*

RIVERSIDE CLINIC

* The arrows in the organization chart depict the provision of service by the three service departments. For example, the Personnel Department serves the Patient Records Department, but not vice versa.

Exhibit 18–2
Provision of Services by Service Departments in 20x1: Riverside Clinic

A. Percentage of Service Output Consumed by Using Departments

User of Service		Provider of Service: Patient Records	Provider of Service: Personnel	Provider of Service: Administration and Accounting
Service departments	Patient Records	—	5%	—
	Personnel	—	—	5%
	Administration and Accounting	—	20%	—
Direct-patient-care departments	Orthopedics	30%	25%	35%
	Internal Medicine	70%	50%	60%

B. Allocation Bases

Service Department	Allocation Base
Patient Records	Annual patient load
Personnel	Number of employees
Administration and Accounting	Size of department (measured in square feet of space)

C. Service Department Costs

Service Department	Variable Cost	Fixed Cost	Total Cost to Be Allocated
Patient Records	$24,000	$ 76,000	$100,000
Personnel	15,000	45,000	60,000
Administration and Accounting	47,500	142,500	190,000
Total	$86,500	$263,500	$350,000

bases, which are used to determine the proportions shown in panel A. Further explanation of the information in Exhibit 18–2 follows.

Patient Records The service output of the Patient Records Department is consumed only by the Orthopedics and Internal Medicine Departments. *Annual patient load* is the *allocation base* used to determine that 30 percent of the Patient Records Department's services were consumed by Orthopedics and 70 percent by Internal Medicine.

Personnel The Personnel Department serves each of the clinic's other departments, including the other two service departments and the two direct-patient-care departments. The *allocation base* used to determine the proportions of the Personnel Department's output consumed by the four using departments is the *number of employees* in the using departments. For example, 5 percent of the clinic's employees (excluding those in the Personnel Department) work in the Patient Records Department.

Administration and Accounting This service department provides services only to the Personnel Department, the Orthopedics Department, and the Internal Medicine Department. A variety of services are provided, such as computer support, patient billing, and general administration. Since greater amounts of these services are provided to the larger departments, departmental size is the allocation base used to determine the proportion of service output consumed by each department. Since the space devoted to each department is a convenient measure of departmental size, square footage is the measure used in Exhibit 18–2. For example, 5 percent of the

Exhibit 18–3
Direct Method of Service Department Cost Allocation: Riverside Clinic

		Direct-Patient-Care Departments Using Services			
		Orthopedics		Internal Medicine	
Provider of Service	**Cost to Be Allocated**	**Proportion**	**Amount**	**Proportion**	**Amount**
Patient Records.	$100,000	3/10	$ 30,000	7/10	$ 70,000
Personnel.	60,000	25/75	20,000	50/75	40,000
Administration and Accounting. . . .	190,000	35/95	70,000	60/95	120,000
Total.	$350,000		$120,000		$230,000

Grand total = $350,000

clinic's space (excluding that occupied by Administration and Accounting and Patient Records) is devoted to the Personnel Department.

Panel C of Exhibit 18–2 shows the total budgeted cost of each service department that is to be allocated among the using departments.

There are two widely used methods of service department cost allocation, the direct method and the step-down method. These methods are discussed and illustrated next, using the data for Riverside Clinic.

Direct Method

Under the **direct method,** each service department's costs are allocated among *only the direct-patient-care departments* that consume part of the service department's output. This method ignores the fact that some service departments provide services to other service departments. Thus, even though Riverside Clinic's Personnel Department provides services to two other service departments, none of its costs are allocated to those departments. Exhibit 18–3 presents Riverside Clinic's service department cost allocations under the direct method.

Notice that the proportion of each service department's costs to be allocated to each direct-patient-care department is determined by the *relative proportion* of the service department's output consumed by each direct-patient-care department. For example, a glance at Exhibit 18–2 shows that the Personnel Department provides 25 percent of its services to Orthopedics and 50 percent to Internal Medicine. Summing these two percentages yields 75 percent. Thus, 25/75 is the fraction of Personnel's cost allocated to Orthopedics and 50/75 is the fraction allocated to Internal Medicine.

Step-Down Method

As stated above, the direct method ignores the provision of services by one service department to another service department. This shortcoming is overcome partially by the **step-down method** of service department cost allocation. Under this method, the managerial accountant first chooses a sequence in which to allocate the service departments' costs. A common way to select the first service department in the sequence is to choose the one that serves the largest number of other service departments. The service departments are ordered in this manner, with the last service department being the one that serves the smallest number of other service departments.[3] Then the managerial accountant allocates each service department's costs among the direct-patient-care departments and all of the other service departments that follow it in the sequence. Note

[3]A tie occurs when two or more service departments serve the same number of other service departments. Then the sequence among the tied service departments usually is an arbitrary choice.

that the ultimate cost allocations assigned to the direct-patient-care departments will differ depending on the sequence chosen.

The step-down method is best explained by way of an illustration. Riverside Clinic's Personnel Department serves two other service departments: Patient Records, and Administration and Accounting. The Administration and Accounting Department serves only one other service department: Personnel. Finally, the Patient Records Department serves no other service departments. Thus, Riverside Clinic's service department sequence is as follows:

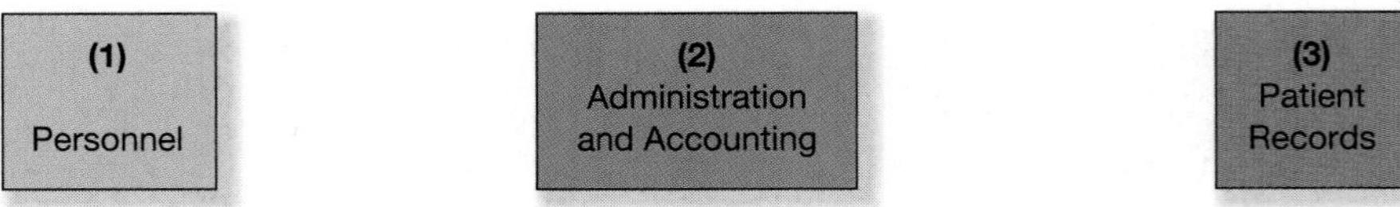

In accordance with this sequence, each service department's costs are allocated to the other departments as follows:

Cost Allocated from This Service Department ⟶	To These Departments
Personnel	Administration and Accounting
	Patient Records
	Orthopedics
	Internal Medicine
Administration and Accounting	Orthopedics
	Internal Medicine
Patient Records	Orthopedics
	Internal Medicine

"Allocating service department costs to the academic units serves a variety of purposes. For one thing, it makes the [academic] units aware that their activities result in those costs being incurred behind the scenes."(18b)
Cornell University

Notice that even though Administration and Accounting serves Personnel, there is no cost allocation in that direction. This results from Personnel's placement before Administration and Accounting in the allocation sequence. Moreover, no costs are allocated from Patient Records to either of the other service departments, because Patient Records does not serve those departments.

Exhibit 18–4 presents the results of applying the step-down method at Riverside Clinic. First, the Personnel Department's $60,000 in cost is allocated among the four departments using its services. Second, the cost of the Administration and Accounting Department is allocated. The total cost to be allocated is the department's original $190,000 *plus* the $12,000 allocated from the Personnel Department. The new total of $202,000 is allocated to the Orthopedics and Internal Medicine Departments according to the *relative proportions* in which these two departments use the services of the Administration and Accounting Department. Finally, the Patient Records Department's cost is allocated.

Reciprocal-Services Method

The direct method and the step-down method both ignore the fact that the Administration and Accounting Department serves the Personnel Department. Neither of these methods allocates any of the costs incurred in Administration and Accounting back to Personnel.

Review the relationships between the service departments depicted in Exhibit 18–1. Notice that the Administration and Accounting Department and the Personnel Department *serve each other.* This mutual provision of service is called **reciprocal service.** A more accurate method of service department cost allocation, called the **reciprocal-services method,** fully accounts for the mutual provision of services. This method, which is more complex than the direct and step-down methods, is covered in the appendix at the end of this chapter.

	Service Department			Direct-Patient-Care Department	
	Personnel	**Administration and Accounting**	**Patient Records**	**Orthopedics**	**Internal Medicine**
Costs prior to allocation	$60,000	$190,000	$100,000		
Allocation of Personnel Department costs	$60,000 →	12,000 (20/100)†	3,000 (5/100)	$ 15,000 (25/100)	$ 30,000 (50/100)
Allocation of Administration and Accounting Department costs		$202,000 →		74,421* (35/95)	127,579* (60/95)
Allocation of Patient Records Department costs			$103,000 →	30,900 (30/100)	72,100 (70/100)
Total cost allocated to each department				$120,321	$229,679
Total cost allocated to direct-patient-care departments				$350,000	

*Rounded.

†Fractions in parentheses are relative proportions of service department's output consumed by departments to which costs are allocated.

Exhibit 18–4

Step-Down Method of Service Department Cost Allocation: Riverside Clinic

Fixed versus Variable Costs

In our allocation of Riverside Clinic's service department costs, we did not distinguish between fixed and variable costs. Under some circumstances, this simple approach can result in an unfair cost allocation among the using departments. To illustrate, we will use the data about Riverside Clinic's fixed and variable costs given in panel C of Exhibit 18–2. Consider the cost data for the Patient Records Department, which serves only the Orthopedics and Internal Medicine departments. Under the *direct method* of service department cost allocation, the Patient Records Department's costs were allocated as follows:

Cost Allocation for 20x1: Direct Method

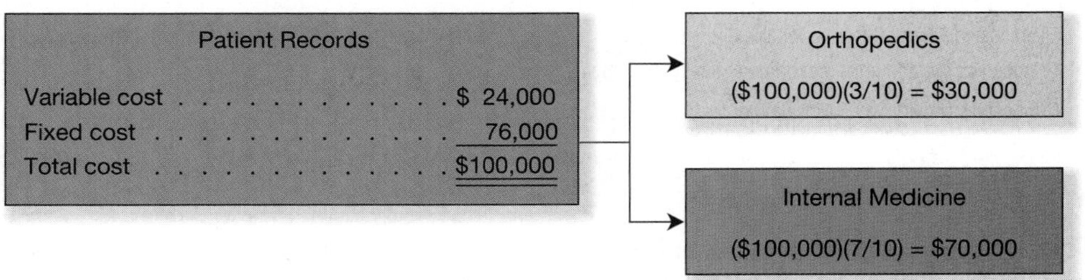

The allocation base used in this cost allocation is the annual patient load in the Orthopedics and Internal Medicine departments. Let's assume the following patient loads in 20x1, the year for which the cost allocation has been done.

Department	Patient Load		Proportion of Total
Orthopedics	30,000		(30,000/100,000) = 3/10
Internal Medicine	70,000		(70,000/100,000) = 7/10
Total	100,000		

Now suppose the projections for 20x2 are as follows:

Department	Projected Patient Load		Projected Proportion of Total
Orthopedics	30,000		(30,000/80,000) = 3/8
Internal Medicine	50,000		(50,000/80,000) = 5/8
Total	80,000		

Department	Budgeted Variable Cost	Budgeted Fixed Cost	Budgeted Total Cost
Patient Records	$19,200	$76,000	$95,200

The projections for 20x2 include a stable patient load in the Orthopedics Department but a decline in the patient load of the Internal Medicine Department. Since the projected total patient load is lower for 20x2, the projected variable cost in the Patient Records Department is lower also.

What will be the effect of these changes on the 20x2 allocation of the Patient Records Department's costs? Using the direct method, we obtain the following allocation.

Cost Allocation for 20x2: Direct Method

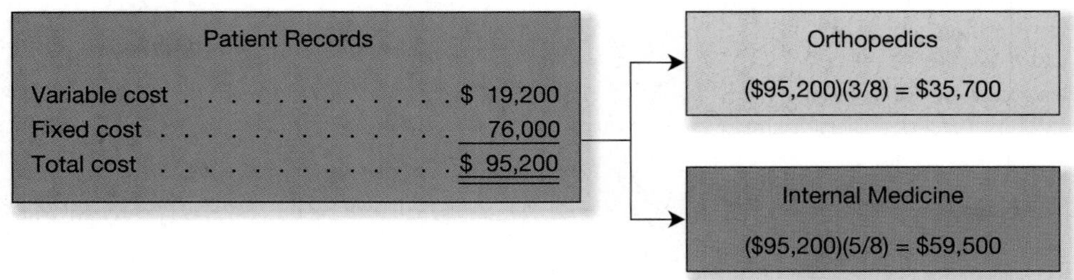

Compare the costs allocated to the two direct-patient-care departments in 20x1 and 20x2. Notice that the cost allocated to the Orthopedics Department *increased by* $5,700 (from $30,000 to $35,700), even though Orthopedics' patient load is projected to remain constant. What has happened here? The projected decline in the Internal Medicine Department's volume resulted in lower budgeted variable costs for the Patient Records Department, but the budgeted *fixed* costs did not change. At the same time, the lower projected patient load in Internal Medicine resulted in a higher proportion of the total projected patient load for Orthopedics (from 3/10 in 20x1 up to 3/8 in 20x2). As the following analysis shows, this results in an increased allocation of fixed costs to the Orthopedics Department in 20x2.

	20x1	20x2
Fixed cost in Patient Records Department	$76,000	$76,000
Orthopedics Department's proportion of total patient load	× 3/10	× 3/8
Orthopedics Department's allocation of fixed cost	$22,800	$28,500

Difference = $5,700

This difference of $5,700 is equal to the increase in the Orthopedics Department's total cost allocation from the Patient Records Department in 20x2.

To summarize, the projected decline in Internal Medicine's 20x2 patient load will result in an increased cost allocation from the Patient Records Department to the Orthopedics Department in 20x2. The cause of this increased allocation is our failure to distinguish between fixed and variable costs in the allocation process.

Dual Cost Allocation

LO 2

Use the dual approach to service department cost allocation.

The problem illustrated in the preceding section can be resolved by allocating fixed and variable costs separately. This approach, called **dual cost allocation,** works with either the direct method or the step-down method of allocation. Under dual cost allocation, *variable costs* are allocated on the basis of *short-run usage* of the service department's output; *fixed costs* are allocated on the basis of *long-run average usage* of the service department's output. The rationale for this approach is that fixed costs are capacity-producing costs. When service departments are established, their size and scale usually are determined by the projected long-run needs of the using departments.

Exhibit 18–5
Provision of Services by Service Departments: Long-Run Average Usage, Riverside Clinic

User of Service		Provider of Service		
		Patient Records	Personnel	Administration and Accounting
Service departments	Patient Records	—	10%	—
	Personnel	—	—	10%
	Administration and Accounting	—	10%	—
Direct-patient-care departments	Orthopedics	40%	20%	45%
	Internal Medicine	60%	60%	45%

To illustrate dual cost allocation for Riverside Clinic, we need estimates of the long-run average usage of each service department's output by each using department. These estimates are given in Exhibit 18–5.

Management Accounting Practice

Medicare

COST MANAGEMENT IN THE HEALTH CARE INDUSTRY

In the past, most healthcare providers operated on a retrospective payment basis that set prices based on the cost of providing healthcare services. About 25 years ago, Medicare implemented a prospective payment system based on diagnosis related groups (DRG) to control soaring healthcare costs. Under this system, a flat amount of fees was paid to a healthcare provider for a given category of illness (per case or DRG). In recent years, managed care plans have emerged to integrate financing and delivery of healthcare services and to provide healthcare in a cost-effective manner. Under managed care plans, treatment providers receive a fixed payment per plan member (patient) regardless of the treatments provided or resources consumed by individual plan members. In such a challenging new environment, accurate costing of healthcare services and cost management have become critically important for healthcare providers to remain profitable under the fixed payment plans. An appropriate cost system can help reduce treatment cost distortion, increase cost effectiveness, and improve decision making in the healthcare industry.

To combine the dual-allocation approach with either the direct method or the step-down method, we simply apply the allocation method twice, as follows:

Costs to Be Allocated	Basis for Allocation	Allocation Method	
Variable costs in 20x1 (Exhibit 18–2, panel C)	Short-run usage in 20x1 (Exhibit 18–2, panel A)	Direct method	Step-down method
		OR	
Fixed costs in 20x1 (Exhibit 18–2, panel C)	Long-run average usage (Exhibit 18–5)	Direct method	Step-down method

After both of these allocation procedures have been completed, the resulting variable- and fixed-cost allocations for each direct-patient-care department are summed. Exhibit 18–6 presents the allocation computations when the dual approach is combined with the direct method. Compare the final direct allocations with those in Exhibit 18–3, where the dual approach was not used. Notice that the final allocations are different. Exhibit 18–7 presents the computations for the step-down method. Compare the final step-down allocations with those in Exhibit 18–4, where the dual approach was not used. Again, the final allocations are different.

A Behavioral Problem Dual cost allocation prevents a change in the short-run activity of one using department from affecting the cost allocated to another using

Exhibit 18–6
Dual Allocation Combined with Direct Method: Riverside Clinic

		Direct-Patient-Care Department Using Services			
		Orthopedics		Internal Medicine	
Provider of Service	**Cost to Be Allocated**	**Proportion**	**Amount**	**Proportion**	**Amount**
I. Variable Costs					
Patient Records.	$ 24,000	3/10	$ 7,200	7/10	$ 16,800
Personnel.	15,000	25/75	5,000	50/75	10,000
Administration and Accounting. . . .	47,500	35/95	17,500	60/95	30,000
Total variable cost.	$ 86,500		$ 29,700		$ 56,800
II. Fixed Costs					
Patient Records.	$ 76,000	4/10	$ 30,400	6/10	$ 45,600
Personnel.	45,000	20/80	11,250	60/80	33,750
Administration and Accounting. . . .	142,500	45/90	71,250	45/90	71,250
Total fixed cost	$263,500		$112,900		$150,600
Total cost (variable + fixed).	$350,000		$142,600		$207,400

Grand total = $350,000

Exhibit 18–7
Dual Allocation Combined with Step-Down Method: Riverside Clinic

	Service Department			Direct-Patient-Care Department	
	Personnel	**Administration and Accounting**	**Patient Records**	**Orthopedics**	**Internal Medicine**
I. Variable Costs					
Variable cost prior to allocation	$15,000	$ 47,500	$24,000		
Allocation of Personnel Department costs.	$15,000	3,000 (20/100)†	750 (5/100)	$ 3,750 (25/100)	$ 7,500 (50/100)
Allocation of Administration and Accounting Department costs. . . .		$ 50,500		18,605* (35/95)	31,895* (60/95)
Allocation of Patient Records Department costs.			$24,750	7,425 (30/100)	17,325 (70/100)
Total variable cost allocated to each department				$ 29,780	$ 56,720
II. Fixed Costs					
Fixed cost prior to allocation	$45,000	$142,500	$76,000		
Allocation of Personnel Department costs.	$45,000	4,500 (10/100)	4,500 (10/100)	$ 9,000 (20/100)	$ 27,000 (60/100)
Allocation of Administration and Accounting Department costs		$147,000		73,500 (45/90)	73,500 (45/90)
Allocation of Patient Records Department costs.			$80,500	32,200 (40/100)	48,300 (60/100)
Total fixed cost allocated to each department				$114,700	$148,800
Total cost allocated to each department (variable + fixed)				$144,480	$205,520

Grand total = $350,000

*Rounded.

†Fractions in parentheses are relative proportions of service department's output consumed by departments to which costs are allocated. Variable costs allocated on basis of short-run proportions. Fixed costs allocated on basis of long-run average proportions.

department. However, the approach sometimes presents a problem of its own. In order to implement the technique, we need accurate projections of the long-run average usage of each service department's output by each using department. This is the information in Exhibit 18–5. Typically, these estimates come from the managers of the departments that consume the services. The problem is that the higher a manager's estimate of the department's long-run average usage is, the greater will be the department's allocation of fixed service department costs. This creates an incentive for using-department managers to understate their expected long-run service needs. Ultimately, such understatements can result in building service facilities that are too small.

How can we prevent this behavioral problem? First, we can rely on the professionalism and integrity of the managers who provide the estimates. Second, we can reward managers through promotions and pay raises for making accurate estimates of their departments' service needs.

> "Our clients are realizing to an ever-greater extent that they have to understand and manage their support service costs." (18c)
>
> **American Management Systems**

Allocate Budgeted Costs

When service department costs are allocated to production departments, such as the direct-patient-care departments of Riverside Clinic, *budgeted* service department costs should be used. If actual costs are allocated instead, any operating inefficiencies in the service departments are passed along to the using departments. This reduces the incentive for service department managers to control the costs in their departments. The proper approach is as follows:

1. Compare budgeted and actual service department costs and compute any variances.
2. Use these variances to help control costs in the service departments.
3. Close out the service department cost variances against the period's income.
4. Allocate the service departments' budgeted costs to the departments that directly produce goods or services.

Today's Advanced Manufacturing Environment

In traditional manufacturing environments, service department costs are allocated to production departments to ensure that all manufacturing costs are assigned to products. For example, the costs incurred in a machine-maintenance department typically are allocated to the other service departments and the production departments that use maintenance services. Service department cost allocation continues to be used in the new manufacturing environment, characterized by the JIT philosophy and CIM systems. However, the extent of such allocations is diminished in advanced manufacturing systems, because more costs are directly traceable to product lines. In a flexible manufacturing system, almost all operations are performed in the FMS cell. Even machine maintenance is done largely by the FMS cell operators rather than a separate maintenance department. Inspection often is performed by FMS cell operators, eliminating the need for a separate inspection department. In short, as more and more costs become directly traceable to products, the need for allocation of indirect costs declines.

The Rise of Activity-Based Costing

LO 3

Explain the difference between two-stage cost allocation with departmental overhead rates and activity-based costing (ABC).

Service department cost allocation is one type of allocation procedure used in two-stage allocation with departmental overhead rates. (See Exhibit 3–12 on page 101). Under this approach, costs first are distributed to *departments;* then they are allocated from service *departments* to production *departments.* Finally, they are assigned from production *departments* to products or services. *Departments* play a key role as intermediate cost objects under this approach.

Milk processing provides an example of joint product cost allocation in the agriculture industry. The cost of producing raw milk must be allocated among such joint products as heavy cream, light cream, whole milk, 2 percent milk, and skim milk.

In an activity-based costing (ABC) system, on the other hand, the key role is played by *activities,* not departments. (See Exhibit 3–13 on page 107). First, the costs of various *activities* are assigned to *activity* cost pools; then these costs are assigned to products or services.

The breakdown of costs by activity in an ABC system is much finer than a breakdown by departments. For example, under the service department cost allocation approach, the Purchasing Department might be one of the service departments identified. However, under ABC, the various activities engaged in by purchasing personnel would be separately identified. Activities such as part specification, vendor identification, vendor selection, price negotiation, ordering, expediting, receiving, inspection, and invoice paying might be identified separately under ABC. Then the costs of each of these activities would be assigned to products or services on the basis of the appropriate cost drivers. The ABC approach generally will provide a much more accurate cost for each of the organization's products or services.[4]

Section 2: Joint Product Cost Allocation

LO 4

Allocate joint costs among joint products using each of the following techniques: physical-units method, relative-sales-value method, and net-realizable-value method.

A **joint production process** results in two or more products, which are termed **joint products.** The cost of the input and the joint production process is called a *joint product cost.* The point in the production process where the individual products become separately identifiable is called the **split-off point.** To illustrate, International Chocolate Company produces cocoa powder and cocoa butter by processing cocoa beans in the joint production process depicted in Exhibit 18–8.

As the diagram shows, cocoa beans are processed in 1-ton batches. The beans cost $500 and the joint process costs $600, for a total *joint cost* of $1,100. The process results in 1,500 pounds of cocoa butter and 500 pounds of cocoa powder. Each of these two joint products can be sold at the split-off point or processed further. Cocoa butter can be separately processed into a tanning cream, and cocoa powder can be separately processed into instant cocoa mix.

Allocating Joint Costs

LO 5

Describe the purposes for which joint cost allocation is useful and those for which it is not.

For product-costing purposes, a joint product cost usually is allocated to the joint products that result from the joint production process. Such allocation *is necessary* for inventory valuation and income determination, among other reasons.[5] As we discussed in Chapter 14, however, joint cost allocation is *not useful* for making substantive economic decisions about the joint process or the joint products. For example, Chapter 14 shows that joint cost allocation is not useful in deciding whether to process a joint

Topic 18–2

[4]Activity-based costing is introduced conceptually in Chapter 3 and covered extensively in Chapter 5.

[5]The purposes of product costing are covered in Chapter 3.

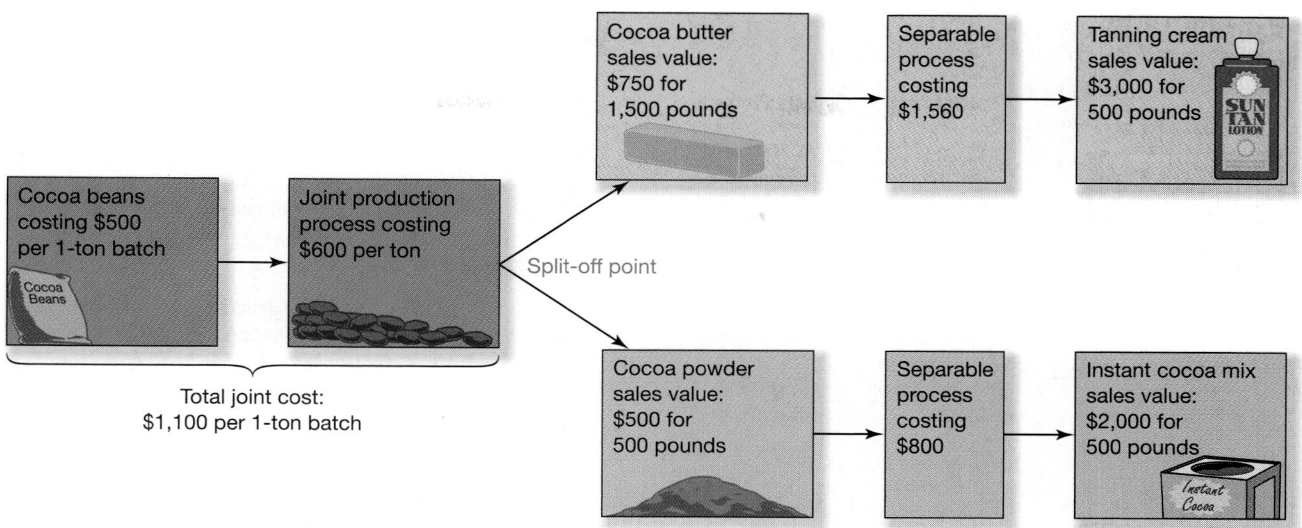

Exhibit 18–8
Joint Processing of Cocoa Beans: International Chocolate Company

product further. (See pages 599–601.) There are three commonly used methods for allocating joint product costs. Each of these is explained next.

Physical-Units Method The **physical-units method** allocates joint product costs on the basis of some physical characteristic of the joint products at the split-off point. Panel A of Exhibit 18–9 illustrates this allocation method for International Chocolate Company using the *weight* of the joint products as the allocation basis.

Relative-Sales-Value Method The **relative-sales-value method** is based on the relative sales value of each joint product *at the split-off point.* In the International Chocolate Company illustration, these joint products are cocoa butter and cocoa powder. This method is illustrated in Exhibit 18–9 (panel B).

Net-Realizable-Value Method Under the **net-realizable-value method,** the relative value of the final products is used to allocate the joint cost. International Chocolate Company's final products are tanning cream and instant cocoa mix. The **net realizable value** of each final product is its sales value less any separable costs incurred *after* the split-off point. The joint cost is allocated according to the relative magnitudes of the final products' net realizable values. Panel C of Exhibit 18–9 illustrates this allocation method.

Notice how different the cost allocations are under the three methods, particularly the physical-units method. Since the physical-units approach is not based on the *economic* characteristics of the joint products, it is the least preferred of the three methods.

> "Joint costing problems crop up more often than you might think. They're among the thornier [cost management] issues our clients have to deal with." (18d)
> **A. T. Kearney**

By-Products A joint product with very little value relative to the other joint products is termed a **by-product.** For example, whey is a by-product in the production of cheese. A common practice in accounting is to subtract a by-product's net realizable value from the cost of the joint process. Then the remaining joint cost is allocated among the major joint products.

An alternative procedure is to inventory the by-product at its sales value at split-off. Then the by-product's sales value is deducted from the production cost of the main products.

Exhibit 18–9
Methods for Allocating Joint Product Costs

A. Physical-Units Method

Joint Cost	Joint Products	Weight at Split-off Point	Relative Proportion	Allocation of Joint Cost
$1,100	Cocoa butter	1,500 pounds	3/4	$ 825
	Cocoa powder	500 pounds	1/4	275
	Total joint cost allocated			$1,100

B. Relative-Sales-Value Method

Joint Cost	Joint Products	Sales Value at Split-off Point	Relative Proportion	Allocation of Joint Cost
$1,100	Cocoa butter	$750	3/5	$ 660
	Cocoa powder	500	2/5	440
	Total joint cost allocated			$1,100

C. Net-Realizable-Value Method

Joint Cost	Joint Products	Sales Value of Final Product	Separable Cost of Processing	Net Realizable Value	Relative Proportion	Allocation of Joint Cost
1,100	Tanning cream	$3,000	$1,560	$1,440*	6/11†	$ 600
	Instant cocoa mix	2,000	800	1,200*	5/11†	500
	Total joint cost allocated					$1,100

*Sales value of final product	−	Separable cost of processing	=	Net realizable value
$3,000	−	$1,560	=	$1,440
2,000	−	800	=	1,200

†Calculation of relative proportions:

$1,440	+	$1,200	=	$2,640
1,440	÷	2,640	=	6/11
1,200	÷	2,640	=	5/11

Management Accounting Practice

Exxon

JOINT COST ALLOCATION IN THE PETROLEUM INDUSTRY

One of the most complicated problems in joint cost allocation routinely occurs in the petroleum industry. When an oil company, such as Exxon, drills a successful oil well, the well almost always produces natural gas in addition to crude oil. Moreover, the crude oil produced by a typical oil well is of various grades. Lighter crude oils suitable for production of such products as gasoline are generally near the top of an oil reservoir, while the heavier crudes are near the bottom. The heavier crude oils are used to make such products as fuel oil for heating homes and businesses and for the generation of electricity.

All of these products obtained from a successful oil well are joint products: the various grades of crude oil and the natural gas. Most of these products will require further processing before they will be salable products such as gasoline, diesel fuel, or home heating oil. Thus, substantial separable costs will be incurred in processing the joint products in addition to the joint costs incurred in the oil field operations. Millions of dollars of joint costs are incurred in the development of an off-shore oil field. The costs of locating the oil field, building the drilling platforms, and the drilling itself are all joint costs. Then there are the costs of crewing the oil rigs and the ongoing costs of bringing oil and natural gas to the surface.

Oil companies such as Exxon typically use the net realizable value of the products manufactured as the basis for allocating the joint production costs. The full costs of the company's various products then become the basis for pricing and product-mix decisions.

The next time you pump gas for your automobile, think about the salaries of the helicopter pilots who bring food and other supplies to the many off-shore oil platforms. Those costs comprise a part of the joint cost allocated to the gasoline you obtain from the pump.

Chapter Summary

Service departments are not involved directly in producing an organization's final output of goods or services, but they do provide essential services in an organization. Thus, in order to determine the full cost of the organization's final services or goods, service department costs are allocated to the departments directly involved in producing the organization's final output. Two methods are used commonly in practice, the direct method and the step-down method. Either of these methods may be combined with the dual-allocation approach, in which variable and fixed costs are allocated separately.

A joint production process results in two or more joint products, which become separately identifiable at the split-off point. The joint costs of production are allocated in order to determine the complete cost of manufacturing the joint products. Three methods are used for this purpose: the physical-units method, the relative-sales-value method, and the net-realizable-value method. Joint cost allocation is useful for product-costing purposes, but the allocated costs should not affect substantive economic decisions.

Key Terms

For each term's definition, refer to the indicated page or turn to the glossary at the end of the text.

Appendix to Chapter 18

Reciprocal-Services Method

The reciprocal-services method of service department cost allocation fully accounts for the mutual provision of services among all the service departments. The relationships between Riverside Clinic's three service departments are portrayed in the following diagram.

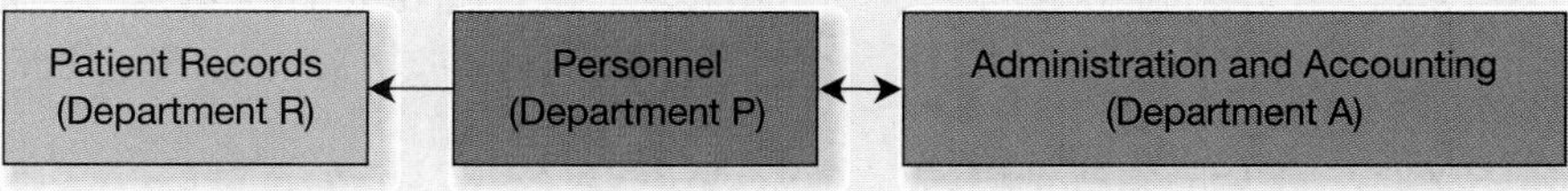

LO 1

Allocate service department costs using the direct method, step-down method, or reciprocal-services method (appendix).

The first step in the technique is to specify a set of equations that express the relationships between the departments. The following equations, which express these relationships for Riverside Clinic, are based on the data in Exhibit 18–2 on page 754.

$$R = 100{,}000 + .05P \quad (1)$$

$$P = 60{,}000 + .05A \quad (2)$$

$$A = 190{,}000 + .20P \quad (3)$$

where R denotes the total cost of the Patient Records Department
P denotes the total cost of the Personnel Department
A denotes the total cost of the Administration and Accounting Department

Equation (1) says that the *total cost* of operating the Patient Records Department (*R*) is $100,000 *plus* 5 percent of the total cost of operating the Personnel Department (*P*). The $100,000 comes from Exhibit 18–2 (panel C) and is the total cost *traceable* to the Patient Records Department. We add to this amount 5 percent of the total cost of operating the Personnel Department. Why? Because Exhibit 18–2 (panel A) tells us that the Patient Records Department used 5 percent of the Personnel Department's services. Similar explanations underlie equations (2) and (3).

The second step in the reciprocal-services method is to solve the simultaneous equations.[6] Let's begin by substituting the expression for *A* from equation (3) into equation (2), and solving for *P* as follows:

$$\begin{aligned} P &= 60{,}000 + .05(190{,}000 + .20P) \\ &= 60{,}000 + 9{,}500 + .01P \\ .99P &= 69{,}500 \\ P &= 70{,}202 \text{ (rounded)} \end{aligned}$$

Then we substitute the value for *P* we just obtained into equation (3), and solve for *A* as follows:

$$\begin{aligned} A &= 190{,}000 + .20P \\ &= 190{,}000 + (.20)(70{,}202) \\ &= 204{,}040 \text{ (rounded)} \end{aligned}$$

Now we can solve for *R* by substituting the value for *P* into equation (1) as follows:

$$\begin{aligned} R &= 100{,}000 + .05P \\ &= 100{,}000 + (.05)(70{,}202) \\ &= 103{,}510 \text{ (rounded)} \end{aligned}$$

Thus, we have determined that $P = 70{,}202$, $A = 204{,}040$, and $R = 103{,}510$.

The final step in the reciprocal-services method is to allocate the *total cost* of operating each service department (*R, P,* and *A*) to the various departments that use its services. For example, we will allocate the total cost of operating the Personnel Department (*P*) among all four of Riverside Clinic's other departments, because they all use Personnel's services. This allocation is made in proportion to the use of Personnel's services by the other departments, as given in Exhibit 18–2 (panel A).

The allocations are shown in Exhibit 18–10. Focus on the second row of numbers, which refers to the Personnel Department. The $70,202 shown in parentheses in the Personnel column is that

Exhibit 18–10
Reciprocal-Services Method of Service Department Cost Allocation: Riverside Clinic

	Service Department			Direct-Patient-Care Department	
	Personnel	**Administration and Accounting**	**Patient Records**	**Orthopedics**	**Internal Medicine**
Traceable costs	$60,000	$190,000	$100,000		
Allocation of Personnel Department costs	(70,202)	14,040* (.20)	3,510* (.05)	$ 17,551* (.25)	$ 35,101 (.50)
Allocation of Administration and Accounting Department costs	10,202 (.05)†	(204,040)	-0- (0)	71,414 (.35)	122,424 (.60)
Allocation of Patient Records Department costs	-0- (0)	-0- (0)	(103,510)	31,053 (.30)	72,457 (.70)
Total cost allocated to each direct-patient-care department				$120,018	$229,982
Total costs allocated				$350,000	

*Rounded.
†Percentages in parentheses are relative proportions of a service department's output consumed by departments to which costs are allocated (from Exhibit 18–2, panel A).

[6]Simultaneous equations are more quickly solved by computers than by people. Numerous software packages are available for this purpose.

department's total cost, as computed using the simultaneous equations. This $70,202 total cost is allocated as follows:

- 20 percent (or $14,040) to Administration and Accounting, because that department uses 20 percent of Personnel's services
- 5 percent (or $3,510) to Patient Records, because that department uses 5 percent of Personnel's services
- 25 percent (or $17,551) to Orthopedics, because that department uses 25 percent of Personnel's services
- 50 percent (or $35,101) to Internal Medicine, because that department uses 50 percent of Personnel's services.

A similar explanation underlies the Administration and Accounting row and the Patient Records row in Exhibit 18–10.

The total costs allocated to Riverside Clinic's two direct-patient-care departments are as follows: $120,018 to Orthopedics and $229,982 to Internal Medicine. Notice that these two amounts add up to $350,000, which is the total of the original traceable costs for the three service departments. Thus, all service department costs have been fully allocated.

The reciprocal-services method is more accurate than the direct and step-down methods, because it fully accounts for reciprocal services. To make the reciprocal-services method even more accurate, it can be combined with the dual-allocation approach. In this approach, variable and fixed costs are allocated separately. This method is explored in Problem 18–34.

Review Questions

18–1. Distinguish between a service department and a production department. Give an example of the counterpart of a manufacturer's "production" department in a bank.

18–2. Define the term *reciprocal services.*

18–3. Explain briefly the main differences between the direct, step-down, and reciprocal-services methods of service department cost allocation.

18–4. How does the managerial accountant determine the department sequence in the step-down method? How are ties handled?

18–5. Why does the dual-allocation approach improve the resulting cost allocation?

18–6. What potential behavioral problem can result when the dual approach is used?

18–7. Should actual or budgeted service department costs be allocated? Why?

18–8. Explain the difference between two-stage allocation with departmental overhead rates and activity-based costing. Which approach generally results in more accurate product costs?

18–9. Define the following terms: joint production process, joint costs, joint products, split-off point, separable costs, and by-product.

18–10. Briefly explain how to use the physical-units method of joint cost allocation.

18–11. Describe the relative-sales-value method of joint cost allocation.

18–12. Define the term *net realizable value,* and explain how this concept can be used to allocate joint costs.

18–13. Are joint cost allocations useful? If they are, for what purpose?

18–14. For what purpose should the managerial accountant be careful not to use joint cost allocations?

Exercises

Exercise 18–15
Direct Method of Service Department Cost Allocation; Bank
(LO 1)

Aurora National Bank has two service departments, the Personnel Department and the Computing Department. The bank has two other departments that directly service customers, the Deposit Department and the Loan Department. The usage of the two service departments' output for the year is as follows:

	Provider of Service	
User of Service	**Personnel**	**Computing**
Personnel	—	15%
Computing	10%	—
Deposit	60%	50%
Loan	30%	35%

The budgeted costs in the two service departments for the year are as follows:

Personnel	$459,000
Computing	688,500

Required: Use the direct method to allocate the budgeted costs of the Personnel and Computing departments to the Deposit and Loan departments.

Exercise 18–16
Step-Down Method of Service Department Cost Allocation; Bank
(LO 1)

Refer to the data given in the preceding exercise.

Required: Use the step-down method to allocate the budgeted costs of the Personnel and Computing departments to the Deposit and Loan departments. Aurora National Bank allocates the costs of the Personnel Department first.

Exercise 18–17
Service Department Cost Allocation; Use of Internet
(LO 1)

Visit the website of one of the following organizations, or a different organization of your choosing.

Allstate	www.allstate.com
Gallo Winery	www.gallo.com
Mayo Clinic	www.mayo.edu
Sheraton Hotels	www.sheraton.com
Walt Disney Studios	www.disney.com

Required: Read about the organization's activities and operations. Then list three activities that you think the organization would need that would likely be established as service departments. For what purposes would it be relevant to allocate those service department costs to nonservice departments within the organization?

Exercise 18–18
Direct Method of Service Department Cost Allocation; College
(LO 1)

Bay State Community College enrolls students in two departments, Liberal Arts and Sciences. The college also has two service departments, the Library and the Computing Services Department. The usage of these two service departments' output for the year is as follows:

	Provider of Service	
User of Service	**Library**	**Computing Services**
Library	—	20%
Computing Services	—	—
Liberal Arts	60%	30%
Sciences	40%	50%

The budgeted costs in the two service departments for the year are as follows:

Library	$900,000
Computing Services	360,000

Required: Use the direct method to allocate the budgeted costs of the Library and Computing Services Department to the college's Liberal Arts and Sciences departments.

Exercise 18–19
Step-Down Method of Service Department Cost Allocation; College
(LO 1)

Refer to the data given in the preceding exercise.

Required: Use the step-down method to allocate Bay State Community College's service department costs to the Liberal Arts and Sciences departments.

Exercise 18–20
Physical-Units Method; Joint Cost Allocation
(LO 4)

Breakfasttime Cereal Company manufactures two breakfast cereals in a joint process. Cost and quantity information is as follows:

Joint Cost	Cereal	Quantity at Split-Off Point	Sales Price per Kilogram
$90,000	Yummies	12,000 kilograms	$6.00
	Crummies	8,000 kilograms	7.50

Required: Use the physical-units method to allocate the company's joint production cost between Yummies and Crummies.

Exercise 18–21
Relative-Sales-Value Method; Joint Cost Allocation
(LO 4)

Refer to the data given in the preceding exercise.

Required: Use the relative-sales-value method to allocate Breakfasttime Cereal Company's joint production cost between Yummies and Crummies.

Exercise 18–22
Net-Realizable-Value Method; Joint Cost Allocation
(LO 4)

Refer to the data given in Exercise 18–20. Breakfasttime Cereal Company has an opportunity to process its Crummies further into a mulch for ornamental shrubs. The additional processing operation costs $1.50 per kilogram, and the mulch will sell for $10.50 per kilogram.

Required:

1. Should Breakfasttime's management decide to process Crummies into the mulch? Why?
2. Suppose the company does process Crummies into the mulch. Use the net-realizable-value method to allocate the joint production cost between the mulch and the Yummies.

Exercise 18–23
Reciprocal-Services Method; Bank (Appendix)
(LO 1)

Refer to the data given in Exercise 18–15 for Aurora National Bank.

Required: Use the reciprocal-services method to allocate the budgeted costs of the Personnel and Computing departments to the Deposit and Loan departments.

Problems

Problem 18–24
Service Department Cost Allocation
(LO 1)

Glass Creations Company is developing departmental overhead rates based on direct-labor hours for its two production departments, Etching and Finishing. The Etching Department employs 20 people and the Finishing Department employs 80 people. Each person in these two departments works 2,000 hours per year. The production-related overhead costs for the Etching Department are budgeted at $400,000, and the Finishing Department costs are budgeted at $640,000. Two service departments, Maintenance and Computing, directly support the two production departments. These service departments have budgeted costs of $96,000 and $500,000, respectively. The production departments' overhead rates cannot be determined until the service departments' costs are allocated. The following schedule reflects the use of the Maintenance Department's and Computing Department's output by the various departments.

	Using Department			
Service Department	**Maintenance**	**Computing**	**Etching**	**Finishing**
Maintenance (maintenance hours)	0	1,000	1,000	8,000
Computing (minutes)	240,000	0	840,000	120,000

Required:

1. Calculate the overhead rates per direct-labor hour for the Etching Department and the Finishing Department. Use the direct method to allocate service department costs.
2. Calculate the overhead rates per direct-labor hour for the Etching Department and the Finishing Department. Use the step-down method to allocate service department costs. Allocate the Computing Department's costs first.

(CMA, adapted)

Problem 18–25
Direct and Step-Down Methods of Service Department Cost Allocation
(LO 1)

Jacksonville Instrument Company manufactures gauges for construction machinery. The company has two production departments: Machining and Finishing. There are three service departments: Human Resources (HR), Maintenance, and Design. The budgeted costs in Jacksonville Instrument Company's service departments during the year are as follows:

	HR	Maintenance	Design
Variable	$ 50,000	$ 80,000	$ 50,000
Fixed	200,000	150,000	300,000
Total	$250,000	$230,000	$350,000

The usage of these service departments' output during the year just completed is as follows:

Provision of Service Output (in hours of service)			
	Provider of Service		
User of Service	HR	Maintenance	Design
HR	—	—	—
Maintenance	500	—	—
Design	500	500	—
Machining	4,000	3,500	4,500
Finishing	5,000	4,000	1,500
Total	10,000	8,000	6,000

Required:

1. Use the direct method to allocate Jacksonville Instrument Company's service department costs to its production departments.
2. Determine the proper sequence to use in allocating the firm's service department costs by the step-down method.
3. Use the step-down method to allocate the company's service department costs.

Problem 18–26
Dual Allocation of Service Department Costs
(LO 1, 2)

Refer to the data given in the preceding problem. When Jacksonville Instrument Company established its service departments, the following long-run needs were anticipated.

Long-Run Service Needs (in hours of service)			
	Provider of Service		
User of Service	HR	Maintenance	Design
HR	—	—	—
Maintenance	500	—	—
Design	1,000	800	—
Machining	3,500	4,800	4,800
Finishing	5,000	2,400	1,200
Total	10,000	8,000	6,000

Required: Use the dual approach in conjunction with each of the following methods to allocate Jacksonville Instrument Company's service department costs: (1) direct method, and (2) step-down method.

Problem 18–27
Service Department Cost Allocation; Plantwide versus Departmental Overhead Rates; Cost Drivers
(LO 1, 3)

Travelcraft, Inc. manufactures a complete line of fiberglass suitcases and attaché cases. The firm has three manufacturing departments: Molding, Component, and Assembly. There are also two service departments: Power and Maintenance.

The sides of the cases are manufactured in the Molding Department. The frames, hinges, and locks are manufactured in the Component Department. The cases are completed in the Assembly Department. Varying amounts of materials, time, and effort are required for each of the cases. The Power Department and Maintenance Department provide services to the three manufacturing departments.

Travelcraft has always used a plantwide overhead rate. Direct-labor hours are used to assign overhead to products. The predetermined overhead rate is calculated by dividing the company's total estimated overhead by the total estimated direct-labor hours to be worked in the three manufacturing departments.

Karen Mason, director of cost management, has recommended that Travelcraft use departmental overhead rates. The planned operating costs and expected levels of activity for the coming year have been developed by Mason and are presented by department in the following schedules. (All numbers are in thousands.)

	Manufacturing Departments		
	Molding	Component	Assembly
Department activity measures:			
Direct-labor hours	500	2,000	1,500
Machine hours	875	125	-0-

(continues)

Departmental costs:			
Direct material	$24,800	$ 60,000	$ 2,500
Direct labor	7,000	40,000	24,000
Variable overhead	7,000	20,000	33,000
Fixed overhead	35,000	12,400	12,200
Total departmental costs	$73,800	$132,400	$71,700
Use of service departments:			
Maintenance:			
Estimated usage in labor hours for the coming year	90	25	10
Power (in kilowatt-hours):			
Estimated usage for the coming year	360	320	120
Maximum allotted capacity	500	350	150

	Service Departments	
	Power	Maintenance
Departmental activity measures:		
Maximum capacity	1,000 kilowatt-hours	Adjustable
Estimated usage for the coming year	800 kilowatt-hours	125 hours
Departmental costs:		
Materials and supplies	$10,000	$3,000
Variable labor	2,800	4,500
Fixed overhead	24,000	500
Total service department costs	$36,800	$8,000

Required:

1. Calculate the plantwide overhead rate for Travelcraft, Inc. for the coming year using the same method as used in the past.
2. Karen Mason has been asked to develop departmental overhead rates for comparison with the plantwide rate. The following steps are to be followed in developing the departmental rates.
   a. The Maintenance Department costs should be allocated to the three manufacturing departments using the direct method.
   b. The Power Department costs should be allocated to the three manufacturing departments using the dual method combined with the direct method. Fixed costs are to be allocated according to maximum allotted capacity, and variable costs are to be allocated according to planned usage for the coming year.
   c. Calculate departmental overhead rates for the three manufacturing departments using a machine-hour cost driver for the Molding Department and a direct-labor-hour cost driver for the Component and Assembly departments.
3. As Karen Mason's assistant, draft a memo for her to send to Travelcraft's president recommending whether the company should use a plantwide rate or departmental rates to assign overhead to products.

(CMA, adapted)

Problem 18–28
Joint Costs; Allocation and Production Decisions
(LO 4, 5)

Le Monde Company is a manufacturer of chemicals for various purposes. One of the processes used by Le Monde produces HTP–3, a chemical used in hot tubs and swimming pools; PST–4, a chemical used in pesticides; and RJ–5, a product that is sold to fertilizer manufacturers. Le Monde uses the net-realizable-value method to allocate joint production costs. The ratio of output quantities to input quantities of direct material used in the joint process remains consistent from month to month. Le Monde Company uses FIFO (first-in, first-out) in valuing its finished-goods inventories.

Data regarding operations for the month of October are as follows. During this month, Le Monde incurred joint production costs of $1,360,000 in the manufacture of HTP–3, PST–4, and RJ–5.

	HTP–3	PST–4	RJ–5
Finished goods inventory in gallons (October 1)	18,000	52,000	3,000
October sales in gallons	650,000	325,000	150,000
October production in gallons	700,000	350,000	170,000
Additional processing costs	$699,200	$652,800	$48,000
Final sales value per gallon	$3.20	$4.80	$4.00

Required:

1. Determine Le Monde Company's allocation of joint production costs for the month of October. (Carry calculation of relative proportions to four decimal places.)
2. Determine the dollar values of the finished-goods inventories for HTP–3, PST–4, and RJ–5 as of October 31. (Round the cost per gallon to the nearest cent.)
3. Suppose Le Monde Company has a new opportunity to sell PST–4 at the split-off point for $3.04 per gallon. Prepare an analysis showing whether the company should sell PST–4 at the split-off point or continue to process this product further.

(CMA, adapted)

Problem 18–29
Joint Cost Allocation; Missing Data
(LO 4)

Gleed Company manufactures products Alpha, Beta, and Gamma from a joint process. Production, sales, and cost data for July follow.

	Alpha	Beta	Gamma	Total
Units produced	4,000	2,000	1,000	7,000
Joint cost allocation	$46,800	?	?	$78,000
Sales value at split-off	?	?	$19,500	$130,000
Additional costs if processed further	$9,100	$6,500	$3,900	$19,500
Sales value if processed further	$91,000	$32,500	$26,000	$149,500

Required:

1. Assuming that joint costs are allocated using the relative-sales-value method, what were the joint costs allocated to products Beta and Gamma?
2. Assuming that joint costs are allocated using the relative-sales-value method, what was the sales value at split-off for product Alpha?
3. Use the net-realizable-value method to allocate the joint production costs to the three products.

(CPA, adapted)

Problem 18–30
Joint Costs
(LO 4, 5)

Allegheny River Sawmill manufactures two lumber products from a joint milling process. The two products developed are mine support braces (MSB) and unseasoned commercial building lumber (CBL). A standard production run incurs joint costs of $750,000 and results in 60,000 units of MSB and 90,000 units of CBL. Each MSB sells for $5, and each unit of CBL sells for $10.

Required:

1. Calculate the amount of joint cost allocated to commercial building lumber (CBL) on a physical-units basis.
2. Calculate the amount of joint cost allocated to the mine support braces (MSB) on a relative-sales-value basis.
3. Assume the commercial building lumber is not marketable at split-off but must be further planed and sized at a cost of $1,000,000 per production run. During this process, 10,000 units are unavoidably lost; these spoiled units have no value. The remaining units of commercial building lumber are saleable at $25.00 per unit. The mine support braces, although saleable immediately at the split-off point, are coated with a tarlike preservative that costs $250,000 per production run. The braces are then sold for $12.50 each. Using the net-realizable-value basis, compute the completed cost assigned to each unit of commercial building lumber.
4. If Allegheny River Sawmill chose not to process the mine support braces beyond the split-off point, the contribution from the joint milling process would increase or decrease by what amount?
5. Did you use the joint cost allocation results in answering requirement (4)? If so, how? Why did you use or not use the allocation results?

(CMA, adapted)

Problem 18–31
Joint Products; Sell or Process Further
(LO 4, 5)

Wyalusing Chemicals uses a joint process to produce MJ-4, a chemical used in the manufacture of paints and varnishes; HD-10, a chemical used in household cleaning products; and FT-5, a by-product that is sold to fertilizer manufacturers. Joint production costs are allocated to the main products on the basis of net realizable value. The by-product is inventoried at its net realizable value, and this value is used to reduce the joint production cost before allocation to the main products.

During the month of November, Wyalusing incurred joint production costs of $3,136,000. Data regarding Wyalusing's November operations are as follows:

	MJ-4	HD-10	FT-5
November production in gallons	600,000	320,000	85,000
Sales value per gallon at split-off	None	$6.00	$1.80*
Separable processing cost	$1,440,000	$1,840,000	None
Final sales value per gallon	$8.00	$12.75	None
Finished-goods inventory in gallons on November 30 (all produced during November)	9,000	26,000	1,500

*Disposal costs of $.20 per gallon will be incurred in order to sell the by-product.

Required:

1. Define the terms *joint costs* and *split-off point.*
2. Determine the dollar values of Wyalusing Chemicals' finished-goods inventories on November 30 for MJ-4 and HD-10.
3. Wyalusing Chemicals has an opportunity to sell HD-10 for its sales value at the split-off point. Determine if management should sell HD-10 at the split-off point or continue to process it further.

(CPA, adapted)

Problem 18–32
Joint Costs; Allocation and Production Decisions; Ethics
(LO 4, 5)

Chemco, Inc. manufactures two products out of a joint process: Compod and Ultrasene. The joint costs incurred are $750,000 for a standard production run that generates 120,000 gallons of Compod and 80,000 gallons of Ultrasene. Compod sells for $6.00 per gallon while Ultrasene sells for $9.75 per gallon.

Required:

1. If there are no additional processing costs incurred after the split-off point, calculate the amount of joint cost of each production run allocated to Compod on a physical-units basis.
2. If there are no additional processing costs incurred after the split-off point, calculate the amount of joint cost of each production run allocated to Ultrasene on a relative-sales-value basis.
3. Suppose the following additional processing costs are required beyond the split-off point in order to obtain Compod and Ultrasene: $.30 per gallon for Compod and $3.30 per gallon for Ultrasene.
   a. Calculate the amount of joint cost of each production run allocated to Ultrasene on a physical-units basis.
   b. Calculate the amount of joint cost of each production run allocated to Compod on a net-realizable-value basis.
4. Assuming the same data as in requirement (3), suppose Compod can be processed further into a product called Compodalene, at an additional cost of $1.20 per gallon. Compodalene will be sold for $7.80 per gallon by independent distributors. The distributors' commission will be 10% of the sales price. Should Chemco sell Compod or Compodalene?
5. Independent of your answer to requirement (4), suppose Christine Dalton, the assistant controller, has completed an analysis showing that Compod should not be processed further into Compodalene. Before presenting her analysis to top management, however, she got a visit from Jack Turner, Chemco's director of research. Turner was upset upon learning that Compodalene, a product he had personally developed, would not be manufactured.

   Turner: "The company's making a big mistake if it passes up this opportunity. Compodalene will be a big seller and get us into new markets."

   Dalton: "But the analysis shows that we'd be losing money on every gallon of Compod that we process further."

   Turner: "I know, Christine, but that's a temporary problem. Eventually, we'll bring down the cost of making Compodalene."

   Dalton: "Can you find me some estimates on the cost reduction you expect?"

Turner: "I don't have a crystal ball, Christine. Look, if you could just fudge the numbers a little bit to help me get approval to produce some Compodalene, I can get this product off the ground. I know the cost reduction will come."

Comment on the ethical issues in this scenario. What should Christine Dalton do?

6. Assume the same data as given in requirements (3) and (4). The industrial chemical industry has experienced a downturn, which has left Chemco with idle capacity. Suppose Chemco can sell only half of the Compod made in each production run, but the remainder could be sold as Compodalene. Should Chemco process the remaining Compod into Compodalene?

(CMA, adapted)

Problem 18–33
Reciprocal-Service Method (Appendix)
(LO 1)

Refer to the data given in Problem 18–24 for Glass Creations Company.

Required:

1. Calculate the overhead rates per direct-labor hour for the Etching Department and the Finishing Department. Use the reciprocal-services method to allocate service department costs.
2. Which of the three methods of service department cost allocation results in the most accurate overhead rates? Why?

Problem 18–34
Reciprocal-Services Method; Dual Allocation (Appendix)
(LO 1, 2)

Refer to the data for Riverside Clinic given in Exhibits 18–2 and 18–5.

Required: Use the reciprocal-services method in combination with the dual-allocation approach to allocate Riverside's service department costs. Hint: You will need to apply the reciprocal-services method twice. First, allocate the three service departments' variable costs using the short-run usage proportions in Exhibit 18–2 (panel A). Second, allocate the three service departments' fixed costs using the long-run average usage proportions in Exhibit 18–5. Finally, add the variable costs and fixed costs allocated to each direct-patient-care department.

Cases

Case 18–35
Joint Cost Allocation; By-Product
(LO 4)

Tropics Fruit Company, based on Oahu, grows, processes, cans, and sells three main pineapple products: sliced, crushed, and juice. The outside skin is cut off in the Cutting Department and processed as animal feed. The feed is treated as a by-product. The company's production process is as follows:

- Pineapples first are processed in the Cutting Department. The pineapples are washed and the outside skin is cut away. Then the pineapples are cored and trimmed for slicing. The three main products (sliced, crushed, juice) and the by-product (animal feed) are recognizable after processing in the Cutting Department. Each product then is transferred to a separate department for final processing.
- The trimmed pineapples are sent to the Slicing Department, where the pineapples are sliced and canned. Any juice generated during the slicing operation is packed in the cans with the slices.
- The pieces of pineapple trimmed from the fruit are diced and canned in the Crushing Department. Again, the juice generated during this operation is packed in the can with the crushed pineapple.
- The core and surplus pineapple generated from the Cutting Department are pulverized into a liquid in the Juicing Department. There is an evaporation loss equal to 8 percent of the weight of the good output produced in this department which occurs as the juices are heated.
- The outside skin is chopped into animal feed in the Feed Department.

Tropics Fruit Company uses the net-realizable-value method to assign the costs of the joint process to its main products. The net realizable value of the by-product is subtracted from the joint cost before the allocation.

A total of 540,000 pounds were entered into the Cutting Department during June. The following schedule shows the costs incurred in each department, the proportion by weight transferred to the four final processing departments, and the selling price of each end product.

Processing Data and Costs for June

Department	Costs Incurred	Proportion of Product by Weight Transferred to Departments	Selling Price per Pound of Final Product
Cutting	$240,000	—	None
Slicing	18,800	35%	$1.20
Crushing	42,320	28	1.10
Juicing	13,000	27	.60
Animal feed	2,800	10	.20
Total	$316,920	100%	

Required: Compute each of the following amounts.

1. The number of pounds of pineapple that result as output for pineapple slices, crushed pineapple, pineapple juice, and animal feed.
2. The net realizable value at the split-off point of the three main products.
3. The amount of the cost of the Cutting Department allocated to each of the three main products.

(CMA, adapted)

Case 18–36
Comprehensive Case on Joint Cost Allocation
(LO 4, 5)

Edmonton Chemical Company manufactures two industrial chemical products in a joint process. In May, 10,000 gallons of input costing $180,000 were processed at a cost of $450,000. The joint process resulted in 8,000 pounds of Resoline and 2,000 pounds of Krypto. Resoline sells for $75 per pound and Krypto sells for $150 per pound. Management generally processes each of these chemicals further in separable processes to produce more refined chemical products. Resoline is processed separately at a cost of $15 per pound. The resulting product, Resolite, sells for $105 per pound. Krypto is processed separately at a cost of $45 per pound. The resulting product, Kryptite, sells for $285 per pound.

Required:

1. Draw a diagram similar to Exhibit 18–8 to depict Edmonton Chemical Company's joint production process.
2. Allocate the company's joint production costs for May using:
   a. The physical-units method.
   b. The relative-sales-value method.
   c. The net-realizable-value method.
3. Edmonton's management is considering an opportunity to process Kryptite further into a new product called Omega. The separable processing will cost $120 per pound. Packaging costs for Omega are projected to be $18 per pound, and the anticipated sales price is $390 per pound. Should Kryptite be processed further into Omega? Why?
4. In answering requirement (3), did you use your joint cost allocation from requirement (2)? If so, how did you use it?

Current Issues in Managerial Accounting

Issue 18–37
Service Department Costs

"Norfolk Southern Is Revamping Its Rail Freight Network," ***The Wall Street Journal,*** **March 28, 2002, p. B3, Daniel Machalaba.**

Overview

Norfolk Southern "implements new train schedules and bypasses yards to reduce delays."

Suggested Discussion Questions

The scheduling operation is a service activity at Norfolk Southern. How did the company reduce the costs of its rail operations? How would you allocate the scheduling department's costs to its rail transportation services?

Appendix I

Compound Interest and the Concept of Present Value

After completing this appendix, you should be able to:

1 Explain the importance of the time value of money in capital-budgeting decisions.

2 Compute the future value and present value of cash flows occurring over several time periods.

Before we can study the methods used to make capital-budgeting decisions, we must examine the basic tools used in those methods. The fundamental concept in a capital-budgeting decision analysis is the *time value* of money. Would you rather receive a $100 gift check from a relative today, or would you rather receive a letter promising the $100 in a year? Most of us would rather have the cash now. There are two possible reasons for this attitude. First, if we receive the money today, we can spend it on that new sweater now instead of waiting a year. Second, as an alternative strategy, we can invest the $100 received today at 10 percent interest. Then, at the end of one year, we will have $110. Thus, there is a time value associated with money. A $100 cash flow today is not the same as a $100 cash flow in 1 year, 2 years, or 10 years.

LO 1

Explain the importance of the time value of money in capital-budgeting decisions.

Topic I–1

Compound Interest Suppose you invest $100 today (time 0) at 10 percent interest for one year. How much will you have after one year? The answer is $110, as the following analysis shows.

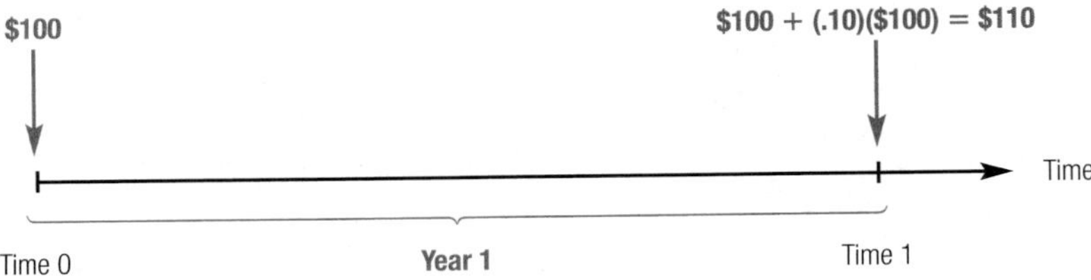

The $110 at time 1 (end of one year) is composed of two parts, as shown below.

LO 2

Compute the future value and present value of cash flows occurring over several time periods.

Principal, time 0 amount	$100
Interest earned during year 1 (.10 × $100)	10
Amount at time 1	$110

Thus, the $110 at time 1 consists of the $100 at time 0, called the **principal,** plus the $10 of interest earned during the year.

Now suppose you leave your $110 invested during the second year. How much will you have at the end of two years? As the following analysis shows, the answer is $121.

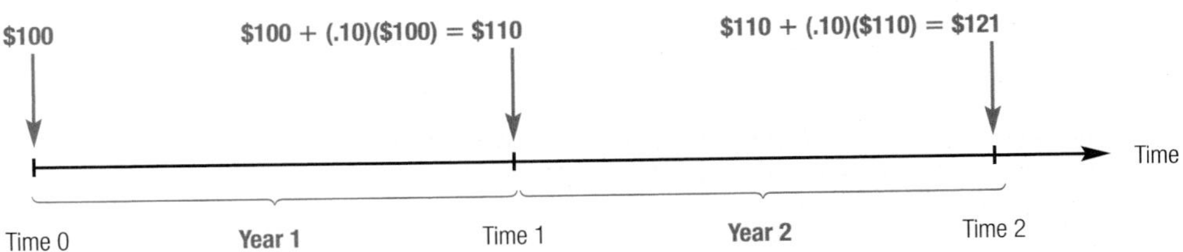

We can break down the $121 at time 2 into two parts as follows:

Amount at time 1	$110
Interest earned during year 2 (.10 × $110)	11
Amount at time 2	$121

Notice that you earned more interest in year 2 ($11) than you earned in year 1 ($10). Why? During year 2, you earned 10 percent interest on the original principal of $100 *and* you earned 10 percent interest on the year 1 interest of $10. Interest earned on prior periods' interest is called **compound interest.** Exhibit I–1 shows how your invested funds grow over the five-year period of the investment. As the exhibit shows, the **future value** of your initial $100 investment is $161.05 after five years.

As the number of years in an investment increases, it becomes more cumbersome to compute the future value of the investment using the method in Exhibit I–1.

Exhibit I–1
Compound Interest and Future Value

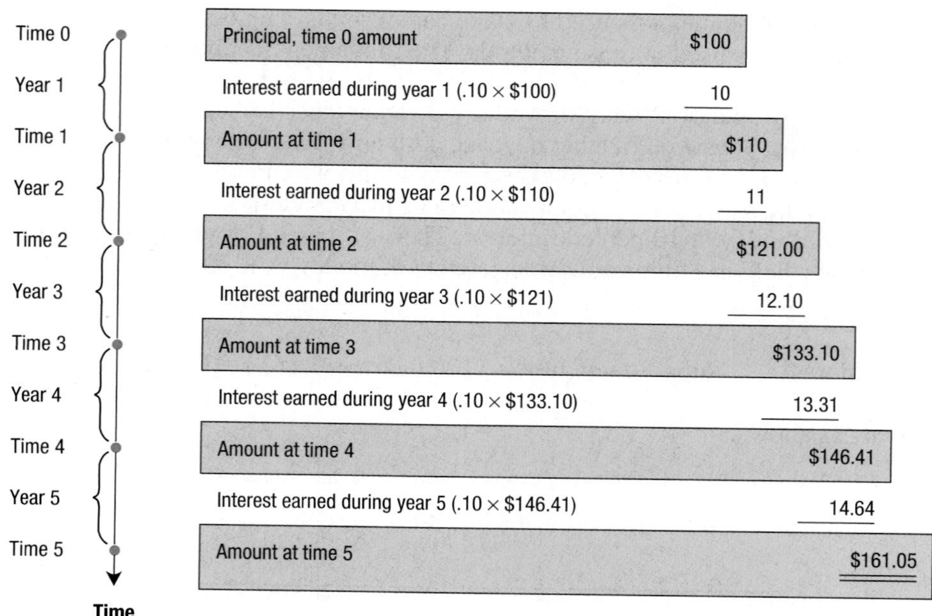

Fortunately, the simple formula shown below may be used to compute the future value of any investment.

$$F_n = P(1 + r)^n \qquad (1)$$

where P denotes principal
r denotes interest rate per year
n denotes number of years

Using formula (1) to compute the future value after five years of your $100 investment, we have the following computation.

$$\begin{aligned} F_n &= P(1 + r)^n \\ &= \$100(1 + .10)^5 \\ &= \$100(1.6105) = \$161.05 \end{aligned}$$

The value of $(1 + r)^n$ is called the **accumulation factor.** The values of $(1 + r)^n$, for various combinations of r and n, are tabulated in Table I of Appendix A to Chapter 16, which appears on page 707.

Use formula (1) and the tabulated values in Table I to compute the future value after 10 years of an $800 investment that earns interest at the rate of 12 percent per year.[1]

Present Value In the discussion above, we computed the future value of an investment when the original principal is known. Now consider a slightly different problem. Suppose you know how much money you want to accumulate at the end of a five-year investment. Your problem is to determine how much your initial investment needs to be in order to accumulate the desired amount in five years. To solve this problem, we start with formula (1):

$$F_n = P(1 + r)^n$$

[1]Using formula (1): $F = \$800\,(1 + .12)^{10}$. From Table I, $(1 + .12)^{10} = 3.106$. (Note that the values in Table I are rounded.) Thus, the future value of the investment is ($800)(3.106) = $2,484.80. Compound interest will more than triple the original $800 investment in 10 years.

Now divide each side of the preceding equation by $(1 + r)^n$

$$P = F_n \left(\frac{1}{(1 + r)^n}\right) \tag{2}$$

In formula (2), P denotes what is commonly referred to as the **present value** of the cash flow F_n, which occurs after n years when the interest rate is r.

Let's try out formula (2) on your investment problem, which we analyzed in Exhibit I–1. Suppose you did not know the value of the initial investment required if you want to accumulate \$161.05 at the end of five years in an investment that earns 10 percent per year. We can determine the present value of the investment as follows:

$$\begin{aligned} P &= F_n \left(\frac{1}{(1 + r)^n}\right) \\ &= \$161.05 \left(\frac{1}{(1 + .10)^5}\right) \\ &= \$161.05(.6209) = \$100 \end{aligned}$$

Thus, as we knew already, you must invest \$100 now in order to accumulate \$161.05 after five years in an investment earning 10 percent per year. The *present value* of \$100 and the *future value* of \$161.05 at time 5 are *economically equivalent,* given that the annual interest rate is 10 percent. If you are planning to invest the \$100 received now, then you should be indifferent between receiving the present value of \$100 now or receiving the future value of \$161.05 at the end of five years.

When we used formula (2) to compute the present value of the \$161.05 cash flow at time 5, we used a process called *discounting.* The interest rate used when we discount a future cash flow to compute its present value is called the **discount rate.** The value of $1/(1 + r)^n$, which appears in formula (2), is called the *discount factor.* Discount factors, for various combinations of r and n, are tabulated in Table III of Appendix A to Chapter 16.

Suppose you want to accumulate \$18,000 to buy a new car in four years, and you can earn interest at the rate of 8 percent per year on an investment you make now. How much do you need to invest now? Use formula (2) and the discount factors in Table III of Appendix A to Chapter 16 (p. 708) to compute the present value of the required \$18,000 amount needed at the end of four years.[2]

Present Value of a Cash-Flow Series The present-value problem we just solved involved only a single future cash flow. Now consider a slightly different problem. Suppose you just won \$5,000 in the state lottery. You want to spend some of the cash now, but you have decided to save enough to rent a beach condominium during spring break of each of the next three years. You would like to deposit enough in a bank account now so that you can withdraw \$1,000 from the account at the end of each of the next three years. The money in the bank account will earn 8 percent per year. The question, then, is how much do you need to deposit? Another way of asking the same question is, what is the *present value* of a series of three \$1,000 cash flows at the end of each of the next three years, given that the discount rate is 8 percent?

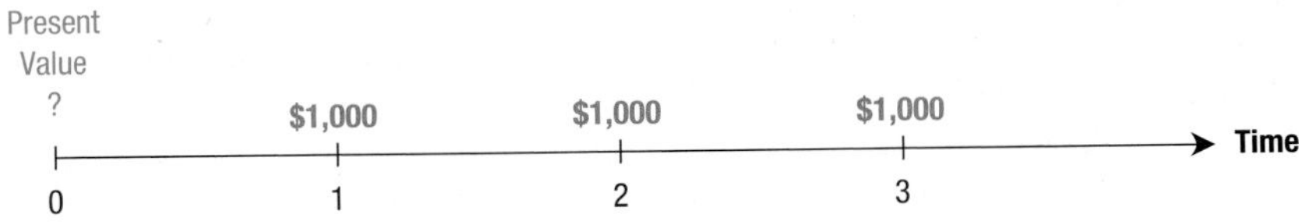

[2]Using formula (2): $P = \$18{,}000 \times [1/(1 + .08)^4]$. From Table III, $1/(1 + .08)^4 = .735$. (Note that the values in Table III are rounded.) Thus, the present value of the required \$18,000 amount is (\$18,000)(.735) = \$13,230. An investment of \$13,230 made now, earning annual interest at 8 percent, will accumulate to \$18,000 at the end of four years.

Exhibit I–2
Present Value of a Series of Cash Flows

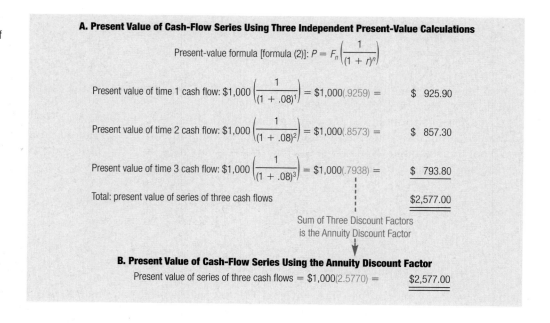

A. Present Value of Cash-Flow Series Using Three Independent Present-Value Calculations

Present-value formula [formula (2)]: $P = F_n\left(\frac{1}{(1+r)^n}\right)$

Present value of time 1 cash flow: $\$1,000\left(\frac{1}{(1+.08)^1}\right) = \$1,000(.9259) =$		\$ 925.90
Present value of time 2 cash flow: $\$1,000\left(\frac{1}{(1+.08)^2}\right) = \$1,000(.8573) =$		\$ 857.30
Present value of time 3 cash flow: $\$1,000\left(\frac{1}{(1+.08)^3}\right) = \$1,000(.7938) =$		\$ 793.80
Total: present value of series of three cash flows		\$2,577.00

Sum of Three Discount Factors is the Annuity Discount Factor

B. Present Value of Cash-Flow Series Using the Annuity Discount Factor

Present value of series of three cash flows = \$1,000(2.5770) = \$2,577.00

One way to figure out the answer to the question is to compute the present value of each of the three \$1,000 cash flows and add the three present-value amounts. We can use formula (2) for these calculations, as shown in panel A of Exhibit I–2. Notice that the present value of each of the \$1,000 cash flows is different, because the timing of the cash flows is different. The earlier the cash flow will occur, the higher is its present value.

Examine panel A of Exhibit I–2 carefully. We obtained the \$2,577 total present value by adding three present-value amounts. Each of these amounts is the result of multiplying \$1,000 by a discount factor. Notice that we can obtain the same final result by adding the three discount factors first, and then multiplying by \$1,000. This approach is taken in panel B of Exhibit I–2. The sum of the three discount factors is called an *annuity discount factor,* because a series of equivalent cash flows is called an **annuity.** Annuity discount factors for various combinations of r and n are tabulated in Table IV of Appendix A to Chapter 16 (p. 708).

Now let's verify that \$2,577 is the right amount to finance your three spring-break vacations. Exhibit I–3 shows how your bank account will change over the three-year period as you earn interest and then withdraw \$1,000 each year.

Future Value of a Cash-Flow Series To complete our discussion of present-value and future-value concepts, let's consider the series of \$1,000 condo rental payments from the condo owner's perspective. Suppose the owner invests each \$1,000 rental payment in a bank account that pays 8 percent interest per year. How much will the condo owner accumulate at the end of the three-year period? An equivalent question is, What is the future value of the three-year series of \$1,000 cash flows, given an annual interest rate of 8 percent? Exhibit I–4 answers the question in two ways. In panel A of the exhibit, three separate future-value calculations are made using formula (1). Notice that the \$1,000 cash flow at time 1 is multiplied by $(1.08)^2$, since it has two years to earn interest. The \$1,000 cash flow at time 2 has only one year to earn interest, and the time 3 cash flow has no time to earn interest.

In panel B of the exhibit, the three-year *annuity accumulation factor* is used. This factor is the sum of the three accumulation factors used in panel A of the exhibit. The annuity accumulation factors for various combinations of r and n are tabulated in Table II of Appendix A to Chapter 16 (p. 707).

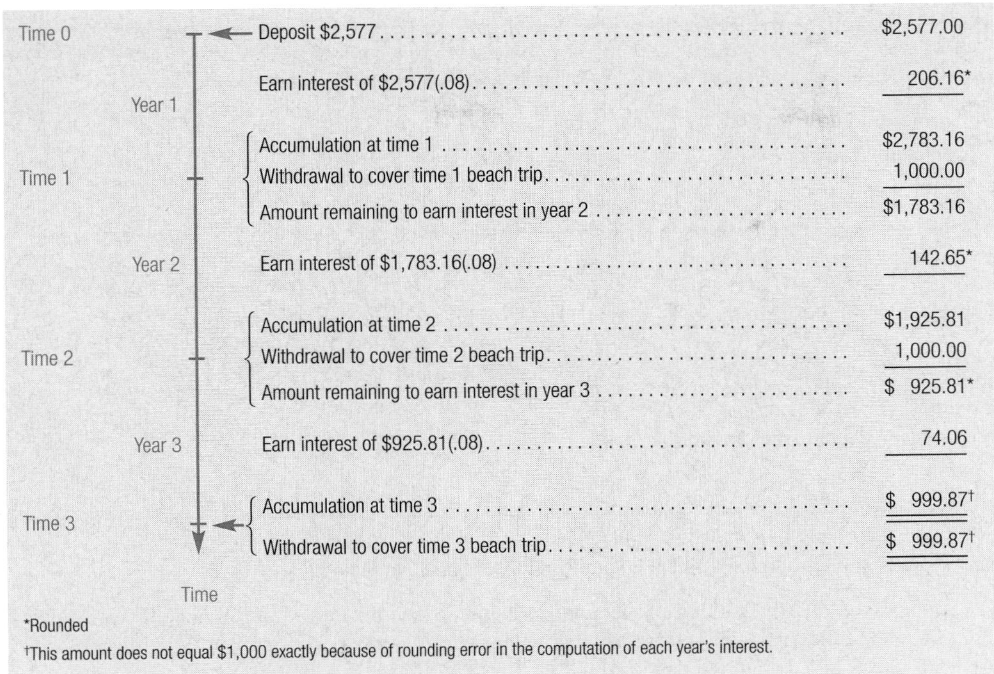

Time 0		Deposit $2,577	$2,577.00
	Year 1	Earn interest of $2,577(.08)	206.16*
Time 1		Accumulation at time 1	$2,783.16
		Withdrawal to cover time 1 beach trip	1,000.00
		Amount remaining to earn interest in year 2	$1,783.16
	Year 2	Earn interest of $1,783.16(.08)	142.65*
Time 2		Accumulation at time 2	$1,925.81
		Withdrawal to cover time 2 beach trip	1,000.00
		Amount remaining to earn interest in year 3	$ 925.81*
	Year 3	Earn interest of $925.81(.08)	74.06
Time 3		Accumulation at time 3	$ 999.87†
		Withdrawal to cover time 3 beach trip	$ 999.87†

Time

*Rounded

†This amount does not equal $1,000 exactly because of rounding error in the computation of each year's interest.

Exhibit I–3
Verification of Present-Value Calculation for Cash-Flow Series

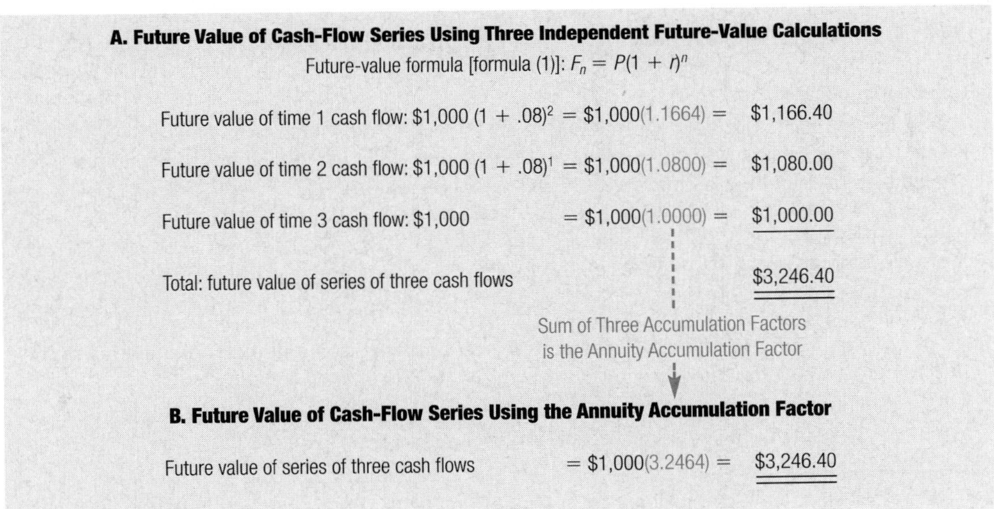

A. Future Value of Cash-Flow Series Using Three Independent Future-Value Calculations

Future-value formula [formula (1)]: $F_n = P(1 + r)^n$

Future value of time 1 cash flow: $1,000 $(1 + .08)^2$	= $1,000(1.1664) =	$1,166.40
Future value of time 2 cash flow: $1,000 $(1 + .08)^1$	= $1,000(1.0800) =	$1,080.00
Future value of time 3 cash flow: $1,000	= $1,000(1.0000) =	$1,000.00
Total: future value of series of three cash flows		$3,246.40

Sum of Three Accumulation Factors is the Annuity Accumulation Factor

B. Future Value of Cash-Flow Series Using the Annuity Accumulation Factor

Future value of series of three cash flows	= $1,000(3.2464) =	$3,246.40

Exhibit I–4
Future Value of a Series of Cash Flows

Using the Tables Correctly When using the tables in Appendix A to Chapter 16 (pp. 707, 708) to solve future-value and present-value problems, be sure to select the correct table. Table I is used to find the *future value* of a *single* cash flow, and Table III is used to find the *present value* of a *single* cash flow. Table II is used in finding the *future value* of a *series* of identical cash flows; Table IV is used in finding the *present value* of a *series* of identical cash flows. Be careful not to confuse future value with present value or to confuse a single cash flow with a series of identical cash flows.

If you have a calculator that will exponentiate (raise a number to a power), you can forget the tables altogether. Just use the pertinent formula and compute the appropriate factor yourself.

Key Terms

For each term's definition, refer to the indicated page or turn to the glossary at the end of the text.

accumulation factor, 778
annuity, 780
compound interest, 777
discount rate, 779
future value, 777
present value, 779
principal, 777

Review Questions

I–1. What is meant by the term *compound interest?*

I–2. Explain in words the following future-value formula: $F_n = P(1 + r)^n$.

I–3. Define the term *present value.*

I–4. "The greater the discount rate, the greater the present value of a future cash flow." True or false? Explain your answer.

I–5. "If the interest rate is 10 percent, a present value of $100 and a future value of $161.10 at the end of five years are *economically equivalent.*" Explain.

I–6. What is an *annuity?*

Exercises

Exercise I-7
Future Value and Present Value
(LO 1, 2)

Answer each of the following independent questions. Ignore personal income taxes.

1. Suppose you invest $2,500 in an account bearing interest at the rate of 14 percent per year. What will be the future value of your investment in six years?
2. Your best friend won the state lottery and has offered to give you $10,000 in five years, after he has made his first million dollars. You figure that if you had the money today, you could invest it at 12 percent annual interest. What is the present value of your friend's future gift?
3. In four years, you would like to buy a small cabin in the mountains. You estimate that the property will cost you $52,500 when you are ready to buy. How much money would you need to invest each year in an account bearing interest at the rate of 6 percent per year in order to accumulate the $52,500 purchase price?
4. You have estimated that your educational expenses over the next three years will be $13,000 per year. How much money do you need in your account now in order to withdraw the required amount each year? Your account bears interest at 10 percent per year.

Exercise I-8
Continuation of Preceding Exercise
(LO 1, 2)

Refer to the answers given for the preceding exercise.

Required:

1. Refer to requirement (1) of the preceding exercise. Prepare a display similar to Exhibit I–1 to show how your accumulation grows each year to equal $5,487.50 after six years.
2. Refer to requirement (4) of the preceding exercise. Prepare a display similar to Exhibit I–3 to verify that $32,331 is the amount you need to fund your educational expenses.

Exercise I-9
Future Value and Present Value
(LO 1, 2)

You plan to retire at age 40 after a highly successful but short career. You would like to accumulate enough money by age 40 to withdraw $225,000 per year for 40 years. You plan to pay into your account 15 equal installments beginning when you are 25 and ending when you are 39. Your account bears interest of 12 percent per year.

Required:

1. How much do you need to accumulate in your account by the time you retire?
2. How much do you need to pay into your account in each of the 15 equal installments?
3. Is this a future-value problem or a present-value problem? Explain.

References for Management Accountants: In Their Own Words

Chapter One

(1a)* Gary Siegel and James E. Sorensen, principal investigators for the Gary Siegel Organization, *Counting More, Counting Less: Transformations in the Management Accounting Profession* (Montvale, NJ: Institute of Management Accountants, 1999).

(1b) Ibid.

(1c) Ibid.

(1d) Ibid.

(1e) Ibid.

(1f) William Fouvielle an Lawrence P. Carr, "Gaining Strategic Alignment: Making Scorecards Work," *Management Accounting Quarterly,* Fall 2001, p. 8.

(1g) Gary Siegel and James E. Sorensen, principal investigators for the Gary Siegel Organization, *Counting More, Counting Less: Transformations in the Management Accounting Profession* (Montvale, NJ: Institute of Management Accountants, 1999).

(1h) Ibid.

(1i) Ibid.

(1j) Ibid.

(1k) Ibid.

Chapter Two

(2a) Gary Siegel and James E. Sorensen, principal investigators for the Gary Siegel Organization, *Counting More, Counting Less: Transformations in the Management Accounting Profession* (Montvale, NJ: Institute of Management Accountants, 1999).

(2b) Gary Siegel, project director, *The Practice Analysis of Management Accounting* (Montvale, NJ: Institute Of Management Accountants, 1996) pp. 17, 18.

(2c) Ibid., p. 14.

(2d) Ibid., p. 19.

(2e) *Activity-Based Management: Part I,* a management education video (Boston: President and Fellows of Harvard College, 1993).

(2f) Gary Siegel, project director, *The Practice Analysis of Management Accounting* (Montvale, NJ: Institute of Management Accountants, 1996), p. 18.

(2g) Interview with a Delta Air Lines accountant conducted during research by the author.

(2h) Gary Siegel and James E. Sorensen, principal investigators for the Gary Siegel Organization, *Counting More, Counting Less: Transformations in the Management Accounting Profession* (Montvale, NJ: Institute of Management Accountants, 1999).

Chapter Three

(3a) *The Management Accounting Video,* a management education video (New York: McGraw-Hill, 1997).

(3b) Gary Siegel and James E. Sorensen, principal investigators for the Gary Siegel Organization, *Counting More, Counting Less: Transformations in the Management Accounting Profession* (Montvale, NJ: Institute of Management Accountants, 1999).

(3c) *The Management Accounting Video,* a management education video (New York: McGraw-Hill, 1997). *Note:* Since this video was made MICRUS was sold to Phillips.

(3d) Interview with a DaimlerChrysler accountant conducted during research by the author.

(3e) Interview with an accountant for The Walt Disney Company conducted during research by the author.

(3f) Interview with a DaimlerChrysler accountant conducted during research by the author.

(3g) Gary Siegel, project director, *The Practice Analysis of Management Accounting* (Montvale, NJ: Institute of Management Accountants, 1996), p. 17.

(3h) Interview with a Cornell University accountant conducted during research by the author.

(3i) *The Management Accounting Video,* a management education video (New York: McGraw-Hill, 1997).

(3j) *Activity-Based Management: Part II,* a management education video (Boston: The President and Fellows of Harvard College, 1993).

Chapter Four

(4a) Gary Siegel and James E. Sorensen, principal investigators for the Gary Siegel Organization, *Counting More, Counting Less: Transformations in the Management Accounting Profession* (Montvale, NJ: Institute of Management Accountants, 1999).

(4b) Steve Player and Carol Cobble, *Cornerstones of Decision Making: Profiles of Enterprise ABM* (Greensboro, NC: Oakhill Press, 1999), p. 161.

(4c) Ibid., p. 12.

(4d) Ibid., p. 168.

Chapter Five

(5a) *Activity-Based Management: Part I,* a management education video (Boston: The President and Fellows of Harvard College, 1993).

(5b) Joyce R. Ochs and Kenneth L. Parkinson, "Moving to Activity-Based Cost Analysis," *Business Finance* 5, no. 11 (November 1999), p. 101.

(5c) Steve Player and Carol Cobble, *Cornerstones of Decision Making: Profiles of Enterprise ABM* (Greensboro, NC: Oakhill Press, 1999), p. 167.

(5d) Ibid., p. 164.

(5e) Tad Leahy, "The A to Z of ABC Dictionaries," *Business Finance* 5, no. 12 (December 1999), p. 82.

(5f) Steve Player and Carol Cobble, *Cornerstones of Decision Making: Profiles of Enterprise ABM* (Greensboro, NC: Oakhill Press, 1999), p. 119.

(5g) *The Management Accounting Video,* a management education video (New York: McGraw-Hill, 1997).

(5h) Steve Player and Carol Cobble, *Cornerstones of Decision Making: Profiles of Enterprise ABM* (Greensboro, NC: Oakhill Press, 1999), p. 79.

*The references are organized by chapter. Thus, reference (1a) relates to the first quote in Chapter 1, and so forth.

Chapter Six

(6a) Gary Siegel and James E. Sorensen, principal investigators for the Gary Siegel Organization, *Counting More, Counting Less: Transformations in the Management Accounting Profession* (Montvale, NJ: Institute of Management Accountants, 1999).

(6b) Ibid.

(6c) Ibid.

(6d) Steve Player and Carol Cobble, *Cornerstones of Decision Making: Profiles of Enterprise ABM* (Greensboro, NC: Oakhill Press, 1999), p. 151.

(6e) Ibid., p. 226.

(6f) Scott Smith, in Steve Player and Carol Cobble, *Cornerstones of Decision Making: Profiles of Enterprise ABM* (Greensboro, NC: Oakhill Press, 1999), p. 187.

Chapter Seven

(7a) Paulo Salgado, Margarida Bajanca, and Nuno Belo, in Steve Player and Carol Cobble, *Cornerstones of Decision Making: Profiles of Enterprise ABM* (Greensboro, NC: Oakhill Press, 1999), p. 172.

(7b) Steve Player and Carol Cobble, *Cornerstones of Decision Making: Profiles of Enterprise ABM* (Greensboro, NC: Oakhill Press, 1999), p. 214.

(7c) Interview with a Ford Motor Company accountant conducted during research by the author.

(7d) Steve Player and Carol Cobble, *Cornerstones of Decision Making: Profiles of Enterprise ABM* (Greensboro, NC: Oakhill Press, 1999), p. 78.

(7e) Interview with a Cornell University accountant conducted during research by the author.

(7f) Gary Siegel, project director, *The Practice Analysis of Management Accounting* (Montvale, NJ: Institute of Management Accountants, 1996), p. 18.

Chapter Eight

(8a) Gary Siegel and James E. Sorensen, principal investigators for the Gary Siegel Organization, *Counting More, Counting Less: Transformations in the Management Accounting Profession* (Montvale, NJ: Institute of Management Accountants, 1999).

(8b) Interview with a Cornell University accountant conducted during research by the author.

(8c) Interview with a Delta Air Lines accountant conducted during research by the author.

(8d) Gary Siegel and James E. Sorensen, principal investigators for the Gary Siegel Organization, *Counting More, Counting Less: Transformations in the Management Accounting Profession* (Montvale, NJ: Institute of Management Accountants, 1999).

(8e) Steve Player and Carol Cobble, *Cornerstones of Decision Making: Profiles of Enterprise ABM* (Greensboro, NC: Oakhill Press, 1999), p. 78.

Chapter Nine

(9a) *The Management Accounting Video,* a management education video (New York: McGraw-Hill, 1997). Best Foods introduced several well-known brands, such as Skippy peanut butter, Hellman's mayonnaise, and Thomas' English Muffins. Best Foods has been acquired by Unilever.

(9b) Ibid.

(9c) Gary Siegel and James E. Sorensen, principal investigators for the Gary Siegel Organization, *Counting More, Counting Less: Transformations in the Management Accounting Profession* (Montvale, NJ: Institute of Management Accountants, 1999).

(9d) Jay Collins, "Advanced Use of ABM: Using ABC for Target Costing, Activity-Based Budgeting, and Benchmarking," in *Activity-Based Management: Arthur Andersen's Lessons from the ABM Battlefield,* Steve Player and David E. Keys, ed. (New York: John Wiley & Sons, 1999), p. 153.

(9e) James A. Brimson and John Antos, *Driving Value Using Activity-Based Budgeting* (New York: John Wiley & Sons, 1999), p. 10.

(9f) Steve Hornyak, "Budgeting Made Easy," *Management Accounting* 80, no. 4, pp. 18–23.

Chapter Ten

(10a) *The Management Accounting Video,* a management education video (New York: McGraw-Hill, 1997).

(10b) Gary Siegel and James E. Sorensen, principal investigators for the Gary Siegel Organization, *Counting More, Counting Less: Transformations in the Management Accounting Profession* (Montvale, NJ: Institute of Management Accountants, 1999).

(10c) *The Management Accounting Video,* a management education video (New York: McGraw-Hill, 1997).

(10d) David Johnsen and Parvez Sopariwala, "Standard Costing Is Alive and Well at Parker Brass," *Management Accounting Quarterly* 1, no. 2 (Winter 2000), p. 13.

(10e) *The Management Accounting Video,* a management education video (New York: McGraw-Hill, 1997).

(10f) *The Balanced Scorecard,* a management education video (Boston: The President and Fellows of Harvard College, 1993).

(10g) Mark Green, Jeanine Garrity, Andra Gumbus, and Bridget Lyons, "Pitney Bowes Calls for New Metrics," *Strategic Finance* 83, no. 11, (May 2002), p. 34.

Chapter Eleven

(11a) Gary Siegel and James E. Sorensen, principal investigators for the Gary Siegel Organization, *Counting More, Counting Less: Transformations in the Management Accounting Profession* (Montvale, NJ: Institute of Management Accountants, 1999).

(11b) Interview with an A. T. Kearney consultant conducted during research by the author.

(11c) Steve Player and Carol Cobble, *Cornerstones of Decision Making: Profiles of Enterprise ABM* (Greensboro, NC: Oakhill Press, 1999), p. 79.

(11d) Cynthia Beier Greeson and Mehmet C. Kocakulah, "Implementing an ABC Pilot at Whirlpool." *Journal of Cost Management* 11, no. 2 (March/April 1997), pp. 16–21.

(11e) Interview with an A. T. Kearney consultant conducted during research by the author.

Chapter Twelve

(12a) Interview with a DaimlerChrysler accountant conducted during research by the author.

(12b) Gary Siegel and James E. Sorensen, principal investigators for the Gary Siegel Organization, *Counting More, Counting Less: Transformations in the Management Accounting Profession* (Montvale, NJ: Institute of Management Accountants, 1999).

(12c) Ibid.

(12d) Interview with an American Management Systems consultant conducted during research by the author.

(12e) Gary Siegel and James E. Sorensen, principal investigators for the Gary Siegel Organization, *Counting More, Counting Less: Transformations in the Management Accounting Profession* (Montvale, NJ: Institute of Management Accountants, 1999).

(12f) Michael Arndt, "Quality Isn't Just for Widgets," *Business Week,* July 22, 2002, p. 72.

Chapter Thirteen

(13a) Gary Siegel and James E. Sorensen, principal investigators for the Gary Siegel Organization, *Counting More, Counting Less: Transformations in the Management Accounting Profession* (Montvale, NJ: Institute of Management Accountants, 1999).

(13b) Thomas P. Kunes, "Environmental Cost Management," *Strategic Finance,* February 2001, p. 83.

(13c) *Current Practices, Perceptions and Trends: Transfer Pricing—1997 Global Survey* (Chicago: Ernst & Young, 1997), p. 1.

(13d) Ibid., p. 4.

(13e) Ibid., p. 11.

(13f) Ibid., p. 11.

Chapter Fourteen

(14a) Gary Siegel and James E. Sorensen, principal investigators for the Gary Siegel Organization, *Counting More, Counting Less: Transformations in the Management Accounting Profession* (Montvale, NJ: Institute of Management Accountants, 1999).

(14b) Ibid.

(14c) Ibid.

(14d) Ibid.

(14e) Ibid.

Chapter Fifteen

(15a) Gary Siegel and James E. Sorensen, principal investigators for the Gary Siegel Organization, *Counting More, Counting Less: Transformations in the Management Accounting Profession* (Montvale, NJ: Institute of Management Accountants, 1999).

(15b) Ibid.

(15c) Steve Player and Carol Cobble, *Cornerstones of Decision Making: Profiles of Enterprise ABM* (Greensboro, NC: Oakhill Press, 1999), p. 80.

(15d) Ibid., p. 80.

(15e) Presentation by U.S. Navy Acquisition Center, *The Second Annual International Conference on Target Costing,* sponsored by the Consortium for Advanced Manufacturing—International, Arthur Andersen, Ernst & Young, and the University of Akron (Washington, DC: CAM-I, 1998).

(15f) Presentation by Eastman Kodak Company, *The Second Annual International Conference on Target Costing,* sponsored by the Consortium for Advanced Manufacturing—International, Arthur Andersen, Ernst & Young, and the University of Akron (Washington, DC: CAM-I, 1998).

(15g) Presentation by Honda of America, *The Second Annual International Conference on Target Costing,* sponsored by the Consortium for Advanced Manufacturing—International, Arthur Andersen, Ernst & Young, and the University of Akron (Washington, DC: CAM-I, 1998).

(15h) Ibid.

Chapter Sixteen

(16a) Interview with a Ford Motor Company accountant conducted during research by the author.

(16b) Interview with a Hewlett-Packard accountant conducted during research by the author.

(16c) Interview with a Cornell University accountant conducted during research by the author.

(16d) Interview with a Boeing Company accountant conducted during research by the author.

(16e) Interview with an A. T. Kearney consultant conducted during research by the author.

Chapter Seventeen

(17a) Steve Player and Carol Cobble, *Cornerstones of Decision Making: Profiles of Enterprise ABM* (Greensboro, NC: Oakhill Press, 1999), p. 168.

Chapter Eighteen

(18a) Interview with a DaimlerChrysler accountant conducted during research by the author.

(18b) Interview with a Cornell University accountant conducted during research by the author.

(18c) Interview with an American Management Systems consultant conducted during research by the author.

(18d) Interview with an A. T. Kearney consultant conducted during research by the author.

Glossary

absorption costing (or **full costing**) A method of product costing in which both variable and fixed manufacturing overhead are included in the product costs that flow through the manufacturing accounts (i.e., Work-in-Process Inventory, Finished-Goods Inventory, and Cost of Goods Sold).

Accelerated Cost Recovery System (ACRS) The depreciation schedule specified by the United States tax code. Since it has been modified by recent tax law changes, the system also is called the Modified Accelerated Cost Recovery System (MACRS).

acceptance-or-rejection decision A decision as to whether or not a particular capital investment proposal should be accepted.

account-classification method (also called **account analysis**) A cost-estimation method involving a careful examination of the ledger accounts for the purpose of classifying each cost as variable, fixed, or semivariable.

accounting rate of return A percentage formed by taking a project's average incremental revenue minus its average incremental expenses (including depreciation and income taxes) and dividing by the project's initial investment.

accumulation factor The value of $(1 + r)^n$, in a future value calculation, where r denotes the interest rate per year and n denotes the number of years.

accurate information Precise and correct data.

activity A measure of an organization's output of goods or services.

activity accounting The collection of financial or operational performance information about significant activities in an enterprise.

activity analysis The detailed identification and description of the activities conducted in an enterprise.

activity base (or **cost driver**) A measure of an organization's activity that is used as a basis for specifying cost behavior. The activity base also is used to compute a predetermined overhead rate. The current trend is to refer to the activity base as a volume-based cost driver.

activity-based budgeting (ABB) The process of developing a master budget using information obtained from an activity-based costing (ABC) analysis.

activity-based costing (ABC) system A two-stage procedure used to assign overhead costs to products or services produced. In the first stage, significant activities are identified, and overhead costs are assigned to activity cost pools in accordance with the way resources are consumed by the activities. In the second stage, the overhead costs are allocated from each activity cost pool to each product line in proportion to the amount of the cost driver consumed by the product line.

activity-based flexible budget A flexible budget based on several cost drivers rather than on a single, volume-based cost driver.

activity-based management (ABM) Using an activity-based costing system to improve the operations of an organization.

activity-based responsibility accounting A system for measuring the performance of an organization's people and subunits, which focuses not only on the cost of performing activities but on the activities themselves.

activity cost pool A grouping of overhead costs assigned to various similar activities identified in an activity-based costing system.

activity dictionary A complete listing of the activities included in an organization's ABC analysis.

actual costing A product-costing system in which actual direct-material, direct-labor, and *actual* manufacturing-overhead costs are added to Work-in-Process Inventory.

actual manufacturing overhead The actual costs incurred during an accounting period for manufacturing overhead. Includes actual indirect material, indirect labor, and other manufacturing costs.

actual overhead rate The rate at which overhead costs are actually incurred during an accounting period. Calculated as follows: actual manufacturing overhead ÷ actual cost driver (or activity base).

administrative costs All costs associated with the management of an organization as a whole.

after-tax cash flow The cash flow expected after all tax implications have been taken into account.

after-tax net income An organization's net income after its income-tax expense is subtracted.

aggregate (or **total) productivity** Total output divided by total input.

allocation base A measure of activity, physical characteristic, or economic characteristic that is associated with the responsibility centers that are the cost objects in an allocation process.

annuity A series of equivalent cash flows.

applied manufacturing overhead The amount of manufacturing-overhead costs added to Work-in-Process Inventory during an accounting period.

appraisal costs Costs of determining whether defective products exist.

attention-directing function The function of managerial-accounting information in pointing out to managers issues that need their attention.

automated material-handling system (AMHS) Computer-controlled equipment that automatically moves materials, parts, and products from one production stage to another.

average cost per unit The total cost of producing a particular quantity of product divided by the number of units produced.

avoidable expenses Expenses that will no longer be incurred if a particular action is taken.

balanced scorecard A model of business performance evaluation that balances measures of financial performance, internal operations, innovation and learning, and customer satisfaction.

bar code technology The use of symbolic codes, which are scanned automatically and read into a computer, to record the use of labor and materials, track work in process and finished goods, and record other production-related information.

base budgeting The initial budget for each of an organization's departments is set in accordance with a base package under an approach called base budgeting.

base package An initial budget that includes the minimal resources needed for a subunit to exist at an absolute minimal level.

batch-level activity An activity that must be accomplished for each batch of products rather than for each unit.

batch manufacturing High-volume production of several product lines that differ in some important ways but are nearly identical in others.

before-tax income An organization's income before its income-tax expense is subtracted.

benchmarking (or **competitive benchmarking)** The continual search for the most effective method of accomplishing a task, by comparing existing methods and performance levels with those of other organizations or with other subunits within the same organization.

best practices The most effective methods of accomplishing various tasks in a particular industry, often discovered through benchmarking.

bill of activities (for a product or service) A complete listing of the activities required for that product or service to be produced.

bill of materials A list of all the materials needed to manufacture a product or product component.

break-even point The volume of activity at which an organization's revenues and expenses are equal. May be measured either in units or in sales dollars.

budget A detailed plan, expressed in quantitative terms, that specifies how resources will be acquired and used during a specified period of time.

budget administration The procedures used to prepare a budget, secure its approval, and disseminate it to the people who need to know its contents.

budgetary slack The difference between the budgetary projection provided by an individual and his or her best estimate of the item being projected. (For example, the difference between a supervisor's expected departmental utility cost and his or her budgetary projection for utilities.)

budget committee A group of top-management personnel who advise the budget director during the preparation of the budget.

budget director (or **chief budget officer)** The individual designated to be in charge of preparing an organization's budget.

budgeted balance sheet Shows the expected end-of-period balances for the company's assets, liabilities, and owners' equity.

budgeted financial statements (or **pro forma financial statements)** A set of planned financial statements showing what an organization's overall financial condition is expected to be at the end of the budget period if planned operations are carried out.

budgeted income statement Shows the expected revenue and expenses for a budget period, assuming that planned operations are carried out.

budgeted schedule of cost of goods manufactured and sold Details the direct material, direct labor, and manufacturing overhead costs to be incurred and shows the cost of the goods to be sold during a budget period.

budgeted statement of cash flows A budget schedule providing information about the expected sources and uses of cash for operating activities, investing activities, and financing activities during a particular period of time.

budgeting system The set of procedures used to develop a budget.

budget manual A set of written instructions that specifies who will provide budgetary data, when and in what form the data will be provided, how the master budget will be prepared and approved, and who should receive the various schedules constituting the budget.

budget period The time period covered by a budget.

by-product A joint product with very little value relative to the other joint products.

CAD/CAM system See **computer-aided design** and **computer-aided manufacturing.**

capital budget A long-term budget that shows planned acquisition and disposal of capital assets, such as land, building, and equipment.

capital-budgeting decision A decision involving cash flows beyond the current year.

capital-intensive A production process accomplished largely by machinery.

capital-rationing decision A decision in which management chooses which of several investment proposals to accept to make the best use of limited investment funds.

capital turnover Sales revenue divided by invested capital.

cash bonus See **pay for performance.**

cash budget Details the expected cash receipts and disbursements during a budget period.

cash disbursements budget A schedule detailing expected cash payments during a budget period.

cash equivalents Short-term, highly liquid investments that are treated as equivalent to cash in the preparation of a statement of cash flows.

cash provided by (or **used by) operations** The difference between the cash receipts and cash disbursements that are related to operating activities.

cash receipts budget A schedule detailing the expected cash collections during the budget period.

cellular manufacturing The organization of a production facility into FMS cells.

Certified Management Accountant (CMA) An accountant who has earned professional certification in managerial accounting.

change champion An individual who recognizes the need for change and seeks to bring it about through his or her own effort.

chief financial officer (CFO) An organization's top managerial and financial accountant. (Also see **controller.**)

coefficient of determination A statistical measure of goodness of fit; a measure of how closely a regression line fits the data on which it is based.

committed cost A cost that results from an organization's ownership or use of facilities and its basic organization structure.

common costs Costs incurred to benefit more than one organizational segment.

common-size financial statements Financial statements prepared in terms of percentages of a base amount.

comparative financial statements Financial statements showing the results of two or more successive years.

competitive benchmarking See **benchmarking.**

competitive bidding A situation where two or more companies submit bids (prices) for a product, service, or project to a potential buyer.

compound interest The interest earned on prior periods' interest.

computer-aided design (CAD) system Computer software used by engineers in the design of a product.

computer-aided manufacturing (CAM) system Any production process in which computers are used to help control production.

computer-integrated manufacturing (CIM) system The most advanced form of automated manufacturing, in which virtually all parts of the production process are accomplished by computer-controlled machines and automated material-handling equipment.

computer-numerically-controlled (CNC) machines Stand-alone machines controlled by a computer via a numerical, machine-readable code.

constraints Algebraic expressions of limitations faced by a firm, such as those limiting its productive resources.

consumption ratio The proportion of an activity consumed by a particular product.

continuous improvement The constant effort to eliminate waste, reduce response time, simplify the design of both products and processes, and improve quality and customer service.

contribution income statement An income statement on which fixed and variable expenses are separated.

contribution margin Sales revenue minus variable expenses. The amount of sales revenue, which is left to cover fixed expenses and profit after paying variable expenses.

contribution margin per unit The difference between the unit sales price and the unit variable expense. The amount that each unit contributes to covering fixed expenses and profit.

contribution-margin ratio The unit contribution margin divided by the sales price per unit. May also be expressed in percentage form; then it is called the contribution-margin percentage.

controllability The extent to which managers are able to control or influence a cost or cost variance.

controllable cost A cost that is subject to the control or substantial influence of a particular individual.

controller (or **comptroller**) The top managerial and financial accountant in an organization. Supervises the accounting department and assists management at all levels in interpreting and using managerial-accounting information. (Also, see **chief financial officer.**)

controlling Ensuring that an organization operates in the intended manner and achieves its goals.

conversion costs Direct-labor cost plus manufacturing-overhead cost.

cost The sacrifice made, usually measured by the resources given up, to achieve a particular purpose.

Cost Accounting Standards Cost-accounting procedures specified by the Cost Accounting Standards Board, an agency of the federal government.

Cost Accounting Standards Board (CASB) A federal agency chartered by Congress in 1970 to develop cost-accounting standards for large government contractors.

cost accounting system Part of the basic accounting system that accumulates cost for use in both managerial and financial accounting.

cost allocation The process of assigning costs in a cost pool to the appropriate cost objects. Also see **cost distribution.**

cost behavior The relationship between cost and activity.

cost center A responsibility center whose manager is accountable for its costs.

cost distribution (sometimes called **cost allocation**) The first step in assigning manufacturing-overhead costs. Overhead costs are assigned to all departmental overhead centers.

cost driver A characteristic of an activity or event that results in the incurrence of costs by that activity or event.

cost estimation The process of determining how a particular cost behaves.

cost management system (CMS) A management planning and controlling system that measures the cost of significant activities, identifies non-value-added costs, and identifies activities that will improve organizational performance.

cost objects Responsibility centers, products, or services to which costs are assigned.

cost of capital The cost of acquiring resources for an organization, either through debt or through the issuance of stock.

cost of goods manufactured The total cost of direct material, direct labor, and manufacturing overhead transferred from Work-in-Process Inventory to Finished-Goods Inventory during an accounting period.

cost of goods sold The expense measured by the cost of the finished goods sold during a period of time.

cost-plus pricing A pricing approach in which the price is equal to cost plus a markup.

cost pool A collection of costs to be assigned to a set of cost objects.

cost prediction Forecast of cost at a particular level of activity.

cost structure The relative proportions of an organization's fixed and variable costs.

cost variance The difference between actual and standard cost.

cost-volume-profit (CVP) analysis A study of the relationships between sales volume, expenses, revenue, and profit.

cost-volume-profit (CVP) graph A graphical expression of the relationships between sales volume, expenses, revenue, and profit.

cross-elasticity The extent to which a change in a product's price affects the demand for substitute products.

curvilinear cost A cost with a curved line for its graph.

customer-acceptance measures The extent to which a firm's customers perceive its product to be of high quality.

customer profitability analysis Using the concepts of activity-based costing to determine the activities, costs, and profit associated with serving particular customers.

customer profitability profile A graphical portrayal of a company's customer profitability analysis.

cycle time See **throughput time.**

decentralization A form of organization in which subunit managers are given authority to make substantive decisions.

decision making Choosing between alternatives.

decision variables The variables in a linear program about which a decision is made.

delivery cycle time The average time between the receipt of a customer order and delivery of the goods.

demand curve A graph of the relationship between sales price and the quantity of units sold.

departmental overhead center Any department to which overhead costs are assigned via overhead cost distribution.

departmental overhead rate An overhead rate calculated for a single production department.

departmental production report The key document in a process-costing system. This report summarizes the physical flow of units, equivalent units of production, cost per equivalent unit, and analysis of total departmental costs.

dependent variable A variable whose value depends on other variables, called *independent variables.*

depreciation tax shield The reduction in a firm's income-tax expense due to the depreciation expense associated with a depreciable asset.

differential cost The difference in a cost item under two decision alternatives.

direct cost A cost that can be traced to a particular department or other subunit of an organization.

direct-exchange (or **noncash**) **transaction** A significant investing or financing transaction involving accounts other than cash, such as a transaction where land is obtained in exchange for the issuance of capital stock.

directing operational activities Running an organization on a day-to-day basis.

direct labor The costs of compensating employees who work directly on a firm's product. Should include wages, salary, and associated fringe benefits.

direct-labor budget A schedule showing the number of hours and cost of direct labor to be used in production of services or goods during a budget period.

direct-labor cost The cost of salaries, wages, and fringe benefits for personnel who work directly on the manufactured products.

direct-labor efficiency variance The difference between actual and standard hours of direct labor multiplied by the standard hourly labor rate.

direct-labor rate variance The difference between actual and standard hourly labor rate multiplied by the actual hours of direct labor used.

direct material Raw material that is physically incorporated in the finished product.

direct-material budget A schedule showing the number of units and the cost of material to be purchased during a budget period.

direct-material price variance (or **purchase price variance**) The difference between actual and standard price multiplied by the actual quantity of material purchased.

direct-material quantity variance The difference between actual and standard quantity of materials allowed, given actual output, multiplied by the standard price.

direct method (of preparing the statement of cash flows) A method of preparing the operating activities section of a statement of cash flows. A cash-basis income statement is constructed in which operating cash disbursements are subtracted from operating cash receipts.

direct method (of service department cost allocation) A method of service department cost allocation in which service department costs are allocated directly to the production departments.

discounted-cash-flow analysis An analysis of an investment proposal that takes into account the time value of money.

discount rate The interest rate used in computing the present value of a cash flow.

discretionary cost A cost that results from a discretionary management decision to spend a particular amount of money.

distribution cost The cost of storing and transporting finished goods for sale.

dual cost allocation An approach to service department cost allocation in which variable costs are allocated in proportion to short-term usage and fixed costs are allocated in proportion to long-term usage.

e-budgeting An electronic and enterprise-wide budgeting process in which employees throughout the organization can submit and retrieve budget information electronically via the Internet.

economic order quantity (EOQ) The order size that minimizes inventory ordering and holding costs.

economic value added (EVA) An investment center's after-tax operating income minus the investment center's total assets (net of its current liabilities) times the company's weighted-average cost of capital.

electronic data interchange (EDI) The direct exchange between organizations of data via a computer-to-computer interface.

empowerment The concept of encouraging and authorizing workers to take the initiative to improve operations, reduce costs, and improve product quality and customer service.

engineered cost A cost that results from a definitive physical relationship with the activity measure.

engineering method A cost-estimation method in which a detailed study is made of the process that results in cost incurrence.

environmental cost management Strategies for reducing, eliminating, or otherwise controlling environmental costs.

environmental costs Costs incurred in dealing with environmental issues.

equivalent unit A measure of the amount of production effort applied to a physical unit of production. For example, a physical unit that is 50 percent completed represents one-half of an equivalent unit.

estimated manufacturing overhead The amount of manufacturing-overhead cost expected for a specified period of time. Used as the numerator in computing the predetermined overhead rate.

expected value The sum of the possible values for a random variable, each weighted by its probability.

expense The consumption of assets for the purpose of generating revenue.

experience curve A graph (or other mathematical representation) that shows how a broad set of costs decline as cumulative production output increases.

external failure costs Costs incurred because defective products have been sold.

facility (or **general-operations) level activity** An activity that is required for an entire production process to occur.

feasible region The possible values for decision variables that are not ruled out by constraints.

FIFO (first-in, first-out) method A method of process costing in which the cost assigned to the beginning work-in-process inventory is not added to current-period production costs. The cost per equivalent unit calculated under FIFO relates to the current period only.

financial accounting The use of accounting information for reporting to parties outside the organization.

financial budget A schedule that outlines how an organization will acquire financial resources during the budget period (for example, through borrowing or sale of capital stock).

financial leverage The concept that a relatively small increase in income can provide a proportionately much larger increase in return to the common stockholders.

financial planning model A set of mathematical relationships that expresses the interactions among the various operational, financial, and environmental events that determine the overall results of an organization's activities.

financing activities Transactions involving a company's debt or equity capital.

finished goods Completed products awaiting sale.

firewall A computer or information router placed between a company's internal network and the Internet to control and monitor all information between the outside world and the company's local network.

fixed cost A cost that does not change in total as activity changes.

fixed-overhead budget variance The difference between actual and budgeted fixed overhead.

fixed-overhead volume variance The difference between budgeted and applied fixed overhead.

flexible budget A budget that is valid for a range of activity.

flexible manufacturing system (FMS) A series of manufacturing machines, controlled and integrated by a computer, which is designed to perform a series of manufacturing operations automatically.

FMS cell A group of machines and personnel within a flexible manufacturing system (FMS).

full (or **absorption) cost** A product's variable cost plus an allocated portion of fixed overhead.

future value The amount to which invested funds accumulate over a specified period of time.

gain-sharing plan An incentive system that specifies a formula by which the cost savings from productivity gains achieved by a company are shared with the workers who helped accomplish the improvements.

goal congruence A meshing of objectives, where managers throughout an organization strive to achieve the goals set by top management.

goodness of fit The closeness with which a regression line fits the data upon which it is based.

grade The extent of a product's capability in performing its intended purpose, viewed in relation to other products with the same functional use.

high-low method A cost-estimation method in which a cost line is fit using exactly two data points—the high and low activity levels.

homogeneous cost pool A grouping of overhead costs in which each cost component is consumed in roughly the same proportion by each product line.

horizontal analysis An analysis of the year-to-year change in each financial statement item.

hurdle rate The minimum desired rate of return used in a discounted-cash-flow analysis.

hybrid product-costing system A system that incorporates features from two or more alternative product-costing systems, such as job-order and process costing.

idle time Unproductive time spent by employees due to factors beyond their control, such as power outages and machine breakdowns.

imperfect competition A market in which a single producer or group of producers can affect the market price.

incentive compensation See **pay for performance.**

incremental cost The increase in cost from one alternative to another.

incremental package A budget detailing the additional resources needed to add various activities to a base package.

independent variable The variable upon which an estimate is based in least-squares regression analysis.

indirect cost A cost that cannot be traced to a particular department.

indirect labor All costs of compensating employees who do not work directly on the firm's product but who are necessary for production to occur.

indirect-labor budget A schedule showing the amount and cost of indirect labor to be used during a budget period.

indirect materials Materials that either are required for the production process to occur but do not become an integral part of the finished product, or are consumed in production but are insignificant in cost.

indirect method (or **reconciliation method**) A method of preparing the operating activities section of a statement of cash flows, in which the analyst begins with net income. Then adjustments are made to convert from an accrual-basis income statement to a cash-basis income statement.

information overload The provision of so much information that, due to human limitations in processing information, managers cannot effectively use it.

in-process quality controls Procedures designed to assess product quality before production is completed.

inspection time The time spent on quality inspections of raw materials, partially completed products, or finished goods.

internal auditor An accountant who reviews the accounting procedures, records, and reports in both the controller's and treasurer's areas of responsibility.

internal control system The set of procedures designed to ensure that an organization's employees act in a legal, ethical, and responsible manner.

internal failure costs Costs of correcting defects found prior to product sale.

internal rate of return The discount rate required for an investment's net present value to be zero; also known as the *time-adjusted rate of return.*

inventoriable cost Cost incurred to purchase or manufacture goods. Also see **product cost.**

inventoriable goods Goods that can be stored before sale, such as durable goods, mining products, and some agricultural products.

inventory budgets Schedules that detail the amount and cost of finished-goods, work-in-process, and direct-material inventories expected at the end of a budget period.

investing activities Transactions involving the extension or collection of loans, acquisition or disposal of investments, and purchase or sale of productive, long-lived assets.

investment center A responsibility center whose manager is accountable for its profit and for the capital invested to generate that profit.

investment opportunity rate The rate of return an organization can earn on its best alternative investments that are of equivalent risk.

ISO 9000 standards International quality-control standards issued by the International Standards Organization.

job-cost record A document that records the costs of direct material, direct labor, and manufacturing overhead for a particular production job or batch. The job-cost record is a subsidiary ledger account for the Work-in-Process Inventory account in the general ledger.

job-order costing system A product-costing system in which costs are assigned to batches or job orders of production. Used by firms that produce relatively small numbers of dissimilar products.

joint cost The cost incurred in a joint production process before the joint products become identifiable as separate products.

joint production process A production process that results in two or more joint products.

joint products The outputs of a joint production process.

just-in-time (JIT) inventory and production management system A comprehensive inventory and manufacturing control system in which no materials are purchased and no products are manufactured until they are needed.

just-in-time (JIT) purchasing An approach to purchasing management in which materials and parts are purchased only as they are needed.

kaizen costing The process of cost reduction during the manufacturing phase of a product. Refers to continual and gradual improvement through small betterment activities.

labor-intensive A production process accomplished largely by manual labor.

lag indicators Measures of the final outcomes of earlier management decisions.

lead indicators Performance measures that identify future nonfinancial and financial outcomes to guide management decision making.

lead time The time required to receive inventory after it has been ordered.

learning curve A graphical expression of the decline in the average labor time required per unit as cumulative output increases.

least-squares regression method A cost-estimation method in which the cost line is fit to the data by statistical analysis. The method minimizes the sum of the squared deviations between the cost line and the data points.

line positions Positions held by managers who are directly involved in providing the goods or services that constitute an organization's primary goals.

make-or-buy (or **outsourcing**) **decision** A decision as to whether a product or service should be produced in-house or purchased from an outside supplier.

management by exception A managerial technique in which only significant deviations from expected performance are investigated.

management by objectives (MBO) The process of designating the objectives of each subunit in an organization and planning for the achievement of these objectives. Managers at all levels participate in setting goals, which they then will strive to achieve.

managerial accounting The process of identifying, measuring, analyzing, interpreting, and communicating information in pursuit of an organization's goals.

manufacturing The process of converting raw materials into finished products.

manufacturing costs Costs incurred in a manufacturing process, which consist of direct material, direct labor, and manufacturing overhead.

manufacturing cycle efficiency (MCE) The ratio of process time to the sum of processing time, inspection time, waiting time, and move time.

manufacturing cycle time The total amount of production time (or throughput time) required per unit.

manufacturing overhead All manufacturing costs other than direct-material and direct-labor costs.

manufacturing-overhead budget Shows the cost of overhead expected to be incurred in the production process during the budget period.

manufacturing-overhead variance The difference between actual overhead cost and the amount specified in the flexible budget.

marginal cost The extra cost incurred in producing one additional unit of output.

marginal cost curve A graph of the relationship between the change in total cost and the quantity produced and sold.

marginal revenue curve A graph of the relationship between the change in total revenue and the quantity sold.

marketing cost The cost incurred in selling goods or services. Includes order-getting costs and order-filling or distribution costs.

mass customization A manufacturing environment in which many standardized components are combined to produce custom-made products to customer order.

master budget (or **profit plan**) A comprehensive set of budgets that covers all phases of an organization's operations for a specified period of time.

material-requirements planning (MRP) An operations-management tool that assists managers in scheduling production in each stage of a complex manufacturing process.

material requisition form A document used by the production department supervisor to request the release of raw materials for production.

merchandise cost The cost of acquiring goods for resale. Includes purchasing and transportation costs.

merchandising The business of acquiring finished goods for resale, either in a wholesale or a retail operation.

merit pay See **pay for performance.**

mixed cost See **semivariable cost.**

Modified Accelerated Cost Recovery System (MACRS) The depreciation schedule specified by the United States tax code, as modified by recent changes in the tax laws.

move time The time spent moving raw materials, subassemblies, or finished products from one production operation to another.

multiple regression A statistical method in which a linear (straight-line) relationship is estimated between a dependent variable and two or more independent variables.

multistage cost allocation The three-step process in which costs are assigned to products or services: (1) cost distribution (or allocation), (2) service department cost allocation, and (3) cost application.

net present value The present value of a project's future cash flows less the cost of the initial investment.

net realizable value A joint product's final sales value less any separable costs incurred after the split-off point.

net-realizable-value method A method in which joint costs are allocated to the joint products in proportion to the net realizable value of each joint product.

nominal dollars The measure used for an actual cash flow that is observed.

nominal interest rate The real interest rate plus an additional premium to compensate investors for inflation.

non-value-added activities Operations that are either (1) unnecessary and dispensable or (2) necessary, but inefficient and improvable.

non-value-added costs The costs of activities that can be eliminated without deterioration of product quality, performance, or perceived value.

normal costing A product-costing system in which actual direct-materials, actual direct-labor, and applied manufacturing-overhead costs are added to Work-in-Process Inventory.

normal equations The equations used to solve for the parameters of a regression equation.

normalized overhead rate An overhead rate calculated over a relatively long time period.

objective function An algebraic expression of the firm's goal.

off-line quality control Activities during the product design and engineering phases that will improve the manufacturability of the product, reduce production costs, and ensure high quality.

oligopolistic market (or **oligopoly**) A market with a small number of sellers competing among themselves.

operating activities All activities that are not investing or financing activities. Generally speaking, operating activities include all cash transactions that are involved in the determination of net income.

operating expenses The costs incurred to produce and sell services, such as transportation, repair, financial, or medical services.

operating leverage The extent to which an organization uses fixed costs in its cost structure. The greater the proportion of fixed costs, the greater the operating leverage.

operating leverage factor A measure of operating leverage at a particular sales volume. Computed by dividing an organization's total contribution margin by its net income.

operational budgets A set of budgets that specifies how operations will be carried out to produce an organization's services or goods.

operation costing A hybrid of job-order and process costing. Direct material is accumulated by batch of products using job-order costing methods. Conversion costs are accumulated by department and assigned to product units by process-costing methods.

opportunity cost The potential benefit given up when the choice of one action precludes selection of a different action.

organizational culture The mindset of employees, including their shared beliefs, values, and goals.

outlier A data point that falls far away from the other points in a scatter diagram and is not representative of the data.

out-of-pocket costs Costs incurred that require the expenditure of cash or other assets.

outsourcing (or **make-or-buy**) **decision** A decision as to whether a product or service should be produced in-house or purchased from an outside supplier.

overapplied overhead The amount by which the period's applied manufacturing overhead exceeds actual manufacturing overhead.

overhead application (or **absorption**) The third step in assigning manufacturing-overhead costs. All costs associated with each production department are assigned to the product units on which a department has worked.

overhead budget A schedule showing the cost of overhead expected to be incurred in the production of services or goods during a budget period.

overhead cost performance report A report showing the actual and flexible-budget cost levels for each overhead item, together with variable-overhead spending and efficiency variances and fixed-overhead budget variances.

overtime premium The extra compensation paid to an employee who works beyond the normal period of time.

padding the budget The process of building budgetary slack into a budget by overestimating expenses and underestimating revenue.

partial (or **component) productivity** Total output (in dollars) divided by the cost of a particular input.

participative budgeting The process of involving people throughout an organization in the budgeting process.

payback period The amount of time required for a project's after-tax cash inflows to accumulate to an amount that covers the initial investment.

pay for performance A one-time cash payment to an investment-center manager as a reward for meeting a predetermined criterion on a specified performance measure.

penetration pricing Setting a low initial price for a new product in order to penetrate the market deeply and gain a large and broad market share.

percentage of completion The extent to which a physical unit of production has been finished with respect to direct material or conversion activity.

perfect competition A market in which the price does not depend on the quantity sold by any one producer.

perfection (or **ideal) standard** The cost expected under perfect or ideal operating conditions.

performance report A report showing the budgeted and actual amounts, and the variances between these amounts, of key financial results for a person or subunit.

period costs Costs that are expensed during the time period in which they are incurred.

physical unit An actual item of production, fully or partially completed.

physical-units method A method in which joint costs are allocated to the joint products in proportion to their physical quantities.

planning Developing a detailed financial and operational description of anticipated operations.

plantwide overhead rate An overhead rate calculated by averaging manufacturing-overhead costs for the entire production facility.

pool rate The cost per unit of the cost driver for a particular activity cost pool.

postaudit (or **reappraisal)** A systematic follow-up of a capital-budgeting decision to see how the project turned out.

practical (or **attainable) standard** The cost expected under normal operating conditions.

predatory pricing An illegal practice in which the price of a product is set low temporarily to broaden demand. Then the product's supply is restricted and the price is raised.

predetermined overhead rate The rate used to apply manufacturing overhead to Work-in-Process Inventory, calculated as: estimated manufacturing overhead cost ÷ estimated amount of cost driver (or activity base).

present value The economic value now of a cash flow that will occur in the future.

prevention costs Costs of preventing defective products.

price discrimination The illegal practice of quoting different prices for the same product or service to different buyers, when the price differences are not justified by cost differences.

price elasticity The impact of price changes on sales volume.

price takers Firms whose products or services are determined totally by the market.

prime costs The costs of direct material and direct labor.

principal The amount originally invested, not including any interest earned.

process A set of linked activities.

process-costing system A product-costing system in which production costs are averaged over a large number of product units. Used by firms that produce large numbers of nearly identical products.

process (or **functional) layout** A method of organizing the elements of a production process, in which similar processes and functions are grouped together.

process time The amount of time during which a product is actually undergoing conversion activity.

process value analysis (PVA) Another term for *activity analysis,* which is the detailed identification and description of the activities conducted in an enterprise.

product cost Cost associated with goods for sale until the time period during which the products are sold, at which time the costs become expenses. See also **inventoriable cost.**

product-costing system The process of accumulating the costs of a production process and assigning them to the products that constitute the organization's output.

production budget A schedule showing the number of units of services or goods that are to be produced during a budget period.

production department A department in which work is done directly on a firm's products.

production Kanban A card specifying the number of parts to be manufactured in a particular work center.

product life-cycle costing The accumulation of costs that occur over the entire life cycle of a product.

product-sustaining-level activity An activity that is needed to support an entire product line, but is not always performed every time a new unit or batch of products is produced.

profitability index (or **excess present value index)** The present value of a project's future cash flows (exclusive of the initial investment), divided by the initial investment.

profit center A responsibility center whose manager is accountable for its profit.

profit plan (or **master budget)** A comprehensive set of budgets that cover all phases of an organization's operations during a specified period of time.

profit-volume graph A graphical expression of the relationship between profit and sales volume.

project costing The process of assigning costs to projects, cases, contracts, programs, or missions in nonmanufacturing organizations.

proration The process of allocating underapplied or overapplied overhead to Work-in-Process Inventory, Finished-Goods Inventory, and Cost of Goods Sold.

pull method A method of coordinating stages in a production process. Goods are produced in each stage of manufacturing only as they are needed in the next stage.

qualitative characteristics Factors in a decision analysis that cannot be expressed easily in numerical terms.

quality of conformance The extent to which a product meets the specifications of its design.

quality of design The extent to which a product is designed to perform well in its intended use.

quick assets Cash, marketable securities, accounts receivable, and current notes receivable. Excludes inventories and prepaid expenses, which are current assets but not quick assets.

raw material Material entered into a manufacturing process.

real dollars A measure that reflects an adjustment for the purchasing power of a monetary unit.

real interest rate The underlying interest rate in the economy, which includes compensation to an investor for the time value of money and the risk of an investment.

reciprocal service The mutual provision of service by two service departments to each other.

reciprocal-services method A method of service department cost allocation which accounts for the mutual provision of reciprocal services among all service departments.

reengineering The complete redesign of a process, with an emphasis on finding creative new ways to accomplish an objective.

regression line A line fit to a set of data points using least-squares regression.

relative-sales-value method A method in which joint costs are allocated to the joint products in proportion to their total sales values at the split-off point.

relevant information Data that are pertinent to a decision.

relevant range The range of activity within which management expects the organization to operate.

repetitive production The manufacture of large numbers of identical or very similar products in a continuous flow.

research and development (R&D) costs Costs incurred to develop and test new products or services.

residual income Profit minus an imputed interest charge, which is equal to the invested capital times an imputed interest rate.

responsibility accounting Tools and concepts used by managerial accountants to measure the performance of an organization's people and subunits.

responsibility center A subunit in an organization whose manager is held accountable for specified financial results of its activities.

return on investment (ROI) Income divided by invested capital.

return-on-investment pricing A cost-plus pricing method in which the markup is determined by the amount necessary for the company to earn a target rate of return on investment.

revenue center A responsibility center whose manager is accountable for its revenue.

rolling budget (also **revolving** or **continuous budget)** A budget that is continually updated by adding another incremental time period and dropping the most recently completed period.

safety margin Difference between budgeted sales revenue and break-even sales revenue.

safety stock Extra inventory consumed during periods of above-average usage in a setting with fluctuating demand.

sales budget A schedule that shows the expected sales of services or goods during a budget period, expressed in both monetary terms and units.

sales forecasting The process of predicting sales of services or goods. The initial step in preparing a master budget.

sales margin Income divided by sales revenue.

sales mix Relative proportion of sales of each of an organization's multiple products.

sales-price variance The difference between actual and expected unit sales price multiplied by the actual quantity of units sold.

sales-volume variance The difference between actual sales volume and budgeted sales volume multiplied by the budgeted unit contribution margin.

scatter diagram A set of plotted cost observations at various activity levels.

schedule of cost of goods manufactured A detailed schedule showing the manufacturing costs incurred during an accounting period and the change in work-in-process inventory.

schedule of cost of goods sold A detailed schedule showing the cost of goods sold and the change in finished-goods inventory during an accounting period.

segmented income statement A financial statement showing the income for an organization and its major segments (subunits).

selling, general, and administrative (S, G, & A) expense budget A schedule showing the planned amounts of selling, general, and administrative expenses during a budget period.

selling costs Costs of obtaining and filling sales orders, such as advertising costs, compensation of sales personnel, and product promotion costs.

semivariable (or **mixed) cost** A cost with both a fixed and a variable component.

sensitivity analysis A technique for determining what would happen in a decision analysis if a key prediction or assumption proves to be wrong.

separable processing cost Cost incurred on a joint product after the split-off point of a joint production process.

sequential production process A manufacturing operation in which partially completed products pass in sequence through two or more production departments.

service department cost allocation The second step in assigning manufacturing-overhead costs. All costs associated with a service department are assigned to the departments that use the services it produces.

service departments Subunits in an organization that are not involved directly in producing the organization's output of goods or services.

service industry firm A firm engaged in production of a service that is consumed as it is produced, such as air transportation service or medical service.

shareholder value analysis Calculation of the residual income associated with a major product line, with the objective of determining how the product line affects a firm's value to its shareholders.

simple regression A regression analysis based on a single independent variable.

Six Sigma An analytical method that aims at achieving near-perfect results in a production process.

skimming pricing Setting a high initial price for a new product in order to reap short-run profits. Over time, the price is reduced gradually.

source document A document that is used as the basis for an accounting entry. Examples include material requisition forms and direct-labor time tickets.

split-off point The point in a joint production process at which the joint products become identifiable as separate products.

staff positions Positions held by managers who are only indirectly involved in producing an organization's product or service.

standard cost A predetermined cost for the production of goods or services that serves as a benchmark against which to compare the actual cost.

standard-costing system A cost-control and product-costing system in which cost variances are computed and production costs are entered into work-in-process inventory at their standard amounts.

standard direct-labor quantity The number of labor hours normally needed to manufacture one unit of product.

standard direct-labor rate Total hourly cost of compensation, including fringe benefits.

standard direct-material price The total delivered cost, after subtracting any purchase discounts taken.

standard direct-material quantity The total amount of material normally required to produce a finished product, including allowances for normal waste and inefficiency.

standard quantity allowed The standard quantity per unit of output multiplied by the number of units of actual output.

statement of cash flows A major financial statement that shows the change in an organization's total cash and cash equivalents and explains that change in terms of the organization's operating, investing, and financing activities during a period.

static budget A budget that is valid for only one planned activity level.

statistical control chart A plot of cost variances across time, with a comparison to a statistically determined critical value.

step-down method A method of service department cost allocation in which service department costs are allocated first to service departments and then to production departments.

step-fixed cost A cost that remains fixed over wide ranges of activity, but jumps to a different amount for activity levels outside that range.

step-variable cost A cost that is nearly variable, but increases in small steps instead of continuously.

storage time The time during which raw materials or finished products are stored in stock.

storyboarding A procedure used to develop a detailed process flowchart, which visually represents activities and the relationships among the activities.

strategic cost analysis A broad-based managerial-accounting analysis that supports strategic management decisions.

strategic cost management Overall recognition of the cost relationships among the activities in the value chain, and the process of managing those cost relationships to a firm's advantage.

summary cash budget A combination of the cash receipts and cash disbursements budgets.

sunk costs Costs that were incurred in the past and cannot be altered by any current or future decision.

supply chain The flow of all goods, services, and information into and out of an organization.

sustainable development Business activity that produces the goods and services needed in the present without limiting the ability of future generations to meet their needs.

target cost The projected long-run product cost that will enable a firm to enter and remain in the market for the product and compete successfully with the firm's competitors.

target costing The design of a product, and the processes used to produce it, so that ultimately the product can be manufactured at a cost that will enable a firm to make a profit when the product is sold at an estimated market-driven price. This estimated price is called the *target price,* the desired profit margin is called the *target profit,* and the cost at which the product must be manufactured is called the *target cost.*

target net profit (or **income**) The profit level set as management's objective.

task analysis Setting standards by analyzing the production process.

theory of constraints A management approach that focuses on identifying and relaxing the constraints that limit an organization's ability to reach a higher level of goal attainment.

throughput costing A product-costing system that assigns only the unit-level spending for direct costs as the cost of products or services.

throughput time The average amount of time required to convert raw materials into finished goods ready to be shipped to customers.

time and material pricing A cost-plus pricing approach that includes components for labor cost and material cost, plus markups on either or both of these cost components.

timely information Data that are available in time for use in a decision analysis.

time record A document that records the amount of time an employee spends on each production job.

total contribution margin Total sales revenue less total variable expenses.

total cost curve Graphs the relationship between total cost and total quantity produced and sold.

total quality control (TQC) A product-quality program in which the objective is complete elimination of product defects.

total quality management (TQM) The broad set of management and control processes designed to focus an entire organization and all of its employees on providing products or services that do the best possible job of satisfying the customer.

total revenue curve Graphs the relationship between total sales revenue and quantity sold.

transaction-based costing system A product-costing system in which multiple cost drivers are identified, and costs of activities are assigned to products on the basis of the number of transactions they generate for the various cost drivers.

transfer price The price at which products or services are transferred between two divisions in an organization.

transferred-in costs Costs assigned to partially completed products that are transferred into one production department from a prior department.

treasurer An accountant in a staff position who is responsible for managing an organization's relationships with investors and creditors and maintaining custody of the organization's cash, investments, and other assets.

trend analysis A comparison across time of three or more observations of a particular financial item, such as net income.

two-dimensional ABC model A combination of the cost assignment view of the role of activity-based costing with its process analysis and evaluation role. Two-dimensional ABC is one way of depicting activity-based management.

two-stage cost allocation A two-step procedure for assigning overhead costs to products or services produced. In the first stage, all production costs are assigned to the production departments. In the second stage, the costs that have been assigned to each production department are applied to the products or services produced in those departments.

unavoidable expenses Expenses that will continue to be incurred even if a subunit or activity is eliminated.

underapplied overhead The amount by which the period's actual manufacturing overhead exceeds applied manufacturing overhead.

unit contribution margin Sales price minus the unit variable cost.

unit-level activity An activity that must be done for each unit of production.

value analysis See **value engineering.**

value chain An organization's set of linked, value-creating activities, ranging from securing basic raw materials and energy to the ultimate delivery of products and services.

value engineering (or **value analysis)** A cost-reduction and process improvement technique that utilizes information collected about a product's design and production processes and then examines various attributes of the design and processes to identify candidates for improvement efforts.

variable cost A cost that changes in total in direct proportion to a change in an organization's activity.

variable costing (or **direct costing)** A method of product costing in which only variable manufacturing overhead is included as a product cost that flows through the manufacturing accounts (i.e., Work-in-Process Inventory, Finished-Goods Inventory, and Cost of Goods Sold). Fixed manufacturing overhead is treated as a period cost.

variable-overhead efficiency variance The difference between actual and standard hours of an activity base (e.g., machine hours) multiplied by the standard variable-overhead rate.

variable-overhead spending variance The difference between actual variable-overhead cost and the product of the standard variable-overhead rate and actual hours of an activity base (e.g., machine hours).

velocity The number of units produced in a given time period.

vertical analysis An analysis of the relationships among various financial items on a particular financial statement. Generally presented in terms of common-size financial statements.

visual-fit method A method of cost estimation in which a cost line is drawn through a scatter diagram according to the visual perception of the analyst.

volume-based cost driver (or **activity base)** A cost driver that is closely associated with production volume, such as direct-labor hours or machine hours.

volume-based (or **throughput-based) costing system** A product-costing system in which costs are assigned to products on the basis of a single activity base related to volume (e.g., direct-labor hours or machine hours).

waiting time The time during which partially completed products wait for the next phase of production.

weighted-average cost of capital (WACC) A weighted average of the after-tax cost of debt capital and the cost of equity capital.

weighted-average method A method of process costing in which the cost assigned to beginning work-in-process inventory is added to the current-period production costs. The cost per equivalent unit calculated under this process-costing method is a weighted average of the costs in the beginning work in process and the costs of the current period.

weighted-average unit contribution margin Average of a firm's several products' unit contribution margins, weighted by the relative sales proportion of each product.

withdrawal Kanban A card sent to the preceding work center indicating the number and type of parts requested from that work center by the next work center.

working capital Current assets minus current liabilities.

work in process Partially completed products that are not yet ready for sale.

work measurement The systematic analysis of a task for the purpose of determining the inputs needed to perform the task.

zero-base budgeting A budgeting approach in which the initial budget for each activity in an organization is set to zero. To be allocated resources, an activity's continuing existence must be justified by the appropriate management personnel.

Photo Credits

Chapter One

p. 3, © Steve Vidler/SuperStock; **p. 11,** © Lisette Le Bon/SuperStock; **p. 11,** © Susan Van Etten/PhotoEdit; **p. 16,** © Gabriel M. Covian/Imagebank/Getty; **p. 16,** Courtesy of Hertz; **p. 16,** © 2001 Quinones, Lisa/Stockphoto.com; **p. 16,** © Larry Chiger/SuperStock; **p. 16,** © David Young-Wolff/PhotoEdit; **p. 16,** © Flash! Light/Stock Boston; **p. 19,** © SuperStock; **p. 19,** © Srulik Haramaty/PhotoTake; **p. 25,** © Romilly Lockyer/Imagebank/Getty; **p. 25,** © Jeff Greenberg/PhotoEdit; **p. 25,** © Bill Aron/PhotoEdit; **p. 25,** © David Young-Wolff/PhotoEdit; **p. 25,** © Mark Richards/PhotoEdit.

Chapter Two

p. 35, © Jules Frazier/PhotoDisc/Getty; **p. 41,** © Gamma; **p. 41,** © Michael Abramson/Woodfin Camp & Associates; **p. 41,** © VLADIMIR PCHOLKIN/Taxi/Getty; **p. 41,** © Dell; **p. 41,** © Jeff Greenberg/Unicorn Stock Photos; **p. 48,** © Didier Dorval/Masterfile; **p. 53,** © SuperStock.

Chapter Three

p. 77, © Thomas Hallstein/Outsight Photography; **p. 81,** © Robert Holmgren/Peter Arnold, Inc; **p. 81,** © Justin Sullivan/Getty Images; **p. 81,** © Tim Boyle/Getty Images; **p. 89,** © Dean Abramson/Stock Boston; **p. 103,** © Stock Trek/PhotoDisc; **p. 104,** © Ovak Arslanian

Chapter Four

p. 131, © 2001 Running, John/Stockphoto.com; **p. 136,** © Jan Suttle/PhotoDisc; **p. 136,** © Dave Thompson/Life/PhotoDisc.

Chapter Five

p. 167, © STEPHEN SIMPSON/Taxi/Getty; **p. 169,** © Kim Steele/PhotoDisc; **p. 175,** © Corbis; **p. 176,** © Andy Sacks/Stone/Getty; **p. 181,** © Tony Cordoza; **p. 183,** © Michael Newman/PhotoEdit; **p. 185,** © Keith Brofsky/PhotoDisc.

Chapter Six

p. 217, © Chris McElcheran/Masterfile; **p. 218,** © Courtesy of Ford Motor Company; **p. 223,** © Tom Carroll/International Stock/Image State; **p. 232,** © Michael Newman/PhotoEdit; **p. 233,** © Kevin Horan/Stone/Getty; **p. 235,** © Makoto Iwafuji/Stock Market/Corbis.

Chapter Seven

p. 255, © Felicia Martinez/PhotoEdit; **p. 256,** © Mark Richards/PhotoEdit; **p. 265,** © 2001 McIntyre, David/Stockphoto.com; **p. 266,** © Sonda Dawes / The Image Works; **p. 268,** © 1998 Stockphoto.Com/Stockphoto.com; **p. 268,** © Ed Young / Photo Researchers, Inc.; **p. 275,** © Steve Vidler/SuperStock.

Chapter Eight

p. 299, © Clive Barda / PAL / Topham/The Image Works. **p. 301,** © Daniel Bosler/Stone/Getty; **p. 301,** © Sergio Piumatti; **p. 310,** © Reuters NewMedia Inc./CORBIS; **p. 314,** © George Hall/CORBIS; **p. 323,** © Lonnie Duka/Stone/Getty.

Chapter Nine

p. 347, © C. Moore/CORBIS; **p. 349,** © Kelly-Mooney Photography/CORBIS; **p. 352,** © Ron Sherman/Stone/Getty; **p. 373,** © Jeff Greenberg/PhotoEdit; **p. 375,** © William Taufic/Stock Market/Corbis; **p. 375,** © William Taufic/Stock Market/Corbis.

Chapter Ten

p. 407, © E. Dygas /Taxi/Getty; **p. 411,** © Dan McCoy/Rainbow; **p. 421,** © Charlie Westerman; **p. 425,** Courtesy of Texas Instruments; **p. 430,** © James Schnepf/Liaison Agency; **p. 433,** © Malcom Fife/PhotoDisc.

Chapter Eleven

p. 459, © Bill Aron/PhotoEdit; **p. 460,** © Adam Crowley/PhotoDisc; **p. 466,** © Michael Wicke / The Image Works; **p. 466,** © Peter Yates/CORBIS; **p. 476,** © Spencer Grant/Stock Boston.

Chapter Twelve

p. 501, © Joe Carini / The Image Works; **p. 504,** © Andy Sacks/Photographer's Choice/Getty; **p. 504,** © Jose Pelaez/Stock Market/Corbis; **p. 504,** © Jeff Greenberg/PhotoEdit; **p. 504,** © Streichan/Zefa/Masterfile.

Chapter Thirteen

p. 541, © 2003 Fritz, Gerard/Stockphoto.com; **p. 547,** © Robert Nickelsberg/Liaison/Getty Images; **p. 547,** © Paul A. Souders/CORBIS; **p. 556,** © Peter Yates/CORBIS; **p. 565,** © D. & I. MacDonald/Index Stock Imagery.

Chapter Fourteen

p. 583, © Didier Dorval/Masterfile; **p. 588,** © Tony Freeman/PhotoEdit; **p. 595,** © PhotoLink/PhotoDisc; **p. 595,** © Bob Mahoney/The Image Works; **p. 595,** © John Madere/CORBIS; **p. 599,** © Etienne De Malglaive/Gamma.

Chapter Fifteen

p. 633, © Royalty-Free/CORBIS; **p. 636,** © Benjamin Rondel/Stock Market/Corbis; **p. 636,** © Spencer Grant/PhotoEdit.

Chapter Sixteen

p. 673, © John Elk/Stock Boston; **p. 684,** © R. Ian Lloyd/Masterfile; **p. 689,** © Jack Spratt/The Image Works, Inc.

Chapter Seventeen

p. 725, © Mug Shots/CORBIS; **p. 727,** © Matthew McVay/Getty; **p. 732,** © Day Williams/Photo Researchers Inc.

Chapter Eighteen

p. 751, © JIM CUMMINS/Taxi/Getty; **p. 753,** © Robert Landau/CORBIS; **p. 762,** © Tardos Camesi/Stock Market/Corbis.

Index of Companies and Organizations

Index of Subjects

Name and Type of Organization Used in Main Illustration of Each Chapter

Chapter Title	Organization Used in Main Illustration	Organization Logo	Type of Organization
1. The Changing Role of Managerial Accounting in a Dynamic Business Environment	The Walt Disney Company	Walt Disney Company	Entertainment company
2. Basic Cost Management Concepts and Accounting for Mass-Customization Operations	Comet Computer; Southwest Airlines, Wal-Mart. and Caterpillar	Comet Cometcomp.com SOUTHWEST AIRLINES® A SYMBOL OF FREEDOM WAL★MART ALWAYS LOW PRICES. ALWAYS WAL-MART. Always CATERPILLAR®	Computer manufacturer with heavy reliance on Internet sales; airline, retailer, and manufacturer,respectively
3. Product Costing and Cost Accumulation in a Batch Production Environment	Adirondack Outfitters	ADIRONDACK OUTFITTERS	Manufacturer of canoes and small boats
4. Process Costing and Hybrid Product-Costing Systems	MVP Sports Equipment Company	MVP Sports Equipment Company	Manufacturer of baseball gloves
5. Activity-Based Costing and Cost Management Systems	Aerotech Corporation	AEROTECH CORPORATION	Manufacturer of circuit boards for aircraft radar and communications equipment
6. Activity-Based Management and Today's Advanced Manufacturing Environment	Aerotech Corporation	AEROTECH CORPORATION	Manufacturer of circuit boards for aircraft radar and communications equipment
7. Activity Analysis, Cost Behavior, and Cost Estimation	Tasty Donuts, Inc.	TASTY DONUTS	Food service; restaurants in Toronto, Ontario, Canada
8. Cost-Volume-Profit Analysis	Seattle Contemporary Theater	SEaTtLe CONTEMPORARY THEATER	Nonprofit arts organization
9. Profit Planning, Activity-Based Budgeting, and e-Budgeting	Cozycamp.com	cozycamp.com	Manufacturer of backpacking tents, with heavy reliance on Internet sales
10. Standard Costing, Operational Performance Measures and the Balanced Scorecard	DCdesserts.com	DC desserts	Producer of fresh fancy desserts, with complete reliance on e-commerce for both sales and purchasing